EVIDENCE-BASED
OTITIS MEDIA
SECOND EDITION

Richard M. Rosenfeld, MD, MPH

Professor of Otolaryngology, SUNY Downstate Medical Center
Director, Division of Pediatric Otolaryngology,
Long Island College Hospital
and University Hospital of Brooklyn
Brooklyn, New York

Charles D. Bluestone, MD

Eberly Professor of Pediatric Otolaryngology,
University of Pittsburgh School of Medicine
Director, Department of Pediatric Otolaryngology,
Children's Hospital of Pittsburgh
Pittsburgh, Pennsylvania

2003
BC Decker Inc
Hamilton • London

BC Decker Inc
P.O. Box 620, L.C.D. 1
Hamilton, Ontario L8N 3K7
Tel: 905-522-7017; 800-568-7281
Fax: 905-522-7839; 888-311-4987
E-mail: info@bcdecker.com
www.bcdecker.com

03 04 05 06/ FP / 9 8 7 6 5 4 3 2 1

ISBN 1-55009-254-5

Printed in Canada

Sales and Distribution

United States
BC Decker Inc
P.O. Box 785
Lewiston, NY 14092-0785
Tel: 905-522-7017; 800-568-7281
Fax: 905-522-7839; 888-311-4987
E-mail: info@bcdecker.com
www.bcdecker.com

Canada
BC Decker Inc
20 Hughson Street South
P.O. Box 620, LCD 1
Hamilton, Ontario L8N 3K7
Tel: 905-522-7017; 800-568-7281
Fax: 905-522-7839; 888-311-4987
E-mail: info@bcdecker.com
www.bcdecker.com

Foreign Rights
John Scott & Company
International Publishers' Agency
P.O. Box 878
Kimberton, PA 19442
Tel: 610-827-1640
Fax: 610-827-1671
E-mail: jsco@voicenet.com

Japan
Igaku-Shoin Ltd.
Foreign Publications Department
3-24-17 Hongo
Bunkyo-ku, Tokyo, Japan 113-8719
Tel: 3 3817 5680
Fax: 3 3815 6776
E-mail: fd@igaku-shoin.co.jp

U.K., Europe, Scandinavia, Middle East
Elsevier Science
Customer Service Department
Foots Cray High Street
Sidcup, Kent
DA14 5HP, UK
Tel: 44 (0) 208 308 5760
Fax: 44 (0) 181 308 5702
E-mail: cservice@harcourt.com

*Singapore, Malaysia, Thailand, Philippines,
Indonesia, Vietnam, Pacific Rim, Korea*
Elsevier Science Asia
583 Orchard Road
#09/01, Forum
Singapore 238884
Tel: 65-737-3593
Fax: 65-753-2145

Australia, New Zealand
Elsevier Science Australia
Customer Service Department
STM Division
Locked Bag 16
St. Peters, New South Wales, 2044
Australia
Tel: 61 02 9517-8999
Fax: 61 02 9517-2249
E-mail: stmp@harcourt.com.au
www.harcourt.com.au

Mexico and Central America
ETM SA de CV
Calle de Tula 59
Colonia Condesa
06140 Mexico DF, Mexico
Tel: 52-5-5553-6657
Fax: 52-5-5211-8468
E-mail:
editoresdetextosmex@prodigy.net.mx

Argentina
CLM (Cuspide Libros Medicos)
Av. Córdoba 2067 - (1120)
Buenos Aires, Argentina
Tel: (5411) 4961-0042/(5411) 4964-0848
Fax: (5411) 4963-7988
E-mail: clm@cuspide.com

Brazil
Tecmedd
Av. Maurílio Biagi, 2850
City Ribeirão Preto – SP – CEP: 14021-000
Tel: 0800 992236
Fax: (16) 3993-9000
E-mail: tecmedd@tecmedd.com.br

Notice: The authors and publisher have made every effort to ensure that the patient care recommended herein, including choice of drugs and drug dosages, is in accord with the accepted standard and practice at the time of publication. However, since research and regulation constantly change clinical standards, the reader is urged to check the product information sheet included in the package of each drug, which includes recommended doses, warnings, and contraindications. This is particularly important with new or infrequently used drugs. Any treatment regimen, particularly one involving medication, involves inherent risk that must be weighed on a case-by-case basis against the benefits anticipated. The reader is cautioned that the purpose of this book is to inform and enlighten; the information contained herein is not intended as, and should not be employed as, a substitute for individual diagnosis and treatment.

*To the children and families who have taught us
and to those who may benefit from these efforts.*

It is a capital mistake to theorize before one has data.
Sir Arthur Conan Doyle

Contents

Foreword

How Many More Treatment Trials in Otitis Media?
Gunnar Stickler (Am J Dis Child 1973;125:403)

From the time of that lament 30 years ago, we have learned a great deal about treating and preventing otitis media. Since 1973, hundreds of articles have been published on the epidemiology, diagnosis, and management of acute otitis media and its consequent otitis media with effusion. The results of many of these studies are conflicting and difficult to interpret and implement for practicing physicians. Day care for infants and widespread use of antibiotics have resulted in multidrug resistance among otitic pathogens, especially the pneumococci, complicating treatment. Each year, there are approximately 30 million office visits for the diagnosis of otitis media and more than 24 million antimicrobial prescriptions. The published data on appropriate treatment are confusing, often illogical, and frequently incorrect.

Until recently, physicians were not taught, in medical school or residency training, how to interpret appropriately published data and to implement evidence-based results from properly planned and executed clinical therapeutic trials. Rarely was there a distinction made between evidence-based and traditional subjective writing in assessing data and conclusions from studies. This was clearly a shortcoming in our education that until recently was unrecognized. Nowhere was this more apparent than in diagnosing and treating otitis media.

This problem was systematically and thoroughly addressed in the first edition of *Evidence-Based Otitis Media* published in 1999. The book presented in great detail the rationale for considering evidence-based information for formulating appropriate management strategies and, most importantly, for selecting optimal antibiotic therapy for infants and children with recurrent acute otitis media or treatment failure. This second edition, again prepared expertly by Dr. Rosenfeld and Dr. Bluestone, is even better, if that is possible, in detailing the importance of evidence-based data in interpreting the ever-enlarging body of literature on otitis media. The editors have assembled an impressive group of experts on all aspects of otitis media and addressed comprehensively many issues related to methodology, clinical management, and consequences of this disease.

For the uninitiated, the eight chapters comprising the methodology section provide the necessary background and detail to allow physicians and other health care professionals to understand and appreciate the value of evidence-based medicine. This framework sets the stage for evaluating each of the excellent chapters on clinical management and consequences of otitis media. Most importantly, those who develop guidelines or offer recommendations to practicing physicians should read this book from cover to cover to garner objective data on the natural history of untreated disease, on the real differences in effectiveness of antibiotics for treatment of acute otitis media, and on the medical and surgical options for preventing recurrent disease and sequelae. In my opinion, this is the only means by which to provide appropriate advice for managing infants and children with otitis media.

George H. McCracken Jr, MD
Professor of Pediatrics
GlaxoSmithKline Distinguished Professor
  of Pediatric Infectious Diseases
The Sarah M. and Charles E. Seay Chair
  in Pediatric Infectious Diseases
University of Texas Southwestern Medical Center
  at Dallas

Preface

Much has changed in 4 years since the first edition of *Evidence-Based Otitis Media*. New studies abound on surgery, basic science, vaccine prevention, judicious antibiotic use, topical antibiotic therapy, and developmental sequelae. The number of systematic reviews and meta-analyses has more than doubled, including several professional evidence reports sponsored by governmental agencies. Evidence-based medicine (EBM) has also matured, with improved methodology, better perspective, and broader clinician acceptance. The melding of otitis media and EBM is an evolving concept, whose progress is mirrored by this state-of-the-art text.

The second edition has greater polish and maturity than its predecessor. Eleven new chapters have been added, including evidence-based medicine, professional evidence reports, molecular and translational research, complementary and alternative medicine, bacteriologic efficacy of antimicrobials, vaccine prevention, international management perspectives, meta-analysis of speech and language sequelae, suppurative complications, host susceptibility to sequelae, and judicious use of systemic and topical antimicrobials. Existing chapters have been updated to incorporate new original research, systematic reviews, and evidence reports. Maturation of EBM as a foundation for clinical care is reflected throughout the revised text.

Contributors are always more important than content. We are blessed to have exceeded the prior edition with the incredible scope, quality, and expertise of our distinguished contributing authors. The authorship constitutes a "who's who" in clinical otitis media, spanning the disciplines of pediatrics, otolaryngology, infectious disease, family practice, allied health, audiology, speech and language pathology, clinical research, biostatistics, health policy analysis, and evidence-based medicine. International authorship for the second edition has also been expanded. Fortunately, we have not had to settle for second best on any chapter; all contributors are leading voices of experience and wisdom in their areas of expertise.

Evidence-Based Otitis Media offers one-stop shopping for the best current evidence to guide management decisions at the individual, organizational, and societal levels. Extensive evidence tables summarize study characteristics and quantitative outcomes for clinically relevant end points. Systematic review and meta-analysis are used throughout to integrate source articles, reconcile conflicting results, and to explore heterogeneity among related studies. Evidence gaps have been identified and plugged with international expert opinion. Our contributing authors are clearly the most qualified for this task because they have personally written or co-written much of the best evidence cited throughout the text.

Sir William Osler once reminded medical students:

A distressing feature in the life which you are about to enter, a feature which will press hardly upon the finer spirits among you and ruffle their equanimity, is the uncertainty which pertains not alone to our science and art, but to the very hopes and fears which make us men. In seeking absolute truth, we aim at the unattainable, and must be content with finding broken portions.

Consider this second edition, therefore, a compendium of the finest broken portions available, bound with the glue of EBM and insights from a cadre of world-renowned experts. As new portions become available, and the quality of the glue improves, we look forward to future editions.

Richard M. Rosenfeld
Charles D. Bluestone
April 2003

Acknowledgments

We are deeply indebted to our contributing authors, whose generous donation of time and expertise brings the evidence in this book to life. Of course, without the tireless efforts of researchers who publish articles about otitis media, there would be no evidence to write about. We are privileged to have such a rich and wonderful legacy to draw on.

In any effort as time consuming as this, the authors' families, friends, and colleagues must provide support—and ours have made this task easier by their understanding and encouragement throughout. We wish to acknowledge Billy Tang and Deborah Hepple for their secretarial support and for their help in collating the references and manuscripts. The patient support of Tricia Bindner and the staff at BC Decker has also been invaluable.

Contributors

Richard E. Besser, MD
Chief, Epidemiology Section, Respiratory Diseases Branch,
Division of Bacterial and Mycotic Diseases, National
 Center for Infectious Diseases,
Centers for Disease Control and Prevention
Atlanta, Georgia

Charles D. Bluestone, MD
Eberly Professor of Pediatric Otolaryngology, University
 of Pittsburgh School of Medicine
Director, Department of Pediatric Otolaryngology,
 Children's Hospital of Pittsburgh
Pittsburgh, Pennsylvania

Cora Collette Breuner, MD, MPH
Assistant Professor, Adolescent Medicine Section,
Department of Pediatrics, Children's Hospital and
 Medical Center
Seattle, Washington

Martin J. Burton, MA, DM
Consultant Otolaryngologist, The Radcliffe Infirmary
Honorary Senior Clinical Lecturer, University of Oxford
Coordinating Editor, Cochrane Ear, Nose & Throat
 Disorders Group
Oxford, United Kingdom

Linda H. Carlson, MS, CPNP
Pediatric Educational Consultant
Statesboro, Georgia

Randal D. Carlson, PhD
Associate Professor of Instructional Technology,
 Georgia Southern University
Statesboro, Georgia

Margaretha L. Casselbrant, MD, PhD
Professor of Otolaryngology, University of Pittsburgh
 School of Medicine
Director of Clinical Research and Education, Department
 of Pediatric Otolaryngology
Children's Hospital of Pittsburgh
Pittsburgh, Pennsylvania

Linda S. Chan, PhD
Professor of Research, Departments of Pediatrics, Surgery,
 and Emergency Medicine,
Keck School of Medicine, University of Southern California
Division of Biostatistics and Outcomes Assessment
Los Angeles, California

Ron Dagan, MD
Professor and Director, Pediatric Infectious Diseases Unit,
 Soroka Medical Center
Beer Sheva, Israel

Joseph E. Dohar, MD, MS
Associate Professor of Otolaryngology, University of
 Pittsburgh School of Medicine
Department of Pediatric Otolaryngology, Children's Hospital
 of Pittsburgh
Pittsburgh, Pennsylvania

Garth D. Ehrlich, PhD
Professor and Vice Chairman, Department of Human Genetics,
Professor and Director of Research, Department of
 Otolaryngology,
Drexel University College of Medicine
Executive Director, Center for Genomic Sciences,
Allegheny Singer Research Institute, Allegheny
 General Hospital
Pittsburgh, Pennsylvania

George A. Gates, MD
Professor of Otolaryngology Head & Neck Surgery,
University of Washington School of Medicine
Director, Virginia Merrill Bloedel Hearing Research Center
Seattle, Washington

Judith S. Gravel, PhD
Professor of Communication Sciences, Hunter College
 of the City University of New York
Visiting Professor of Otolaryngology and Pediatrics,
 Albert Einstein College of Medicine
New York, New York

Mark P. Haggard, PhD
Medical Research Council ESS Team in Children's
 Middle Ear Disease
MRC Cognition and Brain Sciences Unit
Cambridge, United Kingdom

Carla T. Herrerias, BS, MPH
Senior Health Policy Analysis, American Academy of
 Pediatrics
Elk Grove Village, Illinois

Glenn Isaacson, MD
Professor of Otolaryngology, Temple University School
 of Medicine
Chairman, Department of Otolaryngology,
 Temple University Children's Medical Center
Philadelphia, Pennsylvania

Jennifer Jacobs, MD, MPH
Clinical Assistant Professor, Department of Epidemiology
School of Public Health and Community Medicine,
  University of Washington
Seattle, Washington

David Kay, MD
Fellow, Department of Pediatric Otolaryngology
University of Pittsburgh School of Medicine, Children's
  Hospital of Pittsburgh
Pittsburgh, Pennsylvania

Jerome O. Klein, MD
Professor of Pediatrics and Vice Chair for Academic Affairs,
  Boston University School of Medicine
Division of Pediatric Infectious Diseases, Boston
  Medical Center
Boston, Massachusetts

Janet L. Levatin, MD
Private Practice, Pediatrics and Homeopathy
Brookline, Massachusetts

Anthony E. Magit, MD
Assistant Clinical Professor of Otolaryngology and
  Pediatrics, UCSD School of Medicine
Children's Hospital and Health Center of San Diego
San Diego, California

Ellen M. Mandel, MD
Associate Professor of Otolaryngology and Pediatrics,
  University of Pittsburgh School of Medicine
Research Pediatrician, Department of Pediatric
  Otolaryngology, Children's Hospital of Pittsburgh
Pittsburgh, Pennsylvania

Colin D. Marchant, MD
Associate Professor of Pediatrics, Boston University School
  of Medicine,
Division of Pediatric Infectious Diseases, Boston
  Medical Center
Boston, Massachusetts

Adele W. Miccio, PhD
Associate Professor of Communication Sciences and Disorders,
College of Health and Human Development, Pennsylvania
  State University
University Park, Pennsylvania

Elaine E. Nicholls, PhD
Medical Research Council ESS Team in Children's Middle
  Ear Disease
MRC Cognition and Brain Sciences Unit
Cambridge, United Kingdom

Stephen Ira Pelton, MD
Professor of Pediatrics, Boston University School of Medicine
Director, Division of Pediatric Infectious Diseases,
  Boston Medical Center
Boston, Massachusetts

J. Christopher Post, MD, PhD
Professor of Otolaryngology, Drexel University College
  of Medicine
Director, Pediatric Otolaryngology, Allegheny General Hospital
Medical Director, Center for Genomic Sciences, Allegheny
  Singer Research Institute
Pittsburgh, Pennsylvania

Patricia Reitz, MA
Audiologist, Frank Porter Graham Child Development
  Institute, University of North Carolina
Chapel Hill, North Carolina

Joanne E. Roberts, PhD
Senior Scientist and Professor of Pediatrics and Speech and
  Hearing Sciences,
Frank Porter Graham Child Development Institute,
University of North Carolina
Chapel Hill, North Carolina

Howard E. Rockette, PhD
Professor and Chairperson, Department of Biostatistics,
Graduate School of Public Health, University of Pittsburgh
Pittsburgh, Pennsylvania

Richard M. Rosenfeld, MD, MPH
Professor of Otolaryngology, SUNY Downstate
  Medical Center
Director, Division of Pediatric Otolaryngology,
Long Island College Hospital and University Hospital
  of Brooklyn
Brooklyn, New York

Maroeska M. Rovers, PhD
Julius Center for Health Sciences and Primary Care,
University Medical Center Utrecht
Utrecht, The Netherlands

Robert J. Ruben, MD
Distinguished University Professor, Albert Einstein College
  of Medicine
Department of Otolaryngology, Montefiore Medical Center
Bronx, New York

Anne G.M. Schilder, MD, PhD
Department of Pediatric Otorhinolaryngology, University
  Medical Center Utrecht
Wilhelmina Children's Hospital
Utrecht, The Netherlands

Seth R. Schwartz, MD, MPH
Resident, Department of Otolaryngology Head & Neck Surgery
University of Washington School of Medicine
Seattle, Washington

Kai Shen, MD, PhD
Research Fellow, Center for Genomic Sciences
Allegheny Singer Research Institute, Allegheny General
  Hospital
Pittsburgh, Pennsylvania

Sarah C. Smith, PhD
Research Fellow, London School of Hygiene and Tropical
  Medicine, University of London
London, United Kingdom

Glenn S. Takata, MD, MS
Assistant Professor of Pediatrics, Keck School of Medicine,
  University of Southern California
Division of General Pediatrics, Children's Hospital of
  Los Angeles
Los Angeles, California

Lynne Vernon-Feagans, PhD
William C. Friday Distinguished Professor Child
  Development and Family Studies,
School of Education and the Frank Porter Graham Child
  Development Institute
Head, Doctoral Program in Early Childhood, Families
  and Literacy
University of North Carolina at Chapel Hill
Chapel Hill, North Carolina

Xue Wang, MD
Research Assistant Professor, Department of Microbiology
  and Immunology,
Drexel University College of Medicine
Director of Animal Models, Center for Genomic Sciences,
Allegheny Singer Research Institute, Allegheny General
  Hospital
Pittsburgh, Pennsylvania

Kristine M. Yont, PhD
Graduate School of Education, Harvard University
Cambridge, Massachusetts

Susan A. Zeisel, EdD
Investigator, Frank Porter Graham Child Development
  Institute, University of North Carolina
Chapel Hill, North Carolina

Editorial Method

Common sense dictates that *Evidence-Based Otitis Media* be based firmly on principles of evidence-based medicine (EBM). EBM, however, is a work in progress, whose rules and principles vary greatly, depending on the particular definition employed. From a purist perspective, EBM encourages the explicit, judicious, and conscientious use of current best evidence from medical research in reaching decisions about the care of individual patients. Nonetheless, distinguishing evidence-based writing from traditional narrative writing is at best an imperfect science. For practical purposes, we asked our contributing authors to follow the principles outlined in the table below.

Our contributing authors were selected based on the basis of both their clinical expertise and their ability to write for an evidence-based text. Every chapter is written for maximum clinical impact and utility. The text is framed by introductory learning objectives and a concluding table of pointers and pitfalls. In between are all the facts and figures necessary for evidence-based management of otitis media. The book is accompanied by a CD-ROM that permits computerized search of the all references and text.

Evidence-Based Otitis Media offers an uncommon perspective on a common childhood disorder. System-atic review and meta-analysis are used, whenever possible, for quantitative estimates of effect size. Statistical significance (or lack thereof) is qualified by discussions of generalizability and clinical importance. Objective outcomes are supplemented with new information about subjective health status and disease-specific quality of life. Existing practice guidelines and evidence reports are reviewed, focusing on impact and future developments. New clinical pathways are offered for managing acute otitis media and otitis media with effusion, emphasizing natural history, comorbid conditions, and diagnostic certainty.

Like EBM, we consider this book a work in progress. Norman Mailer once remarked that writing books "is the closest men ever come to childbearing," and some of our authors may have felt similarly when adopting an evidence-based style. We are, however, ecstatic with the second edition, which has exceeded our initial expectations. Of course you, the reader, are the ultimate judge, and we welcome your comments and criticisms. We look forward to your feedback and to ongoing otitis media research as a basis for future editions.

Richard M. Rosenfeld
Charles D. Bluestone

Evidence-Based Writing versus Traditional Narrative Writing

	Evidence-Based Writing	*Traditional Narrative Writing*
Editorial tone	Objective and numeric	Subjective and descriptive
Tabular presentation	Strongly emphasized	Emphasis varies
Presentation of study results	Includes significance, magnitude, and clinical importance	Usually limited to statistical significance
Degree of reader empowerment	Empowers readers to make decisions based on best evidence	Limits decisions to those made in advance by the expert author
Selection of references	Emphasizes best available published studies	Liberal selection, often without regard to study quality
Number of references	Selective listing	Exhaustive listing
Expert opinion	Used to fill knowledge gaps	Used without limitation

CHAPTER 1

Evidence-Based Medicine

Martin J. Burton, MA, DM

Evidence-based medicine is the conscientious, explicit, and judicious use of current best evidence in making decisions about the care of individual patients.
David Sackett and colleagues[1]

OBJECTIVES

On completing this chapter, the reader will be able to
1. Define and understand the term "evidence-based medicine."
2. Understand "levels of evidence" and grades of recommendation.
3. Recognize the importance of "critical appraisal skills."
4. Have a framework for critically appraising reports of the most important types of studies.

At the beginning of the 21st century, the term "evidence-based medicine (EBM)" is being widely used. Widely used and widely misused, for while it is well understood by some, it is also misunderstood by many. Some of the problems arise because of the ways in which the term has been used. It has been used as if synonymous with high-quality medicine, implying that it alone can reach this standard. Another view equates it with financially restricted public medicine. Yet others have suggested that it is all about treating populations of patients and that it fails to deal with individuals—so it is seen as promoting depersonalized health care. These are just a few of the more extreme views.

All clinicians, whether caring for individual patients in day-to-day practice, or populations of patients in the public heath setting, aim to use their personal knowledge and expertise as wisely as possible. To this end, consciously or subconsciously, they integrate their personal clinical expertise with information obtained from external sources. Sources can be as diverse as an article read the previous day in a peer-reviewed journal, a recalled chance comment made by a respected teacher 10 years earlier, or a note made during a paper presentation at one of last year's major national meetings. The well-intentioned physician might have an excellent filing system to collect this information, a phenomenal memory, and an impeccable record of "continuing professional development"; nonetheless, it is unlikely that he or she is completely up to date with all the information that might impact on the care of the individual patient.

Each year, over two million articles are published in the biomedical literature in over 30,000 journals. As the amount of "knowledge" in the public domain expands exponentially, the practitioner must acknowledge that new techniques of "knowledge management" must replace traditional methods of "keeping up to date." Moreover, she must also acknowledge that the best quality information may not be readily available—it may be written in a foreign language and be published in a place that is not easily accessible.

WHAT IS EVIDENCE-BASED MEDICINE?

The origins of EBM go to a time well before the explosion in knowledge mentioned above, and can be traced back to 19th century France. But the key features of the practice of EBM are inextricably linked with the knowledge explosion of more recent times.

Sackett and colleagues define EBM as the "...conscientious, explicit and judicious use of current best evidence in making decisions about the care of individual patients."[1] This definition encapsulates the important elements of EBM. In this section, the elements of this definition will be examined in turn.

EBM Relates to Individual Patients

It may seem strange to begin at the end of this definition. But note that EBM is concerned with the care of "individual" patients. Because a lot of "evidence" is derived from data pertaining to groups of patients, critics have sometimes criticized EBM for not addressing the needs of the individual. The author has often been told, "Ah yes, but I deal with patients as individuals," as if EBM was not applicable in these situations.

The clinician is in a unique position to be able to elicit a patient's history and perform a clinical examination. He can understand their condition in relation to their general physical and mental well being and has intimate knowledge of their values, beliefs, and circumstances. With his knowledge of the pathophysiologic processes underlying their disease state, he can help the patient make choices about therapy or diagnostic procedures in light of their particular circumstances. This is particularly important when the available "evidence" might relate to groups of patients whose disease or clinical demographic status differs slightly (or even significantly) from the patient's own. Clinical expertise helps decide whether "evidence" is applicable to an individual patient, and, if so, how it can be integrated into clinical decision making. Hence, one criticism of EBM—that it is "cook book medicine"—is unfounded.

When one or more studies provide good evidence that a particular intervention is effective, the practitioner of EBM must ask an important question relating to his individual patient. That is, "Is my patient so different from the patients in the study that I can reasonably *not* recommend treatment?" Conversely, with treatments that a study suggests are ineffective, he should ask,"Is my patient so different that I would reasonably expect them to respond differently, that is, respond positively, to the treatment?"

This issue of "generalizability"—the application of evidence derived from particular, and sometimes very specific, groups of patients to wider groups of patients in general, and the practitioner's patient in particular—is an important issue in EBM.

EBM Is Conscientious

The conscientious practitioner is driven by the desire to do what is right. He adopts a careful, methodic, measured, and diligent approach. Muir Gray has emphasized the difference between "doing things right" (that is, doing them better, more efficiently, or cheaper) and "doing the right thing" (that is, doing more good than harm—having an understanding of the strength of evidence underlying a management decision).[2] In the context of the new management agenda in health care, he concludes that optimal practice consists of "doing the right things right."

The conscientious practitioner and the health care system in which he works must always ask, "Am I doing more good than harm, and am I doing it in the best and most efficient way?" It will also become apparent that the practice of EBM necessitates that certain strategies be followed with the same conscientiousness that the laboratory-based scientist applies to the different stages in any bench experiment.

EBM Is Explicit

The "explicit" use of evidence suggests clarity and detail, with no room for confusion or doubt. It is one of the tenets of evidence-based practice that the methods by which evidence is to be sought, validated, and graded are specified a priori. This helps minimize bias and forces the practitioners to be clear about their intentions and aims. Being explicit and open promotes transparency and aids reproducibility. It also encourages the sorts of comments and criticism that should improve quality. For example, when a writer declares and publishes in advance the protocol that he is going to use to prepare a systematic review, others can criticize the methodology, and, thus, valid criticisms and suggestions can be incorporated into the review at an early stage. Similarly, quality can be improved post hoc, when new information becomes available or as a result of argument and debate. As an example, if a systematic review has specifically excluded a certain type of study or a particular individual study, these may be included at a later stage following re-evaluation based on informed discussion by readers and others.

Explicitness is important in other areas as well. An evidence-based review stating that a search would be made for all high-quality evidence published since 1995 and available in English would at the very least be explicit about its intentions. Whether or not these were appropriate is a different question. The particular example would produce at least two criticisms or questions: What rationale is there to (1) ignore work done before 1995 and (2) work published in languages other than English? Whereas one can conceive of an answer to the first (perhaps a new technology or drug was only introduced in 1995), the second is almost always impossible to justify. By ignoring (1) unpublished work and (2) work reported or undertaken in languages other than English, publication and language biases are introduced. Yet, it is better to make some explicit statement about methods and allow it to be criticized, than to indulge in obfuscation. Just as the basic scientist describes in her proposal those methods that she aims to employ in her study, the EBM practitioner must be explicit in how he aims to locate, appraise, and synthesize the information he needs to answer his "research" question.

Another important area of explicitness in EBM practice is that required when discussing with patients the strength of evidence underlying management options. This is particularly important when the levels of evidence (see below) are low.

EBM Is Judicious

The term "judicious" brings us back to the idea of considered decisions and sensible opinions. The former suggest that the practitioner has performed a "weighing" exercise, considering alternatives in light of the evidence, while the latter suggest that "common sense" has not been ignored. Again, both these place great emphasis on the clinical skills and experience of the practitioner and his knowledge of disease processes and the patient's circumstances. The slavish application of inappropriate evidence and data is to be rigorously avoided.

EBM Uses Current Best Evidence

The rapid rise in the volume of medical information has already been highlighted. As electronic means of communication change the face of medical publishing, the "currency" of any available evidence—how "up to date" is it?—becomes increasingly important. In one regard, the nature of modern communications helps us address this issue. Whereas paper-based publications may be out of date as soon as they are printed, electronic formats provide an unparalleled opportunity for updating information periodically. In addition, they can facilitate the type of feedback from information "consumers" (patients, practitioners, and so on), which allows constant improvement in quality.

A commitment to practice EBM necessitates that the clinician has specific skills in identifying evidence that is both "current" and "best."

IDENTIFYING INFORMATION THAT IS UP TO DATE

Despite acknowledging that the printed word can be "out of date" almost as soon as it has been printed, print-based journals and textbooks are still produced. The contents of the good ones will at least continue to form the starting point for further inquiry, and the best will draw their readers' attention to parallel electronic resources. The modern EBM practitioner must be fully conversant with the latest techniques for "searching" the literature. This includes not only the ability to search the traditional electronic databases, such as MEDLINE and EMBASE, efficiently but also knowledge of other sources of up-to-date information.

It is likely that all but the most enthusiastic clinician will remain an amateur searcher. There is now a wide professional field of information and knowledge management, drawing on much of the skill and expertise of librarians and others working in the library environment. The advisability of "making friends with your librarian" has rarely been truer. Many of these individuals have been trained in effective and comprehensive search techniques. A comprehensive literature has developed around this, on the basis of the indexing systems of the various databases, making effective and comprehensive searching a very complex matter. Simply entering a term, such as "otitis media" into a MEDLINE search engine is unlikely to be useful.

Among the increasing number of EBM resources are some that aim to take the "pain" out of searching. For example, if one is searching specifically for randomized controlled trials (RCTs) of therapeutic interventions, the *Cochrane Database of Trials*, published quarterly and electronically in the Cochrane Library, aims to be the world's most comprehensive database of these studies. This knowledge will save the clinician who is seeking this specific type of study an enormous amount of time and effort. The database not only includes trials published in MEDLINE-indexed journals, it also includes unpublished studies and those reported in abstract form only. Moreover, the range of languages covered by the Cochrane database is broad—it attempts to include trials in any language. This contrasts with the more limited language spread of the journals indexed in the MEDLINE database.

Some other resources of up-to-date evidence are listed in Table 1-1. This comprises not only resources including databases of citations of individual studies (eg, the Cochrane Library) but also records of formal systematic reviews (see below) and other "evidence-based" reviews. They are all regularly updated electronic resources.

Table 1-1 Evidence-Based Medicine Resources

Bandolier	http://www.jr2.ox.ac.uk/bandolier/index.html
Evidence-based on-call	http://www.eboncall.co.uk/
Clinical evidence	http://www.clinicalevidence.com
Evidence-based medicine	http://ebm.bmjjournals.com/
Cochrane Library	http://www.update-software.com/Cochrane/default.HTM
Centre for EBM, Oxford— The EBM Toolbox	http://minerva.minervation.com/cebm

Table 1-2 Levels of Evidence for Studies Evaluating Therapy, Prevention, Etiology, or Harm

Level	Therapy/Prevention, Etiology/Harm
1a	Systematic review (with homogeneity) of RCTs*
1b	Individual RCT (with narrow confidence interval)
1c	All or none†
2a	Systematic review (with homogeneity) of cohort studies*
2b	Individual cohort study (including low quality RCT; eg, < 80% follow-up)
2c	"Outcomes" research
3a	Systematic review (with homogeneity) of case-control studies*
3b	Individual case-control study
4	Case-series (and poor-quality cohort and case-control studies)
5	Expert opinion without explicit critical appraisal, or based on physiology, bench research, or "first principles"

RCT = randomized controlled trial.

* That is, one in which there are no worrying variations in either the direction or magnitude of the results of individual studies.

† This condition is met when either all patients died before the new treatment and now some survive or some died and now none die.

IDENTIFYING "BEST" EVIDENCE

The term "best evidence" implies that there is a hierarchy of quality in evidence. We need to be able to answer the question—how confident can we be that an estimate of a treatment effect, association, or test result is correct? The strata in the hierarchy of quality and the degree to which we can be confident about our estimates are often referred to as "levels of evidence."

Fletcher and Sackett[3] working for the Canadian Task Force on the Periodic Health Examination initially developed the concept of "levels of evidence" over 20 years ago. The levels they produced (in this case for the value of preventive maneuvers) were linked with "grades of recommendation." Subsequently, these levels and grades have been refined and revised, and the most recent version can be found on the Web site of the Centre for Evidence-Based Medicine in Oxford.[4] Table 1-2 describes the levels of evidence for studies evaluating therapy, prevention, etiology or harm and Table 1-3 the levels of evidence for studies evaluating diagnostic tests. In Table 1-4, the relationship between "grade of recommendation" and levels of evidence is given.

One of the most popular misconceptions about EBM is that it is all about RCTs—nothing could be further from the truth. Although the individual RCT and systematic reviews of multiple RCTs rightly have a place at the top of the hierarchy of evidence, all other types of studies are also considered. In many situations, the "best evidence" we have is level 4 or 5 evidence. This can and should be incorporated into day-to-day clinical practice. But we cannot be complacent, and it must be accepted that, whenever possible, we should be striving to improve the quality of "current best evidence" by conducting appropriate, high-quality research. In areas of particular importance, we should be aiming for new evidence from RCTs.

A second misconception is that the absence of evidence of effectiveness equates evidence of ineffectiveness. This is untrue. Practitioners must be aware that there are many interventions for which we have little high-quality evidence. Some should probably be stopped until such time as they are proven to be effective because the pathophysiologic basis for them is weak. Others are based on stronger foundations but still should be subjected to appropriate scrutiny. It is often said that in the field of surgery, RCTs are difficult to perform. Although undoubtedly true to a degree, they are not impossible to perform, and where true doubt exists about the validity of the intervention, the difficulties should be surmounted, if at all possible. Particular difficulties in undertaking surgical trials are those of blinding and handling patient expectations.

Returning to levels of evidence, the highest level for therapy (1a) is that provided by a "systematic review" of RCTs. The process of systematic review is a quite specific one (see Chapter 4, "Meta-analysis and Systematic Literature Review") and contrasts sharply with the usual process of "reviewing the literature," so often seen in older journals and still published today. It applies a specific, robust scientific process to locating, appraising, and synthesizing information from previously performed studies. This is designed to render the review free from bias, in the same way in which stringent efforts should be, and are, made to ensure that primary studies are similarly free from bias.

Table 1-3 Levels of Evidence for Studies Evaluating Diagnostic Tests

Level	Diagnosis
1a	Systematic review (with homogeneity) of level 1 diagnostic studies*; or CDR† with 1b studies from different clinical centers
1b	Validating cohort study (tests quality of a specific diagnostic test, based on prior evidence) with good reference standards; or CDR† tested in one clinical center
1c	Absolute SpPins and SnNouts‡
2a	Systematic review with homogeneity of level > 2 diagnostic studies*
2b	Exploratory cohort study (trawls data and collects information to find factors that are "significant") with good reference standards; CDR† after derivation, or validated only on database or "split-sample" (all information is collected in a single tranche, then artificially divided into "derivation" and "validation" samples)
3a	Systematic review with homogeneity of level 3b and better diagnostic studies*
3b	Nonconsecutive study; or without consistently applied reference standard
4	Case-control study, poor or nonindependent reference standard
5	Expert opinion without explicit critical appraisal, or based on physiology, bench research or "first principles"

* That is, one in which there are no worrying variations in either the direction or magnitude of the results of individual studies.
† Clinical Decision Rule (CDR) = algorithm or scoring system that leads to a prognostic estimation or a diagnostic category.
‡ Absolute SpPin = a diagnostic finding where specificity is so high that a positive result rules *in* the diagnosis. Absolute SnNout = a diagnostic finding where sensitivity is so high that a negative result rules *out* the diagnosis.

Table 1-4 Grades of Recommendation

Grade	Description
A	Consistent level 1 studies
B	Consistent level 2 or 3 studies or extrapolation* from level 1 studies
C	Level 4 studies or extrapolation* from level 2 or 3 studies
D	Level 5 evidence or troublingly inconsistent or inconclusive studies of any level

* Extrapolation: where data are used in a situation in which there are clinically important differences from the original study.

The process of a systematic review aims to separate the salient and significant from the unreliable and redundant. Full details of this process of systematic review are beyond the scope of this chapter, but a number of the salient features are given in Table 1-5. Several key features should be noted. The process seeks to avoid publication and language bias by searching for studies as comprehensively as possible. The importance of this has been highlighted above. In the English-speaking world, language bias is rife. It must be accepted, without irritation, that there is nothing inherently wrong with studies published in non-

Table 1-5 Features of a Systematic Review

Locates, appraises, and synthesizes evidence from scientific studies.

Adheres to a strict scientific design to make it comprehensive, minimize bias, and ensure reliability.

Addresses a focused question that
  1. addresses decisions people (patients and health care professionals) face.
  2. addresses outcomes that are meaningful to people making decisions.

Critically appraises studies looking at applicability and validity.

Incorporates validity assessments into the review.

Uses statistical methods, when appropriate, to derive meaningful conclusions from data and prevent errors of interpretation.

Does not use statistical methods when inappropriate to do so.

Helps interpret strength of evidence and applicability of results.

Clarifies important "trade-offs" between benefits, harms, and costs.

Table 1-6 Critical Appraisal Skill Resources

Centre for EBM, Oxford	Critical appraisal tools	http://minerva.minervation.com/cebm
New Zealand Guidelines Group	Resources for critical appraisal	http://www.nzgg.org.nz/tools/ resource_critical_appraisal.cfm
The CASP International Network	Resources for critical appraisal	http://www.caspinternational.org.uk

Table 1-7 Outline Worksheet for Appraising a Therapeutic Trial

1. Are the results of this trial valid?

Was the assignment of patients to treatments randomized? If so, was the randomization list concealed?

Were all the patients who entered the trial accounted for at its conclusion? If so, were they analyzed in the groups to which they were randomized?

Were patients and clinicians kept "blind" to which treatments they received?

Were the groups treated equally, apart from the experimental treatment?

Were the groups similar at the start of the trial?

2. Are the valid results of this trial important?

How large was the treatment effect?

How precise was the estimate of the treatment effect? What are the 95% confidence intervals

Were all the clinically important outcomes considered? If not, does it matter?

3. Can this valid, important evidence about a treatment be applied to caring for my patient?

Do these results apply to my patient?
 Is the patient so different from those in the trial that its results cannot be of help?
 How great would the benefit of therapy actually be in my patient?

Does the treatment regimen satisfy my patient's values and preferences?
 Are the patient's values and preferences clear to me?
 Are they met by this management regimen and its consequences?
 Are the benefits worth the harms and costs for my patient?

English journals. Difficulties with translation may exist, but this does not detract from the potential quality of the study. However, it would be naive to assume that all studies are good studies, even if they are based on RCTs. For this reason, the process of undertaking a systematic review includes a blinded (again to avoid bias) assessment of quality against a set of predefined quality criteria.

CRITICALLY APPRAISING THE LITERATURE

Many high-quality systematic reviews of otitis media have already been published (see Chapter 4, "Meta-analysis and Systematic Literature Review"), but not all aspects of management have enough source articles to justify data synthesis. Therefore, the practitioner of EBM often needs to appraise primary studies and, develop and practice critical appraisal skills. A number of helpful "tools" are available (Table 1-6), several of which make use of a framework outlined by Sackett and colleagues.[5]

This asks three important questions about any study:
1. Is the evidence about the therapy/diagnostic test/ prognosis/harm *valid*?
2. Is the evidence *important*?
3. Is this *valid, important* evidence *applicable* in caring for my patient?

The questions are elaborated on in Tables 1-7 and 1-8. These are based on a series of "worksheets" pro-

Table 1-8 Outline Worksheet for Appraising a Diagnostic Study

---

1. Are the results of this diagnostic study valid?

Was there an independent, blind comparison with a reference ("gold") standard? Would this reference test be the best available in the circumstances?

Was the diagnostic test evaluated in an appropriate spectrum of patients (like those in whom it would be used in practice)?

Was the reference standard applied regardless of the diagnostic test result?

---

2. Are the results of this study important?

What are the "properties" of the test?

  What is the likelihood ratio for a positive and negative result?

How precise are the results?

---

3. Can this valid, important diagnostic test be applied to caring for my patient?

When used in my health care setting, is the diagnostic test—

  available?

  affordable?

  accurate?

  precise?

Can I generate a clinically sensible estimate of my patient's pretest probability (from practice data, personal experience, the report itself or clinical speculation)?

Will the resulting post-test probabilities affect management and help the patient?

  Could it move the patient across a test–treatment threshold?

  Would the patient be willing to carry it out?

  Would the consequences of the test help my patient?

---

duced by the Centre for EBM in Oxford (See item 1, Table 1-6).[6] Other worksheets are available for use with studies looking at prognosis, harm and etiology, economic analysis, guidelines, and systematic review.

The secondary questions help the reader answer each of the three main questions. In the case of question 1, they are based on empiric evidence about those features of individual studies that have been shown to be associated with minimum bias. Consider the example of a study about therapy. The secondary questions address the confidence issue again—how confident we can be about the effect shown in the study. Note that the levels and grade of evidence outlined above address only this first question. The second question looks at the issues of "effect size"—how big is the effect? A well-conducted study may show a statistically significant effect but of such a small size that it has no practical clinical significance.

Although all three questions are important, the third is worthy of particular note because it highlights again how well-practiced EBM focuses on the care of the *individual* patient. A therapeutic effect, of a clinically important size, may still be inappropriate in the care of an

Table 1-9 Pointers and Pitfalls

When properly defined and understood, evidence-based practice is seen to be an important and acceptable tool in providing high-quality medical care.

Developing personal "knowledge management skills" is vital in practicing medicine in the 21st century.

Learning to be a critical appraiser of evidence takes time and discipline.

The absence of good evidence of effectiveness is not the same as evidence of ineffectiveness.

Optimal medical practice is always likely to be evidence and wisdom based, but it is not wise to ignore good evidence.

"individual patient" because that patient differs in an important way from the study patients or because his or her preference is that the associated "harms" (risks or side-effects, for example) are not acceptable.

CONCLUSION

When properly understood, there can be little argument that EBM should play a pivotal role in modern health care. But when the "best evidence" is poor, what then? If "the essence of wisdom is the ability to make the right decision on the basis of inadequate evidence," there will always be a need to be able to practice "wisdom-based medicine." This author suggests that optimal medical practice is both "evidence" and "wisdom" based (Table 1-9).

REFERENCES

1. Sackett DL, Rosenberg WMC, Gray JAM, et al. Evidence-based medicine: what it is and what it isn't. BMJ 1996;312:71–2.
2. Gray JAM. Evidence-based healthcare. How to make health policy and management decisions. 1st ed. New York: Churchill Livingstone; 1997.
3. Canadian Task Force on the Periodic Health Examination. The periodic health examination. Can Med Assoc J 1979;121:1193–254.
4. Oxford Centre for Evidence-Based Medicine. Levels of Evidence (May 2001). Available at http://minerva.minervation.com/cebm/docs/levels.html#levels (accessed February 5, 2003).
5. Sackett DL, Richardson WS, Rosenberg W, Haynes RB. Evidence-based medicine. How to practice and teach EBM. Edinburgh, UK: Churchill Livingstone; 1998.
6. Oxford Centre for Evidence-Based Medicine. A set of worksheets for critical appraisal of articles on therapy, diagnosis, prognosis, harm, economic analysis, decision analysis and guidelines. Available at http://www.minervation.com/cebm/documents/worksheets.pdf. (accessed February 5, 2003).

CHAPTER 2

Critical Evaluation of Journal Articles

Richard M. Rosenfeld, MD, MPH

*It is astonishing with how little reading a doctor can practice medicine,
but it is not astonishing how badly he may do it.*
William Osler

OBJECTIVES

On completing this chapter, the reader will be able to
1. Appreciate the need for critical self-assessment of articles about otitis media (OM).
2. Rapidly identify articles worthy of in-depth analysis.
3. Use five questions to interpret any journal article.
4. Understand the profound impact of study design on evidence interpretation.
5. Recognize common statistical deceptions that appear in the medical literature.

Evidence-based medicine (EBM) and peer review have matured since the first edition of this chapter in 1999,[1,2] but the basic principles of critical literature review remain unchanged. These principles are the essence of applied EBM because the methodologic quality (internal validity) and generalizability (external validity) of original research relate directly to informed clinical decisions. For OM, most management decisions are elective and nonurgent. Therefore, issues of effect size, generalizability, and risk–benefit ratio become paramount when applying research evidence to patients. These issues will be emphasized with new examples. Our focus herein is the critical analysis of original otitis media research; Chapter 1 surveys the broader expanse of EBM and Chapter 4 discusses more throughly issues relevant to systematic review and meta-analysis.

Evidence-based medicine begins with *evidence*. Enlightened clinicians have two choices in evidence management: Do it yourself, or let some "expert" do it for you. Unfortunately, relying on experts can be hazardous: Peer review is sadly imprecise, review articles and book chapters are fraught with bias, practice guidelines belie hidden political agendas, and new research proliferates at a mind-numbing rate.[1] The question is not *if* you need to become a self-designated evidence-management guru, but *when*.

Nearly all evidence relevant to clinical care begins with articles in peer-reviewed medical journals. Unfortunately, the process of editorial peer review is largely untested and its effects are uncertain.[3] Manuscript assessment, like most sophisticated diagnostic tests, has a certain sensitivity and specificity; worthy articles may be unappreciated (and unpublished), or worthless ones may pass undetected to the printing press.[4] Peer reviewers may be biased, unqualified, or possess widely discrepant opinions about a study. The bottom line? Caveat lector: beware of what you read even in excellent medical journals.

Of more concern to clinicians than the inadequacies of peer review, however, is that the medical literature generally serves science, rather than medical practice.[5] Peer-reviewed publications facilitate communication from scientist to scientist, not necessarily from scientist to clinician. Most published studies are nondefinitive tests of hypotheses and innovations, only a very small percentage of which may warrant routine clinical application. Whereas the science may be sound, the idea has not progressed beyond the laboratory or preliminary field studies. Definitive studies constituting true scientist to clinician communication are rare in medical journals and must be identified by critical appraisal.

Clinicians can use the medical literature to support clinical decisions in two complementary ways: regular surveillance (or browsing) and problem-oriented searches. While the latter mode is more effective for learning, both are necessary for continuing clinical competence. Both methods require an appreciation of the purposes of the medical literature and a basic understanding of the strengths and weaknesses of the features of various studies for providing valid and clinically applicable information. This chapter is a first step toward achieving this understanding. The brief time spent digesting this information should be richly rewarded the next time you peruse the otitis media literature.

How to Identify Articles Worth Reading

The first step in analyzing a journal article is to determine if it is worthy of analysis. Some articles merit no more than a quick glance at the title; others merit in-depth analysis as described in the following section. Whether to glance through or analyze depends on the relative appeal and quality of the work. Put simply, limit your efforts to useful and interesting articles of apparent high quality.

Articles worthy of in-depth analysis have enticing titles and abstracts, which espouse innovative, controversial, or clinically relevant ideas. The article generally appears as original research in the main section of a peer-reviewed journal. Methods and results sections, which represent the heart and soul of the article, should be appropriately detailed and lengthy. Enough details should be provided for you to reproduce the study on your own, if desired, with a reasonable chance of obtaining the same results. A quick review of the paper in general should disclose many of the signs of grandeur in Table 2-1.

Articles unworthy of in-depth analysis may have enticing titles and abstracts but have no ability to support the lofty claims and conclusions therein. The article may appear in a non–peer-reviewed (throwaway) journal or in an industry-funded supplement to the main section (which generally implies lower quality).[6] Signs of decadence (see Table 2-1) are readily apparent when perusing the article's main sections. The methods and results sections are vague and sparse, overshadowed by a verbose discussion section with unsupported opinions and creative misinterpretations. Do not waste any time analyzing an unworthy article, unless the premise is so novel and important that it overshadows the obvious weaknesses.

Journal articles may be compared with gourmet meals.[7] Abstracts offer a useful taste of study contents but are rarely sufficient to make a meal in themselves. A well-crafted introduction section provides a nourishing appetizer before the main course of the paper and may, in itself, make the reading worthwhile. The methods and results sections constitute the main bill of fare, worthy of careful digestion and analysis. If the meal was delicious (eg, full of useful and high-quality evidence), you may wish to sample the desert, or the discussion section. Discussion sections are full of creative ingredients, ranging from speculation to apologies, which can make them the most enjoyable part of the meal (but hardly the most nourishing).

Five Basic Questions for Interpreting Journal Articles

Just as an expert clinician considers something abnormal until they examine it and prove otherwise, a connoisseur of medical evidence considers a journal article to be laden with flaws, distortions, and omissions, until proven to the contrary. The five basic questions in Table 2-2 will allow you to rapidly taste an article, with the same proficiency that a grand sommelier bestows on a glass of wine. Each of the questions is discussed below, with special emphasis on study design (question 1) because it is the most critical component of the process. The information herein is based on established principles of data analysis[8] and literature interpretation.[9]

Table 2-1 Signs of Grandeur and Decadence in Journal Articles

Section	Signs of Grandeur	Signs of Decadence
Abstract	Structured summary of goals, methods, results, and significance	Unstructured qualitative overview of study; contains more wish than reality
Introduction	Clear, concise, and logical; ends with study rationale or purpose	Rambling, verbose literature review; no critical argument or hypothesis
Methods	Specific enough for the reader to reproduce the study; offers too much detail, rather than too little	Vague or incomplete description of subjects, sampling, outcome criteria; no mention of statistical analysis
Results	Logical blend of numbers and narrative with supporting tables and figures	Difficult to read, with overuse or underuse of statistical tests; no tables
Discussion	Puts main results in context; reviews supporting and conflicting literature; discusses strengths and weaknesses	Full of fantasy and speculation; rambling and biased literature review; does not acknowledge weaknesses
References	Demonstrates clearly that work of others has been considered	Key articles are conspicuously absent; excessively brief

Table 2-2 Five Basic Questions for Interpreting Journal Articles

Question	Why It Is Important	Underlying Principles
How was the study performed?	Study design has a profound impact on interpretation; scrutinize the data collection, degree of investigator control, use of control groups, and direction of inquiry	Bias, research design, placebo effect, causality, confounding
What are the results?	Results should be summarized with appropriate descriptive statistics; positive results must be qualified by the chance of being wrong, and negative results by the chance of having missed a true difference	Measurement scale, association, *p* value, power, effect size, clinical importance
Are the results valid within the study?	Proper statistical analysis and data collection ensures valid results for the subjects studied; measurements must be accurate and reproducible	Internal validity, accuracy, statistical tests
Are the results valid outside the study?	Results can be generalized when the sampling method is sound, subjects are representative of the target population, and sample size is large enough for adequate precision	External validity, sampling, confidence intervals, precision
Are the results strong and consistent?	A single study is rarely definitive; results must be viewed relative to their plausibility, consistency with past efforts, and by the strength of the study methodology	Research integration, level of evidence, systematic review

Question 1: How Was the Study Performed?

Study Design

Despite the befuddling array of study designs espoused in the epidemiologic literature, the savvy evidence analyst need only address a few basic design considerations (Table 2-3). These considerations relate to (1) how the data were gathered, (2) what degree of control the investigator had over study conditions, (3) whether a control or comparison group was used, and (4) what direction of inquiry was followed. Answers to these questions can be found in the article's methods section.

Data collected specifically for research (see Table 2-3) are likely to be unbiased—they reflect the true value of the attribute being measured. In contrast, data collected during routine clinical care will vary in quality depending on the specific methodology applied.[10] *Experimental* studies, such as randomized trials, often yield high-quality data because they are performed under carefully controlled conditions. In *observational* studies, however, the investigator is simply a bystander who records the natural course of health events during clinical care. Although more reflective of "real life" than a contrived experiment, observational studies are more prone to bias. Comparing randomized trials with outcomes studies highlights the difference between experimental and observational research (Table 2-4).

The presence or absence of a *control group* has a profound influence on data interpretation. An uncontrolled study—no matter how elegant—is purely descriptive.[11] Nonetheless, authors of case series often delight in unjustified musings on efficacy, effectiveness, association, and causality. Without a control or comparison group, treatment effects cannot be distinguished from other causes of clinical change (Table 2-5). Some of these causes are found in Figure 2-1, which depicts change in health status after a healing encounter as a complex interaction of three primary factors:

1. *What was actually done.* Specific effect(s) of therapy, including medications, surgery, physical manipulations, and alternative or integrative approaches.
2. *What would have happened anyway.* Spontaneous resolution, including natural history, random fluctuations in disease status, and regression to a mean symptom state.
3. *What was imagined to be done.* Placebo response, defined as a change in health status resulting from the symbolic significance attributed by the patient (or proxy) to the encounter itself.[12,13] A placebo response is most likely to occur when the patient receives a meaningful and personalized explanation, feels care and concern expressed by the healer, and achieves control and mastery over illness (or believes that the healer can control the illness).

Table 2-3 Effect of Study Design on Data Interpretation

Aspect of Study Design	Effect on Data Interpretation
How were the data originally collected?	
Specifically for research	Interpretation is facilitated by quality data collected according to an a priori protocol
During routine clinical care	Interpretation is limited by the consistency, accuracy, availability, and completeness of the source records
Is the study experimental or observational?	
Experimental study with conditions under direct control of the investigator	Low potential for systematic error (bias); bias can be reduced further by randomization and masking (blinding)
Observational study without intervention other than to record, classify, analyze	High potential for bias in sample selection, treatment assignment, measurement of exposures and outcomes
Is there a comparison or control group?	
Comparative or controlled study with two or more groups	Permits analytic statements concerning efficacy, effectiveness, and association
No comparison group present	Permits descriptive statements only because of improvements from natural history and placebo effect
What is the direction of study inquiry?	
Subjects identified prior to an outcome or disease; future events recorded	Prospective design measures incidence (new events) and causality (if comparison group included)
Subjects identified after an outcome or disease; past histories are examined	Retrospective design measures prevalence (existing events) and causality (if comparison group included)
Subjects are identified at a single time point, regardless of outcome or disease	Cross-sectional design measures prevalence (existing events) and association (if comparison group included)

Table 2-4 Comparison of Randomized Clinical Trials and Outcomes Studies

Characteristic	Randomized Clinical Trial	Outcomes Study
Level of investigator control	Experimental	Observational
Treatment allocation	Random assignment	Routine clinical care
Patient selection criteria	Restrictive	Broad
Typical setting	Hospital or university based	Community based
End point definitions	Objective health status	Subjective quality of life
End point assessment	Masked (blinded)	Unmasked
Statistical analysis	Comparison of groups	Multivariate regression
Potential for bias	Low	Very high
Generalizability	Potentially low	Potentially high

The placebo response differs from the traditional definition of placebo as an inactive medical substance. Whereas a placebo can elicit a placebo response, the latter can occur without the former. A placebo response results from the psychological or symbolic importance attributed by the patient to any nonspecific event in a healing environment. These events include touch, words, gestures, local ambiance, and social interactions.[14] Many of these factors are encompassed in the term *caring effects*,[15] which have been central to

Table 2-5 Explanations for Favorable Outcomes in Treatment Studies

Explanation	Definition	Solution
Bias	Systematic variation of measurements from their true values; may be intentional or unintentional	Accurate, protocol-driven data collection
Chance	Random variation without apparent relation to other measurements or variables (eg, getting lucky)	Control or comparison group
Natural history	Course of a disease from onset to resolution; may include relapse, remission, and spontaneous recovery	Control or comparison group
Regression to the mean	Symptom improvement independent of therapy, as sick patients return to a mean level after seeking care	Control or comparison group
Placebo effect	Beneficial effect caused by the expectation that the regimen will have an effect (eg, power of suggestion)	Control or comparison group with placebo
Halo effect	Beneficial effect caused by the manner, attention, and caring of a provider during a medical encounter	Control or comparison group treated similarly
Confounding	Distortion of an effect by other prognostic factors or variables for which adjustments have not been made	Randomization or multivariate analysis
Allocation (susceptibility) bias	Beneficial effect caused by allocating subjects with less severe disease or better prognosis to treatment group	Randomization or comorbidity analysis
Ascertainment (detection) bias	Favoring the treatment group during outcome analysis (eg, rounding up for treated subjects, down for controls)	Masked (blinded) outcome assessment

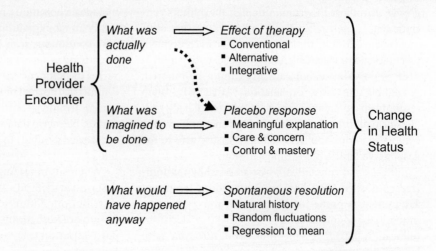

Figure 2-1 Model depicting change in health status after a healing encounter. Dashed arrow shows that a placebo response may occur from symbolic significance of the specific therapy given or from interpersonal aspects of the encounter.

medical practice in all cultures throughout history.

The extremely favorable natural history of untreated OM (see Chapter 12, "Natural History of Untreated Otitis Media") tends to accentuate placebo response and diminish the role of active therapy. Indeed, a large part of managing OM involves watchful waiting to see if middle ear effusion (MEE) or recurrent infections will diminish as the child's immune system matures and the Eustachian tube develops. These factors have resulted in a huge market for alternative therapy of OM (homeo-pathic, chiropractic, and naturopathic), whose benefits stem more likely from placebo response and spontaneous resolution than from direct therapeutic effects.

Assessing Causality

When data from a comparison or control group are available, statistics may be used to test hypotheses and measure associations. Causality may also be assessed when the study has a time-span component, either retrospective or prospective (see Table 2-3). Prospective studies measure *incidence* (new events), whereas retrospective studies measure *prevalence* (existing events). Unlike time-span studies, cross-sectional inquiries (surveys, screening programs, evaluations of diagnostic tests) measure association, not causality.

The relationship between study type and methodology is illustrated in Table 2-6 and explored further in Table 2-7 with hypothetical studies to determine if ice cream causes acute otitis media (AOM). A case series (examples 1 and 2) can have either a prospective or a retrospective direction depending on how subjects are identified. Only the controlled studies (examples 3 to 7) can measure associations, and only the controlled studies with a time-span component (examples 4 to 7) can assess causality. The nonrandomized studies (examples 3 to 6), however, require adjustment for potential confounding variables—baseline prognostic factors that may be associated with both ice cream and AOM (eg, day-care attendance) and, therefore, influence results. Randomization ensures balanced allocation of prognostic factors among groups, and thereby avoids the issue of confounding.

A more concrete example involves a study of gastric juice and MEE in children.[16] Using a cross-sectional design, the investigators found in MEE an 83% prevalence of pepsin/pepsinogen concentrations up to 1,000-fold greater than those in serum. Although the authors conclude that "…anti-reflux treatment could prevent otitis media with effusion," the lack of a time-span component precludes such a statement. A high prevalence of pepsin in MEE is provocative, but causality cannot be inferred. A credible alternative explanation is that MEE often results from a patulous Eustachian tube (see Chapter 11, "Eustachian Tube Function and Dysfunction"), which could also permit transient reflux of gastric acid in the nasopharynx into a pre-existing effusion.

Efficacy and causality are best assessed by randomized controlled trials because nonrandom treatment assignment is prone to innate distortions caused by individual judgments and other selective decisions (allocation bias).[17] A dangerous habit, however, is to label all randomized trials as high quality and all observational studies (eg, outcomes research) as substandard. Randomization cannot compensate for imprecise selection criteria, poorly defined end points, inadequate follow-up, or low compliance with treatment. More meaningful data would come from a protocol-driven, controlled, observational study with unambiguous selection criteria, valid and reliable outcome definitions, and uniform follow-up.

The best randomized trials make special effort to ensure the adequacy of randomization (eg, random numbers generated by the pharmacy), conceal treatment allocation from subjects and investigators (double-blind method), and analyze results by intention-to-treat (instead of including only compliant patients).[18] The intention-to-treat analysis is essential to maintain treatment groups that are similar apart from random variation, which may not occur if the analysis is performed only using subjects who complied with treatment (on-treatment analysis).[19] Readers interested in a more in-depth discussion of quality standards for randomized trials should consult the Consolidated Standards of Reporting Trials (CONSORT) statement, published in 1996 and revised in 2001.[20]

Question 2: What Are the Results?

Most study results are summarized with some combination of descriptive statistics (percentiles, mean, standard deviation), measures of association (odds ratio, rate difference, Pearson's correlation), and analytic statistics (hypothesis tests, *p* values). An understanding of the rationale and interpretation of these procedures is essential for enlightened evidence management.

Descriptive Statistics

Describing results begins by defining the *measurement scale* that best suits the observations. Categoric (qualitative) observations fall into one or more categories and include dichotomous, nominal, and ordinal scales (Table 2-8). Numeric (quantitative) observations are measured on a continuous scale and are further classified by the underlying *frequency distribution* (plot of observed values versus the frequency of each value). Numeric data with a symmetric (normal or Gaussian) distribution are evenly placed around a central crest or trough (bell-shaped curve). Numeric data with an asymmetric distribution are skewed (shifted) to one side of the center or contain unusually high or low outlier values.

When summarizing numeric data (Table 2-9), the descriptive method varies according to the underlying distribution. Numeric data with a symmetric distribution are best summarized with the mean and standard deviation (SD), because 68% of the observations fall within the mean ± 1 SD and 95% fall within the mean ± 2 SD. In contrast, asymmetric numeric data are best summarized with the median because even a single outlier can strongly influence the mean. For example, if five patients are followed after tympanostomy tubes for 10, 12, 15, 16, and 48 months, the mean duration of follow-up is 20 months, but the median is only 15 months. In this case, a single outlier, 48 months, distorts the mean.

A special form of numeric data is called *censored* (see Table 2-8). Data are censored when (1) the study direction is prospective, (2) the outcome is time related, and (3) some subjects die, are lost to follow-up, or have not

Table 2-6 Relationship of Study Type to Study Methodology

Study Type	How Were the Data Originally Collected?	Is There a Control or Comparison Group?	What Is the Direction of Study Inquiry?
Experimental Studies			
Basic science study	Research	Yes or no	Prospective or cross-sectional
Clinical trial	Research	Yes or no	Prospective or cross-sectional
Randomized trial	Research	Yes	Prospective
Observational Studies			
Cohort study	Clinical care or research	Yes or no	Prospective
Historic cohort study	Clinical care	Yes	Prospective
Outcomes research	Clinical care or research	Yes or no	Prospective
Case-control study	Clinical care	Yes	Retrospective
Case series	Clinical care	Yes or no	Retrospective or prospective
Survey study	Clinical care or research	Yes or no	Cross-sectional
Diagnostic test study	Clinical care or research	Yes or no	Cross-sectional

Table 2-7 Determining if Ice Cream Causes AOM: Study Design vs. Interpretation*

Study Design	Study Execution	Interpretation
1. Case series, retrospective	A group of children with AOM are asked whether or not they recently had ice cream	Measures prevalence of ice cream consumption in children with AOM; cannot assess association or causality
2. Case series, prospective	A group of children eating ice cream are examined later for AOM	Measures incidence of AOM after ice cream consumption; cannot assess association or causality
3. Cross-sectional study	A group of children are examined for AOM and simultaneously asked about recent ice cream consumption	Measures prevalence of AOM and ice cream consumption and their association; cannot assess causality
4. Case-control study	A group of children with AOM and a group without AOM are asked about recent ice cream consumption	Measures prevalence of ice cream consumption and association with AOM; limited ability to assess causality
5. Historic cohort study	A group of children who ate ice cream last week and a comparison group who did not are examined for AOM	Measures incidence of AOM and association with ice cream consumption; can assess causality, if adjusted for confounding variables
6. Cohort study (longitudinal)	A group of children about to eat ice cream and an ice cream–free comparison group are examined later to see if AOM develops	Measures incidence of AOM and association with ice cream consumption can assess causality, if adjusted for confounding variables
7. Randomized controlled trial	A group of children are randomly assigned to have ice cream or no ice cream and are examined later to see if AOM develops	Measures incidence of AOM and association with ice cream consumption; can assess causality despite baseline confounding variables

AOM = acute otitis media

*Studies are listed in order of increasing ability to establish causal relationship.

Table 2-8 Measurement Scales for Describing and Analyzing Data

Scale	Definition	Examples
Dichotomous	Classification into either of two mutually exclusive categories	Breast feeding (yes/no), gender (male/female)
Nominal	Classification into unordered qualitative categories	Race, religion, country of origin
Ordinal	Classification into ordered qualitative categories but with no natural (numeric) distance between their possible values	Hearing loss (none, mild, moderate), patient satisfaction (low, medium, high), age group
Numeric	Measurements with a continuous scale or a large number of discrete ordered values	Temperature, age in years, hearing level in decibels
Numeric (censored)	Measurements on subjects lost to follow-up or in whom a specified event has not yet occurred at the end of a study	Survival rate, recurrence rate, or any time-to-event outcome in a prospective study

Table 2-9 Descriptive Statistics

Descriptive Measure	Definition	When to Use It
Central Tendency		
Mean	Arithmetic average	Numeric data that are symmetric
Median	Middle observation; half the values are smaller, and half are larger	Ordinal data; numeric data with an asymmetric distribution
Mode	Most frequent value	Nominal data; bimodal distribution
Dispersion		
Range	Largest value minus smallest value	Emphasizes extreme values
Standard deviation	Spread of data about their mean	Numeric data that are symmetric
Percentile	Percentage of values that are equal to or below that number	Ordinal data; numeric data with an asymmetric distribution
Interquartile range	Difference between the 25th percentile and 75th percentile	Ordinal data; numeric data with an asymmetric distribution
Outcome		
Survival rate	Proportion of subjects surviving, or with some other outcome, after a time interval (1 year, 5 year, etc)	Numeric (censored) data in a prospective study
Odds ratio	Odds of a disease or outcome in subjects with a risk factor divided by odds in controls	Dichotomous data in a retrospective or prospective controlled study
Relative risk	Incidence of a disease or outcome in subjects with a risk factor divided by incidence in controls	Dichotomous data in a prospective controlled study
Rate difference*	Event rate in treatment group minus event rate in control group	Compares success or failure rates in clinical trial groups
Correlation coefficient	Degree to which two variables have a linear relationship	Numeric or ordinal data

*Also called the absolute risk reduction.

yet had the outcome when the study ends. Interpreting censored data is called *survival analysis* because of its use in cancer studies, where survival is the outcome of interest. Survival analysis permits full use of censored observations, by including them in the analysis up to the time the censoring occurred. If censored observations are instead excluded from analysis (eg, exclude all patients with less than 1 year follow-up), the resulting survival rates will be biased and the sample size will be unnecessarily reduced.

Nominal and dichotomous data (see Table 2-8) are best described using ratios, proportions, and rates. A ratio is the value obtained by dividing one quantity by another, both of which are separate and distinct. In an OM treatment study, for example, the ratio of children with clinical resolution after 10 days to those remaining symptomatic might be 80/20 or 4:1. In contrast, a proportion is a type of ratio in which the numerator is included in the denominator. In the previously mentioned study, the proportion with clinical resolution would be 80/100 or 0.80. Alternatively, this could be multiplied by 100 and expressed as a percentage (80%).

Rates are similar to proportions except that a multiplier is used (eg, 1,000 or 100,000), and they are computed over time. For example, a study might report a rate of 110 physician office visits per 100 children. Incidence density is a special form of rate that describes incidence (new events) over a person-time interval. Recurrent OM is often reported as incidence density (see Chapter 13, "Clinical Efficacy of Medical Therapy"), in terms of episodes per child-month or episodes per child-year. For example, an intervention that prevented 0.10 episodes of AOM per child-month would require treating one child for 10 months, or 10 children for 1 month, to prevent a single ear infection.

The odds ratio, relative risk, and rate difference (see Table 2-9) are useful for comparing two groups of dichotomous data.[21] A study of OM and ice cream might report an *odds ratio* of 1.6, indicating that a child who developed OM was 1.6 times more likely to have eaten ice cream than a child with healthy ears. In contrast, a *relative risk* of 1.6 means that the incidence of OM was 1.6 times higher in children who ate ice cream versus controls who did not. Because the relative risk measures incidence, it should be used only in prospective (cohort) studies. When the frequency of events is low, however, the relative risk and odds ratio are nearly equivalent. An odds ratio or relative risk approaching unity (1.0) would suggest no association between ice cream consumption and OM.

The *rate difference* (also called risk reduction) may be expressed in absolute or relative terms. Suppose that OM develops in 20% (A) of ice cream eaters and 10% (B) of controls. The *absolute* rate difference, A − B, between groups is only 10%, but the *relative* rate difference, (A − B) / B, is 100%. As a measure of clinical importance, the absolute rate difference is preferred because it is easier to interpret and takes into account the baseline risk. Relative rate differences can be deceptive, especially when event rates are low. A new antibiotic may be touted as causing 75% less gastric upset than an established standard (relative rate difference), but we are less likely to be impressed if rates decreased from 1% to 0.25% (absolute rate difference of only 0.75%).

Two groups of ordinal or numeric data are compared with a *correlation coefficient* (see Table 2-9). A coefficient (r) from 0 to .24 indicates little or no relationship, from .25 to .49 a fair relationship, from .50 to .74 a moderate to good relationship, and greater than .75 a good to excellent relationship. A perfect linear relationship would yield a coefficient of 1. When one variable varies directly with the other, the coefficient is positive; a negative coefficient implies an inverse association. Sometimes the correlation coefficient is squared (R^2) to form the *coefficient of determination,* which estimates the percentage of variability in one measure that is predicted by the other. For example, if hearing levels show an excellent correlation with duration of middle ear fluid (r = .80), then we could predict 64% (R^2) of the variability in hearing levels by knowing the fluid duration.

Analytic Statistics

A single medical study with several groups treated differently will almost always show some difference in group outcomes. If we conclude the groups are different, we may be mistaking chance variations for treatment effects. If we conclude the groups are equivalent, we may have missed a true difference.[22] In statistical lingo (Table 2-10), we begin with some testable *hypothesis* about the groups under study, such as "Gibberish levels in group A differ from those in group B." Rather than keep it simple, we now invert this to form a *null hypothesis*: "Gibberish levels in group A are equal to those in group B." Next, we fire up a computer, enter the gibberish levels for the subjects in both groups, choose an appropriate statistical test, and wait for the omnipotent *p* value to emerge.

The *p value* tells us the probability of making a *type I error*: rejecting a true null hypothesis. In other words, if p = .10 we have a 10% chance of being wrong (false positive) when we declare that group A differs from group B. Alternatively, there is a 10% probability that the difference in gibberish levels is explainable by random error—we cannot be certain that uncertainty is not the cause. Uncertainty is present in all data because of the inherent variability in biologic systems and our ability to assess them in a reproducible fashion. Since we can never avoid uncertainty entirely in measurements and observations,

Table 2-10 Glossary of Statistical Terms Encountered When Testing Hypotheses

Term	Definition
Hypothesis	A supposition, arrived at from observation or reflection, that leads to predictions that can be tested and refuted
Null hypothesis	Results observed in a study, experiment, or test are no different from what might have occurred due to chance alone
Statistical test	Procedure used to reject or accept a null hypothesis; statistical tests may be parametric or nonparametric (distribution-free)
Type I (alpha) error	Rejecting a true null hypothesis (false-positive error); declaring that a difference exists when, in fact, it does not
p value	Probability of making a type I error; $p < .05$ indicates a statistically significant result that is unlikely to be cause by chance
Type II (beta) error	Accepting a false null hypothesis (false-negative error); declaring that a difference does not exist when, in fact, it does
Power	Probability that the null hypothesis will be rejected if it is, indeed, false; mathematically, power is 1 minus type II error

we instead estimate the probability (p value) that observed results are consistent with unavoidable random variations or fluctuations.

In medicine, $p < .05$ is generally considered low enough to safely reject the null hypothesis. Conversely, when $p > .05$, we accept the null hypothesis of equivalent gibberish levels. Nonetheless, we may be making a *type II error* by accepting a false null hypothesis (false negative). For example, the gibberish levels may really be different, but we studied too few subjects to have a reasonable chance of overcoming the random fluctuations that inevitably exist. Rather than state the probability of a type II error directly, we state it indirectly by specifying *power* (see Table 2-10). Power of 80% or greater is sufficient to be reasonably certain that a true difference was not overlooked.

As an example of statistical inference, consider a prospective study of 40 children to find out if ice cream causes OM. Suppose that OM develops in 80% of ice cream eaters (16 of 20) but in only 50% of controls (10 of 20), producing an absolute rate difference of 30% (80 minus 50). If we infer that on the basis of these results in 40 specific patients, ice cream causes OM *in general*, what is our probability of being wrong (type I error)? Because $p = .10$ (Fisher's exact test) there is a 10% chance of type I error, so we are reluctant to associate ice cream with OM on the basis of this single study.

Intuitively, however, a rate difference of 30% seems meaningful, so what is our chance of being wrong when concluding it is not? The probability of a type II error is 48% (same as saying 52% power), which means we may, indeed, be wrong in accepting the null hypothesis.[23]

Our study was flawed: the sample size of 40 children was too small to detect a meaningful difference (if, indeed, it existed) and too small exclude a real difference (assuming the groups were truly different). Now, suppose we repeat this study with twice as many children, and OM again develops in 80% of ice cream eaters (32 of 40) and 50% of controls (20 of 40). The rate difference is still 30%, but now $p = .01$. Increasing the number of children studied allowed us to exclude chance variations as being responsible for the observed findings.

Studies with "negative" findings should be interpreted by their statistical power, not by p values. There is a big difference between *observing* nothing in a study and *proving* that nothing really happened.[24] Most often, not enough patients were studied to offer a reasonable chance of not missing differences of up to 50% between groups.[25] Calculating sample size before beginning a study ensures that the planned number of observations will offer a reasonable chance (power) of obtaining a clear answer at the end.[26,27] The basic ingredients needed to calculate sample size include the smallest difference that must be detected between the groups, the variability (standard deviation) of this difference (if the measurement scale is numeric), the limit of tolerance for a type I error (typically 5% or 1%), and the limit of tolerance for a type II error (typically 20% or 10%).[28,29]

Statistical Significance versus Clinical Importance

The next logical question after "Is there a difference?" (statistical significance) is: "How big a difference is there?" (*clinical significance*). For example, a randomized trial of nonsevere AOM found amoxicillin superior to placebo as initial treatment ($p = .009$).[30] Before we accept the authors' recommendation for routine amoxicillin therapy, let us look more closely at the magnitude of clinical effect. Initial treatment success occurred in 96% of amoxicillin-treated children versus 92% of controls, yielding a 4% rate difference (96% to 92%) favoring drug therapy. Is this clinically important? Although statistically significant, the rate difference seems small; intuitively, we suspect that many children will need treatment to benefit only a few. The next few paragraphs reveal exactly how many.

Statistically significant results must be accompanied by a measure of *effect size*, which reflects the magnitude of difference between groups.[31] Otherwise, findings with minimal clinical importance may become statistically significant when a large number of subjects are studied. In the above example, the 4% difference in success rates was highly statistically significant because over 1,000 episodes of OM were analyzed. Large numbers provide high precision (repeatability), which, in turn, reduces the likelihood of a type I error. The final result is a hypnotically tiny *p* value, which may reflect a clinical difference of trivial importance. A *p* value of .000001 with a rate difference of 5% is much less clinically relevant than a *p* value of .01 with an absolute rate difference of 25%.

A highly useful measure of effect size is the *number needed to be treated* (NNT), which is simply the reciprocal of the absolute rate difference (or risk reduction).[31] The NNT reflects the amount of clinical effort that must be expended to achieve one additional treatment success and is easily calculated by dividing 100 by the absolute rate difference. For example, in the study cited above, the NNT would be 25 (100% divided by 4%). Consequently, we must treat 25 children, on average, with amoxicillin to increase the resolution rate of nonsevere AOM by one child above what would occur from placebo alone. Because we cannot predict with certainty which one of the 25 children will benefit, we must treat all 25 patients.

The NNT can also be used to estimate the magnitude of effort needed to prevent one adverse event. For example, a population-based review[32] found mastoiditis rates of about 4 per 100,000 person-years (py) in countries with restrictive antibiotic use for AOM versus 2 per 100,000 py in countries with liberal policies. Although the relative reduction is 50%, the absolute risk reduction from liberal antibiotics is only 2 per 100,000 py, or 0.002%. The authors note an NNT of 2,500 antibiotics to prevent one mastoiditis. Liberal treatment would yield 7,800 additional antibiotic prescriptions per 100,000 py, with about 1,600 adverse drug reactions (allergic and gastrointestinal). The purpose herein is not to judge antibiotic prescribing policies but to encourage evidence-based decisions using NNTs.

What constitutes an important NNT magnitude depends on disease severity and treatment side effects. An NNT of 25 might be extremely important in cancer therapy but less exciting in AOM management. Further, if the treatment had relatively minor side effects, we might be willing to accept a higher NNT to justify its routine use. Antimicrobial therapy is presently considered optional therapy for otitis media with effusion (OME) because systematic reviews suggest a relatively modest NNT of 7.

Relative measures of effect size (relative risk, odds ratio, relative rate difference) provide limited information in clinical trials because they do not reflect changes in baseline risk. For example, a relative risk of 50% may mean that the treatment decreases the chance of an unfavorable outcome from 4 to 2% or from 60 to 30%. Conversely, the absolute rate difference and NNT reflect both the baseline risk and degree of relative risk reduction. In the AOM trial above,[30] the absolute decrease in treatment failures because of amoxicillin therapy was only 4% using the rate difference but an impressive 50% using the relative risk! Not surprisingly, most clinicians rate the effectiveness of an intervention lower when presented in absolute terms, rather than using relative measures.[33] Since published trials rarely provide an NNT or rate difference, readers will often have to calculate it on their own on the basis of the absolute difference in group outcomes.[34]

Question 3: Are the Results Valid within the Study?

A measurement is valid if it is unbiased (free of systematic error) and reflects what it is intended to measure. For example, an audiometer that is not properly calibrated may consistently give readings that are off by 15 decibels. The readings are precise (repeatable) but inaccurate (biased). Scrutinize the article's methods section to be sure that means for diagnosing disease, documenting therapy, and recording outcome are valid. Was an algorithm or test of known sensitivity and specificity used to document middle ear effusion? Were measures employed to document compliance with intended therapy? Are the outcome measures clear and meaningful? Do surveys or questionnaires have psychometric validity? If any of the above are in question, so is the validity of the results.

A study has *internal validity* when the design is appropriate for the area of investigation, the measurements are valid, and the data are analyzed with appropriate statistical test(s). Elements of design have been previously discussed (see Tables 2-3 to 2-6) and will not be repeated here. All statistical tests have a common purpose (to measure error), which cannot be fulfilled unless the right

Table 2-11 Statistical Tests for Independent Samples

Situation	Parametric Test	Nonparametric Test
Comparing Two Groups of Data		
Numeric scale	t-test	Mann-Whitney U,* median test
Numeric (censored) scale	Mantel-Haenszel life table	Wilcoxon, log-rank, Mantel-Cox
Ordinal scale	—	Mann-Whitney U,* median test, chi-square test for trend
Nominal scale	—	Chi-square, log-likelihood ratio
Dichotomous scale	—	Chi-squared, Fisher's exact test, odds ratio, relative risk
Comparing Three or More Groups of Data		
Numeric scale	One-way ANOVA	Kruskal-Wallis ANOVA
Ordinal scale	—	Kruskal-Wallis ANOVA, chi-square test for trend
Dichotomous or nominal scale	—	Chi-square, log-likelihood ratio
Associating an Outcome with Predictor Variables		
Numeric outcome, 1 predictor	Pearson correlation	Spearman rank correlation
Numeric outcome, 2 or more predictor variables	Multiple linear regression, Two-way ANOVA	—
Numeric (censored) outcome	Proportional hazards (Cox) regression	—
Dichotomous outcome	Discriminant analysis	Multiple logistic regression
Nominal or ordinal outcome	Discriminant analysis	Log-linear model

ANOVA = analysis of variance.
*The Mann-Whitney U test is equivalent to the Wilcoxon rank-sum test.

test is used for the data being analyzed. To determine if the right statistical test was used you must first check (1) whether the observations come from independent or related samples, (2) whether the purpose is to compare groups or to associate an outcome with one or more predictor variables, and (3) the measurement scale of the variables. Tables 2-11 and 2-12 can then be used to find the right statistical test for valid analysis.

Two events are independent if the occurrence of one is in no way predictable from the occurrence of the other. A common example of *independent samples* is two or more parallel (concurrent) groups in a clinical trial or observational study. Conversely, *related samples* include paired organ studies, subjects matched by age and gender, and repeated measures on the same subjects (eg, before and after treatment). Sometimes the situation is unclear, as when ears (not patients) are the unit of analysis. Although each ear is a separate entity, they share common parameters, such as Eustachian tube function, nasopharynx microflora, and host immune

system. Therefore, to analyze ears as independent samples (which often occurs to inflate sample size) may severely bias results.

The tests in Tables 2-11 and 2-12 labeled as "parametric" assume an underlying symmetric distribution for the data or a relatively large sample size (about 20 or more observations per group). If the data are sparse, asymmetric, or ordinal, then a "nonparametric" test must be used. Nonparametric tests rank the observations in order of magnitude and then compare the ranks, not the measurements themselves. Nonparametric tests are often called "distribution-free" tests because they may be applied to skewed or asymmetric data.

Here are some brief examples to illustrate statistical test selection. Assume we are comparing patient satisfaction for two different OM treatments using a four-point outcome scale (poor, fair, good, excellent). According to Table 2-11, the correct test for two groups of independent ordinal data is the Mann-Whitney U test (Wilcoxon rank sum is equivalent). If the inves-

Table 2-12 Statistical Tests for Related (Matched, Paired, or Repeated) Samples

Situation	Parametric Test	Nonparametric Test
Comparing Two Groups of Data		
Dichotomous scale	—	McNemar test,
Ordinal scale	—	Sign test, Wilcoxon signed rank test
Numeric scale	Paired *t*-test	Sign test, Wilcoxon signed rank test
Comparing Three or More Groups of Data		
Dichotomous scale	—	Cochran Q test, Mantel-Haenszel chi-square
Ordinal scale	—	Friedman ANOVA
Numeric scale	Repeated measures ANOVA	Friedman ANOVA

ANOVA = analysis of variance.

tigators instead used a *t*-test, results might be invalid. Now, suppose we wish to compare hearing levels (numeric scale) before and after tympanostomy tubes for 50 children with OME. Using Table 2-12 (we are dealing with a matched sample), we note that a paired *t*-test or Wilcoxon signed rank test could be used. Finally, if we wanted to associate time until tympanostomy tube extrusion (a censored outcome) with several predictor variables (eg, type of tube, tube location, child age) we would use proportional hazards (Cox) regression (see Table 2-11).

Proper selection of statistical tests can never compensate for flaws in study design. Suppose we measure intelligence quotient (IQ) in 200 children before and after tympanostomy tubes and find a mean IQ increase of 10 points per child. We *can* conclude that the improvement is unlikely to be fortuitous ($p = .01$, matched *t*-test), but we *cannot* be certain as to what caused it. Stated differently, improvement *after* surgery (or any intervention) does not necessarily imply improvement *because* of surgery. More likely the change in IQ was not a real increase but a bias caused by learning from the first test. Without a control group, we cannot determine what part of the change (if any) was caused by the tubes.

A fundamental assumption underlying all statistical tests is that the hypothesis under study was fully developed before the data were examined in any way. When hypotheses are formulated *post hoc*—after even the briefest glance at the data—the basis for probability statements is invalidated. Consider, for example, the Texas sharpshooter who shoots an arrow at a barn wall, then meticulously draws a bulls eye around it. When his friends later arrive, they applaud his incredible accuracy. Similarly, we have no way of knowing at which stage of the research process a hypothesis was

developed. Data that are tortured sufficiently will eventually confess to something—for example, a post hoc hypothesis is born.

Question 4: Are the Results Valid outside the Study?

Having first determined that the investigator's conclusions correctly describe what happened inside the study (question 3), the next task is to determine if they can be applied (generalized) to the universe outside the study. Unfortunately, not all well-conducted, internally valid studies have external validity (generalizability or applicability). This distinction is nontrivial because the key question from the clinician's viewpoint is: "Can I apply the results of this study to the patients I see in my practice?" For the answer to be "yes," the sampling method must be sound, the subjects studied must be representative of the target population, and the sample size must be large enough for adequate precision.

Sampling a Population

When we interpret medical data, we ultimately seek to make inferences about some target population on the basis of the results in a smaller study sample (Table 2-13). Rarely is it possible to study every subject with the condition of interest. Nor is it necessary—statistics allow us to generalize from the few to the many, provided that the few *represent* the many. However, representative samples rarely arise from divine providence. Review carefully the inclusion and exclusion criteria (check the article's methods section) to be sure that the subjects studied are representative of those in whom you wish to apply the results. A study with vague subject selection criteria may yield fascinating results, but we have no way of knowing to whom they apply.

Table 2-13 Glossary of Statistical Terms Related to Sampling and Validity

Term	Definition
Target population	Entire collection of items, subjects, patients, observations, etc, about which we want to make inferences; defined by the selection criteria (inclusion and exclusion criteria) for the study
Accessible population	Subset of the target population that is accessible for study, generally because of geographic or temporal considerations
Study sample	Subset of the accessible population that is chosen for study
Sampling method	Process of choosing the study sample from the larger accessible population
Selection bias	Error caused by systematic differences between a study sample and target population; examples include studies on volunteers and those conducted in clinics or tertiary care settings
Internal study validity	Degree to which conclusions drawn from a study are valid for the study sample; results from proper study design, unbiased measurements, and sound statistical analysis
External study validity (generalizability)	Degree to which conclusions drawn from a study are valid for a target population (beyond the subjects in the study); results from representative sampling and appropriate selection criteria

Consider, for example, a new antibiotic with 96% efficacy for AOM after 4 to 6 days.[35] Will 96% of your patients respond similarly if you use the drug? Yes, if you select patients and judge outcomes the same way the investigators did. Of 521 children enrolled in the study above, 166 were immediately excluded because no pathogens were isolated on tympanocentesis and 175 were excluded later because their second tympanocentesis (day 4 to 6) was not evaluable. The remaining 180 children (35% of the initial sample) were used to judge bacteriologic efficacy. Since most clinicians do not restrict their AOM practice to children with proven bacterial pathogens and double tympanocentesis, the 96% success rate may not be generalizable. Moreover, most clinicians judge outcomes by clinical efficacy (relief of signs and symptoms), not bacteriologic efficacy (sterilization of MEE). Nonetheless, the study provides important data about the value of the new antibiotic in children with specific or resistant pathogens.

Here is another example. In a randomized trial of early versus delayed insertion of tympanostomy tubes for persistent OM, the authors concluded that early tube insertion did not improve developmental outcomes at 3 years of age.[36] To whom do these results apply? The 429 randomized children with persistent effusion were culled from a birth cohort of 6,350 healthy infants examined at least monthly for 3 years; if not included in the study, many of these children would never have received tubes because their MEE was transient, asymptomatic, or unilateral. In contrast, study participants received tubes solely on the basis of cumulative MEE prevalence (identified with regular, intensive screening), not on that of hearing levels or other OM signs and symptoms. Therefore, the ability to generalize these results beyond asymptomatic, otherwise healthy infants identified with aggressive surveillance is unknown.

Having determined that the target population and subject selection criteria are meaningful, the next step in judging external validity is to assess how the study sample was selected. Investigators typically have access to only a small subset of the target population because of geographic, temporal, or demographic constraints. When they choose an even smaller subset of this *accessible population* to study (see Table 2-13), the method of choosing (sampling method) affects their ability to make inferences about the original target population. Unless an appropriate sampling method is used, the study sample may differ systematically from the intended target population (selection bias).

The best sampling method is to randomly select members of the accessible population. Bias is minimized because all subjects have a known (and equal) probability of selection, but random sampling is rarely feasible in most clinical research studies. Fortunately, a consecutive or systematic sample offers a relatively good approximation. Consecutive samples are common and include all subjects over a specified time interval or until a specified sample size is reached. Systematic samples are obtained using some simple, systematic rule, such as day of the week, date of birth, or first letter of the last name. The worst sampling method occurs when subjects are chosen by the investigators on the basis of convenience or subjective judgments about eligibility. Convenience (grab) sampling should be assumed to have taken place when no other method is specified.

Random allocation of patients to treatment groups differs from random sampling of a population. Randomization improves internal validity by reducing allocation bias (see Table 2-5) but has no impact on external validity. If a randomized trial reports a beneficial impact of adenoidectomy on OM, we can be relatively sure that this effect was not caused by overt (or covert) allocation of children with a better prognosis to the surgical group (if the randomization scheme was sound). Conversely, we are limited in our ability to generalize this result if the study excluded children with cleft palate, Down syndrome, immune deficiency, age less than 4 years, and prior tympanostomy tubes. Unfortunately, the children excluded from study are the ones most likely to have severe OM.

Precision and Confidence Intervals

Another component of external validity is *precision*, which reflects the degree of variability in the observations. Variability must be dealt with when interpreting data, unless the results are meant to apply only to the particular group of patients, animals, cell cultures, deoxyribonucleic acid strands, and so on, in which the observations were initially made. Recognizing this limitation, we call each of the descriptive measures in Table 2-9 a *point estimate*, specific to the data that generated it. In medicine, however, we seek to pass from observations to generalizations, from point estimates to estimates about other populations. When this process occurs with calculated degrees of uncertainty, we call it *inference*.

Here is a brief example of clinical inference. After administering vitamin C to 5 children with AOM, you remark to a colleague that 4 had excellent relief. She asks, "How confident are you of your results, ignoring for the moment the possibility of a placebo response?" "Quite confident," you reply, "there were 5 patients, 4 got better, and that's 80%." "Maybe I wasn't clear," she interjects, "how confident are you that 80% of children with AOM you see in the next few weeks will respond favorably, or that 80% of similar children in my practice will do well with vitamin C?" "In other words," she continues, "can you *infer* anything about the real effect of vitamin C on AOM from only 5 patients?" Hesitatingly you retort "I'm pretty confident about that number 80%, but maybe, I'll have to see a few more patients to be sure."

The real issue, of course, is that a sample of only 5 patients offers low *precision* (repeatability). How likely is it that the same results would be found if 5 new patients were studied? Actually, we can state with 95% confidence that 4 successes out of 5 in a *single* trial is consistent with a range of results from 28 to 99% in *future* trials. This *95% confidence interval* (CI) may be calculated manually or with a statistical program[27,37–39] and tells us the range of results consistent with the observed data. Thus, if this trial were repeated, we could obtain a success rate as low as 28%, not very encouraging compared with the original point estimate of 80%. To make an analogy to a mutual fund prospectus, past performance is no guarantee of future results.

Precision may be increased (uncertainty may be decreased) by using a more reproducible measure, by increasing the number of observations (sample size), or by decreasing the variability among the observations. The most common method is to increase the sample size because we can rarely reduce the variability inherent in the subjects we study. If 50 children (instead of 5) received vitamin C and 40 had resolution of AOM, the 95% CI for success narrows to between 66 and 90%. The point estimate, however, remains 80% (40 of 50). Although we are more confident in our results following this larger trial, we cannot say anything about the *efficacy* of vitamin C without an untreated control group for comparison.

Realizing that uncertainty can never be completely avoided, we use statistics to estimate precision. Thus, when data are described using the summary measures listed in Table 2-9 (odds ratio, relative risk, rate difference, correlation coefficient), a corresponding 95% CI should accompany each point estimate.[37] When the study reports "positive" findings ($p < .05$), the *lower* limit of the interval should be scrutinized; if it is less than what you consider to be a clinically important effect size, then precision is inadequate. When the study reports "negative" findings ($p > .05$), the *upper* limit of the interval should be checked; if it is consistent with a clinically important effect size, then statistical power is inadequate.

As an example of CI interpretation, consider an evidence report on AOM management. The Agency for Healthcare Research and Quality concluded that amoxicillin increased the absolute rate of AOM resolution by 12.3% over no placebo or no treatment (95% CI, 2.8, 21.8%).[40] Since the lower limit of the CI is 2.8%, which may not be clinically important, the precision is less than optimal. The 95% CI for the NNT is easily calculated (see above) as 4.6 to 35.7, which again shows that the results are consistent with the need to treat up to 36 children to benefit one. The findings suggest a significant benefit of antibiotics for some children with AOM (95% CI does not contain zero), but the imprecision and modest NNT argue for selective and judicious therapy.

Question 5: Are the Results Strong and Consistent?

A single study—no matter how elegant or seductive—is rarely definitive. Science is a cumulative process that requires a large body of consistent and reproducible evidence before conclusions can be formed.[41] When reading an exciting article, the cumulative basis of science is often overshadowed by the seemingly irrefutable evidence at hand—at least until a new study, by different investigators in a different environment, adds a new twist.

The first step in assessing strength and consistency is asking, "Do the results make sense?" Significant findings that are biologically implausible or that are inconsistent with other known studies can often be explained by hidden biases or design flaws, which were not initially suspected. Improbable results can become statistically significant through biased data collection, natural history, placebo effects, unidentified confounding variables, or improper statistical analysis. A study with design flaws or improper statistical analysis has low internal validity and should be reanalyzed or discarded.

At the next level of integration, we compare the study design that produced the current data with the design of other published studies. The *level of evidence* generally increases as we progress from observational studies (case reports, case series) to controlled experiments (randomized trials).[42] For example, if several randomized efficacy trials have already been published about the topic of interest, an uncontrolled study is unlikely to provide any new insights. Conversely, for populations in which randomization is unethical, a well-designed cohort study may be the best attainable evidence.[43] When a certain level of evidence has been accumulated, causation may be inferred. *Causation* is an epidemiologic concept based on the consistency, strength, specificity, and temporal relationship of the association between a factor and a particular disease or its outcome.[44]

When assessing the level of evidence, readers must realize that certain study designs are more suited than others to answer specific clinical questions. *Therapy* questions, which seek to determine the effect of different treatments on outcomes, are best answered with randomized controlled trials. These trials are also ideal for questions about *harm*, but an observational study may have to suffice if randomized exposure is unethical or impractical. Questions about *diagnosis* are best answered using cross-sectional designs in which patients with and without the condition of interest undergo both the new diagnostic test and an established gold (criterion) standard. Last, *prognosis* questions are addressed by observing groups of patients with and those without baseline risk factors over time in a prospective cohort design.

Excellence in study design cannot substitute for consistency. Consider a randomized trial of Eustachian tube autoinflation for OME that suggests a novel device to be efficacious.[45] Enthusiasm for the product, however, must be tempered by inconsistency with other well-designed randomized trials suggesting no benefit to autoinflation.[46] In contrast, despite consistent randomized trials showing no impact of decongestants on OME resolution, they remain popular.[47] Why does this practice continue? Perhaps the consistent benefits suggested by the initial observational studies left a lasting impression (really placebo effect and regression to the mean), or the emotional appeal of "drying up the fluid" exceeds the logical conclusion of no benefit. As observed by the 19th century French satirist Anatole, "If 50 million people do a foolish thing, it is still a foolish thing."

Beware of the article's discussion section as a source of information on consistency and integration.[48] Efforts are rarely made to systematically describe evidence related to the investigators' own findings. Instead, anecdotal reporting of other work is often the norm. Moreover, a research paper rarely represents the full range of opinions of those scientists whose work it claims to report. Evidence exists of censored criticism; obscured views about the meaning of research findings; incomplete, confused, and sometimes biased assessment of the implications of a study; and frequent failure to indicate directions for future research. Use of a structure discussion has been proposed to circumvent these problems.[48]

The consistency of randomized controlled trials may also be assessed on a quantitative level with systematic review or meta-analysis.[49] The "bottom line" typically includes a summary measure of effect size (eg, rate difference), a 95% CI, and a statistical test for heterogeneity among source articles. The best systematic reviews include a comprehensive search for relevant articles and explicit criteria for rating relevance and merit. Only about 10% of controlled trials, however, make reference to relevant systematic reviews, and even fewer attempt to integrate the present results with an existing review, either qualitatively or quantitatively.[50] Consequently, the task of placing new results in the context of previous trials is again transferred to the reader.

FROM PRINCIPLES TO PRACTICE

Throughout this chapter, emphasis has been placed on fundamental *principles* of journal reading, rather than on specific *practices* that apply to only certain types of articles. These principles are listed in the last column of Table 2-2 and embody the broad concepts of EBM. Readers who take the time to master and apply these principles are well along the path to evidence mastery. Obviously, this chapter can serve only as a first step on what may become a life-long journey. Additional guidance can be found in the many superb

Table 2-14 Pointers and Pitfalls for Critical Appraisal of Journal Articles

1. The peer-reviewed medical literature generally serves science, not medical practice; critical appraisal is needed to locate clinically relevant and valid evidence.

2. Critical appraisal begins with the principles outlined in Tables 2-1 and 2-2, with emphasis on the magnitude, clinical relevance, and generalizability of the main results.

3. Articles about *therapy* should have random allocation of patients to comparison groups and clinically important outcome measures; beware if follow-up is less than 80%.

4. Articles about *diagnosis* should have clearly defined comparison groups (one without the disorder) and an objective or reproducible diagnostic ("gold") standard applied to all participants; beware if investigators are not masked (blinded) to test results.

5. Articles about *prognosis* should have an inception cohort early in the disorder and an objective or reproducible assessment of clinically important outcomes; beware if follow-up is less than 80%.

6. Articles about *causation* should have a clearly identified comparison group for those at risk of, or having, the outcome of interest; beware if observers of outcome are not masked to exposure, or observers of exposure are not masked to outcome.

7. No amount of statistical wizardry can compensate for flawed study design and biased outcome assessment; save your intellectual energy for well-designed studies worthy of interpretation

principle-based books[1,7,51,52] and journal articles[53–56] that are readily available.

Interpretation of evidence-based literature requires knowledge of both principles and practices. The wide variety of descriptive measures and statistical tests in Tables 2-9, 2-11, and 2-12 apply only to certain specific situations (practices), but the rationale behind their selection and interpretation is similar (principles). Journal readers will find Last's *Dictionary of Epidemiology*[57] an invaluable guide to deciphering the endless practices encountered. A wonderful series of users' guides to the medical literature are also available for nearly any type of article, including clinical trials,[58] outcomes studies,[59,60] practice guidelines,[61,62] decision analysis,[63,64] diagnostic tests,[65,66] economic analysis,[67,68] and general health issues.[69–72] The complete set of users' guides has been updated and summarized in a single text.[1]

The journal reader who rarely ventures beyond an abstract often blames his or her timidity on the needless complexities of statistics and epidemiology. Hopefully, this chapter has made the subject matter less daunting and more palatable. Some key elements are summarized in Table 2-14, along with additional pointers on critical appraisal of the literature.[73]

ACKNOWLEDGMENT

I am indebted to R. Brian Haynes, MD, Ph.D, for his critical review of the first edition of this chapter and for his invaluable insights concerning the principles and practice of evidence-based medicine.

REFERENCES

1. Guyatt G, Rennie D, editors. Users' guides to the medical literature: a manual for evidence-based clinical practice. Chicago (IL): AMA Press; 2002.
2. Rennie D. Fourth international congress on peer review in biomedical publication. JAMA 2002;287:259–60.
3. Jefferson T, Alderson P, Wager E, Davidoff F. Effects of editorial peer review: a systematic review. JAMA 2002;287:2784–6.
4. Kassirer JP, Campion EW. Peer review: crude and understudied, but indispensable. JAMA 1994;272:96–7.
5. Haynes RB. Loose connections between peer-reviewed clinical journals and clinical practice. Ann Intern Med 1990;113:724–8.
6. Bero LA, Galbraith A, Rennie D. The publication of sponsored symposiums in medical journals. N Engl J Med 1992;327:1135–40.
7. Gehlbach SH. Interpreting the medical literature. 4th ed. Norwalk (CT): Appleton & Lange; 2002.
8. Rosenfeld RM. The seven habits of highly effective data users. Otolaryngol Head Neck Surg 1998;118:144–58.
9. Oxman AD, Sackett DL, Guyatt GH. Users' guides to the medical literature. I. How to get started. JAMA 1993; 270:2093–7.
10. Sackett DL. Bias in analytic research. J Chron Dis 1979;32:51–63.
11. Moses LE. The series of consecutive cases as a device for assessing outcome of intervention. N Engl J Med 1984;311:705–10.
12. Brody H. The placebo response: how you can release the body's inner pharmacy for better health. New York (NY): Cliff Street Books; 2000.
13. Novack DH. Therapeutic aspects of the clinical encounter. J Gen Intern Med 1987;2:346–55.

14. de Saintonge DMC, Herxheimer A. Harnessing placebo effects in health care. Lancet 1994;344:995–8.

15. Hart JT, Dieppe P. Caring effects. Lancet 1996;347: 1606–8.

16. Tasker A, Dettmar PW, Panetti M, et al. Reflux of gastric juice and glue ear in children. Lancet 2002; 359:493.

17. Feinstein AR. Fraud, distortion, delusion, and consensus: the problems of human and natural deception in epidemiologic science. Am J Med 1988;84:475–8.

18. Schulz KF, Chalmers I, Hayes RJ, Altman DG. Empirical evidence of bias. Dimensions of methodological quality associated with estimates of treatment effects in controlled trials. JAMA 1995;273:408–12.

19. Hollis S, Campbell F. What is meant by intention to treat analysis? Survey of published randomized controlled trials. BMJ 1999;319:670–4.

20. Altman DG, Schultz KF, Moher D, et al. The revised CONSORT statement for reporting randomized trials. Ann Intern Med 2001;134:663–94.

21. Brown GW. 2 x 2 tables. Am J Dis Child 1985;139:410–6.

22. Brown GW. Errors, types I and II. Am J Dis Child 1983;137:586–91.

23. Young MJ, Bresnitz EA, Strom BL. Sample size nomograms for interpreting negative clinical studies. Ann Intern Med 1983;99:248–51.

24. Schor S. Statistical proof in inconclusive "negative" trials. Arch Intern Med 1981;141:1263–4.

25. Freiman JA, Chalmers TC, Smith H, Kuebler RR. The importance of beta, the type II error, and sample size in the design and interpretation of the randomized controlled trial. Survey of two sets of "negative" trials. In: Bailar JC, Mosteller F, editors. Medical uses of statistics. 2nd ed. Boston (MA): NEJM Books; 1992. p. 357–74.

26. Florey C. Sample size for beginners. BMJ 1993;306:1181–4.

27. Brown GW. Sample size. Am J Dis Child 1988;142:1213–5.

28. Machin D, Campbell MJ, Fayers PM, Pinol APY. Sample size tables for clinical studies (book and software). 2nd ed. Oxford (UK): Blackwell Science Ltd; 1997.

29. Borenstein M, Rothstein H, Cohen J. Power and precision (user's manual and software). Englewood (NJ): Biostat Inc; 2001.

30. Kaleida PH, Casselbrant ML, Rockette HE, et al. Amoxicillin or myringotomy or both for acute otitis media: results of a randomized clinical trial. Pediatrics 1991;87:466–74.

31. Laupacis A, Sackett DL, Roberts RS. An assessment of clinically useful measures of the consequences of treatment. N Engl J Med 1988;318:1728–33.

32. Van Zuijlen DA, Schilder AGM, Van Balen FAM, Hoes AW. National differences in acute mastoiditis: relationship to prescribing patterns of antibiotics for acute otitis media. Pediatr Infect Dis J 2001;20:140–4.

33. Naylor CD, Chen E, Strauss B. Measured enthusiasm: does the method of reporting trial results alter perceptions of therapeutic effectiveness? Ann Intern Med 1992;117:916–21.

34. Nuovo J, Melnikow J, Chang D. Reporting number needed to treat and absolute risk reduction in randomized controlled trials. JAMA 2002;287:2813–4.

35. Dagan R, Hoberman A, Johnson C, et al. Bacteriologic and clinical efficacy of high dose amoxicillin/clavulanate in children with acute otitis media. Pediatr Infect Dis J 2001;20:829–37.

36. Paradise JL, Feldman HM, Campbell TF, et al. Effect of early or delayed insertion of tympanostomy tubes for persistent otitis media on developmental outcomes at the age of three years. N Engl J Med 2001;344:1179–87.

37. Thomas DG, Gart JJ. A table of exact confidence limits for differences and ratios of two proportions and their odds ratios. J Am Stat Assoc 1977;72:73–6.

38. Gardner MJ, Altman DG. Confidence intervals rather than p values: estimation rather than hypothesis testing. BMJ 1980;292:746–50.

39. Gustafson TL. TRUE EPISTAT reference manual. Richardson (TX): Epistat Services; 1994.

40. Takata GS, Chan LS, Ernst R, et al. Evidence report/technology assessment, No. 15. Management of acute otitis media. Rockville (MD): AHRQ Publication No. 00-E009, U.S. Department of Health and Human Services; 2000.

41. Light RJ, Pillemer DB. Summing up: the science of reviewing research. Cambridge (MA): Harvard University Press; 1984.

42. Oxford Centre for Evidence-Based Medicine. Levels of evidence and grades of recommendations. Available at: http://cebm.jr2.ox.ac.uk/docs/levels.html. (Accessed 2/2/02).

43. Shott SR, Joseph A, Heithaus D. Hearing loss in children with Down syndrome. Int J Pediatr Otorhinolaryngol 2001;61:199–205.

44. Hill AB. The environment and disease: association or causation. Proc R Soc Med 1965;58:295–300.

45. Stangerup SE, Sederberg-Olsen J, Balle V. Autoinflation as a treatment of secretory otitis media: a randomized controlled study. Arch Otolaryngol 1992;118:149–52.

46. Chan KH, Bluestone CD. Lack of efficacy of middle ear inflation: treatment of otitis media with effusion in children. Otolaryngol Head Neck Surg 1989;100:317–22.

47. Stool SE, Berg AO, Berman S, et al. Otitis media with effusion in young children. Clinical practice guideline, Number 12. AHCPR Publication No. 94-0622. Rockville (MD): Agency for Health Care Policy and Research, Public Health Service, U.S. Department of Health and Human Services; July 1994.

48. Horton R. The hidden research paper. JAMA 2002; 287:2775–8.

49. Rosenfeld RM. How to systematically review the medical literature. Otolaryngol Head Neck Surg 1996;115:53–63.

50. Clarke M, Alderson P, Chalmers I. Discussion sections in reports of controlled trials published in medical journals. JAMA 2002;287:2799–801.

51. Lang TA, Secic M. How to report statistics in medicine. Philadelphia (PA): American College of Physicians; 1997.

52. Dawson B, Trapp RG. Basic and clinical biostatistics. 3rd ed. New York (NY): McGaw-Hill Professional Publishing; 2000.

53. Guyatt G, Jaeschke R, Heddle N, et al. Basic statistics for clinicians: 1. Hypothesis testing. Can Med Assoc J 1995;152:27–32.

54. Guyatt G, Jaeshke R, Heddle N, et al. Basic statistics for clinicians: 2. Interpreting study results: confidence intervals. Can Med Assoc J 1995;152:169–73.

55. Jaeschke R, Guyatt G, Shannon H, et al. Basic statistics for clinicians: 3. Assessing the effects of treatment: measures of association. Can Med Assoc J 1995;152:351–7.

56. Guyatt G, Walter S, Shannon H, et al. Basic statistics for clinicians: 4. Correlation and regression. Can Med Assoc J 1995;152:497–504.

57. Last JM, editor. A dictionary of epidemiology. 4th ed. New York (NY): Oxford University Press; 2000.

58. Dans AL, Dans LF, Guyatt GH, Richardson S. User's guides to the medical literature: XIV. How to decide on the applicability of clinical trial results to your patient. JAMA 1998;279:545–9.

59. Naylor CD, Guyatt GH. Users' guides to the medical literature. X. How to use an article reporting variations in the outcomes of health services. JAMA 1996;275:554–8.

60. Guyatt GH, Naylor CD, Juniper E, et al. Users' guides to the medical literature. XII. How to use articles about health-related quality of life. JAMA 1997;277:1232–7.

61. Hayward RS, Wilson MC, Tunis SR, et al. Users' guides to the medical literature. VIII. How to use clinical practice guidelines. A. Are the recommendations valid? JAMA 1995;274:570–4.

62. Wilson MC, Hayward RS, Tunis SR, et al. Users' guides to the medical literature. VIII. How to use clinical practice guidelines. B. What are the recommendations, and will they help you in caring for your patients? JAMA 1995;274:1630–2.

63. Richardson WS, Detsky AS. Users' guides to the medical literature. VII. How to use a clinical decision analysis. A. Are the results of the study valid? JAMA 1995;273:1292–5.

64. Richardson WS, Detsky AS. Users' guides to the medical literature. VII. How to use a clinical decision analysis. B. What are the results, and will they help me in caring for my patients? JAMA 1995;273:1610–3.

65. Jaeschke R, Guyatt G, Sackett DL. Users' guides to the medical literature. III. How to use an article about a diagnostic test. A. Are the results of the study valid? JAMA 1994;271:389–91.

66. Jaeschke R, Guyatt GH, Sackett DL. Users' guides to the medical literature. III. How to use an article about a diagnostic test. B. What are the results and will they help me in caring for my patients? JAMA 1994;271:703–7.

67. Drummond MF, Richardson WS, O'Brien BJ, et al. Users' guides to the medical literature XIII. How to use an article on economic analysis of clinical practice. A. Are the results of the study valid? JAMA 1997;277:1552–7.

68. O'Brien BJ, Heyland D, Richardson WS, et al. Users' guides to the medical literature. XIII. How to use an article on economic analysis of clinical practice. B. What are the results and will they help me in caring for my patients? JAMA 1997;277:1802–6.

69. Guyatt GH, Sackett DL, Cook DJ. Users' guides to the medical literature. II. How to use an article about therapy or prevention. A. Are the results of the study valid? JAMA 1993;270:2598–601.

70. Guyatt GH, Sackett DL, Cook DJ. Users' guides to the medical literature. II. How to use an article about therapy or prevention. B. What were the results, and will they help me in caring for my patients? JAMA 1994;271:59–63.

71. Levine M. Walter S, Lee H, et al. Users' guides to the medical literature. IV. How to use an article about harm. JAMA 1994;271:1615–9.

72. Laupacis A, Wells G, Richardson WS, Tugwell P. Users' guides to the medical literature. V. How to use an article about prognosis. JAMA 1994;272:234–7.

73. Sackett DL, Richardson SR, Rosenberg W, Haynes RB. Evidence-based medicine: how to practice and teach EBM. London (UK): Churchill Livingstone; 1997.

CHAPTER 3

Design Considerations for Clinical Studies

Howard E. Rockette, PhD

An ounce of prevention is worth a pound of cure.
17th century English proverb

OBJECTIVES

On completing this chapter, the reader will
1. Know the general requirements of designing a research study in otitis media (OM).
2. Know the strengths and weaknesses of different study designs in the research literature.
3. Recognize pitfalls associated with poor study design.
4. Be able to select the appropriate design for their specific problem.
5. Have suitable references for additional information on specific types of designs.

The phase of conducting research known as *study design* attempts to provide an objective framework for conducting a clinical investigation. When conducting research, the investigator should seek to reduce or eliminate bias and quantify and reduce errors due to chance. An opportunity to achieve these goals occurs at the design phase of the study. Sophisticated statistical analysis cannot compensate for a poorly designed study. Designing a clinical study usually consists of the following steps:
1. Statement of an appropriate clinical question
2. Selection of the general study design
3. Formalization of the hypothesis
4. Development of data collection instruments
5. Specification of the method of statistical analysis
6. Sample size estimation
7. Outline of secondary analysis

The sound study design should provide a road map of the investigation from beginning to end.

BIAS AND PRECISION

The concepts of bias and precision are fundamental to understanding the general principles of study design. Most experiments attempt to reach conclusions about a specified group of individuals (study population) on the basis of data collected from a subgroup of those individuals (sample). The data from the sample should represent the study population, and the summary statistics from the sample should not differ widely from what would be observed in other samples taken from the same population under similar conditions. Similarity of the summary statistics from different samples is characterized by the repeatability or precision of the sampling procedure. The most common method of ensuring precision is to collect large samples.

Random collection of the sample will ensure it is representative; in studies where two populations are being compared, random allocation of individuals to the groups will eliminate potential bias due to differing patient characteristics. In some clinical studies, randomization is not practical or may be considered unethical. Although these nonrandomized studies may provide useful information, they must be scrutinized for biased conclusions resulting from the fact that the sample is not representative of the total population or that patient characteristics of two samples being compared are not the same.

STATING THE CLINICAL QUESTION

"The clinical researcher is one who investigates formal hypotheses arising from work in the clinic."[1] Although this quotation from Frei[1] was applied to the cancer clinical researcher, it is equally applicable to all clinical specialties. It implies that the clinical researcher must formulate questions of clinical interest in a format conducive to scientific investigation.

Clinically relevant estimates of outcomes should be provided in a clinical study, and it should have the potential for influencing future clinical practice. In research studies of OM, relevant clinical outcomes include
- middle ear status after treatment,
- percentage of time with middle ear effusion,
- number of episodes of acute otitis media (AOM),

- episodes of purulent otorrhea through a tympanostomy tube,
- hearing levels, and
- disease-specific and overall health-related quality of life.

Although many different clinical research questions may be posed, the focus of this chapter is on studies that investigate risk factors or that are designed to improve the management of disease.

The general clinical question must be refined when designing a study by incorporating the practical details involved in conducting it. The investigator must specify which subjects are eligible, describe exclusion criteria, define outcome and method of diagnosis, state the timing of follow-up visits, and describe the duration and intensity of treatment. The description should be sufficiently detailed so that it is clear which patients will be entered into the study and how they will be clinically managed. Such detail is particularly important in multicenter studies where there may be considerable variability in managing patients with the same disease.

SELECTING GENERAL STUDY DESIGNS

There are a variety of study designs the researcher can select from. Table 3-1 summarizes the characteristics, advantages, and disadvantages of different study designs. The nature of the data and availability of resources are major practical problems affecting selection of a study design. Several of these designs are discussed below.

Case Series

Cases of clinical interest are reported in a case series, but no sampling frame is provided, and the number of individuals in the population base the cases were selected from is not specified; the prevalence of the condition being studied can, therefore, not be estimated. Such studies are particularly useful for rare conditions and may lead to hypotheses for more rigorous studies. Church and Gerkin[2] found that in a case series of 14 children with fetal alcohol syndrome, 13 had histories of childhood hearing disorders. The authors suggest that learning disorders may be a previously unrecognized characteristic of fetal alcohol syndrome.

Medical Databases

With increased computerization of information, it is tempting to use existing databases to test hypotheses of clinical interest. These studies are relatively easy and inexpensive to conduct. The researcher using experimental data has control over the amount and format of the data to be collected and has specified the purpose for conducting the investigation in advance. This is not the case with existing medical databases, which are an example of observational data.

Inference from observational data can be problematic because of bias in the comparison groups, nonstandard definition of terms, and changes in definitions over time.[3] Since observational data usually have not been collected for scientific purposes in accordance with a well-defined a priori hypothesis, its overall quality (errors and/or missing information) is usually poorer than that of experimental data. For studies summarizing occurrence of events in a time interval, there may be the additional problem of identifying a common "time zero" for the individuals in the study.[4,5]

Bias between comparison groups is likely to be a more serious problem when evaluating treatment effects.[3–5] Conclusions drawn from observational data for this purpose are almost always questionable. Studies based on computerized databases may, however, provide interesting hypotheses to be tested in better-designed studies. They may also be useful for studies whose primary objective is identifying risk factors, because the bias is likely to be less than when evaluating treatment efficacy.

Cross-Sectional Study

The cross-sectional study is one of the simplest study designs. In this design, two variables are measured at a single point to determine if they are associated. For example, measurements of the hearing level and presence of effusion in children can be obtained during a routine visit to the doctor's office. The distribution of the hearing level in the case of ears with fluid can then be compared with the hearing level in the case of ears without fluid. Another example would be to determine the middle ear status of a child during a routine visit to the doctor's office and the number of smokers in the household to ascertain whether the proportion of children with effusion is higher in households with smokers. Cross-sectional studies have the advantage of being conducted at one point in time and do not require the effort and cost of obtaining follow-up information on patients. They are limited in determining some causal relationships, primarily by the lack of information on duration of conditions and their inability to demonstrate that the hypothesized precedent factor preceded the hypothesized outcome.

Case-Control Study

The case-control study is an important study design in epidemiology, which is particularly useful for studying rare diseases when a database of cases is available.[6,7] The case-control study is retrospective, because it identifies

Table 3-1 Advantages and Disadvantages of Selected Study Designs in Otitis Media

Study Design	Advantages	Disadvantages
Case study	Easy to conduct Useful in calling attention to rare cases May lead to more formal hypotheses in a more rigorous study	Primarily descriptive Cannot obtain prevalence rate May have a biased selection of cases
Medical databases	Relatively inexpensive Data often is already computerized	Study not designed to eliminate bias Often high rates of missing data or errors Definitions may change over time Difficulty in identifying "time zero"
Cross-sectional study	Requires no patient follow-up Efficient way of determining if two factors are associated	Missing temporal component Often weak evidence for cause and effect
Case-control study	Useful in studying a rare disease Requires less sample size than a prospective study Can be conducted in a short period of time	The cases may not be representative Estimates of prevalence cannot be obtained Subject to more biases than a prospective study
Prospective non-randomized study	Investigation is current with data collection providing opportunity to obtain high-quality data Factors precede outcome in time Opportunity to collect additional data targeted to research question	May be subject to bias due to nonrepresentativeness of study group or differences in patient characteristics in two groups being compared Usually requires a large amount of resources and a long time to conduct
Randomized trial	Eliminates potential bias due to differences in patient characteristics More believable—this is the accepted "gold standard" of clinical research Randomization is usually specified as a prerequisite for standard statistical tests	Costly to do, requires a long time Sometimes cannot be done for ethical reasons Those entering the study may not be representative of the clinical population
Nested case-control study	Well-defined population from which cases and controls are selected Permits investigation of risk factors not feasible to collect on large number of patients Estimates of prevalence and relative risk can be obtained	Requires much longer time than case-control study because prospective follow-up must be completed May not be feasible for rare diseases
Cross-over design	Each patient serves as their own control Usually requires less sample size than standard clinical trial	Presumes there are no "carryover effects" Inefficient if patients do not receive both treatments
Case cross-over study	Can be applied to relate intermittent risk factors to rare outcomes Each subject serves as their own control	Requires adequate records to identify intermittent risk factors May be difficult to identify the appropriate "control" time period
Matched-ear design	Each patient serves as their own control May require less sample size	Cannot be used unless the treatment is ear specific Requires bilateral disease

Table 3-1 Advantages and Disadvantages of Selected Study Designs in Otitis Media (continued)

Study Design	Advantages	Disadvantages
Equivalence studies	Provides a formal mechanism to declare treatments similar in outcome Provides a mechanism to replace older therapies with newer ones that are cheaper or have less side effects	Studies must be interpreted cautiously, because similarity of outcomes can result from poor compliance Approach is not as well established as usual hypothesis testing approach
Meta-analysis	Increases the sample size by combining across a large number of studies Attempts to include all studies on a topic, rather than a selected few Maybe representative of a broader clinical population than can be obtained in a single study	Subject to several types of bias May not lead to a well-defined clinical course of action Potential problems when combining non-randomized studies and/or studies of varying quality

individuals with different outcomes and compares prior (potentially causal) variables among the various outcome groups. In a case-control study[8] to investigate the effect of home environment air pollutants on OM, 125 children with two or more office visits for OM between October 1986 and May 1987 were identified as cases, and 237 randomly selected children seen during the same time interval for routine health maintenance were identified as controls. Information on household environmental conditions, including age of heating system, presence of air conditioning, cigarette smoking habits of household members, and type of cooking stove, was obtained by parental questionnaires. Environmental conditions were compared for cases and controls.

Case-control studies are subject to biases that are usually absent in a prospective study. The control group should be selected by the researcher with the intent that it is comparable with the case group for factors not being investigated, which may be related to both disease and the precedent factor being investigated. The researcher sometimes attempts to achieve comparability by matching on these factors. Common matching factors in OM research include age, gender, and socioeconomic status. Inadequate selection of the control group may bias the comparison in that a precedent factor appearing to be associated with disease outcome can result because the precedent factor is associated with other patient characteristics, which are distributed differently in the case and control groups. To better address this potential bias, researchers sometimes include several control groups in their design.

Another potential source of bias results from measuring the precedent factor. If it is determined by questionnaires, cases and controls may not recall the information with the same degree of accuracy, because the presence of the disease may alter the importance of prior events that subjects consider related to their

disease. Bias in case-control studies may also occur in more subtle ways, such as when precedent factors have an impact on disease diagnosis or when perceptions of the clinician affect the questions raised during the interview.[6] For example, if young male children were seen more frequently than females because of gender being a suspected risk factor for middle ear effusion, then the increased number of examinations may bias toward more identification of asymptomatic OM with effusion in males than in females.

Case-control studies are also limited by the fact that the population the cases were selected from is usually not well defined, meaning disease prevalence cannot be estimated. Similarly, the relative risk—that is, the ratio of the probability that those with the risk factor develop disease and the probability that those without the risk factor develop disease—cannot generally be estimated in case-control studies. Case-control studies typically use the odds ratio, an alternative measure of risk, as the primary summary index of disease. However, if the disease is rare, the odds ratio provides an approximation to the relative risk. Case-control studies that are constructed within a well-defined population or cohort eliminate some of the problems inherent in the design.

Despite its limitations, the case-control study provides an efficient, cost-effective method of testing a wide range of hypotheses. It may be the only practical method of studying precedent factors related to rare diseases.

Prospective Nonrandomized Study

Often, a group of individuals is monitored prospectively with the objective of relating selected factors of interest to disease outcome. In a study of 2,253 infants followed from birth to age 2 years, Paradise and colleagues[9] investigated the effects of gender, race, indices of socioeconomic status, birth weight, number of smokers in the household, and participation in day care on the proportion of days with middle ear effusion. Prospective studies have an advantage over retrospective study designs in that more effort can be made to have high-quality complete data. There is also clear documentation that the factors being investigated precede outcome. Because there is a well-defined population being followed, disease prevalence and relative risk can also be estimated.

The factors of interest in some prospective studies may include differing modalities of treatment. If the intent of a prospective study is evaluating treatment management, it is preferable to use a control group that is followed concurrently with the treated group (internal controls), rather than a control group that uses historic data or expectations obtained from the medical literature (external controls). Bailar and colleagues[10] discuss methods of improving the strength of externally controlled studies.

Even when concurrent controls are used in a prospective study, the failure to randomly allocate patients may result in differences in patient characteristics among treatment groups and a subsequent bias when evaluating treatment effect. Although statistical models that attempt to adjust for differences in patient characteristics are available, they are not an adequate substitute for randomization. In situations where randomization is not feasible, however, a prospective nonrandomized study often provides the best alternative.

Nested Case-Control Study

A nested case-control study is one that is embedded in a cohort or population-based registry.[11] It avoids many of the problems associated with a standard case-control study. Specifically, ascertainment of cases is usually more complete and less biased, and there is usually better information available on risk factors, because they can be obtained prospectively, rather than retrospectively. Because a population at risk is available, estimates of prevalence and relative risk can be obtained. Controls clearly have the same underlying population as the cases and can be randomly selected from the population at risk.

Typically, for a nested case-control study within a cohort, disease free controls are randomly selected from the subpopulation immediately prior to the time the case developed disease. Thus, a case could serve as their own control, and an individual who subsequently develops disease can serve as a control.[12] Selection of controls in this manner results in estimates of risk with desirable statistical properties. If risk factors vary or accumulate over time, they are evaluated only up to the time their corresponding case developed disease.

The smaller number of study subjects in a nested case-control study compared with a prospective study permits investigation of more detailed and expensive risk factors. Thus, precedent factors obtained from detailed medical histories or biologic markers become feasible to investigate. Palmu and colleagues[13] used a nested case-control design to study the association of negative pressure tympanograms occurring with OM with the type of bacteriologic pathogen present in the middle ear.

Randomized Trial

The randomized trial continues to be the "gold standard" among available study designs for comparing different treatment modalities.[14–16] In a randomized trial, patients are assigned to one of several treatment groups by a random mechanism and followed up prospectively. The randomization tends to avoid bias stemming from different patient characteristics in the two groups. Randomized trials are considered more credible; randomization is, in fact, the assumption required for most statistical procedures.

To further reduce the potential for bias, a blinded (masked) study should be conducted. In a double-blind trial, neither the patient nor the physician knows what treatment has been given to individual patients. When a drug is being compared with "no treatment," an inert pill indistinguishable from the active drug should be given to the patient to maintain the blinded nature of the trial; such a pill is called a "placebo." There are numerous examples of a "placebo effect" whereby patients who think they are receiving a potentially helpful drug do better than those receiving no treatment. The purpose of a placebo is to distinguish the pharmacologic effect of a drug from its psychological effect and to eliminate any patient or observer bias.[17]

Although the randomization process will balance a patient characteristic "on average" among treatment groups, sometimes, an investigator requires additional assurance that important factors will be balanced. In addition, there are planned subset analyses in some trials for which it is desirable that there be an equal number of patients in each treatment for the subgroups of interest. Stratification variables are factors where, by design, the number of patients receiving each treatment is balanced for each level of the factor. Zelen[18] discusses various methods of implementing randomization in clinical trials employing stratification variables.

The long completion time of many trials has raised the issue of conducting interim analyses. However, the investigator should be aware that without careful planning for interim analyses in clinical studies, there may be too many instances where the null hypothesis is falsely rejected.[19] In most present-day clinical trials, the timing and frequency of interim analysis is part of the study design. Various strategies have been suggested for interim evaluations of a study in order that the number of false rejections is adequately controlled.[15,16,20–22] A detailed discussion of the various methods is beyond the scope of this chapter, but it has been summarized in a recent book.[23] The usual clinical implication of ignoring appropriate methods of interim hypothesis testing is that a new therapy may be wrongly declared beneficial.

Analysis by the "intent-to-treat" principle is a clinically nonintuitive practice in planning analysis of randomized trials. This principle specifies that once randomized to a specific treatment regimen, a patient will be analyzed in that treatment group, even if the patient does not receive the assigned therapy or receives therapy appropriate for another treatment arm. The comparability of patient characteristics obtained by random assignment to treatment is preserved, otherwise there is no assurance that patients who refuse assigned therapy in a given treatment group have the same patient characteristics as patients who comply. The practice of analyzing by intent to treat may, however, result in considerable decrease in the ability to detect a difference in treatment, if there are even a modest number of patients who refuse therapy. Although many clinicians continue to question this practice, all randomized trials should include an analysis by intent to treat. Many medical journals state this in their statistical guidelines. Analysis by intent to treat does not preclude additional analyses where patients are grouped by the treatment they actually receive.

The randomized clinical trial does have some limitations:

- Execution and conduct of a large randomized clinical trial is expensive and time consuming, particularly if patients are recruited from multiple sites.
- Issues that often must be addressed in a large-scale trial include obtaining informed consent, developing study handbooks and manuals of operations, training data managers, selecting an external data monitoring committee, and data security and storage.
- If a large number of patients withdraw after randomization, which would result in unevaluable outcome measures, then analysis based on the evaluable patients could be biased.
- Overly restrictive eligibility criteria in a randomized trial may mean that conclusions are not generalizable to the clinical population.
- In some circumstances, ethical issues may preclude randomizing patients. Ethical concerns about the effects of randomization, blinding, and interim monitoring on the physician–patient relationship continue to be debated.[15,16,24–26]

Several comprehensive textbooks that address the practical, administrative, and ethical aspects of large-scale randomized trials in addition to the statistical issues are available.[16,27]

Crossover Trial

The crossover trial can provide an efficient alternative to other prospective designs, if the conditions for its use are satisfied. In the most common crossover trial, a patient receives two treatments in sequence. The order of treatment is randomly assigned, with some patients receiving one sequence and others receiving its reverse. The sequences are not of interest, and the objective is to study differences between the treatments that comprise the sequences. The advantage of such studies is that each patient serves as their own control, thus eliminating differences in patient characteristics that may exist in studies where different patients receive the two treatments. The sample size required is usually considerably reduced. Crossover trials could be considered in OM when comparing the effect of drug treatments given for short duration and when an immediate response is expected.

Crossover trials must be used cautiously. It may be difficult to separate treatment from time effects or from effects carried over from the previous treatment period.[28,29] Although the assumption of no carryover effect can be tested, there is usually low probability of detecting it with the sample sizes used in most studies. Furthermore, several authors have been critical of the practice of conducting a formal test for carryover, because it may introduce bias.[30,31] In particular, a two-stage design is frequently used where carryover effects are formally tested in the first stage.[32] This procedure has been shown to have a higher overall probability of rejecting than the nominal $\alpha = .05$, and is now not generally recommended.[33,34] A practical way to handle a possible carryover effect of short duration is to incorporate a "washout" period after the first treatment of interest is completed prior to initiating the second treatment.

Crossover studies should not be planned unless a high percentage of patients are expected to receive both treatments. For example, if the first episode of AOM is treated with treatment A and the second episode with treatment B, the episodes of AOM may be far apart and there is potential for a high drop-out rate between the first and second episodes. Efficiencies gained by using a crossover study may be reduced or eliminated if there are a large number of dropouts. A basic text devoted to the crossover design and written to include an audience of clinicians has been recently published.[31]

Case Crossover Design

A case crossover study[35] is the application of a case-control design to only cases and is particularly applicable to short exposures that may change the risk of rare cases of acute disease. Risk factors immediately preceding the acute event are compared with risk factors of the same subject during time periods not preceding an acute episode. It is similar to a crossover design, except that subjects or nature and not the experimenter determines exposure, and the study approach is retrospective rather than prospective.

The case crossover design has some advantages in that each subject serves as their own control, and that it is uniquely designed to address situations where the risk factor is intermittent, the effect of the risk factor is immediate and transient, and the outcome is abrupt.[36] Limitations of the method include difficulty in selection of the appropriate "control period"[37] and the requirement that records that adequately identify the transient risk factors be available. Determining the risk of acute episodes of OM associated with upper respiratory tract infection is an example where such a study design may be applicable.

Matched-Ear Study

Because most studies in OM entail measurements in both ears, there are at least two measurements taken on each child. Such repeated measures are often referred to as "clustered," that is, ear measures are a cluster of observations within each child. Developments in statistical methodology and the software to analyze clustered data have provided more flexibility in the analytic tools available for studies in OM.[38–41] A special design that takes advantage of the clustered ear measurements for each child is one where different treatments are administered to each ear.[42] For example, in a study to evaluate the safety and efficacy of a single dose of ototopical antibiotic, 50 children receiving bilateral tympanostomy tubes also received the antibiotic treatment in a randomly assigned ear.[42] Hearing loss and postoperative otorrhea were primary outcomes.

Matched-ear studies have the advantage of each patient serving as their own control so that patient characteristics possibly affecting outcome or incidence of disease are equal in the two groups. Controlling for this source of variability should result in decreased sample size requirements. Matched-ear studies can be considered a special case of clustered data, since the outcomes for two ears are measured for each child. Unfortunately, the relative efficiency of a matched-ear design compared with one in which patients have been randomized to two treatment groups has not been adequately investigated. Matched-ear designs are often not feasible, because they require bilateral disease and cannot be used for evaluation of systemic therapy.

Equivalence Studies

There is growing interest in studies designed to show equivalence in the effectiveness of a new treatment compared with an existing therapy, rather than attempting to establish its superiority.[43,44] This may be appropriate if the new treatment has fewer side effects, is less expensive, or is more convenient. The inferential approach to equivalence trials is different from conventional trials. In a typical clinical trial, we assume a priori "no treatment difference" and attempt to collect data that will lead to the rejection of the a priori assumption and the declaration that one of the treatments is superior. In an equivalence trial, we attempt to demonstrate that the two treatments are similar for a particular outcome, where similarity is quantified by specifying a priori bounds on the differences that would be considered equivalent.

Although many of the strategies for the design of the equivalence study are still evolving, the general approach is similar in many respects to the usual clinical trial. Some notable differences are that interpretation of the parameters needed for sample size estimation is different,[45,46] the intent-to-treat principle no longer provides a conservative approach,[44,47] and results and analysis are more appropriately presented as confidence intervals.[44,47]

Meta-analysis

Meta-analysis provides a method of combining and synthesizing results from multiple studies that address a similar question.[48,49] Although meta-analysis can be applied to nonrandomized studies, the methods are most applicable to combining randomized studies. The primary problem in the randomized trial is possible lack of precision, rather than bias. Combining the results from multiple studies improves precision because of the increased sample size. In nonrandomized studies, the possibility exists that all the studies have a similar bias and that a combined statistic would share this bias. Meta-analyses, where the investigators obtain the actual data from individual studies, are preferable, because issues of quality control can be directly assessed and there is a greater likelihood of having more standardized outcome measures across studies.

Although precision is almost always improved in a meta-analysis, problems remain. Limitations of meta-analysis include publication bias (the greater likelihood that positive studies are more likely to be published), combining of studies of varying quality and/or differing designs, and justification of the criteria for inclusion and exclusion. Meta-analysis has been applied specifically to the area of OM,[50–52] and several recent books have been published that address the application of meta-analysis to the biomedical area.[53,54] Meta-analysis is covered in detail in Chapter 4, Meta-analysis and Systematic Literature Review.

FORMALIZING THE HYPOTHESIS

Once the clinical question is appropriately specified, it is necessary in designing a study to determine the general framework of the scientific investigation. The hypothesis-testing format is the most common method of conducting a biomedical study. This is the approach generally presented in standard textbooks in statistics.

The design of a clinical study using a hypothesis-testing approach requires the following six steps:
1. Specifying the null hypothesis
2. Specifying the alternative hypothesis
3. Selecting the appropriate statistical test
4. Computing the test statistic from the data
5. Computing the appropriate p value or significance level
6. Rejecting or failing to reject the null hypothesis

Although only the first three components of hypothesis testing are part of the design of the study, we briefly review all six components because of the importance of the general approach to the conduct of a clinical investigation.

Hypothesis testing usually selects as the null hypothesis an assertion that the investigator is attempting to reject (an equivalence study is an exception to this practice). For example, in a trial to evaluate the efficacy of amoxicillin as a prophylaxis for recurrent middle ear effusion, children who were effusion free but had a history of chronic or recurrent effusion were randomly assigned to receive either amoxicillin or placebo for 1 year.[55] The null hypothesis for this study was that there is no difference in the average number of episodes of middle ear effusion for the two treatment groups. Rejecting the null hypothesis would then be consistent with a finding that the amoxicillin prophylaxis has a different treatment effect from placebo.

The alternative hypothesis summarizes the conclusion that will be accepted if the null hypothesis is rejected. The alternative hypothesis can be stated either as a one-sided hypothesis or a two-sided hypothesis. The former states that one of the treatment regimens is inferior to the other, while the latter states that the two treatment effects are unequal but does not specify which treatment is better.

Selecting the appropriate statistical test is based on the type of outcome measure and the properties of the data. This aspect of design will be discussed in a later section. The next two steps in hypothesis testing entail applying the statistical procedure to the data and obtaining the significance level or p value associated with the test statistic. The p value is defined as the probability that a summary statistic as extreme or more extreme is obtained under the assumption that the null hypothesis is true. Achieving a low p value indicates evidence consistent with rejecting the null hypothesis. Investigators, somewhat arbitrarily, often reject the null hypothesis for p values less than .05.

Clinical researchers should remember that statistical significance does not necessarily imply clinical significance. Trials with large samples may find small differences in treatment outcome to be statistically significant. However, whether a small difference is clinically significant depends on the adverse side effects of treatment and the seriousness of the disease condition being evaluated.

DEVELOPING DATA COLLECTION INSTRUMENTS

The design of the data forms is an important consideration in a clinical study. Data collection instruments should be carefully scrutinized and formally validated because various persons completing the form may interpret ambiguous or vague questions differently. This is particularly true in trials conducted at multiple sites. If questions are not properly stated, then data forms may contain items where the designated answers are not exhaustive and mutually exclusive. This creates problems for analysis. In a prospective study of twins,[56] the data form used for entry information requested the number of siblings. The format of the data form had been used successfully in several previous studies and the specific question regarding the number of siblings was worded in the same manner. However, for the twin study, some interviewers counted the co-twin when answering the question and others did not. This inconsistency had to be resolved prior to analysis.

SPECIFYING STATISTICAL PROCEDURES

Once the type of design is selected and the outcome and hypothesis are specified, the appropriate statistical procedures can be described (see also Chapter 2, "Critical Evaluation of Journal Articles," Tables 2–11 and 2–12). The statistical procedures used in studies of OM are similar to those used in other areas of biomedical research; there are several textbooks summarizing the more common of these statistical procedures.[57–60] Rosner[60] provides numerous examples from otolaryngology. In many research studies, proper analysis of the data requires addressing more complex situations that are generally not discussed in standard textbooks. The clinical researcher should consult a biostatistician when selecting the appropriate statistical procedures for a study.

ESTIMATING SAMPLE SIZE

Sample size estimation is a component of good study design.[61] Sample size estimation indicates the number of patients required to answer the primary study question. Sample size estimates depend on the statistical procedure being used, whether the alternative hypothesis is one-sided or two-sided, and the variability of the data: the type I error (α), the type II error (β), and the minimum clinically important difference (δ). The dependence of sample size on multiple parameters suggests that it is sometimes useful to estimate sample sizes over a range of possible values for some of the parameters. This type of investigation is sometimes called a sensitivity analysis.

Type I error is defined as the probability that the null hypothesis will be falsely rejected when it is true and type II error is the probability that it will be falsely accepted when the alternative is true. Statistical power is defined as 1–type II error (Table 3-2). Type II error depends on which point in the alternative is actually true. Studies should be designed to have low type I error with sufficient sample size to have high statistical power of detecting a difference that is clinically important. The clinical difference that the study is designed to detect is selected by the investigator. Type I error is often set at .05, and the statistical power of the desired detectable difference should be at least .80. Unfortunately, in many published clinical studies, the number of patients is too small to have adequate statistical power of detecting important clinical differences.[62–65]

For many studies, recruiting an adequate number of subjects to achieve sample size requirements is a serious problem. Sample size requirements increase if the type I error is lower, the statistical power is higher, the minimum clinically important difference is lower, or the data variability is higher. Two-sided hypotheses require larger sample sizes than corresponding one-sided hypotheses. Adjustments should be made for the expected number of patient withdrawals when planning sample size for a study. If the primary objective of the study requires testing several hypotheses, then it may be appropriate to decrease the type I error associated with each hypothesis in order to control the overall rate of false rejection of any of the several null hypotheses. This will result in an increase in sample size. In a trial comparing the efficacy of amoxicillin prophylaxis with placebo,[55] the planned sample size of 212 resulted in .90 power to detect a 50% reduction in the average number of episodes of middle ear effusion in the 1-year period. This calculation

Table 3-2 Errors in Hypothesis Testing

	Null Hypothesis	
Decision	True	False
Reject null hypothesis	Type I error	Correct decision (power)
Accept null hypothesis	Correct decision	Type II error

assumed a two-sided type I error of .05, a 25% dropout rate, and a baseline rate of .96 episodes per person in the placebo group.

Sample size estimation requires investigators to be specific about the primary hypothesis. The requirement of providing a sample size estimate for a study, therefore, has the indirect benefit of requiring more detail in specifying the primary hypothesis. In trials of OM, there are a variety of outcome variables and corresponding testable hypotheses that can be selected for a trial. Recent computer software packages provide sample size estimates for some of the statistical procedures[66,67] needed to test these hypotheses.

SECONDARY END POINTS

For many studies, all the questions of interest cannot be contained in a single primary hypothesis. These additional questions can be formulated as secondary hypotheses. The most important of these secondary hypotheses should be stated in advance so the appropriate questions are included in the data collection instruments. In addition, sample size considerations for these secondary hypotheses should be provided. For many trials, however, there may not be sufficient sample size to have high statistical power for all the secondary hypotheses. Some common secondary hypotheses in trials in OM include comparing the effect of treatment in selected patient subgroups, hearing levels, rates of surgical complications, drug side effects, and microbiologic assessments of the middle ear.

One problem that arises in studies with a large number of secondary end points is the increased likelihood of rejecting the null hypothesis by chance. The type I error, usually set at .05, restricts the probability of a random rejection of a single null hypothesis to 1 in 20. However, if multiple hypotheses are tested, the probability of at least one false rejection (sometimes called the experiment-wise error rate) can be much higher than 0.05.

Investigators must decide at the design phase whether to adjust for the elevated false rejection rate,

Table 3-3 Pointers in Clinical Study Design

The goal of experimental design is to reduce or eliminate bias and quantify and reduce errors due to chance.

A clinical study should provide clinically relevant estimates of outcomes and have the potential for influencing future clinical practice.

The double-blind randomized clinical trial is the "gold standard" in clinical research.

Although nonrandomized trials are subject to bias, they have an important role in otitis media research.

A case-control study is particularly appropriate if the disease is rare and a database of cases is available.

A nested case-control study combines some of the advantages of a prospective study and of a classic case-control study.

Trials to demonstrate that a new treatment is equivalent to a standard therapy should be designed as an equivalence trial.

Meta-analysis provides an important tool to synthesize results from different studies addressing a common question.

Data collection instruments should be developed and validated prior to initiation of the study.

Sample size estimation and specification of the procedures for interim analyses are part of good study design.

A biostatistician should be consulted to assist in the design of the study.

Methods of data collection and analysis related to secondary end points should be included in the planning of a study.

Table 3-4 Pitfalls in Clinical Study Design

Use of existing medical databases can result in substantial bias when used to evaluate treatment efficacy.

Crossover trials should not be considered if there is a likely "carryover" effect. Formal testing of a carryover effect has severe limitations.

Unless planned appropriately, interim evaluations of an ongoing trial can lead to an increase in the probability of falsely rejecting the null hypothesis.

Negative studies often do not have sufficient statistical power to eliminate the possibility of clinically important differences.

Nonrandomized studies are subject to a wide range of potential biases that may lead to misinterpretation of results if the study limitations are not recognized.

Summary

The design phase of a study is important, because poor judgment in design or inadequacy of data collection instruments often cannot be corrected after the data are collected. There is a wide range of study designs available in OM research, and each one has specific advantages and disadvantages. Although it is not possible to cover all the issues of study design in one chapter, the references should be used as a supplement to the material presented here. Tables 3-3 and 3-4 summarize pointers and pitfalls of study design in OM research.

References

1. Frei III E. Clinical cancer research: an embattled species. Cancer 1993;50:1979–92.
2. Church MW, Gerkin KP. Hearing disorders in children with fetal alcohol syndrome: findings from case reports. Pediatrics 1988;82:147–54.
3. Byar DP. Why databases should not replace randomized clinical trials. Biometrics 1980;36:337–42.
4. Green SB, Byar DP. Using observational data from registries to compare treatments: the fallacy of omnimetrics. Stat Med 1984;3:361–70.
5. Byar DP. On combining information: historical controls, overviews and comprehensive cohort studies. Recent Results Cancer Res 1987;111:95–8.
6. Fletcher RH, Fletcher SW, Wagner EH, editors. Clinical epidemiology: the essentials. Baltimore (MD): Williams and Wilkins; 1982. p. 171–84.
7. Kahn HA, Sempos CT, editors. Statistical methods in epidemiology. New York: Oxford University Press; 1989. p. 45–71.

which can be done by lowering the a priori threshold for a type I error. One simple approach, which is conservative, is to divide the original type I error (usually $\alpha = .05$) by the number of hypotheses being tested. If this is done, the probability of at least one hypothesis being rejected remains less than α. For some statistical hypotheses, exact methods are available to appropriately adjust the a priori in order to achieve a specified experiment-wise error rate. Note, however, that there is no general agreement on the desirability to adjust a priori. If the number of hypotheses being tested is large, the resultant sample size may not be feasible. However, if adjustment for multiple tests of hypotheses is not made at the design phase, the investigator should consider the increased likelihood of false rejections in the interpretation and discussion of results.

8. Daigler GE, Markello SJ, Cummings M. The effect of indoor air pollutants on otitis media and asthma in children. Laryngoscope 1991;101:293–6.

9. Paradise JL, Rockette HE, Calborn K, et al. Otitis media in 2253 Pittsburgh-area infants: prevalence and risk factors during the first two years of life. Pediatrics 1997;99:318–33.

10. Bailar JC, Louis TA, Lavori PW, Polonsky M. Studies without internal controls. N Engl J Med 1984;311:156–62.

11. Lubin JH, Gail MH. Biased selection of controls for case control analysis of cohort studies. Biometrics 1987;40:63–75.

12. Robins JM, Gail MH, Lubin JH. More on "biased selection of controls for case-control analysis of cohort studies." Biometrics 1986;42:293–9.

13. Palmu A, Syrjanen R, Kilpi T, et al. Negative pressure tympanograms in children less than two years of age—different bacteriological findings in otitis media by tympanometric results. Int J Pediatr Otorhinolaryngol 2001;61:61–9.

14. Byar DP, Simon RM, Friedewald WT, et al. Randomized clinical trials: perspective on some recent ideas. N Engl J Med 1976;295:74–80.

15. Pocock SJ. Clinical trials: a practical approach. New York: John Wiley and Sons; 1983.

16. Piantadosi S. Clinical trials: a methodological perspective. New York: John Wiley and Sons; 1997.

17. Beecher HK. The powerful placebo. JAMA 1955;159:1602–6.

18. Zelen M. The randomization and stratification of patients to clinical trials. J Chron Dis 1974;27:365–75.

19. McPherson K. Statistics: the problem of examining accumulating data more than once. N Engl J Med 1974;290:501–2.

20. Geller NL, Pocock SJ. Interim analyses in randomized clinical trials: ramifications and guidelines for practitioners. Biometrics 1987;43:213–23.

21. Pocock SJ. Interim analyses for randomized clinical trials: the group sequential approach. Biometrics 1982;38:153–62.

22. Fleming TR, Harrington DP, O'Brein PC. Designs for group sequential tests. Control Clin Trials 1984;5:348–61.

23. Jennison C, Turnbull BW. Group sequential methods with applications to clinical trials. New York: Chapman & Hall; 2000.

24. Chalmers TC. Ethical aspects of clinical trials. Am J Ophthalmol 1975;79:753–8.

25. Lebacqz K. Controlled clinical trials: some ethical issues. Control Clin Trials 1980;1:29–36.

26. Baum M, Houghton J, Abrams K. Early stopping rules—clinical perspectives and ethical considerations. Stat Med 1994;13:1459–69.

27. Meinert CL. Clinical trials: design, conduct and analysis. New York: Oxford University Press; 2000.

28. Hill M, Armitage P. The two-period cross-over clinical trial. Br J Clin Pharmacol 1979;8:7–20.

29. Brown BW Jr. The crossover experiment for clinical trials. Biometrics 1980;36:69–79.

30. Fleiss JL. A critique of recent research on the two-treatment crossover design controlled clinical trials. Control Clin Trials 1989;10:237–3.

31. Senn SJ. Cross-over trials in clinical research. Chichester, England: John Wiley & Sons; 2000.

32. Grizzle JE. The two-period change-over design and its use in clinical trials. Biometrics 1965;21:467–80.

33. Freeman PR. The performing of the two-state analysis of two-treatment, two period cross-over trials. Stat Med 1989;8:1421–32.

34. Senn SJ. Problems with the two-stage analysis of cross-over trials. Br J Clin Pharmacol 1991;32:133.

35. Maclure M. The case-crossover design: a method of studying transient effects on the risk of acute events. Am J Epidemiol 1991;133:144–53.

36. Maclure M, Mittleman MA. Should we use a case-crossover design? Ann Rev Public Health 2000;21:193–221.

37. Mittleman MA, Maclure M, Robins JM. Control sampling strategies for case-crossover studies: an assessment of relative efficiency. Am J Epidemiol 1995;142:91–8.

38. Rosner B. Multivariate methods in ophthalmology with applications to other paired data situations. Biometrics 1984;40:1025–35.

39. Le CT. Testing for trends in proportions using correlated otolaryngology or ophthalmology data. Biometrics 1998;44:299–303.

40. Le CT, Lindgren BR. Statistical methods for determining risk factors of chronic otitis media with effusion. Stat Med 1990;9:1495–500.

41. Meester SG, MacKay J. A parametric model for cluster correlated categorical data. Biometrics 1994;50:954–63.

42. Welling DB, Forrest LA, Goll F III. Safety of otopical antibiotics. Laryngoscope 1995;105:472–4.

43. U.S. Food and Drug Administration. Statistical procedures for bioequivalence studies using a standard two treatment crossover design. Washington: Department of Health and Human Services, (US), Public Health Service, Food and Drug Administration; 1992.

44. Jones B, Jarvis P, Lewis JA, Ebbutt AF. Trials to assess equivalence: the importance of rigorous methods. BMJ 1996;313:36–9.

45. Machin D, Campbell MJ, Farjers PM, Pinol A, editors. Demonstrating equivalence. In: Sample size tables for clinical studies. 2nd ed. Malden (MA): Blackwell Science; 1997.

46. Makuch R, Simon R. Sample size requirements for evaluating a conservative therapy. Cancer Treat Rep 1978;62:1037–40.

47. Makuch R, Johnson M. Issues in planning and interpreting active control equivalence studies. J Clin Epidemiol 1989;42:503–11.

48. Olkin T. Meta-analysis: reconciling the results of independent studies. Stat Med 1995;14:457–72.

49. Thacker SB. Meta-analysis: a quantitative approach to research integration. JAMA 1988;259:1685–9.

50. Rosenfeld RM, Post JC. Meta-analysis of antibiotics for the treatment of otitis media with effusion. Otolaryngol Head Neck Surg 1992;106:378–85.

51. Rosenfeld RM, Vertrees JE, Carr J, et al. Clinical efficacy of antimicrobial drugs for acute otitis media: meta-analysis of 5400 children from 33 randomized trials. J Pediatr 1994;124:355–67.

52. Rosenfeld RM, Mandel EM, Bluestone CD. Systemic steroids for otitis media with effusion in children. Arch Otolaryngol Head Neck Surg 1991;177:984–9.

53. Sutton AJ, Abrams KR, Jones DR, et al. Methods for meta-analysis in medical research. Chichester, England: John Wiley & Sons; 2000.

54. Pettiti DB. Meta-analysis, decision analysis and cost effectiveness analysis: methods for quantitative synthesis in medicine. New York: Oxford University Press; 2000.

55. Mandel EM, Casselbrant CL, Rockette HE, et al. Efficacy of antimicrobial prophylaxis for recurrent middle-ear effusion. Pediatr Infect Dis J 1996;15:1074–82.

56. Casselbrandt ML, Mandel EM, Fall PA, et al. The heredi-tability of otitis media: a twin and triplet study. JAMA 1999;282:2125–30.

57. Colton T. Statistics in medicine. Boston (MA): Little Brown and Company; 1974.

58. Brown BW Jr, Holander M. Statistics: a biomedical introduction. New York: John Wiley and Sons; 1977.

59. Ingelfinger JA, Mosteller FM, Thibodeau LA,Ware JH. Biostatistics in clinical medicine. New York: Macmillian; 1987.

60. Rosner B. Fundamentals of biostatistics. Belmont (CA): Wadsworth; 1995.

61. Lieber RL. Statistical significance and statistical power in hypothesis testing. J Orthop Res 1990;8:304–9.

62. Frieman JA, Chalmers TC, Smith H Jr, Keubler RR. The importance of beta, the Type II error and sample size in the design and interpretation of the randomized clinical trial: survey of 71 "negative trials." N Engl J Med 1978; 299:690–4.

63. Edlund MJ, Overall JE, Rhoades HM. Beta, or Type II error in psychiatric controlled clinical trials. J Psychiatr Res 1985;19:563–7.

64. Brown CG, Kelen GD, Ashton JJ, Werman HA. The beta error and sample size determination in clinical trials in emergency medicine. Ann Emerg Med 1987;16:183–7.

65. Ottenbacher KJ, Barrett KA. Statistical conclusion validity of rehabilitation research: a quantitative analysis. Am J Phys Med Rehab 1990;69:102–7.

66. Hintz JL. PASS user's guide: power analysis of sample size for Windows. Kaysville (UT): NCSS; 1996.

67. Elashoff JD. Query advisor release 2.0: study-planning software. Cork: Statistical Solutions Ltd; 1997.

CHAPTER 4

Meta-analysis and Systematic Literature Review

Richard M. Rosenfeld, MD, MPH

Knowledge is a process of piling up facts; wisdom lies in their simplification.
Martin H. Fischer

OBJECTIVES

On completion of this chapter, the reader should be able to

1. Distinguish a systematic review from a traditional narrative review.
2. Understand the role of meta-analysis in evidence-based medicine.
3. Critically appraise a meta-analysis and apply results to patient care.
4. Appreciate the breadth and scope of published otitis media (OM) meta-analyses.
5. Identify the inherent limitations and pitfalls in meta-analyses and systematic reviews.

What a difference four years make! In the brief time lapse since the first edition of this chapter, the quantity and quality of OM reviews have increased dramatically. The second edition boasts 26 meta-analyses, compared with only eight in the first. These studies address a broad range of OM issues, including screening, diagnosis, therapy, surgery, and sequelae. Moreover, a greater percentage of reviews are being conducted or sponsored by professional organizations. The methodology for meta-analysis has matured, with better statistical packages and increased attention to bias, heterogeneity, and external validity. This chapter discusses these new developments in detail and offers a unique quantitative overview of key meta-analysis results for clinicians and policy makers.

Meta-analyses are increasingly prominent features of the medical literature. Clinicians with an interest in OM can access, among other information resources, an expanding corpus of meta-analyses conducted by professional organizations[1–11] and independent researchers.[12–26] These integrative articles facilitate clinical decisions and also serve as the policy foundation for evidence-based practice guidelines, economic evaluations, and future research agendas.[27] This chapter introduces the principles and practice of meta-analysis in the context of acute otitis media (AOM) and otitis media with effusion (OME).

THE TWO FACES OF LITERATURE REVIEW

Most readers are familiar with traditional narrative reviews, once ubiquitous in peer-reviewed medical journals and still thriving in throwaway publications. Despite their continuing popularity, narrative reviews are an inefficient and biased way to extract useful information, particularly when the number of source articles on the topic of interest is large.[28] A good starting point for understanding meta-analysis is to contrast the technique with traditional narrative reviews (Table 4-1).

Narrative Literature Review

Traditional narrative reviews have several problems that meta-analyses may overcome.[29] A narrative review typically presents a series of studies, with strengths and weaknesses discussed selectively and informally by one or more acknowledged experts. Narrative reviews are subjective and bias prone. Without a protocol for choosing articles, an investigator may preferentially select those that support or contradict a particular viewpoint. Independent reviewers frequently disagree about which studies to include and how to balance the quantitative evidence. The frequency of citation of clinical trials is often related to outcome, with studies in line with the prevailing opinion quoted more often than contradictory ones.[30]

If the reviewer's bias is explicitly stated, the reader can take it into account and form appropriate conclusions. For example, an analysis of 106 review articles on passive smoking found that 37% of reviewers reported no harmful effects.[31] Of these "negative" reviews, 74% were written by authors with tobacco-industry affiliations, which

Table 4-1 Comparison of Narrative (Traditional) Reviews and Meta-analyses

	Narrative Review	*Meta-analysis*
Research design	Free form	A priori protocol
Classification	Publication type	Research discipline
Literature search	Convenience sample of articles deemed important by author	Systematic sample using explicit and reproducible article selection criteria
Focus	Broad; summarizes a large body of information	Narrow; tests specific hypotheses and focused clinical questions
Emphasis	Narrative; qualitative summary	Numbers; quantitative summary
Validity	Variable; high potential for bias in article selection and interpretation	Good, provided articles are of adequate quality and combinability
Bottom line	Broad recommendations, often based on personal opinion	Estimates of effect size, based on statistical pooling of data
Utility	Provides a quick overview of a subject area	Provides summary estimates for evidence-based medicine
Appeal to readers	Usually very high	Varies; often low

were not always appropriately disclosed. The only factor associated with concluding that passive smoking is not harmful was author affiliation with the tobacco industry (logistic regression odds ratio .88, $p < .001$); no association was found regarding article quality, peer review status, article topic, or year of publication.

Narrative reviews in peer-reviewed journals are an endangered species, which more likely reflects awareness of narrative review shortcomings, rather than a lack of eager authors. Conversely, throwaway journals, which do not subject articles to peer review, are laden with narrative reviews. These enticing summaries grab the reader's eye with more color, tables, figures, and photographs than similar articles in peer-reviewed journals and are considered more clinically relevant, practical, and interesting.[32] Despite their appeal to readers, review articles in throwaway journals are plagued by poor methodologic and reporting quality, which greatly limits their influence on evidence-based management decisions.

Meta-analysis and Systematic Review

Meta-analysis is a form of literature review in which studies are systematically assembled, appraised, and combined using explicit and predetermined methods to reduce bias.[27] Hence the term "systematic review," which is used interchangeably with "meta-analysis" in this chapter. Purists note, however, that *systematic review* relates more to identifying and appraising relevant studies, whereas *meta-analysis* relates to statistically combining them to estimate effect size.[33,34] This

distinction is made because the simple act of statistically combining studies does not ensure validity or reliability. Historically, methods to reduce statistical imprecision using quantitative synthesis (meta-analysis) were developed before methods to reduce bias using qualitative techniques (systematic review).[35]

A properly performed systematic review is tedious (Table 4-2).[36,37] The intensity of effort involved, combined with the lack of recognition afforded by most academic institutions to clinicians who engage in this form of research,[35] explains the relative paucity of high-quality systematic reviews by independent investigators. In response, several professional organizations have begun to prepare systematic reviews regarding the benefits and risks of health care interventions. These include the Cochrane Collaboration (<http://www.cochrane.co.uk>), Agency for Health Care Policy and Research (<http://www.ahrq.gov>), and the University of York National Health Service Centre for Reviews and Dissemination (<http://www.york.ac.uk/inst/crd/>). The Cochrane Library is a rich source of regularly updated reviews with high methodologic rigor.[38,39]

Although any type of journal article can be included in a meta-analysis, the approach is most applicable to randomized controlled trials (RCTs). Randomized trials often involve greater expense and planning than other types of studies and are more likely to get published in high-quality, peer-reviewed medical journals. Moreover, study end points in RCTs tend to be more consistent and, therefore, more suitable for statistical combining than those recorded in observational studies. Systematic

Table 4-2 Steps in Performing a Meta-analysis

	Action	Purpose	Comment
1.	Prepare a detailed a priori research protocol	Defines study scope, objectives, hypotheses, and methodology	A good meta-analysis requires as much effort to produce as the source articles under study
2.	Specify unambiguous selection criteria for inclusion and exclusion of source articles	Ensures that source articles are similar enough to be statistically combined	Criteria should define patients, exposures, outcomes, and methodology of interest
3.	Search the literature and clearly document the search strategy	Identifies all potential articles and data sources	Computer search is incomplete without manual cross-checks
4.	Determine which articles meet predefined inclusion criteria; keep a log of rejected trials	Limits selection bias, the Achilles heel of traditional narrative review articles	At least two reviewers should be used to minimize bias; also helpful if reviewers are blinded to results
5.	Assess the quality of articles to be combined	Provides quality scores for sensitivity analysis (below)	At least two reviewers should be used to minimize bias
6.	Extract data from included articles for predetermined treatment end points	Obtains accurate and precise numeric data from source articles for statistical pooling	At least two reviewers should abstract the data, with checks for interobserver agreement
7.	Statistically combine the data, where appropriate, to estimate the main effect(s) under study	Improves precision and statistical power by increasing overall sample size	Results should include 95% confidence intervals, a forest plot, and a test for heterogeneity
8.	Perform a qualitative summary, if data are too sparse, low quality, or heterogeneous for pooling	Avoids inflated treatment effects caused by citation bias or heterogeneity	The process of conduct and reporting should be rigorous and explicit
9.	Perform a sensitivity analysis to test the robustness of results and possibility of bias	Shows how results vary by study quality, diagnostic criteria, or outcome choice	May include subgroup analyses, funnel plots, discussions of bias (citation, language, publication)
10.	Discuss clinical significance and policy implications	Formulates caveats by putting results into proper perspective	Proposal of a future research agenda is helpful

reviews of observational studies are gaining popularity but remain risky because of the numerous additional biases that may arise.[40,41] A reporting checklist has been proposed to improve the validity of observational meta-analyses.[42]

Meta-analyses are encountered increasingly in the medical literature. In 1989, the National Library of Medicine acknowledged the importance of systematic reviews by designating "meta-analysis" a medical subject heading (MeSH). MEDLINE articles containing "meta-analysis" as a keyword or subject heading increased from about 250 in 1989, to 390 in 1993, to 820 in 1997, to 1,260 in 2001. A review of MEDLINE from 1980 to 2000 identified 3,025 probable meta-analyses, with a definite upward trend over time (generally linear) and no evidence of leveling off or decreasing.[43] In addition, the number of editorials and reviews of meta-analysis methodology have increased dramatically.[37]

HOW TO APPRAISE AND INTERPRET A META-ANALYSIS

Interpreting the Narrative of a Meta-analysis

Despite all its statistical alchemy,[44] meta-analysis remains a prime candidate for "garbage in, garbage out." A prospective protocol (see Table 4-2) must be followed so that source articles are selected without bias, and that they are of adequate quality and combinability for statistical pooling.[36,37] The authors should state explicitly the information sources searched (electronic and manual), source article selection criteria (target population, intervention, principal outcomes, and study design), methods for abstracting data, and the characteristics of included studies (design, participant characteristics, intervention details, outcome definitions).[27] A good meta-analysis is rarely single authored; at least two independent reviewers are necessary to select articles and extract data in an accurate and unbiased manner.

Quality is best assessed by review of the source article's methods section, without knowledge of the study results. A technician blots out the results section and all references to authorship to ensure adequate blinding. Quality scores are assigned using explicit checklists completed by multiple reviewers.[45] Including only RCTs improves quality, but variations may still occur in blinding, dropout rates, and the adequacy of randomization. Whereas studies with major flaws should be excluded, less severe quality variations are generally not associated with outcomes.[46]

Combinability is more difficult to assess. Studies should have patient demographics, diagnostic criteria, and treatment end points that are similar enough to justify statistical pooling. Inadequate combinability (heterogeneity) can be disastrous—a proverbial mixing of apples and oranges. Sources of variability in OM trials include patient age, disease burden (frequency, duration, and severity of OM), diagnostic criteria (clinical symptoms, pneumatic otoscopy, tympanometry, or audiometry), treatment regimen (specific drug used and duration of therapy), outcome assessment (timing and methodology), criteria for success (clinical versus bacteriologic, unilateral versus bilateral, improvement versus cure), unit of analysis (ears versus patients), and confounding factors (tympanocentesis, compliance rates, day care attendance). Explicit criteria for article selection and data extraction help increase combinability.

Interpreting the Numbers of a Meta-analysis

Statistical analysis is where a systematic review differs most from a traditional review article.[47] When data from a group of logically related studies are combined, the process is often referred to as "pooling." The steps involved in pooling data for a systematic review are the following[36]:

1. Choose a measure of effect size.
2. Choose a statistical model for combining the data.
3. Pool the data; calculate a point estimate for effect size and a 95% confidence interval.
4. Create a graphic display of results.
5. Perform a statistical test for heterogeneity.
6. Do a sensitivity analysis.
7. Assess for bias.

Several computer programs are available that perform many or all of the above statistical analyses. A useful stand-alone program is *Comprehensive Meta-Analysis*, which includes a wide variety of computational options and graphic displays.[48] This program was used for all calculations and graphics in the second edition of this book.

The absolute *rate difference* (RD) is the preferred measure of clinical benefit for systematic reviews of RCTs. Also called the absolute risk reduction or risk difference, the RD is the difference in event rates between the control and treatment groups. The advantage of the RD as an outcome measure is that it can be easily used to calculate the number of patients a clinician needs to treat with a particular therapy to prevent one clinical event (number needed to treat [NNT]).[49] The NNT is simply the reciprocal of the RD. For example, an absolute RD of .20 (eg, 20%) implies a need to treat five patients to avoid one clinical failure. Directly related to NNT is the NNH, or number needed to harm. The NNH applies to studies of adverse events, such as sequelae of tympanostomy tubes.

Other measures of clinical benefit include the odds ratio (OR) and relative risk (RR), which are encountered in meta-analyses of observational studies (cohort or case-control) and in some meta-analyses of RCTs. For RCTs, however, the RD is preferred because the reciprocal gives the NNT. When results are expressed using the OR, the NNT can be calculated by entering the author's individual study data into a computer program and determining the pooled RD. Alternatively, the NNT can be approximated from the patient's expected event rate (PEER) without therapy by using a nomogram[50] or by direct calculation with the following formula[51]:

$$NNT = \frac{\left(1 - \{1 - [PEER \times (1 - OR)]\}\right)}{[(1 - PEER) \times PEER \times (1 - OR)]}$$

Calculating the pooled RD, OR, or RR for a group of studies can be done using a fixed-effect or a random-effect model.[52] The *fixed-effect model* assumes that there is one true effect size and that all included studies would show exactly the same result except for random variation, confounding variables, and artifacts. Conversely, the *random-effect model* assumes a population (distribution) of true effect sizes, with each source article representing one member of this population. Results are expected to vary from study to study, with differences caused by experimental error *and* differences in populations (between-study variability). Although the random-effect computations are more complex, they are readily available in meta-analysis software.

When a fixed-effect model is used, a statistical *test of heterogeneity* must be done to confirm that the underlying assumption of a fixed effect has been satisfied. If the test is significant ($p < .05$) a random-effect model should be substituted. Unfortunately, the test of heterogeneity has low power, meaning that significant variations may exist even with a nonsignificant result.[53] An alternative is to always use a random-effect model because the studies are not assumed to come from a single homogeneous population. When heterogeneity is found, an attempt should be made to identify associations between study or patient characteristics and outcome measures. Subgroup analyses, when performed post hoc, should be adjusted for multiple comparisons to avoid false-positive findings.

A 95% *confidence interval* (CI) must accompany whatever measure of clinical benefit is chosen.[54] The 95% CI tells clinicians what to expect 95% of the time when treating patients outside the study, if the study could be repeated and repeated. Alternatively, the 95% CI can be viewed as a reasonable range for the magnitude of the outcome. Because the CI reflects precision, it varies inversely with total sample size: the more patients and studies included in the meta-analysis, the narrower is the CI. Further, the 95% CI for effect size tends to be broader (less precise) with random-effects analysis but approaches the fixed-effects result when the studies are homogeneous. When a 95% CI is provided, *p* values are optional; the RD is significant at *p* < .05 if the CI does not contain zero.

An example of data pooling is shown in Table 4-3, which estimates the efficacy of amoxicillin versus placebo or no drug for AOM.[4] A clinician viewing these data may ask three questions: (1) What is the mean benefit of treatment? (2) Is the benefit statistically significant? and (3) Are the studies similar enough to justify combining the data? The last row of the table answers these questions. Antibiotics reduce AOM failure rates at 2 to 7 days on average by 12.3% over no treatment (*p* = .016), with a 95% CI of 2.8 to 21.8%. Although statistically significant, the level of clinical benefit is modest—about eight patients (NNT) must be treated (reciprocal

of .123) to achieve a single additional cure. The significant heterogeneity seen in the fixed-effects analysis suggests that a random-effects model is more appropriate.

A graphic display of meta-analysis results is a useful adjunct to numeric results. The *forest plot* (Figure 4-1) is a widely used form of presentation that plots point estimates (black squares) from different studies along with their error bars (horizontal lines).[35,54] Because the eye is drawn to longer error bars, data from smaller studies have a relatively greater visual effect. To compensate for this distortion, boxes are drawn proportional to the study sample size. The combined result is depicted below the studies with a black diamond spanning the 95% CI. The combined RD of .12 in Figure 4-1 (95% CI, .02, .22) is statistically significant (*p* = .016) because the 95% CI does not include zero. The study by Kaleida, however, does not contain the overall RD in its 95% CI, suggesting heterogeneity among the studies. This is confirmed by a statistically significant *p* value (< .001) in the test of heterogeneity.

Checking a Meta-analysis for Bias

Sensitivity analysis is an essential part of a systematic review. The credibility of a pooled estimate is proportional to its stability; if minor changes in the method of analysis (inclusion or exclusion of specific trials) produce large changes in results, credibility will suffer. For example, assume a systematic review shows a beneficial RD of .50 when data from 12 studies are pooled. However, when the data are re-analyzed for the six studies in which a double-blind protocol was followed, the RD falls to .20. This suggests that the initial perceived efficacy may be caused more by bias than by truth.

Table 4-3 Meta-analysis of Amoxicillin vs. Placebo or No Drug for AOM Failure at 2–7 days*

First Author, Year	Clinical Failure Rate (%) Antibiotic	Placebo	RD (95% CI)	
Halsted 1967	10/30 (33)	7/27 (26)	.074	(−.162, .310)
Howie 1972	19/36 (53)	92/116 (79)	−.265	(−.444, −.086)
Laxdal 1980	5/49 (10)	18/48 (37)	−.273	(−.434, −.112)
Kaleida 1991[†]	19/488 (4)	38/492 (8)	−.038	(−.067, −.009)
Burke 1991	2/114 (2)	17/118 (14)	−.127	(−.194, −.059)
Combined[‡]			−.123	(−.218, −.028)[§]

AOM = acute otitis media; RD = absolute rate difference; CI = confidence interval.

*Data extracted from studies selected by Marcy M et al.[4]

[†]Includes only nonsevere episodes of AOM.

[‡]Random effects meta-analysis (fixed effects heterogeneity *p* < .001).

[§]Significant at *p* = .016; number needed to treat (NNT) = 8 (95% CI, 5 to 36).

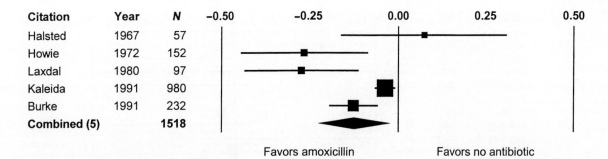

Citation	Year	N					
Halsted	1967	57					
Howie	1972	152					
Laxdal	1980	97					
Kaleida	1991	980					
Burke	1991	232					
Combined (5)		**1518**					

Favors amoxicillin   Favors no antibiotic

Figure 4-1 Random effects meta-analysis of amoxicillin versus placebo or no antibiotic for acute otitis media clinical failure at 2 to 7 days. Forest plot shows absolute rate difference and 95% confidence intervals for individual studies *(squares)* and combined result *(diamond)*. Study symbols are proportion to sample size. Combined result indicates a 12.3% reduction in clinical failures (95% CI, 2.8, 21.8%) attributable to amoxicillin therapy. Data abstracted from Marcy M et al.[4]

A sensitivity analysis should also be performed to see how results vary relative to study quality (patient compliance, dropouts, adequacy of randomization), outcome measure, and clinical variables (disease duration or severity, choice and duration of treatment, and so on).[55]

An example of a sensitivity analysis is shown in Table 4-4. The choice of outcome measure and study design appear to influence study results, although the overlap of the 95% CIs suggests that differences are not statistically significant. The authors of this meta-analysis could not explain the variations observed but noted that most analyses (including some not shown here) yielded a small but statistically significant benefit for antibiotic therapy. Final results were reported using the "all blinded studies" subgroup, which presumably contained data from the highest-quality articles.

Citation bias is potentially the greatest threat to meta-analysis validity. Recognizing the essential relationship between article selection and meta-analysis results, the Quality of Reporting of Meta-Analyses (QUOROM) conference proposed that all systematic reviews contain a flow chart describing the following stages of article selection[27]:

1. Potentially relevant RCTs identified and screened for retrieval (*n* = …) and those excluded with reasons (*n* = …)
2. RCTs retrieved for more detailed evaluation (*n* = …) and those excluded with reasons (*n* = …)
3. Potentially appropriate RCTs to be included in the meta-analysis (*n* = …) and those excluded with reasons (*n* = …)
4. RCTs included in the meta-analysis (*n* = …) and those withdrawn from data pooling, by outcome, with reasons (*n* = …)
5. RCTs with usable information by outcome (*n* = …)

The *funnel plot* is a simple visual tool to examine whether a meta-analysis is based on a biased sample of studies.[56] For example, an industry-funded meta-analysis (Figure 4-2) showed equivalence of azithromycin 3 to 5 days versus another antibiotic 10 days for AOM clinical failure (OR 1.12, 95% CI .81, 1.54).[24] Although the forest plot suggests homogeneity, which is confirmed statistically (*p* = .319), the study selection may have been biased by industry funding. There is no evidence of selection bias, however, in the funnel plot

Table 4-4 Example of Sensitivity Analysis for a Systematic Review: Clinical Efficacy of Antibiotics versus Placebo or No Drug for Otitis Media with Effusion in Children*

Study Types Included in Meta-analysis	No. of Studies	RD (95% CI)
All blinded studies	10	14.0 (3.6, 24.2)
All studies with outcomes measured at 4 to 6 weeks	9	23.4 (9.8, 36.1)
All studies with outcomes measured at 10 to 14 days	7	16.0 (3.7, 28)
Blinded studies using tympanometric outcomes	4	30.8 (20.1, 40.7)
Blinded studies using otoscopic and tympanometric outcomes	4	2.8 (−4.6, 10.3)

CI = confidence interval; RD = absolute rate difference (%).

*Data extracted from studies selected by Stool SE et al.[2]

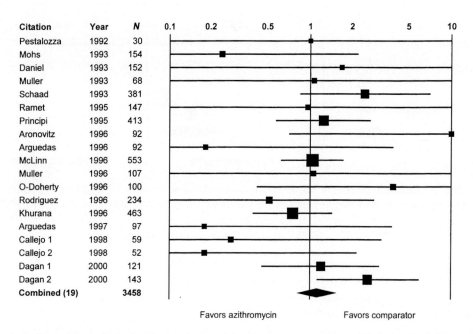

Figure 4-2 Fixed effects meta-analysis of azithromycin (3 to 5 days) versus comparator antibiotic (10 days) for acute otitis media clinical failure at 7 to 14 days (heterogeneity $p = .318$). Forest plot of odds ratios shows no significant combined effect. Data abstracted from Ioannidis JPA et al.[24]

Figure 4-3 Funnel plot of precision versus effect size for the meta-analysis in Figure 4-2. Study symbols (circles) are proportional to sample size. Vertical line is the combined odds ratio and curved lines show the inverted funnel distribution expected by an unbiased study sample. The actual distribution appears unbiased.

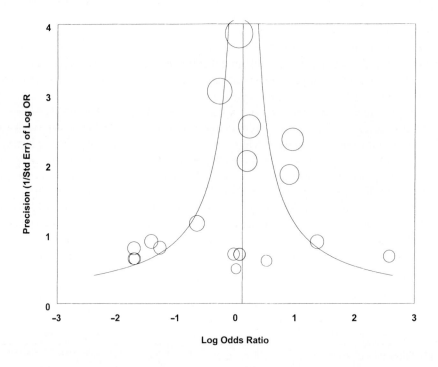

(Figure 4-3), which shows a symmetric scatter of study effect size (log odds ratio) versus study precision (inverse of standard error). Conversely, any gaps in the inverted funnel shape (curved lines in Figure 4-3) would indicate that some studies may not have been published, located, or included.[54]

Individual studies in a funnel plot (see Figure 4-3) are ideally depicted with circles proportional to sam-

ple size. Because large studies estimate effect size more precisely than smaller studies, they tend to lie in a narrow band at the top of the scatterplot, while the smaller studies, with more variation in results, fan out over the larger area at the bottom. An unbiased study sample yields a symmetric funnel centered over the combined effect estimate. In contrast, consider a meta-analysis (Figure 4-4) suggesting that ototopical anti-

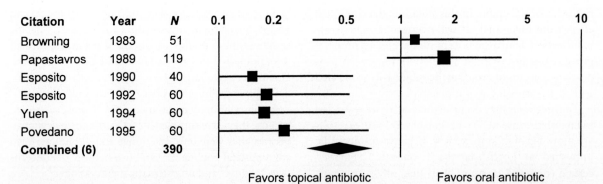

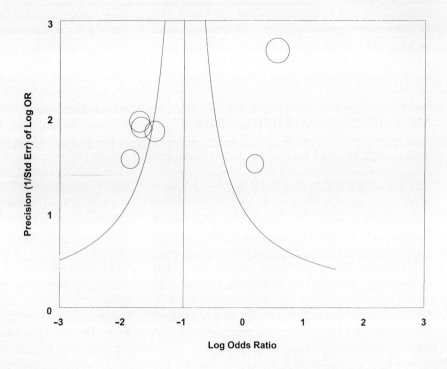

Figure 4-4 Fixed effects meta-analysis of topical versus systemic antimicrobials for control of persistent otorrhea caused by chronic suppurative otitis media (heterogeneity $p < .001$). Forest plot of odds ratios shows a significant combined effect of .46 (95% CI, .30, .69), suggesting a 54% reduction in otorrhea attributable to topical therapy. Data abstracted from Acuin J et al.[6]

Figure 4-5 Funnel plot of precision versus effects size for the meta-analysis in Figure 4-4. The asymmetric study distribution suggests a biased, and potentially invalid, combined result.

biotics are more likely than oral antibiotics to control chronic suppurative otitis media (CSOM) (fixed-effects OR .46, 95% CI .30, .69).[6] The studies, however, are heterogeneous ($p < .001$), and the funnel plot (Figure 4-5) is asymmetric with the largest study suggesting a contrary effect. Further, there is only one symmetric "negative" counterpart to the four "positive" studies on the left. Consequently, validity is compromised.

Publication bias derives from selective publishing of studies with statistically significant or directionally positive results, which can inflate efficacy estimates in meta-analyses. Although many assume the problem stems mainly from preferential publishing of "positive" manuscripts by journal editors, the magnitude of bias is much greater among researchers who preferentially

write and submit positive study results.[57] Publication bias can be sought by statistically determining the number of unpublished negative studies necessary to refute the published evidence[58] or by examining the 95% CI; a broad CI that approaches zero (RD) or unity (odds ratio or relative risk) is suspicious. Alternatively, unpublished data (if available) could be included in sensitivity analysis to assess for stability of the results.

Small study effects describe a trend for the smaller studies in a meta-analysis to show larger treatment benefits.[59] This trend results from a combination of citation bias, publication bias, and the poor methodologic design that often characterizes small studies relative to larger trials. Small study effects produce an asymmetric appearance of the funnel plot, with a gap in the bottom right side of the graph. In this situation, the combined effect from meta-analysis will overestimate the treatment's effect. Statistical tests of funnel plot asymmetry, using regression or rank correlation, have been proposed as a means of avoiding the subjectivity associated with visual assessment of funnel plots.

Language bias may occur in meta-analyses restricted to English because RCTs with statistically positive results are more likely than those with negative results to be published in English-language journals.[60] Further, certain countries are more likely than others to report RCTs with positive results.[61] Despite these theoretical concerns, language-restricted versus language-inclusive meta-analyses do not differ with respect to the estimate of benefit of the effectiveness of an intervention.[62] An analysis of several Cochrane Reviews also found that excluding non–English language trials had little effect on summary treatment effect estimates, but that these trials had fewer participants, poorer methodology, and more positive results than English language studies.[63]

META-ANALYSIS AND OTITIS MEDIA

Otitis media is an ideal topic for meta-analysis because of a large number of published trials assessing logically related diseases and treatment end points. Since the first RCTs were published in the 1940s, more than 100,000 randomized and controlled trials have appeared in print.[64] Several hundred of these studies relate to pharmacologic therapy for AOM and OME, raising the inevitable question "What does it all mean?" Some answers can be found in the plethora of RCT meta-analyses published by professional organizations and individual investigators. Meta-analyses of observational studies are less common but provide valuable summary information about OM sequelae, risk factors, and diagnostic methods.

In preparing this section, systematic reviews and meta-analyses were identified using established search strategies.[65,66] A search term of "otitis media" was used in the following electronic databases: Cochrane Library (<http://www.cochrane.org>), Agency for Healthcare Research and Quality (AHRQ), (<http://www.AHRQ.gov>), Clinical Evidence (<http://www.clinicalevidence.com>), and Evidence-Based Medicine Reviews (<http://www.ovid.com>). MEDLINE (<http://www.ovid.com>) was searched using a medical subject heading of "otitis media" plus publication type meta-analysis (exp otitis media/ and meta-analysis.pt). When an article reported a statistically significant treatment effect but did not provide the NNT, the NNT was calculated as the reciprocal of the random effects absolute RD.[48]

The electronic literature search identified 26 OM systematic reviews[1–26] as of July 2002, of which 11 were conducted by professional organizations (Table 4-5) and 15 by independent investigators (Table 4-6). Specific results of these studies are discussed below. About half were published in 1999 or later and half prior to 1999. No further systematic reviews were identified after manual review of Clinical Evidence[67,68] or source article bibliographies. Three meta-analyses[69–71] were excluded because they were superseded by Cochrane Reviews, two because they were only descriptive and did not perform any statistical pooling,[72,73] and two because of concerns over validity[74] and unsystematic methodology.[75]

Meta-analyses of Otitis Media Natural History

The extremely favorable natural history of untreated AOM is apparent in the meta-analyses listed in Table 4-7. Three independent meta-analyses,[3,9,17] with varying sample sizes and methods of data pooling, conclude that approximately 80% of children with AOM have spontaneous clinical relief within 2 to 14 days, with a 95% CI of about 70 to 90%. The rate for children under age 2 years is likely somewhat lower because not all source articles contained young children and studies restricted to this population suggest spontaneous resolution of only about 30% after a few days.[21,76] Therefore, the meta-analysis results are most applicable to children aged 2 years or older.

Only one published meta-analysis[5] has dealt with spontaneous resolution of OME, although the issue is discussed more fully in the first, and current, editions of this book (see Chapter 12, "Natural History of Untreated Otitis Media"). About 40 to 45% of tympanograms normalize after 6 to 12 weeks, with rates about 50% poorer at 12 weeks when stricter criteria for resolution are applied (tympanogram B to A versus B/C to A). The 95% confidence intervals are wide and overlapping, suggesting a need for additional study and greater precision. Further, the applicability of these rates to young children is unknown because all children in the source articles were age 3 years or older.

Meta-analyses of Antimicrobials for Treating or Preventing AOM

Four meta-analyses[3,9,17,21] have addressed the clinical efficacy of antibiotics for AOM (Table 4-8), of which three note a significant benefit at 2 to 14 days (NNT 7 to 17). The only analysis[21] to conclude no benefit had a small sample size (children under 2 years of age only), producing low statistical power and inconclusive results. Several of the source articles in the three positive analyses[3,9,17] excluded children who had severe AOM or were younger than 2 years of age, which limits the ability to generalize results. The exact target population for these data is

Table 4-5 Systematic Reviews of Otitis Media by Professional Organizations

Year	First Author	Topic	Major Analyses	No. of Studies	Organization
1992	Univ. York[1]	OME	Surgery	19 RCT	NHS-CRD
1994	Stool[2]	OME	Pharmacologic therapy	31 RCT	AHCPR
1998	NZHTA[3]	OME	Preschool and school entry screening	—	NZHTA
2001	Marcy[4]	AOM	Natural history, antibiotic therapy, antibiotic vs. antibiotic	82 RCT 6 CCC	AHRQ
2002	Takata[5]	OME	Natural history, diagnosis, speech and language delay, hearing loss	113 CCC	AHRQ
2002	Acuin[6]	CSOM	Aural toilet, systemic antibiotic, ototopical antibiotic	24 RCT	Cochrane
2002	Butler[7]	OME	Systemic or intranasal steroid	10 RCT	Cochrane
2002	Flynn[8]	AOM	Decongestant, antihistamine	13 RCT	Cochrane
2002	Glasziou[9]	AOM	Antibiotic therapy	10 RCT	Cochrane
2002	Kozyrskyj[10]	AOM	Antibiotic therapy, short vs. long	32 RCT	Cochrane
2002	Straetemans[11]	AOM	Pneumococcal vaccine	10 RCT	Cochrane

AHCPR = Agency for Health Care Policy and Research; AHRQ = Agency for Health Care Research and Quality; AOM = acute otitis media; CCC = cohort, case-control, or cross-sectional study; CSOM = chronic suppurative otitis media; NHS-CRD = National Health Service Centre for Reviews and Dissemination; NZHTA = New Zealand Health Technology Assessment; OME = otitis media with effusion; RCT = randomized controlled trial.

Table 4-6 Systematic Reviews of Otitis Media by Independent Investigators

Year	First Author	Topic	Major Aanalyses	No. of Studies
1991	Rosenfeld[12]	OME	Oral steroid ± antibiotic	6 RCT
1992	Bonati[13]	AOM	Antibiotic prophylaxis	8 RCT
1992	Rosenfeld[14]	OME	Antibiotic therapy	10 RCT
1993	Williams[15]	AOM, OME	Antibiotic therapy and prophylaxis	27 RCT
1994	Garcia[16]	Tube otorrhea	Ototopical antibiotic	5 RCT
1994	Rosenfeld[17]	AOM	Natural history, antibiotic therapy	33 RCT
1996	DiFranza[18]	Otitis media	Environmental tobacco smoke	32 CCC
1996	Pignataro[19]	OME	Mucolytic (carbocysteine) therapy	10 RCT
1996	Uhari[20]	AOM	Epidemiologic risk factors	22 CCC
1998	Damoiseaux[21]	AOM	Antibiotic therapy under age 2 years	6 RCT
1999	Lee[22]	Tube otorrhea	Swimming without ear protection	1 RCT, 4 CCC
1999	Reidpath[23]	OME	Nasal autoinflation	6 RCT
2001	Ioannidis[24]	AOM	Azithromycin vs. other antibiotic	25 RCT
2001	Kay[25]	Tube sequelae	Sequelae incidence	64 RCT, 70 CCC
2001	Rosenfeld[26]	Surgery	MEE prevalence, AOM incidence	7 RCT

AOM = acute otitis media; CCC = cohort, case-control, or cross-sectional study; MEE = middle ear effusion; OME = otitis media with effusion; RCT = randomized controlled trial.

Table 4-7 Meta-analyses of Otitis Media Natural History

Year	First Author	N*	Outcome	Time	Result %[†], (95% CI)	Comment
1994	Rosenfeld[17]	33	AOM clinical cure	7–14 d	81 (69, 94)	Weighted regression
2001	Marcy[4]	5	AOM clinical success[††]	1–7 d	81 (72, 90)	Random effects
2001	Marcy[4]	3	AOM clinical success[††]	3–7 d	78 (66, 90)	Random effects
2002	Glasziou[9]	3	AOM pain free	24 h	62 (56, 67)	Binomial proportion
2002	Glasziou[9]	8	AOM pain free	2–7 d	79 (77, 82)	Binomial proportion
2002	Takata[5]	3	OME tymp B/C → A	< 6 wk	42 (24, 61)	Age 3 yr or older
2002	Takata[5]	3	OME tymp B → A	< 6 wk	37 (2, 73)	Age 3 yr or older
2002	Takata[5]	4	OME tymp B/C → A	< 3 mo	43 (29, 56)	Age 3 yr or older
2002	Takata[5]	4	OME tymp B → A	< 3 mo	23 (6, 39)	Age 3 yr or older

AOM = acute otitis media; OME = otitis media with effusion.
*Number of studies contributing data.
[†]Rate of spontaneous resolution for placebo controls or an untreated cohort.
[††]Reported originally as clinical failure; transformed for consistency with other studies.

Table 4-8 Meta-analyses of Antimicrobials for Treating or Preventing AOM

Year	First Author	N*	Outcome, Comparison	Time	Result[†] (95% CI)	NNT[‡]
1994	Rosenfeld[17]	4	Clinical cure, abx vs. no abx[††]	7–14 d	RD 0.14 (.09, .19)	7
1998	Damoiseaux[21]	4	Clinical improvement, abx vs. placebo	≤ 7 d	OR 1.31 (.83, 2.08)	NS
2001	Marcy[4]	5	Clinical failure, amoxicillin vs. no abx[††]	2–7 d	RD −0.12 (−.22, −.03)	8
2002	Glasziou[9]	3	Persistent pain, abx vs. placebo	24 h	OR 1.03 (.76, 1.39)	NS
2002	Glasziou[9]	8	Persistent pain, abx vs. placebo	2–7 d	OR 0.61 (.48, .77)	17
2002	Glasziou[9]	3	Abnormal tymp, abx vs. placebo	1 mo	OR 0.91 (.62, 1.32)	NS
2002	Glasziou[9]	3	Contralateral AOM, abx vs. placebo	—	OR 0.57 (.36, .91)	[§]15
2002	Glasziou[9]	5	Recurrent AOM, abx vs. placebo	—	OR 1.00 (.78, 1.27)	NS
1992	Bonati[13]	8	Any AOM in trial, abx prophylaxis	2–6 mo	OR 0.23 (.16, .34)	3
1993	Williams[15]	9	AOM/child-month, abx prophylaxis	10 wk–2 yr	RD 0.11 (.03, .19)	9
1993	Williams[15]	5	AOM/child-month, sulfisox prophylaxis	10 wk–2 yr	RD 0.20 (.07, .32)	5

abx = antibiotic; AOM = acute otitis media; CI = confidence interval; NNT = number needed to treat; NS = not significant; OR = odds ratio; RD = absolute rate difference; sulfisox = sulfisoxazole; tymp = tympanogram.
*Number of studies contributing data.
[†]The outcome is more common in the antibiotic group when the RD > 0 or the OR > 1.
[‡]Number needed to treat to achieve one successful outcome; relevant only if $p < .05$ (95% CI for the RD does not include zero, or the 95% CI for the OR does not include one).
[††]All studies, except one, were placebo controlled.
[§]NNT calculated as reciprocal of random effects RD using raw data provided by authors.

somewhat unclear but most likely represents older children with nonsevere AOM, in whom placebo therapy would be considered ethical.[77] Further, all source articles were restricted to initial therapy of uncomplicated AOM, and many excluded recurrent episodes.

Rosenfeld and colleagues[17] pooled data from four RCTs to show a 14% increase in clinical cures over placebo or no drug (see Table 4-8). Although statistically significant, seven children (NNT) must receive antibiotics to cure one. Marcy and coworkers[4] obtained similar results (NNT of 8) in the AHRQ evidence report, using five RCTs (see Table 4-3) employing ampicillin or amoxicillin versus placebo or no drug. Although Glasziou and colleagues[9] also found a significant antibiotic benefit, the magnitude of effect was much lower (NNT of 17). This difference relates to less restrictive inclusion criteria (8 RCTs) compared with the other two analyses (4 to 5 RCTs) and to using pain as the outcome instead of clinical resolution.

Equally important in Table 4-8 are the "negative" meta-analysis results. Compared with placebo, initial antibiotic therapy for AOM does not relieve pain at 24 hours, prevent AOM recurrence, or resolve middle ear effusion at 1 month (normal tympanogram).[9] Conversely, initial antibiotics do reduce contralateral AOM by 43% (OR .57), but 15 children with unilateral AOM would need treatment to prevent one new contralateral episode. The meta-analyses in Table 4-8 argue strongly for realistic and modest expectations regarding the impact of antibiotics on AOM resolution, and for selective treatment of children most likely to benefit (eg, infants and young children with severe AOM who are most at risk for persistent symptoms and suppurative complications).[78]

In a meta-analysis by Williams and colleagues,[15] antimicrobial prophylaxis of recurrent AOM reduced the rate of subsequent recurrence by 0.11 episodes per patient-month (see Table 4-8). Therefore, preventing a single AOM episode requires 9 months of prophylaxis for the average child. Further, the rate of AOM per patient-month observed in the control group (0.19) was much less than the baseline rate, suggesting that most resolution was related to natural history not antimicrobial therapy. Bonati and colleagues[13] also noted a significant benefit of prophylaxis on recurrent AOM, but did not adjust for study duration when pooling. No pooled data are available regarding the impact of prolonged antibiotics on bacterial resistance, but the risk of this event, balanced against the small clinical benefits achieved, suggests a very limited role for antibiotic prophylaxis in managing children with recurrent AOM.

Several subgroups were identified by Williams and colleagues[15] that showed a trend toward increased efficacy of antibiotic prophylaxis. Children who received sulfisoxazole had a mean reduction of 0.20 episodes per

patient-month versus 0.04 for those using other medications (ampicillin, amoxicillin, or co-trimoxazole). Studies with a high rate of AOM recurrence in the control group had a mean reduction of 0.25 episodes per patient-month versus 0.06 for those with infrequent AOM in controls (less than 0.2 episodes per month). Neither of these trends, however, was statistically significant.

Meta-analyses of Comparative Antimicrobial Efficacy for Treating AOM

Meta-analyses[3,10,17,24] of comparative antimicrobial efficacy for treating AOM have shown almost no significant differences in clinical failure rates based on drug choice or duration (Table 4-9). This is not surprising, given the favorable natural history of untreated AOM (see Table 4-7) and the small absolute benefit of antibiotic therapy (see Table 4-8). Although longer courses of therapy (8 to 10 days) are statistically more effective than shorter courses (5 days or less), a NNT of up to 20 children (see Table 4-9) questions clinical importance. Further, the effect is no longer significant after 20 to 30 days, and there are no differences in AOM resolution, relapse, or recurrence for 3 months following long versus short treatment.

Before concluding that drug choice and duration for AOM should be arbitrary, several caveats are in order. First, the impact of child age on outcomes is unclear, with newer evidence suggesting that infants and young children benefit more from full course (7 to 10 day) therapy.[79–82] Second, the optimal method for evaluating comparative drug efficacy is with double-tap bacteriologic studies (see Chapter 16, "Bacteriologic Efficacy of Antimicrobial Agents") because clinical criteria alone can mask potential differences.[83] Nonetheless, the negative findings in Table 4-9, combined with additional negative drug comparisons that are not listed,[3,17] imply that the average clinician need not fret excessively about initial drug choice for sporadic, uncomplicated AOM. This leads to the third caveat; results should not be generalized to children with recurrent, persistent, or complicated AOM because they are excluded from most RCTs. These children are more likely to harbor resistant bacterial pathogens, which have varying sensitivities to commonly used AOM antibiotics.

Meta-analyses of Antimicrobials or Steroids for Treating OME

Three meta-analyses[2,14,15] show a beneficial *short-term* effect of antibiotics on OME resolution (Table 4-10), defined as complete clearance of middle ear effusion (MEE) from all affected ears. The NNT of 6 to 7 suggests a modest effect size within 1 to 2 months,[2,15] but the impact loses statistical significance with follow-up beyond 6 weeks.[15] Publication bias is unlikely because

Table 4-9 Meta-analyses of Comparative Antimicrobial Efficacy for Treating AOM

Year	First Author	N*	Antimicrobial Comparison	Time	AOM Clinical Failure[†] (95% CI)	NNT[‡]
1994	Rosenfeld[17]	3	Penicillin vs. ampicillin	7–14 d	RD 0.07 (−.02, .15)	NS
2001	Marcy[4]	3	Penicillin vs. amox or ampicillin	7–14 d	RD 0.04, (−.02, .11)	NS
2001	Ioannidis[24]	18	Azithro 3–5 d vs. other abx 10 d	7–14 d	OR 1.12 (.81, 1.54)	NS
2001	Marcy[4]	5	Azithro < 5 d vs. amox-clav 7–10 d	10–14 d	RD 0.02 (−.01, .05)	NS
2002	Kozyrskyj[10]	10	Azithro 3–5 d vs. other abx 10 d	10–14 d	OR 1.11 (.82, 1.51)	NS
2001	Marcy[4]	3	Ceftriaxone IM 1 d vs. amox 7–10 d	5–10 d	RD 0.03 (−.02, .08)	NS
2002	Kozyrskyj[10]	3	Ceftriaxone IM 1 d vs. other abx 10 d	≤ 1 mo	OR 1.25 (.90, 1.72)	NS
2002	Kozyrsky[10]	5	Any abx 5 d vs. any abx 8–10 d	8–19 d	OR 1.52 (1.17, 1.98)	13
2002	Kozyrskyj[10]	9	Any abx 5 d vs. any abx 8–10 d	20–30 d	OR 1.22 (.98, 1.54)	NS
2002	Kozyrskyj[10]	7	Same abx 5 d vs. 8–10 d	≤ 1 mo	OR 1.54 (1.21, 1.95)	[§]20

abx = antibiotic; amox = amoxicillin; azithro = azithromycin; AOM = acute otitis media; CI = confidence interval; clav = clavulanate; NNT = number needed to treat; NS = not significant; OR = odds ratio; RD = absolute rate difference; IM = intramuscular.
*Number of studies contributing data.
[†]The rate of clinical failure is more common with the first antibiotic regimen when the RD > 0 or the OR > 1.
[‡]Number needed to treat to achieve one successful outcome; relevant only if $p < .05$ (95% CI for the RD does not include zero, or the 95% CI for the OR does not include one).
[§]NNT calculated as reciprocal of random effects RD using raw data provided by authors.

Table 4-10 Meta-analyses of Antimicrobials or Steroids for Treating OME

Year	First Author	N*	Treatment vs. Control	Time	OME Complete Resolution[†] (95% CI)	NNT[‡]
1992	Rosenfeld[14]	10	Abx vs. placebo or no drug	10 d–2 mo	RD 0.23 (.10, .35)	4
1993	Williams[15]	12	Abx vs. placebo	≤ 1 mo	RD 0.16 (.03, .29)	6
1993	Williams[15]	8	Abx vs. placebo	6 wk–11 mo	RD 0.06 (−.03, .14)	NS
1994	Stool[2]	10	Abx vs. placebo	2 wk–2 mo	RD 0.14 (.04, .24)	7
1991	Rosenfeld[12]	3	Oral steroid vs. placebo	≤ 2 wk	RD 0.20 (−.03, .42) [††]	NS
1994	Stool[2]	3	Oral steroid vs. placebo	≤ 2 wk	RD 0.18 (−.03, .39)	NS
2002	Butler[7]	2	Oral steroid vs. placebo	≤ 2 wk	OR 2.56 (.60, 11.11)	NS
1991	Rosenfeld[12]	3	Oral steroid + abx vs. abx alone	≤ 2 wk	RD 0.31 (−.09, .71) [††]	NS
1994	Stool[2]	4	Oral steroid + abx vs. abx alone	≤ 2 wk	RD 0.25 (−.01, .50)	NS
2002	Butler[7]	4	Oral steroid + abx vs. abx alone	≤ 2 wk	OR 3.13 (1.92, 5.00)	[§]3

abx = antibiotic; CI = confidence interval; OME = otitis media with effusion; NNT = number needed to treat; NS = not significant; OR = odds ratio; RD = absolute rate difference.
*Number of studies contributing data.
[†]The rate of OME resolution is more common with treatment when the RD > 0 or the OR > 1.
[‡]Number needed to treat to achieve one successful outcome; relevant only if $p < .05$ (95% CI for the RD does not include zero, or the 95% CI for the OR does not include one).
[††]Recalculated as random-effects RD using raw data provided by authors.
[§]NNT calculated as reciprocal of random effects RD using raw data provided by authors.

nearly 400 unpublished studies with null results are needed to offset the short-term effects seen in these analyses. The NNT of 4 obtained by Rosenfeld and Post[14] is somewhat higher but is inflated by several unblinded studies, which, if excluded, produce in an NNT consistent with other analyses. In contrast, the impact of antibiotics on OME resolution was deemed nonsignificant in an unsystematic review.[75]

Three meta-analyses[2,7,12] have addressed the efficacy of oral steroids for OME (see Table 4-10). The results are most promising for combination steroid-antimicrobial therapy and achieve statistical significance with an NNT of 3 in the analysis by Butler and van der Hoort.[7] This last analysis, however, has significant heterogeneity and includes a study[84] that uses partial OME resolution (eg, one of two affected ears) as a successful outcome, in contrast to the other analyses that required complete resolution in all affected ears for success. Excluded from all analyses is a recent RCT of steroid-antimicrobial therapy that is larger than prior studies ($N = 135$) and showed a significant benefit at 2 weeks (RD 17%, $p = .03$) but not at 4 weeks.[85] Cumulative meta-analysis would likely show an overall significant short-term benefit.

Considering that antibiotic therapy of OME achieves, at best, only a modest transient short-term benefit, the role of active therapy for most children should be limited. Adding an oral steroid may boost short-term efficacy, but the lack of a long-term effect is disappointing, and potential side effects of steroid therapy cannot be ignored. Until a long-term effect can be obtained, either by applying specific patient selection criteria or by an alternative therapeutic regimen, the potential adverse effects of antimicrobial or steroid therapy appear to outweigh any transient benefit in most children with OME.

Meta-analyses of Nonantibiotic Therapy for AOM or OME

A pot-pourri of meta-analyses of nonantibiotic therapy for AOM or OME are listed in Table 4-11. The pneumococcal polysaccharide vaccine (PPV) reduces AOM incidence by 17% (RR 0.83) in children aged 2 years or older,[11] but the NNT of 125 implies a trivial impact for the average child with sporadic AOM. The vaccine showed no effect below age 2 years, but the newer heptavalent conjugate reduced recurrent AOM by 9% in two studies (data not suitable for pooling).[86,87] Whether these vaccines (polysaccharide or conjugate) have greater efficacy in high-risk (otitis-prone) populations is being investigated.

Antihistamines or decongestants, alone or in combination, are not efficacious for AOM or OME (see Table 4-11).[2,8] Although combination therapy reduced AOM failures by 24% (RR .76) in five RCTs, the authors

Table 4-11 Meta-analyses of Nonantibiotic Interventions for AOM or OME

Year	First Author	N*	Outcome, Intervention	Time	Result† (95% CI)		NNT‡
2002	Straetemans[11]	5	AOM/child-month, PPV, age > 24 mo	—	RR	0.83 (.63, 97)	§125
2002	Flynn[8]	6	AOM failure, antihistamine (AH)	2 wk	RR	0.99 (.83, 1.18)	NS
2002	Flynn[8]	7	AOM failure, decongestant (DC)	2 wk	RR	1.00 (.83, 1.21)	NS
2002	Flynn[8]	10	AOM failure, AH, DC, or AH/DC	2 wk	RR	0.90 (.79, 1.03)	NS
2002	Flynn[8]	5	AOM failure, AH/DC combination	2 wk	RR	0.76 (.60, .96)	11
1994	Stool[2]	4	OME resolution, AH, DC, or AH/DC	—	RD	−0.01 (−.04, .05)	NS
1996	Pignataro[19]	4	OME tymp improved, carbocysteine	15 d–3 mo	OR	2.25 (.97, 5.22)	NS
1996	Pignataro[19]	6	OME improved, carbocysteine	15 d–3 mo	OR	2.31 (1.28, 4.20)	7
1999	Reidpath[23]	6	OME resolution, nasal autoinflation	—	OR	1.85 (1.22, 2.80)	§14

AOM = acute otitis media; CI = confidence interval; NNT = number needed to treat; NS = not significant; OME = otitis media with effusion; OR = odds ratio; PPV = pneumococcal polysaccharide vaccine; RD = absolute rate difference; RR = relative risk; tymp = tympanogram.
*Number of studies contributing data.
†The outcome is more common in the intervention group when the RD > 0 or the OR > 1.
‡Number needed to treat to achieve one successful outcome; relevant only if $p < .05$ (95% CI for the RD does not include zero, or the 95% CI for the OR does not include one).
§NNT calculated as reciprocal of random effects RD using raw data provided by authors.

Table 4-12 Meta-analyses of Surgery and Surgical Sequelae

Year	First Author	N*	Outcome, Comparison	Time	Result[†] (95% CI)	NNT[‡]
2001	Rosenfeld[26]	5	AOM/child-yr, tube vs. no tube	12 mo	RR 0.44 (.24, .79)	1
2001	Rosenfeld[26]	3	MEE days/child-yr, tube vs. no tube	12 mo	RR 0.33 (.23, .46)[††]	—
2001	Kay[25]	10	Atrophy/retraction, tube vs. no tube	—	RR 1.7 (1.1, 2.7)	9
2001	Kay[25]	13	Tympanosclerosis, tube vs. no tube	—	RR 3.5 (2.6, 4.9)	3
2001	Kay[25]	8	Perforation, long- vs. short-term tube	—	RR 3.5 (1.5, 7.1)	14
2001	Kay[25]	6	Cholesteatoma, long vs. short tube	—	RR 2.6 (1.5, 4.4)	77
1994	Garcia[16]	3	Tube otorrhea, postop ototopical abx	≤ 1 mo	OR 0.12 (.04, .37)	[§]6
1999	Lee[22]	5	Tube otorrhea, swimming vs. none	—	RD −0.05 (−.12, .02)	NS

AOM = acute otitis media; CI = confidence interval; MEE = middle ear effusion; NNT = number needed to treat; NS = not significant; OR = odds ratio; RD = absolute rate difference; RR = relative risk.

*Number of studies contributing data.

[†]The outcome is more common in the first group when the RD > 0 or the OR > 1.

[‡]Number needed to treat to achieve one outcome (or sequelae); relevant only if $p < .05$ (95% CI for the RD does not include zero, or the 95% CI for the OR does not include one).

[§]NNT calculated as reciprocal of random effects RD using raw data provided by authors.

[††]Absolute reduction of 115 MEE days/child-year (95% CI, 11, 220).

do not recommend this regimen because the NNT (11) is high and the NNH for drug side effects only slightly higher (17); lower-quality studies found higher benefits (suggesting a design bias), and the subgroup result was no longer significant after adjustment for multiple comparisons.[8] The evidence for OME is clearer, with four RCTs showing a consistent lack of effect.[2] Neither of these analyses were able to assess the modifying effect of allergies on efficacy, but for OME, the tight 95% CI makes such an effect unlikely.

One meta-analysis[19] showed a promising effect of mucolytic therapy (carbocysteine) on OME with an OR of 2.31 (NNT 7). This result has low validity because the trials were heterogeneous, had diverse outcome measures, and used partial resolution as an end point (which tends to give optimistic results versus complete resolution in all ears). Further, the impact of therapy was no longer significant with tympanometry as an outcome (four trials) versus the "relaxed" criteria of clinical improvement (six trials).

Nasal autoinflation for OME was studied in one meta-analysis.[23] The statistically significant but modest NNT of 14 must be viewed with skepticism because the trials were unblinded, heterogeneous, and of varying methodologic quality (some were unpublished). Moreover, all studies employed short-term outcome measures; the likelihood of a long-term benefit is extremely small, given the lack of a similar demonstrable benefit with other interventions (eg, antibiotics or steroids).

Meta-analyses of Surgery and Sequelae

A meta-analysis[26] of tympanostomy tubes showed relative differences of 56% less AOM and 67% less MEE for 12 months after surgery compared with no tube or myringotomy (Table 4-12). The NNT of 1 for AOM probably understates the effect because any tube otorrhea counted as an AOM episode. The absolute reduction of MEE was 115 days/child-year. Although several RCTs have addressed the impact of adenoidectomy on OM, the data were not suitable for pooling. Another meta-analysis of surgery for OME (not listed in Table 4-12) reported that tubes improved hearing levels by 12 dB (no confidence interval provided) and that adenoidectomy added less than 3 dB additional benefit.[1]

Kay and colleagues[25] studied tympanostomy tube sequelae in 64 RCTs and 70 observational studies. Simple pooling of binomial results showed postoperative otorrhea in 16% of patients, delayed otorrhea in 26%, recurrent otorrhea in 7.4%, and chronic otorrhea in 3.8%. Sequelae after tube extrusion included tympanosclerosis (32%), focal atrophy (25%), retraction pocket (3.1%), and perforation (2.2% with short-term tubes, 16.6% with long-term tubes). Meta-analysis results in Table 4-12 show a NNH of 9 for atrophy/retraction and 3 for tympanosclerosis. Compared with short-term tubes, long-term tubes (eg, t-tubes) have an NNH of 14 for perforation and 77 for cholesteatoma.

Table 4-13 Meta-analyses of Otitis Media Risk Factors

Year	First Author	N*	Outcome, Risk Factor	Result† (95% CI)
1996	Uhari[20]	2	AOM, positive family history	RR 2.63 (1.86, 3.72)
1996	Uhari[20]	6	AOM, day care outside the home	RR 2.45 (1.51, 3.98)
1996	Uhari[20]	3	AOM, parental smoking	RR 1.66 (1.33, 2.06)
1996	Uhari[20]	2	AOM, pacifier use	RR 1.24 (1.06, 1.46)
1996	Uhari[20]	6	AOM, breast feeding ≥ 3 mo	RR .87 (.79, .95)
1996	DiFranza[18]	4	AOM incidence, ETS exposure	RR 1.19 (1.05, 1.35)
1996	DiFranza[18]	7	AOM prevalence, ETS exposure	OR 1.58 (1.11, 2.24)
1996	DiFranza[18]	4	Tympanostomy tube insertion, ETS exposure	OR 1.38 (1.02, 1.85)

AOM = acute otitis media; CI = confidence interval; ETS = environmental tobacco smoke; OR = odds ratio; RR = relative risk.
*Number of studies contributing data.
†The outcome is more common with the risk factor if the RR or OR > 1, and is statistically significant ($p < .05$) if the 95% CI does not contain one.

Garcia and colleagues[16] found an NNT of 6 to prevent postoperative tube otorrhea by administering ototopical antibiotics in the perioperative period. The trials were heterogeneous, however, and the event rate in the control group was only 18%. Lee and coworkers[22] assessed the impact of swimming without ear protection versus nonswimming on tympanostomy tube otorrhea. There was no significant impact of water precautions, and results tended to favor the swimmers. Selection bias is a potential problem because four of the five included trials were not randomized.

Meta-analyses of Otitis Media Risk Factors

Two meta-analyses[18,20] have pooled data from observational studies to identify epidemiologic risk factors for OM (Table 4-13). Uhari and coworkers[20] found a negative association with breast feeding for 3 months or longer and positive associations with pacifier use, parental smoking, positive family history, and day care outside the home. The last two factors conferred the largest relative risk (2.45 and 2.63, respectively). In contrast to this study, which combined data from cohort and case-control studies, DiFranza and Lew[18] stratified their analyses by study type. Exposure to environmental tobacco smoke increased AOM incidence by 19% in cohort studies, AOM prevalence by 58% in case-control studies, and tympanostomy tube insertion by 38% in case-control studies. Although statistically significant, the lower ends of the confidence limits cannot exclude the possibility of an almost trivial impact.

Miscellaneous Otitis Media Meta-Analyses

Diagnostic methods for OME were studied in one meta-analysis using myringotomy as the gold standard comparison (Table 4-14).[5] Among the nine diagnostic methods reviewed, pneumatic otoscopy offered the optimal balance of sensitivity (94%) and specificity (80%). Professional tympanometry using a B or C2 curve as abnormal had comparable sensitivity (94%) but tympanometry using static compensated acoustic admittance at 0.1 had the best specificity (95%). Overall, study quality was considered poor because many investigators did not describe qualifications of the testers, reproducibility of test results, or representativeness of the patient sample. The data available were insufficient to evaluate audiometry, binocular microscopy, and nonpneumatic otoscopy as diagnostic methods.

The same investigators[5] studied the relationship of early-life OME (positive OM history prior to 3 years of age) to later developmental outcomes. No associations were found for expressive language, receptive language, or cognitive verbal intelligence (see Table 4-14), but heterogeneity and wide 95% CIs cannot exclude that an effect was missed (low power). Further caution is required when extrapolating these results because only one study focused specifically on persistent bilateral OME and none specifically assessed children who already had speech, language, or developmental delays. The data available were insufficient to assess the impact of early-life OME on speech development. Stool and colleagues[2] reviewed potential developmental sequelae of OME but did not pool data.

Table 4-14 Miscellaneous Otitis Media Meta-analyses

Year	First Author	N*	Outcome, Intervention or Factor	Result† (95% CI)		NNT‡
2002	Takata[5]	7	OME diagnosis, pneumatic otoscopy vs. myringotomy	SE	0.94 (.91, .96)	—
				SP	0.80 (.75, .86)	
2002	Takata[5]	6	OME diagnosis, tympanogram type B or C2 vs. myringotomy	SE	0.94 (.91, .96)	—
				SP	0.62 (.41, .82)	
2002	Takata[5]	16	OME diagnosis, tympanogram type B vs. myringotomy	SE	0.81 (.76, .86)	—
				SP	0.74 (.67, .82)	
2002	Takata[5]	4	OME diagnosis, tympanogram admittance ≤ 0.1 vs. myringotomy	SE	0.33 (.17, .49)	—
				SP	0.95 (.88, 1.00)	
2002	Takata[5]	4	Conductive HL age 6–10y, early OM+ vs. OM–	RD	0.11 (.03, .19)	9
2002	Takata[5]	3	Expressive language age > 3 y, early OM+ vs. OM–	SD	0.15 (–.49, .20)	NS
2002	Takata[5]	4	Receptive language age > 3 y, early OM+ vs. OM–	SD	0.10 (–.29, .50)	NS
2002	Takata[5]	3	Cognitive verbal intelligence age > 3 y, early OM+ vs. OM–	SD	0.23 (–.20, .65)	NS
2002	Acuin[6]	5	CSOM, ototopical quinolone vs. nonquinolone	OR	0.26 (.16, .41)	§3
2002	Acuin[6]	6	CSOM, ototopical abx vs. systemic abx	OR	0.46 (.30, .69)	§4
2002	Acuin[6]	6	CSOM, ototopical abx + aural toilet vs. toilet alone	OR	0.31 (.23, .43)	§3

abx = antibiotic; CI = confidence interval; CSOM = chronic suppurative otitis media; HL = hearing loss; NNT = number needed to treat; NS = not significant; OM = otitis media; OME = otitis media with effusion; OR = odds ratio; RD = absolute rate difference; SD = standardized mean difference.

*Number of studies contributing data.

†SD or RD > 0 favors the OM negative group; OR < 1 favors the first intervention listed.

‡Number needed to treat to achieve one outcome (or sequelae); relevant only if $p < .05$. (95% CI for the SD does not include zero, or the 95% CI for the OR does not include one).

§NNT calculated as reciprocal of random effects RD using raw data provided by authors.

In contrast to the nonsignificant relationships for developmental sequelae, children with early-life OME were 11% more likely (absolute RD) than controls to have conductive hearing loss at age 6 to 10 years (see Table 4-14).[5] Although the four studies were statistically homogeneous, their populations have limited generalizability: one cohort was from Finland, another from Sweden, another included primarily Native Americans, and another primarily Inuit. Study quality was also variable and often poor. The data available were insufficient to assess the impact of early-life OME on permanent (sensorineural) hearing loss.

One meta-analysis[6] compared interventions for CSOM, defined as persistent otorrhea with a nonintact tympanic membrane. Significant benefits were found for ototopical antibiotics versus systemic antibiotics, ototopical antibiotics versus aural toilet, and for ototopical quinolones versus other antibiotics (see Table 4-14). The NNTs are favorable (3 to 4), but generalizability is limited because most subjects were adults, children with tympanostomy tubes were excluded, and significant heterogeneity was present among studies.

The effectiveness of preschool and school entrant screening programs for OME and conductive hearing loss was assessed in one systematic review.[3] Only a few relevant studies were identified, which did not demonstrate screening efficacy. Results were deemed inconclusive, however, because of deficiencies in source article methodology.

Limitations and Pitfalls of Meta-analysis

Meta-analysis benefits must be balanced against limitations (Table 4-15).[88,89] The main benefit relates to recognizing meta-analysis as a research discipline, not simply a publication type. Compared with traditional narrative reviews, the potential for bias is greatly reduced with an a priori systematic protocol. Further, the pooled results achieve increased precision and statistical power compared with individual studies. If studies are heterogeneous, however, a proverbial mixing of apples and oranges may result. Diversity is both a limitation and a

Table 4-15 Pointers and Pitfalls

1. Systematic reviews use explicit and reproducible criteria to assemble, appraise, and combine articles with a minimum of bias.

2. Meta-analysis is a form of systematic review that uses statistical techniques to derive quantitative estimates of the magnitude of treatment effects and their associated precision.

3. Valid systematic reviews address focused questions, use appropriate criteria to select articles, assess the quality and combinability of selected articles, and can be generalized to a meaningful target population.

4. Otitis media is an ideal topic for meta-analysis because of a large number of randomized trials; however, caution is required when combining studies because of variations in diagnostic methods, disease severity, treatment protocols, and outcome definitions.

5. The rate difference, or absolute risk reduction, is the preferred measure of clinical effect size; the reciprocal tells the number needed to treat for one additional favorable outcome.

6. The benefits of meta-analysis over individual trials include greater precision, increased statistical power, and the ability to identify and explore diversity among studies. Threats to validity include heterogeneity, citation bias, publication bias, language bias, and variations in study quality.

7. Meta-analysis defines rational treatment expectations at a population level; it is an adjunct to, not a substitute for, clinical judgment in the care of individual patients.

benefit for meta-analysis; if mishandled or unrecognized, the pooled results may be erroneous. Conversely, meta-analysis offers a unique opportunity to investigate sources of diversity, beyond what is capable in single studies.[90]

Diversity among studies can result from (1) clinical differences in patients, interventions, or outcomes; (2) methodologic differences in study designs or control over bias; or (3) statistical differences suggesting that variation in treatment effects between trials are beyond that compatible with chance alone (eg, heterogeneity $p < .05$).[91] Random-effects models offer a partial solution but do not explain why heterogeneity exists. Explanations may result from subgroup analysis and regression analysis of source articles (meta-regression) or of pooling of individual patient data, if obtainable. Subgroup analyses must be viewed cautiously because they can generate spuriously significant p values (multiple comparison problem) and bias may result if the grouping was post hoc (not done prior to randomization).[89]

Diversity is also the reason why meta-analyses and large RCTs tend to disagree about 10 to 25% of the time, beyond chance variations.[92] The differences are most apparent when small trials are pooled and relate to variations in design, selection of studies, and methods of analysis. Meta-analyses of small RCTs (which is often the case for OM) are best viewed as means to generate hypotheses for large clinical trials, not a substitute for further research.[93] Rigorously designed large RCTs remain the gold standard for deriving efficacy data and identifying prognostic factors. In contrast, meta-analyses of large RCTs could obtain an unbiased population estimate of treatment effect and explore interactions among subgroups.

The ability to generalize meta-analysis results based on RCTs can be limited. Phase III drug trials, which are typically double-blind RCTs, provide useful information on what may be achieved under near ideal conditions. For example, most OM RCTs use explicit diagnostic criteria, monitor compliance, and assess outcome with criteria that are more often objective and reproducible than patient based. Moreover, the very children excluded from these studies are the ones most likely to have OM (eg, children with syndromes, craniofacial defects, immune deficiency). Large pragmatic real-world trials are optimally needed to estimate how well the potential benefits seen in RCTs (or meta-analyses of RCTs) can be realized in routine clinical care. Unfortunately, research of this type is rarely performed or available.[89]

Another issue of generalizability is raised by the NNT as a measure of effect size. NNTs are sensitive to factors that change the baseline risk, such as the clinical setting, patients' characteristics, and secular trends in incidence. For interventions with small treatment effects (eg, NNTs > 100), the NNT should be calculated from the OR using the expected baseline risk in the target population.[94] Conversely, most OM interventions show relatively large treatment effects (eg, NNT < 20), which are insensitive to baseline risk and do not require adjustment.[95] For meta-analyses of AOM prevention, however, the method for calculating the NNT must be scrutinized. Data should be pooled using events (AOM episodes) per time interval (eg, patient-months or patient-years), not simply by events per patient.[89,96] The latter method yields an NNT that is difficult to interpret if studies had different follow-up periods.

Several limitations of meta-analysis relate specifically to policy formulation. Results of systematic reviews apply to populations but may be of less use in treating individual patients. An NNT of 8 cannot tell in advance which one of the eight treated will benefit, regardless of the precision in the associated 95% confidence interval. Further, side effects of treatment, which are important to both patients and policy makers, are not routinely discussed in many systematic reviews.[97] The issue of harm is dealt with more explicitly in some evidence reports.[2,3,67,68] Policy makers should also appreciate that authors of systematic reviews tend to be optimists; they are about 40% more likely than independent readers to conclude that a treatment has a positive effect or a possibly positive effect.[97] Even optimists occasionally produce discordant reviews, which require careful analysis in the context of policy making.[98]

A final drawback of meta-analysis is the effort required for validity (see Tables 4-2 and 4-8). The OME clinical practice guideline incurred about $1,000,000 in direct costs,[2] and subsequent evidence reports on AOM and OME cost approximately $250,000 each.[4–5] Nonetheless, meta-analysis is an invaluable bridge between past and future research efforts, which not only integrates prior work but illuminates research gaps and priorities for future research.[99] New analyses will result from continued refinements in methodology and from ongoing efforts by independent researchers and professional organizations. Meta-analysis has already contributed greatly to our understanding of otitis media risk factors, diagnosis, and management. We look forward to including new meta-analyses in subsequent editions of this book.

References

1. University of York. Centre for Reviews and Dissemination. The treatment of persistent glue ear in children. Effective Health Care 1992;1(4):1–16.
2. Stool SE, Berg AO, Berman S, et al. Otitis media with effusion in young children. Clinical practice guideline, Number 12. AHCPR Publication No. 94-0622. Rockville (MD): Agency for Health Care Policy and Research, Public Health Service, US Department of Health and Human Services; July 1994.
3. New Zealand Health Technology Assessment (NZHTA). Report 3: Screening programmes for the detection of otitis media with effusion and conductive hearing loss in pre-school and new entrant school children: a critical appraisal of the literature. Christchurch (NZ): NZHTA Clearing House; 1998. p. 1–61.
4. Marcy M, Takata G, Shekelle P, et al. Management of acute otitis media. Evidence report/technology assessment No. 15 (Prepared by the Southern California Evidence-based Practice Center under Contract No. 290-97-0001). AHRQ Publication No. 01-E010. Rockville (MD): Agency for Healthcare Research and Quality; May 2001.
5. Takata GS, Chan LS, Shekelle P, et al. Diagnosis, natural history, and late effects of otitis media with effusion. Evidence report/technology assessment: Number 55. AHRQ Publication Number 02-E026. Rockville (MD): Agency for Healthcare Research and Quality; June 2002.
6. Acuin J, Smith A, Mackenzie I. Interventions for chronic suppurative otitis media (Cochrane Review). In: The Cochrane Library, Issue 2, 2002. Oxford (UK): Update Software; 2002.
7. Butler CC, van der Voort JH. Oral or topical nasal steroids for hearing loss associated with otitis media with effusion in children (Cochrane Review). In: The Cochrane Library, Issue 2, 2002. Oxford (UK): Update Software; 2002.
8. Flynn CA, Griffin G, Tudiver F. Decongestants and antihistamines for acute otitis media in children (Cochrane Review). In: The Cochrane Library, Issue 2, 2002. Oxford (UK): Update Software; 2002.
9. Glasziou PP, Del Mar CB, Sanders SL, Hayem M. Antibiotics for acute otitis media in children (Cochrane Review). In: The Cochrane Library, Issue 2, 2002. Oxford (UK): Update Software; 2002.
10. Kozyrskyj AL, Hildes-Ripstein GE, Longstaffe SEA, et al. Short course antibiotics for acute otitis media (Cochrane Review). In: The Cochrane Library, Issue 2, 2002. Oxford (UK): Update Software; 2002.
11. Straetemans M, Sanders EAM, Veenhoven RH, et al. Pneumococcal vaccines for preventing otitis media (Cochrane Review). In: The Cochrane Library, Issue 2, 2002. Oxford (UK): Update Software; 2002.
12. Rosenfeld RM, Mandel EM, Bluestone CD. Systemic steroids for otitis media with effusion in children. Arch Otolaryngol Head Neck Surg 1991;117:984–9.
13. Bonati M, Marchetti F, Pistotti V, et al. Meta-analysis of antimicrobial prophylaxis for recurrent acute otitis media. Clin Trials Meta-Analysis 1992;28:39–50.
14. Rosenfeld RM, Post JC. Meta-analysis of antibiotics for the treatment of otitis media with effusion. Otolaryngol Head Neck Surg 1992;106:378–86.
15. Williams RL, Chalmers TC, Stange KC, et al. Use of antibiotics in preventing recurrent acute otitis media and in treating otitis media with effusion: a meta-analytic attempt to resolve the brouhaha. JAMA 1993; 270:1344–51.
16. Garcia P, Gates GA, Schechtman KB. Does topical antibiotic prophylaxis reduce post-tympanostomy tube otorrhea? A meta-analysis. Ann Otol Rhinol Laryngol 1994;103:54–8.
17. Rosenfeld RM, Vertrees JE, Carr J, et al. Clinical efficacy of antimicrobial drugs for acute otitis media: meta-analysis of 5400 children from thirty-three randomized trials. J Pediatr 1994;124:355–67.
18. DiFranza JR, Lew RA. Morbidity and mortality in children associated with the use of tobacco products by other people. Pediatrics 1996;97:560–8.

19. Pignataro O, Pignataro LD, Gallus G, et al. Otitis media with effusion and S-carboxymethylcysteine and/or its lysine salt: a critical overview. Int J Pediatr Otorhinolaryngol 1996;35:231–41.

20. Uhari M, Mäntysaari K, Niemelä M. A meta-analytic review of the risk factors for acute otitis media. Clin Infect Dis 1996;22:1079–83.

21. Damoiseaux RAMJ, van Balen FAM, Hoes AW, de Melker RA. Antibiotic treatment of acute otitis media in children under two years of age: evidence based? Br J Gen Pract 1998;48:1861–4.

22. Lee D, Youk A, Goldstein NA. A meta-analysis of swimming and water precautions. Laryngoscope 1999;109:536–40.

23. Reidpath DD, Glasziou PP, Del Mar C. Systematic review of autoinflation for treatment of glue ear in children. BMJ 1999;318:1177–8.

24. Ioannidis JPA, Contopoulos-Ioannidis DG, Chew P, Lau J. Meta-analysis of randomized controlled trials on the comparative efficacy and safety of azithromycin against other antibiotics for upper respiratory tract infections. J Antimicrob Chemother 2001;48:677–89.

25. Kay D, Nelson M, Rosenfeld RM. Meta-analysis of tympanostomy tube sequelae. Otolaryngol Head Neck Surg 2001;124:374–80.

26. Rosenfeld RM. Surgical prevention of otitis media. Vaccine 2001;19:S134–9.

27. Moher D, Cook DJ, Eastwood S, et al. Improving the quality of reports of meta-analyses of randomised controlled trials: the QUOROM statement. Lancet 1999;354:1896–900.

28. Light RJ, Pillemer DB. Summing up: the science of reviewing research. Cambridge (MA): Harvard University Press; 1984. p. 3–6.

29. Egger M, Smith GD. Meta-analysis: potentials and promise. BMJ 1997;315:1371–4.

30. Götzsche PC. Reference bias in reports of drug trials. BMJ 1987;295:654–6.

31. Barnes DE, Bero LA. Why review articles on the health effects of passive smoking reach different conclusions. JAMA 1998;279:1566–70.

32. Rochon PA, Bero LA, Bay AM, et al. Comparison of review articles published in peer-reviewed and throw-away journals. JAMA 2002;287:2853–6.

33. Cook DJ, Sackett DL, Spitzer WO. Methodologic guidelines for systematic reviews of randomized control trials in health care from the Postdam consultation on meta-analysis. J Clin Epidemiol 1995;48:167–71.

34. Klassen TP, Jadad AR, Moher D. Guides for reading and interpreting systematic reviews. I. Getting started. Arch Pediatr Adolesc Med 1998;152:700–4.

35. Chalmers I, Hedges LV, Cooper H. A brief history of research synthesis. Eval Health Prof 2002;25:12–37.

36. Rosenfeld RM. How to systematically review the medical literature. Otolaryngol Head Neck Surg 1996;115:53–63.

37. Sutton AJ, Jones DR, Abrams KR, et al. Systematic reviews and meta-analysis: a structured review of the methodological literature. J Health Serv Res Policy 1999;4:49–55.

38. Jadad AR, Haynes RB. The Cochrane Collaboration—advances and challenges in improving evidence-based decision making. Med Decis Making 1998;18:2–9.

39. Jadad AR, Cook DJ, Alison J, et al. Methodology and reports of systematic reviews and meta-analyses: a comparison of Cochrane reviews with articles published in paper-based journals. JAMA 1998;280:278–80.

40. Egger M, Schneider M, Smith GD. Spurious precision? Meta-analysis of observational studies. BMJ 1998;316:410–4.

41. Blettner M, Sauerbrei W, Schlehofer B, et al. Traditional reviews, meta-analyses and pooled analyses in epidemiology. Int J Epidemiol 1999;28:1–9.

42. Stroup DF, Berlin JA, Morton SC, et al. Meta-analysis of observational studies. A proposal for reporting. JAMA 2000;283:2008–12.

43. Lee W, Bausell RB, Berman BM. The growth of health-related meta-analyses published from 1980 to 2000. Eval Health Prof 2001;24:327–35.

44. Feinstein AR. Meta-analysis: statistical alchemy for the 21st century. J Clin Epidemiol 1995;48:71–9.

45. Chalmers TC, Smith H Jr, Blackburn B, et al. A method for assessing the quality of a randomized control trial. Control Clin Trials 1981;2:31–49.

46. Emerson JD, Burdick E, Hoaglin DC, et al. An empirical study of the possible relation of treatment differences to quality scores in controlled randomized clinical trials. Control Clin Trials 1990;11:339–52.

47. Jones DR. Meta-analysis: weighing the evidence. Stat Med 1995;14:137–49.

48. Borenstein M, Rothstein H. Comprehensive meta-analysis: a computer program for research synthesis (v. 1.0.25). Englewood (NJ): Biostat Inc; 2000.

49. Sackett DL. Applying overviews and meta-analyses at the bedside. J Clin Epidemiol 1995;48:61–6.

50. Chatellier G, Zapletal E, Lemaitre D, et al. The number needed to treat: a clinically useful nomogram in its proper context. BMJ 1996;321:426–9.

51. Sackett DL, Richardson WS, Rosenberg W, Haynes RB. Evidence-based medicine: how to practice & teach EBM. New York (NY): Churchill Livingstone; 1997.

52. DerSimonian R, Laird N. Meta-analysis in clinical trials. Control Clin Trials 1986;7:177–88.

53. Sutton AJ, Abrams KR, Jones DR. An illustrated guide to the methods of meta-analysis. J Eval Clin Pract 2001;7:135–48.

54. Borenstein M. The case for confidence intervals in controlled clinical trials. Control Clin Trials 1994;15:411–8.

55. Emerson JD, Burdick E, Hoaglin DC, et al. An empirical study of the possible relation of treatment differences to quality scores in controlled randomized clinical trials. Control Clin Trials 1990;11:339–52.

56. Ferrer RL. Graphical methods for detecting bias in meta-analysis. Fam Med 1998;30:579–83.

57. Olson CM, Rennie D, Cook D, et al. Publication bias in editorial decision making. JAMA 2002;287:2825–8.

58. Rosenthal R. The "file drawer problem" and tolerance for null results. Psychol Bull 1979;86:638–41.

59. Sterne JAC, Gavaghan D, Egger M. Publication and related bias in meta-analysis: power of statistical tests and prevalence in the literature. J Clin Epidemiol 2000;53:1119–29.

60. Egger M, Zellweger-Zahner T, Schneider M, et al. Language bias in randomized controlled trials published in English and German. Lancet 1997;350:326–9.

61. Vickers A, Goyal N, Harland R, Rees R. Do certain countries produce only positive results? A systematic review of controlled trials. Control Clin Trials 1998;19:159–66.

62. Moher D, Pham B, Klassen TP, et al. What contributions do languages other than English make on the results of meta-analyses? J Clin Epidemiol 2000;53:964–72.

63. Juni P, Holenstein F, Sterne J, et al. Direction and impact of language bias in meta-analyses of controlled trials: empirical study. Int J Epidemiol 2002;31:115–23.

64. Mulrow CD, Cook DJ, Davidoff F. Systematic reviews: critical links in the great chain of evidence. Ann Intern Med 1997;126:389–91.

65. McKibbon A, Hunt D, Richardson S, et al. Finding the evidence. In: Guyatt G, Rennie D, editors. Users' guides to the medical literature: a manual for evidence-based clinical practice. Chicago (IL): AMA Press; 2002. p. 13–47.

66. Siwek J, Gourlay MI, Slawson D, Shaughnessy AF. How to write an evidence-based clinical review article. Am Fam Phys 2002;65:251–8.

67. Williamson I. Otitis media with effusion. Clin Evid 2002;7:469–76.

68. O'Neill P. Acute otitis media. Clin Evid 2002;7:236–43.

69. Del Mar C, Glasziou P, Hayem M. Are antibiotics indicated as initial treatment for children with acute otitis media? A meta-analysis. BMJ 1997;314:1526–29.

70. Korzyskyj AL, Hildes-Ripstein G, Longstaffe SEA, et al. Treatment of acute otitis media with a shortened course of antibiotics. A meta-analysis. JAMA 1998;279:1736–42.

71. Butler CC, van de Voort JH. Steroids for otitis media with effusion: a systematic review. Arch Pediatr Adolesc Med 2001;155:641–7.

72. Marchant C, Shurin. Antibacterial therapy for acute otitis media: a critical analysis. Rev Infect Dis 1982;4:506–13.

73. Bodner EE, Browning GG, Chalmers FT, Chalmers TC. Can meta-analysis help uncertainty in surgery for otitis media in children? J Laryngol Otol 1991;105:812–9.

74. Witmer A, Wells AM, Seymour RJ. A comparison of the effectiveness of pharmacologic treatment of otitis media with effusion in children: integrative and meta-analysis. Online J Knowl Syn Nurs [Serial Online] 1998;5(4). http://www.st.iupui.edu/library/ojksn/case_study/050004.pdf (accessed Aug, 2002).

75. Cantekin EI, McGuire TW. Antibiotics are not effective for otitis media with effusion: reanalyses of meta-analyses. Otorhinolaryngol Nova 1998;8:214–22.

76. Damoiseaux RAMJ, van Balen FAM, Hoes AW, et al. Primary care based randomised double blind trial of amoxicillin versus placebo for acute otitis media in children aged under 2 years. BMJ 2000;320:350–4.

77. Burke P, Bain J, Robinson D, Dunleavey J. Acute red ear in children: controlled trial of nonantibiotic treatment in general practice. BMJ 1991;303:558–62.

78. Rosenfeld RM. Observation option toolkit for acute otitis media. Int J Pediatr Otorhinolaryngol 2001;58:1–8.

79. Paradise JL. Short-course antimicrobial treatment for acute otitis media: not best for infants and young children. JAMA 1997; 278:1640–2.

80. Hoberman A, Paradise JL, Burch DJ, et al. Equivalent efficacy and reduced occurrence of diarrhea from a new formulation of amoxicillin/clavulanate potassium (Augmentin) for treatment of acute otitis media in children. Pediatr Infect Dis J 1997;16:463–70.

81. Cohen R, Levy C, Boucherat M, et al. A multicenter, randomized, double-blind trial of 5 versus 10 days of antibiotic therapy for acute otitis media in young children. J Pediatr 1998;133:634–9.

82. Cohen RC, Levy C, Boucherat M, et al. Five vs. ten days of antibiotic therapy for acute otitis media in young children. Pediatr Infect Dis J 2000;19:458–63.

83. Marchant CD, Carlin SA, Johnson CE, Shurin PA. Measuring the comparative efficacy of antibacterial agents for acute otitis media: the "Polyanna phenomenon." J Pediatr 1992;120:72–7.

84. Hemlin C, Carenfelt C, Papatziamos G. Single dose of betamethasone in combined medical treatment of secretory otitis media. Ann Otol Rhinol Laryngol 1997;106:359–63.

85. Mandel EM, Casselbrant ML, Rockette HE, et al. Systemic steroid for chronic otitis media with effusion in children. Pediatrics 2002;110:1071–80.

86. Black S, Shinefield H, Fireman B, et al. Efficacy, safety, and immunogenicity of heptavalent pneumococcal conjugate vaccine in children. Northern California Kaiser Permanente Vaccine Study Center Group. Pediatr Infect Dis J 2000;19:187–95.

87. Eskola J, Kilpi T, Palmu A, et al. Efficacy of a pneumococcal conjugate vaccine against acute otitis media. N Engl J Med 2990;344:403–9.

88. Ioannidis JPA, Lau J. Pooling research results: benefits and limitations of meta-analysis. J Qual Improv 1999;25:462–9.

89. Freemantle N, Mason J, Eccles M. Deriving treatment recommendations from evidence within randomized trials. The role and limiation of meta-analysis. Int J Technol Assess Health Care 1999;15:304–15.

90. Lau J, Ioannidis JPA, Schmid CH. Summing up evidence: one answer is not always enough. Lancet 1998;351:123–7.

91. Higgins J, Thompson S, Deeks J, Altman D. Statistical heterogeneity in systematic reviews of clinical trials: a critical appraisal of guidelines and practice. J Health Services Res Policy 2002;7:51–61.

92. Ioannidis JPA, Cappelleri JC, Lau J. Issues in comparisons between meta-analyses and large trials. JAMA 1998;279:1089–93.

93. Pogue J, Yusuf S. Overcoming the limitations of current meta-analysis of randomised controlled trials. Lancet 1998;351:47–52.

94. Smeeth L, Haines A, Ebrahim S. Numbers needed to treat derived from meta-analyses—sometimes informative, usually misleading. BMJ 1999;318:1548–51.

95. Moore A, McQuay H. NNT is a tool, to be used appropriately. BMJ 1999;319:1290.

96. Rosenfeld RM. What to expect from medical therapy. In: Rosenfeld RM, Bluestone CD, editors. Evidence-based otitis media. Hamilton (ON). BC Decker Inc; 1999. p. 179–206 .

97. Ezzo J, Bausell B, Moerman DE, et al. Reviewing the reviews. How strong is the evidence? How clear are the conclusions? Int J Technol Assess Health Care 2001;17: 457–66.

98. Jadad AR, Cook DJ, Browman GP. A guide to interpreting discordant systematic reviews. Can Med Assoc J 1997;156:1411–6.

99. Chan LS, Takata GS, Shekelle P, et al. Evidence assessment of management of acute otitis media II. Research gaps and priorities for future research. Pediatrics 2001;108:248–54.

CHAPTER 5

Professional Evidence Reports

Glenn S. Takata, MD, MS, and Linda S. Chan, PhD

The beginning of wisdom is:
Acquire wisdom; and with all your acquiring, get understanding.
Proverbs 4:7

OBJECTIVES

On completion of this chapter, the reader should understand the

1. Agency for Healthcare Research and Quality's evidence-based practice initiative.
2. Process of evidence report development.
3. Scope and significance of findings of the acute otitis media (AOM) evidence report.
4. Scope and significance of findings of the otitis media with effusion (OME) evidence report.

AHRQ EVIDENCE-BASED PRACTICE INITIATIVE

The Agency for Health Care Policy and Research, presently the Agency for Healthcare Research and Quality (AHRQ), established 12 Evidence-Based Practice Centers (EPCs) in 1997.[1] The EPCs were charged to promote evidence-based practice in the everyday care of clinical conditions that are common, expensive, or significant for the Medicare and Medicaid populations.[2] With a broad network of experts in clinical, behavioral, organizational, and economic topics, they developed evidence reports and technology assessments based on rigorous systematic reviews and, when needed, supplemental meta-analyses or cost analyses that facilitate the translation of evidence-based research into clinical practice. In June 2002, AHRQ awarded 5-year contracts for 13 EPC II centers (EPC IIs) to continue development of evidence reports and technology assessments and expand on the work of the original group of EPCs by

- updating prior evidence reports;
- providing technical assistance to professional organizations, employers, providers, policy makers, and others to facilitate translation of reports into quality improvement tools, evidence-based curricula, and reimbursement policies; and
- undertaking methods research.

The topics addressed by the original EPCs and the EPC IIs are listed in Table 5-1.[2]

AHRQ's initiative is intended to provide evidence to individuals, such as clinicians, researchers, and policy makers, and to public and private groups, such as medical, professional, and consumer organizations, health purchasers, and health plans. It was hoped that the evidence would help create quality improvement tools, for example, practice guidelines, performance measures, review criteria, and educational programs, and make rational decisions about the use of new technologies, such as medical devices and procedures.[2] The AHRQ regularly solicits nominations for topics for evidence analyses and technology assessments related to "the prevention, diagnosis, treatment, and management of common diseases and clinical conditions, as well as topics relating to organization and financing of health care" through *Federal Register* announcements.[3] Those nominating topics become "partners of AHRQ and the EPCs" and are expected to "serve as resources to EPCs" and as peer reviewers of the draft evidence report or technology assessment and to use the evidence report or technology assessment in their own clinical practice.

AHRQ lists the following selection criteria for topics[2]:

- High incidence or prevalence in the general population and in special populations, including women, racial and ethnic minorities, pediatric and elderly populations, and those of low socioeconomic status
- Significance for the needs of the Medicare, Medicaid, and other Federal health programs
- High costs associated with a condition, procedure, treatment, or technology, whether due to the number of people needing care, high unit cost of care, or high indirect costs
- Controversy or uncertainty about the effectiveness or relative effectiveness of available clinical strategies or technologies
- Impact potential for informing and improving patient or provider decision making
- Impact potential for reducing clinically significant variations in the prevention, diagnosis, treatment,

Table 5-1 AHRQ Supported EPCs and Assigned Topics

Evidence-Based Practice Center	*Topic Assigned—Year Assigned*
Blue Cross and Blue Shield Association, Technical Evaluation Center (TEC), Chicago, IL	Role of endoscopic retrograde cholangiopancreatography (ERCP) in clinical practice—2001 Management of chronic asthma—1999 Use of erythropoietin in hematology and oncology—1998 Testosterone suppression treatment for prostatic cancer—1997
Duke University, Durham, NC	Effect of seasonal allergies on working populations—2001 Management of post-term pregnancy—2000 Treatment of pulmonary disease following spinal cord injury—1999 Treatment of fibroids—1999 Management of acute chronic obstructive pulmonary disease—1998 Evaluation of cervical cytology—1997
ECRI, Plymouth Meeting, PA	Treatment-resistant epilepsy—2001 Repetitive motion disorders, diagnosis, and treatment—2000 Treatment of degenerative lumbar spinal stenosis—1999 Criteria for determining disability in patients with end-stage renal disease (ESRD)—1998 Diagnosis and treatment of dysphagia/swallowing problems in the elderly—1997
Johns Hopkins University, Baltimore, MD	Management of hepatitis C—2001 Management of venous thrombosis—2001 Use of glycohemoglobin and microalbuminuria in diagnosis and monitoring of diabetes mellitus—2001 Bioterrorism: training for rare public health event—2000 Blood pressure monitoring, outside of clinic setting—2000 Treatment of coexisting cataract and glaucoma—1999 Treatment of acne—1998 Anesthesia management during cataract surgery—1998 Evaluation and treatment of new onset of atrial fibrillation in the elderly—1997
McMaster University, Hamilton, Ontario, Canada	Diffusion and dissemination of evidence-based cancer control interventions—2001 Impact of cancer-related decision aids—2000 Management of neurogenic/neuropathic pain following spinal cord injury—1999 Criteria for weaning from mechanical ventilation—1998 Treatment of attention deficit/hyperactivity disorder—1997
MetaWorks, Inc., Boston, MA	Medical and scientific research related to disability from chronic fatigue syndrome—2001 Diagnosis and management of Parkinson's disease—2000 Criteria for the referral of patients with epilepsy—1999 Management of breast disease—1999 Diagnosis of sleep apnea—1997
New England Medical Center, Boston, MA	Management of cancer symptoms—2002 Management of clinically inapparent adrenal mass—2001 Quality of life: management of cancer-associated pain and related symptoms—2001 Neonatal hyperbilirubinemia—2001 Management of allergic rhinitis—2000 Criteria to determine disability for infant/childhood impairments—2000 Evaluation of technologies for identifying acute cardiac ischemia in the emergency department—1999 Management of cancer pain—1998 Diagnosis and treatment of acute bacterial sinusitis—1997

Table 5-1 AHRQ Supported EPCs and Assigned Topics (continued)

Evidence-Based Practice Center	Topic Assigned—Year Assigned
Oregon Health & Science University, Portland, OR	Hyperbaric oxygen therapy: treatment for brain injury and stroke—2001 Preventing adolescent criminal and other health-risking social behavior—2001 Vaginal birth following C-section—2001 Effect of health care working conditions on patient safety—2001 Echocardiography and carotid ultrasound in evaluation and management of stroke—2000 Diagnosis and management of osteoporosis—1999 Medical informatics and telemedicine coverage under the Medicare Program—1999 Rehabilitation of persons with traumatic brain injury—1997
Research Triangle Institute and University of North Carolina at Chapel Hill, NC	Management of bronchiolitis—2001 Methods to rate strength of scientific evidence—2000 Criteria to determine disability for speech/language disorders—2000 Efficacy of behavioral dietary interventions to reduce cancer risk—1999 Management of preterm labor—1998 Pharmacotherapy for alcohol dependence—1997
Southern California Evidence-Based Practice Center-RAND, Santa Monica, CA	Clinical efficacy and side effects of ephedra—2001 Ayurvedic treatments for diabetes mellitus—2000 Diagnosis and treatment of congestive heart failure—2000 Utilization of physician services—2000 **Otitis media with effusion—1999** Mind-body interventions for gastrointestinal conditions—1999 **Management of acute otitis media—1998** Prevention of venous thromboembolism after injury—1998 Prevention and management of urinary complications in paralyzed persons—1997
University of Alberta, Edmonton, Alberta, Canada	Newly added center
University of California, San Francisco and Stanford University, Stanford, CA	Management of coronary heart disease in women (phase 1)—2001 Making health care safer: critical analysis of patient safety practices—2001 Autopsy as ultimate outcome measure—2000 Bioterrorism: decision support systems in disease management—2000 Refinement of HCUP Quality Indicators—1999 Management of unstable angina—1998 Management of stable angina—1997
University of Minnesota, Minneapolis, MN	Newly added center
University of Ottawa, Ottawa, Canada	Newly added center
University of Texas Health Science Center, San Antonio, TX	Defining and managing chronic fatigue syndrome—2000 Medical harms workshop—2000 Use of garlic for cardiovascular disease—1999 Use of silybum marianum in treatment of liver disease and cirrhosis—1999 Management of chronic hypertension during pregnancy—1998 Depression treatment with new drugs—1997

AHRQ = Agency for Healthcare Research and Quality; EPC = evidence-based practice center; HCUP = Healthcare Cost and Uitilization Project.

or management of a disease or condition; in the use of a procedure or technology; or in the health outcomes achieved

- Availability of scientific data to support the systematic review and analysis of the topic
- Submission of the nomination organization's plan to incorporate the report into its managerial or policy decision making, as defined above
- Submission of the nominating organization's plan to disseminate derivative products to its members and plan to measure members' use of these products, and the resultant impact of such use on clinical practice

THE PROCESS OF EVIDENCE REPORT DEVELOPMENT

AHRQ, AOM, and OME

Emphasizing AOM and OME as important medical conditions in children, the American Academy of Family Physicians (AAFP), the American Academy of Pediatrics (AAP), and the American Academy of Otolaryngology–Head and Neck Surgery Foundation (AAO-HNS) nominated both as topics for evidence analysis by the AHRQ. Both were subsequently chosen by the AHRQ as candidates for competitive funding to conduct evidence analysis and later awarded to the Southern California Evidence-Based Practice Center at RAND.

It was the expressed purpose of AHRQ that both evidence analyses answer specific questions about the management of AOM and of OME. It was not AHRQ's intent, nor ours, to develop clinical practice guidelines as had been done previously with OME.[4,5] Sackett and colleagues (1996)[6] describe evidence-based medicine as the melding of individual clinical expertise and external clinical evidence. Individual clinical expertise is described as effective and efficient diagnosis in combination with thoughtful and compassionate consideration of patient preferences on the part of individual practitioners. External clinical evidence is research findings pertinent to the clinical question being addressed. Our aim was to provide answers to well-defined clinical questions on the basis of the available evidence in order to provide the existent external clinical evidence necessary for an evidence-based approach to the management of AOM and OME.

Overview of the Process

Our approach to developing the evidence analyses for AOM and OME followed standard methodologic considerations for an evidence analysis or systematic review and included the following steps:

1. Appointing a technical expert panel
2. Defining the condition, that is, AOM and OME, respectively
3. Topic assessment and refinement and identification of key questions
4. Stating the hypotheses relative to the causal pathways
5. Identification and refinement of causal pathways, study populations, practice settings, and target audience
6. Searching the literature
7. Screening retrieved literature citations for relevance
8. Assessing the quality of retrieved literature citations
9. Extracting relevant data from pertinent articles
10. Organizing relevant data into evidence tables
11. Conducting supplemental analyses, such as meta-analysis
12. Conducting peer review of the draft evidence report and responding to critiques
13. Submitting the final evidence report to the AHRQ

The following discussion focuses on key elements of these steps.

The Technical Expert Panel

The technical expert panel for both AOM and OME evidence analyses were multidisciplinary groups representing all viewpoints in the health care system. Both technical expert panels advised their respective project staff on major clinical content and methodologic issues. The members appointed to the technical expert panels were nominated by the partner organizations to the project, the AAFP, AAP, and AAO-HNS. Nominations were also sought and obtained from the following professional organizations whose members also manage the care of children with AOM and OME:
- National Association of Pediatric Nurse Associates and Practitioners
- American Speech-Language-Hearing Association
- American Academy of Audiology
- Society for Ear, Nose, Throat Advances in Children

The Ambulatory Pediatric Association was also asked for nominations for the OME evidence analysis. In addition, the consumer and payer viewpoints were needed on the technical expert panels, and nominations were sought from the following organizations:
- Foundation for Accountability
- Family Voices
- Various health plans, including a solicitation of the American Association of Health Plans

Through frequent conference calls and electronic and traditional postal communications, the technical expert panels together with their project staff developed definitions of AOM and OME, the study questions, the causal pathways, the scope of the analyses, and the literature search strategies.

Defining AOM and OME

An important but difficult-to-resolve topic that was addressed early in the course of both evidence analyses was the definition and diagnostic criteria for AOM and OME. Without definitions, we felt we would have difficulty determining if particular studies were reporting on AOM or OME and whether the diagnostic criteria were appropriate. A review of the literature did not lead to common definitions of AOM or OME but revealed a multitude of definitions and diagnostic criteria.[4,5,7–11] Through a thoughtful and deliberate consensus process, the technical expert panels for AOM and OME agreed on definitions and diagnostic criteria for both evidence analyses.

Topic Assessment and Refinement and Identification of Key Questions

In each evidence analysis, study questions were proposed by the nominating professional organizations, that is, the AAFP, AAP, AAO-HNS, the technical expert panel, and the project staff. Proposed AOM study questions focused on natural history, definition and physician diagnosis, antibiotic treatment, antibiotic regimen, nonantibiotic pharmaceutical treatment, follow-up strategies, and prevention. Proposed OME study questions focused on allergens, natural history, speech and language, diagnostic methods, surgical interventions, hearing, antibiotics, steroids, antihistamines and decongestants, and alternative or complementary therapies.

As part of the study selection process, the project staff developed conceptual frameworks and causal pathways for management of AOM and OME, linking the conditions to influencing factors, interventions, and outcomes, that were reviewed and approved by the technical expert panel. After extensive discussion and clarification of the questions, the technical expert panel then ranked potential questions to be addressed in the evidence analyses using a voting process. Hypotheses followed naturally from the specification of the questions.

Delineating the Scope of the Analysis and Searching the Literature

As with any rigorous study, the scope of both evidence analyses, in terms of target condition, population of interest, and practice settings of interest, were set prior to the literature search, and before data collection and analysis. The literature search itself was defined by time periods, literature sources, languages of interest, and study designs. The required study designs were dictated by the study questions chosen, that is, randomized controlled trials (RCTs) for therapeutic questions, cohort studies or placebo arms of RCTs for natural history or prognostic questions, and cross-sectional studies for diagnostic questions.

Screening for Relevance and Assessing the Quality of Retrieved Literature Citations

The citations identified by the literature search were then screened for relevance by clinician reviewers. Two reviewers were used to reduce selection bias. Inclusion and exclusion criteria were developed prior to the screening process, and the citation had to be relevant in terms of the specified intervention, if applicable, influencing factors, and outcome. All discrepancies between the two reviewers were discussed and resolved.

The quality of the studies was assessed, because study quality may be associated with study outcomes. It has been found that studies of lower documented quality reported larger effect sizes than did studies of higher documented quality.[12,13] In both the AOM and OME evidence analyses, to assess RCTs, we used the Jadad quality scale[14] that was based on the adequacy of

- randomization,
- blinding procedures, and
- accounting of study withdrawals and dropouts.

In both the AOM and OME evidence analyses, to assess natural history studies, we used quality components suggested by experts in the field:[15–18]

- Prospective
- Outcome clearly defined
- Clearly defined outcome measurement times
- No intervention
- Blind assessment
- Points estimates with variability measures

For prospective cohort studies, we used the following:
- Presence or absence of a clear definition of the study cohort
- Early inception point
- Clear pathway of patient entry
- Complete follow-up
- Description of dropouts
- Objective outcome criteria
- Blind outcome assessment
- Adjustment for extraneous factors

To assess diagnostic studies, we used the following:
- Appropriate reference standard

- Independent assessment of test results and reference standard
- Blind assessment
- Appropriate spectrum of the condition
- Precision and observer variation reported
- Sufficient description of the test

Two reviewers assessed study quality independently. Discrepancies were discussed and resolved by consensus.

Extracting Data and Organizing Data into Evidence Tables

Data extraction involved a similar process with two reviewers abstracting information on sample size, number of nonevaluable subjects, definition and diagnostic criteria, interventions, influencing factors, and outcomes. Discrepancies were discussed and resolved. The extracted data for each study question was then organized into individual evidence tables that included the following information:

- Study name
- Author
- Year of publication
- Study design
- Study quality
- AOM or OME definition
- Sample size
- Time and place of the study
- Inclusion criteria
- Exclusion criteria
- Influencing factors
- Intervention descriptions, if applicable
- Outcome descriptions, if applicable
- Diagnostic method description, if applicable
- Findings

Conducting Supplemental Analyses

Supplemental analyses were specific to each study question. For each outcome of interest, we derived a pooled estimate using meta-analytic techniques. We conducted meta-analyses for estimates that involved three or more studies. To prepare for a meta-analysis, data were abstracted from the evidence table, one meta-analysis for each outcome measure. Prior to all analyses, we obtained a distribution of studies stratified by the population characteristics, type of outcome measures, and nontreatment factors. This step provided us with an overview of the emphasis of past research in this area and an opportunity to identify gaps and areas for future research.

In addition to deriving pooled estimates and their 95% confidence intervals (CI), we also conducted tests of heterogeneity, subgroup analyses, and sensitivity analyses to assess the impact of possible heterogeneity on the conclusions.

Peer Review and Publication

The draft evidence report that described the methods, results, including evidence tables and meta-analyses, conclusions, and priorities for future research regarding the study questions on AOM and OME was then subjected to peer review. Peer review included the technical expert panel and additional individuals nominated by the same organizations that nominated members to the technical expert panel, as well as individuals, including content experts and methodologists, suggested by the AHRQ and the project staff. All comments received from the peer reviewers were reviewed and acted on by the project staffs. Appropriate revisions and responses were made. Comments from peer reviewers and actions/responses were included in the final evidence report.

The final evidence reports on AOM and OME were submitted to the AHRQ. The AOM evidence report has been published by AHRQ.[19] The OME evidence report is in preparation for publication by AHRQ. It is the intent of AHRQ and the project staff that the final evidence reports provide information on specific aspects of AOM and OME management, provide information for use in clinical practice guidelines, provide impetus for research in areas with apparent gaps in knowledge, and provide impetus to better design and reporting of studies on AOM and OME. Both evidence reports are being used by the AAP in its development of individual clinical guidelines for AOM and OME.

AHRQ encourages publications of the findings from evidence reports in peer-reviewed journals or other relevant forums. Results of the AOM evidence analysis have been published.[20,21]

EVIDENCE REPORT FOR MANAGING AND TREATING AOM

Key Questions and Scope

After careful deliberation and refinement of the potential questions addressing various aspects of AOM management, the AOM technical expert panel selected the following questions for evidence analysis:

1. What is the natural history of AOM without antibiotic treatment?
2. Are antibiotics effective in preventing clinical failure?
3. What is the relative effectiveness of specific antibiotic regimens? The regimens analyzed were the following:

- Amoxicillin or trimethoprim-sulfamethoxazole versus other antibiotics
- Oral fluoroquinolones
- Sixty milligrams or higher per kilogram per day of amoxicillin or amoxicillin-clavulanate versus the standard 40 milligrams per kilogram per day
- High-dose amoxicillin therapy twice a day versus three times a day
- Short-term versus long-term antibiotic therapy

The scope of these questions was specified by the AOM technical expert panel. First, the definitions for AOM required much discussion and consensus to achieve the following:

- AOM: Presence of middle ear effusion as demonstrated by (1) the actual presence of fluid in the middle ear, as diagnosed by tympanocentesis or the physical presence of liquid in the external ear canal as a result of tympanic membrane perforation; or (2) limited or absent mobility of the tympanic membrane, as diagnosed by pneumatic otoscopy, tympanogram, or acoustic reflectometry with or without the following: (a) opacification, not including erythema, (b) a full or bulging tympanic membrane, or (c) hearing loss, and rapid onset (ie, up to 48 hours from the onset of acute signs or symptoms first noted by the parent or guardian to the time of contact with the health system) of one or more of the following signs or symptoms, with or without anorexia, nausea, or vomiting: (i) otalgia (or pulling of ear in an infant), (ii) otorrhea, (iii) irritability in the infant or toddler, or (iv) fever
- Uncomplicated AOM: AOM limited to the middle ear cleft. An episode of uncomplicated AOM was considered distinct from a previous episode of AOM and eligible for initial treatment if the most recent course of antibiotic ended 4 weeks prior to the episode of AOM in question or if there was documentation by an examiner that a prior episode of AOM had been cleared.

Outcome indicators were established a priori as well.
1. Presence or absence of signs and symptoms within 48 hours, at 3 to 7 days, 7 to 14 days, 14 days to 3 months, and over 3 months.
2. In addition to those for indicator 1, presence or absence of adverse effects from antibiotic treatment and presence or absence of bacteria and/or resistant bacteria.

Selection criteria for articles that were used in the literature search and manual screening process included human studies addressing a key question about AOM in children between the ages of 4 weeks and 18 years. Excluded were case reports, editorials, letters, reviews, practice guidelines, and studies on patients with immunodeficiencies or craniofacial deficiencies, including cleft palate. Placebo arms of RCTs and prospective and retrospective comparative cohort studies were included for the question on natural history. Only RCTs were used to address the questions on the effectiveness of antibiotics. From a long list of potential risk factors, the AOM technical expert panel selected age (under and over 2 years) and otitis-prone state as being of greatest interest for possible subgroup analysis, in addition to study quality for sensitivity analysis. The otitis-prone child was defined as the child who has had three or more episodes of AOM in a 6-month period or four or more episodes of AOM in a 12-month period.

Literature searches were done of the following electronic databases: MEDLINE (1966–March 1999), the Cochrane Library (through March 1999), HealthSTAR (1975–March 1999), International Pharmaceutical Abstracts (1970–March 1999), Cumulative Index to Nursing & Allied Health Literature (1982–March 1999), BIOSIS (1970–March 1999), and EMBASE (1980–March 1999). The initial module of search statements included an explode of "om" (otitis media), which included the headings "om, mastoiditis," "om w/effusion," "om, suppurative" with the subheading "drug therapy." The next module included the explode of "om" and "om" as a textword. The anti-infectives module used an explode of the mesh heading for anti-infective agents, including antibiotics and other drug groups and the text words antibiotic, antimicrobial, antibacterial, and specific names of antibiotics. Combinations of these modules were used for the literature search.

The search was limited to human or undesignated studies and to infant, child, preschool child, adolescent, or undesignated subjects. For the natural history search, "natural history," "natural course," "untreated," "spontaneous," and "self-limited" were added as key words. Additional articles were identified by review of reference lists in proceedings, published articles, reports, and guidelines.

Summary of Findings

Our search yielded a total of 3,461 citations, of which 760 (22%) were accepted for further review. Seventy-four of the 760 citations, excluding duplicates, were accepted for analysis. Of the 760 studies accepted for further review, 487 had been published in English and 273 in non-English languages. Of the 487 studies published in English, 72 (15%) met our inclusion criteria.

Natural History of AOM
- In children with AOM who were not initially treated with antibiotics, a previous evidence analysis showed

a clinical failure rate of 7.7% at 24 to 48 hours, and another showed a failure rate of 26% at 24 to 72 hours—that is, clinical resolution was 92.3% at 24 to 48 hours and 74% at 24 to 72 hours. The pooled estimate of failure at 1 to 7 days was 18.9 % (95% CI, 9.9 to 28.0%) and at 4 to 7 days was 22.2 % (95% CI, 10.1 to 34.3%).

- A previous evidence analysis estimated that 59% (95% CI, 53 to 65%) of children not treated with antibiotics had resolution of pain and fever within 24 hours of diagnosis of AOM, 87% (95% CI, 84 to 89%) of children had resolution of pain and fever by 2 to 3 days, and 88% (95% CI, 85 to 91%) of children had resolution of pain and fever by 4 to 7 days.

- The available evidence on the natural history of AOM shows that in studies with close follow-up, few episodes of mastoiditis or other suppurative complications were reported in children with AOM not initially treated with antibiotics and that the pooled random effects estimate of the incidence of mastoiditis among 1,211 children in nine studies was 1 per 1,000 (95% CI, 0 to 5).

Effects of Antibiotics on AOM

- Meta-analysis demonstrated a reduction in the clinical failure rate within 2 to 7 days of 12.3% (95% CI, 2.8 to 21.8%) in favor of ampicillin or amoxicillin therapy compared with placebo or observational treatment. This result was generally robust to sensitivity analysis. Eight children with AOM would need to be treated with ampicillin or amoxicillin, rather than no antibiotic treatment, to avoid a case of clinical failure (Table 5-2).[22–49]

- Previous meta-analyses have demonstrated minimal to modest benefits of antibiotics compared with observational intervention without antibiotics during the initial treatment of AOM for the following outcomes: pain and fever resolution at 2 days, pain

Table 5-2 Summary of Meta-Analyses for Use of Antibiotics for AOM

Comparison, Reference	Outcome Indicator	Number of Subjects Gp 1, Gp 2	Absolute Rate Difference in % (95% CI)	Number NNT (95% CI)
Amp/Amox vs. Placebo[22–26]	Failure at 2–7 d	717, 801	–12 (–22, –3)*	–8 (–36, –5)
Pen vs. Amox/Amp[26–28]	Failure at 7–14 d	241, 250	4 (–2, 11)	ND
Cefa vs. Amox/Amp[28,29,31,39]	Failure at 3–7 d	90, 95	–5 (–15, 4)	ND
Cefa vs. Amox/Amp[28,29,31,35,39]	Failure at 5–21 d	154, 161	1 (–6, 7)	ND
Cefi vs. Amox/Amp[34,36,38,40]	Failure at 10–15 d	274, 265	0 (–4, 4)	ND
Cefi vs. Amox/Amp[32,36,40]	Recurrence at 3–5 wk	70, 74	2 (–5, 8)	ND
Cefi vs. Amox/Amp[32,34,36,38,40]	Incidence of diarrhea	380, 374	8 (4, 13)	12 (8, 27)
Cefi vs. Amox/Amp[32,34,36,38,40]	Incidence of vomiting	380, 374	2 (0, 4)	ND
Cefi vs. Amox/Amp[32,34,36,38]	Incidence of rash	360, 354	6 (–2, 14) *	ND
Cefa vs. TMP-SMX[26,27,37]	Failure at 14 d	161, 167	6 (–2, 13)	ND
Ceft (1 dose) vs. Amox (7–10 d)[30,33,41]	Failure at 5–10 d	152, 154	3 (–2, 8)	ND
Azith (< 5 d) vs. Amox-Clav (7–10 d)[42,44,47,48,49]	Failure at 10–14 d	560, 485	2 (–1, 5)	ND
Azith (5 d) vs. Amox-Clav (7–10 d)[43,45,46]	Any adverse events	688, 678	–19 (–29, –9) *	–5 (–11, –3)
Azith (5 d) vs. Amox-Clav (7–10 d)[43,45,46]	GI related adverse events	688, 678	–18 (–28, –8) *	–6 (–13, –4)

Amp = ampicillin; Amox = amoxicillin; Amox/Clav = amoxicillin/clavulanic acid; Azith = azithromycin; Cefa = cefaclor; Cefi = Cefixime; Ceft = ceftriaxone; CI = confidence interval; GI = gastrointestinal; Gp = group; ND = not done due to nonsignificant result; NNT = number needed to treat; Pen = penicillin; TMP-SMX = trimethoprim-sulfamethoxazole.

* Test of heterogeneity *p* value < .05.

resolution at 2 to 7 days, contralateral OM, and 7- to 14-day clinical resolution rate. The following outcomes did not appear to be affected by antibiotic use: pain resolution at 24 hours, pain and fever resolution at 4 to 7 days, tympanic membrane perforation, vomiting/diarrhea/rash, 1-month tympanometry, or recurrent AOM.

Relative Effects of Different Antibiotic Regimens
- Meta-analyses did not demonstrate a significant rate difference in clinical failure rates between children with AOM treated with ampicillin or amoxicillin compared with children treated with penicillin, cefaclor, or cefixime.
- Meta-analyses did not demonstrate a significant difference in clinical failure rates between children treated with trimethoprim-sulfamethoxazole compared with children treated with cefaclor for AOM.
- Meta-analyses demonstrated that children treated with cefixime had an 8.4% greater rate of diarrhea (95% CI, 3.8 to 13.1%) than children treated with ampicillin or amoxicillin. Twelve children with AOM would need to be treated with ampicillin or amoxicillin, rather than cefixime to avoid a case of diarrhea.
- No comment can be made on the effect of oral fluoroquinolones compared with other antibiotics, because no comparative RCTs were found that addressed this question.
- Though not establishing equivalency of effect, a single study demonstrated no difference in clinical effect of high-dose amoxicillin-clavulanate versus standard-dose amoxicillin-clavulanate.
- Though not establishing equivalency of effect, a single study did not demonstrate a difference in clinical effect of taking high-dose amoxicillin two times a day versus three times a day.
- Meta-analyses did not demonstrate a difference in clinical effect between short-duration therapy and long-duration therapy when comparing single-dose ceftriaxone therapy to 7- to 10-day amoxicillin therapy and azithromycin therapy for less than 5 days to 7- to 10-day amoxicillin-clavulanate therapy.
- A previous meta-analysis demonstrated that short-acting oral antibiotic therapy of less than 2 days was not as effective as therapy lasting 7 days or longer.
- A meta-analysis demonstrated that children treated with 7- to 10-day amoxicillin-clavulanate had a 19.2% (95% CI, 9.2 to 29.2%) greater rate of overall adverse effects and 12.9% (95% CI, 4.5 to 21.2%) greater rate of gastrointestinal adverse effects than did children treated with 5-day azithromycin. Eight children would need to be treated with azithromycin, rather than amoxicillin-clavulanate, to avoid a gastro-

intestinal adverse event. (Though not reported in the studies, the clavulanate concentration was most likely 31.25 milligrams per 125 milligrams of amoxicillin, that is, original formulation.)

Because the intent of the AOM evidence report was to present the evidence available to address the specific questions, without comment on recommendations for clinical practice as would be made by a clinical guideline, we allowed the readers to judge the significance of the findings without influence on our part. However, we did advise that on the basis of the exclusion factors of the investigations used in this analysis, the study findings were most applicable to children without comorbidities and with AOM of lesser severity. The reader should also keep in mind the time period analyzed for the evidence report.

Limitations of the Literature

We noted several limitations in the literature that presented difficulties in analysis. First, the diagnostic criteria for AOM were not uniform across studies. Although some studies were of high quality, about half of the studies were not of adequate quality. The AOM outcomes varied among the studies, and the definition of common outcomes, such as clinical failure, were not uniform. This inconsistency made it difficult to compare results across studies. The power of the studies to detect a difference appeared to be insufficient in most cases, although this fact was less important, because the treatment effect sizes were generally less than 10%, that is, an effect size that some clinicians might consider insignificant.

Although many studies had significant numbers of children younger and older than 2 years old, we could not do subgroup analysis, because most of the studies did not report outcome by age. We were, therefore, unable to focus the findings of this study to children in specific age groups. Several studies suggested greater caution be taken with children younger than 2 years old; however, these studies did not definitively answer this question. Because most of the studies did not report outcomes by otitis-prone status, we were unable to do subgroup analysis by this influencing factor.

Future Research

Our recommendations for future AOM research based on the evidence focused primarily on validity issues. Randomized controlled studies of high internal validity and adequate generalizability might still be useful to adequately address the clinical questions asked at the start of the evidence analysis, including the question of the role of antibiotics in the treatment of uncomplicated AOM. Placebo-controlled trials of adequate power with sufficient patient variation for subgroup analysis would be of particular importance. Close monitoring of patients in these studies with a priori plans for appropriate intervention should allay any concerns about suppurative complications, which appear to be few, and should also be a focus of research.

Future AOM research should specifically
- establish uniform definitions of AOM and relevant outcomes, clinical, bacteriologic, and societal;
- establish uniform diagnostic criteria for AOM;
- strengthen internal and external validity;
- address relevant influencing factors, such as age and otitis-prone state; and
- measure long-term as well as short-term outcomes.

Although not addressed in this evidence-based analysis, future AOM research should also consider the impact of bacterial resistance on AOM outcomes. Finally, information on patient preferences for different AOM outcomes, as well as on the alternative management options and the probability of their outcomes, is needed to make rationale clinical decisions.

EVIDENCE REPORT FOR DIAGNOSIS, NATURAL HISTORY, AND LATE EFFECTS OF OME

Key Questions and Scope

After extensive discussions and refinement of the potential questions addressing the spectrum of OME management issues, the OME technical expert panel selected the following questions for evidence analysis:
1. What is the natural history of OME?
2. What are the long-term effects of early-life OM, defined as positive OM history at less than 3 years of age, on speech and language development?
3. What are the long-term effects of early-life OM on hearing?
4. What are the operating characteristics of various methods of diagnosing OME?

Although the focus of the evidence analysis was initially OME, it was decided by the technical expert panel of this evidence analysis that the questions on long-term impact should study the effects of OM in general, rather than OME specifically.

The scope of the evidence analysis was specified by the OME technical expert panel. First, the definition for OME. OME is "…fluid in the middle ear without signs or symptoms of ear infection."

Outcome indicators were established a priori as well:
1. Partial OME resolution, complete OME resolution, relapse/recurrence (dynamic course or fluctuation), AOM
2. Speech and/or language development, expressive or receptive, verbal measures of intelligence
3. Long-term hearing level, unilateral or bilateral
4. Sensitivity and specificity

Selection criteria for OME articles that were used in the literature search and manual screening process were similar to those for AOM. Selection criteria included human studies that addressed a key question about OME in children with exclusion criteria the same as for AOM. Used for the natural history question were prospective cohort(s) studies on untreated subjects, from which outcome data were abstractable for children up through age 12 years. Used for the speech and language and hearing questions were prospective cohort studies that fulfilled the following criteria: (1) the degree of OM was determined during the first three years of life, upper age limit was 22 years, (2) the degree of OM was graded in some way, and (3) the outcome was measured when the child was older than age 3 years. Used for the diagnostic methods question were prospective studies on children up through 12 years of age that fulfilled four criteria: the diagnostic procedure of interest (1) was performed within 24 hours of the reference standard, (2) was not an algorithm or combination of multiple diagnostic procedures, (3) used one of the acceptable reference standards specified in the scope, and (4) produced abstractable data.

Literature searches were limited to MEDLINE (1966–January 2000), the Cochrane Library (through January 2000), and EMBASE (1980–January 2000). On the basis of the experience with the AOM evidence analysis, the project staff did not feel that searching other electronic databases or for articles written in non-English languages would add value to the search. Additional articles were identified by review of reference lists in proceedings, published articles, reports, and guidelines. The search strategy included search terms for otitis media with effusion combined with search terms for natural history, speech and language development, hearing, and diagnosis.

The otitis media module included otitis media, otitis media with effusion, suppurative otitis media, allergic otitis media, fluid ear, glue ear, middle ear effusion, mucoid otitis media, nonsuppurative otitis media, secretory otitis media, and serous otitis media. The natural history terms included natural course, natural history, placebo, placebos, resolution, self-limited, self-limiting, and untreated, as well as a variety of terms for spontaneous resolution. The speech and language module included speech and language, speech and language disorders, child language, communication, communication disorders, language development and tests, voice, and voice disorders. The hearing module included hearing and hearing disorders, hearing aids and tests, and the text word hearing. The diagnosis module used diagnosis and diagnostic techniques and procedures, as well as the text words audiometry, diagnosis, diagnostic, otoscopy, and tympanometry.

Summary of Findings

Of the 4,882 titles/abstracts identified, 141 articles addressed the natural history question, 87 addressed the speech and language question, 161 addressed the hearing question, and 75 addressed the diagnostic methods question.

Natural History of OME

These following estimates must be viewed with caution due to the clinical heterogeneity evident in the data synthesized and due to the weaknesses of design or documentation of the study cohorts. In particular, half the investigators did not document whether subjects had received medical or surgical treatment during the course of the study that could affect OME outcome or how compliance with nontreatment was established. Of those investigators who reported how many children received treatment, the majority did not stratify their findings by treatment status (Table 5-3).[50–55]

- For the over-3-years age group, two sets of meta-analyses showed that 22.5% (95% CI, 5.9 to 39.0%) to 42.7% (95% CI, 29.3 to 56.1%) of ears with OME cumulatively resolved over a period of 3 months, depending on the definition of OME resolution. No meta-analyses for children under 3 years of age were possible because we could identify only two studies each for the less than 6 months and the 3 months to 3 years age groups.
- Another finding was the inclusion of what we called noncumulative resolution rates in some studies. A noncumulative resolution rate was the % of ears without OME 6 weeks after the inception point evaluation, without regard to ear status during the intervening period. For example, for the over-3-years age group, two sets of meta-analyses showed that 37.2% (95% CI, 1.8 to 72.5%) to 42.3% (95% CI, 24.1 to 60.6%) of ears with OME at the inception point did not have OME at 6-week follow-up. What we traditionally would consider the resolution rate of a condition, as reported in the bullet above, we called the cumulative resolution rate (percent of ears with resolution of OME at any point within the follow-up period after the inception point evaluation).
- A few studies analyzed OME resolution by such influencing factors as gender, care at home versus day care, season, side of affected ear, race or ethnicity, or diagnostic instrument. Because of the paucity of such studies, quantitative synthesis was not possible, and we refrained from making any conclusions regarding the effect of these influencing factors on resolution.

Early-Life OM and Long-Term Speech and Language Development

Studies that addressed the effects of early-life OM on long-term speech and language development among children differed considerably with respect to risk factors studied, type of outcome measured, method of measurement, unit of measurement, age at outcome determination, and study design (Table 5-4).[56–61]

- The meta-analyses that could be conducted on long-term expressive language, receptive language, and cognitive verbal intelligence showed no effect of early OM as measured during the first 3 years of life.
- These findings may not be generalizable, since five of the six cohorts that were included in these three meta-analyses focused primarily on children from specific ethnic/racial groups or from particular socioeconomic groups. Furthermore, the results of these studies cannot be applied to children with craniofacial defects, primary mucosal disorders, immunodeficiency disorders, genetic conditions, or pre-existing developmental disorders because children with these conditions were excluded from this analysis.
- Only one of the studies included in these meta-analyses focused solely on persistent bilateral OM as opposed to unspecified unilateral or bilateral OM.

Early-Life OM and Long-Term Hearing

We advised caution in interpreting the following results because the findings were based on four homogeneous but very different populations: one from Finland, another from Sweden, one primarily of Native American children, and another primarily of Inuit children. The four studies also differed on the definition and collection of OM history and exclusion factors (Table 5-5).[62–64]

- Of the eight cohort studies analyzed, one set of four studies reported percentage of conductive hearing loss at 6 to 10 years of age. For this analysis, the threshold for conductive hearing loss was defined as greater than or equal to 20 dB at any frequency, with or without treatment of OM.
- The pooled risk of conductive hearing loss at 6 to 10 years among 346 children who had a positive history of early-life OM was 22% (95% CI, 7 to 36%). In contrast, the pooled risk of conductive hearing loss at 6 to 10 years of age among 237 children with no history of early-life OM was 6% (95% CI, 1 to 12%).

Table 5-3 Meta-Analyses for Resolution Rate for Newly Diagnosed OME of Unknown Duration in Children Older Than 3 Years of Age

A. < 6 Weeks Resolution; Tympanometry Diagnostic Criteria: Type B or C to A

Author, Year	Diagnostic Criterion	Age at Diagnosis	Number Ears Resolved	Total Number Ears	Noncumulative Resolution Rate[†] in %
Sly et al, 1980[50]	B or C to A	5 yr	18	32	56.3
Sly et al, 1980[50]	B or C to A	5 yr	11	22	50.0
Lamothe et al, 1981[51]	Otoscopy	6 yr	25	53	47.2
Total			48	107	44.9

Random effects pooled estimate (95% CI) 42.3 (24.1, 60.6); heterogeneity $p = .02$.

B. < 6 Weeks Resolution; Tympanometry Diagnostic Criteria: Type B to A

Author, Year	Diagnostic Criterion	Age at Diagnosis	Number Ears Resolved	Total Number Ears	Noncumulative Resolution Rate[†] in %
Sly et al, 1980[50]	B to A	5 yr	6	9	66.7
Sly et al, 1980[50]	B to A	5 yr	0	5	0.0
Lamothe et al, 1981[51]	Otoscopy	6 yr	25	53	47.2
Total			31	67	46.3

Random effects pooled estimate (95% CI) 37.2 (1.8, 72.5); heterogeneity $p = .001$.

C. < 3 Months Resolution; Tympanometry Diagnostic Criteria: Type B or C to A

Author, Year	Diagnostic Criterion	Age at Diagnosis	Number Ears Resolved	Total Number Ears	Noncumulative Resolution Rate[†] in %
Fiellau-Nikolajsen 1979[52]	B or C to A	3–4 yr	154	348	44.3
Fiellau-Nikolajsen 1979[53]	B or C to A	3–4 yr	83	200	41.5
Tos et al, 1981[54]	B or C to A	4 yr	103	393	26.2
Renvall et al, 1982[55]	Otoscopy	4 yr	86	144	59.7
Total			426	1085	39.3

Random effects pooled estimate (95% CI) 42.7 (29.3, 56.1); heterogeneity $p = .001$.

D. < 3 Months Resolution; Tympanometry Diagnostic Criteria: Type B to A

Author, Year	Diagnostic Criterion	Age at Diagnosis	Number Ears Resolved	Total Number Ears	Noncumulative Resolution Rate[†] in %
Fiellau-Nikolajsen 1979[52]	B to A	3–4 yr	22	91	24.2
Fiellau-Nikolajsen 1979[53]	B to A	3–4 yr	16	62	25.8
Tos et al, 1981[54]	B to A	4 yr	3	87	3.4
Renvall et al, 1982[55]	Otoscopy	4 yr	16	40	40.0
Total			57	280	20.4

Random effects pooled estimate (95% CI) 22.5 (5.9, 39.0); heterogeneity $p = .001$.

[†]Noncumulative resolution rate: the percent of ears without OME < 6 weeks after the inception point evaluation without regard to ear status during the intervening period.

[*]Cumulative resolution rate: the % of ears with resolution of OME at any point < 6 weeks after the inception point evaluation.

Table 5-4 Meta-Analyses for Expressive and Receptive Language Development and Cognitive Verbal Intelligence

A. Expressive Language Development

Author, Year	Positive OM History			Negative OM History			Standardized Mean Difference (95% CI)
	N	Mean	SD	N	Mean	SD	
Fischler et al, 1985[56]	33	60.0	20.4	71	64.8	28.8	−0.18 (−0.59, 0.23)
Gravel et al, 1992[57]	8	36.0	5.2	12	39.0	6.2	−0.49 (−1.40, 0.42)
Paul et al, 1993[58]	8	57.8	3.8	13	54.6	10.7	0.35 (−0.54, 1.24)

Random effects estimate −0.14 (−0.49, 0.20); heterogeneity p = .412.

B. Receptive Language Development

Author, Year	Positive OM History			Negative OM History			Standardized Mean Difference (95% CI)
	N	Mean	SD	N	Mean	SD	
Black et al, 1993[59]	21	83	17	10	72	18	0.62 (−0.15, 1.39)
Fischler et al, 1985[56]	33	67	28	71	73	32	−0.19 (−0.61, 0.22)
Gravel et al, 1992[57]	8	36	5	13	38	5	−0.38 (−1.27, 0.51)
Teele et al, 1990[60]	52	101	17	80	96	15	0.31 (−0.04, 0.67)

Random effects estimate 0.10 (−0.29, 0.49); heterogeneity p = .102.

C. Cognitive Intelligence

Author, Year	Positive OM History			Negative OM History			Standardized Mean Difference (95% CI)
	N	Mean	SD	N	Mean	SD	
Black et al, 1993[59]	21	46.7	11.5	10	41.0	10.7	0.49 (−0.27, 1.26)
Gravel et al, 1992[57]	9	88.3	15.9	13	84.3	9.4	0.31 (−0.55, 1.17)
Roberts et al, 1986[61]	19	52.0	8.0	19	52.0	9.0	0.00 (−0.64, 0.64)

Random effects estimate 0.23 (−0.20, 0.65); heterogeneity p = .609.

CI = confidence interval; N = number of subjects; OM = otitis media; SD = standard deviation.

- The pooled rate difference of conductive hearing loss at 6 to 10 years of age between children with a positive OM history and those with a negative OM history was 11% (95% CI, 3 to 19%). Neither the studies pooled for the rate difference nor the studies pooled for the risk ratio showed significant heterogeneity in the outcomes.

Diagnostic Methods for OME
On the basis of our evaluation of 52 diagnostic studies, we were able to assess the ability of the following methods to diagnose middle ear effusion in OME at a single point in time: acoustic reflectometry at < 5 or ≥ 5 reflective units (RU); pneumatic otoscopy; portable tympanometry; professional tympanometry using acoustic reflex at 500 or 1,000 Hz; professional tympanometry using static compensated acoustic admittance at 0.1, 0.2, and 0.3; professional tympanometry using B curve as abnormal; and professional tympanometry using B or C2 curves as abnormal. All comparisons used myringotomy as the reference standard (Table 5-6).[5–94]

- Among the eight diagnostic methods, we used the receiver-operator characteristic points (plotting sensitivity against 1 minus specificity) to demonstrate that

Table 5-5 Meta-analysis for Effects of Early-Life Otitis Media on Long-Term Conductive Hearing Loss

Author, Year	Positive OM History		Negative OM History		Rate Difference in % (95% CI)
	Number of Subjects	Percent Had Hearing Loss	Number of Subjects	Percent Had Hearing Loss	
Sorri et al, 1995[62]	64	51.6	35	20.0	31.6 (13.5, 49.6)
Fischler et al, 1985[56]	96	9.4	70	1.4	7.9 (1.5, 14.4)
Harsten et al, 1993[63]	24	8.3	56	5.4	3.0 (−9.6, 15.5)
Kaplan et al, 1973[64]	162	19.8	76	7.9	11.9 (3.2, 20.5)

Random effects pooled estimates 11.3 (3.3, 19.3); heterogeneity $p = .064$.

Random effects pooled estimates excluding article by Sorri 8.4 (3.6, 13.2); heterogeneity $p = .508$.

OM = otitis media; CI = confidence interval.

Note: Hearing loss was measured at > 20–25 dB threshold at any frequency with or without treatment measured at 6 to 10 years of age. Sorri, Fischler, and Harsten did not specify type of pure-tone test used in defining hearing loss. Kaplan used air and bone conduction. OM history was obtained prospectively by Harsten, retrospectively by Fischler, prospectively and retrospectively by Kaplan, and without documentation by Sorri.

pneumatic otoscopy was closest to the optimal operating point where both sensitivity and specificity would be 100%. However, tester qualifications were reported inconsistently, and training was not specified.

- The pooled sensitivity for pneumatic otoscopy was 94% (95% CI, 91 to 96%) and the pooled specificity was 80% (95% CI, 75 to 86%). These findings were based on 2,694 children from seven studies that reported a pooled prevalence of OME of 63% (95% CI, 58 to 67%). The prevalence rate ranged from 56 to 71%, which indicated significant heterogeneity among outcomes ($p < .001$).

Table 5–6 summarizes results of the meta-analyses that compare sensitivity, specificity, and prevalence rate for eight diagnostic methods, which we presented to the readers of the evidence report to assess. A summary of the evidence report on OME has been published.[95] The final report is awaiting publication. As with the AOM evidence report, all findings in the OME evidence report were presented without specific clinical recommendations because our intent was to present the evidence and not standards of care.

Limitations of the Literature

Literature on the natural history of OME was difficult to interpret because of its generally poor quality, the lack of control for therapeutic interventions, the inability to distinguish persistent from recurrent OME due to the length of follow-up intervals, and the varied criteria for continued follow-up from examination to examination. Differing definitions of OME resolution and diagnostic

methods made comparison difficult. Few studies considered the child or the episode as the unit of analysis, included younger children, or assessed types of OME other than newly diagnosed OME of unknown duration. In addition, few studies addressed the possible effects of influencing factors on OME resolution.

The literature on the long-term effects of early-life OM on speech and language development diverged considerably with respect to methodology. As a result, findings could not be combined easily. Although the literature on the long-term effects of early-life OM on hearing was abundant, few studies used a prospective cohort study design. Because of the limited nature of this evidence and because the rate of intervention is highly dependent on the threshold hearing level adopted, as well as the other cautions mentioned above, the findings of this analysis should be applied with caution. Nine comparisons of diagnostic methods enabled derivations of pooled estimates of diagnostic accuracy. However, more comparisons could not be made, including those that would have evaluated clinical signs and/or symptoms, air and/or bone threshold audiometry, binaural microtympanoscopy, and nonpneumatic otoscopy. Diagnostic methods that use algorithms or aggregated scorings may be important but were not included in this evidence assessment.

Future Research

Future research on the natural history of OME must focus on improving study quality. In particular, control of therapeutic interventions during the study and the distinction between OME persistence and recurrence need to be addressed. In addition, researchers, in con-

Table 5-6 Summary of Meta-Analyses for Comparison of Diagnostic Methods with Myringotomy

Measure	Diagnostic Method[†] versus Myringotomy	No. Articles (References)	No. Cases	Random Effect Estimate % (95% CI)		Test of Heterogeneity p Value
Sensitivity	Acoustic reflectometry (≥ =5 vs. < 5)	3[65–67]	308	64.2	(57.0, 71.5)	.168
	Pneumatic otoscopy	7[68–74]	1,732	93.8	(91.4, 96.3)	< .001
	Portable tympanometry	6[67,75–79]	774	84.5	(76.0, 93.1)	<.001
	Professional tympanometry (using static compensated acoustic admittance at 0.1)	3[80–82]	358	33.9	(12.7, 55.0)	< .001
	Professional tympanometry (using static compensated acoustic admittance at 0.2)	3[80–82]	359	52.2	(39.5, 64.8)	.005
	Professional tympanometry (using static compensated acoustic admittance at 0.3)	3[75,80,81]	222	65.4	(39.1, 91.7)	< .001
	Professional tympanometry (using flat or B curve as abnormal)	16[73–75,77,83–94]	2,853	80.9	(76.1, 85.7)	< .001
	Professional tympanometry (using flat or B or C2 curve as abnormal)	6[75,77,81,86,90,91]	892	93.8	(91.1, 96.4)	.093
Specificity	Acoustic reflectometry (≥ =5 vs. < 5)	3[65–67]	212	80.4	(65.0, 95.9)	< .001
	Pneumatic otoscopy	7[68–74]	962	80.5	(75.1, 86.0)	< .001
	Portable tympanometry	6[67,75–79]	506	64.4	(44.3, 84.4)	< .001
	Professional tympanometry (using static compensated acoustic admittance at 0.1)	3[80–82]	278	94.1	(83.9, 100)	.001
	Professional tympanometry (using static compensated acoustic admittance at 0.2)	3[80–82]	278	87.7	(76.8, 98.5)	< .001
	Professional tympanometry (using static compensated acoustic admittance at 0.3)	3[75,80,81]	191	48.6	(10.2, 87.0)	< .001
	Professional tympanometry (using flat or B curve as abnormal)	16[73–75,77,83–94]	931	74.5	(66.9, 82.0)	< .001
	Professional tympanometry (using flat or B or C2 curve as abnormal)	6[75,77,81,86,90,91]	320	61.8	(41.5, 82.1)	< .001
Prevalence	Acoustic reflectometry (≥ =5 vs. < 5)	3[65–67]	520	59.6	(52.5, 66.7)	.067
	Pneumatic otoscopy	7[68–74]	2,694	62.8	(58.3, 67.2)	< .001
	Portable tympanometry	6[67,75–79]	1,280	58.5	(40.3, 76.7)	< .001
	Professional tympanometry (using static compensated acoustic admittance at 0.1)	3[80–82]	636	56.3	(52.5, 60.2)	.510
	Professional tympanometry (using static compensated acoustic admittance at 0.2)	3[80–82]	636	56.3	(52.5, 60.2)	.510
	Professional tympanometry (using static compensated acoustic admittance at 0.3)	3[75,80,81]	413	53.8	(49.0, 58.6)	.811
	Professional tympanometry (using flat or B curve as abnormal)	16[73–75,77,83–94]	3,784	73.6	(69.1, 78.1)	< .001
	Professional tympanometry (using flat or B or C2 curve as abnormal)	6[75,77,81,86,90,91]	1,212	67.3	(56.3, 78.2)	< .001

Portable tympanometry = tympanometry performed on a portable device; professional tympanometry = tympanometry performed by a clinical professional in tympanometry usage.

junction with clinicians, should agree upon standard procedures for follow-up, including intervals of follow-up, definition of OME resolution, and diagnostic methods so that resolution rates are, indeed, comparable.

More research is needed on the role of influencing factors on the natural history of OME so that the clinician on a particular day in a particular setting can make a better decision when assessing a particular child with particular characteristics. Future research must also focus on refining the search to establish the effect of OM on long-term outcomes, such as speech, language, and hearing. The justification for intervention is dependent on OM having a negative long-term impact on the child. Evaluation of long-term effects of early-life OM on speech, language, or hearing requires a coordinated systematic approach that uses a rational conceptual framework to address risk factors, interventions, and outcome measures in an integrated fashion.

We also suggest that future research focus on the child, rather than an ear, as the unit of analysis, because the outcomes of ultimate interest, such as speech, language, and hearing, are functional requirements of a child and not just an ear. Literature on findings should report both univariate and multivariate findings to enhance understanding of the patient and study characteristics and to allow pooling of data. An integrated approach is also important for the evaluation of diagnostic methods. Such an approach will provide guidance for future studies. Future studies of diagnostic assessments of OME should also consider cost-effectiveness analysis, which can take into account the variable proficiency of clinicians in performing pneumatic otoscopy as well as the consequences of testing and patient preferences for the various OME outcomes.

REFERENCES

1. Agency for Healthcare Research and Quality (AHRQ). AHCPR announces 12 evidence-based practice centers. Rockville (MD): AHRQ; 1997. http://www.ahcpr.gov/news/press/12epcpr.htm (accessed Feb18, 2003).
2. Agency for Healthcare Research and Quality (AHRQ). Evidence-based practice centers: synthesizing scientific evidence to improve quality and effectiveness in health care. Rockville (MD): AHRQ; 2002a. http://www.ahcpr.gov/clinic/epc/epc.html (accessed Feb18, 2003).
3. Agency for Healthcare Research and Quality (AHRQ). Nominations of topics for evidence-based practice centers. Rockville (MD): AHRQ; 2002b. http://www.ahcpr.gov/fund/fr/fr021402.htm (accessed Feb18, 2003).
4. Stool SE, Berg AO, Berman S, et al. Otitis media with effusion in young children. Clinical practice guideline, Number 12. Rockville (MD): Agency for Health Care Policy and Research, Public Health Services, U.S. Department of Health and Human Services. July 1994a. AHCPR Publication No. 94-0622.
5. Stool SE, Berg AO, Berman S, et al. Managing otitis media with effusion in young children. Quick reference guide for clinicians. Rockville (MD): Agency for Health Care Policy and Research, Public Health Service, U.S. Department of Health and Human Services; July 1994b. AHCPR Publication No. 94-0623.
6. Sackett DL, Rosenberg WMC, Gray JAM, et al. Evidence based medicine: what it is and what it isn't. BMJ 1996;312:71–2.
7. Senturia BH, Paparella MM, Lowery HW, et al. Report of the ad hoc committee on definitions and classification of otitis media and otitis media with effusion. Ann Otol Rhinol Laryngol 1980;39 Suppl 68:3–4.
8. Hayden GF. Acute suppurative otitis media in children. Clin Pediatr (Phila) 1981;20(2):99–104.
9. Paparella MM, Bluestone CD, Arnold W, et al. Definition and classification. Ann Otol Rhinol Laryngol 1985;94 Suppl 116:8-9.
10. Chow AW, Hall CB, Klein JO, et al. General guidelines for the evaluation of new anti-infective drugs for the treatment of respiratory tract infections. Clin Infect Dis 1992;15 Suppl 1:S62–S88.
11. Bluestone CD, Klein JO. Otitis media, atelectasis, and eustachian tube dysfunction. In: Bluestone CD, Stool SE, Kenna MA, editors. Pediatric otolaryngology. Philadelphia (PA): WB Saunders; 1996. p. 388–582.
12. Moher D, Jones A, Cook DJ, et al. Does quality of reports of randomized trials affect estimates of intervention efficacy reported in meta-analyses? Lancet 1998;352:609–13.
13. Schulz KF, Chalmers I, Hayes RJ, Altman DJ. Empirical evidence of bias: dimensions of methodological quality associated with estimates of treatment effects in controlled trials. J Am Med Assoc 1995;273:408–12.
14. Jadad AR, Moore A, Carroll D, et al. Asessing the quality of reports of randomized clinical trials: is blinding necessary? Control Clin Trials 1996;17:1–12.
15. Jaeschke R, Guyatt G, Sackett DL. Users' guides to the medical literature: III. How to use an article about diagnostic test: A. Are the results of the study valid? J Am Med Assoc 1994;271:389–91.
16. Sackett DL. How to read clinical journals. V: To distinguish useful from useless or even harmful therapy. Can Med Assoc J 1981;124:1156–62.
17. Trout KS. How to read clinical journals: IV. To determine etiology or causation. Can Med Assoc J 1981;124:985–90.
18. Tugwell P. How to read clinical journals: III. To learn the clinical course and prognosis of disease. Can Med Assoc J 1981;124:869–72.
19. Takata GS, Chan LS, Shekelle PG, et al. Management of acute otitis media. Evidence report/technology assessment No. 15 (Prepared by the Southern California Evidence-based Practice Center under Contract No. 290-97-0001). AHRQ Publication No. 01-E010. Rockville (MD): Agency for Healthcare Research and Quality; May 2001.

20. Takata GS, Chan LS, Shekelle P, et al. Evidence assessment of management of acute otitis media: I. The role of antibiotics in treatment of uncomplicated acute otitis media. Pediatrics 2001;108:239–47.

21. Chan LS, Takata GS, Shekelle P, et al. Evidence assessment of management of acute otitis media: II. Research gaps and priorities for future research. Pediatrics 2001;108:248–54.

22. Burke P, Bain J, Robinson D, Dunleavey J. Acute red ear in children: controlled trial of non-antibiotic treatment in general practice. BMJ (Clin Res Ed) 1991;303 (6802):558–62.

23. Halsted C, Lepow ML, Balassanian N, et al. Otitis media. Clinical observations, microbiology, and evaluation of therapy. Am J Dis Child 1968;115:542–51.

24. Howie VM, Ploussard JH. Efficacy of fixed combination antibiotics versus separate components in otitis media. Effectiveness of erythromycin estolate, triple sulfonamide, ampicillin, erythromycin estolate-triple sulfonamide, and placebo in 280 patients with acute otitis media under two and one-half years of age. Clin Pediatr (Phila) 1972;11(4):205–14.

25. Kaleida PH, Casselbrant ML, Rockette HE, et al. Amoxicillin or myringotomy or both for acute otitis media: results of a randomized clinical trial. Pediatrics 1991;87(4):466–74.

26. Laxdal OE, Merida J, Jones RH. Treatment of acute otitis media: a controlled study of 142 children. Can Med Assoc J 1970;102(3):263–8.

27. Bass JW, Cashman TM, Frostad AL, et al. Antimicrobials in the treatment of acute otitis media. A second clinical trial. Am J Dis Child 1973;125(3):397–402.

28. Berman S, Lauer BA. A controlled trial of cefaclor versus amoxicillin for treatment of acute otitis media in early infancy. Pediatr Infect Dis J 1983;2:30–3.

29. Giebink GS, Batalden PB, Russ JN, Le CT. Cefaclor v. amoxicillin in treatment of acute otitis media. Am J Dis Child 1984;138(3):287–92.

30. Green SM, Rothrock SG. Single-dose intramuscular ceftriaxone for acute otitis media in children. Pediatrics 1993;91(1):23–30.

31. Jacobson JA, Metcalf TJ, Parkin JL, et al. Evaluation of cefaclor and amoxycillin in the treatment of acute otitis media. Postgrad Med J 1979;55 Suppl 4:39–41.

32. Johnson CE, Carlin SA, Super DM, et al. Cefixime compared with amoxicillin for treatment of acute otitis media. J Pediatrics 1991;119(1 Pt 1):117–22.

33. Kara CO, Ozuer MZ, Kilic I, et al. Comparison of amoxicillin with second and third generation cephalosporins in the treatment of acute otitis media. Infez Med 1998;6(2):93–5.

34. Leigh AP, Robinson D, Millar ED. A general practice comparative study of a new third-generation oral cephalosporin, cefixime, with amoxicillin in the treatment of acute paediatric otitis media. Br J Clin Pract 1989;43(4):140–3.

35. McLinn SE. Cefaclor in treatment of otitis media and pharyngitis in children. Am J Dis Child 1980;134(6): 560–3.

36. McLinn SE. Randomized open label multicenter trial of cefixime compared with amoxicillin for treatment of acute otitis media with effusion. Pediatr Infect Dis 1987;6(10):997–1001.

37. Nilson BW, Poland RL, Thompson RS, et al. Acute otitis media: treatment results in relation to bacterial etiology. Pediatrics 1969;43(3):351–8.

38. Owen MJ, Anwar R, Nguyen HK, et al. Efficacy of cefixime in the treatment of acute otitis media in children. Am J Dis Child 1993;147(1):81–6.

39. Ploussard JH. Evaluation of five days of cefaclor vs. ten days of amoxicillin therapy in acute otitis media. Curr Ther Res 1984;36(Oct):641–5.

40. Principi N, Marchisio P. Cefixime vs amoxicillin in the treatment of acute otitis media in infants and children. Drugs 1991;42 Suppl 4:25–9.

41. Varsano I, Frydman M, Amir J, Alpert G. Single intramuscular dose of ceftriaxone as compared to 7-day amoxicillin therapy for acute otitis media in children. A double-blind clinical trial. Chemotherapy 1988;34 Suppl 1:39–46.

42. Arguedas A, Loaiza C, Herrera M, Mohs E. Comparative trial of 3-day azithromycin versus 10-day amoxicillin/clavulanate potassium in the treatment of children with acute otitis media. Int J Antimicrob Agents 1996;6:233–8.

43. Aronovitz G. A multicenter, open label trial of azithromycin vs. amoxicillin/clavulanate for the management of acute otitis media in children. Pediatr Infect Dis J 1996;15:S15–9.

44. Daniel RR. Comparison of azithromycin and co-amoxiclav in the treatment of otitis media in children. J Antimicrob Chemother 1993;31 Suppl E:65–71.

45. Khurana CM. A multicenter, randomized, open label comparison of azithromycin and amoxicillin/clavulanate in acute otitis media among children attending day care or school. Pediatr Infect Dis J 1996;15 (9 Suppl):S24–9.

46. McLinn S. A multicenter, double blind comparison of azithromycin and amoxicillin/clavulanate for the treatment of acute otitis media in children. Pediatr Infect Dis J 1996;15(9 Suppl):S20–3.

47. Pestalozza G, Cioce C, Facchini M. Azithromycin in upper respiratory tract infections: a clinical trial in children with otitis media. Scand J Infect Dis Suppl 1992;83:22–5.

48. Principi N. Multicentre comparative study of the efficiency and safety of azithromycin compared with amoxicillin/clavulanic acid in the treatment of paediatric patients with otitis media. Eur J Clin Microbinfect Dis 1995;14:669–76.

49. Schaad UB. Multicentre evaluation of azithromycin in comparison with co-amoxiclav for the treatment of acute otitis media in children. J Antimicrob Chemother 1993;31 Suppl E:81–8.

50. Sly RM, Zambie MF, Fernandes DA, Frazer M. Tympanometry in kindergarten children. Ann Allergy 1980;44:1–7.

51. Lamothe A, Boudreault V, Blanchette M, et al. Serous

otitis media: a six week prospective study. J Otolaryngol 1981;10:371–9.

52. Fiellau-Nikolajsen M. Tympanometry in 3-year-old children. Type of care as an epidemiological factor in secretory otitis media and tubal dysfunction in unselected populations of 3-year-old children. ORL J Otorhinolaryngol Relat Spec 1979;41:193–205.

53. Fiellau-Nikolajsen M, Lous J. Tympanometry in three-year-old children. A cohort study on the prognostic value of tympanometry and operative findings in middle ear effusion. ORL J Otorhinolaryngol Relat Spec 1979;41:11–25

54. Tos M, Holm-Jensen S, Sorensen CH. Changes in prevalence of secretory otitis from summer to winter in four-year-old children. Am J Otol 1981;2:324–7.

55. Renvall U, Aniansson G, Liden G. Spontaneous improvement in ears with middle ear disease. Int J Pediatr Otorhinolaryngol 1982;4:245–50.

56. Fischler RS, Todd NW, Feldman CM. Otitis media and language performance in a cohort of Apache Indian children. Am J Dis Child 1985;139:355–60.

57. Gravel JS, Wallace IF. Listening and language at 4 years of age: effects of early otitis media. J Speech Hear Res 1992;35:588–95.

58. Paul R, Lynn TF, Lohr-Flanders M. History of middle ear involvement and speech/language development in late talkers. J Speech Hear Res 1993;36:1055–62.

59. Black MM, Sonnenschein S. Early exposure to otitis media: a preliminary investigation of behavioral outcome. J Dev Behav Pediatr 1993;14:150–5.

60. Teele DW, Klein JO, Chase C, et al. Otitis media in infancy and intellectual ability, school achievement, speech, and language at age 7 years. Greater Boston Otitis Media Study Group. J Infect Dis 1990;162:685–94.

61. Roberts JE, Sanyal MA, Burchinal MR, et al. Otitis media in early childhood and its relationship to later verbal and academic performance. Pediatrics 1986;78:423–30.

62. Sorri M, Maki-Torkko E, Alho OP. Otitis media and long-term follow-up of hearing. Acta Otolaryngol (Stockh) 1995;109:811–6.

63. Harsten G, Nettelbladt U, Schalen L, et al. Language development in children with recurrent acute otitis media during the first three years of life. Follow-up study from birth to seven years of age. J Laryngol Otol 1993;107:407–12.

64. Kaplan GJ, Fleshman JK, Bender TR, et al. Long-term effects of otitis media: a ten-year cohort study of Alaskan Eskimo children. Pediatrics 1973;52:577–85.

65. Fried M, Kelly J, Zubick H, et al. Acoustic reflectivity for diagnosis of middle ear effusions: comparison with results of myringotomy. New Dimensions Otorhinolaryngol Head Neck Surg 1985;2:931–2.

66. Macknin ML, Skibinski C, Beck G, et al. Acoustic reflectometry detection of middle ear effusion. Pediatr Infect Dis J 1987;6:866–8.

67. Babonis TR, Weir MR, Kelly PC. Impedance tympanometry and acoustic reflectometry at myringotomy [published erratum appears in Pediatrics 1991:87(6):945]. Pediatrics 1991;87:475–80.

68. Paradise JL, Smith CG, Bluestone CD. Tympanometric detection of middle ear effusion in infants and young children. Pediatrics 1976;58:198–210.

69. Cantekin EI, Beery QC, Bluestone CD. Tympanometric patterns found in middle ear effusions. Ann Otol Rhinol Laryngol Suppl 1977;86:16–20.

70. Bluestone CD, Cantekin EI. Design factors in the characterization and identification of otitis media and certain related conditions. Ann Otol Rhinol Laryngol Suppl 1979;88:13–28.

71. Karma PH, Penttila MA, Sipila MM, Kataja MJ. Otoscopic diagnosis of middle ear effusion in acute and non-acute otitis media. I. The value of different otoscopic findings. Int J Pediatr Otorhinolaryngol 1989;17:37–49.

72. Mains BT, Toner JG. Pneumatic otoscopy: study of inter-observer variability. J Laryngol Otol 1989;103:1134–5.

73. Toner JG, Mains B. Pneumatic otoscopy and tympanometry in the detection of middle ear effusion. Clin Otolaryngol Allied Sci 1990;15:121–3.

74. Finitzo T, Friel-Patti S, Chinn K, Brown O. Tympanometry and otoscopy prior to myringotomy: issues in diagnosis of otitis media. Int J Pediatr Otorhinolaryngol 1992;24:101–10.

75. Orchik DJ, Dunn JW, McNutt L. Tympanometry as a predictor of middle ear effusion. Arch Otolaryngol 1978;104:4–6.

76. Rees GL, Freeland AP. The effect of anaesthesia on tympanograms of children undergoing grommet insertion [see comments]. Clin Otolaryngol Allied Sci 1992;17:200–2.

77. Vaughan-Jones R, Mills RP. The Welch Allyn Audioscope and Microtymp: their accuracy and that of pneumatic otoscopy, tympanometry and pure tone audiometry as predictors of otitis media with effusion. J Laryngol Otol 1992;106:600–2.

78. van Balen FA, de Melker RA. Validation of a portable tympanometer for use in primary care. Int J Pediatr Otorhinolaryngol 1994;29:219–25.

79. Koivunen P, Alho OP, Uhari M, et al. Minitympanometry in detecting middle ear fluid. J Pediatr 1997;131: 419–22.

80. Fiellau-Nikolajsen M. Serial tympanometry and middle ear status in 3-year-old children. ORL J Otorhinolaryngol Relat Spec 1980;42:220–32.

81. Nozza RJ, Bluestone CD, Kardatzke D, Bachman R. Identification of middle ear effusion by aural acoustic admittance and otoscopy. Ear Hear 1994;15:310–23.

82. Barnett ED, Klein JO, Hawkins KA, et al. Comparison of spectral gradient acoustic reflectometry and other diagnostic techniques for detection of middle ear effusion in children with middle ear disease. Pediatr Infect Dis J 1998;17:556–9, discussion 580.

83. Shaw JO, Stark EW, Gannaway SD. The influence of nitrous oxide anaesthetic on middle-ear fluid. J Laryngol Otol 1978;92:131–5.

84. Johnson LP, Parkin JL, Stevens MH, et al. Action of general anesthesia on middle ear effusions. Arch Otolaryngol 1980;106:100–2.

85. Ben-David J, Podoshin L, Fradis M. Tympanometry and audiometry in diagnosis of middle-ear effusions. Ear Nose Throat J 1981;60:120–3.

86. Kennedy TL, Gore LB. Middle ear effusions and the nitrous oxide myth. Laryngoscope 1982;92:169–72.

87. Gersdorff M, Scholtes JL, Yousif A, Robillard TH. Secretory otitis media, tympanometry and general anesthesia. In: Sade J, editor. Acute and secretory otitis media. Amsterdam: Kugler Publications; 1986. p. 39–44.

88. Park IY, Kim HN, Chung MH, et al. Diagnostic reliability of impedance audiometry in case of otitis media with effusion. Proceedings of the Fourth International Symposium: Recent Advances in Otitis Media with Effusion. Hamilton: BC Decker; 1988. p. 52–4.

89. Mitchell DB, Ford GR, Albert D, Waldron J. Acoustic reflectometry as an aid to the diagnosis of glue ear. Br J Clin Pract 1990;44:557–9.

90. Ovesen T, Paaske PB, Elbrond O. Accuracy of an automatic impedance apparatus in a population with secretory otitis media: principles in the evaluation of tympanometrical findings. Am J Otolaryngol 1993;14:100–4.

91. Sassen ML, van Aarem A, Grote JJ. Validity of tympanometry in the diagnosis of middle ear effusion. Clin Otolaryngol Allied Sci 1994;19:185–9.

92. Tom LW, Tsao F, Marsh RR, et al. Effect of anesthetic gas on middle ear fluid. Laryngoscope 1994;104:832–6.

93. Renvall U, Berg U. Reliability of tympanogram. Proceedings of the Sixth International Symposium: Recent Advances in Otitis Media with Effusion. Hamilton: BC Decker; 1996. p. 143–6.

94. Watters GW, Jones JE, Freeland AP. The predictive value of tympanometry in the diagnosis of middle ear effusion. Clin Otolaryngol Allied Sci 1997;22:343–5.

95. Diagnosis, natural history, and late effects of otitis media with effusion. Summary, evidence report/ technology assessment: Number 55. AHRQ Publication Number 02-E026, June 2002. Rockville (MD): Agency for Healthcare Research and Quality: 2002.

CHAPTER 6

Clinical Practice Guidelines

Anthony E. Magit, MD, and Carla T. Herrerias, BS, MPH

Although everyone wants practice guidelines to improve the quality of care,
only patients care exclusively about clinical outcomes.
Steven H. Woolf

OBJECTIVES

On completion of this chapter, the reader should be able to

1. Understand the definition of a *clinical guideline* as compared to a *standard* or *option*.
2. Appreciate the limitations of clinical practice guidelines.
3. Recognize the forces driving the creation of clinical guidelines.
4. Understand the approach to creating clinical guidelines using the "explicit" method.
5. Recognize the potential role of guidelines in litigation.

Many attempts have been made to create clinical guidelines to assist in delivering health care. An overwhelming amount of information concerning otitis media (OM) must be incorporated into an accessible and meaningful guideline. The 1994 Clinical Practice Guideline for Otitis Media with Effusion in Young Children, sponsored by the United States Department of Health and Human Services, is an important example of this process. The context in which this guideline was created and the methods used to create it reflect the conflicting approaches to managing OM. This chapter will present the forces behind OM clinical guideline development and provide information on the most recent guideline efforts.

Significant effort has been expended to determine the impact of clinical guidelines on physician behavior and patient outcomes in general and subsequent to creating the OM clinical practice guidelines. Important lessons have been learned concerning the integration of clinical guidelines into clinical practice. This chapter will discuss the success of clinical guidelines and impediments to their implementation.

HISTORIC BACKGROUND OF CLINICAL PRACTICE GUIDELINES

In a broad sense, formal medical teaching can be considered a series of clinical practice guidelines. Historic equivalents of clinical guidelines include clinical pearls and rules of thumb. For the purposes of this discussion, *clinical guidelines* refer to official statements of policies of organizations or agencies. Defined this way, guidelines have been a part of organized medicine for at least the past five decades. Synonyms for contemporary clinical guidelines include practice standards, recommendations, protocols, practice parameters, and practice options. Expert panels or individuals have developed these guidelines from information disseminated in the medical literature and through the publications of specialty societies, government agencies, and health policy organizations.

The American Academy of Pediatrics guidelines for infectious diseases (the Red Book) published in 1938 is an early example of a national medical society being actively involved in guideline development.[1] By 1989, more than 35 physician organizations and national medical societies had developed some form of practice guideline according to a survey conducted that year.[2]

The federal government of the United States has also been an active participant in guideline development through the National Institutes of Health, the Centers for Disease Control, the Food and Drug Administration, and other agencies within the Public Health Service.[3] Congress introduced legislation in 1989 to support expanded federal funding for effectiveness research and the development and dissemination of practice guidelines. Several physician organizations ultimately supported the emphasis on guideline development as an alternative to strict enforcement of government expenditure targets that would potentially restrict necessary medical services.

The creation of the Agency for Health Care Policy and Research (AHCPR), now the Agency for Healthcare Research and Quality (AHRQ), included in the Omnibus Reconciliation Act of 1989 was a milestone in government participation in guideline development.[4] The AHCPR division responsible for the development, review, and update of practice guidelines was the Office of the Forum for Quality and Effectiveness in Health Care. The Office of the Forum was charged with creating three guidelines by January 1, 1991. Areas in which guideline efforts were directed include benign prostatic hypertrophy, pain management, pressure sores, cataracts, urinary incontinence, sickle cell disease, depression, and otitis media with effusion (OME).[5]

Although the AHRQ does not develop clinical practice guidelines, they support academic centers to conduct research through evidence-based medicine on selected topics. Currently, there are several centers in the United States and Canada (evidence-based practice centers) working with the federal government that are charged with developing the evidence base for clinical conditions. The reports from these centers are then used by other organizations to develop clinical policies and practice guidelines. Insurers were also involved in guideline development prior to the expanded activities of government and nongovernmental organizations. Insurance companies developed most guidelines internally, although some were the result of collaborations between insurers and physician organizations.

Independent research centers with experience in health care assessment have continued to be involved in developing guidelines. The RAND Corporation, with its history of involvement in evaluating clinical appropriateness and in its relationship with the Health Care Financing Administration (HCFA), continues to contribute to guideline development.

DEFINITIONS OF CLINICAL PRACTICE POLICIES AND GUIDELINES

Clinical policies are intended to ensure that a certain level of clinical practice will result in the best patient outcomes, given the current knowledge. Clinical policies should be reproducible to the extent that different groups of physicians would have similar recommendations for appropriate management of a given clinical situation. Policies should be easy to use and realistically appreciate the limitations of patient–physician encounters. Patients should be the focus of the policies, with patient preferences emphasized. Risks and benefits of diagnostic and therapeutic interventions must be addressed. The clinical guideline is one form of clinical policy.

The Institute of Medicine defines clinical practice guidelines as "systematically developed statements to assist practitioner and patient decisions about appropriate health care for specific clinical circumstances." Other terms that have been used to refer to guidelines are "practice parameters," "appropriateness indicators," "care maps," and "critical pathways."

The term "clinical guidelines" can have a broad meaning. Given the emphasis on evidence-based recommendations, the general area of clinical policies can be subdivided into three classes: standards, guidelines, and options.

- *Standards* exist when the consequences of a clinical alternative are well known and there is virtual unanimity among physicians regarding the preferred approach to a specific clinical situation and benefits/harms are clear.
- *Guidelines* imply that the outcomes of a clinical strategy are sufficiently understood to permit decisions.
- *Options* are a list of alternatives for a given situation with the likelihood of outcomes not clearly characterized, and the benefits and harms are unclear.

The decision to proceed with a guideline implies that sufficient information is available regarding the effectiveness of therapeutic interventions or the predictive value of a diagnostic test. Guidelines are created to help physicians make decisions about managing individual patients and may be directed toward screening, preventive care, diagnostic alternatives, or therapeutic interventions. The guideline may address the full gamut of clinical care, including the specific requirements of a clinical setting, the qualifications of the practitioner, and the appropriate use of a particular diagnostic or therapeutic intervention.

FORCES BEHIND GUIDELINE DEVELOPMENT

The explosion in clinical guideline development can be tied to identifiable forces. While it is true that the proliferation of medical information makes it difficult for physicians to stay current with the medical literature, this is not the primary force behind the need to create evidence-based guidelines. Guidelines can be important educational tools, but it is more likely that financial pressures and an interest in standardizing clinical care are driving clinical guideline development.

Rising health care costs, variations in clinical practice, reports of inappropriate care, and delays in incorporating new scientific information into clinical care are stimulating interest in clinical guidelines. Guideline development is seen as a means of organizing medicine and tying specific clinical outcomes to clinical interventions in response to the above.

Health care expenditures in the United States increased to more than 12% of the gross national product in the late 1980s. With 60% of the federal government budget for health care being spent on the Medicare program and physician payments comprising the majority of Part B Medicare expenditures, the government sought to identify areas where services could be reduced.[6]

Researchers led by Wennberg and colleagues[7] investigated variation in the rates of specific interventions performed by physicians in different geographic areas.

Significant variations in practice behavior were demonstrated in similar populations. Although evidence as to the cause of these differences was inconclusive, it was suggested that physician uncertainty about the appropriate indications for specific interventions might have been responsible. Clinical practice guidelines are considered as a potential means to reduce variation in clinical behavior.

Concerns have been raised about inappropriate care as information related to clinical outcomes becomes more widely available. Studies designed to examine the appropriateness of procedures suggest that many medical procedures lie outside the recommendations of expert panels.[8] Clinical practice guidelines used prospectively may be a solution to curtailing unnecessary clinical practices.

MEDICOLEGAL ASPECTS OF CLINICAL GUIDELINES

Introducing a clinical guideline by a provider organization potentially shifts some of the exposure to liability away from the independent physician and to the organization implementing a guideline intended to affect physician behavior. An organization that uses a guideline to influence physician practice, through either a reward or penalty system, can make the organization solely or jointly liable in a malpractice case.[9] Health care organizations that inadequately monitor physician practice with regard to guideline recommendations may be subject to liability because of the corporate negligence doctrine.

Physician liability when practicing under the auspices of a clinical guideline is theoretically reduced, given the assumption that an appropriately created guideline makes the standard of care physicians are expected to meet regarding appropriate practice more explicit. To support this claim, under common law, most states allow a practice parameter to be used as evidence of standard of care when the parameter is applicable to the clinical situation.[10,11] However, the legal system tends to incorporate many factors in determining appropriate care, and courts have determined that even if clinical practice was consistent with a clinical guideline, medical judgment determines the standard of care and not third-party payers' decisions based on economics.[12] Guidelines not reflecting current scientific knowledge can expose physicians to liability if the courts consider that the clinical practice was not based on current and relevant information.

Evidence exists supporting the claim that clinical practice guidelines have been used more by plaintiffs than physicians in malpractice litigation. Hyams and colleagues[13] presented a survey of 259 malpractice claims, with 17 claims between 1990 and 1992 involving practice guidelines, 12 used to implicate the physicians, and 4 used for evidence for the defendant physicians. In some situations, clinical guidelines have provided motivation for attorneys to bring a lawsuit; however, guidelines may dissuade attorneys from initiating malpractice litigation. In this same report, 26% of attorneys surveyed reported that practice guidelines influenced their decision not to take a case.[13] The state of Maine has legislation in which compliance with a guideline provides exculpatory evidence to help protect a physician from a legal action.[14]

The role of clinical guidelines in malpractice litigation is complicated. In the current legal environment, clinical guidelines do not uniformly protect or threaten physicians. Physicians must balance the pressure to use guidelines on the part of health care organizations against a physician's responsibility to weigh the value of specific guidelines based on evidence-based recommendations and clinical judgment.

METHODS OF CLINICAL GUIDELINE DEVELOPMENT

Clinical guidelines may be created by informal consensus development, formal consensus development, evidence-based guideline development, or explicit guideline development.[15]

Informal consensus development relies on expert opinion, with guidelines typically released by specialty societies, federal agencies, or disease-oriented task forces. Consensus is achieved primarily through open discussion, with little analysis of the medical literature. Guidelines produced using this methodology usually provide general recommendations with no formal discussion of the process by which the guideline was created. Their lack of explicitness makes them suspect. Individual opinions and biases may sway the consensus statement of an expert panel's recommendation, especially if the panel comprises a group of specialists who support an approach favorable to their specialty. The major benefit of this approach is that the guideline can be created quickly, often as the result of a single discussion. For this reason, informal consensus remains the most common method of generating clinical practice guidelines.

Formal consensus development uses a structured approach, often requiring several days to complete a clinical guideline. The National Institutes of Health Consensus Development Program introduced an approach in 1977 that created a guideline in a closed session after a plenary session and open discussion.[16] The American Medical Association has conducted appropriateness assessments through the Diagnostic and Therapeutics Technology Assessment program. For a specific topic, questionnaires are mailed to experts, and the results are tabulated and presented in the *Journal of the American Medical Association.* This form of formal consensus lacks panel discussion interaction and represents a simple vote.

The RAND Corporation, for example, assumed an active role in guideline development in the 1980s with the two-step Delphi approach. This involves presenting an expert panel with several potential indications for performing a procedure.[17] Panel members are asked prior to meeting to assess the appropriateness of a procedure using a nine-point scale, with 1 representing extremely inappropriate and 9 extremely appropriate. Scores are reviewed during a subsequent panel meeting, then revised on the basis of the discussion. Appropriateness scores produced using the Delphi approach have been widely used commercially by firms, hospitals, health plans, and insurers. The RAND panels consider scientific evidence, although the methodology does not explicitly state the relationship between recommendations and the quality of evidence.

Evidence-based guidelines tie recommendations to the quality of supporting information. In the majority of evidence-based guidelines, expert panels are used to evaluate the quality of supporting evidence. Given the strict reliance on quality evidence, many guidelines created using this approach cannot be used to make recommendations in the absence of quality evidence. When this is the case, a neutral recommendation or clinical option is commonly presented. This provides little assistance to practicing clinicians, who are usually confronted with clinical situations where rigorously tested scientific evidence supporting specific interventions is lacking.

Explicit guideline development evolved, under the leadership of Eddy,[18,19] to fill gaps in quality scientific information that can result in neutral recommendations from strict evidence-based guidelines. The benefits, harms, and costs of interventions are described in detail, and the probability of each outcome is estimated using scientific evidence and, where possible, formal analytic methods. Expert opinion is used to generate estimates of outcomes that are placed in a "balance sheet" with the assumptions used. This "balance sheet" permits patients, clinicians, and policy makers to examine the implications of various interventions. The relative value of various outcomes is judged with an emphasis on patient preferences.

Explicitly derived guidelines are meant to combine the scientific rigor of evidence-based guidelines while filling gaps in scientifically proven evidence with expert opinion. It is hoped that the result will be guidelines that are more comprehensive in scope and reflect realistic clinical situations. The explicit approach requires an extensive review of information available on a particular subject, as well as an organized and committed expert panel.

GUIDELINE DEVELOPMENT: STEP BY STEP

Creating any guideline, regardless of underlying methodology, requires organization and planning. The time spent and level of detail required for each step depend on the method chosen and the extent of resources. The steps in guideline development as outlined by Woolf are introductory decisions, assessments of clinical appropriateness, assessment of public policy issues, and guideline document development and evaluation.[15] Guideline development can be broken down into a series of tasks (Table 6-1).

Introductory decisions include the selection of a topic, either a disease or presenting complaint. The focus may be on prevention, diagnosis, treatment, or rehabilitation. Once the topic is chosen, a panel is assembled, and one of its initial tasks is to narrow and clarify the topic.

Table 6-1 Methodologic Issues to Address in Guideline Documents*

Selection of topic

Clarification of purpose

Clarification of clinical benefits and harms
    Assessment of scientific evidence
        Admissible evidence
        Review process
        Evaluation of scientific evidence
    Assessment of expert opinion

Assessment of public policy issues
    Resource limitations
    Feasibility issues

Drafting of document

Peer review

Pretesting

Recommendations of other groups

Recommendations for research

Disclaimers

References

*Adapted from Woolf SH.[15]

The second step in creating a guideline is assessing clinical harms and benefits, focusing initially on the practices that produce the best clinical outcomes and secondarily on such factors as cost, feasibility, and malpractice. This assessment is based on a review of scientific evidence and on expert opinion. Review of scientific information proceeds from retrieval of the evidence to evaluation of individual studies to synthesis of the data. Supporting scientific evidence can be analyzed by various means, ranging from narrative or visual descriptions of the evidence to more formal analytic techniques, including meta-analysis and decision analysis. Expert opinion is a critical component of most guidelines. Expert panels can assess evidence informally with open discussions and voting or use more complex processes, such as the Delphi method discussed above.

The third step in creating a guideline is to summarize benefits and harms associated with anticipated outcomes to construct a model for predicting the results of specific interventions. Putting recommendations in clinical perspective requires placing individual practices into one of three categories: appropriate, inappropriate, or uncertain appropriateness, commonly referred to as the "gray zone." The handling of gray-zone practices distinguishes between traditional evidence-based guidelines and the more flexible explicit approach. Uncertainty in clinical guidelines is unavoidable where scientific evidence is absent or incomplete for specific practices. Unlike pure evidence-based guidelines, where no recommendation can be made when information is lacking, explicit methods allow expert opinion to bridge gaps in evidence. Explicitly reporting the quality and origin of support for specific recommendations, whether based on scientific evidence or expert opinion, allows guidelines to acknowledge patient preferences and reasonable differences in opinion in the medical literature or among members of an expert panel. The "cookbook" approach to clinical medicine is thereby avoided.

The completed guideline reflects an ideal situation, with patient outcomes as the primary concerns. Guidelines affecting a large number of patients constitute public policy and may potentially have significant social impact. Meaningful and realistic guidelines must address issues related to resource limitations and cost and reflect awareness that resources may be shifted away from established practices if the guidelines are implemented. Guidelines must be appropriate for the intended clinical situations and fit within the constraints of "real-world" practice conditions. These conditions include time pressures, available staff and equipment, reimbursement, malpractice liability, patient preferences, and access to medical services.

The successful guideline becomes integrated into clinical practice and should be considered dynamic. The written guideline document is often combined with educational programs when disseminated. In this atmosphere, suggestions for changes may be elicited. Investigating changes in clinical practices and patient outcomes subsequent to introducing the guideline is the only means of establishing the impact of clinical guidelines. The guideline must be updated as new information becomes available.

Clinical guidelines can prevent stagnation in medical progress and direct research support by identifying areas deficient in scientific evidence. Directing research may be one of the most important functions of a clinical practice guideline. Without including recommendations for research, strict reliance on guidelines would tend to restrict innovations in clinical practice.

DEVELOPING A GUIDELINE FOR OTITIS MEDIA

The purpose of this section is to present clinical guidelines relevant to OME. Presenting a complete handbook for clinical guideline development is beyond the scope of this chapter.

The Otitis Media Clinical Guideline was one of several developed by the AHCPR (now AHRQ).[20] This agency was presented with the task of creating guidelines for diseases with broad clinical and financial impact for the American population, and OME clearly fits these criteria. The development of this guideline will serve as a model for explicit guideline development.

Prior to the OM guideline, the federal government tended to create the infrastructure for establishing a guideline with assistance from outside experts. The OM guideline was unique in that after an application process, the guideline was awarded to a consortium of nongovernmental organizations consisting of the American Academy of Pediatrics (AAP), the American Academy of Family Physicians (AAFP), and the American Academy of Otolaryngology–Head and Neck Surgery (AAO–HNS). Physicians may have been more likely to implement such a guideline developed by their own professional organizations, rather than one presented to them by a federal agency.

Constructing the Panel

The AHCPR, through the Federal Register and the consortium organizations, assembled a panel representing the spectrum of individuals involved in managing OME. It consisted of pediatricians, family physicians, otolaryngologists, a pediatric psychologist, a pediatric audiologist, a pediatric nurse practitioner, a maternal and child health expert, a speech-language pathologist, an infectious disease specialist, an economist and health policy analyst, and a consumer representative. Consortium support staff consisted of a health policy methodologist, a health policy coordinator, and a project manager.

Choosing the Topic

For a feasible guideline to be developed with limited resources, there must be a specific focus. Creating a comprehensive guideline for all forms of OM would be a nearly impossible task. The panel chose OME rather than acute otitis media (AOM) or recurrent OM. Among the many factors involved in choosing this form of otitis media (OM) was the desire to address the indications for tympanostomy tube placement as a major intervention. Also, OME is prevalent among the pediatric population and its management is controversial.

After selecting the general topic, the panel chooses the specific subjects related to the disease. Some panels may severely limit the scope of the guideline, analyzing only diagnostic or therapeutic interventions, for example. The OM panel chose to address the natural history of OME, diagnosis and hearing evaluation, functional impairments that may result, control of environmental risk factors, and medical and surgical interventions.

The "Target" Children

Creating a "target" patient to anchor a guideline is one tool to assist in accumulating and analyzing evidence when the body of scientific literature and expert opinion is vast. Identifying a target patient is crucial for such a disease as OME because of the variety of short- and long-term outcomes related to the stage of a patient's physical, emotional, social, and psychological development.

The relationship between hearing loss associated with OME and speech and language development provides a striking example of this aspect of the target patient. Hearing loss associated with a middle ear effusion (MEE) would be expected to be more detrimental to a preschool-aged child in the period of rapid language acquisition than to a school-aged child without a history of OM or previous hearing loss. Emphasizing patient outcomes in a clinical guideline mandates that the target of the guideline be explicitly described. For specific practices, however, the nature of the intervention and quality of evidence may allow a particular recommendation to be applied to patients other than the target patient.

The target patient for the OME clinical guideline is a child aged 1 through 3 years with no craniofacial or neurologic abnormalities or sensory deficits, who is otherwise healthy except for OME. The target setting and audience for the guideline must also be determined. The panel intended the guideline to be widely applicable and used in any setting in which children at risk for OME would be identified or treated, including physician offices, outpatient clinics, hospital emergency departments, urgent care centers, and schools or childcare facilities. The guideline is intended for use by providers of health care to young children, including primary care and specialist physicians, professional nurses and nurse practitioners, physician assistants, audiologists, speech-language pathologists, child development specialists, and consumers.

Accumulating the Evidence

Developing a comprehensive body of evidence for a clinical guideline requires an extensive and critical literature review. The literature search for the 1994 OME guideline used the National Library of Medicine and 10 specialized databases. Using multiple search terms, 3,578 bibliographic citations were identified and 1,362 abstracts were evaluated. On the basis of a review of the abstracts using the target patient and areas of interest for the guideline, 378 articles were selected for data extraction using a form developed by the methodologist and panel. Alternative citations were identified through review of literature reference lists, updated on-line searches, requests to professionals, and suggestions from experts. Unpublished research was elicited through announcements in professional journals and communications with professional organizations.

The panel sought to reduce the likelihood that relevant information would be presented after the guideline was created. To reduce this possibility and to give individuals not included on the panel an opportunity to contribute to the guideline, an open meeting was held, which gave individuals the opportunity to provide testimony to the panel. The meeting was announced in the Federal Register and selected professional journals. Twelve individuals presented data and opinions to the panel.

Evaluating the Evidence

Data abstracted from the chosen citations were entered into a computer database. The panel reviewed evidence in the database and assessed its scientific merit, focusing on randomized, blinded, and controlled studies, when available. Appropriate literature addressing outcomes of interest was combined using meta-analyses.

The panel based recommendations regarding diagnostic and therapeutic interventions on evidence from the database and meta-analyses, when available. Expert opinions were solicited in making decisions regarding specific interventions when evidence was limited. Consensus was sought on all decisions. When consensus could not be reached, votes were taken. The majority recommendation was presented without minority comment. Dissenting panel members commented on specific recommendations in the appendix to the guidelines' technical report and in professional journals.

Presenting the structure of the panel, including the literature retrieval and review, is central to the explicit approach to the guideline development. The panel used a grading scale to rate individual recommendations based on the quality and quantity of evidence and the strength of expert opinion. There were three categories of recommendations used: (1) strong recommendations, (2) moderate recommendations, and (3) recommendations. Less compelling recommendations were presented as clinical opinions, and no recommendation was made if evidence was lacking.

Prerelease Review

Prior to public release, the panel and AHCPR hoped to anticipate criticism and fine-tune the guideline. This prerelease review was accomplished by having a draft of the guidelines reviewed by approximately 75 experts involved with OM.

THE OTITIS MEDIA CLINICAL PRACTICE GUIDELINE

The complete OM guideline was available through the U.S. Department of Health and Human Services until 2001 but is still currently available through the specialty societies in the Consortium. This publication explicitly described the outcomes addressed by the guideline and a summary of the evidence used in making specific recommendations.[20] The guideline also provides a Quick Reference Guide for Clinicians, a complete technical report, and abbreviated patient pamphlet.

Aspects of the algorithm are worthy of discussion to highlight assumptions and recommendations made by the panel in creating the guideline. The patient enters the algorithm after being diagnosed with OME by pneumatic otoscopy, with tympanometry reserved to confirm the diagnosis. Pneumatic otoscopy is considered more predictive of the presence or absence of a MEE than is static otoscopy. Tympanometry is not recommended routinely because limited resources make it unlikely that a tympanometer would be available in all target settings.

Throughout the guideline, decongestants, antihistamines, and oral steroids are not recommended for treatment. The decision to not recommend antihistamines and decongestants is based on literature demonstrating their lack of efficacy in clearing MEEs. The general panel did not recommend steroids, although a dissenting minority was in favor of using steroids. Environmental

risk factor control is presented as a safe educational intervention. Passive exposure to cigarette smoke is considered a well-defined risk factor for OM. Bottle feeding versus breast feeding and placement in a childcare setting are associated with OME. There is, however, a lack of studies proving a reduction in OME subsequent to limiting these risk factors.

The absence of adenoidectomy as a surgical intervention at any point in the algorithm is an example of excluding literature because of using a target child. Because studies supporting adenoidectomy for OME addressed children older than the target patient, the panel was reluctant to extrapolate this information to a younger child. Tonsillectomy is not recommended because of its lack of efficacy for managing OME in children of any age.

The emphasis on hearing assessment is a pivotal component of the algorithm. By design, the target child is asymptomatic, with the major emphasis on long-term outcomes, primarily speech and language development. The relationship between hearing impairment and speech and language development is discussed at length, with a hearing threshold of 20 decibels or poorer for the better-hearing ear being a reason for concern. Many options are presented for the hearing assessment. The algorithm is appropriate for clinical settings possessing differing levels of audiology services because of the flexibility in the method of hearing evaluation. These include pure-tone threshold audiometry measuring air and bone conduction, speech reception threshold audiometry, speech awareness threshold audiometry, behavioral observations audiometry, and auditory brainstem recording evaluation.

Recommendations for specific antibiotics were not included as the panel analyzed multiple studies of a variety of antibiotics.

IMPACT OF THE OTITIS MEDIA CLINICAL GUIDELINE

Examining physician behavior following the publication of the Otitis Media Clinical Practice Guideline provides insight into the impact this guideline has had on clinical behavior. Stewart and coworkers[21] surveyed 1,167 otolaryngologists, pediatricians, and pediatric otolaryngologists in an attempt to determine the utilization of the OME Clinical Practice Guideline. Forty-eight percent of the physicians returned a six-item questionnaire seeking information about practice patterns and treatment preferences for managing OM in young children. Only eight physicians answered all six questions in agreement with the practice guideline.

Agreement with components of the practice guideline varied among the specialties. No difference was seen between the groups with regard to the best diagnostic combination to detect OME, which was pneumatic otoscopy and tympanometry. Otolaryngologists and pediatric otolaryngologists were less likely to treat newly diagnosed OME with 6 weeks of observation than were pediatricians. With regard to being aware that antihistamines and decongestants have been shown to be ineffective adjuvants to treating OME, this question was answered correctly by most of the pediatric otolaryngologists and fewest of the pediatricians.

The information garnered from this study must be viewed cautiously as a physician's response to a survey is likely to differ from actual clinical practice.

Awareness of the OME clinical practice guideline has been less than anticipated. Three hundred of 555 eligible pediatricians returned an American Medical Association survey assessing awareness and attitudes about four clinical practice guidelines, including the OME guideline.[22] Only 50% were aware of the OME guideline, and 28% of respondents reported that they had changed patient management because of the guideline. The AAP received responses from 627 general pediatricians for a questionnaire investigating attitudes, beliefs, and practices about clinical practice guidelines.[23] Of the more than 100 practice guidelines used by pediatricians, 19% of the physicians use an OME guideline compared with 77% using an asthma guideline.

The AAP survey cited that common reasons for using a guideline were standardization of care (17%) and helpfulness (10%). Problems identified for guidelines included failure to allow for clinical judgment (54%), use in litigation (16%), and limitation of autonomy (5%).

REVISING THE OTITIS MEDIA CLINICAL PRACTICE GUIDELINE

New guidelines are being developed (December 2002) by the AAP, AAFP, and AAO-HNS for managing AOM and OME. The AOM guideline is a completely new document. The OME guideline updates the 1994 AHCPR report with new information on developmental outcomes and the impact of tympanostomy tube insertion. Unlike the 1994 document, the new OME guideline targets children aged 2 months to 12 years, with or without developmentally disabilities or underlying conditions that predispose to OM.

The evidence-based approach to guideline development is unique because of the levels at which the evidence is identified, criticized, and summarized, and the explicit ways in which evidence strength is linked to the quality of recommendations. Evidence grading assumes that highest quality comes from well-designed clinical trials, followed by other prospective trials. Lower quality evidence may be obtained from case reports and data that could be extrapolated from populations outside the intended target population.

An additional factor that influences the strength of recommendations is the balance of benefits and harms. Strong recommendations can be made on the basis of when there are clear benefits to an intervention and, perhaps, minimal harms. There can also be stronger recommendations made against an intervention if the harms present an off-balance argument. This model was used in developing the new OM guidelines.

The two multidisciplinary panels that were convened to develop clinical practice guidelines on AOM and OME used several structured literature reviews to provide data for guideline recommendations.

- The AOM practice guideline focuses on standardizing the definition; identifying appropriate methods for diagnosis; initial treatment of uncomplicated AOM (including selective use of nonantibiotic management); and issues regarding treatment failure and ensuring follow-up.
- The updated practice guideline on OME addresses issues related to accurately diagnosing middle ear fluid; medical management; defining associated morbidity; surgical interventions; and follow-up.

These nested guidelines complement each other in reaffirming the importance of appropriate diagnosis before implementing a treatment strategy.

PHYSICIAN ACCEPTANCE OF CLINICAL GUIDELINES

A well-constructed clinical practice guideline is of little use if it is rejected or ignored by physicians. Physician resistance to implementing clinical guidelines has been studied with the purpose of addressing these barriers in future guideline development. Seventy-six published studies investigating barriers to adherence to clinical guidelines led Cabana and colleagues[24] to identify seven categories of barriers. These categories are lack of awareness, lack of familiarity, lack of agreement, lack of self-efficacy, lack of outcome expectancy, inertia of previous practice, and external barriers.

- *Lack of awareness* for a guideline and lack of familiarity for the content of a guideline are straightforward concepts. Lack of agreement with a guideline includes differences in interpreting evidence, believing that the benefits of a recommendation do not outweigh the risk and that the guideline oversimplifies the problem.

- *Lack of self-efficacy* means that an individual cannot or is unlikely to perform a behavior. An example is that a physician is likely to prescribe a medication if the physician believes that the patient will be compliant. Conversely, a physician may be reluctant to engage in health education and counseling if he or she believes that the patient will not be able to adhere to the recommendations.
- *Lack of outcome expectancy* reflects the belief that the desired outcome will not be reached if the guideline is followed. Preventive health counseling and education guidelines are often cited as areas in which physicians have little confidence that these interventions will positively affect patient outcomes. One explanation for this belief is that physicians tend to assess outcomes on the basis of individuals and not on a population level. If a population's outcome is improved significantly, but with a small percentage, the physician may not recognize this degree of improvement in his or her clinical practice.
- *Inertia of previous practice* may be caused by an inability to change or a lack of motivation. The first step to change is a priming phase. Behavior change is a series of steps involving precontemplation, contemplation, preparation, action, and maintenance.
- *External barriers* include guideline-related barriers, patient-related barriers, and environment-related barriers. Guideline-related barriers include inconvenience. Guidelines that promote a new behavior may be easier to implement than those that attempt to eliminate a behavior. Patient-related barriers reflect the lack of reconciling a recommendation with patient preferences. Environment-related barriers include the need to acquire new resources or facilities to implement a guideline.

Barriers to guideline implementation are well recognized through formal study and clinical experience. Guideline development is dependent on anticipating barriers either before or during development. Once a guideline is created, barriers cannot be ignored and the guideline must to altered to address the barriers.

Conclusion

Clinical practice guidelines have become integrated into clinical practice because of forces both external to and within medicine. Their potential benefits are great, including an educational role for physicians and a means to integrate new scientific information into "frontline" clinical practices. The explicit approach to guideline development uses rigorous analytic methods while employing expert opinion to keep recommenda-

---

Table 6-2 Pointers and Pitfalls

1. The otitis media clinical practice guideline was created using a "target" child. Extrapolation of a specific recommendation to other children must be done on the basis of relevant evidence.

2. Strictly evidence-based guidelines will necessarily have areas with "no recommendation" because of gaps in scientific information.

3. Clinical practice guidelines are patient-centered policies emphasizing clinical outcomes.

4. Expert opinion plays a large role in explicit guideline development. The composition of the expert panel is an important component of biases influencing recommendations.

5. Clinical guidelines can be created for any aspect of a condition, including diagnostic and therapeutic interventions.

6. Recommendations of clinical guidelines reflect realistic clinical situations with the ideal management of a patient tempered by limitations of resources.

---

tions feasible and realistic. The explicitly derived guideline is costly, however, both financially and in terms of human resources.

Criticism of any guideline is expected because of the reliance on expert opinion and the inherent differences in evaluating scientific evidence. The method used to create a guideline can be as important as the specific recommendations. Any guideline effort is undertaken with an appreciation for sound methodology and potential problem areas (Table 6-2).

Guidelines cannot be created in a vacuum. Despite having supporting evidence for interventions with desired outcomes, guidelines work in a world of potential conflict. Guidelines are dynamic in that the information supporting their recommendations and the barriers to their implementation may change over time.

References

1. American Academy of Pediatrics. Report of the committee on immunization procedures of the AAP. Evanston (IL): AAP; 1938.
2. American Medical Association. QA Rev 1989;1:7.
3. Woolf SH. Practice guidelines: a new reality in medicine I. Recent developments. Arch Intern Med 1990;150: 1811–8.
4. U.S. House of Representatives. Omnibus Budget Reconciliation Act of 1989: conference report to accompany HR 3299. Washington (DC): US Congress; November 21, 1989.

5. Magit AE, Stool SE. Clinical guideline development for otitis media: a report on the methodology. Otolaryngol Head Neck Surg 1993;109:478–81.

6. Iglehart JK. Payment of physicians under Medicare. N Engl J Med 1988;318:863–8.

7. Wennberg JE, Perrin JM, Homer CJ, et al. Variations in rates of hospitalization of children in three urban communities. N Engl J Med 1989;320:1183–7.

8. Roark R, Petrofski J, Berson E, Berman S. Practice variations among pediatricians and family physicians in the management of otitis media. Arch Pediatr Adolesc Med 1995;1149:839–44.

9. Merritt TA, Palmer D, Bergman DA, Shiono PH. Clinical practice guidelines in pediatric and newborn medicine: implications for their use in practice. Pediatrics 1997; 99:100–14.

10. American Medical Association. Legal implications of practice parameters. Chicago (IL): American Medical Association; 1990.

11. Hirshfeld E. Practice parameters and the malpractice liability of physicians. JAMA 1990;263:1556–62.

12. Wickline v. State of California, 192 Ca App 3d at p.1633, (239 Cal Rept 810) 1986.

13. Hyams AL, Brandenberg JA, Lipsitz SR, et al. Practice guidelines and malpractice litigation: a two-way street. Ann Intern Med 1995;122:450–5.

14. Maine Public Law, PL1989, Chapter 931, 1990.

15. Woolf SH. Practice guidelines: a new reality in medicine II. Methods of developing guidelines. Arch Intern Med 1992;152:946–52.

16. Institute of Medicine, Council on Health Care Technology. Consensus development at the NIH: improving the program. Washington (DC): National Academy Press; 1990.

17. Park RE, Fink A, Brook RH, et al. Physician ratings of appropriate indications for six medical and surgical procedures. Am J Public Health 1985;76:766–72.

18. Eddy DM. Practice policies, guidelines for methods. JAMA 1990;263:1839–41.

19. Eddy DM. Guidelines for policy statements: the explicit approach. JAMA 1990;263:2240–3.

20. Stool SE, Berg AO, Berman S, et al. Otitis media with effusion in young children. Clinical practice guideline, number 12. Rockville (MD): Agency for Health Care Policy and Research, Public Health Service, U.S. Department of Health and Human Services; July 1994. AHCPR Publication No.94-0622.

21. Stewart MG, Manolidis S, Wynn R, Bautista M. Practice patterns versus practice guidelines in pediatric otitis media. Otolaryngol Head Neck Surg 2001;124:489–95.

22. Christakis DA, Rivera FP. Pediatricians' awareness of and attitudes about four clinical practice guidelines. Pediatrics 1998;101:825–30.

23. Flores G, Lee M, Bauchner H, Kastner B. Pediatricians' attitudes, beliefs, and practices regarding clinical practice guidelines: a national survey. Pediatrics 2000;105:496–501.

24. Cabana MD, Rand PC, Powe NR, et al. Why don't physicians follow clinical practice guidelines? A framework for improvement. JAMA 1999;282:1458–65

CHAPTER 7

Molecular and Translational Research

Kai Shen, MD, PhD, Xue Wang, MD, J. Christopher Post, MD, PhD, and Garth D. Ehrlich, PhD

If you work at it hard enough, you can grind an iron rod into a needle.
Chinese Proverb

OBJECTIVES

On completion of this chapter, the reader should be able to

1. Know common molecular diagnostic methods for detecting otitis media (OM) pathogens.
2. Understand the principles behind various molecular diagnostics and be able to choose correct methods for diagnosis in clinical practice.
3. Recognize animal models used to study OM and their research applications.
4. Appreciate phenotypic and genotypic complexities of bacterial life in vitro and in vivo and the differences between planktonic and biofilm growth forms.
5. Understand diversity, genomic plasticity, the "Distributed Genome Hypothesis," and the terms "supragenome" and "supravirulence" with respect to OM pathogens.

EDITORIAL COMMENT

The first edition of this book did not contain any information on molecular or translational research, which was, in retrospect, a significant omission. Whereas basic research is often considered the weakest level of evidence to support clinical decisions, the search for certainty (eg, research) is often the springboard for paradigm shifts and practice-changing clinical trials. This chapter emphasizes molecular, animal, and translational research because they are the techniques most likely to lead from the bench to the bedside. Please accept this chapter as an intellectual bridge for clinicians wishing to understand the cutting-edge research most likely to revolutionize future management of OM.

MOLECULAR METHODS OF DETECTION

Genes and their cognate ribonucleic acid (RNA) and protein products can be directly assayed with a battery of technologies collectively referred to as molecular diagnostics. Molecular methods provide direct evidence of bacteria and other pathogens in infectious diseases by identifying pathogenic genes and their products.

The Polymerase Chain Reaction and Related Amplification Methodologies

Modern polymerase chain reaction (PCR) was invented in 1983 by Kary B. Mullis, for which he was awarded the 1993 Nobel Prize in Chemistry. A research group led by Professor Khorana, however, had posited the general concept of in vitro reciprocal primer-directed deoxyribonucleic acid (DNA) replication that would result in the exponential accumulation of product. PCR is a rapid, cyclic, in vitro, enzymatic DNA amplification process that results in a 2^n accumulation of target DNA sequences where n equals the number of amplification cycles.[1] The primitive method quickly blossomed into a family of PCR-based assay systems, with such enhancements as thermostable DNA polymerases, tandem enzymes, and automation.[2]

The exponential amplification process imbues PCR-based assays with an exquisite sensitivity that enables very small amounts (down to a single copy) of input DNA (and RNA) to be repeatedly replicated and then detected. The method also achieves unparalleled specificity by using type-specific oligonucleotide primers that, through complementary DNA base pairing, anneal only to the target sequence. The primers that flank the double-stranded (ds) DNA sequence of interest are oriented so that on denaturation of the dsDNA, they will hybridize to opposite strands of the target DNA with their 3′ ends facing each other.

Hybridizing a specific primer to its complementary sequence within the target DNA forms a template-primer complex, which is recognized as a substrate by a DNA polymerase. This allows simultaneous copying of both strands of the DNA segment between the primers because all DNA polymerases add nucleotides to the 3′ end of a growing chain (Figure 7-1). If the target sequence is

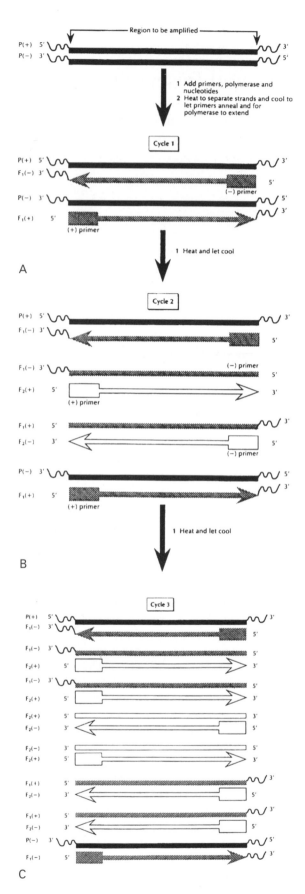

Figure 7-1 Diagrammatic representation of the enzymatic polymerase chain reaction deoxyribonucleic acid (PCR DNA) amplification process. The thick black lines represent the input target DNA sequence (P); the stippled lines represent the first generation of amplified DNA molecules (F_1); the open bars represent the second and subsequent generations of amplified DNA products (F_2); the boxes a the 5′ ends of the DNA strands represent the specific oligonucleotide primers used to initiate DNA chain elongation. *A, Top*, target DNA and flanking sequences; *bottom*, first cycle of amplification. *B*, Cycle 2 of amplification; note that the F_1 DNAs synthesized in the first cycle serve as templates for future DNA synthesis in the second cycle, hence the name polymerase chain reaction. *C*, Cycle 3 of PCR amplification; note that F_2-type molecules with discrete 5′ and 3′ ends serve as templates for additional F_2-type molecules, thus resulting in the exponential accumulation of amplimers bounded and included by the two primers. Reproduced with permission from Ehrlich GD, Sirko DA. PCR and its role in clinical diagnostics. In: Ehrlich GD, Greenberg ST, editors. PCR based diagnostics in infectious disease. Boston: Blackwell Scientific Publications; 1994. p. 8–9.

absent, the primers will not anneal, no matter how much nontarget DNA is present, and there will be no resultant amplification. Conversely, if the target sequence is present, the primers can support amplification in a 10^{15}-fold excess of nontarget DNA (this is equivalent to detecting one infected cell in a million as each cell contains $> 10^9$ bp of DNA).

With PCR-based assays as an effective and powerful diagnostic tool, almost any infectious agent can be detected quickly and precisely by amplifying in vitro minute quantities of DNA. RNA can be detected if prior to amplifying, a reverse transcriptase (RT) step is added to generate cDNA as a template for the thermal-stable DNA polymerase. PCR is much faster than most traditional culture-based methods because in PCR the DNA replication time is measured in seconds instead of minute or hours. Thus, it is possible to provide clinically useful information to the physician sooner. This benefit of timeliness adds to advantages in sensitivity and specificity.

The availability of PCR-based assays facilitates rapid diagnosis, which, in turn, permits earlier pathogen-specific treatment. PCR-based tests for *Mycobacterium tuberculosis* (TB),[3] human immunodeficiency virus (HIV),[4] *Borrelia burgdorferi* (the causative agent of Lyme disease),[5] and mycal infections[6] are typical successes when compared with classic laboratory-based methods of culture. PCR, combined with RT, can also detect pathogen gene expression, by designing primers for specific genes. Gene-specific studies can determine the metabolic state of the pathogen and guide therapy based on the prevailing bacterial phenotype.

With all the benefits associated with PCR, it is important to be vigilant and to remember that this technology is not a panacea in all circumstances. In those diagnostic situations where the specimens must be screened for a large number of different pathogenic species, a PCR-based test or multiplex assay must exist for each and every potential pathogen in order to provide data equivalent to what would be obtained by culture. The decision of whether or not to apply a PCR-based assay must be made after considering matters of patient benefit, the adequacy of existing testing modalities, and cost.

PCR-Based Pathogen Detection

Detection of DNA identifies bacteria without culture. Culture is inadequate in many situations, including (1) specimens obtained from patients already receiving antibiotics; (2) fastidious pathogens that are difficult or impossible to grow in culture; (3) phenotypically diverse envirovars, such as biofilm bacteria, which do not grow well in planktonic culture.

Background

Traditional laboratory methods for identifying infectious organisms have many disadvantages, primarily the low success rates for culture from chronic infections and specimens obtained from persons on antimicrobials. The dichotomy between acute and chronic infections is well illustrated by comparing the results obtained in the study of otitis media (OM). In acute OM (AOM), the generally reported culture-positive rate is 65 to 75%, and, if using blind broth subcultures, the positive culture rate can exceed 90%.[7,8] In contrast, bacterial culture techniques applied to chronic otitis media with effusion (OME) detect pathogenic bacteria in only ~30% of specimens.[9]

The importance of positive bacterial cultures for making a diagnosis was so high that even though indirect methods of bacterial detection indicated bacteria in culture-negative effusions, the dogma (prior to developing and applying molecular diagnostic methods) was that chronic OME was a noninfectious, inflammatory process. Indirect lines of evidence supporting a bacterial etiology for chronic OME included gram stain; detection of specific metabolites, such as proteoglycan, neuraminidase, and endotoxin; immunoelectrophoresis for bacterial-specific antigens; and measuring bacterial-specific antibodies.[10]

The first infectious disease PCR-based assay was developed by a team, including one of the authors (GDE), in 1985 for HIV.[11,12] The current authors were subsequently the first to apply this methodology to middle ear disease in 1991.[13] Since conventional simplex PCR-based assays detect only a single infectious agent and many clinical diseases have multiple pathogens involved, developing multiplex PCR-based assays is the most efficient way to simultaneously detect different pathogens associated with syndromic illness.

Methods

Clinical samples relevant to middle ear disease can be prepared from middle ear effusions (MEEs), otorrheic specimens, adenoidal tissue, tonsillar tissue, nasopharyngeal washings, resected mastoid tissue, and cholesteatoma. Animal samples can be prepared from MEEs of infected chinchillas, rats, gerbils, and monkeys. The tissue specimens all require homogenization and proteinase K digestion for preparation.[14] Purified bacterial genomic DNA can also be prepared using standard methodology.[15]

Oligonucleotide primers and probes are obtained (1) from the literature; (2) designed from published DNA sequences; or (3) designed from DNA sequences available through on-line public sequence depository databases, such as Genbank available through the National Center for Biotechnology Information (NCBI) Web site. Primers and probes should be designed such that their GC content is equivalent to the GC content of the gene or organism to be detected.

All PCR reagents (buffer, Mg^{2+}, *Taq* polymerase, primers, probes, control DNAs and dilutions, deoxyribonucleoside triphosphates, and water) used in PCR amplifications should be produced under rigorous quality assurance protocols. These procedures, originally developed by one of the authors (GDE), have been largely incorporated into National Committee for Clinical Laboratory Standards (NCCLS) <http://www.nccls.org/> for clinical molecular biology laboratories. Multiple methods exist for detecting the amplified product, but, for clinical verification purposes, it should include a hybridization step to ensure specificity.

All diagnostic runs should include dilution series of positive control DNAs from pure culture bacteria, negative controls with DNA from unrelated bacterial species, and blank controls without any DNA template, to ensure the sensitivity and specificity of the assay and to detect cross contamination by amplified DNA "carryover." If any of the negative control tests positive, the entire run should be discarded and should be repeated using new reagents.

Clinical Results

We used PCR-based detection methods to investigate bacterial DNA in clinical samples of chronic OME.

Haemophilus influenzae is a small, pleomorphic, gram-negative coccobacillus that exists as either encapsulated or nonencapsulated strains. The encapsulated strains are designated type *a* to type *f* and differ in their polysaccharide capsular composition. Other types include nonencapsulated and nontypeable (NT) strains.

Table 7-1 *Haemophilus influenzae* Primers and Probes

Primer (Polarity)	Probe (Polarity)	Gene	Sequence No.	Sequences (5'-3')
HI-IV (+)		P6	103–122	ACT TTT GGC GGT TAC TCT GT
	HI-VI(+)	P6	217–243	TGC TGA TCT TCA ACA ACG TTA CAA TAC CGT
HI-V (–)		P6	356–375	TGT GCC TAA TTT ACC AGC AT
HI/6-2 (+)		P6	131–170	TCCTCTAACAACGATGCTGCAGGCAATGGTGCTGCTCAAA
	HI/6-2 (+)	P6	321–360	TAGAAGGTAATACTGATGAACGTGGTACACCAGAATACAA
HI/6-2 (–)		P6	480–519	ACGATGAAGCTGCATATTCTAAAAACCGTCGTGCAGTGTT
HIP61 (+)		P6	15–37	CCAGCTTGGTCTCCATACTTAAC
	HIP63 (+)	P6	115–150	GCATTAGCGGCTTGTAGTTCCTCTAACAACGATGCT
HIP62 (–)		P6	149–169	TTGAGCAGCACCATTCCCTGC

Reproduced with permission from Magit AE et al.[10]

P6 is a 16 kDa peptidoglycan-associated lipoprotein that is highly conserved in all strains of *H. influenzae.* Therefore, the *P6* gene sequence was chosen as a target for designing primers and probes for PCR-based assays of *H. influenzae* (Table 7-1).[14,16] All strains of *H. influenzae,* including type *b* and nontypeable isolates, can be detected using a P6 PCR-based system.

Similarly, primers and probes for *Streptococcus pneumoniae* and *Moraxella catarrhalis* were designed from conserved sequences, and the simplex assays developed from these oligonucleotides proved sensitive and specific. None of the three species-specific amplification-detection systems evidenced any cross-reactivity when tested with a panel of DNAs from other human pathogens and commensal bacteria.

These assays were applied to 140 chronic OME samples and the results compared with standard culture methods (Table 7-2).[17] Although 34 (24.3%) of the specimens were culture positive for one or more of the three organisms, 100 (71.4%) samples tested PCR-positive. None of the culture-positive specimens were PCR-negative, whereas 66 of the PCR-positive specimens were culture-negative for the three tested species. The difference between the proportion of culture-positive and PCR-positive specimens for all three organisms individually and collectively was highly significant ($p < .0001$).

Table 7-2 Comparative Evaluation of Culture and PCR-Based Detection Methods for Identification of the Bacterial Pathogens *Haemophilus influenzae, Streptococcus pneumoniae,* and *Moraxella catarrhalis* for 140 Adult and Pediatric Middle Ear Specimens

Bacteria	PCR +/ Culture + n	%	PCR +/ Culture – n	%	PCR –/ Culture – n	%	PCR –/ Culture + n	%	Total Culture +* n	%	Total PCR +* n	%	p Value
H. influenzae	25	18.0	40	28.6	75	53.6	0	0	25	18.0	69	49.3	< .0001
S. pneumoniae	9	6.4	40	28.6	92	65.7	0	0	9	6.4	49	35	< .0001
M. catarrhalis	5	3.6	40	28.6	95	67.9	0	0	5	3.6	45	32.1	< .0001
One or more of the target species	34	24.0	66	47.1	40	28.6	0	0	34	24.3	100	71.4	< .0001

Reproduced with permission from Post JC et al.[17]

*1 df comparing total culture-positive specimens with total PCR-positive specimens.

Table 7-3 Characteristics of the Primers and Probes Used to Support and Detect Amplification of DNA from the Upper Respiratory Tract Bacterial Pathogens *Haemophilus influenzae, Streptococcus pneumoniae,* and *Moraxella catarrhalis* in a Multiplex PCR-Liquid Hybridization Format

Primer (Polarity)	Probe (Polarity)	Gene	Sequence No.	Sequences (5'-3')	Amplimer Size
H. influenzae					
HI-IV (+)		P6	103–122	ACT TTT GGC GGT TAC TCT GT	
	HI-VIB (+)	P6	123–152	TGC TGA TCT TCA ACA ACG TTA CAA TAC CGT	273 bp
HI-V (–)		P6	375–356	TGT GCC TAA TTT ACC AGC AT	
S. pneumoniae					
JM201 (+)		PBP2B	1805–1825	ATG CAG TTG GCT CAG TAT GTA	
	JM204 (+)	PBP2B	1836–1865	CA AAT AAT GGT GTT CGT GTG GCT CCT CGT A	87 bp
JM202 (–)		PBP2B	1891–1872	CAC CCA GTC CTC CCT TAT CA	
M. catarrhalis					
MCAT51 (+)		NadR	148–167	GTC GCA CGC CAA CAC TTG CT	
	MCAT53 (+)	NadR	173–212	CGG TGC GTT GGG TTC AGA TGG CTT GTC AAT CAT TTG GTT T	197 bp
MCAT52 (–)		NadR	344–325	ATT GTC GTA TGA GCG GTA AT	

Reproduced with permission from Post JC et al.[17]

Simultaneous Detection of Multiple Bacterial Species using Multiplex PCR

Detecting one or more pathogens simultaneously from clinical specimens requires methods to amplify and discriminate among more than one amplimer within a single reaction.

We developed a multiplex PCR-based detection system for *H. influenzae, S. pneumoniae,* and *M. catarrhalis.*[17,18] The *H. influenzae* primer sets HI-IV/HI-V were derived from the DNA sequence coding for the outer membrane protein *P6*; the *S. pneumoniae* primer sets JM201/JM202 were designed from the penicillin-binding protein 2B (*PBP2B*) gene based on the published sequence; and the *M. catarrhalis* primer sets MCAT51/MCAT52 were designed from cloning and characterizing an *N*-terminal segment of the *M. catarrhalis* homologue of the *Salmonella typhimurium nadR* gene (Table 7-3).

Autoradiographic exposure following multiplex PCR and liquid hybridization of a combined dilution series of the three target DNAs maintains sensitivity, as compared with the simplex and duplex assays (data not shown), plus the ability to distinguish each of the amplified products from the others based on their relative mobilities in the gel (Figure 7-2).[17]

Strain-Specific PCR Detection Using Allele-Specific Discrimination

All members of a given bacterial species are not genetically identical, and recent work from our laboratory indicates enormous levels of genomic plasticity among chronic OME-inducing bacteria within a species (including *H. influenzae, S. pneumoniae,* and *Pseudomonas aeruginosa*). This diversity is not limited to different alleles of the same gene but also shows that different strains of the same bacteria have a different genomic compliment of genes. Taken collectively, these observations form the experimental basis for developing a novel theoretical framework for understanding the pathogenesis of chronic bacterial infections.

Distributed Genome Hypothesis

This hypothesis postulates that chronic infections are maintained by continuous reassortment of genetic information among multiple infecting strains of a given species (ie, a natural infecting population is not monogenic), each with its own set of distributed genes from a species-wide supragenome. The size of the supragenome (on a worldwide basis) may be several times the size of the genome for any single bacterium, and the degree of

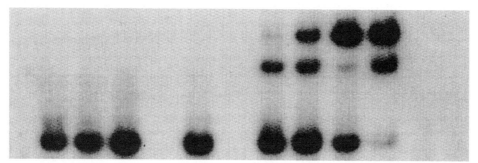

Figure 7-2 Representative autoradiography of multiplex polymerase chain reaction (PCR) products following liquid hybridization and gel retardation analysis. Lanes 1–6: sonicates of chinchilla middle ear effusions and lavages from chinchilla set 2 displaying only *S. pneumoniae* positivity; lane 7: negative control PCR reagent blank; lanes 8–11: dilution series of three positive control bacterial DNA templates; lane 8–10 pg of genomic DNA from *H. influenzae*, *S. pneumoniae*, and *M. catarrhalis*; lane 9: 1 pg of genomic DNA from *H. influenzae*, *S. pneumoniae*, and *M. catarrhalis;* lane 10: 100 fg of genomic DNA from *H. influenzae*, *S. pneumoniae*, and *M. catarrhalis;* lane 11: 10 fg of genomic DNA from *H. influenzae*, *S. pneumoniae*, and *M. catarrhalis;* lanes 12 and 13: negative control PCR reagent blanks. Increased signal intensity of *H. influenzae* DNA at lower input levels is due to artifact of liquid hybridization whereby concentration of amplified DNA at high DNA input levels is so great that two strands of amplified DNA effectively compete with probe in liquid hybridization reaction. Reproduced with permission from Aul JJ et al.[18]

genetic diversity varies greatly among species. Thus, it is important for epidemiologic, nosocomial, and evolutionary studies to discriminate among many strains of the same species.

One general methodology for this type of discrimination is PCR-based DNA fingerprinting, which, not surprisingly, has produced much of the supporting evidence for the Distributed Genome Hypothesis. DNA fingerprinting creates DNA signatures corresponding to each isolate by using short arbitrary primers to amplify a unique set of binding sites from each strain; this methodology does not require the a priori knowledge of any DNA sequence information. Alternatively, if DNA sequence information is available, and the idea is to detect a specific strain (eg, *H. influenzae* type b [Hib]), then a strain-specific set of primers can be developed.

Approaches

Strain-specific discrimination can be achieved by strain-specific PCR (or detection) or by more generic molecular fingerprinting methods, such as randomly amplified polymorphic DNA (RAPD) analysis. Each approach has benefits and disadvantages, but all are useful in following nosocomial infections or performing other molecular epidemiology studies. The benefit of strain-specific assays is direct analysis of clinical material without culture, whereas the generic methods require preliminary culturing and extracting strain-specific DNA. Conversely, a single generic method assay can be applied across a wide range of

organisms and discriminate among scores of strains as opposed to just two.

Strain-specific assays use DNA sequence data for designing (1) gene- or allele-specific primers or (2) gene- or allele-specific probes. In the former case, the discrimination occurs during amplification, whereas in the latter, discrimination occurs when detecting generically amplified products. In either case, one or more of the oligonucleotides for amplification or detection are designed such that they will hybridize to the DNA of one strain but not other strains. RAPD PCR also provides the ability to distinguish among genetically different strains of a bacterial species (or between species) but does not need unique DNA sequence information.

Methods

We use the RAPD method of discriminating among different bacterial strains.[19] The bacterial strains to be studied are grown in pure culture after their isolation from clinical specimens. The bacteria are then harvested and genomic DNA is extracted and purified as described above, then assessed for integrity by agarose gel electrophoresis.

Multiple RAPD primers of 8 to 12 bases are designed and screened for their ability to detect discriminatory polymorphisms using 20 ng of control DNA isolated from known strains of the bacteria. Primers that can reproducibly generate unique DNA fingerprints are chosen for the formal study, and the RAPD PCR mixtures are then prepared.

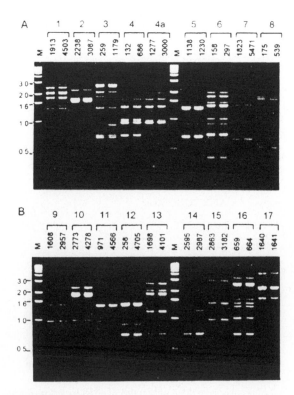

Figure 7-3 *Psuedomonas aeruginosa* cystic fibrosis (CF) isolate randomly amplified polymorphic DNA (RAPD) polymorphisms amplified by primer 272. The fingerprint patterns of 34 strains of 17 RAPD types are shown; type 1 to 8 *(A)* and type 9 to 17 *(B)* are shown. The strain number and RAPD type are indicated above each lane. Molecular size markers were run in lanes M, and their sizes (in kilobases) are indicated to the left of the gels. Reproduced with permission from Mahenthiralingham E et al.[19]

Clinical Results

This example (Figure 7-3) shows the RAPD typing of *P. aeruginosa* isolates recovered from chronically colonized patients with cystic fibrosis (CF).[19] From 100 primers (10-mers) of arbitrary sequences, eight were found to reproducibly generate DNA fingerprints. Primer 272 was used to type the CF isolates described in the study, and primer 208 was used for confirmation.

Strategies for Elucidating Unknown Bacteria

The bacterial *16S* rDNA locus is about 1,400 to 1,500 bases long[20] and is required by all bacterial species for protein synthesis. Consequently, gene mutations accumulate only very slowly. Stability of the *16S* gene makes it useful for detecting unknown organisms because primers made to highly conserved portions of this gene will support amplification from almost any bacteria. Nearly universal eubacterial primers can be constructed

from this locus to amplify rDNA at the bacterial domain level, making it useful for characterizing unclassified bacterial pathogens.[21] Some primers designed to amplify bacterial rDNA are shown in Table 7-4. PCR amplicons are sequenced, and the sequence data are analyzed by phylogenetic comparison.

With this method, unknown and nonculturable bacteria can be detected. Examples of important pathogens first recognized by application of this technique include *Rochalimaea henselae,* which causes bacillary angiomatosis, WABO (similar to *Rhodococcus equi*), which causes Whipple's disease, and *Ehrlichia chaffeensis,* which causes human ehrlichiosis.[22–25]

Gene Distribution Studies

PCR-based assays can determine the distribution of bacterial contingency genes and virulence genes among different strains within a species or across multiple related species in the analysis of species or genera-based supragenomes (defined above). This is a particularly timely application of molecular diagnostics because only recently has it been determined that genomic plasticity, combined with high rates of horizontal gene transfer within and among bacterial species, likely serves as a supravirulence factor for chronic infections. This permits an almost endless reassortment of genes from within a population-based supragenome.

Background

The genomic plasticity observed among different isolated strains of numerous pathogenic bacterial species leads to the question of the prevalence of each of the various novel genes and classes of genes among clinical isolates in general. If a novel gene is detected in one clinical strain, it is important to determine what percentage of clinical strains overall carry the gene in order to help assess its time of entry into the species and its importance in terms of selection.

To answer these questions requires a series of studies, including (1) establishing a pooled genomic library that contains DNA from each strain of the bacterial strains to be studied, (2) sequencing of the clones, (3) identifying the unique clones, and (4) developing gene-specific PCR-based assays for each of the unique genes. The gene-specific PCR-based assays are then used to determine the distribution of the new gene among the component members of the library and among other clinical isolates (see below).

Methods

A pooled *P. aeruginosa* genomic library composed of 12 strains was constructed and used to array over 240,000 clones (Sayeed and colleagues, personal communication,

Table 7-4 Oligonucleotides Complementary to Bacterial 16S RNA and Used to Amplify Bacterial rDNA in PCR

Strand Primed	Gene	Sequence No. (*Escherichia coli*)	Sequences (5′–3′)
Sense*	*p13p*	1389–1370	AGGCCCGGGAACGTATTCAC
Antisense*	*P11P*	1173–1192	GAGGAAGGTGGGGATGACGT
Sense**	*pH*	1542–1522	AAGGAGGTGATCCAGCCGCA
Antisense**	*pA*	8–28	AGAGTTTGATCCTGGCTCAG
Sense†	*OX2*	1542–1520	AAGGAGGTGATCCANCCNCACC
Antisense†	*OX1*	8–29	AGAGTTYGATCCTGGCTAGG
Sense‡	*PC5*	1507–1492	TACCTTGTTACGACTT
Antisense‡	*P3mod*	787–806	ATTAGATACCCTDGTAGTCC
Sense‡	*PC3mod*	787–806	GGACTACHAGGGTATCTAAT
Antisense‡	*P0mod*	8–22	AGAGTTTGATCMTGG

Reproduced with permission from Wilson KH. Characterization of novel bacterial pathogens by amplification and sequencing of 16S ribosomal RNA genes. In: Ehrlich GD, Greenberg SJ, editors. PCR-based diagnostics in infectious disease. Boston: Blackwell Scientific Publications; 1994.

*, ** Probes contain significant mismatches with numerous eubacteria. Although successfully used, suggest low stringency conditions.

† Essentially the same as the primers of * but designed to have a cyanobacterial bias.

‡ The primer for the positive strand is nearly universally conserved, mismatching eukaryotic rRNA only at the 5′ end. However, used with P3, it does not amplify mammalian rDNA. Mitochondrial rDNA from higher plants, but not from animals, is also amplified.

February 2003). About 1,200 clones were randomly chosen for DNA sequence analysis. Homology searches using BLAST identified about 160 clones with unique sequences when compared with the genome of the standard laboratory strain of *P. aeruginosa*, PA01.[26] PCR-based assays were developed for each of 87 of these clones to investigate the distribution pattern of these unique sequences among the 12 component strains (Shen and colleagues, unpublished observations, February 2003).

To investigate the distribution of these gene sequences in different isolates, primers were designed for PCR amplification using specialized software. Sheared genomic DNAs prepared from each of the component clinical strains of *P. aeruginosa* (used to construct the pooled library) served as templates.

Clinical Results

Sequence analysis of clone (97_B7) showed that it had 84% (286/334 bp) homology with the sequence of a gene from strain 9a5c of *Xylella fastidiosa* (a plant pathogen). Another clone (515_A13) demonstrated 82% (353/426 bp) DNA sequence homology with the bacteriophage D3. Both clones displayed no detectable homology with any sequence within the published genome of PA01. The image shows the distribution pattern of these two genes across 11 clinical isolates of *P. aeruginosa* (Figure 7-4).

RT-PCR of Pathogens

Reverse transcriptase-PCR (RT-PCR) detects RNA species by incorporating a cDNA synthesis step into the amplification reaction prior to PCR. cDNA is prepared using the retroviral RT enzyme that recognizes RNA as a template for producing a DNA copy. RT-PCR can be used in a myriad of applications including (1) determining if pathogens are metabolically active, (2) determining if a specific gene is active during infection, (3) comparing levels of gene expression among conditions—quantitative PCR (real time or limiting dilution PCR).

Background

RT-PCR is a multistep enzymatic process that includes reverse transcribing RNA into its complementary DNA and then using the cDNA as the template in the PCR. Following RT-PCR, the reaction products can be assessed using the same analysis methods described for PCR.

Detecting microorganisms using extracted DNA as templates in a PCR-based system demonstrated bacterial DNA in a high percentage of culture-negative (sterile) effusions.[27] Whether these DNA molecules were from metabolically active pathogens or whether they merely represented "fossilized remains" of a no-longer-viable bacterial population was unknown. Circumstantial evidence using the chinchilla model of OM, however,

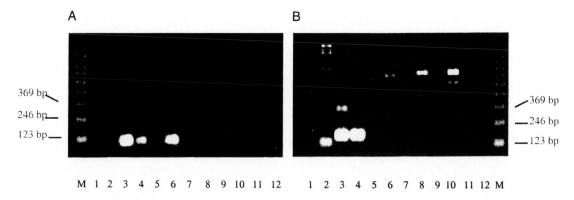

Figure 7-4 Gene distribution study in 11 strains of *Psuedomonas aeruginosa*. Polymerase chain reaction (PCR) was performed using primers designed from sequences of clone (A) 97_B7 and clone (B) 515_A13. Lane 1–11: genomic DNA from eleven strains of isolated *P. aeruginosa*; lane 12: negative control PCR reagent blank; M, marker. Panel A, positive target band of 98 bp observed in: strain Pitt D (lane 3), stain Pitt E (lane 4), and strain 27853 (lane 6). Panel B, positive target band of 190 bp observed in: strain Pitt D (lane 3) and strain Pitt E (lane 4).

showed that DNA from viable, intact bacteria could be detected by PCR-based assays for up to 22 days after antibiotics without culturability. This finding contrasted the inability to detect DNA after 24 hours from heat-killed bacteria or purified DNA that had been inoculated simultaneously with the viable organisms.[27]

To provide definitive evidence that culture-negative chronic MEEs harbor viable, metabolically active bacteria, the existence of bacterial messenger RNA (mRNA) needed to be proved. Detecting bacterial mRNA is prima facie evidence of metabolic activity because bacterial mRNAs have extremely short half-lives, seconds to minutes depending on the gene of origin, and, therefore, will not be detected without a live and intact organism.

Methods

Clinical and animal specimens were collected and prepared with special attention to minimize RNA degradation. In all cases, the MEEs were collected into liquid N_2 or a dry ice-ethanol bath in the operating room to prevent any RNA degradation. RNA was subsequently extracted from the MEE specimen.

Deoxyribonuclease (DNAse) I treatment of the RNA is a critical step prior to RT-PCR amplification. This treatment ensures that any positive results are attribut-able only to mRNA and not to contaminating bacterial DNA. Before using the DNAse-treated RNA in an RT-PCR, it must first be assayed in a PCR-only reaction to ensure that it does not amplify without an RT step. A positive PCR test indicates that sufficient residual DNA remains for amplification, and the DNAse treatment must be repeated. The specimen is again checked for the absence of DNA prior to use in an RT-PCR assay for mRNA detection.

As with the diagnostic amplification protocol, it is imperative that positive and negative controls be included with each set of assays. If any negative control gives a positive result, the data are unreliable.

Clinical Results

RT-PCR can show bacterial metabolic activity in the absence of culturability. We developed a PCR primer-probe set from on-line DNA sequence information, corresponding to the *H. influenzae* glyceraldehyde-3-phosphate dehydrogenase (*GAPDH*) gene, an essential component of glycolytic metabolism (Table 7-5).[28] These oligonucleotides were used in an RT-PCR–based assay to detect *H. influenzae GAPDH* mRNA from MEE specimens in children having outpatient tympanostomy tube insertion for OME lasting 3 months or longer.

Table 7-5 Primers and Probes Used for the Detection of *Haemophilus influenzae*–Specific mRNA in Middle Ear Effusions from Pediatric Patients with Chronic Otitis Media with Effusion

Primer	Probe	Sequence (5'–3')
H. influenzae		
Hflu *GAPDH*	upper 410	ACG CAT ACG CAG GTC AAG ATA
	Hflu 589	GGC CGC GGT GCA TCA CAA AAC ATC
Hflu *GAPDH*	lower 677	CAC GGA AAG CCA TAC CAG TTA

Reproduced with permission from Rayner MG et al.[28]

Table 7-6 Comparison of Culture and RT-PCR Results from 93 Pediatric Middle Ear Effusions Analyzed for *Haemophilus influenzae*

Culture Results	RT-PCR +	RT-PCR –	Total
+	11	0	11
–	29	53	82
Total	40	53	93

Reproduced with permission from Rayner MG et al.[28]

Sensitivity testing showed the primers could detect 100 femtograms of *H. influenzae* DNA (50 genomic equivalents). Specificity examinations detected no amplification in 100 ng (in excess of 30 million genomic equivalents) of DNA prepared from pure cultures of a panel of highly related bacterial species and other upper respiratory pathogens and commensal flora, including *Neisseria mucosa*, *Neisseria* spp, *Escherichia coli*, *Acinetobacter* spp, *P. aeruginosa*, *M. catarrhalis*, *Haemophilus parainfluenzae*, *Streptococcus pyogenes*, the viridans group of streptococci, *S. pneumoniae*, streptococcus group C, *Enterococcus* spp, *Staphylococcus epidermidis*, *Staphylococcus aureus*, and *Candida albicans*.

RT-PCR results were compared with PCR and culture results. There was 100% correlation between PCR-positivity (DNA presence) and RT-PCR positivity (RNA presence), but when RT-PCR was compared with traditional culture methods (Table 7-6), there was a highly significant tendency for *H. influenzae* culture-negative specimens to test positive by RT-PCR ($p < .001$). Figure 7-5 shows the positive RT-PCR results for 14 specimens that were PCR positive/culture negative.[28]

These data provide convincing evidence that bacterial DNA-positivity in MEEs, as detected by PCR-based molecular diagnostics, is a valid surrogate marker for live metabolically active pathogens that are culture negative. This observation provided one of the pillars on which the biofilm paradigm of chronic OME was advanced (see below).

RT-PCR and ELISA for Determining Host Expression Profiles

Cytokines mediate and regulate the host's immune and inflammation systems, whereas growth factors regulate the host's tissue repairing and wound healing response. RT-PCR–based evaluations of the hosts' expression can determine the response to infection and compare effective versus ineffective responses. RT-PCR–based methods have the advantage of revealing the transcriptional activities of the cells expressing cytokines or growth factors in the mucosa and submucosal cells of the middle ear cavity, whereas enzyme-linked immunosorbent assay (ELISA) is better used to detect the results of cellular activity within the middle ear effusion itself.

Background
The expression levels of many cytokines and growth factors will be significantly altered in response to pathogen challenge.

Host resistance against invasion by foreign organisms, such as bacteria or viruses, is, in part, controlled by cytokine-mediated immune and inflammatory reactions. The levels of various cytokines reflect the status of the host defense systems. The relevant target cells for each cytokine may be the same cell that secretes the cytokine (autocrine), a nearby cell (paracrine), or, like hormones, a distant cell that is stimulated via cytokines that have been secreted into the circulation (endocrine). These

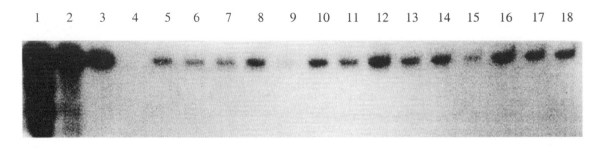

Figure 7-5 Reverse transcriptase–polymerase chain reaction (RT-PCR) amplification of *Haemophilus influenzae* mRNA. Autoradiographic exposure after RNAse-free DNAse I digestion, RT-PCR, and liquid hybridization of: Lanes 1–3: a dilution series (10^{-4}–10^{-6}) of control mRNA extracted from cultured *H. influenzae*; Lane 4: a reagent blank into which no exogenous template was added (a test for carryover); and Lanes 5–18: mRNA extracted from patient samples, each showing a positive signal for mRNA. Reproduced with permission from Rayner MG et al.[28]

effector cells have corresponding surface receptors that make them sensitive to activation by circulating or local sources of cytokines. Although inflammatory cytokines and related proteins play critical roles in a variety of cellular processes, their roles in clearing or maintaining effusions in the middle ear are not well elucidated.

Growth factors and their receptors are part of the host's tissue repair system following damage associated with pathogen challenge. Growth factors and other mediators regulate the repairing and remodeling of the tissue and organ structure by the process of mitosis, necrosis, and apoptosis. In most complex organisms, cellular proliferation is controlled, in part, by polypeptide growth factors.

Clinical Results

AOM caused by *S. pneumoniae* in the chinchilla model was previously used to characterize, by ELISA, the local inflammatory response during the first 72 hours following inoculation. The MEEs were monitored to determine the concentrations of interleukin-1β (IL-1β), interleukin-6 (IL-6), interleukin-8 (IL-8), and tumor necrosis factor-α (TNF-α) using the ELISA method.[29] The levels of all four of these cytokines were found to increase significantly during the observation period and correlated well with the observed increase in the concentration of neutrophils and other inflammatory cells in the middle ear space. *H. influenzae*–induced AOM in the guinea pig model showed similar results.[30]

Kita and Himi,[31] using RT-PCR and ELISA to study the effects of gram-positive exotoxin (lipoteichoic acid) on cytokine levels, showed increased protein level in rat MEE of growth-regulated gene product/cytokine-induced neutrophil chemoattractant-1 (GRO/CINC-1). The mRNA expressions of GRO/CINC-1, TNF-α, and interleukin-10 (IL-10) in the middle ear mucosa were stimulated. This study showed that for fluid specimens, the results of ELISA and RT-PCR are similar, but that for assaying tissue specimens there may be an advantage of RT-PCR over ELISA-based methods, as RNA purifications are more generic than those for proteins.

Palacios and colleagues[32] measured alteration of middle ear mucosal growth factor levels in rat MEE induced by *H. influenzae* using RT-PCR assays. Hepatocyte growth factor and epidermal growth factor receptor (EGFR) were not detected in the normal middle ear mucosa but were upregulated following infection, whereas keratinocyte growth factor and hepatocyte growth factor receptor were present at all time points tested (0, 6, 24, 48, and 72 hours). Betacellulin and neuregulin-a products were also detected up to 48 hours. These results suggest that growth factors function in the middle ear mucosa during OM. Other growth factors and their receptors, including fibroblast growth factor, fibroblast growth factor receptor 1, and vascular endothelial growth factor, also cause mucosal changes in animals with OM.[33,34]

Cytokines and epidermal growth factor (EGF) are thought to regulate bone resorption in chronic OM. Yetiser and colleagues[35] performed a controlled, blinded, prospective study to compare EGF, IL-1α, and TNF-α expression in chronic OM, with or without cholesteatoma. Using ELISA, tissue biopsy samples were analyzed from 16 OME patients, 23 patients with cholesteatoma and 21 normal subjects (external auditory canal skin samples). Cholesteatoma epithelium had higher levels of EGF, IL-1α, and TNF-α, confirming that keratinocytes produce the cytokines and EGF responsible for destructive behavior. Antibiotics did not alter cytokine levels, but otorrhea and infectious symptoms regressed in some patients, suggesting that antibiotic-resistant bacterial biofilms were present and maintained the hosts' inflammatory response. Chole and Faddis[36] have recently produced transmission electron micrographic evidence that cholesteatomas contain extensive biofilms.

In Situ Hybridization

This technique visualizes genes and their expression in situ, thereby permitting direct observation of genomes, discrete genomic elements, and gene expression changes (both of the host and the pathogen) under numerous normal and abnormal physiologic conditions.

Background

In situ hybridization involves hybridizing a nucleic acid probe to denatured DNA or RNA of a fixed cell or tissue section. Probe labeling is accomplished using radioactive isotopes or nonisotopic reporter groups, such as fluorescent dye molecules. Fluorescent probes are safer and offer better resolution when compared with radioactive probes.[37]

Fluorescence in situ hybridization (FISH) combines the precision of molecular genetics with the visual information of microscopy, allowing simultaneous visualization, identification, enumeration, and localization of individual microbial cells. FISH can also identify specific gene expression patterns. FISH has been successfully used in detecting nonencapsulated, nontypeable *H. influenzae* in cryosectioned clinical respiratory tract samples.[38] FISH has also been used to detect other pathogens, including *P. aeruginosa*, *Burkholderia cepacia*, *Stenotrophomonas maltophilia*, *S. aureus*, and so on.[39]

Methods

Oligonucleotide probes for bacterial FISH can be designed that complement any species-specific gene, including type-specific regions of the 16S rRNA, which is present at many copies within the bacterial cell and, therefore, makes for a high sensitivity target. The probe is labeled at its 5′ termini by a fluorescent dye, such as fluorescein isothiocyanate (FITC) or Cy3.

Specimen preparation includes tissue fixation (usually 4% paraformaldehyde) and paraffin embedding. The wax blocks are then used for sectioning. Alternatively, fresh frozen tissue can be used and sectioned with a cryostat. In either case, the tissue sections are then mounted on glass slides.

Clinical Results

Clinical specimens from CF patients were fixed and evaluated for 10 pathogenic bacterial species/strains using fluorescein-labeled oligonucleotide probes designed to hybridize with respective ribosomal RNAs. FISH analyses of specimens from these patients provided evidence of *P. aeruginosa*, *B. cepacia*, *S. maltophilia*, *S. aureus*, and *H. influenzae* in both sputum and throat swab samples.[39] Similar approaches are currently being used to study *H. influenzae* in chronic OME.

Radioimmunoprecipitation Assays to Identify de Novo Protein Biosynthesis

Radioimmunoprecipitation assays (RIPAs) demonstrate active translation of mRNA into protein and are, therefore, useful in studying gene expression and the control of gene expression.

Background

Bacterial *biofilms* account for greater than 99.9% of the total bacterial mass in all natural environments that have been ecologically studied. This observation, combined with molecular diagnostic data identifying metabolically active bacteria in culture-negative OME, led the authors to propose a biofilm paradigm of OME and other chronic infections.[28,40] This hypothesis states that bacteria establish a chronic infection by metabolic metamorphosis from a *planktonic mode of existence* to a *mucosal biofilm*. In this state, the bacteria are viable but not culturable, due to a shift in metabolic states from a free-living (planktonic) mode to a sessile attached mode.

Bacteria in biofilms behave analogous to cells in a primitive tissue by using specialized ligands and receptors for intercellular communication. Moreover, recent studies indicate that the bacteria differentiate within the biofilm and multiple phenotypes coexist.[41,42] A cardinal feature of biofilm growth and differentiation is *quorum sensing*, an intercellular communication system that permits bacteria to assess population density and then, when high enough, to organize into three-dimensional structures composed of the bacteria and a secreted matrix. The matrix, which represents about 90% of the biofilm volume, provides structural support for the biofilm bacteria and serves a defense role by minimizing phagocytosis and by trapping immunoglobulins and complement.

RIPA identifies de novo protein (antigen) biosynthesis, making it a useful technique to study the metabolism of biofilm cells that cannot be easily cultured. The first phase of RIPA, metabolic labeling of newly synthesized proteins, is accomplished by adding radioactively labeled amino acids (AA) (usually sulfur 35 [^{35}S]-tagged cysteine and methionine) to the MEE. These tagged AA are then incorporated without bias into nascent protein chains at the ribosomes, effectively labeling the newly synthesized proteins. After the incorporation phase, the bacterial cells are lysed and the bacterial proteins are immunoprecipitated using bacterial-specific antisera. Various recovered antigens are then separated by size using a polyacrylamide gel and visualized using fluorography or phosphor imaging.

Methods

Specimens can be prepared using either MEE from myringotomy (ex vivo) or by establishing an effusion using the chinchilla model and inoculating the radioactive AA directly into the tympanic bullae. In the latter case, MEEs can be induced by transbullar inoculation of the chinchillas using a virulent strain of bacteria (eg, *H. influenzae*) isolated from patients with OM. Aliquots of the MEE are used for (1) culture on agar plates, (2) PCR to detect bacterial DNA, (3) RT-PCR to detect bacterial RNA, and (4) RIPA using lysates of the effusions to test for bacterial de novo protein synthesis.

Clinical Results

The studies described include RIPA performed on a cohort of six chinchillas experimentally infected with *H. influenzae* and analysis of 36 pediatric effusions for *H. influenzae*. Laemmli gel analysis of protein lysates prepared from the effusions revealed detectable levels of labeled proteins for all labeling conditions, but there was a significant drop in signal intensity below 750 μCi. Therefore, all subsequent labeling experiments for both the in vivo chinchilla effusions and ex vivo pediatric effusions were performed using 750 μCi of the Expre^{35}S.

MEEs were collected from children via myringotomy prior to tube placement. Aliquots of each effusion were placed in RPMI 1640 selectamine-media lacking methionine and cysteine. To this culture, 750 μCi/specimen of the Expre^{35}S labeling reagent was added and incubation was continued for 4 hours. Metabolically labeled *H. influenzae* proteins were immunoprecipitated using purified polyclonal anti–*H. influenzae* immunoglobulin G (IgG) (Figure 7-6).

A parallel analysis of these effusions was performed using PCR-based and RT-PCR–based assays to detect

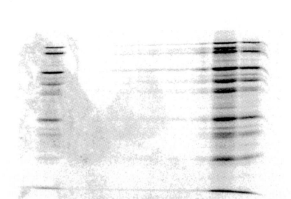

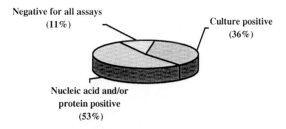

Figure 7-7 Analysis of 36 pediatric effusions for evidence of *Haemophilus influenzae* using culture, molecular diagnostics, and radioimmunoprecipitation analyses (RIPA). All culture-positive samples were also nucleic acid positive and protein RIPA positive.

Figure 7-6 Radioimmunoprecipitation analyses (RIPA) to detect de novo protein biosynthesis within culture-negative pediatric middle ear effusions. Phosphor imaging of a Laemmli gel of *Haemophilus influenzae*–specific antigens following metabolic labeling of pediatric middle ear effusions with ³⁵S-labeled amino acids (methionine and cysteine) followed by precipitation with *H. influenzae*–specific antibodies. Lane 1: MW markers; lanes 2–3: RIPA of effusions using nonimmune serum; lanes 4–9: RIPAs of pediatric effusions using *H. influenzae*–specific antiserum.

for green fluorescent protein (GFP) and its many derivatives have been used to monitor gene expression, as GFP expression is readily observed without the performance of any enzymatic step.

GFP and Derivatives

GFP is a luminescent photoprotein originally isolated from the jellyfish, *Aequorea victoria*. GFP fluoresces green and requires only oxygen to mature; that is, no external compounds need to be added to organisms expressing GFP to detect green fluorescence.[43]

The cloned "wild type" GFP has properties similar to that of the original form and folds very slowly into the actively fluorescent state over hours. Modulation of the wild-type *GFP* gene to induce more rapid protein folding has reduced chromophore production to minutes. Some of the mutant proteins are also more fluorescent, more resistant to photobleaching, and more soluble than the wild-type protein, enabling it to be an ideal reporter system for gene expression in real time at the single-cell level.[44] GFP mutants have also been prepared with shifted emission spectra, including blue (BFP), cyan (CFP), yellow (YFP), and red (RFP) variants, and are still in continuous development for practical visualization.[45] This permits the possibility of monitoring more than one gene at a time.

There are additional *GFP* mutants that are unstable and degrade at different rates inside a cell. A number of *GFP* genes derived from *GFPMUT3* have been constructed, each of which encodes proteins with different half-lives ranging from 40 minutes to a few hours.[46] These can assess when a gene is turned off as well as on making them very useful for studying developmental processes, such as maturation of a bacterial biofilm.

Bacterial biofilms have extensive phenotypic heterogeneity with respect to local environments, which may result in unique spatial and temporal patterns of gene expression. GFP reporters coupled with confocal microscopy have been invaluable tools for disclosing biofilm structure.

H. influenzae DNA and mRNA. Comparison of the results demonstrated that 36% of the specimens were culture positive, all of which were also nucleic acid positive and protein positive (Figure 7-7). An additional 53% of these specimens were positive for *H. influenzae* de novo protein biosynthesis and most of these were also nucleic acid positive.

In vivo Gene Reporter Systems

In vivo gene reporter systems can demonstrate unequivocally that a specific gene is turned on under a specific set of environmental conditions without having to destroy the specimen—thus allowing serial monitoring.

Background

The chloramphenicol acetyl transferase (*CAT*) gene has historically been used to monitor the promoter function in eukaryotes. The level of the enzymatic activity corresponds to the amount of enzyme that was made, which, in turn, indicates the level of expression driven by the promoter under the prevailing environmental conditions. Another reporter gene, *lacZ*, that codes for β-galactosidase (an enzyme) which cleaves a chromogenic substrate, has been extensively used in both prokaryotes and eukaryotes. Recently, however, the gene

Methods

An example of spatial patterns of gene expression in bacterial biofilm grown in flow-chambers is presented. In this series of experiments, a growth- rate-regulated *E. coli* promoter rrnBP1 was fused to destabilized *GFP* variants in *Pseudonomas putida*.[47]

Biofilms were cultivated in four-channel flow cells, inoculated with an overnight culture of *P. putida* strains JB156, SM1639, or SM1699. After inoculation, the medium flow was arrested for 1 hour, and then restarted, and the substrate was pumped through the flow cells at a constant rate. Embedding and 16S rRNA hybridization of hydrated biofilm samples were performed to detect biofilm cells in situ as the positive control, by using a probe specific for *P. putida* group A.

Clinical Results

The strain SM1639, which expressed stable *GFP*MUT3*b that fused to the *rrn*BP1 promoter, showed reduced signal intensity as the growth rate was reduced; however, the strain SM1669, which expressed *GFP*(AAV), decreased more with decreasing growth rate than the corresponding signals obtained from the rRNA hybridizations. When the bacterial colonies in the flow channels reached a critical size, the light emitted by the SM1669 cells decreased in the center of the colony, indicating that the growing activity of these cells was reduced compared with that of cells in the periphery of the colony.

These results demonstrate that the actively growing cells expressed GFP, whereas quiescent cells did not, and the short half-life of the *GFP* variants ensured that the GFP signal was lost once expression was turned off. This confirms spatial heterogeneity in the growth state of *P. putida* within a mature biofilm.[47] Similar strain construction experiments are underway with respect to middle ear pathogens *P. aeruginosa* and *H. influenzae* to monitor gene expression of putative biofilm-expressed virulence genes in vivo.

ANIMAL MODELS OF OTITIS MEDIA

Animal models provide the most easily controlled research subjects, which facilitate developing prospective, blinded, and randomized studies.

Chinchilla

The chinchilla *(Chinchilla laniger)* is a good model for studying the pathogenesis of OM and biofilms because of a large middle ear space enclosed in the tympanic bullae, a bony prominence equivalent to the human mastoid bone.

Background

The chinchilla is a small (500 to 1,000 g) fur-bearing rodent in the squirrel family. Its anatomic features facilitate pathogen inoculation and specimen collection, as well as otoscopic, tympanometric, and endoscopic examination of the middle ear space. Importantly, it does not have a high incidence of spontaneous OM (as opposed to the rat model), which helps ensure that observed results arise from experimental manipulation.

Although the immunogenetics of the chinchilla are not well known, there are tools for detecting immunoglobulin levels.[48] Bacteria, such as *S. pneumoniae, S. pyogenes, H. influenzae, S. aureus, M. catarrhalis,* and *P. aeruginosa,* are frequently used to induce AOM in animal models for studying immune responses, immunoglobulin protection, antibiotic treatment, and new vaccine prophylaxis.[49–51] Animal models also facilitate molecular diagnostics and bacterial biofilm studies of OM.[18,28,52]

The chinchilla model has long been used to study AOM,[49] but inoculation with virulent bacterial strains can result in an unacceptably high mortality. For this reason, and to mimic the human treatment regimen, the chinchillas are usually treated with antibiotics for 3 to 4 days beginning on day 3 following inoculation. We have found that most chinchillas will maintain an effusion for 3 to 5 weeks before clearing. This provides a useful model of early stage OME but is inadequate for modeling human chronic OME persisting for months or years.

Recent theoretic work in our laboratory, based on population genomic studies (see above), suggests that to establish truly chronic infections it may require multiple strains of the same bacterial species. This provides sufficient genomic plasticity within the bacterial population to produce large numbers of unique recombinants during infection, some of which will have a selective survival advantage under the prevailing environmental conditions. This genomic reassortment of the distributed genes from the population supragenome is called a *supravirulence factor* because it requires "cooperation" from multiple strains (ie, survival of the population depends on the supragenome, not the genome of a single strain).

Methods

The chinchilla model used to characterize molecular diagnostic assays and to study bacterial biofilm formation is described. Research grade chinchillas (obtained commercially as culls from local ranches) weighing 400 to 600 g are allowed to acclimate to their new environment for several days. After determining that they are free of middle ear disease by otoscopy and tympanometry, they can be used in experimental OM protocols.

On day 0, anesthesia is induced and inoculation is performed, usually bilaterally, using a transbullar

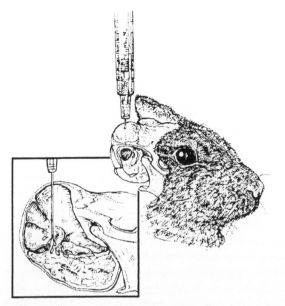

Figure 7-8 Procedure for transbullar inoculation of chinchillas using a bacterial preparation to induce experimental otitis media. Animals are anesthetized, and the injection is made into the middle ear space through the thin bony covering of the roof of the tympanic bullae. Reproduced with permission from Post JC.[68]

Table 7-7 Persistence of *Haemophilus influenzae* in Chinchilla Middle Ear

Time	H. influenzae PCR (%)	H. influenzae Culture (%)	No. of Animals
Day 0*	0	0	5
Day 3	100	100	2
Day 4	100	80	10
Day 7	80	100	10
Day 14	85	77	13
Day 21	30	30	10
Day 28	20	20	15
Day 35	14	14	14

Reproduced with permission from Aul JJ et al.[18]

approach with a tuberculin syringe (Figure 7-8). Intramuscular ampicillin is given twice daily for 3 to 5 days beginning day 3 or 4 after inoculation. Each animal is sampled only once to prevent cross-contamination among specimens. For specimen collection, the chinchillas are deeply anesthetized and then euthanized.

Effusion and middle ear lavage specimens are collected via a midline ventral incision through the roof of the tympanic bullae. Mucosal specimens are harvested by longitudinally splitting the dorsal (roof) and ventral (floor) halves of the bullae. The specimens are processed according to the specific protocol.

Clinical Results

Chinchillas were injected with ampicillin-resistant *H. influenzae*, with ampicillin treatment initiated on day 3 and continued for 3 days. This protocol was conducted to determine the ability of the chinchillas to control the infectious process. Of 95 total animals, 21 died (22%), demonstrating their inability to control the infection locally.

PCR-based diagnostics were compared with culture for all effusions (Table 7-7), which were observed by day 2 in nearly all animals and persisted for a minimum of 2 weeks in almost all surviving animals. Both cultura-

bility and PCR positivity of *H. influenzae* were highly correlated with an observable effusion at the time of euthanasia for the time points beyond 14 days.[18]

Rat

The anatomic structure of the rat *(Ratus norvegicus)* middle ear and Eustachian tube is similar to that of humans. In addition, the middle ear mucosa in rats and humans has similar histologic characteristics, both in terms of cell type and cilliary clearance tracts.

Background

The rat is an inexpensive and readily available animal model of OM. A chief advantage is the highly defined immunology of the rat, for which there are many well-characterized investigative tools. Models for both acute and chronic OM have been established using various bacteria and bacterial components and have yielded useful histopathologic, immunologic, and metabolic response data.

The rat model has significant limitations: (1) reaction to a pathogen or immunogen can vary greatly, especially with chronic OME because different strains of rats have different genetic predispositions[53]; (2) rats are coprophagic and have a high incidence of spontaneous OM; (3) the small size of the middle ear limits the volume of effusion and mucosa that can be obtained from a single animal; and (4) surgical obstruction of the Eustachian tube is a difficult procedure. To overcome the disadvantages of natural infection, specific pathogen-free rats can be used but are expensive to purchase, handle, and maintain.[54–56]

Methods

Rats tolerate unilateral Eustachian tube obstruction (ETO) better than bilateral obstruction.[56] Animals are anesthetized and checked by otomicroscopy to ensure they are free of middle ear disease. Under an operating microscope, the Eustachian tube is exposed via a midline incision and a hole drilled at a 75-degree angle midway between the beginning and end of the bony portion. The membranous cover under the bone is opened with a sharp dissector ear instrument, and small pieces of an inert dental material, gutta-percha, are placed into the defect and melted with an electrocautery to conform.

After obstructing the Eustachian tube, bacteria or their components are inoculated into the ipsilateral bulla and the skin is sutured. Animals are treated with ampicillin for 5 days. Otomicroscopy is performed bilaterally on a weekly basis, with tympanic membrane position (retracted, normal, or bulging), effusion status (absent or present), and effusion type (serous, seromucoid, or purulent) being recorded.

AOM develops during the first week and can be detected otoscopically. If the animals are treated with antibiotics, most will develop chronic OME. Specimen collection is performed under deep anesthesia or following euthanasia. For histologic studies, the skulls are decalcified, divided into anterior and posterior bullar halves, and processed separately.

Clinical Results

Piltcher and coworkers[56] subjected 164 specific pathogen-free rats to surgical ETO. Animals ($n = 108$) were divided into seven time groups to identify dynamic changes after *S. pneumoniae* infection. The remaining animals served as uninfected controls. Animals were sacrificed on days 1, 2, 7, 21, 35, 56, and 112. Fourteen rats died of surgical complications, and 9 resolved their effusion within 2 weeks. Infected rats had acute macroscopic and microscopic inflammation within the first 14 days, which later became chronic.

Monkeys

Using a primate research model more closely approximates the human condition in terms of structure and immune function.

Background

The high degree of similarity among all primates makes small monkey species, such as the cynomolgus monkeys (*Macaca fascicularis*) and rhesus monkeys (*Macaca mulatta*), good models to study OM, especially the treatment. However, there are drawbacks to the monkey model, including cost and resistance to many pathogens associated with OME in humans.

Otitis media redistributes the component volumes within the middle ear because the effusion effectively reduces the air space.[57] Although inflation, via the Eustachian tube, was developed to treat OM more than 90 years ago, controlled clinical studies always resulted in discrepant effects. This occurred because intra- and interstudy variations could not be adequately controlled, including the type of the inflationary maneuver; the frequency, duration and compliance in performing the maneuver; the criteria for including and excluding study subjects; and the demographics of the studied populations. The monkey model permitted good control over these confounding factors.[58]

In monkey studies of Eustachian tube inflation, botulinum toxin was injected to paralyze the right tensor veli palatini muscle and induce functional obstruction, whereas the left side muscle was injected with saline as a control. Repeated argon gas inflation via the nose and Eustachian tube to the right ear daily did not prevent inflammation and MEE. However, more frequent air inflation (twice a day) prevented 50% of OME but had to be continued to maintain efficacy. Magnetic resonance imaging (MRI), tympanometry, and otoscopy revealed displaced MEE in the mastoid and petrous air cells, creating a false impression of clinical improvement.[58,59] Thus, the monkey model helped put to rest a potentially dangerous mode of treatment.

In another cynomolgus monkey study, chronic OME with perforation and otorrhea was induced by *P. aeruginosa* to test topical therapy of tobramycin and dexamethasone, which rapidly resolved otorrhea and eradicated *P. aeruginosa*. Both drugs were ototoxic free individually or in a combination. Dexamethasone enhanced tobramycin by accelerating the resolution of otorrhea.[60] In addition, current work in our laboratory employs the monkey model of otorrhea to study gene expression of *P. aeruginosa* growing as a biofilm and to assess the efficacy of antibiotics.

Methods

Cynomolgus monkeys are a useful model for chronic suppurative otitis media (CSOM).[61] Under anesthesia, the right tympanic membrane is perforated, a baseline auditory brainstem response (ABR) obtained, and the middle ear inoculated with *P. aeruginosa*. Three days later, a second inoculation is made using the same or a different strain of *P. aeruginosa*. The left serves as a control. Resulting otorrhea is collected, measured, and cultured. Observations and specimen collection are continued twice weekly to assess otorrhea and tympanic membrane status (intact versus perforated). After 3 to 4 weeks without treatment, the ears are suctioned twice weekly. If the tympanic membrane heals, it is reperforated to at least 50% of the tympanic area.

Clinical Results

Ciprofloxacin was tested for its safety and efficacy in treating CSOM using the model just described.[61] Forty adult cynomolgus monkeys of both sexes were randomly assigned to 4 groups: (1) saline (negative control), (2) Cortisporin otic suspension (neomycin, polymyxin B sulfate, and hydrocortisone; Burroughs Wellcome; positive control), (3) ciprofloxacin 0.2% (experimental group), or (4) vehicle (potassium sorbate, polysorbate 20, sodium acetate trihydrate, glacial acetic acid, glycerin, methocel A4M, and purified water; pH 4.75).

After establishing the CSOM model, ototopical therapy was given twice daily for 4 weeks. Biweekly culture and suctioning of the ears was continued over the 4-week period of treatment. Histopathologic data showed no statistically significant difference in the amount of outer hair cell loss for the ciprofloxacin group as compared with the control and other treatment groups. Therefore, the drug was determined not to be ototoxic. Ciprofloxacin and the positive control Cortisporin were both effective in eradicating *P. aeruginosa* more rapidly from CSOM as compared with saline, but did not resolve the drainage.

Other Models

Mouse (Mus musculus)

The murine *(Mus musculus)* model benefits from the extraordinary genetic and immunologic tools that are available for the mouse. Its limitations include the small size of the middle ear, less sample (effusion, exudates, and tissue), and difficulty of manipulation.

A study by Johnson and colleagues[62] illustrates the utility of the mouse model in OM pathogenesis. Interleukin-8 found in chronically inflamed human MEE led to the question of what role this cytokine plays in initiating or maintaining effusion. The authors injected ICR mice transtympanically with human IL-8, heat-killed *S. pneumoniae*, or normal saline. Temporal bones of IL-8-injected ears demonstrated thickening of the epithelial layer and the subepithelial space, with inflammatory cell infiltration peaking at 4 to 8 hours and resolving by 48 hours. Dead bacteria-injected ears demonstrated findings similar to, although not as extensive as, those found in IL-8-injected ears. These results support the hypothesis that IL-8 may be one of the key cytokines in leukocyte recruitment and inflammation.

In other examples using the mouse model, in situ hybridization showed that cells producing IL-2 and IL-4, but not IL-5, appeared during AOM. In chronic OME, IL-2–positive and IL-4–positive cells were less prevalent, but IL-5–positive cells were numerous.[63] These findings suggest that locally produced IL-2 and IL-4 augment IgG production in AOM, whereas IL-5

contributes to increased IgA production in chronic OME. A mouse model for virally-induced OM has also been developed.[64]

Specific pathogen-free mice without spontaneous OM are suitable to study the effects of bacterial metabolites, such as lipopolysaccharide (LPS) and endotoxin. Male BALB/c mice inoculated intratympanically with endotoxin derived from nontypeable *H. influenzae* and treated by anti–IL-1 receptor antibodies, induced the expression of IL-1β mRNA in the epithelium of the middle ear mucosa.[65] BALB/c mice were also used to evaluate an intranasal immunization protocol using the outer membrane protein P6 of nontypeable *H. influenzae*.[66]

Guinea Pig, Gerbil, and Pig

Such animals as the guinea pig *(Cavia porcellus)*, gerbil *(Meriones unguliculatus)*, and pig *(Sus scrofa)* have also been used as models for OM.[67] These species have been used to examine etiology, pathophysiologic changes, immune responses, vaccine production, and antimicrobial treatment.

IMAGING METHODOLOGIES

Scanning Electron Microscopy

Scanning electron microscopy (SEM) can directly image fixed specimens with very high degrees of magnification and resolution. This technology has recently demonstrated bacterial biofilms on tympanostomy tubes and on the middle ear mucosal surfaces of chinchillas (see below).

Confocal Laser Scanning Microscopy

Confocal laser scanning microscopy (CLSM), like electron microscopy, can directly image middle ear structures, including various pathogenic conditions such as biofilms and cholesteatoma; however, it has the advantage of not requiring fixation of the specimens, thus allowing samples to be viewed without the artifacts inherent in dehydration and fixation. Moreover, the ability to view live specimens permits using vital dyes to ascertain if culture-negative bacteria are actually viable.

Background

Although most AOM effusions are culture positive for bacteria (predominantly *H. influenzae, S. pneumoniae, M. catarrhalis,* and *Alliococcus otitis*), the majority of chronic effusions are culture negative, refractory to antibiotic treatment, and positive for a variety of inflammatory mediators. Therefore, chronic OME was previously

Figure 7-9 Scanning electron microscopy (SEM) of the chinchilla middle ear mucosa following formaldehyde fixation and dehydration. *A*, Control at ×4,300 original magnification. The specimen was obtained at time 0 in an animal that was not inoculated with *Haemophilus influenzae*; *B*, *H. influenzae* microcolonies on middle ear mucosa 24 hours after inoculation at ×4,000 original magnification; *C*, developing biofilm 48 hours after inoculation at ×5,000 original magnification. Reproduced with permission from Post JC.[68]

thought to be a sterile, inflammatory process directed against residual bacterial metabolites. However, several recent observations cannot be explained by this paradigm.

1. Most sterile effusions from children contain bacterial DNA.
2. Pasteurized bacteria and purified bacterial DNA are cleared within hours from the middle ear space of chinchillas, but DNA from live infectious bacteria persists in sterile effusions for up to 4 weeks after antimicrobial therapy.
3. Bacterial mRNA is present in culture-negative, DNA-positive effusions from children, demonstrating that the bacteria are intact and metabolically active.
4. Bacteria synthesize proteins in culture-negative effusions.

The mucosal biofilm hypothesis suggests that chronic OME is the result of a bacterial biofilm forming directly on the surface of the middle ear mucosa. Bacteria growing as a biofilm display a different phenotype than free-living bacteria, have greatly reduced metabolic rates that render them nearly impervious to antibiotic treatment, have an exopolysaccharide matrix that resists phagocytosis and other host defense mechanisms, rely on complex intercellular communication systems for organized growth, and resist standard culture techniques because of altered metabolism.

The reduced metabolic and divisional rates of biofilm bacteria largely explain the failure of antibiotic treatment to eliminate infections in patients who have biofilm-colonized indwelling medical devices, primarily because nondividing bacteria largely escape antibiotic killing. Antibiotic treatment of biofilms kills bacteria on the periphery, but deep organisms persist and act as a nidus for regrowth and periodic planktonic showers, which can result in systemic infection.

Methods

To obtain direct morphologic evidence of biofilm formation in middle ear infections, SEM and CLSM were chosen as the best means to achieve convincing data. Two sets of chinchilla experiments were performed: one to obtain samples for SEM and the other for CLSM.[68,69] For each series of experiments, a cohort of 21 animals was inoculated at time 0 and another 3 animals served as negative controls. Two infected animals at each time point (3, 6, 12, and 24 hours and 2, 4, 5, 10, 16, and 22 days) following inoculation were euthanized for specimen collection. One additional animal for each set of experiments was inoculated to account for expected mortality, for a total of 48 animals in the study. Bilateral MEEs and mucosal specimens were collected after harvesting the temporal bullae.

Clinical Results

Representative SEM images are shown in Figure 7-9, demonstrating images of control mucosa and mucosa with attached biofilms.[68]

PATHOGEN DIVERSITY ASSESSMENT

Pathogen diversity assessment can determine genetic heterogeneity (different alleles of the same gene in different individuals) and genomic plasticity (different sets of contingency genes in different stains of a species). The following material is abstracted from the authors' work "Distributed Genome Hypothesis and Supra-Virulence Corollary (in preparation)."

Since the DNA sequence data from multiple strains of a single bacterial species have now become available, the extent of genomic diversity within species is higher than what could have been predicted on the basis of prior concepts of a species. For instance, the strain 86-028NP, a nontypeable *H. influenzae*, has an ~1.83×10^6 genome size. This equals the size of a published Rd strain genome sequence,[70] but the overall nucleotide sequences of these two same species strains differ by more than 25%! This is astonishing when compared with humans and chimpanzees, two *different* species sharing nearly 98% nucleotide identity. Nor is this observation an isolated event; our unpublished observations indicate that 15% of the genes of each strain of *P. aeruginosa* are unique with respect to the published PA01 sequence.

Genomic diversity among different strains of a bacterial species prompted us to question the clinical relevance of defining the single genome of one laboratory strain as the reference standard. Conversely, each strain's genome is better thought of as a subset or unique component of the *supragenome*, which is a theoretic construct including all of the genes and alleles present in the multitude of strains making up the species.[71] Numerous biologic and clinical ramifications result from this paradigm shift in genomic diversity. Because of diversity observed in such bacteria as *H. influenzae* and *P. aeruginosa*, attempts to comprehensively catalogue their supragenomes need international organization comparable with the human genome effort.

The supragenome concept and the ongoing establishment of the "supragene pool" provides advantages for further functional and evolutionary studies, such as investigating virulence gene sets that might distribute differently in different geographic locales or cause supervirulence if more virulent genes are present and expressed in a given strain. This modeling should benefit our understanding of chronic bacterial pathogenic mechanisms by helping elucidate the complex interspecies relationships, including bacterial pathogenicity, biofilm formation, and bacterial communal cooperation. Establishing a supragenome database requires obtaining and sequencing as many isolated strains of a bacterial species as possible and then constructing genomic libraries for all the stains for DNA sequencing.

Genomic Library Construction

Genomic library construction is the first step in establishing a supragenomic database, which is required for identifying all the distributed contingency genes of a species and for identifying genes associated with specific phenotypic traits.

Background

Genomic library construction means to clone an entire genome, by first breaking the genome into fragments of a manageable size and then inserting the fragments into a cloning vector to generate a population of molecular chimeras. The whole process is referred to as a shotgun experiment. The number of random fragments that must be cloned to ensure a high probability that every sequence of the genome is represented in at least one chimeric plasmid decreases with the fragment size and increases with the genome size and the desired probability of inclusion.[72]

Selection of the unique genomic clones from the library to be sequenced is accomplished by one or more differential hybridization techniques. The simplest is colony hybridization, in which bacterial colonies carrying chimeric vectors generated above are lysed on nitrocellulose or nylon filters. DNA is denatured in situ and fixed on the filter, which is hybridized with radioactively labeled probes representing all known genes for the species under study. Nonhybridizing clones are candidates for containing unique genes, which are then subjected to DNA sequence analysis. Another method of identifying unique genes is by suppression-subtraction-hybridization-PCR (SSH-PCR), which uses multiple rounds of liquid hybridization for common sequence depletion and PCR to amplify the unique sequences.

Methods

Low-passage clinical strains are preferable for all genomic and pathogenic studies because strains in long-term culture often lose virulence genes that are not under selective pressure when grown in artificial media. In the study described, clinical strains of bacteria were isolated and cultured for one passage before being stored frozen in liquid nitrogen as glycerol stocks. For DNA preparation, the glycerol stocks were used to inoculate overnight cultures in which bacteria were grown in broth culture. Bacteria were lysed and DNA extracted as previously described.[73] The purified cellular DNA was tested for quantity and quality by ultraviolet (UV) absorbance at 260/280 nm and agarose gel electrophoresis, respectively.

The purified DNA was fragmented into small sizes averaging ~1.4 kb, and a shotgun subcloning kit was used to construct pooled genomic DNA libraries. Fragmented DNA from each strain was pooled, followed by DNA end repairing and dephosphorylation prior to ligation into the pCR4Blunt-TOPO vector. Bulk ligations were performed using 250 ng vector DNA with 5 μg of fragmented bacterial DNA to generate an expected ~100,000 recombinant colonies. After ligation, the DNA was precipitated, purified, and resuspended in deionized water.

Using the purified ligated DNA, *Escherichia coli* TOP10 cells were transformed by electroporation, plated, and incubated until ready for picking (~1 mm diameter). A simple formula was used to calculate the number of colonies required:

$$N = \ln(1-p) / \ln(1-1/n)$$

where N is the number of clones needed to have a probability, p, of finding any particular sequence in the library, when the ratio of the combined genome size of the strains to the average cloned fragment size is n.[74] For example, to obtain a $p > .995$ for any given *H. influenzae* DNA sequence from 10 genomes, a minimum of 63,000 colonies would need to be collected. Therefore, 76,800 colonies were collected based on 80 to 90% cloning efficiency of the shotgun cloning system.

The collected colonies were grown overnight, replicated, and stored. Recombinant plasmids were isolated and tested for quantity and quality by UV absorbance at 260/280 nm. From each plasmid preparation, approximately 500 ng DNA was subjected to restriction enzyme analysis. The cloning site of the pCR4Blunt-TOPO vector was surrounded by two *EcoR* I restriction enzyme recognition sites, making it is possible to estimate the insert size of the genomic clones by agarose gel electrophoresis of the *EcoR* I digested DNA.[71]

Clinical Results

A genomic library was prepared by pooling the DNA from 10 strains of *H. influenzae* that had been isolated from pediatric OM patients that contained 76,800 colonies.[71] Two clones were picked randomly from each of the 200 replica-plates of this *H. influenzae* genomic library to test their characteristics. The apparent average molecular weight of the genomic inserts in the pooled *H. influenzae* genomic library is 1.4 kb (Figure 7-10).

Characterization of Bacterial Supragenomes through DNA Sequence Analysis of Genomic Libraries

The rationale for this process is to assess the quality of the genomic libraries (ie, percent of clones with inserts, percent with bacterial inserts, percent with unique inserts); obtain sequence data for homology searches to estimate the extent of the species-wide supragenome, and the degree to which unique genes are distributed across strains; and determine genes that are differentially expressed under various environmental conditions.

Background

The genomic plasticity of bacteria is attributable to the very large number of ways in which horizontal gene transfer can occur among prokaryotes, including natural competence and transformation, viral transduction,

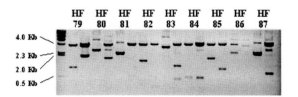

Figure 7-10 Restriction analysis of *Haemophilus influenzae* genomic DNA clones. Clones were picked into 384-deep well plates using a robotic colony picker, the QBot. The plasmid DNAs of two randomly selected clones from each plate were isolated and digested with the restriction enzyme *EcoR* I, and then analyzed on ethidium bromide–stained agarose gels. The numbers at the top of the figure correspond to array plates from which the clones were chosen.

and conjugation and mating. The lack of a meiotic step in the replication cycle of prokaryotes frees them from the restraint of having to pair homologous chromosomes, which, in turn, means there is no discrete physical constraint on their genome size. This lack of control provides the bacteria with a much greater degree of genomic dynamics than is available to eukaryotes.

The natural transformation systems of pathogens, which permits the bacterial cells to take up environmental DNA sequences, is one of the mechanistic lynch pins supporting the *distributed genome hypothesis*. Such phenomena would not have evolved and become fixed in the populations of so many pathogens (both gram-negative and gram-positive) had they not conferred a substantial survival advantage. Knowing that each strain of a species has a unique complement of genes from the supragenome, a species can be thought of as a group of organisms that share a common core set of genes, with each strain or isolate having a unique complement of contingency genes. Genomic plasticity can arise both through intraspecies genetic exchange and interspecies transfers (Antalis and colleagues, personal communication, February 2003).

H. influenzae is typical of bacteria that can take up DNA from the environment or (preferably) from other *Haemophilus*. The latter is insured because *Haemophilus* contains an uptake signal sequence (USS) repeated 1,400 times throughout the genome (~ once/gene) and targeted by the transformation machinery.[75] Chronic persistence in the host may contribute to the genetic diversity, probably by resorting distributed genes among multiple infecting strains. Modern sequencing technologies provide fast, precise, and reliable means to obtain genetic information.

Methods

To examine the degree of genomic plasticity among pathogenic strains of *H. influenzae*, we sequenced selected clones from our pooled genomic library prepared from the DNA of multiple clinical isolates. Plasmid DNA templates were prepared for sequencing by digesting the plasmid DNAs, followed by analysis on ethidium bromide–stained 1% agarose gels in tris-acetate EDTA buffer. Only those constructs containing inserts of DNA larger than 0.5 kb were used as sequencing templates. We used three different automated fluorescence sequencing systems, all based on the dideoxy terminator method, to analyze these clones.

DNA sequence similarity searches were performed using the basic BLAST and BLASTx algorithms available through the NCBI Web site (<http://www.ncbi.nlm.nih.gov/>).[76] Putative open reading frames were analyzed for codon usage and compared with published codon usage tables.[77]

Clinical Results

From the *H. influenzae* pooled genomic library (see above), 771 clones were randomly chosen for sequencing. Most clones were sequenced at least twice using both forward and reverse primers, with an average read length of 650 bases from each end of the clone. This provided ~90% of the complete sequence for the average-sized (1.4 kb) clone.

After comparing the sequences with the published sequence of *H. influenzae* strain Rd,[70] unique sequences were found in over 9% of the clones. About one-third of the unique clones also contained sequences homologous to those in the Rd strain, indicating a chromosomal origin. The remaining unique clones displayed no homology to Rd, indicating a chromosomal insertion size of greater than the clone or that they were of episomal origin (Antalis and colleagues, unpublished results, February 2003).

Cross-Hybridization Studies

The rationale for cross-hybridization studies is to determine the unique set of genes for each strain of bacteria within a species.

Background

Comparative analysis of the two *H. influenzae* genomes that have been fully sequenced demonstrate ~25% diversity between the two strains. Thus, there are most likely similar levels of plasticity among the many clinical isolates.

Methods

After establishing genomic libraries from clinical strains (and a reference strain), the next step is to identify the unique clones in each clinical strain (ie, not possessed by the reference strain). This can be achieved by pairwise cross-hybridizations, in which probes prepared from an unknown strain are hybridized against an arrayed genomic library of the reference strain. Conversely, probes prepared from the known strain can be hybridized against an arrayed genomic library of the uncharacterized clinical strain. In the former case, genes unique to the reference strain will be identified; in the latter case, clones unique to the clinical isolate will be identified.

To identify clones within the individual strain libraries that contain both unique sequences and the reference strain–like sequences, a strategy based on subtractive hybridization is used. The subtraction reagent is made by taking size-fractionated DNA from the reference strain, heat denaturing, quenching on ice, and biotinylating using the photobiotinylation kit. This substituted DNA is then reacted with streptavidin-coated paramagnetic beads to bind the DNA. The DNA-coated beads are subjected to denaturing conditions to eliminate any hybridizing complementary strands to prepare the ssDNA capture reagent.

Genomic DNA from each of the strains is hydrosheared to produce randomly sheared DNAs in the 200- to 300-bp size range. A high percentage of DNA fragments of this size that contain unique (non-Rd) sequences contain only unique sequences and, therefore, are not captured by the subtraction reagent. Those sequences that do not hybridize are recovered and subjected to two more rounds of subtraction to ensure removing all homologous sequences.

COMPARATIVE GENE EXPRESSION STUDIES

All of life is dependent on the organism's ability to adapt to its environment, which is accomplished by changing which genes are expressed. Ribonucleic acid evolved to interact immediately with the environment and still serves this dual role of genotype and phenotype. Conversely, DNA evolved later as an archival molecule to conserve energy by removing the genotype from the phenotype (this separation of functions permitted the evolution of differential gene expression and ultimately metazoan life).

By assessing which RNAs are present during various stages of development (as with a biofilm) or under a given set of environmental conditions (such as when antibiotics are added to a culture), it is possible to ascertain what genes are active. Determining specific bacterial gene activities associated with a given clinical condition provides targets for potential interventional therapies to combat infection.

Bacteria in chronic infections often adopt a biofilm mode of existence. Moreover, when living in biofilms, individual bacteria within the biofilm express different phenotypes, as the environment throughout the biofilm varies dramatically with respect to pH, oxygen, and nutrient availability, from the exposed surface of the biofilm to the attachment substrate. Thus, the bacterial phenotype is plural, not uniform.

Phenotypic plurality acts as a supravirulence factor for maintaining chronic infections in that any host defense system, or any exogenous antimicrobial will have limited effectiveness against the population as a whole. One stratagem may kill bacteria of a single phenotype but leave the nidus of the biofilm intact. Thus, the biofilm as a population gains a survival advantage because of the phenotypical plurality of the component member bacteria. If the biofilm survives, it is able to continue as a chronic infection, making phenotypical plurality a chronic supravirulence factor.

RNA Extraction and Probe Production

Messenger RNA is the link between the genome (DNA) and the expressed phenotype of the organism. Thus, the most facile means to learn about an organism's expressome is to study the pattern of gene expression through mRNA analyses.

Background

Messenger RNA is very labile because the 2′ hydroxyl group on the ribose residues of RNA makes the sugar–phosphate bonds comparatively unstable chemically. Moreover, all organisms maintain high levels of RNA degradative enzymes, RNAses, to promote rapid turnover of RNAs so that expression of a gene does not continue after the environmental conditions no longer warrant the continued production of its cognate protein.

Great care must be taken to ensure mRNA is not degraded during the extraction process. Thus, it is important to work at low temperatures and to use protective agents when extracting RNA, including chaotropic agents, which prevent proper folding of degradative enzymes, and specific RNAse inhibitors. Once mRNA is purified, it should be converted into a cDNA probe for performing the hybridization experiments. During or after the cDNA conversion process, a reporter group can be added to the probe to facilitate visualization of hybridizing clones.

Methods

These methods are adapted from the RNA extraction and probe labeling protocols found in *Short Protocols in Molecular Biology*.[15]

For RNA extraction from tissue culture cells, gentle detergents are used to lyse the cells; for plant cells, phenol and sodium dodecyl sulfate (SDS) are used for lysis. Since guanidinium isothiocyanate and guanidinium hydrochloride are both lysis reagents and very strong inhibitors of RNAse, guanidinium-based methods have become the choice for tissues that have high levels of endogenous RNAse. The hot-phenol method also works consistently for extracting bacterial mRNA from complex clinical specimens. We have also developed specific protocols for extracting bacterial RNA from MEEs.

Probe labeling can be achieved either isotopically or nonisotopically. In most cases, labeling is achieved by incorporating nucleotides that have the reporter group covalently attached during the polymerization process into the nascent probe. Radiolabeled probes (usually radioactve phosphorus [^{32}P or ^{33}P]) have high sensitivity and specificity, but care must be taken to prevent environmental contamination with radioactive isotopes. With nonisotopic labeling, biotin, digoxigenin, and fluorescent dye are used most frequently.

Clinical Results

Examples can be found in the PCR and related nucleic acid amplification methodologies section of this chapter.

Macroarrays

Macroarrays are two-dimensional matrices, usually configured on nylon or nitrocellulose membranes, that provide a discrete address for each of tens to hundreds of thousands of bacterial clones or their chimeric plasmids. All addresses must be simultaneously probed with any cDNA or genomic DNA probe to investigate gene expression profiles or issues of genomic diversity, respectively, thus permitting massive parallel interrogation of entire expressomes and genomes.

Background

Macroarray technology is based on developing robotic devices that can automatically print clones onto membranes. The macroarrays are made by printing either growing bacterial colonies (which contain within them plasmid DNA clones) or by printing purified plasmid DNAs that have been previously recovered from the individual bacterial clones onto positively charged (DNA is negatively charged) nylon membranes. The plasmid clones may contain either cDNAs (an expressed sequence tag library) or genomic fragments. Probing is accomplished using radiolabeled or colorimetrically-labeled (not fluorescent) probes that are produced from either reverse transcription of extracted RNA (cDNA) or are derived from genomic libraries.

After autoradiography or phosphor imaging for radiolabeled probes, or densitometric scanning for chromogenic probes, the images are scanned and analyzed. By comparing the densities of the hybridization spots, gene expression profiles (for expression studies) and unique genes (for distributed genome studies) can be determined. Macroarrays that are hybridized with radiolabeled probes can often be rehybridized multiple times by stripping off the label, using either heat or alkali to denature the heteroduplexes, thus permitting comparative studies to be performed on the same membrane. This reduces membrane-to-membrane variation and cost.[78]

Planktonic bacteria and biofilm bacteria have different phenotypes and, thus, are hypothesized to have substantially different expressomes. To identify genes that are uniquely expressed in biofilms and are, therefore, expressed during chronic infectious processes, such as chronic OME, the macroarray provides a useful means to collect large-scale comparative gene expression data.

Methods

E. coli clones containing the individual genomic fragments from the *H. influenzae* and *P. aeruginosa* pooled genomic libraries were initially grown in 384-deep well plates and then transferred into 96-deep well plates containing Luria-Bertani medium. The individual plasmid DNAs were prepared and purified robotically, then dried, resuspended in nuclease-free water, and transferred back to 384-deep well plates. Macroarrays were produced by spotting the purified plasmid DNA onto nylon membranes. Denatured ^{33}P-labeled probes from either planktonic or biofilm cDNA were then added to the prehybridization solution for overnight incubation. Membranes were washed, partially dried, and exposed to x-ray film. Autoradiographs were scanned under high resolution, and the inverted images (negatives) were digitally stored for further analysis (Sayeed and colleagues, personal communication, February 2003).

Clinical Results

From the pooled *P. aeruginosa* genomic library, 13,056 clones were randomly chosen for macroarray production. Plasmid DNAs were spotted in duplicate, and the position of each clone on the membrane was recorded according to its address in the 384-deep well plate. Some clones showed differential expression between planktonic and biofilm envirovars, such as the clone PA13_O16 (Sayeed and colleagues, unpublished result, February 2003) (Figure 7-11).

Microarray

Developing glass slide microarrays that could be simultaneously hybridized with multiple probes, each labeled with its own unique fluorescent tag, permits the simultaneous quantitative comparison of the expression levels of thousands of genes under different environmental conditions.

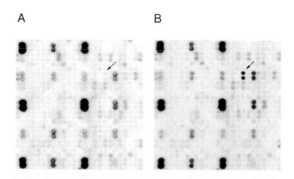

A   B

Figure 7-11 Identical sections of a macroarray membrane (containing plasmid DNAs prepared from a *Pseudomonas aeruginosa* library composed of 12 clinical isolates) comparatively hybridized with ^{33}P-labeled probes prepared from *(A)* planktonic and *(B)* biofilm cDNA. Each plasmid was spotted in duplicate. The arrows identify duplicate spots demonstrating upregulated expression of the clone PA13_O16 in biofilm bacteria.

Background

Microarray technology offers a powerful platform by which large sets of genes can be examined simultaneously. Thousands of gene sequences affixed in an *x*-by-*y* matrix to a glass slide substrate are hybridized to fluorescently labeled cRNA or cDNA probes, and the amount of bound fluorescence yields quantitative information about the relative level of gene expression in each probe.[79] The printed spots can contain PCR-derived double-strand amplicons, or single-strand synthetic oligonucleotides, corresponding to known or putative open reading frames (ORFs). Additional control spots are added to monitor the printing and hybridization steps.

The system allows two (or more depending on the number of excitation lasers the scanner has) populations of cDNA to be differentially labeled with different fluorochromes, such as Cy3- and Cy5-dUTP, during a first-strand RT reaction using random hexamers as primers.[80] The labeled cDNAs are usually derived from RNA prepared from the same organism cultivated under, or exposed to, two contrasting conditions. A mixture of equal amounts of the two labeled probe populations are applied to the microarray slide for hybridization, after which the slide array is scanned using a laser scanner, and the emission intensity of each label for each clone is quantified. Images of the slide are processed to derive values for all spots, which yield ratios of the relative degree of expression or repression of each clone for each condition under study.

The expanding number of genome sequence databases of pathogenic bacteria and their hosts provides an unprecedented chance to study pathogenesis from a whole-genome perspective through microarray technology. Two bacterial genomes can be compared at the ORF-content level of resolution by hybridizing labeled DNA from a nonsequenced strain to a DNA microarray containing representations of each ORF from a sequenced, reference strain. The result discloses genes common to both strains and genes that are present in the reference strain but absent in the experimental strain. The limitation is that genes present in the experimental strain but absent in the reference strain would not be detected using this methodology.

Currently, the number of microarray studies published investigating the expression profiles of pathogenic bacteria under in vivo conditions is very small, and the information available from these studies is also limited.[81] Thus, it is important that a common, shared public database be created for researchers to deposit, analyze, and retrieve microarray data for bacterial pathogens in order to promote and accelerate this type of research.[82]

Method

The example given here is based on a study investigating the interaction of *P. aeruginosa* with epithelial cells.[83] To identify critical host responses during infection, a DNA microarray containing 1,506 human cDNA clones was used to monitor gene expression in a lung pneumocyte cell line during exposure to *P. aeruginosa*. Readers are referred to the source article for details regarding preparation of the microarray.[83]

Clinical Results

Human lung carcinoma cells were either exposed to *P. aeruginosa* strain PAK or the nonpiliated (NP) strain PAK-NP. Cellular RNA was extracted from the cultured cells after a brief exposure (time 0) or after incubating with bacteria for 3 hours. During a 3-hour exposure to strain PAK, 22 genes displayed more than a twofold increase in the levels of transcript, and only two genes were down-regulated more than twofold. In contrast, the 3-hour infection with strain PAK-NP increased expression more than twofold in 16 genes. One of the genes with differential expression was *IRF-1*, a transcription factor shown to mediate the expression of interferon (IFN)-responsive genes, which demonstrated a 2.5-fold increase when exposed to strain PAK versus strain PAK-NP.[81]

Analyses of Macroarrays and Microarrays

Sophisticated automated software-based methods of analysis are needed to interpret the immense amount of data provided by simultaneously interrogating tens of thousands of clones. The software must be able to acquire, analyze, filter, and present the data through an easily interpretable graphic interface. Moreover, it should also be able to instruct laboratory-based automated systems in the redesigning and rearraying of libraries on the basis of the results from previous experiments, thus freeing the operators from time-intensive tasks.

Background

Macroarrays and microarrays generate huge amounts of information that require rapid and efficient analysis. In competitively hybridized microarrays, the processed data from one spot on the slide contains dozens of values. Therefore, a single microarray containing 20,000 spots would produce on the order of a million data points.[82] To relieve the burden of processing and analyzing the data, various kinds of software have been developed.

The software principles used for analyzing macro- and microarrays are similar. Both begin with the images being scanned and stored digitally to indicate the signal intensities of each probe for each spot. The background value (itself a very complex computation based on local, regional, and array-wide values) is subtracted and ratios of the signal intensities between control and experimental specimens are generated and compared. At least three replicates of each experiment should reach a reliable conclusion. The combined use of experimental replicates and appropriate statistical instruments are two means to ensure that observed differences are significant.[84]

Although several software packages exist for array analysis, detailed discussion of the relative advantages and disadvantages is beyond the scope of this chapter.

COMPARATIVE PROTEOMIC STUDIES

Proteomics is the protein equivalent of genomics and expressomics, wherein the expression levels of all proteins expressed by an organism (cell or tissue) are assessed simultaneously. Comparative proteomics permits simultaneous characterization of the expression profiles of thousands of proteins from multiple environmental conditions. The application of proteomics to compare expression profiles between planktonic and biofilm envirovars of *P. aeruginosa* has revealed hundred of proteins that are differentially expressed[42] but were not detected in parallel microarray experiments. Thus, it is insufficient to study only RNA when performing expression studies because there are numerous post-transcriptional regulatory mechanisms that factor into the ultimate phenotype.

Background

Observations of *P. aeruginosa* biofilm growth in vitro have revealed five-stages of development: (1) reversible attachment, (2) irreversible attachment, (3) maturation-1 (several bacterial layers thick), (4) maturation-2 (cell

A. Chemostat B. Biofilm, 1 d C. Biofilm, 3 d D. Biofilm, 6 d E. Biofilm, 12 d

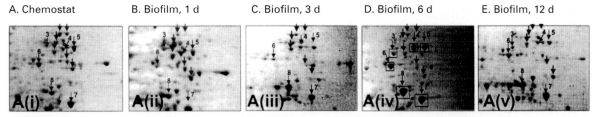

Figure 7-12 Enlarged partial two-dimensional gels showing crude protein extracts of *Pseudonomas aeruginosa* strain PAO1 grown planktonically in a chemostat *(A)* and for 1 day *(B)*, 3 days *(C)*, 6 days *(D)*, and 12 days *(E)* in a biofilm. Proteins that were identified by MS analysis are indicated by boxes. The spot numbers correlate with the proteins that have been analyzed further. The gels were stained with Coomassie brilliant blue R-350. Reproduced with permission from Sauer K et al.[42]

clusters reaching maximum thickness), and (5) dispersion.[42] In vivo experiments with *H. influenzae*–induced OM in the chinchilla have demonstrated a similar progression of bacterial biofilm development.[69]

The phenotypic difference among planktonic and the various stages of biofilm bacteria are believed to be the result of transitions in gene expression and ultimately protein production. Proteomic methods enable the comparison of protein expression between planktonic and biofilm bacteria among various strains of a bacterial species or among different species.

Methods

A flow through silicon tube system was used to cultivate biofilm bacteria.[42] Cultures of bacteria were grown in chemostats prior to inoculating the silicone tubing by syringe injection. After various times (ie, up to 12 days), the biofilm was harvested from the interior surface by pinching the tube along its entire length, resulting in extrusion of the cell material from the lumen. The resulting cell paste was collected and centrifuged for crude protein extraction.

Total protein concentration was determined by the modified method of Lowry and colleagues,[85] with experiments for each time point repeated at least five times. Two-dimensional gel electrophoresis of the extracted

proteins was conducted with mass spectrometry (MS) for protein spot identification performed on differentially expressed proteins. Protein spots of interest were excised from the gel and analyzed by matrix-assisted laser desorption ionization-time of flight. Peptide mass fingerprints were searched using appropriate software.[42]

Clinical Results

Figure 7-12 shows the differential protein expression among planktonic bacteria and the various stage of biofilm development for *P. aeruginosa* strain PA01. Protein MS analysis of selected differentially expressed protein spots indicated changes in the expression patterns of proteins involved in many metabolic processes, including amino acid biosynthesis, membrane signaling proteins, and oxidative stress response proteins (Table 7-8).[42]

CONCLUSION

A wide variety of animal models and molecular techniques exist to study OM pathogenesis and treatment. Pointers and pitfalls are summarized in Table 7-9. Greater clinician familiarity with these exciting and rapidly developing techniques should facilitate translating basic research into clinically relevant management tools.

Table 7-8 Differential Expression Patterns in Planktonic Cells and in Biofilm Cells after Various Times of Biofilm Growth*

Expression Pattern	% of Proteins					
	Chemo/1 d	1 d/3 d	3 d/6 d	Chemo/6 d	1 d/6 d	6 d/12 d
Constant	71	91	61	43	61	63.5
Up-regulated	25	4.5	36	51	36	1.5
Down-regulated	4	4.5	3	6	3	35.0

Reproduced with permission frm Sauer K et al.[42]

Chemo = planktonic cells grown in a chemostat; 1 d, 3 d, 6 d, and 12 d = biofilm cells grown for 1, 3, 6, and 12 days as a biofilm.

*The comparative analysis between different growth conditions was carried out using the software Melanie 3.0 from GenBio.

Table 7-9 Pointers and Pitfalls

1. Molecular methods used in the diagnosis of pathogens causing chronic OM produced a paradigm shift in our understanding of chronic bacterial processes in general. It is now understood that many chronic infectious processes result from bacteria adopting a biofilm mode of growth. This, in turn, led to the concept of "phenotypic plurality" as a chronic supravirulence factor. Supravirulence factors are those that require a population of bacteria for their expression and, therefore, are not invested in single organisms.

2. Comparative genomic analyses among multiple clinical isolates of common bacterial pathogens associated with COME and CSOM have revealed extensive genetic heterogeneity and genomic plasticity among the strains of each species. These observations gave rise to the genomic plurality paradigm which embodies the distributed genome hypothesis and the concepts of the supragenome and supravirulence. Each of these postulates supposes that chronic pathogenicity (at least in part) derives from complex bacterial populations and the reassortment of genes among the bacteria within these populations. It should be remembered, however, that these hypotheses still need to be subjected to rigorous testing.

3. Understanding the principles of the various detection methodologies is essential to choosing the right means for aiding in a clinical diagnosis.

4. The conditions for each diagnostic method and each pathogen need to be optimized before the introduction of such a test as a clinical assay.

5. PCR-based assays can identify infectious organisms with greater rapidity and better sensitivity and specificity than traditional culture methods; however, they are not suitable for broad-scale screening when specimens must be simultaneously evaluated for a large number of pathogenic species.

6. RNA-based analyses and de novo protein biosynthesis experiments have revealed actively metabolizing bacterial pathogens in culture-negative pediatric middle ear effusions and culture-negative experimentally induced chinchilla middle ear effusions. Such experiments are technically challenging, however, and great care must be taken to ensure that the RNA is not degraded and that contaminating DNA moieties are digested prior to RT-PCR.

7. Comparative global gene expression analyses have indicated substantial differences between the expressomes and proteomes of planktonic bacteria and biofilm bacteria growing on inert surfaces. Application of these technologies to mucosal biofilms should provide targets for future interventional strategies.

8. Microscopic imaging methods (SEM and CLSM) have provided direct evidence of *H. influenzae*'s ability to form mucosal biofilms in the chinchilla model of middle ear disease. Similar experiments need to be performed in the human but must await the development of an endoscopic CLSM.

9. In vivo gene reporter systems based on green fluorescent protein can be used to confirm the expression of virulence genes under pathogenic conditions.

10. Host responses to pathogen invasion indirectly affect the occurrence of OM, and additional studies are needed to establish the host's role in the development and maintenance of OM.

11. Each animal model has its own advantages and disadvantages with respect to prior pathogen exposure, pathogen susceptibility, immunology, and similarity of anatomy and physiology to the human condition

CLSM = confocal laser scanning microscopy; COME = chronic otitis media with effusion; CSOM = chronic serous otitis media; OM = otitis media; PCR = polymerase chain reaction; RT = reverse transcriptase; SEM = scanning electron microscopy.

References

1. Mullis KB, Faloona FA. Specific synthesis of DNA in vitro via a polymerase-catalyzed chain reaction. Methods Enzymol 1987;155:335–50.

2. Saiki RK, Gelfand DH, Stoffel S, et al. Primer-directed enzymatic amplification of DNA with a thermostable DNA polymerase. Science 1988;239(4839):487–91.

3. Ehrlich GD. Caveats of PCR. Clin Micro News 1992; 13:149–51.

4. Laure F, Courgnaud V, Rouzioux C, et al. Detection of HIV1 DNA in infants and children by means of the polymerase chain reaction. Lancet 1988;2:538–41.

5. Golightly MG, Thomas JA, Viciana AL. The laboratory diagnosis of Lyme borreliosis. Lab Med 1990;21: 299–304.

6. Vilgalys R, Hester M. Rapid genetic identification and mapping of enzymatically amplified ribosomal DNA from several *Cryptococcus* species. J Bacteriol 1990;172:4238–46.

7. Bluestone CD, Klein J. Otitis media, atelectasis, and eustachian tube dysfunction. In: Bluestone CD, Stool SE, Sceetz M, editors. Pediatric otolaryngology. Vol 1. Philadelphia (PA): WB Saunders; 1990. p. 320.

8. Del Beccaro MA, Mendelman PM, Inglis AF et al. Bacteriology of acute otitis media: a new perspective. J Pediatr 1992;120:81–4

9. Stephenson JS, Martin LM, Kardatzke D, Bluestone CD. Prevalence of bacteria in middle ear effusion for the 80s. In: Lim DJ, Bluestone CD, Klein JO, et al. editors. Proceedings of the Fifth International Symposium of Recent Advances in Otitis Media; 1991 May 20–24, Ft Lauderdale, USA. Hamilton: BC Decker; 1993.

10. Magit AE, Ehrlich GD, Post JC. Applications of PCR to the diseases of the ears, nose, and throat. In: Ehrlich GD, Greenberg SJ, editors. PCR-based diagnostics in infectious disease. Boston (MA): Blackwell Scientific Publications; 1994. p. 193–211.

11. Abbott MA, Poiesz BJ, Byrne BC, et al. Enzymatic gene amplification: qualitative and quantitative methods for detecting proviral DNA amplified in vitro. J Infect Dis 1988;158:1158–69.

12. Ehrlich GD, Glaser JB, LaVigne K, et al. Prevalence of human T-cell leukemia/lymphoma virus (HTLV) type II infection among high-risk individuals: type-specific identification of HTLVs by polymerase chain reaction. Blood 1989;74:1658–64.

13. Post JC, Magit AE, Eagle LR, et al. The polymerase chain reaction for identification of bacterial DNA in middle-ear effusions [abstract]. Association of Research in Otolaryngology, 15th Midwinter Meeting; 1992 February 5; St Petersburg Beach, USA. 1992.

14. Post JC, Larkins-Pettigrew MD, Magit AE, et al. PCR-based strategies for the detection of *H. influenzae* and *Str. pneumoniae* DNA associated with diseases of the ear, nose, and throat. In: Ehrlich GD, Greenberg SJ, editors. PCR-based diagnostics in infectious disease. Boston (MA): Blackwell Scientific Publications; 1994. p. 593–607.

15. Ausubel FM, Brent R, Kingston RE, et al, editors. Short protocols in molecular biology. 3rd ed. New York (NY): Greene Publishing Associates and Wiley Interscience, John Wiley and Sons; 1997.

16. van Ketel RJ, de Wever B, van Alphen L. Detection of *Haemophilus influenzae* in cerebrospinal fluids by polymerase chain reaction DNA amplification. J Med Microbiol 1990;33:271–6.

17. Post JC, White GJ, Aul JJ et al. Development and validation of a multiplex PCR-based assay for the upper respiratory tract bacterial pathogens *Haemophilus influenzae*, *Streptococcus pneumoniae*, and *Moraxella catarrhalis*. Mol Diagn 1996;1:29–39.

18. Aul JJ, Anderson KW, Wadowsky RM, et al. Comparative evaluation of culture and PCR for the detection and determination of persistence of bacterial strains and DNAs in the *Chinchilla laniger* model of otitis media. Ann Otol Rhinol Laryngol 1998;107:508–13.

19. Mahenthiralingam E, Campbell ME, Foster J, et al. Random amplified polymorphic DNA typing of *Pseudomonas aeruginosa* isolates recovered from patients with cystic fibrosis. J Clin Microbiol 1996;34:1129–35.

20. Gutell RR, Weiser B, Woese CR, Noller HF. Comparative anatomy of 16-S-like ribosomal RNA. Prog Nucleic Acid Res Mol Biol 1985;32:155–216.

21. Wilson KH. Characterization of novel bacterial pathogens by amplification and sequencing of 16S ribosomal RNA genes. In: Ehrlich GD, Greenberg SJ, editors. PCR-based diagnostics. Boston (MA): Blackwell Scientific Publications; 1994. p. 649–63.

22. Welch DF, Pickett DA, Slater LN, et al. *Rochalimaea henselae* sp. nov., a cause of septicemia, bacillary angiomatosis, and parenchymal bacillary peliosis. J Clin Microbiol 1992;30:275–80.

23. Regnery RL, Anderson BE, Clarridge JE III, et al. Characterization of a novel *Rochalimaea* species, *R. henselae* sp. nov., isolated from blood of a febrile, human immunodeficiency virus-positive patient. J Clin Microbiol 1992;30:265–74.

24. Relman DA, Schmidt TM, MacDermott RP, Falkow S. Identification of the uncultured bacillus of Whipple's disease. N Engl J Med 1992;327:293–301.

25. Anderson BE, Sumner JW, Dawson JE, et al. Detection of the etiologic agent of human ehrlichiosis by polymerase chain reaction. J Clin Microbiol 1992;30:775–80.

26. Stover CK, Pham XQ, Erwin AL, , et al. Complete genome sequence of *Pseudomonas aeruginosa* PA01, an opportunistic pathogen. Nature 2000;406:959–64.

27. Post JC, Aul JJ, White GJ et al. PCR-based detection of bacterial DNA after antimicrobial treatment is indicative of persistent, viable bacteria in the chinchilla model of otitis media. Am J Otolaryngol 1996;17:106–11.

28. Rayner MG, Zhang Y, Gorry MC, et al. Evidence of bacterial metabolic activity in culture-negative otitis media with effusion. JAMA 1998;279:296–9.

29. Sato K, Liebeler CL, Quartey MK, et al. Middle ear fluid cytokine and inflammatory cell kinetics in the chinchilla otitis media model. Infect Immun 1999;67:1943–6.

30. Sato K, Kawana M, Nonomura N, Nakano Y. Course of IL-1beta, IL-6, IL-8, and TNF-alpha in the middle ear fluid of the guinea pig otitis media model induced by nonviable *Haemophilus influenzae*. Ann Otol Rhinol Laryngol 1999;108:559–63.

31. Kita H, Himi T. Cytokine and chemokine induction using cell wall component and toxin derived from gram-positive bacteria in the rat middle ear. Acta Otolaryngol 1999;119:446–52.

32. Palacios SD, Pak K, Rivkin AZ, et al. Growth factors and their receptors in the middle ear mucosa during otitis media. Laryngoscope 2002;112:420–3.

33. Koutnouyan HA, Baird A, Ryan AF. Acidic and basic FGF mRNA expression in the middle ear mucosa during experimental acute and chronic otitis media. Laryngoscope 1994;104(3 Pt 1):350–8.

34. Jung HH, Kim MW, Lee JH, et al. Expression of vascular endothelial growth factor in otitis media. Acta Otolaryngol 1999;119:801–8.

35. Yetiser S, Satar B, Aydin N. Expression of epidermal growth factor, tumor necrosis factor-alpha, and interleukin-1alpha in chronic otitis media with or without cholesteatoma. Otol Neurotol 2002;23:647–52.

36. Chole RA, Faddis BT. Evidence for microbial biofilms in cholesteatomas. Arch Otolaryngol Head Neck Surg 2002;128(10):1129–33.

37. DeLong EF, Wickham GS, Pace NR. Phylogenetic stains: ribosomal RNA-based probes for the identification of single cells. Science 1989;243:1360–3.

38. Forsgren J, Samuelson A, Ahlin A, et al. *Haemophilus influenzae* resides and multiplies intracellularly in human adenoid tissue as demonstrated by in situ hybridization and bacterial viability assay. Infect Immun 1994;62:673–9.

39. Hogardt M, Trebesius K, Geiger AM, et al. Specific and rapid detection by fluorescent in situ hybridization of bacteria in clinical samples obtained from cystic fibrosis patients. J Clin Microbiol 2000;38:818–25.

40. Post JC, Ehrlich GD. The impact of the polymerase chain reaction in clinical medicine. JAMA 2000;283:1544–6.

41. Sauer K, Camper AK. Characterization of phenotypic changes in *Pseudomonas putida* in response to surface-associated growth. J Bacteriol 2001;183:6579–89.

42. Sauer K, Camper AK, Ehrlich GD, et al. *Pseudomonas aeruginosa* displays multiple phenotypes during development as a biofilm. J Bacteriol 2002;184:1140–54.

43. Chalfie M, Tu Y, Euskirchen G, et al. Green fluorescent protein as a marker for gene expression. Science 1994;263:802–5.

44. Cormack, BP, Valdivia RH, Falkow S. FACS-optimized mutants of the green fluorescent protein (GFP). Gene 1996;173:33–8.

45. Lansford R, Bearman G, Fraser SE. Resolution of multiple green fluorescent protein color variants and dyes using two-photon microscopy and imaging spectroscopy. J Biomed Opt 2001;6:311–8.

46. Andersen JB, Sternberg C, Poulsen L, et al. New unstable variants of green fluorescent protein for studies of transient gene expression in bacteria. Appl Environ Microbiol 1998;64:2240–6.

47. Sternberg C, Christensen BB, Johansen T, et al. Distribution of bacterial growth activity in flow-chamber biofilms. Appl Environ Microbiol 1999;65:4108–17.

48. Konietzko S, Koskela M, Erdmann G, Giebink GS. Isotype-specific rabbit antibodies against chinchilla immunoglobulins G, M, and A. Lab Anim Sci 1992;42:302–6.

49. Giebink GS, Payne EE, Mills EL, et al. Experimental otitis media due to *Streptococcus pneumoniae*: immunopathogenic response in the chinchilla. J Infect Dis 1976;134:595–604.

50. Giebink GS. Otitis media: the chinchilla model. Microb Drug Resist 1999;5:57–72.

51. Bakaletz LO, Kennedy BJ, Novotny LA, et al. Protection against development of otitis media induced by nontypable *Haemophilus influenzae* by both active and passive immunization in a chinchilla model of virus-bacterium superinfection. Infect Immun 1999;67:2746–62.

52. Post JC, Preston RA, Aul JJ, et al. Molecular analysis of bacterial pathogens in otitis media with effusion. JAMA 1995;273:1598–604.

53. Clark JM, Brinson G, Newman MK, et al. An animal model for the study of genetic predisposition in the pathogenesis of middle ear inflammation. Laryngoscope 2000;110:1511–5.

54. Russell JD, Giles SJ. Persistent otitis media with effusion: a new experimental model. Laryngoscope 1998;108:1181–4.

55. Wielinga EW, Peters TA, Tonnaer EL, et al. Middle ear effusions and structure of the tympanic membrane. Laryngoscope 2001;111:90–5.

56. Piltcher OB, Swarts JD, Magnuson K, et al. A rat model of otitis media with effusion caused by eustachian tube obstruction with and without *Streptococcus pneumoniae* infection: methods and disease course. Otolaryngol Head Neck Surg 2002;126:490–8.

57. Doyle WJ, Alper CM. A model to explain the rapid pressure decrease after air-inflation of diseased middle ears. Laryngoscope 1999;109:70–8.

58. Alper CM, Doyle WJ. Repeated inflation does not prevent otitis media with effusion in a monkey model. Laryngoscope 1999;109(7 Pt 1):1074–80.

59. Alper CM, Swarts JD, Doyle WJ. Prevention of otitis media with effusion by repeated air inflation in a monkey model. Arch Otolaryngol Head Neck Surg 2000;126:609–14.

60. Alper CM, Dohar JE, Gulhan M, et al. Treatment of chronic suppurative otitis media with topical tobramycin and dexamethasone. Arch Otolaryngol Head Neck Surg 2000;126:165–73.

61. Dohar JE, Alper CM, Rose EA, et al. Treatment of chronic suppurative otitis media with topical ciprofloxacin. Ann Otol Rhinol Laryngol 1998;107(10 Pt 1):865–71.

62. Johnson M, Leonard G, Kreutzer DL. Murine model of interleukin-8-induced otitis media. Laryngoscope 1997;107:1405–8.

63. Bikhazi P, Ryan AF. Expression of immunoregulatory cytokines during acute and chronic middle ear immune response. Laryngoscope 1995;105:629–34.

64. Meek RB 3rd, McGrew BM, Cuff CF, et al. Immunologic and histologic observations in reovirus-induced otitis media in the mouse. Ann Otol Rhinol Laryngol 1999;108:31–8.

65. Watanabe T, Hirano T, Suzuki M, et al. Role of interleukin-1 beta in a murine model of otitis media with effusion. Ann Otol Rhinol Laryngol 2001;110:574–80.

66. Sabirov A, Kodama S, Hirano T, et al. Intranasal immunization enhances clearance of nontypable *Haemophilus influenzae* and reduces stimulation of tumor necrosis factor alpha production in the murine model of otitis media. Infect Immun 2001;69:2964–71.

67. Alper CM, Andalibi A, Bakaletz LO, et al. Recent advances in otitis media. 4. Anatomy, cell biology, pathology, and animal models. Ann Otol Rhinol Laryngol Suppl 2002;188:36–51.

68. Post JC. Direct evidence of bacterial biofilms in otitis media. Laryngoscope 2001;111:2083–94.

69. Ehrlich GD, Veeh R, Wang X et al. Mucosal biofilm formation on middle-ear mucosa in the chinchilla model of otitis media. JAMA 2002;287:1710–5.

70. Fleischmann RD, Adams MD, White O, et al. Whole-genome random sequencing and assembly of *Haemophilus influenzae* Rd. Science 1995;269:496–512.

71. Geza E, Sayeed S, Antalis P, et al. Development and

characterization of a pooled *Haemophilus influenzae* genomic library for the evaluation of gene expression changes associated with mucosal biofilm formation. Int J Pediatr Otol. [In press]

72. Lewin B. Genes. 6th ed. Cambridge (MA): Oxford University Press; 1997.

73. Woo TH, Cheng AF, Ling JM. An application of a simple method for the preparation of bacterial DNA. Biotechniques 1992;13:696–8.

74. Sambrook J, Fritsch EF, Maniatis T. Molecular cloning. 2nd ed. Cold Spring Harbor (NY): Cold Spring Harbor Laboratory Press; 1989.

75. Smith HO, Tomb JF, Dougherty BA, et al. Frequency and distribution of DNA uptake signal sequences in the *Haemophilus influenzae* Rd genome. Science 1995;269: 538–40.

76. Altschul SF, Gish W, Miller W, et al. Basic local alignment search tool. J Mol Biol 1990;215:403–10.

77. Nakamura Y, Gojobori T, Ikemura T. Codon usage tabulated from international DNA sequence databases: status for the year 2000. Nucleic Acids Res 2000;28:292.

78. Tao H, Bausch C, Richmond C, et al. Functional genomics:

expression analysis of *Escherichia coli* growing on minimal and rich media. J Bacteriol 1999;181:6425–40.

79. Schena M, Shalon D, Davis RW, Brown PO. Quantitative monitoring of gene expression patterns with a complementary DNA microarray. Science 1995;270:467–70.

80. Eisen MB, Brown PO. DNA arrays for analysis of gene expression. Methods Enzymol 1999;303:179–205.

81. Schoolnik GK. Microarray analysis of bacterial pathogenicity. Adv Microb Physiol 2002;46:1–45.

82. Sherlock G, Hernandez-Boussard T, Kasarskis A, et al. The Stanford microarray database. Nucleic Acids Res 2001;29:152–5.

83. Ichikawa JK, Norris A, Bangera MG, et al. Interaction of *Pseudomonas aeruginosa* with epithelial cells: identification of differentially regulated genes by expression microarray analysis of human cDNAs. Proc Natl Acad Sci U S A 2000;97:9659–64.

84. Schoolnik GK. Microarray analysis of bacterial pathogenicity. Adv Microb Physiol 2002;46:1–45.

85. Peterson GL. A simplification of the protein assay method of Lowry et al. Which is more generally applicable? Anal Biochem 1977;83:346–56.

CHAPTER 8

Definitions, Terminology, and Classification

Charles D. Bluestone, MD

The purpose of a classification schema is to classify and simplify the nomenclature and to derive acceptable terminology for the various facets of otitis media for the purpose of communication. In the past there has been a confusion of terms in part because of a failure to distinguish conceptually between the disease process, otitis media, and one of the manifestations of that disease process, namely otitis media with effusion. Otitis media is dynamic and at any one time should be considered a single point in a continuum of the disease process.

Ben H. Senturia

OBJECTIVES

On completing this chapter, the reader will be able to
1. Understand that definitions and terminology of otitis media (OM) and related conditions must be consistent and based on general consensus so that information can be disseminated for clinical and investigation purposes.
2. Use terminology to describe the various stages and grades of OM, such as *acute otitis media* and *otitis media with effusion*, that is consistent with our current understanding of the pathogenesis and pathology of the disease.
3. Employ a classification of complications and sequelae of OM based on our current understanding of the pathogenesis and pathology of the disease, rather than on outdated or inappropriate terms that are potentially misleading and confusing.
4. Use a *grading* and *staging system* for many of the complications and sequelae of OM so that its natural history can be precisely studied, outcomes of intervention can be appropriately evaluated, and management decisions can be based on evidence, rather than on preconceived ideas and personal bias.

We are indebted to the late Ben H. Senturia for organizing a small task force of clinicians and scientists to meet with him in St. Louis in 1978 to reach a consensus on definitions, terminology, and a classification of OM. His purpose in convening this meeting is stated in the introductory quote above, which was published with the task force's report in the proceedings of the Second International Symposium on Recent Advances in Otitis Media.[1]

Although controversy lingers, there is now general consensus on the terminology and definitions used to describe the various stages of otitis media. It is important that agreement be reached about these issues so that health care professionals can communicate with one another, both clinically and scientifically.

NEED FOR CLASSIFICATION, GRADING, AND STAGING

The 1978 task force did not grade acute otitis media (AOM) and otitis media with effusion (OME) on the basis of severity or classify the complications and sequelae of OM and related conditions. This chapter addresses these omissions, including those facets of the disease that would seem reasonable on the basis of our current knowledge of its pathogenesis and pathology. Many of the terms employed by the task force were defined prior to the advent of modern otology, which affords the opportunity to examine patients with the operating microscope in the ambulatory setting and at the time of otologic surgery. The more recent availability of radiologic imaging technology has also allowed practitioners to visualize the contents of temporal bone and the intracranial cavity in a way that the pioneers in otology could not.

There is a need for consensus on classifying the complications and sequelae of OM, as the 1978 task force did in defining AOM and OME. There are also no acceptable staging systems for these complications and sequelae. Such staging systems would improve our ability to study the natural history of OM and more uniformly conduct and evaluate research, resulting in more effective management of patients. Developing evidence-based information in the future requires a universally acceptable classification as well as grading and staging systems for many of the otogenic complications and sequelae. The *grade* of OM and related diseases and disorders relates to the severity, whereas a *stage* is a period or distinct phase in the course of OM or one of its complications or sequelae.

Many of the following terms, definitions, and classifications of OM and its complications and sequelae have been used in international symposia, conferences, guidelines, and textbooks related to the disease.[2–8] Also, a research meeting of international experts reached consensus on the terminology that follows,[8] but the definitions of these and other terms await future deliberations.

TERMINOLOGY AND DEFINITIONS

Definitions of the terms most commonly used in relation to OM are given below:
- *OM* is an inflammation of the middle ear without reference to etiology or pathogenesis.
- *AOM* is the rapid onset of signs and symptoms, such as otalgia and fever, of acute infection within the middle ear.
- *OME* is an inflammation of the middle ear with liquid collected in the middle ear space. The signs and symptoms of acute infection are absent, and there is no perforation of the tympanic membrane.
- *Middle ear effusion* (MEE) designates liquid in the middle ear but not etiology, pathogenesis, pathology, or duration. The effusion may be serous—a thin, watery liquid; mucoid—a thick, viscid, mucus-like liquid; purulent—a pus-like liquid; or a combination of these. An effusion can result from either AOM or OME. It can be of recent onset, acute, or more long lasting, subacute, or chronic.
- *Otorrhea* is a discharge from the ear, originating at one or more of the following sites: the external auditory canal, middle ear, mastoid, inner ear, or intracranial cavity.

CLASSIFICATION

Table 8-1 demonstrates a classification derived from our present knowledge of the disease and its complications and sequelae. Terms used in this classification are defined below.

Complications and sequelae of OM are classified into *intratemporal* (extracranial) complications and sequelae, those that occur within the temporal bone, and those that occur within the intracranial cavity (*intracranial* complications). Several conditions may be complications or sequelae of a related condition. Several conditions may be complications or sequelae not of OM

but of a related condition, such as mastoiditis.[9] An example of this would be the presence of a retraction pocket of the tympanic membrane, in which a discontinuity of the ossicular chain occurs or an acquired cholesteatoma develops.[10–11]

This author has grouped and presented the intratemporal complications and sequelae of OM and related disorders, such as the atelectasis of the middle ear with retraction pocket, followed by adhesive OM, and then cholesteatoma, because we believe cholesteatoma frequently progresses in this order. Also, the suppurative complications, such as mastoiditis, petrositis, labyrinthitis, and facial paralysis, are grouped.[8]

ACUTE OTITIS MEDIA

The rapid and short onset of signs and symptoms of inflammation in the middle ear are characteristic of AOM. Acute suppurative or purulent OM are synonyms still used by some but are not recommended terms. One or more local or systemic signs are present: otalgia (or pulling of the ear in the young infant), otorrhea, fever, recent onset of irritability, anorexia, vomiting, or diarrhea. The tympanic membrane is full or bulging, is opaque, and has limited or no mobility to pneumatic otoscopy, all of which indicate MEE. Erythema of the eardrum is found inconsistently. The acute onset of ear pain, fever, and a purulent discharge (otorrhea) through a perforation of the tympanic membrane (or tympanostomy tube) would also be evidence of AOM. This is known as *acute otitis media with perforation*, a complication that is discussed below.

Grading System Based on Severity

There may be some advantage to grading the severity of AOM because the outcome of treatment, or no treatment, may vary. Kaleida and colleagues[12] graded AOM in infants and children who were entered into a clinical trial of the efficacy of antibiotics or myringotomy, or both, in subjects who had acute, "severe" OM. The efficacy of antibiotic compared with placebo was investigated in subjects judged to have acute, "nonsevere" OM.[12] Enrollment criteria were based on an otalgia scoring system that took into account estimated parental anxiety and reliability. Each hour of otalgia or apparent discomfort (ear pulling or irritability in infants) rated as mild, moderate, or severe was assigned 1, 3, or 12 points, respectively. An episode of AOM was classified as "severe" if the subject's temperature had reached 39°C orally or 39.5°C rectally in the 24-hour period before presentation or if the child attained an otalgia point score equal to or greater than

Table 8-1 Classification of Otitis Media and its Complications and Sequelae

1 Acute OM

2 Otitis media with effusion
   2.1 acute (short duration)
   2.2 subacute
   2.3 chronic

3 Eustachian tube dysfunction

4 Intratemporal (extracranial) complications and sequelae
   4.1 hearing loss
      4.1.1 conductive
      4.1.2 sensorineural
   4.2 perforation of tympanic membrane
      4.2.1 acute perforation
         4.2.1.1 without otitis media
         4.2.1.2 with OM (AOM with perforation)
            4.2.1.2.1 without otorrhea
            4.2.1.2.2. with otorrhea
      4.2.2 chronic perforation
         4.2.2.1 without OM
         4.2.2.2 with OM
            4.2.2.2.1 AOM
               4.2.2.2.1.1 without otorrhea
               4.2.2.2.1.2 with otorrhea
            4.2.2.2.2 chronic OM (and mastoiditis)
            (CSOM)
               4.2.2.2.2.1 without otorrhea
               4.2.2.2.2.2 with otorrhea
   4.3 mastoiditis
      4.3.1 acute
         4.3.1.1 acute mastoiditis without periosteitis/ osteitis
         4.3.1.2 acute mastoiditis with periosteitis
         4.3.1.3 acute mastoiditis with osteitis
            4.3.1.3.1 without subperiosteal abscess
            4.3.1.3.2 with subperiosteal abscess
      4.3.2 subacute
      4.3.3 chronic
         4.3.3.1 without CSOM
         4.3.3.2 with CSOM
   4.4 petrositis
      4.4.1 acute
      4.4.2 chronic

   4.5 labyrinthitis
      4.5.1 acute
         4.5.1.1 serous
            4.5.1.1.1 localized (circumscribed)
            4.5.1.1.2 generalized
         4.5.1.2 suppurative
            4.5.1.2.1 localized
            4.5.1.2.2 generalized
      4.5.2 chronic
         4.5.2.1 labyrinthine sclerosis
   4.6 facial paralysis
      4.6.1 acute
      4.6.2 chronic
   4.7 external otitis
      4.7.1 acute
      4.7.2 chronic
   4.8 atelectasis of the middle ear
      4.8.1 localized
         4.8.1.1 without retraction pocket
         4.8.1.2 with retraction pocket
      4.8.2 generalized
   4.9 adhesive OM
   4.10 cholesteatoma
      4.10.1 without infection
      4.10.2 with infection
         4.10.1.1 acute
            4.10.1.1.1 without otorrhea
            4.10.1.1.2 with otorrhea
         4.10.1.2 chronic (cholesteatoma with CSOM)
            4.10.1.2.1 without otorrhea
            4.10.1.2.2 with otorrhea
   4.11 tympanosclerosis
   4.12 cholesterol granuloma
   4.13 ossicular discontinuity
   4.14 ossicular fixation

5 Intracranial complications
   5.1 meningitis
   5.2 extradural abscess
   5.3 subdural empyema
   5.4 focal otitic encephalitis
   5.5 brain abscess
   5.6 dural sinus thrombosis
   5.7 otitic hydrocephalus

AOM = acute otitis media; CSOM = chronic suppurative otitis media; OM = otitis media

12 points. Episodes of AOM not meeting these criteria were classified as "nonsevere."

The following grading can be used:

- *Acute severe otitis media:* presence of moderate-to-severe otalgia, or fever equal to or higher than 39°C orally or 39.5°C rectally, or both.
- *Acute nonsevere otitis media:* mild otalgia and fever less than 39°C orally or 39.5°C rectally, or no fever present.

In the earliest stage of AOM, only inflammation of the mucous membrane and tympanic membrane of the middle ear will be present without a MEE, that is, *acute otitis media without effusion.* Pneumatic otoscopy may reveal only myringitis in the appearance of the tympanic membrane, in which there is usually erythema and opacification of the eardrum but relatively normal mobility in response to applied positive and negative pressure. Blebs or bullae may be present when the disease is acute, and positive pressure may be present within the middle ear; positive middle ear pressure can be visualized with the pneumatic otoscope or identified by tympanometry. Children who have functioning tympanostomy tubes in place may present to their physician very early at the acute onset of fever and otalgia and with an erythematous tympanic membrane but no otorrhea.

Evidence for the existence of this type of OM, which may also be chronic, has been provided by examining histopathologic specimens of temporal bone.[13, 14] The absence of a MEE when a tympanocentesis is performed in the presence of AOM—the child is symptomatic and tympanic membrane is thick and opaque—has provided clinical proof that this condition exists in certain cases, especially when pathogenic bacteria are isolated following irrigation and aspiration of the middle ear with non-bactericidal saline.

Persistent Middle Ear Effusion

The term *persistent middle ear effusion* can be used to describe an asymptomatic MEE persisting for weeks to months following the onset of AOM. It should be defined, however, since this stage of AOM is clinically and pathologically indistinguishable from OME.

OTITIS MEDIA WITH EFFUSION

There are many synonyms for a relatively asymptomatic effusion developing in the middle ear, such as secretary, nonsuppurative, or serous OM, but the most acceptable term is *otitis media with effusion.* Because the effusion may be serous (transudate), the term "secretory" may not be correct in all cases. The term "nonsuppurative" may not always be correct as asymptomatic MEE often contains bacteria and may even be purulent.[15–17] The term "serous otitis media" has been used if an amber or bluish effusion can be visualized through a translucent tympanic membrane but is not recommended. Also, the most frequent otoscopic finding is opacification of the tympanic membrane, which prevents the above assessments of effusion type.

Pneumatic otoscopy frequently reveals either a retracted or convex tympanic membrane with impaired mobility. Fullness or bulging may be visualized in some patients. An air-fluid level, bubbles, or both may be observed through a translucent tympanic membrane. The most important distinction between OME and AOM is that the signs and symptoms of acute infection (eg, otalgia and fever) are lacking in the former. Hearing loss is usually present in both conditions.

Grading System Based on Severity and Duration

As with AOM, there may be an advantage to grading OME according to severity because the natural history, effect of treatment, or both, may vary. One system proposes treating young children who have chronic OME associated with a bilateral hearing loss of 20 dB hearing threshold or worse in the better-hearing ear. Children who have better hearing, a unilateral effusion, or both, would be candidates for observation.[4] An alternative grading method is to use a tympanometric pattern classification. For example, patients showing a flat pattern would be considered to have a more severe case than those showing any degree of gradient. Otitis media with effusion could also be graded according to otoscopic appearance. For example, patients with a completely opaque tympanic membrane that is immobile to pneumatic otoscopy would be considered to have a more severe case than those with a tympanic membrane that is translucent and mobile to pneumatic otoscopy, with bubbles, an air-fluid level, or both, visible through the eardrum.

The following staging system distinguishes among mild, moderate, and severe, on the basis of one or more of otoscopic appearance, tympanometric patterns, or hearing thresholds as well as duration (not severity) of the effusion. Acute would be less than 3 weeks, subacute 3 weeks to 3 months, and chronic longer than 3 months:

1. Acute mild, moderate, or severe OME
2. Subacute mild, moderate, or severe OME
3. Chronic mild, moderate, or severe OME

EUSTACHIAN TUBE DYSFUNCTION

Eustachian tube dysfunction is a middle ear disorder that can have symptoms similar to OM, such as hearing loss, otalgia, and tinnitus, but with no MEE. The dysfunction may be related to a Eustachian tube that is too closed (ie, obstructed) or too open (ie, patulous). The latter condition is most frequently associated with symptoms of autophony (see Chapter 11, "Eustachian Tube Function and Dysfunction").

Grading of Severity and Duration

The severity of this condition can be graded into those patients with mild, moderate, or severe symptoms on the basis of the frequency, duration, and severity of symptoms. The degree of disability caused by the symptoms, such as tinnitus, otalgia, autophony, disequilibrium or vertigo, and hearing loss are also considered, as is duration (acute, subacute, or chronic as delineated above in grading OME).

The following grading system can be used:
1. Acute mild, moderate, or severe Eustachian tube dysfunction
2. Subacute mild, moderate, or severe Eustachian tube dysfunction
3. Chronic mild, moderate, or severe Eustachian tube dysfunction

INTRATEMPORAL (EXTRACRANIAL) COMPLICATIONS AND SEQUELAE OF OTITIS MEDIA

The following intratemporal complications and sequelae are classified into complications and sequelae; some, however, may be both a complication and sequela, such as hearing loss. Another disease or disorder concurrent with OM is considered a complication, whereas a sequela of OM is a disease or disorder that follows, is a consequence of, or is caused by OM. Also, a complication or sequela may also cause another complication or sequela, for example, a cholesteatoma may cause facial paralysis.

Many of the complications and sequelae of OM can also be iatrogenic, such as those that may follow tympanostomy tube insertion, tympanoplasty, or tympanomastoidectomy. These can include tympanosclerosis, adhesive OM, ossicular discontinuity or fixation, or cholesteatoma, all of which, in turn, may cause conductive hearing loss.

Hearing Loss

Hearing loss is the most common complication and sequela of OM and can be conductive, sensorineural, or both. When conductive, the loss may be either transient or permanent. When sensorineural in origin, the impairment is usually permanent.

Conductive Hearing Loss

Fluctuating or persistent loss of hearing is present in most children who have MEE due to AOM or OME. It may be either mild or moderate, with the maximum loss being no greater than 60 dB. The loss is usually between 15 and 40 dB. When due to OME, there is an average loss of 27 dB.[18]

Hearing usually returns to normal thresholds when the MEE resolves. Permanent conductive hearing loss can occur, however, as a result of recurrent, acute or chronic inflammation due to adhesive OM, ossicular discontinuity, or fixation. Negative pressure in the ear, in the absence of MEE, can also be a cause of conductive loss.[19] Patients with Eustachian tube dysfunction and intermittent or persistent high negative pressure may have an associated conductive hearing impairment.

Although a debated subject, hearing loss caused by chronic and recurrent MEEs may be associated with delay or impairment of speech, language, and cognition in young children, which may or may not affect performance in school.[20–22]

Sensorineural Hearing Loss

Sensorineural hearing loss caused by OM may result from AOM, OME, or another complication or sequela of OM, such as chronic suppurative otitis media (CSOM). Sensorineural hearing loss can be mild, moderate, severe, or profound. Reversible sensorineural hearing impairment is generally attributed to the effect of increased tension and stiffness of the round window membrane. Permanent sensorineural hearing loss is most likely due to the spread of infection or products of inflammation through the round window membrane into the labyrinth, development of a perilymphatic fistula in the oval or round window, or a suppurative complication such as labyrinthitis.[23–29]

Perforation of Tympanic Membrane

Perforation of the tympanic membrane may be acute or chronic; OM may or may not be present; and, when it is, otorrhea may or may not be present. Classification of perforation should include the site, extent, and duration of the perforation. No classification exists that has received widespread acceptance. The following seems reasonable:
- *Site:* (1) pars tensa—anterosuperior, anteroinferior, posterosuperior, or posteroinferior quadrant; and (2) pars flaccida

- *Extent:* (pars tensa): (1) limited to one quadrant (less than 25%); (2) involving two or more quadrants but not total; and (3) total perforation, that is, all four quadrants
- *Duration:* (1) acute; and (2) chronic
- *Acute perforation* of the tympanic membrane is most commonly associated with OM (with or without otorrhea) but may also occur without OM. Otorrhea indicates OM when there is a perforation.

Acute perforations without OM most commonly follow acute perforation with OM; the middle ear inflammation resolves but the perforation persists. Such perforations will either spontaneously heal or progress to a chronic state. Although relatively uncommon compared with the above pathogenesis, a perforation of the tympanic membrane can occur in the absence of OM. This may result from penetrating trauma, as a complication of extreme changes in middle ear pressures (eg, barotrauma), or more rarely, longstanding severe atelectasis.

One of the most common complications of AOM is perforation of the tympanic membrane, accompanied by acute drainage (otorrhea) through the defect. This is known as *acute otitis media with perforation*. Also, an acute perforation can be present in which there is OM but no evidence of otorrhea (see Table 8-1). Acute otitis media with perforation was more frequently encountered prior to the widespread use of antimicrobial therapy. It is still prevalent in the developing countries where primary health care is inadequate.[30] An acute perforation can occur, however, as a complication of chronic OME, as has been reported in Australian Aborigines.[31]

When an attack of AOM is complicated by a perforation, usually accompanied by otorrhea, one of four outcomes is possible: resolution of the AOM and healing of the tympanic membrane defect; resolution of the AOM but the perforation becomes chronic; the perforation and OM persist to become chronic (ie, CSOM); or a suppurative complication of OM develops (Figure 8-1).

Chronic perforation occurs when an acute perforation of the tympanic membrane fails to heal after 3 months or more. It may be present with or without OM; the former condition may or may not be associated with otorrhea. Some clinicians have termed chronic perforation without otorrhea as "inactive" CSOM and chronic perforation with otorrhea as "active" CSOM.[32] This classification is not only confusing but is inappropriate in some cases, such as when there is a chronic perforation and the middle ear does not become infected. Grouping chronic perforations under the term "chronic otitis media" irrespective of the status of the middle ear should be avoided. The term is confusing and potentially misleading and should not be used.

When a chronic perforation is not associated with AOM or CSOM, it usually does not heal spontaneously. The middle ear is susceptible to AOM,

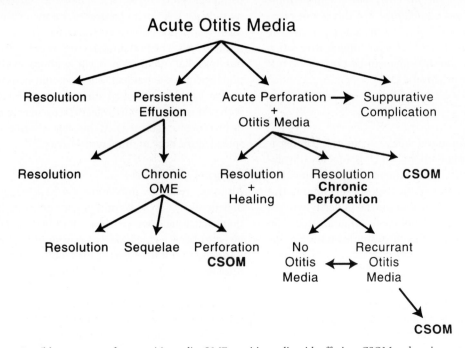

Figure 8-1   Possible outcomes of acute otitis media. OME = otitis media with effusion; CSOM = chronic suppurative otitis media.

however, and subsequently CSOM when a perforation is present. This can result from contamination of the middle ear through the external auditory canal or by reflux of nasopharyngeal secretions into the middle ear.

When a chronic perforation is associated with OM, the middle ear (and mastoid) infection may be either acute or chronic. The mastoid gas cell system is invariably involved when the inflammatory process is chronic. Otorrhea may or may not be evident when either AOM or CSOM is present (see Table 8-1). The OM, with or without otorrhea, will have one of the following four courses: (1) AOM occurs but resolves without progressing to the chronic stage; (2) recurrent AOM occurs but does not progress to the chronic stage; (3) AOM persists into the chronic stage (ie, CSOM); or (4) recurrent AOM and CSOM occur periodically over time.[30]

Chronic perforation with chronic otitis or, more commonly, *chronic suppurative otitis media* is a stage of ear disease in which there is chronic inflammation of the middle ear cleft (*middle ear cleft* is a term frequently used for the middle ear, Eustachian tube, and mastoid gas cells) and there is a chronic perforation of the tympanic membrane. Mastoiditis is invariably a part of the pathologic process. The condition has been called *chronic otitis media*, but this term can be confused with chronic otitis media with effusion, in which no perforation is present. It is also called *chronic suppurative otitis media and mastoiditis, chronic purulent otitis media*, and *chronic otomastoiditis*. The most descriptive term is *chronic otitis media with perforation, discharge, and mastoiditis*,[1] but this is not commonly used. When a cholesteatoma is also present, the term *cholesteatoma with chronic suppurative otitis media* is used; cholesteatoma can be present even if there is no acute or chronic OM.

Mastoiditis

Mastoiditis may or may not be a suppurative complication of OM, since both AOM and OME may also involve the mastoid. It may be acute, subacute, or chronic. The following classification of the stages of this suppurative complication is a revision based on an understanding of the pathogenesis and pathology of mastoiditis and on the more recent availability of computed tomographic (CT) scans.[33]

Acute Mastoiditis

Acute mastoiditis can be staged as follows:
1. Acute mastoiditis–without periosteitis/osteitis
2. Acute mastoiditis with periosteitis
3. Acute mastoid osteitis

Acute mastoiditis–without periosteitis/osteitis may be a natural extension and part of the pathologic process of acute middle ear infection. Most patients with AOM probably have extension of the middle ear disease into the mastoid gas cell system; this stage of acute mastoiditis, however, is not strictly a complication of OM. It can, nevertheless, be misinterpreted as a complication of OM, especially when CT scans are obtained for other reasons during an episode of OM, for example, following head trauma. Specific signs or symptoms of mastoid infection, such as protrusion of the pinna, postauricular swelling, tenderness, pain, or erythema, are not present in this most common type of mastoiditis. This stage of mastoiditis may either resolve, as it most commonly does, or progress to a true complication of OM, that is, *acute mastoiditis with periosteitis*. This, in turn, can progress to *acute mastoid osteitis*.

Acute mastoiditis with periosteitis may develop when infection within the mastoid spreads to the periosteum covering the mastoid process. The route of infection from the mastoid cells to the periosteum is by venous channels, usually the mastoid emissary vein. This stage of acute mastoiditis should not be confused with the presence of a subperiosteal abscess. Acute mastoiditis with periosteitis is characterized by erythema, mild swelling, and tenderness in the postauricular area. The pinna may or may not be displaced inferiorly and anteriorly, with loss of the postauricular crease. Sagging of the posterior external auditory canal is infrequently present.[9]

Acute mastoid osteitis has also been termed acute coalescent mastoiditis or acute surgical mastoiditis, but the pathologic process is osteitis. When infection within the mastoid gas cell system progresses, rarefying osteitis can cause destruction of the bony trabeculae that separate the mastoid cells. The postauricular area is usually involved, but mastoid osteitis can occur without evidence of postauricular involvement. The signs and symptoms are similar to those described above for acute mastoiditis with periosteitis; a subperiosteal abscess may or may not be present (see Table 8-1). At this stage, the infection can spread to the neck or intracranial cavity.[9, 34]

Subacute Mastoiditis

Although relatively uncommon, subacute mastoiditis may develop if an acute middle ear and mastoid infection fail to totally resolve within 10 to 14 days. This stage has also been termed *masked mastoiditis*. The classic signs and symptoms of acute mastoiditis, such as pinna displacement, postauricular erythema, or subperiosteal abscess, are usually absent, but otalgia with postauricular pain and fever may be present. Diagnosis is made by CT. In this stage, the infection in the mastoid can progress into another intratemporal complication or even an intracranial complication.

Many cases of subacute mastoiditis occur in patients with persistent signs and symptoms of AOM, who, if initially administered antimicrobial treatment, are considered "treatment failures." Tympanocentesis for diagnosis of the causative organism and myringotomy for drainage of the middle ear and mastoid in conjunction with culture-directed antimicrobial therapy will usually cure this condition without the need for mastoidectomy. If no MEE is present, the aditus ad antrum may be obstructed and the patient may require more aggressive management, such as mastoidectomy.

Chronic Mastoiditis

Chronic infection of the mastoid is usually due to CSOM with a chronic perforation of the tympanic membrane. Chronic mastoiditis may also occur in the absence of CSOM. Patients with relatively asymptomatic chronic OME frequently have some or all of the mastoid gas cell system involved in the chronic disease process. This is commonly visualized on CT scans of the temporal bones. Chronic infection may be present in the mastoid, even in the absence of middle ear disease, due to obstruction of the aditus ad antrum; the OM will resolve, but the disease in the mastoid will not. Symptoms can include low-grade fever and chronic otalgia and tenderness over the mastoid process.

Petrositis

When infection spreads from the middle ear and mastoid gas cells into the petrosal gas cells, the resulting complication is variously termed *apical petrositis*, *petrous apicitis*, or *petrositis*. This suppurative complication may be either acute or chronic and may result from AOM or chronic ear disease. When the latter is the cause, CSOM and/or cholesteatoma is usually responsible and can extend into the intracranial cavity or the neck.[35]

Labyrinthitis

When infection spreads from the middle ear, mastoid gas cells, or both, into the cochlear and vestibular apparatus, the resulting complication is termed *labyrinthitis*. The classification proposed by Schuknecht is appropriate, describing the complication as either serous labyrinthitis (also termed toxic labyrinthitis) or suppurative labyrinthitis.[36] Labyrinthitis may also be due to meningitis, which may or not be a complication of OM. Serous and suppurative labyrinthitis may be acute or chronic, or circumscribed or generalized, respectively. The end stage of chronic labyrinthitis is termed labyrinthine sclerosis.

Facial Paralysis

Facial paralysis caused by OM or one of its complications or sequelae may be acute or chronic. It may result from AOM or chronic middle ear and mastoid disease, such as cholesteatoma, CSOM, or both.[37] The grading system of the degree of injury to the face proposed by House and Brackmann is generally accepted and correlates with recovery (Table 8-2).[38]

External Otitis

Acute otitis media with perforation and otorrhea or CSOM can cause an infection of the external auditory canal termed *external otitis*; also termed infectious *eczematoid external otitis*. An infection in the mastoid may also erode the bone of the ear canal or the postauricular area, resulting in dermatitis. The skin of the ear canal is erythematous, edematous, filled with purulent drainage, and yellow-crusted plaques may be present. The organisms involved are usually the same as those found in a middle ear mastoid infection, but the flora of the external canal usually contribute to the infectious process.

Classification is based on duration, as follows:

- *Acute external otitis:* duration of the external auditory canal infection is less than 3 months
- *Chronic external otitis:* duration of the external auditory canal infection is 3 or more months

Atelectasis of the Middle Ear

Atelectasis of the middle ear is a sequela of OM, or Eustachian tube dysfunction, or both. Retraction or collapse of the tympanic membrane is characteristic of the condition. Collapse implies passivity (absence of high negative middle ear pressure), whereas retraction implies active pulling inward of the tympanic membrane, usually from negative middle ear pressure due to Eustachian tube dysfunction. Middle ear effusion is usually absent in atelectasis. The condition may be acute or chronic, localized (with or without a retraction pocket) or generalized, and mild, moderate, or severe.

Sadé has classified atelectasis on the basis of the position of the tympanic membrane, as follows:

- *Stage 1.* Slightly retracted
- *Stage 2.* Retracted onto the incus
- *Stage 3.* Retracted onto the promontory
- *Stage 4.* Adherent in the sinus tympani with accumulation of keratin (ie, cholesteatoma)[39]

This system does not provide mutually exclusive staging or include all anatomic sites or duration.

Table 8-2 House-Brackmann Facial Nerve Grading System[38]

Grade	Description	Characteristics
I	Normal	Normal facial function in all areas

II	Mild dysfunction	Slight weakness noticeable on close inspection; may have very slight synkinesis
		Normal symmetry and tone at rest
		Motion
		    Forehead: moderate to good function
		    Eye: complete closure with minimum effort
		    Mouth: slight asymmetry

III	Moderate dysfunction	Obvious, but not disfiguring, difference between two sides; noticeable but not severe synkinesis, contracture, or hemifacial spasm
		Normal symmetry and tone at rest
		Motion
		    Forehead: slight to moderate movement
		    Eye: complete closure with effort
		    Mouth: slightly weak with maximum effort

IV	Moderately severe dysfunction	Obvious weakness or disfiguring asymmetry
		Normal symmetry and tone at rest
		Motion
		    Forehead: none
		    Eye: incomplete closure
		    Mouth: asymmetric with maximum effort

V	Severe dysfunction	Only barely perceptible motion
		Asymmetry at rest
		Motion
		    Forehead: none
		    Eye: incomplete closure
		    Mouth: slight movement

VI	Total paralysis	No movement

Atelectasis can be classified, graded, and staged on the basis of extent and duration. Such a classification follows.

Localized Atelectasis

Localized atelectasis of the tympanic membrane may or may not be a retraction pocket because the depth of the retraction may be mild, moderate, or severe. When localized (with or without a retraction pocket), it may be found in one of the four quadrants of the pars tensa (anterosuperior, anteroinferior, posterosuperior, posteroinferior); in the pars flaccida; or in two or more of these anatomic sites. Localized atelectasis results from recurrent or chronic moderate-to-severe underpressure in the middle ear due to Eustachian tube dysfunction. *Localized atelectasis without retraction pocket* occurs when one or more, but not all, quadrants of the pars tensa are atelectatic. The atelectatic area can be mild, moderate, or severe, and acute or chronic. When severe, a retraction pocket is usually present.

Localized Atelectasis with Retraction Pocket

This is marked by a retraction pocket characterized by a localized area of atelectasis of the tympanic membrane. An indrawing of the membrane forms borders (edges or margins) most frequently at the site of an osseous anatomic structure (eg, the notch of Rivinus, scutum, or the malleus). The retraction pocket can be in one or more of the four quadrants of the pars tensa or in the pars flaccida. It may be acute or chronic and reversible or irreversible.

Sadé has classified posterosuperior retraction pockets on the basis of the condition of the pocket, as follows:
- *Stage 1.* Slightly retracted and self-cleansing
- *Stage 2.* Deeper and needing cleansing
- *Stage 3.* Deeper still and partly hidden, requiring excision
- *Stage 4.* So deep the pocket can only be removed by exposing the scutum and the rest of the framework (ie, retraction pocket cholesteatoma)[39]

Table 8-3 Staging of Retraction Pockets: Designate Site(s) on Tympanic Membrane

	Duration		Relation to ME Structures		Expands with Pressure	Extent Visualized and Self-Cleansing
	Acute	Chronic	Approximates	Adherent		
Stage	1a	1c	No	No	Yes	Yes
	2a	2c	Yes	No	Yes	Yes
	3a	3c	Yes	Yes	No	Yes
	4a	4c	Yes	Yes	No	No

ME = middle ear.

This staging system is helpful but does not include duration, presence or absence of adhesive changes, which relates to reversibility, or other sites.

Persistent and progressive localized atelectasis with retraction pocket can lead to sequelae commonly attributed to OM, such as hearing loss, ossicular chain discontinuity, and cholesteatoma.

The four stages of retraction pockets may be subclassified as *acute* (less than 3 months duration) or *chronic* (3 months or longer duration) (Table 8-3). Key factors affecting the progression of a retraction pocket from stage 1 to stage 4 are (1) *relation to middle ear structures*: does or does not approximate (touch) or is or is not adherent to one or more ossicles (ie, adhesive OM), including the incus, incudostapedial joint, stapes, head of malleus, and incudomalleolar joint (or other middle ear structure, such as promontory of the cochlea); (2) *expands with pressure*: entire pocket does or does not easily expand to the normal position when negative pressure is applied with a pneumatic otoscope or with the Bruening otoscope with a nonmagnifying lens under the otomicroscope, or when positive pressure is applied when the patient is anesthetized with nitrous oxide; (3) *extent visualized*: the entire pocket is visualized or parts are not seen even after pressure is applied. This is because the pocket extends beyond the visible portion of the middle ear space (eg, sinus tympani, facial recess, epitympanum, or medial to other parts of the tympanic membrane); and (4) *retraction pocket is self-cleansing and free of infection*: epithelial debris, crusting, or purulent material is or is not within the pocket.

Combining the above classifications, the following staging system may be used:

- *Stage 1a. Acute mild retraction pocket:* membrane of pocket neither approximates nor is adherent to any middle ear structure and expands with pressure. The entire contents of the pocket are readily visible, and it is self-cleansing.
- *Stage 1c. Chronic mild retraction pocket:* same as stage 1a but chronic.

- *Stage 2a. Acute moderate retraction pocket:* membrane of pocket is applied to one or more middle ear structures but is not adherent. The pocket expands with pressure, its extent can be visualized, and it is self-cleansing without infection.
- *Stage 2c. Chronic moderate retraction pocket:* same as stage 2a but chronic.
- *Stage 3a. Acute severe retraction pocket:* tympanic membrane is adherent to one or more middle ear structures, its extent is visualized, and it is without infection. It cannot be expanded with pressure.
- *Stage 3c. Chronic severe retraction pocket:* same as stage 3a but chronic.
- *Stage 4a. Acute retraction pocket cholesteatoma:* tympanic membrane is adherent to one or more middle ear structures. Its extent cannot be visualized, and it is not self-cleansing or free of infection.
- *Stage 4c. Chronic retraction pocket cholesteatoma:* same as stage 4a but chronic.

Generalized Atelectasis

This may be acute (duration less than 3 months) or chronic (3 months or longer). It involves all four quadrants of the pars tensa, with or without involvement of the pars flaccida and can be staged as follows:

- *Stage 1a. Acute generalized mild atelectasis:* middle ear aerated.
- *Stage 1c. Chronic generalized mild atelectasis:* same as stage 1a but chronic.
- *Stage 2a. Acute generalized severe atelectasis:* middle ear not aerated (ie, no apparent middle-ear space).
- *Stage 2c. Chronic generalized severe atelectasis:* same as stage 2a but chronic.

Adhesive Otitis Media

Adhesive OM is a result of healing following chronic inflammation of the middle ear and mastoid. The mucous membrane is thickened by proliferation of fibrous tissue, which frequently impairs movement of the ossicles to result in conductive hearing loss. The pathologic process is a proliferation of fibrous tissue within the middle ear and mastoid termed *fibrous sclerosis*.[36] When cystic spaces are present, the condition is called *fibrocystic sclerosis*; when there is new bone growth in the mastoid, it is termed *fibro-osseous sclerosis*.

In addition to fixation of the ossicles, adhesive OM may be the cause of ossicular discontinuity and conductive hearing loss due to rarefying ossicular osteitis, especially of the long process of the incus. Severe localized atelectasis (a retraction pocket) in the posterosuperior portion of the pars tensa of the tympanic membrane may cause adhesive changes to bind the tympanic membrane to the incus, stapes, and other surrounding middle ear structures, causing resorption of the ossicles. The development of a cholesteatoma then becomes possible.

Adhesive OM may be staged as follows:
- *Stage 1.* Adhesive OM within the middle ear, mastoid, or both, with no functional deficit secondary to the adhesive changes (ie, hearing loss). The middle ear remains aerated.
- *Stage 2.* Adhesive OM within the middle ear (with or without mastoid involvement) with mild hearing loss secondary to adhesive pathology. This may involve fixation, discontinuity, or both, of the ossicular chain (see "Ossicular Discontinuity" and "Ossicular Fixation," below), limited tympanic membrane compliance, or both. The middle ear remains aerated.
- *Stage 3.* Similar to stage 2 but with maximum conductive hearing loss secondary to ossicular pathology. No middle ear space is present. Both conditions are due to extensive adhesive OM.

Cholesteatoma

Cholesteatoma occurs when keratinizing stratified squamous epithelium accumulates in the middle ear or other pneumatized portions of the temporal bone. The term "aural" distinguishes this type of cholesteatoma from a similar pathologic entity occurring outside the temporal bone. The term "acquired" identifies it as a sequela of OM or related conditions (eg, retraction pocket of the tympanic membrane), distinct from aural congenital cholesteatomas. Although the term is a misnomer—keratoma is more consistent with the pathology—cholesteatoma is in common usage and is, therefore, accepted.[40]

Cholesteatoma may be classified as congenital or acquired.[41] The latter may be subclassified as a sequela of OM and certain related conditions or as a result of implantation (iatrogenic or due to trauma). Otitis media

may also be involved in the pathogenesis of congenital cholesteatoma. *Congenital cholesteatoma* is not a sequela of OM, whereas *acquired cholesteatoma* is. Despite a recent alternative acquired pathogenetic theory,[42] classically, *congenital cholesteatoma* develops as a congenital rest of epithelial tissue within the temporal bone in the absence of a defect in the tympanic membrane. Aural acquired cholesteatoma develops from a retraction pocket in the pars tensa or pars flaccida (see above), migration of epithelium through a pre-existing defect of the tympanic membrane (eg, perforation), or more rarely, metaplasia of the middle ear–mastoid mucous membrane. The middle ear, mastoid, or both may be involved in a cholesteatoma, which may or may not extend beyond the temporal bone.

Cholesteatoma may or may not be associated with OM and mastoiditis. When OM is present, the infection may be acute or chronic, and otorrhea may or may not be present. The cholesteatoma may be a cyst-like structure with no signs of infection. When present in association with chronic inflammation of the middle ear and mastoid, the condition is defined as *cholesteatoma with chronic suppurative otitis media.* Cholesteatoma may or may not be associated with CSOM. Cholesteatoma, in the absence of an associated infection, such as CSOM, should not be considered a form of chronic OM.

Aural acquired cholesteatoma can be staged under the following broad categories of presence and duration of OM, or its absence:
- *Cholesteatoma without infection:* cholesteatoma that is not associated with infection within the cholesteatoma or in any other portion of the middle ear cleft (can be further classified by site and extent).
- *Cholesteatoma with infection:* the infection may be acute (with or without otorrhea) or CSOM.

The following staging system can be used:
- *Stage 1.* Cholesteatoma is confined to the middle ear (hypo- or mesoepitympanum) with no erosion of ossicular chain
- *Stage 2.* Same as stage I but with erosion of one or more ossicles.
- *Stage 3.* Middle ear and mastoid gas cell system involved without erosion of ossicles.
- *Stage 4.* Same as stage 3 but with erosion of one or more ossicles.
- *Stage 5.* Extensive cholesteatoma of the middle ear, mastoid, and other portions of the temporal bone and not totally accessible to surgical removal (eg, medial to labyrinth), with one or more ossicles involved. Fistula of the labyrinth may or may not be present.
- *Stage 6.* Same as stage 5, but cholesteatoma extends beyond the temporal bone.

Cholesterol Granuloma

Cholesterol granuloma is a relatively uncommon sequela of OM. It has often been termed "idiopathic hemotympanum," but this is a misnomer, since there is no evidence of blood in the middle ear.[43] The blue coloration of the tympanic membrane is likely due to light reflected from the thick liquid (granuloma) within the middle ear. The tissue is composed of chronic granulations with foreign body giant cells, foam cells, and cholesterol crystals within the middle ear, mastoid, or both.[44]

Staging of cholesterol granuloma is based on the site and extent of the cholesterol granuloma, as follows:

- *Stage 1.* Cholesterol granuloma localized to one portion of the mastoid gas cell system or middle ear
- *Stage 2.* Cholesterol granuloma involving entire middle ear cleft

Tympanosclerosis

Tympanosclerosis is marked by whitish plaques in the tympanic membrane and nodular deposits in the submucosal layers of the middle ear. The pathologic process occurs in the lamina propria in the tympanic membrane and affects the basement membrane if within the middle ear. Hyalinization is followed in both sites by deposition of calcium and phosphate crystals. Conductive hearing loss may occur if the ossicles become embedded in the deposits. Tympanosclerosis is usually a sequela of chronic middle ear disease (chronic OME or chronic suppurative OM) but is also associated with trauma, such as following tympanostomy tube insertion. Conductive hearing loss secondary to tympanosclerosis involving only the tympanic membrane is rare, although scarring of the eardrum at the site of tympanostomy tube insertion is common.[45–47]

Tympanosclerosis can be staged as follows:

- *Stage 1.* Tympanosclerosis limited to the tympanic membrane (ie, little or no involvement of the middle ear) and the hearing is unaffected; the term *myringosclerosis* is also acceptable.

  This stage can be subclassified as follows: stage 1–1: tympanosclerosis limited to one quadrant of the pars tensa; stage 1–2: tympanosclerosis limited to two or more quadrants but not total involvement of the tympanic membrane; and stage 1–3: tympanic membrane is totally involved.

- *Stage 2.* Same as stage 1 (designate subclass) but hearing loss secondary to tympanosclerosis occurs.
- *Stage 3.* Tympanosclerosis involving the middle ear only with no hearing loss.
- *Stage 4.* Same as stage 3 but with hearing loss. This stage can be subclassified on the basis of the ossicle or

joint involved (see "Ossicular Fixation," below).

- *Stage 5.* Tympanosclerosis involving the tympanic membrane (designate subclass) and middle ear, with no hearing loss
- *Stage 6.* Extensive tympanosclerosis involving both the tympanic membrane (stage 1–3) and middle ear (designate ossicle or joint involved) with hearing loss.

Ossicular Discontinuity

Ossicular discontinuity, a sequela of OM and certain related conditions, is the result of rarefying osteitis caused by inflammation; a retraction pocket or cholesteatoma can also cause resorption of ossicles. The most commonly involved ossicle is the incus, its long process usually eroding to cause a disarticulation of the incudostapedial joint. The second most commonly eroded ossicle is the stapes, with the crural arches often initially involved. The malleus may also become eroded, but not as commonly as the incus and stapes.

Ossicular discontinuity can be classified on the basis of the site of pathology, as follows: (1) stapes crura; (2) incudostapedial joint; (3) incus; (4) incudomalleolar joint; and (5) malleus.

Ossicular Fixation

The ossicles can become fixed as a sequela of chronic middle ear inflammation, usually by fibrous tissue, caused by adhesive OM, tympanosclerosis, or both. Each of these has a staging system for extent and presence or absence of hearing loss. The ossicle itself or one or both of the joints (ie, incudostapedial or incudomallealar) may be fixed.

Ossicular fixation can be classified on the basis of the site of pathology, as follows: (1) stapes footplate; (2) incudostapedial joint; (3) incus; (4) incudomalleolar joint; and (5) malleus.

INTRACRANIAL COMPLICATIONS OF OTITIS MEDIA

There are seven intracranial suppurative complications of OM. These may also be caused by an intratemporal complication, such as mastoiditis or labyrinthitis, or one or more of the other complications of OM with the intracranial cavity.[48]

Meningitis

Meningitis is an inflammation of the meninges, which, when a suppurative complication of OM or certain related conditions (eg, labyrinthitis), is usually caused by a bacterium associated with infections of the middle ear, mastoid, or both. The infection may spread directly from the middle ear–mastoid through the dura and extend to the pia-arachnoid, causing generalized meningitis. Suppurative complications in an adjacent area, such as a subdural abscess, brain abscess, or lateral sinus thrombophlebitis, may also cause an inflammation of the meninges.

Extradural Abscess

Extradural abscess, also termed *epidural abscess*, is an infection that occurs between the dura of the brain and the cranial bone. It usually results from the destruction of bone adjacent to the dura by cholesteatoma, CSOM, or both. This occurs when granulation tissue and purulent material collect between the lateral aspect of the dura and the adjacent temporal bone. Dural granulation tissue within a bony defect is much more common than an actual accumulation of pus. When an abscess is present, a dural sinus thrombosis or, less commonly, a subdural or brain abscess, may also be present.

Subdural Empyema

Subdural empyema occurs when purulent material collects within the potential space between the dura externally and the arachnoid membrane internally. Since the pus collects in a preformed space, it is correctly termed empyema, rather than abscess. Subdural empyema may develop as a direct extension or, more rarely, by thrombophlebitis through venous channels.

Focal Otitic Encephalitis

Focal otitic encephalitis, also termed *cerebritis*, is a potential suppurative complication of AOM, cholesteatoma, or CSOM. It may also be a complication of one or more of the suppurative complications of these disorders, such as an extradural abscess or dural sinus thrombophlebitis, in which a focal area of the brain is edematous and inflamed. The signs and symptoms of this complication are similar to those associated with a brain abscess but suppuration within the brain is not present.

Brain Abscess

Otogenic *brain abscess* is a potential intracranial suppurative complication of cholesteatoma, CSOM, or both. It may also be caused by AOM or acute mastoiditis.[49] An intratemporal complication, such as labyrinthitis or apical petrositis, may be the focus or the abscess may follow development of an adjacent intracranial otogenic suppurative complication, such as lateral sinus thrombophlebitis or meningitis.

Brain abscesses can be classified on the basis of the (1) site in the brain (eg, temporal lobe or cerebellum); (2) number of lesions (solitary or multiple); and (3) definition (well-defined versus ill-defined [cerebritis]). This is related to management and outcome.

Dural Sinus Thrombosis

Lateral and *sigmoid sinus thrombosis* or *thrombophlebitis* arise from inflammation in the adjacent mastoid. The superior and petrosal dural sinuses are also intimately associated with the temporal bone but are rarely affected. This suppurative complication can occur as a result of AOM, an intratemporal complication (eg, acute mastoiditis or apical petrositis), or another intracranial complication of OM.

Otitic Hydrocephalus

Otitic hydrocephalus describes a complication of OM, in which there is increased intracranial pressure without abnormalities of cerebrospinal fluid. The pathogenesis of the syndrome is unknown, but because the ventricles are not dilated, the term "benign intracranial hypertension" also seems appropriate. The disease is usually associated with lateral sinus thrombosis.

CONCLUSION

This classification makes it clear that the clinician or investigator must define the specific disease or disorder being managed or studied. Universal consensus regarding the definitions, grading, and staging of many of these disease entities must be established. Table 8-4 presents pointers and pitfalls related to terminology, which will hopefully initiate discussion and, ultimately, consensus.

Table 8-4 Pointers and Pitfalls

1. When conducting and reporting studies of OM, the specific disease being investigated should be precisely defined.

2. Grading and staging of OM, its complications, and sequelae are important for studies and for clinical management.

3. The definition of *acute otitis media* is distinctly different from the definition of *otitis media with effusion*. This has clinical implications related to the need to treat or not treat and the incidence of complications and sequelae of each condition.

4. The term *otitis media with effusion* is preferable to other terms, such as secretary, serous, or nonsuppurative OM.

5. The term *middle ear effusion* does not distinguish between effusions due to AOM and effusions due to OME.

6. Despite the lack of a MEE, *Eustachian tube dysfunction* is a disorder of the ear with signs and symptoms similar to those present when there is an effusion in the middle ear.

7. Perforations of the tympanic membrane should be classified on the basis of site, extent, and duration.

8. The term *chronic otitis media* is confusing, potentially misleading, and should not be used. Some consider it to mean chronic OM with effusion, others CSOM, and others include cholesteatoma under this term.

9. The terms "inactive" and "active" CSOM are not recommended because the disease can be a chronic perforation with or without acute or chronic OM. *Chronic suppurative otitis media* means a chronic perforation with chronic OM.

10. In the absence of signs and symptoms of mastoid infection, an effusion in the mastoid visualized on CT does not necessarily indicate a need for mastoidectomy. The effusion may be the natural extension of disease in the middle ear, such as an AOM or OM with effusion.

11. The term *subacute mastoiditis* is preferable to "masked mastoiditis." The condition should not be confused with an attack of AOM that does not improve symptomatically despite antimicrobial therapy (ie, AOM treatment failure).

12. Such terminology as "coalescent mastoiditis" and acute "surgical" mastoiditis should not be used because they do not appropriately describe the pathology—especially to nonotolaryngologists—when acute mastoiditis with osteitis is present.

13. The grading system proposed by House and Brackmann is recommended when facial paralysis occurs as a complication of otitis media.[38]

14. An appropriate staging system for atelectasis of the middle ear should be related to the following factors: duration (acute versus chronic); localized versus generalized; and presence or absence of a retraction pocket.

15. An appropriate staging system for a retraction pocket should be related to the following conditions: whether or not it approximates or is adherent to middle ear structures; whether it expands with positive or negative pressure; whether its extent can be fully visualized; and whether it is self-cleansing and free of infection.

16. The term *cholesteatoma with chronic suppurative otitis media* is appropriate when there is chronic infection in the middle ear cleft but not when OM is absent.

17. Cholesteatoma should be staged related to the following conditions: extent; presence or absence of ossicular erosion (and number of ossicles); and whether or not the disease is completely amenable to surgical removal.

18. Sequelae, such as cholesterol granuloma, adhesive OM, and tympanosclerosis, should also be staged.

AOM = acute otitis media; CSOM = chronic suppurative otitis media; MEE = middle ear effusion; OM = otitis media.

REFERENCES

1. Senturia BH, Bluestone CD, Klein JO, et al. Report of the ad hoc committee on definition and classification of otitis media with effusion. Ann Otol Rhinol Laryngol 1980;89:3–4.
2. Bluestone CD. Definitions and classifications: state of the art. In: Lim DJ, Bluestone CD, Klein JO, Nelson JD, editors. Recent advances in otitis media with effusion. Proceedings of the Third International Symposium. Philadelphia (PA): BC Decker; 1984. p. 1–4.
3. Lim DJ, Bluestone CD, Klein JO, et al, editors. Recent advances in otitis media. Proceedings of the Fifth International Symposium. Hamilton (ON): Decker Periodicals; 1993.
4. Stool SE, Berg AO, Berman S, et al. Managing otitis media with effusion in young children. Quick reference guide for clinicians. Rockville (MD): Agency for Health Care Policy and Research, Public Health Service (US). Department of Health and Human Services; 1994 AHCPR Publication No. 94-0623.
5. Lim DL, Bluestone CD, Casselbrant ML, et al, editors. Recent advances in otitis media. Proceedings of the Sixth International Symposium. Hamilton (ON): BC Decker; 1996. p. 1–579.
6. Bluestone CD. Definitions, terminology, and classification. In: Rosenfeld RM, Bluestone CD, editors. Evidence-based otitis media. Hamilton (ON): BC Decker, 1999; p. 85–103.
7. Bluestone CD, Klein JO, editors. Otitis media in infants and children. 3rd ed. Philadelphia (PA): WB Saunders; 2001.
8. Bluestone CD, Gates GA, Klein JO, et al. Definitions, terminology, and classification of otitis media. Ann Otol Rhinol Laryngol 2002; III Suppl 188:8–18.
9. Goldstein NA, Casselbrant ML, Bluestone CD, Kurs-Lasky M. Intratemporal complications of acute otitis media in infants and children. Otolaryngol Head Neck Surg 1998;119:444–54.
10. Bluestone CD, Cantekin EI, Beery QC, et al. Functional eustachian tube obstruction in acquired cholesteatoma and related conditions. In: McCabe BF, Sadé J, Abramson M, editors. Eustachian tube, cholesteatoma. First International Congress. Birmingham (AL): Aesculapius; 1977.
11. Bluestone CD, Cantekin EI, Beery QC, Stool SE. Function of the eustachian tube related to surgical management of acquired aural cholesteatoma in children. Laryngoscope 1978;88:1155–64.
12. Kaleida PH, Casselbrant ML, Rockette HE, et al. Amoxicillin or myringotomy or both for acute otitis media: results of a randomized clinical trial. Pediatrics 1991;87:466–74.
13. Paparella MM, Goycoolea MV, Meyerhoff WL. Inner ear pathology and otitis media: a review. Ann Otol Rhinol Laryngol 1980;89:249–53.
14. Paparella MM, Schachern P, daCosta SS, et al. Clinical and pathologic correlates of silent (subclinical) otitis media. In: Lim DJ, Bluestone CD, Klein JO, et al, editors. Recent Advances in Otitis Media—Proceedings from the Fifth International Symposium. Hamilton (ON): BC Decker; 1993. p. 319–22.
15. Post JC, Preston RA, Aul JJ, et al. Molecular analysis of bacterial pathogens in otitis media with effusion. JAMA 1995;273:1598–604.
16. Rayner MG, Zhang Y, Gorry MC, et al. Evidence of bacterial metabolic activity in culture-negative otitis media with effusion. JAMA 1998;279:296–9.
17. Riding KH, Bluestone CD, Michaels RH, et al. Microbiology of recurrent and chronic otitis media with effusion. J Pediatr 1978;93:739–43.
18. Fria TJ, Cantekin EI, Eichler JA. Hearing acuity of children with otitis media with effusion. Arch Otolaryngol Head Neck Surg 1985;111:10–6.
19. Finkelstein Y, Zohar Y, Talmi YP, et al. Effects of acute negative middle car pressure on hearing. Acta Otolaryngol (Stockh) 1992;112:88–95.
20. Paradise JL. Long-term effects of short-term hearing loss: menace or myth? Pediatrics 1983;71:647–8.
21. Teele DW, Klein JO, Rosner B. Otitis media with effusion during the first three years of life and development of speech and language. Pediatrics 1984;74:282–7.
22. Paradise JL, Feldman HM, Campbell TF, et al. Effect of early or delayed insertion of tympanostomy tubes for persistent otitis media on developmental outcomes at age of three years. New Engl J Med 2001;344:1179–87.
23. Morizono T, Giebink GS, Paparella MM, et al. Sensorineural hearing loss in experimental purulent otitis media due to Streptococcus pneumoniae. Arch Otolaryngol 1985;111:794–8.
24. Paparella MM, Oda M, Hiraide F, Brady D. Pathology of sensorineural hearing loss in otitis media. Ann Otol Rhinol Laryngol 1972;81:632–47.
25. Johansson U, Hellstrom S, Anniko M. Round window membrane in serous and purulent otitis media. Structural study in the rat. Ann Otol Rhinol Laryngol 1993;102:227–35.
26. Lundman L, Juhn SK, Bagger-Sjoback D, Svanborg C. Permeability of the normal round window membrane to Haemophilus influenzae type b endotoxin. Acta Otolaryngol (Stockh) 1992;112:524–9.
27. Grundfast KM, Bluestone CD. Sudden or fluctuating hearing loss and vertigo in children due to perilymph fistula. Ann Otol Rhinol Laryngol 1978;87:761–71.
28. Supance JS, Bluestone CD. Perilymph fistulas in infants and children. Otolaryngol Head Neck Surg 1983;91:663–71.
29. Weber PC, Perez BA, Bluestone CD. Congenital perilymphatic fistula and associated middle-ear abnormalities. Laryngoscope 1993;103:160–4.
30. Bluestone CD. Epidemiology and pathogenesis of chronic suppurative otitis media: implications for prevention and treatment. Int J Pediatr Otorhinolaryngol 1998a;42:207–23.
31. Boswell JB, Nienhuys TG. Patterns of persistent otitis media in the first year of life in aboriginal and non-aboriginal Australian infants. Ann Otol Rhinol Laryngol 1996;105:893–900.

32. Browning GG, Gatehouse D. The prevalence of middle-ear disease in the adult British population. Clin Otolaryngol 1992;17:317–21.

33. Bluestone CD. Acute and chronic mastoiditis and chronic suppurative otitis media. Semin Pediatr Infect Dis 1998;9:12–26.

34. Marioni G, de Filippis C, Tregnaghi A, et al. Bezold's abscess in children: case report and review of the literature. Int J Pediatr Otorhinolaryngol 2001;61:173–7.

35. Somers TJ, De Foer B, Govaerts P, et al. Chronic petrous apicitis with pericarotid extension into the neck in a child. Ann Otol Rhinol Laryngol 2001;110:988–91.

36. Schuknecht HF. Pathology of the ear. 2nd ed. Philadelphia (PA): Lea & Febiger; 1993. p. 191–234.

37. Shapiro NM, Schaitken BM, May M. Facial paralysis in children. In: Bluestone CD, Stool SE, Kenna MA, editors. Pediatric otolaryngology. 3rd ed. Philadelphia (PA): WB Saunders; 1996. p. 325–6.

38. House JW, Brackmann DE. Facial nerve grading system. Otolaryngol Head Neck Surg 1985;93:146–7.

39. Sadé J. Treatment of cholesteatoma and retraction pockets. Eur Arch Otorhinolaryngol 1993;250:193–9.

40. Ferlito A. A review of the definition, terminology, and pathology of aural cholesteatoma. J Laryngol Otol 1993;107:483–8.

41. Fisch U. Tympanoplasty and mastoidectomy. New York (NY): Theime; 1994.

42. Tos M. A new pathogenesis of mesotympanic (congenital) cholesteatoma. Laryngoscope 2000:110; 1890–7.

43. Sadé J, Halevy A, Klajman A, Mualem T. Cholesterol granuloma. Acta Otolaryngol (Stockh) 1980;89: 233–9.

44. Miura M, Sando I, Orita Y, Hirsch BE. Histopathological study of the temporal bones and eustachian tubes in children with cholesterol granuloma. Ann Otol Rhinol Laryngol 2002;111:609–15.

45. Kokko E. Chronic secretary otitis media in children: a clinical study. Acta Otolaryngol (Stockh) 1974;327 Suppl:1–44.

46. Lildholdt T. Ventilation in secretary otitis media. A randomized, controlled study of the course, the complications, and the sequelae of ventilation tubes. Acta Otolaryngol (Stockh) 1983;398:5–28.

47. Asiri S, Hasham A, Anazy FA, et al. Tympanosclerosis: review of literature and incidence among patients with middle-ear infection. J Laryngol Otol 1999:113: 1076–80.

48. Go C, Bernstein JM, de Jong AL, et al. Intracranial complications of acute mastoiditis. Int J Pediatr Otorhinolaryngol 2000;52:143–8.

49. Sennaroglu L, Sozeri B. Otogenic brain abscess: review of 41 cases. Otolaryngol Head Neck Surg 2000; 123:751–5.

CHAPTER 9

Diagnosis

Linda H. Carlson, MS, CPNP, and Randal D. Carlson, PhD

*In all affairs it's a healthy thing now and then to hang a question mark
on the things you have long taken for granted.*
Bertrand Russell

OBJECTIVES

On completing this chapter, the reader will be able to
1. Discuss the importance of proper diagnosis as the basis of management of otitis media (OM).
2. Describe the significance of symptoms related to acute otitis media (AOM).
3. Explain the use of pneumatic otoscopy and recognize its benefits and deficiencies.
4. Describe the use of tympanometry as an adjunct to diagnosis.
5. Determine the appropriate use of audiometry in diagnosis.
6. Discuss acoustic reflectometry from current literature.

Proper diagnosis of OM is critically important in managing this frequently occurring childhood disorder. As concern for the appropriate use of antibiotics continues to grow, correct diagnosis is being advocated as a means of addressing the problem of resistant organisms.[1,2] The Agency for Healthcare Research and Quality (AHRQ) evidence-based reports on AOM and otitis media with effusion (OME) emphasize appropriate diagnosis.[3] Diagnosis was one of four key questions addressed in the AHRQ evidence-based report on OME.[4]

Diagnosis is often not easily accomplished, and physicians have reported concerns about diagnostic certainty. Questionnaire results from general practitioners involved in the International Primary Care Network, which consists of several countries, including Australia, Belgium, the United Kingdom, Israel, The Netherlands, New Zealand, Canada, Switzerland, and the United States, showed self-reported diagnostic uncertainty for AOM. The diagnostic certainty was inversely related to the age of the child: 58% for ages 0 to 12 months, 66% for ages 13 to 30 months, and 73% for ages 31 months or older.[5]

A more recent study consisting of a questionnaire mailed to a convenience sample of private offices, clinics, and emergency departments included data from physicians (63%) and nurse practitioners and physician assistants (37% combined). The AHRQ criteria for accurate diagnosis of AOM as well as self-reported certainty were discussed in the findings. Although the survey response rate was low (27%), clinicians reported diagnostic certainty for 90% of the episodes (122 of 135) but only 70% (95 of 135) fulfilled the diagnostic criteria for AOM stated in the AHRQ report.[6]

Although the correct diagnosis of OM has been repeatedly stressed,[1,7] formalized diagnostic training is often lacking in residency and professional training programs. In a recent mail survey of accredited American and Canadian pediatric residency training programs with a response rate of 64% (144 of 224), only 59% had some type of formalized education in diagnosing and managing OM. These curricula primarily consisted of lectures by general pediatricians fewer than three times per year.[8] There were no studies discussing the types of training in otoscopy in family practice, nurse-practitioner, and physician-assistant educational programs. Assessment of these programs warrants further investigation.

The presumptive diagnosis of OM is usually made by the use of an otoscope with an insufflator and may be confirmed by tympanocentesis or myringotomy. Diagnosis by the subjective method of pneumatic otoscopy may be aided by the use of objective measures, including tympanometry and audiometry, which have been recommended as adjuncts to diagnosis.[7] Another objective measure, the acoustic reflectometer, was redesigned in the late 1990s.

In spite of the available instrumentation, diagnosis often remains a challenge. Correct diagnosis requires an accurate understanding of both the subjective and objective measures. Information from evidence-based literature will be presented in this text. Expert opinion will be provided in cases where evidence gaps exist.

SYMPTOMS

Much has been written about the symptoms associated with OM, but objective evidence is scarce. The focus of this section will be AOM, because it is the condition with the most evidence.

Earache has often been described as a common and specific symptom of AOM. This is not clearly stated by the literature, however. Varying criteria to define ear pain and imprecise methods of data collection make it difficult to interpret results. Much of the data available has been obtained through practice survey questionnaires and reported in descriptive studies that may not be reliable or valid. Ear pain can be reported by the patient if the child is older than 2 years of age but can be difficult to assess in a child younger than 2 years.

In a descriptive study of 313 children with 335 episodes of AOM in a private pediatric practice, pneumatic otoscopy was used to confirm diagnosis and a parent questionnaire provided information on symptoms.[9] Earache in children younger than 2 years was evidenced by pain, fussiness, sleep problems, and additional areas that were not described. Earache was reported in 83% of episodes, significantly higher in children older than 2 years versus younger children (93% versus 75%, $p < .001$). While the lack of consistency in defining this symptom adds to confusion about its occurrence in children with AOM, best evidence suggests that ear pain most likely occurs in 50 to 75% of children with the disease and that reports of ear pain are more common in children over the age of 2 years.[9–11] Ear pain can be a positive predictor of AOM, but its absence does not rule out the disease.

Fever is another symptom frequently discussed in relation to AOM. Reported incidences of fever associated with AOM have ranged from 21% ($N = 335$)[9] to 30% ($N = 811$)[12] to 45.5% ($N = 354$).[11] Although fever occurs in approximately one-half or less of the children in these studies, it is not a good predictor of AOM. The importance of fever was discussed in a recent study, and the question of whether to use fever as an appropriate indication to begin treatment immediately compared with a period of watchful waiting of up to 3 days of this symptom is absent.[13] Further studies are needed in this area.

Sensitivity, specificity, positive predictive value, and negative predictive value of several symptoms commonly associated with AOM were examined in two studies (Table 9-1).[11,14] *Sensitivity* can be defined as the probability that the symptom is present when the

child does in fact have AOM; *specificity* is the probability that the symptom is absent when the child does not have AOM; *positive predictive value* is the probability that the child has AOM when the symptom is present; and *negative predictive value* is the probability that the child does not have AOM when the symptom is absent. Although none of the symptoms or signs in Table 9-1 is optimal for AOM diagnosis, earache is the best single predictor.

AOM is often preceded by or occurs concurrently with upper respiratory infection.[10,15–17] Additional symptoms that have been described in AOM include loss of appetite, vomiting, diarrhea, and increased fatigue. These are vague symptoms, however, which in the majority of circumstances have not been analyzed according to strict criteria. Since these symptoms may occur in a variety of conditions, they should not be used as criteria in diagnosing AOM or OME.

Dizziness has also been described as occurring in some children with OM. Casselbrant and colleagues[18] demonstrated that children with OME had a significantly higher velocity of postural sway than normal children. This has been frequently reported anecdotally, and many clinicians have noted improvement in balance after myringotomy and tympanostomy tube placement.

Most of the symptoms associated with AOM are vague and diagnosis should never be made on the basis of these alone. Ear pain traditionally thought to be specific to AOM may occur in children without AOM because of teething, viral myringitis, and external otitis or as referred pain from tonsillitis or temporomandibular disorders. Therefore, it is important to conduct a thorough examination of the ear using subjective/objective instruments to confirm the presence or absence of the disease.

PNEUMATIC OTOSCOPY

The vast majority of authors and clinicians advocate pneumatic otoscopy as a subjective measure of tympanic membrane (TM) and middle ear status. There is a shortage of evidence-based literature regarding what has commonly been believed to be the most important and readily available tool. The strong recommendation for the use of pneumatic otoscopy from The Agency for Health Care Policy and Research, *Otitis Media with Effusion in Young Children: Clinical Practice Guideline No. 12*, was based on limited scientific evidence.[7] The AHRQ evidence report on OME, however, recently reaffirmed pneumatic otoscopy as the best diagnostic option for most clinicians.[3] Among the nine methods reviewed, pneumatic otoscopy offered the optimal balance of sensitivity (94%) and specificity (80%).

Table 9-1 Symptoms Related to the Presence or Absence of AOM

Study	Symptom	Age < 2 years				Age ≥ 2 years				All			
		SNS	SPC	PPV	NPV	SNS	SPC	PPV	NPV	SNS	SPC	PPV	NPV
			N =	150			N =	204			N =	354	
Niemela[11]													
	Earache	36	94	92	45	72	76	72	75	54	82	78	60
	Rubbing	59	74	80	51	25	94	77	59	42	87	79	56
	Crying	71	43	69	45	39	83	66	61	55	69	68	57
	Rhinitis	73	52	73	52	78	39	52	67	75	57	61	60
	Coughing	41	48	58	31	54	56	46	52	47	55	50	42
	Fever	45	50	61	34	36	52	37	46	40	52	48	41
			N = 141				N = 161				N = 302		
Heikkinen[14]													
	Earache									60	92	83	78
	Restless									64	51	46	68
	Rhinitis									96	8	41	74
	Cough									83	17	40	61
	Fever									69	23	38	53

AOM = acute otitis media; NPV = negative predictive value; PPV = positive predictive value; restless = restless sleeping; SNS = sensitivity; SPC = specificity; tugging = tugging at ears.

The otoscope has been described in detail in only one narrative article.[19] The handle often has a 2.5- or 3.5-volt rechargeable battery in it, or the unit operates from a wall transformer. Some pocket models use disposable batteries. The head contains a two- or three-power magnifying lens and a funnel-shaped disposable or reusable speculum. Nondisposable specula with an elastomer tip provide a better seal for performing insufflation, which is accomplished with a rubber insufflator bulb attached to the head of the otoscope.

Proper otoscopic examination requires a correctly functioning instrument. Optimal visualization of the TM requires 100 foot-candles of light output. Light output of 221 instruments in a variety of settings including private offices, hospitals, and emergency departments, was checked by Barriga and colleagues (Table 9-2).[20] Nearly 25% of the instruments did not meet the 100 foot-candle of light output criterion recommended. Bulbs were inadequate in some cases. In others, batteries were expired by as much as 5 years. Changing the bulb had more effect on increasing light output than changing the battery, with a mean difference of 32.1 versus 21.9 foot-candles for disposable batteries and 10.7 for rechargeable ones. This study highlights the importance of checking and properly maintaining equipment.

According to one manufacturer, the nickel cadmium rechargeable battery is guaranteed for 2 years, but it lasts much longer in most cases. This claim was substantiated by Barriga and coworkers.[20] The halogen bulb is designed to last for 25 to 30 hours of continuous clinical use. The xenon bulb used in a pocket-sized unit is reported by the manufacturer to last for 25 hours.

Clark and colleagues[21] studied the amount of pneumatic pressure used and frequency of the pulse pressure, but the sample was too small (N = 20) for inferential statistics. The pressure required to move a normal tympanic membrane ranged from 10 to 15 mm of water pressure. Conversely, the pressure needed to move the TM when a serous or purulent effusion was present was 40 and 160 mm, respectively. Although movement was not obtained in abnormal ears at 200 mm pressure, the examiners used pressures ranging from 70 to 500 mm.[21] Another study by a single observer demonstrated a range from 378 to 1,134 mm

Table 9-2 Light Output of Otoscopes*

Light Output (foot-candles)	Rating	Number of Otoscopes	Percentage
0–19	Not acceptable	6	3
20–49	Minimum to see landmarks	13	6
50–99	Minimum for color	29	13
≥ 100	Optimal	173	78
Total		221	100

*Data from Barriga F et al.[20]

pressure using the bulb and 378 to 729 mm using the mouthpiece.[22] Using both the bulb and the mouthpiece, pressures far in excess of those needed to move the normal TM were used. Health care practitioners report anecdotally that one of the reasons they do not use pneumatic otoscopy more frequently is that it causes pain or discomfort to the patient. These two studies suggest that pressure far exceeding that required to move the TM is responsible.

The earliest description of the systematic examination of the ear examination was published in 1909 by Adam Politzer.[23] Findings from otoscopic examinations have been defined in a variety of terms and confusion has ensued at times. The use of a mnemonic, "COMPLETES," published in 1997 provides a detailed method of observing and documenting otoscopic findings.[24] Although there is no objective evidence supporting the use of this mnemonic, it may prove useful in both teaching and clinical practice to ensure that a thorough examination has been completed. The mnemonic is detailed in Table 9-3.

The competency of the clinician in diagnosing AOM may vary, and the skill level may not be high. Several studies have shown the sensitivity, specificity, positive predictive value, and negative predictive value for otoscopists conducting the research. These data are important for the reader evaluating study results. Results of several studies reporting the accuracy of otoscopists using pneumatic otoscopy versus middle ear effusion (MEE) confirmed at myringotomy are presented in Table 9-4.[25–29]

Few institutions have reported carrying out a program to assess the accuracy of otoscopists. One validation program was conducted over a 10-year period at a large children's hospital extensively involved in research. Participants in the program included otolaryngologists, pediatricians, and nurse practitioners. Most participants

Table 9-3 COMPLETES: Mnemonic for Otoscopic Examinations

Color	Gray, white, yellow, amber, pink, red, blue
Other conditions	Fluid level, bubbles, perforation, retraction pocket, atrophic area, otorrhea, bullae, tympanosclerosis, cholesteatoma
Mobility	4+, 3+, 2+, 1+
Position	Neutral, bulging, retracted
Lighting	Battery charged, halogen or bulb
Entire surface	Visualize all quadrants: anterosuperior, posterosuperior, anteroinferior, posteroinferior
Translucency	Translucent or opaque
External auditory canal and auricle	Inflammation, foreign body, displacement, deformed
Seal	Appropriate sized speculum Airtight pneumatic system

Adapted from Kaleida PH.[24]

Table 9-4 Accuracy of Otoscopists Using Pneumatic Otoscopy Compared with MEE at Myringotomy

Study	Observer*	Sensitivity %	Specificity %	PPV %	NPV %
Cantekin[25]	A (370 ears)	97	81	90	94
Cantekin[25]	B (350 ears)	88	81	86	83
Finitzo[26]	C (163 ears)	93	56	84	78
Karma[27]	D (593 ears)	99	90	96	97
Karma[27]	E (499 ears)	94	71	88	83
Nozza[28]	F (249 ears)	85	71	78	79
Paradise[29]	G (213 ears)	99	75	88	97

MEE = middle ear effusion; NPV = negative predictive value; PPV = positive predictive value.
*Observers A, B, and C were pediatric otolaryngologists; observer D was an otolaryngologist; observer F was a pediatric nurse practitioner; observers E and G were pediatricians.

were required to examine a minimum of 100 ears of children in the same day surgical unit prior to myringotomy with or without tubes. At the completion of the validation process, mean sensitivity scores ranged from 87 to 88% and mean specificity scores from 73 to 75%.[30]

Another validation study was conducted in a medical center training program for otolaryngology–head and neck surgery residents (postgraduate year 2). Residents received both formalized didactic and clinical instructions. Children's ears were examined in the holding area of the ambulatory surgical center prior to myringotomy. Sensitivity scores ranged from 82 to 100% and specificity scores 70 to 86% during the second half of the study period.[31] Because of the time requirement and difficulty of setting up these types of validation programs, they are rarely carried out.

A recent study compared the otoscopic findings of pediatric residents with those of pediatric otolaryngologists (gold standard). Repeated observation and performance improved the residents' diagnostic skill, despite the lack of MEE at myringotomy.[32] Notwithstanding a lack of published scientific evidence, anecdotal reports suggest that the majority of health care providers learn otoscopy by trial and error and may not be properly trained. An option that could aid the practitioner in learning and assessing otoscopic findings is a videotape of TMs showing both normal and abnormal conditions, including TM mobility.[33] Attending educational workshop programs and internet resources are also ways of enhancing diagnostic skills.

The presence of cerumen, which may partially or completely obstruct the ear canal and TM, is a frequent source of frustration to those providing health care. Most studies do not report whether cerumen removal was attempted or performed, casting doubt on the reli-

ability of the reported diagnosis. Cerumen removal may not have been attempted because of resistance of the child, lack of time on the part of the provider, and concern about damaging the ear canal or TM. In one study, removing cerumen mechanically was required in 29% of children for adequate TM visualization.[34] Among infants aged 2 to 6 months of age, 70% required cerumen removal. Believing that AOM will cause the cerumen to become soft and sticky was not supported in this study and should serve as a reminder that cerumen removal enhances diagnostic accuracy.

Recommendations for preparing for pneumatic otoscopy are summarized in Table 9-5. These recommendations are based on available research as well as expert opinion. Achieving diagnostic competency and skill with the pneumatic otoscope should be a priority for all those who provide care to children with middle ear disease.

TYMPANOMETRY

Tympanometry has been an important adjunct to diagnosing OM for many years. It is an objective, quantitative method of assessing TM mobility and middle ear function. Tympanometry is defined as measuring acoustic immitance of the ear as a function of ear canal air pressure.[35] The procedure involves inserting a probe tone (standard frequency, 226 Hz, but multifrequency units are now available) into the ear canal and measuring the amount of sound energy reflected back. Prior to 1987, there was variability in instruments due to the lack of standards. In 1987, American National Standards Institute (ANSI) specifications were released.[36] While many studies have attempted to correlate tympano-

Table 9-5 Hints for Preparing for Pneumatic Otoscopy

1. Inspect otoscope to ensure proper functioning: battery fully charged (check expiration date), use halogen or xenon bulb, change as needed.

2. Check that pneumatic seal can be obtained with instrument by compressing insufflator bulb, placing finger over the tip, and releasing. If system is sealed, the bulb will stay compressed.

3. Use proper size speculum to obtain a seal.

4. Visually inspect auricle and posterior auricular area.

5. Remove cerumen, if present, to obtain clear view of entire tympanic membrane.

metric results with the presence or absence of MEE, evidence has been difficult to evaluate in light of the variations in classifications used.[7] Differing classifications include Jerger,[37] Paradise and colleagues,[29] and others.

The majority of studies have used a type B or C2 tympanogram curve to indicate MEE. Using these criteria, sensitivity and specificity of tympanometry compared with findings of MEE at myringotomy in a study sample scheduled for surgery are reported in Table 9-6.[38–44] These findings may differ from a more representative sample, that is those with a lower prevalence of OM. Of interest, the results obtained by the general practitioner using a screening tympanometer were similar to those obtained by the audiologist and a more sophisticated instrument. Use of a hand held tympanometer, however, may reduce accuracy compared with a professional unit.[4]

Tympanometry results have often been described as curve patterns (A, B, C1, C2). This system uses the following definitions: type A, peak pressure > -100 mm H_2O

(effusion in 3% of ears at myringotomy); type B, flat curve without an impedance minimum (effusion in 85 to 100%); type C1, pressure -100 to -199 mm H_2O (effusion in 17%); or type C2, pressure -200 to -400 mm H_2O (effusion in up to 55%).[45,46] The AHRQ evidence report for OME recently assessed the accuracy of tympanometry curves versus myringotomy for detecting MEE.[4] A type B tympanogram offered 81% sensitivity and 74% specificity compared with 94% sensitivity and 62% specificity for a type B/C2 tympanogram (eg, B or C2 curve).

Although tympanometric curve patterns are often cited, most experts prefer quantitative immittance variables. These variables are obtained directly from the tympanometer, thereby avoiding the need for interpretation. Five variables have been described[47]:

1. Static admittance (peak Y) is the measurement in acoustic millimhos (mmho) of the height of the admittance-magnitude tympanogram relative to the tail value.[47] It has also been defined as the peak compensated static acoustic admittance.[36] A mmho is

Table 9-6 Type B or Flat Tympanograms Compared with MEE at Myringotomy

Study	Instrument	Sensitivity %	Specificity %	PPV %	NPV %
Babonis[38] (220 ears)	Microtymp	78	82	84	76
Finitzo[26] (163 ears)	MacroScreening 610 Immitance Bridge	90	86	99	73
Kemaloglu[39] (300 ears)	Interacoustics AZ7 electroacoustic impedancemeter	96	92	92	96
Koivunen[40] (97 ears)	Microtymp	79	78	58	91
Orchik[41] (50 ears)	Madsen ZO-72	54	95	91	66
Ovesen[42] (393 ears)	Madsen ZS330	91	73	96	54
Toner[43] (222 ears)	Rexton Tymp 82	86	93	94	84
Watters[44] (955 ears)	Grayson Stadler GSI 133	91	79	93	72

MEE = middle ear effusion; NPV = negative predictive value; PPV = positive predictive value.

Table 9-7 ASHA Recommended Initial Tympanometric Screening Test Criteria

	Infants	One Year to School Age
Peak admittance (Y_{tm})	< 0.2 mmho	< 0.3 mmho
	OR	
Tympanometric width (TW)	> 235 daPa	> 200 daPa

Adapted from American Speech-Language-Hearing Association 1997.[48]
daPa = decaPaschal; mmho = millimho.

equivalent to cm³ at a frequency of 226 hz. This number has been used as the basis for categorizing the shape of tympanograms.[47]

2. Equivalent ear canal volume (Vec) is the estimate of the air volume between the front of the probe and the tympanic membrane. Ear canal volume outside the range of 0.3 to 0.9 cm in children between the ages of 1 and 7 years can be an indication of a perforation of the TM or a patent tympanostomy tube.[48]

3. Tympanometric width (TW) is a gradient measurement increasingly considered to be a good indicator of middle ear disease.

4. Tympanometric peak pressure (TPP) indirectly measures the air pressure within the middle ear space. It is not believed to be a good indicator of middle ear disease and not recommended as a criterion for audiologic or medical referral.[47] As noted above, classifications of tympanometric curve patterns rely heavily on TPP.

5. Acoustic reflex (AR) is not recommended for referral criteria because of a large number of false positives in studies.

Two of the above variables have been included in the most recent American Speech-Language-Hearing Association (ASHA) guidelines[48]: peak compensated static acoustic admittance (Y_{tm} or peak Y) and the TW. Recommendations for initial tympanometric screening criteria are presented in Table 9-7 and the interim norms for tympanometric results in Table 9-8. Values in Table 9-7 are recommended for screening of children and may differ in children with a history of chronic MEE. In a study of 171 children (249 ears) scheduled for tympanostomy tube placement. Nozza and colleagues[28] suggested that for children with a history of chronic or recurrent OM, the criteria may need to be changed to Y_{tm} < 0.3 mmho or TW > 300 daPa. Results of this study are presented in Table 9-9.

AUDIOMETRY

MEE is associated with varying degrees of hearing loss.[7] While pure tone hearing screening is not recommended for screening children to identify those at risk for middle ear disease,[49] it may be useful in determining hearing loss in the child with OME. Conductive hearing loss has been documented in children with OME.[50,51] Concern about its effects on the development of the child contributed to the commissioning of the expert panel to develop national guidelines for the management of OME in children.[7]

Practitioners should consider using audiometry to detect hearing loss in cases where middle ear disease has been detected by other measures. Audiologic testing may include pure-tone threshold audiometry, speech reception threshold audiometry, speech awareness audiometry, behavioral observation audiometry, and auditory brainstem response (ABR). Audiometry will be discussed in further detail in Chapter 22.

Table 9-8 Suggested Interim Norms for Tympanometric Results*

	Peak Y (mmho or cm³)		TW (daPa)	
	Mean	90% Range	Mean	90% Range
Children	0.5	0.2–0.9	100	60–150
Adults	0.8	0.3–1.4	80	50–110

*Adapted from Margolis RN and Heller JW[49]; American Speech-Language-Hearing Association[48]; Appendix A, p. 22.
daPa = decaPaschal; mmho = millimho; TW = tympano metric width.

Table 9-9 Sensitivity, Specificity, and Predictive Values as Determined by Myringotomy*

Variable	Criterion	SNS %	SPC %	PPV %	NPV %
Y_{tm}	≤ 0.2	46	92	88	58
Peak Y	≤ 0.3	70	80	81	69
TW	> 200	89	47	67	78
	> 300	77	85	86	75

*Data reproduced from Nozza RJ et al.[28]

NPV = negative predictive value; PPV = positive predictive value; SNS = sensitivity; SPC = specificity.

ACOUSTIC REFLECTOMETRY

Acoustic reflectometry, another objective measure of middle ear status, was redesigned to include a spectral gradient analysis (SG-AR) and approved by the Food and Drug Administration (FDA) in 1997. The probability of fluid within the middle ear space is determined by measuring the response of the TM to a 1.8 to 4.4 kHz frequency sweep spectrum. There is no airtight seal required at the opening of the ear canal, which is a benefit of the procedure.[52] The sum of a sound tone is emitted into the ear canal and its reflection are analyzed by a microprocessor. Results are depicted as a curve on a graph. The slopes of this curve represent the spectral gradients, indicating probability of effusion within the middle ear space. Results in both the professional and parent model are reported according to the spectral gradient angle ranging from low (1) to high (5) risk of disease.

Prior to the redesign of the instrument, study results were conflicting and the national guidelines did not recommend its use.[7] Few studies have been published since

the instrument was redesigned to include spectral gradient analysis. In two studies comparing the results of SG-AR with the results of myringotomy, the samples were highly selective for MEE, since all subjects had been referred to the otolaryngology department for evaluation of chronic or frequent episodes of OM. In the first study, 58% of the children had MEE at the time of surgery.[53] The second study was even more selective, with 90% having MEE at surgery.[54] A third study intended to validate the instrument used SG-AR to evaluate the ears of a relatively healthy population. MEE was documented by validated otoscopists and reported in 20% of the sample. Only 5% of the subjects were age 6 to 11 months, 49% 1 to 5 years, 30% 6 to 10 years, and 15% 11 to 18 years.[55] As the incidence of OM is greatest in children 2 years or younger, it is impossible to generalize these results.

Sensitivity, specificity, positive predictive value, and negative predictive value, from all studies are listed in Table 9-10.[53–55] These results represent a highly selected sample. It is unknown what the results will be

Table 9-10 Comparison of Accoustic Reflectometry Risk Indication with MEE

Study	High-Risk Indication*	Low-Risk Indication	SNS %	SPC %	PPV %	NPV %
Barnett 1998[53]	Levels 2–5	Level 1	95	31	66	83
MEE by surgery	Level 5	Levels 1–4	38	93	88	52
(299 ears)						
Barnett 1998[53]	Levels 2–5	Level 1	94	30	77	67
MEE by pneumatic otoscopy	Level 5	Levels 1–4	36	94	93	37
(274 ears)						
Block 1998[55]	Levels 3–5	Levels 1–2	67	87	57	91
MEE by pneumatic otoscopy						
(870 ears)						
Block 1999[54]	Levels 3–5	Levels 1–2	86	75	96	42
MEE by tympanocentesis	Levels 2–5[†]	Level 1	93	25	89	36
(127 ears)	Level 5[†]	Levels 1–4	25	88	93	14

MEE = middle ear effusion; NPV = negative predictive value; PPV = positive predictive value; SNS = sensitivity; SPC = specificity.

*Level 1 > 95°, Level 2 = 70–95°, Level 3 = 60–69°, Level 4 = 49–59°, Level 5 < 49°.

[†]From data reported in Table 9-1 by Block SL et al.[54]

Table 9-11 Pointers and Pitfalls

1. Symptoms such as ear pain, fever, and rhinitis are frequently associated with AOM. However, lack of symptoms does not indicate absence of disease.

2. Pneumatic otoscopy is the recommended subjective method of diagnosis. The otoscope must be functioning properly, including adequate light source, sealed pneumatic system, and the correct amount of pressure delivered. Cerumen removal is imperative for proper visualization in nearly all cases.

3. Tympanometry is an important adjunct to pneumatic otoscopy in diagnosis of OM. Terminology should be standardized to avoid confusion among clinicians and researchers.

4. Not all tympanometers are created equal. ANSI standards were not available until 1987. Check to see that the machine is either validated or meets ANSI standards. Instruments must be calibrated on a regular basis according to the manufacturer's recommendation.

5. Audiometry can determinine the effects of OME on hearing levels but is not recommended for diagnosis.

6. Acoustic reflectometry with spectral gradient analysis warrants further investigation by researchers, with an emphasis on generalizable studies.

7. The development of additional technology to aid in diagnosis of AOM and OME is needed.

ANSI = American National Standards Institute; AOM = acute otitis media; OM = otitis media; OME = otitis media with effusion.

in a more generalizable sample. The instrument is handheld and fairly easy to use, making studies of larger samples feasible. The outcomes from a larger, not so highly selected sample, of children aged 2 years or younger should better guide practitioners. Adding spectral gradient analysis may show promise in improving the diagnostic accuracy; however, further research is warranted (Table 9-11).

ACKNOWLEDGMENT

The authors are indebted to Sylvan Stool, MD, for his expert assistance in providing critical insight in reviewing this chapter and providing expert opinion in areas where the evidence is lacking.

REFERENCES

1. Dowell SF, Marcy SM, Phillips WR, et al. Principles of judicious use of antimicrobial agents for pediatric upper respiratory tract infections. Pediatrics 1998;101:163–84.

2. Rosenfeld RM. Evidence-based approach to treating otitis media. Pediatr Otolaryngol 1996;43:1165–81.

3. Marcy M, Takata G, Shekelle P, et al. Management of acute otitis media. Evidence Report/Technology Assessment No. 15 (Prepared by the Southern California Evidence-based Practice Center under Contract No. 290-97-0001). Rockville (MD): Agency for Healthcare Research and Quality; 2001 May. AHRQ Publication No. 01-E010. Available at: http://hsat.nlm.nih.gov/hq/Hquest/db/3639/screen/DocTitle/odas/1/s/36034 (accessed Feb 12, 2003).

4. Takata GS, Chan LS, Shekelle P, et al. Diagnosis, natural history, and late effects of otitis media with effusion. Summary, Evidence Report/Technology Assessment: Number 55. Rockville (MD): Agency for Healthcare Research and Quality; 2002 June. AHRQ Publication Number 02-E026.

5. Froom J, Culpepper L, Grob P, et al. Diagnosis and antibiotic treatment of acute otitis media: report from International Primary Care Network. BMJ 1990;300 (6724):582–6.

6. Rosenfeld RM. Diagnostic certainty for acute otitis media. Int J Pediatr Otorhinolaryngol 2002;64:89–95.

7. Stool SE, Berg AD, Berman S, et al. Otitis media with effusion in young children. Clinical practice guideline No. 12. Rockville (MD): Agency for Health Care Policy and Research, Public Health Service, U.S. Department of Health and Human Services; 1994 July. AHCPR Publication No. 94-0622.

8. Steinbach WJ, Sectish TC. Pediatric resident training in the diagnosis and treatment of acute otitis media. Pediatrics 2002;109:404–8.

9. Hayden GF, Schwartz RH. Characteristics of earache among children with acute otitis media. Am J Dis Child 1985;139:721–3.

10. Pitkaranta A, Virolainen A, Jero J, et al. Detection of rhinovirus, respiratory syncytial virus, and coronavirus infections in acute otitis media by reverse transcriptase polymerase chain reaction. Pediatrics 1998;102:291–5.

11. Niemela M, Uhari M, Jounio-Ervasti K, et al. Lack of specific symptomatology in children with acute otitis media. Pediatr Infect Dis J 1994;13:765–8.

12. Medellin G, Roark R, Berman S. The usefulness of symptoms to identify otitis media. Arch Pediatr Adolesc Med 1996;150:98.

13. Little P, Gould C, Moore M, et al. Predictors of poor

outcome from antibiotics in children with acute otitis media: pragmatic randomized trial. BMJ 2002;325:22–5.

14. Heikkinen T, Ruuskanen O. Signs and symptoms predicting acute otitis media. Arch Pediatr Adolesc Med 1995;149:26–9.

15. Pukander J. Clinical features of acute otitis media among children. Acta Otolaryngol 1983;95:117–25.

16. Ruuskanen O, Heikkenen T. Otitis media: etiology and diagnosis. Pediatr Infect Dis J 1994;13:S23–6.

17. Chonmaitree T, Owen MJ, Patel JA, et al. Effect of viral respiratory tract infection on outcome of acute otitis media. J Pediatr 1992;120:856–62.

18. Casselbrant ML, Furman JM, Rubensteing E, Mandel EM. Effects of otitis media on the vestibular system in children. Ann Otol Rhinol Laryngol 1995;104:620–4.

19. Stool, SE, Anticaglia J. Electric otoscopy—a basic pediatric skill. Clin Pediatr 1973;12:420–6.

20. Barriga F, Schwartz RH, Hayden GF. Adequate illumination for otoscopy. Am J Dis Child 1986;140:1237–40.

21. Clarke LR, Wiederhold ME, Gates GA. Quantitation of pneumatic otoscopy. Otolaryngol Head Neck Surg 1987;96:199–24.

22. Cavanaugh RM. Pediatricians and the pneumatic otoscope: are we playing it by ear? Pediatrics 1989;84:362–4.

23. Politzer A. Diseases of the ear. 5th ed. London (UK): Bailliere, Tinsdall & Cox; 1909.

24. Kaleida PH. The COMPLETES exam for otitis. Contemp Pediatr 1997;4:93–101.

25. Cantekin EJ, Bluestone CD, Fria TJ, et al. Identification of otitis media with effusion in children. Ann Otol Rhinol Laryngol 1988;Supp 68:190–5.

26. Finitzo T, Friel-Patti S, Chinn K, Brown O. Tympanometry and otoscopy prior to myringotomy: issues in diagnosis of otitis media. Int J Pediatr Otorhinolaryngol 1992;24:101–10.

27. Karma PH, Penttila MA, Sipilä MM, Kataja MJ. Otoscopic diagnosis of middle ear effusion in acute and nonacute otitis media. I. The value of different otoscopic findings. Int J Pediatr Otorhinolaryngol 1989;17:37–49.

28. Nozza RJ, Bluestone CD, Kardatzke D, Bachman R. Identification of middle ear effusion by aural acoustic immittance and otoscopy. Ear Hear 1994;15:310–23.

29. Paradise JD, Smith CG, Bluestone CD. Tympanometric detection of middle ear effusion in infants and young children. Pediatrics 1976;58:198–210.

30. Kaleida PH, Stool SE. Assessment of otoscopists' accuracy regarding middle-ear effusion: otoscopic validation. Am J Dis Child 1992;146:433–5.

31. Silva AB, Hotaling AJ. A protocol for otolaryngology-head and neck resident training in pneumatic otoscopy. Int J Pediatr Otorhinolaryngol 1997;40:125–31.

32. Steinbach WJ, Sectish TC, Benjamin DK, et al. Pediatric residents' clinical diagnostic accuracy of otitis media. Pediatrics 2002;109:993–8.

33. Kaleida PH, Hoberman A, Smith CG. Videotaped otoendoscopic examinations in clinical education and research. Pediatr Res 1992;31:123A.

34. Schwartz RH, Rodriguez WJ, McAveny W, Grundfast KM. Cerumen removal. Am J Dis Child 1983;137:1064–5.

35. Margolis RH, Hunter LL, Giebink GS. Tympanometric evaluation of middle ear function in children with otitis media. Ann Otol Rhinol Laryngol 1994;103:34–8.

36. American National Standards Institute. American national standards specifications for instruments to measure acoustic impedance and admittance (aural acoustic immittance) (ANSI 53.39–1987). New York (NY): ANSI; 1987.

37. Jerger J. Clinical experience with impedance audiometry. Arch Otolaryngol 1970;92:311–24.

38. Babonis TR, Weir MR, Kelly PC. Impedance tympanometry and acoustic reflectometry at myringotomy [published erratum appears in Pediatrics 1991;87(6): 945]. Pediatrics 1991;87:475–80.

39. Kemaloglu YK, Sener T, Beder L, et al. Predictive value of acoustic reflectometry (angle and specificity) and tympanometry. Int J Pediatr Otorhinolaryngol 1999;48: 137–42.

40. Koivunen P, Alho OP, Uhari M, et al. Minitympanometry in detecting middle ear fluid. J Pediatr 1997;131: 419–22.

41. Orchik DJ, Morff R, Dunn JW. Middle ear status at myringotomy and its relationship to middle ear immittence measurements. Ear Hear 1980;1:324–8.

42. Ovesen T, Paaske PB, Elbrond O. Accuracy of an automatic impedance aparatus in a population with secretory otitis media: principles in the evaluation of tympanometrical findings. Am J Otolaryngol 1993;14:100–4.

43. Toner JG, Mains B. Pneumatic otoscopy and tympanometry in the detection of middle ear effusion. Clin Otolaryngol Allied Sci 1990;15:121–3.

44. Watters GW, Jones JE, Freeland AP. The predictive value of tympanometry in the diagnosis of middle ear effusion. Clin Otolaryngol Allied Sci 1997;22:343–5.

45. Fiellau-Nikolajsen M. Epidemiology of secretory otitis media: a descriptive cohort study. Ann Otol Rhinol Laryngol 1983;92:172–7.

46. Tos M. Epidemiology and natural history of secretory otitis. Am J Otol 1984;5:459–62.

47. American Speech-Language-Hearing Association. Guidelines for screening for hearing impairment and middle-ear disorders. ASHA 1990;32:17–24.

48. American Speech-Language-Hearing Association. Guidelines for audiologic screening. ASHA 1997 Audiologic Assessment Panel 1996.

49. Margolis RN, Heller JW. Screening tympanometry: criteria for medical referral. Audiology 1987;26:197–208.

50. Fria TJ, Cantekin EI, Eichler A. Hearing acuity of children with otitis media with effusion. Arch Otolaryngol 1985;111:1–6.

51. Friel-Patti S, Finitzo T. Language learning in a prospective study of otitis media with effusion in the first two years of life. J Speech Hear Res 1990;33:188–94.

52. Kimball S. Acoustic reflectometry: spectral gradient analysis for improved detection of middle ear effusion in children. Pediatr Infect Dis J 1998;17 (Suppl):552–5.

53. Barnett ED, Klein JO, Hawkins KA, et al. Comparison of spectral gradient acoustic reflectometry and other diagnostic techniques for detection of middle ear effusion in

children with middle ear disease. Pediatr Infect Dis J 1998;17 Suppl:556–9.

54. Block SL, Pichichero ME, McLinn S, et al. Spectral gradient acoustic reflectometry: detection of middle ear effusion by pediatricians in suppurative acute otitis media. Pediatr Infect Dis J 1999;18:741–4.

55. Block SL, Mandel E, McLinn S, et al. Spectral gradient acoustic reflectometry for the detection of middle ear effusion by pediatricians and parents. Pediatr Infect Dis J 1998;17 Suppl:560–4.

CHAPTER 10

Epidemiology

Margaretha L. Casselbrant, MD, PhD, and Ellen M. Mandel, MD

Wherever there is number, there is beauty.
Proclus

OBJECTIVES

On completing this chapter, the reader will be able to

1. Explain the frequent occurrence of otitis media (OM).
2. Identify risk factors for OM.
3. Appreciate that variations in study results may be due to differences in study design.

Otitis media is a worldwide pediatric health care problem. In physician office practices in the United States, it is the most common diagnosis made in children under 15 years of age.[1] Although the highest incidence is in young children, acute otitis media (AOM) does occur in older children, adolescents, and adults.[2] Approximately 3 to 15% of patients with OM referred to otolaryngology clinics are adults.[3,4]

INCIDENCE OF OTITIS MEDIA

The incidence rates of middle ear effusion (MEE), that is, AOM and otitis media with effusion (OME), found in different studies are not always comparable because of differences in definitions of disease, case finding

methods, observation intervals, prevalence windows, and population characteristics. Many studies use tympanometry alone to determine middle ear status while otoscopy or pneumatic otoscopy, alone or in combination with tympanometry, are used in others. AOM is diagnosed by tympanocentesis in some studies, which may improve the accuracy of diagnosis. Long intervals between observations may affect the number of episodes identified as well as the time to resolution of the episode. Incidence rates may also reflect such factors as time (year and season) of the study, geographic area, number of patients enrolled, type of population, or any particular circumstance characterizing the study.

Acute Otitis Media

Most children experience at least one episode of AOM during their childhood. The cumulative incidence, by country, of the first episode of AOM is shown in Table 10-1 and is graphically depicted in Figure 10-1. In these various studies, 19 to 62% of children had had at least one episode of AOM by the age of 1 year. By 3 years of age, 50 to 84% had experienced AOM at least once.

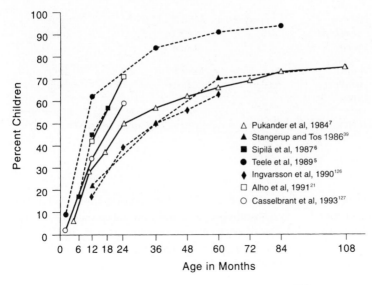

Δ Pukander et al, 1984[7]
▲ Stangerup and Tos 1986[39]
■ Sipilä et al, 1987[6]
● Teele et al, 1989[5]
♦ Ingvarsson et al, 1990[126]
□ Alho et al, 1991[21]
○ Casselbrant et al, 1993[127]

Figure 10-1 Cumulative incidence of first episode of acute otitis media.

Table 10-1 Cumulative Incidence of First Episode of Acute Otitis Media

Authors	Number of Children	City/ Country	Population	Incidence Obtained From	Definition	Tap	Observation Intervals
Pukander et al[7]	4,582	Finland	All with AOM Urban & rural areas	Calculation	MEE & "SXs + signs"	No	None
Stangerup & Tos[39]	729	Denmark	3 cohorts of healthy newborns Urban	Calculation	"SXs + signs"	No	Variable + with events
Sipilä et al[6]	1,642	Finland (three areas)	Control group for vaccine study	Prospective data	MEE & 1 SX + 1 sign or SX + tap	±	With events
Teele et al[5]	498	Boston, MA, USA	Children followed for 7 years; selected from a larger cohort Urban & suburban	Prospective data	MEE + 1 SX	No	With routine visits & events; 4–7 yrs at least q 4 mo
Ingvarsson et al[126]	16,611	Sweden	All children born in Malmo 1971–83 Urban	Prospective data	No standard definition	No	With event
Alho et al[21]	2,431	Northern Finland	Random sample from newborns 1985–86 Rural 10 centers	Retrospective data	MEE & "SXs + signs"	±	Routine visits 3, 6, 12, 24 mo + events
Casselbrant et al[127]	218	Pittsburgh, PA, USA	Normal newborns Urban	Prospective data	MEE & 1 SX & 1 sign	±	Monthly + event
Daly et al[9]	596	Minneapolis, MN, USA	Normal newborns Urban	Prospective data	MEE & 2 signs	No	Monthly + event

AOM = acute otitis media; B = Black; MEE = middle ear effusion by otoscopy; NA = not available; SX = symptom; W = White.
*Rates reported for males.[†]
[†]Rates reported for females.

The peak incidence of AOM was found to occur during the second half of the first year of life in most studies.[5–8] The incidence decreases with age, and by 7 years of age, few children experience AOM episodes.[5]

Recurrent episodes of AOM are common. Two or more episodes of AOM were reported in 20% of infants by 6 months of age.[9] Three or more episodes of AOM by 1 year of age have been reported to occur in 10 to 19% of children.[5,10,11] By ages 3, 5, and 7, three or more episodes of AOM have been documented in 50, 65, and

Age at Entry	Gender	Race	% with Acute Otitis Media (Age in Months)									
			2	6	12	18	24	36	48	60	72	84
All ages	NA	W		(5 mo) 6	(11 mo) 28	(17 mo) 37	50	57	62	66	69	73
NA	NA	W			22		50			70		75
5–9 mo	~ Equal	W		17	45	57						
< 3 mo	~ Equal	97% W	9		62			84		91		95
Birth	~ Equal	W			17* 15+			39* 35†	50* 46†	56* 54†	63* 60†	
Birth	NA	W			42		71					
Birth– 2 mo	~ Equal	33% W 67% B	2		34		59					
Birth	~ Equal	96% W 4% other	10	39								

75% of children, respectively.[5] Howie and colleagues[12] found that 6% of children had six or more episodes of AOM before the age of 6 years, while Teele and colleagues[5] found that 39% had six or more episodes of AOM by the age of 7 years.

Otitis Media with Effusion

It may not be possible to determine the "true" incidence of OME because the disorder is asymptomatic by definition. Furthermore, most screening studies determine the presence of MEE without differentiating between AOM and OME. Short observation intervals are needed to accurately record the onset and the time to resolution of each new OME episode as approximately 65% of episodes in children 2 to 7 years old are resolved within 1 month.[13,14] The spontaneous resolution of recently diagnosed OME of unknown duration, however, is substantially less favorable (see Chapter 12, "Natural History of Untreated Otitis Media").

Since the introduction of tympanometry as a diagnostic tool,[15,16] many screening studies have been done in healthy children to determine the incidence of MEE. Using tympanometry to determine middle ear status, MEE was found at least once in 26% of ears of 278 two-year-old Danish children examined at 3-month intervals (November, February, and May).[17] Tos and colleagues[18] found that 32% of ears of 288 four-year-old Danish children had a type B tympanogram at least once on five screenings during a 1-year period. Fiellau-Nikolajsen[19] documented a 41% incidence of MEE in 404 three-year-old children examined four times from August through February; 17 to 20% of subjects were found to have OM at each screening.

Monthly pneumatic otoscopy and tympanometry examinations of 2- to 6-year-old children in a day care center in Pittsburgh revealed MEE at least once in 53 to 61% of children.[14] Lous and Fiellau-Nikolajsen[13] found an incidence of MEE of 26% in 387 seven-year-old children observed approximately monthly for 1 year using tympanometry to diagnose disease. Casselbrant and colleagues[20] found MEE at least once in 22% of 111 school-age children (5 to 12 years old) examined at monthly intervals by otoscopy and tympanometry.

The point prevalence of MEE from various countries, which includes only AOM and OME, is shown in Table 10-2. As the many studies reveal, there is a wide range in prevalence. Comparing the outcomes from so many studies emphasizes the need to evaluate study methodology and exercise caution when drawing conclusions.

The cumulative incidence of the first episode of MEE from various studies is shown in Table 10-3 and is graphically depicted in Figure 10-2. Nearly all children studied had experienced at least one episode of MEE by the age of 3 years.

RISK FACTORS

Host-related factors (age, gender, race, allergy, immunocompetence, craniofacial abnormalities, genetic predisposition), as well as environmental factors (upper respiratory infection, seasonality, day care, siblings, tobacco-smoke exposure, breast feeding, socioeconomic status), are considered important in the occurrence, recurrence, and persistence of middle ear disease.

Table 10-2 Point Prevalence of Middle Ear Effusion

Authors	N	City/Country	Population	Definition	Age Range	Number of Screenings/ Subject	Month of Peak Prevalence*	Prevalence Range (% Children)†
Zonis[128]	505	Southwest Native American	Total population	Oto	0–8 yr	1	May	1
Virolainen et al[129]	1,207	Finland	School children	Oto	7–8 yr	1	NA	4
Lous & Fiellau-Nikolajsen[13]	387	Denmark	School children	Tymp	7 yr	10	November	9
Sorensen et al[130]	373	Denmark	Normal children	Tymp Oto	4 yr	1	February	20
Halama et al[131]	267	Venda, S. Africa	Rural village	Pneum oto + Tymp (alg)	Birth–15 yr	1	July	1–10
Fiellau-Nikolajsen[19]	404	Denmark	Normal children	Tymp	3 yr	4	February	21
Miller et al[132]	170	Nigeria	Rural village	Pneum oto + Tymp (alg)	5 mo–15 yr	1	July	6–50

Study	Location	N	Population	Method	Age	Alg	Month of peak	Prevalence (%)
Nelson & Berry[133]	Navajo reservation	15,980	School children	Tymp, Oto	4–14 yr	1	NA	2
Casselbrant et al[14]	Pittsburgh, PA, USA	74	Day care children	Tymp Pneum oto	2–6 yr	12	January	33
Holmquist et al[134]	Kuwait	893	School children	Tymp, Oto	7–15 yr	2	January	12
Ogisi[135]	Nigeria	407	School children	Tymp, Oto	5–6 yr	1	NA	1
Cohen & Tamir[136]	Jerusalem	2,664	School children	Pneum oto	8–13 yr	1	NA	1.5
Zielhaus et al[137]	Netherlands	1,439	Normal children	Tymp	2–4 yr	9	NA	28–39
Schilder et al[138]	Netherlands	946	School children	Tymp	7.5–8 yr	1	Sept–Feb	10
Williamson et al[139]	South West Hampshire, UK	856	School children	Tymp	5–8 yr	3	Jan–March	6–20
Bastos et al[140]	Tanzania	449 405	School children Urban Rural	Oto	6–13 yr 6–16 yr	1	April–Nov	0.2 0.7
Moller & Tos[141]	Denmark	51	Normal children	Tymp	3–5.5 yr	1	November	22
Homoe et al[142]	Greenland	325 266	School children	Tymp, Oto	3–5, 8 yr	1	March	9-38
Rushton et al[143]	Hong Kong	177 75	School children Oriental Caucasian	Tymp, Oto	5–6 yr	1	NA	1 10
Marchisio et al[144]	Italy	3,413	School Children	Tymp, Oto	6–7 yr	1	NA	14.2
Renvall et al[145]	Sweden	800	School children	Tymp	7 yr	1	NA	2
Poulsen & Tos[17]	Denmark	240	Normal children	Tymp	2 yr	3	February	15
Tos et al[87]	Denmark	288	Normal children	Tymp	4 yr	5	February	19
Thomsen et al[146]	Denmark	66	Normal children	Tymp	1–4 yr	11	November	19

Alg = algorithm; N = number of children; NA = not available; Oto = otoscopy; Pneum oto = pneumatic otoscopy; Tymp = tympanometry.

*Month of peak prevalence if multiple screenings.

†Range is given if results reported for individual age groups.

Table 10-3 Cumulative Incidence of First Episode of Middle Ear Effusion

Authors	Study Design	Number of Children	City/ State	Population	Definition	Tap
Howie et al[12]	Retrospective	488	Galveston, TX	Private practice	Pneum oto	If AOM
Marchant et al[27]	Prospective	70	Cleveland, OH	Inner city clinic	Tymp Pneum oto	No
Gravel et al[30]	Prospective	46 NICU 19 FT	New York City, NY	Low SES Urban 46 NICU graduates 19 FT	Pneum oto	No
Roland et al[147]	Prospective	483	Dallas, TX	Middle SES	Tymp Pneum oto	No
Stewart[148]	Retrospective	59 (Barrow) 285 (Bethel)	Alaska	Rural 2 Inuit populations	NA	No
Casselbrant et al[127]	Prospective	218	Pittsburgh, PA	Inner city clinic	Tymp Pneum oto (algorithm)	If AOM
Owen et al[149]	Prospective	698	Galveston, TX	Urban	Tymp AR	No
Zeisel et al[150]	Prospective	102	Chapel Hill, NC	Urban Day care center	Tymp Pneum oto	No
Paradise et al[37]	Prospective	634	Pittsburgh, PA	Urban	Pneum oto +/– Tymp	No

AOM = acute otitis media; AR = acoustic reflectometry; Bi = Biracial; B = Black; FT = full term; H = Hispanic; Pneum oto = pneumatic otoscopy; NA = not available; NICU = neonatal intensive care unit; SES = socioeconomic status; Tymp = tympanometry; W = White.

Host-Related Factors

Age

As previously noted, the highest incidence of AOM occurs between 6 and 11 months of age.[5,7,21] Onset of the first episode of AOM before 6 months of age[5,22] or 12 months of age[23] is a powerful predictor for recurrent AOM. Jero and Karma[24] found, in children observed prospectively after an episode of AOM, that those under 2 years of age were more likely to experience a recurrence than were older children.

The risk for persistent MEE after an AOM episode is also inversely correlated with age.[5] Shurin and colleagues[25] found the risk of persistent MEE after AOM to be four times higher in children under 2 years of age than in older children. Marchisio and colleagues[26] followed up 196 Italian children for 3 months after an episode of AOM and found that younger children were significantly more likely to develop chronic MEE than were older children.

Observe Intervals	Age at Entry	Gender	Race	% with Middle Ear Effusion Age in Months					
				2	6	12	18	24	36
All records	Birth	NA	NA			49		61	
5 times	< 2 mo	~ Equal	26 W 44 B	34	73	77			
q mo age 1–6 mo q 2 mo age 7–12 mo	40 wks conceptional age or discharge from NICU		33 B 31 H 1 NA		52	91			
Clinic visits: 6, 9, 12, 18, 24, 36 mo Homevisits: q 6–8 wk, age 6–18 mo q 10–12 wk age > 18 mo	6 mo	NA	NA				74		
All records	Birth	NA		40 NA	71 73	95 74			
q mo + sick visits	Birth–2 mo	~ Equal	60 W 138 B 20 Bi	10		78		92	
q 2 wk birth–18 mo q 4 wk age 18–36 mo	Birth	~ Equal	51 W 35 B 14 H		85	96		98	99
q week entry 16 mo q 2 wk age 16–36 mo	NA	~ Equal	B				99		
q mo	< 2 mo	~ Equal	166 W 438 B 30 NA	61	85			93	

Children experiencing their first episode of MEE before 2 months of age were found to be at higher risk of persistent effusion (3 months or longer) during their first year of life than were children who had their first episode later.[27]

Prematurity

Some studies have found an increased risk of MEE in premature infants, while others have not. Children 2.5 to 6 years of age whose birth weight had been below 2.3 kg were found to have more type B tympanograms at a screening examination than were normal newborns,[28] as were children born 8 to 10 weeks premature.[29] Gravel and colleagues,[30] however, in a prospective study of 49 children who had been in the newborn intensive care unit and 19 full-term infants, did not find any association between gestational age, birth weight, or length of stay in the intensive care unit and percentage of visits with MEE during the first year. Alho and colleagues,[31] examining the records of 2,512 children from birth to

Figure 10-2 Cumulative incidence of first episode of middle ear effusion.

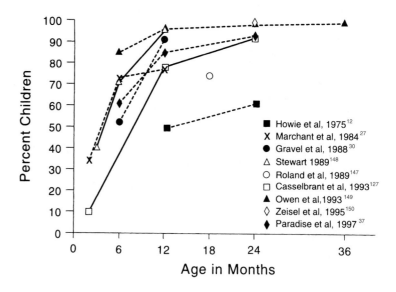

2 years of age, found no association between AOM and low birth weight (< 2,500 g) or prematurity (< 37 weeks).

Engel and colleagues,[32] in a prospective study of 150 full-term and 100 high-risk infants (most preterm or very low birth weight), found higher OME prevalence rates in the high-risk group. Peak prevalence was 59% in the high-risk group versus 49% in the full-term group, which was observed around the age of 10 months in both groups. When they looked at reasons for the increased prevalence in the high-risk group, such factors as nasotracheal, nasopharyngeal, and nasogastric tubes, cranial growth, and neuromotor function did not appear to be significantly related in the 83 infants with available data.[33]

Gender

Most investigators have reported no apparent gender-based difference in the incidence of OME[28,34–36] or in time with MEE.[37] Some studies have found males to have a significantly higher incidence of AOM and more recurrent episodes of AOM than females,[5,23,38,39] but others have not found males to have more episodes of AOM.[40] Males have been reported to be more prone to persistent MEE.[41,42] The reason for the difference in incidence between genders is not known.

Race

Previous studies have suggested a lower incidence of OM in African American children compared with Caucasian American children.[1,25,27,43–45] Kessner and colleagues[43] reported that the prevalence of "ear pathology" (any abnormality in one or both ears, except for fibrotic scarring) in inner-city children aged 6 months to 12 years was 35.6% in 112 Caucasian American children and 19.0% in 2031 African American children.

In a report from the Division of Health Care Statistics, the office visit rate for OM was much lower for African American children compared with that for Caucasian American children.[1] Griffith[44] used tympanometry to screen 126 African American children in one day care center and 148 Caucasian American children in another, finding significantly less OM and middle ear dysfunction in African American than in Caucasian American children. Marchant and colleagues[27] also reported a significantly lower incidence of OM diagnosed by otoscopy in 26 African American children than in 44 Caucasian American children followed up from birth to 12 months of age. The rates of recurrent OM and bilateral chronic MEE in the African American children who developed OM were comparable with those in Caucasian American children.

In a recent prospective study, however, no difference was found between African American and Caucasian American children in their experience with OM when the children were from the same socioeconomic background, were examined at monthly intervals and whenever they developed signs and symptoms of ear disease, and when they received the same treatment for ear disease from birth to 2 years of age.[40] In another prospective study, 2,253 children were followed up from approximately 2 months to 2 years of age with otoscopic examinations every 6 weeks. The mean cumulative percent of days with MEE during the first year was higher in the African American infants than in the Caucasian American infants, but by the second year the rates were equal.[37]

Another study of American school children, ages 6 to 10 years, evaluated with tympanometry as part of an American population-based sample survey, showed that the prevalence for OME was significantly higher for

Hispanic children compared with Caucasian children. The prevalence of OME in this study was not significantly different in African American children compared with Caucasian American children.[46]

Allergy and Immunity

Allergy is a common problem in young children, occurring at a time when respiratory viral infections and OM are both very prevalent. There is still controversy regarding the role of allergy in the pathogenesis of OM. Several mechanisms have been suggested, including the middle ear functioning as a "shock organ," inflammatory swelling of the Eustachian tube, and inflammatory obstruction of the nose and secondary Eustachian tube dysfunction.[47]

Evidence that allergic rhinitis contributes to the pathogenesis of MEE is derived from epidemiologic, mechanistic, and therapeutic lines of investigation. Kraemer and coworkers[48] compared risk factors of persistent MEE among 76 children admitted for bilateral myringotomy and tube insertion and 76 controls matched by age, gender, and season of admission for a general surgical procedure. They showed a nearly fourfold increase in the risk of persistent MEE in children who had atopic symptoms for more than 15 days per month. Pukander and Karma[49] followed 707 children with AOM and found persistence of MEE for 2 months or more to be greater in children with "atopic manifestations" (undefined) than in children without allergy. In another study, however, allergic manifestations were not found to predispose a child to develop AOM.[50]

Tomonaga and colleagues[51] found allergic rhinitis present in 50% of 259 Japanese patients (mean age of 6 years) in whom OME had been diagnosed. Otitis media with effusion was present in 21% of 605 patients (mean age of 9 years) in whom allergic rhinitis had been diagnosed. The incidence of allergic rhinitis, OME, and both of these conditions was 17, 6, and 2%, respectively, among a control group of 108 children (aged 5 to 8 years, mean age of 6 years) in whom neither condition had been previously diagnosed. Bernstein and Reisman[52] similarly determined the allergy status of a group of 200 children who had received one or more tympanostomy tubes. Allergy was diagnosed in 46 children (23%), but the frequency was 35% among the 88 children with multiple tube insertions. In a follow-up study,[53] 77 children aged 2 to 18 years who had chronic MEE and had undergone at least one tube procedure were examined. Middle ear immunoglobulin E (IgE) was increased in 14 of 32 children with allergic rhinitis compared with 2 of 45 children considered nonallergic.

Other investigators have proposed that defective or immature immunologic responses in children with recurrent AOM may contribute to the pathogenesis of the disease.[54] In general, normal serum concentrations of IgG, IgM, and IgA have been demonstrated in children with recurrent AOM.[55] However, there may be more subtle immune deficiencies in otitis-prone children compared with normal children. These might include lower IgG2 levels[56]; a relatively low C1q concentration and low or absent specific IgG antibodies against pneumococcal capsular polysaccharides 6A and 19F[57]; poor response to immunization with *Haemophilus influenzae* capsular polysaccharide–protein conjugate vaccine[58]; and poor response to the outer membrane protein P6 of nontypeable *H. influenzae* and lower concentrations of antibody to P6.[59] Also, children 3 years of age or older with chronic MEE may have a functional antibody deficiency to *Streptococcus pneumoniae*.[60]

Human immunodeficiency virus (HIV)-infected children have a significantly higher recurrence rate of AOM than have normal children[61] or children who have seroconverted.[62] Infected children with a low T4 lymphocyte count had a nearly threefold increased risk for recurrent AOM compared with HIV-infected children with normal lymphocyte counts.

Cleft Palate/Craniofacial Abnormality/ Down Syndrome

Otitis media is present in nearly all infants under 2 years of age with unrepaired clefts of the palate.[63–65] The occurrence of OM was reduced following surgical repair of the palate,[65,66] likely due to improvement of the Eustachian tube function.[67] Otitis media is also common in children with craniofacial abnormalities and Down syndrome.[68,69] The children with Down syndrome have, in addition to poor active opening function of the Eustachian tube, a very low resistance of the tube. Secretions from the nasopharynx can, therefore, easily access the middle ear.[70]

Genetic

The frequency of one episode of OM occurring is so high that a genetic predisposition cannot be expected. However, a predisposition to recurrent episodes of OM and chronic MEE may have a significant genetic component. Anatomic, physiologic, and epidemiologic data suggest this. For example, the degree of pneumatization of the mastoid process, a trait believed to be linked causally to OM, was found to be more similar in monozygotic than dizygotic twins.[71,72] Racial differences in Eustachian tube anatomy and function have also been reported. The shorter, straighter Eustachian tube found in Native Americans is associated with a higher incidence of chronic suppurative OM.[73,74]

The human leucocyte antigen (HLA)-A2 occurred more frequently and HLA-A3 less frequently in children with recurrent AOM than in healthy controls.[75] The frequency of HLA-A2 was significantly lower in children with chronic OME than in children with recurrent AOM.[76] Also, the genetically determined IgG2 marker G2m(23) has shown significant association with recurrent AOM.[77,78] Spivey and Hirschhorn[79] found in a study of Apache Natives adopted into middle-class foster homes that the incidence of most infectious diseases decreased, but OM incidence was comparable with that reported for the reservation.

Familial clustering of OM suggests a genetic component to the disease.[22,45,80,81] Rich and colleagues,[82] using tympanostomy tube placement as the basis for proband identification, estimated that the genetic component accounted for up to 60% of OM liability in a "permissive environment."

Twin and triplet studies have been used to assess heritability for OM. Two retrospective questionnaire studies have been reported. The first study of 2,750 Norwegian twin pairs estimated the heritability at 74% in females and 45% in males.[83] In the second study, the estimated heritability at ages 2, 3 and 4 years for acute infections was on average 57%.[84] In a prospective twin/triplet study from Pittsburgh, with monthly assessment of middle ear status, the heritability estimate for OM at age 2 years was 79% in females and 64% in males.[85]

Environmental Factors

Season and Upper Respiratory Infection

Both epidemiologic evidence and clinical experience strongly suggest that OM is frequently a complication of upper respiratory infection (URI). The incidence of OME is highest during the fall and winter months and lowest in the summer months in both the northern[14] and southern hemispheres,[86] which parallels the incidence of AOM[28,38] and URI.[14,28,87] This supports the hypothesis that an episode of URI plays an important role in the etiology of OM. Experimental studies in animals[88,89] and in humans[90–92] as well as clinical studies[93,94] have shown that viral URI is a risk factor for Eustachian tube dysfunction and development of OM.

Upper respiratory tract infections with respiratory syncytial virus, influenza virus, and adenovirus often precede episodes of AOM.[95,96] Respiratory syncytial virus, rhinovirus, adenovirus, and coronavirus have been isolated in episodes of AOM.[97–99]

Day Care/Home Care

Prevalence of high negative middle ear pressure and flat tympanograms (type B), indicative of MEE, have been shown to be highest in children cared for in day care centers with many children, intermediate in children in family day care with fewer children, and lowest in children cared for at home.[34,100] Another study showed that children cared for in a day care center for at least 12 months during the first 4 years of life had 2.6 times the risk of developing persistent OME compared with children cared for at home.[101]

Alho and colleagues[8] examined responses to questionnaires sent to parents of 2512 Finnish children as well as the children's medical records and found an odds ratio of 2.06 for the develop AOM in children attending day care centers compared with children cared for at home. This increased incidence of AOM in children in day care centers was also found in a case-control study in Finland.[49] Children in day care have also been shown to be more likely to have a tympanostomy tube inserted than children cared for at home.[101,102]

Almost universally, studies identify day care center attendance as a very important risk factor for developing OM, possibly explained by the increased risk for URI in young children in day care centers.[102–106] These children are at increased risk for URI probably because of the large number of susceptible children in close contact.

Siblings

Birth order was associated with the rate of episodes of OM and percentage of time with MEE in a prospective longitudinal study by Casselbrant and co-workers.[40] The study found that firstborn children had a lower rate of AOM and less time with MEE during the first 2 years of life than did children with older siblings. Pukander and colleagues[49] also found children with more siblings most likely to have recurrent episodes of AOM. Having more than one sibling was significantly related to early OM onset.[9] However, Teele and colleagues[5] reported no association between number of siblings and risk of AOM or MEE.

The reason for the higher morbidity is probably the same as for children in day care centers. Paradise and colleagues[37] combined the number of older siblings and day care attendance into a "child exposure index" and found a significant correlation with cumulative time with MEE. The more children in the same place, the greater is the opportunity for exposure to URI, which may cause Eustachian tube dysfunction and increase the likelihood of developing OM.

Environmental Tobacco Smoke

An association between OM and passive exposure to smoking has been reported by many investigators.[48,107–113] The risk of recurrent OM ($\geq$ 6 lifetime episodes) was significantly increased with combined gestational and passive smoke exposure.[106] Other investigators, however, have not been able to demonstrate such an association.[28,35,42,114]

In most studies, information on smoke exposure has been obtained from the parents' report. Strachan and colleagues,[109] however, measured cotinine, a metabolite of nicotine and a marker of passive exposure to smoking, in the saliva of children 6 to 7 years of age and correlated its concentration with middle ear status as determined by tympanometry. They found that increased cotinine concentrations correlated with abnormal tympanograms and number of smokers in the household.

Etzel and colleagues[111] measured serum cotinine concentration in children who attended a day care center. Children exposed to tobacco smoke who had a serum cotinine concentration ≥ 2.5 ng/mL had a 38% higher rate of new episodes of MEE and OM episodes of longer duration. However, Daly and colleagues[9] were not able to show an association between early AOM onset and cotinine:creatinine ratio in urine in children followed from birth to 6 months of age. The difficulty in establishing a conclusive relationship between tobacco-smoke exposure and OM has been reviewed by Blakley and Blakley.[115] More information about the pathogenesis, duration, and intensity of exposure is needed to clarify this association.

Breast-Feeding versus Bottle-Feeding

Most studies have found that breast feeding has a protective effect against middle ear disease. However, there is controversy regarding the duration of breast feeding necessary for protection. Some investigators have found no association between duration of breast-feeding and recurrence rate of AOM,[22,116] but many have reported fewer recurrences of AOM among children who were breast fed exclusively for a prolonged period of time.[5,7,10,11,117,118]

Duncan and colleagues[117] followed up 1,013 infants in a 1-year study and found that infants exclusively breast fed for 4 months or longer had half the mean number of AOM episodes compared with infants who were not breast fed at all and 40% less than infants breast fed for less than 4 months. The recurrence rate in infants exclusively breast fed for 6 months or longer was 10% compared with 20.5% in infants who were breast fed for less than 4 months.

A cohort of 306 normal children enrolled shortly after birth was followed up at well-baby visits for 2 years.[105] The infants were examined with pneumatic otoscopy and tympanometry monthly for the first 6 months, every other month at ages 6 to 12 months, every 3 months ages at 12 to 24 months, and at interim visits after the diagnosis of OM and other recent illnesses. Between 6 and 12 months of age, the cumulative incidence of first OM episodes increased from 25 to 51% in infants exclusively breast fed and from 54 to 76% in infants formula fed from birth. Peak incidence of AOM and OME episodes was inversely related

to rates of breast-feeding beyond 3 months of age. A twofold elevated risk of first episode of AOM or OME was observed in exclusively formula-fed infants compared with infants exclusively breast fed for 6 months.[105] The authors concluded that breast-feeding is a modifiable factor in the onset of AOM and OME.

Saarinen[119] found, in a prospective study of 237 children, that prolonged breast-feeding (6 months or longer) protected the child from recurrent OM not only during the period of breast-feeding but also up to 3 years of age.

The mechanism for the protective effect of breast milk is not known, but several hypotheses have been suggested. The protective mechanism may be through immunologic factors provided through the breast milk, especially secretory IgA, with antibody activity against respiratory tract viruses and bacteria,[120] or it may be through other factors preventing bacterial adhesion.[120,121] Bluestone and colleagues[122] have suggested mechanisms in bottle-fed children that may account for these differences, including allergy to formula or cow's milk, poorer development of facial musculature needed to promote good Eustachian tube function, aspiration of fluids in the middle ear with high intraoral pressures generated by bottle feeding, and the reclining or horizontal position of the infants during feeding possibly causing reflux.

Socioeconomic Status

Socioeconomic status and access to health care are factors that may affect the incidence of OM. It has been generally thought that OM is more common among people in the lower socioeconomic strata due to poor sanitary conditions and crowding.

Paradise and colleagues[37] followed up 2,253 infants for 2 years and found an inverse relationship between the cumulative proportion of days with MEE and socioeconomic status. Castagno and Lavinsky[86] also found a higher prevalence of OME in children in the lower socioeconomic class in southern Brazil. However, many studies revealed no correlation between socioeconomic status of the child's family and incidence of MEE.[5,28,34,41,42] Tos and colleagues[34] found no difference in MEE rates between children living in apartments and those in houses.

Pacifier Use

Niemelä and colleagues[123] found from parental questionnaires that among 938 five-year-old children those who had used pacifiers had a greater risk of having had four or more episodes of AOM than those who had not, while thumb-sucking was not associated with AOM. In a follow-up prospective study of 845 children in day care centers, Niemelä and colleagues[124] found that the use

Table 10-4 Pointers and Pitfalls

1. OM is a worldwide pediatric health care problem.

2. Incidence rates of OM in epidemiologic studies are not always comparable because of differences in methodology, disease definition, and patient populations.

3. Most children have at least one episode of AOM with a peak incidence between 6 and 11 months of age; by age 3, about 50 to 85% of children have had AOM.

4. Recurrent AOM (3 or more episodes) is common, affecting about 10 to 20% of children by 1 year of age; nearly 40% of older children eventually have 6 or more total episodes.

5. The lack of symptoms with OME makes it difficult to estimate prevalence, but the point prevalence of MEE on screening tests is about 20%.

6. By 3 years of age, nearly all children have experienced at least one episode of MEE (includes both AOM and OME).

7. Host-related risk factors for OM include young age, male gender, racial factors, allergic rhinitis, immune deficiency, cleft palate, craniofacial abnormalities, and genetic predisposition.

8. Environmental risk factors for OM include fall/winter season, upper respiratory infection, day care attendance, older siblings, environmental tobacco smoke, not being breast fed, and pacifier use.

AOM = acute otitis media; MEE = middle ear effusion; OM = otitis media; OME = otitis media with effusion.

of a pacifier increased the annual incidence of AOM and calculated that pacifier use was responsible for 25% of AOM episodes in children younger than 3 years.

Warren and colleagues[125] used questionnaires at 6 weeks, 3, 6, 9, and 12 months to determine the relationship between OM and pacifier use. Pacifier-sucking was significantly associated with OM from 6 to 9 months and approached statistical significance at 9 to 12 months ($p = .056$); other time periods showed no significant relationship to OM.

Pointers and pitfalls regarding the epidemiology of otitis media are summarized in Table 10-4.

REFERENCES

1. Schappert SM. Office visits for otitis media: United States, 1975–90. From Vital and Health Statistics of the Centers for Disease Control and Prevention. Adv Data 1992;222:1–20.

2. Bernstein JM, Schatz M, Zeiger R. Immunologic ear disease in adults. Clin Rev Allergy 1984;2:349–76.

3. Sadé J. Secretory otitis media and its sequelae. In: Monograghs in clinical otolaryngology. Vol 1. New York (NY): Churchill Livingston; 1979.

4. Oppenheimer RP. Serous otitis: a review of 922 cases. Eye Ear Nose Throat Month 1975;54:37–40.

5. Teele DW, Klein JO, Rosner B, Greater Boston Otitis Media Study Group. Epidemiology of otitis media during the first seven years of life in children in greater Boston: a prospective, cohort study. J Infect Dis 1989;160(1):83–94.

6. Sipilä M, Pukander J, Karma P. Incidence of acute otitis media up to the age of 1–1/2 years in urban infants. Acta Otolaryngol (Stockh) 1987;104:138–45.

7. Pukander J, Sipilä M, Karma P. Occurrence of and risk factors in acute otitis media. In: Lim DJ, Bluestone CD, Klein JO, Nelson JD, editors. Recent advances in otitis media with effusion. Proceedings of the Third International Symposium. Philadelphia (PA): BC Decker; 1984. p. 9–12.

8. Alho O, Kilkku O, Oja H, et al. Control of the temporal aspect when considering risk factors for acute otitis media. Arch Otolaryngol Head Neck Surg 1993;119:444–9.

9. Daly KA, Brown JE, Lindgren BR, et al. Epidemiology of otitis media onset by six months of age. Pediatrics 1999;103:1158–66.

10. Kero P, Piekkala P. Factors affecting the occurrence of acute otitis media during the first year of life. Acta Paediatr Scand 1987;76:618–23.

11. Sipilä M, Karma P, Pukander J, et al. The Bayesian approach to the evaluation of risk factors in acute and recurrent acute otitis media. Acta Otolaryngol (Stockh) 1988;106:94–101.

12. Howie VM, Ploussard JH, Sloyer J. The "otitis-prone" condition. Am J Dis Child 1975;129:676–8.

13. Lous J, Fiellau-Nikolajsen M. Epidemiology of middle-ear effusion and tubal dysfunction: a one year prospective study comprising monthly tympanometry in 387 non-selected seven-year-old children. Int J Pediatr Otorhinolaryngol 1981;3:303–17.

14. Casselbrant ML, Brostoff LM, Cantekin EI, et al. Otitis media with effusion in preschool children. Laryngoscope 1985;95:428–36.

15. Brooks DN. The use of the electro-acoustic impedance bridge in the assessment of middle-ear function. Int Audiol 1969;8:563–9.

16. Brooks DN. Middle-ear effusion in children. Ann Otol Rhinol Laryngol 1976;25:223–8.

17. Poulsen G, Tos M. Repetitive tympanometric screenings of two-year old children. Scand Audiol 1980;9:21–8.

18. Tos M, Holm-Jensen S, Sorensen CH, Mogensen C. Spontaneous course and frequency of secretory otitis in four-year-old children. Arch Otolaryngol 1982;108:4–10.

19. Fiellau-Nikolajsen M. Epidemiology of secretory otitis media: a descriptive cohort study. Ann Otol Rhinol Laryngol 1983;92:172–7.

20. Casselbrant ML, Brostoff LM, Cantekin EI, et al. Otitis media in children in the United States. Acute and secretory otitis media. Proceedings of the International Conference on Acute and Secretory Otitis Media, Part I. Amsterdam: Kugler Publications; 1996. p. 161–4.

21. Alho O, Koivu M, Sorri M, Rantakallio P. The occurrence of acute otitis media in infants. A lifetable analysis. Int J Pediatr Otorhinolaryngol 1991;21:7–14.

22. Harsten G, Prellner K, Heldrup J, et al. Recurrent acute otitis media. Acta Otolaryngol (Stockh) 1989;107:111–9.

23. Lundgren K, Ingvarsson L, Olofsson B. Epidemiology aspects in children with recurrent acute otitis media. In: Lim DJ, Bluestone CD, Klein JO, Nelson JD, editors. Recent advances in otitis media with effusion. Proceedings of the Third International Symposium. Philadelphia (PA): BC Decker; 1984. p. 19–22.

24. Jero J, Karma P. Prognosis of acute otitis media. Factors associated with the development of recurrent acute otitis media. Acta Otolaryngol (Stockh) 1997;Suppl 529: 30–3.

25. Shurin PA, Pelton SI, Donner A, Klein JO. Persistence of middle-ear effusion after acute otitis media in children. N Engl J Med 1979;300:1121–3.

26. Marchisio P, Bigalli L,Massironi E, Principi N. Risk factors for persisting otitis media with effusion in children. In: Lim DJ, Bluestone CD, Klein JO, Nelson JD, editors. Recent advances in otitis media with effusion. Proceedings of the Fourth International Symposium. Philadelphia (PA): BC Decker; 1988. p. 3–5.

27. Marchant CD, Shurin PA, Turczyk VA, et al. Course and outcome of otitis media in early infancy: a prospective study. J Pediatr 1984;104:826–31.

28. Van Cauwenberge P, Kluyskens P. Some predisposing factors in OME. In: Lim DJ, Bluestone CD, Klein JO, Nelson JD, editors. Recent advances in otitis media with effusion. Proceedings of the Third International Symposium. Philadelphia (PA): BC Decker; 1984. p. 28–32.

29. Van Cauwenberge PB. Relevant and irrelevant predisposing factors in secretory otitis media. Acta Otolaryngol (Stockh) 1984;414:147–53.

30. Gravel JS, McCarton CM, Ruben RJ. Otitis media in neonatal intensive care unit graduates: a 1-year prospective study. Pediatrics 1988;82:44–9.

31. Alho O, Koivu M, Hartikainen-Sorri A, et al. Is a child's history of acute otitis media and respiratory infection already determined in the antenatal and perinatal period? Int J Pediatr Otorhinolaryngol 1990;19:129–37.

32. Engel J, Anteunis L, Volovics A, et al. Prevalence rates of otitis media with effusion from 0 to 2 years of age: healthy-born versus high-risk-born infants. Int J Pediatr Otorhinolaryngol 1999;47:243–51.

33. Engel J, Mahler E, Anteunis L, et al. Why are NICU infants at risk for chronic otitis media with effusion?

Int J Pediatr Otorhinolaryngol 2001;57:137–44.

34. Tos M, Poulsen G, Borch J. Tympanometry in two-year-old children. Otorhinolaryngology 1978;40:77–85.

35. Zielhuis GA, Heuvelmans-Heinen EW, Rach GH, Broek PVD. Environmental risk factors for otitis media with effusion in preschool children. Scand J Prim Health Care 1989;7:33–8.

36. Engel J, Anteunis L, Volovics A, et al. Risk factors of otitis media with effusion during infancy. Int J Pediatr Otorhinolaryngol 1999;48:239–49.

37. Paradise JL, Rockette HE, Colburn K, et al. Otitis media in 2253 Pittsburgh-area infants: prevalence and risk factors during the first two years of life. Pediatrics 1997;99:318–33.

38. Pukander J, Karma P, Sipilä M. Occurrence and recurrence of acute otitis media among children. Acta Otolaryngol 1982;94:479–86.

39. Stangerup SE, Tos M. Epidemiology of acute suppurative otitis media. Am J Otolaryngol 1986;7:47–54.

40. Casselbrant ML, Mandel EM, Kurs-Lasky M, et al. Otitis media in a population of black American and white American infants, 0–2 years of age. Int J Pediatr Otorhinolaryngol 1995;33:1–16.

41. Stewart I, Kirkland C, Simpson A, et al. Some factors of possible etiologic significance related to otitis media with effusion. In: Lim DJ, Bluestone CD, Klein JO, Nelson JD, editors. Recent advances in otitis media with effusion. Proceedings of the Third International Symposium. Philadelphia (PA): BC Decker Inc; 1984. p. 25–7.

42. Birch L, Elbrond O. A prospective epidemiological study of secretory otitis media in young children related to the indoor environment. Otorhinolaryngology 1987;49:253–8.

43. Kessner DM, Snow CK, Singer J. Assessment of medical care for children.Washington (DC): Institute of Medicine, National Academy of Sciences; 1974.

44. Griffith TE. Epidemiology of otitis media: an interracial study. Laryngoscope 1979;89:22–30.

45. Teele DW, Klein JO, Rosner BA. Epidemiology of otitis media in children. Ann Otol Rhinol Laryngol 1980; 68:5–6.

46. Hoffman HJ, MacTurk RH, Gravel JS, et al. Epidemiological risk factors for otitis media and hearing loss in school age children based on NHANES III, 1988–1994. Proceedings of the Seventh International Symposium. Recent Advances in Otitis Media with Effusion [book on CD-ROM]. Hamilton (ON): BC Decker; 2002.

47. Bluestone CD. Eustachian tube function: physiology, pathophysiology, and role of allergy in pathogenesis of otitis media. J Allergy Clin Immunol 1983;72:242–51.

48. Kraemer MJ, Richardson MA, Weiss NS, et al. Risk factors for persistent middle-ear effusions—otitis media, catarrh, cigarette smoke exposure, and atopy. JAMA 1983;249:1022–5.

49. Pukander JS, Karma PH. Persistence of middle-ear effusion and its risk factors after an acute attack of otitis media with effusion. In: Lim DJ, Bluestone CD, Klein JO, Nelson JD, editors. Recent advances in otitis media. Proceedings of the Fourth International Symposium. Toronto (ON): BC Decker Inc; 1988. p. 8–11.

50. Pukander J, Luotonen J, Timonen M, Karma P. Risk factors affecting the occurrence of acute otitis media among 2–3-year-old urban children. Acta Otolaryngol (Stockh) 1985;100:260–5.

51. Tomonaga K, Kurono Y, Mogi G. The role of nasal allergy in otitis media with effusion: a clinical study. Acta Otolaryngol (Stockh) 1988;458 Suppl:41–7.

52. Bernstein JM, Reisman RE. The role of acute hypersensitivity in secretory otitis media. Trans Am Acad Ophthalmol Otolaryngol 1974;78:120–7.

53. Bernstein JM, Lee J, Conboy K, et al. The role of IgE mediated hypersensitivity in recurrent otitis media with effusion. Am J Otol 1983;5:66–9.

54. Rynnel-Dagoo B, Freijd A. Immunodeficiency. In: Bernstein J, Ogra P, editors. Otitis media in immunology of the ear. New York (NY): Raven Press; 1987. p. 363–80.

55. Berman S, Lee B, Nuss R, et al. Immunoglobulin G, total and subclass, in children with or without recurrent otitis media. J Pediatr 1992;121:249–51.

56. Freijd A, Oxelius V, Rynnel-Dagöö B. A prospective study demonstrating an association between plasma IgG2 concentrations and susceptibility to otitis media in children. Scand J Infect Dis 1985;17:115–20.

57. Prellner K, Kalm O, Harsten G, et al. Pneumococcal serum antibody concentrations during the first three years of life: a study of otitis-prone and non-otitis prone children. Int J Pediatr Otorhinolaryngol 1989;17:267–79.

58. Pelton SI, Teele DW, Earle R, Breña AW. Pediatrics. Impaired response to *Haemophilus* capsular polysaccharide-protein conjugate vaccine in children with otitis media. In: Lim DJ, Bluestone CD, Klein JO, Nelson JD, editors. Recent advances in otitis media with effusion. Proceedings of the Fifth International Symposium. Hamilton (ON): Decker Periodicals; 1993. p. 167–8.

59. Yamanaka N, Faden H. Antibody response to outer membrane protein of nontypeable *Haemophilus influenzae* in otitis-prone children. J Pediatr 1993;122:212–8.

60. Sigurdardottir S, Otte W, Casselbrant M, Fireman P. Abnormal immune responsiveness in older children with chronic otitis media with effusion. Pediatr Res 1991;29:163A.

61. Principi N, Marchisio P, Tornaghi R, et al. Acute otitis media in human immunodeficiency virus-infected children. Pediatrics 1991;88:566–71.

62. Barnett ED, Klein JO, Pelton SI, Luginbuhl LM. Otitis media in children born to human immunodeficiency virus-infected mothers. Pediatr Infect Dis J 1992;11:360–4.

63. Stool SE, Randall P. Unexpected ear disease in infants with cleft palate. Cleft Palate J 1967;4:99–103.

64. Paradise JL, Bluestone CD, Felder H. The universality of otitis media in 50 infants with cleft palate. Pediatrics 1969;44:35–42.

65. Frable MA, Brandon GT, Theogaraj SD. Velar closure and ear tubings as a primary procedure in the repair of cleft palates. Laryngoscope 1985;95:1044–6.

66. Paradise JL, Bluestone CD. Early treatment of the universal otitis media of infants with cleft palate. Pediatrics 1974;53:48–54.

67. Doyle WJ, Reilly JS, Jardini L, Rovnak S. Effect of palatoplasty on the function of the eustachian tube in children with cleft palate. Cleft Palate J 1986;23:63–8.

68. Schwartz DM, Schwartz RH. Acoustic impedance and otoscopic findings in young children with Down's syndrome. Arch Otolaryngol 1978;104:652–6.

69. Balkany TJ, Downs MP, Jafek BW, Krajicek MJ. Otologic manifestations of Down syndrome. Surg Forum 1978;29:582–5.

70. White BL, Doyle WJ, Bluestone CD. Eustachian tube function in infants and children with Down's syndrome. In: Lim DJ, Bluestone CD, Klein JO, Nelson JD, editors. Recent advances in otitis media with effusion. Proceedings of the Third International Symposium. Philadelphia (PA): BC Decker; 1984. p. 62–6.

71. Dahlberg G, Diamant M. Hereditary character in the cellular system of the mastoid process. Acta Otolaryngol (Stockh) 1945;33:378–89.

72. Diamant H, Diamant M. The mastoid air cells. In: McCabe BF, Sadé J, Abramson M, editors. Cholesteatoma First International Conference. Birmingham (UK): Aesculapius Publishing Co; 1977. p. 319–23.

73. Doyle WJ. A functional-anatomic description of eustachian tube vector relations in four ethnic populations: an osteologic study [PhD dissertation]. Pittsburgh (PA): University of Pittsburgh; 1977.

74. Beery QC, Doyle WJ, Bluestone CD, et al. Eustachian tube function in an American Indian population. Otol Rhinol Laryngol 1980;89:28–33.

75. Kalm O, Johnson U, Prellner K, Ninn K. HLA frequency in patients with recurrent acute otitis media. Arch Otolaryngol Head Neck Surg 1991;117:1296–9.

76. Kalm O, Johnson U, Prellner K. HLA frequency in patients with chronic secretory otitis media. Int J Pediatr Otorhinolaryngol 1994;30:151–7.

77. Prellner K, Hallbert T, Kalm O, Magnusson B. Recurrent otitis media: genetic immunoglobulin markers in children and their parents. Int J Pediatr Otorhinolaryngol 1985;9:219–25.

78. Kelly KM. Correspondence. Int J Pediatr Otolaryngol 1993;25:279–80.

79. Spivey GH, Hirshhorn N. A migrant study of adopted Apache children. Johns Hopkins Med J 1977;1210: 43–6.

80. Seiff E. Genetic and environmental basis of otitis media with effusion: a preliminary study [masters thesis]. Pittsburgh (PA): University of Pittsburgh; 1979.

81. Stenström C, Ingvarsson L. Otitis-prone children and controls: a study of possible predisposing factors. I. Heredity, family background and perinatal period. Acta Otolaryngol (Stockh) 1997;117: 87–93.

82. Rich SS, Savona K, Giebink GS, Daly K. Familial aggregation and risk factors for chronic/recurrent otitis media. Am J Hum Gen 1994;55:942.

83. Kvaerner KJ, Harris JR, Tambs K, Magnus P. Distribution and heritability of recurrent ear infections. Ann Otol Rhinol Laryngol 1997;106:624–32.

84. Rovers M, Haggard M, Gannon M, et al. Heritability of symptom domains in otitis media: a longitudinal study of 1,373 twin pairs. Am J Epidemiol 2002;155:958–64.

85. Casselbrant ML, Mandel EM, Fall PA, et al. The heritability of otitis media: a twin and triplet study. JAMA 1999;282:2125–30.

86. Castagno LA, Lavinsky L. Otitis media in children: seasonal changes and socioeconomic level. Int J Pediatr Otorhinolaryngol 2002;62:129–34.

87. Tos M, Holm-Jensen S, Sorensen CH. Changes in prevalence of secretory otitis from summer to winter in four-year-old children. Am J Otol 1981;2(4):324–7.

88. Giebink GS, Ripley ML,Wright PF. Eustachian tube histopathology during experimental influenza A virus infection in the chinchilla. Ann Otol Rhinol Laryngol 1987;96:199–206.

89. Rarey KE, DeLacure MA, Sandridge SA, Small PA Jr. Effect of upper respiratory infection on hearing in the ferret model. Am J Otolaryngol 1987;8:161–70.

90. Doyle WJ, McBride TP, Swarts JD, et al. The response of the nasal airway, middle ear, and eustachian tube to experimental rhinovirus infection. Am J Rhinol 1988;2: 149–54.

91. McBride TP, Doyle WJ, Hayden FG, Gwaltney JM. Alterations of the eustachian tube, middle ear, and nose in rhinovirus infection. Arch Otolaryngol Head Neck Surg 1989;115:1054–9.

92. Buchman CA, Doyle WJ, Skoner D, et al. Otologic manifestations of experimental rhinovirus infection. Laryngoscope 1994;104:1295–9.

93. Bylander A. Upper respiratory tract infection and eustachian tube function in children. Acta Otolaryngol (Stockh) 1984;97:343–9.

94. Sanyal MA, Henderson FW, Stempel EC, et al. Effect of upper respiratory tract infection on eustachian tube ventilatory function in the preschool child. Pediatrics 1980;97:11–5.

95. Henderson FW, Collier AM, Sanyal MA et al. A longitudinal study of respiratory viruses and bacteria in the etiology of acute otitis media with effusion. N Engl J Med 1982;306:1379–83.

96. Sarkkinen H, Ruuskanen O, Meurman O, et al. Identification of respiratory virus antigens in middle ear fluids of children with acute otitis media. J Infect Dis 1985; 151:444–8.

97. Chonmaitree T, Howie VM, Truant AL. Presence of respiratory viruses in middle ear fluids and nasal wash specimens from children with acute otitis media. Pediatrics 1986;77:698–702.

98. Arola M, Ziegler T, Ruuskanen O, et al. Rhinovirus in acute otitis media. J Pediatr 1988;113:693–5.

99. Pitkäranta A, Virolainen A, Jero J, et al. Detection of rhinovirus, respiratory syncytial virus, and coronavirus infections in acute otitis media by reverse transcriptase polymerase chain reaction. Pediatrics 1998; 102:291–5.

100. Fiellau-Nikolajsen M. Tympanometry in three-year old children. Type of care as an epidemiological factor in secretory otitis media and tubal dysfunction in unselected populations of three-year old children. Otorhinolaryngology 1979;41:193–205.

101. Rasmussen F. Protracted secretory otitis media. The impact of familial factors and day-care center attendance. Int J Pediatr Otorhinolaryngol 1993;26:29–37.

102. Wald ER, Dashefsky B, Byers C, et al. Frequency and severity of infections in day care. J Pediatr 1988;112: 540–6.

103. Strangert K. Infection in younger children attending day-care centers [thesis]. Stockholm: University of Stockholm; 1976.

104. Ståhlberg MR. The influence of form of day care on occurrence of acute respiratory tract infections among young children. Acta Paediatr Scand 1980;Suppl 282: 1–87.

105. Duffy LC, Faden H, Wasielewski R, et al. Exclusive breastfeeding protects against bacterial colonization and day care exposure to otitis media. Pediatrics 1997; 100(4):e7.

106. Lieu JE, Feinstein AR. Effect of gestational and passive smoke exposure on ear infections in children. Arch Pediatr Adolesc Med 2002;156:147–54.

107. Ståhlberg MR, Ruuskanen O, Virolainen E. Risk factors for recurrent otitis media. Pediatr Infect Dis 1986;5:30–2.

108. Reed BD, Lutz LJ. Household smoking exposure-association with middle-ear effusions. Fam Med 1988;20:426–30.

109. Strachan DP, Jarvis MJ, Feyerabend C. Passive smoking, salivary cotinine concentrations, and middle ear effusion in 7 year old children. BMJ 1989;298:1549–52.

110. Hinton AE. Surgery for otitis media with effusion in children and its relationship to parental smoking. J Laryngol Otol 1989;103:559–61.

111. Etzel RA, Pattishall EN, Haley NJ, et al. Passive smoking and middle-ear effusion among children in day care. Pediatrics 1992;90:228–32.

112. Stenstrom R, Bernard PAM, Ben-Simhon H. Exposure to environmental tobacco smoke as a risk factor for recurrent acute otitis media in children under the age of five years. Int J Pediatr Otorhinolaryngol 1993;27:127–36.

113. Maw AR, Parker AJ, Lance GN, Dilkes MG. The effect of parental smoking on outcome after treatment for glue ear in children. Clin Otolaryngol 1992;17:411–4.

114. Vinther B, Elbrønd O, Brahe Pedersen C. A population study of otitis media in childhood. Acta Otolaryngol 1979;360:135–7.

115. Blakley BW, Blakley JE. Smoking and middle-ear disease: are they related? A review article. Otolaryngol Head Neck Surg 1995;112:441–6.

116. Tainio VM, Savilahti E, Salmenpera L, et al. Risk factors for infantile recurrent otitis media: atopy but not type of feeding. Pediatr Res 1988;23:509–12.

117. Duncan B, Ey J, Holberg CJ, et al. Exclusive breastfeeding for at least 4 months protects against otitis media. Pediatrics 1993;91:867–72.

118. Aniansson G, Alm B, Andersson B, et al. A prospective cohort study on breast-feeding and otitis media in Swedish infants. Pediatr Infect Dis J 1994;13:183–8.

119. Saarinen UM. Prolonged breast-feeding as prophylaxis for recurrent otitis media. Acta Paediatr Scand 1982;71: 567–71.

120. Andersson B, Porras O, Hanson LA, et al. Inhibition of attachment of *Streptococcus pneumoniae* and *Haemo-*

philus influenzae by human milk and receptor oligosac-charides. J Infect Dis 1986;153:232–7.

121. Hanson LA, Andersson B, Carlsson B, et al. Defense of mucous membranes by antibodies, receptor analogues, and nonspecific host factors. Infection 1985;13 Suppl 2: S166–70.

122. Bluestone CD, Klein JO, Flaherty MR, et al. Otitis media in infants and children. Philadelphia (PA): WB Saunders; 1995. p. 49–51.

123. Niemelä M, Uhari M, Hannuksela A. Pacifiers and dental structure as risk factors for otitis media. Int J Pediatr Otorhinolaryngol 1994;29:121–7.

124. Niemelä M, Uhari M, Möttönen M. A pacifier increases the risk of recurrent acute otitis media in children in day-care centers. Pediatrics 1995;96:884–8.

125. Warren JJ, Levy SM, Kirchner HL, et al. Pacifier use and the occurrence of otitis media in the first year of life. Pediatr Dent 2001;23:103–7.

126. Ingvarsson L, Lundgren K, Stenstrom C. Occurrence of acute otitis media in children: cohort studies in an urban population. In: Bluestone CD, Casselbrant ML, editors. Workshop on epidemiology of otitis media. Ann Otol Rhinol Laryngol 1990;99 Suppl 149:17–8.

127. Casselbrant ML, Mandel EM, Rockette HE, Bluestone CD. Incidence of otitis media and bacteriology of acute otitis media during the first two years of life. In: Lim DJ, Bluestone CD, Klein JO, Nelson JD, editors. Recent advances in otitis media with effusion. Proceedings of the Fifth International Symposium. Philadelphia (PA): BC Decker; 1993. p. 1–3.

128. Zonis RD. Chronic otitis media in the Southwestern American Indian. I. Prevalence. Arch Otolaryngol 1968; 88:360–5.

129. Virolainen E, Puhakka H, Aantaa E, et al. Prevalence of secretory otitis media in seven to eight year old school children. Ann Otol Rhinol Laryngol 1980;89 Suppl 68: 7–10.

130. Sørensen CH, Jensen SH, Tos M. The post-winter prevalence rate of middle-ear effusion in four-year-old children, judged by tympanometry. Int J Pediatr Otorhinolaryngol 1981;3:119–28.

131. Halama AR, Musgrave GM. Prevalence of otitis media in children in a black rural community in Venda (South Africa). Int J Pediatr Otorhinolaryngol 1986;11:73–7.

132. Miller SA, Omene JA, Bluestone CD, Torkelson DW. A point prevalence of otitis media in a Nigerian village. Int J Pediatr Otorhinolaryngol 1983;5:19–29.

133. Nelson SM, Berry RI. Ear disease and hearing loss among Navajo children—a mass survey. Laryngoscope 1984;94:316–23.

134. Holmquist J, Fadala SA, Qattan Y. Prevalence of secretory otitis media among school children in Kuwait. J Laryngol Otol 1987;101:116–9.

135. Ogisi FO. Impedance screening for otitis media with effusion in Nigerian children. J Laryngol Otol 1988;102: 986–8.

136. Cohen D, Tamir D. The prevalence of middle-ear pathologies in Jerusalem school children. Am J Otol 1989;10:456–9.

137. Zielhuis GA, Rach GH, van den Broek P. The occurrence of otitis media with effusion in Dutch pre-school children. Clin Otolaryngol 1990;15:147–53.

138. Schilder AGM, Zielhuis GA, Van Den Broek P. The otological profile of a cohort of Dutch 7.5–8-year-olds. Clin Otolaryngol 1993;18:48–54.

139. Williamson IG, Dunleavey J, Bain J, Robinson D. The natural history of otitis media with effusion—a three-year study of the incidence and prevalence of abnormal tympanograms in four South West Hampshire infant and first schools. J Laryngol Otol 1994;108:930–4.

140. Bastos I, Mallya J, Ingvarsson L, et al. Middle-ear disease and hearing impairment in northern Tanzania. A prevalence study of schoolchildren in the Moshi and Monduli districts. Int J Pediatr Otorhinolaryngol 1995;32:1–12.

141. Møller H, Tos M. Point and period prevalence of otitis media with effusion evaluated by daily tympanometry. J Laryngol Otol 1995;104:1937–41.

142. Homøe P, Christensen RB, Bretlau P. Prevalence of otitis media in a survey of 591 unselected Greenlandic children. Int J Pediatr Otorhinolaryngol 1996;36: 215–30.

143. Rushton HC, Tong MC, Yue V, et al. Prevalence of otitis media with effusion in multicultural schools in Hong Kong. J Laryngol Otol 1997;111:804–6.

144. Marchisio P Principi N, Passali D, et al. Epidemiology and treatment of otitis media with effusion in children in the first year of primary school. Acta Otolaryngol (Stockh) 1998;118:557–62.

145. Renvall U, Liden G, Jungert S, Nilsson E. Impedance audiometry in the detection of secretory otitis media. Scand Audiol 1975;4:119–24.

146. Thomsen J, Tos M, Hancke AB, Melchoirs H. Repetitive tympanometric screenings in children followed from birth to age four. Acta Otolaryngol 1982;386:155–7.

147. Roland PS, Finitzo T, Friel-Patti S, et al. Otitis media: incidence, duration and hearing status. Arch Otolaryngol Head Neck Surg 1989;115:1049–53.

148. Stewart JL. Otitis media in the first year of life in two Eskimo communities. Ann Otol Rhinol Laryngol 1989; 98:200–1.

149. Owen MJ, Baldwin CD, Luttman D, Howie VM. Otitis media with effusion detected by tympanometry on frequent home visits in Galveston, Texas. In: Lim DJ, Bluestone CD, Klein JO, Nelson JD, editors. Recent advances in otitis media. Proceedings of the Fifth International Symposium. Hamilton (ON): Decker Periodicals; 1993. p. 17–20.

150. Zeisel SA, Roberts JE, Gunn EB et al. Prospective surveillance for otitis media with effusion among black infants in group child care. J Pediatr 1995;127:875–80.

CHAPTER 11

Eustachian Tube Function and Dysfunction

Charles D. Bluestone, MD

It is beyond doubt that sometimes in excessive swelling of the tubal mucous membrane and impermeability of the Eustachian tube, there occurs in consequence of the consecutive rarefaction of the air in the tympanum, a transudation of serous fluid.
Adam Politzer

OBJECTIVES

On completing this chapter, the reader will be able to
1. Realize that the Eustachian tube is an organ within a system of connected organs.
2. Become familiar with the latest studies that have detailed the anatomy of the tube related to function.
3. Understand the physiology of the tube related to its functions of regulation of pressure, protection, and clearance of the middle ear.
4. Know a more simplified approach to the dysfunctions of the tube that can be explained to patients and their families.
5. Become familiar with the latest studies that have demonstrated the role of the tube in the pathogenesis of otitis media (OM).
6. Apply this knowledge when evaluating and managing patients with OM.

EDITORIAL COMMENT

Since the publication of the first edition of this book there has been further evidence from studies of human temporal bone specimens, experiments in animal models, and clinical studies to not only define normal and abnormal structure and function of the Eustachian tube but to establish the role of the Eustachian tube in the pathogenesis of OM. This chapter provides the details of these investigations.

ANATOMY

Much of the current information regarding the anatomy of the Eustachian tube has been recently determined by assessment of three-dimensional computer-reconstructed human temporal bone specimens ranging in age from fetal to adult. These studies reveal marked developmental differences between the anatomy of the

infant and young child compared with older children and adults, which most likely has a bearing on the high frequency of OM in the young. Using the same methodology, specimens from individuals with cleft palate and Down syndrome were compared with specimens from those without these disorders. Valuable clues as to the extraordinarily high prevalence of OM when these malformations occur were provided.

EUSTACHIAN TUBE AS AN ORGAN WITHIN A SYSTEM

The Eustachian tube is not just a tube but an organ consisting of a lumen with its mucosa, cartilage, surrounding soft tissue, peritubal muscles (ie, tensor veli palatini, levator veli palatini, salpingopharyngeus, and tensor tympani), and its superior bony support, the sphenoid sulcus (Table 11-1). An analogy can be made to the larynx, which is not only a conduit for air to pass from the pharynx to the lungs but also an organ consisting of a mucosal-lined tubelike structure, cartilage support, and muscles.[1] Like the larynx, the Eustachian tube is not in isolation but is part of a system of contiguous organs. The anterior end of the Eustachian tube is in continuity with the nasopharynx, nasal cavities, and palate. Its posterior end is in continuity with the middle ear and mastoid gas cells. The anatomy of the Eustachian tube is intimately related to its physiology and pathophysiology, which is, in turn, related to the pathogenesis of middle ear disease.

DEVELOPMENTAL DIFFERENCES

Studies of human temporal bone specimens reveal that the infant Eustachian tube is anatomically different from the adult tube, which contributes to the increased incidence of OM in this age group. Table 11-2[2–16] summarizes some of the known differences.

Table 11-1 Eustachian Tube and Associated Structures Constituting an Organ

Lumen

Mucosal lining

Mucociliary system

Cartilage

Osseous portion

Surrounding soft tissue

Vascular supply

Innervation

Lymphatics

Peritubal muscles

    Tensor veli palatini

    Levator veli palatini

    Salpingopharyngeus

    Tensor tympani

Sphenoid bony sulcus

Table 11-2 Developmental Differences between Infants and Adults in Anatomy of the Eustachian Tube*

Anatomic Features of the Eustachian tube Adult	Feature in Infant Compared with
Length of tube[2]	Shorter
Ratio of cartilaginous to osseous portion[3]	8:1 vs. 4:1
Angle of tube to horizontal plane[3,4]	Straight vs. angled
Angle of tensor veli palatini to cartilage[5,6]	Variable vs. stable
Connective tissue lateral to tube[7]	Less
Cartilage cell density[8]	Greater
Elastic at hinge portion of cartilage[9]	Less
Ostmann's fat pad[10]	Relatively wider
Lumen size and volume[11,12]	Smaller
Goblet cells in lumen[13]	Fewer
Serous glands in lumen[14]	Fewer
Mucosal folds in lumen[15]	Greater

*Adapted from Bluestone CD and Klein JO.[16]

The Eustachian tube lengthens rapidly during early childhood, essentially reaching its adult length by age 7 years.[2] The infant Eustachian tube is about half as long as that of the adult. Because the infant (and young child) has a shorter Eustachian tube than the older child and adult, nasopharyngeal secretions can reflux more readily into the middle ear through the shorter tube and result in OM.[17] In the infant, the direction of the tube varies from horizontal to an angle of about 10 degrees to the horizontal, and the tube is not angulated at the isthmus but merely narrows. In the adult, the tube is approximately 45 degrees related to the horizontal plane.[4] The angular relationship between the tensor veli palatini muscle and the cartilage varies in the infant but is relatively stable in the adult.[5] These differences may help explain the inefficient opening—due to contraction of the tensor veli palatini muscle—found in youngsters.[18,19]

Cartilage mass increases from birth to puberty. The density of elastin in the cartilage is less in the infant, but the cartilage cell density is greater.[8,9] Ostmann's fat pad is less in volume in the infant, but the width is similar between the two age groups.[10] The lumen is smaller in its cross-sectional dimension and volume in the infant compared with that in the adult.[11,12] Within the lumen, there are fewer goblet cells and serous glands in the infant compared with those in the adult.[13,14] Also, there are more folds in the mucosa of the lumen in the infant compared with that in the adult. These findings may explain the increased compliance (floppiness) of the tube in the infant compared with that of the adult.[17]

A recent finding from temporal bone specimens revealed that calcification and atrophy of the tensor veli palatini muscle increased with the aging process, which may be one explanation for the occurrence of OM in the elderly.[20] Also, in a study in humans, Eustachian tube compliance (floppiness) was found to increase with advancing age.[21]

ANATOMIC ABNORMALITIES IN SPECIAL POPULATIONS

Studies of human temporal bones of specimens from individuals with cleft palate and Down syndrome have revealed that they have several anatomic differences in their Eustachian tubes compared with specimens from those without these malformations. These studies have confirmed that the Eustachian tube of cleft palate patients is not anatomically obstructed, pointing to functional (ie, failure of the opening mechanism), rather than mechanical, obstruction as the underlying defect.[22]

Table 11-3[23–29] compares the anatomic abnormalities in the Eustachian tube of cleft palate specimens with those of histologic specimens without cleft palate. Sadler-

Kimes and associates compared the temporal bones of children with cleft palate with those of age-matched controls (without cleft palate) below the age of 6 years and reported that the Eustachian tube was statistically shorter in the specimens from those with clefts.[2] This team also compared the length of the Eustachian tube in specimens from children who had Down syndrome and found their tubes were also statistically shorter than control specimens. The relatively short Eustachian tube may explain the frequently recurrent and chronic otitis media, and especially troublesome otorrhea following tympanostomy tube placement, in these special populations of children. Nasopharyngeal secretions would be more likely to reflux into the middle ear through a Eustachian tube that is too short than one that is of normal length.

Other anatomic findings, such as abnormal cartilage and lumen, insertion ratio of the tensor veli palatini muscle into the cartilage, deficient attachment of the tensor veli palatini muscle into the lateral lamina of the cartilage, and deficient elastin at the hinge portion of the cartilage, most likely explain the functional obstruction (ie, failure of the opening mechanism) identified by radiographic and manometric Eustachian tube function tests.[22,25–31] In addition, patients with cleft palate have been found to have craniofacial skeletal abnormalities that could affect the anatomy of the Eustachian tube.[32] More rare conditions, such as trisomy 22, oculoauriculovertebral spectrum, Townes' syndrome, and oral-facial-digital syndrome, cause anatomic deformities of the Eustachian tube and other portions of the temporal bone.[33–35]

In a study of temporal bones of infants and children who had histopathologic evidence of OM, mucosa-

Table 11-3 Abnormalities of Eustachian Tube Anatomy*

Abnormality Compared with Specimens without Cleft Palate†

1. Length of tube shorter[2,23]

2. Angle between cartilage and tensor veli palatini larger[24]

3. Cartilage cell density greater[25]

4. Ratio of lateral and medial laminae area of cartilage smaller[26]

5. Immaturity of lateral lamina of cartilage[27]

6. Curvature of lumen less[26]

7. Elastin at hinge portion of cartilage less[28]

8. Insertion ratio of tensor veli palatini to cartilage less[29]

*In extended temporal bone specimens from infants and young children with cleft palate.
†Adapted from Bluestone CD and Klein JO.[16]

Table 11-4 Classification of Function and Dysfunction of Eustachian Tube

Functions
  Pressure regulation (ventilatory function)
  Protection
    Anatomic
    Immunologic and mucociliary defense
  Clearance (drainage)
    Mucociliary clearance
    Muscular clearance (pumping action)
  Surface tension factors

Dysfunctions
  Impairment of pressure regulation
    Anatomic obstruction
      Intraluminal
      Periluminal
      Peritubal
    Failure of opening mechanism (functional obstruction)
  Loss of protective function
    Abnormal patency
    Short tube
    Abnormal gas pressures
      Intratympanic
      Nasopharyngeal
    Nonintact middle ear–mastoid
  Impairment of clearance
    Mucociliary
    Muscular

associated lymphoid tissue (MALT) was identified in the Eustachian tubes, middle ears, and mastoids, which indicated to the investigators that MALT could be a mechanism involved in a local immune reaction to recurrent OM.[36] Also, a recent histopathologic study of temporal bone specimens from patients who had chronic renal failure revealed ossification of the Eustachian tube cartilage and Ostmann's fatty tissue.[37]

FUNCTIONS

There are three physiologic functions attributed to the Eustachian tube: (1) pressure regulation ("ventilation") of the middle ear to equilibrate gas pressure in the middle ear with atmospheric pressure; (2) protection of the middle ear from nasopharyngeal sound pressure and secretions; and (3) clearance (drainage) of secretions produced within the middle ear into the nasopharynx. Table 11-4 shows a proposed classification of the physiology and pathophysiology of the Eustachian tube.

Pressure Regulation ("Ventilatory") Function

The most important function of the Eustachian tube is regulation of pressure within the middle ear, because hearing is optimum when the middle ear gas pressure is relatively the same as the air pressure in the external auditory canal (ie, when tympanic membrane and middle ear compliance is optimal).

Normally, the intermittent active opening of the Eustachian tube, due to contraction of the tensor veli palatini muscle during swallowing, maintains nearly ambient pressures in the middle ear.[38–41] Under physiologic conditions, the fluctuations in ambient pressure are bidirectional (ie, either to or from the middle ear), relatively small in magnitude, and not readily appreciated.[42] These fluctuations reflect the rise and fall in barometric pressures associated with changing weather conditions and/or elevation. The changes in middle ear pressure show mass directionality, can achieve appreciable magnitudes, and can result in pathologic changes. These conditions result primarily from the fact that the middle ear–mastoid gas cell system is a relatively rigid (ie, noncollapsible) gas pocket that is surrounded by a mucous membrane in which gases are exchanged between the middle ear space and the mucosa. (The mastoid gas cells probably act as a gas reserve for the middle ear, as opposed to having a pressure regulating function.[43])

Differential pressure exceeds 54 mm Hg between the middle ear space at atmospheric pressure and the microcirculation in the mucous membrane. This represents a diffusion-driven gradient from the middle ear cavity to the mucosa that can produce an underpressure (relative to ambient pressure) in the middle ear of more than 600 mm H_2O during equilibration. A mathematic model describing the gas exchange between the middle ear and microcirculation of the middle ear mucosa has been described.[44,45]

Normal Eustachian tube function has been determined, using a pressure chamber, in Swedish children and adults who were considered to be otologically normal. The study revealed that 35.8% of the children could not equilibrate applied negative intratympanic pressure by swallowing, whereas only 5% of the adults were unable to perform this function.[46] Children aged 3 to 6 years had worse function than those aged 7 to 12 years. The conclusion from these studies is that even in apparently otologically normal children, Eustachian tube function is not as good as in adults, which is most likely related to the higher incidence of middle ear disease in the younger population.

Inefficient active tubal opening in children probably explains the frequent finding—by otoscopy and tympanometry—of relatively high negative middle ear pressure in this age group, even though they have no otologic symptoms or OM. Since infants have an inefficient active opening mechanism, they most likely compensate in some way to regulate pressure within the middle ear. Crying is one possible compensatory mechanism, because high positive pressure is apparent by otoscopy and tympanometry when some infants are crying during these examinations. Also, this mechanism could explain why infants tend to cry in a descending airplane.

Protective Function

The Eustachian tube protects the middle ear and mastoid gas cell system through the functional anatomy of the Eustachian tube–middle ear and by immunologic and mucociliary defense of the mucous membrane lining.

Protection of the middle ear from abnormal nasopharyngeal sound pressures and secretions depends primarily on the normal structure and function of the Eustachian tube and the integrity of the middle ear and mastoid air cell system, which maintains a "gas cushion." To determine the protective function of the tube, studies employing radiographic techniques were used.[17,22,47,48] In these studies, radiopaque material was instilled into the nose and nasopharynx of children who had OM and compared with those of children who were otologically healthy. In the physiologic state, contrast material entered the nasopharyngeal end of the Eustachian tube during swallowing activity but did not enter the middle ear. By contrast, the dye did reflux into the middle ear in some patients who had middle ear disease, especially during closed-nose swallowing.

At rest, the normal Eustachian tube is collapsed and the tubal lumen is closed, thus preventing liquid—and abnormal nasopharyngeal sound pressures—from entering the nasopharyngeal end of the tube. During swallowing, when the proximal end (ie, cartilaginous portion) opens, liquid can enter this part of the tube but does not gain entrance into the middle ear, due to the narrow midportion of the tube, the isthmus. The entire Eustachian tube–middle ear system is similar in this function to a flask with a long, narrow neck—the mouth of the flask represents the nasopharyngeal end; the narrow neck, the isthmus; and the bulbous portion, the middle ear and mastoid air-cell system.[17,49]

Protection of the middle ear–mastoid is also provided by the respiratory epithelium of the Eustachian tube lumen by means of its local immunologic defense, as well as mucociliary defense, that is, clearance.

Clearance Function

There are two physiologic methods of clearance (drainage) of secretions from the middle ear into the nasopharynx: (1) mucociliary clearance, and (2) muscular clearance. The mucociliary system of the Eustachian tube and some areas of the middle ear mucous membrane clear secretions from the middle ear, and the "pumping action" of the Eustachian tube during closing provides muscular clearance.

Mucociliary clearance function has been studied (1) by instilling radiopaque material into the middle ear of children whose tympanic membranes were not intact or when the material entered the middle ear (intact tympanic membrane) from the nasopharynx, and (2) following insertion of foreign material into the middle ear of animal models.[17,47,50,51] Such material will flow toward the middle ear portion of the Eustachian tube and out of the tube. This movement is related to ciliary activity that occurs in the Eustachian tube and parts of the middle ear. Ciliated cells in the middle ear are more active the more distal than they are to the opening of the Eustachian tube.[52]

The "pumping action" of the Eustachian tube to drain middle ear fluid was first reported by Honjo and colleagues.[53,54] In a series of experiments in both animal models and humans, the Eustachian tube, during closing, was shown to "pump" instilled radiographic contrast material out of the middle ear and into the nasopharynx. The passive closing process of the Eustachian tube begins at the middle ear end of the tube and progresses toward the nasopharyngeal end, thus "pumping out" secretions.

Surface Tension Factors

Surface tension factors have been identified that have been thought to be involved in normal Eustachian tube function.

Birkin and Brookler isolated surface tension-lowering substances from washings of Eustachian tubes of dogs.[55] They postulated that these substances could act to enhance Eustachian tube functions, as surfactant does in the lung. Rapport and colleagues described a similar substance and demonstrated the effect of washing out the Eustachian tube on the opening pressure in the experimental animal; others have also demonstrated a surfactant-like phospholipid in the middle ears and Eustachian tubes of animals and humans.[56–59] In a recent study in gerbils, Fornadley and Burns produced middle ear effusions (MEEs) by injecting killed *Streptococcus pneumoniae* into the middle ear through the tympanic membrane, which increased the opening pressure of the Eustachian tube.[60] When the investigators introduced exogenous surfactant, the opening pressure dropped.

It is apparent from these studies that the clearance function of the Eustachian tube–middle ear system is important in maintaining a healthy middle ear. Because OM is so common in humans, efficient removal of MEEs must depend, to a large extent, on these functions.

DYSFUNCTIONS

Simplified terms to describe the abnormal dysfunctional Eustachian tube might be "too closed," "won't open," "too floppy," "too open," "too short," "too stiff," or, at either end of the Eustachian tube system, "too closed," "too open," or "has abnormal pressures." More precisely, the pathophysiology can be classified into impairment of pressure regulation, loss of protective function, and impairment of clearance. These types of dysfunction are described in detail below.

Impairment of Pressure Regulation

Impairment of the regulation of pressure within the middle ear (and mastoid) can be due to either anatomic obstruction of the Eustachian tube ("too closed") or failure of the opening mechanism of the Eustachian tube ("won't open").

Anatomic Obstruction of Eustachian Tube

Anatomic (ie, "mechanical") obstruction in the tube can be either intraluminal, periluminal, or peritubal. Obstruction of the lumen or within the periluminal tissues (ie, intrinsic obstruction) can be due to inflammation secondary to infection or allergy.[61–64] Obstruction within the bony portion (ie, middle ear end) of the tube is usually due to acute or chronic inflammation of the mucosal lining, which may also be associated with polyps or a cholesteatoma. Total obstruction may be present at the middle ear end of the tube. Stenosis of the Eustachian tube has also been diagnosed but is a rare finding. Peritubal obstruction (ie, extrinsic obstruction) could be the result of compression caused by a tumor or possibly an adenoid mass.[46,65]

Failure of Opening Mechanism of Eustachian Tube ("Functional Obstruction")

Opening failure may be due to persistent collapse of the Eustachian tube due to increased tubal compliance (ie, a lack of stiffness, or being "too floppy"), an inefficient active opening mechanism, or both defects coexisting. This has also been termed "functional obstruction" of the Eustachian tube—the tube is not anatomically (ie, mechanically) obstructed, but it is functionally obstructed. It was first described in infants with unrepaired palatal clefts who had had chronic OM with effusion.[22] Failure of the opening mechanism of the Eustachian tube is common in infants and younger children without cleft palate or history of middle ear disease but more common in those children with middle ear disease.[17,19,66–71] Failure of an active muscle opening of the Eustachian tube has also been identified in adults with middle ear disease.[72]

There is now evidence that failure of the opening mechanism of the Eustachian tube may be due to persistent collapse of the tubal cartilage. Because the amount of cartilage is less in the infant than in older children and adults and the cell density of the cartilage decreases with advancing age, the stiffness of the tubal cartilage in the infant and young child could be affected.[2,8] If the tubal cartilage lacks stiffness (is "too floppy"), then the lumen may not open in response to contraction of the tensor veli palatini muscle. Also, the density of elastin in the cartilage is less in the infant, and Ostmann's fat pad is less in volume in the infant than in the adult.[9,10]

There is evidence that failure of the opening mechanism of the Eustachian tube may be due to an inefficient tensor veli palatini muscle. This poor muscle opening may be due to the marked age differences in the craniofacial base. The angle of the tube in the child is different from that of the adult. In the adult, the tube is approximately 45 degrees related to the horizontal plane but only 10 degrees in infants.[4] This difference in the angle has been thought by some to be related to possible clearance problems in children, but this hypothesis has not been confirmed. It is more likely that the difference in angulation has an effect on the function of the active opening mechanism (ie, tensor veli palatini muscle contraction). Swarts and Rood found that the angular relationship between the tensor veli palatini muscle and the cartilage varies in the infant but is relatively stable in the adult.[5]

Loss of Protective Function

There are four possible dysfunctions of the Eustachian tube system that could result in loss of protective function: (1) the tube has abnormal patency ("too open"), (2) the tube is relatively short ("too short"), (3) abnormal gas pressures develop at either end of the tube ("too closed" at the proximal end of the tube), or (4) there is a nonintact middle ear (eg, perforation of the tympanic membrane or tympanostomy tube) resulting in a loss of the middle ear gas pocket or cushion ("too open" at the middle ear end of the Eustachian tube).

Abnormal Patency of Eustachian Tube

The Eustachian tube may be abnormally open, and when extreme, that is, when open even at rest, it is patulous. Lesser degrees of abnormal patency result in a semipatulous Eustachian tube that is closed at rest but has low resistance in comparison with the normal tube.[73] Increased patency of the tube may be due to abnormal tube geometry or to a decrease in the peritubal pressure, such as occurs after weight loss or possibly as a result of periluminal factors. Because the Eustachian tube has been found to be highly compliant in infants and young children, this increase in distensibility of the tube may result in abnormal patency, especially when there is high nasopharyngeal pressure. The patulous tube, however, has been found to be "too stiff" in teenagers and adults compared with normal tubal compliance.[74]

A patulous Eustachian tube usually permits gas to flow readily from the nasopharynx into the middle ear, which, effectively regulates middle ear pressure. Unwanted secretions from the nasopharynx can more readily gain access, that is, reflux, into the middle ear when the tube is abnormally patent. Certain special populations have been found to have patulous or semipatulous Eustachian tubes, such as Native Americans and patients who have Down syndrome and middle ear disease.[75,76] Failure of the passive closing mechanism of the Eustachian tube (the tube is "too open") has been postulated to be related to "sniff-induced" middle ear disease (see "Other Causes of Eustachian Tube Dysfunction," below).[77]

The Short Eustachian Tube

As described above, one of the most important differences in the structure of the Eustachian tube between infants and young children, and older children and adults, is the length of the tube—the tube is shorter in children below the age of 7 years (see Table 11-2).[2] Young children with a cleft palate have Eustachian tubes that are statistically shorter than in age-matched controls below the age of 6 years (see Table 11-3). The tube is also shorter in children with Down syndrome.[2]

The shorter the tube, the more likely it is that secretions can reflux into the middle ear. An analogy can be made to the length of the urethra: females of all ages have more urinary tract infections than males, because the urethra is shorter in the female. This may be one explanation for the frequent occurrence of troublesome otorrhea in infants and young children, especially those who have a cleft palate or Down syndrome, when the tympanic membrane is not intact.

Abnormal Gas Pressures at Either End of the System

Nonphysiologic pressures that develop at either end of the Eustachian tube system can result in a loss of protective function. At the distal end, development of high negative middle ear pressure, secondary to obstruction of the Eustachian tube, due to either anatomic obstruction, failure of active opening, or both, may result in aspiration of nasopharyngeal secretions into the middle ear. The process has been modeled in the chinchilla (WJ Doyle, PhD, unpublished data, 1989).

At the proximal end of the system, high positive nasopharyngeal pressures can result in insufflation of secretions into the middle ear. This may occur during blowing of the nose, when the infant is crying, or when nasal obstruction is present. Swallowing when the nose is obstructed by inflammation or enlarged adenoids results in an initial positive nasopharyngeal air pressure followed by a negative pressure phase. The ferret animal model of complete nasal obstruction has resulted in persistent high positive middle ear pressures, most likely secondary to insufflation of air into the middle ear during swallowing activity.[78] When the tube is pliant, positive nasopharyngeal pressure might insufflate infected secretions into the middle ear, especially when the middle ear has high negative pressure. With negative nasopharyngeal pressure, a pliant tube could be prevented from opening and could be further obstructed functionally. This has been referred to as the "Toynbee phenomenon."[66,79,80]

Rapid changes in ambient pressures during swimming, diving, air travel, and when receiving hypobaric pressure treatments may also result in the aspiration or insufflation of nasopharyngeal secretions. Indeed, Eustachian tube function tests have been helpful in predicting dysfunctional tubes in scuba divers who were susceptible to barotrauma during diving.[81]

Also, at the proximal end of the Eustachian tube, abnormal negative pressures can be transmitted to the middle ear. It has been reported that sniffing causes abnormal middle ear negative pressures in patients, which was postulated to be involved in the pathogenesis of middle ear effusions.[82,83] Mucosal surface area may be involved in determining middle ear pressure response following sniff-induced middle ear negative pressures.[84] A recent report indicated that bottle-feeding of infants instead of breast-feeding resulted in high negative middle ear pressures, which was attributable to conventional nonventilated and underventilated bottles that create negative pressure during sucking. The investigators postulated that this could be a mechanism causing OM, which is more common in bottle-fed infants than in those who are breast fed.[85] During bottle feeding, it is probable that the negative pressure in the pharynx is transmitted to the middle ear.

Nonintact Middle Ear and Mastoid

Secretions from the nasopharynx are prevented from entering the middle ear when the structure of the Eustachian tube is normal and because of the cushion of gas that is within the intact middle ear and mastoid air cell system. The gas pocket is lost when a perforation of the tympanic membrane is present; a tympanostomy tube is in place; or in the extreme condition when a radical mastoidectomy is present (the eardrum is absent, and the middle ear, mastoid, and ear canal communicate forming a single cavity). When this is the case, secretions from the nasopharynx reflux into the middle ear.[17,67]

Impairment of Clearance Function

Several conditions can occur in the Eustachian tube and middle ear that can adversely affect clearance of secretions. Ohashi and colleagues, in studies conducted in guinea pigs, demonstrated that bacteria, their toxins, and irradiation can impair ciliary function.[86] Park and associates demonstrated that influenza A virus alters the ciliary activity and dye transport function in the Eustachian tube of the chinchilla.[87] Recently, tobacco smoke and histamine were found to interfere with the normal clearance function and opening pressures of the Eustachian tube in a rat animal model.[88] Most investigators consider impairment of clearance function to be related to failure to resolve MEEs, rather than being the primary cause of the disease.[89] However, patients who have ciliary dysmotility in their upper respiratory tract mucous membrane have been observed to have chronic MEEs.[90] Also, tubal pumping action is most likely ineffective when the opening mechanism is inadequate and has been demonstrated to be impaired when negative pressure was present within the middle ear.[91,92]

Dysfunction Related to Cleft Palate

There is longstanding evidence that OM is universally present in infants with an unrepaired cleft palate.[93,94] Palate repair appears to improve middle ear status, but middle ear disease, nonetheless, often continues or recurs after palate repair.[95,96]

Failure of the opening mechanism in infants with an unrepaired cleft palate is the primary cause of dysfunction.[22,31,96] As described above, histopathologic temporal bone studies have confirmed that the Eustachian tube of cleft palate patients is not anatomically obstructed. This gives credence to failure of the opening mechanism, that is, functional, as opposed to anatomic, obstruction as the underlying defect. Other anatomic findings, such as abnormal cartilage and lumen, insertion ratio of the tensor veli palatini muscle into the cartilage, deficient attachment of the tensor veli palatini muscle into the lateral lamina of the cartilage, and deficient elastin at the hinge portion of the cartilage, most likely explain the functional obstruction identified by radiographic and manometric Eustachian tube function tests (see Table 11-3).[25,26,29,31] Also, OM with effusion developed in animals whose palates had been surgically split.[96–98]

From these studies in humans and animals, it appears that the high incidence of OM in children with cleft palate is related to failure of the opening mechanism and may also be related to the deficient length of the Eustachian tube. If infants with intact palates are able to inflate their middle ears during crying, as a physiologic compensatory mechanism for their ineffective active tubal opening, then infants with unrepaired cleft palates have an additional handicap (the proximal end of the Eustachian tube system is "too open").

Dysfunction Related to Allergy

The effect of allergy and inflammatory mediators on the function of the Eustachian tube has been evaluated in adult volunteers. Nasal and Eustachian tube function were assessed before and after intranasal challenge of allergic antigens and mediators. These studies were conducted in subjects with and without allergy because upper respiratory tract allergy has been implicated in the pathogenesis of middle ear disease.

The role of allergy in the etiology and pathogenesis of OM has been postulated to be one or more of the following mechanisms: middle ear mucosa functioning as a "shock (target) organ," inflammatory swelling of the mucosa of the Eustachian tube, inflammatory obstruction of the nose, that is, Toynbee phenomenon, or aspiration of bacteria-laden allergic nasopharyngeal secretions into the middle ear cavity.[64,99–101] Another possible mechanism has been proposed on the basis of the possible increase in circulating anti-inflammatory mediators as the result of local allergic reactions in the mucosa of the nose or stomach.[102] These could alter the middle ear mucosal permeability and result in altered gas exchange.

The effect of allergy on the Eustachian tube has been evaluated in humans. Studies involving adult volunteers have shown that there is an adverse effect on Eustachian tube function, in subjects who were hypersensitive to the antigen when there were changes in the nose, but OM did not develop in any of the subjects in these studies.[64,103–109] Histamine exposure of the Eustachian tube in a rat animal model also resulted in impairment of mucociliary clearance time and opening pressures.[110] In another rat animal model study, Hardy and colleagues demonstrated that late-phase allergy could impair Eustachian tube dysfunction when the rats were sensitized to ovalbumin and later challenged in the middle ear.[111]

It is possible that MEE would develop with repeated challenge with antigen over a prolonged period of time in individuals who are not only hypersensitive to the specific antigen but who also have pre-existing poor Eustachian tube function.

Other Causes of Eustachian Tube Dysfunction

Dysfunction of the Eustachian tube has also been reported to be associated with deviation of the nasal septum ("too closed" at the proximal end of the system); trauma induced by nasogastric and nasal endotracheal tubes ("too closed"); trauma to the palate, pterygoid bone, or tensor veli palatini muscle ("won't open"); injury to the trigeminal nerve or, more specifically, to the mandibular branch of this nerve ("won't open"); and trauma associated with surgical procedures, such as palatal or maxillary resection for tumor ("won't open" or "too open" at proximal end of the system).[112–117] Benign or malignant neoplastic disease invading the palate, pterygoid bone, or tensor veli palatini muscle can cause OM, which can be caused by failure of the opening mechanism of the tube ("won't open")[117–120]

Recently, a study of pepsin concentrations in middle ear effusions of children showed that most effusions had up to 1,000-fold greater concentrations than the serum. This indicated to the investigators that gastric reflux may be a pathogenic mechanism in OM. They postulated that the gastric juice "refluxes" into the middle ear.[121] If this finding is confirmed from other studies, the acid could also cause mechanical obstruction within the Eustachian tube and/or be aspirated in the middle ear during periods of high middle ear negative pressure. Indeed, a recent study in a rat animal model showed that exposure of the middle ear to pepsin and hydrochloric acid results in elevated opening pressures and impairment of the active opening mechanism of the Eustachian tube.[122]

Individuals who are "habitual sniffers" can create underpressure within the middle ear by this act.[77] This mechanism is uncommon in children, however. In a study from Japan, Sakakihara and coworkers evaluated 17 subjects with a mean age of 16 years who had "sniff-induced" OM and found that their Eustachian tubes were excessively patent ("too open") with poor active opening mechanisms ("won't open").[75]

ROLE IN PATHOGENESIS OF OTITIS MEDIA

Recent studies in animal models and adult human volunteers have confirmed the hypothesis that dysfunction of the Eustachian tube is, indeed, involved in the pathogenesis of certain types of middle ear disease. Several clinical studies in which adult volunteers had an intranasal challenge of virus have convincingly demonstrated the sequence of events from a viral upper respiratory tract infection to Eustachian tube obstruction to negative middle ear pressures to OM. The details of these studies follow.

Animal Models

Middle-ear effusion has been produced in animal models using a variety of methods. Table 11-5 summarizes these studies.

Table 11-5 Animal Models of High Negative Middle Ear Pressure and Middle Ear Effusion

Experiment Number	Year (Reference)	Animal	Diagnostic Method	Method	Outcomes		
					HNP	MEE	Resolved Long-term
1	1977 (123)	Monkey	Otomic and tymp	TVP excised	Yes	Yes	No
2	1980 (124)	Monkey	Otomic and tymp	TVP: excised transected transposed	Yes Yes Yes Yes	Yes Yes Yes Yes	No No No/yes Yes
3	1988 (41)	Monkey	Otomic and tymp	Botulinum into TVP	Yes	Yes	Yes
4	1995 (126)	Ferret	Otomic and tymp	Influenza A nasal inoculation	Yes	No	Yes
5	1995 (127)	Monkey	MRI	CO_2 insuf into ME	Yes	Yes	NA
6	1997 (125)	Monkey	MRI	Botulinum into TVP	Yes	Yes	Yes

CO_2 = carbon dioxide; HNP = high negative middle ear pressure; insuf = insufflation; ME = middle ear; MEE = middle ear effusion; MRI = magnetic resonance imaging; NA = not applicable (acute experiment); otomic = otomicroscope; tymp = tympanometry; TVP = tensor veli palatini muscle.

Experiments have provided ample evidence that inactivation of the tensor veli palatini muscle prevents active opening of the Eustachian tube, which results in negative middle ear pressure followed by middle ear effusion. When the tensor veli palatini muscle was surgically altered or inactivated, negative pressure and effusion developed in the middle ear. In one experiment, excision of a portion of the tensor veli palatini muscle at the pterygoid hamulus in the palate resulted in negative pressure in the middle ear followed by an effusion.[123] Comparable results were produced in a similar experiment in which the muscle was either completely excised, the superficial muscle bundle transected, or transposition of the tendon of the tensor medial to the hamular process.[124] Complete excision resulted in middle ear underpressures followed by persistent effusion; transection of the muscle resulted in negative middle ear pressures, or effusion, or both (and in some animals the middle ear returned to normal after healing of the muscle). When the tendon of the tensor was transposed, outcomes were similar to surgical alteration, but the middle ear rapidly returned to normal. Using a noninvasive method, Casselbrant and associates injected botulinum toxin into the tensor muscle, which resulted in negative pressure and then effusion.[41] The middle ear returned to normal when the effect of the botulinum toxin resolved.

In these earlier studies, middle ear status was diagnosed with the aid of otomicroscopy and tympanom-

etry. More recently, Alper and colleagues also injected botulinum toxin into the tensor veli palatini muscle of monkeys, which resulted in an opening failure of the Eustachian tube, middle ear underpressures, and effusion. This was assessed using magnetic resonance imaging (MRI) of the middle ear cleft and by tympanometry.[125] In ears that developed underpressures within the middle ear, increased vascular permeability was observed on the MRI (Figure 11-1). These experiments created a functional obstruction of the Eustachian tube (ie, impairment of active opening of the tube), which impeded pressure regulation of the middle ear and which subsequently resulted in an effusion. When the botulinum toxin resolved, the middle ear status returned to normal.

Using a different animal model, the ferret, Buchman and colleagues evaluated the effect of influenza A virus nasal challenge on the function of the Eustachian tube (assessed by forced-response and inflation-deflation tests) and middle ear status (evaluated by otomicroscopy and tympanometry).[126] All 10 animals involved in the experiment became infected, and all had Eustachian tube dysfunction associated with middle ear underpressures, but no MEE developed. However, the investigation showed that even though the Eustachian tube does not become totally obstructed, abnormally high negative pressures develop within the middle ear.

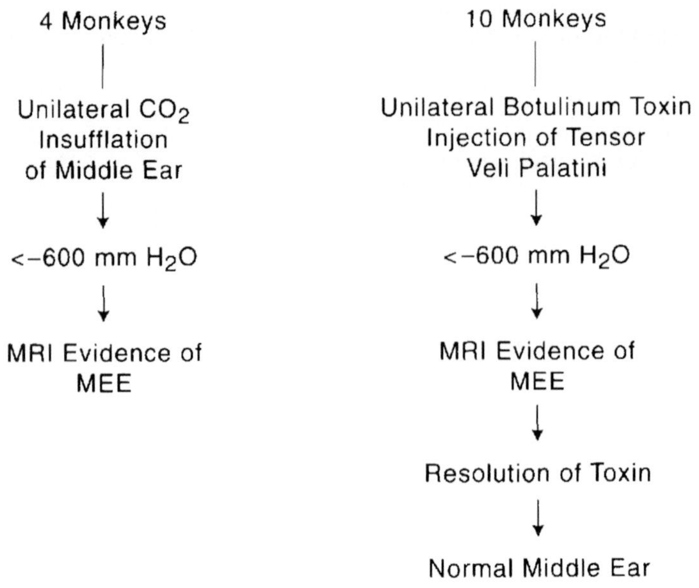

4 Monkeys

|

Unilateral CO_2
Insufflation
of Middle Ear

↓

<−600 mm H_2O

↓

MRI Evidence of
MEE

10 Monkeys

|

Unilateral Botulinum Toxin
Injection of Tensor
Veli Palatini

↓

<−600 mm H_2O

↓

MRI Evidence of
MEE

↓

Resolution of Toxin

↓

Normal Middle Ear

Figure 11-1 Flow diagrams of two experiments in monkeys using magnetic resonance imaging (MRI) showing the pathogenesis of middle ear effusion (MEE) following induced high negative middle ear pressures (supports hydrops ex vacuo theory of MEE pathogenesis). Adapted from Swarts JD et al.[127] and Alper CM et al.[125]

Employing a different approach, Swarts and associates were also able to produce unilateral MEE in the monkey shortly after inducing middle ear negative pressure by inflating the middle ear with carbon dioxide (CO_2). Increased vascular permeability was identified on the MRI using a contrast agent (see Figure 11-1).[127] None of these changes was found in the contralateral control ear. When the middle ear cleft was flushed with oxygen, lesser middle ear underpressures developed, but no MEE or other changes on the MRI scan were noted. Even though the Eustachian tube was not altered in this experiment, the effect of middle ear negative pressure in the development of MEE was not shown.

The above experiments provide convincing evidence for the role of the Eustachian tube in the development of OM in animal models. There is now equally convincing evidence from studies in adult volunteers.

Clinical Viral Challenge Studies

Five intranasal viral challenge studies in adult volunteers provide support for the role the Eustachian tube plays in the pathogenesis of OM, including AOM. These investigations are summarized in Table 11-6.

The first clinical study to show the effect of an upper respiratory tract infection (ie, a cold) on the function of the Eustachian tube and the status of the middle ear in humans was conducted by Doyle and associates.[128] Rhinovirus was inoculated into the noses of 40 adult volunteers—these viruses can be isolated in approximately 40% of individuals with an upper respiratory tract infection, that is, a cold. All participants were

found to be infected after inoculation, but only 80% developed the signs and symptoms of a clinical illness. Eustachian tube function was assessed before and periodically after the nasal challenge with rhinovirus, using sonotubometry and the nine-step test, middle ear pressure employing tympanometry, and nasal patency using active posterior rhinometry. All subjects with a cold had decreased nasal patency, 50% had Eustachian tube obstruction, and 30% had abnormal negative middle ear pressure for approximately 1 week after the inoculation. These outcomes completely resolved within 16 days, and none of the volunteers developed a MEE.

McBride and colleagues recruited 32 adult volunteers in a design similar to the first study.[62] Abnormal findings were limited to the 24 subjects (75%) who developed clinical signs and symptoms of infection after challenge with rhinovirus. After 2 days of the illness, 80% had Eustachian tube obstruction, 50% had high negative middle ear pressure, and 46% had decreased nasal patency. Again, none of the subjects developed a MEE. These abnormal findings resolved in 6 to 10 days after the challenge.

In a similar investigation by Buchman and coworkers that involved 60 adult volunteers, 95% became infected after nasal inoculation with rhinovirus, and 60% had a clinical cold.[63] Prior to the nasal challenge, three (5%) volunteers had abnormal middle ear pressure, and two of these subjects developed a MEE. Of the 60 subjects, 22 (39%) had high negative middle ear pressure. None of the subjects who had normal middle ear pressure before the challenge developed an effusion, which would indicate that a rhinovirus infection

Table 11-6 Effect of Nasal Virus Challenge on Eustachian Tube and Middle Ear Status in Volunteers

Experiment Number	Year (Reference)	Number Subjects	Virus	Outcomes (%)			
				ET OBS	HNP	MEE	AOM
1	1988 (128)	40	Rhinovirus	50	30	0	0
2	1989 (62)	32	Rhinovirus	80	50	0	0
3	1994 (63)	60	Rhinovirus	NT	39	3	0
4	1994 (109)	33	Influenza A	80	80	23	0
5	1995 (126)	27	Influenza A	NT	59	25	4

AOM = acute otitis media; ET OBS = Eustachian tube obstruction; HNP = high negative pressure; MEE = middle-ear effusion; NT = not tested.

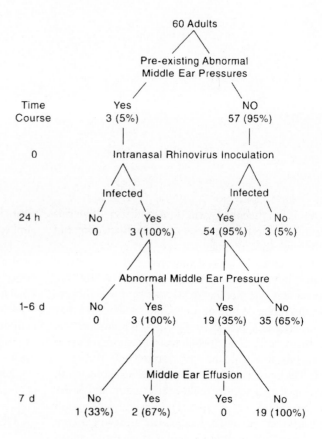

Figure 11-2 Flow diagram showing that pre-existing abnormal negative middle ear pressure predisposes to MEE following intranasal inoculation of rhinovirus in 60 adult volunteers. Adapted from Buchman CA et al.[63]

may result in a MEE if the patient has a pre-existing dysfunction of the Eustachian tube (Figure 11-2).

In another related study, Doyle and colleagues performed Eustachian tube function tests on 18 adult volunteers both before and after nasal challenge with influenza A virus. This study showed that those individuals with inefficient Eustachian tube function prior to the challenge were prone to abnormal middle ear pressures after the challenge, whereas those whose pre-existing tubal function was good were less likely to have otologic complications.[129] Doyle and colleagues also reported that intranasal challenge with influenza A virus in 33 healthy adult volunteers resulted in 80% demonstrating Eustachian tube obstruction and 80% having negative middle ear pressure. Five (23%) of 21 subjects infected with this virus also developed a MEE.[109]

Figure 11-3 Flow diagram of the effect of intranasal inoculation of influenza A virus in 27 adult volunteers, in which one subject developed acute otitis media. Adapetd from Buchman CA et al.[126] *Middle ear aspirate = PCR-positive virus + *Streptococcus pneumoniae.*

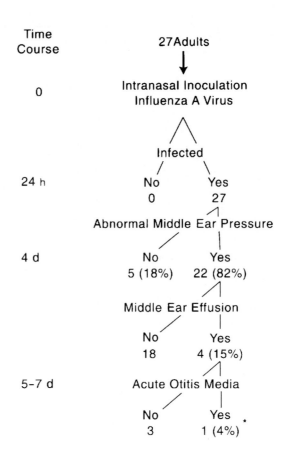

Most likely, influenza A virus is more virulent than rhinovirus in the pathogenesis of Eustachian tube and middle ear abnormalities.

These clinical studies demonstrated the role played by the Eustachian tube in the development of MEE, but there is now evidence that AOM has a similar pathogenesis. In a recent important study conducted by Buchman and colleagues, this cascade of events was reproduced for the first time in 27 adult volunteers, in whom influenza A was inoculated into the nose (Figure 11-3).[126] All subjects developed a nasal infection, 22 (82%) subsequently developed high negative middle ear pressure, and, in one subject, AOM was present. The middle ear aspirate revealed the virus and *S. pneumoniae* using polymerase chain reaction; traditional viral and bacterial culture methods failed to grow these organisms from the MEE. It is possible that these microorganisms were aspirated from the nasopharynx into the middle ear cavity due to the high negative middle ear pressure.

Analyzing the outcomes of the challenge studies of three viruses—rhinovirus type 39, rhinovirus strain hanks, and influenza A virus—revealed that even although middle ear underpressures were common in subjects who were infected and reported illness, these abnormal pressures were also found in subjects who were infected but did not have clinical symptoms of an upper respiratory tract infection.[130]

The results of these challenge studies support the causal relationship between upper respiratory tract infection, partial Eustachian tube obstruction, abnormal middle ear underpressures, and OM. Also, this cascade of events was confirmed in a prospective study in children using daily tympanometry, which also showed that negative middle ear pressures were documented prior to the onset of clinical symptoms of a naturally occurring upper respiratory tract infection.[131]

CONCLUSION

We now have sufficient evidence from studies of human temporal bone specimens, experiments in animal models, and clinical studies in humans to conclude that the Eustachian tube plays an important role in the development of OM (Table 11-7). Even although there are many other factors involved in the pathogenesis of OM, such as immunologic status and possibly allergy, pre-existing Eustachian tube dysfunction appears to be a critical risk factor in developing OM with effusion, especially during exposure to a viral upper respiratory tract infection.

Table 11-7 Pointers and Pitfalls

1. Knowledge of the developmental anatomy and physiology of the Eustachian tube should provide evidence, in addition to other factors (eg, immature immunity), that most infants and young children will have fewer episodes of OM with advancing age.

2. Instituting aggressive preventive measures that are not based on evidence are not warranted because most infants and children grow out of their susceptibility for OM.

3. Those older children and adults who have persistent middle ear disease most likely have dysfunction of the Eustachian tube.

4. There are many reasons why the Eustachian tube may be dysfunctional, and the clinician should try to determine the most likely etiology to direct management decisions.

5. As there is now evidence that upper respiratory tract infections can precede an episode of either AOM or OM with effusion, management should be focused on prevention of these viral infections.

AOM = acute otitis media; OM = otitis media.

REFERENCES

1. Bluestone CD, Cantekin EI. Current clinical methods, indications and interpretation of Eustachian tube function tests. Ann Otol Rhinol Laryngol 1981;90:552–62.

2. Sadler-Kimes D, Siegel MI, Todhunter JS. Age-related morphologic differences in the components of the eustachian tube/middle ear system. Ann Otol Rhinol Laryngol 1989;98:854–8.

3. Ishijima K, Sando I, Balaban C, et al. Length of the eustachian tube and its postnatal development: computer-aided three-dimensional reconstruction and measurement study. Ann Otol Rhinol Laryngol 2000;109:542–8.

4. Proctor B. Embryology and anatomy of the eustachian tube. Arch Otolaryngol 1967;86:503–14.

5. Swarts JD, Rood SR. Preliminary analysis of the morphometry of the infant eustachian tube. In: Lim DJ, Bluestone CD, Klein JO, et al, editors. Recent advances in otitis media. Proceedings of the Fifth International Symposium. Toronto (ON): Decker Periodicals; 1993. p. 111–3.

6. Suzuki C, Sando I, Balaban C, et al. Differences in attachment of the tensor veli palatini muscle to the eustachian tube cartilage with age. Ann Otol Rhinol Laryngol 2003. [In press]

7. Orita Y, Sando I, Miura M, Hasebe S. Postnatal change of the connective tissue in the region lateral to the eustachian tube: its possible relationship to the function of the eustachian tube. Presented at the Festschrift in Honor of Isamu Sando, MD, University of Pittsburgh School of Medicine, Pittsburgh (Pa), May 18, 2001.

8. Yamaguchi N, Sando I, Hashida Y, et al. Histologic study of eustachian tube cartilage with and without congenital anomalies: a preliminary study. Ann Otol Rhinol Laryngol 1990a;99:984–7.

9. Matsune S, Sando I, Takahashi H. Comparative study of elastic at the hinge portion of eustachian tube cartilage in normal and cleft palate individuals. In: Lim DJ, Bluestone CD, Klein JO, et al, editors. Recent advances in otitis media. Proceedings of the Fifth International Symposium. Burlington (ON): Decker Periodicals; 1993. p. 4–6.

10. Aoki H, Sando I, Takahashi H. Anatomic relationships between Ostmann's fatty tissue and eustachian tube. Ann Otol Rhinol Laryngol 1994;103:211–4.

11. Suzuki C, Balaban C, Sando I, et al. Postnatal development of eustachian tube: a computer aided 3-D reconstruction and measurement study. Acta Otolaryngol (Stockh) 1998;118:837–43.

12. Ishijima K, Sando I, Balaban C, et al. Postnatal development of static volumes of the eustachian tube: a computer-aided three dimensional reconstruction and measurement study. Ann Otol Rhinol Laryngol 2002;111:832–5.

13. Tos M, Bak-Pedersen K. Goblet cell populations in the normal middle ear and eustachian tube of children and adults. Ann Otol Rhinol Laryngol 1976;85 Suppl 25: S44–50.

14. Orita Y, Sando I, Hirsch BE, et al. Postnatal development of the eustachian tube glands. Presented at the 4th Extraordinary International Symposium on Recent Advances in Otitis Media; April 16–20;2001 Miyagi, Japan. Laryngoscope 2002;112:1647–52.

15. Sudo M, Sando I, Ikui A. Narrowest (isthmus) portion of eustachian tube: a computer-aided 3-D reconstruction and measurement study. Ann Otol Rhinol Laryngol 1997;106:583–8.

16. Bluestone CD, Klein JO. Otitis media and eustachian tube dysfunction. In: Bluestone CD, Stool SE, Kenna MA, editors. Pediatric otolaryngology. 4th ed. Philadelphia (PA): WB Saunders; 2003. p. 498–501.

17. Bluestone CD, Paradise JL, Beery QC. Physiology of the eustachian tube in the pathogenesis and management of middle ear effusions. Laryngoscope 1972a;82:1654–70.

18. Bylander A, Tjernstrom O. Changes in eustachian tube function with age in children with normal ears. A longitudinal study. Acta Otolaryngol (Stockh) 1983;96: 467–77.

19. Bylander A, Tjernstrom O, Ivarsson A. Pressure opening and closing functions of the eustachian tube by inflation and deflation in children and adults with normal ears. Acta Otolaryngol (Stockh) 1983;96:255–68.

20. Takasaki K, Sando I, Balaban CD, et al. Histopathological changes of the eustachian tube cartilage and tensor veli palatini muscle with aging. Laryngoscope 1999;109: 1679–83.

21. Kaneko A, Hosoda Y, Doi T, et al. Tubal compliance—changes with age and in tubal malformation. Auris Nasus Larynx 2001;28:121–4.

22. Bluestone CD. Eustachian tube obstruction in the infant with cleft palate. Ann Otol Rhinol Laryngol 1971;80:1–30.

23. Siegel MI, Sadler-Kimes D, Todhunter JS. Eustachian tube cartilage shape as a factor in the epidemiology of otitis media. In: Lim DJ, Bluestone CD, Klein JO, Nelson JD, editors. Recent advances in otitis media. Proceedings of the Fourth International Symposium. Philadelphia & Toronto: BC Decker; 1988. p. 114–7.

24. Sadler-Kimes D, Siegel, MI, Todhunter JS. Eustachian tube-tensor veli palatini relationship and its implications for otitis media. In: Lim, DJ, Bluestone CD, Klein JO, et al, editors. Recent advances in otitis media. Proceedings of the Fifth International Symposium. Burlington (ON): Decker Periodicals; 1993. p. 114–8.

25. Shibahara Y, Sando I. Histopathologic study of eustachian tube in cleft palate patients. Ann Otol Rhinol Laryngol 1988;97:403–8.

26. Matsune S, Sando I, Takahashi H. Abnormalities of lateral cartilaginous lamina and lumen of eustachian tube in cases of cleft palate. Ann Otol Rhinol Laryngol 1991a;100:909–13.

27. Takasaki K, Sando I, Balaban CD, Ishijima K. Postnatal development of eustachian tube cartilage. A study of normal and cleft palate cases. Int J Pediatr Otorhinolaryngol 2000a;52:31–6.

28. Matsune S, Sando I, Takahashi H. Elastin at the hinge portion of eustachian tube cartilage in specimens from normal subjects and those with cleft palate. Ann Otol Rhinol Laryngol 1992;101:163–7.

29. Matsune S, Sando I, Takahashi H. Insertion of the tensor veli palatini muscle into the eustachian tube cartilage in cleft palate cases. Ann Otol Rhinol Laryngol 1991b;100:439–46.

30. Kitajiri M, Sando I, Hashida Y, Doyle WJ. Histopathology of otitis media in infants with cleft and high arched palates. In: Lim DJ, Bluestone CD, Klein JO, et al, editors. Recent advances in otitis media with effusion. Toronto (ON): BC Decker; 1984. p. 195–8.

31. Bluestone CD, Wittel RA, Paradise JL. Roentgenographic evaluation of the eustachian tube function in infants with cleft and normal palates. Cleft Palate J 1972b;9:93–100.

32. Kemaloglu YK, Kobayashi T, Nakajima T. Analysis of the craniofacial skeleton in cleft children with otitis media with effusion. Int J Pediatr Otorhinolaryngol 1999;47:57–69.

33. Miura M, Sando I, Takasaki K, et al. Histopathological study on temporal bone and eustachian tube in trisomy 22. Int J Pediatr Otorhinolaryngol 2000;56:191–8.

34. Miura M, Sando I, Haginomori S-I, Casselbrant ML. Histopathological study of temporal bone and eustachian tube in oculoauriculovertebral spectrum. Ann Otol Rhinol Laryngol 2001;110:922–7.

35. Miura M, Sando I, Hirsch BE, Orita Y. Anomaly of the tube and its associated structures in patients with multiple congenital malformation: a histopathological and morphometric study. Int J Pediatr Otorhinolaryngol 2002b. [In press]

36. Kamimura M, Balaban CD, Sando I, et al. Cellular distribution of mucosa-associated lymphoid tissue with otitis media in children. Ann Otol Rhinol Laryngol 2000;109:467–72.

37. Takasaki K, Thompson SW, Sando I. Ossification of eustachian tube cartilage and Ostmann's fatty tissue in chronic renal failure. Otolaryngol Head Neck Surg 2000b;122:567–71.

38. Cantekin EI, Doyle WJ, Reichert TJ, et al. Dilation of the eustachian tube by electrical stimulation of the mandibular nerve. Ann Otol Rhinol Laryngol 1979;88:40–51.

39. Honjo I, Okazaki N, Kumazawa T. Experimental study of the eustachian tube function with regard to its related muscles. Acta Otolaryngol (Stockh) 1979;87:84–9.

40. Rich AR. A physiological study of the eustachian tube and its related muscles. Bull Johns Hopkins Hosp 1920;31:305–10.

41. Casselbrant ML, Cantekin EI, Dirkmaat DC, et al. Experimental paralysis of tensor veli palatini muscle. Acta Otolaryngol (Stockh) 1988;106:178–85.

42. Doyle WJ, Seroky JT. Middle ear gas exchange in rhesus monkeys. Ann Otol Rhinol Laryngol 1994;103:636–45.

43. Doyle WJ. Experimental results do not support a gas reserve function for the mastoid. Int J Pediatr Otorhinolaryngol 2000a;52:229–38.

44. Doyle WJ. Increases in middle ear pressure resulting from counter-diffusion of oxygen and carbon dioxide into the middle ear of monkeys. Acta Otolaryngol (Stockh) 1998;117:708–13.

45. Doyle WJ. Mathematical model explaining the sources of error in certain estimates of the gas exchange constants for the middle ear. Ann Otol Rhinol Laryngol 2000b;109:533–41.

46. Bylander A. Comparison of eustachian tube function in children and adults with normal ears. Ann Otol Rhinol Laryngol 1980;89:20–4.

47. Bluestone CD, Wittel RA, Paradise JL, Felder H. Eustachian tube function as related to adenoidectomy for otitis media. Trans Am Acad Ophthalmol Otolaryngol 1972;76:1325–39.

48. Wittenborg MH, Neuhauser EB. Simple roentgenographic demonstration of eustachian tubes and abnormalities. Am J Roentgenol Rad Ther Nucl Med 1963;89:1194–200.

49. Bluestone CD, Klein JO, editors. Management. In: Otitis media in infants and children. 3rd ed. Philadelphia (PA): WB Saunders; 2001. p. 180–298.

50. Albiin N, Hellstrom S, Stenfors LE. Clearance of effusion material from the attic space—an experimental study in the rat. Int J Pediatr Otorhinolaryngol 1983;5:1–10.

51. Stenfors LE, Hellstrom S, Albiin N. Middle ear clearance in eustachian tube function: physiology and role in otitis media. Ann Otol Rhinol Laryngol 1985;94:30–1.

52. Ohashi Y, Nakai Y, Koshimo H, Esaki Y. Ciliary activity in the in vitro tubotympanum. Arch Otorhinolaryngol 1986;243:317–9.

53. Honjo I. Experimental study of the pumping function

of the eustachian tube. Acta Otolaryngol (Stockh) 1981;91:85–91.

54 Honjo I, Hayashi M, Ito S, Takahashi H. Pumping and clearance function of the eustachian tube. Am J Otolaryngol 1985;6:241–4.

55 Birkin EA, Brookler KH. Surface tension lowering substance of the canine eustachian tube. Ann Otol Rhinol Laryngol 1972;81:268–71.

56 Rapport PN, Lim DJ, Weiss HJ. Surface active agent in eustachian tube function. Arch Otolaryngol 1975;101: 305–11.

57 Hagen WE. Surface tension lowering substance in eustachian tube function. Laryngoscope 1977;87:1033–45.

58 White P. Effect of exogenous surfactant on eustachian tube function in the rat. Am J Otolaryngol 1989;10:301–4.

59 Karchev T, Watanabe N, Fujiyoshi T, et al. Surfactant-producing epithelium in the dorsal part of the cartilaginous eustachian tube of mice. Acta Otolaryngol (Stockh) 1994;114:64–9.

60 Fornadley JA, Burns JK. The effect of surfactant on eustachian tube function in a gerbil model of otitis media with effusion. Otolaryngol Head Neck Surg 1994;110:110–4.

61 Bluestone CD, Cantekin EI, Beery QC. Effect of inflammation on the ventilatory function of the eustachian tube. Laryngoscope 1977;87:493–507.

62 McBride TP, Doyle WJ, Hayden FG, Gwaltney JM. Alterations of the eustachian tube, middle ear, and nose in rhinovirus infection. Arch Otolaryngol 1989;115:1054–9.

63 Buchman CA, Doyle WJ, Skoner D, et al. Otologic manifestations of experimental rhinovirus infection. Laryngoscope 1994;104:1295–9.

64 Friedman RA, Doyle WJ, Casselbrant ML, et al. Immunologic-mediated eustachian tube obstruction: a double-blind crossover study. J Allergy Clin Immunol 1983;71:442–7.

65 Bluestone CD, Cantekin EI, Beery QC. Certain effects of adenoidectomy on eustachian tube ventilatory function. Laryngoscope 1975;85:113–27.

66 Bluestone CD, Beery QC, Andrus WS. Mechanics of the eustachian tube as it influences susceptibility to and persistence of middle ear effusions in children. Ann Otol Rhinol Laryngol 1974;83:27–34.

67 Bluestone CD, Cantekin EI, Beery QC, Stool SE. Function of the eustachian tube related to surgical management of acquired aural cholesteatoma in children. Laryngoscope 1978;88:1155–64.

68 Stenstrom C, Bylander-Groth A, Ingvarsson L. Eustachian tube function in otitis-prone and healthy children. Int J Pediatr Otorhinolaryngol 1991;21:127–38.

69 Iwano T, Hamada E, Kinoshita T et al. Passive opening pressure of the eustachian tube. In: Lim DJ, Bluestone CD, Klein JO, et al, editors. Recent advances in otitis media. Proceedings of the Fifth International Symposium. Burlington (ON): Decker Periodicals; 1993. p. 76–8.

70 Bylander A, Tjernstrom O. Changes in eustachian tube function with age in children with normal ears. A longitudinal study. Acta Otolaryngol (Stockh) 1983;96:467–77.

71 van Heerbeek N, Ingels KJAO, Snik AFM, Zielhuis GA. Reliability of manometric eustachian tube function tests in children. Otol Neurotol 2001;22:183–7.

72 Poe DS, Pyykko I, Valtonen H, Silvola J. Analysis of eustachian tube function by video endoscopy. Am J Otol 2000;21:602–6.

73 Bluestone CD. Management of the abnormally patulous eustachian tube. In: Myers E, editor. Advances in otolaryngology-head and neck surgery. St. Louis (MO): Mosby; 1998. p. 201–29.

74 Sakakihara J, Honjo I, Fujita A, et al. Compliance of the patulous eustachian tube. Ann Otol Rhinol Laryngol 1993;102:110–2.

75 Beery QC, Doyle WJ, Cantekin EI, et al. Eustachian tube function in an American Indian population. Ann Otol Rhinol Laryngol 1980;89:28–33.

76 White BL, Doyle WJ, Bluestone CD. Eustachian tube function in infants and children with Down syndrome. In: Lim DJ, Bluestone CD, Klein JO, et al, editors. Recent advances in otitis media with effusion. Toronto (ON): BC Decker; 1984. p. 62–6.

77 Falk B, Magnuson B. Eustachian tube closing failure in children with persistent middle ear effusion. Int J Pediatr Otorhinolaryngol 1984;7:97–106.

78 Buchman CA, Doyle WJ, Swarts JD, Bluestone CD. Effects of nasal obstruction on eustachian tube function and middle ear pressure. Acta Otolaryngol (Stockh) 1999;119:351–5.

79 Jorgensen F, Holmquist J. Toynbee phenomenon and middle ear disease. Am J Otolaryngol 1984;4:291–4.

80 Thompson AC, Crowther JA. Effect of nasal packing on eustachian tube function. J Laryngol Otol 1991;105: 539–40.

81 Uzun C, Adali MK, Koten M, et al. Use of the nine-step inflation/deflation test as a predictor of middle ear barotrauma in sports scuba divers. Br J Audiol 2000;34:153–63.

82 Magnuson B. On the origin of the high negative pressure in the middle ear space. Am J Otolaryngol 1981;2:1–12.

83 Bunne M, Magnuson B, Falk B, Hellstrom S. Eustachian tube function varies over time in children with secretory otitis media. Acta Otolaryngol 2000;120:716–23.

84 Doyle WJ. Mucosal surface area determines the middle ear pressure response following establishment of sniff-induced underpressures. Acta Otolaryngol (Stockh) 1999;119:694–702.

85 Brown CE, Magnuson B. On the physics of the infant feeding bottle and middle ear sequela: ear disease in infants can be associated with bottle feeding. Int J Pediatr Otorhinolaryngol 2000;54:13–20.

86 Ohashi Y, Nakai Y, Furuya H, et al. Mucociliary diseases of the middle ear during experimental otitis media with effusion induced by bacterial endotoxin. Ann Otol Rhinol Laryngol 1989;98:479–84.

87 Park K, Bakaletz LO, Coticchia JM, Lim DJ. Effect of influenza A virus on ciliary activity and dye transport function in the chinchilla eustachian tube. Ann Otol Rhinol Laryngol 1993;102:551–8.

88. Dubin MG, Pollock HK, Ebert CS, et al. Eustachian tube dysfunction after tobacco smoke exposure. Otolaryngol Head Neck Surg 2002;126:14–9.

89. Mogi G, Kawauchi H, Kurono Y. Tubal dysfunction or infection? Role of bacterial infection and immune response. In: Mogi G, editor. Recent advances in otitis media. Proceedings of the Second Extraordinary International Symposium on Recent Advances in Otitis Media. New York (NY): Kugler Publications; 1993. p. 73–7.

90. Shikowitz MJ, Ilardi CF, Gero, M. Immotile cilia syndrome associated with otitis media with effusion: a case report. In: Lim DJ, Bluestone CD, Klein JO, Nelson JD, editors. Recent advances in otitis media. Proceedings of the Fourth International Symposium. Philadelphia (PA): BC Decker; 1988. p. 304–7.

91. Nozoe T, Okazaki N, Koda Y, et al. Fluid clearance of the eustachian tube. In: Lim DJ, Bluestone CD, Klein JO, et al, editors. Recent advances in otitis media with effusion. Toronto (ON): BC Decker; 1984. p. 66–8.

92. Takahashi H, Honjo I, Hayashi M, Fujita A. Clearance function of eustachian tube and negative middle ear pressure. Ann Otol Rhinol Laryngol 1992;101:759–62.

93. Stool SE, Randall P. Unexpected ear disease in infants with cleft palate. Cleft Palate J 1967;4:99–103.

94. Paradise JL, Bluestone CD, Felder H. The universality of otitis media in fifty infants with cleft palate. Pediatrics 1969;44:35–42.

95. Paradise JL, Bluestone CD. Early treatment of the universal otitis media of infants with cleft palate. Pediatrics 1974;53:48–54.

96. Doyle WJ, Cantekin EI, Bluestone CD. Eustachian tube function in cleft palate children. Ann Otol Rhinol Laryngol 1980;89:34–40.

97. Doyle WJ, Ingraham AS, Saad M, Cantekin EI. A primate model of cleft palate and middle ear disease: results of a one-year postcleft follow-up. In: Lim DJ, Bluestone CD, Klein JO, et al, editors. Recent advances in otitis media with effusion. Toronto (ON): BC Decker; 1984a. p. 215–8.

98. Odoi H, Proud GO, Toledo PS. Effects of pterygoid hamulotomy upon eustachian tube function. Laryngoscope 1971;81:1242–4.

99. Miglets A. The experimental production of allergic middle ear effusions. Laryngoscope 1973;83:1355–84.

100. Bernstein JM, Lee J, Conboy K, et al. Further observations on the role of IgE-mediated hypersensitivity in recurrent otitis media with effusion. Otolaryngol Head Neck Surg 1985;93:611–5.

101. Bluestone CD. Eustachian tube function and allergy in otitis media. Pediatrics 1978;61:753–60.

102. Doyle WJ. Panel on etiology of otitis media with effusion: role of allergy and tubal function. In: Mogi G, editor. Recent advances in otitis media: Proceedings of the Second Extraordinary International Symposium on Recent Advances in Otitis Media. Amsterdam: Kugler Publications; 1994. p. 53–60.

103. Ackerman MN, Friedman RA, Doyle WJ, et al. Antigen-induced eustachian tube obstruction: an intranasal provocative challenge test. J Allergy Clin Immunol 1984;73:604–9.

104. Doyle WJ, Friedman RA, Fireman P, Bluestone CD. Eustachian tube obstruction after provocative nasal antigen challenge. Arch Otolaryngol 1984b;110:508–11.

105. Skoner DP, Doyle WJ, Chamovitz AH, Fireman P. Eustachian tube obstruction after intranasal challenge with house dust mite. Arch Otolaryngol 1986;112:840–2.

106. Stillwagon PK, Doyle WJ, Fireman P. Effect of an antihistamine/decongestant on nasal and eustachian tube function following intranasal pollen challenge. Ann Allergy 1987;58:442–6.

107. Skoner DP, Doyle WJ, Fireman P. Eustachian tube obstruction (ETO) after histamine nasal provocation—a double-blind dose-response study. J Allergy Clin Immunol 1987;79:27–31.

108. Doyle WJ, Boehm S, Skoner DP. Physiologic responses to intranasal dose-response challenges with histamine, methacholine, bradykinin, and prostaglandin in adult volunteers with and without nasal allergy. J Allergy Clin Immunol 1990;86:924–35.

109. Doyle WJ, Skoner DP, Hayden F, et al. Nasal and otologic effects of experimental influenza A virus infection. Ann Otol Rhinol Laryngol 1994;103:59–69.

110. Downs BW, Butehorn JF, Prazma J, et al. Action of histamine on eustachian tube function. Otolaryngol Head Neck Surg 2001;123:414–20.

111. Hardy SM, Heavner SB, White DR, et al. Late-phase allergy and eustachian tube dysfunction. Otolaryngol Head Neck Surg 2001;125:339–45.

112. McNicoll WD, Scanlon SG. Submucous resection: the treatment of choice in the nose-ear distress syndrome. J Laryngol Otol 1979;93:357–67.

113. McNicoll WD. Remediable eustachian tube dysfunction in diving recruits: assessment, investigation, and management. Undersea Biomed Res 1982;9:37–43.

114. Tos M, Bonding P. Middle ear pressure during and after prolonged nasotracheal and/or nasogastric intubation. Acta Otolaryngol (Stockh) 1977;83:353–9.

115. Wake M, McCullough DE, Binnington JD. Effect of nasogastric tubes on eustachian tube function. J Laryngol Otol 1990;104:17–9.

116. Perlman HB. Observations on the eustachian tube. Arch Otolaryngol 1951;53:370–85.

117. Myers EN, Beery QC, Bluestone CD, et al. Effect of certain head and neck tumors and their management on the ventilatory function of the eustachian tube. Ann Otol Rhinol Laryngol 1984;93 Suppl 114:3–16.

118. Weiss MH, Liberatore LA, Kraus DH, Budnick AS. Otitis media with effusion in head and neck cancer patients. Laryngoscope 1994;104:5–7.

119. Takahara T, Sando I, Bluestone CD, Myers EN. Lymphoma invading the anterior eustachian tube: temporal bone histopathology of functional tubal obstruction. Ann Otol Rhinol Laryngol 1986;95:101–5.

120. Yamaguchi N, Sando I, Hashida Y, et al. Histopathologic study of otitis media in individuals with head and neck tumors. Ann Otol Rhinol Laryngol 1990b;99:827–32.

121. Tasker A, Dettmar PW, Panetti M, et al. Reflux of

gastric juice and glue ear in children. Lancet 2002; 359:493.

122. Heavner SB, Hardy SM, White DR, et al. Function of the eustachian tube after weekly exposure to pepsin/hydrochloric acid. Otolaryngol Head Neck Surg 2001;125:123–9.

123. Cantekin EI, Bluestone CD, Saez CA, et al. Normal and abnormal middle ear ventilation. Ann Otol Rhinol Laryngol 1977;86:1–15.

124. Cantekin EI, Phillips DC, Doyle WJ, et al. Effect of surgical alterations of the tensor veli palatini muscle on eustachian tube function. Ann Otol Rhinol Laryngol 1980;89:47–53.

125. Alper CM, Tabari R, Seroky JT, Doyle WJ. Magnetic resonance imaging of the development of otitis media with effusion caused by functional obstruction of the eustachian tube. Ann Otol Rhinol Laryngol 1997;106: 422–31.

126. Buchman CA, Doyle WJ, Skoner DP, et al. Influenza A virus-induced acute otitis media. J Infect Dis 1995;172: 1348–51.

127. Swarts JD, Alper CM, Seroky JT, et al. In vivo observation with magnetic resonance imaging of middle ear effusion in response to experimental underpressures. Ann Otol Rhinol Laryngol 1995;104:522–8.

128. Doyle WJ, McBride TP, Skoner DP, et al. A double-blind placebo-controlled clinical trial of the effect of chlorpheniramine on the response of the nasal airway, middle ear, and eustachian tube to provocative rhinovirus challenge. Pediatr Infect Dis J 1998;7:229–38.

129. Doyle WJ, Seroky JT, Angelini BL, et al. Abnormal middle ear pressures during experimental influenza A virus infection—role of eustachian tube function. Auris Nasus Larynx 2000;27:323–6.

130. Doyle WJ, Alper CM, Buchman CA, et al. Illness and otological changes during upper respiratory tract virus infection. Laryngoscope 1999;109:324–8.

131. Moody SA, Alper CM, Doyle WJ. Daily tympanometry in children during the cold season: association of otitis media with upper respiratory tract infections. Int J Pediatr Otorhinolaryngol 1998;45:143–50.

CHAPTER 12

Natural History of Untreated Otitis Media

Richard M. Rosenfeld, MD, MPH, and David Kay, MD

The art of medicine consists in amusing the patient while nature cures the disease.
Voltaire

OBJECTIVES

On completing this chapter, the reader will be able to

1. Appreciate the favorable natural history of untreated otitis media (OM).
2. State the expected clinical course of acute otitis media (AOM) when antibiotics are withheld.
3. State the expected prognosis of recurrent AOM.
4. State the expected resolution rates for untreated otitis media with effusion (OME).
5. Understand how disease and outcome definition impact effusion resolution.
6. Use information about natural history to guide interpretation of treatment results.

EDITORIAL COMMENT

Compared with the first edition of this chapter, the second edition features random-effects meta-analysis, heterogeneity statistics, and a variety of outcomes for OME (cure, resolution, improvement). Validity of data abstraction has been ensured by two independent reviewers and by comparison with evidence tables from the Agency for Healthcare Research and Quality.[1,2] The resulting overview of OM natural history is the most comprehensive currently available.

INTRODUCTION

Rational management of OM begins with a firm understanding of the natural history of untreated disease. Only when rates of spontaneous resolution are known can the incremental benefits of therapies be judged and prognoses formulated to guide selection of treatment alternatives. Hippocrates noted first that "natural forces are the healers of disease," and Galen later cautioned physicians to serve as "nature's assistant."[3] This chapter

offers an inventory of nature's accomplishments in resolving OM, which can then serve as a basis for evidence-based management decisions.

Information about the natural history of untreated OM is plentiful but is not organized for ready access by clinicians. Despite hundreds of published clinical trials and epidemiologic studies, most book chapters and review articles draw conclusions on the basis of a convenience sample of a few often-cited references. Conclusions are plagued by selection bias and vary widely among authors, although most agree that spontaneous resolution is very common. Resolution rates are provided for a restricted number of time points and are rarely qualified by 95% confidence intervals (CIs) or discussions of combinability and generalizability. Consequently, the clinical utility of most published material is limited.

Meta-analysis is a form of literature review in which studies are systematically assembled, appraised, and combined using explicit and reproducible methods to reduce bias (see Chapter 4, "Meta-analysis and Systematic Literature Review").[4] Although several meta-analyses have examined treatment or prevention of OM,[5–16] none have focused exclusively on the natural history of untreated disease. Instead, the emphasis has been on determining the rate difference (risk reduction), which is the difference in event rates between the control and treatment groups.[17] Whereas knowing the incremental benefits of therapies is important, it is equally (if not more) important to quantitatively describe the impact of natural history alone. Limited information on OM natural history is available in one unsystematic review[18] and two recent systematic reviews.[1,2]

In contrast to traditional epidemiologic studies of AOM and OME, this chapter focuses sharply on natural history and spontaneous resolution. Evidence about OM incidence, prevalence, and risk factors is also important, but peripheral, to the topic at hand. The present discussion strives to answer a single question: What can clinicians expect from nature alone as a remedy for AOM, recurrent AOM, or OME? Alternatively, this could be phrased as the "efficacy" of placebo, doing nothing, or watchful waiting.

PROTOCOL AND METHODS

AOM was defined as middle ear effusion with recent onset of signs and symptoms of middle ear inflammation, and OME was defined as asymptomatic middle ear effusion. An a priori research protocol was developed on the basis of established methodology for meta-analysis and systematic literature review,[19,20] with emphasis on techniques appropriate for observational studies.[21] Evidence was drawn from (1) epidemiologic (surveillance) studies of healthy children, (2) untreated control groups in randomized clinical trials (RCTs), and (3) cohort studies with a restrictive approach to antimicrobial therapy for AOM. Nonrandomized comparative studies were excluded because of allocation bias when deciding which children should receive no therapy, and retrospective studies were excluded because of recall bias and limitations imposed by chart review.

Source articles were identified by MEDLINE search from 1966 through August 2002 using separate strategies for cohort studies and randomized controlled trials. Both strategies began with a main grouping of OM articles, which combined the exploded MeSH (medical subject heading) term "otitis media" with the keywords (.mp. modifier) "glue ear OR secretory otitis media OR otitis media with effusion OR middle ear effusion OR serous otitis media OR acute otitis media." Relevant cohort studies were identified by combining the main otitis media set with the keywords "natural history OR natural course OR placebo OR placebos OR resolution OR self limited OR untreated OR spontaneous OR observation." Relevant RCTs were identified by combining the main otitis media set first with the MeSH terms "randomized controlled trials OR controlled clinical trials OR comparative study" and subsequently with the MeSH terms "placebos OR double-blind method and the keywords "untreated OR placebo OR placebos."

The initial MEDLINE data set was reduced by limiting the results to human studies, age group children (0 to 18 years), and English language. Although this could result in language bias (positive results are more likely than negative ones to appear in English-language journals),[22] we did not consider the impact significant because the goals of this study were descriptive and excluding non–English language trials generally has little effect on meta-analysis results.[23] The search set was then purged of editorials, letters, reviews, practice guidelines, reviews of reported cases, and consensus development conferences. The MEDLINE search was supplemented with electronic searches of CINAHL (Cumulative Index to Nursing and Allied Health Literature) and the Cochrane Library (through August 2002). Lastly, a manual search was conducted of published OM meta-analyses and OM evidence tables prepared by the Agency for Healthcare Research and Quality (AHRQ).[1,2]

Titles and abstracts of identified articles were screened by two reviewers and complete articles obtained for all considered potentially relevant. Criteria for study inclusion were defined a priori as follows:

- AOM criteria: (1) cohort study or RCT of antimicrobial treatment, (2) group or subgroup receiving placebo or no drug, and (3) clinically relevant outcomes reported by patients (not ears).
- Recurrent AOM criteria: (1) cohort study or RCT of antimicrobial prophylaxis, (2) group or subgroup receiving placebo or no prophylaxis, and (3) clinically relevant outcomes reported by patients.
- OME inclusion criteria (for OME of new onset or unknown prior duration): (1) cohort study or RCT enrollment cohort (children with OME observed prospectively before randomization), (2) unilateral or bilateral OME diagnosed by tympanometry (type B curve) or using an algorithm containing tympanometry, and (3) cumulative OME resolution over time reported by patients or ears.
- OME inclusion criteria (for chronic bilateral OME): (1) cohort study or RCT of surgery, (2) group or subgroup managed with watchful waiting, (3) prospective documentation of bilateral OME for 3 months or longer, and (4) cumulative OME resolution over time reported by patients or ears.

The AOM and recurrent AOM criteria are based on the principle that control groups in RCTs can serve as proxies for natural history because subjects are monitored closely and followed up similar to the active therapy group. For recurrent AOM the active therapy was restricted to antimicrobial prophylaxis because these RCTs generally have longer follow-up and more homogeneous selection criteria and outcome measures than do studies of other interventions (eg, vaccines, xylitol). Conversely, the OME criteria emphasize prospective cohort studies, not RCTs. Randomized trials of OME interventions tend to be short term and extremely heterogeneous, unless they relate to surgical therapy of chronic OME.

Data were abstracted from studies independently by two investigators, and discrepancies were resolved by mutual consensus. The accuracy of data abstraction was further verified by comparison with results obtained in prior meta-analyses and the detailed evidence tables in the AHRQ evidence reports on AOM and OME. The data abstraction end points for the clinical disorders were as follows:

- AOM end points: (1) clinical success, defined as resolution or improvement of AOM signs and symptoms (excluding middle ear effusion), (2) symptomatic relief as defined by the study authors, (3) resolution of middle ear effusion, (4) incidence of suppurative complications (mastoiditis, meningitis), and (5) proportion of cohort managed without antibiotics (does not apply to RCTs).
- AOM diagnostic certainty: (1) high certainty, defined as diagnosis using tympanometry, pneumatic otoscopy, otomicroscopy, needle aspiration, or otolaryngology referral, or (2) low certainty, defined as diagnosis using nonpneumatic otoscopy and clinical symptoms.
- Recurrent AOM end points: (1) AOM incidence density, defined as total new AOM episodes per patient-month of observation in the study, (2) proportion with no further AOM during study, and (3) proportion with recurrent AOM during study (3 or more episodes).
- OME end points: cumulative resolution rates over time (by ears and by patients) for (1) newly detected OME of unknown duration present at the start of a cohort study, (2) OME of known onset while enrolled in a cohort study, and (3) chronic bilateral OME. Tympanometric resolution was the preferred outcome, followed by OME algorithm or clinical examination (pneumatic otoscopy).

Although more recent studies emphasize static admittance and tympanometric width for OME diagnosis,[24] all studies relevant to this analysis used tympanometric patterns (A, C1, C2, B). Natural history of OME was, therefore, determined using several tympanometric criteria, including change from B to A (OME cure), change from B to A/C1 (OME resolution), or change from B to non-B or A/C1/C2 (OME improvement). Patterns were classified as type A, peak pressure > -100 mm H_2O (effusion in 3% of ears at myringotomy); type B, flat curve without an impedance minimum (effusion in 85 to 100%); type C1, pressure -100 to -199 mm H_2O (effusion in 17%); or type C2, pressure -200 to -400 mm H_2O (effusion in up to 55%).[25,26]

Data from individual studies were combined (pooled) whenever results were available from two or more source articles for a particular end point and outcome time. Pooling was done using a random-effects model of meta-analysis, which assumes a population (distribution) of true effect sizes with each source article representing one member of this population.[27] Under this model, results are expected to vary from study to study, with differences caused by experimental

error and differences in populations (between-study variability). Because of this additional variability, the 95% CI for the pooled result is wider (less precise) than for a fixed-effect model.

Statistical analysis was performed using Comprehensive Meta-Analysis,[28] a computer program for research synthesis developed with funding from the National Institutes of Health. The program weights study results by the inverse of variance and calculates a random effects estimate of the combined effect and 95% CI. A test of heterogeneity is performed using the Q statistic to evaluate constancy of effect across strata. Significant heterogeneity exists if $p < .05$, although the test has low power and important variations may be present even with a nonsignificant result.[29] For this reason, the random effects model is used, regardless of the test of heterogeneity, although test results are still stated and explored.

SYSTEMATIC LITERATURE REVIEW

MEDLINE search identified 560 cohort studies and 109 potentially relevant RCTs. Review and screening of initial articles plus manual cross-checks identified 63 source articles that met inclusion criteria and had extractable data. The source articles included 11 RCTs of AOM antibiotic versus placebo or no drug,[30–40] one RCT of AOM homeopathy versus placebo,[41] 9 cohort studies of restrictive antibiotics for AOM,[42–50] 14 RCTs of recurrent AOM antimicrobial prophylaxis versus placebo or no drug,[51–64] 1 cohort study of recurrent AOM natural history,[65] 18 cohort studies of OME natural history,[66–83] 2 RCT enrollment cohorts of OME therapy,[84,85] and 7 cohorts or RCT control groups of chronic OME natural history.[86–92]

The median publication year was 1986 (range 1958 to 2001), with 25% of articles published prior to 1981 and 25% after 1993. There were 19 studies from the United States, 10 from Denmark, 9 from England, 7 from the Netherlands, 4 from Sweden, 4 from Israel, 2 from Canada, 2 from Italy, 1 each from Brazil, Finland, New Zealand, Scotland, and Switzerland, and 1 multinational study. Several articles that appeared promising after initial screening were later excluded, including 2 RCTs of antibiotic prophylaxis versus placebo for children with sporadic (not recurrent) AOM considered "at risk" for recurrent AOM,[93,94] 2 OME cohort studies in neonates followed up for less than 6 months,[95,96] 3 OME cohort studies that included type C tympanograms in their definition of OME,[97–99] 10 OME studies with cohorts already reported in other source articles,[100–109] and 3 OME studies for which data were not extractable.[110–112]

Spontaneous Resolution of AOM

Meta-analysis Results

Most observational cohort studies (Table 12-1) included a broad age range of children and had low diagnostic certainty for AOM. The incidence of nonantibiotic therapy ranged from 3 to 95%, with an overall random-effects estimate of 59% (95% CI, 31 to 87%) and significant heterogeneity. Clinical success rates for the nonantibiotic group of 97%, 90%, and 88% were reported by three authors but are difficult to interpret because of selection bias.[45,47,49] Little and colleagues[50] noted a 76% antibiotic prescription fill rate for children randomized to initial observation of AOM. Acute mastoiditis was reported after 6 of 2,530 AOM episodes (0.24%) in 7 studies that explicitly discussed complications (see Table 12-1). Of the 6 episodes, 4 had initially received antibiotics, and 2 occurred after observation alone.

The natural history of AOM in 11 untreated RCT control groups is shown in Table 12-2. All trials except one[31] were placebo controlled, and all had close follow-up, with provisions to begin antibiotics for observation failures (typically after 48 to 72 hours). Most children received symptomatic therapy, including analgesics, nose drops, or antihistamine-decongestant preparations. Three studies[34,35,37] excluded children under age 2 years and two others[32,40] were limited to infants or young children. Most trials concerned initial empiric therapy of uncomplicated AOM, but Appleman and colleagues[36] studied only recurrent episodes, and Howie and colleagues[32] limited their sample to children with middle ear effusion on tympanocentesis. Kaleida and Ploussard[38] was the only study that restricted placebo to children with nonsevere illness, as defined by otalgia and fever scores at initial presentation.

Within 24 hours of AOM diagnosis, 61% of children managed without antibiotics (see Table 12-2) had symptomatic relief (95% CI, 50 to 72%). By 2 to 3 days, the rate of spontaneous resolution increased to 80% (95% CI, 69 to 90%), with a slight decrease to 74% at 4 to 7 days (95% CI, 64 to 85%). The rate of complete clinical resolution was 70% at 7 to 14 days (95% CI, 49 to 92%) because of more stringent outcome criteria (eg, otorrhea without pain and fever would pass for

Table 12-1 Observational Studies of Nonantibiotic Treatment of AOM

Year First Author	Country	Age Range	Diagnostic Certainty*	Managed without Antibiotics, n/N (%)	Acute Mastoiditis
1958 Fry[42]	England	< 20 yr	Low (o)	387/497 (78)	None
1964 Townsend[43]	USA	NS	Low (o)	243/335 (73)	1 in antibiotic group
1979 Thomsen[44]	Denmark	6 mo–10 yr	High (e,o)	76/93 (82)	—
1985 van Buchem[45]	Netherlands	2–12 yr	Low (o)	465/490 (95)	None†
1988 Ostfeld[46]	Israel	NS	High (n,p)	397/693 (57)	5; 3 in antibiotic group
1990 Froom[47]	Various (9)	NS	Low (o)	419/2,982 (14)	None
1991 Bollag[48]	Switzerland	< 16 yr	Low (o)	211/230 (92)	None
1997 Tilyard[49]	New Zealand	< 16 yr	Low (o)	74/2,441 (3)	—
2001 Little[50]	England	6 mo–10 yr	Low (o)	114/285 (40)	None
RANDOM-EFFECTS META-ANALYSIS					
Combined sample size				8,101	—
Estimate of combined rate, (95% CI)		.59 (.31, .87)			
Test for heterogeneity, Q statistic				11,803.7, df = 8	
Test for heterogeneity, *p* value				< .001	

AOM = acute otitis media; CI = confidence interval; df = degrees of freedom; NS = not stated.

*Studies with high certainty confirmed diagnosis of AOM with tympanometry (t), pneumatic otoscopy (p), otomicroscopy (m), needle aspiration (n), or referral to an ear, nose, and throat specialist (e); low certainty studies relied on nonpneumatic otoscopy (o) and clinical symptoms.

†In a larger series, two cases of mastoiditis were observed for an *estimated* 4,860 children treated without initial antibiotics.

Table 12-2 Natural History of AOM in Children Randomized to Placebo or No Drug in Clinical Trials

Year First Author	Country	Age Range	Diagnostic Certainty*	Symptomatic Relief of AOM, N (%)[†]			Clinical Resolution[‡]
				24 hours	2–3 days	4–7 days	
1968 Halsted[30]	USA	2 mo–6 yr	Low (o)	—	20/27 (74)	—	21/21 (100)
1970 Laxdal[31]	Canada	< 14 yr	Low (o)	—	—	30/48 (62)	22/48 (46)
1972 Howie[32]	USA	< 2.5 yr	High (o,n)	—	—	116/116 (100)	—
1981 Mygind[33]	Denmark	1–10 yr	High (e,o)	—	48/77 (62)	53/77 (69)	53/77 (69)
1981 van Buchem[34]	Netherlands	2–12 yr	High (e,o)	29/40 (73)	—	34/38 (89)	—
1986 Thalin[35]	Sweden	2–15 yr	High (e,m)	96/158 (61)	133/158 (84)	156/158 (99)	146/158 (92)
1991 Appleman[36]	Netherlands	6 mo–12 yr	High (e,o)	—	44/54 (81)	—	—
1991 Burke[37]	England	3–10 yr	Low (o)	61/117 (52)	—	85/114 (75)	101/118 (86)
1991 Kaleida[38]	USA	7 mo–12 yr	High (p,t)	—	454/492 (92)	—	—
2000 Damoiseaux[40]	Netherlands	6 mo–2 yr	Low (o)	—	—	34/123 (28)	36/120 (30)
2001 Jacobs[41]	USA	18 mo–6 yr	Low (o)	—	—	26/38 (68)	—
RANDOM-EFFECTS META-ANALYSIS							
Combined sample size				315	808	712	542
Estimate of combined rate, (95% CI)				.61 (.50, .72)	.80 (.69, .90)	74 (.64, .85)	.70 (.49, .92)
Test for heterogeneity, Q statistic				6.1, df = 2	45.9, df = 4	417.3, df = 7	236.1, df = 5
Test for heterogeneity, p value				.048	< .001	< .001	< .001

AOM = acute otitis media; CI = confidence interval; df = degrees of freedom.

*Studies with high certainty confirmed diagnosis of AOM with tympanometry (t), pneumatic otoscopy (p), otomicroscopy (m), needle aspiration (n), or referral to an ear, nose, and throat specialist (e); low certainty studies relied on nonpneumatic otoscopy (o) and clinical symptoms.

[†]Symptomatic relief implies absence of fever and relief of otalgia; some authors[34,35,37] did not mention fever or considered it a separate end point.

[‡]Absence of all presenting signs and symptoms of middle ear infection within 7 to 14 days after therapy started; some authors further required an improved appearance of the tympanic membrane.[30,40]

symptomatic relief, but not complete resolution). All analyses had significant heterogeneity. One placebo-treated child developed meningitis, but the incidence of suppurative complications in children managed without antibiotics (1 of 843, 0.12%) was comparable with that observed after initial antibiotic treatment (2 of 932, 0.21%).

Sensitivity analysis was performed to evaluate the impact of diagnostic certainty, child age, and illness severity on results. Quantitative analysis by diagnostic certainty was not performed because review of Table 12-2 does not show a consistent association (positive or negative) between certainty and outcome. Analysis of symptomatic relief at 4 to 7 days included two studies[32,40] of children under 2.5 years of age, one of which was primarily a bacteriologic study with limited clinical outcome data.[32] Excluding these studies had a minimal impact on results (78% versus 74%) and did not elimi-

nate heterogeneity. Similarly, excluding the one study[38] at 2 to 3 days limited to nonsevere AOM episodes had a minimal impact on results (76% versus 80%) and did not eliminate heterogeneity.

Persistent asymptomatic middle ear effusion (OME) after nonantibiotic management of AOM was common (Table 12-3), and reported in 41% of children at 4 weeks (95% CI, 32 to 50%) and 54% at 6 weeks (95% CI, 40 to 68%). Results were heterogeneous, and overlap of the CIs does not suggest significant differences at the 4-week versus 6-week end points. Conversely, only 26% had persistent OME after 12 weeks (95% CI, 20 to 32%), and results were homogeneous. Initial antibiotic therapy has not been shown to alter the course of persistent OME after AOM.[15]

Teele and colleagues reported the prevalence of OME after *antibiotic-treated* AOM for a cohort of 2,565 children under 3 years of age.[113] Prevalence rates decreased

Table 12-3 Persistence of OME after Initial AOM Episode in Children Randomized to Placebo

Year First Author	Country	Age Range	Persistence of OME, N (%)		
			4 Weeks	6 Weeks	12 Weeks
1981 Mygind[33]	Denmark	1–10 yr	25/77 (32)	—	18/77 (23)
1986 Thalin[35]	Sweden	2–15 yr	68/158 (43)	—	—
1991 Burke[37]	England	3–10 yr	41/116 (35)	—	31/111 (28)
1991 Kaleida[38]	USA	7 mo–12 yr	—	169/328 (52)	—
1994 Claessen[39]	Netherlands	6 mo–12 yr	25/45 (56)	—	—
2000 Damoiseaux[40]	Netherlands	6 mo–2 yr	—	70/105 (67)	—
2001 Jacobs[41]	USA	18 mo–6 yr	—	16/39 (41)	—
RANDOM-EFFECTS META-ANALYSIS					
Combined sample size			396	472	188
Estimate of combined rate, (95% CI)			.41 (.32, .50)	.54 (.40, .68)	.26 (.20, .32)
Test for heterogeneity, Q statistic			8.1, df = 3	11.1, df = 2	0.5, df = 1
Test for heterogeneity, *p* value			.044	.004	.479

AOM = acute otitis media; CI = confidence interval; df = degrees of freedom; OME = otitis media with effusion.

gradually from 70% after 2 weeks to 40% after 1 month, 20% after 2 months, and only 10% after 3 months. These rates are comparable with those for placebo-treated children for the first month but are significantly better after 3 months (10% versus 26%). The reason for this discrepancy is unknown but may reflect differences in child age, inclusion criteria, and diagnostic certainty. Initial antibiotic therapy has not been shown to alter the prevalence of OME after an episode of AOM.

Generalizability of AOM Findings

Children who receive placebo or no therapy in randomized trials *are not* a random subset of children at risk for AOM; they tend to be older, have less severe symptoms, and have parents who consent to withholding antibiotic therapy. Although only Kaleida and colleagues[38] explicitly withheld placebo from children with severe illness, Burke and colleagues[37] note clearly the possibility of selection bias:

"...children included in the study did not represent a cross-section of all those with *acute earache* [emphasis by editor] but were selected on the basis that treatment with placebo would raise no ethical problems, and their inclusion was subject to informed parental consent...Excluded children

may have been more severely affected...The children in the study are typical, however, of those with moderate symptoms and signs, whose treatment presents general practitioners with a dilemma."[37]

Considering the above, the rates in Table 12-2 *may not apply* to all children aged 2 years or younger, particularly those with severe symptoms or high fever. None of the studies reporting outcomes at 24 hours included young children,[34,35,37] and the only recent trial limited to this age group reported only 28% symptomatic relief with placebo at 4 to 7 days.[40] The risk of suppurative complications when antibiotics are initially withheld from very young or ill children is unknown, but the only reported complication with placebo for RCTs in our analyses was in a young child.[40]

The words "acute earache" in the above quotation and "acute red ear" in the article title[37] highlight the issue of diagnostic certainty for AOM. The variability in diagnostic criteria in Table 12-2, however, probably increases generalizability because it mimics the uncertainty inherent in everyday practice. Although low certainty could inflate spontaneous resolution with false-positive AOM diagnoses, no relationship between outcomes and certainty was observed. Paradoxically, AOM studies with highest certainty (eg, double-tap studies) may apply least to everyday practice because they exclude children without bacterial pathogens on the initial tympanocentesis tap. The resulting "pure" sample of bacteriologic AOM is ideal for comparing antimicrobial efficacy but differs greatly from AOM diagnosed clinically by primary-care physicians.

Clinical versus bacteriologic efficacy must be considered when generalizing AOM results. Although children with clinical cure (symptomatic relief) are more likely to have bacteriologic cure (sterilization of middle ear effusion), the two are frequently discordant.[114] For example, Howie and Ploussard[32] reported 100% symptomatic relief for 166 children with AOM after 7 days of placebo, yet 53% of middle ear aspirates had persistent pathogenic bacteria. Similarly, Dagan and co-workers[115] noted that 63% of children with persistent middle ear pathogens after 3 to 4 days of antibiotic treatment, nonetheless, had clinical improvement or resolution. The practical significance of bacteriologic failure in children with clinical success is unclear because higher rates of AOM recurrence or suppurative complications have not been documented.

SPONTANEOUS RESOLUTION OF RECURRENT AOM

Meta-analysis Results

The expected course of recurrent AOM is more properly described in terms of prognosis, not spontaneous resolution. Resolution implies disappearance of a history, which is a more abstract concept when diagnosis is based on recurrence (eg, three episodes of AOM in 6 to 12 months), rather than a single event (sporadic AOM or OME). Moreover, children in placebo-controlled studies of recurrent AOM, nonetheless, receive antibiotic therapy for subsequent AOM episodes. This facilitates ethical study conduct and discourages biased opting out of the control group. In contrast, placebo-controlled studies of sporadic AOM withhold antibiotics unless acute symptoms persist or progress (as discussed earlier).

The prognosis of recurrent AOM is summarized in Table 12-4 for 14 RCTs[51-64] comparing antimicrobial prophylaxis to placebo and 1 observational cohort.[65] The mean baseline rate of AOM recurrence was at least 0.46 episodes/patient-month ($\geq$ 5.5 annual AOM per child). During the study, the cumulative recurrence rate was 0.23 AOM episodes/patient-month (2.8 annual AOM per child) with a 95% CI of 0.18 to 0.28. In the four studies that specified a baseline rate of AOM,[52,55,59,61] the incidence decreased by a mean of 0.21 episodes per patient-month during the study (2.5 annual AOM per child). For the studies in which a minimum baseline rate of AOM could be calculated from entry criteria, the incidence decreased by at least 0.11 episodes/patient-month ($\geq$ 1.4 annual AOM per child).[54,56-58,60,62-65]

During a median observation period of 6 months (range 10 weeks to 2 years), 41% of children had no further AOM (95% CI, 32 to 51%) and 83% had fewer than three episodes (95% CI, 74 to 91%). Alternatively, only 17% of children had remained otitis prone (three or more total AOM episodes). Sensitivity analysis did not suggest an impact of study duration on prognosis estimates. For example, when studies of less than 6 months duration were excluded, the combined estimate for no further AOM was 36% (95% CI, 23 to 49%), and the combined estimate for fewer than three AOM episodes was 81% (95% CI, 71 to 91%). Estimates for AOM episodes/patient-month would not be affected by study duration because duration is accounted for in the denominator.

Generalizability of Recurrent AOM Findings

Results for the prognosis of recurrent AOM can be generalized to a broad range of children because few restrictions were placed on AOM severity or child age. Unlike studies of AOM *therapy*, where withholding antibiotics raises ethical concerns for children who are very young or very ill, children on placebo *prophylaxis* still receive antibiotics for individual AOM episodes. Consequently, the spontaneous improvement noted in Table 12-4 has the implicit assumption that each child may still receive several discrete courses of antibiotic therapy.

Many studies excluded children with baseline OME, so results should be extrapolated to this population with caution. Children were also generally excluded if they had immune deficiency, cleft palate, craniofacial anomalies, or Down syndrome. Unfortunately, these are also the children most likely to develop recurrent AOM. Spontaneous rates of improvement are likely to be lower in populations with baseline OME or with underlying predisposing factors for AOM or OME.

SPONTANEOUS RESOLUTION OF OME

Meta-analysis Results

The validity of longitudinal (cohort) studies depends on the adequacy and completeness of follow-up. Most studies in Tables 12-5 to 12-8 had less than 10 to 20% loss to follow-up in the first year, but several had greater than 30% attrition after several years. Incomplete follow-up is more likely for OME that develops late in the study because the likelihood of complete follow-up decreases with the passage of time. To limit bias in OME resolution rates, the data in Tables 12-5 to 12-8 reflect only OME present at study inception. This also mimics actual office practice, where clinicians routinely see chil-

Table 12-4 Prognosis of Recurrent AOM in Children Receiving Interval Placebo or No Antibiotic

Year First Author	Country	Entry Rate*	Study Duration	AOM Episodes, N(%)[†]		AOM/Patient-Month (Rate)[‡]	
				None	2 or Fewer	Baseline	During Study
1972 Maynard[51]	Alaska	NS	1 yr	115/191 (60)	171/191 (90)	—	141/2,292 (.06)
1974 Perrin[52]	USA	3/18; 5	3 mo	33/54 (61)	—	(.31)	28/162 (.17)
1982 Gaskins[53]	USA	3/18; 5	6 mo	3/11 (27)	11/11 (100)	—	8/66 (.12)
1983 Liston[54]	USA	3/6	3 mo	14/34 (41)	27/34 (79)	($\geq$ .50)	43/102 (.42)
1983 Schuller[55]	USA	4/12	2 yr	—	—	(.45)	118/288 (.41)
1985 Perisco[56]	Israel	3/6	6 mo	7/48 (15)	19/48 (40)	($\geq$ 1.00)	—
1985 Varsano[57]	Israel	3/6	10 wk	12/32 (38)	—	($\geq$ .50)	36/74 (.49)
1986 Gonzalez[58]	USA	3/6; 5/18	6 mo	3/20 (15)	—	($\geq$ .28)	40/120 (.33)
1989 Principi[59]	Italy	3/6	6 mo	11/30 (37)	—	(.52)	25/180 (.14)
1992 Casselbrant[60]	USA	3/6; 4/12	2 yr	32/80 (40)	61/80 (76)	($\geq$ .33)	173/1,920 (.09)
1993 Sih[61]	Brazil	3/12	3 mo	10/20 (50)	19/20 (95)	(.50)	14/60 (.23)
1994 Prellner[62]	Sweden	3/6	5 mo	—	—	($\geq$ .50)	78/186 (.42)
1996 Alho[65]	Finland	3/6; 4/12	2 yr	85/214 (40)	188/214 (88)	($\geq$ .33)	227/1,284 (.18)
1996 Mandel[63]	USA	3/12	1 yr	24/51 (47)	46/51 (90)	($\geq$ .25)	46/531 (.09)
1997 Roark[64]	USA	3/6	NS	37/59 (63)	NS	($\geq$ .50)	20/92 (.22)
RANDOM-EFFECTS META-ANALYSIS							
Combined sample size				844	648	—	7,357
Estimate of combined rate (95% CI)				.41 (.32, .51)	.83 (.74, .91)		.23 (.18, .28)
Test for heterogeneity, Q statistic				88.5, df = 12	59.1, df = 7		445.3, df = 13
Test for heterogeneity, *p* value				< .001	< .001		< .001

AOM = acute otitis media; CI = confidence interval; df = degrees of freedom; NS = not stated.

*Baseline rate of AOM recurrence to enter study in episodes/month or total episodes.

[†]Number of children with specified number of AOM episodes divided by the total number of children in placebo group.

[‡]Rate of occurrence of AOM episodes per patient-month of observation (incidence density); baseline rate is listed (if stated by authors) or calculated from entry criteria when possible.

dren with OME of varying or unknown prior duration, not necessarily of recent onset.

Using a *strict* outcome criterion (B to A tympanogram), combined *cure* rates (see Table 12-5) were 20% by 3 months (95% CI, 7 to 34%), rising to 28% by 6 months (95% CI, 17 to 40%). Using a *relaxed* outcome criterion (B to A/C1 tympanogram), combined *resolution* rates (see Table 12-6) showed minimal change by 3 months (22 to 28%) but increased to 42% by 6 months (95% CI, 35 to 49%) and 56% by 9 months (95% CI, 30 to 82%). Using a *liberal* outcome criterion (B to A/C1/C2 or non-B

tympanogram), combined *improvement* rates (see Table 12-7) were 56% by 3 months (95% CI, 51 to 61%), 72% by 6 months (95% CI, 68 to 76%), and 81% by 9 months (95% CI, 77 to 85%). Similar improvement rates were achieved with patient-based outcomes (see Table 12-8) after the first month.

Resolution rates for OME present at cohort inception were rarely provided beyond 12 months of observation. Thomsen and Tos[73] noted an increase in improvement (B to non-B tympanogram) from 81% by 9 months to 88% by 15 months to 98% by 27 months. Fiellau-Nikolajsen and Lous[100] reported 3-year cure

Table 12-5 Spontaneous Resolution by Ear (B to A Tympanogram)* of Newly Diagnosed OME

Year First Author	Country	Age	Rate of B to A Tympanogram Change, N(%)[†]			
			4–6 Weeks	3 Months	6 Months	9 Months
1979 Fiellau-Nikolajsen[66]	Denmark	3 yr	14/91 (15)	22/91 (24)	32/91 (35)	—
1979 Fiellau-Nikolajsen[67]	Denmark	3 yr	7/64 (11)	16/62 (26)	—	—
1980 Sly[68]	USA	4–5 yr	4/14 (29)	—	—	—
1980 Tos[69]	Denmark	2 yr	—	6/51 (12)	16/51 (31)	24/51 (47)
1982 Renval[74]	Sweden	2 yr	10/40 (25)	16/40 (40)	—	—
1982 Tos[75]	Denmark	4 yr	—	3/87 (3)	17/87 (20)	—
1988 Robinson[79]	USA	6–13 mo	10/25 (40)	—	—	—
RANDOM-EFFECTS META-ANALYSIS						
Combined sample size			234	331	229	—
Estimate of combined rate (95% CI)			.21 (.11, .30)	.20 (.07, .34)	.28 (.17, .40)	
Test for heterogeneity, Q statistic			10.3, df = 4	44.4, df = 4	6.2, df = 2	
Test for heterogeneity, p value			.036	< .001	.045	

CI = confidence interval; df = degrees of freedom; OME = otitis media with effusion.

*Outcome using strict criterion for OME resolution: conversion of type B tympanogram (flat curve without an impedance minimum) to type A (peak pressure > –100 mm H_2O).

[†]Number of ears with clearance of OME at the specified time period divided by the total number of evaluable ears.

Table 12-6 Spontaneous Resolution by Ear (B to A/C1 Tympanogram)* of Newly Diagnosed OME

Year First Author	Country	Age	Rate of B to A/C1 Tympanogram Change, N(%)[†]			
			1 month	3 Months	6 Months	9 Months
1979 Fiellau-Nikolajsen[66]	Denmark	3 yr	20/91 (22)	30/91 (33)	41/91 (45)	—
1979 Fiellau-Nikolajsen[67]	Denmark	3 yr	14/64 (22)	25/62 (40)	—	—
1980 Tos[69]	Denmark	2 yr	—	13/51 (26)	24/51 (47)	34/51 (67)
1982 Tos[75]	Denmark	4 yr	—	12/87 (14)	31/87 (36)	37/82 (45)
RANDOM-EFFECTS META-ANALYSIS						
Combined sample size			153	291	229	133
Estimate of combined rate (95% CI)			.22 (.16, .29)	.28 (.14, .41)	.42 (.35, .49)	.56 (.30, .82)
Test for heterogeneity, Q statistic			6.6, df = 1	17.8, df = 3	12.9, df = 2	6.3, df = 1
Test for heterogeneity, p value			.930	< .001	.302	.012

CI = confidence interval; df = degrees of freedom; OME = otitis media with effusion.

*Outcome using relaxed criterion for OME resolution: conversion of type B tympanogram (flat curve without an impedance minimum) to type A (peak pressure > –100 mm H_2O) or type C1 (pressure –100 to –199 mm H_2O).

[†]Number of ears with clearance of OME at the specified time period divided by the total number of evaluable ears.

Table 12-7 Spontaneous Resolution by Ear (B to Non-B Tympanogram)* of Newly Diagnosed OME

Year First Author	Country	Age	Rate of B to non-B Tympanogram Change, N(%)[†]				
			4–6 Weeks	*3 Months*	*6 Months*	*9 Months*	*12 Months*
1979 Fiellau-Nikolajsen[67]	Denmark	3 yr	22/64 (34)	35/62 (57)	—	—	—
1980 Tos[69]	Denmark	2 yr	—	27/51 (53)	34/51 (67)	44/51 (86)	—
1981 Lamothe[71]	Canada	6–7 yr	38/53 (47)	—	—	—	—
1981 Thomsen[73]	Denmark	2 yr	—	25/48 (52)	30/48 (62)	39/48 (81)	—
1982 Renvall[74]	Sweden	4 yr	27/40 (68)	28/40 (70)	—	—	—
1982 Tos[75]	Denmark	4 yr	—	51/87 (59)	62/87 (71)	60/82 (73)	64/82 (78)
1988 Robinson[79]	USA	6 mo–13 yr	13/25 (52)	—	—	—	—
1990 Zielhuis[80]	Netherlands	2 yr	—	172/330 (52)	244/330 (74)	275/330 (83)	295/330 (89)
1994 Williamson[82]	England	5–8 yr	—	—	—	52/67 (78)	61/67 (91)

RANDOM-EFFECTS META-ANALYSIS

Combined sample size			182	618	516	578	479
Estimate of combined rate (95% CI)			.56 (.35, .78)	.56 (.51, .61)	.72 (.68, .76)	.81 (.77, .85)	.87 (.80, .94)
Test for heterogeneity, Q statistic			16.0, df = 3	6.2, df = 5	3.2, df = 3	5.2, df = 4	6.0, df = 2
Test for heterogeneity, *p* value			< .001	.292	.367	.266	.049

CI = confidence interval; df = degrees of freedom; OME = otitis media with effusion.

*Outcome using liberal criterion for OME resolution: conversion of type B tympanogram (flat curve without an impedance minimum) to non-B (peak pressure > –400 mm H_2O, including types A, C1, and C2).

[†]Number of ears with clearance of OME at the specified time period divided by the total number of evaluable ears.

rates of 51% (B to A tympanogram), resolution rates of 65% (B to A/C1 tympanogram), and improvement rates of 77% (B to non-B tympanogram). Unfortunately, no information was recorded between 6 months and 3 years of follow-up, during which time many children had surgery for persistent OME.

Two studies described natural history by ear for OME of defined onset *during* the study.[72,77] Resolution rates defined using an algorithm[72] or improvement (B to non-B tympanogram)[77] were 67 to 72% by 1 month, 86 to 95% by 3 months, and 98 to 100% by 6 months. These rates are dramatically higher than those in Tables 12-5 to 12-8, which reflect OME present at cohort inception but of unknown prior duration. Conversely, another study reported resolution rates by child for bilateral OME that began during the study and persisted for 4 months or longer.[83] Resolution rates for one or both ears using liberal criterion were 16% by 1 month, 47% by 3 months, and 65% by 6 months.

Spontaneous resolution rates for chronic OME (Table 12-9) are initially comparable with rates obtained for newly diagnosed OME of unknown duration using strict criterion (see Table 12-5). By 3 months, 19% of ears with chronic OME no longer had effusions (95% CI, 13 to 24%), increasing to 25% by 6 months (95% CI, 17 to 34%), and stabilizing at 31 to 33% by 1 to 2 years. Longer-term rates were reported by Maw and Bawden,[92] who observed 59% resolution with pneumatic otoscopy at 4 years (35 of 59 ears), 69% at 5 years (38 of 55 ears), 85% at 7 years (34 of 40 ears), and 95% at 10 years (19 of 21 ears). The median duration of untreated OME was a staggering 6.1 years by otoscopic assessment and 7.8 years by tympanometry.[116]

Generalizability of OME Findings

The ability to generalize OME results relate to the definitions of disease and outcome. Resolution rates in clin-

Table 12-8 Spontaneous Resolution by Child (B to non-B Tympanogram)* of Newly Diagnosed OME[†]

Year First Author	Country	Age	Rate of B to Non-B Tympanogram Change, N(%)[‡]			
			1–2 months	3 Months	6–8 Months	12 Months
1983 Fiellau-Nikolajsen[76]	Denmark	3 yr	28/78 (35)	46/78 (58)	53/78 (68)	—
1985 Reves[78]	England	3 mo–6 yr	—	40/68 (58)	—	—
1992 Mills[81]	England	1–14 yr	57/192 (30)	—	—	—
1994 Williamson[82]	England	5–8 yr	—	—	38/50 (76)	45/50 (90)
1995 Zeisel[83]	USA	6 mo–2 y	18/57 (32)	27/57 (47)	37/57 (65)	51/57 (89)
1996 van Balen[84]	Netherlands	6 mo–6 yr	—	210/433 (48)	—	—
1998 Marchisio[85]	Italy	5–7 yr	—	331/451 (73)	—	—
RANDOM-EFFECTS META-ANALYSIS						
Combined sample size			327	1,087	185	107
Estimate of combined rate (95% CI)			.31 (.26, .36)	.58 (.43, .72)	.70 (.63, .76)	.90 (.84, .96)
Test for heterogeneity, Q statistic			1.0, df = 2	66.9, df = 4	1.8, df = 2	0.1, df = 1
Test for heterogeneity, p value			.620	< .001	.413	.929

CI = confidence interval; df = degrees of freedom; OME = otitis media with effusion.

*Outcome using liberal criterion for OME resolution: conversion of type B tympanogram (flat curve without an impedance minimum) to non-B (peak pressure > –400 mm H_2O, including types A, C1, and C2).

[†]Duration of prior OME unknown for all studies except Zeisel (> 3 months prior duration).

[‡]Number of children with clearance of OME at the specified time period divided by the total number of evaluable children.

Table 12-9 Spontaneous Resolution by Ear of Chronic OME Documented for 3 Months or Longer

Year First Author	Country	Age	Resolution rate, N(%)*				
			< 3 Months	6 Months	1 Year	2 Years	3 Years
1984 Ernstson[86]	Sweden	1–11 yr	11/72 (15)	—	—	—	—
1985 Maw[87]	England	2–9 yr	10/52 (19)	13/52 (25)	14/52 (27)	—	—
1986 Lieberman[88]	Israel	2–10 yr	—	—	—	49/158 (31)	—
1991 Buckley[89]	England	1–14 yr	17/75 (23)	20/52 (39)	16/32 (50)	—	—
1993 Dempster[91]	Scotland	3.5–12 yr	—	7/35 (21)	11/35 (32)	—	—
1994 Maw[92]	England	2–9 yr	—	14/71 (20)	17/79 (22)	27/73 (37)	32/65 (49)
RANDOM-EFFECTS META-ANALYSIS							
Combined sample size			199	210	198	231	—
Estimate of combined rate (95% CI)			.19 (.13, .24)	.25 (.17, .34)	.31 (.19, .43)	.33 (.27, .39)	
Test for heterogeneity, Q statistic			1.3, df = 2	5.8, df = 3	8.4, df = 3	0.8, df = 1	
Test for heterogeneity, p value			.513	.124	.039	.376	

CI = confidence interval; df = degrees of freedom; OME = otitis media with effusion.

*Number of ears with clearance of OME divided by the total number of evaluable ears (Maw and Dempster based results on ear randomly selected not to receive a tympanostomy tube).

ical practice probably exceed those in Tables 12-5 to 12-7 because the diagnostic criteria are more liberal: otoscopy or pneumatic otoscopy, with or without tympanometric confirmation. We limited our analyses to type B tympanograms, which have the highest specificity for OME (to avoid inflated estimates caused by including otoscopy results), or type C tympanograms, which have higher sensitivity but poor specificity for OME. Results are based on newly diagnosed OME of unknown duration at cohort inception, which often mirrors the situation in clinical practice. As noted above, resolution rates for OME of defined onset, whether de novo or following AOM, are much higher.

Data concerning the long-term resolution of untreated OME are rare (see Table 12-9) and may be unfavorably biased by systematically higher revisit rates for the most serious cases. Maw and Bawden[92] provide unique insights into OME resolution after 10 years of observation, but the initial sample of 79 ears at year 1 dwindles to only 21 remaining ears at year 10. The resulting 73% attrition rate may yield an unduly pessimistic prognosis for the type of child defined at study entry. Until new data are forthcoming, however, their estimates remain the best available for the long-term natural history of untreated OME.

The extremely dynamic nature of OME must also be considered when assessing spontaneous resolution. About 30 to 40% of children have recurrent OME over several years,[72,77,108,117] although episode duration is similar, regardless of the episode being initial or recurrent.[112] Further, repetitive screenings of healthy children show enormous variability in tympanogram types: 25% of ears improve or deteriorate between consecutive months[72] and more than 50% change type within 3 months.[118] Transient improvement of OME followed by relapse occurs in 30 to 45% of children (B tympanogram to C2 to B), making it inappropriate to equate improvement (C2 tympanogram) with resolution or cure.[67,118] Last, OME *first* detected in May through August has the best prognosis, whereas OME detected in September through February has the worst.[72,73,118]

CLINICAL IMPLICATIONS

At some point during the accumulation of knowledge, it is useful to pause and reflect on what has already been learned. Clinicians who treat children with OM are fortunate to have more than 30 years of prospective evidence from which to draw conclusions about the spontaneous resolution of AOM and OME. Although much of this evidence was not originally collected for the specific goal of documenting natural history (eg, control groups in randomized trials), it, nonetheless, serves admirably. In an

era of evidence-based medicine, quantitative estimates of natural history provide an invaluable benchmark against which medical, surgical, or alternative (complementary) therapies can be effectively judged.

Systematic review of published evidence reveals favorable rates of spontaneous resolution for AOM (Table 12-10). Within 24 hours, 61% of placebo-treated children have symptomatic relief (95% CI, 50 to 72%), increasing to 80% after 2 to 3 days (95% CI, 69 to 90%). By 7 to 14 days, 70% of children experience complete clinical resolution of AOM (95% CI, 49 to 92%), exclusive of middle ear effusion. Suppurative complications are comparable whether initial antibiotics are withheld (0.12%) or provided (0.24%). Although children with recurrent AOM enter clinical trials with a mean baseline rate of 5.5 or more annual episodes, they average only 2.8 annual episodes while on placebo (95% CI, 2.2 to 3.4). Further, 41% have no additional episodes of AOM while on placebo for a median duration of 6 months (95% CI, 32 to 51%), and 83% have only 2 or fewer episodes (95% CI, 74 to 91%).

The spontaneous resolution of OME is also favorable but varies by population and outcome (Table 12-11). Children with OME after an episode of untreated AOM have 59% resolution by 1 month (95% CI, 50 to 68%) and 74% resolution by 3 months (95% CI, 68 to 80%). Children with newly diagnosed OME of unknown duration still do well, with resolution rates (B tympanogram to A/C1) increasing from 28% by 3 months (95%, CI 14 to 41%), to 42% by 6 months (95% CI, 35 to 49%). Rates show a relative decrease of about 30%, however, with strict criterion for cure (B tympanogram to A). Conversely, success rates nearly double with a criterion of tympanometric improvement (B to non-B): 56% by 3 months (95% CI, 51 to 61%), 72% by 6 months (95% CI, 68 to 76%), and 87% by 1 year (95% CI, 80 to 94%). Even higher resolution rates occur for OME of defined onset, reaching 90% by 3 months.

Our data are consistent with findings by other investigators. Clinical resolution of AOM without antibiotics has been reported as 62% by 24 hours,[15] 81% at 1 to 7 days (95% CI, 72 to 90%),[1] and 81% by 7 to 14 days (95% CI, 69 to 94%).[9] The AHRQ evidence report on AOM also concluded that suppurative complications were not increased if antibiotics were withheld, but close follow-up was provided.[1] A subsequent AHRQ report on OME noted 23% resolution (95% CI, 6 to 39%) by 3 months (B tympanogram to A) and higher resolution (43%) with more inclusive outcome criterion (B/C tympanogram to A).[2] Lastly, a review of antimicrobial prophylaxis for recurrent AOM noted 0.19 episodes per patient-month in controls (95% CI, 0.13 to 0.26).[7]

Spontaneous resolution of AOM most likely results from the child's immune response and clearance of secre-

Table 12-10 Summary of Spontaneous Resolution Rates for AOM

Clinical Situation	Time Point	N[†]	Rate[‡]	(95% CI)
Symptomatic relief of pain and fever caused by AOM in children randomized to placebo (see Table 12-2)	24	3	.61	(.50,.72)
	2–3 d	5	.80	(.69, .90)
	4–7 d	8	.74	(.64, .85)
Complete clinical resolution of AOM in children randomized to placebo or no drug* (see Table 12-2)	7–14 d	6	.70	(.49, .92)
Resolution of OME persisting after AOM in children randomized to placebo or no drug (see Table 12-3)	4 wk	4	.59	(.50, .68)
	6 wk	3	.46	(.32, .60)
	12 wk	2	.74	(.68, .80)
Future incidence of AOM episodes/month for children with a history of recurrent AOM (see Table 12-4)	up to 2 yr	14	.23	(.18, .28)
Future chance of having no AOM episodes for children with recurrent AOM (see Table 12-4)	6 mo median	13	.41	(.32, .51)
Future chance of having two or fewer AOM episodes for children with recurrent AOM (see Table 12-4)	6 mo median	8	.83	(.74, .91)

AOM = acute otitis media; CI = confidence interval.

*Absence of all presenting signs and symptoms, exclusive of middle ear effusion, within 7 to 14 days after therapy started.

[‡]Estimate based on random-effects meta-analysis.

[†]Number of studies from which data were combined to derive the overall resolution rate.

tions through a patulous Eustachian tube. Complete clearance of middle ear effusion, however, often lags behind symptom relief because of persistent inflammation and mucosal edema. Improvement in recurrent AOM is more gradual, most likely related to immune maturation, Eustachian tube growth, and regression to a mean symptom state (eg, children enter clinical trials when symptoms are most prominent, and the next likely event, irrespective of management, is improvement to a mean level). Resolution of OME is most likely a combination of drainage and absorption as the Eustachian tube matures and the local immune response gradually declines.

The favorable natural history of OM suggests that most children will improve (eventually) irrespective of management. Rather than endorse nihilism, our data suggest a careful need to balance nature's accomplishments against potential therapeutic benefits. For example, although antimicrobials have proven efficacy for AOM, initial observation of selected children can also achieve excellent outcomes (see Table 12-2).[119] Similarly, delaying interventions for recurrent AOM by 6 months will often provide relief (see Table 12-4). OME in otherwise healthy children should be documented for 3 months prior to surgery,[8] but extending this to 6 months achieves a relative increase of 30 to 50% in spontaneous resolution (see Tables 12-5 to 12-7). This also applies to children with baseline chronic OME, but longer periods of observation are often disappointing (see Table 12-9).

Any decision for prolonged observation must be balanced against the potential adverse impact of persistent OME on a child's hearing, speech, overall development, and school performance.

Significant heterogeneity was noted in most of the meta-analyses, which raises the issue of whether combining the studies was justifiable. The random effects model presupposes a heterogeneous population of studies, which results in broader confidence limits on effect estimates. Nonetheless, it is inappropriate to combine grossly different studies. The only situation where this may apply is for Table 12-1, which describes prevalence of antibiotic treatment in AOM observational cohorts. This end point, however, was a minor outcome provided for descriptive and historic purposes. In contrast, the study quality, definitions of disease, and outcome end points in the other tables are sufficiently similar to justify random-effects pooling. Moreover, the AHRQ concluded in two evidence reports[1,2] that meta-analysis of AOM control groups and OME cohort studies was appropriate to study natural history.

Meta-analysis results are useful in formulating public policy or practice guidelines but may be of less use in treating individual patients. Although we can predict that on average 80% of children with sporadic AOM will improve spontaneously in a few days, we cannot identify a priori the 20% likely to remain symptomatic. Similarly, knowing that 83% of children with recurrent AOM will

Table 12-11 Summary of Spontaneous Resolution Rates for OME

Clinical Situation	Time Point	N[†]	Rate[‡]	(95% CI)
Resolution of OME persisting after AOM in children	4 wk	4	.59	(.50, .68)
randomized to placebo or no drug (see Table 12-3)	6 wk	3	.46	(.32, .60)
	12 wk	2	.74	(.68, .80)
Cure (B to A tympanogram*) of newly diagnosed OME of	4–6 wk	5	.21	(.11, .30)
unknown duration by ear (see Table 12-5)	3 mo	5	.20	(.07, .34)
	6 mo	3	.28	(.17, .40)
Resolution (B to A/C1 tympanogram*) of newly diagnosed	1 mo	2	.22	(.16, .29)
OME of unknown duration by ear (see Table 12-6)	3 mo	4	.28	(.14, .41)
	6 mo	3	.42	(.35, .49)
	9 mo	2	.56	(.30, .82)
Improvement (B to A/C1/C2 tympanogram*) of newly	4–6 wk	4	.56	(.35, .78)
diagnosed OME of unknown duration by ear (see Table 12-7)	3 mo	6	.56	(.51, .61)
	6 mo	4	.72	(.68, .76)
	9 mo	5	.81	(.77, .85)
	12 mo	3	.87	(.80, .94)
Improvement (B to A/C1/C2 tympanogram*) of newly	1–2 mo	3	.31	(.26, .36)
diagnosed OME by child (see Table 12-8)	3 mo	5	.58	(.43, .72)
	6–8 mo	3	.70	(.63, .76)
	12 mo	2	.90	(.84, .96)
Clinical resolution of documented OME lasting 3 months	< 3 mo	3	.19	(.13, .24)
or longer by ear (see Table 12-9)	6 mo	4	.25	(.17, .34)
	12 mo	4	.31	(.19, .43)
	24 mo	2	.33	(.27, .39)

CI = confidence interval; OME = otitis media with effusion.

*Tympanometric patterns defined as: type A, peak pressure > –100 mm H_2O (effusion in 3% of ears at myringotomy); type B, flat curve without an impedance minimum (effusion in 85–100%); type C1, pressure –100 to –199 mm H_2O (effusion in 17%); or type C2, pressure –200 to –400 mm H_2O (effusion in up to 55%).

[†]Number of studies from which data were combined to derive the overall resolution rate.

[‡]Estimate based on random-effects meta-analysis.

likely experience two or fewer episodes over the next 6 months offers little solace to the 17% who remain otitis prone. A narrow CI in meta-analysis reflects certainty about effects in populations, not patients. Meta-analysis cannot substitute for judgment in deciding whom to treat (or observe), but it can define realistic treatment expectations based on best evidence synthesis. Optimal management of individual patients is ultimately based on a combination of best evidence, expert judgment, and patient preferences.

Although existing evidence offers some intriguing insights into the natural history of untreated OM, there is ample room for future research. A major need relates to the influence of baseline prognostic factors on outcome, such as the impact of child age on AOM resolution and risk of suppurative complications. Ideally, patient-related factors would be incorporated into esti-

mates of natural history or treatment benefits to facilitate evidence-based management decisions. Data concerning the natural history of OME using newer immittance measures (static admittance and gradient width) would also be helpful, because existing large cohorts relied on less accurate classifications of tympanometric peak pressure (A, C1, C2). Large cohort studies of recurrent AOM prognosis are also needed because of the favorable changes in epidemiology anticipated from universal administration of the conjugate pneumococcal vaccine.[120]

The favorable natural history of OM (Table 12-12) suggests a need for clinicians to critically examine existing and new therapies. No intervention can be deemed effective simply because it works; to do so may rob nature alone of the credit for resolution or symptomatic relief. To endorse a completely nihilistic or overly critical

Table 12-12 Pointers and Pitfalls

1. Rates of spontaneous resolution for OM are favorable; most children are likely to improve, regardless of compliance with therapy, medications, or follow-up.

2. About 60% of children with AOM initially managed without antibiotics are symptom-free in 24 hours; by 2 to 3 days, 80% are without residual symptoms (excluding MEE).

3. Suppurative complications from AOM are comparable, whether antibiotics are initially withheld or provided, if children are followed closely and observation failures receive antibiotic therapy.

4. All clinical trials that initially withheld antimicrobials for children with AOM had provisions to begin therapy if symptoms persisted or progressed; no study proposed to simply "not treat" AOM.

5. Residual MEE after untreated AOM is the rule, not the exception; MEE prevalence gradually declines from about 65% at 2 weeks, to 40% at 1 month, and 25% at 3 months.

6. Children with recurrent AOM are likely to have 1.5 to 2.5 fewer episodes the next year; 40% will have no AOM over a median period of 6 months, and over 80% will have two or fewer episodes.

7. Although most OME resolves within a few months, the prognosis is inversely related to duration; new onset OME does extremely well, but OME lasting weeks or months does poorly.

8. About 22% of newly detected OME resolves by 1 month, 28% by 3 months, 42% by 6 months, and 56% by 9 months; rates of improvement (not resolution) are substantially higher.

9. Documented OME of 3 months duration or longer resolves spontaneously in only about 33% of children after 1 to 2 years; longer periods of observation provide only marginal benefits.

10. Treatments for OM cannot be endorsed simply because they yield good results; comparative studies are needed to demonstrate significant benefits beyond natural history.

AOM = acute otitis media; MEE = middle ear effusion; OM = otitis media; OME = otitis media with effusion.

approach to management, however, is also unjustified. Clearly, a middle ground is desirable, the limits of which will vary on the basis of provider experience and individual patient preference. Perhaps we should offer the words of British biologist Hans Krebs (1900–1981) to children with OM: "You and your family must clearly understand that the great ultimate healer is always nature itself and that the drug, the physician, and the patient can do no more than assist nature, by providing the very best conditions for your body to defend and heal itself."[3]

References

1. Marcy M, Takata G, Shekelle P, et al. Management of acute otitis media. Evidence Report/Technology Assessment No. 15 (Prepared by the Southern California Evidence-based Practice Center under Contract No. 290-97-0001). Rockville(MD): Agency for Healthcare Research and Quality; 2001 May AHRQ Publication No. 01-E010.

2. Takata GS, Chan LS, Shekelle P, et al. Diagnosis, natural history, and late effects of otitis media with effusion. Evidence Report/Technology Assessment: Number 55. Rockville (MD): Agency for Healthcare Research and Quality; 2002 June. AHRQ Publication Number 02-E026.

3. Brallier JM. Medical wit and wisdom: from Hippocrates to Groucho Marx. Philadelphia (PA): Running Press; 1993. p. 63–5.

4. Egger M, Smith GD, Phillips AN. Meta-analysis: principles and procedures. BMJ 1997;315:1533–7.

5. Rosenfeld RM, Post JC. Meta-analysis of antibiotics for the treatment of otitis media with effusion. Otolaryngol Head Neck Surg 1992;106:378–86.

6. Bonati M, Marchetti F, Pistotti V, et al. Meta-analysis of antimicrobial prophylaxis for recurrent acute otitis media. Clin Trials Meta Analy 1992;28:39–50.

7. Williams RL, Chalmers TC, Stange KC, et al. Use of antibiotics in preventing recurrent acute otitis media and in treating otitis media with effusion: a meta-analytic attempt to resolve the brouhaha. JAMA 1993;270:1344–51.

8. Stool SE, Berg AO, Berman S, et al. Otitis media with effusion in young children. Clinical Practice Guideline, Number 12. Rockville (MD): Agency for Health Care Policy and Research, Public Health Service, U.S. Department of Health and Human Services; 1994 July. AHCPR Publication No. 94-0622.

9. Rosenfeld RM, Vertrees JE, Carr J, et al. Clinical efficacy of antimicrobial drugs for acute otitis media: meta-analysis of 5400 children from thirty-three randomized trials. J Pediatr 1994;124:355–67.

10. Pignataro O, Pignataro LD, Gallus G, et al. Otitis media with effusion and S-carboxymethylcysteine and/or its lysine salt: a critical overview. Int J Pediatr Otorhinolaryngol 1996;35:231–41.

11. Damoiseaux RAMJ, van Balen FAM, Hoes AW, de Melker RA. Antibiotic treatment of acute otitis media in children under two years of age: evidence based? Br J Gen Pract 1998;48:1861–4.

12. Rosenfeld RM. Surgical prevention of otitis media. Vaccine 2001;19:S134–9.

13. Flynn CA, Griffin G, Tudiver F. Decongestants and antihistamines for acute otitis media in children (Cochrane Review). In: The Cochrane Library, Issue 2, 2002. Oxford (UK): Update Software; 2002

14. Straetemans M, Sanders EAM, Veenhoven RH, et al. Pneumococcal vaccines for preventing otitis media (Cochrane Review). In: The Cochrane Library, Issue 2, 2002. Oxford (UK): Update Software; 2002.

15. Glasziou PP, Del Mar CB, Sanders SL, Hayem M. Antibiotics for acute otitis media in children (Cochrane Review). In: The Cochrane Library, Issue 2, 2002. Oxford (UK): Update Software; 2002.

16. Kozyrskyj AL, Hildes-Ripstein GE, Longstaffe SEA, et al. Short course antibiotics for acute otitis media (Cochrane Review). In: The Cochrane Library, issue 2, 2002. Oxford (UK): Update Software; 2002.

17. Sackett DL. Applying overviews and meta-analyses at the bedside. J Clin Epidemiol 1995;48:61–6.

18. Rosenfeld RM. Natural history of untreated otitis media. In: Rosenfeld RM, Bluestone CD, editors. Evidence-based otitis media. Hamilton (ON): BC Decker; 1999.

19. Rosenfeld RM. How to systematically review the medical literature. Otolaryngol Head Neck Surg 1996;115:53–63.

20. Sutton AJ, Jones DR, Abrams KR, et al. Systematic reviews and meta-analysis: a structured review of the methodological literature. J Health Serv Res Policy 1999; 4:49–55.

21. Stroup DF, Berlin JA, Morton SC, et al. Meta-analysis of observational studies in epidemiology. A proposal for reporting. JAMA 2000;283:2008–12.

22. Egger M, Zellweger-Zahner T, Schneider M, et al. Language bias in randomized controlled trials published in English and German. Lancet 1997;350:326–9.

23. Juni P, Holenstein F, Sterne J, et al. Direction and impact of language bias in meta-analyses of controlled trials: empirical study. Int J Epidemiol 2002;31:115–23.

24. Brookhouser PE. Use of tympanometry in office practice for diagnosis of otitis media. Pediatr Infect Dis J 1998;17:544–51.

25. Fiellau-Nikolajsen M. Epidemiology of secretory otitis media: a descriptive cohort study. Ann Otol Rhinol Laryngol 1983;92:172–7.

26. Tos M. Epidemiology and natural history of secretory otitis. Am J Otol 1984;5:459–62.

27. DerSimonian R, Laird N. Meta-analysis in clinical trials. Control Clin Trials 1986;17:177–88.

28. Borenstein M, Rothstein H. Comprehensive meta-analysis: a computer program for research synthesis (v. 1.0.25). Englewood (NJ): Biostat Inc; 2000.

29. Sutton AJ, Abrams KR, Jones DR. An illustrated guide to the methods of meta-analysis. J Eval Clin Pract 2001; 7:135–48.

30. Halsted C, Lepow ML, Balassanian N, et al. Otitis media: clinical observations, microbiology, and evaluation of therapy. Am J Dis Child 1968;115:542–51.

31. Laxdal OE, Merida J, Trefor Jones RH. Treatment of acute otitis media: a controlled study of 142 children. Can Med Assoc J 1970;102:263–8.

32. Howie VM, Ploussard JH. Efficacy of fixed combination antibiotics versus separate components in otitis media: effectiveness of erythromycin estolate, triple sulfonamide, ampicillin, erythromycin estolate-triple sulfonamide, and placebo in 280 patients with acute otitis media under two and one-half years of age. Clin Pediatr 1972;11:205–14.

33. Mygind N, Meistrup-Larsen KI, Thomsen J, et al. Penicillin in acute otitis media: a double-blind, placebo-controlled trial. Clin Otolaryngol 1981;6:5–13.

34. van Buchem FL, Dunk JHM, van't Hof MA. Therapy of acute otitis media: myringotomy, antibiotics, or neither: a double blind study in children. Lancet 1981;2:883–7.

35. Thalin A, Densert O, Larsson A, et al. Is penicillin necessary in the treatment of acute otitis media? In: Proceedings of the International Conference on Acute and Secretory Otitis Media, Part 1; 1985 Nov 17–22; Jerusalem, Israel. Amsterdam: Kugler Publications, 1986. p. 441–6.

36. Appelman CLM, Claessen JQPJ, Touw-Otten FWMM, et al. Coamoxiclav in recurrent acute otitis media: placebo-controlled study. BMJ 1991;303:1450–2.

37. Burke P, Bain J, Robinson D, Dunleavey J. Acute red ear in children: controlled trial of nonantibiotic treatment in general practice. BMJ 1991;303:558–62.

38. Kaleida PH, Casselbrant ML, Rockette HE, et al. Amoxicillin or myringotomy or both for acute otitis media: results of a randomized clinical trial. Pediatrics 1991;87: 466–74.

39. Claessen JQPJ, Appelman CLM, Touw-Otten FWMM, et al. Persistence of middle ear dysfunction after recurrent acute otitis media. Clin Otolaryngol 1994;19:35–40.

40. Damoiseaux RAMJ, van Balen FAM, Hoes AW, et al. Primary care based randomised double blind trial of amoxicillin versus placebo for acute otitis media in children aged under 2 years. BMJ 2000;320:350–4.

41. Jacobs J, Springer DA, Crothers D. Homeopathic treatment of acute otitis media in children: a preliminary randomized placebo-controlled trial. Pediatr Infect Dis J 2001;20:177–83.

42. Fry J. Antibiotics in acute tonsillitis and acute otitis media. BMJ 1958;2:883–6.

43. Townsend EH. Otitis media in pediatric practice. N Y State J Med 1964;64:1591–7.

44. Thomsen J, Mygind N, Meistrup-Larsen KI, et al. Oral decongestant in acute otitis media: results of a double-blind trial. Int J Pediatr Otorhinolaryngol 1979;1:103–8.

45. van Buchem FL, Peeters MF, van't Hof MA. Acute otitis media: a new treatment strategy. BMJ 1985;290:1033–7.

46. Ostfeld E, Segal J, Kaufstein M, Gelernter I. Management of acute otitis media without primary administration of systemic antimicrobial agents. In: Lim DJ, Bluestone CD, Klein JO, Nelson JD, editors. Proceedings of the Fourth International Symposium Recent Advances in Otitis Media; 1987 June 1–4; Bal Harbour (FL). Toronto: BC Decker Inc; 1988. p. 235–9.

47. Froom J, Culpepper L, Grob P, et al. Diagnosis and antibiotic treatment of acute otitis media: report from International Primary Care Network. BMJ 1990;300: 582–6.

48. Bollag U, Bollag-Albrecht E. Recommendations derived from practice audit for the treatment of acute otitis media. Lancet 1991;338:96–9.

49. Tilyard MW, Gurr E, Dovey SM, Walker SA. Otitis media treatment in New Zealand general practice. N Z Med J 1997;25:143–5.

50. Little P, Gould C, Williamson I, et al. Pragmatic randomised controlled trial of two prescribing strategies for childhood acute otitis media. BMJ 2001;322:336–42.

51. Maynard JE, Fleshman JK, Tschopp CF. Otitis media in Alaskan Eskimo children: prospective evaluation of chemoprophylaxis. JAMA 1972;219:597–9.

52. Perrin JM, Charney E, MacWhinney JB Jr, et al. Sulfisoxazole as chemoprophylaxis for recurrent otitis media: a double-blind crossover study in pediatric practice. N Engl J Med 1974;291:664–7.

53. Gaskins JD, Holt RJ, Kyong CU, et al. Chemoprophylaxis of recurrent otitis media using trimethoprim/ sulfamethoxazole. Drug Intell Clin Pharm 1982;16:387–9.

54. Liston TE, Foshee WS, Pierson WD. Sulfisoxazole chemoprophylaxis for frequent otitis media. Pediatrics 1983;71:524–30.

55. Schuller DE. Prophylaxis of otitis media in asthmatic children. Pediatr Infect Dis 1983;2:280–3.

56. Perisco M, Podoshin L, Fradis M, et al. Recurrent acute otitis media—prophylactic penicillin treatment: a prospective study. Part I. Int J Pediatr Otorhinolaryngol 1985;10:37–46.

57. Varsano I, Volvitz B, Mimouni F. Sulfisoxazole prophylaxis of middle ear effusion and recurrent acute otitis media. Am J Dis Child 1985;139:632–5.

58. Gonzalez C, Arnold JE, Woody EA, et al. Prevention of recurrent acute otitis media: chemoprophylaxis versus tympanostomy tubes. Laryngoscope 1986;96:1330–4.

59. Principi N, Marchisio P, Massironi E, et al. Prophylaxis of recurrent acute otitis media and middle-ear effusion: comparison of amoxicillin with sulfamethoxazole and trimethoprim. Am J Dis Child 1989;143:1414–8.

60. Casselbrant ML, Kaleida PH, Rockette HE, et al. Efficacy of antimicrobial prophylaxis and of tympanostomy tube insertion for prevention of recurrent acute otitis media: results of a randomized clinical trial. Pediatr Infect Dis J 1992;11:278–86.

61. Sih T, Moura R, Caldas S, Schwartz B. Prophylaxis for recurrent acute otitis media: a Brazilian study. Int J Pediatr Otorhinolaryngol 1993;25:19–24.

62. Prellner K, Foglé-Hansson M, Jørgensen F, et al. Prevention of recurrent acute otitis media in otitis-prone children by intermittent prophylaxis with penicillin. Acta Otolaryngol (Stockh) 1994;114:182–7.

63. Mandel EM, Casselbrant ML, Rockette HE, et al. Efficacy of antimicrobial prophylaxis for recurrent middle ear effusion. Pediatr Infect Dis J 1996;15:1074–82.

64. Roark R, Berman S. Continuous twice daily or once daily amoxicillin prophylaxis compared with placebo for children with recurrent acute otitis media. Pediatr Infect Dis J 1997;16:376–81.

65. Alho O, Läärä E, Oja H. What is the natural history of recurrent acute otitis media in infancy? J Fam Pract 1996;43:258–64.

66. Fiellau-Nikolajsen M, Lous J. Prospective tympanometry in 3-year old children. A study of the spontaneous course of tympanometry types in a nonselected population. Arch Otolaryngol 1979;105:461–6.

67. Fiellau-Nikolajsen M. Tympanometry in 3-year-old children. Type of care as an epidemiological factor in secretory otitis media and tubal dysfunction in unselected populations of 3-year-old children. ORL J Otorhinolaryngol Relat Spec 1979;41:193–205.

68. Sly RM, Zambie MF, Fernandes DA, Frazer M. Tympanometry in kindergarten children. Ann Allergy 1980; 44:1–7.

69. Tos M. Spontaneous improvement of secretory otitis and impedance screening. Arch Otolaryngol 1980;106: 345–9.

70. Fiellau-Nikolajsen M. Tympanometry in three-year-old children. The 3-year follow-up of a cohort study. ORL J Otorhinolaryngol Rel Spec 1981;43:89–103.

71. Lamothe A, Boudreault V, Blanchette M, et al. Serous otitis media: a six week prospective study. J Otolaryngol 1981;10:371–9.

72. Lous J, Fiellau-Nikolajsen M. Epidemiology of middle ear effusion and tubal dysfunction. A one-year prospective study comprising monthly tympanometry in 387 non-selected 7-year-old children. Int J Pediatr Otorhinolaryngol 1981;3:303–17.

73. Thomsen J, Tos M. Spontaneous improvement of secretory otitis: a long-term study. Acta Otolaryngol 1981;92: 493–9.

74. Renvall U, Aniansson G, Lidén G. Spontaneous improvement in ears with middle ear disease. Int J Pediatr Otorhinolaryngol 1982;4:245–50.

75. Tos M, Holm-Jensen S, Sorensen CH, Mogensen C. Spontaneous course and frequency of secretory otitis in 4-year old children. Arch Otolaryngol 1982;108:4–10.

76. Fiellau-Nikolajsen M. Epidemiology of secretory otitis media. A descriptive cohort study. Ann Otol Rhinol Laryngol 1983;92:172–7.

77. Casselbrant ML, Brostoff LM, Cantekin EI, et al. Otitis media with effusion in preschool children. Laryngoscope 1985;95:428–36.

78. Reves R, Budgett R, Miller D, et al. Study of middle ear disease using tympanometry in general practice. BMJ 1985;290:1953–6.

79. Robinson DO, Allen DV, Root LP. Infant tympanometry: differential results by race. J Speech Hear Disord 1988; 53:341–6.

80. Zielhuis GA, Rach GH, van den Broek P. The natural course of otitis media with effusion in preschool children. Eur Arch Otorhinolaryngol 1990;247:215–21.

81. Mills R, Vaughan-Jones R. A prospective study of otitis media with effusion in adults and children. Clin Otolaryngol Allied Sci 1992;17:271–4.

82. Williamson IG, Dunleavey J, Bain J, Robinson D. The natural history of otitis media with effusion—a three-year study of the incidence and prevalence of abnormal tympanograms in four South West Hampshire infant and first schools. J Laryngol Otol 1994;108:930–4.

83. Zeisel SA, Roberts JE, Gunn EB, et al. Prospective surveillance for otitis media with effusion among black infants in group child care. J Pediatr 1995;127:875–80.

84. van Balen FAM, de Melker RA, Touw-Otten FWMM. Double-blind randomised trial of co-amoxiclav versus placebo for persistent otitis media with effusion in general practice. Lancet 1996;348:713–6.

85. Marchisio P, Principi N, Passali D, et al. Epidemiology and treatment of otitis media with effusion in children in the first year of primary school. Acta Otolaryngol (Stockh) 1998;118:557–62.

86. Ernstson S, Sundberg L. Erythromycin in the treatment of otitis media with effusion (OME). J Laryngol Otol 1984;98:767–9.

87. Maw RA. The long term effect of adenoidectomy on established otitis media with effusion in children. Auris Nasus Larynx 1985;12 Suppl 1;S234–6.

88. Lieberman A, Bartal N. Untreated persistent middle ear effusion. J Laryngol Otol 1986;100:875–8.

89. Buckley G, Hinton A. Otitis media with effusion in children shows a progressive resolution with time. Clin Otolaryngol 1991;16:354–7.

90. Mandel EM, Rockette HE, Bluestone CD, et al. Myringotomy with and without tympanostomy tubes for chronic otitis media with effusion. Arch Otolaryngol Head Neck Surg 1989;115:1217–24.

91. Dempster JH, Browning GG, Gatehouse SG. A randomized study of the surgical management of children with persistent otitis media with effusion associated with a hearing impairment. J Laryngol Otol 1993;107:284–9.

92. Maw RA, Bawden R. The long term outcome of secretory otitis media in children and the effects of surgical treatment: a ten year study. Acta Otorhinolaryngol Belg 1994;48:317–24.

93. Foglé-Hansson M, White P, Hermansson A, Prellner K. Short-term penicillin-V prophylaxis did not prevent acute otitis media in infants. Int J Pediatr Otorhinolaryngol 2001;59:119–23.

94. Teele DW, Klein JO, Work BM, et al. Antimicrobial prophylaxis for infants at risk for recurrent acute otitis media. Vaccine 2001;19 Suppl:S140–3.

95. Poulsen G, Tos M. Screening tympanometry in newborn infants and during the first six months of life. Scand Audiol 1978;7:159–66.

96. Roberts DG, Johnson CE, Carlin SSA, et al. Resolution of middle ear effusion in newborns. Arch Pediatr Adolesc Med 1995;149:873–7.

97. Renvall U, Liden G, Jungert S, Nilsson E. Long-term observation of ears with reduced middle ear pressure. Acta Otolaryngol 1978;86:104–9.

98. Portoian-Shuhaiber S, Cullinan TR. Middle ear disease assessed by impedance in primary school children in south London. Lancet 1984;1:1111–2.

99. Holmquist J, Al Fadala S, Qattan Y. Prevalence of secretory otitis media among school children in Kuwait. J Laryngol Otol 1987;101:116–9.

100. Fiellau-Nikolajsen M, Lous J. Tympanometry in three-year-old children. A cohort study on the prognostic value of tympanometry and operative findings in middle ear effusion. ORL J Otorhinolaryngol Rel Spec 1979;41:11–25.

101. Fiellau-Nikolajsen M. Tympanometry in three-year-old children: prevalence and spontaneous course of MEE. Ann Otol Rhinol Laryngol 1980;89 Suppl:223–7.

102. Fiellau-Nikolajsen M. Tympanometry and middle ear effusion: a cohort-study in three-year old children. Int J Pediatr Otorhinolaryngol 1980;2:39–49.

103. Fiellau-Nikolajsen M. Serial tympanometry and middle ear status in 3-year-old children. ORL J Otorhinolaryngol Relat Spec 1980;42:220–32.

104. Fiellau-Nikolajsen M, Falbe-Hansen J, Knudstrup P. Tympanometry in three-year-old children. III. Correlation between tympanometry findings at paracentesis in a prospectively followed population of otherwise healthy children aged 3-4 years. Scand Audiol 1980;9:49–54.

105. Tos M, Poulsen G, Hancke AB. Screening tympanometry during the first year of life. Acta Otolaryngol 1979;88:388–94.

106. Poulsen G, Tos M. Repetitive tympanometric screenings of two-year-old children. Scand Audiol 1980;9:21–8.

107. Holme-Jensen S, Sorensen CH, Tos M. Repetitive tympanometric screenings in 4-year-old children. Seasonal influence on secretory otitis and tubal dysfunction. ORL J Otorhinolaryngol Relat Spec 1981;43:164–74.

108. Zielhuis GA, Straatman H, Rach GH, van den Broek P. Analysis and presentation of data on the natural course of otitis media with effusion in children. Int J Epidemiol 1990;19:1037–44.

109. Zielhuis GA, Rach GH, van den Broek P. Screening for otitis media with effusion in preschool children. Lancet 1989;1:311–4.

110. Birch L, Elbrond O. Prospective epidemiological investigation of secretory otitis media in children attending day-care centers. ORL J Otorhinolaryngol Relat Spec 1984;46:229–34.

111. Casselbrant ML, Brostoff LM, Cantekin EI, et al. Incidence, prevalence, and natural history of otitis media in children in Pittsburgh. Ann Otol Rhinol Laryngol 1990;99:28–9.

112. Hogan SC, Stratford KJ, Moore DR. Duration and recurrence of otitis media with effusion in children from birth to 3 years: prospective study using monthly otoscopy and tympanometry. BMJ 1997;314:350–5.

113. Teele DW, Klein JO, Rosner BA. Epidemiology of otitis media in children. Ann Otol Rhinol Laryngol 1980;68 Suppl:5–6.

114. Marchant CD, Carlin SA, Johnson CE, Shurin PA. Measuring the comparative efficacy of antibacterial agents for acute otitis media: the "Pollyanna phenomenon." J Pediatr 1992;120:72–7.

115. Dagan R, Leibovitz E, Greenberg D, et al. Early eradication of pathogens from middle ear fluid during antibiotic treatment of acute otitis media is associated with improved clinical outcome. Pediatr Infect Dis J 1998;17:776–82.

116. Maw R, Bawden R. Spontaneous resolution of severe chronic glue ear in children and the effect of adenoidectomy, tonsillectomy, and insertion of ventilation tubes (grommets). BMJ 1993;306:756–60.

117. Tos M. Epidemiology and natural history of secretory otitis. Am J Otol 1984;5:459–62.

118. Tos M. Epidemiology and spontaneous improvement of secretory otitis. Acta Otorhinolaryngol Belg 1983;37:31–43.

119. Rosenfeld RM. Observation option toolkit for acute otitis media. Int J Pediatr Otorhinolaryngol 2001;58:1–8.

120. Black S, Shinefield H, Fireman B, et al. Efficacy, safety and immunogenicity of heptavalent pneumococcal conjugate vaccine in children: Northern California Kaiser Permanente Vaccine Study Center Group. Pediatr Infect Dis J 2000;19:187–95.

CHAPTER 13

Clinical Efficacy of Medical Therapy

Richard M. Rosenfeld, MD, MPH

The desire to take medicine is perhaps the greatest feature that distinguishes man from animals.
William Osler

OBJECTIVES

On completing this chapter, the reader will be able to

1. State the quantitative impact of medical therapy on otitis media (OM).
2. Appreciate the modest benefits of antibiotic therapy and prophylaxis for acute otitis media (AOM).
3. Appreciate the modest, short-term benefit of antibiotic therapy for otitis media with effusion (OME).
4. Understand why antihistamine-decongestant therapy is ineffective for OME.
5. Use evidence synthesis from randomized trials to establish realistic treatment expectations.
6. Recognize the limitations of current best evidence regarding medical therapy.

EDITORIAL COMMENT

Whereas only two new randomized trials are added to the second edition of this chapter, major changes have been made throughout. All meta-analyses now include forest plots and tests of heterogeneity, and many include funnel plots to assess for study selection bias. The accuracy of data abstraction has been verified by recomparison with source articles and with evidence tables from the Agency for Healthcare Research and Quality (AHRQ) evidence report on AOM.[1] Meta-analyses of AOM antibiotic prophylaxis and OME antibiotic therapy are now restricted to placebo-controlled studies to avoid inflated efficacy estimates. Last, the sensitivity analysis for AOM antibiotic prophylaxis has been expanded to identify children most likely to benefit from treatment.

INTRODUCTION

Enlightened management of OM requires knowing what to expect from medical therapy.[2] When managing OM, expectations relate to the incremental benefits of a specific intervention above and beyond natural history

(see Chapter 12, "Natural History of Untreated Otitis Media"). Therapeutic benefits for acute otitis media (AOM) include symptomatic relief, clinical resolution, prevention of suppurative complications, clearance of residual middle ear fluid, and reduced incidence of future episodes. Therapeutic benefits for otitis media with effusion (OME) are often more narrowly defined in terms of effusion resolution, although the impact of OME on child and parent quality of life has received increasing attention.[3]

Randomized controlled trials (RCTs) are ideal for defining treatment benefits. Subjects in a RCT are *randomly* allocated into groups, usually called *study* and *control* groups, to receive or not to receive an experimental preventive or therapeutic intervention. Random assignment helps avoid *allocation bias*, an apparent beneficial effect of therapy caused when investigators allocate subjects (consciously or unconsciously) with less severe disease or a better prognosis to the study group. Trial results are assessed by comparing disease, recovery, or other appropriate outcomes in study and control groups, respectively. Randomized controlled trials are the most rigorous method of hypothesis testing available in clinical research.[4]

When studying a disease with high rates of spontaneous resolution (eg, OM), the most useful RCTs for defining treatment expectations are those in which the study group receives an active drug and the control group receives placebo (inert medication). When the placebo is indistinguishable from the active drug, the study can be *masked* (blinded). Masking reduces bias by preventing patients and caregivers from knowing who is in the study group and who is in the control group during outcome assessment and analysis. Otherwise, the experimenter's and participant's expectations may unfairly favor the study group producing an *ascertainment bias*. Consequently, this chapter will emphasize blind RCTs as a gold standard for defining treatment expectations.

The best method of quantifying treatment expectations is to statistically combine RCT results using a method of systematic literature review called *meta-analysis*.

Numerous meta-analyses regarding AOM and OME therapy have already been published (see Chapter 4, "Meta-analysis and Systematic Literature Review"), and this author's intent herein is not to simply repeat their conclusions.[1,5–18] Rather, the RCTs and methodologic framework established by these investigators will be used as a foundation for fresh interpretation of OM treatment expectations. Issues and controversies will be discussed, and new RCTs will be added to older studies for more contemporary estimates of treatment effect. Numerous tables of raw study data are provided for motivated readers interested in performing their own analyses.

METHODS

Source articles were identified by a computerized MEDLINE search from 1966 through August 2002. A modified version of an optimal search strategy for identifying RCTs was used,[19] which included (1) medical subject heading (MeSH) terms "randomized controlled trials," "random allocation," "double-blind method," "single-blind method," and "placebos"; (2) publication type "randomized controlled trial"; and (3) text words (title or abstract) of "placebo$" or "random$" (the "$" is a truncation symbol). Search results were combined with the MeSH term "otitis media" (exploded). Manual search included review of symposium proceedings, published OM meta-analyses, book chapters, and retrieved article bibliographies.

Data were extracted from the tables and results sections of all source articles and checked for accuracy. Most of the source articles were thoroughly analyzed in prior meta-analyses or evidence reports, permitting additional cross-checks for the accuracy of data extraction. When an RCT compared two or more antimicrobials with placebo therapy, data were combined into a single group to increase sample size. The validity of this approach is based on the absence of demonstrable differences in clinical outcomes based on antimicrobial selection in all published OM meta-analyses.

Data from individual studies were combined (pooled) whenever results were available from two or more source articles for a particular end point and outcome time. Pooling was done using a random-effects model of meta-analysis, which assumes a population (distribution) of true effect sizes with each source article representing one member of this population.[20] Under this model, results are expected to vary from study to study, with differences caused by experimental error and differences in populations (between-study variability). Because of this additional variability, the 95% confidence interval (CI) for the pooled result is wider (less precise) than for a fixed-effect model.

Statistical analysis was performed using Comprehensive Meta-Analysis,[21] a computer program for research synthesis developed with funding from the National Institutes of Health. The program weights study results by the inverse of variance and calculates a random effects estimate of the combined effect and 95% CI. A test of heterogeneity is performed using the Q statistic to evaluate constancy of effect across strata. Significant heterogeneity exists if $p < .05$, although the test has low power and important variations may be present even with a nonsignificant result.[22] For this reason, the random effects model is used, regardless of the test of heterogeneity, although test results are still stated and explored.

Results are interpreted using an abbreviated version of the approach outlined in Chapter 2, "Critical Evaluation of Journal Articles". For each clinical entity (AOM, recurrent AOM, and OME), three questions are posed regarding the pooled study data for spontaneous resolution: (1) What are the results (clinical significance)? (2) Are the results valid for the subjects studied (internal validity)? and (3) To whom do the results apply (external validity)?[23] Assessment for validity includes comparison with published meta-analysis results for similar clinical conditions and treatment outcomes.

HOW TO INTERPRET THE TABLES

This section offers a brief overview on interpreting meta-analysis results. Readers interested in a more comprehensive treatment of this subject are referred to Chapter 4.

Quantitative outcomes are best suited to a tabular presentation of results. For each outcome assessed, the primary source articles are listed with columns in the table for the first author, year of publication, country of origin, pertinent clinical characteristics, and treatment results for the study and control groups. The last column shows the *absolute rate difference* (RD), defined as the absolute difference in successful outcomes between the study group and the control group. For example, if clinical resolution of AOM occurs for 95% of children in the study group and for 80% in the control group, the RD is 15% (.15). A large RD implies a large treatment effect, but an RD less than zero implies better outcomes in the control group.

The RD is a useful measure of clinical importance because it reflects the absolute increase in successful outcomes attributable to therapy.[24] When the control group receives placebo or no active drug (which applies to all RCTs in this chapter), the RD shows the impact of treatment above and beyond spontaneous resolution. Another advantage of the RD is that its reciprocal—the number needed to treat (NNT)—reflects the amount of clinical effort that must be expended to achieve one additional treatment success. The NNT is easily calculated by dividing the RD into 100. For example, an RD of .10 requires treating about 10 children (1/.10) to improve one. Because we cannot predict which one of the 10 children will benefit, all must be treated.

The RD gives the magnitude of the treatment effect, but the 95% (CI) determines credibility[25] and provides the range of results consistent with the data (eg, what the reader could expect 95% of the time if the study could be repeated and repeated). For example, consider the van Buchem study with an RD of zero and 95% CI of –.19 to .19. Although the RD suggests equivalence of antibiotic and placebo for the *sample* of children studied, the data are consistent with an actual value as low as –.19 or as high as .19. Because only a limited number of children were studied, we do not know exactly where in this range the true RD lies. The 95% CI for the overall RD (last row of each table) is always narrower than the individual studies that produced it because the combined sample size produces larger precision.

The RD is statistically significant ($p < .05$) when the 95% CI does not contain zero. When the RD is statistically significant, a *narrow* CI is most interesting. For example, an RD of .25 (95% CI, .22, .28) is clinically more important than an RD of .25 (95% CI, .02, .48). With the latter treatment, the broad CI means the data are consistent with a true RD as low as 2%, which may not justify therapy. Conversely, when the RD is not statistically significant, a *broad* CI is most interesting. An RD of .25 (95% CI, –.02, .52) suggests a true difference as high as 52%, which may be clinically important. The broad CI means the overall sample size may have been too small to detect a meaningful difference, even if one existed (low statistical power). Hence there is a need for more studies before treatment can be deemed ineffective. In contrast, an RD of .03 (95% CI, –.02, .07) argues strongly for no clinically significant impact of therapy.

All combined RDs in this chapter are random effects estimates, which have broader 95% CI than those obtained with a fixed effects model (see Chapter 4). Although this compensates (in part) for potential heterogeneity between studies, a test of heterogeneity is provided for all analyses as the last table end note. For example, the five studies in Table 13-3 appear homogeneous (Q = 3.61, $p = .461$), but differences among the six studies listed in Tables 13-4 and 13-5 exceed what can be expected from sampling error ($p < .001$ and $p = .005$, respectively). Significant heterogeneity does not necessarily imply that combining the studies is invalid but should prompt a critical examination of results. Heterogeneity may stem from variations in diagnosis, therapy, end point definition, outcome assessment, or study methodology.

All meta-analyses in this chapter include a *graphic display* of results to aid interpretation. The *forest plot* is a widely used form of presentation that plots point esti-

mates (black squares) from different studies along with their error bars (horizontal lines).[26,27] Because the eye is drawn to longer error bars, data from smaller studies have a relatively greater visual effect. To compensate for this distortion, boxes are drawn proportional to the study sample size. The combined result is depicted below the studies with a black diamond spanning the 95% CI. Results are statistically significant ($p < .05$) when the combined 95% CI does not include zero. When most or all of the individual study 95% CIs contain the combined RD (center of the black diamond), the studies are relatively homogeneous.

Analyses with statistically significant results also include a *funnel plot*, which is a simple visual tool to assess for a biased sample of studies.[28] Individual studies in funnel plots are depicted with circles proportional to sample size. Because large studies estimate effect size more precisely than smaller studies, they tend to lie in a narrow band at the top of the plot, while the smaller studies, with more variation in results, fan out over the larger area at the bottom. An unbiased study sample yields a symmetric funnel centered over the combined effect estimate. Any gaps in the inverted funnel shape (particularly at the bottom) suggest that some studies may not have been published, located, or included.

ANTIMICROBIAL THERAPY OF AOM

What are the results?

Nine RCTs were found comparing antibiotic versus placebo or no drug as *initial* therapy for AOM (Table 13-1).[29–37] The word "initial" is emphasized because all children received antibiotics if fever and otalgia persisted despite watchful waiting (typically after 48 to 72 hours). Antibiotics were administered for 7 to 14 days and consisted of penicillin or an aminopenicillin, alone or in combination with sulfisoxazole or clavulanate. Most studies were published in the decade from 1981 to 1991; only two[29,30] were published prior and only one[37] in the last decade. Diagnostic certainty for AOM was generally high, but four studies[29,30,35,37] relied only on clinical symptoms plus otoscopy by the primary care practitioner. All studies reported symptomatic relief of AOM by 2 to 7 days, and most reported clinical resolution at 7 to 14 days, which usually reflected more stringent outcome criteria (see Table 13-1).

Initial antibiotic therapy did not relieve AOM symptoms by 24 hours (Table 13-2, Figure 13-1), but provided 4% greater relief (95% CI, .02, .07) by 2 to 3 days (see Table 13-3 and Figure 13-2). The funnel plot (Figure 13-3) does not suggest study selection bias. Antibiotic-treated children had 9% greater symptom relief (95% CI,

Table 13-1 Diagnostic and Outcome Criteria for AOM Source Articles

Author Year	Diagnostic Certainty*	AOM Outcome Criteria Used in Meta-analyses	
		Symptomatic Relief	*Clinical Resolution*
Halsted[29] 1968	Low (o)	No fever, less pain 24–72 h	No fever, less pain; normal TM 14–18 d
Laxdal[30] 1970	Low (o)	Improved AOM symptoms 7 d	No signs of middle ear infection 14 d
Mygind[31] 1981	High (e,o)	No AOM symptoms 2 d, 7 d	No symptoms, otorrhea, contralateral AOM 7 d
van Buchem[32] 1981	High (e,o)	No pain 24 h, 7 d	—
Thalin[33] 1986	High (e,m)	No pain, otorrhea 24 h, 3 d, 7 d	No pain, fever, infection 7 d
Appelman[34] 1991	High (e,o)	No pain, fever 3 d	—
Burke[35] 1991	Low (o)	No pain 24 h, 5–7 d	No symptoms or other antibiotic 7 d
Kaleida[36] 1991	High (p,t)	Minimal pain, fever 2 d	—
Damoiseaux[37] 2000	Low (o)	No pain, fever, crying, irritability or other antibiotic 4 d	No pain, fever, crying, irritability; improved appearance TM 11 d

AOM = acute otitis media; TM = tympanic membrane.

*Studies with high certainty confirmed diagnosis of AOM with tympanometry (t), pneumatic otoscopy (p), otomicroscopy (m), or referral to an ear, nose, and throat specialist (e); low certainty studies relied on nonpneumatic otoscopy (o) and clinical symptoms.

Table 13-2 Antibiotic versus Placebo for Symptomatic Relief of AOM by 24 Hours

Author Year	Country	Age Range	Drug and Duration	Symptom Relief by 24 h, N (%)[†]		Absolute RD[††] (95% CI)
				Antibiotic	*Placebo*	
van Buchem[32] 1981	Netherlands	2–12 yr	AMX 7 d	34/47 (72)	29/40 (72)	0 (–.19, .19)
Thalin[33] 1986	Sweden	2–15 yr	PCN 7 d	97/159 (61)	96/158 (61)	0 (–.11, .11)
Burke[35] 1991	England	3–10 yr	AMX 7 d	59/112 (53)	61/117 (52)	.01 (–.12, .13)
Combined*				190/318 (60)	186/315 (59)	0 (–.07, .08)

AMX = amoxicillin; AOM = acute otitis media; CI = confidence interval; PCN = penicillin; RD = rate difference.

*Combined $p = .942$; test for heterogeneity $Q = .01$, df $= 2$, $p = .998$.

[†]Number of children with positive outcome divided by total number of evaluable children.

[††]Absolute change in symptom relief attributable to therapy; positive values favor the antibiotic group.

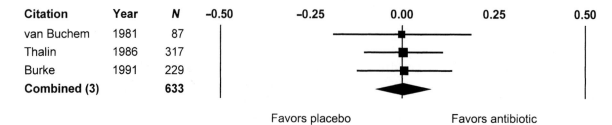

Figure 13-1 Random effects meta-analysis of antibiotic versus placebo for symptomatic relief of AOM by 24 hours (see Table 13-2 for study details). Forest plot shows absolute rate difference and 95% confidence intervals for individual studies (*squares* proportional to study size) and combined result (*diamond*). Combined result indicates no significant impact of antibiotic therapy.

Table 13-3 Antibiotic versus Placebo for Symptomatic Relief of AOM by 2 to 3 Days

Author Year	Country	Age Range	Drug and Duration	Symptom Relief by 2–3 d, N (%)[†]		Absolute RD[‡] (95% CI)
				Antibiotic	Placebo	
Halsted[29] 1968	USA	2 mo–6 yr	AMP or PCN/SSX 10 d	45/62 (73)	20/27 (74)	−.01 (−.21, .18)
Mygind[31] 1981	Denmark	1–10 yr	PCN 7 d	57/72 (79)	48/77 (62)	.17 (.02, .31)[‖]
Thalin[33] 1986	Sweden	2–15 yr	PCN 7 d	143/159 (91)	133/158 (84)	.06 (−.02, .13)
Appelman[34] 1991	Netherlands	6 mo–12 yr	AMX/CLV 7 d	56/67 (84)	44/54 (81)	.02 (−.12, .16)
Kaleida[36] 1991[§]	USA	7 mo–12 yr	AMX 14 d	469/488 (96)	454/492 (92)	.04 (.01, .07)[‖]
Combined*				770/848 (91)	699/808 (87)	.04 (.02, .07)[‖]

AMP = ampicillin; AMX = amoxicillin; AOM = acute otitis media; CI = confidence interval; CLV = clavulanate; PCN = penicillin; RD = rate difference; SSX = sulfasoxazole.

*Combined $p = .001$; test for heterogeneity $Q = 3.61$, df = 4, $p = .461$.

[†]Number of children with positive outcome divided by total number of evaluable children.

[‡]Absolute change in symptom relief attributable to therapy; positive values favor the antibiotic group.

[§]Includes only "nonsevere" episodes of AOM, defined as mild-moderate symptoms for less than 12 hours with maximum rectal temperature less than 39.5°C in prior 24 hours.

[‖]$p < .05$ when the 95% CI does not contain zero.

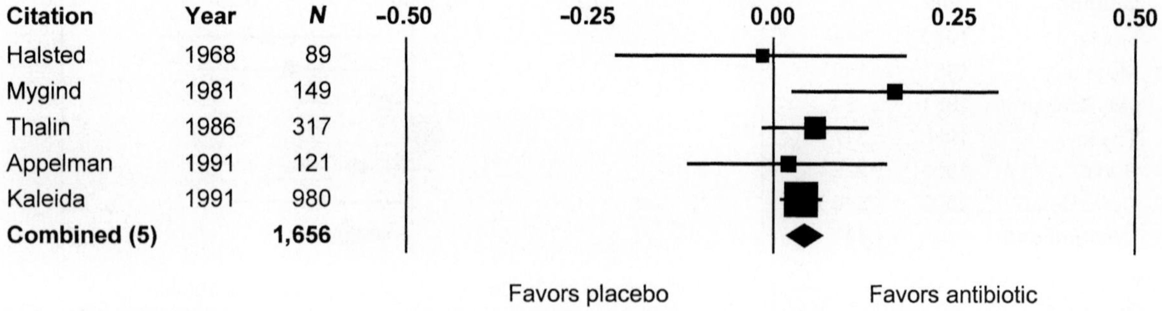

Citation	Year	N
Halsted	1968	89
Mygind	1981	149
Thalin	1986	317
Appelman	1991	121
Kaleida	1991	980
Combined (5)		**1,656**

Favors placebo   Favors antibiotic

Figure 13-2 Random effects meta-analysis of antibiotic versus placebo for symptomatic relief of AOM by 2 to 3 days (see Table 13-3 for study details). Forest plot shows absolute rate difference (RD) and 95% confidence intervals for individual studies (*squares* proportional to study size) and combined result (*diamond*). Combined result indicates a small impact of therapy (RD .04), implying a need to treat 25 children to improve one.

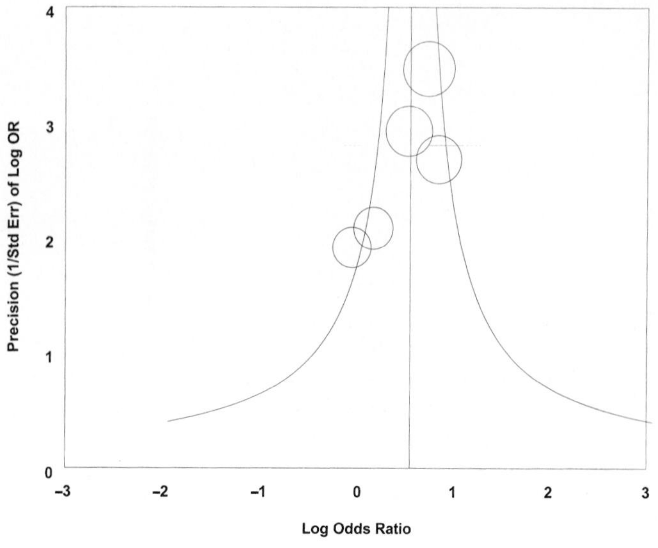

Figure 13-3 Funnel plot of precision versus effect size for the meta-analysis in Figure 13-2. Study symbols (*circles*) are proportional to sample size. Vertical line is the combined effect and curved lines show the inverted funnel distribution expected by an unbiased study sample. Despite asymmetry for the smaller studies, the actual distribution appears unbiased because the asymmetry is skewed toward negative outcomes.

Table 13-4 Antibiotic versus Placebo or No Antibiotic for Relief of AOM by 4 to 7 Days

Author Year	Country	Age Range	Drug and Duration	Symptom Relief by 4–7 d, N (%)[†] Antibiotic	No Antibiotic	Absolute RD[‡] (95% CI)
Laxdal[30] 1970	Canada	< 14 yr	AMP or PCN 7 d	78/94 (83)	30/48 (62)	.21 (.05, .36)[§]
Mygind[31] 1981	Denmark	1–10 yr	PCN 7 d	62/72 (86)	53/77 (69)	.17 (.04, .30)[§]
van Buchem[32] 1981	Netherlands	2–12 yr	AMX 7 d	43/46 (93)	34/38 (90)	.04 (–.08, .16)
Thalin[33] 1986	Sweden	2–15 yr	PCN 7 d	154/159 (97)	156/158 (99)	–.02 (–.05, .01)
Burke[35] 1991	England	3–10 yr	AMX 7 d	91/111 (82)	85/114 (75)	.07 (–.03, .18)
Damoiseaux[37] 2000	Netherlands	6 mo–2 yr	AMX 10 d	48/117 (41)	34/123 (28)	.13 (.01, .25)
Combined, placebo only (excludes Laxdal)				398/505 (79)	362/510 (71)	.07 (–.02, .16)
Combined, placebo or no antibiotic*				476/599 (79)	392/558 (70)	.09 (.01, .18)[§]

AMP = ampicillin; AMX = amoxicillin; AOM = acute otitis media; CI = confidence interval; PCN = penicillin; RD = rate difference.
*Combined p = .043; test for heterogeneity Q = 20.62, df = 5, p = .001.
[†]Number of children with positive outcome divided by total number of evaluable children; all studies were placebo controlled except for Laxdal 1970.
[‡]Absolute change in symptom relief attributable to therapy; positive values favor the antibiotic group.
[§]p < .05 when the 95% CI does not contain zero.

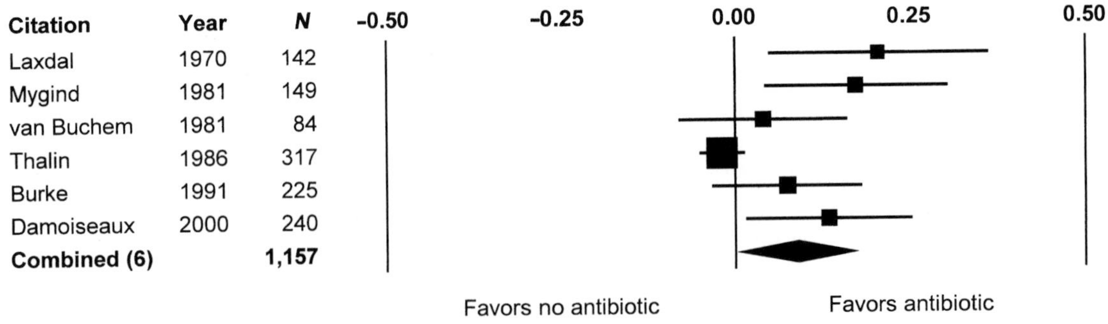

Figure 13-4 Random effects meta-analysis of antibiotic versus no antibiotic for symptomatic relief of AOM by 4 to 7 days (see Table 13-4 for study details). Forest plot shows absolute rate difference (RD) and 95% confidence intervals for individual studies (*squares* proportional to study size) and combined result *(diamond)*. Combined result indicates a small impact of therapy (RD .09), implying a need to treat 11 children to improve one.

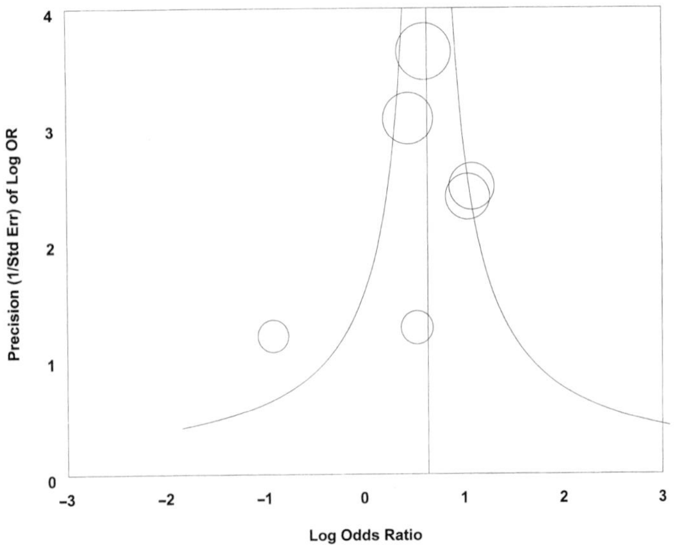

Figure 13-5 Funnel plot of precision versus effect size for the meta-analysis in Figure 13-4. Study symbols *(circles)* are proportional to sample size. Vertical line is the combined effect and curved lines show the inverted funnel distribution expected by an unbiased study sample. The asymmetry is skewed toward negative outcomes and does not suggest selection bias.

.01, .18) by 4 to 7 days (Table 13-4, Figure 13-4), but after excluding the only unblinded study,[30] the combined effect was not significant (RD .07; 95% CI, −.02, .16). Moreover, there was a significant impact of diagnostic certainty for AOM on outcomes (ANOVA, $p = .001$): studies with high certainty (see Table 13-1) had a nonsignificant effect by 4 to 7 days (RD .05, 95% CI, −.07, .17), but those with low certainty had a moderate effect (RD .12; 95% CI, .05, .19). The funnel plot (Figure 13-5) for all studies in Table 13-4 does not suggest selection bias.

The efficacy of antimicrobials for clinical resolution of AOM, exclusive of middle ear effusion (MEE), within 7 to 14 days is shown in Table 13-5 and Figure 13-6. Excluding the only unblind study[30] again reduced the combined effect to a nonsignificant RD of .07 (95% CI, −.01, .14). Conversely, there was no difference in outcomes when studies were stratified by diagnostic certainty (ANOVA, $p = .825$). The funnel plot (Figure 13-7) for all studies in Table 13-5 does not suggest selection bias.

Suppurative complications of AOM for the nine source articles are summarized in Table 13-6. Two studies[29,33] did not explicitly mention complications and were excluded from the meta-analysis. For the remaining seven articles (1,495 children), there were three suppurative complications: meningitis in a placebo-treated child,[37] acute mastoiditis in an antibiotic-treated child,[31] and transient facial paralysis in an antibiotic-treated child.[36] The combined complication rate (see Table 13-6) was equivalent for antibiotic versus no antibiotic (RD .001; 95% CI, −.007, .008). The overall incidence of .20% (3 of 1,495) suggests that about one complication will occur for every 500 children with AOM who are followed up carefully. As noted previously, *all* children who were initially observed received antibiotics if an irregular clinical course ensued.

The impact of initial antibiotic therapy for AOM on resolution of residual OME is shown in Tables 13-7 and 13-8. Included in this data set are resolution rates reported by Claessen and colleagues[38] for children in the RCT by Appelman and colleagues.[34] Asymptomatic OME may persist for weeks to months after AOM, and resolution by 4 to 6 weeks (see Table 13-7 and Figure 13-8) and by 3 months (see Table 13-8, Figure 13-9) is comparable with or without antibiotics. The studies are homogeneous ($p = .772$ for 4 to 6 weeks, $p = .199$ for 3 months), and review of Figures 13-8 and 13-9 suggests a low probability of missing a true clinically relevant effect. The prevalence of OME does, however, gradually decreases over time.

Are the Results Valid?

Three meta-analyses[1,8,15] have addressed the efficacy of antibiotics for AOM. Rosenfeld and colleagues[15] reported an RD of .14 (95% CI, .08, .19) for clinical resolution of AOM by 7 to 14 days. This exceeds the RD of .08 in Table 13-5 because two studies with small effects[33,37] were not included. Glasziou and colleagues[8] later reported on symptomatic relief and found no benefit for antibiotics by 24 hours, but a small benefit by 2 to 7 days (NNT = 17). The results in Tables 13-3 and 13-4 are comparable, with an NNT of 25 by 2 to 3 days and 11 by 4 to 7 days. Last, the AHRQ report[1] found an RD of .12 (95% CI, .03, .22) by 2 to 7 days, but the results may be inflated by the large study[39] (280 children) with a very favorable RD (.22). Moreover, because all children had baseline tympanocentesis the outcome (exudate or otorrhea) was not comparable with other studies.

The studies in Table 13-1 are generally of high quality, so results are likely to be valid *for the children studied.* Note, however, that several studies[32,33,35] excluded children under 2 years of age, which has important implications for external validity as discussed in the next section. Most children received penicillin or an aminopenicillin, although choice of antibiotic is unrelated to clinical resolution of AOM.[1,15] All the studies were randomized, and all, except for Laxdal and colleagues,[30] were blinded (placebo controlled). When the analyses in Tables 13-4 and 13-5 were restricted to only blinded studies, the results were no longer statistically significant. This suggests potential bias in outcome assessment with an unblinded protocol.

Accurate diagnosis of AOM implies MEE plus acute symptoms, but MEE can be difficult to diagnose in clinical practice. When diagnostic certainty is low, the true impact of therapy may be understated, if large numbers of children with earache or red ear (without MEE) dilute the population of children with true AOM.[40] Most studies (see Table 13-1) confirmed MEE with tympanometry,[36] pneumatic otoscopy,[36] or specialist referral,[31–34] but some relied on nonpneumatic otoscopy.[29,30,35,37] Paradoxically, studies with low diagnostic certainty showed greater impact of antibiotic therapy on symptom relief by 4 to 7 days. Conversely, no relationship was observed with clinical resolution by 7 to 14 days. Nonetheless, diagnostic certainty must always be considered when interpreting AOM trials, and clinicians must be cognizant of their own levels of certainty when extrapolating study results to their own patients.

To Whom Do the Results Apply?

Nearly all trials excluded children with immune deficiencies, cleft palate, craniofacial anomalies, pre-existing OME, complicated AOM (eg, facial paralysis), and concurrent bacterial infections (sinusitis, bronchitis); therefore, results cannot be extrapolated to these subgroups. Furthermore, some trials excluded children

Table 13-5 Antibiotic versus Placebo or No Antibiotic for Relief of AOM by 4 to 7 Days

Author Year	Country	Age Range	Drug and Duration	Clinical Resolution 7–14 d, N (%)[†]		Absolute RD[‡] (95% CI)
				Antibiotic	No Antibiotic	
Halsted[29] 1968	USA	2 mo–6yr	AMP or PCN/SSX 10 d	46/50 (92)	21/21 (100)	−.07 (−.17, .03)
Laxdal[30] 1970	Canada	< 14 yr	AMP or PCN 7d	59/94 (63)	22/48 (46)	.17 (0, .34)
Mygind[31] 1981	Denmark	1–10 yr	PCN 7 d	62/72 (86)	53/77 (69)	.17 (.04, .30)[§]
Thalin[33] 1986	Sweden	2–15 yr	PCN 7 d	155/159 (97)	146/158 (92)	.05 (.01, .10)[§]
Burke[35] 1991	England	3–10 yr	AMX 7 d	112/114 (98)	101/118 (86)	.13 (.06, .19)[§]
Damoiseaux[37] 2000	Netherlands	6 mo–2 yr	AMX 10 d	40/112 (36)	36/120 (30)	.06 (−.06, .18)
Combined, placebo only (excludes Laxdal)				415/507 (82)	357/494 (72)	.07 (−.01, .14)
Combined, placebo or no antibiotic*				474/601 (79)	379/542 (70)	.08 (.01, .14)[§]

AMP = ampicillin; AMX = amoxicillin; AOM = acute otitis media; CI = confidence interval; PCN = penicillin; RD = rate difference; SSX = sulfasoxazole.

*Combined p = .027; test for heterogeneity Q = 14.09, df = 5, p = .015.

[†]Number of children with positive outcome divided by total number of evaluable children; all studies were placebo controlled except for Laxdal 1970.

[‡]Absolute change in clinical resolution attributable to therapy; positive values favor the antibiotic group.

[§]p < .05 when the 95% CI does not contain zero.

Citation	Year	N	-0.50	-0.25	0.00	0.25	0.50
Halsted	1968	71					
Laxdal	1970	142					
Mygind	1981	149					
Thalin	1986	317					
Burke	1991	232					
Damoiseaux	2001	232					
Combined (6)		**1,143**					

Favors no antibiotic   Favors antibiotic

Figure 13-6 Random effects meta-analysis of antibiotic versus no antibiotic for clinical resolution of AOM by 7 to 14 days (see Table 13-5 for study details). Forest plot shows absolute rate difference (RD) and 95% confidence intervals for individual studies (*squares* proportional to study size) and combined result *(diamond)*. Combined result indicates a small impact of therapy (RD .08), implying a need to treat 12 children to improve one.

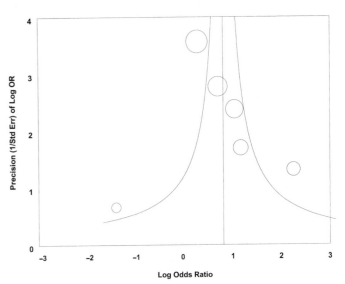

Figure 13-7 Funnel plot of precision versus effect size for the meta-analysis in Figure 13-6. Study symbols *(circles)* are proportional to sample size. Vertical line is the combined effect and curved lines show the inverted funnel distribution expected by an unbiased study sample. The sample is unbiased.

Table 13-6 Incidence of Suppurative Complications after Antibiotic versus No Antibiotic for AOM

Author Year	Country	Age Range	Suppurative Complications, N (%) Antibiotic	No Antibiotic	Absolute RD† (95% CI)
Halsted[29] 1968	USA	2 mo–6 yr	NS	NS	—
Laxdal[30] 1970	Canada	< 14 yr	0/94 (0)	0/48 (0)	0 (−.037, .027)
Mygind[31] 1981	Denmark	1–10 yr	1/72 (1.38)	0/77 (0)	.014 (−.023, .051)
van Buchem[32] 1981	Netherlands	2–12 yr	0/47 (0)	0/40 (0)	0 (−.046, .042)
Thalin[33] 1986	Sweden	2–15 yr	0/159 (0)	0/158 (0)	0 (−.012, .012)
Appelman[34] 1991	Netherlands	6 mo–12 yr	NS	NS	—
Burke[35] 1991	England	3–10 yr	0/110 (0)	0/111 (0)	0 (−.017, .018)
Kaleida[36] 1991‡	USA	7 mo–12 yr	1/169 (0.59)	0/170 (0)	.006 (−.010, .022)
Damoiseaux[37] 2000	Netherlands	6 mo–2 yr	0/117 (0)	1/123 (0.81)	−.008 (−.030, .015)
Combined*			2/768 (0.26)	1/727 (0.14)	.001 (−.007, .008)

AOM = acute otitis media; CI = confidence interval; NS = not stated explicitly.
*Combined p = .867; test for heterogeneity Q =1.61, df = 6, p = .952.
†Absolute change in complications attributable to therapy; negative values favor the antibiotic group.
‡Includes only "nonsevere" episodes of AOM, defined as mild-moderate symptoms for less than 12 hours with maximum rectal temperature less than 39.5°C in prior 24 hours.

under 2 years of age, those with recurrent AOM, or those with severe symptoms. None of the trials reporting outcomes at 24 hours (see Table 13-2) included infants or very young children, which makes generalization of results to this age group unjustified. Damoiseaux and coworkers,[37] however, found a greater antibiotic benefit at 4 to 7 days (RD .13) for children under age 2 years compared with studies[32,33,35] limited to older children (RD −.02 to .07).

Children in RCTs are not a random sample of children with AOM but may represent a select group with less severe symptoms. Kaleida and coworkers,[36] for example, gave placebo to children with only nonsevere illness. Whereas other listed studies did not explicitly exclude children on the basis of severity, Burke and colleagues[35] noted that "…children included in the study did not represent a cross section of all those with acute earache, but were selected on the basis that treatment with placebo would raise no ethical problems, and their inclusion was subject to informed parental consent…Excluded children may have been more severely affected…The children in the study are typical, however, of those with moderate symptoms and signs, whose treatment presents general practitioners with a dilemma."

Considering the above selection biases, results from AOM RCTs *cannot* be broadly extrapolated to children

with AOM. They most likely *can* be applied to children aged 2 years or older with nonsevere AOM, and most likely *cannot* be applied to infants with severe symptoms (since several trials excluded this subgroup, and others considered it unethical to withhold initial antimicrobial therapy). The applicability to older children with severe AOM is also uncertain. The low incidence of acute mastoiditis (0.20%) noted above must be extrapolated with similar caution because it may reflect, in part, selection of older children with less severe AOM. Of note, the only suppurative complication of AOM without antibiotics (see Table 13-6) occurred in a very young child.[37]

A final concern when generalizing AOM results relates to the difference between clinical and bacteriologic efficacy. Although children who experience clinical cure (symptomatic relief) are more likely to have bacteriologic cure (sterilization of MEE), the two are frequently discordant.[39,41] Marchant and coworkers[41] reported AOM clinical cure rates of 93% (95% CI, .89, .96) in children with bacteriologic cure, and 63% (95% CI, .46, .77) in children with bacteriologic failure. When no bacteria were found on initial tympanocentesis (eg, viral AOM), the clinical cure rate was 80% (95% CI, .73, .86). The authors concluded that nonbacterial factors were the most common cause of persistent symptoms after initial antibiotic therapy for AOM.

Table 13-7 Antibiotic versus Placebo for AOM: Resolution of Residual OME by 4 to 6 Weeks

Author Year	Country	Age Range	Drug and Duration	OME Resolution by 4–6 wk, N(%)[†] Antibiotic	Placebo	Absolute RD[‡] (95% CI)
Mygind[31] 1981	Denmark	1–10 yr	PCN 7 d	49/72 (68)	52/77 (68)	0 (–.15, .16)
Thalin[33] 1986	Sweden	2–15 yr	PCN 7 d	94/159 (59)	93/158 (59)	0 (–.11, .11)
Burke[35] 1991	England	3–10 yr	AMX 7 d	71/112 (63)	75/116 (65)	–.01 (–.14, .11)
Claessen[38] 1991	Netherlands	6 mo–12 yr	AMX/CLV 7 d	30/51 (59)	20/45 (44)	.14 (–.06, .34)
Kaleida[36] 1991[§]	USA	7 mo–12 yr	AMX 14 d	178/329 (54)	159/328 (48)	.06 (–.02, .13)
Damoiseaux[37] 2000	Netherlands	6 mo–2 yr	AMX 10 d	38/107 (36)	35/105 (33)	.02 (–.11, .15)
Combined*				460/830 (55)	434/829 (52)	.03 (–.02, .08)

AMX = amoxicillin; AOM = acute otitis media; CI = confidence interval; CLV = clavulanate; OME = otitis media with effusion; PCN = penicillin; RD = rate difference.

*Combined p = .188; test for heterogeneity Q = 2.53, df = 5, p = .772.

[†]Number of children with positive outcome divided by total number of evaluable children.

[‡]Absolute change in OME resolution attributable to therapy; positive values favor the antibiotic group.

[§]Includes only "nonsevere" episodes of AOM, defined as mild-moderate symptoms for less than 12 hours with maximum rectal temperature less than 39.5°C in prior 24 hours.

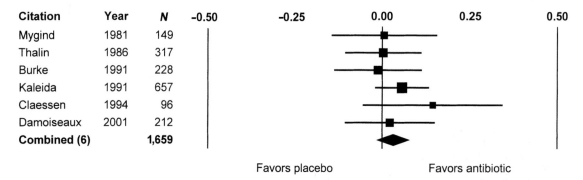

Figure 13-8 Random effects meta-analysis of antibiotic versus placebo for acute otitis media on resolution of otitis media with effusion by 4 to 6 weeks (see Table 13-7 for study details). Forest plot shows absolute rate difference and 95% confidence intervals for individual studies (*squares* proportional to study size) and combined result (*diamond*). Combined result indicates no significant impact of antibiotic therapy.

Whereas clinical efficacy should guide clinical management, bacteriologic efficacy is more properly used to compare new drugs to established therapeutic standards or to establish efficacy for specific pathogens. The dual aspirate protocol developed by Howie and Ploussard[42] permits drug evaluation with reduced sample size,[41] but the techniques employed (and the patients studied) differ greatly from those encountered in routine clinical care. Furthermore, the significance of viable bacteria (bacteriologic failure) after clinical success is unclear and has not been correlated with higher rates of relapse or complication.

ANTIMICROBIAL PROPHYLAXIS OF AOM

What Are the Results?

Ten RCTs (Table 13-9) that compared antimicrobial prophylaxis to placebo for preventing recurrent AOM were found.[43–52] To limit bias in outcome assessment, 3 trials were excluded that were not placebo controlled,[53–55] 2 that administered prophylaxis only during upper respiratory infections were excluded,[56,58] and 1 was excluded with entry criteria of only one prior AOM.[58] Most children experienced three or more episodes of AOM over the preceding 6 to 12 months.

Table 13-8 Antibiotic versus Placebo for AOM: Resolution of Residual OME by 3 Months

Author Year	Country	Age Range	Drug and Duration	OME Resolution by 3 mo, N(%)[†]		Absolute RD[‡] (95% CI)
				Antibiotic	Placebo	
Mygind[31] 1981	Denmark	1–10 yr	PCN 7 d	54/72 (75)	59/77 (77)	−.02 (−.15, .12)
Burke[35] 1991	England	3–10 yr	AMX 7 d	91/111 (82)	80/111 (72)	.10 (−.01, .21)
Combined*				145/183 (79)	139/188 (74)	.05 (−.08, .17)

AMX = amoxicillin; AOM = acute otitis media; CI = confidence interval; OME = otitis media with effusion; PCN = penicillin; RD = rate difference.

*Combined p = .456; test for heterogeneity Q = 1.65, df = 1, p = .199.

[†]Number of children with positive outcome divided by total number of evaluable children.

[‡]Absolute change in OME resolution attributable to therapy; positive values favor the antibiotic group.

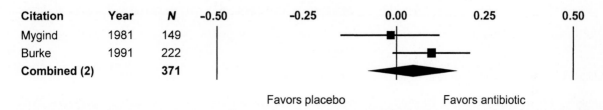

Citation	Year	N	-0.50	-0.25	0.00	0.25	0.50
Mygind	1981	149					
Burke	1991	222					
Combined (2)		**371**					

Favors placebo   Favors antibiotic

Figure 13-9 Random effects meta-analysis of antibiotic versus placebo for acute otitis media on resolution of otitis media with effusion by 3 months (see Table 13-8 for study details). Forest plot shows absolute rate difference and 95% confidence intervals for individual studies (*squares* proportional to study size) and combined result (*diamond*). Combined result indicates no significant impact of antibiotic therapy.

Study duration ranged from several months to 2 years (median of 6 months), during which time children in the study group received daily antimicrobial therapy at one-half the usual dosage for AOM. Amoxicillin (or ampicillin) was used most often, followed by sulfasoxazole, trimethoprim-sulfamethoxazole, and penicillin. AOM episodes, if they occurred, were treated with a therapeutic dosage of an alternative antibiotic.

The overall absolute decrease in AOM recurrence (see Table 13-9 and Figure 13-10) attributable to antibiotic prophylaxis was −.09 (95% CI, −.12, −.05) episodes per patient-month or 1.1 annual episodes (95% CI, 0.6, 1.4). As noted above, this estimate (in contrast to the first edition of this chapter) is based solely on blinded trials. If two unblinded prophylaxis trials[53,54] are included the RD is −.12 (95% CI, −.16, −.08), suggesting a mean annual decrease of 1.4 AOM episodes per child (27% higher than the blinded trials estimate). The unblinded trials alone produced a larger RD of −.20 (95% CI, −.48, .08), which differed significantly from the blinded estimate (ANOVA, p < .0001).

Studies with the longest follow-up in Figure 13-10 (largest black squares) had lower efficacy. Moreover, Figure 13-11 shows three small studies at the funnel base with large effects favoring prophylaxis that are not offset by corresponding studies with negative results.

Whether this represents study selection bias or a real association between study duration and outcomes is unclear because sensitivity analysis (Table 13-10) shows similar findings: the RD for studies with less than 6 months follow-up was −.16 compared with −.05 for longer follow-up studies (p < .0001). Similarly, there were significant differences that favored increased efficacy for children receiving sulfisoxazole, with entry AOM rates of 0.5 per month or higher, or with study AOM rates of 0.2 per month or higher. The meaning of these associations is difficult to assess because many of the factors were interrelated among studies.

An RD of −.09 (95% CI, −.12, −.05) AOM episodes per patient-month (see Table 13-9) implies an NNT of 11 (95% CI, 8, 19). Therefore, preventing a single AOM episode requires treating one child for 11 months or 11 children for 1 month. Less effort may be needed (see Table 13-10) when sulfisoxazole is used for prophylaxis, the duration of prophylaxis is under 6 months, or when children have a history of 6 or more annual AOM episodes at study entry. For comparison, the mean reduction in AOM recurrence from baseline in the placebo group (natural history) was 0.21 episodes/patient-month (2.5 annual episodes) in the four studies[44,48,50,54] that specified a baseline AOM rate and at least 0.11 episodes/patient-month (≥ 1.4 annual

Table 13-9 Antibiotic Prophylaxis versus Placebo for Recurrent AOM: Incidence Density

Author Year	Country	Entry Rate[†]	Drug and Duration	AOM/Patient-Month(Rate)[‡] Prophylaxis	Placebo	Absolute RD[#] (95% CI)
Maynard[43] 1972	USA	NS	AMP 1 yr	73/2,076 (.04)	141/2,292 (.06)	−.03 (−.04, −.01)[ǁ]
Perrin[44] 1974	USA	3/18; 5	SSX 3 mo	4/162 (.02)	28/162 (.17)	−.15 (−.21, −.09)[ǁ]
Liston[45] 1983	USA	3/6	SSX 3 mo	25/102 (.25)	43/102 (.42)	−.18 (−.30, −.05)[ǁ]
Varsano[46] 1985	Israel	3/6	SSX 10 wk	9/74 (.12)	36/74 (.49)	−.37 (−.50, −.23)[ǁ]
Gonzalez[47] 1986	USA	3/6; 5/18	SSX 6 mo	29/126 (.23)	40/120 (.33)	−.10 (−.22, .01)
Principi[48] 1989	Italy	3/6	AMX or TMP /SMX 6 mo	20/396 (.05)	25/180 (.14)	−.09 (−.14, −.03)[ǁ]
Casselbrant[49] 1992	USA	3/6; 4/12	AMX 2 yr	103/2,064 (.05)	173/1,920 (.09)	−.04 (−.06, −.02)[ǁ]
Sih[50] 1993	Brazil	3/12	AMX or TMP /SMX 3 mo	8/120 (.07)	14/60 (.23)	−.17 (−.28, −.05)[ǁ]
Mandel[51] 1996	USA	3/12[§]	AMX 1 yr	14/610 (.02)	46/531 (.09)	−.06 (−.09, −.04)[ǁ]
Roark[52] 1997	USA	3/6	AMX 45 d	36/146 (.25)	20/92 (.22)	.03 (−.08, .14)
Combined*				321/8,576 (.06)	566/5,533 (.10)	−.09 (−.12, −.05)[ǁ]

AMP = ampicillin; AMX = amoxicillin; AOM = acute otitis media; CI = confidence interval; PCN = penicillin; RD = rate difference; SSX = sulfasoxazole; SMX = sulfamethoxazole; TMP = trimethoprim.

*Combined $p < .001$; test for heterogeneity Q = 55.28, df = 9, $p < .001$.

[†]Baseline rate of AOM recurrence to enter study in episodes/month or total episodes.

[‡]Rate of occurrence of AOM episodes per patient-month of observation (incidence density).

[§]Eligibility based on recurrent middle ear effusion, not just recurrent AOM.

[ǁ]$p < .05$ when the 95% CI does not contain zero.

[#]Absolute change in AOM episodes/patient-month attributable to therapy; negative values favor prophylaxis.

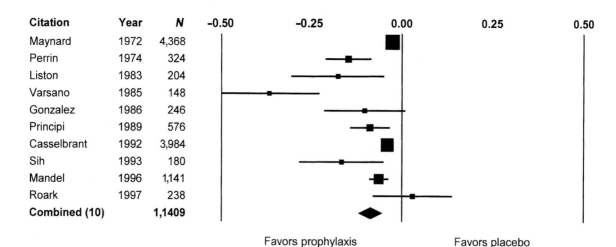

Figure 13-10 Random effects meta-analysis of antibiotic prophylaxis versus placebo for AOM incidence density (see Table 13-9 for study details). Forest plot shows absolute rate difference (RD) and 95% confidence intervals for individual studies (*squares* proportional to study size) and combined result (*diamond*). Combined result indicates a small impact of therapy (RD −.09), implying a need to treat one child for 12 months to prevent one AOM episode.

Figure 13-11 Funnel plot of precision versus effect size for the meta-analysis in Figure 13-10. Study symbols *(circles)* are proportional to sample size. Vertical line is the combined effect and curved lines show the inverted funnel distribution expected by an unbiased study sample. Asymmetry at the funnel base, with less precise studies showing greater treatment effects, suggests a biased sample.

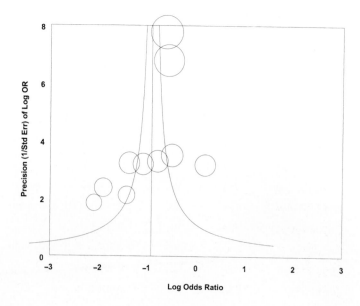

Table 13-10 Sensitivity Analysis of Antibiotic Prophylaxis versus Placebo for Recurrent AOM

Comparison	Groups	Studies	RD (95% CI)*	p Value†
Antibiotic administered	Sulfisoxazole	4	−.19 (−.29, −.09)	< .0001
	Any other antibiotic	6	−.05 (−.07, −.03)	
AOM rate at study entry	≥ 0.5 AOM/patient-month	5	−.15 (−.26, −.03)	< .0001
	< 0.5 AOM/patient-month	4	−.08 (−.12, −.04)	
AOM rate in controls during study	≥ 0.2 AOM/patient-month	5	−.15 (−.28, −.02)	.0003
	< 0.2 AOM/patient-month	5	−.06 (−.09, −.03)	
Study duration	≥ 6 months total follow-up	5	−.05 (−.07, −.03)	< .0001
	< 6 months total follow-up	5	−.16 (−.28, −.05)	

AOM = acute otitis media; CI = confidence interval; RD = rate difference.
*Absolute change in AOM episodes/patient-month attributable to therapy; negative values favor prophylaxis.
†Between-group analysis of variance; $p < .05$ indicates significant differences.

episodes) in studies with a minimum baseline rate calculable from entry criteria (see Chapter 12).

Antimicrobial prophylaxis increased the likelihood of having no further AOM (Table 13-11 and Figure 13-12) during the median study period of 6 months by 21% (95% CI, .13, .30). The studies were heterogeneous ($p = .026$) and the funnel plot (Figure 13-13) suggested small study bias. Similarly, the likelihood of having less than three further AOM episodes during the study period was significantly reduced by therapy (Table 13-12 and Figure 13-14). The RD, however, was only 8% (95% CI, .04, .12), making it necessary to treat 12 children to prevent frequent AOM in one. Although the studies were homogeneous ($p = .587$) the funnel plot (Figure 13-15) showed a conspicuous absence of small studies with a reduced effect size.

Are the Results Valid?

Two meta-analyses[12,14] have addressed the efficacy of antimicrobial prophylaxis for preventing recurrent AOM. Bonati and colleagues[12] did not assess incidence density, but noted that prophylaxis increased the chance of remaining otitis free (odds ratio .23; 95% CI, .16, .34). Williams and colleagues[14] reported a slightly higher overall RD for incidence density than in Table 13-9 (.11 versus .09) with a 95% CI more than twice as broad. The reasons for this discrepancy are twofold. First, Williams and colleagues[14] incorrectly pooled data using AOM episodes *per patient* instead of *per patient-month* (personal communication, July 1998), which decreases precision because study duration is ignored. Second, three of the RCTs[50–52] in Table 13-9 were published subsequent to their analysis.

Table 13-11 Antibiotic Prophylaxis versus Placebo for Recurrent AOM: Chance of No Further AOM

Author Year	Country	Entry Rate[†]	Drug and Duration	No AOM Episodes, N(%)[‡]		Absolute RD[#] (95% CI)
				Prophylaxis	Placebo	
Maynard[43] 1972	USA	NS	AMP 1 yr	131/173 (76)	115/191 (60)	.15 (.06, .25)[§]
Perrin[44] 1974	USA	3/18; 5	SSX 3 mo	50/54 (93)	33/54 (61)	.31 (.17, .46)[§]
Liston[45] 1983	USA	3/6	SSX 3 mo	18/35 (51)	14/34 (41)	.10 (−.13, .34)
Varsano[46] 1985	Israel	3/6	SSX 10 wk	25/32 (78)	12/32 (38)	.41 (.19, .63)[§]
Gonzalez[47] 1986	USA	3/6; 5/18	SSX 6 mo	5/21 (24)	3/20 (15)	.09 (−.15, .33)
Principi[48] 1989	Italy	3/6	AMX or TMP/SMX 6 mo	48/66 (73)	11/30 (37)	.36 (.16, .56)[§]
Casselbrant[49] 1992	USA	3/6; 4/12	AMX 2 yr	50/86 (58)	32/80 (40)	.18 (.03, .33)[§]
Sih[50] 1993	Brazil	3/12	AMX or TMP/SMX 3 mo	33/40 (82)	10/20 (50)	.33 (.08, .57)[§]
Mandel[51] 1996	USA	3/12[‖]	AMX 1 yr	42/55 (76)	24/51 (47)	.29 (.12, .47)[§]
Roark[52] 1997	USA	3/6	AMX 45 d	62/99 (63)	37/59 (63)	0 (−.16, .16)
Combined*				464/661 (70)	291/571 (51)	.21 (.13, .30)[§]

AMP = ampicillin; AMX = amoxicillin; AOM = acute otitis media; CI = confidence interval; PCN = penicillin; RD = rate difference; SSX = sulfasoxazole; SMX = sulfamethoxazole; TMP = trimethoprim.

*Combined $p < .001$; test for heterogeneity Q = 18.92, df = 9, $p < .026$.

[†]Baseline rate of AOM recurrence to enter study in episodes/month or total episodes.

[‡]Number of children with no AOM during study (median duration 6 mo) divided by total number of evaluable children.

[§]$p < .05$ when the 95% CI does not contain zero.

[‖]Eligibility based on recurrent middle ear effusion, not just recurrent AOM.

[#]Absolute change in rate of no further AOM attributable to therapy; positive values favor prophylaxis.

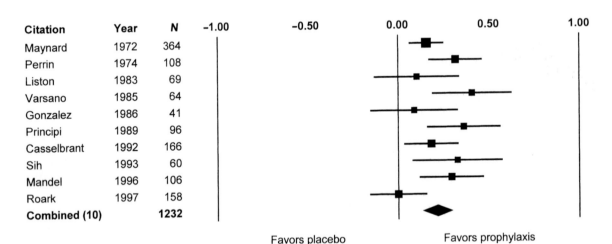

Figure 13-12 Random effects meta-analysis of antibiotic prophylaxis versus placebo for chance of no further AOM episodes (see Table 13-11 for study details). Forest plot shows absolute rate difference (RD) and 95% confidence intervals for individual studies (*squares* proportional to study size) and combined result *(diamond)*. Combined result indicates a moderate impact of therapy (RD .21), implying a need to treat 5 children to benefit one.

The studies in Tables 13-9 through 13-12 are all randomized, placebo controlled, and of adequate quality for an acceptable level of internal validity. Variations occur in the randomization process, duration of follow-up, and adequacy of follow-up but are unlikely to significantly impact the validity of pooled estimates derived from this data set. All studies except one[43] provided sufficient direct or indirect information regarding the baseline rate of AOM recurrence. All studies administered continuous, low-dose antimicrobial prophylaxis to the treatment

Figure 13-13 Funnel plot of precision versus effect size for the meta-analysis in Figure 13-12. Study symbols *(circles)* are proportional to sample size. Vertical line is the combined effect and curved lines show the inverted funnel distribution expected by an unbiased study sample. Asymmetry at the funnel base, with less precise studies showing greater treatment effects, suggests a biased sample.

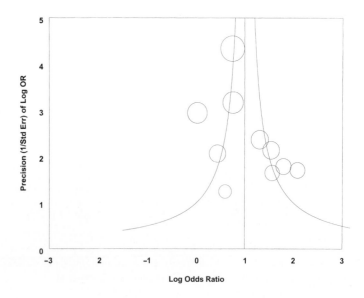

group; trials were excluded that used intermittent prophylaxis only during upper respiratory infections.

The funnel plots in Figures 13-11, 13-13, and 13-15 suggest a potentially biased sample of studies, which may compromise validity of the pooled estimates. All the plots show an excess of lower precision studies with large treatment effects. The problem is particularly evident in Figure 13-15. Including unpublished or unidentified smaller precision studies with small treatment effects would result in lower efficacy than suggested by the above analyses.

To Whom Do the Results Apply?

Results can be generalized to a broad range of children because few restrictions were placed on AOM severity or child age when defining study eligibility. Unlike placebo controlled studies of AOM *therapy*, where withholding antibiotics raises ethical concerns for children who are very young or very ill, children on placebo *prophylaxis* still receive antibiotics for individual AOM episodes. The impact of changing bacterial resistance patterns of antimicrobial efficacy is unclear because the majority of AOM (and recurrent AOM) improves spontaneously. The discouraging results reported by Roark and Berman,[52] however, suggest that amoxicillin may not be the prophylactic agent of choice in an era of multidrug resistant *Pneumococcus*.

Many RCTs of antibiotic prophylaxis excluded children with baseline OME, so results should be extrapolated to this population with caution. Children were also generally excluded if they had immune deficiency, cleft palate, craniofacial anomalies, or Down syndrome. Unfortunately, these are also the children most likely to develop recurrent AOM. If we cautiously extrapolate the

above finding that prophylaxis is most effective in studies where placebo-treated children had high recurrence rates, then children with syndromes or OM predispositions may benefit from therapy.

MEDICAL THERAPY OF OME

What Are the Results?

Antimicrobial Therapy

Nine placebo-controlled RCTs were found (Table 13-13) that assessed the efficacy of antimicrobial therapy for OME.[59–67] To avoid bias in outcome assessment, four unblinded studies[68–71] in which the control group received no drug instead of placebo were excluded. These unblinded studies were included in the first edition of this chapter, but inflated the combined RD by 47% over the estimate obtained using only masked studies. Also excluded were 1 nonrandomized study of antimicrobial therapy,[72] 3 randomized trials that used a *prophylactic* dose of antibiotic (one-half of the recommended daily therapeutic dosage),[46,73,74] and 1 controversial reanalysis[75] of data originally published by Mandel and coworkers.[60]

Review of Table 13-13 and Figure 13-16 shows that 7 of the 9 RCTs had results favoring antimicrobial therapy (RD greater than zero), of which 6 were statistically significant. The overall RD was 15% (95% CI, .06, .24) producing an NNT of 7 children. There was significant heterogeneity among studies ($p < .001$), with results ranging from an RD of .37 to −.09 (negative results favor placebo). The study[63] with the poorest result used erythromycin as single-agent therapy. The funnel plot (Figure 13-17) suggests a slight excess

Table 13-12 Antibiotic Prophylaxis versus Placebo for Recurrent AOM: Chance of Less than 3 Further AOM

Author Year	Country	Entry Rate[†]	Drug and Duration	< 3 AOM Episodes, N(%)[‡]		Absolute RD[#] (95% CI)
				Prophylaxis	Placebo	
Maynard[43] 1972	USA	NS	AMP 1 yr	165/173 (95)	171/191 (90)	.06 (.01, .11)[§]
Liston[45] 1983	USA	3/6	SSX 3 mo	34/35 (97)	27/34 (79)	.18 (.03, .32)[§]
Casselbrant[49] 1992	USA	3/6; 4/12	AMX 2 yr	75/86 (87)	61/80 (76)	.11 (−.01, .23)
Sih[50] 1993	Brazil	3/12	AMX or TMP/SMX 3 mo	40/40 (100)	19/20 (95)	.06 (−.06, .17)
Mandel[51] 1996	USA	3/12[‖]	AMX 1 yr	55/55 (100)	46/51 (90)	.10 (.01, .18)[§]
Combined[*]				369/389 (95)	324/376 (86)	.08 (.04, .12)[§]

AMP = ampicillin; AMX = amoxicillin; AOM = acute otitis media; CI = confidence interval; PCN = penicillin; RD = rate difference; SSX = sulfasoxazole; SMX = sulfamethoxazole; TMP = trimethoprim.

[*]Combined $p < .001$; test for heterogeneity Q = 2.83, df = 4, $p = .587$.

[†]Baseline rate of AOM recurrence to enter study in episodes/month or total episodes.

[‡]Number of children with no AOM during study (median duration 6 mo) divided by total number of evaluable children.

[§]$p < .05$ when the 95% CI does not contain zero.

[‖]Eligibility based on recurrent middle ear effusion, not just recurrent AOM.

[#]Absolute change in rate of no further AOM attributable to therapy; positive values favor prophylaxis.

Citation	Year	N						
			−0.50	−0.25	0.00		0.25	0.50
Maynard	1972	364						
Liston	1983	69						
Casselbrant	1992	166						
Sih	1993	60						
Mandel	1996	106						
Combined (5)		**765**						

Favors placebo   Favors prophylaxis

Figure 13-14 Random effects meta-analysis of antibiotic prophylaxis versus placebo for chance of less than three further AOM episodes (see Table 13-12 for study details). Forest plot shows absolute rate difference (RD) and 95% confidence intervals for individual studies (*squares* proportional to study size) and combined result *(diamond)*. Combined result indicates a small impact of therapy (RD .08), implying a need to treat 8 children to benefit one.

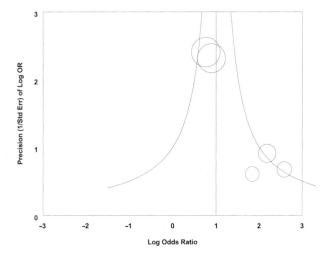

Figure 13-15 Funnel plot of precision versus effect size for the meta-analysis in Figure 13-14. Study symbols *(circles)* are proportional to sample size. Vertical line is the combined effect and curved lines show the inverted funnel distribution expected by an unbiased study sample. Marked asymmetry at the funnel base suggests a biased sample.

of smaller studies with favorable results but does not have marked asymmetry.

Whereas other meta-analyses[5,14] of OME have included RCTs with a prophylactic dosage of antimicrobial,[46,73,74] these studies were excluded from Table 13-13 because a subtherapeutic level of drug could unfavorably bias results. Prophylaxis studies generally administer one-half of the recommended therapeutic drug dosage, which might reduce clinical efficacy. As shown in Table 13-14 and Figure 13-18, the overall impact of antimicrobial prophylaxis on OME resolution is not statistically significant (RD .12, 95% CI, –.11, .35). Only one study[73] showed a significant benefit, but the sample size was too low to define the magnitude of benefit with an acceptable degree of clinical certainty (95% CI, .06, .56).

Corticosteroid Therapy

Three RCTs were found (Table 13-15 and Figure 13-19) that compared corticosteroids with placebo for resolution of OME in all ears.[71,76,77] The overall RD at 2 weeks was 20% (95% CI, –.05, .45), which is not statistically significant but suggests a trend toward short-term steroid efficacy and possible low statistical power (the combined sample size was only 108 children). As with antimicrobial therapy, however, blinded studies showed poorer outcomes. The only nonblinded study[71] had the largest RD (.39) and was the only one of the three to reach statistical significance.

Five RCTs were found (Table 13-16 and Figure 13-20) that compared corticosteroid-antibiotic therapy with placebo-antibiotic therapy for resolution of OME in all ears.[64,78–81] All of the included studies were blinded. Excluded from Table 13-16 are two non-randomized studies,[82,83] and a randomized study[84] in which cure was defined as OME resolution in any ear (not in all ears). The combined RD of 25% is statistically significant, and is difficult to interpret because of heterogeneity ($p < .001$) and a wide 95% CI (.02, .47). Moreover, the largest and most recent study[81] in this group noted the effect to be only transient, with no significant difference between groups by 4 weeks, even if antibiotics were continued after steroid therapy. Last, the funnel plot (Figure 13-21) suggests a biased selection of low precision studies.

Antihistamine-Decongestant Preparations

Three RCTs were found (Table 13-17 and Figure 13-22) that compared antihistamine-decongestant preparations with placebo for OME.[85–87] All of the listed studies showed no significant benefit to therapy, including an unlisted study by Mandel and coworkers,[60] in which all children also received amoxicillin. The overall RD was 0% (–07, .07), suggesting no efficacy and no evidence of heterogeneity ($p = .712$) or inadequate statistical power.

Are the Results Valid?

Three published meta-analyses[5,13,14] have shown that antibiotic therapy confers a modest but statistically significant short-term benefit for resolution of OME. Rosenfeld and Post[13] obtained a higher RD than in Table 13-13 (.23 versus .15) because they included several unblinded studies that inflated the treatment effect. Conversely, Stool and colleagues[5] emphasized blinded studies, but their effect size was slightly lower (RD .14; 95% CI, .04, .24) because one RCT[67] was unpublished and three included studies[47,88,89] that used a *prophylactic* dosage of antibiotic. The same observations apply to Williams and coworkers,[14] who obtained an RD of 16% (95% CI, .03, .29) with some unblinded studies included.

The earlier RCT by Mandel and colleagues[60] in Table 13-13 was the subject of considerable controversy because a dissenting analysis[75] using tympanometry as an outcome measure reduced the RD to 8% (51 of 309 successes in the study group and 13 of 150 successes in the placebo group). Because of this controversy, Williams and colleagues[14] used the dissenting analysis and Stool and colleagues[5] used neither. When viewed in perspective as only one link in a chain of RCT evidence (see Table 13-13), however, the impact of this controversy on meta-analysis results is extremely small. When recalculated using data from the dissenting analysis, the RD in Table 13-13 decreases by one percentage point to 14% (95% CI, .05, .23).

Validity of the corticosteroid RCTs in Tables 13-14 and 13-15 is limited by small sample size, low precision (wide 95% CIs), and low statistical power. The overall estimates have broad 95% CIs (up to 60 percentage points), in part caused by heterogeneity among studies. Although the impact of steroid-antibiotic therapy was statistically significant, the lower limit of the 95% CI cannot exclude a trivial effect and the funnel plot suggests sampling bias. Validity of the antihistamine-decongestant RCTs in Table 13-17 appears adequate to conclude no impact of therapy on OME resolution. The studies were all blinded, and the combined result does not indicate heterogeneity or low statistical power.

To Whom Do the Results Apply?

Most of the children in RCTs of medical therapy for OME have established, pre-existing effusion(s) lasting weeks to months (see Table 13-13, column 3). Consequently, results may not apply to OME of very recent onset or of lesser duration. The cause of OME is generally unknown but more often of spontaneous onset rather than persistent effusion after a discrete episode of AOM. As in most OM RCTs, children who had immune deficiency, cleft palate, craniofacial anomalies, prior tympanostomy

Table 13-13 Antibiotic Therapy for Resolution of OME at 10 Days to 8 Weeks (Median 4 Weeks)

Author Year	Country	Duration (Diagnosis)[†]	Drug and Duration[‖]	Complete Resolution, N (%)[‡]		Absolute RD[#] (95% CI)
				Antibiotic	Placebo	
Marks[59] 1981	England	NS (t)	TMP/SMX 28 d	16/25 (64)	7/26 (27)	.37 (.12, .63)[§]
Mandel[60] 1987	USA	most ≥ 4 wk (a)	AMX 14 d	96/318 (30)	22/156 (14)	.16 (.09, .24)[§]
Schloss[61] 1988	Canada	NS (o,t)	ERY/SSX 14 d	6/25 (24)	8/27 (30)	−.06 (−.30, .18)
Thomsen[62] 1989	Denmark	12 wk (t)	AMX/CLV 30 d	69/111 (62)	34/110 (31)	.31 (.19, .44)[§]
Møller[63] 1990	Norway	12 wk (o,t)	ERY 14 d	12/69 (17)	19/72 (26)	−.09 (−.23, .05)
Podoshin[64] 1990	Israel	8 wk (t)	AMX 14 d	20/49 (41)	5/37 (14)	.27 (.10, .45)[§]
Daly[65] 1991	USA	NS (o,t)	TMP/SMX 14 d	5/21 (24)	2/21 (10)	.14 (−.08, .36)
Mandel[66] 1991	USA	most ≥ 4wk (a)	VAR 14 d	59/236 (25)	11/78 (14)	.11 (.01, .20)[§]
van Balen[67] 1996	Netherlands	12 wk (t)	AMX/CLV 14 d	18/79 (23)	5/74 (7)	.16 (.05, .27)[§]
Combined*				301/933 (32)	113/60 (19)	.15 (.06, .24)[§]

AMP = ampicillin; AMX = amoxicillin; AOM = acute otitis media; CEF = cefaclor; CI = confidence interval; CLV = clavulanate; ERY = erythromycin; OME = otitis media with effusion; PCN = penicillin; RD = rate difference; SSX = sulfasoxazole; SMX = sulfamethoxazole; TMP = trimethoprim; VAR = various antibiotics (AMX, CEF, or ERY/SSX).

*Combined p = .001; test for heterogeneity Q = 27.00, df = 8, p < .001.

[†]Minimum duration of OME to enter study and method of diagnosis: algorithm (a), otoscopy (o), or tympanometry (t).

[‡]Number of children with clearance of OME from all initially affected ears divided by the total number of evaluable children.

[§]p < .05 when the 95% CI does not contain zero.

[‖]Outcomes are reported at completion of therapy for all studies except Podoshin 1990 (who reported 6 weeks later) and for Mandel 1987 and Møller 1990 (who reported 2 weeks later).

[#]Absolute change in OME complete resolution attributable to therapy; positive values favor the antibiotic group.

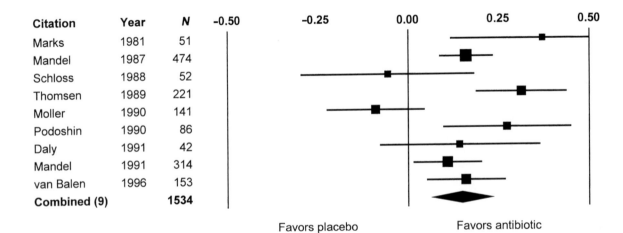

Figure 13-16 Random effects meta-analysis of antibiotic therapy for complete resolution of otitis media with effusion (see Table 13-13 for study details). Forest plot shows absolute rate difference (RD) and 95% confidence intervals for individual studies (*squares* proportional to study size) and combined result (*diamond*). Combined result indicates a modest impact of therapy (RD .15), implying a need to treat 7 children to resolve effusion in one.

Figure 13-17 Funnel plot of precision versus effect size for the meta-analysis in Figure 13-16. Study symbols *(circles)* are proportional to sample size. Vertical line is the combined effect and curved lines show the inverted funnel distribution expected by an unbiased study sample. There is slight asymmetry at the funnel base, but no indication of marked bias.

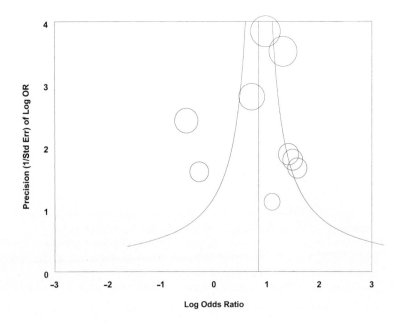

Table 13-14 Antibiotic Prophylaxis versus Placebo for Resolution of OME

Author Year	Country	Duration (Diagnosis)[†]	Drug and Duration[‡]	Blind Study	Complete Resolution, N (%)[‡]		Absolute RD[∥] (95% CI)
					Prophylaxis	No Prophylaxis	
deCastro[73] 1982	USA	NS (t)	SSX	Y	5/15 (33)	0/15 (0)	.31 (.06, .56)[§]
Schwartz[74] 1982	USA	≤ 15 d (t)	TMP/SMX	N	19/33 (58)	21/36 (58)	−.01 (−.24, .23)
Varsano[46] 1985	Israel	NS (o)	SSX	Y	10/19 (53)	8/16 (50)	.03 (−.31, .36)
Combined*					34/67 (51)	29/67 (43)	.12 (−.11, .35)

CI = confidence interval; OME = otitis media with effusion; SSX = sulfasoxazole; SMX = sulfamethoxazole; TMP = trimethoprim; RD = rate difference.

*Combined p = .323; test for heterogeneity Q = 3.77, df = 2, p = .152.

†Minimum duration of OME to enter study and method of diagnosis: algorithm (a), otoscopy (o), or tympanometry (t).

‡Number of children with clearance of OME from all initially affected ears divided by the total number of evaluable children.

∥Absolute change in OME complete resolution attributable to therapy; positive values favor the prophylaxis group.

§p < .05 when the 95% CI does not contain zero.

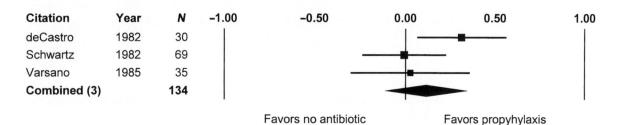

Figure 13-18 Random effects meta-analysis of antibiotic prophylaxis for complete resolution of otitis media with effusion (see Table 13-14 for study details). Forest plot shows absolute rate difference (RD) and 95% confidence intervals for individual studies *(squares* proportional to study size) and combined result *(diamond)*. Combined result indicates no significant benefit.

Table 13-15 Corticosteroid Therapy versus Placebo or No Steroid for Resolution of OME at 2 Weeks

Author Year	Country	Duration (diagnosis)[†]	Drug and Duration	Blind Study	Complete Resolution, N (%)[‡]		Absolute RD[∥] (95% CI)
					Steroid	No Steroid	
Niederman[76] 1984	USA	8 wk (t)	DEX 13 d	Y	3/12 (25)	0/10 (0)	.22 (−.05, .49)
Macknin[77] 1985	USA	3 wk (a)	DEX 13 d	Y	3/26 (12)	2/23 (9)	.03 (−.14, .20)
Giebink[71] 1990	USA	8 wk (a)	PRD 14 d	N	8/18 (44)	1/19 (5)	.39 (.14, .64)[§]
Combined*					14/56 (25)	3/52 (6)	.20 (−.05, .45)

CI = confidence interval; DEX = dexamethasone; OME = otitis media with effusion; PRD = prednisone; RD = rate difference.
*Combined p = .113; test for heterogeneity Q = 5.85, df = 2, p = .054.
[†]Minimum duration of OME to enter study and method of diagnosis: algorithm (a), otoscopy (o), or tympanometry (t).
[‡]Number of children with clearance of OME from all initially affected ears divided by the total number of evaluable children.
[§]p < .05 when the 95% CI does not contain zero.
[∥]Absolute change in OME complete resolution attributable to therapy; positive values favor the steroid group.

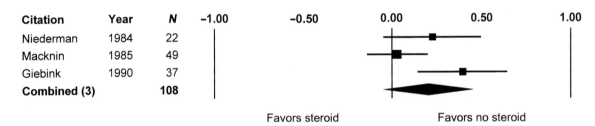

Figure 13-19 Random effects meta-analysis of corticosteroid therapy for complete resolution of otitis media with effusion (see Table 13-15 for study details). Forest plot shows absolute rate difference (RD) and 95% confidence intervals for individual studies (*squares* proportional to study size) and combined result (*diamond*). Combined result indicates no significant benefit.

Table 13-16 Corticosteroid-Antibiotic versus Placebo-Antibiotic for Resolution of OME

Author Year	Country	Duration (Diagnosis)[†]	Drug and Duration	Complete Resolution, N (%)[‡]		Absolute RD[∥] (95% CI)
				Steroid-Abx	Placebo–Abx	
Schwartz[78] 1980	USA	3 wk (o)	PRD, SSX 7 d	15/24 (63)	1/17 (6)	.57 (.34, .79)[§]
Lambert[79] 1986	USA	8 w k(a)	PRD, AMX 14 d	14/32 (44)	14/28 (50)	−.06 (−.32, .19)[§]
Berman[80] 1990	USA	6 wk (a)	PRD, TMP/SMX 30 d	20/26 (77)	8/27 (30)	.47 (.24, .71)[§]
Podoshin[64] 1990	Israel	8 wk (t)	PRD, AMX 14 d	20/50 (40)	15/49 (31)	.09 (−.09, .28)
Mandel[81] 2002	USA	2 mo (a)	PRD, AMX 14 d	23/69 (33)	11/66 (17)	.17 (.02, .31)
Combined*				92/241 (38)	49/187 (26)	.25 (.02, .47)

Abx = antibiotic; AMX = amoxicillin; CI = confidence interval; OME = otitis media with effusion; PRD = prednisone; RD = rate difference; SSX = sulfasoxazole; SMX = sulfamethoxazole; TMP = trimethoprim.
*Combined p = .030; test for heterogeneity Q = 20.66, df = 4, p < .001.
[†]Minimum duration of OME to enter study and method of diagnosis: algorithm (a), otoscopy (o), or tympanometry (t).
[‡]Number of children with clearance of OME from all initially affected ears divided by the total number of evaluable children.
[§]p < .05 when the 95% CI does not contain zero.
[∥]Absolute change in OME complete resolution attributable to therapy; positive values favor the prophylaxis group.

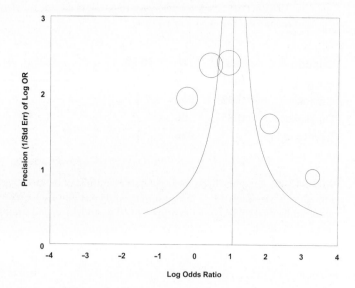

Citation	Year	N
Schwartz	1980	41
Lambert	1986	60
Berman	1990	53
Podoshin	1990	99
Mandel	2002	135
Combined (5)		**388**

Favors placebo-antibiotic   Favors steroid-antibiotic

Figure 13-20 Random effects meta-analysis of corticosteroid-antibiotic for complete resolution of otitis media with effusion (see Table 13-16 for study details). Forest plot shows absolute rate difference (RD) and 95% confidence intervals for individual studies (*squares* proportional to study size) and combined result *(diamond)*. Combined result indicates a large impact of therapy (RD .25), but the broad confidence intervals indicate low precision. Heterogeneity is pronounced.

Figure 13-21 Funnel plot of precision versus effect size for the meta-analysis in Figure 13-20. Study symbols *(circles)* are proportional to sample size. Vertical line is the combined effect and curved lines show the inverted funnel distribution expected by an unbiased study sample. There is asymmetry at the funnel base suggesting bias.

tubes, Down, or other syndromes were often excluded. Meta-analysis results may not apply to these populations.

The modest 15% increase in OME resolution attributable to antimicrobial therapy must be viewed in the context of a *short-term* benefit; the impact on *long-term* resolution is smaller, if not negligible, on the basis of the limited evidence available. Mandel and colleagues[60] reported an RD of 16% at 2 weeks, but only 6% at 4 weeks. Giebink and colleagues[71] reported RD's of 55% and 18%, respectively, at similar time points. Similarly, Williams and coworkers[14] reported no significant intermediate or long-term benefits to antimicrobial therapy for OME in their meta-analysis. The same trend is observed with corticosteroid therapy, alone or in combination with an antibiotic.[5,81]

Clinicians should also recall that data in Tables 13-13 through 13-17 are for *complete* resolution of OME in all initially affected ears, which excludes partial resolution of bilateral OME in only one ear. Rates for partial reso-

lution of OME, however, can be substantially higher. For example, van Balen and colleagues[67] obtained an RD of 16% for complete resolution but a more impressive RD of 27% for partial resolution. Similarly, Butler and van der Voort[6] found a promising impact of steroid-antibiotic therapy in a meta-analysis that included one study[84] using partial resolution (RD .24). Unfortunately, the highly variable nature of OME (see Chapter 12) makes partial resolution rates less meaningful. Most children with OME have frequent relapse and recurrence, which greatly limits the significance of unilateral resolution of bilateral effusions.

ADVERSE EFFECTS OF MEDICAL THERAPY

The benefits of medication must be balanced against potential adverse effects when deciding for or against treatment. Antibiotics increase the risk of vomiting, diarrhea, or rashes

Table 13-17 Antihistamine-Decongestant Therapy versus Placebo for Resolution of OME

Author Year	Country	Duration (Diagnosis)[†]	Drugs and Duration	Complete Resolution, N (%)[‡]		Absolute RD[††] (95% CI)
				Therapy	Placebo	
Haugeto[85] 1981	Norway	NS (t)	PPL, BPM 4 wk	15/55 (27)	8/22 (36)	−.09 (−.32, .14)
Cantekin[86] 1983	USA	8 wk mean (a)	PSE, CPM 4 wk	68/278 (24)	66/275 (24)	0 (−.07, .08)
Dusdieker[87] 1985	USA	NS (o,t)	PSE, CPM 12 wk	19/42 (45)	10/24 (42)	.04 (−.21, .28)
Combined*				102/375 (27)	84/321 (26)	0 (−.07, .07)

CI = confidence interval; BPM = brompheniramine maleate; CPM = chlorpheniramine maleate; NS = not specified; OME = otitis media with effusion; PPL = phenylpropanolamin; PSE = pseudoephedrine; RD = rate difference.

*Combined p = .980; test for heterogeneity Q = .680, df = 2, p = .712.

[†]Minimum duration of OME to enter study and method of diagnosis: algorithm (a), otoscopy (o), or tympanometry (t).

[††]Absolute change in OME complete resolution attributable to therapy; positive values favor therapy.

[§]p < .05 when the 95% CI does not contain zero.

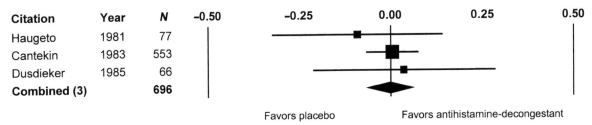

Citation	Year	N
Haugeto	1981	77
Cantekin	1983	553
Dusdieker	1985	66
Combined (3)		**696**

Favors placebo   Favors antihistamine-decongestant

Figure 13-22 Random effects meta-analysis of antihistamine-decongestant therapy for complete resolution of otitis media with effusion (see Table 13-17 for study details). Forest plot shows absolute rate difference (RD) and 95% confidence intervals for individual studies (*squares* proportional to study size) and combined result *(diamond)*. Combined result indicates no significant benefit.

by about 5 to 10% compared with control, but the incidence of these symptoms is unrelated to long versus short therapy.[90] The choice and duration of drug, however, may influence bacterial resistance (see Chapters 26, "Bacterial Resistance and Antimicrobial Drug Selection" and 27, "Judicious Use of Systemic Antimicrobials"). Further, prescribing antibiotics for minor illness encourages further consultations.[91] As noted earlier, initial nonantibiotic therapy of AOM does not increase suppurative complications when children are followed up closely.[1] Short courses of steroids can produce behavioral changes, increased appetite, and weight gain. Idiosyncratic reactions may occur, including fatal varicella infection and avascular necrosis of the femoral head. Adverse effects of antihistamines include hyperactivity, insomnia, drowsiness, behavioral change, blood pressure variability, and seizures.[92]

CLINICAL IMPLICATIONS

Medical therapy of OM is likely to be most rewarding when clinicians and parents have realistic expectations. Knowing in advance what to expect from therapy minimizes frustration and disappointment with treatment results. Tables 13-18 and 13-19 summarize the impact of medical therapy, emphasizing two related measures of clinical importance: (1) the RD, or absolute increase in resolution rates attributable to therapy, and (2) its reciprocal, the NNT, which defines the number needed to treat for one additional successful outcome beyond natural history. The 95% confidence limits offer a range of results consistent with the available data.

A pervasive theme in Tables 13-18 and 13-19 is the relatively modest impact of antimicrobial therapy on AOM, OME, and recurrent AOM. Unless treatment expectations are correspondingly modest, clinicians and familes are likely to be disappointed with the outcomes achieved. Despite antibiotic therapy, some children with AOM will remain symptomatic, many children with recurrent AOM will have future episodes (but slightly less frequently), and many children with OME will retain persistent effusions in one or both ears. Expectations of complete and lasting cure are destined for disappointment. Continued growth and development are the only cures for OM; antimicrobial therapy is at best a means for temporary control and preventing complications.

Table 13-18 Summary of What to Expect from Medical Therapy for AOM

Clinical Situation and Outcome	Time Point	N*	RD†	(95% CI)	NNT‡ (95% CI)
Symptomatic relief of AOM in RCTs of antibiotic vs. placebo or no drug (Tables 13-2 to 13-4)	24 h	3	0	(−.07, .08)	—
	2–3 d	5	.04	(.02, .07)§	25 (14,50)
	4–7 d	6	.09	(.01, .18)§	11 (6, 333)
Complete clinical resolution of AOM in RCTs of antibiotic vs. placebo or no drug (Table 13-5)	7–14 d	6	.08	(.01, .14)§	13 (7,111)
Incidence of suppurative complications of AOM in RCTs of antibiotic vs. placebo or no drug (Table 13-6)	7–14 d	9	.001	(−.007, .008)	—
Resolution of persistent OME after treatment of AOM in RCTs of antibiotic vs. placebo (Tables 13-7 to 13-8)	4–6 wk	6	.03	(−.02, .08)	—
	3 mo	2	.05	(−.08, .17)	—
Incidence of AOM episodes/patient-month in RCTs of antibiotic prophylaxis vs. placebo (Table 13-9)	Up to 2 yr	10	−.09	(−.12, −.05)§	11 (8, 19)
Having no further AOM episodes in RCTs of antibiotic prophylaxis vs. placebo (Table 13-11)	6 mo median	10	.21	(.13, .30)§	5 (3, 8)
Having 2 or fewer AOM episodes in RCTs of antibiotic prophylaxis vs. placebo (Table 13-12)	6 mo median	5	.08	(.04, .12)§	13 (8, 24)

AOM = acute otitis media; OME = otitis media with effusion; CI = confidence interval; RCT = randomized controlled trial; RD = absolute rate difference; NNT = number needed to treat.

*Number of studies from which data were combined to derive the overall treatment effect.

†RD is the absolute change in outcome for treatment vs. control groups.

‡NNT is the number of children who must be treated for one additional successful outcome and is relevant only for statistically significant outcomes.

§$p < .05$ when the 95% CI does not contain zero.

Table 13-19 Summary of What to Expect from Medical Therapy for OME

Clinical Situation and Outcome	Time Point	N*	RD†	(95% CI)	NNT‡ (95% CI)
Resolution of persistent OME after treatment of AOM in RCTs of antibiotic vs. placebo (Tables 13-7 to 13-8)	4–6 wk	6	.03	(−.02, .08)	—
	3 mo	2	.05	(−.08, .17)	—
Complete resolution of OME in blinded RCTs of antibiotic therapy vs. placebo (Table 13-13)	4 wk median	9	.15	(.06, .24)§	7 (4, 17)
Complete resolution of OME in RCTs of antibiotic prophylaxis vs. placebo (Table 13-14)	4 wk median	3	.12	(−.11, .35)	—
Complete resolution of OME in RCTs of steroid vs. placebo or no drug (Table 13-15)	2 wk	3	.20	(−.05, .45)	—
Complete resolution of OME in RCTs of steroid & antibiotic vs. placebo & antibiotic (Table 13-16)	Up to 2 mo	5	.25	(.02, .47)§	4 (2, 43)
Complete resolution of OME in RCTs of antihistamine & decongestant vs. placebo (Table 13-14)	1–3 mo	3	0	(−.07, .07)	—

OME = otitis media with effusion; CI = confidence interval; RCT = randomized controlled trial; RD = (absolute) rate difference; NNT = number needed to treat.

*Number of studies from which data were combined to derive the overall treatment effect.

†RD is the absolute change in outcome for treatment vs. control groups.

‡NNT is the number of children who must be treated for one additional successful outcome and is relevant only for statistically significant outcomes.

§$p < .05$ when the 95% CI does not contain zero.

Table 13-20 Potential Modifiers of Clinical Response for Children with Otitis Media

Host factors	Effectiveness of the local and systemic immune reaction
	Severity and duration of the local inflammatory reaction
	Ability of the Eustachian tube to clear middle ear fluid
	Degree of mastoid air cell development and aeration
	Adenoidal reservoir of pathogenic bacteria
	Underlying syndrome, illness, or genetic predisposition
Infectious factors	Antibiotic consumption
	Frequency and duration of viral upper respiratory infections
	Prevalence of bacterial pathogens in the middle ear
	Prevalence of viral pathogens or co-pathogens in the middle ear
	Bacterial colonization of the nasopharynx
Environmental factors	Group day care attendance
	Environmental tobacco smoke exposure
	Early infant feeding practices
	Pacifier use
	Food or inhalant allergies

Validity of the meta-analysis results in this chapter may be compromised by heterogeneity, low precision, and sampling bias. Most of the analyses had significant heterogeneity among source articles, which is only partially addressed by using a random-effects model for the combined effect. A consequence of this model is wider CIs (lower precision), which decreases certainty for the magnitude of effect size. For example, the lower limits of the confidence intervals in Tables 13-3 through 13-5 cannot exclude a potentially trivial impact of antibiotic therapy on AOM symptom relief or clinical resolution. The same applies to results obtained for treatment of OME and prophylaxis of recurrent AOM. Last, many of the statistically significant results had funnel plots that suggested sampling bias for the less precise studies.

The modest magnitude of clinical effect results from the favorable history of untreated OM (see Chapter 12), which makes it difficult to demonstrate impressive therapeutic benefits. Similarly, when dealing with small treatment effects it is unlikely that choice of antibiotic or duration of therapy will perceptibly influence results. Clinicians and parents must remember that medical therapy is only one of myriad factors that influence clinical outcomes (Table 13-20). Host, infectious, and environmental factors may be important modifiers of the clinical response to therapeutic or prophylactic antibiotics observed in a particular child. Some of these factors can be altered with medications, surgery, or environmental modifications; others are beyond the control of physicians or families.

The modest impact of antimicrobial therapy on OM outcomes raises the question of whether treatment should be offered at all. Decisions to withhold therapy, however, must always be balanced against the attendant risk. Suppurative complications of AOM were rare (0.20%) and statistically equivalent for placebo and antibiotic, but some studies excluded children under 2 years of age or those with severe symptoms. Despite the modest impact of antibiotics on symptomatic relief, withholding therapy from young or severely ill children risks a return to the once prevalent suppurative complications of the preantibiotic era. Conversely, untreated OME carries little serious risk, making aggressive antimicrobial therapy difficult to justify, given the modest short-term benefits.

Science is a cumulative process, in which each new study builds on an existing base of gradually acquired knowledge. This fundamental principle guides the analyses in this chapter, which in many instances builds on earlier meta-analyses by integrating subsequently published RCTs into the overall estimates of treatment effect. Further, the tabular presentations of raw data permit easy integration of future RCTs as they are published. New RCTs must be judged not as entities unto themselves but relative to their impact on the cumulative results of existing RCTs. Heterogeneity among studies should be embraced because it may help identify clinical or demographic factors associated with particular outcomes.

Evidence-based management of OM means blending expert judgment and patient preference with the best available external evidence. Systematic review of the evidence (Table 13-21) defines rational treatment expectations, which facilitates informed patient decisions. The modest incremental benefits of antimicrobials for OM make expert judgment paramount in deciding whom to treat. Meta-analysis, systematic literature review, and clinical practice guidelines help define what to expect *in general* but can never substitute for clinical judgment

Table 13-21 Pointers and Pitfalls

1. Statistical significance alone does not justify therapy; the number needed to treat (NNT) for one additional successful outcome should also reflect a reasonable level of clinical effort.

2. Initial antibiotic therapy of AOM does not reduce symptoms by 24 hours compared with placebo, but no study reporting outcomes at this time point included children below age 2 years.

3. Initial antibiotic therapy of AOM reduces symptoms by 2 to 3 days (NNT 25) and by 4 to 7 days (NNT 11); clinical resolution at 7 to 14 days is also improved (NNT 13).

4. About one suppurative complication will occur for every 500 children with AOM (0.20%); complications are not increased by initial nonantibiotic therapy if children are followed up carefully.

5. Initial antibiotic therapy of AOM does not affect resolution of persistent OME.

6. Antimicrobial prophylaxis reduces the incidence or recurrent AOM by 0.09 episodes per patient-month, which implies that 11 months are required to prevent one episode (NNT 11).

7. Antimicrobial prophylaxis of recurrent AOM slightly reduces the chance of having no further AOM episodes (NNT 5) or having less than three further AOM episodes (NNT 13) during therapy.

8. Antibiotic therapy of OME lasting weeks to months has a modest impact on short-term complete resolution (NNT 7) but may not alter long-term outcome.

9. Steroid-antibiotic therapy of OME facilitates complete short-term resolution (NNT 4) but relapse of effusion is common after several weeks.

10. Complete resolution of OME is not significantly affected by steroid therapy (without concurrent antibiotic) or by antihistamine-decongestant therapy.

11. Meta-analysis results were often imprecise, and the 95% confidence interval could not exclude a trivial effect; many analyses were heterogeneous with sampling bias suggested by funnel plots.

AOM = acute otitis media; OME = otitis media with effusion.

when managing *individual* patients. Later chapters in this book use the evidence presented herein as a basis for enlightened and individualized decision making.

REFERENCES

1. Marcy M, Takata G, Shekelle P, et al. Management of acute otitis media. Evidence Report/Technology Assessment No. 15 (Prepared by the Southern California Evidence-based Practice Center under Contract No. 290-97-0001). Rockville (MD): Agency for Healthcare Research and Quality; 2001 May. AHRQ Publication No. 01-E010.

2. Rosenfeld RM. What to expect from medical treatment of otitis media. Pediatr Infect Dis J 1995;14:731–8.

3. Rosenfeld RM, Goldsmith AJ, Tetlus L, Balzano A. Quality of life for children with otitis media. Arch Otolaryngol Head Neck Surg 1997;123:1049–54.

4. Last JM. A dictionary of epidemiology. 3rd ed. Oxford (UK): Oxford University Press; 1995. p. 139–40.

5. Stool SE, Berg AO, Berman S, et al. Otitis media with effusion in young children. Clinical practice guideline, Number 12. Rockville (MD): Agency for Health Care Policy and Research, Public Health Service, U.S. Department of Health and Human Services; 1994 July. AHCPR Publication No. 94-0622.

6. Butler CC, van der Voort JH. Oral or topical nasal steroids for hearing loss associated with otitis media with effusion in children (Cochrane Review). In: The Cochrane Library, Issue 2, 2002. Oxford (UK): Update Software; 2002.

7. Flynn CA, Griffin G, Tudiver F. Decongestants and antihistamines for acute otitis media in children (Cochrane Review). In: The Cochrane Library, Issue 2, 2002. Oxford (UK): Update Software; 2002.

8. Glasziou PP, Del Mar CB, Sanders SL, Hayem M. Antibiotics for acute otitis media in children (Cochrane Review). In: The Cochrane Library, Issue 2, 2002. Oxford (UK): Update Software; 2002.

9. Kozyrskyj AL, Hildes-Ripstein GE, Longstaffe SEA, et al. Short course antibiotics for acute otitis media (Cochrane Review). In: The Cochrane Library, Issue 2, 2002. Oxford (UK): Update Software; 2002.

10. Straetemans M, Sanders EAM, Veenhoven RH, et al. Pneumococcal vaccines for preventing otitis media (Cochrane Review). In: The Cochrane Library, Issue 2, 2002. Oxford (UK): Update Software; 2002.

11. Rosenfeld RM, Mandel EM, Bluestone CD. Systemic steroids for otitis media with effusion in children. Arch Otolaryngol Head Neck Surg 1991;117:984–9.

12. Bonati M, Marchetti F, Pistotti V, et al. Meta-analysis of antimicrobial prophylaxis for recurrent acute otitis media. Clin Trials Meta Anal 1992;28:39–50.

13. Rosenfeld RM, Post JC. Meta-analysis of antibiotics for the treatment of otitis media with effusion. Otolaryngol Head Neck Surg 1992;106:378–86.

14. Williams RL, Chalmers TC, Stange KC, et al. Use of antibiotics in preventing recurrent acute otitis media and in treating otitis media with effusion: a meta-analytic attempt to resolve the brouhaha. JAMA 1993;270:1344–51.

15. Rosenfeld RM, Vertrees JE, Carr J, et al. Clinical efficacy of antimicrobial drugs for acute otitis media: meta-analysis of 5400 children from thirty-three randomized trials. J Pediatr 1994;124:355–67.

16. Pignataro O, Pignataro LD, Gallus G, et al. Otitis media with effusion and S-carboxymethylcysteine and/or its lysine salt: a critical overview. Int J Pediatr Otorhinolaryngol 1996;35:231–41.

17. Damoiseaux RAMJ, van Balen FAM, Hoes AW, de Melker RA. Antibiotic treatment of acute otitis media in children under two years of age: evidence based? Br J Gen Pract 1998;48:1861–4.

18. Ioannidis JPA, Contopoulos-Ioannidis DG, Chew P, Lau J. Meta-analysis of randomized controlled trials on the comparative efficacy and safety of azithromycin against other antibiotics for upper respiratory tract infections. J Antimicrob Chemother 2001;48:677–89.

19. Dickersin K, Scherer R, Lefebvre C. Identifying relevant studies for systematic reviews. BMJ 1994;309:1286–91.

20. DerSimonian R, Laird N. Meta-analysis in clinical trials. Control Clin Trials 1986;17:177–88.

21. Borenstein M, Rothstein H. Comprehensive Meta-Analysis: a computer program for research synthesis (v. 1.0.25). Englewood (NJ): Biostat Inc; 2000.

22. Sutton AJ, Abrams KR, Jones DR. An illustrated guide to the methods of meta-analysis. J Eval Clin Pract 2001;7:135–48.

23. Oxman AD, Sackett DL, Guyatt GH. Users' guides to the medical literature. I. How to get started. JAMA 1993;270:2093–7.

24. Laupacis A, Sackett DL, Roberts RS. An assessment of clinically useful measures of the consequences of treatment. N Engl J Med 1988;318:1728–33.

25. Borenstein M. The case for confidence intervals in controlled clinical trials. Control Clin Trials 1994;15:411–28.

26. Chalmers I, Hedges LV, Cooper H. A brief history of research synthesis. Eval Health Prof 2002;25:12–37.

27. Sutton AJ, Abrams KR, Jones DR. An illustrated guide to the methods of meta-analysis. J Eval Clin Pract 2001;7:135–48.

28. Ferrer RL. Graphical methods for detecting bias in meta-analysis. Fam Med 1998;30:579–83.

29. Halsted C, Lepow ML, Balassanian N, et al. Otitis media: clinical observations, microbiology, and evaluation of therapy. Am J Dis Child 1968;115:542–51.

30. Laxdal OE, Merida J, Trefor Jones RH. Treatment of acute otitis media: a controlled study of 142 children. Can Med Assoc J 1970;102:263–8.

31. Mygind N, Meistrup-Larsen KI, Thomsen J, et al. Penicillin in acute otitis media: a double-blind, placebo-controlled trial. Clin Otolaryngol 1981;6:5–13.

32. van Buchem FL, Dunk JHM, van't Hof MA. Therapy of acute otitis media: myringotomy, antibiotics, or neither: a double-blind study in children. Lancet 1981;2:883–7.

33. Thalin A, Densert O, Larsson A, et al. Is penicillin necessary in the treatment of acute otitis media? In: Proceedings of the International Conference on Acute and Secretory Otitis Media, Part 1; 1985 November 17–22; Jerusalem, Israel. Amsterdam: Kugler Publications; 1986. p. 441–6.

34. Appelman CLM, Claessen JQPJ, Touw-Otten FWMM, et al. Coamoxiclav in recurrent acute otitis media: placebo-controlled study. BMJ 1991;303:1450–2.

35. Burke P, Bain J, Robinson D, Dunleavey J. Acute red ear in children: controlled trial of nonantibiotic treatment in general practice. BMJ 1991;303:558–62.

36. Kaleida PH, Casselbrant ML, Rockette HE et al. Amoxicillin or myringotomy or both for acute otitis media: results of a randomized clinical trial. Pediatrics 1991;87:466–74.

37. Damoiseaux RAMJ, van Balen FAM, Hoes AW, et al. Primary care based randomised double blind trial of amoxicillin versus placebo for acute otitis media in children aged under 2 years. BMJ 2000;320:350–4.

38. Claessen JQPJ, Appelman CLM, Touw-Otten FWMM, et al. Persistence of middle ear dysfunction after recurrent acute otitis media. Clin Otolaryngol 1994;19:35–40.

39. Howie VM, Ploussard JH. Efficacy of fixed combination antibiotics versus separate components in otitis media: effectiveness of erythromycin estolate, triple sulfonamide, ampicillin, erythromycin estolate-triple sulfonamide, and placebo in 280 patients with acute otitis media under two and one-half years of age. Clin Pediatr 1972;11:205–14.

40. Browning GG, Bain J. Controversies in therapeutics. Child otalgia: acute otitis media. BMJ 1990;300:1005–7.

41. Marchant CD, Carlin SA, Johnson CE, Shurin PA. Measuring the comparative efficacy of antibacterial agents for acute otitis media: the "Polyanna phenomenon." J Pediatr 1992;120:72–7.

42. Howie VM, Ploussard JH. The "in vivo sensitivity test"—bacteriology of middle ear exudate, during antimicrobial therapy in otitis media. Pediatrics 1969;44:940–4.

43. Maynard JE, Fleshman JK, Tschopp CF. Otitis media in Alaskan Eskimo children: prospective evaluation of chemoprophylaxis. JAMA 1972;219:597–9.

44. Perrin JM, Charney E, MacWhinney JB Jr, et al. Sulfisoxazole as chemoprophylaxis for recurrent otitis media: a double-blind crossover study in pediatric practice. N Engl J Med 1974;291:664–7.

45. Liston TE, Foshee WS, Pierson WD. Sulfisoxazole chemoprophylaxis for frequent otitis media. Pediatrics 1983;71:524–30.

46. Varsano I, Volvitz B, Mimouni F. Sulfisoxazole prophylaxis of middle ear effusion and recurrent acute otitis media. Am J Dis Child 1985;139:632–5.

47. Gonzalez C, Arnold JE, Woody EA, et al. Prevention of recurrent acute otitis media: chemoprophylaxis versus

tympanostomy tubes. Laryngoscope 1986;96:1330–4.

48. Principi N, Marchisio P, Massironi E, et al. Prophylaxis of recurrent acute otitis media and middle-ear effusion: comparison of amoxicillin with sulfamethoxazole and trimethoprim. Am J Dis Child 1989;143:1414–8.

49. Casselbrant ML, Kaleida PH, Rockette HE, et al. Efficacy of antimicrobial prophylaxis and of tympanostomy tube insertion for prevention of recurrent acute otitis media: results of a randomized clinical trial. Pediatr Infect Dis J 1992;11:278–86.

50. Sih T, Moura R, Caldas S, Schwartz B. Prophylaxis for recurrent acute otitis media: a Brazilian study. Int J Pediatr Otorhinolaryngol 1993;25:19–24.

51. Mandel EM, Casselbrant ML, Rockette HE, et al. Efficacy of antimicrobial prophylaxis for recurrent middle ear effusion. Pediatr Infect Dis J 1996;15:1074–82.

52. Roark R, Berman S. Continuous twice daily or once daily amoxicillin prophylaxis compared with placebo for children with recurrent acute otitis media. Pediatr Infect Dis J 1997;16:376–81.

53. Gaskins JD, Holt RJ, Kyong CU, et al. Chemoprophylaxis of recurrent otitis media using trimethoprim/ sulfamethoxazole. Drug Intel Clin Pharm 1982;16:387–9.

54. Schuller DE. Prophylaxis of otitis media in asthmatic children. Pediatr Infect Dis 1983;2:280–3.

55. Perisco M, Podoshin L, Fradis M, et al. Recurrent acute otitis media—prophylactic penicillin treatment: a prospective study. Part I. Int J Pediatr Otorhinolaryngol 1985;10:37–46.

56. Prellner K, Foglé-Hansson M, Jørgensen F, et al. Prevention of recurrent acute otitis media in otitis-prone children by intermittent prophylaxis with penicillin. Acta Otolaryngol (Stockh) 1994;114:182–7.

57. Foglé-Hansson M, White P, Hermansson A, Prellner K. Short-term penicillin-V prophylaxis did not prevent acute otitis media in infants. Int J Pediatr Otorhinolaryngol 2001;59:119–23.

58. Teele DW, Klein JO, Work BM, et al. Antimicrobial prophylaxis for infants at risk for recurrent acute otitis media. Vaccine 2001;19 Suppl:S140–3.

59. Marks NJ, Mills RP, Shaheen OH. A controlled trial of cotrimoxazole therapy in serous otitis media. J Laryngol Otol 1981;95:1003–9.

60. Mandel EM, Rockette HE, Bluestone CD, et al. Efficacy of amoxicillin with and without decongestant-antihistamine for otitis media with effusion in children: results of a double-blind randomized trial. N Engl J Med 1987;316:432–7.

61. Schloss MD, Dempsey EE, Rishikof E, et al. Double blind study comparing erythromycin-sulfisoxazole (Pediazole) t.i.d. to placebo in chronic otitis media with effusion. In: Lim DJ, Bluestone CD, Klein JO, Nelson JD, editors. Proceedings of the Fourth International Symposium on Recent Advances in Otitis Media; 1987 June 1–4; Bal Harbour (FL). Toronto: BC Decker, 1988. p. 261–3.

62. Thomsen J, Sederberg-Olsen J, Balle V, et al. Antibiotic treatment of children with secretory otitis media: a randomized, double-blind, placebo-controlled study. Arch Otolaryngol Head Neck Surg 1989;115:447–51.

63. Møller P, Dingsør G. Otitis media with effusion: can erythromycin reduce the need for ventilating tubes? J Laryngol Otol 1990;140:200–2.

64. Podoshin L, Fradis M, Ben-David Y, Faraggi D. The efficacy of oral steroids in the treatment of persistent otitis media with effusion. Arch Otolaryngol Head Neck Surg 1990;116:1404–6.

65. Daly K, Giebink GS, Batalden PB, et al. Resolution of otitis media with effusion with the use of a stepped treatment regimen of trimethoprim-sulfamethoxazole and prednisone. Pediatr Infect Dis J 1991;10:500–6.

66. Mandel EM, Rockette HE, Paradise JL, et al. Comparative efficacy of erythromycin-sulfisoxazole, cefaclor, amoxicillin or placebo for otitis media with effusion in children. Pediatr Infect Dis J 1991;10:899–906.

67. van Balen FAM, de Melker RA, Touw-Otten FWMM. Double-blind randomised trial of co-amoxiclav versus placebo for persistent otitis media with effusion in general practice. Lancet 1996;348:713–6.

68. Healy GB. Antimicrobial therapy of chronic otitis media with effusion. Int J Pediatr Otorhinolaryngol 1984;8:13–7.

69. Ernstson S, Anari M. Cefaclor in the treatment of otitis media with effusion. Acta Otolaryngol (Stockh) 1985; Suppl 424:17–21.

70. Corwin MJ, Weiner LB, Daniels D. Efficacy of oral antibiotics for the treatment of persistent otitis media with effusion. Int J Pediatr Otorhinolaryngol 1986;11: 109–12.

71. Giebink GS, Batalden PB, Le CT, et al. A controlled trial comparing three treatments for chronic otitis media with effusion. Pediatr Infect Dis J 1990;9:33–40.

72. Sundberg L. Antibiotic treatment of secretory otitis media. Acta Otolaryngol (Stockh) 1984;Suppl 407:26–9.

73. deCastro FJ, Jaeger RW, Martin L, et al. Serous otitis media: a double-blind trial with sulfisoxazole. Mo Med 1982;79:629–30.

74. Schwartz RH, Rodriguez WJ. Trimethoprim-sulfamethoxazole treatment of persistent otitis media with effusion. Pediatr Infect Dis 1982;1:333–5.

75. Cantekin EI, McGuire TW, Griffith TL. Antimicrobial therapy for otitis media with effusion ('secretory' otitis media). JAMA 1991;266:3309–17.

76. Niederman LG, Walter-Bucholtz V, Jabalay T. A comparative trial of steroids versus placebos for treatment of chronic otitis media with effusion. In: Lim DJ, Bluestone CD, Klein JO, Nelson JD, editors. Proceedings of the 3rd International Symposium on Recent Advances in Otitis Media. Burlington (ON): BC Decker Inc; 1984. p. 273–5.

77. Macknin ML, Jones PK. Oral dexamethasone for treatment of persistent middle ear effusion. Pediatrics 1985;75:329–35.

78. Schwartz RH, Puglese J, Schwartz DM. Use of a short course of prednisone for treating middle ear effusion: a double-blind crossover study. Ann Otol Rhinol Laryngol 1980;89 Suppl 68:296–300.

79. Lambert PR. Oral steroid therapy for chronic middle ear effusion: a double-blind crossover study. Otolaryngol Head Neck Surg 1986;95:193–9.

80. Berman S, Grose K, Nuss R, et al. Management of chronic middle ear effusion with prednisone combined with trimethoprim-sulfamethoxazole. Pediatr Infect Dis J 1990;9:533–8.

81. Mandel EM, Casselbrant ML, Rockette HE, et al. Systemic steroid for chronic otitis media with effusion in children. Pediatrics; 2002;110:1071–80.

82. Perisco M, Podoshin L, Fradis M. Otitis media with effusion: a steroid and antibiotic therapeutic trial before surgery. Ann Otol 1987;87:191–5.

83. Rosenfeld RM. Nonsurgical management of surgical otitis media with effusion. J Laryngol Otol 1995;109:811–6.

84. Hemlin C, Carenfelt C, Papatziamos G. Single dose of betamethasone in combined medical treatment of secretory otitis media. Ann Otol Rhinol Laryngol 1997;106:359–63.

85. Haugeto OK, Schrøder, Mair IWS. Secretory otitis media, oral decongestant and antihistamine. J Otolaryngol 1981;10:359–62.

86. Cantekin EI, Mandel EM, Bluestone CD, et al. Lack of efficacy of a decongestant-antihistamine combination for otitis media with effusion ("secretory" otitis media) in children: results of a double-blind, randomized trial. N Engl J Med 1983;308:297–301.

87. Dusdieker LB, Smith G, Booth BM, et al. The long-term outcome of nonsuppurative otitis media with effusion. Clin Pediatr 1985;24:181–6.

88. deCastro FJ, Jaeger RW, Martin L, et al. Serous otitis media: a double-blind trial with sulfisoxazole. Mo Med 1982;79:629–30.

89. Schwartz RH, Rodriguez WJ. Trimethoprim-sulfamethoxazole treatment of persistent otitis media with effusion. Pediatr Infect Dis 1982;1:333–5.

90. O'Neill P. Acute otitis media. Clin Evid 2002;7:236–43.

91. Little R, Gould C, Williamson I, et al. Reattendance and complications in a randomized trial of prescribing strategies for sore throat: the medicalising effect of prescribing antibiotics. BMJ 1997;315:350–2.

92. Williamson I. Otitis media with effusion. Clin Evid 2002;7:469–76.

CHAPTER 14

Clinical Efficacy of Surgical Therapy

Richard M. Rosenfeld, MD, MPH, and Charles D. Bluestone, MD

The feasibility of an operation is not the best indication for its performance.
Henry, Lord Cohen of Birkenhead

A possible apprehension now is that the surgeon be sometimes tempted to supplant instead of aiding Nature.
Henry Maudsley

OBJECTIVES

On completing this chapter, the reader will be able to

1. Know the indications for surgery in patients with acute otitis media (AOM), recurrent AOM, or otitis media with effusion (OME), on the basis of the available evidence from randomized trials.
2. Learn when tympanocentesis is indicated in selected patients who have AOM.
3. Learn the role of myringotomy for AOM on the basis of the available clinical trials.
4. State the quantitative impact of tympanostomy tubes on AOM incidence and OME prevlance.
5. State the quantitative impact of adenoidectomy on AOM incidence, OME prevalence, and incidence of future tube insertion.
6. Use the best available published evidence to guide clinical decisions for or against surgery to treat and prevent otitis media (OM) in children.

EDITORIAL COMMENT

This chapter offers a somewhat myopic view of surgical therapy because it emphasizes objective outcomes: clinical resolution, AOM incidence, OME prevalence, and tube reoperation. Consequently, recommendations for surgery, which are driven more by values than objective evidence, are minimized. Surgical indications are fully discussed in the clinical pathways for AOM and OME (see Chapters 18 and 19, respectively), in which objective benefits are used to facilitate evidence-based decisions. We do not wish to imply that other surgical outcomes are unimportant (eg, hearing, speech, language, behavior, cognition, quality of life), but they are less useful in assessing efficacy because they are multifactorial and difficult to measure with adequate internal and external validity. These topics are thoroughly discussed in the chapters dealing with consequences and sequelae (see Chapters 22 through 25).

Increasing concerns over drug-resistant bacteria mandate that alternative methods of treatment and prevention, including surgery, be considered to reduce antibiotic usage for OM. There are many randomized control trials (RCTs) of various treatment options for AOM and OME. There is general agreement on some treatment algorithms but many unresolved issues remain. This confusion in using published studies to help select the best treatment is due to the limitations of the individual studies. Systematic review and meta-analysis (see Chapter 4, "Meta-analysis and Systematic Literature Review") may overcome some of these limitations.

In an attempted meta-analysis of surgical management of OME, Bodner and colleagues[1] found that fewer than 10% of the studies had adequate statistical analysis. Only one-third of studies specified the management strategies. A meta-analysis was not possible due to the variable and inconsistent entry criteria, outcome assessment, data presentation, blinding protocol, and statistical analysis. Similarly, a systematic review by the University of York[2] found extensive heterogeneity among RCTs of surgery for AOM and OME. They were unable to pool data but stated that tympanostomy tubes improved hearing up to 12 dB in three trials. More recently, Rosenfeld pooled data from seven RCTs to estimate the impact of surgery on AOM incidence and middle ear effusion (MEE) prevalence.[3]

In this chapter, we review and critique the currently available evidence for selecting operations, such as myringotomy, tympanostomy tube insertion, and adenoidectomy, in managing children recurrent AOM or chronic OME. Whenever possible, trial results are statistically combined using meta-analysis for quantitative estimates of effect size. We also present the evidence, and offer suggestions, for selecting patients with AOM who are most likely to benefit from tympanocentesis and myringotomy. Specific details of surgical technique are not discussed but may be readily found elsewhere.[4]

METHODS

Articles were selected with a combination of MEDLINE searches, review of book chapters, and discussions with experts in the field. The computerized MEDLINE searches ranged from 1966 to September 2002. The medical subject heading (MeSH) "otitis media" (exploded) and the keywords "otitis media" in the title, abstract, and registry word number were examined. This was combined with a similar search with MeSH terms "surgical therapy" and "randomized controlled trials," and the keywords "randomized controlled trials" in the title, abstract, and registry. Articles were included if the unit of analysis was patients and involved only children under the age of 18 years.

Indications for tympanocentesis and myringotomy were assessed by qualitative comparison because available studies are not suitable for statistical pooling. Conversely, surgical benefits for recurrent AOM and chronic OME were assessed through meta-analysis of parallel group RCTs comparing tympanostomy tubes or adenoidectomy versus no surgery for recurrent AOM or chronic OME. To maximize validity, we emphasized parallel group RCTs of surgery versus nonsurgical controls. Articles were excluded if the primary intervention was not effective for OM (eg, tonsillectomy or myringotomy alone), a nonsurgical comparison group was not included (eg, control subjects received myringotomy alone), or if the comparison used was the contralateral ear instead of a concurrent control group.

Primary outcomes for the meta-analyses were AOM incidence density (episodes per child-year) and MEE prevalence (days per child-year). Data from individual studies were combined (pooled) whenever results were available from two or more source articles for a particular endpoint and outcome time. Pooling was done using a random-effects model of meta-analysis, which assumes a population (distribution) of true effect sizes with each source article representing one member of this population.[5] Under this model, results are expected to vary from study to study, with differences caused by experimental error and differences in populations (between-study variability). Because of this additional variability, the 95% confidence interval (CI) for the pooled result is wider (less precise) than for a fixed-effect model.

Statistical analysis was performed using Comprehensive Meta-Analysis,[6] a computer program for research synthesis developed with funding from the National Institutes of Health. The program weights study results by the inverse of variance and calculates a random effects estimate of the combined effect and 95% CI. A test of heterogeneity is performed using the Q statistic to evaluate constancy of effect across strata. Significant heterogeneity exists if $p < .05$, although the test has low power and important variations may be present even with a nonsignificant result.[7] For this reason, the random effects model is used, regardless of the test of heterogeneity, although test results are still stated and explored.

Data are limited or conflicting in some of the following topics. For these topics, we present an analysis of the studies and present our opinion for optimal management.

ACUTE OTITIS MEDIA

Empiric treatment of AOM with antimicrobial agents is based on the presumption that the three major bacterial pathogens—*Streptococcus pneumoniae*, *Haemophilus influenzae*, and *Moraxella catarrhalis*—are most likely present.[8] However, these organisms may be resistant to standard therapy, such as amoxicillin, or there may be other bacterial pathogens present. Tympanocentesis, that is, diagnostic middle ear aspiration, is indicated in certain patients to determine the causative pathogen. Myringotomy to provide drainage of the middle ear is also required in some patients.

Tympanocentesis

About 70 to 90% of AOM episodes will improve clinically within 48 to 72 hours (see Chapter 13, "Clinical Efficacy of Medical Therapy). If signs and symptoms of infection progress despite initial antibiotic therapy, that is, treatment failure, the patient should be re-evaluated within 24 hours, since a suppurative complication or a concurrent serious infection (eg, an infant may have meningitis) may have developed. Persistent or recurrent otalgia, fever, or both, during treatment would also be a treatment failure. Effective management of a child who is a treatment failure should include tympanocentesis to obtain an aspirate of the middle ear effusion for Gram stain, culture, and susceptibility testing. Selection of another antibiotic at this stage would depend on the results of these tests.

With the emergence of antibiotic-resistant bacterial organisms causing OM, such as beta-lactamase–producing *H. influenzae*, *M. catarrhalis*, and now multidrug-resistant *Pneumococcus*, tympanocentesis is an increasingly important diagnostic procedure. RCTs that prove the effectiveness of this procedure are lacking, since the currently accepted indications for performing tympanocentesis would make a control group less than ethical. Lack of evidence notwithstanding, Table 14-1 lists our indications for performing tympanocentesis.[9] Also, with the current problem with resistant bacteria, routine aspiration of acute middle ear effusions in one or two pediatric practices in the community, to determine the prevalence of these bacteria, could be informative, since prevalence rates vary from community to community.

Table 14-1 Indications for Tympanocentesis*

1. OM in children who have severe otalgia, are seriously ill, or appear toxic

2. Unsatisfactory response to antimicrobial therapy

3. Onset of OM in a patient who is receiving antimicrobial therapy

4. OM associated with a confirmed or potential suppurative complication

5. OM in a newborn, sick neonate, or immunologically deficient patient, any of whom might harbor an unusual organism

OM = otitis media.
*Reproduced with permission from Bluestone CD and Klein JO.[9]

Myringotomy

Myringotomy is performed to drain the MEE, whereas tympanocentesis is used to identify the offending microbial pathogens. There have been several studies that have assessed the effect of routinely performing myringotomy in children with AOM (Table 14-2).[10–17] The outcomes of these trials do not provide convincing evidence that myringotomy (with or without antibiotic) provides any statistical advantage over antibiotic alone for either symptomatic relief or for earlier resolution of the MME in subjects with uncomplicated episodes of AOM.[18]

Only two published trials, by Puhakka and colleagues[13] and by Qvarnberg and Palva,[15] have shown statistically improved outcomes by adding myringotomy. These two studies, however, did not systematically document the characteristics of the patient population, provide inclusion or exclusion criteria, or describe the randomization procedure. Moreover, no uniform outcome measures were used. Without standardization in these areas, it is impossible to exclude bias as causing the significant results.

Two well-designed and executed clinical trials convincingly demonstrated no difference in outcome by adding myringotomy. Englehard and colleagues[16] randomized 105 Israeli children to receive amoxicillin-clavulanate, amoxicillin-clavulanate and myringotomy, or myringotomy and placebo. Both antibiotic groups were more effective than myringotomy without antibiotic, and there was no statistical advantage found by adding myringotomy to the antibiotic (Table 14-3). Kaleida and coworkers[17] found that children who had episodes of "severe" AOM, and who had been randomized to receive myringotomy with antibiotic, had similar outcomes to those children who had been randomized to receive only an antimicrobial agent (Table 14-4). Similar to the Israeli study, myringotomy without antibiotic had a worse outcome than either antibiotic group.

Several other studies have also found no benefit from adding myringotomy to antibiotic therapy as compared with antibiotic therapy alone.[19,20] These studies are not included because of vague inclusion criteria, concomitant topical therapy, and inconsistent diagnostic criteria. Nevertheless, myringotomy is indicated to relieve severe otalgia, when suppurative complications are present or suspected, or at any time a tympanocentesis is warranted (see Table 14-1).

RECURRENT ACUTE OTITIS MEDIA

Even though antimicrobial prophylaxis is efficacious for preventing AOM (see Chapter 13), the absolute benefit is small, and long-term therapy is associated with the resistant *Pneumococcus* in infants and young children; thus, preventing recurrent middle ear infections by surgery must also be an option.[21]

Myringotomy and Tympanostomy Tube

Five RCTs have shown tympanostomy tube insertion to be effective for preventing recurrent AOM in children with recurrent AOM or with baseline chronic OME.[22–26] Four of the five studies showed significantly fewer AOM episodes after tube placement (Table 14-5), with the largest impact observed for children with recurrent AOM, with or without OME at study entry. Random effects meta-analysis suggests a combined absolute reduction of 1.03 AOM episodes per child-year attributable to tubes (95% CI, .40, 1.66), but significant heterogeneity was noted among the studies ($p < .0001$). Using relative risk reduction as the outcome, tubes reduced the incidence of new AOM by 56% (95% CI, 17, 77). Efficacy was higher when limited to the first 6 months to 1 year after tube insertion (see Table 14-5).

The heterogeneity noted when combining the studies in Table 14-5 suggests a need for more in-depth analysis of individual source articles. Gebhart evaluated 95 otitis-prone infants and young children in Columbus, Ohio, who were randomized to tube insertion versus no surgery.[22] Tubes reduced AOM incidence by 3.01 episodes per child-year (95% CI, 2.18, 3.84), but

Table 14-2 Persistent Middle Ear Effusion Following Initial Myringotomy and Antimicrobial Therapy versus Antimicrobial Therapy Alone for Acute Otitis Media

First Author Year	Procedure	N	Persistent Middle Ear Effusion, %			p Value < .05?
			10–14 Days	4 Weeks	6 Weeks	
Roddey[10] 1966	Abx	121	35	7	2	No
	Abx-Mx	94	24	9	1	
Herberts[11] 1971	Abx	81	10	—	—	No
	Abx-Mx	91	18	—	—	
Lorentzen[12] 1977	Abx	190	16	6	—	No
	Abx-Mx	164	20	6	—	
Puhakka[13] 1978	Abx	90	78	29	—	Yes
	Abx-Mx	68	29	10	—	
Schwartz[14] 1980	Abx	361	47	—	—	No
	Abx-Mx	415	51	—	—	
Qvarnberg[15] 1980	Abx	151	50	—	—	Yes
	Abx-Mx	97	28	—	—	
Engelhard[16] 1989	Abx	55	40	—	—	No
	Abx-M	53	40	—	—	
Kaleida[17] 1991	Abx	167	61	—	56	No
	Abx-Mx	104	56	—	52	

Abx = antibiotic; Abx-Mx =antibiotic and myringotomy.
Reproduce with permission from Bluestone CD and Klein JO.[18]

Table 14-3 Outcomes after 105 Episodes of Acute Otitis Media in Israeli Children*

	Antibiotic Alone	Antibiotic and Myringotomy	Placebo and Myringotomy	p Value
Number of subjects				
Recovered, %	60	60	23	< .01
Persistent infection, %	7	17	70	< .001
Number of ears				
Recovered, %	64	65	31	< .001
Persistent infection, %	4	13	64	< .001
Middle ear effusion, %	31	23	6	> .05
Nonclosure of myringotomy, %	—	6	21	< .04
Otorrhea at myringotomy site, %	—	4	17	< .04

*Data from Engelhard D et al;[16] antibiotic was amoxicillin-clavulanate.

some children had MEE, and follow-up was limited to 6 months. Gonzalez and coworkers[23] enrolled 65 otitis-prone children in a multicenter study conducted in the United States Army. Similar to the Gebhart trial, children were entered with and without MEE, were not stratified, and were followed up for only 6 months. Tubes reduced overall AOM incidence by 2.27 episodes per child-year (95% CI, 1.03, 3.51), but attack rates were not reduced significantly for children without MEE at the time of randomization.

Table 14-4 Outcomes after 122 Episodes of Severe Acute Otitis Media in Pittsburgh Children*

	Antibiotic Alone	Antibiotic and Myringotomy	Placebo and Myringotomy	p *Value*
Initial treatment failure, %	4	3	24	.006
Effusion at 2 weeks, %	54	54	52	.37
Effusion at 6 weeks, %	63	55	35	.15
Recurrence at 2–6 weeks, %	32	31	17	.30

*Data from Kaleida PH et al;[17] antibiotic used was amoxicillin.

Table 14-5 Efficacy of Tympanostomy Tubes in Reducing AOM Incidence

First Author Year	Age Range	Entry Criteria[†]	Follow-up Time	AOM/Child-Year (n)[‡]		Rate Difference[‖] (95% CI)
				Tubes	No Surgery	
Gebhart[22] 1981	6 mo–3 yr	AOM 3/6 MEE allowed	6 mo	1.33 (54)	4.34 (41)	−3.01 (−3.84, −2.18)[§]
Gonzalez[23] 1986	6 mo–10 yr	AOM 3/6, 5/18 MEE allowed	6 mo	1.73 (22)	4.00 (20)	−2.27 (−3.51, −1.03)[§]
Casselbrant[24] 1992	7 mo–3 yr	AOM 3/6, 4/12 MEE excluded	2 yr	1.02 (77)	1.08 (80)	−.06 (−.28, .15)
Mandel[25] 1989	7 mo–12 yr	OME ≥ 2 mo	3 yr	.18 (30)	.38 (29)	−.20 (−.36, −.05)[§]
Mandel[26] 1992	7 mo–12 yr	OME ≥ 2 mo	1 yr	.23 (36)	.95 (35)	−.72 (−1.07, −.38)[§]
Combined, first 6 mo to 1 yr of follow-up only						−1.97 (−3.80, −.13)[§]
Combined, all studies*						−1.03 (−1.66, −.40)[§]

AOM = acute otitis media; MEE = middle ear effusion; OME = otitis media with effusion; RD = rate difference.
NB: All studies classify tube-related otorrhea as AOM except Mandel 1989 and Mandel 1992.
*Combined p = .001; test for heterogeneity Q = 62.60, df = 4, p < .0001.
[†]Baseline rate of recurrent AOM to enter study in episodes/month.
[‡]Rate of occurrence of AOM episodes per child-year of observation (number of subjects).
[§]p < .05 when the 95% CI does not contain zero.
[‖]Absolute change in AOM episodes per child-year; negative values favor tubes.

Casselbrant and colleagues[24] randomly assigned 264 Pittsburgh children, 7 to 35 months of age, with recurrent AOM but no MEE to amoxicillin prophylaxis (20 mg/kg/d in one dose at bedtime), myringotomy and tube insertion, or placebo (Table 14-6). Subjects were followed up monthly, and whenever an ear, nose, and throat illness intervened, for 2 years. Tubes did not reduce overall AOM incidence, but infections (eg, tube otorrhea) were usually asymptomatic. When time with OM of any type (ie, AOM, otorrhea, or OME) was evaluated, however, the tube group had only 6.6% prevalence (95% CI, 4.1, 9.2) compared with 10% (95% CI, 7.3, 12.7) for the amoxicillin group, 15.0%

(95% CI, 12.1, 17.9) for subjects who received placebo. The differences between the tube group and the amoxicillin and the placebo groups reflect 26 and 61 fewer days, respectively, with OM over 2 years.

The implications of counting tube otorrhea as an AOM episode deserves comment. Tube otorrhea is common but is generally benign and can be managed expectantly or with topical therapy alone.[27,28] Considering that most studies included tube otorrhea in AOM rates, the potential reduction in systemic antimicrobial use would, therefore, be greater than that suggested by a per episode analysis. Moreover, frequent use of oral antibiotics can induce bacterial resistance,

Table 14-6 Prophylaxis versus Tubes versus Placebo for Recurrent AOM in 264 Pittsburgh Children*

Outcome Measure	Group 1 Amoxicillin	Group 2 Placebo	Group 3 Tubes	p *Value Groups* 1 vs. 2	3 vs. 2	1 vs. 3
Incidence of AOM or otorrhea per child-year	0.60	1.08	1.02	< .001	NS	.001
Mean percent time with OM over 2 years	10.0	15.0	6.6	.03	< .001	NS
Median months to first episode AOM or otorrhea	22.1	8.2	11.2	.002	NS	—

AOM = acute otitis media; NS = not significant; OM = otitis media.
*Adapted from Casselbrant ML et al.[24]

Table 14-7 Efficacy of Adenoidectomy in Reducing AOM Incidence

First Author Year	Age Range	Entry Criteria[†]	Study Year	AOM/Child-Year (n)[‡] Adenoidectomy	Control	Rate Difference[∥] (95% CI)
Paradise[29] 1990	1–15 yr	Recurrent OM after prior tube extrusion	1	1.06 (48)	1.45 (38)	−.39 (−.84, .07)
			2	1.09 (45)	1.67 (27)	−.44 (−1.12, −.04)[§]
			3	0.89 (37)	0.87 (15)	.02 (−.52, 0.57)
			1–3*			−.32 (−.60, −.04)[§]
Paradise[31] 1999	3–15 yr	Recurrent AOM[#] without prior tubes	1	1.84 (61)	2.09 (79)	−.25 (−.68, .17)
			2	1.64 (53)	1.20 (59)	.44 (.02, .85)[§]
			3	1.29 (34)	1.45 (47)	−.15 (−.64, .34)
			1–3*			.04 (−.23, .29)

AOM = acute otitis media; MEE = middle ear effusion; OM = otitis media.
*Study years 1, 2, and 3 combined using fixed-effects meta-analysis.
[†]Baseline rate of recurrent AOM to enter study in episodes/month.
[‡]Rate of occurrence of AOM episodes per child-year of observation (number of subjects).
[§]$p < .05$ when the 95% CI does not contain zero.
[∥]Absolute change in AOM episodes per child-year; negative values favor adenoidectomy.
[#]Recurrent AOM (93% of study sample) defined as 3 in past 6 months or 4 in past 12 months; about 7% had persistent MEE only (180 days in past year).

but repetitive use of topical antibiotic drops has not been associated with similar problems because of the higher concentrations of active drug achieved by direct application to the middle ear.

Adenoidectomy

Paradise and coworkers[29] demonstrated a significant decrease in the attack rate of AOM in Pittsburgh children who received an adenoidectomy with tube placement (Table 14-7). The rate of recurrent AOM was not significantly decreased after 1 year, but it was after 2 years (−.44 episodes per child year, 95% CI, −1.12, −.04). Over the 2-year follow-up period, these children had over 31% less AOM (28% in the first year and 35% in the second year) and 42% less time with OM as compared with the control group. Adenoidectomy also decreased the need for tympanostomy tubes by 55%

in the first year and by 50% in the second year compared with controls.

Van Cauwenberge and colleagues[30] found a decrease in AOM per child-year of .39 episodes in the first year after adenoidectomy (1.75 episodes per child for the adenoidectomy group, 2.14 episodes per child for the control group). This corresponds to the effect size seen by Paradise and coworkers,[29] but, as with their results, the effect was not statistically significant.

Another RCT evaluated the efficacy of adenoidectomy or adenotonsillectomy for preventing recurrent AOM in children without prior tympanostomy tubes.[31] The design and method were similar to those described above in the previous trial conducted by the same research team, except that none of the subjects had previous tubes, and a third group was included (adenotonsillectomy). A total of 461 Pittsburgh children aged 3 to 15 years were enrolled in two parallel trials: 305 subjects enrolled (266 followed up) without recurrent throat infection or tonsillar hypertrophy (ie, three-way trial), and 157 subjects enrolled (144 followed up) who had such conditions were randomized to either adenotonsillectomy or control groups (ie, two-way trial). All subjects had had three or more AOM episodes in the prior 6 months or at least four in the prior 12 months, with at least one attack being of recent onset.

As shown in Table 14-7, there was no benefit of adenoidectomy on AOM incidence in any of the three trial years. There was, however, a statistically significant ($p = .03$) decrease of 22 mean days with OM in the first year attributable to adenoidectomy. The largest differences were observed in year 1 of the trial for adenotonsillectomy versus control (data not shown in Table 14-7): mean annual AOM episodes per child, 1.4 versus 2.1 ($p < .001$); and mean percentage of time with OM, 19% versus 30% ($p = .002$). In contrast to the earlier trial, there was no impact of surgery on future rates of tympanostomy tubes (very few children required additional surgery).

The above RCTs support adenoidectomy as a reasonable intervention for recurrent AOM following extrusion of tympanostomy tubes. In this population, adenoidectomy reduces OM incidence by about 33% and the need for subsequent tubes by about 50%. As a note of caution, adenoidectomy in infants should be recommended selectively (such as in those who also have severe nasal obstruction due to adenoid hyperplasia), because the operation carries some degree of increased risk in this age group. Conversely, the efficacy of adenoidectomy or adenotonsillectomy for recurrent AOM in children without prior tubes is short term and modest. Neither procedure is recommended as a first surgery for children who have not received a previous tube insertion and whose only indication for either operation is recurrent AOM.

OTITIS MEDIA WITH EFFUSION

Myringotomy, with tympanostomy tube placement, and adenoidectomy and myringotomy, with and without tube insertion, have been demonstrated to be effective in children with chronic effusions that had been unresponsive to a trial of antibiotics.

Myringotomy and Tympanostomy Tube

Three parallel group RCTs[25,26,32] have assessed the efficacy of tympanostomy tubes versus no surgery or myringotomy alone for persistent OME despite antimicrobial therapy. In all trials, tube insertion produced a clinically and statistically significant reduction in MEE

prevalence. Results of these studies, individually and in aggregate, are summarized in Tables 14-8 and 14-9 and discussed further below.

Gates and associates[32] randomly assigned children into one of four surgical treatment groups: (1) myringotomy, (2) myringotomy and tympanostomy tube insertion, (3) adenoidectomy and myringotomy, and (4) adenoidectomy and myringotomy and tympanostomy tube insertion. The study did not include a control group of no surgery, but all three of the other treatments did statistically better than myringotomy without tube placement. The prevalence of MEE for children randomized to tubes ($n = 129$) versus myringotomy alone ($n = 107$) was 35% versus 49%, resulting in 102 fewer days with effusion for intubated children during the 2-year follow-up ($p < .001$). Three children had persistent tympanic membrane (TM) perforation after tube extrusion, and three had tube displacement into the middle ear requiring repeat myringotomy for removal and insertion of a new tube.

Mandel and coworkers[25] randomly assigned 109 children with OME to receive one of three treatments: (1) myringotomy, (2) myringotomy and tympanostomy tube, or (3) no surgery (control). Children were randomized to no surgery only if they did not have otalgia, vertigo, or significant hearing loss (> 20 dB if bilateral OME, > 40 dB if unilateral OME). Myringotomy and tube placement provided more effusion-free time (see Tables 14-8 and 14-9) and better short-term hearing than either myringotomy without tube insertion, or no surgery. Two children developed persistent tube otorrhea, and one subject had persistent TM perforation after tube extrusion. Interpretation of the trial results, however, was rendered difficult by the short time until repeat surgery in some children and by the lack of uniform treatment failure criteria. Therefore, the protocol was revised and a second clinical trial was conducted.

Mandel and colleagues[26] subsequently randomized 111 children into the same groups: (1) myringotomy, (2) myringotomy and tympanostomy tube, and (3) no surgery (control). Similar outcomes were observed in this trial as were reported in the first study (see Tables 14-8 and 14-9). Patients who underwent myringotomy and tube placement had an overall 76% fewer episodes of AOM in the first year as compared with patients who had no surgery. Over the same period, they had 47% less time with MEE. These results are similar when comparing the efficacy of myringotomy and tube placement with that of only myringotomy for OME. Two children developed persistent tube otorrhea, and three subjects had persistent TM perforation after tube extrusion.

Tympanostomy tubes remain functional (patent) for a median of 12 to 14 months,[24–26] but myringotomy

Table 14-8 Efficacy of Tympanostomy Tubes versus No Surgery in Reducing MEE Prevalence

First Author Year	Age Range	Entry Criteria	Follow-up Time	Time with MEE (n)[‡]		Rate Difference[†] (95% CI)
				Tubes	No Surgery	
Mandel[25] 1989[ǁ]	7 mo–12 yr	OME ≥ 2 mo	1 yr	.16 (27)	.56 (18)	−.40 (−.66, −.13)[§]
Mandel[26] 1992	7 mo–12 yr	OME ≥ 2 mo	1 yr	.17 (36)	.64 (35)	−.47 (−.67, −.27)[§]
Combined*						−.44 (−.60, −.28)[§]

MEE = middle ear effusion; OME = otitis media with effusion.
*Combined p <.001; heterogeneity Q = .18, df = 1, p =.667.
[†]Absolute change in proportion of time with MEE during study; negative values favor tubes.
[‡]Mean proportion of time with MEE (AOM, OME, or otorrhea) and number of children (n).
[§]p < .05 when the 95% CI does not contain zero.
[ǁ]Excludes children with otalgia, vertigo, or hearing loss (> 20 dB if bilateral, > 40 dB if unilateral).

Table 14-9 Efficacy of Tympanostomy Tubes versus Myringotomy in Reducing MEE Prevalence

First Author Year	Age Range	Entry Criteria[†]	Follow-up Time	Time with MEE (n)[‡]		Rate Difference[†] (95% CI)
				Tubes	No Surgery	
Gates[32] 1987	4–8 yr	OME ≥ 2 mo	2 yr	.35 (129)	.49 (107)	−.14 (−.26, −.01)[§]
Mandel[25] 1989a[ǁ]	7 mo–12 yr	OME ≥ 2 mo	1 yr	.16 (27)	.57 (24)	−.40 (−.63, −.17)[§]
Mandel[25] 1989b[ǁ]	7 mo–12 yr	OME ≥ 2 mo	1 yr	.10 (10)	.57 (12)	−.47 (−.81, −.14)[§]
Mandel[26] 1992	7 mo–12 yr	OME ≥ 2 mo	1 yr	.17 (36)	.61 (38)	−.44 (−.64, −.24)[§]
Combined, first year of follow-up only					−.44 (−.57, −.30)[§]	
Combined, all studies*						−.35 (−.55, −.14)[§]

MEE = middle ear effusion; OME = otitis media with effusion.
*Combined p = .001; heterogeneity Q = 10.07, df = 3, p = .018.
[†]Absolute change in proportion of time with MEE during study; negative values favor tubes.
[‡]Mean proportion of time with MEE (AOM, OME, or otorrhea) and number of children (n).
[§]p < .05 when the 95% CI does not contain zero.
[ǁ]Mandel 1989a only asymptomatic OME; Mandel 1989b only symptomatic OME defined as OME with otalgia, vertigo, hearing levels > 20 dB if bilateral, or hearing levels > 40 dB if unilateral.

alone offers only several days of middle ear ventilation. Myringotomy patency can be extended to several weeks by using a laser, prompting some investigators to suggest that laser-assisted myringotomy (LAM) may obviate a need for tube placement.[33–38] There are no RCTs, however, to support this theory, and methodologically sound RCTs of traditional myringotomy (see Table 14-9) show a conclusive lack of benefit versus tube insertion. Conversely, existing studies of LAM have inconsistent inclusion criteria, limited and incomplete follow-up, and use historic (external) controls instead of randomized parallel groups. Although the efficacy of LAM for chronic OME is unproven, the procedure is feasible in an office setting and costs less than myringotomy performed under a general anesthetic.[39,40]

Tympanostomy tubes for persistent OME reduce relative AOM incidence and MEE prevalence by about 50 to 75% in the year following tube placement compared with no surgery (see Tables 14-5 and 14-8). The absolute prevalence of MEE decreases by 44% (95% CI, 28, 60), which equates to 161 MEE days (95% CI, 102, 219). Mean hearing levels improve by up to 12 dB at 6 months but diminish over time.[2] In deciding for or against intubation, clinicians and parents must determine whether benefits of this magnitude exceed the risks of tube insertion (see Chapter 29, "Tympanostomy Tube Care and Consequences"). Modifying factors in this decision include effusion chronicity, likelihood of spontaneous resolution, associated symptoms (otalgia, vertigo, recurrent AOM), hearing levels, and, most importantly, the individual child's characteristics (intelligence, behavior, development).

The existing evidence *does not* support myringotomy alone, either traditional or laser-assisted, as effective for OME. Laser-assisted myringotomy should be considered experimental and of uncertain benefit (and risk).

Adenoidectomy and Tonsillectomy

Adenoidectomy and myringotomy, with or without tube placement, have been shown to be effective for chronic OME in several clinical trials. Most of the studies, however, are not of high quality and use inconsistent outcome measures. Bulman and colleagues[41] primarily used audiometric outcomes, which do not always correlate with MEE prevalence. Roydhouse[42] and Black and colleagues[43] both used individual ears as the unit of analysis, with neither study having a control group with no surgery. Dempster and coworkers[44] also analyzed ears without nonsurgical controls. Widemar and associates[45] used patients as the unit of analysis, but they also did not have a nonsurgical control group.

Studies by Maw and Parker[46,47] show efficacy of adenoidectomy, but not tonsillectomy, for chronic OME. We excluded these studies, however, because the unit of analysis was the ear, and there were no independent (parallel) comparison groups. Further, the data were presented graphically, making it difficult to quantify the differences in treatment versus control ears at the marked time intervals. Maw and Bawden[48] later reported up to 12-year follow-up of these children, suggesting sustained

efficacy (by ear) of adenoidectomy, including less need for future tube insertion. However, the patients who had tonsillectomy and adenoidectomy were combined with the adenoidectomy patients, and the indications for repeat tubes were unclear (including OME in contralateral unoperated ear).

Three well-designed and executed studies have shown the efficacy of adenoidectomy for OME (Tables 14-10 and 14-11). Gates and colleagues[32] followed up children aged 4 to 8 years with chronic OME for 2 years, and found 19% less MEE (absolute RD) after adenoidectomy and 49% less future surgery. Paradise and coworkers[29] studied children aged 1 to 15 years with recurrent OM after prior tubes and reported significantly less MEE after adenoidectomy in years 1 and 2 of follow-up (24% and 11%, respectively). Tube insertions were not significantly reduced in any single study year (see Table 14-11) but were significantly reduced (12%) for all years combined. Paradise and colleagues[31] later studied children aged 3 to 15 years with recurrent AOM or chronic OME *without* prior tubes, finding only limited and short-term efficacy of adenoidectomy. For example, future tube insertion was significantly reduced for all 3 study years combined (see Table 14-11), but the magnitude of effect (6%) was almost trivial.

There are important differences in the design of the studies in Tables 14-10 and 14-11 that preclude statistical pooling of results with meta-analysis. All studies have subjects with different age ranges and inclusion criteria. Moreover, the interventions varied greatly. Gates and colleagues[32] compared adenoidectomy plus

Table 14-10 Efficacy of Adenoidectomy in Reducing MEE Prevalence

First Author Year	Age Range	Entry Criteria[†]	Study Year	Time with MEE (n)[‡]		Rate Difference[‖] (95% CI)
				Adenoidectomy	Control	
Gates[32] 1987	4–8 yr	OME ≥ 2 mo	1–2	.30 (130)	.49 (107)	−.19 (−.31, −.07)[§]
Paradise[29] 1990	1–15 yr	Recurrent OM after prior tube extrusion	1	.15 (48)	.29 (38)	−.14 (−.26, −.02)[§]
			2	.18 (45)	.28 (27)	−.11 (−.19, −.03)[§]
			3	.15 (37)	.17 (15)	−.02 (−.14, .10)
			1–3*			−.09 (−.16, −.03)[§]
Paradise[31] 1999	3–15 yr	Recurrent AOM[#] without prior tubes	1	.22 (16)	.30 (79)	−.08 (−.15, 0)
			2	.20 (53)	.20 (59)	.00 (−.08, .07)
			3	.19 (34)	.17 (47)	.03 (−.06, .12)

AOM = acute otitis media; MEE = middle ear effusion; OM = otitis media; OME = otitis media with effusion.

*Study years 1, 2, and 3 combined using fixed-effects meta-analysis.

[†]Baseline rate of recurrent AOM to enter study in episodes/month.

[‡]Mean proportion of days with MEE (number of subjects).

[§]$p < .05$ when the 95% CI does not contain zero.

[‖]Absolute change in MEE prevalence; negative values favor adenoidectomy.

[#]Recurrent AOM (93% of study sample) defined as 3 in past 6 months or 4 in past 12 months; about 7% had persistent MEE only (180 days in past year).

Table 14-11 Efficacy of Adenoidectomy in Reducing Need for Subsequent Tympanostomy Tubes

First Author Year	Age Range	Entry Criteria[†]	Study Year	Tube Insertions/Child (n)[‡] Adenoidectomy	Control	Rate Difference[‖] (95% CI)
Gates[32] 1987	4–8 yr	OME ≥ 2 mo	1–2	.13 (130)	.62 (107)	−.49 (−.60, −.38)[§]
Paradise[29] 1990	1–15 yr	Recurrent OM after prior tube extrusion	1	.13 (48)	.29 (38)	−.16 (−.34, .01)
			2	.13 (45)	.26 (27)	−.13 (−.32, .07)
			3	.08 (37)	.13 (15)	−.05 (−.25, .14)
			1–3*			−.12 (−.23, −.01)[§]
Paradise[31] 1999	3–15 yr	Recurrent AOM[#] without prior tubes	1	.03 (61)	.10 (79)	−.07 (−.15, .01)
			2	.02 (53)	.07 (59)	−.05 (−.12, .03)
			3	.00 (34)	.06 (47)	−.06 (−.14, .03)
			1–3*			−.06 (−.10, −.01)[§]

AOM = acute otitis media; MEE = middle ear effusion; OM = otitis media; OME = otitis media with effusion.

*Study years 1, 2, and 3 combined using fixed-effects meta-analysis.

[†]Baseline rate of recurrent AOM to enter study in episodes/month.

[‡]Tube insertions per child after study entry (number of subjects).

[§]$p < .05$ when the 95% CI does not contain zero.

[‖]Absolute change in tube insertions per child; negative values favor adenoidectomy.

[#]Recurrent AOM (93% of study sample) defined as 3 in past 6 months or 4 in past 12 months; about 7% had persistent MEE only (180 days in past year).

myringotomy versus myringotomy alone (data reported in Tables 14-10 and 14-11) but also had parallel groups comparing adenoidectomy plus tubes versus tubes alone (data not shown). In the first study by Paradise and colleagues,[29] children were made "effusion free" at the time of adenoidectomy by inserting tubes for baseline OME (71% of adenoidectomy group, 66% of control group). In the later study,[31] children with baseline OME instead received myringotomy alone (63% of adenoidectomy group, 50% of control group).

The above RCTs suggest that adenoidectomy (with myringotomy) is efficacious as first-line surgery for children aged 4 to 8 years with chronic OME and as second-line surgery for children aged 3 years or older with OM relapse after prior tube extrusion (Paradise and colleagues[29] performed adenoidectomy on only one child below age 2 years, but 31% were aged 3 to 4 years). Benefits include a moderate reduction in MEE prevalence (about 50 to 70 days per year for 2 years) and at least a 50% relative reduction in subsequent need for tube surgery. Conversely, adenoidectomy is not appropriate as a first surgical intervention in children whose only indication is recurrent AOM (without chronic OME).[31]

Adenoid size is unrelated to outcomes, suggesting that the beneficial effect on OM is more related to eliminating a bacterial reservoir than to reducing Eustachian tube obstruction. Therefore, adenoidectomy *should not* be limited only to children with hyperplastic tissue or overt signs of nasal airway obstruction. Tonsillectomy does not improve outcomes beyond adenoidectomy alone and is not recommended for primary or secondary therapy of OME. [29,30,47]

ADVERSE EFFECTS OF SURGERY

Anesthesia mortality is about 1:50,000 for ambulatory surgery,[49] but the current fatality rate is estimated as 1:250,000.[50] Laryngospasm and bronchospasm occur more often in children receiving anesthesia than in adults. Tympanostomy tube sequelae are common but are generally transient (otorrhea) or cosmetic (tympanosclerosis, focal atrophy, or shallow retraction pocket).[51] Tympanic membrane perforations, which may require repair, are seen in 2.2% of children after short-term (grommet-type) tubes and 16.6% after long-term (t-type) tubes. Sequelae of tubes are discussed in detail in Chapter 29. Adenoidectomy has a 0.2% incidence of hemorrhage[52] and a 2.4% incidence of transient velopharyngeal insufficiency.[29] Other potential risks, such as nasopharyngeal stenosis and persistent velopharyngeal insufficiency, are extremely rare and can be minimized with appropriate patient selection and surgical technique.

CLINICAL IMPLICATIONS

Table 14-12 summarizes what to expect from tympanostomy tubes and adenoidectomy on the basis of random effects meta-analysis of parallel group RCTs. The tympanostomy tube results (first three rows) are derived from pooling between two and five studies, but the adenoidectomy results (last five rows) are based on single studies. For the data abstracted from Paradise and colleagues,[29,31] however, data from each study year are combined using fixed effects meta-analysis to estimate the overall impact over a 3-year time period. Although significant heterogeneity is present in most of the analyses, the summary estimates, nonetheless, provide clinically useful estimates of effect size to guide evidence-based management. RCTs with paired organ controls (different treatment by ear) provide additional information but are excluded because of methodologic concerns and difficulties in interpretation.

Tympanostomy tubes significantly reduce AOM incidence and MEE prevalence (see Table 14-12). The

absolute decrease (RD) of about 1.0 AOM episode per child-year doubles to 2.0 AOM episode per child-year when confined to the usual period of tube patency (6 months to 1 year). On a relative risk (RR) basis, each child with tubes has only 33% the incidence of AOM as do nonintubated controls (95% CI, 25 to 44%). Further, children with tubes have 44% less absolute time (161 days) with MEE during the first year of intubation than do children with no tubes or myringotomy (95% CI, 102 to 219 days). The RR of .28 indicates 72% less overall time with MEE (95% CI, 50 to 84%). Myringotomy alone is ineffective for OME.

Adenoidectomy offers more modest absolute reductions in AOM incidence and MEE prevalence than tympanostomy tubes (see Table 14-12), but on a relative basis, the reductions are still clinically important (26 to 39%). The main benefit of adenoidectomy is to significantly reduce the chance of future tube insertions. About two children (95% CI, 1 to 3) aged 4 to 8 years with chronic OME need adenoidectomy to prevent one future tube insertion (NNT), corresponding to a rela-

Table 14-12 Summary of What to Expect from Surgery for OM Based on Parallel Group RCTs

Clinical Situation and Outcome	Time	N[†]	RD[∥] (95% CI)	RR[‡] (95% CI)[∥]
Tube vs. no tube for RAOM or OME ≥ 2 mo: AOM/child–year (see Table 14-5)	6 mo–3 yr	5	−1.03 (−1.66, −.40)[§]	.44 (.23, .83)[§]
	6 mo–1 yr	3	−1.97 (−3.80, −.13)[§]	.33 (.25, .44)[§]
Tube vs. no tube for OME ≥ 2 mo: MEE prevalence (see Table 14-8)	1 yr	2	−.44 (−.60, −.28)[§]	.28 (.16, .50)[§]
Tube vs. myringotomy for OME ≥ 2 mo: MEE prevalence (see Table 14-9)	1–2 yr	3	−.35 (−.55, −.14)[§]	.38 (.18, .79)[§]
	1 yr	2	−.44 (−.57, −.30)[§]	.27 (.16, .47)[§]
Adenoidectomy vs. control for any OM after tube extrusion: AOM/child-year (see Table 14-7)	3 yr	*1	−.32 (−.60, −.04)[§]	.74 (.58, .94)[§]
Adenoidectomy vs. control for any OM after tube extrusion: MEE prevalence (see Table 14-10)	3 yr	*1	−.09 (−.16, −.03)[§]	.62 (.45, .84)[§]
Adenoidectomy-Mx vs. Mx alone for OME ≥ 2 mo: MEE prevalence (see Table 14-10)	2 yr	1	−.19 (−.31, −.07)[§]	.61 (.44, .85)[§]
Adenoidectomy vs. control for any OM after tube extrusion: future tubes/child (see Table 14-11)	3 yr	*1	−.12 (−.23, −.01)[§]	.48 (.26, .90)[§]
Adenoidectomy-Mx vs. Mx alone for OME ≥ 2 mo: future tubes/child (see Table 14-11)	2 yr	1	−.49 (−.60, −.38)[§]	.21 (.13, .34)[§]

AOM = acute otitis media; CI = confidence interval; MEE = middle ear effusion; Mx = myringotomy; OM = otitis media; OME = otitis media with effusion; RAOM = recurrent AOM; RCT = randomized controlled trial; RD = absolute rate difference; RR = relative risk.
*Study years 1, 2, and 3 combined using fixed-effects meta-analysis.
[†]Number of studies from which data were combined to derive the overall treatment effect.
[‡]Relative risk for outcome for surgery vs. control groups; values less than unity favor surgery.
[§]$p < .05$ when the RD 95% CI does not contain zero or the RR 95% CI does not contain unity.
[∥]Absolute change in outcome for surgery vs. control groups; negative values favor surgery.

Table 14-13 Pointers and Pitfalls

1. Well-designed and conducted RCTs are available of clinically relevant outcomes for OM; these studies compare patients (not ears) with nonsurgical controls, have clear diagnostic and outcome criteria, and have adequate patient follow-up.

2. Tympanocentesis is appropriate for diagnosing unusual or resistant middle ear pathogens in select children (see Table 14–1); conversely, therapeutic efficacy for tympanocentesis is unproven.

3. Myringotomy is appropriate for AOM with severe otalgia, suppurative complications, or as an adjunct to tympanocentesis; myringotomy does not hasten resolution of MEE or clinical symptoms for children with uncomplicated AOM.

4. Surgical treatment of recurrent AOM avoids prolonged or repetitive courses of antibiotics, which may induce bacterial resistance. Children with tympanostomy tubes avoid 2.0 AOM episodes/child-year, have 67% less AOM than controls, and can generally be managed with topical (not systemic) antimicrobials. When performed after tube extrusion, adenoidectomy reduces relative AOM incidence by 26% over the next 3 years and relative MEE prevalence by 38%.

5. Surgical treatment of chronic OME reduces MEE prevalence and AOM incidence. Children with tympanostomy tubes have 161 fewer days with effusion during the first year of intubation, a relative decrease of 72% versus no surgery or myringotomy alone. Adenoidectomy plus myringotomy as primary therapy in children age 4 years or older reduces MEE prevalence by 139 days over 2 years versus myringotomy alone.

6. Adenoidectomy significantly reduces the chance of future tube insertions for children age 4 years or older with chronic OME (79% relative decrease) and for children age 2 years or older with recurrent OM after tube extrusion (relative decrease of 52%). The benefits of adenoidectomy are independent of adenoid size.

7. Tonsillectomy is ineffective for OM and not recommended as primary or secondary therapy, unless other compelling reasons exist (severe recurrent throat infection, severe obstruction).

8. Multiple or prolonged course of antimicrobial agents should not be administered in an effort to prevent surgery. Judicious surgery for recurrent AOM or chronic OME can reduce AOM incidence, antibiotic burden, prevalence, and lessen the need for future tube insertions.

AOM = acute otitis media; MEE = middle ear effusion; OM = otitis media; OME = otitis media with effusion; RCT = randomized controlled trial.

tive decrease of 79% (RR .21). The NNT for children aged 2 years with recurrent OM after tube extrusion is 8 (95% CI, 4 to 91), with a relative decrease of 52% (RR .48). Approximately the same results (RR .50, $p < .001$) were found in a records-based review of 37,000 Canadian children.[53] Adenoidectomy is not recommended as initial surgery for recurrent AOM in children without prior tubes because of limited and short-term efficacy.

Results of RCTs are generalizable to a broad range of children, but care must be taken to ensure that target children are comparable with those studied. Consequently, all tables include brief descriptions of entry criteria, child age, and study duration. In particular, adenoidectomy results have limited generalizability below age 4 years because only two studies[29,31] included this age range and the one[29] showing efficacy enrolled only 16 children aged 3 to 4 years in the surgical group. A records-based study found adenoidectomy benefits to be age related, apparent at age 2 years but greatest for children aged 3 years or older.[53] Further restrictions in generalizability arise because most

studies excluded children with syndromes, cleft palate, immune deficiency, or structural changes of the TM, and some considered it unethical to include children with "significant" hearing loss or developmental delays.

Surgical management of patients with OM is going through a period of re-evaluation because of several factors, including (1) the steadily increasing incidence of the disease calling for methods of prevention; (2) the dramatic emergence of multidrug-resistant bacterial pathogens, which makes judicious use of antibiotics imperative; and (3) the growing financial impact in today's cost-conscious climate. Despite the heterogeneity of existing evidence, enough RCTs are available to estimate the impact of surgery on objective outcomes (AOM incidence, MEE prevalence, future tube insertion) and to identify interventions that are ineffective (myringotomy, tonsillectomy) or unproven (laser-assisted myringotomy). The quantitative estimates of surgical efficacy in this chapter (see Tables 14-12 and 14-13) should facilitate evidence-based decisions for or against surgery on an individualized basis.

REFERENCES

1. Bodner EE, Browning GG, Chalmers FT, Chalmers TC. Can meta-analysis help uncertainty in surgery for otitis media in children. J Laryngol Otol 1991;105:812–9.

2. University of York. Centre for Reviews and Dissemination. The treatment of persistent glue ear in children. Effect Health Care 1992;1(4):1–16.

3. Rosenfeld RM. Surgical prevention of otitis media. Vaccine 2001;19:S134–9.

4. Bluestone CD, Rosenfeld RM. Surgical atlas of pediatric otolaryngology. Hamilton (ON): BC Decker; 2002.

5. DerSimonian R, Laird N. Meta-analysis in clinical trials. Control Clin Trials 1986;17:177–88.

6. Borenstein M, Rothstein H. Comprehensive Meta-Analysis: a computer program for research synthesis (v. 1.0.25). Englewood (NJ): Biostat Inc; 2000.

7. Sutton AJ, Abrams KR, Jones DR. An illustrated guide to the methods of meta-analysis. J Eval Clin Pract 2001; 7:135–48.

8. Bluestone CD, Stephenson JS, Martin LM. Ten-year review of otitis media pathogens. Pediatr Infect Dis J 1992;8:S7–11.

9. Bluestone CD, Klein JO. Otitis media in infants and children. 2nd ed. Philadelphia (PA): WB Saunders; 1995. p. 145–240.

10. Roddey OF, Earle R, Haggerty R. Myringotomy in acute otitis media. JAMA 1966;197(11):849–53.

11. Herberts G, Jeppsson PH, Nylen O, Branefors-Helander P. Acute otitis media: etiological and therapeutical aspects on acute otitis media. Pract Oto Rhino Laryngol 1971;33:191–202.

12. Lorentzen P, Haugsten P. Treatment of acute suppurative otitis media. J Larynol Otol 1977;91(4):331–40.

13. Puhakka H, Virolainen E, Aantaa E, et al. Myringotomy in the treatment of acute otitis media in children. Duodecim 1978;94:850–5.

14. Schwartz RH, Schwartz DM. Acute otitis media: diagnosis and drug therapy. Drugs 1980;19:107–18.

15. Qvarnberg Y, Palva T. Active and conservative treatment of acute otitis media: prospective studies. Ann Otol Rhinol Laryngol 1980;S3:269–70.

16. Engelhard D, Cohen D, Strauss N, et al. Randomised study of myringotomy amoxycillin/clavulanate or both for acute otitis media in infants. Lancet 1989;5:141–3.

17. Kaleida PH, Casselbrant ML, Rockette HE, et al. Amoxicillin or myringotomy or both for acute otitis media: results of a randomized clinical trial. Pediatrics 1991;87:466–74.

18. Bluestone CD, Klein JO. Otitis media, atelectasis and eustachian tube dysfunction. In Bluestone CD, Stool SE, Kenna MA, editors. Pediatric otolaryngology. 3rd ed. Philadelphia (PA): WB Saunders; 1996. p. 388–582.

19. Roddey OF, Earle R, Haggerty R. Myringotomy in acute otitis media. JAMA 1966;197(11):849–53.

20. Herberts G, Jeppsson PH, Nylen O, Branefors-Helander P. Acute otitis media: etiological and therapeutical aspects on acute otitis media. Pract Oto Rhino Laryngol 1971;33:191–202.

21. Guillemot D, Carbon C, Balkau B, et al. Low dosage and long treatment duration of beta-lactam: risk factors for carriage of penicillin-resistant *Streptococcus pneumoniae*. JAMA 1998;279:365–70.

22. Gebhart DE. Tympanostomy tubes in the otitis media prone child. Laryngoscope 1981;91:849–66.

23. Gonzalez C, Arnold JE, Woody EA, et al. Prevention of recurrent acute otitis media: chemoprophylaxis versus tympanostomy tubes. Laryngoscope 1986;96:1330–4.

24. Casselbrant ML, Kaleida PH, Rockette HE, et al. Efficacy of antimicrobial prophylaxis and of tympanostomy tube insertion for prevention of recurrent acute otitis media: results of a randomized clinical trial. Pediatr Infect Dis J 1992;11:278–86.

25. Mandel EM, Rockette HE, Bluestone CD, et al. Myringotomy with and without tympanostomy tubes for chronic otitis media with effusion. Arch Otolaryngol Head Neck Surg 1989;115:1217–24.

26. Mandel EM, Rockette HE, Bluestone CD, et al. Efficacy of myringotomy with and without tympanostomy tubes for chronic otitis media with effusion. Pediatr Infect Dis J 1992;11:270–7.

27. Goldblatt EL, Dohar J, Nozza RJ, et al. Topical ofloxacin versus systemic amoxicillin/clavulanate in purulent otorrhea in children with tympanostomy tubes. Int J Pediatr Otorhinolaryngol 1998;46:91–101.

28. Dohar JE, Garner ET, Nielsen RW, et al. Topical ofloxacin treatment of otorrhea in children with tympanostomy tubes. Arch Otolaryngol Head Neck Surg 1999;125:537–45.

29. Paradise JL, Bluestone CD, Rogers KD, et al. Efficacy of adenoidectomy for recurrent otitis media in children previously treated with tympanostomy-tube placement: results of parallel randomized and nonrandomized trials. JAMA 1990;263:2066–73.

30. Van Cauwenberge PB, Bellusi L, Maw AR, et al. The adenoid as a key factor in upper airway infections. Int J Pediatr Otorhinolaryngol 1995;32:S71–80.

31. Paradise JL, Bluestone CD, Colborn DK, et al. Adenoidectomy and adenotonsillectomy for recurrent acute otitis media: parallel randomized clinical trials in children not previously treated with tympanostomy tubes. JAMA 1999;282:945–53.

32. Gates GA, Avery CS, Prihoda TJ, Cooper JC Jr. Effectiveness of adenoidectomy and tympanostomy tubes in the treatment of chronic otitis media with effusion. N Engl J Med 1987;317:1444–51.

33. Siegel G, Brodsky L, Waner M, et al. Office based laser assisted tympanic membrane fenestration in adults and children: pilot data to support an alternative to traditional approaches to otitis media. Int J Pediatr Otorhinolaryngol 2000;53:111–20.

34. Brodsky L, Cook S, Deutsch E, et al. Optimizing effectiveness of laser tympanic membrane fenestration in chronic otitis media with effusion: clinical and technical considerations. Int J Pediatr Otorhinolaryngol 2001;58: 59–64.

35. Cohen D, Sheckter Y, Slatkin M, et al. Laser myringotomy in different age groups. Arch Otolaryngol Head Neck Surg 2001;127:260–4.

36. Cook SP, Brodsky L, Reilly J, et al. Effectiveness of adenoidectomy and laser tympanic membrane fenestration. Laryngoscope 2001;111:251–4.

37. Garin P, Ledeghen S, Van Prooyen-Keyser V, Remacle M. Office-based CO_2 laser-assisted tympanic membrane fenestration addressing otitis media with effusion. J Clin Laser Med Surg 2001;19:185–7.

38. Silverstein H, Jackson LE, Rosenberg SI, Conlon WS. Pediatric laser-assisted tympanostomy. Laryngoscope 2001;111:905–6.

39. Brodsky L, Brookhauser P, Chait D, et al. Office-based insertion of pressure equalizing tubes: the role laser-assisted tympanic membrane fenestration. Laryngoscope 1999;109:2009–14.

40. Friedman O, Deutsch ES, Reilly JS, Cook SP. The feasibility of office-based laser-assisted tympanic fenestration with tympanostomy tube insertion: the DuPont Hospital experience. Int J Pediatr Otolaryngol 2002; 62:31–5.

41. Bulman CH, Brook SJ, Berry MG. A prospective randomized trial of adenoidectomy versus grommet insertion in the treatment of glue ear. Clin Otolaryngol 1984;9:67–75.

42. Roydhouse N. Adenoidectomy for otitis media with mucoid effusion. Ann Otol Rhinol Laryngol 1980; S89:312–5.

43. Black NA, Sanderson CFB, Freeland AP, Vessey MP. A randomised controlled trial of surgery for glue ear. BMJ 1990;300:1551–6.

44. Dempster JH, Browning GG, Gatehouse SG. A randomized study of the surgical management of children with persistent otitis media with effusion associated with a hearing impairment. J Laryngol Otol 1993;107:284–9.

45. Widemar L, Svensson C, Rynnel-Dagoo B, Schiratzki H. The effect of adenoidectomy on secretory otitis media: a 2 year controlled prospective study. Clin Otolaryngol 1985;10:345–50.

46. Maw AR. Chronic otitis media with effusion and adeno-tonsillectomy: a prospective randomized controlled study. Int J Pediatr Otorhinolaryngol 1983;6:239–46.

47. Maw AR, Parker A. Surgery of the tonsils and adenoids in relation to secretory otitis media in children. Acta Otolaryngol 1988;454:202–7.

48. Maw R, Bawden R. Spontaneous resolution of severe chronic glue ear in children and the effect of adenoidectomy, tonsillectomy and insertion of ventilation tubes (grommets). BMJ 1993;306(6880):756–60.

49. Holzman RS. Morbidity and mortality in pediatric anesthesia. Pediatr Clin North Am 1994;41:239–56.

50. Cotrell JE, Golden S. Under the mask: a guide to feeling secure and comfortable during anesthesia and surgery. New Brunswick (NJ): Rutgers University Press; 2001.

51. Kay DJ, Nelson M, Rosenfeld RM. Meta-analysis of tympanostomy tube sequelae. Otolaryngol Head Neck Surg 2001;124:374–80.

52. Crysdale WS, Russel D. Complications of tonsillectomy and adenoidectomy in 9409 children observed overnight. CMAJ 1986;135:1139–42.

53. Coyte PC, Croxford R, McIsaac W, et al. The role of adjuvant adenoidectomy and tonsillectomy in the outcome of insertion of tympanostomy tubes. New Engl J Med 2001;344:1188–95.

Clinical Effectiveness of Complementary and Alternative Therapies

Jennifer Jacobs, MD, MPH, Janet L. Levatin, MD, and Cora Collette Breuner, MD, MPH

*Sometimes a normal problem, one that ought to be resolvable by known rules and procedures,
resists the reiterated onslaught of the ablest members of the group within whose competence it falls...
Then begin the extraordinary investigations that lead the profession at last to a new set of
commitments, a new basis for the practice of science.*

T.S. Kuhn

OBJECTIVES

On completing this chapter, the reader will be able to

1. Understand the extent to which consumers and physicians are using complementary and alternative medical (CAM) therapies and the extent of this use in children.
2. Know for which CAM modalities there has been research in the treatment of otitis media (OM) and related conditions, and understand, in brief, the theoretic bases of these therapies.
3. Understand the limitations of the existing research on CAM modalities of OM.
4. Feel competent discussing with parents the relative risks and benefits of using various complementary and alternative therapies for their children with OM.

The field of CAM is broad and diverse, comprising numerous therapeutic modalities.[1,2] Research supporting the use of CAM in treating OM and related conditions is limited. There are a number of good reasons, however, for conventional physicians to learn about CAM practices and products and to develop collegial relationships with competent CAM practitioners in their areas. As used in this chapter, the word "physicians" applies not only to physicians but also to other primary care providers, such as nurse practitioners and physician assistants. Some physicians may want to take the further step of studying selected CAM modalities and including them directly in their practices.

One important reason for physicians to learn about CAM therapies is that consumers are seeking and using these forms of treatment (see the following section). Many consumers view CAM as an adjunct or complement to conventional treatment. There also are a significant number of people who rely primarily on CAM therapies (or a particular CAM modality) to meet most of their health care needs.[3,4] Understanding patient or parental choices and supporting them inasmuch as they are safe demonstrates the physician's respect for the health care choices made by patients.[5]

Many cases of untreated acute otitis media (AOM) and otitis media with effusion (OME) resolve spontaneously (see Chapter 12, "Natural History of Untreated Otitis Media") and antimicrobials offer only incremental benefits (see Chapter 13, "Clinical Efficacy of Medical Therapy"). Moreover, there may be negative consequences to the injudicious use of antimicrobials, both for the individual patient and for the global community at large (see Chapters 20, "International Perspective on Management" and 27 "Judicious Use of Systemic Antimicrobials"). Confronted with a child in distress and concerned parents, a CAM therapy might provide the clinician with an opportunity to recommend a treatment to relieve the symptoms and possibly alter the course of the illness and/or prevent recurrences.

In this chapter, the research evidence on the use of CAM modalities for the treatment or prevention of OM will be reviewed. If CAM treatments for OM are found to be effective and safe over time, some may become standard practice.

THE RISE IN INTEREST IN COMPLEMENTARY AND ALTERNATIVE MEDICINE

CAM is gaining popularity among consumers and professionals. In 1993, Harvard researchers published a study documenting that more than one-third of Americans used "unconventional" therapies in 1990.[6] A second study by the same researchers found that between 1990 and 1997, this number increased by 38%, from 60 million to 83 million individuals annually. Expenditures for visits to alternative medicine providers in 1997 were estimated as

$21.2 billion, $12.2 billion of which was paid out of pocket. This exceeded the estimated out-of-pocket expenditures for all primary-care physician services in the United States in the same year. Nearly 1 in 5 individuals taking prescription medicines was also taking herbs or high-dose vitamin supplements.[7]

Partly in response to these trends, the number of courses containing content on CAM has increased dramatically at American medical schools. In 1997, 64% of American medical schools reported including such courses in their elective or required curricula.[8] Increased interest in CAM among family physicians has also been reported.[9] The number of CAM practitioners is projected to increase by 88% between the years 1994 and 2010 and that the number of allopathic (conventional) physicians using CAM will increase by 16% in the same time period.[10]

Both Harvard studies found that a large majority of patients did not disclose their use of CAM therapies to their conventional health care providers. If patients conceal their use of CAM products, there is increased risk for adverse interactions between CAM substances and conventional drugs. If the use of CAM services is not disclosed to conventional physicians, there is no possibility for physician coordination of the two types of treatments. This may lead to confusion in patients, undermine doctor–patient relationships, and decrease adherence to medical advice and prescriptions. Therefore, all health care providers should recognize CAM modalities and inquire regularly about their use when taking medical histories.

USE OF COMPLEMENTARY AND ALTERNATIVE THERAPIES IN CHILDREN

A survey administered to a clinic population in Canada in 1994 showed that 11% of children had seen one or more CAM practitioners.[11] The therapies most frequently used were, in order of prevalence, chiropractic, homeopathy, naturopathy, acupuncture, osteopathy, and oligotherapy (trace mineral supplementation). The first four therapies accounted for 84% of CAM use in children. Demographic characteristics of the pediatric CAM users included older patient age, a higher level of maternal education, and parental use of CAM. The medical conditions cited most often by parents seeking CAM for their children were respiratory, ear-nose-and-throat, musculoskeletal, skin, gastrointestinal conditions, and allergies. Parents also sought preventive care from CAM practitioners. The reasons parents gave for seeking CAM included word-of-mouth recommendations, fear of drug side effects, chronic medical problems that parents thought were not improving with

standard treatment, dissatisfaction with conventional medicine, and parental perception that CAM providers provided more personalized attention.

A cross-sectional survey in the District of Colombia evaluated prevalence and reasons for CAM use among children receiving conventional pediatric services.[12] Although most parents reported being satisfied with their children's conventional medical care, 21% had treated their children with some form of CAM (vitamins, herbs, supplements, and dietary modifications were the most common treatments reported). Conditions for which parents most often sought alternative therapy were frequent acute respiratory illnesses, asthma, headaches, and nosebleeds. Eighty-one percent of parents treating their children with CAM indicated that they would have liked to discuss it with their pediatricians, although only 36% reported having done so. Parents who included CAM in their own medical care were more likely to use it for their children.[13]

At the same time that more parents are seeking CAM therapies for their children, CAM practitioners are treating children more frequently in their practices. According to a survey published by Harvard researchers in the year 2000, almost one-third of patient visits to CAM providers were by children.[13]

CLASSIFICATION OF COMPLEMENTARY AND ALTERNATIVE THERAPIES

Complementary and alternative modalities are defined as those medical practices that are not currently being widely used in conventional medical practice. These practices have been categorized by the National Institutes of Health (NIH) National Center on Complementary and Alternative Medicine (NCCAM) into five major groups (Table 15-1).[14]

1. *Alternative medical systems* are complete systems of medical theory and practice that have evolved separately from the conventional biomedical approach, such as homeopathy, naturopathy, and Ayurvedic medicine.
2. *Mind-body interventions* include a variety of techniques that are designed to use the interconnectedness of mind and body to improve health and to mobilize the mind's ability to affect physical symptoms and functions of the body.
3. *Biologically based therapies* include treatments with specific substances thought to have general effects on overall health, or specific therapeutic effects targeted at particular tissues or organ systems. These therapies involve ingestion or injection of substances not generally accepted as efficacious by mainstream medicine, such as shark cartilage or bee pollen.

Table 15-1 Classification of Complementary and Alternative Medicine[14]

Alternative medical systems

Traditional oriental medicine (including acupuncture, herbal therapy, massage, qigong)

Homeopathy

Naturopathy

Ayurveda

Other traditional medical systems (African, Native American, Tibetan, Middle Eastern)

Mind-body interventions

Hypnosis

Meditation

Prayer

Dance, art, and music therapy

Biofeedback

Biologically based therapies

Herbal medicine (phytotherapy)

Special diets (Atkins, Ornish, Pritikin, etc)

Vitamins, nutritional supplements, other orthomolecular therapies, such as melatonin

Shark cartilage/glucosamine

Bee pollen

Manipulative and body-based methods

Chiropractic practice

Osteopathic medicine

Massage

Craniosacral manipulation

Energy therapies

Qigong (a major branch of traditional Chinese medicine)

Therapeutic touch/laying on of hands

Reiki

Bioelectromagnetic therapies using magnets or alternating and direct currents

4. *Manipulative and body-based methods* are techniques involving physical manipulation at the level of the tissues and organs. Practitioners of manipulative therapies believe that structure and function are interrelated and that a properly aligned body will function optimally.

5. *Energy therapies* are believed, by their practitioners, to work by altering the energy fields that purportedly surround and penetrate the human body. These therapies include the use of electric fields and magnetic currents that are applied directly to or in the vicinity of the body.

A number of CAM therapies are not well understood because the explanations for their modes of action sometimes lie outside the current understanding provided by biologic and physical sciences. While physiologic mechanisms for some of the therapeutic effects have been proposed, much more research is needed to thoroughly explicate these theories.[15]

RESEARCH IN CAM

Until recently, there was very little research in the area of CAM, due largely to lack of funding for studies of nonpharmaceutical modalities. In response to constituents' demands, Congress mandated that the NIH establish the Office of Alternative Medicine in 1993. In 1998, this agency was elevated to the level of a center and renamed the National Center for Complementary and Alternative Medicine. The mission of the center is to sponsor research in the various CAM fields. Funding for research in CAM has increased dramatically since the founding of NCCAM (their budget was over $100 million in 2002), but because of the large number of CAM modalities, the number of studies on particular treatments for specific illnesses has been limited.

A few pilot studies suggest that specific CAM therapies may be efficacious in treating acute and chronic OM. These therapies include homeopathy; chiropractic; xylitol, a type of nutritional supplement; and elimination diets for food allergies. Additionally, there are pilot studies sponsored by NCCAM now underway evaluating the use of craniosacral osteopathic manipulation and botanic (herbal) treatment of recurrent OM.[14] Because the research evidence on CAM treatments for OM is limited, this chapter will also include research evidence on treating conditions related to OM, such as upper respiratory illness with CAM therapies, including acupuncture and herbs. Such studies are included because they indicate areas to consider for further research on OM.

RESEARCH EVIDENCE ON CAM AND OTITIS MEDIA

Homeopathic Medicine

General Overview

Homeopathy is a system of medicine that was developed in the late 18th century by the German physician Samuel Hahnemann. It was widely practiced in the United States by the late 1800s, but its use declined dramatically during the early 20th century. Recently, there has been a resurgence of interest in homeopathy around the world. In some European countries as many as 30 to 40% of patients and physicians use homeopathy,[16–18] while in the United States, there were almost five million visits to homeopathic providers in 1990.[6] The percentage of the population who used homeopathy increased from 0.7% in 1990, to 3.4% in 1997,[7] and retail sales of homeopathic medicines increased from $100 million in 1988, to $250 million in 1996.[19,20]

Homeopathic medicines are prepared according to standardized methods, as specified by the Homeopathic Pharmacopoeia of the United States (HPUS),[21] which was mandated by Congress to regulate the manufacture of homeopathic medicines as part of the Food, Drug, and Cosmetics Act of 1939. Most homeopathic products are derived from plant, mineral, and animal sources. Homeopathic medicines are generic and, therefore, inexpensive and are available in bottles of 100 tablets for $5 to $10 in the United States. Most carry an over-the-counter classification.

Principles of Homeopathy

Homeopathy is based on the "principle of similars," which states that highly dilute preparations of substances that can cause certain symptoms in healthy volunteers are found to stimulate healing in ill patients who have similar symptoms.[22] For example, the homeopathic medicine *Allium cepa*, which is made from the red onion, could be used to treat symptoms of the common cold, such as sneezing, lacrimation, and a clear nasal discharge, which are similar to those caused by exposure to onions.

Homeopathic medications are individually prescribed for each patient by matching the signs and symptoms of the patient with those known to be associated with a specific homeopathic medicine. As a result, two or more patients with the same medical diagnosis may receive completely different medications, based on the specific signs and symptoms of each case. A child with AOM may be prescribed one of several different medicines commonly used for this illness, on the basis of such factors as the child's mood, type of pain, amount of thirst, and the time aggravation of symptoms (Table 15-2).

Homeopathic medications are prepared by a process of serial dilution and succussion (shaking), and are defined by the number of times the medicine is diluted in a water/alcohol solution. For example, a 30C potency is a medicine that has been diluted by a factor of 1:100 thirty successive times. Homeopathy is thought to enhance the immune response and other auto-regulatory systems of the body.[23,24] Although a definitive explanation for the mechanism of action of the highly diluted substances does not presently exist, there are several theories. The most widely held is the "memory of water" theory, which postulates that in the process of serial dilution and succussion, the structure of the water molecules of the solvent are altered.[25]

Because it uses highly diluted medicines, homeopathy is one of the most controversial of the CAM therapies. Many critics claim that because of the extreme dilution of homeopathic medications, any positive clinical results must be due to the placebo effect.[26] However, a recent meta-analysis of 89 blinded, placebo-controlled clinical trials in homeopathy found a combined odds ratio of 2.45 (95% CI 2.05, 2.93) in favor of homeopathy and concluded that the effects of homeopathy cannot entirely be explained by placebo.[27]

Research on Homeopathy for Otitis Media

For the past 100 years, homeopathic practitioners have advocated homeopathy as an effective treatment for AOM on the basis of anecdotal evidence. Until recently, however, there were no published studies documenting these claims. In a 1992 survey of medical doctors using homeopathy, OM was reported as the third most frequent illness treated.[28] Since 1996, there have been three published studies on the use of homeopathy for AOM.

The first study, by a group of German researchers, was a prospective study comparing conventional treatment with homeopathic treatment for AOM.[29] Treatment outcomes of 103 children, ages 1 to 11 years, treated with individualized homeopathic medicines and 28 children treated by decongestant nose drops, antibiotics, secretolytics, and/or antipyretics were compared. The authors reported pain duration for 2 days in the homeopathy group versus 3 days in the group receiving conventional medications. They also found fewer relapses within 1 year in children treated with homeopathy (29.3%) as compared with the conventional treatment group (43.5%). No adverse effects were reported in either group. This study was not randomized, there was no blinding, and the number of participants in each arm was not balanced. It should be seen as preliminary to future studies to be done with a more rigorous approach.

Table 15-2 Common Homeopathic Medicines for Acute Otitis Media with Associated Symptoms

Pulsatilla (Windflower)

Mood	**Weepy, clingy, whiny.** Wants to be held and carried
	Changeable moods, one minute happy, the next crying
	Needs attention and reassurance
Generals	Worse in a warm room
	Symptoms improve (pain, weeping) when outside and in fresh air
	Thirstless—refuses to drink
Ears	**Earache begins in the middle of the night**
	External ear and meatus are red. Decreased hearing
	Earache following a cold

Chamomilla (German chamomile)

Mood	Irritable, quarrelsome, nothing pleases child
	Asks for something, then rejects it, striking out
	Sensitive to pain, moaning, frenzied
	Symptoms improve when being carried
Generals	**One cheek red, the other pale**
	Thirsty for cold drinks
	Symptoms are worse in the evening, until midnight
Ear	**Unbearable pain, screaming from pain.** Ears feel stopped

Sulfur (elemental sulfur)

Mood	Emotionally irritable and/or sluggish
Generals	**Symptoms worse when overheated.** Kicks covers off in bed
	Fever with sweating and shivering. Restless sleep
	Thirsty for cold drinks, little appetite
	Symptoms are worse in the early morning, around 5:00 am
Ear	Sharp pains, worse on the left
	Redness of external ear. Enlarged cervical lymph nodes
	Earache with painful ringing in the ears

Belladonna (deadly nightshade)

Mood	Crying loudly. Appears to be in severe pain
	Nightmares causing the child to cry out
Generals	**Sudden, intense onset of pain**
	Face flushed and hot with dilated pupils
	Fever > 102°F
Ear	**Throbbing, pulsating ear pain,** decreased hearing
	Enlarged cervical lymph nodes, **pain worse at night**

Items in bold are keynotes for that remedy. Adapted from Jonas W et al[22] and Jacobs J et al.[31]

Barnett reported on a case series of 24 children ages 8 to 77 months who were treated by two Boston-area physicians who regularly use homeopathy as the primary treatment modality for AOM.[30] Rigorous diagnostic criteria for AOM, including pneumatic otoscopy, tympanometry, and acoustic reflectometry, were used. Patients were treated with homeopathic single medicines, which were changed during the study period as clinically indicated. Follow-up phone calls were made on days 1, 2, and 3 after diagnosis and patients were seen at office visits at 2 and 4 weeks. By the end of 1 month, there were 2 patients (8%) who were considered treatment failures and had received antibiotics, 1 on day 13, and 1 on day 28. No adverse effects were reported. This study is important in that it traces the natural history of AOM treated with homeopathy. Without a placebo group, however, it is difficult to know if the children improved because of the homeopathic treatment, or if they recovered spontaneously.

A randomized, double-blind, placebo-controlled pilot study of 75 children ages 18 months to 6 years with middle ear effusion and ear pain and/or fever was conducted in Seattle, Washington.[31] Children were randomized to receive either an individualized homeopathic medicine or a placebo. Outcome measures included treatment failure, defined as (1) any ear pain and/or fever > 38°C orally any time after the first 48 hours of treatment; or (2) severe ear pain and/or a fever of 39°C after 24 hours. A daily symptom score diary also was used. Results showed less symptoms after 24 hours in the homeopathy group ($p < .05$). There also were fewer treatment failures after 5 days in children who received homeopathy (19.4%) versus placebo (30.8%), but the difference was not statistically significant. On the basis of the treatment failure rates at 5 days, sample size calculations found that 242 children in each of two treatment groups would be needed for significant results. A larger study using this design would be justified.

Safety Considerations and Treatment Recommendations

Because of the highly dilute nature of the homeopathic preparations, they are generally regarded as free of side effects. A systematic review of the literature on homeopathic medications concluded that side effects are rare.[32] There is a phenomenon reported in the homeopathic literature known as an "aggravation of symptoms," wherein 10 to 20% of patients are said to have an initial worsening of symptoms after taking a homeopathic medicine.[22] This aggravation generally lasts no more than a few hours and is usually followed by alleviation of symptoms.

As with other CAM modalities, the biggest danger with homeopathy is that it will be used in situations where more aggressive medical therapy is indicated. In the hands of trained health care providers, however, homeopathy should be considered for symptomatic relief during the early "watch and wait" period of AOM. Parents using homeopathy for self-care of their children with AOM should be encouraged to seek medical care if danger signs appear, such as fever > 38.5°C (101.3°F) or pain persisting for more than 24 hours. Indications for some of the most common homeopathic medications for AOM can be found in Table 15-2.

Chiropractic

General Overview

Chiropractic was founded in the mid-1880s by Daniel David Palmer (1845–1961), who reportedly cured a man of long-term deafness by physically adjusting his thoracic vertebrae. Chiropractic has become quite popular in the United States as well as in other countries, including Mexico, Japan, Taiwan, and a number of European countries. As of 1999, chiropractic was the third largest health profession in the United States, after medicine and dentistry, with over 55,000 practicing chiropractors and approximately 12,000 students of chiropractic. There are 12 accredited colleges and 4 accredited universities of chiropractic. Many insurance plans, including state and federal worker's compensation systems, Medicare, and Medicaid, cover chiropractic. Chiropractors treat many conditions, including low back pain, cervical pain, headache, dysmenorrhea, and carpal tunnel syndrome, in addition to OM.[33–35]

Chiropractic Principles

Chiropractic is based on the idea that the human body is self-healing, maintaining health and balance through its own homeostatic mechanisms (*vis medicatrix naturae*, or "the healing power of nature"). Early chiropractic theory stated that all disease could be traced to malpositioned bones in the spinal column, called "subluxations," which lead to the entrapment of spinal nerves. This interferes with the optimal functioning of tissues and organs innervated by the corresponding nerve roots, producing symptoms of disease. It is believed that restoring proper alignment of the spine via physical adjustments relieves these nerve entrapments and restores health. The functioning of viscera and the immune system are thought by chiropractors to be affected by these mechanisms.[32]

Chiropractors assess spinal dysfunction by evaluating pain and tenderness; asymmetry; abnormalities of range of motion; and abnormalities of tissue, tone, texture, and temperature. The main therapeutic tool of chiropractic is the chiropractic adjustment, which involves manual delivery of a rapid thrust to the subluxed joint. Within the profession, there are a number of schools of thought espousing a variety of specific adjustment techniques.[36] Some techniques use little or no force, while others deliver higher-velocity forces of larger magnitude to areas being treated.[32]

Misalignment of the atlanto-occipital joint is thought by chiropractors to cause inadequate drainage through the Eustachian tube (ET), which can cause or contribute to the development of acute or chronic OM.[36,37] Chiropractors use specific examination techniques to diagnose anatomic problems associated with OM and administer physical manipulations to alter ET anatomy, which improves drainage and leads to resolution of acute or chronic middle ear effusion.

Research on Chiropractic for Otitis Media

There are three published studies of chiropractic treatment of OM: one retrospective case series, one prospective case series, and one single-blind feasibility study.

The case series' were conducted in private chiropractic practices, and the feasibility study was conducted at a chiropractic college.

Froehle reported on 46 consecutive patients aged 5 years or less, representing 95 discrete episodes of OM.[38] Patients received manipulative treatment until they improved: three visits the first week, two the second, and one the third. Treatment techniques used included blocking and modified kinesiology (nonforce techniques), in addition to adjustment of subluxations, which was usually done with an activator (a small device that delivers a calibrated, high-velocity thrust to the tissues). Ninety-two of these episodes were treated without concurrent use of antibiotics. Of these episodes, 85 (92.4%) showed definite clinical improvement; the remainder were unchanged after three treatments or fewer, at which time the parents sought other treatment. Improvement was seen in 10 days or fewer in 63 (74%) of those episodes. There were significant limitations to this study, including lack of standard diagnostic criteria and the fact that patient improvement was determined clinically, by parental report, again without standardized objective criteria.

Fallon conducted a more rigorous study and reported it in greater detail. Three hundred fifteen children with various forms of OM were treated with spinal manipulation on the basis of a standardized chiropractic assessment.[36] Diagnosis of OM was confirmed with otoscopy and tympanometry. All children received an occipital adjustment using manual adjustment techniques, and all received soft tissue effleurage (stroking of the sternocleidomastoid muscle toward the anterior). The frequency of treatments varied, with three times per week being typical. One hundred twenty-seven children were diagnosed with AOM. They averaged 6.7 days to normalization of otoscopy and 8.4 days to normalization of tympanometry. Their 6 month recurrence rate was 11%. One hundred four children were diagnosed with OME. They averaged 8.6 days to normalization of otoscopy and 10.1 days to normalization of tympanometry. Their 6-month recurrence rate was 16.3%. A significant limitation to interpretation of the data is that it was unclear whether the subjects received antibiotics during their courses of chiropractic treatment. Additionally, only 221 of the subjects had baseline and follow-up tympanometry.

Finally, a single-blind, randomized feasibility study of active chiropractic spinal manipulation versus placebo ("sham") spinal manipulation in the treatment of OM in 20 children 6 months to 6 years of age was conducted.[39] Otitis media was diagnosed by otoscopy and tympanometry, and 10 spinal adjustments were given over the course of 4 weeks. The ears then were reassessed. No conclusions about the effectiveness of the treatment were drawn, as the sample of 20 subjects was far too small to permit any conclusions about treatment efficacy. The authors did conclude, however, that it is feasible to conduct a placebo-controlled study of chiropractic treatment for OME.

Manipulative Techniques That Can Be Done by Parents

A recent review suggests several manipulative techniques that can be used for OM, which are relatively easy for parents to learn and to use with their children (Table 15-3).[40] The rationale of these techniques is based on the anatomy and physiology of the Eustachian tube, and they are unlikely to cause harm unless done with inappropriate force. They might reasonably be considered as adjunctive therapies when poor drainage is thought to be

---

Table 15-3 Manipulative Techniques for Enhancing Middle Ear Drainage[40]

Auricular adjusting

Traction on or rapid movement of the external ear to improve drainage of the middle ear via movement of the tympanic fascia

Soft tissue manipulations

"Milking the ET" by applying deep pressure as fingers are moved along the anterior border of the sternocleidomastoid muscle or gently massaging the neck to enhance lymphatic flow away from the inflamed area

Intraoral massage of nasopharyngeal muscle

Use of fingers to apply downward pressure on the tissues inferior to the medial orifice of the ET

Tympanic ventilation

Correction of negative pressure in the middle ear by having the patient do a Valsalva's maneuver with the nostrils occluded or by blowing air into the nose as the patient swallows (the latter technique is feasible with children too young to perform the former)

ET = Eustachian tube.

an important etiologic factor; in cases of chronic OME; and in other cases where antimicrobial therapy is deemed inappropriate, but there is a strong need on the parents' part to do something active.

Safety Considerations of Manipulative Therapies

Reviews of complication rates after chiropractic and osteopathic treatment reveal a wide range in incidence. Mild, transient, adverse effects were reported as often as 10% of the time. Serious adverse effects were reported anywhere from 1 in 40,000 treatment sessions to 1 in 4,000,000. Risk factors contributing to the likelihood of complications occurring include manipulation of the upper cervical spine, misdiagnosis by the practitioner, presence of a bleeding disorder, presence of a herniated disc, and improper manipulative technique.[41]

Advice on Using Manipulative Therapies

In the absence of definitive evidence, it can be said that the manipulative therapies show some degree of promise in the treatment of OM. Parents will want to consider the costs of such treatment, which are unproven, if payment will be out of pocket. When seeking chiropractic care for a child, it is crucial to identify a practitioner with experience in treating children. Nonforce and low-force techniques may be more appropriate for use in children.

Xylitol

Finnish researchers have found that xylitol, a five-carbon polyol sugar alcohol, is an effective prophylactic medication for reducing the incidence of AOM. The research was carried out after the observation was made that xylitol reduced the growth of *Streptococcus mutans*, the main bacterium responsible for dental caries. Growth of *Streptococcus pneumoniae* was also found to be inhibited, in vitro, in the presence of xylitol, although in vivo tests did not show a difference in the nasopharyngeal carriage rate of pneumococcus.[42] Xylitol may work by reducing the ability of pneumocci and other bacteria to adhere to receptors on pharyngeal epithelial cells.[43]

Research

Two clinical studies have been done to test the efficacy of xylitol in preventing AOM. In one study, xylitol gum was given to children five times daily (total daily dose of 8.4 grams) for a 2-month study period.[42] In the second study, xylitol gum was given five times daily to older children (mean age 4.6 years old) who were able to chew gum, and xylitol syrup was given five times daily to children too young to chew gum (mean age 2.2 years old). Xylitol lozenges were also given to a group of subjects.[44] Daily doses of xylitol were either 8.4 or 10 grams daily.

Findings of the research are presented in Table 15-4. Rates of OM were found to be lower when xylitol was given prophylactically in either the gum or the syrup form. It was found, however, that if xylitol administration was started at the onset of an acute respiratory infection, it was no better than the control preparations at preventing the occurrence of AOM.[45]

Complications/Precautions

There were very few complications associated with xylitol ingestion in these studies. Some subjects experi-

Table 15–4   Results of Xylitol Studies for OM

Substance	No. of Subjects	Mean Age, yr (SD)	Dose of Active Substance	% with Prior OM	Total OM Episodes	Total Antibiotic Courses
1996 Study						
Xylitol gum[42]	157	4.9 (1.5)	8.4 g/d	12.1	22	34
Sucrose (control) gum[42]	149	5.0 (1.4)	None	20.8	43	60
1998 Study						
Xylitol syrup[44]	159	2.2 (1.0)	10 g/d	29	69	110
Control syrup[44]	165	2.2 (1.1)	0.5 g/d xylitol	41	114	163
Xylitol gum[44]	179	4.6 (1.4)	8.4 g/d	16	44	44
Control gum[44]	178	4.6 (1.3)	0.5 g/d xylitol	28	72	72
Xylitol lozenges[44]	176	4.7 (1.3)	10 g/d	22	52	52

OM = otitis media.

enced diarrhea and abdominal discomfort, especially if the xylitol was ingested too quickly, but these symptoms were not common or severe. Several problems with this research have been raised. One is that the mean age of the children tested with xylitol syrup, the easiest form of the substance to administer, was 2.2 years; thus testing was not done on infants in the age range when OM is most likely to occur. Also, the dosing regimen of five times daily, which must be maintained in an ongoing, prophylactic fashion, is impractical for most families. Additionally, xylitol is not yet readily available in the United States as it is in Europe.[46,47]

Elimination Diets for Food Allergies

The upper respiratory tract can be a target of IgE-mediated food allergy, with symptoms including nasal congestion, rhinorrhea, sneezing, and pruritus. Whole foods as well as additives often are implicated, including common dietary allergens such as eggs, milk, nuts, wheat, fish, and soy. The gold standard for diagnosing food allergies is a food challenge. In a food challenge, the implicated food is completely withheld from the diet for the trial period of 1 to 2 weeks. The symptoms attributed to ingestion of the eliminated food should resolve and then reappear when the food is re-introduced. Importantly, any food thought capable of provoking an anaphylactic reaction should not be rein-troduced at home.[48]

Research

One study has suggested food allergy as a possible cause for recurrent OM, with results showing a favorable response with individualized elimination diets.[48] In this study, 104 patients (ages 1.5 to 9 years) with serous OM were tested for food allergy. Those who were allergic (81 of 104), as determined by skin prick testing, food challenge, or with specific IgE tests, were given an elim-ination diet for 16 weeks followed by a 16-week, non-blinded food challenge test. Tympanometry, audiom-etry, and clinical observation were used for outcome evaluations. The investigators reported that 70 of 81(86%) patients improved with the elimination diet, and of these, 66 of 70 (94%) showed recurrence of the serous OM with re-introduction of the food. Others in the field feel that while food allergy may play a role in the etiology and treatment of serous OM more research needs to be performed.[50]

Complications/Contraindications

If certain foods are eliminated over a lengthy period of time, dietary substitutions should be used to prevent nutritional deficiencies, such as providing another calcium source when the child is allergic to diary products. The

Food Allergy Network (<http://www.foodallergy.org>) offers nutritional support services and recommendations for diagnostic procedures to limit the list of foods to be avoided when a food allergy is diagnosed.[51]

RESEARCH EVIDENCE ON CONDITIONS RELATED TO OTITIS MEDIA

Herbal Medicines

Overview

Herbal medicines have been used for hundreds of thou-sands of years by most cultures of the world. Herbs con-tinue to be used today by many people around the world for their healing properties; they also may be used in spir-itual ceremonies. Because herbal products are sold in many grocery stores and health food stores, they are con-sidered by many consumers to be safe and natural. However, the U.S. Food and Drug Administration (FDA) is not mandated to approve packaging or marketing infor-mation before a herbal product reaches the market. Although they cannot be marketed for the diagnosis, treat-ment, cure, or prevention of disease, the United States Dietary Supplement Health and Education Act of 1994 does allow herbal products to be labeled as supplements and marketed with broad, nonspecific health claims.

Herbs are marketed as pills, capsules, or tinctures, often with advertisements promoting their efficacy and safety. Consumers have essentially no protection against misleading or fraudulent claims made by herbal prod-uct manufacturers. Product quality and composition vary substantially, with some containing little or none of the purported active ingredients.

Echinacea (E. angustifolia, E. pallida, and E. purpurea)

Echinacea is a plant native to North America and was used by the plains Indians to treat fever and respiratory infections. A paste made of the mashed plant was used topically to treat snake bites, stings, burns, and swelling of the lymph glands. *E. angustifolia* was used in the 1800s as an all purpose "blood purifier" and, at one time, was the most commonly used plant-derived rem-edy in the United States.[52] Its use declined beginning in the 1920s, although European demand remains high.

The primary active ingredients of *Echinacea* are the polysaccharides arabinogalactan and echinacin, which are believed to have immune-modulating effects on the body.[53] Glycosides, alkaloids, alkylamides, poly-acetylenes, and fatty acids also are thought to have effects on the immune system by enhancing phagocy-tosis, improving the motility of human granulocytes, and inhibiting viral replication.[54,55] *Echinacea* may also increase antibody-dependent cellular cytotoxicity and natural killer cell activity as well as enhance interferon levels.[50] Researchers at the University of Arizona have published a review of the various formulations and doses of *Echinacea* used for children as well as a description of an ongoing study on the use of *Echinacea* in the prevention of recurrent OM.[56]

Prevention of Upper Respiratory Infections

A randomized, placebo-controlled trial in 301 volunteers compared *E. angustifolia* extract, *E. purpurea* root extract, and placebo for prevention of upper respiratory infection (URI). The percentage of subjects in each group who developed URI and the time to occurrence of the URI were not found to be significantly different in the three groups.[57] In a similar study, Grimm and Muller compared *E. purpurea* root extract with placebo in an 8-week trial and found no effect on the incidence, duration, and severity of URIs in 109 patients.[58] *Echinacea* was found in another study to be ineffective in preventing infection in volunteers who were exposed to rhinovirus experimentally.[59]

Treatment of Upper Respiratory Infections

Many studies have been published on the use of *Echinacea* in the treatment of URIs. In a randomized, placebo-controlled, double-blind trial of 180 adults who received 900 mg of *E. purpurea* root daily, there was a statistically significant improvement in such symptoms as chills, sore throat, and headache in the treatment group.[60] In 100 adults with an acute flu-like illness who took 30 mL of *Echinacea* extract for 2 days, followed by 15 mL for 4 days, there was more symptom resolution than in those who took the placebo.[61]

Treatment with 900 mg of *E. pallida* root extract significantly decreased the average length of infection, as well as decreasing symptom scores, in 160 patients with URIs.[62] A Cochrane review of 16 trials with 3,396 total participants concluded that some *Echinacea* preparations might be better than placebo in the treatment of upper respiratory symptoms.[63]

Complications

Reported adverse effects of *Echinacea* include allergic reactions to *Echinacea* ointment and shivering, fever, and muscle weakness from parenteral administration.[64,65] *Echinacea* is not recommended for patients with progressive systemic diseases, such as multiple sclerosis, tuberculosis, systemic lupus erythematosus (SLE), autoimmune diseases, and human immunodeficiency virus (HIV) infection, because of the possibility that it may exacerbate abnormalities in the immune system.[66] German guidelines recommend that *Echinacea* not be used for more than 8 weeks at a time because of possible hepatotoxicity or immunosuppression.[67]

Naturopathic Ear Drops

Sarrell studied a naturopathic herbal extract containing *Allium sativum*, *Verbascum thapsus*, *Calendula officinalis*, and *Hypericum perforatum* in olive oil and compared it with anesthetic ear drops containing ametocaine and phenozone in glycerin for the management of ear pain associated with OM. In the 110 children enrolled in the study (ages 6 to 18 years), 61 received the naturopathic extract and 54 the anesthetic. There was a statistically significant improvement in ear pain score in both groups but no difference between the herbal-extract and anesthetic-eardrop groups. No antibiotic treatment was used in either group. Unfortunately, there was no control group in this study.[68]

Chinese Herb: *Shuang Huang Lian*

Shuang huang lian is a Chinese herb used in traditional Chinese medicine. Kong and colleagues randomized 96 children in China with bronchiolitis to receive *Shuang huang lian* alone, *Shuang huang lian* and antibiotics, or antibiotics alone in a randomized, single-blind trial.[69] The groups that received *Shuang huang lian*, either alone or in combination with antibiotics, had a decrease in the mean duration of symptoms, including rhinorrhea and fever, from 8.6 to 6.2 days, as compared with those children who received antibiotics alone. There was also a decrease in the duration of fever, cough, wheezing, and crackles in the herb-treated groups.

Acupuncture

Overview

Acupuncture originated in China approximately 5,000 years ago, with written records dating back almost 2,000 years.[1,2,70] It is one of the disciplines within the complex system of traditional Chinese medicine. Acupuncture is used widely in adults and children.[9,71,72] In 1991, an estimated $14 billion was spent out of pocket for acupuncture therapy.[6]

Principles of Acupuncture

Acupuncture is based on the premise that energy, or *Qi* (pronounced chi), flows through the body along channels, known as meridians, connected by acupuncture points.[73] If the flow of *Qi* is obstructed, imbalance results; restoration of the energy flow eliminates or reduces that imbalance. The flow of *Qi* is manipulated by insertion of fine needles at acupuncture points along the involved meridians.

A practitioner diagnoses illness after extensive discussion with and examination of the patient. This includes an examination of the shape, color, and coating of the tongue and the strength, rhythm, and character of the radial pulses. Once a diagnosis has been made, the specific treatment may take a number of forms, including solid needle placement, moxibustion (the practice of burning dried herbs over acupuncture points), acupressure, or cupping.[74,75]

In 1997, an NIH consensus conference concluded that acupuncture was effective for treating certain types of pain in adults, such as dental pain, migraine headaches, back pain, and dysmenorrhea. The conference also concluded that acupuncture was effective in the treatment of adult postoperative and chemotherapy-related nausea and vomiting and probably for nausea of pregnancy.[76]

Research Evidence on Acupuncture

There have been no studies, to date, looking at the use of acupuncture in the treatment or management of OM in children. Because acupuncture is such an important alternative treatment, studies evaluating the use of acupuncture for symptoms associated with OM, such as upper respiratory infections and pain, will be discussed.

In one study of nasal congestion, nasal airway resistance (NAR), as measured by posterior rhinomanometry, and subjective sensation of nasal airflow measured on a visual analog scale (VAS) were evaluated after an acupuncture point in the nose associated with these symptoms was massaged. Twenty patients were randomized into two groups. One group self-massaged the point for 30 seconds while the other group, acting as controls, did not do nasal massage. The NAR and VAS were measured at baseline and again at 2 and 10 minutes after the massage. At the end of the study, patients were asked to score any change in their nasal congestion. There was no statistically significant difference between the two groups in percentage change in the NAR or VAS from baseline at any time during the study. More patients in the treatment group felt subjectively that their nasal congestion was improved ($p < .005$). The results of this study suggest that acupuncture point massage may provide some symptomatic relief from nasal congestion.[77] Clinical observation of 46 cases of recurrent respiratory tract infections in infants treated by mild moxibustion over acupuncture points on the back showed a possible reduction in symptoms, including rhinorrhea, fever, and sore throat, although further study is warranted.[78]

Acupuncture has been found to be useful in treating pain in children with illnesses other than OM and might be considered for symptomatic treatment of AOM. In one cross-over study, 10 patients with sickle cell anemia received either acupuncture point or sham

site treatments during 16 painful crises in the two extremities. In 15 of these 16 patients, equal pain relief, as determined by a standard pain questionnaire, was obtained from subjects receiving sham and real acupuncture. The investigators concluded that needling at either acupuncture or sham sites may be an effective tool for alleviating pain.[79]

In another study, acupuncture and hypnotherapy were compared in the treatment of chronic pain in children. Thirty-one children received acupuncture along with a 20-minute hypnotherapy session over a 6-week period of time. Patient and parent reports of pain-associated disability (physical activity, social interactions) and patients' pain ratings were assessed before and after each of the 6 weekly sessions. The study subjects experienced an average of 46% reduction in pain and a 32% reduction in pain-related disability.[80] A limitation of this study was that acupuncture and hypnotherapy were not evaluated individually and there was no control group.

When perceived efficacy and acceptance of acupuncture in 47 pediatric patients were reviewed, it was found that 70% of patients (average age 16 years, 79% female) interviewed found the treatments helped the symptoms, and 67% rated the therapies as pleasant.[81] The predominant presenting problems in this population were migraines, endometriosis, and reflex sympathetic dystrophy. Research is recommended on the use of acupuncture for the pain suffered by children with OM.

Contraindications/Complications

One of the advantages of acupuncture is that the incidence of adverse effects is substantially lower than that of many drugs used for the same conditions. The single reported fatality from acupuncture was from toxic shock syndrome.[82] In a prospective study involving 32,000 acupuncture consultations, an incidence of 684 adverse events per 10,000 consultations was found. Serious adverse events, including pneumothorax, angina, septic sacroilitis, epidural abscess, and temporomandibular abscess, were noted in only 11 out of the 32,000 treatments.[83]

In a review of nine surveys on the safety of acupuncture, Ernst reported that the most common adverse effects from acupuncture were pain (1 to 45% of treatments), fatigue (2 to 41%), and bleeding (0.03 to 38%).[84] A Japanese review reported that more adverse events occurred when those performing acupuncture were poorly trained.[85] Setting standards for practice, education, and ongoing certification in acupuncture are important in order to minimize complications and promote safety and acceptance of this important therapeutic tool.

ADVICE TO DOCTORS: TALKING TO PATIENTS AND PARENTS ABOUT CAM

Be open-minded when talking to patients or parents. Most patients are reluctant to share information about their use of CAM therapies because they are concerned that their physicians will disapprove. By remaining open minded, you can learn much about your patients' use of unconventional therapies. Start by asking questions and listen to what your patients tell you. All patients should be asked about their use of alternative therapies during routine history taking. One approach is simply to inquire, "Are you doing anything else for this condition?" This open-ended question gives the patient an opportunity to tell you about his or her use of other health care providers or therapies. Another approach is to ask, "Are you currently taking, or have you taken, any over-the-counter remedies such as vitamins or herbs?" Avoid using the words "alternative therapy," at least initially. Also avoid the temptation to denigrate a therapy with which you are not acquainted. These measures demonstrate that you are open minded and nonjudgmental.

Do not summarily dismiss any therapy as worthless or "just a placebo." If a patient tells you about a therapy with which you are unacquainted, make a note of it in the patient's record and schedule a follow-up visit after you have learned more. At that time, you will be in a better position to discuss the therapy with the patient. If you determine that the therapy might be harmful, you have an obligation to advise the patient to stop using it. If it is not harmful and the patient feels better using it, you may want to consider incorporating the therapy into your care plan.

One recommended approach in relation to CAM therapies is to "protect, permit, promote, and partner." This includes the following: (1) protect patients against dangerous practices, products, and practitioners; (2) permit practices that are harmless and that contribute to comfort or palliation; (3) promote and use those practices that are found to be safe and effective; and (4) partner with patients by discussing the use of specific CAM therapies and products with them.[6]

In discussing CAM therapies with patients and parents, remember that you may be in the position to recommend a therapy for which thorough research evidence is not available. Kemper recommends the conservative approach of not referring children for therapies which may be costly and for which there is not yet enough evidence of efficacy.[86] Loo, on the other hand, encourages physicians to consider therapies that may be safe and effective but for which thorough evidence is lacking, especially if this approach supports the health care philosophy of the involved family.[87]

It is beneficial to discuss providers as well as therapies. One way to help your patients negotiate the maze of alternative therapies is by stressing that they see appropriately trained and licensed providers and by developing a referral network in your area. Studdert and colleagues recommend referring to practitioners licensed in their fields and further recommends knowing the particular practitioner to whom you are referring patients.[88] These measures will help increase the likelihood that a referral will be appropriate and have a positive outcome.

Encourage your patients to ask alternative providers about their background and training and the treatment modalities they use (Table 15-5). By doing so, your patients will be better equipped to make educated decisions about their health care. Discuss CAM therapies with your patients at every visit. Charting the details of their use will remind you to raise the issue. It may also help alert you to potential complications before they occur.

Table 15-6 outlines the pointers and pitfalls regarding the use of CAM therapies for OM. It is appropriate to use a CAM therapy alone for OM in children who are not extremely ill, particularly those who are not in severe pain, experiencing high fevers, and do not have concurrent conditions such as pneumonia or sinusitis. These are children for whom a "watch-and-wait" period is appropriate prior to prescribing antibiotics. For more seriously ill patients, conventional therapy alone or conventional therapy in combination with a CAM therapy are indicated. As with all medical interventions, following up on any worsening of illness is essential.

ACKNOWLEDGMENT

Dr. Levatin acknowledges Dr. Barry S. Fogel's assistance in preparing the section on chiropractic.

Table 15-5 Questions for the Patient to Ask the CAM Provider

Is there any research evidence of efficacy of the treatment?

What is the provider's experience and training with the CAM treatment?

Approximately how many treatments will be needed over what period of time?

What is a reasonable expectation for the outcome of the treatment?

What are the costs, and are they reimbursed by insurance?

What are the toxicity and safety risks or adverse effects of the treatment?

Is the CAM provider willing to work together with the patient's conventional physician?

Adapted from Chez RA et al.[5]
CAM = complimentary and alternative medicine.

Table 15-6 Pointers and Pitfalls in CAM Therapies for Otitis Media

1. CAM therapies are becoming increasingly popular in both the adult and pediatric populations of the United States.

2. Research evidence about the use of most CAM therapies for the treatment of OM is limited.

3. Recent research suggests that homeopathic medicines may be useful for symptomatic relief in AOM during the "watch-and-wait" period.

4. Chiropractic techniques show promise in the treatment of OM, but further research needs to be carried out before treatment recommendations can be made.

5. Xylitol gum or syrup appears to reduce the incidence of AOM episodes when used prophylactically, although the practical aspects about its use have been questioned.

6. Herbal medicines and acupuncture have been found to be effective in treating conditions related to OM, such as upper respiratory infections and pain.

7. Physicians should query their patients about the use of CAM therapies and provide information on the benefits and limitations of these modalities.

AOM = acute otitis media; CAM = complementary and alternative medicine; OM = otitis media.

REFERENCES

1. Jonas WB, Levin JS, editors. Essentials of complementary and alternative medicine. Philadelphia (PA): Lippincott Williams & Wilkins; 1999.

2. Micozzi MS, Koop CE, editors. Fundamentals of complementary and alternative medicine. 2nd ed. New York (NY): Churchill Livingstone; 2001.

3. Furnham A, Forey J. The attitudes, behaviors and beliefs of patients of conventional vs complementary (alternative) medicine. J Clin Psychol 1994;50:458–69.

4. Astin JA. Why patients use alternative medicine. JAMA 1998;279:1548–53.

5. Chez RA, Jonas WB, Eisenberg D. The physician and complementary and alternative medicine. In: Jonas WB, Levin JS, editors. Essentials of complementary and alternative medicine. Philadelphia (PA): Lippincott Williams & Wilkins; 1999.

6. Eisenberg DM, Kessler RC, Foster C, et al. Unconventional medicine in the United States. N Engl J Med 1993;328:246–52.

7. Eisenberg DM, Davis RB, Ettner SL, et al. Trends in alternative medicine use in the United States, 1990–1997. JAMA 1998;280:1569–75.

8. Wetzel MS, Eisenberg DM, Kaptchuk TJ. Courses involving complementary and alternative medicine at United States medical schools. JAMA 1998;280:784–7.

9. Berman B, Singh B, Lao L, et al. Physicians' attitudes toward complementary or alternative medicine. J Am Board Fam Pract 1995;8:361–6.

10. Cooper RAK, Stoflet SJ. Trends in the education and practice of alternative medicine clinicians. Health Aff (Millwood) 1996;17:226–38.

11. Spigelblatt L, Laine–Ammara G, Pless IB, Guyver A. The use of alternative medicine by children. Pediatrics 1994;94:811–4.

12. Ottolini MC, Hamburger EK, Loprieato JO, et al. Complementary and alternative medicine use among children in the Washington, DC area. Ambul Pediatr 2001;1(2):122–5.

13. Lee ACC, Kemper KJ. Homeopathy and naturopathy. Arch Pediatr Adolesc Med 2000;154:78–80.

14. United States Department of Health and Human Services. NCCAM Five Year Strategic Plan. Bethesda (MD): National Insititutes of Health; 2000. NIH Publication No. 01–5001.

15. Benford MS, Schwartz GER, Russek LGS, Boosey S. Exploring the concept of energy in touch–based healing. In: Novey DW, editor. Clinician's complete reference to complementary and alternative medicine. St. Louis (MO): Mosby; 2000. p. 483–93.

16. Bouchayer F. Alternative medicines: a general approach to the French situation. Complement Med Res 1990;4:4–8.

17. Wharton R, Lewith G. Complementary medicine and the general practitioner. BMJ 1986;292:1498–500.

18. Ernst E, Kaptchuck TJ. Homeopathy revisited. Arch Int Med 1996;156:2162–4.

19. Swander H. Homeopathy: medical enigma attracts renewed attention. Am Acad Fam Pract Rep 1994; XXI(6):1–2.

20. Harvard University. Complementary therapies: homeopathy. Harvard Women's Health Watch 1997;4. p. 2.

21. Homeopathic Pharmacopoeia Convention of the United States. Homeopathic Pharmacopoeia of the United States. Washington: The Convention; 1988.

22. Jonas W, Jacobs J. Healing with homeopathy: the complete guide. New York (NY): Warner Books, Inc; 1996.

23. Bellavite P, Signorini, A. Homeopathy: a frontier in medical science. Berkeley (CA): North Atlantic Books; 1995.

24. Van Wijk R, Wiegant FAC. The Similia principle as a therapeutic strategy: a research program on stimulation of self-defense in disordered mammalian cells. Altern Ther 1997;3:33–8.

25. Resch G, Gutmann V. Scientific foundations of homeopathy [English ed]. Germany: Barthel & Barthel Publishing; 1987.

26. Sampson W, London W. Homeopathic treatment of childhood diarrhea [special article]. Pediatrics 1995:96: 961–4.

27. Linde K, Clausius N, Ramirez G, et al. Are the clinical effects of homeopathy placebo effects? A meta-analysis of placebo-controlled trials. Lancet 1997;350:834–43.

28. Jacobs J, Chapman EH, Crothers D. Patient characteristics and practice patterns of physicians using homeopathy. Arch Fam Med 1998;7:537–40.

29. Friese KH, Druse S, Moeller H. Acute otitis media in children. Comparison between conventional and homeopathic therapy. HNO 1996;44:462–6.

30. Barnett ED, Levatin JL, Chapman EH, et al. Challenges of evaluating homeopathic treatment of acute otitis media. Pediatr Infect Dis J 2000;19:273–5.

31. Jacobs J, Springer DS, Crothers D. Homeopathic treatment of acute otitis media in children: a preliminary randomized controlled trial. Pediatr Infect Dis J 2001;20:177–83.

32. Dantes F, Rampes H. Do homeopathic medicines provoke adverse effects? A systematic review. Br Homeopath J 2000;89:S35–8.

33. Lawrence DJ. Chiropractic medicine. In: Jonas WB, Levin JS, editors. Essentials of complementary and alternative medicine. Philadelphia (PA): Lippincott Williams & Wilkins; 1999. p.275–88

34. Coughlin P. Manual therapies. In: Micozzi MS, Koop CE, editors. Fundamentals of complementary and alternative medicine. 2nd ed. New York (NY): Churchill Livingstone; 2001. p. 100–27.

35. Hansen TJJ. Chiropractic. In: Novey DW, editor. Clinician's complete reference to complementary and alternative medicine. St. Louis (MO): Mosby; 2000. p. 310–24.

36. Fallon JM. The role of the chiropractic adjustment in the care and treatment of 332 children with otitis media. J Clin Chiro Pediatr 1997;2:167–83.

37. Schmidt MA. Healing childhood ear infections. Berkeley (CA): North Atlantic Books; 1996.

38. Froehle RM. Ear infection: a retrospective study examining improvement from chiropractic care and analyzing for influencing factors. J Manipulative Physiol Ther 1996;19:169–77.

39. Sawyer CE, Evans RL, Boline PD, et al. A feasibility study of chiropractic spinal manipulation versus sham spinal manipulation for chronic otitis media with effusion in children. J Manipulative Physiol Ther 1999;22:292–8.

40. Lamm L, Ginter L. Otitis media: a conservative chiropractic management protocol. Top Clin Chiro 1998;5:18–28.

41. Ernst, E. Adverse effects of spinal manipulation. In: Jonas WB, Levin JS, editors. Essentials of complementa-

ry and alternative medicine. Philadelphia (PA): Lippincott Williams & Wilkins; 1999. p. 176–9.

42. Uhari M, Kontiokari T, Koskela M, Miemela M. Xylitol chewing gum in prevention of acute otitis media: double blind randomized trial. BMJ 1996;313: 1180–3.

43. Kontiokari T, Uhari M, Koskela M. Antiadhesive effects of xylitol on otophatogenic bacteria. J Antimicrob Chemother 1998;41:563–5.

44. Uhari M, Kontiokari T, Niemela M. A novel use of xylitol sugar in preventing acute otitis media. Pediatrics 1998;102:879–84.

45. Tapiainen T, Luotonen L, Kontiokari T, et al. Xylitol administered only during respiratory infections failed to prevent acute otitis media. Pediatrics 2002;109:e19.

46. Wright PF. Xylitol sugar and acute otitis media. Pediatrics 1998;102:971–2.

47. Mitchell AA. Xylitol prophylaxis for acute otitis media: *toute de suite*? Pediatrics 1998;102:974–5.

48. Sicherer SH. Manifestation of food allergy: evaluation and management. Am Fam Phys 1999;59:415–24.

49. Nsouli TM, Nsouli SM, Linde RE, et al. Role of food allergy in serous otitis media. Ann Allergy 1994;73:215–9.

50. Fireman P. Otitis media and Eustachian tube dysfunction: connection to allergic rhinitis. J Allergy Clin Immunol 1997;99:S787–97.

51. Spergel JM, Pawlowski NA. Food Allergy: mechanisms, diagnosis and management in children. Pediatr Clin North Am 2002;49:73–96 .

52. Awang DVC, Kindack DG. Herbal medicine: *Echinacea*. Can Pharm J 1991;124:512–6.

53. Goldhaber–Fiebert S, Kemper K. *Echinacea*. The Longwood Herbal Task Force 1999. Available at: http://www.mcp.edu/herbal (accessed February 28, 2003).

54. Stotsem CD, Hungerland U, Mengs U. Influence of *Echinacea purpurea* in the phagocytosis of human granulocytes. Med Sci Res 1992;20:719–20.

55. Turner RB. Ineffectiveness of echinacea for prevention of experimental rhinovirus colds. Antiviral Res 2001;49:1–14.

56. Mark JD, Grant KL, Barton LL. The use of dietary supplements in pediatrics: a study of echinacea [see comments]. Clin Pediatr 2001;40:265–9.

57. Melchart D , Walther E, Linde, K, et al. Echinacea root extracts for the prevention of upper respiratory tract infections: a double blind placebo controlled randomized trail. Arch Fam Med 1998;7:541–5.

58. Grimm W, Muller HH. A randomized controlled trial of the effect of fluid extract of *Echinacea purpurea* on the incidence and severity of colds and respiratory infections. Am J Med 1999;106:138–43.

59. Turner RB. Ineffectiveness of echinacea for prevention of experimental rhinovirus colds. Antimicrob Agents Chemother 2000;44:1708–9.

60. Braunig B, Dorn M, Limburg E. Enhancement of resistance in common cold by *Echinacea purpura* radix. J Phytother 1992;13:7–13.

61. Schulz V, Hansel R, Tyler VE. Rational phytotherapy: a physicians' guide to herbal medicine. Berlin: Springer; 1997. p. 306.

62. Dorn M, Knick E, Lewith G. Placebo–controlled double blind study of *Echinacea pallidae* in upper respiratory infections. Complement Ther Med 1997;3:40–2.

63. Melchart D, Linde K, Fischer P, Kaesmayr J. Echinacea for the preventing and treating the common cold. Cochrane Database of Systematic Review 2002; Issue 2.

64. Mullins RJ, Heddle R. Adverse reactions associated with echinacea: the Australian experience [see comments]. Ann Allergy Asthma Immunol 2002;88:42–51.

65. Parnham MJ. Benefit–risk assessment of the squeezed sap of the purple cornflower (*Echinacea purpurea*) for long-term oral immunostimulation. Phytomedicine 1996;3(1):95–102.

66. Brinker FJ. Herb contraindication and drug interactions: with appendices addressing specific conditions and medicines. Sandy (OR): Eclectic Institute; 1997. p. 146.

67. Blumenthal M. The complete German Commission E monographs: therapeutic guide to herbal medicines. Austin (TX): American Botanical Council; 1998.

68. Sarrell EM, Mandelberg A, Cohen HA. Efficacy of naturopathic extracts in the management of ear pain associated with acute otitis media. Arch Pediatr Adolesc Med 2001;155:796–9.

69. Kong XT. Treatment of acute bronchiolitis with Chinese herbs. Arch Dis Child 1993;68:468–71.

70. Kaptchuk T. The web that has no weaver. New York (NY): Congdon and Weed; 1983.

71. Drivdahl CE, Miser WF. The use of alternative health care by a family practice population. J Am Board Fam Pract 1998;11:193–9.

72. Blanc PD. Alternative therapies among adults with a reported diagnosis of asthma or rhinosinusitis: data from a population-based survey. Chest 2001;120:1461–7.

73. Helms JM. Acupuncture energetics. Berkely (CA): Medical Acupuncture Publishers; 1995. p. 19–34.

74. Sung J, Liao M, Lee K. Principles and practice of contemporary acupuncture. New York (NY): Marcel Dekker, Inc; 1994.

75. Stux G, Pomeranz B. Basics of acupuncture. Germany: Springer Verlag; 1998.

76. NIH consensus Conference. Acupuncture. JAMA 1998;280:1518–24.

77. Takeuchi H. The effects of nasal massage of the "ying xiang" acupuncture point on nasal airway resistance and sensation of nasal airflow in patients with nasal congestion associated with acute upper respiratory tract infection. Am J Rhinol 1999;13:77–9

78. Long X. Clinical observation on 46 cases of infantile repeated respiratory tract infection treated by mild-moxibustion over acupoints on back. J Tradit Chin Med 2001;21(1): 23–6.

79. Co L, Schmitz T, Havdala H, et al. Acupuncture: an evaluation in the painful crisis of sickle cell anemia. Pain 1979;7:181.

80. Waterhouse MW, Stelling C, Poweres M, et al. Acupuncture and hypnotherapy in the treatment of chronic pain in children. Clin Acupunct Orient Med 2001;1:139–50.

81. Kemper KJ, Sarah R, Silver-Highfield E, et al. On pins and needles? Pediatric pain patients' experience with acupuncture. Pediatrics 2000;4:941–7.

82. Onizuka T, Oishi K, Ikeda T, et al. A fatal case of streptococcal toxic shock-like syndrome probably caused by acupuncture. Kansenshogaku Zasshi 1998; 72:776–80.

83. White A, Hayhoe S, Hart A, Ernst E. BMAS and AACP. British Medical Acupuncture Society and Acupuncture Association of Chartered Physiotherapists. Survey of adverse events following acupuncture (SAFA): a prospective study of 32,000 consultations. Acupunct Med 2001;19:84–92.

84. Ernst E. Prospective studies of the safety of acupuncture: a systematic review. Am J Med 2001;110(6): 481–5.

85. Yamashita H, Tsukayama H, White AR, et al. Systematic review of adverse events following acupuncture: the Japanese literature. Complement Ther Med 2001;9: 98–104.

86. Kemper KJ. Otitis media: when parents don't want antibiotics or tubes. Contemp Pediatr 2002;19:47–58.

87. Loo M. Complementary/alternative therapies in select populations: children. In: Spencer JW, Jacobs JJ, editors. Complementary/alternative medicine: an evidence based approach. St Louis (MO): Mosby; 1999. p. 371–90.

88. Studdert DN, Eisenberg DM, Miller FH, et al. Medical malpractice implications of alternative medicine. JAMA 1998;280:1610–5.

CHAPTER 16

Bacteriologic Efficacy of Antimicrobial Agents

Colin D. Marchant, MD, and Ron Dagan, MD

The ultimate test of the efficacy of antibiotic therapy (in acute otitis media)
is its ability to eradicate the organism from the site of infection.
Virgil M. Howie and John H. Ploussard

OBJECTIVES

On completing this chapter, the reader will be able to
1. Distinguish bacteriologic and clinical outcomes in acute otitis media (AOM).
2. Appreciate the limitations of trials with clinical outcomes for distinguishing between antibacterial drugs.
3. Know the strengths and limitations of bacteriologic efficacy data.
4. Understand which antibiotic regimens eradicate pathogens from the middle ear and which do not.
5. Apply bacteriologic efficacy data in clinical decision making.

RATIONALE FOR BACTERIOLOGIC EFFICACY

Antibacterial drugs are selected or designed for their ability to kill bacteria or inhibit their growth. When administered to patients they are distributed to tissues and body fluids and, combined with host defenses, eradicate pathogens from the site of infection, a property known as bacteriologic efficacy. To measure bacteriologic efficacy, cultures are obtained from the site of infection before antibiotic therapy and then again during or at the end of the antibiotic regimen. In clinical trials of antibacterial agents for streptococcal pharyngitis and urinary tract infections, bacteriologic efficacy is widely accepted as a criterion for success. In AOM, this measure of efficacy has been less widely used because tympanocentesis with culture of the middle ear fluid is a brief but painful procedure that is not routinely employed in ordinary clinical practice.

Superficially, it would seem better to assess the effects of antibacterial agents on AOM in trials that measure symptomatic response and/or resolution of physical findings of AOM as the outcome. If all cases of AOM were caused solely by bacterial invasion of the middle ear, evaluating the effects of antibacterial agents by clinical response might be a relatively simple matter. However, AOM is not a simple bacterial disease. Approximately 25% of patients have no live bacteria in the middle ear, and the clinical course is expected to be unaffected by antibiotic therapy.[1]

Increasing evidence suggests that AOM is usually bacterial and viral. Often, AOM is preceded by a presumed viral upper respiratory infection (URI): children with coryza and cough typically develop AOM on the second through fourth day of illness.[2] Polymerase chain reaction and viral antigen assays document a specific viral etiology for AOM in 40 to 60% of patients, and bacterial–viral co-infection is common.[3,4] Consequently, viral URI and bacterial infection of the middle ear may simultaneously cause discomfort to the patient. Moreover, patients with persistent symptoms after 48 hours of antibacterial therapy are more likely to have an identifiable viral pathogen in the middle ear or upper respiratory tract.[5]

Improvement of AOM symptoms may be caused by host defenses eradicating bacterial and/or viral infection, by antibacterial therapy eliminating bacteria, or by both. Conversely, persistent symptoms may reflect persistent bacterial or viral infection. Antipyretics and analgesics may also improve patients' symptoms despite failure of antibacterial therapy. Clinical response may be further modified by psychological factors, including parental expectation. Thus, the clinical effects of antibacterial treatment in AOM are diluted by nonbacterial cases, obscured by concurrent viral infection, augmented by the host's substantial immunologic defenses, aided by concurrent use of medications that relieve pain and fever, and subjectively modified by the human mind. Bacteriologic efficacy in the middle ear is a more direct way of assessing the effects of antibacterial drugs in AOM than clinical outcome.

Howie and Ploussard[6] first assessed the effects of antibacterial drugs in AOM by tympanocentesis and culture of the middle ear during therapy. In a series of clinical trials, they performed tympanocentesis and cultured the middle ear before therapy and again 2 to 7 days later to measure the bacteriologic efficacy of antibiotics.[7] Using this "in vivo sensitivity test," they documented antibacterial effects of host defenses in patients with AOM caused by *Streptococcus pneumoniae* and *Haemophilus influenzae*.[7] Penicillin and erythromycin failed to eradicate *H. influenzae*, but sulfonamides, combined with either penicillin or erythromycin, successfully eradicated *S. pneumoniae* and *H. influenzae*.[7] The ability of their studies to distinguish between antibacterial drugs led other investigators to adopt a similar approach.

This chapter presents evidence for using bacteriologic efficacy to evaluate antibacterial drugs, demonstrates the limitations of clinical trials that use clinical outcomes, and outlines and approach for applying bacteriologic efficacy data to patient management.

BACTERIOLOGIC EFFICACY AND CLINICAL OUTCOME

Evidence Linking Bacteriologic Efficacy and Clinical Outcome

Although Howie and Ploussard[7] showed that some antibacterial drugs had greater bacteriologic efficacy than others, they neither sought nor found any statistically significant differences in clinical outcome between antibiotic regimens. Bacteriologic efficacy would be of only biologic importance, but not clinically meaningful, if there were no relationship between bacteriologic efficacy and clinical outcome. Two studies by subsequent investigators, however, showed that bacteriologic efficacy predicts clinical efficacy (Figure 16-1).

Carlin and coworkers[8] found that after 3 to 6 days of antibiotic therapy, patients in whom bacteria were eliminated from the middle ear experienced a 93% probability of symptomatic relief, while only 62% of those with persistent bacterial infection were symptomatically improved. Dagan and colleagues,[9] using a clinical scoring system based on symptoms and otoscopic signs, similarly demonstrated a correlation between bacteriologic and clinical outcome. If bacteria were eradicated from the middle ear, then the clinical cure rate was 97%, and if bacteria were not eliminated, then 63% were improved.

Consequently, eradicating bacteria from the middle ear increases clinical improvement by about 30% compared with failure to eliminate pathogens from the site of infection, a difference that we judge to be clinically important. The above studies demonstrate that the goal of antibacterial therapy, eradication of pathogens from the site of infection, has clinical validity.

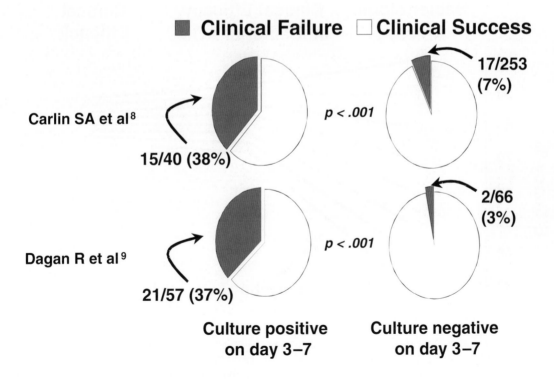

Figure 16-1 Correlation between clinical and bacteriologic outcome in acute otitis media.

Implications of Bacteriologic Efficacy Data

Data showing that eradicating bacteria from the middle ear predicts symptom resolution provides further evidence of the favorable effect of antibiotics demonstrated in randomized placebo-controlled trials (see Chapter 13, "Clinical Efficacy of Medical Therapy"). The data also validate bacteriologic outcome as a surrogate measure of clinical effect. An antibacterial drug that eliminates bacteria from the middle ear can be expected to produce a favorable clinical outcome, whereas one with a lower eradication rate will be less effective clinically.

The incomplete correlation between clinical and bacteriologic outcomes may disappoint those who consider AOM a simple bacterial disease but is not surprising, given the complexities of AOM. In a multifactorial situation, the correlation between only one factor (bacteriologic eradication) and the outcome of interest (clinical improvement) will be imperfect. Concurrent viral infection causes, at least in part, persistent symptoms despite bacterial eradication.[5] In contrast, the cause (or causes) of clinical improvement with persistent infection is less clear. Reducing bacterial load by antibiotic therapy may afford clinical improvement. Also unknown is whether patients with persistent bacterial growth but improved symptoms are at increased risk of recurrent AOM. These unknown factors and outcomes, however, do not detract from the well-documented correlation (albeit imperfect) between bacteriologic and clinical outcomes.

The discrepancies between clinical and bacteriologic outcomes have implications for designing clinical trials to assess the comparative efficacy of antibiotic therapy. Data for the relationship between clinical and bacteriologic outcomes in bacterial AOM (see Figure 16-1) and data from the same series of clinical trials showing an 80% symptomatic response of nonbacterial AOM, were used to calculate, for various levels of bacteriologic efficacy, the clinical efficacy in trials using clinical response as the outcome (Figure 16-2).[10] Bacteriologic efficacy was compared with clinical efficacy in patients with bacterial AOM (single tympanocentesis trial) or with all patients with clinical AOM (clinical trial with no tympanocenteses).

Patients with persistent symptoms despite bacterial eradication make excellent drugs appear worse than they really are in trials that measure only clinical outcomes (see Figure 16-2). Similarly, those with clinical improvement despite failure of a poor antibiotic to eradicate bacterial pathogens make a poor drug appear clinically effective when it is not. The predominant effect is that drugs with poor bacteriologic efficacy can, nonetheless, appear to be effective clinically (see Figure 16-2).[10] This "Pollyanna phenomenon" was named in reference to the blindly optimistic heroine of the novel Pollyanna, by E.H. Porter.

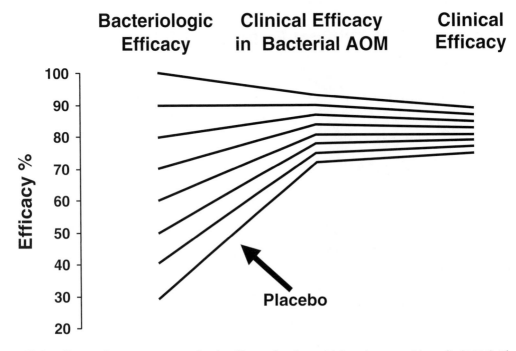

Figure 16-2 Pollyanna phenomenon: measuring the efficacy of antibacterial drugs in acute otitis media (AOM). Three strategies for assessing antibiotic efficacy are compared: bacteriologic efficacy (double tympanocentesis), efficacy using clinical response in patients with proven bacterial AOM (single tympanocentesis), and clinical response in clinical AOM (no tympanocentesis). The lines connect corresponding efficacy rates for various levels of bacteriologic efficacy. Data from Marchant CD et al.[10]

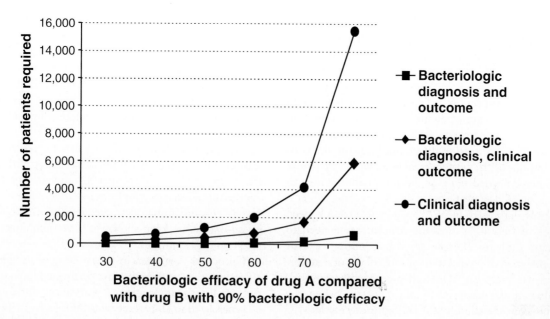

Figure 16-3 Sample sizes required to detect differences between antibacterial drugs for acute otitis media. Bacteriologic versus clinical outcomes are compared in a trial of two drugs with varying bacteriologic efficacy (half the patients would be in each arm of the study). Data from Marchant CD et al.[10]

There is a further implication of these data and the Pollyanna phenomenon. When differences between one treatment and another are small, large sample sizes are required to protect against falsely concluding that two treatments are similar when they are not. When two drugs for AOM have substantially different bacteriologic effects and are compared in trials with clinical outcomes, the differences in clinical effects will be small. So, unless large numbers of patients with AOM are enrolled in a trial with clinical outcomes, there is a high probability of concluding that two drugs are equivalent when they are not.

When planning a trial with clinical outcomes, several hundred patients are required to ensure that differences between an effective drug and a placebo are detected (Figure 16-3). When comparing two drugs, each with some antibacterial activity, several thousand patients are usually required to detect differences. Comparative trials of antibacterial drugs with clinical outcomes as the end point have enrolled too few patients to distinguish between poor drugs and excellent drugs: most have not been large enough to distinguish between a good drug and a placebo. In contrast, comparative bacteriologic efficacy of antibiotics can be assessed with sample sizes of fewer than 200 patients with bacterial AOM to distinguish between an antibiotic with 90% bacteriologic efficacy and one with 70% bacteriologic efficacy. Because trials with clinical end points have had inadequate statistical power, the most revealing data for making clinical choices among antibacterial agents has been bacteriologic efficacy data.

Some antibiotics with inferior efficacy have been, nonetheless, widely prescribed because they were licensed and promoted with inadequate data based on clinical outcomes. Considering that millions of prescriptions are written each year for AOM, the impact is not inconsequential. For every million prescriptions with a drug that has 20% lower bacteriologic efficacy than alternatives, 40,000 children will experience clinical symptoms that would otherwise experience relief.[10]

Advantages and Limitations of Bacteriologic Efficacy Data

Some of the advantages of bacteriologic efficacy data have been cited above: direct assessment of antibacterial effect in vivo, validated surrogate measures of clinical response, and the ability to reveal differences between antibiotics with relatively small numbers of patients. Bacteriologic efficacy data can also determine efficacy of antibiotic regimens for specific pathogens, at least for the three most common bacterial species: *S. pneumoniae, H. influenzae,* and occasionally *Moraxella catarrhalis.*

Double tympanocentesis studies have also been able to examine the relationship between levels of pathogen antimicrobial susceptibility and bacteriologic efficacy of the regimen. For example, Dagan and colleagues[11] demonstrated that cefuroxime axetil did not eradicate *S. pneumoniae* with intermediate levels of susceptibility to penicillin from the middle ear. Further, bacteriologic efficacy data in AOM has been used to establish pharmacokinetic–pharmacodynamic (PK-PD) parameters that relate antimicrobial susceptibility of the bacterial pathogen, the time-concentration characteristics of the oral antibiotic regimen, and bacteriologic cure. Microbiologists typically measure the susceptibility of a bacterial pathogen to an antibacterial drug by measuring the lowest concentration of antibiotic required to inhibit bacterial growth in the test tube—the minimum inhibitory concentration (MIC). To further apply this information to treating infections, knowing the concentrations of the antibiotic achieved with a particular regimen is needed, but even this information is insufficient for valid predictions.

How high does antimicrobial concentration need to be or how long does the concentration need to remain high for effective microbial killing in vivo? Animal models predict that for most of the oral antibiotics used to treat AOM (all except azithromycin), killing of the bacterial pathogen occurs when the serum concentrations of the antibiotic exceed the MIC of the pathogen for 40 to 50% of the dosing interval.[12] Craig and Andes[13] validated the 40 to 50% criterion in humans by correlating bacteriologic efficacy data from AOM trials with the time serum concentration exceeds the MIC for *S. pneumoniae* and *H. influenzae*. Bacteriologic efficacy data validated experimental concepts and criteria with clinically relevant data in humans. With this validation, PK-PD concepts can be applied to future antibiotic regimens to predict dosing for clinical success.

Bacteriologic efficacy trials have some disadvantages and limitations. Because tympanocentesis is not routinely performed, few investigators have been willing to perform a second tympanocentesis to measure bacteriologic efficacy. Accordingly, the bacteriologic efficacy of some licensed antibiotic regimens is unknown. For some antibiotics, the efficacy data are limited to a small number of patients, and clinical efficacy cannot be predicted. Thus, an important limitation of bacteriologic efficacy data is that there are not enough of them. Fortunately, there are sufficient data for most of the commonly prescribed antibiotics.

Antibiotic regimens have commonly been, arbitrarily, 10-day regimens. Bacteriologic efficacy studies have been performed, arbitrarily, in the 2 to 7 days, typically 3 to 6 days, after therapy was initiated. The 3- to 6-day time point for repeat tympanocentesis may not be optimal. Perhaps another time point, or more precise timing, would produce a better correlation between bacteriologic and clinical response. Nonetheless, the studies that have been performed have been validated, and further studies will be required to determine if there is a more optimal time for assessing bacteriologic efficacy.

Also, it is possible that tympanocentesis itself has an effect on the symptoms, clinical course, and possibly bacterial clearance in AOM. The clinical and bacteriologic response rates may be altered by the technique used to measure efficacy in these studies. While this is possible, the data correlating bacteriologic efficacy and clinical outcome support the assertion that if there are such effects of tympanocentesis, they are not large enough to obscure the important relationship between clinical and bacteriologic events.

The use of bacteriologic efficacy data to predict clinical outcome assumes that antibacterial drugs exert their effects by antibacterial properties and do not have appreciable effects on symptoms by other mechanisms, such as anti-inflammatory or analgesic effects. To date, no antibiotic has been shown to have such effects in AOM, so the assumption remains valid.

Caution is warranted in interpreting bacteriologic efficacy studies because they are performed in younger patients, mostly younger than 2 years of age, and cannot be generalized to all patients with AOM in a strict scientific sense. In children under age 2 years, however, the population at highest risk of bacteriologic and clinical failure, these data apply. Further, there is no compelling biologic evidence or rationale to suggest that the efficacy, or lack thereof, of an antibiotic in young patients will differ qualitatively in older patients.

REVIEW OF PUBLISHED BACTERIOLOGIC EFFICACY STUDIES

There are some differences among reported studies of bacteriologic efficacy. In the studies by Howie and colleagues[6,7,14–18] a repeat culture was not performed if there was no middle ear exudate at the follow-up visit, and these patients were considered to have eradication of their pathogens. In other published studies, follow-up tympanocenteses were performed during therapy in all patients with bacterial AOM.[19–29]

In some, but not all, studies, there were randomized double-blind comparisons between drug regimens. Ideally, there should be comparative trials between each new antibiotic and a standard regimen, for example, amoxicillin, or with an optimal regimen. There are several drugs for which bacteriologic efficacy data have not been obtained, and there are even fewer "head to head" comparisons between drugs that enable optimal comparisons between drugs. Because of these limitations, we believe that it is most instructive to examine the bacteriologic efficacy for each drug against the three major pathogens, rather than to evaluate each comparative study. The interested reader is directed toward the references for review of the specific comparisons. Also selected comparative trials are cited in the text below.

Method and Caveats

Reported bacteriologic efficacy studies are reviewed and presented for the various drug classes. Studies where repeat tympanocentesis was performed only in some patients with persistent symptoms have been excluded. Studies with the double tympanocentesis design have been included, except for the early studies by Howie and Ploussard that were not performed with a systematic protocol, a series of patients treated with trimethoprim-sulfamethoxazole that excluded patients on the basis of antimicrobial sensitivity tests, and data with antibiotics that are no longer used and also have minimal historic interest.

The data for patients given placebo by Howie and Ploussard[7] provide a historic control for assessing the bacteriologic efficacy of antibiotics for *S. pneumoniae* and *H. influenzae.* At that time, *M. catarrhalis* was not considered a pathogen. *Moraxella catarrhalis* accounted for 16 of 25 "nonpathogens" in initial middle ear aspirates and 13 of 21 in follow-up cultures. These data suggest that *M. catarrhalis* often persists in the middle ear without antibiotic therapy, leading the authors to state, "*M. catarrhalis* seems to persist in continuing exudates as often as *H. influenzae* when patients are treated with placebo." It is not possible, however, to definitively establish a spontaneous bacteriologic cure rate for *M. catarrhalis.* The data from the placebo study are presented in Tables 16-1 to 16-5 to facilitate comparisons for *S. pneumoniae* and *H. influenzae.*

Ninety-five percent confidence intervals have been calculated to account for statistical variation and facilitate comparison between drugs. This allows the reader to assess statistical significance of the data. If the 95% confidence intervals of two bacteriologic cure rates do not overlap, then the data are statistically significant at the $p < .05$ level.

The reader is cautioned that the comparisons with placebo, or other comparisons between drugs, are not usually from concurrent randomized trials and, therefore, do not have the scientific strengths of the randomized controlled design. Further, these studies have been performed during different time periods, and there have been changes in the antimicrobial susceptibility of the three major pathogens from 1969 to the present.

- From the mid-1970s onward, there has been a slow, but steady, increase in beta-lactamase–producing *H. influenzae,* making them less susceptible to penicillins and some cephalosporins.[30]
- *Moraxella catarrhalis* were uniformly sensitive to penicillin in the 1960s, but by the early 1980s, more than 80% produced beta-lactamase, and there is no clear documentation of the trajectory of this change.[31]
- From the 1970s onward, there has been an increase in

S. pneumoniae resistant to penicillins, cephalosporins, macrolides, and trimethoprim-sulfamethoxazole.

We present data for the three major pathogens for each drug used by individual study, rather than combine the results of the same-drug studies, because changes in pathogen susceptibility have not been documented precisely in relationship to all studies of bacteriologic efficacy. The reader should keep in mind that studies from earlier decades may not apply to current or future practice. The reader should also be aware that although some of these studies measured patient compliance with the antibiotic regimen, none of these methods is entirely satisfactory, and, in some individual cases, noncompliance could be a factor in bacteriologic failures.

Penicillins and Amoxicillin Combined with a Beta-Lactamase Inhibitor

In the mid-1970s, phenoxymethyl penicillin (penicillin G) was found to be efficacious for *S. pneumoniae,* but not for *H. influenzae,* although the numbers of patients with *H. influenza* were too small for definitive conclusion in comparison with placebo treated patients (see Table 16-1).[15] Compared with ampicillin, however, phenoxymethyl penicillin is significantly inferior for eradicating *H. influenzae,* so concluding that phenoxymethyl penicillin has less than optimal efficacy against this organism appears warranted.[7,14,15] In the 1970s, ampicillin and amoxicillin were found to be effective against both *S. pneumoniae* and *H. influenzae.* Amoxicillin displaced ampicillin because of similar efficacy but lower incidence of diarrhea.

Also in the mid-1970s, strains of *H. influenzae* began to hydrolyze amoxicillin and some cephalosporins because of an ability to produce the enzyme beta-lactamase. Resistant *H. influenzae* appeared in cases of AOM and increased slowly over the ensuing decades. The numbers of *H. influenzae* treated with amoxicillin in bacteriologic efficacy studies that produce beta-lactamase have been small, but only half of the 24 subjects with beta-lactamase–producing *H. influenzae* cleared the bacteria from their middle ear on amoxicillin therapy, a rate consistent with placebo. Data for *M. catarrhalis* are limited, and it is not possible from bacteriologic efficacy studies to conclude whether beta-lactamase strains have an impact in AOM treated with amoxicillin.

Adding the beta-lactamase inhibitor clavulanate to amoxicillin was designed to inhibit beta-lactamase–producing strains of *H. influenzae.* Bacteriologic efficacy data support the efficacy of amoxicillin-clavulanate for these pathogens.[23,25] Eradication rates are available for beta-lactamase–producing *M. catarrhalis* with amoxicillin-clavulanate, but it is not possible to conclude that it is superior to amoxicillin.[16,20,23,25]

Table 16-1 Bacteriologic Efficacy of Penicillins and Amoxicillin Combined with a Beta-Lactamase Inhibitor

Drug Dosage; Interval	Years	Streptococcus pneumoniae		Haemophilus influenzae		Moraxella catarrhalis	
		Eradicated/ Treated	Percent (95% CI)[†]	Eradicated/ Treated	Percent (95% CI)[†]	Eradicated/ Treated	Percent (95% CI)[†]
Placebo[7]	1968–70	11/57	19 (10, 31)	12/25	48 (27, 68)	NA	—
Phenoxymethyl penicillin[15] 20–40 mg/kg/d; qid	1974–75	17/19	89 (67, 98)	7/17	41 (18, 67)	NA	—
Ampicillin[7] 36–73 mg/kg/d; qid	1969	11/11	100 (72, 100)*	11/12	92 (61, 99)	NA	—
Ampicillin[14] 50–70 mg/kg/d; qid	1972–73	18/21	86 (64, 97)	28/31	90 (74, 98)	NA	—
Ampicillin[15] 50–70 mg/kg/d; qid	1976–77	21/25	84 (64, 95)	29/33	88 (72, 96)	NA	—
Amoxicillin[14] 12–31 mg/kg/d; tid	1972–73	27/32	84 (67, 94)	14/17	82 (56, 96)	NA	—
Amoxicillin[16,17] dose NA	1985–87	17/18	94 (73, 99)	3/8 BL+ 13/13 BL– 16/21 total	38 (8, 75) 100 (75, 100)* 76 (53, 92)	9/12 BL+ 0 BL– 9/12 total	75 (43, 95) 75 (43, 95)
Amoxicillin[18] 40 mg/kg/d; tid	1987–88	29/31	94 (78, 99)	26/35	74 (56, 87)	13/21	62 (38, 82)
Amoxicillin[21] 40 mg/kg/d; tid	1991	14/15	93 (68, 99)	1/3 BL+ 7/10 BL– 8/13 total	33 (1, 99) 70 (35, 93) 61 (32, 86)	6/7 BL+ 1/1 BL– 7/8 total	86 (42, 99) 100 (2, 100)* 88 (47, 99)
Amoxicillin[29] 80 mg/kg/d; bid	1999– 2001	6/6 PSSP 16/18 PNSP 22/24 total	100 (54, 100)* 89 (65, 98) 92 (73, 99)	8/13 BL+ 21/24 BL– 29/37 total	62 (32, 86) 87 (68, 97) 78 (61, 90)	NA	—
Amoxicillin- clavulanate[20] 40/mg/kg/d; tid	1986	21/21	100 (83, 100)*	0 BL+ 14/15 BL– 14/15 total	93 (68, 99) 9 (68, 99)	4/4 BL+ 3/3 BL– 7/7 total	100 (39, 100)* 100 (29, 100)* 100 (59, 100)*
Amoxicillin- clavulanate[16] dose NA	1988–91	40/42	95 (84, 99)	33/43	76 (61, 88)	21/23 BL+	91 (71, 98)
Amoxicillin- clavulanate[23] 45–6.4 mg/kg/d; bid	1997–98	PSSP 18/20 PNSP 9/9 Total 27/29	90 (68, 99) 27 (66, 100)* 93 (77, 99)	8/9 BL+ 22/30 BL– 30/39 total	89 (53, 98) 73 (58, 96) 77 (61, 88)	4/4 BL+	100 (39, 100)*
Amoxicillin- clavulanate[25] 90–6.4 mg/kg/d; bid	1999	88/88 MIC ≤ 1.0 31/34 MIC >1.0 109/122 total	100 (96, 100) 91 (76, 98) 89 (82, 94)	25/28 BL+ 53/55 BL– 78/83 total	89 (71, 98) 96 (82, 98) 93 (86, 98)	3/3	100 (29, 100)*

BL+ = beta-lactamase–producing strains; BL– = non-beta-lactamase–producing strains; CI = confidence interval; MIC = minimal inhibitory concentration in µg/mL; NA = not available; PNSP = penicillin-nonsusceptible *Streptococcus pneumoniae*; PSSP = penicillin-susceptible *Streptococcus pneumoniae*.

*One-sided, 97.5% CI.

[†]Binomial exact 95% CI.[35]

The recent increase in the prevalence of *S. pneumoniae* not susceptible to penicillin led to a recommendation to increase the dose of amoxicillin, alone or combined with clavulanate, from 40 to 50 mg/kg/d to 80 to 90 mg/kg/d. Bacteriologic efficacy studies with higher doses of amoxicillin, alone or combined with clavulanate, demonstrate eradication of *S. pneumoniae* not susceptible to penicillin.[25,29]

Cephalosporins

Among the oral cephalosporins, cefaclor, cefixime, cefuroxime axetil, and cefpodoxime have been studied in double tympanocentesis trials, and there are limited data with cefprozil (see Table 16-2). There are no bacteriologic efficacy data for loracarbef, cefdinir, or ceftibuten. For cefaclor, three separate trials found reduced bacteriologic efficacy of cefaclor for all the three major pathogens combined compared with comparator drugs: amoxicillin/ ampicillin, trimethoprim-sulfamethoxazole, and amoxicillin-clavulanate.[16,19,20] In two further reports, cefaclor produced low eradication rates for *S. pneumoniae* not susceptible to penicillin and beta-lactamase–producing *H. influenzae.*[11,22]

Cefixime is a beta-lactamase–stable cephalosporin that is very active in vitro against *H. influenzae.* A pooled analysis of three trials comparing cefixime versus amoxicillin found that eradication rates for *H. influenzae* were superior in cefixime-treated patients, but eradication rates for *S. pneumoniae* were better with amoxicillin.[17,18,21] Cefuroxime axetil eradicated *H. influenzae* and penicillin-susceptible *S. pneumoniae* from the middle ear, but eradication rates for more resistant isolates with cefuroxime MICs > 0.5 µg/mL were lower than for isolates with MICs ≤ 0.5 µg/mL.[11,16] Cefpodoxime proxetil was efficacious for *H. influenzae* and *S. pneumoniae,* but definitive conclusions for eradication of *M. catarrhalis* cannot be made because of limited sample size.[16] Last, cefprozil has limited data suggesting effective elimination of *S. pneumoniae* but probably not *H. influenzae.*[16]

Ceftriaxone is the only parenteral cephalosporin used to treat AOM. A single 50 mg/kg intramuscular dose is highly efficacious for *H. influenzae.* For *S. pneumoniae* with reduced susceptibility to penicillin, a single dose had only a 52% eradication rate, but the same dose on 3 consecutive days achieved 92% eradication.[26,27]

Macrolides

A very limited early study of erythromycin suggested efficacy for eradicating *S. pneumoniae* but not *H. influenzae* (see Table 16-3).[7] Similarly, a small study of clarithromycin found a high eradication rate for *S. pneumoniae* but not *H. influenzae.*[16] Azithromycin is the most comprehensively studied macrolide. In two trials,[22,23] azithromycin eradication rates for *H. influenzae* were no better than historic placebo control.[7] In a comparative study with amoxicillin-clavulanate, azithromycin had inferior bacterial eradication rates for all bacterial isolates, including *H. influenzae.*[23] Moreover, patient numbers in this study were adequate to demonstrate the clinical inferiority of azithromycin.[23]

H. influenzae intrinsically resists macrolides at clinically achievable concentrations because of an efflux pump that is almost universal in this bacterial species. Macrolides have been efficacious for *S. pneumoniae* in all bacteriologic efficacy trials; however, increases in the prevalence of macrolide-resistant strains may force revision of this viewpoint.

Sulfonamides

Data with triple sulfonamide are too limited to draw conclusions, but it appears to improve bacteriologic efficacy for *H. influenzae* when combined with penicillin or erythromycin(see Table 16-4).[7,15] These data may have reduced applicability today because of increasing resistance of *H. influenzae* to sulfonamides. The erythromycin-sulfonamide combination, however, is still licensed for use in the United States.

Bacteriologic efficacy of trimethoprim-sulfamethoxazole appeared less than optimal in a small study in the 1970s, but efficacy was shown against all major pathogens in a trial in the 1980s.[15,19] Since that time, there has been increasing in vitro resistance to trimethoprim-sulfamethoxazole among strains of *S. pneumoniae* and *H. influenzae.* A trial in the 1990s showed failure to eliminate many strains of *S. pneumoniae* and *H. influenzae* with in vitro resistance.[24]

Quinolones

Quinolones have not been licensed for use in pediatrics because of toxicity concerns. Gradually, evidence that these agents can be safely used in children has emerged, and members of this class of antibiotics are being evaluated in clinical trials (see Table 16-5). The first quinolone that has been studied, gatifloxacin, has high bacteriologic efficacy against *S. pneumoniae* and *H. influenzae.*[28]

CLINICAL APPLICATION OF BACTERIOLOGIC EFFICACY DATA

After the clinician has diagnosed AOM and decided to use an antibiotic, which antibiotic should be chosen? Drug efficacy, safety, cost, and other factors need to be balanced. Data on the clinical efficacy of antibiotics have

Table 16-2 Bacteriologic Efficacy of Cephalosporins

Drug Dosage; Interval	Years	*Streptococcus pneumoniae* Eradicated/ Treated	Percent (95% CI)[†]	*Haemophilus influenzae* Eradicated/ Treated	Percent (95% CI)[†]	*Moraxella catarrhalis* Eradicated/ Treated	Percent (95% CI)[†]
Placebo[7]	1968–70	11/57	19 (10, 31)	12/25	48 (27, 68)	NA	—
Cefaclor[16] 40–50 mg/kg/d; qid	1979–80	8/17	47 (23, 72)	18/30	60 (40, 77)	NA	—
Cefaclor[19] 40 mg/kg/d; bid	1984	16/20	80 (56, 94)	10/18	55 (31, 78)	8/8	100 (63, 100)*
Cefaclor[20] 40 mg/kg/d; tid	1986	12/14	85 (47, 98)	2/2 BL+ 8/12 BL– 10/14 total	100 (15, 100)* 66 (34, 90) 71 (41, 91)	5/7 BL+ 0 BL– 5/7 total	71 (29, 96) 71 (29, 96)
Cefaclor[11, 22] 40 mg/kg/d; tid	1995–98	24/25 PSSP 5/12 PNSP 29/37 total	96 (79, 99) 41 (15, 72) 78 (62, 90)	37/41 MIC < 1.0 11/29 MIC ≥ 1.0	90 (77, 97) 38 (21, 57)	NA	—
Cefixime[17,18] 8 mg/kg/d; bid, qid	1985–87	33/45	73 (58, 85)	57/61	93 (84, 98)	25/28	86 (68, 96)
Cefixime[18] 8 mg/kg/d; qd	1987–88	21/26	81 (61, 93)	31/34	91 (76, 98)	10/10	100 (69, 100)*
Cefixime[21] 8 mg/kg/d; bid, qid	1991	12/16	75 (47, 93)	1/1 BL+ 9/9 BL– 10/10 total	100 (2, 100)* 100 (66, 100)* 100 (69, 100)*	5/6 BL+ 1/1 BL– 6/7 total	83 (35, 99) 100 (2, 100) 85 (42, 99)
Cefuroxime axetil[11] 30 mg/kg/d; bid	1995–96	20/22 PSSP 15/19 PNSP 35/41 total	91 (71, 99) 79 (54, 94) 85 (71, 94)	39/46	85 (71, 94)	NA	—
Cefuroxime axetil[16] dose NA	1987–88	11/11	100 (71, 100)	4/5	80 (28, 99)	3/3	100 (29, 100)
Cefpodoxime[16] dose NA	1986–91	20/24	83 (62, 95)	21/22	95 (77, 99)	9/15	60 (32, 83)
Cefprozil[16] 30 mg/kg/d; bid	1987–88	12/13	92 (64, 99)	6/14	42 (17, 71)	—	75 (19, 99)
Ceftriaxone[26] 50 mg/kg IM; qd for 1 day	1998–99	3/3 PSSP 14/27 PNSP 17/30 total	100 (29, 100)* 52 (32, 71) 56 (37, 75)	27/27	100 (87, 100)*	3/3	100 (29, 100)*
Ceftriaxone[26,27] 50 mg/kg IM; qd for 3 days	1995–99	14/14 PSSP 63/68 PNSP 77/82 total	100 (76, 100)* 92 (84, 86) 94 (86, 98)	92/92	100 (96, 100)*	2/3	67 (18, 98)

BL+ = beta-lactamase–producing strains; BL– = non-beta-lactamase–producing strains; CI = confidence interval; MIC = minimal inhibitory concentration in μg/mL; NA = not available; PNSP = penicillin-nonsusceptible *Streptococcus pneumoniae*; PSSP = penicillin-susceptible *Streptococcus pneumoniae*.

*One-sided, 97.5% CI.

[†]Binomial exact 95% CI.[35]

Table 16-3 Bacteriologic Efficacy of Macrolides

Drug Dosage; Interval	Years	Streptococcus pneumoniae		Haemophilus influenzae		Moraxella catarrhalis	
		Eradicated/ Treated	Percent (95% CI)[†]	Eradicated/ Treated	Percent (95% CI)[†]	Eradicated/ Treated	Percent (95% CI)[†]
Placebo[7]	1968–70	11/57	19 (10, 31)	12/25	48 (27, 68)	NA	—
Erythromycin estolate[7]	1969–70	6/7	85 (42, 99)	2/8	25 (3, 65)	NA	—
Clarithromycin[16] dose NA	1990–91	12/12	100 (73, 100)	3/15	20 (6, 57)	4/5	80 (28, 99)
Azithromycin[22] 10 mg/kg/d; QD for 3 days	1995–96	12/12 MIC ≤ .06 0/6 MIC ≥ 32	100 (73, 100) 0 (0, 46)	13/33	39 (23, 57)	5/8	63 (24, 91)
Azithromycin[23] 10 mg/kg/d day 1, then 5 mg/kg/d days 2–5; qd	1997–98	23/25 MIC ≤ .25 3/8 MIC ≥ 2 26/33 total	92 (74, 99) 38 (9, 76) 79 (61, 91)*	14/30	47 (28, 66)	NA	—

CI = confidence interval; MIC = minimal inhibitory concentration in μg/mL; NA = not available.
*One-sided, 97.5% CI.
[†]Binomial exact 95% CI.[35]

Table 16-4 Bacteriologic Efficacy of Sulfonamides Alone and Combined with Other Antibiotics

Drug Dosage; Interval	Years	Streptococcus pneumoniae		Haemophilus influenzae		Moraxella catarrhalis	
		Eradicated/ Treated	Percent (95% CI)[†]	Eradicated/ Treated	Percent (95% CI)[†]	Eradicated/ Treated	Percent (95% CI)[†]
Placebo[7]	1968–70	11/57	19 (10,31)	12/25	48 (27, 68)	NA	—
Triple sulfonamide[7] 72–144 mg/kg/d; qid	1969–70	10/13	76 (46, 94)	1/2	50 (1, 98)	NA	—
Triple sulfonamide[15] 72–144 mg/kg/d plus phenoxymethyl penicillin[15] 18–36 mg/kg/d; qid	1974–75	41/50	82 (68, 91)	24/32	75 (56, 88)	NA	—
Triple sulfonamide[7] 72–144 mg/kg/d plus erythromycin estolate[7] 18–36 mg/kg/d; qid	1969–70	29/29	100 (88, 100)	24/25	96 (79, 99)	NA	—
TMP-SMX[15] 8/40 mg/kg/d; bid	1973–74	7/9	77 (39, 97)	12/21	57 (34, 78)	NA	—
TMP-SMX[19] 8/40 mg/kg/d; bid	1998–99	19/19	100 (82, 100)*	13/14	92 (66, 99)	9/9	100 (66, 100)*
TMP-SMX[24] 8/40 mg/kg/d; bid	1998–99	9/9 MIC ≤ .5 4/15 MIC > .5 13/24 total	100 (66, 100)* 27 (8, 55) 54 (33, 74)	28/28 MIC ≤ .5 6/12 MIC > .5 34/40 total	100 (88, 100)* 50 (21, 79) 85 (70, 94)	NA	—

CI = confidence interval; MIC = minimal inhibitory concentration in μg/mL; NA = not available; TMP-SMX = trimethoprim-sulfamethoxazole.
*One-sided, 97.5% CI.
[†]Binomial exact 95% CI.[35]

Table 16-5 Bacteriologic Efficacy of Quinolones

Drug Dosage; Interval	Years	Streptococcus pneumoniae		Haemophilus influenzae		Moraxella catarrhalis	
		Eradicated/ Treated	Percent (95% CI)*	Eradicated/ Treated	Percent (95% CI)*	Eradicated/ Treated	Percent (95% CI)*
Placebo[7]	1968–70	11/57	19 (10,31)	12/25	48 (27, 68)	NA	—
Gatifloxacin[8] 10 mg/kg/d; qd	2000–01	28/30	93 (78, 99)	59/59	100 (93, 100)	NA	—

CI = confidence interval; NA = not available.
*Binomial exact 95% CI.[35]

Table 16-6 Pointers and Pitfalls

1. Bacteriologic efficacy is measured by culturing the site of infection (tympanocentesis) before antibiotic therapy and again during or at the end of the antibiotic regimen.

2. Clinical effects of antibacterial treatment in AOM are diluted by nonbacterial cases, obscured by viral co-infection, augmented by the host's substantial immunologic defenses, and aided by concurrent analgesics and antipyretics. Bacteriologic efficacy in the middle ear is the most direct outcome measure.

3. Eradicating bacteria from the middle ear increases clinical improvement by about 30% compared with failure to eliminate pathogens from the site of infection (see Figure 16-1).

4. Antibiotic comparisons using clinical outcomes are subject to the "Pollyanna phenomenon," by which clinical improvement, despite bacteriologic failure, can make a poor drug appear clinically effective when it is not (see Figure 16-2).

5. Bacteriologic efficacy data can reveal differences between antibiotics with relatively small numbers of patients and can also determine the efficacy of an antibiotic regimen for specific bacterial pathogens.

6. Data are available (see Tables 16-1 to 16-5) regarding the bacteriologic efficacy of common antimicrobial classes for major otitis media pathogens, including *S. pneumoniae*, *H. influenzae*, and *M. catarrhalis*.

7. When a clinician diagnoses AOM and decides to use an antibiotic, bacteriologic efficacy data should guide drug selection.

AOM = acute otitis media.

been inadequate. This has led to the licensure and widespread use of antibiotic regimens that are convenient and palatable, believed by clinicians to be efficacious, but that have inferior efficacy bacteriologically and, ultimately, clinically. Cefaclor and azithromycin have been striking examples of this phenomenon.

The clinician's best guide to antibiotic efficacy is bacteriologic efficacy data (Table 16-6). The Drug-resistant *Streptococcus pneumoniae* Therapeutic Working Group, convened by the Centers for Disease Control, formulated guidelines for selecting antibiotics in AOM.[32–34] They relied heavily on bacteriologic efficacy data to formulate these recommendations. Unfortunately, bacteriologic efficacy data are sometimes unavailable or based on limited numbers of patients. In these cases, the clinician still cannot rely on data from clinical trials with clinical outcomes; efficacy can only be an intelligent guess based on in vitro antimicrobial activity pharmacokinetic data, including drug concentrations at the site of infection.

Bacteriologic efficacy studies, however, have revealed that the criteria for in vitro antimicrobial susceptibility may be inappropriate.[11] The emerging field of PK-PD analysis holds the promise of improved clinical prediction with subclinical data and may have increasing application in the future. Unless clinical trials are improved, the clinician should still look to bacteriologic efficacy data as the best guide for judging efficacy and making informed clinical decisions.

REFERENCES

1. Bluestone CD, Stephenson JS, Martin LM. Ten-year review of otitis media pathogens. Pediatr Infect Dis J 1992;11:S7–11.
2. Heikkinen T. Temporal development of acute otitis media during upper respiratory tract infection. Pediatr Infect Dis J 1994;13:659–61.
3. Heikkinen T, Thint M, Chonmaitree T. Prevalence of various respiratory viruses in the middle ear during acute otitis media. N Engl J Med 1999;340:260–4.
4. Pitkaranta A, Virolainen A, Jero J, et al. Detection of rhinovirus, respiratory syncytial virus, and coronavirus infections in acute otitis media reverse transcriptase polymerase chain reaction. Pediatrics 1998;102:400–1.

5. Arola M, Ziegler T, Ruuskanen O. Respiratory virus infection as a cause of prolonged symptoms in acute otitis media. J Pediatr 1990;116:697–701.

6. Howie VM, Ploussard JH. The "in vivo sensitivity test"—bacteriology of middle ear exudates. Pediatrics 1969;44:940–4.

7. Howie VM, Ploussard JH. Efficacy of fixed combination, antibiotics versus separate components in otitis media. Effectiveness of erythromycin estolate, triple sulfonamide, ampicillin, erythromycin estolate-triple sulfonamide, and placebo in 280 patients with acute otitis media under two and one-half years of age. Clin Pediatr 1972; 211:205–14.

8. Carlin SA, Marchant CD, Shurin PA, et al. Host factors and early therapeutic responses in acute otitis media: does symptomatic response correlate with bacterial outcome? J Pediatr 1991;118:178–83.

9. Dagan R, Leibovitz E, Greenberg D, et al. Early eradication of pathogens from middle ear fluid during antibiotic treatment of acute otitis media is associated with improved clinical outcome. Pediatr Infect Dis J 1998;17:776–82.

10. Marchant CD, Carlin SA, Johnson CE, Shurin PA. Measuring the comparative efficacy of antibacterial agents for acute otitis media: the "Pollyanna phenomenon." J Pediatr 1992;120:72–7.

11. Dagan R, Abramson O, Leibovitz E, et al. Bacteriologic response to oral cephalosporins: are established susceptibility breakpoints appropriate in the case of acute otitis media? J Infect Dis 1997;176:1253–9.

12. Andes D, Craig WA. Animal model pharmacokinetics and pharmacodynamics: a critical review. Int J Antimicrob Agents 2002;19:261–8.

13. Craig WA, Andes D. Pharmacokinetics and pharmacodynamics of antibiotics in otitis media. Pediatr Infect Dis J 1996;15:255–9.

14. Howie VM, Ploussard JH, Sloyer J. Comparison of ampicillin and amoxicillin in the treatment of otitis media in children. J Infect Dis 1974;129: S181–4.

15. Howie VM, Ploussard JH. The "in vivo sensitivity test": bacteriology of middle ear exudates during antimicrobial therapy in otitis media. Pediatrics 1969;44:940–4.

16. Howie VM. Eradication of bacterial pathogens from middle ear infections. Clin Infect Dis 1992;14:S209–11.

17. Howie VM, Owen MJ. Bacteriologic and clinical efficacy of cefixime compared with amoxicillin in acute otitis media. Pediatr Infect Dis J 1987;6:989–91.

18. Owen MJ, Anwar R, Nguyen HK, et al. Efficacy of cefixime in the treatment of acute otitis media in children. Am J Dis Child 1993;147:81–6.

19. Marchant CD, Shurin PA, Turcyzk VA, et al. A randomized, controlled trial of cefaclor compared with trimethoprim-sulfamethoxazole for treatment of acute otitis media. J Pediatr 1984;105:633–8.

20. Marchant CD, Shurin PA, Johnson CE, et al. A randomized controlled trial of amoxicillin plus clavulanate compared with cefaclor for treatment of acute otitis media. J Pediatr 1986;109:891–6.

21. Johnson CE, Carlin SA, Super DM, et al. Cefixime compared with amoxicillin for treatment of acute otitis media. J Pediatr 1991; 119:117–22.

22. Dagan R, Leibovitz E, Fliss DM, et al. Bacteriologic efficacy of oral azithromycin and oral cefaclor in the treatment of acute otitis media in infants and young children. Antimicrob Agents Chemother 2000;44:43–50.

23. Dagan R, Johnson C, McLinn S, et al. Bacteriologic and clinical efficacy of amoxicillin-clavulanate versus azithromycin in acute otitis media. Pediatr Infect Dis J 2000;19:95–104.

24. Leiberman A, Leibovitz E, Piglansky L, et al. Bacteriologic and clinical efficacy of trimethoprim/sulfamethoxazole for treatment of acute otitis media. Pediatr Infect Dis J 2001;20:260–4.

25. Dagan R, Hoberman A, Johnson C, et al. Bacteriologic and clinical efficacy of high dose amoxicillin/clavulanate in children with acute otitis media. Pediatr Infect Dis J 2001;20:829–37.

26. Leibovitz E, Piglansky L, Raiz S, et al. Bacteriologic and clinical efficacy of one day vs. three day intramuscular ceftriaxone for treatment of nonresponsive acute otitis media in children. Pediatr Infect Dis J 2000;19:1040–5.

27. Leibovitz E, Piglansky L, Raiz S, et al. Bacteriologic efficacy of a three-day intramuscular ceftriaxone regimen in nonresponsive acute otitis media. Pediatr Infect Dis J 1998;17:1126–31.

28. Leibovitz E, Piglansky L, Raiz S, et al. Bacteriological efficacy of gatifloxacin in the treatment of recurrent/non-responsive acute otitis media. (G-1558a). 41st Interscience Conference on Antimicrobial Agents and Chemotherapy; 2001 December 16–19; Chicago, IL.

29. Piglansky L, Leibovitz E, Raiz S, et al. The bacteriologic and clinical efficacy of high-dose amoxicillin as first-line therapy for acute otitis media in children. Pediatr Infect Dis J. (In press)

30. Shurin PA, Pelton SI, Scheifele D, Klein JO. Otitis media caused by non-typable, ampicillin-resistant strains of *Haemophilus influenzae*. J Pediatr 1976;88:646–9.

31. Shurin PA, Marchant CD, Kim CH, et al. Emergence of beta-lactamase–producing strains of *Branhamella catarrhalis* as important agents of acute otitis media. Pediatr Infect Dis J 1983;2:34–8.

32. Jacobs MR, Koornhoff HJ, Robins-Browne RM, et al. Emergence of multiply resistant pneumococci. N Engl J Med 1978;299:735–40.

33. Jacobs MR, Dagan R, Appelbaum PC, Burch DJ. Prevalence of antimicrobial-resistant pathogens in middle ear fluid: multinational study of 917 children with acute otitis media. Antimicrob Agents Chemother 1998;42:589–95.

34. Dowell SF, Butler JC, Giebink GS, et al. Acute otitis media: management and surveillance in an era of pneumococcal resistance—a report from the Drug-resistant *Streptococcus pneumoniae* Therapeutic Working Group. Pediatr Infect Dis J 1999;18:1–9.

35. Fleiss L. Statistical methods for rates and proportions. 2nd ed. New York (NY): John Wiley & Sons; 1981.

CHAPTER 17

Vaccine Prevention

Stephen Ira Pelton, MD

The physician is Nature's assistant.
Galen

OBJECTIVES

On completing this chapter, the reader will be able to

1. Identify the priciples necessary to achieve effective immunoprophylaxis of acute otitis media (AOM).
2. Detail results of efficacy trials of vaccines for prevention of AOM (influenza trivalent inactivated and pneumococcal conjugate vaccine).
3. Provide perspective on the benefit of immunizations with currently available vaccines for prevention of AOM.

PATHOGENESIS OF ACUTE OTITIS MEDIA

Acute otitis media (AOM) in children begins early and recurs frequently.[1] Day care attendance has increased the burden of disease early in life, but AOM incidence decreases after age 3 years.[2] These observations have led to two alternative explanations. First, Eustachian tube function is the critical correlate for developing AOM, and the decline in episodes in most children reflects improved Eustachian tube function. An alternative, although not mutually exclusive, explanation is that immunologic maturation is the critical process leading to the relative protection from AOM observed with increasing age. Supporters of the latter hypothesis suggest that maturation of the immune system and exposure to viral and bacterial respiratory pathogens early in life results in host defenses capable of protecting against middle ear disease.

Children with immunologic impairments (human immunodeficiency virus [HIV] infection, immunoglobulin [Ig]G or IgG subclass deficiency, or impaired response to polysaccharide antigens) have an increased frequency of AOM episodes, and this lasts beyond the first few years of life, suggesting that immune dysfunction contributes to AOM susceptibility.[3–5] Alternatively, it is widely accepted that ET dysfunction, as observed in children with cleft palate or induced in adult volunteers following challenge with respiratory virus, leads to altered middle ear ventilation that precedes the nearly universal development of

AOM in the first group and AOM in a subset of challenged adults.[6,7] Supporters of immunologic naïveté as a primary hypothesis suggest that inducing protective antibody and/or immunologic memory will prevent AOM, similar to the reduction in *Haemophilus* or pneumococcal invasive disease caused by conjugate bacterial vaccines.

Viral and bacterial pathogens, most often in concert, are critical for AOM onset.[8,9] Tympanocentesis shows that *Streptococcus pneumoniae*, nontypeable *Haemophilus influenzae*, and *Moraxella catarrhalis* are the predominant pathogens worldwide.[10,11] Viral copathogens are often involved resulting in a seasonal variation of AOM, highest in winter, paralleling viral upper respiratory infections (URIs) in the community.[9,12] Further, the high incidence of AOM in children under 2 years of age is when respiratory infections prevail. Prospective clinical studies of children with viral URIs identify a peak attack rate for AOM beginning 3 to 4 days after onset.[13,14] AOM is associated with specific viruses in the middle ear and nasopharynx (Tables 17-1 and 17-2), including respiratory syncytial virus (RSV), influenza A and B virus, and adenovirus (see Table 17-1).[15,16]

Viral respiratory tract infection changes ET function (epithelial cell damage, ciliary dysfunction, and negative middle ear pressure), alters human host defense mechanisms (decreased polymorphonuclear cell function), and increases the density of nasopharyngeal colonization with bacterial AOM pathogens.[17–20] Viruses are also found in the middle ear of children with AOM as a sole pathogen or, more often, with bacterial otopathogens. These studies provide sufficient evidence to hypothesize that preventing respiratory infection caused by viral pathogens has implications for preventing AOM. The pathogenesis of AOM (Figure 17-1) provides multiple opportunities for immunoprophylaxis by targeting viral respiratory pathogens and bacterial otopathogens. This chapter will focus on the evidence from experimental animal and clinical (pediatric) studies that establishes the necessary principles for successful immunoprophylaxis in children, as well as the efficacy and limitations of current immunization strategies.

Table 17-1 Spectrum of Viral Respiratory Infection in 456 Children with AOM*

Virus	Infected, n (%)	Virus in MEF, n (%)[†]
Respiratory syncytial virus	65 (14)	48 (74)
Parainfluenza virus	29 (6)	15 (52)
Influenza virus	24 (5)	10 (42)
Enterovirus	27 (6)	3 (11)
Adenovirus	23 (5)	1 (4)

AOM = acute otitis media; MEF = middle ear fluid.
*Data from Heikkinen T et al.[15]
[†]Specific viral infection with recovery from MEF.

Table 17-2 Viral Detection by RT-PCR in 92 Children with AOM*

Virus	Middle Ear Fluid, c (%)	Nasopharynx, n (%)
Human rhinovirus	22 (24)	28 (30)
Respiratory syncytial virus	17 (18)	21 (23)
Human coronavirus	7 (8)	14 (15)
TOTAL	44 (48)	57 (62)

AOM = acute otitis media; RT-PCR = reverse transcriptase-polymerase chain reaction.
*Data from Pitkäranta A et al.[16]

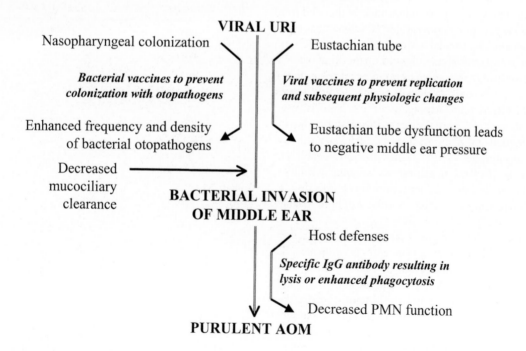

Figure 17-1 Schema of events in viral-bacterial pathogenesis of acute otitis media (AOM) with potential vaccine targets *(italics).* IgG = immunoglobin G; PMN = polymorphonuclear leukocyte; URI = upper respiratory infection.

MICROBIAL TARGETS FOR VACCINE STRATEGIES

Spectrum and Diversity of Bacterial Otopathogens

S. pneumoniae and H. influenzae are the predominant pathogens recovered from the middle ear of children with AOM. The same pathogens are important for recurrent disease; however, when isolates from consecutive episodes are examined, identical pathogens are rarely recovered.[21,22]

Suetake and colleagues[21] identified a change in the bacterial isolate recovered from the nasopharynx or middle ear (otorrhea) in 150 of 202 consecutive episodes in Japanese children. Even in cases from which a penicillin-sensitive or penicillin-intermediate isolate was recovered from the two consecutive episodes, the isolates differed in 68% of the episodes as determined by detailed analysis of serotype, analysis of penicillin binding proteins, or other genetic markers. Similarly, Leibovitz and colleagues[22] reported that recurrent episodes of AOM, within 30 days of antimicrobial therapy, were caused by a nonidentical isolate (from the initial episode) in more than 75% of children. The authors used polyacrylamide gel techniques, routine microbiology, and beta-lactamase production to compare identity among consecutive isolates.

Otitis media (OM) recurs because of the diversity of isolates within the bacterial species, not from failure to develop type-specific immunity to a specific bacterial pathogen.[23–25] Shurin and colleagues[24] and Bernstein and colleagues[25] observed independently that children with AOM caused by nontypeable H. influenzae developed serum bactericidal activity following infection. Bernstein and coworkers[25] showed further that when a new episode of AOM caused by nontypeable H. influenzae occurred, bactericidal activity against the first isolate was not effective in vitro against the second isolate. These observations are consistent with animal studies of experimental OM demonstrating bactericidal antibody following middle ear infection with nontypeable H. influenzae, protection against rechallenge with the homologous isolates, and susceptibility to infection at rechallenge with a heterologous isolates of nontypeable H. influenzae.[26]

Current evidence implies that the immune response following middle ear infection with H. influenzae is directed at strain-specific epitopes and not those conserved across the species. This represents perhaps the major challenge in developing efficacious vaccines—identifying conserved epitopes that are surface exposed and are critical for virulence for each of the bacterial pathogens. We reported efficacy using the P1 protein from the outer membrane of nontypeable H. influenzae as a vaccine candidate in our experimental animal model; however, it was neither conserved, as challenge with heterologous isolates resulted in OM, nor critical for virulence, as an otherwise isogenic P1-deficient mutant was capable of producing middle ear infection.[27]

Vaccines for preventing disease cause by S. pneumoniae have focused on the capsule as a critical virulence feature, even though each of the described 90 serotypes has a unique polysaccharide composition with limited cross-reaction among serotypes. One reason for targeting the capsule is its capacity to protect S. pneumoniae from host defenses and the low pathogenicity of unencapsulated isolates (at least for invasive disease). Further, consensus is lacking about alternative targets that fulfill the requirements for potential vaccine candidates: conservation of the antigen across the species and critical for virulence. Last, repeated infection with the same serotype of S. pneumoniae is uncommon.[28]

After identifying the capsule as a candidate vaccine target, two challenges remained for a successful pneumococcal polysaccharide vaccine for AOM in children. First, polysaccharide antigens are poorly immunogenic in young children. Second, multiple serotypes are required to prevent a significant proportion of AOM. Consequently, a conjugate vaccine, linking type-specific polysaccharides to a protein carrier, would be required

Table 17-3 Prevalence of Pneumococcal Serotypes in Middle Ear Fluid*

Serotype	Frequency (%)
19F	16.1
23F	14.9
14	13.1
6B	10.1
6A	7.3
19A	6.6
9V	4.6
3	4.0
15	2.1
1	1.6
18C	1.4
11	1.3
5	1.0
7	0.8
4	0.7

*Data from Hausdorff W et al[33]: United States (3 samples), Israel, Greece, France, Finland, Argentina, and other countries.

to overcome the relative lack of immunogenicity of the polysaccharide antigen in the target population (< 2 years).[29,30]

A limited number of serotypes cause more than 80% of invasive pneumococcal disease in in children in the United States, resulting in a heptavalent conjugate vaccine with greater than 75% efficacy after licensure.[31,32] For OM, however, the spectrum of serotypes producing disease is broader and varies by age (Table 17-3).[33] A large multinational compilation of isolates from more than 3,200 episodes of AOM identified serotypes 19F and 23F as most common, comprising 13 to 25% of cases, followed by types 14 and 6B, accounting for 6 to 18% of disease, and 6A, 19A, and 9V, each causing 5 to 10%. These seven serotypes were prominent in the 6- to 59-month age group despite the broad geographic diversity of the nine different data sets. For children age < 6 months or > 60 months, serotypes 1, 3, and 5 were relatively more important than at other ages.

The broad diversity of serotypes capable of producing AOM in children creates a challenge for vaccines that rely on immunity to type-specific capsular polysaccharide. Although currently the polysaccharide capsule is the focus of clinical trials for preventing pneumococcal disease, identifying a conserved target critical for virulence among all isolates of *S. pneumoniae* remains a goal for future efforts.

Principles of Vaccine Development for Preventing Bacterial Otitis Media

Recurrent OM, pneumonia, and sinusitis occur frequently in children with immunoglobulin and immunoglobulin subclass deficiency, suggesting that immune dysfunction may predispose to AOM. Hotomi and colleagues[34] showed a reduced response to bacterial polysaccharide and protein antigens in otitis-prone children; however, other studies fail to identify immune dysfunction in a significant proportion of afflicted children. Immunologic naïveté, as evidenced by a lack of specific antibody to pathogens recovered from the middle ear, is a clear risk feature but does not differentiate whether local or humoral antibody is the critical protective mechanism. Clarifying the role of humoral versus local antibody in middle ear infection is a critical concept for future vaccine development.

Animal studies suggest that the humoral antibody can prevent AOM caused by *S. pneumoniae* or nontypeable *H. influenzae*. After unilateral middle ear infection and recovery, both ears are protected at rechallenge with the homologous isolate because of a humoral immune response to outer membrane protein antigens.[26] Protection against ipsilateral and contralateral rechallenge following middle ear infection with pneumococcal serotype

3 in a rat model has also been reported.[35] Rats were rechallenged after the initial rise in serum antibody concentrations declined to preimmune levels, suggesting that local responses may have been protective. Although local immune responses following initial middle ear infection could protect the contralateral ear, the role of local versus humoral immunity could not be distinguished.

Passive immunization studies in animals and children suggest that humoral antibody is protective, even without mucosal antibody. Shurin and colleagues[36] demonstrated that a specially prepared bacterial polysaccharide immune globulin (created by immunizing adults with pneumococcal, meningococcal, and *Haemophilus* polysaccharide vaccines), administered intraperitoneally, protects against middle ear infection caused by serotype 12F *S. pneumoniae* in animals. Similar protection has been observed for nontypeable *H. influenzae* infection after passive immunization with convalescent chinchilla sera or immune serum globulin.[37] These studies are consistent with others[23–25] showing that acute sera from children with AOM lacks bactericidal antibody against the specific isolate of nontypeable *H. influenzae* recovered from the middle ear, yet convalescent sera demonstrate specific bactericidal activity. As noted above, these bactericidal antibodies appear strain specific because recurrence is frequently caused by heterologous isolates of nontypeable *H. influenzae* that are not susceptible to the initial bactericidal antibodies. Therefore, the absence of strain-specific antibody is an important risk feature for susceptibility to bacterial AOM.

High-dose RSV immune globulin (RSVIG), given to prevent RSV disease, decreases AOM episodes by almost 80%, showing that passive immunization and serum antibody alone can prevent disease.[38] Antibacterial activity as the cause for observed AOM reduction, is suggested by antibodies to bacterial otopathogens in RSVIG and no reduction in RSV replication in the upper respiratory tract. This interpretation is strengthened by studies of RSV monoclonal antibodies (which have no activity against bacterial otopathogens) that show protection from serious RSV lower respiratory disease but no reduction in AOM episodes.[39] These studies establish specific humoral antibody as sufficient to prevent AOM.

VACCINATION FOR VIRAL URIs TO REDUCE AOM INCIDENCE

Using antigen detection, serology, or polymerase chain reaction, co-infection with respiratory viruses has been identified in more than 60% of children with AOM. Parainfluenza, RSV, and influenza A and B (see Tables 17-1 and 17-2) are most commonly identified, but recent studies using advanced techniques to identify rhinovirus and coronaviruses suggest that these latter viruses may be more important in causing AOM than previously recognized.[15,16] Currently, vaccines for preventing respiratory tract infection caused by RSV, parainfluenza, and adenovirus are in clinical development (phase I). However, both animal and human studies support the efficacy of influenza vaccines in preventing AOM as a complication of influenza infection in children and suggest principles for future respiratory vaccine development.

Giebink[40] reported that a cold-adapted influenza A virus vaccine (CAIV) reduced the attack rate of experimental OM in chinchillas cochallenged with wild-type influenza A and pneumococcus. They compared immunization with intranasal CAIV and intramuscular inactivated influenza vaccine. Although seroconversion rates were similar with each formulation, CAIV significantly reduced the density of influenza virus and pneumococcus recovered from the nasopharynx versus controls and the inactivated influenza vaccine cohort. Only 18% of the CAIV group had OM, compared with 41% and 39% in the control and inactivated vaccine groups, respectively. The greater efficacy of intranasal CAIV versus inactivated vaccine in reducing intranasal replication of wild-type influenza virus is consistent with human studies showing decreased viral recovery after intranasal challenge with live, attenuated influenza vaccine virus in children with and without serologic evidence of humoral response to prior immunization with CAIV.[41]

The prototypic studies of preventing viral URI and the effect of vaccination on AOM have been reported for influenza vaccines. Three investigators (Table 17-4) found about a 35% decline in AOM episodes during influenza season, following immunization with trivalent inactivated influenza vaccine or live attenuated influenza vaccine.[42–44] AOM episodes associated with influenzae respiratory infection, however, represented only a minority of episodes even during influenza season and only a small fraction of annual cases (Tables 17-5 and 17-6). Hoberman and colleagues[45] reported that inactivated influenza vaccine administered to children aged 6 to 24 months reduced the attack of influenza from nearly 16 to 5.5% but failed to reduce the annual burden of AOM. These observations are consistent with finding influenza virus in the nasopharynx for approximately 5% of AOM episodes.[15]

The success of influenza vaccine in reducing influenza respiratory infection and associated AOM, compared with the failure of passively administered RSV monoclonal antibody, establishes several principles for developing vaccines against respiratory viruses. RSV immune globulin was associated with an almost 80% decline in AOM in a cohort of children at high-risk of RSV disease. However, in subsequent studies using RSV monoclonal antibody, no effect on AOM incidence in similar children could be identified. The likely interpretation is that neither RSVIG nor RSV

Table 17-4 Preventing AOM by Influenza Virus Vaccination

Investigator	Age	Influenza Vaccine	Outcome
Clements[42]	6–30 mo	Trivalent, inactivated	32% ↓ in AOM; 28% ↓ in OME
Heikkinen[43]	2.2 yr mean	Trivalent, inactivated	36% ↓ in episodes during season
Belshe[44]	6–18 mo	Live, attenuated	93% ↓ in influenza infection; 36% ↓ in febrile AOM

AOM = acute otitis media; OME = otitis media with effusion.

Table 17-5 Efficacy of CAIV for AOM during the 6-Week Influenza Season*

Clinical outcome	Vaccinees (N =187), n (%)	Controls (N =187), n (%)	Relative Rate Reduction, %
Culture-positive influenza	5 (2.7)	29 (15.5)	83
AOM episodes with influenza	3 (1.6)	19 (10)	—
AOM unrelated to influenza	33 (18)	41 (22)	18
Total AOM episodes	36 (19)	60 (32)	40

AOM = acute otitis media; CAIV = cold-adapted influenza vaccine.

*Children aged 1–3 years; data from Heikkinen T et al.[43]

Table 17-6 Efficacy of CAIV for AOM during the 6-week Influenzae Season*

Clinical Outcome	Vaccinees (N=1070), n (%)	Controls (N=532), n (%)	Relative Rate Reduction, %
Culture-positive influenza	14 (1.3)	94 (17.7)	93
AOM episodes with influenza	1 (7)	20 (21)	—
AOM unrelated to influenza	449 (42)	294 (46)	9
Total febrile AOM	150 (14)	106 (20)	30

AOM = acute otitis media; CAIV = cold-adapted influenza vaccine.
*Children aged 15 to 71 months; data from Belshe RB et al.[44]

monoclonal antibody had a significant effect on upper respiratory tract disease caused by RSV and the resultant increase in susceptibility was caused by ET dysfunction or increased colonization with otopathogens. Viral vaccines must prevent upper respiratory tract replication and disease to reduce AOM. Successful AOM prevention will require vaccines against a spectrum of associated viruses to achieve a substantial impact because no single virus, even RSV, is identified in more than 14% of episodes (see Table 17-1).

POLYSACCHARIDE VACCINES TO PREVENT PNEUMOCOCCAL OTITIS MEDIA

Animal studies provided initial evidence that immunization with pneumococcal polysaccharides could prevent type specific middle ear infection. Giebink and colleagues[46] demonstrated first that animals seroconverting after immunization with serotype 7 polysaccharide had modified experimental OM with fewer pneumococci in their middle ear compared with control or nonseroconverting animals. Immunization also reduced bacteremia. Using an alternative strategy for inducing experimental OM (nasopharyngeal colonization followed by barotrauma instead of direct intrabullar inoculation), Giebink and coworkers[47] found substantial efficacy for immunization with 7F polysaccharide. Protection was associated with high concentrations of serum antibody prior to challenge. These studies established early that high serum antibody concentrations are needed to prevent experimental OM and possibly AOM in children.

Investigators in the late 1970s evaluated multivalent pneumococcal polysaccharide vaccines to prevent pneumococcal AOM in children aged 3 to 83 months.[48–51] Immunogenicity for serotypes 3 and 7 were found to be best, but, in general, those serogroups most frequently associated with AOM (4, 6, 14, 19, and 23) were least immunogenic. These studies reported some evidence for preventing pneumococcal OM, which appeared to correlate with the immunogenicity of the individual serotypes. Protection was not observed in children < 6 months of age, was in general greater in children > 2 years of age, and, in one report, was only present for the first 6 months following immunization. These studies further support that serum antibodies directed at capsular polysaccharide are protective, but that high concentrations of antibody would be essential for success.

Next generation pneumococcal vaccines, linking carrier proteins to pneumococcal polysaccharides, were developed following the success of type b conjugate *Haemophilus* vaccine in preventing invasive disease and nasopharyngeal colonization. Giebink and colleagues[52] found that a tetravalent vaccine, composed of pneumococcal capsular polysaccharides 6B, 14, 19F, and 23F conjugated to an outer membrane complex (Merck), increased type-specific serum IgG by at least twofold in 89 to 96% of animals. Culture-positive experimental AOM occurred in 38% and 0% of immunized animals versus 88% and 100% of control animals challenged with serotype 6B or 19F, respectively. Further, cross-protection against middle ear infection caused by 6A, but not by 19A, was observed. These studies confirmed the theoretic benefit of linking pneumococcal polysaccharides to protein carriers and suggested that at least for some cross-reactive serotypes (immunization with 6B, protection against 6A), protection was likely increasing the proportion of disease that a vaccine with limited serotypes could prevent.

Two clinical trials have validated principles established in animal studies or with the less immunogenic polysaccharide vaccines. Finnish investigators compared the heptavalent pneumococcal conjugate vaccine (PCV7) with hepatitis b vaccine in children aged 6 to 24 months with microbiologic end points as the outcome.[53] Children were immunized at 2, 4, and 6 months of age, and tympanocentesis was performed for each AOM episode. Two hundred and seventy-one episodes of pneumococcal otitis occurred in the PCV7 (Prevnar) cohort versus 414 in the comparison group, a 34% relative reduction

Table 17-7 Efficacy of PCV7 in Preventing AOM*

	AOM Episodes		Vaccine Efficacy
Etiology of AOM	PCV7	Control	RRR (95% CI)
All combined	1251	1345	6 (−4, 16)
All pneumococcal	271	414	34 (21, 45)[†]
Vaccine serotype	107	250	57 (44, 67)[†]
Serotype 4	2	4	49 (−179, 19)
Serotype 6B	9	56	84 (62, 93)[†]
Serotype 9V	5	71	54 (−48, 86)
Serotype 14	8	26	69 (20, 88)[†]
Serotype 18C	7	17	58 (−4, 83)
Serotype 19F	43	58	25 (−14, 51)
Serotype 23F	33	82	59 (35, 75)[†]
Nonvaccine serotype	125	95	−33 (−80, 1)
Haemophilus influenzae	315	287	−11 (−34, 8)

AOM = acute otitis media; CI = confidence interval; PCV7 = pneumococcal conjugate heptavalent vaccine; RRR = relative rate reduction (%).
*Data from Eskola J et al.[53]
[†]p < .05 if the 95% CI does not include zero.

Table 17-8 Efficacy of PCV7 for AOM Caused by Cross-Reactive Serotypes*

Vaccine Serotypes		Cross-Reactive Serotypes	
Serotype	Efficacy, RRR (95% CI)	Serotype	Efficacy, RRR (95% CI)
6B	84 (62, 93)[†]	6A	57 (24, 76)[†]
9V	54 (−48, 86)	9N	75 (−25, 95)
18C	58 (−4, 83)	18B	−103 (−213, 82)
19F	25 (−14, 51)	19A	34 (−26, 65)
23F	59 (35, 75)[†]	23A	75 (−151, 97)

AOM = acute otitis media; CI = confidence interval; PCV7 = pneumococcal conjugate heptavalent vaccine; RRR = relative rate reduction (%).
*Data from Eskola J et al.[53]
[†]p < .05 if the 95% CI does not include zero.

(Table 17-7). The pneumococcal vaccine reduced AOM from vaccine serotypes by 57%, cross-reactive serotypes by 51%, however, a 33% increase in disease due to non-vaccine serotypes was observed. Protection for cross-reactive serotypes 6A and 9N was similar for vaccine serotypes 6B and 9V (Table 17-8). PCV reduced overall AOM episodes by 6%, but the trend was not statistically significant (95% confidence interval [CI], −4, 16%).

Concurrently, the Finnish group evaluated a second polysaccharide protein conjugate vaccine (Merck) for preventing AOM.[54] Children were immunized at 2 and 4 months and received a booster with 23-valent pneumo-coccal polysaccharide vaccine or PncOMPC (pneumo-coccal outer membrane protein complex) at 12 months.

Children boosted with 23-valent polysaccharide vaccine had higher concentrations of antibody to serotype 19F and fewer episodes of disease caused by serotype 19F.[55] These results are consistent with the principle that high serum antibody concentrations result in better protection for AOM.

The Northern California Kaiser Permanente Vaccine Study Group used a "real world" study design to evaluate PCV7 for preventing AOM.[56,57] Nearly 38,000 children were randomized to receive PCV7 or meningococcal con-

Table 17-9 Impact of PCV7 on Otitis Visits for Dose-Defined Intervals*

Follow-up Interval[†]	N	RRR for Otitis Visits (95% CI)
Dose 1 to age 3.5 yr	37,868	7.0 (4.7, 9.1)[‡]
Dose 3 (+14 days) to age 3.5 yr	33,766	7.8 (5.4, 10.2)[‡]
Dose 1 to dose 2	37,584	−1.1 (−7.7, 5.1)
Dose 2 to dose 3	35,872	6.5 (2.0, 10.8)[‡]
Dose 3 to booster dose	34,138	7.9 (5.2, 10.6)[‡]
Booster dose to age 3.5 yr	26,412	7.5 (4.4, 10.6)[‡]

CI = confidence interval; PCV7 = pneumococcal conjugate heptavalent vaccine; RRR = relative rate reduction (%).
*Data from Fireman B et al.[57]
[†]The first row reports an intention-to-treat analysis, including all follow-up in randomized children. For subsequent rows, follow-up was omitted after a protocol violation.
[‡]p < .05 if the 95% CI does not include zero.

jugate vaccine at 2, 4, 6, and 12 to 15 months of age and then followed up for clinical episodes of AOM through age 3.5 years. In contrast to the Finnish study, tympanocentesis was not performed. Children immunized with PCV7 had fewer otitis visits than control children beginning with the second dose of vaccine (Table 17-9). Overall, a 6.6% decrease in episodes and a 7.8% decline in visits were observed. This implies 43 fewer visits with a diagnosis of OM for every 100 children immunized with PCV7, or about 1.7 million preventable visits over three and a half years for each American birth cohort.

Efficacy of PCV7 in the Northern California study was greatest in children aged 15 to 18 months following the booster dose, suggesting that higher antibody concentrations, likely to be present after the booster, resulted in greater protection. Efficacy declined in children 24 to 42 months of age, presumably because of decay in serum antibody concentrations but possibly because of "replacement" disease from nonvaccine serotypes of *S. pneumoniae*. Complex episodes, defined as episodes lasting more than 60 days, declined by 22%. These episodes may have been caused by nonsusceptible otopathogens, specifically multidrug-resistant *S. pneumoniae*. Finally, myringotomy and tympanostomy tube insertion declined 24% in the vaccine cohort.

FUTURE CHALLENGES IN THE IMMUNOPROPHYLAXIS OF AOM

The first challenge in preventing AOM is the broad diversity of isolates of nontypeable *H. influenzae* and *S. pneumoniae* found in the middle ear of children with AOM. Direct sampling of the middle ear, via tympanocentesis or culture of middle ear exudate, has identified more than 16 serogroups of *S. pneumoniae*

as pathogens in children with AOM (Figure 17-2).[58] Although certain serogroups are recovered more frequently, a large spectrum can infect the middle ear. Similarly, strains of nontypeable *H. influenzae* recovered from the middle ear of children with AOM represent a diverse group of isolates as characterized by ribotyping.[27] This diversity of bacterial isolates has important implications for recurrent AOM. Leibovitz and coworkers,[22] for example, reported that most recurrences are caused by new pathogens, rather than the initial organism.

In a chinchilla model, Karasic and colleagues[59] demonstrated that immunization with a pilus vaccine prevented experimental OM caused by the piliated form of the strain from which the vaccine was prepared. Unfortunately, immunization selected for disease caused by a nonpiliated variant of the initial nontypeable *H. influenzae* isolate and failed to prevent against disease caused by a heterologous strain. These studies confirm the diversity of nontypeable *H. influenzae* and its ability to phase vary, thereby escaping the protective effect of immunization.

The Finnish Vaccine trial of PCV7 for preventing AOM in children demonstrates the efficacy of this vaccine for preventing pneumococcal disease, but also highlights the limited impact on overall AOM of a vaccine directed against only a limited spectrum of pathogens.[54] PC7 reduced AOM caused by vaccine or vaccine-related serotypes by greater than 50%; however, a significant increase in disease caused by nonvaccine *S. pneumoniae* and a nonsignificant increase in disease caused by nontypeable *H. influenzae* was observed (see Table 17-7). These results are not surprising because immunization with PCV7 reduces nasopharyngeal carriage of vaccine and vaccine-related pneumococci but increases the prevalence of nonvaccine serotypes.[60–62]

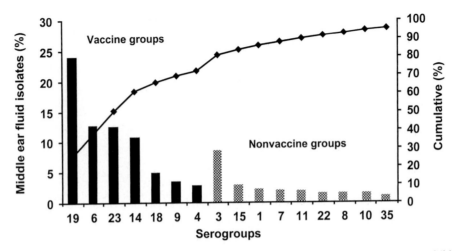

Figure 17-2 Serogroups of *Streptococcus pneumoniae* producing acute otitis media in North American children. Diamonds indicate cumulative percent. Data from Hausdorff W et al.[58]

Table 17-10 Pointers and Pitfalls

1. Vaccination against viral (influenza) and bacterial (*Streptococcus pneumoniae*) pathogens is an established general preventive strategy for acute otitis media (AOM), but preventing respiratory infection caused by a single virus or subpopulation of the major bacterial AOM pathogens is unlikely to have a substantial impact on a specific child.

2. Viral vaccines will need to prevent or limit viral replication in the nasopharynx following exposure to wild type virus.

3. High serum antibody concentrations for specific bacterial pathogens are achievable with conjugate vaccine technologies. Local antibody may be more efficacious in preventing colonization with viral or bacterial respiratory pathogens.

4. Heptavalent pneumococcal conjugate vaccine (PCV7) reduces pneumococcal otitis media, but replacement disease is observed and long-term effects remain uncertain.

5. A 6% absolute decrease in otitis office visits because of PCV7 results in 1.7 million fewer office visits for each American birth cohort. This reduction has a clear public health benefit, however, is difficult to measure for a given individual.

CONCLUSION

The pathogenesis of OM is complex and frequently involves co-infection with viral and bacterial pathogens. Several key targets exist for immunoprophylactic strategies to prevent AOM (see Figure 17-1). Influenza vaccine is a prototype for prevention because it reduces viral replication in the upper respiratory tract and subsequent Eustachian tube and immune dysfunction. These events are the precursors to AOM in a large proportion of infected children. Such strategies as RSV monoclonal antibody, which may be successful in preventing serious lower tract respiratory disease, do not appear to prevent the physiologic changes associated with upper respiratory tract viral infection. Consequently, they do not effectively prevent AOM.

Developing vaccines for the most common respiratory viruses associated with AOM is a future challenge.

Studies of passive and active immunization show that humoral antibody prevents AOM caused by *S. pneumoniae* and nontypeable *H. influenzae*. Pneumococcal conjugate vaccine is a first step in preventing disease caused by the most common *S. pneumoniae* serotypes; however, intervention strategies that target only a selected population of bacterial otopathogens are likely to have limited success (Table 17-10). Disease caused by "escape" populations is likely to be observed and will potentially reduce the benefit of immunization for preventing AOM. In contrast, vaccines that target broadly cross-reactive antigens from *S. pneumoniae* and nontypeable *H. influenzae* are more likely to succeed and are the focus of ongoing research.

REFERENCES

1. Teele DW, Klein JO, Rosner B. Epidemiology of otitis media during the first seven years of life in children in greater Boston: a prospective, cohort study. J Infect Dis 1989;160:83–94.

2. Block SL, Harrison CJ, Hedrick J, et al. Restricted use of antibiotic prophylaxis for recurrent acute otitis media in the era of penicillin non-susceptible *Streptococcus pneumoniae*. Int J Pediatr Otorhinolaryngol 2001;61:47–60.

3. Umetsu DT, Ambrosino DM, Quinti I, et al. Recurrent sinopulmonary infection and impaired antibody response to bacterial capsular polysaccharide antigen in children with selective IgG-subclass deficiency. N Engl J Med 1998;313:1247–51.

4. Barnett ED, Klein JO, Pelton SI, Luginbuhl LM. Otitis media in children born to human immunodeficiency virus-infected mothers. Pediatr Infect Dis J 1992;11:360–4.

5. Epstein MM, Grudkay F. Selective deficiency in pneumococcal antibody response in children with recurrent infections. Ann Allergy Asthma Immunol 1995;75:125–31.

6. Hubbard TW, Paradise JL, McWilliams BJ, et al. Consequences of unremitting middle-ear disease in early life. Otologic, audiologic, and developmental findings in children with cleft palate. N Engl J Med 1985;312:1529–34.

7. Buchman CA, Doyle WJ, Skoner DP, et al. Influenza A virus-induced acute otitis media. J Infect Dis 1995;172:1348–51.

8. Chonmaitree T. Viral and bacterial interaction in acute otitis media. Pediatr Infect Dis J 2000;19 Suppl:S24–30.

9. Henderson FW, Collier AM, Sanyal MA, et al. A longitudinal study of respiratory viruses and bacteria in the etiology of acute otitis media with effusion. N Engl J Med 1982;306:1377–83.

10. Jacobs MR, Dagan R, Appelbaum PC, Burch DJ. Prevalence of antimicrobial-resistant pathogens in middle ear fluid: multinational study of 917 children with acute otitis media. Antimicrob Agents Chemother 1998;42:589–95.

11. Klein JO. Microbiology of otitis media. Ann Otol Rhinol Laryngol 1980;Suppl 89:98–101.

12. Ruuskanen O, Arola M, Putto-Laurila A, et al. Acute otitis media and respiratory virus infections. Pediatric Infect Dis J 1989;8:94–9.

13. Heikkinen T. Temporal development of acute otitis media during upper respiratory tract infection. Pediatr Infect Dis J 1994;13:659–61.

14. Koivunen P, Kontiokari T, Niemla M, et al. Time to development of acute otitis media during an upper respiratory tract infection in children. Pediatr Infect Dis J 1999;18:303–5.

15. Heikkinen T, Thint M, Chonmaitree T. Prevalence of various respiratory viruses in the middle ear during acute otitis media. N Engl J Med 1999;340:260–4.

16. Pitkäranta A, Virolainen A, Jero J, et al. Detection of rhinovirus, respiratory syncytial virus, and coronavirus infections in acute otitis media by reverse transcriptase polymerase chain reaction. Pediatrics 1998;102:291–5.

17. Sanyal MA, Henderson FW, Stempel EC, et al. Effect of upper respiratory tract infection on Eustachian tube ventilatory function in the preschool child. J Pediatr 1980;97:11–5.

18. Patel J, Faden H, Sharma S, Ogra PL. Effect of respiratory syncytial virus on adherence, colonization and immunity of nontypable *Haemophilus influenzae*: implications for otitis media. Int J Pediatr Otorhinolaryngol 1992;23:15–23.

19. Wadowsky RM, Mietzner SM, Skoner DP, et al. Effect of experimental influenza A virus infection on isolation of *Streptococcus pneumoniae* and other aerobic bacteria from the oropharynges of allergic and nonallergic adult subjects. Infect Immunol 1995;63:1153–7.

20. Abramson JS, Giebink GS, Quie PG. Influenza A virus induced polymorphonuclear leukocyte dysfunction in the pathogenesis of experimental pneumococcal otitis media. Infect Immunol 1982;36:289–96.

21. Suetake M, Irimada M, Takahashi S, et al. Identification of bacterial strain at each episode of recurrent acute otitis media. Nippon Jibiinkoka Gakkai Kaiho 2000;103(1):19–23.

22. Leibovitz E, Greenberg D, Porat N, et al. Clinical relapse of otitis media (CR-AOM) within 1 month after completion of treatment (Tx): bacteriologic correlates. Abstract # 1968. Presented at 40th ICAAC (Interscience Conference on Antimicrobial Agents and Chemotherapy); 2000 September 17–20; Toronto, ON. p. 466.

23. Barenkamp SJ, Bodor FF. Development of serum bactericidal activity following nontypable *Haemophilus influenzae* acute otitis media. Pediatr Infect Dis J 1990;9:333–9.

24. Shurin PA, Pelton SI, Tager IB, Kasper DL. Bactericidal antibody and susceptibility to otitis media caused by nontypable strains of *Haemophilus influenzae*. J Pediatr 1980;97:364–9.

25. Bernstein JM, Faden HS, Loos BG, et al. Recurrent otitis media with nontypable *Haemophilus influenzae*: the role of serum bactericidal antibody. Int J Pediatr Otorhinolaryngol 1992;23:1–13.

26. Karasic RB, Trumpp CE, Gnehm HE, et al. Modification of otitis media in chinchillas rechallenged with nontypable *Haemophilus influenzae* and serological response to outer membrane antigens. J Infect Dis 1985;151:273–9.

27. Bolduc GR, Bouchet V, Jiang RZ et al. Variability of outer membrane protein P1 and its evaluation as a vaccine candidate against experimental otitis media due to nontypable *Haemophilus influenzae*: an unambiguous, multifaceted approach. Infect Immunol 2000;68:4505–17.

28. Austrian R, Howie VM, Ploussard JH. The bacteriology of pneumococcal otitis media. Johns Hopkins Med J 1997;141:104–11.

29. Shinefield HR, Black S, Ray P, et al. Safety and immunogenicity of heptavalent pneumococcal CRM197 conjugate vaccine in infants and toddlers. Pediatr Infect Dis J 1999;18:757–63.

30. Rennels MB, Edward KM, Keyserling HL, et al. Safety and immunogenicity of heptavalent pneumococcal vaccine conjugated to CRM197 in United States infants. Pediatrics 1998;101:604–11.

31. Hsu KK, Pelton SI, Heisey-Grove DM, et al. Serotype-specific surveillance for childhood invasive pneumococcal disease 2002. Abstract G-1067, Presented at 42nd ICAAC (Interscience Conference on Antimicrobial Agents and Chemotherapy); 2002 September 27–30; San Diego, CA. p. 246.

32. Whitney CG, Harrison LH, Reingolf A, et al. Ongoing surveillance for effect of conjugate vaccine on invasive pneumococcal disease in the U.S. Abstract G-1068, Presented at 42nd ICAAC (Interscience Conference on Antimicrobial Agents and Chemotherapy); 2002 September 27–30; San Diego, CA. p. 246.

33. Hausdorff W, Yothers G, Dagan R, et al. A multinational study of pneumococcal serotypes causing acute otitis media in children. Pediatr Infect Dis J 2002;21:1008–16.

34. Hotomi M, Yamanaka N, Shimada J, et al. Antibody responses to the outer membrane protein P6 of nontypable *Haemophilus influenzae* and pneumococcal capsular polysaccharides in otitis-prone children. Acta Otolaryngol 1999;119:703–7.

35. Svinhufvud M, Prellner K, Hermansson A, Schalen C. Experimental recurrent pneumococcal otitis media. Protection and serum antibodies. Acta Otolaryngol 1991;111;1083–9.

36. Shurin PA, Giebink GS, Wegman DL, et al. Prevention of pneumococcal otitis media in chinchillas with human bacterial polysaccharide immune globulin. J Clin Microbiol 1988;26:755–9.

37. Barenkamp SJ. Protection by serum antibodies in experimental nontypable *Haemophilus influenzae* otitis media. Infect Immunol 1986;52:572–8.

38. Simoes EA, Groothuis JR, Tristram DA et al. Respiratory syncytial virus-enriched globulin for the prevention of acute otitis media in high risk children. J Pediatr 1996;129:214–9.

39. Englund JA, Glezen WP. Passive immunization for the prevention of otitis media. Vaccine 2000;19 Suppl: S116–21.

40. Giebink GS. Studies of *Streptococcus pneumoniae* and influenza virus vaccines in the chinchilla otitis media model. Pediatr Infect Dis J 1989;8 Suppl:S42–4.

41. Belshe RB, Gruber WC, Mendelman PM, et al. Correlates of immune protection induced by live, attenuated, cold-adapted, trivalent, intranasal influenza virus vaccine. J Infect Dis 2000;181:1133–7.

42. Clements DA, Langdon L, Bland C, Walter E. Influenza A vaccine decreases the incidence of otitis media in 6- to 30-month old children in day care. Arch Pediatr Adolesc Med 1995;149:1113–6.

43. Heikkinen T, Ruuskanen O, Waris M, et al. Influenza vaccination in the prevention of acute otitis media in children. Am J Dis Child 1991;145:445–8.

44. Belshe RB, Mendelman PM, Treanor J et al. The efficacy of live attenuated, cold-adapted, trivalent, intranasal Influenzavirus vaccine in children. N Engl J Med 1998;338:1405–12.

45. Hoberman A, Greenberg DP, Paradise JL, et al. Efficacy of inactivated influenza vaccine in preventing acute otitis media (AOM) in young children. Abstract #906.

Presented at Pediatric Academic Society Meeting; 2002, May 3–6; Baltimore, MD.

46. Giebink GS, Schiffman G, Petty K, Quie PG. Modification of otitis media following vaccination with the capsular polysaccharide of *Streptococcus pneumoniae* in chinchillas. J Infect Dis 1978;138:480–7.

47. Giebink GS, Berzins IK, Schiffman G, Quie PG. Experimental otitis media in chinchillas following nasal colonization with type 7F *Streptococcus pneumoniae*: prevention after vaccination with pneumococcal capsular polysaccharide. J Infect Dis 1979;140:716–23.

48. Sloyer JL, Ploussard JH, Howie VM, Sloyer JL Jr. Efficacy of pneumococcal polysaccharide vaccine in preventing acute otitis media in infants in Huntsville, Alabama. Rev Infect Dis 1981;3 Suppl:S119–23.

49. Karma P, Pukander J, Sipila M, et al. Prevention of otitis media in children by pneumococcal vaccination. Am J Otolaryngol 1985;6:173–84.

50. Makela PH, Sibakov M, Herva E, et al. Pneumococcal vaccine and otitis media. Lancet 1980;2:547–51.

51. Teele DW, Klein JO, Bratton L, et al. Use of pneumococcal vaccine for prevention of recurrent acute otitis media in infants in Boston. The Greater Boston Collaborative Otitis Media Study Group. Rev Infect Dis 1981;3 Suppl:S113–8.

52. Giebink GS, Meier JD, Quartey MK, et al. Immunogenicity and efficacy of *Streptococcus pneumoniae* polysaccharide-protein conjugate vaccines against homologous and heterologous serotypes in the chinchilla otitis media model. J Infect Dis 1996;173:119–27.

53. Eskola J, Kilpi T, Palmu A, et al, for The Finish Otitis Media Study Group. Efficacy of pneumococcal conjugate vaccine against acute otitis media. N Engl J Med 2001;344:403–9.

54. Kilpi T, Palmu A, Leinonen M, et al. FINOM Study Group. Effects of a 7-valent pneumococcal conjugate vaccine (PncIMPC) on acute otitis media (AOM) due to vaccine serotypes after boosting with conjugate or polysaccharide vaccines. Abstract G-2036, Presented at the 41st ICAAC (Interscience Conference on Antimicrobial Agents and Chemotherapy); 2001 December 16–19; Chicago, IL. p. 282.

55. Kilpi T, Palmu A, Leinonen M, Eskola SG, for FINOM. Efficacy of a seven-valent pneumococcal conjugate vaccine (PncOMPC) against serotype-specific acute otitis media (AOM) caused by *Streptococcus pneumoniae* (Pnc). Abstract # 689, Presented at the 40th ICAAC (Interscience Conference on Antimicrobial Agents and Chemotherapy); 2000 September 17–20; Toronto, ON. p. 245.

56. Black S, Shinefield H, Fireman B, et al. Efficacy, safety and immunogenicity of heptavalent pneumococcal conjugate vaccine in children. Northern California Kaiser Permanente Vaccine Study Center Group. Pediatr Infect Dis J 2000;19:187–95.

57. Fireman B, Black S, Shinefield H, et al. The impact of the pneumococcal conjugate vaccine on otitis media. Pediatr Infect Dis J 2003;22:10–16.

58. Hausdorff WP, Bryant J, Kloek C, et al. The contribution

of specific pneumococcal serogroups to different disease manifestations: implications for conjugate vaccine formulation and use (Figure 2 reference). Clin Infect Dis 2000;30:122–40.

59. Karasic RB, Beste DJ, To SC, et al. Evaluation of pilus vaccines for prevention of experimental otitis media caused by nontypable *Haemophilus influenzae*. Pediatr Infect Dis J 1989;8 Suppl:S62–5.

60. Dagan R, Givon-Lavi N, Zamir O, et al. Reduction of nasopharyngeal carriage of *Streptococcus pneumoniae* after administration of a 9-valent pneumococcal conju-

gate vaccine to toddlers attending day care centers. J Infect Dis 2002;185:927–36.

61. Mbelle N, Huebner RE, Wasas AD, et al. Immunogenicity and impact on nasopharyngeal carriage of a nonvalent pneumococcal conjugate vaccine. J Infect Dis 1999;180: 1171–6.

62. Dagan R, Muallem M, Melamed R, et al. Reduction of pneumococcal nasopharyngeal carriage in early infancy after immunization with tetravalent pneumococcal vaccines conjugated to either tetanus toxoid or diptheria toxoid. Pediatr Infect Dis J 1997;16:1060–4.

CHAPTER 18

Clinical Pathway for Acute Otitis Media

Richard M. Rosenfeld, MD, MPH

To learn how to treat disease, one must learn how to recognize it.
The diagnosis is the best trump in the scheme of treatment.
Jean Martin Charcot

OBJECTIVES

On completing this chapter, the reader will be able to

1. Know the time course and natural history of acute otitis media (AOM).
2. Appreciate the critical importance of diagnostic certainty and judicious antibiotic use.
3. Identify children who are—and are not—suitable for the AOM observation option.
4. Realize that antibiotics serve more to prevent complications than to relieve symptoms, whether administered at AOM diagnosis or after a period of initial observation.
5. Recognize that middle ear effusion after AOM is common and rarely needs treatment, unless chronic.
6. Use primary prevention and parent education to achieve optimal outcomes.
7. Understand and choose among management options for recurrent AOM.

EDITORIAL COMMENT

Continuing concerns over multidrug-resistant bacteria, particularly pneumococcus, mandate that clinicians reconsider their approach to everyday AOM management. Three primary themes have emerged since the last edition of this chapter to promote judicious antibiotic use: (1) improved diagnostic certainty to limit false positives, (2) use of the "observation option" in selected children, and (3) targeted antimicrobial therapy based on tympanocentesis. All three have a role in enlightened management, and none is mutually exclusive. Therefore, this author suggests that AOM is managed optimally by (1) increased diagnostic certainty through education, workshops, and use of ancillary measures to assess for middle ear effusion; (2) initial observation of selected cases on the basis of child age, illness severity, and an honest estimate of provider diagnostic certainty; and (3) selective use of tympanocentesis in complicated or
refractory cases to identify causative pathogens. These concepts are thoroughly elaborated below.

CLINICAL PATHWAYS

This chapter offers a framework for thinking about and applying the voluminous evidence summarized elsewhere in this book. The *clinical pathway* is ideal for this purpose because it provides a concise, visual overview of where management efforts should be focused at any point in the course of disease. Clinical pathways exemplify a typical patient's road to recovery on the basis of an optimal sequence of activities and outcomes.[1] Unlike practice guidelines, they follow a time line, with emphasis on treatment outcomes, patient education, and coordination of care. Like guidelines, they seek to minimize delays and resource utilization yet maximize quality. The pathway in this chapter is offered as *one* possible solution for managing AOM, not as the *only* solution.

The basic format of a clinical pathway is the *task-time* matrix, also known as a Gantt chart, which indicates for each time point the corresponding actions and expected outcomes.[2] The time course of AOM may be considered in four phases (Table 18-1): (1) initial diagnosis, (2) symptom relief and prevention of suppurative complications, (3) resolution of persistent middle ear effusion (MEE), and (4) long-term management of recurrent AOM and chronic otitis media with effusion (OME). These phases are divided into clinically relevant intervals or thresholds in the first row of Table 18-2, beginning with AOM onset and ending with recurrent AOM. The first column of Table 18-2 lists the actions, interventions, and outcomes that deserve emphasis at each of the various time points.

Clinical pathways emphasize typical treatment for a typical patient.[3] In real-life practice scenarios, however, few clinicians routinely associate the word "typical" with either their treatments or their patients. Recognizing the

Table 18-1 Management Phases for Acute Otitis Media

Phase	Management Focus
Initial diagnosis	Confirm presence of MEE; reassure and educate family
Symptomatic relief	Judicious use of observation and pharmacologic therapy; prevention and early detection of treatment failures or complications
Resolution of MEE	Primary prevention and risk factor modification; antimicrobial therapy on a selective and individualized basis
Preventing recurrent AOM	Primary prevention and risk factor modification; antimicrobial prophylaxis or surgery on an individualized basis
Resolution of chronic OME	Assess morbidity and surgical candidacy; manage as described in Chapter 19, "Clinical Pathway for Otitis Media with Effusion"

AOM = acute otitis media; MEE = middle ear effusion; OME = otitis media with effusion.

uniqueness of the provider-patient interaction, it bears emphasis that pathways are a source of perspective and balance, not a substitute for individualized management decisions. Pathways may be likened to leadership (deciding to do the right thing) and individual decisions to management (doing things right). Recognizing the importance of both leadership and management, the pathway is supplemented with clinical pearls regarding the most common dilemmas likely to be faced by clinicians when managing AOM.

Much of the evidence and concepts explored in this chapter is considered in greater detail in other parts of this book. For example, there are complete chapters dealing with diagnosis, natural history, medical therapy, surgical therapy, antimicrobial selection, and tympanostomy tube care. The author's purpose here is to provide a unified framework in which to consider this evidence, not to simply repeat material discussed elsewhere. Readers are encouraged to refer liberally to related chapters for more in-depth discussions of selected material.

Managing AOM Episodes

The initial phase of AOM management (first five columns in Table 18-2) concerns symptomatic relief of associated pain and fever and prevention of suppurative complications, such as mastoiditis or meningitis. The pathway in Table 18-2 is not for managing acute earache or "red ear," but for true AOM; therefore, the presence of MEE *must* be confirmed by direct visualization (pneumatic otoscopy)[4] or by indirect assessment of middle ear function (tympanogram, acoustic reflectometry).[5,6] I prefer pneumatic otoscopy because of the low cost and direct visual feedback, with 94% sensitivity (95% CI, 91 to 96%) and 80% specificity (95% CI, 75 to 86%).[7] Tympanometry has comparable sensitivity, but specificity

is lower. Nonpneumatic otoscopy alone has poor sensitivity for diagnosing MEE, unless an obvious purulent effusion or air-fluid level or otorrhea is visualized.

The bottom three rows of Table 18-2 define outcomes in terms of natural history (spontaneous resolution) and the incremental benefit of antimicrobial therapy. More detailed information is provided in Tables 18-3 and 18-4, based on the randomized controlled trials (RCTs) discussed in Chapters 12, "Natural History of Untreated Otitis Media" and 13, "Clinical Efficacy of Medical Therapy". The favorable history of untreated AOM is immediately apparent, but the decrease from about 80% symptom relief at 2 to 3 days to 70% clinical resolution at 7 to 14 days requires comment. Symptomatic relief is a narrower outcome measure than clinical resolution because the latter requires absence of all presenting signs and symptoms exclusive of MEE.[8] An afebrile, pain-free child with otorrhea, a tympanic membrane perforation, or other tympanic membrane abnormality (eg, erythema or persistent bulging) would qualify for symptomatic relief but would not meet the more stringent criteria for clinical resolution.

Do All Children with AOM Require Initial Antibiotics?

In a 1998 consensus report, the American Academy of Pediatrics (AAP) and the Centers for Disease Control (CDC) recommended that all children with a definitive diagnosis of AOM receive initial antibiotic therapy.[9] This recommendation is under revision (November 2002), and the updated guideline will allow for observing selected older children with definitive AOM. The key words in the preceding two sentences are *definitive AOM*, which imply MEE in conjunction with the rapid onset of one or more signs or symptoms of inflammation of the middle ear (Table 18-5).[10] MEE *must* be present to diag-

Table 18-2 Clinical Pathway for Acute Otitis Media

	Onset	24 h	2–3 d	4–7 d	7–14 d	4–6 w	3 mo	OME ≥ 4 mo	AOM ≥ 3/6 mo or 4/12 mo
Diagnostics	Confirm MEE*	Tympanocentesis if toxicity or persistent symptoms despite second antibiotic				Assess for persistent MEE*		Audiometry and tympanometry; examine palate; test for allergies, immune deficiencies, sinusitis	
Antimicrobials	Observation option vs. first-line drug	First-line drug if observation failure; second-line drug if First-line failure				Optional; impact on MEE resolution is short term and modest			Treat AOM episodes; selective use of prophylaxis
Other medications	Analgesics; ototopical drops if otorrhea or perforated TM; no benefit to antihistamines, decongestants, or steroids					No documented benefits to alternative medical therapies or traditional medical therapies (other than antimicrobials)			
Family education	Parent information sheet; dry ear precautions if otorrhea or perforated TM; call if child worsens					May have temporary hearing loss if MEE persists; reassure		Emphasize need for audiometry; encourage primary prevention and risk-factor modification	
Primary prevention	Limit exposure to environmental tobacco smoke; treat comorbid conditions (rhinosinusitis; allergy exacerbations)							Reduce supine bottle-feeding, eliminate pacifiers, consider vaccines; control allergies; group day care alternatives	
Surgical procedures	Routine tympanocentesis is unnecessary; reserve myringotomy for acute suppurative complications					None		Tympanostomy tubes and/or adenoidectomy on an individualized basis	
Desired outcome	Symptomatic relief; prevent complications			AOM cure		MEE resolution	OME resolution	Reduced AOM frequency	
Spontaneous resolution rate†	—	60%	80%	75%	70%	60%	75–90%	Less favorable; risk of reinfection	1.5–2.5 decrease in AOM/yr No AOM in 40% next 6 mo < 3 AOM in 80% next 6 mo
	Complications about 0.2% with initial antibiotics or with antibiotic treatment of initial observation failures								
Antimicrobial benefit‡	—	NS	5%	10%	10%	NS	NS	15% short-term	0.5–1.5 decrease in AOM/yr

AOM = acute otitis media; MEE = middle ear effusion; NS = not statistically significant; OME = otitis media with effusion; TM = tympanic membrane.
*Presence of MEE may be assessed by pneumatic otoscopy, tympanometry, or acoustic reflectometry; nonpneumatic otoscopy alone is insufficient.
†Desired outcomes attributable to spontaneous resolution, rounded to nearest five% (see Chapter 12).
‡Approximate absolute increase in desired outcome attributable to therapy (see Chapter 13).

Table 18-3 Summary of Natural History of AOM and Recurrent AOM*

Clinical Situation	Time Point	N[‡]	Rate[§]	(95% CI)
Symptomatic relief of pain and fever caused by AOM in children randomized to placebo	24 hours	3[‖]	.61	(.50, .72)
	2–3 d	5	.80	(.69, .90)
	4–7 d	8	.74	(.64, .85)
Complete clinical resolution of AOM in children randomized to placebo or no drug[†]	7–14 d	6	.70	(.49, .92)
Resolution of OME persisting after AOM in children randomized to placebo or no drug	4 wk	4	.59	(.50, .68)
	6 wk	3	.46	(.32, .60)
	12 wk	2	.74	(.68, .80)
Future incidence of AOM episodes/month for children with a history of recurrent AOM	Up to 2 yr	14	.23	(.18, .28)
Future chance of having no AOM episodes for children with recurrent AOM	6 mo median	13	.41	(.32, .51)
Future chance of having 2 or fewer AOM episodes for children with recurrent AOM	6 mo median	8	.83	(.74, .91)

AOM = acute otitis media; CI = confidence interval; OME = otitis media with effusion.

*See Chapter 12 for derivation of listed rates.

[†]Absence of all presenting signs and symptoms, exclusive of middle ear effusion, within 7 to 14 days after therapy started.

[‡]Number of studies from which data were combined to derive the overall resolution rate.

[§]Estimate based on random-effects meta-analysis.

[‖]Based on children aged 2 years or older; resolution may be poorer for younger children.

Table 18–4 Summary of What to Expect from Antibiotic Therapy for AOM or Prophylaxis of Recurrent AOM

Clinical Situation and Outcome	Time Point	N[†]	RD[‖]	(95% CI)	NNT[‡]	(95% CI)
Symptomatic relief AOM in RCTs of antibiotic versus placebo or no drug	24 h	3	0	(−.07, .08)	—	
	2–3 d	5	.04	(.02, .07)[§]	25	(14, 50)
	4–7 d	6	.09	(.01, .18)[§]	11	(6, 333)
Complete clinical resolution of AOM in RCTs of antibiotic versus placebo or no drug	7–14 d	6	.08	(.01, .14)[§]	13	(7,111)
Incidence of suppurative complications of AOM in RCTs of antibiotic versus placebo or no drug	7–14 d	9	.001	(−.007, .008)	—	
Resolution of persistent OME after treatment of AOM in RCTs of antibiotic versus placebo	4–6 wk	6	.03	(−.02, .08)	—	
	3 mo	2	.05	(−.08, .17)	—	
Incidence of AOM episodes/patient-month in RCTs of antibiotic prophylaxis versus placebo	Up to 2 yr	10	−.09	(−.12, −.05)[§]	11	(8, 19)
Having no further AOM episodes in RCTs of antibiotic prophylaxis versus placebo	6 mo median	10	.21	(.13, .30)[§]	5	(3, 8)
Having 2 or fewer AOM episodes in RCTs of antibiotic prophylaxis versus placebo	6 mo median	5	.08	(.04, .12)[§]	13	(8, 24)

AOM = acute otitis media; CI = confidence interval; NNT = number needed to treat; OME = otitis media with effusion; RCT = randomized controlled trial; RD = absolute rate difference.

*See Chapter 13 for derivation of listed rate differences.

[†]Number of studies from which data were combined to derive the overall treatment effect.

[‡]NNT is the number of children who must be treated for one additional successful outcome and is relevant only for statistically significant outcomes.

[§]$p < .05$ when the 95% CI does not contain zero.

[‖]RD is the absolute change in outcome for treatment versus control groups.

Table 18-5 Consensus Definition of AOM Used in the AHRQ Evidence Report[10]

Three-part complete* definition of AOM:

1. *AOM is defined* as presence of MEE as demonstrated by the actual presence of fluid in the middle ear as diagnosed by tympanocentesis or the physical presence of liquid in the external ear canal as a result of TM perforation or indicated by limited or absent mobility of the TM as diagnosed by pneumatic otoscopy, tympanogram, or acoustic reflectometry *with or without* the following:
   a. Opacification, not including erythema
   b. A full or bulging TM
   c. Hearing loss

2. *And,* rapid onset (over the course of 48 hours)[†]

3. *Of,* one or more of the following signs or symptoms:
   a. Otalgia (or pulling of ear in an infant)
   b. Otorrhea
   c. Irritability in the infant or toddler[‡]
   d. Fever
   With or without anorexia, nausea, or vomiting

AHRQ = Agency for Healthcare Research and Quality; AOM = acute otitis media; MEE = middle ear effusion; TM = tympanic membrane.
*Abbreviated definition: AOM is the presence of MEE in conjunction with the rapid onset of one or more signs or symptoms of inflammation of the middle ear.
†Rapid onset is defined as less than or equal to 48 hours from the onset of acute signs or symptoms first noted by the parent or guardian to contact with the health system.
‡Irritability in the infant or toddler and fever must be associated with either otalgia or otorrhea to fulfill criterion 3.

nose AOM; an inflamed tympanic membrane *without* MEE (red ear) may represent dilated intratympanic vessels from crying, fever, or viral myringitis.[11] Similarly, acute earache without MEE is unreliable as an indication because most children have referred pain from teething or pharyngitis.[12] About 5 to 8% of nonteething infants have ear rubbing, rising to about 10% on the day of tooth eruption (*p* < .01).[13]

Concerns over bacterial resistance have prompted reconsidering the risks versus the benefits of prescribing antibiotics for all AOM. The impact of antibiotics on symptom relief and clinical resolution in RCTs is significant but modest after 24 hours: between 11 and 25 children need antibiotics to improve one child's condition beyond natural history alone (see Table 18-4).[14–22] Similarly, the number needed to treat (NNT) in published meta-analyses[10,23–25] ranges from 7 to 17 (see Chapter 4, "Meta-analysis and Systematic Literature Review"). Risks of antibiotics include allergic reactions, gastric upset, accelerated bacterial resistance, and unfavorable changes in nasopharyngeal bacterial flora.[26–29] Moreover, antibiotic prescribing has a "medicalizing" effect, increasing revisit rates and the likelihood of seeking medical care for future illness.[30] Initial observation of children with AOM does not increase suppurative complications with appropriate follow-up.[10]

The incremental benefits of antibiotics combined with high rates of spontaneous resolution (Table 18-6) suggest that some children with AOM are suitable for initial observation.[31] Cates reduced the median number of antibiotic prescriptions by 31% versus 12% in a control practice when children with nonsevere AOM were given a "safety-net" prescription (eg, parents were given an antibiotic prescription but asked to redeem it only if the child failed to improve within 2 days).[32] When Little and coworkers randomized 315 children aged 6 months to 10 years with AOM to initial antibiotics versus a safety-net prescription for up to 72 hours, only 24% of the latter group eventually filled the prescription.[33] More recently (September 2002), the New York State Department of Health distributed a toolkit for judicious observation of selected children with AOM.[34] This toolkit is discussed in detail below.

Another response to rising bacterial resistance has been to select antimicrobials on the basis of tympanocentesis results. Whereas routine tympanocentesis can improve diagnostic certainty for AOM, it offers no therapeutic advantage beyond antibiotics alone (see Chapter 14, "Clinical Efficacy of Surgical Therapy"). Moreover, the favorable natural history of uncomplicated AOM makes it difficult to justify an invasive, painful, and potentially harmful intervention for routine initial management. For example, tympanocentesis was performed incorrectly by 17% of 514 participating pediatricians in a training workshop (12% too deep, 5% too superior).[35] Procedural risks include tympanic membrane perforation, ossicular dislocation, and traumatic sensorineural hearing loss.

Table 18-6 Comparative AOM Outcomes for Initial Antibiotic versus Observation Based on Best Evidence

AOM Outcome	Initial Antibiotic	Initial Observation	NNT (95% CI) or p Value	Source
Symptom relief at 24 h*	60%	59%	NS	Chapter 13, Table 13-2
Symptom relief at 2–7 d	92%	79%	8 (5–33)	Marcy[10] 2001
Clinical resolution at 7–14 d	84%	73%	8 (5–13)	Rosenfeld[8] 1994
Pain duration, mean days	2.8	3.3	NS	Burke[20] 1991
Crying duration, mean days	0.5	1.4	$p < .001$	Burke[20] 1991
Analgesic use, mean doses	2.3	4.1	$p = .004$	Damoiseaux[22] 2000
Fever duration, median days	2.0	3.0	$p = .004$	Damoiseaux[22] 2000
Contralateral AOM episode	11%	17%	14 (9–33)	Del Mar[24] 1997
Suppurative complications	0.26%	0.14%	NS	Chapter 13, Table 13-6
Persistent MEE at 4–6 wk	55%	52%	NS	Chapter 13, Table 13-7
Persistent MEE at 3 mo	79%	74%	NS	Chapter 13, Table 13-8
Cost of therapy, 1995 US mean	$20	—	—	Marcy[10] 2001

AOM = acute otitis media; CI = confidence interval; MEE = middle ear effusion; NS = not significant.
*Based on children aged 2 years or older; resolution may be poorer for younger children.

Therefore, tympanocentesis should be limited to the following scenarios on an individualized basis:

- Toxic or highly febrile child
- High-risk neonate with suspected AOM[36]
- Children in intensive care units[37]
- Bulging tympanic membrane with anticipated spontaneous rupture (relative indication)
- Suspected AOM with an acute suppurative complication
- Refractory AOM unresponsive to a second course of antibiotics

Tympanocentesis is also advantageous in research studies requiring microbiologic documentation of conditioning variables or outcomes. Ethical use of the procedure as part of a research protocol, however, would require clearly defined case criteria relative to the above clinical indications.

What Is the "Observation Option" for AOM, and How Can It Be Implemented?

The observation option refers to deferring antibiotic treatment of selected children with uncomplicated AOM for up to 72 hours, during which time, management is limited to analgesics and symptomatic relief.[38] This practice is based on data from RCTs suggesting that most children will improve naturally and that antibiotics provide only a marginal benefit.[14–22] Antibiotic therapy is begun, however, if symptoms persist or worsen during this initial period of observation. The observation option for AOM is an official policy in The Netherlands (children aged 6 months and older) and Sweden (children aged 2 years or older), and an unofficial policy in Denmark and Norway. Complication rates from AOM (eg, mastoiditis) are no greater with the observation option than with initial antibiotic therapy, *provided that* antibiotics are given when symptoms persist or worsen.

Whereas most clinicians agree that *some* children with AOM are suitable for initial observation, there is considerable disagreement about exactly *which* children should be observed. To facilitate decisions for or against initial observation, the New York State Department of Health developed the Observation Option Toolkit.[34,39] Included in the toolkit are (1) an overview of AOM treatment, (2) a health care provider information sheet, (3) a parent or caregiver information sheet (in tear-off pads of 50 each), (4) an annotated bibliography, and (5) a laminated decision aid for clinician reference and patient education. The toolkit is not intended to endorse observation as the preferred method of AOM management, nor is it intended as a rigid practice guideline to supplant clinician judgment. Rather, it gives busy clinicians the tools to implement the observation option should they desire to so.

Children are *unsuitable* for initial observation (Tables 18-7 and 18-8) if they are under age 6 months or are OM treatment failures; if the AOM relapses (within 30 days); or if they have immune deficiency, craniofacial anomalies, or coexisting streptococcal pharyngitis or bacterial sinusitis. For other children, decisions are based on child age, diagnostic certainty, and illness severity. Note that in contrast to the Dutch AOM guideline (see Chapter 20, "International Perspective on Management"), *diagnostic certainty* for AOM is a primary influencing factor. A *certain diagnosis* is a clinical picture suggesting AOM (see Table 18-5) with a *high probability* of MEE. An *uncertain diagnosis* is suspected AOM with anything *less than a high probability* of MEE as a result of obstructing cerumen, child apprehension, or other factors that impair visibility of the tympanic membrane or adequate performance of pneumatic otoscopy.

The issue of diagnostic certainty warrants further comment. An international survey of general practitioners revealed AOM diagnostic certainty of only 58% in infants, 66% in toddlers, and 73% in older children.[40] Conversely, primary-care practitioners in New York expressed 90% certainty (median child age, 2.4 years), but the true prevalence of AOM was only 70% (nearly all false-positives related to absence of MEE).[41] The relative risk of receiving an antibiotic was 1.50 times higher when clinicians expressed certainty, suggesting that 26% of prescriptions were potentially unnecessary. Interobserver reliability for otitis media (OM) is also poor, with only a slight to moderate correlation between clinical diagnostic examinations of pediatric residents, pediatric otolaryngologists, and tympanometry.[42] This, in part, relates to a paucity of formalized resident education in diagnosing OM,[43] but no degree of education—or experience—can eliminate all uncertainty. Therefore, uncertainty should be part of the treatment paradigm.

Initial antibiotic therapy is recommended (see Table 18-8) for all children under 2 years of age with a *certain* diagnosis of AOM because of a poorer natural history[22,44–46] and greater absolute benefit from *full-course* antibiotics (7 to 10 days) than older children.[47–51] Young children cared for outside the home during the day derive even greater benefit from full-course therapy.[49,51] In contrast, older children are the best candidates for initial observation or short-course therapy (5 days), particularly when the illness is nonsevere[21] or the AOM diagnosis is uncertain. Short-course therapy for older children offers easier administration, comparable outcomes to full-course therapy, and reduced incidence of resistant pneumococci after therapy.[50–52]

Which Adjunctive Therapies Are Appropriate for AOM Symptom Relief?

Analgesics are used liberally for 24 hours after AOM diagnosis (especially at bedtime) because about 40% of children remain symptomatic whether initially managed

Table 18-7 Scope of the AOM Observation Option Toolkit[39]

Aspect	Definition
Disease entity	Initial presentation of uncomplicated AOM (as defined in Table 18-5) Excludes AOM treatment failures or relapses (within 30 days), AOM with sinusitis or streptococcal pharyngitis, and children with syndromes, immune deficiency, or craniofacial anomalies
Patient population	Age 2 months to 18 years
Setting	All types of providers and practice settings
Interventions	Initial observation (observation option) Initial short-course antibiotics (5 days) Initial full-course antibiotics (7–10 days)
Influencing factors	Diagnostic certainty for AOM Age under 2 years vs. 2 years or older Illness severity Follow-up availability and reliability Patient or caregiver preference
Outcome measures	Clinical success defined as resolution or improvement of all presenting AOM signs and symptoms, excluding MEE Observation failure defined as worsening or persistence of initial AOM signs and symptoms by 72 hours

AOM = acute otitis media; MEE = middle ear effusion.

Table 18-8 Overview of Initial AOM Management in the Observation Option Toolkit[39]

Child Age	Certain AOM Diagnosis	Uncertain AOM Diagnosis
Under 6 mo	Antibiotics[†]	Antibiotics[†]
6 mo to 2 yr	Antibiotics[†]	Antibiotics[†] if severe* illness Observe[§] if nonsevere* illness
2 yr or older	Antibiotics[‡] if severe* illness Observe[§] if nonsevere* illness	Observe[§]

AOM = acute otitis media.

*Nonsevere illness is mild otalgia and fever < 39°C orally (about 102°F) or < 39.5°C rectally in the past 24 hours; severe illness is moderate to severe otalgia or higher fever or clinician judgment that child is toxic or severely ill.

[†]Children under age 2 years receive full-course antibiotics.

[‡]Children aged 2 years or older may receive short-course antibiotics or full-course antibiotics based on clinician judgment and parental preference.

[§]Observation is appropriate only when follow-up can be assured (by telephone or office visit) and antibiotics started if symptoms worsen or persist by 72 hours.

with antibiotics or not (see Table 18-6). When 219 children aged 1 to 6 years were randomized to ibuprofen, acetaminophen, or placebo, the prevalence of otalgia after 48 hours was 7%, 10%, and 25%, respectively ($p < .05$).[53] Greatest efficacy was observed for ibuprofen versus placebo ($p < .01$), with an absolute rate difference (RD) of 18% (95% CI, 7 to 30%). Symptom relief rises dramatically within several days, but asymptomatic MEE may persist up to several months. Parents are counseled that MEE may cause a transient hearing loss or fullness but that additional antibiotics will not hasten resolution (see Tables 18-4 and 18-6).

When the tympanic membrane is intact, otic solution containing benzocaine will significantly reduce otalgia 30 minutes after administration.[54] The magnitude of clinical benefit, however, is small and has only been documented in children aged 5 years and older. Comparable results were achieved in children aged 6 years and older using ear drops with a naturopathic herbal extract.[55] Consequently, the efficacy of topical drops (allopathic or naturopathic) is unproven in children younger than 5 years. When the tympanic membrane is not intact (spontaneous rupture or indwelling ventilating tube), ototopical antimicrobial medication may be used to control persistent or severe otorrhea. Ofloxacin is an ototopical antimicrobial approved for use with a nonintact tympanic membrane.

Antihistamines or decongestants, alone or in combination, are not recommended for AOM. Although combination therapy reduced AOM failures by 24% (relative risk [RR].76) in one meta-analysis,[56] the authors do not recommend this regimen because the NNT (11) is high, the NNH (number needed to harm) for drug side effects only slightly higher (17), lower quality studies found higher benefits (suggesting a design bias), and the subgroup result was no longer significant when adjusted for

multiple comparisons. There is no convincing evidence to support routine use of systemic corticosteroids, topical corticosteroids, or topical nasal decongestants as adjunctive measures for AOM management.

Can Withholding Initial Antibiotics Predispose to Suppurative Complications?

Routine antibiotic therapy for AOM is often cited as the main reason for infrequent mastoiditis. Rudberg[57] reported a median 21% incidence of surgical mastoiditis after AOM in 16 trials of nonantibiotic therapy from the 1930s and 1940s. By the 1950s, however, the rate decreased to 0.43% for 12,781 children treated with antibiotics and myringotomy.[58] With the increasing popularity of restrictive antibiotic therapy for AOM, concern exists over a possible resurgence of mastoiditis.[59,60] Such concern is based on opinion, not evidence, and is not supported by published data. In contrast, several evidence-based conclusions are apparent from recently published case series of pediatric mastoiditis:

- Acute mastoiditis is most common in infants and young children, and can be the presenting sign of AOM in a patient with no prior middle ear disease[59–69]
- Routine antibiotic treatment of AOM is not an absolute safeguard against complications; most cases (range 36 to 87%) have received prior antibiotic therapy[59,63,67,69–72]
- Antibiotic treatment may mask mastoiditis signs and symptoms, producing a subtle presentation that can delay diagnosis[66,69,71]

Van Zuijlen and colleagues[73] compared national differences in acute mastoiditis rates from 1991 to 1998 for children age 14 years or younger:

- Incidence rates in the United Kingdom, Canada, Australia, and the United States, where antibiotic prescription rates for AOM are all at least 96%, ranged from 1.2 per 100,000 person-years (py) to 2.0 per 100,000 py.
- Incidence rates in the Netherlands, Norway, and Denmark, where antibiotic prescription rates for AOM are 31%, 67%, and 76%, respectively, were higher: 3.8 per 100,000 py, 3.5 per 100,000 py, and 4.2 per 100,000 py, respectively.

These data suggest a *relative* twofold increase in mastoiditis with restrictive antibiotics, but causality cannot be inferred. Norway and Denmark have prescribing rates more than twice that of the Netherlands, yet the mastoiditis rates are statistically equivalent. Further, 1997 discharge data for New York City, Westchester, and Nassau County children showed 3.9 cases per 100,000 py (Robert Ruben, personal communication), which is comparable with the Netherlands. Even if the twofold difference were real, the *absolute* difference is only 2 extra cases of mastoiditis per 100,000 children per year. A restrictive antibiotic policy, however, would create 7,800 fewer antibiotic prescriptions per 100,000 children per year, thereby avoiding 1,600 adverse drug reactions (eg, diarrhea, vomiting, skin rash, allergic reactions, anaphylaxis).[73]

The above evidence suggests that occasional mastoiditis after AOM is likely to persist, even if antibiotics are routinely prescribed. Infants and young children are at highest risk. With appropriate follow-up, initially withholding antibiotics from selected older children with AOM does not appear to increase risk.[10] This observation must be tempered, however, by realizing that some placebo-controlled RCTs were limited to older children or those with nonsevere AOM. Whether restrictive antibiotic use increases mastoiditis rates at the population level is unresolved (see Chapter 20), but the absolute increase (if any) is small and must be weighed against potential adverse effects. In regions where resistant pneumococci are prevalent, for example, antibiotics may not only fail to eradicate the organisms, but they often induce MEE superinfection with resistant pneumococci initially carried in the nasopharynx.[74]

What Factors Influence Initial Antibiotic Choice and Duration of Therapy?

As discussed above, selected children with AOM may benefit from initial observation (see Table 18-8). When prescribing antibiotics, initially or for observation failures, clinicians should choose drugs that are efficacious and cover common AOM pathogens.[75] The suggestions in this section stem primarily from RCTs, or meta-analyses of RCTs (see Chapter 4), that address clinical outcomes after initial antibiotic therapy. Conversely, when a child fails initial therapy or a specific pathogen is suspected, issues of bacteriologic efficacy assume increased importance (see Chapters 16, "Bacteriologic Efficacy of Antimicrobial Agents" and 26, "Bacterial Resistance and Antimicrobial Drug Selection).

Antibiotic treatment of AOM is usually empiric. Tympanocentesis may identify a pathogen in 70 to 80% of cases,[76–78] but risks exceed benefits for routine AOM management (see above). About 35 to 40% of AOM is caused by *Streptococcus pneumoniae*, 30% by non-typeable *Haemophilus influenzae*, and 10% by *Moraxella catarrhalis*, of which 0%, 35 to 70%, and 90 to 100% produce beta-lactamase, respectively.[78,79] Pneumococcus is most virulent, increasing in prevalence from birth and peaking at preschool age.[80] Resistance to penicillin and other drugs has reached 60 to 80% in some areas (see Chapter 20), with antimicrobial use as a major risk factor (especially ongoing, recent, frequent, or prophylactic use of antibiotics).[80–81] The cause of AOM is similar for young children with acute myringitis and for afebrile nontoxic infants.[82,83]

Amoxicillin (40 mg/kg/d) is recommended as first-line therapy for AOM because of its safety, palatability, low cost, and comparable clinical efficacy with other agents (Table 18-9). A higher dose (80 to 90 mg/kg/d) is advised for resistant *S. pneumoniae* related to geographic trends, recent antibiotic use, or group day care attendance.[84,85] For penicillin-allergic children, trimethoprim-sulfamethoxazole and azithromycin are effective. Both drugs, however, are suboptimal for resistant *H. influenzae*, and trimethoprim-sulfamethoxazole has poor efficacy for resistant pneumococcus.[76,86] Second line drugs (see Table 18-9) may be necessary as initial therapy for selected children to maximize compliance through improved taste and more convenient dosing intervals (once or twice daily).[87] Initial therapy with a second-line agent is also appropriate for complicated infections, recently treated AOM (relapse within 30 days), and for children with ipsilateral conjunctivitis suggesting *H. influenzae* infection.[88–90]

The optimum duration of AOM therapy is controversial. Short-course therapy (3 days of azithromycin, 5 days of other antibiotics) is an option for children aged 2 years or older and full-course treatment (5 days of azithromycin, 7 to 10 days of other antibiotics) is better for younger children. Kozyrskyj and colleagues[50] found slightly better short-term outcomes with full-course treatment (odds ratio 1.5), but the NNTs (13 to 20) indicate only a small effect. The impact is more pronounced, however, for children aged 2 years or younger, especially when attending group day care.[48–51] Better outcomes

Table 18–9 Antimicrobials Approved by the FDA for Treating Otitis Media

Class	Generic Name	Brand Name	Dosing Interval
First-line drugs			
PCN	Amoxicillin	Amoxil®	tid
MISC	Trimethoprim-sulfamethoxazole	Bactrim®, Septra®	bid
Second-line drugs			
PCN	Amoxicillin/clavulanate	Augmentin®	bid
CEF2	Cefaclor	Ceclor®	bid or tid
CEF2	Cefprozil	Cefzil®	bid
CEF2	Cefuroxime axetil	Ceftin®	bid
CEF2	Loracarbef	Lorabid®	bid
CEF3	Cefixime	Suprax®	qd
CEF3	Cefpodoxime proxetil	Vantin®	qd or bid
CEF3	Ceftibuten	Cedax®	qd
CEF3	Cefdinir	Omnicef®	qd or bid
CEF3	Ceftriaxone	Rocephin®	qd*
MAC	Azithromycin	Zithromax®	qd
MAC	Clarithromycin	Biaxin®	bid
MISC	Erythromycin-sulfisoxazole	Pediazole®	qd

bid = twice daily; CEF2 = 2nd generation cephalosporins; CEF3 = 3rd generation cephalosporins; FDA = Food and Drug Administration; MAC = macrolides; MISC = miscellaneous; PCN = penicillins; qd = once daily; qid = four times daily; tid = three times daily.
*Intramuscular.

with full-course therapy have also been demonstrated for children with AOM in the preceding month.[91]

Much debate has focused on choosing among the 15 oral antibiotics (see Table 18-9) approved by the U.S. Food and Drug Administration for treating AOM. Nonetheless, no differences have been found in clinical efficacy for AOM or persistent MEE. Rosenfeld and colleagues[8] found no relationship between antibacterial spectrum and AOM outcomes in 33 RCTs: clinical resolution was 92% with a standard-spectrum drug versus 91% with an extended-spectrum agent. Similarly, Berman and coworkers[92] reported that 88% of over 12,000 AOM episodes were successfully treated with a single antibiotic, regardless of the cost or antimicrobial spectrum of the initial drug. Takata and coworkers[93] found no differences in comparative antibiotic efficacy for AOM in a comprehensive meta-analysis, and Ionnidis and colleagues[94] found no differences in a meta-analysis of azithromycin versus other drugs.

The comparable *clinical* efficacy of first- and second-line drugs relates to the high rate of AOM spontaneous resolution, which greatly dilutes any discernible benefit caused by the nuances of antimicrobial selection. For example, when amoxicillin-clavulanate was given to 23 children with AOM caused by highly resistant *S. pneumonia*, 20 (87%) had successful outcomes, although the drug was theoretically ineffective for more than two-thirds of bacterial strains.[95] In routine clinical practice, however, the bacteriology of AOM (for a specific child) is unknown, diagnostic certainty varies, and 15 to 20% of infections may be viral. This further reduces the incremental benefit of antimicrobials seen in RCTs and would make differences nearly impossible to detect in a nonexperimental setting. AOM studies with double-tap tympanocentesis protocols can show significant differences in antibiotic efficacy (see Chapter 16),[96] but generalizability of results to everyday clinical practice is limited (see Chapter 2, "Critical Evaluation of Journal Articles).

Although a single intramuscular dose of ceftriaxone has comparable efficacy to a 7-to 10-day course of first-line therapy,[50,93] its use as *initial* empiric therapy for uncomplicated AOM should be discouraged. Liberal use of ceftriaxone may accelerate bacterial resistance and compromise efficacy as a back-up for suppurative complications (for which oral alternatives do not exist). Further, using such a potent drug for a ubiquitous childhood illness with high spontaneous resolution is difficult to justify. Ceftriaxone is appropriate as initial AOM therapy in the rare instance when intramuscular administration is the only way to ensure compliance but should not be offered simply because parents find a single dose most convenient.

How Should Initial Treatment Failures Be Managed?

All children with AOM require follow-up, but not necessarily after completing the initial course of therapy. Early follow-up may be selectively offered to children whose parents feel the infection has not resolved because parent perceptions of clinical resolution are generally accurate.[97,98] Persistent symptoms are most likely to occur in children who are young or have recurrent infections.[99,100] Routine follow-up of AOM at 10 to 14 days *is not* recommended because 70% of children will have residual MEE that may prompt additional— but unnecessary—antimicrobial therapy. In contrast, a follow-up visit is recommended between 1 and 3 months (see Table 18-2) to detect persistent, asymptomatic MEE that may benefit from parent education and primary prevention measures.

Persistent AOM despite treatment is most often secondary to middle ear inflammation after the bacteria are killed, either by antibiotics or by the host immune response. Other reasons for treatment failure are listed in Table 18-10, many of which do not benefit from antibiotics. Additional therapy is *not indicated* when MEE cannot be documented by pneumatic otoscopy or other diagnostic measures. Most episodes of AOM are associated with common respiratory viruses,[101] which may prolong symptom duration.[102,103] When viral upper respiratory or systemic symptoms overshadow ear-related complaints (particularly in an older child), additional antibiotics may be withheld pending results of symptomatic therapy for 24 to 48 hours.

Since the cause of AOM treatment failure is generally not apparent, antibiotics are indicated to prevent suppurative complications. If the child was initially observed, a first-line antibiotic is begun. For children initially treated with a first-line agent, re-treatment with a second-line antibiotic (see Table 18-9) is more effective, but about 30% of children will, nonetheless, fail additional therapy.[104] If a second-line antibiotic was initially given, an alternative second-line drug should be chosen. Changes in an antibiotic regimen should not be made sooner than 48 to 72 hours after therapy has begun because 40% of children with AOM remain symptomatic after 24 hours (higher for children under age 2 years).

When a child fails to improve after 48 to 72 hours of therapy with the second-line drug, diagnostic tympanocentesis should be considered.[105,106] In about 30 to 60% of cases, however, no pathogens are detected, and in about 20 to 30% of cases, bacteria sensitive to the most recent antibiotic are isolated.[100,107–109] Some studies report sterile taps in less than 30% of children with a rising prevalence of multidrug-resistant organisms (particularly pneumococcus).[106,110] Therefore, tympanocentesis is recommended to help guide therapy in severely ill children with refractory AOM despite several prior antibiotics. Culture of the nasopharynx is easy to perform but correlates poorly with tympanocentesis results.[111]

Table 18–10 Causes of Apparent Initial Treatment Failure for AOM

Cause of Fever, Otalgia, or Other Symptoms	Status of Middle Ear Space	Benefits from Antibiotics?
Residual inflammation	Sterile MEE without viable pathogens	No
Persistent infection	MEE with bacteria sensitive to initial antibiotic	Yes
Persistent infection	MEE with bacteria resistant to initial antibiotic	Yes
Persistent infection	MEE with viral pathogens, no viable bacteria	No
Concurrent viral infection	MEE with delayed bacterial clearance	Possibly
Coexisting URI	MEE, with or without viral pathogens	No
Viral myringitis	Normal, but tympanic membrane inflamed	No
Referred otalgia*	Baseline OME, misdiagnosed as AOM	No
Referred otalgia*	Normal	No

AOM = acute otitis media; MEE = middle ear effusion; OME = otitis media with effusion; URI = upper respiratory infection.
*Pain referred to ear along trigeminal nerve from teeth or pharynx.

A negative culture for antibiotic-resistant *S. pneumoniae*, however, practically rules out its presence in MEE (negative predictive value, 93 to 95%).[112]

Amoxicillin-clavulanate, cefuroxime, and ceftriaxone have been recommended for treating nonresponsive AOM,[9,84] but clinical data are lacking to show improved outcomes with these versus other second-line agents (see Table 18-9). When using amoxicillin-clavulanate, the newer formulation with high-dose amoxicillin (90 mg/kg/d) is advised for increased coverage of resistant pneumococcus.[113] As noted above, ceftriaxone is a potent drug that is best reserved for children who are very ill, have real or impending suppurative complications, or have persistent acute symptoms despite several prior antibiotics. A 3-day course of intramuscular ceftriaxone (50 mg/kg) has greater efficacy for nonresponsive AOM than does 1-day administration (97% versus 57% pneumococcus eradication, $p < .001$).[114] Readers should consult Chapters 16 and 26 for a more comprehensive discussion of antibiotic selection issues for nonresponsive AOM.

MANAGING PERSISTENT MEE

As shown in Tables 18-1 and 18-2, managing AOM does not end with resolution of acute local and systemic symptoms. Asymptomatic MEE commonly persists for an additional 1 to 3 months and may become chronic. Follow-up of AOM should continue until MEE resolves.

What Causes Persistent MEE?

Persistent MEE after resolution of AOM symptoms is expected and *does not* require additional antibiotic therapy.[9] AOM produces an intense local inflammatory reaction, resulting in mucosal edema within the middle ear, mastoid, and Eustachian tube. The corresponding decrease in Eustachian tube function may delay resolution of sterile MEE for weeks or months after symptomatic relief. Consequently, physician and parent expectations should be modified to expect and monitor MEE, rather than express surprise and disappointment when asymptomatic MEE persists. Appropriate expectations will help avoid unnecessary additional antibiotics, which do not benefit MEE, *unless* accompanied by new onset of local or systemic illness suggesting re-infection (AOM).[14,20,21,115]

Persistent asymptomatic MEE after AOM is called otitis media with effusion. OME may also arise without antecedent AOM, but about 50% of OME in infants and young children is caused by direct continuation of an acute episode.[116] Two weeks after an episode of AOM, 60 to 70% of children are expected to have OME,

decreasing to 40% after 1 month, and 25% after 3 months. RCTs generally yield higher estimates of MEE because of the better diagnostic measures and more intense follow-up characteristic of experimental studies. In contrast, the prevalence of MEE in routine clinical scenarios is most likely underestimated. Follow-up may be less than optimal, and MEE is easily overlooked in an asymptomatic child.

Risk factors for delayed resolution of MEE include a prior history of tympanostomy tubes and additional prior episodes of AOM or OME.[116,117] Stated differently, once a child develops AOM or OME, he or she is less likely to recover promptly from future episodes. Bilateral disease and day care attendance also increase the probability of developing persistent OME.[118] Laterality is most likely a severity marker, possibly related to intrinsic host susceptibility. Day care attendance is extrinsic but more directly causal, presumably marking frequency of exposure to viral pathogens.

To summarize, residual MEE is a consequence, not a complication, of AOM. Clinicians who routinely observe transient MEE following AOM can be assured of a relatively high degree of diagnostic certainty concerning the initial episode. Conversely, clinicians who routinely note a normal middle ear status (no MEE) after antimicrobial therapy should reassess their diagnostic accuracy. Properly diagnosed AOM results in a 60 to 70% prevalence of MEE after 2 weeks, which is best viewed as a confirmation of initial diagnosis, not an indication of suboptimal or improper clinical management.

What, if Anything, Should Be Done about Persistent MEE?

Children with AOM should be reassessed after 4 to 6 weeks (see Table 18-2) to detect persistent MEE. If MEE is found, the parents are reassured that it will most likely resolve spontaneously, but that a temporary hearing loss may accompany the effusion. Efforts are also indicated to minimize direct child exposure to environmental tobacco smoke (ETS) and to maximize control of any known inhalant or food allergies. Antibiotics are not prescribed, unless there are local or systemic symptoms to suggest ongoing infection. A follow-up visit is scheduled at approximately 3 months to be sure that the MEE eventually resolves.

Chronic OME is diagnosed when MEE fails to resolve within 3 months of the initial AOM episode. The natural history of chronic OME is subject to seasonal variations, but the chance of spontaneous resolution decreases the longer the effusion persists (see Chapter 12). Antimicrobial therapy is optional and confers a modest short-term benefit of about a 15% increase in absolute cure rates (see Chapter 13). Consequently, about 7 children need treatment to resolve OME in 1 child. Antihistamine and decongestant therapy have no impact on OME resolution, and steroids or mucolytic agents offer inconsistent benefits of questionable significance (see Chapter 13). Considering the disappointing results obtained with all medical therapies, management efforts are best directed at primary prevention and family education (see Table 18-2).

Children with bilateral OME lasting 3 months or longer are referred for complete hearing evaluation by a licensed audiologist.[119] Parent assurance that their child's hearing is "normal" cannot be trusted because parents are often unable to detect the borderline to mild hearing loss caused by most OME.[120] Readers should refer to Chapter 19, "Clinical Pathway for Otitis Media with Effusion" for complete information on managing chronic effusions. Briefly, for most children, a decision must be made regarding timely insertion of tympanostomy tubes versus continued watchful waiting. Some of the primary determinants in this decision process are hearing status, structural integrity of the tympanic membrane, and the overall developmental status of the child. Therefore, in addition to their primary-care physician, an audiologist and otolaryngologist should evaluate all children with chronic OME.

Managing Recurrent AOM

Howie and colleagues[121] coined the term "otitis-prone" in 1975 on the basis of the clinical observation that certain children have a remarkable tendency for recurrent infection. Recurrent AOM can be viewed as one potential long-term outcome of an AOM episode (see Table 18-2). Children with previous OM are more than twice as likely (odds ratio 2.2, 95% CI, 1.5, 3.3) as those without prior attacks to develop recurrent AOM.[122] Although less than one in five children become otitis prone, the condition is distinct from isolated AOM and requires different management strategies as outlined below.

What Is Recurrent AOM?

Recurrent AOM is best defined as three or more *well-documented* and *separate* AOM episodes in the preceding 6 months or four or more episodes in the preceding 12 months.[9] The word "well-documented" is emphasized because issues of diagnostic certainty become paramount when dealing with recurrent infection. Certainty levels of 60 to 75% when diagnosing AOM, which often prevail in general practice,[40,41] will yield an unacceptable level of unnecessary antibiotic prescriptions. Emphasis is also placed on the word "separate" because true recurrent AOM has an *effusion-free inter-*

val between episodes. Persistent OME, with superimposed recurrent acute infection, is a distinct entity, which is managed as described in Chapter 19.

Otoscopic detection of MEE can be difficult in a cooperative child, and cooperation is generally not facilitated by the acute symptoms that accompany AOM. When diagnostic certainty is suboptimal, we strongly recommend adjunctive tympanometry[5] or acoustic reflectometry (with spectral gradient analysis)[6] to document MEE (see Chapter 9, "Diagnosis"). Acoustic reflectometry is equivalent to tympanometry but is less expensive and is easier to use in crying children because an airtight seal is unnecessary and the constant stimulus permits a reading when the child pauses to take a breath. Tympanometry provides additional information about middle ear peak pressures and static compliance.[7] Both instruments can be used with a recorder, which produces a permanent print-out for the child's medical record.

Whether a given child will or will not go on to develop recurrent AOM cannot be predicted accurately after the initial AOM episode. Therefore, the frequency of subsequent infection must be documented, with particular emphasis on the presence or absence of intercurrent MEE. About 15 to 20% of children develop recurrent AOM as defined above, with a mean age of 15 months at the time of diagnosis.[123] Risk factors of recurrent infection include AOM debut before the age of 6 months, day care attendance, exposure to second-hand smoke, short duration of breast feeding, sibling history of recurrent AOM, and possible genetic or immunologic predispositions.[124–126] Additional factors associated with recurrent attack after an initial AOM episode include young age and use of broad-spectrum antibiotics.[122]

Can Recurrent AOM be Prevented?

The first steps in managing recurrent AOM are parent education and primary prevention measures, not surgery or antibiotic prophylaxis. This begins by recognizing the profound impact that recurrent AOM can have on family relationships. Mothers of children who had six or more episodes of AOM in the first 2 years of life rate their children as significantly more demanding than similar children with only one episode.[127] Moreover, they rate themselves as more depressed and less competent than control mothers. Clinicians should reassure parents that OM is an occupational hazard of early childhood, not a reflection of poor parenting, and that time (natural history) is on their side.

When surveyed about OM risk factors, only 11% of 400 Minnesota women recognized that most ear infections got better by themselves.[128] This suggests substantial opportunity for parent education and reassurance. Children who receive *placebo* or *no drug* between episodes of recurrent AOM average 2.8 annual episodes,[129–141] although their baseline rate of AOM was at least 5.6 annual episodes (see Chapter 12). The mean spontaneous reduction in AOM frequency is 1.5 to 2.5 episodes per year. Further, about 40% of children have no further AOM during a median observation period of 6 months, and more than 80% have only 2 or fewer episodes (see Chapter 12). The preceding figures are not offered in support of placebo but, rather, as a means of reassuring anxious parents. Seasonal variations can also be reassuring, given the approximate 50% drop in AOM incidence during the summer.[142]

The favorable natural history of recurrent AOM is related to growth and development of the child's Eustachian tube (see Chapter 11, "Eustachian Tube Function and Dysfunction") and immune system. Children have high levels of maternal immunoglobulin (Ig)G at birth, but a nadir is reached at about 5 to 6 months of age because of gradual degradation.[143] In contrast, levels of endogenous IgG, IgA, and IgM rise gradually after birth and plateau in later childhood. Not coincidentally, this nadir and plateau correspond with the onset and disappearance of AOM in most children.

Whereas little can be done to accelerate immune development, vaccines can modify AOM susceptibility. An influenza vaccine will reduce AOM incidence for children in day care by about 35% during the acute influenza season.[144,145] Children aged 2 years or older can reduce their AOM risk slightly (relative risk .83, 95% CI, .63, .97) by receiving a polysaccharide pneumococcal vaccine.[146] The vaccine showed no effect below age 2 years, but the newer heptavalent conjugate vaccine reduced absolute risk for recurrent AOM (3 in past 6 months or 4 in past year) by 9.1% (95% CI, 4.1, 13.8%).[147] The heptavalent conjugate vaccine is currently recommend for universal use in American children 23 months and younger, to be given concurrently with other vaccines at 2, 4, 6, and 12 to 15 months of age.[148]

All children with recurrent AOM should undergo audiometry and tympanometry to document hearing status and detect OME. Additional diagnostic tests should be considered for selected children, including (1) examination for submucous cleft palate (triad of bifid uvula, palatal muscle diastasis, and a notch in the posterior surface of the hard palate)[149,150]; (2) evaluation for respiratory allergies; (3) immune studies to identify defects in cellular or humoral immunity (particularly in older children or when infections affect more than one site in the respiratory tract); and (4) radiography or computed tomography to detect paranasal sinusitis. Although uncommon (0.05% incidence), submucous cleft palate is an important cause of refractory OM. Children with a submucous cleft palate should be further evaluated for velopharyngeal incompetence.

Infant feeding practices can be modified to prevent AOM. In a prospective study of 400 Swedish infants, the frequency of AOM was significantly lower in breast-fed babies than in children with mixed feeding or those who received other foods only.[150] Further, the first attack of AOM occurred earlier in children who were weaned at a younger age. Whereas it is too late to begin breast feeding by the time most children develop recurrent AOM, parents should be counseled regarding future children. Expectations regarding breast feeding and AOM, however, must be realistic. Although statistically significant, the clinical impact in most studies is relatively modest. In recent studies of infectious diseases, breast feeding as a preventive factor generally does not emerge as strongly as previously thought, probably because of lower socioeconomic status among controls (Mark P. Haggard, personal communication).

Parents who bottle feed are encouraged to use a semiupright position to avoid fluid reflux into the middle ear. In a prospective study of 90 children *without* OM, 60% had abnormal tympanograms after feeding in the supine position versus only 15% when feeding in the semiupright position.[151] Placing the child in a prone or semiupright position for 15 minutes after feeding returned most tympanograms to normal. The impact of positional changes on otitis-prone children is unknown, but some attention to feeding position would appear prudent. When a child must feed in the supine position (for behavioral or other reasons), water or other clear liquids may be less irritating than milk or formula, if reflux into the nasopharynx should occur.

Day care attendance is a well-established risk factor for AOM, but group size, not day care per se, is the mediating factor. Small groups are preferable because AOM risk increases by about 50 to 100% with group sizes of more than 4 to 6 other children.[152,153] Exposing immunologically immature young children to others in close quarters facilitates the spread of respiratory viruses, which initiate most AOM. Removing an otitis prone child from day care, however, is not always effective because having an older sibling at home also increases the viral burden.[153] Instead, parents of young children in day care are urged to choose a setting with as few children as possible and to focus on avoiding pacifier use, which was responsible for 25% of AOM observed in 845 Finnish children.[154] AOM incidence is also 33% higher when children use a pacifier continuously instead of not at all or only when falling asleep.[155] Pacifiers are best restricted to the first 10 months of life, when the need for sucking is strongest.

A final prevention opportunity for children with recurrent AOM concerns exposure to ETS. Passive smoking has a harmful effect on the respiratory health of children and is a risk factor of OM.[156] Exposure to ETS significantly increases AOM incidence, AOM prevalence, and need for tympanostomy tubes (relative risk or odds ratio, 1.2 to 1.6).[157] Parents should be advised of this relationship and asked to discontinue smoking. If smoking cessation is not possible, parents and relatives should restrict smoking to well-ventilated or outdoor areas to limit direct exposure of the child to ETS.

What Management Options Are Available?

Antimicrobial Prophylaxis

Antimicrobial prophylaxis may be considered for *selected* children with recurrent AOM. I emphasize the need for individualized decisions because for most children the risk of accelerated bacterial resistance exceeds the modest benefit of daily antibiotic consumption. Prophylaxis is only appropriate for children with three or more well-documented and separate AOM episodes in the preceding 6 months or four or more episodes in the preceding 12 months (without chronic underlying MEE). Parent expectations for prophylaxis must also be appropriately modest (see Table 18-4 and Chapter 13), reflecting only a 0.09 episode per month decrease in AOM frequency attributable to therapy in placebo-controlled RCTs (about 0.5 to 1.5 AOM per year for 95% of children).[129–135,137,138,140–141] For children with 6 or more AOM episodes in the preceding year the impact may be higher (see Chapter 13).

Sulfisoxazole or amoxicillin are the agents of choice for antibiotic prophylaxis; trimethoprim-sulfamethoxazole (TMP-SMX) is contraindicated,[158] and cephalosporins have not been demonstrated to be effective. Choosing between sulfisoxazole and amoxicillin is largely a matter of personal preference. Sulfisoxazole may be more efficacious (see Chapter 13) and less likely to promote pharyngeal colonization with resistant pneumococci or beta-lactamase–producing bacteria.[159] Amoxicillin, however, is a safe, well tolerated, established standard for treating AOM. Adverse reaction rates for sulfonamides are also favorable, estimated at only 11 events per 100 py at risk among children younger than 2 years of age.[160] Hematologic reactions are related more to TMP-SMX than sulfisoxazole, but concerned clinicians can obtain a baseline complete blood count with platelets.[161]

To minimize the risk of resistant bacteria, prophylactic therapy should be limited to 3 to 6 months.[9] The ideal time for prophylaxis is during the season for upper respiratory tract viruses, which, in the northeastern United States, runs from October through May. Breakthrough episodes of AOM should be anticipated because prophylaxis is unlikely to eliminate all AOM (see Chapter 13). When episodes occur, they are treated with a full therapeutic course of an alternative antimicrobial agent. Two or more breakthrough infections is

the criterion for considering prophylaxis failure. Finally, we want to re-emphasize that instituting antimicrobial prophylaxis is inappropriate if longstanding chronic MEE is present. When this occurs, the child should be managed as described in Chapter 19.

Antimicrobial prophylaxis for recurrent AOM should be offered only to families whose members are likely to comply with therapy and are comfortable with their child receiving a daily dose of antibiotic. The modest benefits of prophylaxis demonstrated under ideal circumstances in RCTs are likely to be smaller in real-life situations, where compliance may be less than optimal. For example, when 80 inner-city children with recurrent AOM were given prophylactic antibiotics, less than half complied with maintenance medication.[162] Greater compliance is achieved with intermittent prophylaxis at the onset of an upper respiratory infection, but RCTs have shown inconsistent benefits.[136,163] I do not recommend intermittent prophylaxis because of decreased efficacy compared with continuous drug administration.[164,165]

Tympanostomy Tubes

Five parallel-group RCTs[129,166–169] have shown tympanostomy tube insertion to be effective for preventing recurrent AOM in children with a history of recurrent AOM or with baseline chronic OME (see Chapter 14). Tubes achieve an absolute reduction of 1.0 AOM episodes per child-year (95% CI, 0.4, 1.5), with a greater effect noted (2.0 AOM per child-year reduction) in the first 6 to 12 months of follow-up (95% CI, 0.1, 3.8). Using relative risk reduction as the outcome, tubes decrease future AOM incidence by 56% (95% CI, 17, 77%). Tympanostomy tubes are effective for recurrent AOM because they directly ventilate the middle ear and bypass the child's immature and poorly functioning Eustachian tube; baseline or intercurrent OME is not a prerequisite for tube efficacy.

Tubes can minimize the antibiotic burden for recurrent AOM because subsequent infections (eg, tube otorrhea) can often be managed topically without systemic antibiotics (see Chapter 29, "Tympanostomy Tube Care and Consequences"). Children with breakthrough AOM episodes while on antibiotic prophylaxis are also tube candidates, although failure of antimicrobial prophylaxis *is not* a mandatory prerequisite for surgery. The relative merits of tubes versus prophylaxis are widely debated, but decision analysis suggests that tubes are preferred when at least two *severe* AOM episodes are anticipated in the next year.[170] A severe episode of AOM is defined as a 3-day course of illness with otalgia, fever, and loss of appetite treated by bed rest and antibiotics. When frequent, but mild, episodes are anticipated, watchful waiting is best. Unfortunately, there is no valid predictor of future episode severity, and the degree of prior severity may be an imperfect surrogate.

Tympanostomy tubes as a rational alternative to a long-term course of antimicrobial prophylaxis in children who *have not* had tube placement in the past. This approach is predicated on growing concerns over resistant bacteria induced by prolonged courses of low-dosage daily antibiotics. Factors that would favor antimicrobial prophylaxis include poor candidacy for general anesthesia and the season during which the child was evaluated. When encountering an infant or young child in the spring, who has had recurrent AOM during the previous fall and winter months, and who would only require the prophylactic regimen for 1 or 2 months, we would favor using prophylaxis. Conversely, children in group day care should avoid prophylaxis to limit nasopharyngeal carriage of resistant pneumococci.

A lower threshold for deciding on tympanostomy tube insertion is appropriate for some children with recurrent AOM. Children with speech delay, developmental delay, baseline sensorineural hearing loss, or behavioral problems are relatively intolerant of the transient conductive hearing loss that accompanies individual AOM episodes. MEE commonly persists for weeks to months after each acute infection, resulting in significant cumulative time with effusion. Although tubes and antibiotic prophylaxis have a comparable impact on AOM frequency (about a 55 to 60% relative decrease), children with tubes have decreased overall time with MEE and less severe AOM episodes.[129,170] Tubes are also preferred in children with severe AOM accompanied by febrile seizures.

Adenoidectomy

Adenoidectomy is an option for selected children with recurrent AOM. When AOM recurs after *prior tube extrusion*, adenoidectomy reduces relative AOM incidence by 26% over the next 3 years, MEE prevalence by 38%, and the need for future tubes by 52% (see Chapter 14).[171] The beneficial effect of adenoidectomy is not size dependent but may be related to a shift in nasopharyngeal microflora away from bacterial pathogens and toward commensal organisms.[172] Small, medium, as well as large adenoids may affect Eustachian tube function because of size changes during upper respiratory infection. Adenoidectomy is most beneficial for children aged 3 years or older.

Re-insertion of tympanostomy tubes is an alternative to adenoidectomy but is more of a temporizing measure than a means of altering child susceptibility. Adenoidectomy is not recommended for *initial* management of AOM, unless there is another primary indication for surgery, such as severe nasal obstruction, refractory rhinosinusitis, or obstructive sleep apnea syndrome. One RCT showed only limited and short-term benefits of adenoidectomy for recurrent AOM in children *without* prior tubes, leading the authors to conclude that surgical risks exceeded benefits for this indication.[173] In contrast, RCTs do support adenoidectomy for initial management of chronic OME (see Chapter 19).

Other Options

Parents of some children with recurrent AOM become frustrated with the modest benefits of antimicrobial prophylaxis (see Table 18-4) and, instead, seek refuge in herbal therapies or complementary (alternative) medicine. Given the favorable natural history of untreated recurrent AOM (see Chapter 12), such treatments seem to be "effective" for many children. Until evidence from RCTs demonstrates benefits beyond spontaneous resolution, however, the true efficacy—if any—of these remedies remains unknown. Although no large randomized trials of AOM are available, no differences were observed in rates of upper respiratory infections or antimicrobial prescriptions for 175 Dutch children randomized to homeopathic medicines versus placebo.[174]

There is insufficient evidence to recommend homeopathy for AOM. Barnett and colleagues[175] reported 92% success for 24 children (8 to 77 months) in a feasibility study of challenges in evaluating homeopathy. Failure of one homeopathic medicine, however, to cure AOM (67% of children) was not viewed as failure of therapy by the homeopathic physicians, if a subsequent one produced a cure. Jacobs and colleagues[176] randomized 75 children (1.5 to 6.0 years) to homeopathy versus placebo and found no significant difference in AOM treatment failures at 5 days or 2 weeks. Because of the small sample size, they concluded that a positive homeopathy effect could not be excluded (low power). Frei and Thurneysen[177] treated 230 Swiss children with homeopathy and noted 39% otalgia control by 6 hours and 72% by 12 hours. Bias cannot be excluded because of absent controls (historic only) and poor description of the study sample, disease definition, and outcome measures.

As noted by Peter Morgan, a medical epidemiologist, "Alternative medicine has become sophisticated, cloaking itself in updated scientific vocabularies, yet at the same time it does not have the scientific research capacity to test its own hypotheses."[178] Homeopathy has been better studied than other complementary or alternative therapies (see Chapter 15, "Clinical Effectiveness of Complementary and Alternative Therapies"), most of which are supported only by anecdote or case series. When patients pursue long-term complementary therapies, clinicians should encourage periodic follow-up to screen for persistent MEE, hearing loss, or tympanic membrane abnormalities. Most complementary medicine specialists are ill equipped to monitor the integrity of a child's tympanic membrane and to determine whether MEE is present. Further, parent perceptions of otologic and hearing status are inaccurate.[120]

Xylitol sugar has reduced the incidence of AOM by about 35% in Finnish children attending group day care.[179,180] Xylitol is a five-carbon polyol found in many plants, which is as sweet as sucrose and metabolized in the liver to glucose. The benefits observed for AOM relate to inhibition of pneumococci growth, decreased pneumococcal virulence, and decreased adhesion of both pneumococci and *H. influenzae* on epithelial cells. Unfortunately, drug concentrations become subtherapeutic within 5 to 10 minutes of drinking xylitol syrup or chewing xylitol gum. Xylitol must, therefore, be consumed regularly (about five times daily) to achieve an effect. In parts of Europe and Scandinavia, xylitol gum is regularly chewed to prevent dental caries, and frequent dosing has been successfully implemented.

Despite the appeal of the impressive *relative* benefits of xylitol consumption, the *absolute* benefits are somewhat less exciting: between 1 and 1.5 *years* of therapy are needed to prevent a single AOM episode. Therefore, to avoid one AOM, the average child must consume about 1,800 teaspoons of xylitol syrup, 5,600 pieces of xylitol chewing gum, or 15,200 xylitol lozenges. Few clinicians or parents are willing to expend this level of effort for such a small absolute benefit, and the effects of high and frequent doses through early childhood have not been studied. Therefore, I do not recommend xylitol for routine prevention of recurrent AOM. Administering xylitol only during acute upper respiratory infections is ineffective in preventing AOM.[181]

PATHWAYS, EVIDENCE, AND PERSONAL SIGNIFICANCE

This chapter has used the clinical pathway as a basis for evidence-based management. Clearly, the level of evidence supporting some decisions is greater than that supporting others. Whereas one can estimate the quantitative impact of antimicrobial therapy and prophylaxis on AOM with reasonable precision (see Table 18-4), much greater uncertainty accompanies decisions about surgery. There are, however, enough methodologically sound RCTs to estimate the impact of surgery on AOM outcomes (see Chapter 14). When evidence gaps exist, expert judgment and clinical consensus have been used. Several of the central principles underlying AOM management are summarized in Table 18-11.

There is no simple answer to the question, "Do all children with AOM require initial antibiotics?" What is clear, however, is that therapeutic nihilism risks a return to the once prevalent suppurative complications of the preantibiotic era. Whereas universal antibiotic prescribing is probably unnecessary, antibiotics do provide incremental benefits (see Table 18-6) and are undoubt-

edly responsible for the present rarity of AOM suppurative complications. The issue, however, is not "to treat or not to treat" with antibiotics but more accurately whether to prescribe or not to prescribe them *initially*. Observation is appropriate *only* when follow-up is assured and antibiotics can be started for persistent or worsening symptoms after 48 to 72 hours. In this context, appropriate tools exist for safe, judicious, and selective use of the AOM observation option (see Table 18-8) by interested clinicians and families.[34,39]

Clinicians must distinguish theory from fact when making evidence-based decisions. Despite the *theoretic* differences in antimicrobial efficacy for AOM based on pharmacologic models, RCTs show no differences in clinical outcomes. Practitioners should not ignore bacteriology but, instead, realize that clinical outcomes depend on more than direct "bug-drug" relationships. Similarly, despite correlations between allergy and OM, no RCTs exist to support a beneficial effect of allergy therapy. Day care attendance and passive smoke have modest epidemiologic links to recurrent AOM, yet many children cared for at home by nonsmokers are otitis prone. Risk factor modification and allergy control "make sense," but the impact on AOM outcomes is unknown.

The physician's contribution to managing AOM is threefold: (1) evaluating research evidence, (2) exploring the patient's philosophy of health, and (3) delivering an opinion based on a synthesis of the two.[182] If patients' priorities are different from those of the clinician, however, the quality of medical evidence matters little—the clinician's advice based on it will be ignored. For example, antibiotic prophylaxis may be the ideal solution to a child's recurrent AOM but will not be accepted by a parent whose priority is to limit drug consumption. Tympanostomy tube insertion, no matter how well suited to a child's problem, will not be embraced by families with fears about anesthesia or misconceptions about tube risks. Therefore, clinicians are urged to consider not just the quality of the message or the pathway behind it, but its personal significance to them and their patients.

ACKNOWLEDGMENT

The author is indebted to Mark P. Haggard, PhD, for his critical review of the first edition of this chapter and for his helpful comments. Dr. Rosenfeld thanks the New York State Department of Health and the New York Region Otitis Project for their continuing efforts in developing and distributing evidence-based materials for judicious use of antibiotics in managing AOM.

Table 18-11 Pointers and Pitfalls

1. Clinical pathways define the time course of disease in a typical patient, with corresponding actions and expected outcomes.

2. Diagnosis of AOM must be distinguished from OME, because OME usually does not require antibiotics or active treatment unless chronic.

3. Children aged 2 years or older with nonsevere AOM may be safely observed for 48 to 72 hours, provided that antibiotics are started if symptoms persist or worsen beyond that time.

4. Adequate analgesia for 24 hours after AOM diagnosis is strongly advised because about 40% of children remain symptomatic; antibiotic benefits are not apparent until after 24 hours.

5. All approved antibiotics have comparable clinical efficacy for initial empiric therapy of AOM; however, initial failures are best re-treated with second-line (extended spectrum) agents.

6. Tympanocentesis is indicated for antibiotic treatment failure; myringotomy, with or without tympanostomy tube insertion, is indicated if suppurative complications are present or suspected.

7. Asymptomatic persistent MEE is expected after an episode of AOM and does not require therapy, unless it fails to subside spontaneously within 3 months.

8. About 15 to 20% of preschoolers develop recurrent AOM, but the natural history is favorable; initial control efforts should emphasize parent education and primary prevention.

9. Children with refractory recurrent AOM benefit from antibiotic prophylaxis (sulfisoxazole is preferred) or tympanostomy tubes; adenoidectomy is of benefit only after prior tubes.

10. Judicious antibiotic use is essential for limiting the spread of multidrug-resistant bacteria; practitioners must strive to improve diagnostic certainty when treating AOM.

AOM = acute otitis media; MEE = middle ear effusion; OME = otitis media with effusion.

REFERENCES

1. Coffey RJ, Othman E, Walters JI. Extending the application of critical path methods. Qual Manag Health Care 1995;3:14–29.

2. Pearson SD, Goulart-Fisher D, Lee TH. Critical pathways as a strategy for improving care: problems and potential. Ann Intern Med 1995;123:941–8.

3. Frommer AG. Benchmarking, monitoring and moving through the continuum of the clinical pathway system. Best Pract Benchmarking Healthcare 1996;1:154–60.

4. Pelton SI. Otoscopy for the diagnosis of otitis media. Pediatr Infect Dis J 1998;17:540–3.

5. Brookhouser PE. Use of tympanometry in office practice for diagnosis of otitis media. Pediatr Infect Dis J 1998;17:544–51.

6. Kimball S. Acoustic reflectometry: spectral gradient analysis for improved detection of middle ear effusion in children. Pediatr Infect Dis J 1998;17:552–5.

7. Takata G, Chan LS, Shekelle P, et al. Diagnosis, natural history, and late effects of otitis media with effusion. Evidence Report/Technology Assessment (Prepared by the Southern California Evidence-based Practice Center under Contract No. 290-97-0001). AHRQ Publication. Rockville (MD): Agency for Healthcare Research and Quality; 2002.

8. Rosenfeld RM, Vertrees JE, Carr J, et al. Clinical efficacy of antimicrobial drugs for acute otitis media: meta-analysis of 5400 children from thirty-three randomized trials. J Pediatr 1994;124:355–67.

9. Dowell SF, Marcy MS, Phillips WR, et al. Otitis media—principles of judicious use of antimicrobial agents. Pediatrics 1998;101 Suppl:165–71.

10. Marcy M, Takata G, Shekelle P, et al. Management of acute otitis media. Evidence Report/Technology Assessment No. 15 (Prepared by the Southern California Evidence-based Practice Center under Contract No. 290-97-0001). AHRQ Publication No. 01-E010. Rockville (MD): Agency for Healthcare Research and Quality; May 2001.

11. Rosenfeld RM, Casselbrant ML, Hannley MT. Implications of the AHRQ evidence report on acute otitis media. Otolaryngol Head Neck Surg 2001;125:440–8.

12. Browning GG. Childhood otalgia: acute otitis media. BMJ 1990;300:1005–7.

13. Macknin ML, Piedmonte M, Jacobs J, Skibinski C. Symptoms associated with infant teething: a prospective study. Pediatrics 2000;105:747–52.

14. Halsted C, Lepow ML, Balassanian N, et al. Otitis media: clinical observations, microbiology, and evaluation of therapy. Am J Dis Child 1968;115:542–51.

15. Laxdal OE, Merida J, Trefor Jones RH. Treatment of acute otitis media: a controlled study of 142 children. Can Med Assoc J 1970;102:263–8.

16. Mygind N, Meistrup-Larsen KI, Thomsen J, et al. Penicillin in acute otitis media: a double-blind, placebo-controlled trial. Clin Otolaryngol 1981;6:5–13.

17. van Buchem FL, Dunk JHM, van't Hof MA. Therapy of acute otitis media: myringotomy, antibiotics, or neither: a double-blind study in children. Lancet 1981;2:883–7.

18. Thalin A, Densert O, Larsson A, et al. Is penicillin necessary in the treatment of acute otitis media? In: Proceedings of the International Conference on Acute and Secretory Otitis Media, Part 1; 1985 17–22 November; Jerusalem, Israel. Amsterdam: Kugler Publications; 1985. p. 441–6.

19. Appelman CLM, Claessen JQPJ, Touw-Otten FWMM, et al. Coamoxiclav in recurrent acute otitis media: placebo-controlled study. BMJ 1991;303:1450–2.

20. Burke P, Bain J, Robinson D, Dunleavey J. Acute red ear in children: controlled trial of nonantibiotic treatment in general practice. BMJ 1991;303:558–62.

21. Kaleida PH, Casselbrant ML, Rockette HE, et al. Amoxicillin or myringotomy or both for acute otitis media: results of a randomized clinical trial. Pediatrics 1991;87:466–74.

22. Damoiseaux RAMJ, van Balen FAM, Hoes AW, et al. Primary care based randomised double blind trial of amoxicillin versus placebo for acute otitis media in children aged under 2 years. BMJ 2000;320:350–4.

23. Rosenfeld RM, Vertrees JE, Carr J, et al. Clinical efficacy of antimicrobial drugs for acute otitis media: meta-analysis of 5400 children from thirty-three randomized trials. J Pediatr 1994;124:355–67.

24. Del Mar C, Glasziou P, Hayem M. Are antibiotics indicated as initial treatment for children with acute otitis media? A meta-analysis. BMJ 1997;314:1526–9.

25. Glasziou PP, Del Mar CB, Sanders SL, Hayem M. Antibiotics for acute otitis media in children (Cochrane Review). In: The Cochrane Library, Issue 2, 2002. Oxford (UK): Update Software; 2002.

26. Gonzales R, Malone DC, Maselli JH, Sande MA. Excessive antibiotic use for respiratory infections in the United States. Clin Infect Dis 2001;33:757–62.

27. Ghaffar F, Muniz LS, Katz K, et al. Effects of large dosages of amoxicillin/clavulanate or azithromycin on nasopharyngeal carriage of Streptococcus pneumoniae, Haemophilus influenzae, nonpneumococcal alpha-hemolytic streptococci, and Staphylococcus aureus in children with acute otitis media. Clin Infect Dis 2002; 34:1301–9.

28. Heikkinen T, Saeed KA, McCormick DP, et al. A single intramuscular dose of ceftriaxone changes nasopharyngeal bacterial flora in children with acute otitis media. Acta Paediatr 2000;89:1316–21.

29. O'Neill P. Acute otitis media. Clin Evid 2002;7:236–43.

30. Little P, Williamson I, Warner G, et al. Reattendance and complications in a randomized trial of prescribing strategies for sore throat: the medicalising effect of prescribing antibiotics. BMJ 1997;315:350–2.

31. Marcy SM. Treatment of otitis media. Pediatr Infect Dis J 2000;19:1032–3.

32. Cates C. An evidence based approach to reducing antibiotic use in children with acute otitis media: controlled before and after study. BMJ 1999;318:715–6.

33. Little P, Gould C, Williamson I, et al. Pragmatic randomised controlled trials of two prescribing strategies for childhood acute otitis media. BMJ 2001;322:336–42.

34. New York Regional Otitis Project. Observation option toolkit for acute otitis media. State of New York: Department of Health, Publication #4894; March 2002. (Can be ordered by writing to: Publications, New York State Dept. of Health, Box 2000, Albany, NY 12220, USA.)

35. Pichichero ME, Poole MD. Assessing diagnostic accuracy and tympanocentesis skills in the management of otitis media. Arch Pediatr Adolesc Med 2001;155:1137–42.

36. Burton DM, Seid AB, Kearns DB, Pransky SM. Neonatal otitis media: an update. Arch Otolaryngol Head Neck Surg 1993;119:672–5.

37. Derkay CS, Bluestone CD, Thompson AE, Kardatske D. Otitis media in the pediatric intensive care unit: a prospective study. Otolaryngol Head Neck Surg 1989;100:292–9.

38. Culpepper L, Froom J. Routine antimicrobial treatment of acute otitis media. Is it necessary? JAMA 1997;278:1643–5.

39. Rosenfeld RM. Observation option toolkit for acute otitis media. Int J Pediatr Otorhinolaryngol 2001;58:1–8.

40. Froom J, Culpepper L, Grob P, et al. Diagnosis and antibiotic treatment of acute otitis media: a report from international primary care network. BMJ 1990;300:582–6.

41. Rosenfeld RM. Diagnostic certainty for acute otitis media. Int J Pediatr Otorhinolaryngol 2002;64:89–95.

42. Steinbach WJ, Sectish TC, Benjamin DK, et al. Pediatric residents' clinical diagnostic accuracy of otitis media. Pediatrics 2002;109:993–8.

43. Steinbach WJ, Sectish TC. Pediatric resident training in the diagnosis and treatment of acute otitis media. Pediatrics 2002;109:404–8.

44. Harsten G, Prellner K, Heldrup J, et al. Treatment failure in acute otitis media: a clinical study of children during their first three years of life. Acta Otolaryngol 1989;108:253–8.

45. Carlin SA, Marchant CD, Shurin PA, et al. Host factors and early therapeutic response in acute otitis media. J Pediatr 1991;118:178–83.

46. Schutzman SA, Petrycki S, Fleisher GR. Bacteremia with otitis media. Pediatric 1991;87:48–53.

47. Paradise JL. Short-course antimicrobial treatment for acute otitis media: not best for infants and young children. JAMA 1997;278:1640–2.

48. Hoberman A, Paradise JL, Burch DJ, et al. Equivalent efficacy and reduced occurrence of diarrhea from a new formulation of amoxicillin/clavulanate potassium (Augmentin) for treatment of acute otitis media in children. Pediatr Infect Dis J 1997;16:463–70.

49. Cohen R, Levy C, Boucherat M, et al. A multicenter, randomized, double-blind trial of 5 versus 10 days of antibiotic therapy for acute otitis media in young children. J Pediatr 1998;133:634–9.

50. Kozyrskyj AL, Hildes-Ripstein GE, Longstaffe SEA et al. Short course antibiotics for acute otitis media (Cochrane Review). In: The Cochrane Library, Issue 2, 2002. Oxford (UK): Update Software; 2002.

51. Cohen RC, Levy C, Boucherat M, et al. Five vs. ten days

of antibiotic therapy for acute otitis media in young children. Pediatr Infect Dis J 2000;19:458–63.

52. Guillemot D, Carbon C, Balkau B, et al. Low dosage and long treatment duration of beta-lactams: risk factors for carriage of penicillin-resistant *Streptococcus pneumoniae*. JAMA 1998;279:365–70.

53. Bertin L, Pons G, d'Athis P, et al. A randomized, double-blind, multicentre controlled trial of ibuprofen versus acetaminophen and placebo for symptoms of acute otitis media in children. Fundam Clin Pharmacol 1996; 10:387–92.

54. Hoberman A, Paradise JL, Reynolds EA, Urkin J. Efficacy of Auralgan for treating ear pain in children with acute otitis media. Arch Pediatr Adolesc Med 1997;151:675–8.

55. Sarrell EM, Mandelberg A, Cohen HA. Efficacy of naturopathic extracts in the management of ear pain associated with acute otitis media. Arch Pediatr Adolesc Med 2001;155:796–9.

56. Flynn CA, Griffin G, Tudiver F. Decongestants and antihistamines for acute otitis media in children (Cochrane Review). In: The Cochrane Library, Issue 2, 2002. Oxford (UK): Update Software; 2002.

57. Rudberg RD. Acute otitis media: comparative therapeutic results of sulphonamide and penicillin administered in various forms. Acta Otolaryngol 1954;Suppl 113:1–79.

58. Palva T, Pulkkinen K. Mastoiditis. J Laryngol Otol 1959;73:573–88.

59. Hoppe JE, Köster S, Bootz F, Niethammer D. Acute mastoiditis—relevant once again. Infection 1994;22:178–82.

60. Bahadori RS, Schwartz RH, Ziai M. Acute mastoiditis in children: an increase in frequency Northern Virginia. Pediatr Infect Dis J 2000;19:212–5.

61. Faye-Lund H. Acute and latent mastoiditis. J Laryngol Otol 1989;103:1158–60.

62. Scott TA, Jackler RK. Acute mastoiditis in infancy: a sequelae of unrecognized acute otitis media. Otolaryngol Head Neck Surg 1989;101:683–7.

63. Nadal D, Herrman P, Bauman A, Fanconi A. Acute mastoiditis: clinical, microbiological, and therapeutic aspects. Eur J Pediatr 1990;149:560–46.

64. Harley EH, Sdralis T, Berkowitz RG. Acute mastoiditis in children: a 12-year retrospective study. Otolaryngol Head Neck Surg 1997;116:26–30.

65. Kaplan SL, Mason EO Jr, Wald ER, et al. Pneumococcal mastoiditis in children. Pediatrics 2000;106:695–99.

66. Kvestad E, Kværner KJ, Mair IWS. Acute mastoiditis: predictors for surgery. Int J Pediatr Otorhinolaryngol 2000;52:149–55.

67. Linder TE, Briner HR, Bischoff T. Prevention of acute mastoiditis: fact or fiction? Int J Pediatr Otorhinolaryngol 2000;56:129–34.

68. Ghaffar FA, Wördemann M, McCracken H Jr. Acute mastoiditis in children: a seventeen-year experience in Dallas, Texas. Pediatr Infect Dis J 2001;20:376–80.

69. Petersen CG, Ovesen T, Pedersen CB. Acute mastoidectomy in a Danish county from 1977 to 1996 with focus on the bacteriology. Int J Pediatr Otorhinolaryngol 1998;45:21–9.

70. Gliklich RE, Eavey RD, Iannuzzi RA, et al. A contempo-

rary analysis of acute mastoiditis. Arch Otolaryngol Head Neck Surg 1996;122:135–9.

71. Dhooge IJM, Albers FWJ, Van Cauwenberge PB. Intratemporal and intracranial complications of acute suppurative otitis media in children: renewed interest. Int J Pediatr Otorhinolaryngol 1999;49:S109–14.

72. Luntz M, Brodsky A, Nusem S, et al. Acute mastoiditis—the antibiotic era: a multicenter study. Int J Pediatr Otorhinolaryngol 2001;57:1–9.

73. Van Zuijlen DA, Schilder AGM, Van Balen FAM, Hoes AW. National differences in acute mastoiditis: relationship to prescribing patterns of antibiotics for acute otitis media. Pediatr Infect Dis J 2001;20:140–4.

74. Dagan R, Leibovitz E, Cheletz G, et al. Antibiotic treatment in acute otitis media promotes superinfection with resistant *Streptococcus pneumoniae* carried before initiation of treatment. J Infect Dis 2001;183:880–6.

75. McCracken GH Jr. Prescribing antimicrobial agents for treatment of acute otitis media. Pediatr Infect Dis J 1999;18:1141–6.

76. Dagan R, Johnson CE, Mclinn S, et al. Bacteriologic and clinical efficacy of amoxicillin/clavulanate vs. azithromycin in acute otitis media. Pediatr Infect Dis J 2000;19:95–104.

77. Lieberman A, Leibovitz E, Piglansky L, et al. Bacteriologic and clinical efficacy of trimethoprim-sulfamethoxazole for treatment of acute otitis media. Pediatr Infect Dis J 2001;20:260–4.

78. Gehanno P, Panajotopoulos, Barry B, et al. Microbiology of otitis media in the Paris, France, area from 1987 to 1997. Pediatr Infect Dis J 2001;20:570–3.

79. Bluestone CD, Stephenson JS, Martin LM. Ten-year review of otitis media pathogens. Pediatr Infect Dis J 1992;11 Suppl;7–11.

80. Dagan R. Clinical significance of resistant organisms in otitis media. Pediatr Infect Dis J 2000;19:378–82.

81. Wald ER, Mason EO Jr, Bradley JS, et al. Acute otitis media caused by *Streptococcus pneumoniae* in children's hospitals between 1994 and 1997. Pediatr Infect Dis J 2001;20:34–9.

82. Palmu AA, Kotikoski MJ, Kaijalainen TH, Puhakka H. Bacterial etiology of acute myringitis in children less than two years of age. Pediatr Infect Dis J 2001;20:607–11.

83. Nozicka CA, Hanly JG, Beste DJ, et al. Otitis media in infants aged 0–8 weeks: frequency of associated serious bacterial disease. Pediatr Emerg Care 1999;15:252–4.

84. Dowell SF, Butler JC, Giebink GS, et al. Acute otitis media: management and surveillance in an era of pneumococcal resistance—a report from the Drug-Resistant *Streptococcus pneumoniae* Therapeutic Working Group. Pediatr Infect Dis J 1999;18:1–9.

85. Canafax DM, Yuan Z, Chonmaitree T, et al. Amoxicillin middle ear fluid penetration and pharmacokinetics in children with acute otitis media. Pediatr Infect Dis J 1998;17:149–56.

86. Lieberman A, Leibovitz E, Piglansky L, et al. Bacteriologic and clinical efficacy of trimethoprim-sulfamethoxazole for treatment of acute otitis media. Pediatr Infect Dis J 2001;20:260–4.

87. Bauchner H, Klein JO. Parental issues in selection of antimicrobial agents for infants and children. Clin Pediatr 1997;36:201–5.

88. Bodor FF. Systemic antibiotics for the treatment of the conjunctivitis-otitis media syndrome. Pediatr Infect Dis J 1989;8:287–90.

89. Harrison CJ, Marks MI, Welch DF. Microbiology of recently treated acute otitis media compared with previously untreated acute otitis media. Pediatr Infect Dis J 1985;4:641–6.

90. Faden H, Bernstein J, Brodsky L, et al. Effect of prior antibiotic on middle ear disease in children. Ann Otol Rhinol Laryngol 1992;101:87–91.

91. Pichichero ME, Marsocci SM, Murphy ML, et al. A prospective observational study of 5-, 7-, and 10-day antibiotic treatment for acute otitis media. Otolaryngol Head Neck Surg 2001;124:381–7.

92. Berman S, Byrns PJ, Bondy J, et al. Otitis media-related antibiotic prescribing patterns, outcomes, and expenditures in a pediatric medicaid population. Pediatrics 1997;100:585–92.

93. Takata GS, Chan LS, Shekelle P, et al. Evidence assessment of management of acute otitis media: I. The role of antibiotics in treatment of uncomplicated acute otitis media. Pediatrics 2001;108:239–47.

94. Ioannidis JPA, Contopoulos-Ioannidis DG, Chew P, Lau J. Meta-analysis of randomized controlled trials on the comparative efficacy and safety of azithromycin against other antibiotics for upper respiratory tract infections. J Antimicrob Chemother 2001;48:677–89.

95. Hoberman A, Paradise JL, Block S, et al. Efficacy of amoxicillin/clavulanate for acute otitis media: relation to *Streptococcus pneumoniae* susceptibility. Pediatr Infect Dis J 1996;15:955–62.

96. Dagan R, Johnson CE, McLinn S, et al. Bacteriologic and clinical efficacy of amoxicillin/clavulanate vs. azithromycin in acute otitis media. Pediatr Infect Dis J 2000;19:95–104.

97. Hathaway TJ, Katz HP, Dershewitz RA, Marx TJ. Acute otitis media: who needs posttreatment follow-up? Pediatrics 1994;94:143–7.

98. Mandel EM, Casselbrant ML, Rockette HE, et al. Efficacy of 20- versus 10-day antimicrobial treatment for acute otitis media. Pediatrics 1995;96:5–13.

99. Berman S, Roark R. Factors influencing outcome in children treated with antibiotics for acute otitis media. Pediatr Infect Dis J 1993;12:20–4.

100. Pichichero ME, McLinn S, Aronovitz G, et al. Cefprozil treatment of persistent and recurrent acute otitis media. Pediatr Infect Dis J 1997;16:471–8.

101. Pitkäranta A, Virolainen A, Jero J, et al. Detection of rhinovirus, respiratory syncytial virus, and corona virus infections in acute otitis media by reverse transcriptase polymerase chain reaction. Pediatrics 1998;102:291–5.

102. Chonmaitree T, Owen MJ, Patel JA, et al. Effect of viral respiratory tract infection on outcome of acute otitis media. J Pediatr 1992;120:856–62.

103. Chonmaitree T, Heikkinen T. Viruses and acute otitis media. Pediatr Infect Dis J 2000;19:1005–7.

104. Pichichero ME, Pichichero CL. Persistent acute otitis media II. Antimicrobial treatment. Pediatr Infect Dis J 1995;14:183–8.

105. Hoberman A, Paradise JL, Wald ER. Tympanocentesis technique revisited. Pediatr Infect Dis J 1997;16:S25–6.

106. Leibovitz E, Raiz S, Piglansky L, et al. Resistance pattern of middle ear fluid isolates in acute otitis media recently treated with antibiotics. Pediatr Infect Dis J 1998;17:463–9.

107. Teele DW, Pelton SI, Klein JO. Bacteriology of acute otitis media unresponsive to initial antimicrobial therapy. J Pediatr 1981;98:537–9.

108. Pichichero ME, Pichichero CL. Persistent acute otitis media I. Causative pathogens. Pediatr Infect Dis J 1995;14:178–83.

109. Block SL, Hedrick JA, Tyler RD, et al. Microbiology of acute otitis media recently treated with aminopenicillins. Pediatr Infect Dis J 2001;20:1017–21.

110. Loundon N, Roger G, VuThien H, et al. Evolution of bacteriologic features of persistent acute otitis media compared with acute otitis media. Arch Otolaryngol Head Neck Surg 1999;125:1134–40.

111. Gehanno P, Lenoir G, Barry B, et al. Evaluation of nasopharyngeal cultures for bacteriologic assessment of acute otitis media in children. Pediatr Infect Dis J 1996;15:329–32.

112. Eldan M, Leibovitz E, Piglansky L, et al. Predictive value of pneumococcal nasopharyngeal cultures for the assessment of nonresponsive acute otitis media. Pediatr Infect Dis J 2000;19:298–303.

113. Dagan R, Hoberman A, Johnson C, et al. Bacteriologic and clinical efficacy of high dose amoxicillin/clavulanate in children with acute otitis media. Pediatr Infect Dis J 2001;20:829–37.

114. Leibovitz E, Piglansky L, Raiz S, et al. Bacteriologic and clinical efficacy of one day vs. three day intramuscular ceftriaxone for treatment of nonresponsive acute otitis media in children. Pediatr Infect Dis J 2000;19:1040–5.

115. Claessen JQPJ, Appelman CLM, Touw-Otten FWMM, et al. Persistence of middle ear dysfunction after recurrent acute otitis media. Clin Otolaryngol 1994;19:35–40.

116. Alho O, Oja H, Koivu M, Sorri M. Chronic otitis media with effusion in infancy: How frequent is it? How does it develop? Arch Otolaryngol Head Neck Surg 1995;121:432–6.

117. Froom J, Culpepper L, Bridges-Webb C, et al. Effect of patient characteristics and disease manifestations on the outcome of acute otitis media at 2 months. Arch Fam Med 1993;2:841–6.

118. Daly K, Giebink GS, Le CT, et al. Determining risk for chronic otitis media with effusion. Pediatr Infect Dis J 1988;7:471–5.

119. Stool SE, Berg AO, Berman S, et al. Otitis media with effusion in young children. Clinical practice guideline, Number 12. AHCPR Publication No. 94-0622. Rockville (MD): Agency for Health Care Policy and Research, Public Health Service, US Department of Health and Human Services; July 1994.

120. Rosenfeld RM, Goldsmith AJ, Madell JR. How accurate is

parent rating of hearing for children with otitis media? Arch Otolaryngol Head Neck Surg 1998;124:989–92.

121. Howie VM, Ploussard JH, Sloyer J. The "otitis-prone" condition. Am J Dis Child 1975;129:676–8.

122. Joki-Erkkilä V, Pukander J, Laippala P. Alteration of clinical picture and treatment of pediatric acute otitis media over the past two decades. Int J Pediatr Otorhinolaryngol 2000;55:197–201.

123. Alho OP, Koivu M, Sorri M. What is an "otitis-prone" child? Int J Pediatr Otorhinolaryngol 1991;21:201–9.

124. Alho OP, Koivu M, Sorri M, Rantakallio P. Risk factors for recurrent acute otitis media and respiratory infection in infancy. Int J Pediatr Otorhinolaryngol 1990;19:151–61.

125. Prellner K, Kalm O, Harsten G. The concept of pronicity in otitis media. Otolaryngol Clin North Am 1991;24:787–94.

126. Teele DW, Klein JO, Rosner, and the Greater Boston Otitis Media Study Group. Epidemiology of otitis media during the first seven years of life in children in greater Boston: a prospective, cohort study. J Infect Dis 1989;160:83–94.

127. Forgays DK, Hasazi JE, Wasserman RC. Recurrent otitis media and parenting stress in mothers of two-year-old children. Dev Behav Pediatr 1992;13:321–5.

128. Daly K, Selvius R, Lindgren B. Knowledge and attitudes about otitis media risk: implications for prevention. Pediatrics 1997;100:931–6.

129. Casselbrant ML, Kaleida PH, Rockette HE et al. Efficacy of antimicrobial prophylaxis and of tympanostomy tube insertion for prevention of recurrent acute otitis media: results of a randomized clinical trial. Pediatr Infect Dis J 1992;11:278–86.

130. Gaskins JD, Holt RJ, Kyong CU, et al. Chemoprophylaxis of recurrent otitis media using trimethoprim/sulfamethoxazole. Drug Intel Clin Pharm 1982;16:387–9.

131. Gonzalez C, Arnold JE, Woody, EA, et al. Prevention of recurrent acute otitis media: chemoprophylaxis versus tympanostomy tubes. Laryngoscope 1986;96:1330–4.

132. Liston TE, Foshee WS, Pierson WD. Sulfisoxazole chemoprophylaxis for frequent otitis media. Pediatrics 1983;71:524–30.

133. Mandel EM, Casselbrant ML, Rockette HE, et al. Efficacy of antimicrobial prophylaxis for recurrent middle ear effusion. Pediatr Infect Dis J 1996;15:1074–82.

134. Maynard JE, Fleshman JK, Tschopp CF. Otitis media in Alaskan Eskimo children: prospective evaluation of chemoprophylaxis. JAMA 1972;219:597–9.

135. Perrin JM, Charney E, MacWhinney JB Jr, et al. Sulfisoxazole as chemoprophylaxis for recurrent otitis media: a double-blind crossover study in pediatric practice. N Engl J Med 1974;291:664–7.

136. Prellner K, Foglé-Hansson M, Jørgensen F, et al. Prevention of recurrent acute otitis media in otitis-prone children by intermittent prophylaxis with penicillin. Acta Otolaryngol (Stockh) 1994;114:182–7.

137. Principi N, Marchisio P, Massironi E, et al. Prophylaxis of recurrent acute otitis media and middle-ear effusion: comparison of amoxicillin with sulfamethoxazole and trimethoprim. Am J Dis Child 1989;143:1414–8.

138. Roark R, Berman S. Continuous twice daily or once daily amoxicillin prophylaxis compared with placebo for children with recurrent acute otitis media. Pediatr Infect Dis J 1997;16:376–81.

139. Schuller DE. Prophylaxis of otitis media in asthmatic children. Pediatr Infect Dis J 1983;2:280–3.

140. Sih T, Moura R, Caldas S, Schwartz B. Prophylaxis for recurrent acute otitis media: a Brazilian study. Int J Pediatr Otorhinolaryngol 1993;25:19–24.

141. Varsano I, Volvitz B, Mimouni F. Sulfisoxazole prophylaxis of middle ear effusion and recurrent acute otitis media. Am J Dis Child 1985;139:632–5.

142. Teele D, Klein JO, Rosner B. Otitis media with effusion during the first three years of life and development of speech and language. Pediatrics 1984;74:282–7.

143. Goldman AS, Goldblum RM. Primary deficiencies in humoral immunity. Pediatr Clin North Am 1977;24:277–91.

144. Heikkinen T, Ruuskanen O, Waris M, et al. Influenza vaccination in prevention of acute otitis media in children. Am J Dis Child 1991;145:445–8.

145. Clements DA, Langdon L, Bland C, Walter E. Influenza A vaccine decreases the incidence of otitis media in 6- to 30-month old children in day care. Arch Pediatr Adolesc Med 1995;149:1113–7.

146. Straetemans M, Sanders EAM, Veenhoven RH, et al. Pneumococcal vaccines for preventing otitis media (Cochrane Review). In: The Cochrane Library, Issue 2. Oxford (UK): Update Software; 2002.

147. Black S, Shinefield H, Fireman B, et al. Efficacy, safety, and immunogenicity of heptavalent pneumococcal conjugate vaccine in children. Northern California Kaiser Permanente Vaccine Study Center Group. Pediatr Infect Dis J 2000;19:187–95.

148. American Academy of Pediatrics Committee on Infectious Diseases. Policy statement: recommendations for the prevention of pneumococcal infections, including the use of pneumococcal conjugate vaccine (Prevnar), pneumococcal polysaccharide vaccine, and antibiotic prophylaxis. Pediatrics 2000;106:362–6.

149. Gosain AK, Conley SF, Marks S, Larson DL. Submucous cleft palate: diagnostic methods and outcomes of surgical treatment. Plast Reconstr Surg 1996;97:1497–509.

150. Aniansson G, Alm B, Andersson B, et al. A prospective cohort study of breast-feeding and otitis media in Swedish infants. Pediatr Infect Dis J 1994;13:183–8.

151. Tully SB, Bar-Haim Y, Bradley RL. Abnormal tympanography after supine bottle feeding. J Pediatr 1995;126:S105–11.

152. Marx J, Osguthorpe D, Parsons G. Day care and the incidence of otitis media in young children. Otolaryngol Head Neck Surg 1995;112:695–9.

153. Kværner KJ, Nafstad P, Hagen JA, et al. Early acute otitis media and siblings' attendance at nursery. Arch Dis Child 1996;75:338–41.

154. Marjo N, Uhari M, Möttönen M. A pacifier increases the risk of recurrent acute otitis media in children in day care centers. Pediatrics 1995;96:884–8.

155. Niemelä M, Pihakari O, Pokka T, et al. Pacifier risk as a factor for acute otitis media: a randomized, controlled trial of parental counseling. Pediatrics 2000;106:483–8.

156. Etzel RA, Balk SJ, Bearer CF, et al. American Academy of Pediatrics Committee on Environmental Health: environmental tobacco smoke: a hazard to children. Pediatrics 1997;99:639–42.

157. DiFranza JR, Lew RA. Morbidity and mortality in children associated with the use of tobacco products by other people. Pediatrics 1996;97:560–8.

158. Physicians' desk reference. 52nd ed. Montvale (NJ): Medical Economics Company; 1998. p. 1081.

159. Brook I, Gober AE. Prophylaxis with amoxicillin and sulfisoxazole for otitis media: effect on recovery of penicillin-resistant bacteria from children. Clin Infect Dis 1996;22:143–5.

160. Uhari M, Nuutinen M, Turtinen J. Adverse reactions in children during long term antimicrobial therapy. Pediatr Infect Dis J 1996;15:404–8.

161. Cunningham MJ. Chemoprophylaxis with oral trimethoprim-sulfamethoxazole in otitis media: relevance of hematologic abnormalities. Clin Pediatr 1990; 29:273–7.

162. Goldstein NA, Sculerati N. Compliance with prophylactic antibiotics for otitis media in a New York City clinic. Int J Pediatr Otorhinolaryngol 1994;28:129–40.

163. Heikkinen T, Ruuskanen O, Ziegler T, et al. Short term use of amoxicillin-clavulanate during upper respiratory tract infection for prevention of acute otitis media. J Pediatr 1995;126:313–6.

164. Berman S, Nuss R, Roark R, et al. Effectiveness of continuous vs. intermittent amoxicillin to prevent episodes of otitis media. Pediatr Infect Dis J 1992;11:63–7.

165. Foglé-Hansson M, White P, Hermansson A, Prellner K. Short-term penicillin-V prophylaxis did not prevent acute otitis media in infants. Int J Pediatr Otorhinolaryngol 2001;59:119–23.

166. Gebhart DE. Tympanostomy tubes in the otitis media prone child. Laryngoscope 1981;91:849–66.

167. Gonzalez C, Arnold JE, Woody EA et al. Prevention of recurrent acute otitis media: chemoprophylaxis versus tympanostomy tubes. Laryngoscope 1986;96: 1330–4.

168. Mandel EM, Rockette HE, Bluestone CD, et al. Myringotomy with and without tympanostomy tubes for chronic otitis media with effusion. Arch Otolaryngol Head Neck Surg 1989;115:1217–24.

169. Mandel EM, Rockette HE, Bluestone CD, et al. Efficacy of myringotomy with and without tympanostomy tubes for chronic otitis media with effusion. Pediatr Infect Dis J 1992;11:270–7.

170. Bergus GR, Lofgren MM. Tubes, antibiotic prophylaxis, or watchful waiting: a decision analysis for managing recurrent acute otitis media. J Fam Pract 1998;46: 304–10.

171. Paradise JL, Bluestone CD, Rogers KD, et al. Efficacy of adenoidectomy for recurrent otitis media in children previously treated with tympanostomy-tube placement: results of parallel randomized and nonrandomized trials. JAMA 1990;263:2066–73.

172. Talaat AM, Baghat YS, El-Ghazzawy E, Elwany S. Nasopharyngeal bacterial flora before and after adenoidectomy. J Laryngol Otol 1989;103:372–4.

173. Paradise JL, Bluestone CD, Colborn DK et al. Adenoidectomy and adenotonsillectomy for recurrent acute otitis media: parallel randomized clinical trials in children not previously treated with tympanostomy tubes. JAMA 1999;282:945–53.

174. de Lange de Klerke ESM, Blommers J, Kuik DJ, et al. Effect of homeopathic medicines on daily burden of symptoms in children with recurrent upper respiratory infections. BMJ 1994;309:1329–32.

175. Barnett ED, Levatin JL, Chapman EH, et al. Challenges of evaluating homeopathic treatment of acute otitis media. Pediatr Infect Dis J 2000;19:273–5.

176. Jacobs J, Springer DA, Crothers D. Homeopathic treatment of acute otitis media in children: a preliminary randomized placebo-controlled trial. Pediatr Infect Dis J 2001;20:177–83.

177. Frei H, Thurneysen A. Homeopathy in acute otitis media in children: treatment effect or spontaneous recovery? Br Homeopathic J 2001;90:180–2.

178. Morgan PP. Homeopathy—will its theory ever hold water? Can Med Assoc J 1992;146:1719–20.

179. Uhari M, Kontiokari T, Koskela M, Niemelä M. Xylitol chewing gum in prevention of acute otitis media: double blind randomised trial. BMJ 1996;313:1180–4.

180. Uhari M, Kontiokari T, Niemelä M. A novel use of xylitol sugar in preventing acute otitis media. Pediatrics 1998;102:879–84.

181. Tapiainen T, Luotonen L, Kontiokari T, et al. Xylitol administered only during respiratory infections failed to prevent acute otitis media. Pediatrics 2002;109:302.

182. Sweeney KG, MacAuley D, Gray DP. Personal significance: the third dimension. Lancet 1998;351:134–6.

CHAPTER 19

Clinical Pathway for Otitis Media with Effusion

Richard M. Rosenfeld, MD, MPH, and Charles D. Bluestone, MD

There are many paths to the top of the mountain, but the view is always the same.
Chinese proverb

OBJECTIVES

On completing this chapter, the reader will be able to
1. Know the time course and natural history of otitis media with effusion (OME).
2. Use primary prevention and parent education to achieve optimal outcomes.
3. Assess the impact of otitis media (OM) with effusion on health status and quality of life.
4. Understand and choose among management options for OME.
5. Recognize how child comorbidity impacts management decisions.

EDITORIAL COMMENT

Considerable uncertainty remains in managing OME. In Ontario, for example, an analysis of small-area variations in tympanostomy tube insertion revealed almost a 10-fold difference between areas with the lowest and highest operative rates.[1] The only procedure with more variability was routine circumcision. New research has also raised uncertainty about the impact of OME on child development. Studies of infants and young children suggest questionable relationships among OME and language outcomes,[2,3] but older children appear susceptible to deficits in language, behavior, and reading ability.[4,5] Meta-analysis of developmental sequelae has proved inconclusive.[6] Consequently, duration-based criteria[7] for surgical intervention have come under increased scrutiny.[8] This chapter summarizes the current state of knowledge (and uncertainty) in OME management and offers guidelines for evidence-based decisions.

CLINICAL PATHWAY FOR OME

This chapter updates the clinical practice guideline released in 1994 by the Agency for Health Research and Quality (AHRQ).[7] Guidelines must have a clear target audience if they are to improve quality,[9] and the AHRQ guideline focuses sharply on OME in an *otherwise healthy* child aged 1 to 3 years with no craniofacial or neurologic abnormalities and no sensory deficits. Unfortunately, this restriction eliminates a large number of children who, nonetheless, have frequent or chronic OME. In contrast, our pathway is applicable to children of all ages with or without comorbidity. We are also more liberal in filling evidence gaps with expert opinion because guideline protocol often mandates "no recommendation" when scientific evidence is lacking.[10]

Our clinical pathway seeks also to address criticisms of the AHRQ guideline,[11] including (1) over-reliance on audiometric hearing levels as an appropriateness indicator for tympanostomy tubes, (2) failure to adjust treatment thresholds by comorbidity (eg, otoscopic abnormalities, sensorineural hearing loss, speech or developmental delays), (3) failure to consider indications for tympanostomy tubes other than bilateral OME (eg, unilateral or recurrent OME), and (4) designation of adenoidectomy as "not recommended" despite efficacy in children with prior tubes. The 1994 guideline is outdated (and out of print) because of new data regarding the timing of tympanostomy tubes and the association of OME with developmental sequelae.[8] These data are summarized in the AHRQ evidence report on OME (see Chapter 5, "Professional Evidence Rports"), which was completed in 2002.[6]

The basic format of a clinical pathway is the *task-time matrix* (Gantt chart), which indicates for each time point the corresponding actions and expected outcomes.[12] Clinical pathways provide a concise, visual overview of where management efforts should be focused at any point in the course of disease.[13] The time course of OME (Table 19-1) may be considered in four phases: (1) initial diagnosis and family education, (2) OME persisting for 1 to 3 months, (3) OME persisting 3 to 6 months (chronic OME), and (4) OME persisting beyond 6 months. These phases are divided into clinically relevant intervals or thresholds in the first row of Table 19-2, beginning with OME diagnosis and ending with chronic OME. The first column of Table 19-2 lists the actions, interventions, and outcomes that deserve emphasis at each of the various time points.

Table 19-3 High-Risk Criteria for Speech or Learning-Language Sequelae from OME

Comorbid Conditions
Cleft palate, overt or submucous[*]
Autism-spectrum disorder or other pervasive developmental disorder
Attention deficit or hyperactivity disorder
Suspected or diagnosed speech or language delays
Syndrome or craniofacial disorder that includes cognitive or linguistic delay
Permanent sensorineural or conductive hearing loss independent of OME
Psychomotor retardation or sensory defects
Intellectual impairment, cognitive deficits, or school problems

OME = otitis media with effusion.
[*]Triad of bifid uvula, palatal muscle diastasis, and notch in posterior surface of hard palate.

"no problem" or "hardly a problem at all" regarding their child's ears.[14] Consequently, absence of symptoms does not equate with absence of OME.

In many situations, the duration of OME prior to diagnosis is unknown because associated symptoms may have been absent or minimal. Some of the situations in which OME may be initially detected include the following:

- Failed screening test at school, doctor's office, or audiology suite
- Routine ear examination during an office visit for another reason
- Delayed resolution of MEE following an episode of AOM
- Primary complaints of hearing loss, speech delay, or poor articulation
- Primary complaint of ear pain, fullness, or rubbing
- Evaluation of restless or irritable child with sleep disruption
- Evaluation of child with unexplained clumsiness, balance problems, or motor delays

Because of the high prevalence of OME in young children (see Chapter 10, "Epidemiology"), we recommend that clinicians consider infants and young children to routinely have bilateral MEE, until proven otherwise. The AHRQ systematically reviewed the sensitivity, specificity, and predictive values of nine diagnostic methods for MEE.[6] Consistent with the 1994 guideline,[7] pneumatic otoscopy had the best overall receiver-operating charac-

teristics. Meta-analysis revealed a pooled sensitivity of 94%, specificity of 80%, and predictive values (positive and negative) of 89% (see Chapter 5). Consequently, we recommend pneumatic otoscopy for primary diagnosis of OME. Nonpneumatic otoscopy may suffice if an obvious air bubble or effusion level is visualized, but less obvious signs of effusion (eg, reduced tympanic membrane mobility) will be missed.

Tympanometry should be an adjunctive measure in diagnosing OME whenever uncertainty exists. A variety of portable and handheld tympanometers can be used easily in the office setting, but professional tympanometry, if available, offers increased accuracy.[6] Professional tympanometry using a type B (no impedance peak) or C2 curve (peak pressure less than -200 mm H_2O) as abnormal has 94% sensitivity (95% confidence interval [CI], 91 to 96%) but only 62% specificity (95% CI, 41 to 82%).[6] Specificity rises to 95% (95% CI, 88 to 100%) using tympanogram admittance ≤ 0.1 mmho, but specificity is poor (33%). Acoustic reflectometry may also be used for confirmatory diagnosis, but studies are heterogeneous, and overall performance is poorer than pneumatic otoscopy or tympanometry (see Chapter 9, "Diagnosis").

Obstructing cerumen *must* be removed before concluding that MEE is absent. All high-risk children and selected low-risk children should be referred to an otolaryngologist when cerumen, ear canal stenosis, or other factors preclude definitive examination in a primary-care setting.

Entering the Clinical Pathway

Unlike the AOM pathway (see Chapter 15, "Clinical Effectiveness of Complementary and Alternative Therapies"), children enter the OME pathway (see Table 19-2) at different points based on prior OME duration. As noted above, when the cause of OME is unknown, clinicians must make an educated guess regarding effusion duration. For low-risk children, we suggest this estimate be conservative, but for high-risk children, we urge a more liberal estimate. A best-guess OME duration of 2 to 4 months would, therefore, become a 2-month estimated duration for a low-risk child but a 4-month estimated duration for a high-risk child. These children would enter the pathway in Table 19-2 in columns 3 and 4, respectively.

Once an entry column is determined, specifics of management are noted in Table 19-2. Unilateral and bilateral OME are managed similarly, except that the threshold for intervention with unilateral disease is higher. Intervention is appropriate for unilateral OME that occurs in high-risk children, persists for 6 months or longer, or is associated with structural defects of the tympanic membrane. Unilateral OME may also cause problems with equilibrium or auditory function (eg, understanding speech when background noise is present). Evaluation of OME-related morbidity is discussed later in the chapter, but we wish to emphasize early that the impact of OME should not be trivialized (which was done to some extent in the Agency for Health Care Policy and Research clinical practice guideline).

Clinicians should note that no active interventions are recommended at the time of OME onset in Table 19-2 (second column). Intervention is limited to OME persisting at least 4 to 6 weeks in selected children, because 20 to 60% initial effusions will have already resolved spontaneously by this time (Table 19-4). The likelihood of spontaneous resolution depends strongly on the type of OME (Table 19-5). OME of new or recent onset, whether de novo or after AOM, has the best prognosis, but OME that is chronic or of unknown prior duration does much poorer. Risk factors for OME persistence after 3 months of watchful waiting include time of year when first seen (July to December), hearing level ≥ 30 dB hearing loss (HL) in the better ear, and a route of referral that includes prior audiometry.[15] Persistence at 3 months is more than 80% when all three factors are present. Of note, parental report of OME duration is unrelated to persistence.

FAMILY EDUCATION AND PRIMARY CONTROL

For most low-risk children with OME, the clinician's role in management can be described in the elegant words of Voltaire: "The art in medicine consists in amusing the patient while nature cures the disease."[16] We suggest that the best form of initial "amusements" are to educate families about the favorable course of most untreated OME and to encourage risk-factor

Table 19-4 Summary of Spontaneous Resolution Rates for OME*

Clinical Situation	Time Point	N[‡]	Rate[§]	(95% CI)
Resolution of OME persisting after AOM in children randomized to placebo or no drug	4 weeks	4	.59	(.50, .68)
	6 weeks	3	.46	(.32, .60)
	12 weeks	2	.74	(.68, .80)
Cure (B to A tympanogram[†]) of newly diagnosed OME of unknown duration by ear	4–6 weeks	5	.21	(.11, .30)
	3 months	5	.20	(.07, .34)
	6 months	3	.28	(.17, .40)
Resolution (B to A/C1 tympanogram[†]) of newly diagnosed OME of unknown duration by ear	1 month	2	.22	(.16, .29)
	3 months	4	.28	(.14, .41)
	6 months	3	.42	(.35, .49)
	9 months	2	.56	(.30, .82)
Improvement (B to A/C1/C2 tympanogram[†]) of newly diagnosed OME of unknown duration by ear	4–6 weeks	4	.56	(.35, .78)
	3 months	6	.56	(.51, .61)
	6 months	4	.72	(.68, .76)
	9 months	5	.81	(.77, .85)
	12 months	3	.87	(.80, .94)
Improvement (B to A/C1/C2 tympanogram[†]) of newly diagnosed OME by child	1–2 months	3	.31	(.26, .36)
	3 months	5	.58	(.43, .72)
	6–8 months	3	.70	(.63, .76)
	12 months	2	.90	(.84, .96)
Clinical resolution of documented OME lasting 3 months or longer by ear	< 3 months	3	.19	(.13, .24)
	6 months	4	.25	(.17, .34)
	12 months	4	.31	(.19, .43)
	24 months	2	.33	(.27, .39)

CI = confidence interval; OME = otitis media with effusion.

*See Chapter 12 for derivation of rates listed in table.

[†]Tympanometric patterns defined as: type A, peak pressure > –100 mm H_2O (effusion in 3% of ears at myringotomy); type B, flat curve without an impedance minimum (effusion in 85 to 100%); type C1, pressure –100 to –199 mm H_2O (effusion in 17%); or type C2, pressure –200 to –400 mm H_2O (effusion in up to 55%).

[‡]Number of studies from which data were combined to derive the overall resolution rate.

[§]Estimate based on random-effects meta-analysis.

Table 19-5 Impact of OME Type and Outcome Definition on Natural History*

OME Type and Definition of Success	Cumulative Successes (%)			
	1 mo	3 mo	6 mo	12 mo
OME of new onset, improvement by ear	70	90	99	100
OME persisting after AOM, resolution by ear	60	75	90	100
OME of unknown duration, improvement by ear	55	55	70	90
OME of unknown duration, improvement by child	30	60	70	90
OME of unknown duration, resolution by ear	20	30	40	50
OME for 3 months or longer, bilateral resolution	—	20	25	30

AOM = acute otitis media; OME = otitis media with effusion.
*Derived from OME cohort studies listed in Chapter 12; rates approximated to nearest 5%.

modification and primary control efforts. Whereas these measures also apply to high-risk children, the threshold for active therapy (medical or surgical) is somewhat lower (see Table 19-2).

Family Education

Most parents of children with OME have three primary concerns: (1) what caused the problem, (2) what effect it will have on the child, and (3) what needs to be done about it. We find the information below to be a useful framework for answering such questions:

- OME may arise after AOM, during a viral upper respiratory infection or because of pressure changes in the middle ear space (which are common in young children); often, OME resolves within several months without active treatment (see Table 19-4).
- The longer OME persists, the less likely it is to resolve promptly. Optimism must be tempered by realism: the median time to effusion resolution was a staggering 6.1 years when children with documented OME for at least 3 months were observed without intervention.[17]
- OME may cause short-term problems related directly to fluid in the middle ear and long-term problems persisting after fluid resolution because of temporary, but prolonged, hearing loss. The mild hearing loss caused by OME is not readily apparent to most parents. Consequently, parental assurance of "normal" hearing does not rule out a hearing problem.
- Short-term problems caused by OME include ear fullness, ear pain (tugging, rubbing, or banging), clumsiness, hearing loss, irritability, fragmented sleep, and worsening of any comorbid conditions (see Table 19-3). Some children, however, have no discernible symptoms despite OME in both ears.

Therefore, absence of symptoms does not necessarily mean absence of OME.
- Long-term problems caused by prolonged OME include speech delay, articulation problems, learning difficulties, school difficulties, and collapse or perforation of the eardrum. The best means of avoiding these problems is through regular follow-up until the OME resolves, either spontaneously or through active intervention.
- What needs to be done about OME depends primarily on the duration of effusion and whether there are associated comorbid conditions (see Table 19-3). Low-risk children with OME are suitable for 3 months of initial watchful waiting. Conversely, a high-risk child with OME may require active intervention much sooner.

Parents may ask if a clinician "believes" in a particular therapy for OME, such as tubes, antibiotics, or alternative medicine. Whereas provider experience is an essential part of evidence-based medicine, beliefs and unsubstantiated opinions rarely contribute to optimal care. The published evidence concerning OM is voluminous (hence this book) but obviously incomplete. We can estimate with some certainty the quantitative impact of tubes (see Chapter 14, "Clinical Efficacy of Surgical Therapy") and antibiotics (see Chapter 13) on outcomes but can say little about the effect of complementary and alternative medicine when no randomized trials exist to support efficacy beyond natural history (see Chapter 12).

Recognizing that some families will pursue alternative medicine despite a lack of documented efficacy, we urge clinicians to emphasize the role of otologic follow-up for all children with newly detected OME. A follow-up visit within 12 weeks is advised (see Table 19-2) and should continue until complete resolution is documented. Most alternative medicine therapists do not have the training or equipment needed to accurately assess middle ear status, and neither the absence of physical symptoms nor the absence of hearing problems necessarily implies resolution of OME.

Preliminary evidence suggests that some families can monitor their child's OME with a consumer version of the acoustic reflectometer, but most parents studied had advanced educational degrees and relatively high incomes.[18] Parental home monitoring of OME is a useful adjunct to professional otologic follow-up, not a replacement for it.

Primary Control and Risk Factor Modification

The AHRQ guideline considered control of environmental risk factors to be an *option* in managing OME, based on limited scientific evidence and strong panel consensus. As noted in the guideline, "Reports were found of research into the association of infant feeding practices, passive smoking, and child-care facility placement with the occurrence of OME...None of the studies reported, however, was designed to test the direction or strength of the linkage between these environmental factors and the incidence or natural history of OM...These finding did not provide information regarding whether intervening to decrease environmental risk factors would make a clinically important difference in the care of otherwise healthy young children with OME."[7]

The designation of environmental control as an "optional" intervention by the AHRQ is best understood by a careful re-reading of the above quotation. At issue are the *strength* and *directionality* of the associations between risk factors and OME. Most studies report odds ratios or relative risks less than 2.0, which indicate small or modest relationships. Although important from a population perspective, such small associations are likely to be imperceptible when managing individual children. Further, nearly all studies are cross-sectional in design and consequently lack the time-span component necessary to suggest causality (see Chapter 2, "Critical Evaluation of Journal Articles"). Reporting a higher *prevalence* of OME among children exposed to environmental tobacco smoke (cross-sectional study) is very different from noting a decreased *incidence* of future OME after exposure is eliminated (prospective study).

Despite the lack of definitive evidence linking environmental control with better OME outcomes, we consider such measures prudent, *to the extent that* families can implement them without undo stress or strain on interpersonal relationships. These measures include (1) breast-feeding,[19,20] (2) reduced exposure to environmental tobacco smoke,[21,22] and (3) small-group alternatives (less than four other children) to large group day care.[23–25] Children in day care are not only more likely to require tympanostomy tubes than those cared for at home but are also over three times more likely to require a second set of tubes.[26] Children with older siblings are also at increased risk of OME until age 3 years.[25] Additional information about OM risk factors can be found in Chapter 10.

Inflammatory or infectious processes in the nose, nasopharynx, or paranasal sinuses, should be controlled because secondary mucosal edema may compromise Eustachian tube function (see Chapter 11, "Eustachian Tube Function and Dysfunction"). Chronic rhinitis, sinusitis, or adenoiditis should be diagnosed, and treated with antibiotics or surgery, when appropriate. Control of known inhalant and food allergies would also seem prudent, although no prospective studies have shown efficacy for OME resolution. Because of insufficient evidence, the AHRQ panel offered no recommendation regarding the role of allergy therapy in OME management.[7] Preliminary studies, however, suggest that nasal allergies and food allergies (particularly milk protein allergy in infants) *may* predispose some children to OME.[27,28]

Autoinflation of the Eustachian tube has been proposed as a method for primary control of OME. Although one study demonstrated improved tympanograms following nasal inflation with a toy balloon,[29] other investigators have found no benefits to this therapy.[30,31] A meta-analysis[32] of six published and unpublished studies found an odds ratio of 1.85 favoring autoinflation (95% CI, 1.2, 2.8), requiring a need to treat 14 children to improve one (see Chapter 4, "Meta-analysis and Systematic Literature Review"). Benefits were considered inconclusive, however, because the trials were unblinded, heterogeneous, and of varying methodologic quality. Autoinflation may be used as a harmless adjunct to watchful waiting, but we suggest that expectations be adjusted to reflect the uncertainty of the procedure's long-term efficacy.

PHARMACOLOGIC THERAPY

The value of pharmacologic therapies for OME is judged by comparing risks versus benefits. In most cases, the balance is unfavorable, suggesting a very limited role in OME management. Benefits are best defined as the incremental effect on resolution rates beyond what would occur from natural history alone (eg, the RD, or rate difference, in Table 19-6). In this section, *resolution* refers to complete *short-term* clearance of OME from all ears. *Long-term* resolution, which has not been associated with medical therapy, results from growth and development that explain the relative

Table 19-6 Summary of What to Expect from Medical Therapy for OME*

Clinical Situation and Outcome	Time Point	N[†]	RD[‖] (95% CI)	NNT[‡] (5% CI)
Resolution of persistent OME after treatment	4–6 wk	6	.03 (−.02, .08)	—
of AOM in RCTs of antibiotic vs. placebo	3 mo	2	.05 (−.08, .17)	—
Complete resolution of OME in blinded RCTs of antibiotic therapy vs. placebo	4 wk median	9	.15 (.06, .24)[§]	7 (4, 17)
Complete resolution of OME in RCTs of antibiotic prophylaxis vs. placebo	4 wk median	3	.12 (−.11, .35)	—
Complete resolution of OME in RCTs of steroid vs. placebo or no drug	2 wk	3	.20 (−.05, .45)	—
Complete resolution of OME in RCTs of steroid and antibiotic vs. placebo and antibiotic	Up to 2 mo	5	.25 (.02, .47)[§]	4 (2, 43)
Complete resolution of OME in RCTs of antihistamine and decongestant vs. placebo	1–3 mo	3	0 (−.07, .07)	—

AOM = acute otitis media; CI = confidence interval; NNT = number needed to treat; OME = otitis media with effusion; RCT = randomized controlled trial; RD = absolute rate difference.

*See Chapter 13 for derivation of rates listed in table.

[†]Number of studies from which data were combined to derive the overall treatment effect.

[‡]NNT is the number of children who must be treated for one additional successful outcome and is relevant only for statistically significant outcomes.

[§]$p < .05$ when the 95% CI does not contain zero.

[‖]RD is the absolute change in outcome for treatment versus control groups.

paucity of OME seen after age 7 years. Readers should also note that resolution (clearance in all ears) differs from *improvement* (clearance in at least one ear); improvement is not considered a "successful" outcome because of a high rate of OME relapse.

The favorable natural history of untreated OME (see Chapter 12) makes it difficult for small studies to demonstrate significant therapeutic benefits. As shown in Tables 19-4 and 19-5, the anticipated natural history depends largely on two factors: the type of OME (eg, newly diagnosed versus unknown prior duration) and the definition of a successful outcome (eg, resolution versus improvement; ears versus children). After 3 months, for example, success rates can range from 20 to 90% and after 6 months from 25 to 99%. Therefore, clinicians must compare "apples with apples" when judging interventions versus natural history, ideally with a double-blind randomized controlled trial (RCT). The self-limited nature of OME is a nuisance for clinicians who conduct RCTs because at least 50% of children improve spontaneously before study enrollment.[15,33]

Natural history is not only the gold standard against which OME interventions must be compared but also a formidable opponent when trying to prove incremental efficacy. Meta-analyses, or systematic reviews, are the best means to demonstrate efficacy because combining multiple studies increases precision and statistical power

(see Chapters 4 and 13). Systematic reviews published by professional organizations[7,34,35] and independent researchers[36–39] are the basis for the evidence-based conclusions summarized in Table 19-7 and discussed further below. The relevance of significant individual RCTs published subsequent to the reviews is also discussed.

Antimicrobials

The rationale for antimicrobial therapy of OME is based on a 30% prevalence of viable bacteria in aspirated effusions and an 80% prevalence of bacterial genomic material.[40,41] Unfortunately, the impact of antimicrobial therapy on OME resolution is less than what might be expected from bacteriologic studies: only about 1 in 7 children derive a short-term therapeutic benefit (see Tables 19-6 and 19-7). Randomized trials with *blinded* outcome assessment[42–50] show only a 15% absolute increase in OME resolution attributable to antimicrobial therapy, which increases to 22% when *nonblinded* trials are also included.[51–54] The latter estimate, however, is artificially high because of bias related to less rigorous study design (no placebo controls). In contrast, antimicrobial *prophylaxis* offers no benefits beyond spontaneous resolution[55–57] and should not be used when managing chronic OME (see below for recurrent OME).

Table 19-7 Implications of Meta-analysis for Treating OME*

Question	Antimicrobial Therapy	Antimicrobial Prophylaxis	Antimicrobial-Steroid Therapy	Antihistamines or Decongestants
1. Is the result statistically significant?	Yes; confirmed by 3 independent meta-analyses	No; unlikely that a true difference was missed	Yes; but significant heterogeneity among studies	No; unlikely that a true difference was missed
2. What are the benefits of therapy?	15% increase in *short-term* resolution	Efficacy comparable with placebo	25% increase in *short-term* resolution	Efficacy comparable with placebo
3. To whom do the results best apply?	Children not recently treated with antibiotics	All children	Children not recently treated with antibiotics	All children
4. What data are available on subgroups?	Limited; no differences in comparative drug efficacy	Not applicable	Steroid plus antimicrobial is better than steroid alone	Equivalent results, with or without concurrent antimicrobial therapy
5. What are the clinical implications?	Short-term NNT of 7, but no long-term benefit; therapy is optional	Antimicrobial prophylaxis should not be used for OME	Short-term NNT of 4, but no long-term benefit; unclear risk vs. benefit profile	Antihistamine-decongestant therapy should not be used for OME

NNT = number needed to treat for one cure beyond natural history; OME = otitis media with effusion.
*Based on data presented in Chapters 4 and 13.

The relatively modest benefit of antimicrobial therapy for OME explains the "brouhaha" that has permeated the medical literature over the past decade.[38] When the focus of attention is only *statistical* significance (see Chapter 2), the results of individual trials appear conflicting, and even a single study[43,58] can yield discrepant conclusions based on the method of outcome assessment (algorithm versus tympanometry). When the focus of attention is *clinical* importance, however, the individual and pooled 95% confidence limits show remarkably consistent findings: a small benefit of antimicrobial therapy that on aggregate is statistically significant. Three independent meta-analyses[7,37,38] support this conclusion, making the brouhaha more of an historic curiosity than a clinically meaningful issue.

We agree with the AHRQ conclusion that antimicrobial therapy is *optional* for most OME[7] but suggest that this "option" be exercised more often in some children than in others. A *single* course of antimicrobial therapy is recommended for (1) high-risk children with OME lasting 4 weeks or longer, (2) surgical candidates who have not had recent prior antibiotics, and (3) selected children with recurrent OME, particularly if high-risk. Whereas no prospective trials demonstrate improved outcomes with this approach, we believe that even a modest short-term reduction in OME persistence may benefit high-risk children and help avoid a small percentage of surgery. There is no definitive

evidence, however, to mandate a trial of antimicrobial therapy before tympanostomy tube placement.

When antimicrobial therapy is considered for a child with OME, clinicians are advised to consider the following:

- Expectations should reflect that only about 1 in 7 children derive a short-term benefit from antimicrobial therapy; hopes for a dramatic and lasting response are likely to yield disappointment.
- A single 5- to 10-day course of therapy is appropriate; no benefits have been documented for prolonged, repetitive, or aggressive therapeutic regimens.
- Prophylactic antimicrobials have no role in managing chronic OME; randomized studies show comparable outcomes with placebo therapy.
- Placebo-controlled studies show no difference in antimicrobial efficacy related to bacterial spectrum of the prescribed drug.[37,38]
- Comparative antimicrobial studies generally show equivalent efficacy between established standards (amoxicillin) and newer, broader-spectrum agents; however, one RCT showed slightly better outcomes with amoxicillin-clavulanate than penicillin V.[59]
- A single intramuscular dose of ceftriaxone is *not* recommended for OME; this agent is approved only for treating AOM, and the efficacy for OME is unknown.

Restrictive antimicrobial use is essential to limit the spread of multidrug-resistant bacteria, particularly

Streptococcus pneumoniae. We agree with recommendations by the American Academy of Pediatrics and Centers for Disease Control and Prevention that antimicrobials are not indicated for *initial* treatment of sporadic OME.[60] We emphasize, however, that there is a role for *judicious* antimicrobial therapy in managing selected children with OME. The guidelines presented above should help target children most likely to benefit from therapy, while preventing excessive antimicrobial use in the general community.

Antimicrobial prophylaxis is an option for selected *effusion-free* children with histories of chronic or recurrent OME. Mandel and colleagues[61] compared the efficacy of amoxicillin prophylaxis with that of placebo for managing recurrent MEE (either AOM or OME) in 111 Pittsburgh children. Inclusion criteria were at least 3 episodes of MEE or 3 cumulative months of MEE during the past year. Amoxicillin prophylaxis reduced AOM incidence by 0.76 episodes/year and OME incidence by 0.62 episodes/year; overall time with MEE was also reduced by 13%. Although statistically significant, clinical benefits of this magnitude may only be relevant for high-risk children with recurrent OME and effusion-free periods.

As noted above, prophylaxis is ineffective as therapy for persistent OME without effusion-free intervals. One later study found that azithromycin prophylaxis of OME for 12 weeks improved middle ear pressures versus decongestant alone, but the clinical relevance is unclear and the duration of benefit (if any) beyond the prophylactic period was unstudied.[62]

Other Medical Therapies

Antihistamine and decongestant therapy for OME continues to enjoy popularity, despite three randomized trials showing comparable efficacy to placebo (see Table 13-17 in Chapter 13).[63–65] Stool and colleagues[7] confirmed this lack of efficacy in a meta-analysis using these trials plus another study[43] in which all children received concurrent antimicrobial therapy. Clinicians *should not* prescribe antihistamines or decongestants for children with OME, unless they are consciously trying to achieve a placebo effect. We consider this practice ill advised because of the potential side effects and drug reactions that may occur. Whereas "drying up the fluid" makes sense, neither antihistamines nor decongestants achieve this goal. Further, topically administered nasal decongestants do not alter middle ear pressure dynamics.[66]

Mucoactive therapy (S-carboxymethyl-cysteine) has a promising impact on OME outcomes, as suggested in a meta-analysis by Pignataro and colleagues.[39] Despite the appeal of the 25% absolute RD observed in their study (based on *improvement*, not resolution), the results had low precision and just missed statistical significance. Similarly, a double-blind RCT conducted after this meta-analysis found an 8.5% RD after 6 weeks of therapy, but the results were not statistically significant.[67] In contrast, direct intratympanic administration of *N*-acetylcysteine during and shortly after tympanostomy tube placement, significantly reduced OME recurrence and tube reinsertions.[68] We consider mucoactive therapy (intratympanic and orally administered) a promising area for future investigation but cannot endorse it at present because of limited data on safety and efficacy.

The efficacy of oral corticosteroids for OME, with or without a concurrent antimicrobial agent, has been assessed in eight RCTs[47,54,69–74] and three meta-analyses[7,34,36] (see Chapters 4 and 13). Combination steroid-antimicrobial therapy increases rates of complete OME resolution by 25% (see Table 19-6). Although statistically significant, this result must be interpreted with caution because of heterogeneity, broad CIs, and potential adverse therapeutic effects. Moreover, the largest and most recent study[74] noted only a transient benefit, even if antibiotics were continued for several weeks.

Rather than completely dismiss steroid therapy, we consider it an option in selected *low-risk* children who are surgical candidates. We do not recommend steroid therapy for *high-risk* children (see Table 19-3) because of a high relapse rate (about 40%) that may unnecessarily delay needed surgical intervention. Children *without* baseline hearing loss or histories of recurrent AOM are likely to have the most favorable outcomes.[75] When antibiotic-steroid therapy is considered for a child with OME, clinicians are advised to consider the following[75,76]:

- Steroid therapy is contraindicated with concurrent acute infection, such as AOM or sinusitis.
- Parents should be told that oral steroid therapy has promising short-term benefits but that long-term benefits have not been demonstrated.
- About 4 children need treatment to benefit one, but 40% will relapse.
- Disseminated varicella has been reported when 2 mg/kg/d of prednisone is given during the viral incubation phase. To eliminate this risk, restrict therapy to children who have had varicella or the varicella vaccine, and limit prednisone dosage to 1 mg/kg/d (tapered over 10 days).
- Concurrent antimicrobial agents are necessary because children with OME treated with steroids alone may be at increased risk of AOM.
- Repeated courses of steroid therapy are contraindicated because most children have depressed adrenal function (serum cortisol less than 10 μg/dL) for up to 3 weeks after treatment; the clinical significance of this transient depression, if any, is unknown.

We do not recommend intranasal steroids or glutathione for treating OME because of limited evidence. When children aged 3 years or older with chronic OME *and* recurrent AOM were randomized to daily amoxicillin prophylaxis, with or without intranasal beclomethasone, resolution rates by child were significantly higher after 8 weeks in the steroid group (42% versus 18%) using tympanometry.[77] At 4 weeks and 12 weeks, however, the differences were not significant, nor were they significant at any time (4, 8, or 12 weeks), by child, using otoscopic criteria. In another RCT, children aged 3 years or older with chronic OME received glutathione by nasal aerosol every 3 or 4 waking hours for 2 weeks.[78] After 3 months, 67% had improved (not resolved) in the glutathione group versus only 8% with placebo. Although promising, the safety and practicality of this approach require further investigation.

MEASURING MORBIDITY

Optimal management of OME involves fitting the punishment to the crime, the "crime" being the objective and subjective impact of OME on the child and their family. The optimal time at which to measure OME-related morbidity is controversial, but we recommend a cutoff point of 3 to 4 months, with a lower threshold for high-risk children (see Table 19-3). Morbidity assessment for OME should include (1) hearing evaluation, preferably using pure-tone audiometry in a soundproof booth, and (2) tympanic membrane integrity evaluation, preferably by an otologist or ear, nose, and throat specialist. Additional assessments that may be used on an individualized basis include (1) auditory function (speech in noise) tests, (2) speech and language evaluation, (3) tests of balance and vestibular function, and (4) disease-specific quality of life surveys.

Tympanic Membrane Integrity

Children with chronic OME are at risk of structural damage of the tympanic membrane.[79] OME invokes a local inflammatory response because the fluid contains leukotrienes, prostaglandins, and arachidonic acid metabolites. Reactive changes eventually occur in the adjacent tympanic membrane and mucosal linings. Otitis-prone children also have Eustachian tubes that are "too short, and too floppy, and won't work" (see Chapter 11), leaving the middle ear vulnerable to pressure swings in the nasopharynx. The effect is similar to repeatedly blowing up and deflating a balloon; eventually the elastic fibers become flaccid and atrophic followed by collapse. Finally, a relative underventilation of the middle ear produces a negative pressure that predisposes to focal retraction pockets and generalized atelectasis of the tympanic membrane.

The impact of OME on tympanic membrane structure is best assessed by an otologist or ear, nose, and throat specialist. A search is made for retraction-type ear disease, which includes focal retraction pockets (pars tensa and pars flaccida), ossicular erosion (myringoincudopexy or myringostapediopexy), and areas of atelectasis or atrophy. Conditions that generally mandate insertion of a tympanostomy tube are (1) posterosuperior retraction pockets, (2) ossicular erosion, (3) adhesive atelectasis, and (4) retraction pockets that accumulate keratin debris (pre-cholesteatoma). The prevalence of atelectasis and attic retraction in ears with persistent OME increases with time, rising from 4% and 2% at 1 year to 7% and 39% at 5 years.[80] Over the same time period, segmental atrophy occurred in 3% of ears, and minor scarring or thickening of the pars tensa was seen in 14%.

Hearing and Auditory Function

The impact of OME on child hearing and auditory function is discussed in Chapter 22, "Hearing and Auditory Function", but certain issues related to clinical decision making deserve re-emphasis and clarification. We recommend that clinicians consider three aspects of auditory assessment: (1) degree of hearing loss, (2) temporal pattern of hearing loss, and (3) impact of hearing loss on everyday child function (eg, speech in noise perception).

Most children with OME have a mild degree of hearing impairment, with mean three-frequency pure tone average hearing levels of 27 dB in infants and 25 dB in older children.[81] The degree of hearing loss relates to the volume of fluid present in the middle ear, not to its viscosity or other physical properties.[82] For both ears combined, the hearing status is usually expressed relative to the better-hearing ear, or with soundfield thresholds in those young children in whom ear-specific testing in not feasible. Broad guidelines for interpreting hearing status for children with OME may be summarized as follows:

- *Hearing levels of 40 dB or higher*, if persistent, mandate early consideration of surgery.
- *Hearing levels of 21 to 39 dB* require individualized management, depending on duration severity, and may include surgery and strategies to optimize the listening-learning environment (see Chapter 22).
- *Hearing levels of 20 dB or lower* are considered "normal," but audiometry should be repeated in 3 to 6 months if OME persists on follow-up evaluation.

Parents or caregivers *cannot* accurately detect hearing impairment caused by OME. Rosenfeld and colleagues[83] first reported a lack of correlation between a global question of child hearing behavior and audiometry results. In a follow-up investigation, Brody and colleagues[84] showed good test-retest reliability and internal consistency for a seven-item hearing survey, but the survey scores did not correlate with actual hearing levels. Stewart and coworkers[85] also demonstrated that parent perception of their child's hearing loss is a poor predictor of audiologic findings, before and after tympanostomy tubes. Last, Anteunis and colleagues[86] showed good negative predictive values (89 to 96%) for parental report on OME-related hearing impairment, but positive predictive values were poor (10 to 27%).

Assessment of hearing status for children with OME often requires serial audiometry because hearing status may change relative to effusion volume. Stephenson and colleagues[87] found that OME is often associated with fluctuating or asymmetric hearing, the impact of which may not be developmentally benign. Mandel and coworkers[88] reported that when children with chronic OME and normal hearing were randomized to nonsurgical management, 50% developed "significant" hearing loss persisting for at least 2 months despite antimicrobial treatment the following year. A "significant" hearing loss was defined as 20 dB pure-tone average hearing level bilaterally, 40 dB unilaterally, or as a speech awareness threshold greater than 20 dB above the age-appropriate level.

High-risk children (see Table 19-3) are more susceptible to the auditory degradation caused by persistent OME, with or without measurable hearing loss. Determining the impact of unilateral or bilateral OME on children with Down syndrome, developmental delays, baseline sensorineural hearing loss, or other global problems is at best an imperfect science, which cannot be reduced to a simple audiometric threshold at a single assessment point. Recognizing that evidence-based medicine rests on a foundation of external evidence, clinician experience, and patient preference, we suggest that the latter two variables take precedence when assessing the auditory impact of OME on high-risk children.

A final consideration in hearing assessment is the relation between hearing levels in a soundproof booth and auditory function in real-life situations. Audiometry alone may underestimate the listening difficulties a child encounters in real life and may provide a sense of false security in postponing or delaying definitive treatment.[89] Rosenfeld and colleagues[90] showed that children with chronic bilateral OME and normal hearing, nonetheless, had substantial difficulties with word recognition at soft-listening levels and in background noise. After tympanostomy tube insertion, children tested at soft-listening levels had an absolute increase in word recognition scores of 66% with competing background noise, and 36% without noise. Speech in noise (auditory function) testing can gener-

ally be accomplished in children aged 3 years or older and is described in detail in Chapter 22.

Speech, Language, Cognition, Behavior, and Balance

Speech and language development can be screened in the office setting,[91] or evaluated more thoroughly by a qualified professional. We do not recommend that all children with OME be evaluated but suggest evaluation for children with suspected delays or articulation problems, particularly those with chronic OME whose parents decline surgery. A Diagnostic and Therapeutic Technology Assessment from the American Medical Association concluded that among "children (ages 1 to 18 years) with impaired speech, language, or learning skills and a prior history of recurrent acute or chronic OME, the effectiveness of speech therapy to improve speech, language, or learning skills is established or promising in those with most types of hearing loss associated with OME."[92]

A brief three-item parent survey has been developed to rapidly screen 2-year-old children for developmental language delay.[93] The three questions are given below:

Q1. Are you worried about your child's language development? (1 = yes, 0 = no)
Q2. How many ear infections has your child had? (enter number reported)
Q3. Does the child use fewer than 50 words *or* no word combinations? (1 = yes, 0 = no)

A screening score is calculated on the basis of the above three questions as: $16(Q1) + Q2 + 16(Q3)$. If the resulting screening score is 28 or more, the child can be considered to be at risk of language delay, with the risk increasing the higher the score. The screening score correlates significantly (−.38 to −.68) with three outcome measures, one based on a language sample (mean length of utterance in morphemes) and two based on a standardized test (receptive and expressive language in the Mullen Scales of Early Learning).

Otitis media with effusion indirectly affects child development, with conductive hearing loss and the quality of the caregiving environment serving as intermediary variables.[94] In one study,[95] the cumulative duration of MEE in their first year of life explained only 1.2 to 2.9% of the variance in receptive vocabulary and verbal cognition at age 3 years beyond sociodemographic variables. These children, however, were otherwise healthy, had intermittent OME, and were identified by intense screening. Placement of tympanostomy tubes did not influence language development for otherwise healthy children with persistent OME identified by screening[3] or intense prospective surveillance.[2] Again, these children were asymptomatic and not representative of the typical child referred for surgery. Conversely, older children (mean age 3 years) with chronic bilateral OME and hearing loss (25 dB HL or poorer) had better expressive language and verbal comprehension with tube insertion versus watchful waiting.[4]

Otitis media with effusion has a direct and reversible impact on the vestibular system.[99–100] Children with chronic OME have significantly poorer vestibular function and gross motor proficiency when compared with non-OME controls. Moreover, the vestibular and motor deficiencies resolve promptly in nearly all children following tympanostomy tube insertion. These findings argue for timely surgical therapy in children with chronic OME who have unexplained clumsiness, balance problems, or delayed motor development. Because most parents do not appreciate the potential relation of these symptoms with OME, clinicians must often ask specific and targeted questions to elucidate the history of symptoms.

Certain behavioral problems occur disproportionately with OME, including distractibility, withdrawal, frustration, and aggressiveness.[101] In a large cohort study, for example, OME severity from age 5 to 9 years correlated with lower intelligence quotient to age 13 years and with hyperactive and inattentive behavior until age 15 years.[5] The largest effects were observed for defects in reading ability between 11 and 18 years. An ongoing area of psychometric research concerns developing a valid, but brief, parent questionnaire to identify OME-specific behavior in young children.[102] Changes after tympanostomy tube insertion are measurable for language and speech behavior and for physical and motor behavior; emotional behavior presents additional measurement difficulties.

Nearly all developmental research in OME has excluded high-risk children as defined in Table 19-3. The negative effects in this population are likely to be magnified relative to their low-risk peers. Parents of children with cerebral palsy, Down syndrome, developmental delays, attention deficit disorder, or pervasive developmental disorder will often notice direct behavioral sequelae of OME that resolve when the effusion clears. Although anecdotal, the parent's perception of OME impact on their child must be considered in surgical decision making.

Quality of Life

Health-related quality of life (QoL) is a patient's subjective perception of his or her health status. For OME, quality of life describes the net consequences of illness on a child's daily activities, physical comfort, social interactions, and emotional well being (see Chapter 25, "Quality of Life and Child Behavior"). In contrast, hearing, otoscopy, and language development are more objective measures of outcome. While important to most health care providers, objective measures may be less relevant to patients and their families. Parents want their children to feel and function better; they are less concerned with hearing levels in a soundproof booth, the beauty of the tympanic membrane (or lack thereof), or the quality and quantity of middle ear fluid.

Parent reports in structured focus groups suggest that chronic OM is a painful and stressful condition for children and their families.[103] Frustration often surrounds issues of cost, medication, lack of information about the illness, and worries about future hearing impairment. Some children had difficulty interacting with others because of hearing or speech problems, and others had difficulty or were easily distracted in noisy group situations. A common concern was developing immunity to medications for treating or preventing OM. Conversely, parents expressed great satisfaction when tubes offered relief from further problems. Generalizability of the above results may be limited because the sample was small (14 families), referral based, and from the suburban Midwest United States.

Clinicians can rapidly measure QoL with a brief, six-item, parent-completed survey, the OM-6 (Figure 19-1). The OM-6 is valid, reliable, and responsive to changes in child health status.[14] Please refer to Table 19-8 for how to score and interpret the OM-6 survey. Once a baseline survey has been completed, follow-up surveys can categorize changes as trivial, small, moderate, or large. When the OM-6 was completed by parents of 248 children (median age 1.4 years) before and after tympanostomy tube insertion, QoL changes before surgery were mostly trivial compared with those observed subsequently.[104] Large, moderate, and small improvements in QoL occurred after surgery in 56%, 15%, and 8% of children, respectively. Physical symptoms, caregiver concerns, emotional distress, and hearing loss were most improved. Predictors of poorer QoL (4% of children) were otorrhea lasting 3 or more days (10% of variance) and decreased satisfaction with surgical decision (3% of variance).

The OM-6 may also help in routine clinical care. Survey results allow clinicians to identify rapidly in what domains (eg, physical, emotional, hearing) parents perceive their children to be most affected by OME. Conversely, clinicians can also identify children with "silent" OME, who have documented MEE but minimal or absent subjective complaints. Parents of children with silent OME are often reluctant to undergo therapy because of the difficulties involved in making asymptomatic patients feel better. While some low-risk children with silent OME can be observed for prolonged periods, many parents must be educated regarding the spectrum of morbidity outlined in this section.

Instructions: Please help us understand the impact of ear infections or fluid on your child's quality of life by checking one box [x] for each question below. Thank you.

PHYSICAL SUFFERING: Ear pain, ear discomfort, ear discharge, ruptured ear drum, high fever, or poor balance. How much of a problem for your child during the past 4 weeks?

[ ] Not present/no problem   [ ] Hardly a problem at all   [ ] Quite a bit of a problem
                                     [ ] Somewhat of a problem   [ ] Very much a problem
                                     [ ] Moderate problem   [ ] Extreme problem

HEARING LOSS: Difficulty hearing, questions must be repeated, frequently says "what," or television is excessively loud. How much of a problem for your child during the past 4 weeks?

[ ] Not present/no problem   [ ] Hardly a problem at all   [ ] Quite a bit of a problem
                                     [ ] Somewhat of a problem   [ ] Very much a problem
                                     [ ] Moderate problem   [ ] Extreme problem

SPEECH IMPAIRMENT: Delayed speech, poor pronunciation, difficult to understand, or unable to repeat words clearly. How much of a problem for your child during the past 4 weeks?

[ ] Not present/no problem   [ ] Hardly a problem at all   [ ] Quite a bit of a problem
     (or not applicable)   [ ] Somewhat of a problem   [ ] Very much a problem
                                     [ ] Moderate problem   [ ] Extreme problem

EMOTIONAL DISTRESS: Irritable, frustrated, sad, restless, or poor appetite. How much of a problem for your child during the past 4 weeks as a result of ear infections or fluid?

[ ] Not present/no problem   [ ] Hardly a problem at all   [ ] Quite a bit of a problem
                                     [ ] Somewhat of a problem   [ ] Very much a problem
                                     [ ] Moderate problem   [ ] Extreme problem

ACTIVITY LIMITATIONS: Playing, sleeping, doing things with friends/family, attending school or day care. How limited have your child's activities been during the past 4 weeks because of ear infections or fluid?

[ ] Not limited at all   [ ] Hardly limited at all   [ ] Moderately limited
                                     [ ] Very slightly limited   [ ] Very limited
                                     [ ] Slightly limited   [ ] Severely limited

CAREGIVER CONCERNS: How often have you, as a caregiver, been worried, concerned, or inconvenienced because of your child's ear infections or fluid over the past 4 weeks?

[ ] None of the time   [ ] Hardly any time at all   [ ] A good part of the time
                                     [ ] A small part of the time   [ ] Most of the time
                                     [ ] Some of the time   [ ] All of the time

Figure 19-1 OM-6 quality of life survey for measuring subjective morbidity and change in health status for children with chronic and recurrent otitis media.

Rovers and colleagues[105] showed that tympanostomy tubes did not improve QoL more than watchful waiting in a RCT of 187 Dutch children. Results must be interpreted with caution, however, because the surveys measured *overall* QoL and were not *disease specific* for OM (as is the OM-6). Overall (general) QoL surveys are not validated to measure longitudinal disease-specific change within individuals and are, therefore, subject to low statistical power. Moreover, the study sample was identified by population-based auditory screening at 9 to 12 months of age, and the operated children were mostly asymptomatic. Conversely, the study reported above with the OM-6 was a symptomatic referral-based sample.[104]

SURGICAL MANAGEMENT

Objective benefits of surgery for OME include improved hearing, reduced MEE prevalence, reduced AOM incidence, and reduced need for reoperation (see Chapter 14). For example, in the first year after tube insertion, children have about 160 fewer days with effusion, a relative decrease of 72% compared with no surgery or myringotomy alone.[88,106,107] The impact of this on a given child, however, is likely to be highly variable. An asymptomatic child may derive no perceptible benefit (or may even be perceived as worse if tube otorrhea develops), but a high-risk child with developmental delays may show large changes. Similarly, the short-term improvement in hearing that accompanies tubes (mean 6 to 12 dB lasting 6 to 12 months) may be dramatic in some but unnoticeable in others.[108,109] By definition, a "mean" improvement of 6 to 12 dB implies that 50% of children derive greater benefit.

Optimal surgical outcomes are most likely to occur if the right child has the right surgery. Selecting the right child is undoubtedly the more difficult, and more important, of these two decisions. The difficulties inherent in assessing surgical candidacy explain the impressive small-area variations in tube insertion rates, which are strongly influenced by opinions of the primary-care physicians.[1] In general, *asymptomatic* children with a persistent OME *identified by screening or intense surveillance* derive minimal benefits from surgery.[2,3] Conversely, *symptomatic children* with OME *who present for evaluation* have larger changes in quality of life and development.[4,104] The impact of surgery on high-risk children (see Table 19-3) with OME has not been assessed in RCTs because of ethical and logistic concerns, but most experts advise aggressive management.[11]

Assessing Surgical Candidacy

Surgical candidacy for OME depends largely on (1) associated symptoms (eg, hearing loss), (2) the child's developmental risk (high versus low as defined in Table 19-3), and (3) the anticipated chance of timely spontaneous resolution of the effusion (see Tables 19-4 and 19-5). *Candidates* for surgery include children with the following:

1. Bilateral OME lasting 3 months or longer, especially if symptomatic
2. Unilateral OME lasting 6 months or longer, especially if symptomatic
3. Recurrent or persistent OME in high-risk children, regardless of symptom status
4. OME and structural damage to the tympanic membrane or middle ear

Decisions regarding surgical intervention for a given child are made using factors known to influence OME prognosis and outcome (Table 19-9). How much the surgical threshold is lowered on the basis of the factors in Table 19-9 is determined by clinician experience and family preference. There are no right or wrong decisions for a given child, and the procedures under consideration are nearly always elective in nature. Families who are hesitant to have surgery, whether for logical or illogical reasons, are best re-evaluated in 1 month, rather than forced into a decision with which they are uncomfortable. Patient satisfaction with decisions is an important aspect of the process of care,[109] which correlates significantly with perceived changes in quality of life after tympanostomy tube insertion.[104]

Most of the factors in Table 19-9 have been previously discussed, but several issues deserve emphasis. When young infants have chronic OME, the threshold for surgery should be lower because they are unable to communicate about their symptoms and are at increased risk of suppurative disease. Earlier intervention should also

---

Table 19-8 How to Use the OM-6 Survey to Measure Health-Related Quality of Life

1. The *target population* is children age 6 months to 12 years, with chronic otitis media with effusion (3 months or longer) or recurrent acute otitis media (3 or more episodes in the past 12 months).

2. The child's *parent or caregiver* completes the OM-6 at baseline. Item responses are scored from 1 to 7, with higher scores indicating more of a problem.

3. The same person who completed the baseline OM-6 completes a second survey after a specific intervention, with a minimum time between surveys of 4 weeks. Item responses are scored from 1 to 7, with higher scores indicating more of a problem.

4. The *follow-up survey score* is calculated as the mean of the six-item scores. The global ear-related quality-of-life rating at the bottom of the survey form is read directly and is not used when calculating the follow-up score.

5. A *change score* is calculated by subtracting the follow-up survey score from the baseline survey score. A positive value indicates clinical improvement, a negative value indicates deterioration. A change score of less than 0.5 indicates trivial change, 0.5 to 0.9 indicates small change, 1.0 to 1.4 indicates moderate change, and 1.5 or greater indicates large change.

Adapted from Rosenfeld RM et al.[14]

Table 19-9 Factors Influencing the Threshold for Surgical Intervention in Children with OME

Prognostic Factor	Lowers Surgical Threshold	Raises Surgical Threshold
Developmentally at-risk child[§]	Yes (major factor)	No
Hearing and auditory function	Abnormal	Normal
Language/academic achievement	Abnormal or delayed	Normal
Tympanic membrane structure	Abnormal[†]	Normal
Recurrent AOM	Present	Absent
Bilateral OME duration	≥ 3 months	< 3 months
Unilateral OME duration	≥ 6 months	< 6 months
Child age	Infant or toddler	Older child
Imbalance, clumsiness, vertigo	Present	Absent
Environment	Unfavorable[‡]	Favorable
Quality of life[*]	Poor	Good

AOM = acute otitis media; OME = otitis media with effusion.

[*]Physical symptoms, sleep disturbance, emotional distress, activity limitations, and so on.

[†]Atelectasis, retraction pocket, or thickened and hypervascular tympanic membrane.

[‡]Environmental tobacco smoke; group day care (4–6 children or higher); less responsive home or childcare environment.

[§]Speech delays, cognitive deficits, or sensorineural hearing loss (see Table 19-3 for complete list).

be considered for children with OME relapse despite prior surgery because of increased risk of persistent or chronic disease with nonsurgical management. Last, an exception to the concept of aggressive OME management in high-risk children concerns primary ciliary dyskinesia because continuous mucoid otorrhea may occur after tube insertion.[111] In this situation, hearing aids are preferred if a hearing loss is present.

Choosing a Surgical Procedure

On the basis of evidence from methodologically sound RCTs (see Chapter 14),[88,106,107,112,113] we recommend the following surgical approach for OME (Table 19-10):
- *Initial surgery*: myringotomy and tympanostomy tube placement; adenoidectomy is withheld unless nasal obstruction is present
- *Repeat surgery*: myringotomy, with or without tube placement, and adenoidectomy (irrespective of adenoid size)
- *Tonsillectomy*: withheld unless other indications for surgery exist, such as frequently recurrent tonsillitis or pharyngeal obstruction

Tympanostomy tubes are recommended for initial surgery because RCTs show a mean 72% relative decrease in effusion prevalence and an absolute decrease

of about 160 effusion days per child during the next year (see Chapter 14). Adenoidectomy plus myringotomy (without tube insertion) has comparable efficacy in children aged 4 years or older[106] but is more invasive with additional surgical and anesthetic risks. Similarly, the added risk or adenoidectomy was felt to outweigh the limited, short-term benefit for children aged 3 years or older without prior tubes.[114] Consequently, adenoidectomy is not recommended for initial OME surgery, unless a distinct indication exists, such as adenoiditis, postnasal obstruction, or chronic sinusitis.

The care and consequences of tympanostomy tubes are discussed in Chapter 29, "Tympanostomy Tube Care and Consequences", but several issues merit attention. First, water precautions are *unnecessary* in young children with tubes who surface swim and do not dive; equivalent outcomes occur whether children use earplugs, antibiotic ear drops, or abstain completely from swimming.[115] Second, a short-acting grommet tube should be used for *initial* therapy (if the ear canal is not stenotic) because long-acting t-tubes have relatively high rates of typanic membrane perforation and structural damage.[116] The functional period of a grommet tube can be maximized by inserting it in a small, radial incision near the annulus anteriorly.[117] Last, we consider it prudent to document hearing before *and* after surgical manipulation in all children, despite a

Table 19-10 Surgical Management Options for Chronic OME

Management Option	Comment
Myringotomy	Ineffective as a sole management option; useful as an adjunct to adenoidectomy
Tympanostomy tubes	Proven efficacy in managing OME; reduces hearing loss, effusion prevalence, and infection incidence while the tube remains patent
Adenoidectomy	Proven efficacy in managing OME, irrespective of adenoid size; limited data below age 4 years
Tonsillectomy	Ineffective for OME; only appropriate for other indications, such as frequently recurrent tonsillitis or pharyngeal obstruction

OME = otitis media with effusion.

lack of demonstrated cost-effectiveness with this approach.[118] This is particularly important in high-risk children with underlying syndromes associated with hearing loss independent of OME.[119]

About 50% of children with tympanostomy tubes need reoperation within 3 years.[88,107] When a child needs repeat surgery for OME, we recommend adenoidectomy because of a 50% reduction in the need for future surgery.[106,112,120] The benefit of adenoidectomy is apparent at age 2 years,[120] is greatest for children aged 3 years or older, and is independent of adenoid size.[106,113,114] Myringotomy, with or without tube placement, is performed concurrent with adenoidectomy. Myringotomy alone is effective for children aged 4 years or older,[106] but tube placement is advised for younger children, when potential relapse of effusion must be minimized (eg, high-risk children) or when pronounced inflammation of the tympanic membrane and middle ear mucosa are present.

Tonsillectomy alone (without adenoidectomy) is not recommended to treat OME. Although tonsillectomy is either ineffective[113] or of limited efficacy,[114–120] all authors concur that the risks of hemorrhage (about 2%) and additional hospitalization outweigh any potential benefits, unless a distinct indication for tonsillectomy exists. Tonsillectomy is performed concurrently with other surgery for OME only when a distinct indication exists (eg, obstruction or severe recurrent infection).

Myringotomy alone (without adenoidectomy or tube insertion) is ineffective for OME[88,107] because removing the fluid does not alter chronic changes in the middle ear and mastoid mucosa. OME induces a chronic inflammatory response, which causes mucosal hyperplasia and forms active mucus-secreting glands.[121] Aeration of the middle ear allows mucosal recovery (disappearance of glands) and opening of the mastoid air cell system but occurs gradually over a *3- to 8-month* period.[122] Myringotomy ventilates the middle ear for only several days, which is insufficient for mucosal recovery. Laser-assisted myringotomy extends the ventilation up to 3 weeks,[123] but efficacy has not been shown in RCTs with concurrent controls (see Chapter 14). In contrast, tubes ventilate the middle ear for 12 to 14 months.[88,107]

Anesthesia mortality is about 1:50,000 for ambulatory surgery,[124] but the current fatality rate is estimated as 1:250,000.[125] Laryngospasm and bronchospasm occur more often in children receiving anesthesia than in adults. Tympanostomy tube sequelae are common but are generally transient (otorrhea) or cosmetic (tympanosclerosis, focal atrophy, or shallow retraction pocket).[116] Tympanic membrane perforations, which may require repair, are seen in 2.2% of children after short-term (grommet-type) tubes and 16.6% after long-term (t-type) tubes. Adenoidectomy has a 0.2% incidence of hemorrhage[126] and 2.4% incidence of transient velopharyngeal insufficiency.[112] Other potential risks, such as nasopharyngeal stenosis and persistent velopharyngeal insufficiency, are extremely rare and can be minimized with appropriate patient selection and surgical technique.

BEYOND PRACTICE GUIDELINES

Optimal management of children with OME requires both art and science. Evidence from methodologically sound scientific studies supplies probabilities to guide clinical care, but probability rarely equates with certainty regarding individual patients. As noted by Osler, "Variability is the law of life, and as no two faces are the same, no two bodies are alike, and no two individuals react alike and behave alike under the abnormal conditions which we know as disease."[127] The guidelines presented in this chapter result from combining probabilities with values and expert consensus. Table 19-11 offers some final pointers and pitfalls for managing OME.

From a practical standpoint, children with OME fall into two categories: those who get better in a few months

Table 19-11 Pointers and Pitfalls

1. Clinical pathways (see Table 19-2) define the time course of disease in a typical patient, with corresponding actions and expected outcomes.

2. OME may be overlooked with nonpneumatic otoscopy; optimal diagnosis requires pneumatic otoscopy supplemented, when necessary, by tympanometry.

3. Management decisions are highly influenced by comorbidity (see Table 19–3); high-risk children have lower thresholds for hearing testing, speech and language assessment, and surgical intervention.

4. Absence of symptoms does not imply absence of OME; similarly, absence of apparent hearing loss by parent report does not provide any assurance that hearing is truly unaffected.

5. Environmental control and risk factor modification are prudent for OME but their efficacy is not supported by prospective studies.

6. A restrictive approach to antimicrobial therapy for OME is advised; no benefits have been shown for prophylactic, prolonged, or repetitive therapy.

7. Surgical candidacy is based on effusion duration, laterality, and associated comorbid conditions (see Table 19–9); flexibility and individualized decisions are essential.

8. Of the surgical methods for managing OME, only tympanostomy tubes assuredly control middle ear effusion and the associated conductive hearing loss.

9. Adenoidectomy is effective for OME in children aged 4 years or older and in children aged 2 to 3 years who have had one or more tympanostomy tube insertions in the past.

10. Tonsillectomy or myringotomy alone are ineffective for OME.

11. OME can have a substantial impact on parent and child quality of life; objective measures of health status alone may underestimate actual OME-related morbidity.

OME = otitis media with effusion.

no matter what you (or they) do, and those who eventually require surgery for timely resolution.[16] The art of management, of course, lies in deciding as soon as possible into which category a child falls. Such decisions are based in large part on clinician experience and patient preference, although the information in Tables 19-2 and 19-9 should also be of use. Patient (parent) preference must be considered because poor satisfaction with decisions results in higher surgical cancelation rates and diminished QoL changes after tube placement.[104,128] We cannot overemphasize the importance of measuring morbidity (see above) as a basis for enlightened management. Many of the manifestations of OME are subtle or subclinical and can be easily overlooked, if not specifically sought.

Watchful waiting alone may be appropriate long-term management for selected low-risk children with chronic OME but satisfactory hearing and minimal associated morbidity. The word "watchful" deserves emphasis because OME is dynamic. Children managed expectantly *must* undergo periodic re-evaluation of their hearing and tympanic membrane status, with continual reassessment of the surgical threshold. If patients opt to pursue unproved alternative or unconventional medical interventions, they should, nonetheless, be cautioned about a need for "conventional" physician follow-up to monitor OME and morbidity. The authors have seen children with asymptomatic OME whose parents delay or avoid timely follow-up, only to return years later with retraction-type ear disease (eg, ossicular erosion or cholesteatoma) that could have been avoided.

In conclusion, we wish to re-emphasize that high-risk children (see Table 19-3) with OME need aggressive management. This recommendation stems from common sense, not evidence, because RCTs of watchful waiting versus early intervention do not (and probably will never) exist in this population. Prolonged observation of OME is ill advised for high-risk children because of increased risk of developmental sequelae from degradation of the auditory signal, with or without measurable hearing loss. Because of the myriad problems faced by high-risk children, tube insertion is unlikely to result in a miracle cure or a "new child." Rather, timely surgery can help maximize their return on time invested in the numerous supportive therapies and services they typically receive.

REFERENCES

1. Coyte PC, Croxford R, Asche CV, et al. Physician and population determinants of rates of middle-ear surgery in Ontario. JAMA 2001;286;2128–35.
2. Paradise JL, Feldman HM, Campbell TF, et al. Effect of early or delayed insertion of tympanostomy tubes for persistent otitis media on developmental outcomes at the age of three years. N Engl J Med 2001;344:1179–87.
3. Rovers MM, Straatman H, Ingels K, et al. The effect of ventilation tubes on language development in infants with otitis media with effusion. A randomized trial. Pediatrics 2000;106:E42.
4. Maw R, Wilks J, Harvey I, et al. Early surgery compared with watchful waiting for glue ear and effect on language development in preschool children: a randomized trial. Lancet 1999;353:960–3.
5. Bennett KE, Haggard MP, Silva PA, Stewart IA. Behaviour and developmental effects of otitis media with effusion into the teens. Arch Dis Child 2001;85:91–5.
6. Takata GS, Chan LS, Shekelle P, et al. Diagnosis, natural history, and late effects of otitis media with effusion. Evidence Report/Technology Assessment: Number 55. AHRQ Publication Number 02-E026. Rockville (MD): Agency for Healthcare Research and Quality; June 2002.
7. Stool SE, Berg AO, Berman S, et al. Otitis media with effusion in young children. Clinical practice guideline, Number 12. AHCPR Publication No. 94-0622. Rockville (MD): Agency for Health Care Policy and Research, Public Health Service, US Department of Health and Human Services; July 1994.
8. Shekelle PG, Ortiz E, Rhodes S, et al. Validity of the Agency for Healthcare Research and Quality clinical practice guidelines: how quickly to guidelines become outdated? JAMA 2001;286:1461–7.
9. Battista RN, Hodge MJ. Clinical practice guidelines: between science and art. Can Med Assoc J 1993;148: 385–9.
10. Eddy DM. A manual for assessing health practices & designing practice policies: the explicit approach. Philadelphia (PA): American College of Physicians; 1992.
11. Bluestone CD, Klein JO. Clinical practice guideline on otitis media with effusion in young children: strengths and weaknesses. Otolaryngol Head Neck Surg 1995;112: 507–11.
12. Pearson SD, Goulart-Fisher D, Lee TH. Critical pathways as a strategy for improving care: problems and potential. Ann Intern Med 1995;123:941–8.
13. Coffey RJ, Othman E, Walters JI. Extending the application of critical path methods. Qual Manag Health Care 1995;3:14–29.
14. Rosenfeld RM, Goldsmith AJ, Tetlus L, Balzano A. Quality of life for children with otitis media. Arch Otolaryngol Head Neck Surg 1997;123:1049–54.
15. MRC Multi-centre Otitis Media Study Group. Clin Otolaryngol 2001;26:147–56.
16. Rosenfeld RM. Amusing parents while nature cures otitis media with effusion. Int J Pediatr Otorhinolaryngol 1998;43:189–92.

17. Maw R, Bawden R. Spontaneous resolution of severe chronic glue ear in children and the effect of adenoidectomy, tonsillectomy, and insertion of ventilation tubes (grommets). BMJ 1993;306:756–60.
18. Block SL, Mandel E, McClinn S, et al. Spectral gradient acoustic reflectometry for the detection of middle ear effusion by pediatricians and parents. Pediatr Infect Dis J 1998;17:560–4.
19. Paradise JL, Elster BA, Tan L. Evidence in infants with cleft palate that breast milk protects against otitis media. Pediatrics 1994;94:853–60.
20. Paradise JL, Rockette HE, Colborn K, et al. Otitis media in 2253 Pittsburgh-area infants: prevalence and risk factors during the first two years of life. Pediatrics 1997;99:318–33.
21. Etzel RA, Pattishall EN, Haley NJ, et al. Passive smoking and middle ear effusion among children in day care. Pediatrics 1992;90:228–32.
22. DiFranza JR, Lew RA. Morbidity and mortality in children associated with the use of tobacco products by other people. Pediatrics 1996;97:560–8.
23. Marx J, Osguthorpe D, Parsons G. Day care and the incidence of otitis media in young children. Otolaryngol Head Neck Surg 1995;112:695–9.
24. Kværner KJ, Nafstad P, Hagen JA, et al. Early acute otitis media and siblings' attendance at nursery. Arch Dis Child 1996;75:338–41.
25. Dewey C, Midgeley E, Maw R. The relationship between otitis media with effusion and contact with other children in a British cohort studied from 8 months to 3½ years. The ALSPAC Study Team. Avon Longitudinal Study of Pregnancy and Childhood. Int J Pediatr Otorhinolaryngol 2000;55:33–45.
26. Postma DS, Poole MD, Wu SM, Tober R. The impact of day care on ventilation tube insertion. Int J Pediatr Otorhinolaryngol 1997;41:253–62.
27. Bernstein JM. The role of IgE-mediated hypersensitivity in the development of otitis media with effusion. Otolaryngol Clin North Am 1992;25:197–211.
28. Bernstein JM. Role of allergy in eustachian tube blockage and otitis media with effusion: a review. Otolaryngol Head Neck Surg 1996;114:562–8.
29. Stangerup SE, Sederberg-Olsen J, Balle V. Autoinflation as at treatment of secretory otitis media: a randomized controlled study. Arch Otolaryngol Head Neck Surg 1992;118:149–52.
30. Chan KH, Bluestone CD. Lack of efficacy of middle-ear inflation: treatment of otitis media with effusion in children. Otolaryngol Head Neck Surg 1989;100:317–23.
31. Brooker DS, McNeice A. Autoinflation in the treatment of glue ear in children. Clin Otolaryngol 1992;17:289–90.
32. Reidpath DD, Glasziou PP, Del Mar C. Systematic review of autoinflation for treatment of glue ear in children. BMJ 1999;318:1177–8.
33. Sederberg-Olsen J, Sederberg-Olsen N, Thomsen J, Balle V. Problems in recruiting patients to controlled trials on children with secretory otitis media. A demographic comparison of excluded versus included patients. Int J Pediatr Otorhinolaryngol 1998;43:229–33.

34. Butler CC, van der Voort JH. Oral or topical nasal steroids for hearing loss associated with otitis media with effusion in children (Cochrane Review). In: The Cochrane Library, Issue 2, 2002. Oxford (UK): Update Software; 2002.

35. Williamson I. Otitis media with effusion. Clin Evid 2002;7:469–76.

36. Rosenfeld RM, Mandel EM, Bluestone CD. Systemic steroids for otitis media with effusion in children. Arch Otolaryngol Head Neck Surg 1991;117:984–9.

37. Rosenfeld RM, Post JC. Meta-analysis of antibiotics for the treatment of otitis media with effusion. Otolaryngol Head Neck Surg 1992;106:378–86.

38. Williams RL, Chalmers TC, Stange KC, et al. Use of antibiotics in preventing recurrent acute otitis media and in treating otitis media with effusion: a meta-analytic attempt to resolve the brouhaha. JAMA 1993;270:1344–51.

39. Pignataro O, Pignataro LD, Gallus G, et al. Otitis media with effusion and S-carboxymethylcysteine and/or its lysine salt: a critical overview. Int J Pediatr Otorhino-laryngol 1996;35:231–41.

40. Post JC, Preston RA, Aul JJ, et al. Molecular analysis of bacterial comments in otitis media with effusion. JAMA 1995;273:1598–604.

41. Hendolin PH, Markkanen A, Ylikoski J, Wahlfors JJ. Use of multiplex PCR for simultaneous detection of four bacterial species in middle ear effusions. J Clin Micro-biol 1997;35:2854–8.

42. Marks NJ, Mills RP, Shaheen OH. A controlled trial of cotrimoxazole therapy in serous otitis media. J Laryngol Otol 1981;95:1003–9.

43. Mandel EM, Rockette HE, Bluestone CD, et al. Efficacy of amoxicillin with and without decongestant-antihistamine for otitis media with effusion in children: results of a double-blind randomized trial. N Engl J Med 1987;316:432–7.

44. Schloss MD, Dempsey EE, Rishikof E, et al. Double blind study comparing erythromycin-sulfisoxazole (Pediazole) t.i.d. to placebo in chronic otitis media with effusion. In: Lim DJ, Bluestone CD, Klein JO, Nelson JD, editors. Proceedings of the Fourth International Symposium on Recent Advances in Otitis Media; 1987 June 1–4; Bal Harbour (FL). Toronto: BC Decker, 1988. p. 261–3.

45. Thomsen J, Sederberg-Olsen J, Balle V, et al. Antibiotic treatment of children with secretory otitis media: a ran-domized, double-blind, placebo-controlled study. Arch Otolaryngol Head Neck Surg 1989;115:447–51.

46. Møller P, Dingsør G. Otitis media with effusion: can erythromycin reduce the need for ventilating tubes? J Laryngol Otol 1990;140:200–2.

47. Podoshin L, Fradis M, Ben-David Y, Faraggi D. The effi-cacy of oral steroids in the treatment of persistent otitis media with effusion. Arch Otolaryngol Head Neck Surg 1990;116:1404–6.

48. Daly K, Giebink GS, Batalden PB, et al. Resolution of otitis media with effusion with the use of a stepped treatment regimen of trimethoprim-sulfamethoxazole and prednisone. Pediatr Infect Dis J 1991;10:500–6.

49. Mandel EM, Rockette HE, Paradise JL, et al. Compara-tive efficacy of erythromycin-sulfisoxazole, cefaclor, amoxicillin or placebo for otitis media with effusion in children. Pediatr Infect Dis J 1991;10:899–906.

50. van Balen FAM, de Melker RA, Touw-Otten FWMM. Double-blind randomised trial of co-amoxiclav versus placebo for persistent otitis media with effusion in general practice. Lancet 1996;348:713–6.

51. Healy GB. Antimicrobial therapy of chronic otitis media with effusion. Int J Pediatr Otorhinolaryngol 1984;8:13–7.

52. Ernstson S, Anari M. Cefaclor in the treatment of otitis media with effusion. Acta Otolaryngol (Stockh) 1985; Suppl 424:17–21.

53. Corwin MJ, Weiner LB, Daniels D. Efficacy of oral anti-biotics for the treatment of persistent otitis media with effusion. Int J Pediatr Otorhinolaryngol 1986;11:109–12.

54. Giebink GS, Batalden PB, Le CT, et al. A controlled trial comparing three treatments for chronic otitis media with effusion. Pediatr Infect Dis J 1990;9:33–40.

55. Varsano I, Volvitz B, Mimouni F. Sulfisoxazole prophy-laxis of middle ear effusion and recurrent acute otitis media. Am J Dis Child 1985;139:632–5.

56. deCastro FJ, Jaeger RW, Martin L, et al. Serous otitis media: a double-blind trial with sulfisoxazole. Mo Med 1982;79:629–30.

57. Schwartz RH, Rodriguez WJ. Trimethoprim-sulfamethoxazole treatment of persistent otitis media with effusion. Pediatr Infect Dis 1982;1:333–5.

58. Cantekin EI, McGuire TW, Griffith TL. Antimicrobial therapy for otitis media with effusion ('secretory' otitis media). JAMA 1991;266:3309–17.

59. Thomsen J, Sederberg-Olsen J, Balle V, Hartzen S. Anti-biotic treatment of children with secretory otitis media. Arch Otolaryngol Head Neck Surg 1997;123:695–9.

60. Dowell SF, Marcy M, Phillips WR, et al. Otitis media—principles of judicious use of antimicrobial agents. Pedi-atrics 1998;101 Suppl:165–71.

61. Mandel EM, Casselbrant ML, Rockette HE, et al. Efficacy of antimicrobial prophylaxis for recurrent middle-ear effusion. Pediatr Infect Dis J 1996;15:1074–82.

62. Safak MA, Kilic R, Haberal I, et al. A comparative study of azithromycin and pseudoephedrine hydrochloride for otitis media with effusion in children. Acta Otolaryn-gol 2001;121:925–9.

63. Cantekin EI, Mandel EM, Bluestone CD, et al. Lack of efficacy of a decongestant-antihistamine combination for otitis media with effusion ("secretory" otitis media) in children: results of a double-blind, randomized trial. N Engl J Med 1983;308:297–301.

64. Dusdieker LB, Smith G, Booth BM, et al. The long-term outcome of nonsuppurative otitis media with effusion. Clin Pediatr 1985;24:181–6.

65. Haugeto OK, Schrøder, Mair IWS. Secretory otitis media, oral decongestant and antihistamine. J Otolaryngol 1981;10:359–62.

66. Turner RB, Darden PM. Effect of topical adrenergic decongestants on middle ear pressure in infants with common colds. Pediatr Infect Dis J 1996;15:621–4.

67. Commins DJ, Koay BC, Bates GJ, et al. The role of Mucodyne in reducing the need for surgery in patients

with persistent otitis media with effusion. Clin Otolaryngol 2000;25:274–9.

68. Oversen T, Felding JU, Tommerup B, et al. Effect of N-acetylcysteine on the incidence of recurrence of otitis media with effusion and re-insertion of ventilation tubes. Acta Otolaryngol 2000;Suppl 543:79–81.

69. Macknin ML, Jones PK. Oral dexamethasone for treatment of persistent middle ear effusion. Pediatrics 1985;75:329–35.

70. Niederman LG, Walter-Bucholtz V, Jabalay T. A comparative trial of steroids versus placebos for treatment of chronic otitis media with effusion. In: Lim DJ, Bluestone CD, Klein JO, Nelson JD, editors. Proceedings of the 4th International Symposium on Recent Advances in Otitis Media. Burlington (ON): BC Decker Inc; 1988. p. 273–5.

71. Berman S, Grose K, Nuss R, et al. Management of chronic middle ear effusion with prednisone combined with trimethoprim-sulfamethoxazole. Pediatr Infect Dis J 1990;9:533–8.

72. Lambert PR. Oral steroid therapy for chronic middle ear effusion: a double-blind crossover study. Otolaryngol Head Neck Surg 1986;95:193–9.

73. Schwartz RH, Puglese J, Schwartz DM. Use of a short course of prednisone for treating middle ear effusion: a double-blind crossover study. Ann Otol Rhinol Laryngol 1980;89 Suppl 68:296–300.

74. Mandel EM, Casselbrant ML, Rockette HE, et al. Systemic steroid for chronic otitis media with effusion in children. Pediatrics 2002;110:1071–80.

75. Rosenfeld RM. Nonsurgical management of surgical otitis media with effusion. J Laryngol Otol 1995;109:811–6.

76. Rosenfeld RM. New concepts for steroid use in otitis media with effusion. Clin Pediatr 1992;31:615–21.

77. Tracy JM, Demain JG, Hoffman KM, Goetz DW. Intranasal beclomethasone as an adjunct to treatment of chronic middle ear effusion. Ann Allergy Asthma Immunol 1998;80:198–206.

78. Testa B, Testa D, Mesolella M, et al. Management of chronic otitis media with effusion: the role of glutathione. Laryngoscope 2001;111:1486–9.

79. Sano S, Kamide Y, Schachern PA, Paparella MM. Micropathologic changes of pars tensa in children with otitis media with effusion. Arch Otolaryngol Head Neck Surg 1994;120:815–9.

80. Maw RA, Bawden R. Tympanic membrane atrophy, scarring, atelectasis and attic retraction in persistent, untreated otitis media with effusion and following ventilation tube insertion. Int J Pediatr Otorhinolaryngol 1994;30:189–204.

81. Fria TJ, Cantekin EI, Eichler JA. Hearing acuity of children with otitis media with effusion. Arch Otolaryngol 1985;111:10–6.

82. Wiederhold ML, Zajtchuk JT, Vap JG, Paggi RE. Hearing loss in relation to physical properties of middle ear effusions. Ann Otol Rhinol Laryngol 1980;89 Suppl 68:185–9.

83. Rosenfeld RM, Goldsmith AJ, Madell JR. How accurate is parent rating of hearing for children with otitis media? Arch Otolaryngol Head Neck Surg 1998;124:989–92.

84. Brody R, Rosenfeld RM, Goldsmith AJ, Madell JR. Parents cannot detect mild hearing loss in children. Otolaryngol Head Neck Surg 1999;121:681–6.

85. Stewart MG, Ohlms LA, Friedman SM, et al. Is parental perception an accurate predictor of childhood hearing loss? A prospective study. Otolaryngol Head Neck Surg 1999;120:340–4.

86. Anteunis LJC, Engel JAM, Hendriks JJT, Manni JJ. A longitudinal study of the validity of parental reporting in the detection of otitis media and related hearing impairment in infancy. Audiology 1999;38:75–82.

87. Stephenson H, Haggard M, Zielhuis G, et al. Prevalence of tympanogram asymmetries and fluctuations in otitis media with effusions: implications for binaural hearing. Audiology 1993;32:164–74.

88. Mandel EM, Rockette HE, Bluestone CD, et al. Myringotomy with and without tympanostomy tubes for chronic otitis media with effusion. Arch Otolaryngol Head Neck Surg 1989;115:1217–24.

89. Gravel JS, Ellis MA. The auditory consequences of otitis media with effusion: the audiogram and beyond. Semin Hear 1995;16:45–59

90. Rosenfeld RM, Madell JR, McMahon A. Auditory function in normal-hearing children with middle ear effusion. In: Lim DJ, Bluestone CD, Casselbrant M, Klein JO, Ogra PL, editors. Recent advances in otitis media. Proceedings of the Sixth International Symposium June 4–8, 1995. Hamilton (ON): BC Decker, Inc; 1996. p. 354–6.

91. Ruben RJ. Language screening as a factor in the management of the pediatric otolaryngic patient: effectiveness and efficiency. Arch Otolaryngol Head Neck Surg 1991;117:1021–5.

92. Glade MJ. Diagnostic and therapeutic technology assessment: speech therapy in patients with a prior history of recurrent acute or chronic otitis media with effusion. JAMA 1996;1–14.

93. Klee T, Pearch K, Carson DK. Improvinjg the predictive value of screening for developmental language disorder. J Speech Lang Hear Res 2000;43:821–33.

94. Roberts JE, Burchinal MR, Zeisel SA, et al. Otitis media, the caregiving environment, and language and cognitive outcomes at 2 years. Pediatrics 1998;102:346–54.

95. Paradise JL, Dollaghan CA, Campbell TF, et al. Language, speech sound production, and cognition in three-year-old children in relation to otitis media in their first three years of life. Pediatrics 2000;105:1119–30.

96. Casselbrant ML, Furman JM, Rubenstein E, Mandel EM. Effect of otitis media on the vestibular system in children. Ann Otol Rhinol Laryngol 1995;104:620–4.

97. Orlin MN, Effgen SK, Handler SD. Effect of otitis media with effusion on gross motor ability in preschool-aged children: preliminary findings. Pediatrics 1997;99:334–7.

98. Golz A, Netzer A, Angel-Yeger B, et al. Effects of middle ear effusion on the vestibular system in children. Otolaryngol Head Neck Surg 1998;119:695–9.

99. Casselbrant ML, Redfern MS, Furman JM, et al. Visual-induced postural sway in children with and without otitis media. Ann Otol Rhinol Laryngol 1998;107:401–5.

100. Koyuncu M, Saka MM, Tanyeri Y, et al. Effects of otitis media with effusion on the vestibular system in chil-

dren. Otolaryngol Head Neck Surg 1999;120:117–21.

101. Haggard MP, Birkin JA, Browning GG, et al. Behavior problems in otitis media. Pediatr Infect Dis J 1994;13: S43–50.

102. Timmerman AA, Anteunis LJC, Meesters CMG. The initial development of an instrument for the description of "otitis media with effusion specific behavior" in young children. Int J Behav Med 2000;6:255–67.

103. Asmussen L, Olson LM, Sullivan SA. 'You have to live it to understand it…' Family experiences with chronic otitis media in children. Ambul Child Health 1999;5:303–12.

104. Rosenfeld RM, Bhaya MH, Bower CM, et al. Impact of tympanostomy tubes on child quality of life. Arch Otolaryngol Head Neck Surg 2000;126:585–92.

105. Rovers MM, Krabbe PF, Straatman H, et al. Randomised controlled trial of the effect of ventilation tubes (grommets) on quality of life at age 1-2 years. Arch Dis Child 2001;84:45–9.

106. Gates GA, Avery CA, Prihoda TJ, Cooper JC Jr. Effectiveness of adenoidectomy and tympanostomy tubes in the treatment of chronic otitis media with effusion. N Engl J Med 1987;317:1444–51.

107. Mandel EM, Rockette HE, Bluestone CD, et al. Efficacy of myringotomy with and without tympanostomy tubes for chronic otitis media with effusion. Pediatr Infect Dis J 1992;11:270–7.

108. University of York. Centre for Reviews and Dissemination. The treatment of persistent glue ear in children. Effect Health Care 1992;1(4):1–16.

109. Rovers MM, Straatman H, Ingels K, et al. The effect of short-term ventilation tubes versus watchful waiting on hearing in young children with persistent otitis media with effusion: a randomized trial. Ear Hear 2001;22:191–9.

110. Holmes-Rovner M, Kroll J, Schmitt N, et al. Patient satisfaction with health care decisions: the satisfaction with decision scale. Med Decis Making 1996;16:58–64.

111. Hadfield PJ, Rowe-Jones JM, Bush A, Mackay IS. Treatment of otitis media with effusion in children with primary ciliary dyskinesia. Clin Otolaryngol 1997; 22:302–6.

112. Paradise JL, Bluestone CD, Rogers KD, et al. Efficacy of adenoidectomy for recurrent otitis media in children previously treated with tympanostomy-tube placement: results of parallel randomized and nonrandomized trials. JAMA 1990;263:2066–73.

113. Maw RA. Chronic otitis media with effusion (glue ear) and adenotonsillectomy: prospective randomised controlled study. BMJ 1983;287:1586–8.

114. Paradise JL, Bluestone CD, Colborn DK, et al. Adenoidectomy and adenotonsillectomy for recurrent acute otitis media: parallel randomized clinical trials in children not previously treated with tympanostomy tubes. JAMA 1999;282:945–53.

115. Salata JA, Derkay CS. Water precautions in children with tympanostomy tubes. Arch Otolaryngol Head Neck Surg 1996;122:276–80.

116. Kay DJ, Nelson M, Rosenfeld RM. Meta-analysis of tympanostomy tube sequelae. Otolaryngol Head Neck Surg 2001;124:374–80.

117. Armstrong BW. Prolonged middle ear ventilation: the right tube in the right place. Ann Otol Rhinol Laryngol 1993;92:582–6.

118. Manning SC, Brown OE, Roland PS, Phillips DL. Incidence of sensorineural hearing loss in patients evaluated for tympanostomy tubes. Arch Otolaryngol Head Neck Surg 1994;120:881–4.

119. Shott SR, Joseph A, Heithaus D. Hearing loss in children with Down syndrome. Int J Pediatr Otorhinolaryngol 2001;61:199–205.

120. Coyte PC, Croxford R, McIsaac W, et al. The role of adjuvant adenoidectomy and tonsillectomy in the outcome of insertion of tympanostomy tubes. N Engl J Med 2001;344:1188–95.

121. Sade J. Pathology and pathogenesis of serous otitis media. Arch Otolaryngol 1966;84:297–305.

122. Neel HB III, Keating LW, McDonald TJ. Ventilation in secretory otitis media. Arch Otolaryngol 1977;103: 228–31.

123. Brodsky L, Cook S, Deutsch E, et al. Optimizing effectiveness of laser tympanic membrane fenestration in chronic otitis media with effusion: clinical and technical considerations. Int J Pediatr Otorhinolaryngol 2001;58:59–64.

124. Holzman RS. Morbidity and mortality in pediatric anesthesia. Pediatr Clin North Am 1994;41:239–56.

125. Cotrell JE, Golden S. Under the mask: a guide to feeling secure and comfortable during anesthesia and surgery. New Brunswick (NJ): Rutgers University Press; 2001.

126. Crysdale WS, Russel D. Complications of tonsillectomy and adenoidectomy in 9409 children observed overnight. Can Med Assoc J 1986;135:1139–42.

127. Osler W. On the educational value of the medical society. In: Aequanimitas. Philadelphia (PA): P. Blakiston's Son & Co.; 1904. p. 348.

128. Parhiscar A, Rosenfeld RM. Can patient satisfaction with decisions predict compliance with surgery? Otolaryngol Head Neck Surg 2002;126:365–70.

CHAPTER 20

International Perspective on Management

Anne G.M. Schilder, MD, PhD, and Maroeska M. Rovers, PhD

Support bacteria…they are the only culture some people have.
Steve Eskes

OBJECTIVES

On completing this chapter, the reader will be able to
1. State the large variation in management of acute otitis media (AOM) across Western countries.
2. Recognize potential reasons for this variety in management.
3. Appreciate international efforts to reduce the use of antibiotics for AOM.
4. Quantify the relationship between antibiotic prescription for AOM and complications such as acute mastoiditis.

International rates of antibiotic prescribing and surgery for AOM vary greatly. With antibiotic resistance rising and more evidence regarding the limited clinical efficacy of antibiotics becoming available, interest in nonantibiotic management of AOM has increased. Rational treatment decisions require knowledge, not only of the efficacy of various treatment options but also of potential complications. In this chapter, we discuss international rates of antibiotic prescription and surgery for AOM, current evidence regarding the efficacy of these treatment options, and their complications, such as bacterial resistance and acute mastoiditis. We also discuss recent international efforts for judicious use of antibiotics in treating AOM.

INTERNATIONAL MANAGEMENT OF AOM

Antibiotic Prescribing

Cars and colleagues[1] recently reported data on outpatient antibiotic sales for the year 1997 in 15 countries of the European Union (Figure 20-1). They showed that the daily-defined dose of antibiotics per 1,000 people, irrespective of the condition for which they were prescribed, varied more than fourfold between European countries,

from 9 in the Netherlands to 37 in France. Obviously, this large variation cannot be explained by differences in frequency of bacterial infections.

In 1986, Froom and colleagues[2] monitored the diagnosis and treatment of AOM in general practice in four European countries, Israel, Australia, New Zealand, and the United States. The percentage of patients given antibiotics for AOM varied from 31% in the Netherlands to 85% in Belgium and more than 90% in other countries (Figure 20-2).

Surgery

No formal comparison of tympanostomy tube insertion rates across countries is available, but for several countries, tympanostomy tube insertion rates have been published (Figure 20-3). In the United Kingdom, about 2 out of 1,000 children younger than 15 years of age receive tympanostomy tubes.[3] In Canada and the United States, this surgical rate is 8 and 9 per 1,000 children, respectively.[4,5] In the Netherlands, where only 1 in 3 children with AOM is treated with antibiotics, 20 per 1,000 children younger than 12 years are treated with tympanostomy tubes annually.[6]

Regarding adenoidectomy, we calculated the 1998 surgical rate in several countries of the European Union, the United States, and Canada as the total number of day care and inpatient procedures, performed in children aged 0 to 14 years, divided by the 1998 mid-year population estimate of children in the same age range. Adenoidectomy rates varied from 17 per 10,000 children in Canada to 101 and 129 per 10,000 children in the Netherlands and Finland, respectively (Figure 20-4).

These data confirm that management strategies for AOM vary considerably. They also suggest that physicians who practice a restrictive policy regarding antibiotics for AOM may conversely be more liberal in their indications for surgery.

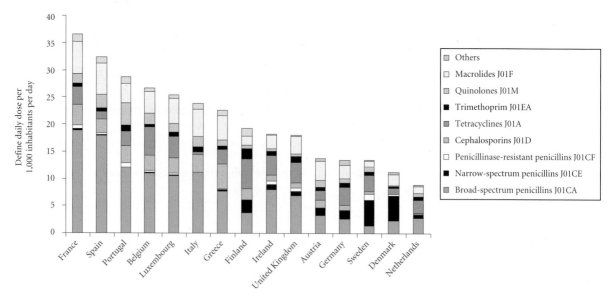

Figure 20-1 Outpatient antibiotic sales in the European Union in 1997. Cars O et al.[1]

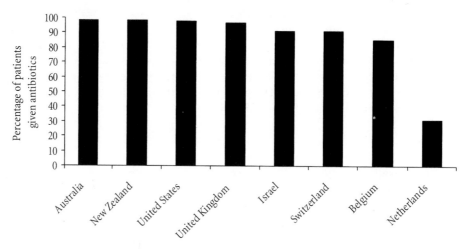

Figure 20-2 International antibiotic prescription rates for acute otitis media in 1986. Froom J et al.[2]

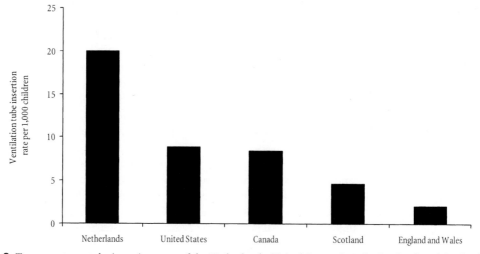

Figure 20-3 Tympanostomy tube insertion rates of the Netherlands, United States, Canada, Scotland, and England and Wales.

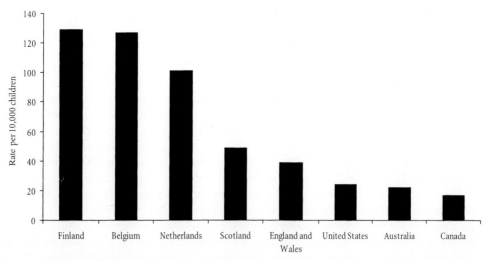

Figure 20-4 International pediatric adenoidectomy rates in 1998.

EFFICACY OF ANTIBIOTICS AND SURGERY

The clinical efficacy of medical and surgical therapies for AOM is described in detail in Chapters 13, "Clinical Efficacy of Medical Therapy" and 14, "Clinical Efficacy of Surgical Therapy". In this chapter, we briefly summarize relevant evidence regarding antibiotic therapy, tympanostomy tube insertion, and adenoidectomy.

Antibiotic Therapy

Recently, three meta-analyses concerning the efficacy of antibiotic therapy in AOM have been published.[7–9] Because criteria for studies to be included in the analyses and definition of AOM and clinical outcomes have not been uniform, the results of these three meta-analyses vary.

Glasziou and colleagues[7] performed a meta-analysis for The Cochrane Collaboration of seven randomized, placebo-controlled trials in children aged 6 months to 15 years. They showed that antibiotics do not reduce pain at 24 hours. At 2 to 7 days, approximately 80% of the children had recovered spontaneously, and antibiotics achieved a further relative reduction in pain of 28% (95% confidence interval [CI], 15, 38%). Overall, 5% fewer children had pain at 2 to 7 days, meaning that about 17 needed to be treated (NNT) to prevent one child having pain after 2 days.

The Agency for Healthcare Research and Quality[8] performed a meta-analysis of five randomized controlled trials (RCTs) in children aged 4 weeks to 18 years. Outcome was defined as failure to resolve or improve clinical signs and symptoms within 2 to 7 days. They showed that ampicillin or amoxicillin reduce the absolute clinical failure rate by 12% (95% CI, –3, 22%)

compared with placebo or observational therapy. This estimate yields an NNT of about 8 children.

Rosenfeld[9] performed a meta-analysis of eight RCTs comparing antibiotics with placebo or no drug as initial therapy for AOM in children aged 6 months to 15 years. Initial antibiotic therapy reduced symptoms of pain and fever by 4% (NNT 25) at 2 to 3 days; at 24 hours and 4 to 7 days of treatment no beneficial effect of antibiotics was found. Complete clinical resolution (exclusive of middle ear effusion [MEE]) was modestly improved by antibiotics (NNT 8) at 7 to 14 days. An updated version of this meta-analysis can be found in Chapter 13.

Tympanostomy Tubes

A meta-analysis of five RCTs[10] of tympanostomy tubes versus no surgery in children aged 6 months to 12 years with recurrent AOM showed that tubes reduce the AOM incidence by a mean of 1.0 episode per child-year (95% CI, 0.4, 1.6); this is a relative decrease of 56% (95% CI, 21, 76%). The greatest benefit was found in the first 6 to 12 months of follow-up. Tympanostomy tubes reduced the prevalence of MEE by 115 days per child-year (95% CI, 11, 220). The validity of this meta-analysis, however, is limited due to heterogeneity and modest sample sizes. An updated version of this meta-analysis can be found in Chapter 14.

Adenoidectomy

On the basis of two trials by Paradise and colleagues,[11,12] Rosenfeld[10] concluded that adenoidectomy reduced the incidence of AOM by 0.3 episodes (95% CI, 0.03, 0.61) per child-year for a period of 3 years in children aged 1 to 15 years who had previously been treated with tympanostomy tubes. Adenoidectomy reduced the relative risk of needing future tubes by 50%. In children without prior tubes, no beneficial effect of adenoidectomy was found. Similarly, Coyte and coworkers[13] examined the hospital records of 37,316 children aged 19 years or younger who received tympanostomy tubes as their first surgical therapy for otitis media (OM). They found that adjuvant adenoidectomy reduced the likelihood of re-insertion of tympanostomy tubes by 50% (relative risk [RR] 0.5; 95% CI, 0.5, 0.6).

Overall, these data indicate that the benefit of both antibiotics and surgery for children with AOM is modest. On an absolute basis, between 8 and 25 children with AOM need antibiotic treatment to achieve a single clinical cure, about 3 to 4 children need adenoidectomy to avoid one AOM episode per year, and about 8 children need adenoidectomy to prevent one future tube insertion.

REASONS FOR INTERNATIONAL VARIETY IN MANAGEMENT

International variations in antibiotic prescribing and surgical interventions exist because guidelines on the management of AOM vary considerably. As a result of insufficient scientific evidence regarding the best strategy in children with AOM, current guidelines are also based on clinical judgment and expert opinions. Given the variety in these opinions, diversity in the resulting guidelines is expected.

Physicians' and patients' perception of the benefit of antibiotics and their expectation of the outcome of a consultation are also important determinants of AOM management. For example, Butler and colleagues[14] showed in a survey of antibiotic prescribing for sore throats that although physicians felt that the patient wanted something done and expected antibiotics, the majority of patients actually consulted for reassurance. They concluded that irrational prescribing is a cultural problem that goes beyond doctors simply not knowing of the evidence.[14]

Finally, disparities in the organization of health care play a role.[15] For example, in the Netherlands, family physicians are considered the gatekeepers of the health care system, and expenses of primary care are covered by national or private insurance. Every family is registered at a local family practice and common conditions, such as AOM, are primarily managed by the family physicians. This system might encourage more frugal prescribing than in many other countries, where AOM is managed primarily by pediatricians or a fee-for-service policy is practiced. Also, the Netherlands has a nationwide structure of family physician peer-review groups, collaborating with local pharmacists, to promote rational prescribing through audit and feedback. Most other countries have no such structure.

INTERNATIONAL EFFORTS TO PROMOTE JUDICIOUS ANTIBIOTIC USE

In the Netherlands, a restrictive use of antibiotics for AOM has been practiced since the early 1990s. A recent update of the guidelines on AOM developed by the Dutch College of General Practitioners[16] recommends initial observation in children older than 6 months of age presenting with AOM. Antibiotics are indicated for recurrent AOM within 12 months and for children with an increased risk of complications, age under 6 months, Down syndrome, craniofacial malformation, or immunodeficiency. Antibiotic therapy is also recommended in children with progressive general illness or earache, poor fluid intake, or no improvement of symptoms after 3 days.

More recently, initiatives to promote judicious use of antibiotics in AOM have been started in other countries as well.[17–20] For example, the "Observation Option Toolkit for AOM," developed by the New York Region Otitis Project (NYROP),[18] recommends initial observation in children aged 2 years or older, particularly when the illness is nonsevere or the AOM diagnosis is uncertain. Initial antibiotic therapy is recommended for all children under 2 years of age with a certain diagnosis of AOM. In children aged 6 months to 2 years, initial observation may be acceptable in case of an uncertain diagnosis and a nonsevere illness but only when follow-up can be assured. It has been estimated that if clinicians would manage AOM according to this NYROP guideline, initial antibiotics would not be prescribed for 29% of AOM episodes.[17]

Little and colleagues[19] have published an open randomized trial in the United Kingdom comparing standard management of AOM (ie, immediate antibiotics) with a 72-hour wait-and-see policy. They demonstrated that immediate prescription of antibiotics for AOM reduced the duration of illness, but the benefit occurred mainly after the first 24 hours, when symptoms were already resolving. They concluded that for children presenting with AOM who are not very unwell systemically, an observational period seems feasible and acceptable to parents. Implementing this policy would result in a 76% reduction in the use of antibiotic prescriptions for AOM in the United Kingdom.

The most recent Norwegian consensus recommends that uncomplicated AOM should not be treated with antibiotics. Antibiotics should only be prescribed to children younger than 1 year of age and to children with recurrent episodes of AOM, that is, children who have had 3 or more episodes of AOM during the previous 6 months or 4 or more episodes during the previous year.[20]

It is important to realize that managing children with AOM without antibiotics should not be confused with

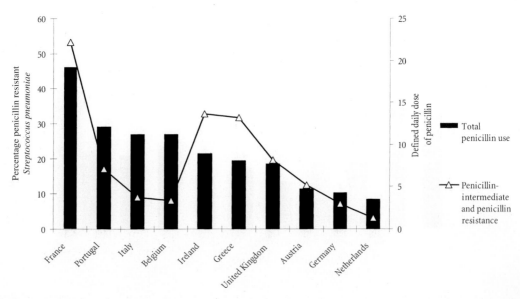

Figure 20-5 Penicillin consumption (1997) and penicillin intermediate and resistance of *Streptococcus pneumoniae* (1998) in Europe. Cars O et al[1] and Schito GC et al.[21]

withholding therapy. Children with AOM should receive medical care. During the initial observation period of 2 to 3 days, children should be given adequate analgesics and symptomatic relief. Parents should be instructed to monitor their child carefully and be informed about the natural course of AOM and signs of complications.

COMPLICATIONS OF ANTIBIOTICS AND SURGERY

The most important complication of antibiotic therapy is accelerated antibiotic resistance. In Figure 20-5, we show the relationship between daily penicillin consumption for 10 countries and the corresponding prevalence of penicillin-resistant *Streptococcus pneumoniae*. The data illustrate an inverse association between antibiotic use and resistance: the 1998 prevalence of penicillin-resistant (intermediate and resistant) *S. pneumoniae* strains ranged from 3% in the Netherlands to 53% in France,[21] while the daily defined dose of broad- and narrow-spectrum penicillin varied from 4 to 19 per 1,000 inhabitants in the Netherlands and France, respectively.[1]

Complications of tympanostomy tubes are described in detail in Chapter 29, "Tympanostomy Tube Care and Consequences". Apart from otorrhea occurring in 50% of children with tympanostomy tubes,[22] tube insertion can induce tympanosclerosis and atrophy of the tympanic membrane. These changes are found in 40 to 65% and 16 to 73% of the ears treated with tubes, as opposed to 0 to 10% and 5 to 31%, respectively, of the ears that have not been treated surgically.[23] The hearing loss

associated with these tympanic abnormalities is small, that is, less than 5 dB.[23] Persistent perforation of the tympanic membrane after short-term tubes occurs in 0.5 to 2% of ears.[24,25]

Apart from postoperative pain, complications of adenoidectomy are very rare. No good estimates of the incidence of scarring of the nasopharynx affecting the airway or Eustachian tube function, or postoperative hemorrhage after adenoidectomy alone are available.[26,27]

RELATIONSHIP BETWEEN ACUTE MASTOIDITIS AND ANTIBIOTIC PRESCRIBING FOR AOM

The alarming rise in antibiotic resistance and the modest benefit of antibiotic therapy for AOM has prompted clinicians and researchers to consider a more selective approach to therapy. What prevents most physicians from not prescribing antibiotics for a child with AOM, however, is a fear of suppurative complications. In the preantibiotic era, the incidence rate of acute mastoiditis as a complication of AOM was estimated at 20%.[28]

Complications of AOM are presently rare, but there is little evidence that antibiotics alone are responsible for this decrease (see also Chapter 18, "Clinical Pathway for Acute Otitis Media"). RTCs, to date, have not shown that withholding antibiotics initially in children with AOM is associated with a higher risk of suppurative complications.[9] In several of these trials, however, very ill children and children younger than 2 years of age were excluded, which may have had implications for external validity.

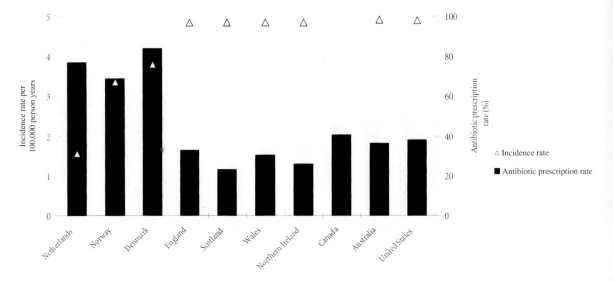

Figure 20-6 Incidence rates of acute mastoiditis in children age 14 years and younger (1991–1998) versus antibiotic prescription rates for AOM. Van Zuijlen DA et al.[29]

Furthermore, due to the low incidence rate of mastoiditis, the power of most RCTs performed so far has not been high enough to obtain a valid and precise risk estimate of this complication.

One way to study the relationship between antibiotic prescription for AOM and the risk of suppurative complications is to compare national incidence rates of acute mastoiditis across countries with varying antibiotic prescription rates. Figure 20-6 shows the results of this comparison,[29] which suggests the following conclusions:

- Incidence rates of acute mastoiditis in children aged 14 years and younger in the period 1991 to 1998 in the United Kingdom, Canada, Australia, and the United States, where antibiotic prescription rates for AOM are all above 96%, ranged from 1.2 (95% CI, 0.9, 1.5) to 2.0 (95% CI, 1.8, 2.2) per 100,000 person years.
- Incidence rates in Norway and Denmark, where antibiotic prescription rates for AOM are 67% and 76%,[29] respectively, and in The Netherlands, where antibiotic prescription is 31%,[2] were considerably higher: 3.5 (95% CI, 2.9, 4.0), 4.2 (95% CI, 3.6, 4.8) and 3.8 (95% CI, 3.5, 4.1) per 100,000 person years, respectively.
- The exact 95% confidence interval of the incidence rate in The Netherlands does not overlap with those of the other countries, except for Norway and Denmark. The incidence rate ratios (RR), with the Netherlands as a reference, ranged from 0.3 in Scotland (95% CI, 0.2, 0.4) to 0.5 in Canada (95% CI, 0.4, 0.6).
- The United States rate ratio was also 0.5. Its CIs could not be calculated because the American data were derived from a random sample of hospitals.
- Norway and Denmark did not differ significantly

from the Netherlands (RR 0.9; 95% CI, 0.8, 1.1; and RR 1.1; 95% CI, 0.9, 1.3, respectively).

These data suggest that initial observation of children with AOM results in 1 to 2 extra cases of acute mastoiditis per 100,000 children per year, although such a causal relationship is not fully supported by these data. Whereas, for example, the incidence rate in Norway and Denmark was comparable with the rate in the Netherlands, antibiotic prescription rates for AOM in Scandinavia are twice as high.[30,31] Also, the 1997 incidence rate in New York City and adjacent counties Westchester and Nassau, a region with a total population of 7.6 million (twice the population of Norway), where antibiotics are prescribed to almost all children with AOM, was comparable with those of The Netherlands, Norway, and Denmark at 4 per 100,000 children (data provided by the Montefiore Medical Center Planning Department, New York).

Assuming that the higher incidence rate of acute mastoiditis in The Netherlands is real, and that it is caused by restricted use of antibiotics for AOM, the question arises whether 2 additional cases of acute mastoiditis per 100,000 children per year compared with other countries warrant abandoning of the initial observation strategy in AOM. The advantages of the Dutch policy of initial observation and restricted use of antibiotics for AOM are obvious: fewer antibiotic prescriptions and, therefore, cost reduction; fewer side effects from antibiotics; and a lower antibiotic resistance rate.

The incidence rate of AOM in Dutch children younger than 15 years of age is 120 per 1,000 children per year.[32] Given the antibiotic prescription rate of 31% in

Table 20-1 Pointers and Pitfalls

1. There are large international differences in management strategies for AOM.

2. This variation can be explained by the lack of uniform evidence-based guidelines, differences in physicians' and patients' expectations of the benefit of antibiotics, and in the organization of health care.

3. The benefit of antibiotic and surgical therapy in AOM is statistically significant in randomized controlled trials, but the effect size is modest and incremental.

4. In countries with low antibiotic prescribing rates, the incidence of acute mastoiditis is slightly higher.

5. The number of antibiotic prescriptions for AOM needed to prevent one episode of acute mastoiditis is high: at least 2,500 but more likely 5,000.

6. The only way to control emerging resistance is a more judicious use of antibiotics.

7. Efforts to limit antibiotic prescription for AOM have been undertaken, not only in The Netherlands but also in other European countries and in the United States.

8. Managing AOM in children without initial antibiotics should not be confused with withholding therapy because antibiotics are still used for observation failures.

9. International debates, with the aim of overcoming cultural differences regarding the management of otitis media and of reaching agreement on AOM guidelines on the basis of current evidence, are necessary.

AOM = acute otitis media.

The Netherlands as opposed to 96% elsewhere,[2] each year 7,800 fewer prescriptions for AOM per 100,000 children are issued. Up to 20% of children receiving antibiotic therapy for OM develop diarrhea, vomiting, or skin rash, and 1 to 5% experience allergic reactions, including anaphylaxis.[33] This adds up to an estimated 1,600 fewer side effects from antibiotic therapy in 100,000 children with AOM annually.

The number of antibiotic prescriptions for AOM that would be needed to prevent one episode of acute mastoiditis is extremely high: at least 2,500, in view of the low estimated incidence of acute mastoiditis in AOM of 0.4 per 1000 AOM episodes.[34] Moreover, not all cases of acute mastoiditis can be prevented by antibiotics. Retrospective studies[35–37] have shown that 36 to 87% of patients have received antibiotics for AOM prior to developing acute mastoiditis. Taking 50 as the percentage of cases of acute mastoiditis prevented by antibiotic therapy of AOM, the NNT could be as high as 5,000.

SYNTHESIS AND NEED FOR FUTURE STUDIES

In this chapter, we have demonstrated large differences in antibiotic prescribing and surgery for AOM across the Western world, and that a restrictive policy regarding antibiotics might coincide with a more liberal policy regarding surgery (Table 20-1). These international differences are possible because of incomplete evidence about the efficacy of antibiotics and surgery and because

uniform management guidelines for childhood AOM are missing. Although the only way to control emerging bacterial resistance is by more judicious use of antibiotics, there is a need for further research to identify subgroups of children who might benefit from antibiotics or surgery and to find alternative management strategies.

Medical professionals, parents, and patients should be educated about the favorable natural course of AOM and the importance of judicious antibiotic use. But they should also be educated to recognize signs of complications, since a restrictive antibiotic policy may result in more cases of acute mastoiditis. Finally, international debates, with the aim of overcoming cultural differences regarding the management of OM and of reaching agreement on guidelines on the basis of current evidence, are necessary.

ACKNOWLEDGMENT

We acknowledge the contribution of Willeke Lok, MD, in preparing this chapter.

REFERENCES

1. Cars O, Molstad S, Melander A. Variation in antibiotic use in the European Union. Lancet 2001;357:1851–3.
2. Froom J, Culpepper L, Grob P, et al. Diagnosis and antibiotic treatment of acute otitis media: report from International Primary Care Network. BMJ 1990; 300:582–6.

3. Mason J, Freemantle N, Browning G. Impact of effective health care bulletin on treatment of persistent glue ear in children: time series analysis. BMJ 2001;323:1096–7.

4. Owings MF, Kozak LJ. Ambulatory and inpatient procedures in the United States, 1996. Vital Health Stat 1998;13:1–119.

5. Coyte PC, Croxford R, Asche CV, et al. Physician and population determinants of rates of middle-ear surgery in Ontario. JAMA 2001;286:2128–35.

6. Engel JAM, Anteunis LJC, Hendriks JJT. Treatment with grommets in the Netherlands: incidence in children from birth to 12 years. In: Tos M, Thomsen J, Balle V, editors. Otitis media today. The Hague/The Netherlands: Kugler Publications; 1999. p. 451–5.

7. Glasziou PP, Del Mar CB, Hayem M, Sanders SL. Antibiotics for acute otitis media in children. Cochrane Database Syst Rev. 2000;CD000219.

8. Marcy M, Takata G, Shekelle P, et al. Management of acute otitis media. Evidence report no. 15 (Prepared by the Southern California evidence-based practice center). AHRQ publication no. 01-E010. Rockville (MD): Agency for Healthcare Research and Quality; 2001.

9. Rosenfeld RM. What to expect from medical therapy. In: Rosenfeld RM, Bluestone CD, editors. Evidence-based otitis media. Hamilton (ON): BC Decker Inc.; 1999. p. 207–22.

10. Rosenfeld RM. Surgical prevention of otitis media. Vaccine. 2000;19 Suppl 1:S134–9.

11. Paradise JL, Bluestone CD, Rogers KD et al. Efficacy of adenoidectomy for recurrent otitis media in children previously treated with tympanostomy-tube placement. JAMA 1990;263:2066–73.

12. Paradise JL, Bluestone CD, Colborn DK, et al. Adenoidectomy and adenotonsillectomy for recurrent acute otitis media: parallel randomized clinical trials in children not previously treated with tympanostomy tubes. JAMA 1999;282:945–53.

13. Coyte PC, Croxford R, McIsaac W, et al. The role of adjuvant adenoidectomy and tonsillectomy in the outcome of the insertion of tympanostomy tubes. N Engl J Med 2001;344:1188–95.

14. Butler CC, Rollnick S, Pill R, et al. Understanding the culture of prescribing: qualitative study of general practitioners' and patients' perceptions of antibiotics for sore throats. BMJ 1998;317:637–42.

15. Coenen S, Kuyvenhoven MM, Butler CC, et al. Variation in European antibiotic use. Lancet 2001;358:1272.

16. Appelman CLM, Van Balen FA, Van de Lisdonk EA, et al. The Dutch College of General Practitioners Practice Guideline "Acute otitis media." E09. 1999. Available at: http://www. artsennet.nl/nhg/guidelines/E09.htm.

17. Rosenfeld RM. Diagnostic certainty for acute otitis media. Int J Pediatr Otorhinolaryngol 2002;64:89–95.

18. Rosenfeld RM. Observation option toolkit for acute otitis media. Int J Pediatr Otorhinolaryngol 2001;58:1–8.

19. Little P, Gould C, Williamson I, et al. Pragmatic randomised controlled trial of two prescribing strategies for childhood acute otitis media. BMJ 2001;322:336–42.

20. Kvaerner KJ, Mair IW. Acute and recurrent otitis media. Prevention and treatment in the light of current knowledge. Tidsskr Nor Laegeforen 1997;117:4096–8.

21. Schito GC, Debbia EA, Marchese A. The evolving threat of antibiotic resistance in Europe: new data from the Alexander Project. J Antimicrob Chemother 2000;46 Suppl T1:3–9.

22. Mandel EM, Casselbrant ML, Kurs-Lasky M. Acute otorrhea: bacteriology of a common complication of tympanostomy tubes. Ann Otol Rhinol Laryngol 1994;103:713–8.

23. Schilder AG. Assessment of complications of the condition and of the treatment of otitis media with effusion. Int J Pediatr Otorhinolaryngol 1999;49 Suppl 1: S247–51.

24. Casselbrant ML, Kaleida PH, Rockette HE, et al. Efficacy of antimicrobial prophylaxis and of tympanostomy tube insertion for prevention of recurrent acute otitis media: results of a randomized clinical trial. Pediatr Infect Dis J 1992;11:278–86.

25. Poole MD. Treatment of otorrhea associated with tubes or perforations. Ear Nose Throat J 1993;72:225–6.

26. Colclasure JB, Graham SS. Complications of outpatient tonsillectomy and adenoidectomy: a review of 3,340 cases. Ear Nose Throat J 1990;69:155–60.

27. Crysdale WS, Russel D. Complications of tonsillectomy and adenoidectomy in 9409 children observed overnight. Can Med Assoc J 1986;135:1139–42.

28. Rudberg R. Acute otitis media: comparative therapeutic results of sulphonamide and penicillin administered in various forms. Acta Otolaryngol 1954;113:S1–79.

29. Van Zuijlen DA, Schilder AG, Van Balen FA, Hoes AW. National differences in incidence of acute mastoiditis: relationship to prescribing patterns of antibiotics for acute otitis media? Pediatr Infect Dis J 2001;20:140–4.

30. Faye-Lund H. Acute and latent mastoiditis. J Laryngol Otol 1989;103:1158–60.

31. Hoppe JE, Koster S, Bootz F, Niethammer D. Acute mastoiditis—relevant once again. Infection 1994;22:178–82.

32. Bruijnzeels MA, Van Suijlekom-Smit LWA, Van der Velden J, Van der Wouden H. The child in general practice [English summary]. Rotterdam: Universiteitsdrukkerij Erasmus Universiteit; 1993.

33. Ruben RJ. Sequelae of antibiotic therapy. In: Rosenfeld RM, Bluestone CD, editors. Evidence-based otitis media. Hamilton (ON): BC Decker Inc.; 1999. p. 303–14.

34. Van Buchem FL, Peeters MF, Van't Hof MA. Acute otitis media: a new treatment strategy. BMJ 1985;290:1033–7.

35. Goldstein NA, Casselbrant ML, Bluestone CD, Kurs-Lasky M. Intratemporal complications of acute otitis media in infants and children. Otolaryngol Head Neck Surg 1998;119:444–54.

36. Harley EH, Sdralis T, Berkowitz RG. Acute mastoiditis in children: a 12-year retrospective study. Otolaryngol Head Neck Surg 1997;116:26–30.

37. Gliklich RE, Eavey RD, Iannuzzi RA, Camacho AE. A contemporary analysis of acute mastoiditis. Arch Otolaryngol Head Neck Surg 1996;122:135–9.

CHAPTER 21

Economic Costs

Seth R. Schwartz, MD, MPH, and George A. Gates, MD

Not everything that can be counted counts, and not everything that counts can be counted.
Albert Einstein

OBJECTIVES

On completing this chapter, the reader will be able to
1. Describe the various forms of cost and outcomes assessment.
2. Identify the key components that make up the direct and indirect costs associated with otitis media (OM).
3. Understand the best current estimates of the costs related to acute and chronic OM and its prevention.
4. Appreciate the need for further studies that directly measure the costs associated with acute and chronic OM and its treatment.

Otitis media is one of the most common childhood disorders. Annual costs in the United States are estimated at $3 to 5 billion.[1,2] Although estimates vary widely, there is little argument about the magnitude of the costs. With the current prevailing economic concerns about the rising costs of health care, the tremendous amount of financial resources consumed in caring for children with OM is of particular concern. In this economic environment, the search for effective and efficient therapies is of great and increasing importance. While this search is relatively new, several efforts stand out. There is still however, no consensus on the actual costs associated with OM and its treatment.

Discussions of cost alone, although they provide estimates of the financial burden of disease, take on greater meaning when they are considered in the context of value (ie, what is purchased for the money spent). In relation to an intervention for OM, this means that the cost of therapy is relative to the outcome of the intervention. One therapy may be more expensive than another, but it may still be a better alternative if it proves more effective than the less expensive intervention. Whereas estimating the effectiveness of various interventions for OM is beyond the scope of this chapter, it should be clear that economic evaluations of health

interventions are inextricably linked to the outcomes of those interventions.

Formal economic evaluation in OM is, however, still in its nascent stages. The bulk of existing studies seek to estimate costs alone. These estimates may ultimately form the numerator for cost-effectiveness ratios in future studies. This chapter will unravel the many components that contribute to the overall cost of OM and summarize several of the better estimates.

FORMS OF ECONOMIC EVALUATION

Formal economic evaluation of health care programs involves assessing the costs of competing programs in terms of the outcomes achieved by each respective program. A ratio of costs (numerator) to outcomes (denominator) is generated for each program.[3] These ratios can then be compared to determine which program offers more benefit for a given amount of money spent. These evaluations take on several forms, depending on how outcomes are assessed.

The simplest form of economic evaluation is the *cost-minimization* study. In this form of evaluation, the interventions compared are found to have equivalent outcomes. For example, two alternative antibiotics used to treat acute otitis media (AOM) may have equal rates of clearing the infection. Because there is no difference in outcome, the overall costs of each intervention can be compared directly. Any of the other forms of economic evaluation described below reduce to a cost-minimization study if the outcomes of the alternative treatments are identical.

Cost-benefit analyses compute both the costs and the outcomes of an intervention in monetary terms. Typical outcomes in this form of analysis are medical expenses averted by the intervention and wages lost as a result of the illness. These analyses are limited by the requirement that all outcomes must be expressed in monetary terms.

Many outcomes, such as parental emotional distress or the quality-of-life impact of illness and reduced hearing, are difficult to express in monetary terms. Nonetheless, these are real determinants that affect medical decisions and parental choices.

Cost-effectiveness analyses do not suffer from this limitation. They assess cost in relation to disease-specific outcomes. The result, therefore, is a ratio of cost to some unit measure of effectiveness (ie, cost per episode of OM averted, or cost per life saved). This form of analysis is quite useful when comparing interventions that act on the same disease entity, but it does not permit comparisons of values across disease states.

Cost-utility analysis applies a more generic outcome unit. Utility is the valuation of health states on a scale of 0 to 1 where 1 corresponds to perfect health and 0 corresponds to a state equivalent to death (estimated utility of AOM is 0.7 for the short episode duration).[1] In a cost-utility analysis, the outcome of interest is the *quality adjusted life-year* (QALY). QALYs are calculated by multiplying the utility score of the health state achieved through an intervention by the duration that affected individuals spend in that health state. The ratio of cost per QALY allows for comparison across disease states (ie, QALYs generated with an OM vaccine versus those generated with a hepatitis vaccine). This is particularly important in making decisions about general resource allocation.

None of these forms of analysis provides direct answers about what treatment to recommend. Rather, they provide information about value, distinguishing which treatment options offer the most benefit for the dollars spent. One option may prove drastically more expensive than another and yet deliver proportionally as much benefit. Both, then, are equally cost-effective options. The user of the information must still decide which treatment option is the better one. This will likely be decided on the basis of other factors, such as available resources or convenience. As a whole, economic evaluations of medical programs, therefore, provide relative, rather than absolute, information to assist in informed medical and policy decision making.

BROAD CONSIDERATIONS IN ESTIMATING COST

Any discussion of the cost of a disease or an intervention must first consider on whom the burden of the cost falls. In the context of economic evaluations, this is called perspective. There are several different perspectives that any study measuring costs can take. The broadest is the societal perspective. In this case, the estimation of cost must account for all costs that accrue to the administrator of the intervention, the patient, the family of the patient, and society at large. All other perspectives are narrower. Other frequently considered perspectives are the health care system, the payer (ie, Medicaid or private insurance), and the patient. The societal perspective, in theory, provides the best estimate of the true cost of an intervention. There is room for error, however, as many of the costs to society are unknowable with the current state of data collection. Additionally, the narrower perspective of the health care system may have direct applications for decision making and resource allocation.

Related to perspective is the issue of how the costs of an intervention are assessed. Studies gather cost information from a plethora of sources. Typical sources include hospital charge records, health care plan databases, and Medicaid reimbursement records. Many economic evaluations make assumptions or guesses about actual cost where actual data are not available. The result of an economic evaluation can vary dramatically, depending on which source of cost estimation is employed or what assumptions are made. For example, Medicaid reimbursement for placement of tympanostomy tubes is frequently less than half of what hospitals charge for the procedure. Readers must be wary as studies comparing similar programs using different data sources for cost estimation can provide widely disparate results.

A final consideration is that of discounting. Discounting refers to adjusting the value of monetary costs to present day value. Because of inflation, the value of money has, on average, decreased over time. This means that one dollar in the year 2000 is not as valuable or could not purchase as many goods as the same dollar in the year 1970. Many studies use data gathered 10 or more years before the evaluation was performed. Therefore, the results of an evaluation may need to be adjusted to present day dollar values to accurately interpret their meaning. Furthermore, dollars spent or saved in the future must be assumed to be worth less than current dollars. This becomes important when considering the value of long-term outcomes. For example, a vaccination may provide lifelong immunity and, therefore, avert medical costs that may accrue many years in the future. When adding that cost savings into a current evaluation, it should be given less value than an equal amount saved or spent in the present.

With these issues covered, we turn to the issue of what is actually considered when costs are evaluated.

THE COMPONENTS OF COST

There are many components that together comprise the entire financial burden of OM and the various interventions employed to treat it. These costs are traditionally broken down into three general categories: (1) direct costs, (2) indirect costs, and (3) intangible costs.[4] Direct costs are considered universally in all economic evaluations and constitute the most easily measured economic consequences of OM. Indirect costs are more difficult to measure directly yet they may significantly contribute to overall costs, particularly when considering the societal perspective. Intangible costs are those that cannot currently be measured using existing data gathering techniques. A discussion of all three components is germane to any discussion of the total cost of OM.

The temporal nature of OM is important when considering cost components. For the purposes of this discussion, OM can be thought of in phases: a prediseases state, where preventing an episode is possible; an acutely infected state (AOM); a chronic state with persistent otitis media with effusion (OME); and a recurrent state, in which risk of further episodes is great and where prophylaxis of further episodes is possible. The components that make up total costs in any study are dependent on the phase of OM under consideration.

Direct Costs

Direct costs are those that accrue as an immediate consequence of the disease state or that are generated by an intervention. Measuring direct costs is typically straightforward. Studies usually gather this information from pharmacy records, Medicaid billing summaries, hospital charge data, and other similar recorded sources. The components of direct costs can be broken down by the phase that is being addressed.

The recently developed conjugate pneumococcal vaccine affords the potential for preventing many episodes of OM in the general population (see Chapter 17, "Vaccine Prevention"). Direct costs from the health care perspective of a vaccine administration program include the actual cost per dose of the vaccine, the cost of clinic visits needed to give the vaccine, and the medical cost of treating adverse reactions to the vaccine. Direct cost savings include all the medical expenses averted by preventing cases of OM, which will be discussed in more detail below.

Direct costs associated with a simple episode of AOM are straightforward. A simple episode can either be treated with antibiotics and other additional medicines or it can be left to resolve spontaneously. If left untreated, there is no direct medical cost. Treating AOM accrues the cost of medicines and multiple physician visits.

Complex episodes of AOM involve cases in which the infection fails to clear, a medical complication occurs (ie, meningitis or mastoiditis), or the effusion fails to clear. In cases of persistent infection, the cost of additional courses of antibiotics, additional physician visits, and the cost of surgery, if needed, is added to the

above direct costs. If complications occur, the medical costs of hospitalization, intravenous antibiotics, and surgical intervention are added. Failure of middle ear effusion to clear after an AOM episode has motivated many of the economic evaluations for OM to date.

OME persisting after an episode of AOM may cause chronic conductive hearing loss and the adhesive ear disease. Debate persists regarding whether there are long-term developmental and cognitive sequelae from OME (see Chapters 23 to 25). Nonetheless, treatment is aimed at reducing the time with effusion to decrease potential sequelae. The myriad treatment options for OME include (see Chapter 19, "Clinical Pathway for Otitis Media with Effusion") antibiotics, steroids, and pressure equalization tubes (PET) with or without adenoidectomy.

Direct costs of medical treatment options for OME are similar to those for AOM. If surgery is undertaken, direct costs include surgeon and anesthesia professional fees, operating room charges, costs of equipment, costs of postoperative visits, costs of perioperative medications, and the costs of treating postoperative complications. Additionally, referral to an otolaryngologist results in a consultation fee and fees for audiologic evaluation.

Young children with a pattern of ear infections are at an increased risk of further infections. There are several options for managing recurrent AOM, including treating each recurrent episode, antibiotic prophylaxis, and PET. Direct costs again include physician visits, medications, and operative and perioperative charges as outlined above.

Indirect Costs

Indirect costs of OM are those that accrue as a secondary result of the infection or of interventions. These are more difficult to measure and frequently require estimation by some means. Studies typically classify indirect cost as those incurred by the family in caring for a sick child.[4] These may consist of the cost of transportation to and from physician visits, wages forfeited as a result of time lost from work, and costs of additional caregivers.

Costs incurred by the family of a child with OM are difficult to measure as they vary widely from family to family depending on the distances necessary to travel, the earning potential of the caregiver, and other factors. Several methods have been used to estimate family expenses. These include telephone surveys and diaries in which families record activities and expenses related to caring for the sick child.[5,6]

Additional indirect costs are particular to the phase of OM under consideration. Preventing OM with a pneumococcal vaccine, in addition to the above-mentioned costs to the family, may have the additional administrative costs of a vaccination program. Indirect cost savings from a vaccine would include the decrease in medical expenses

Table 21-1 Overall Annual United States Costs of Otitis Media

Author Year	Data Source	Cost, $ (billions)
Gates[1] 1996	AHCPR, assumptions	5.00
Bondy[2] 2000	Colorado Medicaid	4.09–4.15 (direct)

AHCPR = Agency for Health Care Policy and Research.

resulting from overall less invasive pneumococcal disease. OME may lead to other indirect costs resulting from the long-term sequelae of effusion and of PET placement. Chronic OME rarely leads to adhesive ear disease that, in turn, may require surgery many years after the inciting infection. Persistent perforation after PET extrusion may also require surgery and the associated costs. These expenses are difficult to measure because the events do not occur for a prolonged time, and yet they clearly follow from the initial condition or the intervention designed to treat it.

Intangible Costs

Other costs of OM and its treatments are even more difficult to measure. Ascribing a dollar value to the pain and suffering of an affected child, the emotional distress of the parent, and the turmoil caused in a family with an affected child is currently not possible. Some attempts have been made to ascribe dollar values to other consequences of OM, such as the decreased lifelong productivity of a child with incrementally lower cognitive power as a result of prolonged OME.[1] The real financial impact of these factors, however, cannot currently be measured. Medical interventions have other impacts that are not measurable. Antibiotic resistance for example, may ultimately lead to untreatable infections that clearly generate economic costs. Vaccinations also have broader impacts with difficult-to-quantify economic benefits, such as herd immunity.

These costs are, by definition, unquantifiable. They are not, therefore, included in the majority of economic evaluations in OM and warrant no further discussion here. It should be noted that these intangible costs may have a profound impact on the ultimate decision to perform a given intervention or initiate a given program. The remainder of this chapter will, however, focus on economic evaluations exploring primarily direct and indirect costs associated with OM and its treatment.

SUMMARY OF THE EVIDENCE

Overall Cost Estimates

The estimated national cost of treating OM in its various forms provides an estimate of the overall burden of disease and creates a financial measure of the scale of the

problem. Given the huge number of diagnosed and undiagnosed cases, the myriad treatments provided, the diversity of settings in which these treatments are offered, and the lack of systematic recording of treatment data, direct measures of total cost are not possible. Despite the impossibility of direct measurement, several authors have attempted to estimate the magnitude of the total cost of OM based on fragmentary pieces of data.

Two principle estimates stand out in the literature (Table 21-1). Gates[1] generated an annual estimate of $3.15 billion for treating AOM in children under age 5 years based on estimates of AOM incidence from the annual report of Vital and Health Statistics from the Centers for Disease Control and Prevention and assumptions of average direct and indirect costs per episode. Estimates of OME prevalence were derived from a cohort of Boston children and cost estimates came from the 1994 Clinical Practice Guideline for OME in young children.[7] From this information, an estimate of $1.85 billion dollars per year was reached for the treatment of OME in children under age 5 years. The cost estimate for OME was very sensitive to changes in the prevalence of chronic OME. Combined, these estimates suggest that direct and indirect costs of AOM and OME annually reach 5 billion dollars.

The second estimate was generated by extrapolation from 1992 Colorado Medicaid claims data for OM treatments in a large cohort of continuously enrolled children.[2] Direct expenditures for Medicaid were obtained from the Medicaid database. Total costs for Colorado were derived from assumptions of the percentage of uninsured children and the degree of inflation of private insurance expenditures above Medicaid (2.42 times for visits and 3.22 times for procedures, based on surveys of private insurers). These estimates were then applied to estimates of the entire national pediatric population up to age 14 years based on information from the 1992 Bureau of the Census. Total cost estimates were between $4.09 and $4.15 billion in 1992 dollars.

While providing general figures for the financial burden of all OM treatment, these estimates are far from perfect. The first estimate had wide variation with altered assumptions about the cost of individual therapies and the prevalence of OME. The second estimate alleviates some of this uncertainty by employing directly meas-

Table 21-2 Costs of Pneumococcal Vaccine

Author Year	Analysis Type	Efficacy Data	Cost Data	Result
Weycker[8] 2000	Cost-benefit	Literature	NEHCP claims data	Cost saving (age 2–5 yr) Cost > benefits (age < 2 yr)
Lieu[9] 2000	Cost-effectiveness	Meta-analysis	NCKP claims data	$80,000/life-year saved $160/AOM averted

AOM = acute otitis media; NCKP = Northern California Kaiser Permanente; NEHCP = New England Health Care Plans.

ured cost data and fewer assumptions, but it ignores indirect costs that account for a substantial fraction of total costs. As more complete cost data become available, these estimates are subject to significant change.

Costs of Pneumococcal Vaccine

The multivalent pneumococcal vaccine provides an opportunity to prevent many infections resulting from *Streptococcus pneumoniae*. This bacterium is still one of the most common causative organisms for OM. Use of the vaccine could, therefore, decrease the incidence of OM. Widespread use of the vaccine is currently under consideration for children under age 5 years. Administration of a vaccination program is costly. The results of cost-effectiveness analyses may influence policy decisions regarding vaccine administration. Two high-quality studies have addressed this issue (Table 21-2).

Weycker and coworkers[8] performed a cost-benefit analysis using vaccine efficacy data from the literature and claims data from a large New England health plan to estimate prevalence of disease, rates of interventions, and costs of therapy. Cost of the vaccine was estimated at $57 per dose. Costs of parental work lost per episode were estimated from the literature as $182 for AOM and $461 for surgically-treated OME. The direct cost of an AOM episode was estimated as $86 to $100 and for tube-related procedures was $1,641 to $2,259. Hypothetical cohorts of 1,000 patients of various ages from less than 7 months to 48 to 59 months were used to calculate costs with and without vaccination from a societal perspective. The analysis also included costs of community-acquired pneumonia, the incidence of which will decrease with vaccination.

Using the base-case estimates, the economic costs of vaccination outweighed the economic benefits for children under age 2 years. Conversely, for children aged 2 to 5 years, the vaccine was found to be cost saving. This difference appeared to result largely from the increased number of doses of vaccine that younger children require. Under all scenarios, administering the

vaccine was never cost saving below age 7 months but was most likely to be cost saving in children aged 2 to 4 years. The analysis was very sensitive to changes in the estimate of vaccine efficacy, prevalence of disease, medical costs, and parental work-loss costs.

Lieu and colleagues[9] used a decision analysis model with a base case derived from data on vaccine efficacy and disease prevalence from a randomized control trial from Northern California Kaiser Permanente (NCKP), from published sources, and from an expert panel. Cost estimates came from claims data from NCKP. Direct costs of AOM ranged from $134 for simple episodes to $389 for complex episodes; indirect costs ranged from $141 to $589 for simple and complex episodes, respectively. Estimates of the cost of PET were $1,869 and $443 for direct and indirect costs, respectively. Vaccine cost of $58 per dose came from the manufacturer with $5 for administration. Estimates of parental wages lost were derived from a prior telephone survey.

These data were then applied to a hypothetical birth cohort of 3.8 million American infants. With the base-case estimate, the cost per life-year saved was $80,000 (societal) and $176,000 (payer), and the cost per episode of AOM averted was $160 ($550 from the payer perspective). Estimates were sensitive to changes in vaccine efficacy, incidence of overall and invasive disease, and estimates of vaccine cost per dose.

These two studies suggest that at current best price estimates for the pneumococcal conjugate vaccine, economic costs will outweigh economic benefits for children under age 2 years (the currently recommended timing of administration based on maximum efficacy) and that the cost per life-year saved is at the high end of the currently acceptable range as determined by decisions to cover other health interventions. While comprehensive, these studies still depend on many assumptions about costs, disease prevalence, and vaccine efficacy. Variability in these parameters significantly altered study results in sensitivity analysis (the equivalent of significance testing) affording limited confidence in the robustness of the results.

Table 21-3 Costs of Acute Otitis Media

Author Year	Data Source	AOM Type	Cost/Episode, $	
			Total	Direct/Indirect
Gates[1] 1996	AHCPR	Any	233	100/133
Kaplan[10] 1997	West Virginia urban	Sporadic Recurrent	108 125	65/43
Capra[5] 2000	NCKP claims	Simple Complex	262 789	132/130 331/458
Alsarraf[6] 1999	Otitis Media Diary	Any	1,331	138/1,193

AHCPR = Agency for Health Care Policy and Research; AOM = acute otitis media; NCKP = Northern California Kaiser Permanente.

Acute and Recurrent Otitis Media

Multiple estimates have been made of the costs of an AOM episode. By convention, most authors tabulate all OM-related costs generated in the 3 months following an episode as being attributable to the episode. A general estimate of $233 ($100 direct, $133 indirect) per episode of AOM was made by the senior author on the basis of the average use of 1.5 courses of amoxicillin and 2.5 clinic visits per episode.[1] Several studies have more directly measured these costs (Table 21-3).

Kaplan and colleagues[10] examined 568 episodes of AOM in children under age 7 years from an urban population in West Virginia and estimated average costs of $116 per episode. Antibiotics accounted for only a small percentage of total costs. The average cost per episode was greater for recurrent episodes than for simple AOM ($125 versus $108). Capra and colleagues[5] had similar results, but cost estimates—based on utilization data from over 100,000 children younger than age 14 years from the NCKP and indirect costs from a telephone survey of parents of OM-affected children—were higher. Total costs for a single AOM episode were estimated as $262. Complex episodes were much more costly because of hospitalization, procedures, and further time lost from work by caregivers.

Bondy and colleagues[2] derived more general cost estimates using the Colorado Medicaid database and the Medicaid reimbursement schedule for children under age 13 years. Direct annual expenditures for OM (not per episode) ranged from $75 for children aged 0 to 6 months to $240 for children aged 19 to 24 months in 1992 dollars. Physician visits accounted for greater than 50% of costs in all age groups. OM-affected children were more than twice as costly to insure as the average age matched Medicaid enrollee ($28 if less than 1 year, $89 to $133 if 1 to 2 years).

Typical estimates of indirect costs of AOM are based on gross assumptions about missed work, lost wages, and the costs of transportation to and from the physician's office. Calculating wages lost due to caring for affected children is a surrogate measure for opportunity cost of time that the caregiver could have spent in other ways (ie, work, housekeeping, leisure activities) but, instead, spent caring for a sick child. This true measure is more difficult to obtain. A validated instrument, the Otitis Media Diary (OMD), more accurately measures the indirect costs related to OM.[6] Using this instrument, a significantly higher estimate of the indirect cost of an episode of AOM was reached ($1,192). In this study, nearly 90% of the cost of an episode of AOM was attributable to indirect costs.

Many children who experience a single episode of AOM will go on to have recurrent AOM. Although the above data suggest that each further episode becomes more costly than the first, there are no systematic studies to estimate the costs of recurrent infections. There are two traditional approaches to managing recurrent AOM: (1) antimicrobial prophylaxis or (2) PET (and related procedures). Chemoprophylaxis is falling out of favor because of concerns over induced antibiotic resistance. Nonetheless, the only study in the literature suggests that chemoprophylaxis is less costly and generates higher utility than PET (Table 21-4).[11] This study used a valid decision-analysis model, but only direct costs were evaluated. Costs were estimated from "local" charges for medications and procedures, and utilities were estimated on the basis of two-clinician consensus. The senior author previously calculated the cost-utility of PET for recurrent AOM as $6,790 per QALY on the basis of different assumptions in which the health status after tubes was better (higher utility) than in those not receiving PET. Additionally, indirect costs were included in this estimate.[1] This cost per

Table 21-4 Costs of Recurrent Acute Otitis Media

Author Year	Data Source	Antibiotic Prophylaxis, $	Myringotomy and Tubes, $
Bissoni[11] 1991	Local costs	281/patient	396/patient
Gates[1] 1996	AHCPR		6,790/QALY

AHCPR = Agency for Health Care Policy and Research; QALY = quality-adjusted life-year.

QALY is well within the range of normally funded medical and surgical interventions.

Even best estimates of AOM cost, which have been described above, have substantial variability (more than 100%). Newer data suggest that the costs of AOM are greater than previously estimated. Moreover, using the $1,192 estimate of indirect costs derived by Alsarraf and colleagues,[6] the estimated national cost of AOM increases nearly fivefold to more than $9 billion annually. This has clear implications for the cost effectiveness of preventive measures, such as the pneumococcal vaccine. Additionally, this suggests that the indirect cost estimates from other studies and for other treatments are undervalued. More research is needed to confirm these findings and to explore indirect costs associated with surgical treatment of AOM and OME.

Otitis Media with Effusion

Otitis media with effusion is an area of even greater controversy with regard to costs and the impact of alternative management strategies. Costs per episode are difficult to calculate because OME is often persistent or chronic, in contrast to the sporadic nature of most AOM. Studies have typically examined the cost-effectiveness of medicine versus surgery in clearing effusion. Whether additional procedures, such as adenoidectomy or tonsillectomy, are indicated remains a point of controversy.

Further, whereas surgery undoubtedly clears effusion faster, the impact on language and cognitive development is controversial.

Stool and colleagues[7] estimated medical and surgical costs on the basis of insurance claims data, standard drug pricing, and parental time lost from work, as part of a Clinical Practice Guideline sponsored by the Agency for Health Care Policy and Research. The mean cost per overall OME episode was $1,330 (Table 21-5). Medical management of OME cost $406; surgical management with PET alone was $2,173; and with PET plus adenoidectomy was $3,334. On the basis of these data and assumptions about the increase in utility by reducing the communication disorder generated by OME over a 2-year period, the senior author calculated a cost per QALY of $2,141 for PET and $2,027 for PET with adenoidectomy.[1]

Only one prospective randomized controlled trial (RCT) exploring the costs of surgery versus nonsurgical management of OME has been published. Hartman and colleagues[12] examined societal costs over 1 year of follow-up after randomizing 187 Dutch children with OME to PET or watchful waiting. Direct costs were measured from hospital costs, and indirect costs were assessed using a diary. Surgery cleared the middle ear effusion in 4.5 months, but there was no statistically significant difference in comprehensive language development between the two groups at the 1-year follow-up.

Table 21-5 Costs of Clearing Otitis Media with Effusion in Dollars*

Author Year	Data Source	Mean Cost	Medical Therapy	Tubes Alone	Tubes and Adenoidectomy
Stool[7] 1994	Lewin-VHI	1,330	406	2,173	3,334
Gates[1] 1996	Lewin-VHI			2,141/QALY	2,027/QALY
Hartman[12] 2001	Hospital cost/ Diary	120	454		
Berman[13] 1994	Colorado Medicaid Private insurance	350 601			

QALY = quality-adjusted life-year; VHI = Value Health Incorporated.

*All studies used a societal perspective.

Table 21-6 Pointers and Pitfalls

1. Costs can be divided into direct, indirect, and intangible, but most analyses only measure or estimate the first two.

2. The cost of an intervention to treat or prevent OM is inextricably linked to the effectiveness of the intervention.

3. Most studies rely on theoretic models and assumptions to estimate costs related to OM while few have directly measured these costs.

4. At current price estimates, the pneumococcal vaccine will cost $80,000 per life-year saved or $160 per episode of AOM averted. Economic costs appear to outweigh the economic benefits for children under age 2 years.

5. Estimates of the cost per episode of AOM from a societal perspective vary widely but range from $108 to $1,330.

6. Cost estimates for OME vary from $120 to $406 for medical management to $2,173 (tubes alone) to $3,334 (tubes plus adenoidectomy) for surgical treatment.

7. Indirect costs of OM have likely been grossly underestimated in most studies because new direct measures of indirect costs suggest they account for 90% of total costs.

8. Future studies are needed that jointly and directly measure the costs and consequences of various treatment options for OM before reliable guidelines can be established for cost-effective management of this common disorder.

AOM = acute otitis media; OM = otitis media, OME = otitis media with effusion.

Over the 12-month study period, average cost for the surgical patients was $454 (in 1998 US dollars) compared with $120 for the watchful waiting group. These estimates are significantly lower than the majority of other studies. The authors attribute this difference to using true cost instead of charge data and failing to include time lost from work. Given the lack of a detected difference in cognitive outcomes, this study reduces to a cost-minimization study and concludes that watchful waiting is less costly than surgery. The short duration of follow up for cognitive outcomes and the failure to account for the bulk of indirect costs make these results suspect. Further, the included children were identified by a population-based screening and had primarily asymptomatic OME.

Berman and colleagues[13] used decision analysis from a societal perspective to assess theoretic cost-effectiveness of management options for persistent OME. Meta-analysis of RCTs provided efficacy data and costs were derived from the 1992 Colorado Medicaid utilization data. A base-case scenario of a child diagnosed with OME requiring three visits was analyzed (6, 9, and 12 weeks after AOM). Treatment options at each visit included observation, antibiotics alone, steroids alone, antibiotics plus steroids, or referral for surgery.

The most cost-effective strategy was antibiotics plus steroids at visit one, additional antibiotics for persistent effusions, and surgery for OME persisting beyond 12 weeks. Average cost to clear effusion was $601 for private insurance and $350 for Medicaid. Conversely, sequential antibiotics followed by surgery generated private and Medicaid costs of $974 and $553, respectively. All estimates are lower than those obtained by Stool and colleagues.[7] When extended over the 6-month follow-up, the optimal strategy cost $1,088 for private insurance and $659 for Medicaid.

Although there remains substantial variability in actual cost estimates, surgery to place PET (with or without adenoidectomy) is more costly than watchful waiting or medical management for OME. Better outcomes data are needed to determine the true developmental consequences of prolonged middle ear effusion before the cost effectiveness of these two treatment strategies can be meaningfully compared.

CONCLUSION

The majority of data about costs incurred in treating OM is still fundamentally based on theoretical models and many assumptions. Recent articles have made efforts to measure direct and indirect costs, but estimates still vary widely (Table 21-6). Very few authors have undertaken prospective measurement of the costs of intervention. In part, this results from the inherent difficulty in accurately measuring those costs. Nonetheless, to resolve many of the as yet unanswered questions about the most cost effective strategies to manage OM, prospective cost and outcome assessment are still required.

REFERENCES

1. Gates GA. Cost-effectiveness considerations in otitis media treatment. Otolaryngol Head Neck Surg 1996;114:525–30.
2. Bondy J, Berman S, Glazner J, Lezotte D. Direct expenditures related to otitis media diagnosis: extrapolations from a pediatric Medicaid cohort. Pediatrics 2000;105:72.

3. Drummond MF, O'Brien B, Stoddart GL, Torrance GW. Methods for the economic evaluation of health care programmes. 2nd ed. New York (NY): Oxford University Press; 1997.

4. Stool SE, Field MJ. The impact of otitis media. Pediatr Infect Dis J 1989;8:S11–4.

5. Capra AM, Lieu TA, Black SB, et al. Costs of otitis media in a managed care population. Pediatr Infect Dis J 2000;19:354–5.

6. Alsarraf R, Jung CJ, Perkins J, et al. Measuring the indirect and direct costs of acute otitis media. Arch Otolaryngol Head Neck Surg 1999;125:12–8.

7. Stool SE, Berg AO, Berman S, et al. Otitis media with effusion in young children. Clinical practice guideline, number 12. Rockville (MD). AHCPR Publication No. 94-0622. 1994.

8. Weycker D, Richardson E, Oster G. Childhood vaccination against pneumococcal otitis media and pneumonia: an analysis of benefits and costs. Am J Managed Care 2000;6 Suppl:S526–35.

9. Lieu TA, Ray GT, Black SB, et al. Projected cost-effectiveness of pneumococcal conjugate vaccination of healthy infants and young children. JAMA 2000;283:1460–8.

10. Kaplan B, Wandstrat TL, Cunningham JR. Overall cost in the treatment of otitis media. Pediatr Infect Dis J 1997;16:S9–11.

11. Bisonni RS, Lawler FH, Pierce L. Recurrent otitis media: a cost-utility analysis of simulated treatment using tympanostomy tubes vs antibiotic prophylaxis. Fam Pract Res J 1991;11:371–8.

12. Hartman M, Rovers MM, Ingels K, et al. Economic evaluation of ventilation tubes in otitis media with effusion. Arch Otolaryngol Head Neck Surg 2001;127:1471–6.

13. Berman S, Roark R, Luckey D. Theoretical cost effectiveness of management options for children with persisting middle ear infections. Pediatrics 1994;93:353–63.

CHAPTER 22

Hearing and Auditory Function

Judith S. Gravel, PhD

*Hearing…the sound of the voice brings language, sets thoughts astir,
and keeps us in the intellectual company of man.*
Helen Keller

OBJECTIVES

On completing this chapter, the reader will be able to
1. Understand the average range and variation of the conductive hearing loss associated with otitis media with effusion.
2. Recognize the effect of conductive hearing loss on speech detection and recognition.
3. Recognize the potential impact of early conductive hearing loss on later auditory function.
4. Appreciate the possible impact of early conductive hearing loss during one or more early periods important for language learning and the development of auditory skills.

Interpreting most studies of otitis media with effusion (OME) and child development is complicated by a striking lack of information about the degree of accompanying hearing loss. Frequently, hearing status has not been evaluated directly, and, therefore, the presence and degree of hearing loss are assumed. Conductive hearing loss that often accompanies OME is frequently considered the mediator of communication and developmental outcomes. Sufficiently large groups of children with continuous bilateral disease and significant bilateral (symmetric and asymmetric) and unilateral conductive hearing loss have not been examined to determine if there are consequences of persistent impairment. Scant attention has been given to possible peripheral and higher-order auditory consequences in the short and long term.

MODELING THE IMPACT OF CONDUCTIVE HEARING LOSS AND OUTCOMES

Figure 22-1 presents a model modified from one suggested by Vernon-Feagans[1] and is predicated on the work of Vernon-Feagans and coworkers[1–3] and Roberts and colleagues.[4,5] Past global models have depicted a direct effect of OME and hearing loss on child outcomes. Current models postulate that while hearing loss mediates outcomes, the effect, however, is moderated by extrinsic factors, such as the language environment in the home, maternal responsiveness, the family's socioeconomic status, and the quality of the day care setting, plus intrinsic variables, such as the child's cognitive capacity and the coexistence of developmental disabilities or sensory deficits.[1,4,6–9]

The model proposed in Figure 22-1 incorporates the "Interactive Language and Attention" and the "Transactional" models proposed by Vernon-Feagans[1] and Roberts and colleagues,[4] respectively, and the "Cumulative Risk" model[10] that suggests one or more risk factors coexisting with chronic otitis media places a child at greater risk (accumulated risk) of adverse outcomes.[1] Added to the present model depicted in Figure 22-1 is the potential moderating influence of atypical auditory electrophysiology and function (eg, delayed auditory brainstem response, impaired binaural processing) that may exist for some children following the spontaneous resolution of middle ear disease and its concomitant conductive hearing loss or the surgical restoration of normal peripheral hearing. In this model, persistent conductive hearing loss in early life, which is the result of OME, mediates early acquisition of language.

In the proposed model, persistent conductive hearing loss in early life is considered a form of auditory deprivation, the short- and long-term consequences of which can be indexed by physiologic, psychoacoustic, and behavioral measures of auditory status. The plasticity of the auditory system and the redundancy of normal auditory input children experience when OME has resolved can result in rapid resolution of any auditory deficits for most children.[11] Or, if any auditory problems do persist, exposure to an ideal acoustic listening environment or a language-rich learning environment, for example, may reduce the impact of any higher-order auditory deficits on a child's functional abilities. For the

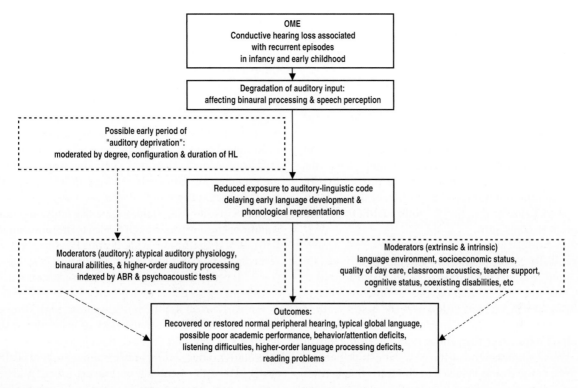

Figure 22-1 Relationship of otitis media with effusion (OME) to hearing loss (HL), auditory function, and developmental outcomes.

child with one or more extrinsic and/or intrinsic risk factors, however, persistent auditory deficits in the presence of normal peripheral hearing may moderate higher-order listening, language, attention, and academic outcomes at later ages.[12]

CHARACTERISTICS OF THE HEARING LOSS ASSOCIATED WITH OME

The conductive hearing loss associated with OME is distinguished by its unique "acoustic signature": the degree, configuration (spectral characteristics and symmetry), and stability of an impairment that results purely from transient episodes of effusion in the middle ear space (conductive) versus a permanent, stable sensory (cochlear) deficit.

Some [2,3,6,12–17] have suggested that the instability of the speech input signal during recurrent OME episodes could make learning the auditory-linguistic code challenging for some children, particularly during the important period of spoken language acquisition in the first 3 years of life when the incidence of OME is highest.[18]

Accurate detection of the acoustic features of the incoming speech signal is critical for accurate perception of spoken language. The hearing loss resulting from middle ear effusion (MEE) may render the acoustic cues

of speech attenuated, distorted, or inaudible,[19] potentially impacting the child's ability to analyze and synthesize the phonemes of spoken language, to develop auditory memory, and to temporally order speech features important for phonologic processing.

Evidence of Instability Associated with OME

Several prospective studies suggest that fluctuations in middle ear state characterize OME in some children. For example, Hogan and colleagues[20] examined duration of unilateral OME (UOME) and bilateral OME (BOME) episodes and changes in middle ear state prospectively. Findings were modeled on data obtained through prospective tympanometry tests collected at home visits from a cohort ($n = 95$) of children enrolled at birth; fewer children at 2 and 3 years of age were actually examined at the time of the study's publication. The modal duration of a UOME or BOME episode was 6 and 9 weeks, respectively, across the age range studied. One-quarter of the cases experienced > 60 weeks without an UOME or BOME episode. At the other end of the OME-experience continuum, only 9 weeks separated a bilateral effusion-free state and a UOME or BOME episode. The model revealed that children had (1) a low probability of changing the affected ear, if diagnosed with a unilateral OME; (2) a high probability of remaining either bilaterally affected or bilaterally OME-free; and (3) normal middle ear function bilaterally approximately half of the time following a UOME diagnosis at the previous visit.

In two reports, Zeisel and colleagues[21,22] in North Carolina, using pneumatic otoscopy as the primary measurement tool, documented middle ear status from 6 months to 5 years of age in a group of African American children. All children were involved in childcare at study onset. Between 6 and 24 months of age, 60 children experienced continuous BOME of 4 months' duration, and 8 children of the 60 experienced a similar duration of continual BOME from age 24 to 60 months.

In a similar prospective study in New York, Gravel and Wallace[23] found that increasing proportions (49, 57, and 75%) of children ($n = 114$) were categorized as BOME free (had normal middle ear function bilaterally at 80% or more of visits) over the first 3 years of life. Overall, the OME experiences of the New York cohort were fewer than those reported in the North Carolina studies; none of the New York study participants, however, was involved in childcare. Stephenson and colleagues[24] examined tympanograms prospectively every 3 months in a cohort of children. In 6.4% of the cases, (1) asymmetric tympanogram types or unilateral flat tympanograms were detected during more than half of the tests, or (2) middle ear state changed from asymmetric to symmetric OME during the observation period.

Examined collectively, longitudinal examinations of children's OME status support a continuum of middle ear experiences, with some experiencing numerous episodes of OME of variable duration and inter-ear symmetry during early life. Characterizing these experiences for the population is difficult, as intrinsic and extrinsic factors, such as age, racial group, childcare attendance, health care delivery systems, and so on, impact the outcome. Overall, studies suggest that

1. the proportion of children with OME decreases with age,
2. middle ear status (UOME, BOME, symmetry versus asymmetry of BOME) varies across relatively short time periods, and
3. duration of OME episodes is affected by persistence (whether children experience a low or high amount of time spent overall with OME).

Evidence of the Impact of MEE on Hearing Sensitivity

The presence of effusion in the middle ear space alters the transmission characteristics of the middle ear mechanism, reduces the admittance at the tympanic membrane, and increases the mass of the middle ear system (tympanic membrane and ossicles).[25] Reduced transmission of energy results in sound reflection back into the external auditory canal (EAC), contrary to the usually efficient transfer of acoustic energy to the cochlea when the middle ear system functions normally.[25,26]

Table 22-1 presents studies of MEE volume, viscosity, and elasticity. Wiederhold and colleagues[27] demonstrated in an animal model (cat) that induced MEE caused maximal hearing loss 3 weeks after a period of negative middle ear pressure, ultimately resulting in a flat, type B tympanogram (at the time the effusion was sampled). Neither viscosity (thin fluid or glue-like effusions) nor volume of effusion was strongly related to the time (duration) spent with effusion. While hearing loss was not correlated with fluid viscosity, it was significantly correlated ($r = 0.74$) with the volume of fluid in the middle ear space (increasing by 3.9 dB for each 0.1 mL of fluid).

Similarly in an animal model (guinea pig), Brown and colleagues[28] demonstrated a lack of association with hearing loss and fluid viscosity. Both high and low viscous fluids produced comparable hearing losses of 30 dB at 0.5 kHz with essentially no hearing loss at 4 kHz. Hearing loss (averaged for the thin and thick fluids) approximated 28, 20, 8, and 0 dB hearing level (HL) at 0.5, 1, 2, and 4 kHz, respectively, and varied (standard error of the mean) by less than 1 dB at all frequencies. In a follow-up study by the same group,[26] mucus injected into the middle ear of guinea pigs resulted in more hearing loss at 2 and 4 kHz (not significant) than found in their previous study. Their conclusions were the same, however: volume, rather than viscosity of the fluid, accounted for the hearing loss associated with MEE.

The results of animal studies[26–29] were similar to studies of humans that also showed no relationship of hearing to fluid viscosity. Using a newer technique (oscillating sphere magnetic rheometer), Majima and colleagues[30] measured the viscoelastic properties of the effusion found in the middle ears of children (mean age = 7.5 years; range = 6 to 13 years) and found that viscosity of the MEE was related to the degree of air-bone gap measured using conventional pure-tone audiometry at 0.5 and 1 kHz, but no relationship between viscosity and degree of conductive hearing loss was found at 2 and 4 kHz. The range of viscosity associated with a 30 dB air-bone gap was wide indicating that viscosity alone did not account for the entire conductive deficit. Elasticity of the MEE was not related to the degree of air-bone gap at any audiometric frequency.

Examined collectively, the studies suggest that it is the volume of effusion in the middle ear space that primarily is related to the degree of hearing loss. Viscosity of the MEE influences the amount of conductive hearing loss for frequencies at and below 1 kHz.

Table 22-1 Relationship of Middle Ear Effusion Properties to Hearing Loss for Air-Conducted Sounds

Author Year	Subjects (N)	Method (Stimulus)	Hearing Loss (Effusion Type)	MEE Property vs. Hearing Loss
Bluestone[77] 1973	Children (58 ears)	Audiometry (tones)	PTA (3-frequency) HL: 0 to ≥ 25 dB HL (40% of ears with mucoid effusions, viscosity > 1k centipoise)	Viscosity: $p = NS$
Wiederhold[27] 1980	Cats (42 ears)	EcoG-CM (clicks)	Mean peak SPL: 31.3 dB (thin effusions, $n = 19$) Mean peak SPL: 29.9 dB (thick effusions, $n = 23$)	Volume: $p < .05$ Viscosity: $p = NS$
Brown[28] 1983	Guinea pigs (5)	EcoG-CM (tones)	Mean HL: ~28, 20, 8, 0 dB @ 0.5, 1, 2 , 4 kHz, respectively (thick and thin effusions)	Volume: $p < .05$ Viscosity: $p = NS$
Marsh[26] 1985	Guinea pigs (5)	EcoG-CM (tones)	Mean HL: ~25, 24, 15, 10 dB @ 0.5, 1, 2 4 kHz, respectively (mucoid effusion; no difference with saline)	Volume: $p < .05$ Viscosity: $p = NS$
Majima[30] 1988	Children (40)	Audiometry (tones)	Mean air-bone gap: 19.2, 25.1, 21.7, 24.4 dB @ 0.5, 1, 2, 4 kHz, respectively (viscosity associated with gap only at 0.5 and 1 kHz)	Viscosity: $p < .05$ Elasticity: NS

EcoG = electrocochleography; CM = cochlear microphonic; dB = decibels; HL = hearing level, kHz = kilohertz; MEE = middle ear effusion; NS = not significant.; PTA = pure-tone average; SPL = sound pressure level.

DETERMINING HEARING LOSS IN CHILDREN WITH OME

Using conventional terminology,[31] the degree of impairment associated with OME (based on the results of pure-tone audiometry) can be "slight" (16 to 24 dB HL), "mild" (25 to 40 dB HL), or "moderate" (41 to 60 dB HL). The convention of providing a descriptive label for the hearing loss associated with OME may or may not convey the magnitude of the auditory dysfunction.[32] Direct audiometric assessment of an individual child's hearing is needed to completely delineate the degree and configuration of any hearing loss associated with an OME episode. Other means of documenting the presence of any hearing impairment, as well as the actual degree of hearing loss, are inaccurate.

For example, mounting evidence suggests that parent perception (assessment/report) of the presence or absence of hearing loss is not highly related to children's actual audiometric status.[33–35] Further, while pneumatic otoscopy and tympanometry are highly accurate for the identification of OME, hearing sensitivity cannot be estimated reliably from these widely used clinical procedures.

Fria and colleagues[36] examined audiometric outcomes associated with various tympanic membrane signs (eg, an air-fluid line) and tympanogram types (eg,

flat, noncompliant) and found that hearing sensitivity could range from normal to moderate degrees of hearing loss for the same otoscopic/tympanometric finding. These inaccuracies are also apparent in cases of more "minor" tympanic membrane abnormalities. Li and colleagues[37] examined audiograms from children (6 to 13 years) who had retractions of the pars tensa or pars flaccida portions of the tympanic membrane. Mild to severe pars tensa retraction resulted in average thresholds (0.25 to 8 kHz) of between 5 to 30 dB HL and 5 to 25 dB HL for the same degree of pars flaccida retraction. Degree of hearing loss was not predictable by otoscopic examination alone.

METHODS FOR CHARACTERIZING HEARING LOSS ASSOCIATED WITH OME

Hearing sensitivity can be measured using behavioral and electrophysiologic test procedures. Table 22-2 lists the types of tests that can be used to obtain a behavioral audiogram (air- and bone-conduction thresholds) for children of various ages. Behavioral tests require a voluntary response from the individual and are potentially influenced by examiner bias and the attention and motivation of the patient.[38]

Table 22-2 Behavioral and Physiologic Tests Used in Audiologic Evaluation

Test	Type (Age)	Response	Characteristics	Measures Hearing?
Visual reinforcement audiometry	Behavioral (~6–24 mo)	Conditioned head-turn	Reliable; thresholds within 10 to 15 dB of adult values; conventional audiometric test signals, air- and bone-conduction assessment and speech detection threshold possible	Yes
Conditioned play audiometry	Behavioral (~24–48 mo)	Conditioned play task (block drop, ring stack, etc)	Reliable; thresholds approximate those of older children; conventional audiometric test signals; air- and bone-conduction assessment and speech detection threshold possible	Yes
Conventional audiometry	Behavioral (> 48 mo)	Hand raise, button push, verbal report	Reliable; thresholds approximate adults; conventional audiometric test signals; air- and bone-conduction assessment and speech detection threshold possible	Yes
Auditory brainstem response	Physiologic (any age)	Identify threshold of wave V	Objective. Requires no response from child. Click threshold in 2 to 4 kHz range or region of best hearing; frequency-specific thresholds related to behavioral thresholds. Air- and bone-conduction assessment possible	Yes (estimate)
Otoacoustic emissions	Physiologic (any age)	Presence-absence of emission	Objective. Evoked using clicks (transients: TEOAE) or two tones close in frequency (distortion product: DPOAE). Amplitude of emission and/or signal-to-noise ratio recorded. Tests functional integrity of outer hair cells of cochlea	No
Tympanogram	Physiologic (any age)	Pattern typed or quantifiable parameters	Objective. Measures middle ear function through assessment of peak admittance and width (gradient) of tympanic membrane, middle ear pressure, and ear canal volume	No
AMEMR	Physiologic (any age)	Threshold level (in dB HL) recorded	Evaluates ipsilateral and crossed (contralateral) acoustic reflex arc. Broadband signal used to broadly estimate degree of HL (AMEMR)	No

AMEMR = acoustic middle ear muscle reflex thresholds; HL=hearing level.

The evoked auditory brainstem response (ABR) provides a reasonably accurate (within 10 to 15 dB of behavioral thresholds) estimate of auditory status.[39] The ABR, however, is not a true test of "hearing" in the global sense, but it is a very beneficial measurement tool when used with infants too young to respond reliably to behavioral tests or with any child unable or unwilling to be assessed using conventional audiometric test procedures. As with standard audiometric procedures, responses to air- and bone-conducted stimuli may be obtained using the ABR. Therefore, the ABR is useful in distinguishing conductive from sensorineural hearing loss.

Other physiologic and acoustic test procedures (see Table 22-2) are useful in comprehensively assessing auditory system integrity. Acoustic immittance measurement (including tympanometry and acoustic middle ear muscle reflex thresholds), suprathreshold (high level/neurologic) click-ABR, and evoked otoacoustic emissions (transient and distortion product) provide some information about the functional status of the middle ear, the cochlea (primarily outer hair cell function), and the neural integrity of the auditory pathway to the level of the brainstem. These tests, however, cannot accurately estimate threshold sensitivity.

The magnitude (degree) of conductive hearing loss can be estimated by several methods, which are listed below and discussed further in subsequent sections:

1. Threshold sensitivity in dB HL for nominal audiometric test frequencies in the conventional (0.25 through 8 kHz) range for air- and bone-conducted signals
2. Thresholds in dB SPL (sound pressure level) for extended high-frequency (> 8 kHz to 16 kHz) test signals beyond the conventional audiometric range
3. Pure-tone average (PTA) in dB HL for three (PTA3: 0.5, 1, and 2 kHz) or four (PTA4: 0.5, 1, 2, and 4 kHz) nominal test frequencies
4. Air-bone gap (air-conduction threshold in dB minus the bone-conduction threshold in dB) at individual test frequencies or for the PTA3 or PTA4
5. Auditory brainstem response thresholds in dB normal hearing level (nHL) for click or tone burst stimuli
6. Speech awareness (SAT) or speech reception/recognition (SRT) threshold in dB HL for air- and bone-conducted signals

Hearing Loss Associated with OME in the Conventional Audiometric Range

Table 22-3 summarizes audiometric outcomes of children with OME. Studies examining hearing sensitivity in children with OME report that 4-frequency PTA (0.5, 1, 2, and 4 kHz) hearing loss ranges from normal hearing to moderate hearing loss (0 to 55 dB HL). The 50th percentile is about 25 to 28 dB HL, while a lesser proportion (approximately 20%) exceed 35 dB HL.[36,40] The mean hearing loss associated with OME in children is about 28 dB HL (SD = 13 dB).[36] Table 22-4 summarizes studies of infants and preschoolers experiencing OME. When the findings across childhood reported in the two tables (see Tables 22-3 and 22-4) are compared, similarities among hearing loss associated with OME are evident.

For groups of children, examining mean threshold values does suggest that the hearing loss associated with OME results in an essentially equal loss of sensitivity across the speech range, at least as depicted on the conventional audiogram.[36,40] Hunter,[41] however, has reported that audiometric configurations associated with OME obtained in the sound field and under earphones can be categorized into five types (the proportions reported here are for infants and children, respectively): (1) flat (47.8%, 32.9%), (2) rising (11.9%, 17.1%), (3) falling (6%, 2.9%), (4) 2kHz peak (20.9%, 41.4%), and (5) other (13.4%, 5.7%). Studies of hearing loss associated with the physical properties of MEE (see

Table 22-1) are consistent with audiometric data on degree and configuration of hearing loss of children with OME (see Tables 22-3 and 22-4).

Otitis media with effusion in infants and children impairs hearing for speech. Children with OME have reduced SAT SRT generally consistent with the estimated PTA.[36,40,42,43] Thresholds for speech ranged from normal to moderate/moderate-severe (60 dB) hearing loss. One study reported that children might experience lower (poorer) SRTs than predicted by their PTAs.[42] For SRT testing, the child must recognize a spondee word accurately in order to respond correctly. Therefore, depending on the configuration of the hearing loss, the resultant SRT may not reflect the PTA, which is derived through a simple and nonlinguistically loaded sound detection task.

Extended High-Frequency Hearing Sensitivity

Longitudinal studies in young participants suggest that children with well-documented histories of OME have significantly poorer hearing sensitivity in the extended high-frequency (EHF) audiometric range (> 8 to 20 kHz) than children who have no history of early, persistent middle ear disease.[44-47]

Hunter and colleagues[45] showed that children aged 3 to 6 years serving as controls (no history of OME) had significantly better EHF thresholds (4.5 to 14.7 dB at 9 to 20 kHz, respectively) than study children with positive histories of middle ear disease (OME+ group). The differences in threshold sensitivity between older (7 to 11 years of age) controls and OME = positive children were larger than in the younger group, ranging from 13.4 dB to 24.6 dB at 9 to 16 kHz, respectively. OME = positive children had repeated visits at which OME was diagnosed and repeated tympanostomy tube insertions (these two predictive factors accounting for 32% of the variance in EHF thresholds).[45]

Laitila and colleagues[47] found poorer EHF thresholds in the 10 to 18 kHz range in children aged 14 years with recurrent otitis media (OM) than in those considered OM free at a similar number of observations. All children had their middle ear status documented at birth, 7 months, 24 months, and 60 months of age.

The EHF loss reported in the aforementioned studies appears to be cochlear in nature because multifrequency tympanometry suggests the loss is not associated with middle ear effects.[44,45] Thus, the presumed basal-end cochlear site of the lesion may result from middle ear pathogens or ototopical medications diffusing across the round window membrane.[45] Recently, Ryding and colleagues[46] also reported similar effects of a history of acute episodes of OM and OME on EHF hearing sensitivity. These authors suggested, however, that middle ear

Table 22-3 Hearing Loss Associated with OME Using Behavioral Audiometry in Children Aged 4 Years or Older

Author Year	Age (N)	OME Diagnosis	Hearing loss, dB HL (SD)				Air Conduction PTA3/4, dB HL (SD)	Bone Conduction PTA3/4, dB HL (SD)	Air-Bone Gap, dB
			0.5 kHz	1 kHz	2 kHz	4 kHz			
Bluestone[77] 1973	NS (91 ears)	MX, TYMP	NS	NS	NS	NS	PTA3: ≤ 24 (53% had OME) PTA3: ≥ 25 (79% had OME)		8.3–45.0
Kokko[40] 1974	4–8.6 yr (161 ears)	OTO	29.6 (12.7)	30.1 (13.8)	23.0 (12.0)	28.8 (14.5)	PTA4: 27.6 (12.8)	PTA4: 3.0 (7.1)	24.6
Fria[36] 1985	2–12 yr (540 ears)*	OTO, AMEMR, TYMP	27.5 (11.6)	26.5 (12.1)	19.6 (12.1)	26.8 (14.9)	PTA4: 24.5 (11.0)† SRT: 22.7 (10.9)†	PTA4: ~6.4 (~6.2)	~20.0

AMEMR = acoustic middle ear muscle reflex thresholds; dB = decibels; HL = hearing level; MX = myringotomy; NS = not stated; OME = otitis media with effusion; OTO = otoscopy; PTA3/4 = pure tone-average, 3 or 4 frequency; SRT = speech reception threshold; TYMP = tympanometry.

*Only one ear reported for each child studied.

†Range of PTA4, 0–55 dB HL; range of SRT, 0–50 dB HL.

Table 22-4 Hearing Loss Associated with OME Using Behavioral Audiometry in Infants and Toddlers under 3 Years of Age

Author Year	Age (N)	OME Diagnosis	Outcome 1	Outcome 2	Measure
Fria[36] 1985	7–24 mo (222)	OTO, TYMP, AMEMR	Bilateral OME: mean dB HL (SD) 7–9 mo (n = 35): 26.1 (11.4) 10–12 mo (n = 35): 25.9 (12.0) 13–15 mo (n = 36): 25.1 (8.8) 16–20 mo (n = 38): 25.5 (13.3) 21–24 mo (n = 19): 24.7 (10.5)	Unilateral OME: mean dB HL (SD) 7–9 mo (n = 10): 27.0 (12.3) 10–12 mo (n = 16): 19.4 (6.8) 13–15 mo (n = 10): 24.5 (13.0) 16–20 mo (n = 17): 21.8 (12.5) 21–24 mo (n = 6): 16.7 (10.3)	SAT-VRA
Roland[43] 1989	12 mo (NS)	OTO	Mean dB HL 27 at 0.5 kHz, 26 at 2 kHz	Mean dB HL SAT=19	VRA SAT-VRA
Roberts[4] 1995	6–12 mo (61)	OTO (1°), TYMP (2°)	Sessions with 50% responses ≥ 25 dB HL 49% at 0.5 kHz, 48% at 2 kHz, 63% at 4 kHz	Percent time with responses ≥ 25 dB HL Never, 6.6%; 1–19% of time, 18%; 20–49% of time, 28%; 50–69% of time, 11%; 70–99% of time, 21%; 100% of time, 15%	VRA
Gravel[23] 2000	7–36 mo (114)	TYMP	Bilateral OME* mean PTA4 dB HL (SD) Year 1 (n = 20): 20 (7.3), range 9.8–36.5 Year 2 (n = 27): 18.3 (4.4), range 9.1–28.4 Year 3 (n = 10): 18.6 (6.2), range 11.3–29.4	Unilateral OME* mean PTA4 dB HL (SD) Year 1 (n = 8): 14.7 (6.3), range 7.9–25.0 Year 2 (n = 1): 23.6 Year 3 (n = 4): 13.5 (2.7)	VRA

AMEMR = acoustic middle ear muscle reflex thresholds; dB = decibels; HL = hearing level; NS = not stated; OME = otitis media with effusion; OTO = otoscopy; PTA4 = pure-tone average, 4 frequency; SAT = speech awareness threshold (sound field); TYMP = tympanometry; VRA = visual reinforcement audiometry (sound field).

*Bilateral OME at ≥ 30% of all visits or unilateral OME at ≥ 50% of all visits.

factors and cochlear dysfunction could account for the elevated EHF thresholds in children with recurrent middle ear disease.

Currently, there is debate over the functional consequences of EHF hearing loss (see Hunter and colleagues [45] for a review). Sensorineural hearing loss in the high-frequency range is not usually evaluated during conventional audiologic assessment but may, nonetheless, affect speech perception in background noise. As yet there is no evidence supporting a relation between EHF hearing loss and a higher likelihood of progressive hearing loss in the higher frequencies of the conventional audiometric range. Longitudinal studies examining these factors would be extremely valuable in clinical management of OME.

Auditory Brainstem Response and Assessment of Children with OME

Fria and Sabo[48] first used ABR to identify and assess hearing loss in children with OME. The sensitivity of delayed latency of ABR waves I and V was 82% and 100%, respectively, for identifying OME in infants and toddlers ($n = 14$) and school-age children ($n = 12$). The authors also found a relation (albeit $p \leq .10$) between wave V latency and actual conductive hearing loss, with the predictive error not exceeding 20 dB. On the basis of ABR latency, 70% of children's measured average audiometric thresholds were within 5 dB of that predicted by the click-ABR, and 95% were within 10 dB (except for 4 kHz).

Owen and colleagues[49] predicted hearing sensitivity by examining the ABR wave V latency-intensity function (LIF). On the basis of ABR wave V LIF, about 38% of ears with effusion ($n = 63$) had moderate hearing loss (27.5 to 50 dB), 16% had normal hearing, and 46% had mild impairments. Stapells and Mackersie[50] later concluded that examining ABR wave I latency was inaccurate for predicting conductive hearing loss. Using two different predictive methods, they found an average prediction error in dB for ears with OME ($n = 55$) of 11 dB (SD = 15.7, range = −19 to 58 dB) and 2 dB (SD = 13.9, range = −25 to 46 dB).

Two early prospective investigations of OME and language development used click-ABR thresholds to estimate hearing sensitivity.[13,14] Wallace and colleagues[13] reported that OME-positive infants had average click-ABR thresholds higher than infants without OME during the same period (33 versus 22 dB nHL). Click-ABR wave V thresholds were 30 to 80 dB nHL because of conductive hearing loss from OME. Similarly, Roland and colleagues[43] performed click-ABR in 328 infants aged 6 months. Only 34%, 64%, 83%, and 92 % of ears with OME had ABR wave V at 20, 30,

40, and 50 dB nHL, respectively. Conversely, 95% of effusion-free ears had detectable responses at 20 dB nHL. Mean click-ABR threshold for ears with and without effusion were 31.2 and 20.6 dB nHL, respectively.

There are significant limitations in using click-ABR to monitor children with OME:

1. Click-ABR is only a gross estimate of hearing sensitivity. The acoustic spectrum of the click delivered through a standard earphone is broadband containing equal energy from 1 to 8 kHz.[39,50]
2. Click-ABR thresholds are most closely associated with regions of best auditory sensitivity and are, therefore, poor predictors of audiometric configuration.[39,50] ABR may be insensitive to mild or low-frequency hearing loss.[50] Frequency-specific air- and bone-conducted ABR procedures can overcome some of these limitations.[39]
3. The infant or young child must sleep (or rest) quietly for extended time periods to obtain reliable ABR threshold recordings.
4. Periodic ABR assessments are necessary to document the degree of hearing loss and the fluctuant nature of auditory thresholds; therefore, the technique is time consuming, expensive, and impractical in clinical practice.[38]
5. Hearing loss configuration cannot be estimated accurately based on ABR wave latency-intensity estimates.[50]

Speech Perception

Traditional Measurement of Speech Recognition

Conventionally, the functional impact of degree of hearing loss is measured by speech recognition ability (sometimes [although inappropriately] termed "speech discrimination"). Generally, a%-correct score is calculated on the basis of the individual's response to lists (25 or 50 items) of phonetically balanced (PB) monosyllabic words presented at an overall sensation level (dB SL) well above the speech threshold. The overall presentation level (dB HL) is intended to "compensate" for the degree of hearing loss, achieving maximum audibility of the monosyllabic words (PB-max).

Speech recognition ability, as measured traditionally, does not reflect the actual consequences of hearing loss on the child's ability to hear speech at a typical conversational level or when the speech signal occurs in challenging listening environments (such as in background noise). Children learning language at home and in the day care or classroom environment encounter these acoustic conditions daily.

Speech recognition tests are not available clinically for infants or children under age 3 years; that is, infants cannot be instructed to "say (or point to) the word." Nozza,[51] however, found that the abilities of infants with normal hearing for simple place feature discrimination depend on the overall intensity level of the phoneme pair. At presentation levels lower than normal conversational speech (at which adult listeners' performance was at 100%), immature listeners' speech discrimination performance was just above chance. Similarly, Penn and colleagues[52] recently suggested that children's speech discrimination abilities are more affected by the same degree of (simulated) conductive hearing loss than are adults'.

Although incomplete, existing evidence suggests that the impact of even a mildly attenuated signal (similar to that associated with mild conductive hearing loss) results in greater speech perception difficulties in infants and children than in adults with established linguistic development.

Measurement of Higher-Order Speech Processing

Some studies of children with OME histories reveal early deficits in discriminating phonologic and morphologic speech features,[53] and in speech-sound discrimination and identification using conventional speech continua and test procedures.[54–57]

Clarkson and colleagues[55] used traditional identification and discrimination tasks to examine speech perception in 5-year-old children with and those without histories of OME. Discrimination of the voicing feature (voice onset time) was poorer in children with early OME histories, but categorization (identification) of the feature was poorer only in children who had coexisting language delay. Another study[56] using a factorial design found that OME and language impairment were related to specific speech perception problems but that the combination (OME and language impairment) was not additive. Children with a language disorder and OME history, however, had the worst results on speech perception tasks.

Mody and colleagues[57] examined two groups of 9-year old children prospectively, with or without OME and conductive hearing loss in the first year of life, using speech perception and short-term memory tasks. Children with early histories of OME and hearing loss did worse on a speech perception task when the test items were phonetically similar but performed comparable with non-OME controls on identification or temporal order recall when speech sounds differed by multiple features.

Studies of speech perception using traditional clinical measures in children with various short- and long-term OME and hearing loss experiences have been reported, but the number of children studied is small. For example, in a single case study, DeMarco and Givens[58] examined a 4-year old with a prolonged history of OME and mild to moderate conductive hearing loss. Before pressure equalization tube (PET) insertion, hearing loss affected discrimination of word pairs differing by a single phoneme. Increasing the overall sensation level of the test stimuli ameliorated some of the effects. Following surgery and normalization of hearing, speech discrimination improved, as expected, from the presurgical results; the misperceptions were clearly the result of an attenuated acoustic input. Interestingly however, some speech discrimination errors persisted at the post-surgery assessment, suggesting that perhaps some perceptual errors had been more firmly established. There was no long-term follow-up to determine whether the errors persisted or were resolved with experience.

Single-subject analyses can provide unique insights into the speech perception deficits of individual children, which are not always apparent in conventional audiometric assessment of word recognition ability.

Speech Perception in Noise and OME

Rosenfeld and colleagues[59] studied a small group of children with bilateral OME, normal hearing, and excellent word recognition scores in quiet conditions. Before PET surgery, word recognition in noise was worse than would be expected, given their audiometric profiles. The most significant improvement in word recognition scores in both quiet and noise following PET insertion and restoration of normal hearing was for lower than average speech levels.

Behavioral studies of larger samples of children with histories of recurrent OME and hearing loss and on children pre- and post-PET insertion indicate that speech perception-in-noise abilities are affected, even when hearing has returned to normal. Jerger and colleagues[60] reported that children's word and sentence recognition performance was significantly poorer in the competition conditions than in quiet, a result found across the 2.5- to 6.0-year age range studied. They suggested that speech perception of children with histories of OME in demanding listening environments might lag behind that of peers with no OME histories.

Gravel and Wallace[61] demonstrated that at 4-years of age, children who were prospectively followed up and who had early histories of OME and hearing loss required a more advantageous signal-to-noise ratio to correctly identify 50% of the sentences presented diotically than did early OME-free peers. The 4 year olds all had normal hearing sensitivity at the time of evaluation. Later, advantage for listening to diotic signals in background competition was associated with teacher's judgments of academic performance and pre-reading abilities.[12] Schilder and her colleagues[62] reported similar findings in a large group of children with or without OME histories when speech and noise level ratios were fixed at +5 dB (speech signal 5 dB louder than the background noise level).

HIGHER-ORDER AUDITORY FUNCTION AND EARLY OME

A growing body of evidence indicates that short- and long-term differences in various aspects of higher-order auditory processing are apparent for many children who experienced early OME and hearing loss. For some children, these differences persist after hearing loss has resolved and peripheral hearing sensitivity has returned to normal. These auditory processing differences have been detected through the use of physiologic and psychoacoustic test procedures.

Auditory Physiology

Auditory Brainstem Response

The ABR provides information about the integrity of the auditory pathway from the cochlea and eighth nerve to the level of the auditory brainstem. Table 22-5 presents studies that have reported ABR waveform abnormalities (eg, prolonged absolute wave latencies and or interpeak and inter-ear latency differences) in children with early histories of recurrent OME.

In the one longitudinal study, to date, Gunnarson and Finitzo[63] prospectively monitored children enrolled in an OME study[43] that used click-ABR to estimate hearing sensitivity at regular intervals from early infancy through age 18 months. Monaural and binaural ABRs at 5 to 7 years of age showed significantly prolonged absolute latencies for ABR waves III and V, and prolonged ABR interpeak I–III and I–V latencies, in children with intermittent or chronic early OME and hearing loss compared with controls. ABRs recorded in infancy revealed precursors to ABR results at age 5 to 7 years: early evidence of increasing absolute latencies of waves III and V with time spent with OME and hearing loss. Children with early chronic OME and hearing loss were also less likely to have a measurable binaural interaction component (BIC) than their early OME-free or intermittent-OME peers.[63] This is of interest because the first site of binaural interaction in the central auditory system is at the level of the medial superior olivary nucleus in the auditory brainstem.[25]

Examined collectively, the evidence in Table 22-5 consistently indicates that children with histories of OME have some type of abnormalities on ABR evaluation compared with peers with no history of OME. All studies except one,[63] however, are not prospective in nature and, thus, OME and hearing loss in early life could not be documented effectively. Delays in absolute latencies of ABR waves III and/or V, plus indications of one or more prolonged ABR interwave intervals (I–III, I–V, III–V) are apparent, although the exact abnormalities are not always consistent among studies. It is unclear

what these findings indicate with regard to underlying auditory brainstem physiology.[64] Nonetheless, the data suggest that experience with OME and, therefore, some degree of transient conductive hearing loss are associated with later atypical findings using an objective marker of auditory brainstem pathway integrity, even although peripheral hearing is normal.

Although it is tempting to suggest that these findings are evidence of early auditory deprivation, there are other potential explanations.[64] Chronic conductive impairments not associated with OME produce the same effects in adults; therefore, the concept of sound deprivation affecting auditory physiology is not exclusive to the developing child.[65] The relationship between atypical ABR findings (including inter-ear asymmetries associated with a history of OME) and functional outcomes remains to be evaluated in cohorts of children who exhibit the electrophysiologic marker and who also are evaluated for functional auditory skills and auditory brainstem integrity at multiple time periods in their development.

Psychoacoustic Measures

Binaural Processing

The ability to efficiently process binaural auditory input allows individuals to detect signals in background noise, to localize sound accurately, and to easily perceive the first of multiple sounds arriving at the ears (precedence effect).[64,66] Researchers have speculated that binaural processing abilities may be impacted by an early history of OME because of the asymmetric or unilateral conductive hearing loss that frequently exists.

Table 22-6 presents the outcomes of psychoacoustic studies that have examined the impact of early OME on binaural skills in infancy through adolescence using multiple tasks. In some instances, history of OME has been well documented, as when children have been studied just prior to, and for periods after, the surgical insertion of PETs.[64,67–70] Other investigators documented OME prospectively[20,66,71] but failed to examine hearing sensitivity over the same time period. Some teams have used parental report to determine the child's OME history.[72] In most (but not all[73]) cases, peripheral hearing was tested prior to psychoacoustic testing, except when concurrent OM and hearing loss were part of the experimental design.

Signal Detection in Noise

The binaural masking level difference (MLD) task has been used extensively in the OME literature as an index of a listener's ability to detect subtle time and amplitude cues arriving at each ear. The MLD is derived by obtaining two different thresholds: (1) noise masker and signal in phase (NoSo), a simple simultaneous masking

Table 22-5 Auditory Processing in Infants and Children with OME Histories Using a Physiologic Test (ABR)

Author Year	Age (N)	OME/Hearing Documentation	Design and Groups	Outcome 1	Outcome 2
Folsom[78] 1983	6–10 yr (30)	OME history by MD/ENT and parent report	2 equal groups: (1) OME group with recurrent OME or PETs, and (2) controls with no reported OME	Group 1 vs. 2 (control) Latency wave I: NS Latency wave III: $p < .05$ Latency wave V: $p < .01$ LIF: $p < .01$	Group 1 vs. 2 (control) IPL waves I–V: NR IPL waves I–III: $p < .05$ IPL waves III–V: $p < .01$
Lenhardt[79] 1985	8 yr (2)	History ENT and repeated PETs	1 group: normal hearing at ABR test	Latency wave I: normal Latency wave III: delayed Latency wave V: delayed Repetitive rate inc: abnormal	IPL waves I–V: NR IPL waves I–III: prolonged IPL waves III–V: normal
Anteby[80] 1986	4–12 yr (205 ears)	Cross-section; otoscopy, tympanometry, history of OME; reported normal hearing at ABR test	5 groups: (1) active OME, (2) recurrent OME, (3) recovered OME with PETs, (4) recovered OME without tubes, and (5) controls without OME	Group 1 vs. 5 (control) IPL waves I–V: $p = NS$ IPL waves I–III: $p = NS$ IPL waves III–V: $p = .05$ Repetitive rate inc: $p = .05$ Group 2 vs. 5 (control) IPL waves I–V: $p = .025$ IPL waves I–III: $p = NS$ IPL waves III–V: $p = .01$ Repetitive rate inc: $p = NS$	Group 3 vs. 5 (control) IPL waves I–V: $p = .025$ IPL waves I–III: $p = NS$ IPL waves III–V: $p = .05$ Repetitive rate inc: $p = .05$ Group 4 vs. 5 (control) IPL waves I–V: $p = .025$ IPL waves I–III: $p = NS$ IPL waves III–V: $p = .025$ Repetitive rate inc: $p = NS$
Chambers[81] 1989	2.4–8.9 yr (36)	History; MD/ENT; parent report; normal SRT at time of ABR	2 equal groups: (1) OME group with 4–11 episodes and no previous PETs and (2) controls with no reported OME	Group 1 vs. 2 (control) Latency wave I: $p = NS$ Latency wave III: $p < .001$ Latency wave V: $p < .02$	Group 1 vs. 2 (control) IPL waves I–V: $p = NS$ IPL waves I–III: $p < .01$ IPL waves III–V: $p = NS$
Gunnarson[63] 1991	5–7 yr (27)	Longitudinal: 3–5 early ABRs (term, 6 wk, 6 mo, 12 mo, 18 mo postterm); normal audiogram: 5–7 yr	3 equal groups: (1) controls, (2) ≤ 1 ABR = 30 dB nHL, and (3) > 1 ABR = 30 dB nHL with severe OME and hearing loss by 18 mo	Latency wave I: NS Latency wave III: $p = .01$ Latency wave V: $p < .001$ LIF: $p = NS$	IPL waves I–V: $p = .02$ IPL waves I–III: $p = .04$ IPL waves III–V: $p = NS$
Owen[49] 1993	Children (52; 98 ears)	PET recipients; medical history of OME (≥ 4 episodes within 6 mo)	4 groups: (1) OME at myringotomy, (2) no OME, (3) dry PETs, and (4) otorrhea	Group 1 Latency wave I: delayed Latency wave III: delayed Latency wave V: delayed	Group 2 (control) vs. 3 Latency wave I: $p < .05$ Latency wave III: $p = NS$ Latency wave V: $p < .05$ IPL waves III–V: $p = NS$
Hall[64] 1993	5.2–9.2 yr (27)	OME group had PE tubes Controls: no OME by chart and parent report	2 groups: (1) OME (n = 14) and (2) controls (n = 13)	Group 1 vs. 2 (control) Latency wave I: $p = NS$ Latency wave III: $p < .05$ Latency wave V: $p < .05$	Group 1 vs. 2 (control) IPL waves I–V: $p = NS$ IPL waves I–III: $p = NS$ IPL waves III–V: $p = NS$

ABR = auditory brainstem response; ENT = otolaryngologist; inc = increase; IPL = interpeak latency difference; LIF = latency-intensity function; ms = milliseconds; NR = not reported; NS = not significant; OME = otitis media with effusion; PET = pressure equalizing tube; SRT = speech recognition threshold.

Table 22-6 Auditory Processing in Infants and Children with OME Histories Using Psychoacoustic Tests (MLD, CMR, and VAL)

Author Year	Age (N); Groups	OME/Hearing Documentation	Binaural Processing Task	Procedure	Outcome
Morrongiello[73] 1989	6–18 mo (28); unilateral OME only	Medical examination, otoscopy	Localization of sound in horizontal plane	Localization: 2-AFT visually reinforced head-turn/eye-movement; test signal shifted (varied degree) off midline	Reduced localization accuracy to OME side at baseline, but no difference after 2 weeks
Pillsbury[70] 1991	5–13 yr (55); control group (25) PET group (30 at 1 mo, 22 at 3 mo)	Controls by history; PET group with hearing loss; postsurgery had normal hearing	Signal detection in background noise	MLD: 3-AFT with 5 kHz pure tone and 0.3 kHz wide noise band masker; threshold for tone for S0 and Sπ conditions; MLD computed	PE tube group at baseline MLD: 8.5 dB (90% < control 95% CI) PE tube group postsurgery MLD at 1 mo: 10.6 dB (70% < control 95% CI) MLD at 3 mo: 11.3 dB (64% < control 95% CI) MLD at 1 mo and 3 mo postsurgery correlated with presurgery HL asymmetry
Hall[67] 1995	5–13 yr (62); control group (40), PET group (22 at 1 y, 14 at 2 yr, 11 at 3 yr, 8 at 4 yr)	Controls by history; PET group had 14 from Pillsbury[70] and 8 new candidates	Signal detection in background noise	MLD: 3-AFT with 5 kHz pure tone and 0.3 kHz wide noise band masker; threshold for tone for S0 and Sπ conditions; MLD computed; normal hearing at time of test	PE tube group postsurgery MLD at 1 yr: 11.4 dB (55% < control 95% CI) MLD at 2 yr: 12.4 dB (21% < control 95% CI) MLD at 3 yr: 13.1 dB (same as controls) MLD at 4 yr: (same as controls) MLD at 3 mo postsurgery correlated with presurgery HL asymmetry, but not degree of HL
Moore[66] 1991	6–12 yr, adults	Documented history	Signal detection in background noise	MLD	MLD reduced in OM+ children versus OM– children and adults
Hutchings[71] 1992	7–10 mo, 7–12 yr, adults	Documented history	Signal detection in background noise	MLD at 0.05 kHz	MLD reduced in OM+ and OM– infants versus children and adults

Table 22-6 Auditory Processing in Infants and Children with OME Histories Using Psychoacoustic Tests (MLD, CMR, and VAL) (continued)

Author Year	Age (N); Groups	OME/Hearing Documentation	Binaural Processing Task	Procedure	Outcome
Hogan[82] 1996	12–18 yr (43); OM+ (26), OM– (17)	Subjects from Moore[66] 6–12 yr later	Signal detection in background noise	MLD	MLD same in OM– controls versus OM+ group (≥ 5 OM episodes below age 5 yr)
Hall[68] 1998a	5.5–11.0 yr (17); OM+ (7), OM– (10)	OM+ group received PETs	Signal detection in noise delayed and "shifted" to various degrees from midline (0°)	MLD: 3-AFT with 0.5 kHz pure tone 0.1 kHz wide noise band masker; threshold for tone S0 and Sπ with noise signal time delayed in μs (approximate phase shifts of −131°, −65°, 65°, 131°, 180°); MLD computed	MLD smaller for OM+ group in 3 shortest noise time delays (3 smallest phase differences) versus OM– controls; all had normal hearing at testing
Hall[69] 1998b	5–11.9 yr (63); OM+ (34), OM– (29)	OM+ group received PETs	Signal detection in simple or complex noise masking background	CMR: one ear tested with 4 masking conditions: (1) on-signal band, (2) comodulated, (3) comodulated +2 codeviant bands, (4) comodulated +8 codeviant bands 25 OM+ tested presurgery and postsurgery (1 mo, 6 mo, 1 yr); 9 OM+ only postsurgery; normal hearing at test time	CMR performance of OM+ group unaffected for simplest task (detection of tone in single noise band). CMR greatest effect and longest recovery time for most complex task (tone detection in background in two independent patterns of modulation)
Besing[72] 1995	Children, adults (15); OM+ (5); OM– (5 adults, 5 children)	Retrospective history, parent report	Localization of speech in quiet and reverberant environments and signal detection in background noise	VAL, MLD: MLD measured at 4 frequencies (0.25, 0.5, 2, and 4 kHz).	VAL: OM+ group greater localization errors (~2 positions away from the actual source) and fewer correct identification of source location than OM– children and adults in both listening environments MLD: smaller for OM+ group only at .25 kHz

CI = confidence interval; CMR = comodulation masking release; MLD = binaural masking level difference; OM = otitis media; 2-AFT = two–alternative forced choice; 3-AFT = three-alternative forced choice; PETs = pressure equalizing tubes; S0 = signal in phase; Sπ = signal out of phase; VAL = virtual auditory localization tasks.

condition; and (2) noise in phase and signal presented 180° out-of-phase (NoSπ). Small MLDs indicate that the individual is receiving less advantage from inter-ear cues.[64]

There is a maturational time course for the developing MLD.[74,75] Nozza and colleagues[74] found that the MLD is smaller in infants than in preschoolers (age 3.5 to 4.5 years) and smaller in preschoolers than in adults. In a normative study of children, Hall and Grose[75] found that by age 6 years, the MLD is within the 95% confidence interval for adults.

The MLD is significantly smaller in children with conductive hearing loss (eg., OME) than in children without hearing loss or a history of MEE and normal-hearing adults.[67,70] After PETs are inserted and audiometrically normal hearing is restored, binaural abilities, as indexed by the MLD, do not immediately return to normal for all children.[67,70] Normalization may first occur months, or even years, after correcting conductive hearing loss.[67,70]

The factor accounting for the lower MLD associated with OME history appears to be a higher masked threshold for the binaural condition (the NoSπ) than in effusion-free controls. The diotic condition (NoSo) is essentially within the range expected for both groups.[60] Thus, children with normal hearing and OME histories benefit less from the binaural difference cue than do peers without OME. The one study of infants with or without OME using an MLD paradigm found that infants with OME histories had smaller MLDs than normal-hearing peers.[71] By adolescence, the same children had normal MLDs, presumably from normal experiences with binaural input following the resolution of OME in early childhood.

Since the hearing loss with OME often is associated with poorer low-frequency thresholds than high, inter-ear asymmetries and unilateral impairments, it is tempting to speculate that these auditory characteristics could impact binaural performance. As such, the MLD task (useful for infants and children) may provide a unique, nonlinguistic, and time-efficient way of examining the course of the recovery or the development of typical binaural abilities during or after the auditory impairment associated with OME.

Sound Localization Abilities

Accurately determining the source of a sound is among the most fundamental of binaural skills. Studies examining infants with or without unilateral OME and children with or without histories of OME suggest that effusion and previous experiences with middle ear disease may negatively affect localization abilities.

Besing and Koehnke[72] examined the effect of OME on binaural abilities using a more complex skill—sound localization. They developed a virtual test of localization, Virtual Auditory Localization task (VAL), which eliminates the need for multiple loudspeaker sound-field testing and for the immobility of the listener during testing. Two groups of five children with or without a reported history of OME and five adults had VAL and MLD testing. Children with histories of OME had more errors on the VAL and smaller MLDs (but only at 250 Hz) than controls. Besing and Koehnke[72] suggested that the more complex localization task might be more sensitive to binaural deficits than the MLD. Thus, there appears to be some relationship between small MLDs and errors in localization ability, indicating that the two tests are sensitive to binaural deficits in children with OME. Whether both tests are equally related to physiologic indicators of binaural processing is unknown.

Examined collectively, the results of current psychoacoustic studies suggest that OME and its accompanying conductive hearing loss may compromise binaural auditory abilities (detecting interaural timing cues) for some children in the short term and for others for longer periods of time (months to years). When followed up prospectively, the proportion of children with normal binaural abilities becomes greater, presumably with increasing time (experience) with normal auditory input.

The extensive studies by Hall and colleagues on both binaural processing (referenced above) and other complex auditory tasks[68,69] suggest that children with histories of OME and conductive hearing loss are at a disadvantage for some period after surgical restoration of normal hearing. Time required to restore or develop age-appropriate binaural abilities differs among individuals, which may be related to the duration, severity, asymmetry, and age at onset of persistent conductive hearing loss. Although normal auditory abilities improve with time spent with normal hearing, it is unclear whether reduced binaural abilities, especially in early life, could deleteriously affect a young child's early abilities to listen efficiently in background noise. Deficits in higher-order auditory processing, combined with a noisy home environment or childcare setting, poor quality of instruction, or reduced language stimulation, might adversely affect a child's abilities to optimally parse and act appropriately on complex auditory inputs.

Combining Psychoacoustic and Physiologic Findings

As yet, there is little evidence about the relationship among psychoacoustic and physiologic indices of auditory processing in children with histories of OME. Hall and Grose[64] examined the MLD and the ABR in children with or without histories of OME, but with normal hearing at both evaluations (Table 22-7). They reported a negative relationship between the MLD and ABR inter-ear interpeak latency asymmetries: greater inter-

Table 22-7 Auditory Function in Children with OME Histories Comparing a Psychoacoustic test (MLD) to Physiologic Measures (ABR, OAE)

Author Year	Age (N); Groups	OME/HL Documentation	Design	Outcome 1	Outcome 2
Hall[64] 1993	5.2–9.2 yr (27); OM+ (14), OM– (13)	OM+ group were PET recipients; OM– had negative medical record and parent report	ABR latencies; MLD (0.5 kHz)	OM+ correlations with MLD *Absolute wave latencies: NS* *Inter-ear asymmetries vs. MLD* Waves I–III: r = –.64, p < .05 Waves I–V: r = –.68, p < .05 Waves III–V: NS	Significant correlations for presurgery threshold asymmetries & several inter-ear asymmetries OM– group No relationship ABR-MLD
Stollman[83] 1996	~12 yr (5); OM+ group only	Otitis media history (mainly unilateral) ages 2–4 yr, untreated	ABR, ABR-BIC, MLD, OAE	No abnormal findings on any measure	OAE-suppression results equivalent to adult norms

ABR = auditory brainstem response; ABR-BIC = auditory brainstem response–binaural interaction component; MLD = binaural masking level difference; NS = not significant; OAE = otoacoustic emissions; OM = otitis media; PETs = pressure equalization tubes.

ear asymmetry on ABR had a smaller MLD. This implies a potentially important relationship between efficiency of the binaural auditory system to detect signals in background noise (MLD) and inter-ear asymmetry at the brainstem level (ABR) in children with histories of OME and conductive hearing loss.

CLINICAL AND RESEARCH IMPLICATIONS

A growing body of intriguing evidence indicates that some children experience short- and long-term auditory consequences of early OME, hearing loss later in childhood, and after surgery for persistent OME. Despite normal peripheral hearing in the conventional audiometric range, long-term higher-order auditory-perceptual sequelae have been detected by electrophysiologic, psychoacoustic, and behavioral test procedures. Whether such deficits have functional consequences for the child in the home and academic environments is uncertain.

Research, to date, suggests that short-term higher-order auditory effects of the conductive hearing loss associated with OME result from a reduced acoustic signal reaching the ear (auditory deprivation). If such atypical indices resolved once hearing became normal, then the hearing loss might be of little consequence. A growing body of evidence, however, shows that some

auditory-perceptual sequelae persist for months or years, even although peripheral hearing becomes normal. Apparently in some children, deficits in basic auditory abilities, including binaural processing of sound, underlying physiology, and higher-order auditory processing of speech, persist for short or longer amounts of time despite normal hearing and neural plasticity.

Future research is needed to clarify host susceptibility, determine comprehensively the degree of adverse impact, and predict what skills are likely to be compromised. Comparing children whose experiences with OME and hearing loss resolved early in life with those with more recent conductive deficits associated with MEE should delineate auditory-perceptual sequelae that are likely to resolve immediately following a period of normal hearing from those that persist. This would considerably help clinicians in counseling and in planning, providing, and timing specific medical, surgical, audiologic, and other interventions.

Collectively, the evidence regarding hearing loss and later auditory function of children with OME suggests the need for more rigorous attention to assessing and delineating any auditory physiologic and functional consequences of the conductive hearing loss associated with OME. Table 22-8 offers some pointers and strategies to help clinicians reduce the risk of poor outcomes in children with OME or significant OME histories.[76]

Table 22-8 Pointers and Strategies to Reduce the Risk of Poor Outcomes in Children with OME*

1. Consider the hearing loss associated with OME as a primary risk condition.

2. Directly assess degree of hearing loss using frequency- and ear-specific (whenever possible) air- and bone-conduction test methods.
   - Speech awareness threshold (SAT) in younger infants and children and speech recognition/reception threshold (SRT) in older children can estimate overall hearing status.
   - SAT and SRT are not a sufficient test of hearing sensitivity for purposes of determining the type, degree, and configuration of hearing loss.

3. Monitor hearing status over time.

4. Evaluate hearing beyond the conventional audiogram, including behavioral, electrophysiologic, and psychoacoustic measures of speech perception in background noise and binaural abilities.

5. Screen for communication development and academic performance.

6. Provide information to parents and caregivers regarding means to improve the acoustic conditions of homes, childcare, and educational settings.

OME = otitis media with effusion.
*Adapted from Gravel JS and Wallace IF.[76]

REFERENCES

1. Vernon-Feagans L. Impact of otitis media on speech, language, cognition and behavior. In: Rosenfeld RM, Bluestone CD, editors. Evidence-based otitis media. Hamilton (ON): BC Decker; 1999. p. 353–73.

2. Feagans LV. Otitis media: a model for long-term effects with implications for intervention. In: Kavanaugh JF, editor. Otitis media and child development. Parkton (MD): York Press; 1986. p. 192–208.

3. Feagans LV, Kipp EK, Blood I. The effects of otitis media on the language and attention skills of daycare attending toddlers. Dev Psychol 1994;30:701–8.

4. Roberts JE, Burchinal MR, Medley LP, et al. Otitis media, hearing sensitivity, and maternal responsiveness in relation to language during infancy. J Pediatr 1995;126:481–9.

5. Roberts JE, Burchinal MR, Zeisel S, et al. Otitis media, the caregiving environment, and language and cognitive outcomes at 2 years. Pediatrics 1998;102:346–53.

6. Roberts JE, Burchinal MR, Collier AM, et al. Otitis media in early childhood and cognitive, academic and classroom performance of the school-aged child. Pediatrics 1989;83:477–85.

7. Wallace IF, Gravel JS, Schwartz R, Ruben RJ. Otitis media, parental linguistic style and language skills at 2-years of age. J Dev Behav Pediatr 1996;17:27–35.

8. Nittrouer S. The relation between speech perception and phonemic awareness: evidence from low-SES children and children with chronic OM. J Speech Hear Res 1996;39:1059–70.

9. Vernon-Feagans L, Emmanuel DC, Blood I. The effect of otitis media and quality of day care and quality of day care on children's language development. J Appl Dev Psychol 1997;18:395–409.

10. Rutter M. Psychosocial resilience and protective mechanisms. Am J Orthopsychiatry 1987;57:316–31.

11. Paradise JL. Otitis media in early life: how hazardous to development? A critical review of evidence. Pediatrics 1981;68:869–73.

12. Gravel JS, Wallace IF. Early otitis media, auditory abilities and educational risk. Am J Speech Language Pathol 1995;4:89–94.

13. Wallace IF, Gravel JS, McCarton CM, et al. Otitis media, auditory sensitivity, and language outcomes at one year. Laryngoscope 1988;8:64–70.

14. Friel-Patti S, Finitzo T. Language learning in a prospective study of otitis media with effusion. J Speech Hear Res 1990;33:188–94.

15. Needleman H. Effects of hearing loss from early recurrent otitis media on speech and language development. In: Jaffe B, editor. Hearing loss in children. Baltimore (MD): University Park Press; 1977. p. 640–9.

16. Skinner MW. The hearing of speech during language acquisition. Otolaryngol Clin North Am 1978;11:631–50.

17. Menyuk P. Predicting speech and language problems with persistent otitis media. In: Kavanaugh J, editor. Otitis media and child development. Parkton (MD): York Press; 1986. p. 192–208.

18. Daly KA. Definition and epidemiology of otitis media. In: Roberts JE, Wallace IF, Henderson FW, editors. Otitis media in young children. Baltimore (MD): Paul H. Brookes Publishing Co. 1997. p. 3–41.

19. Dobie R, Berlin C. Influence of otitis media on hearing and development. Ann Otol Rhinol Laryngol 1979;88:48–53.

20. Hogan SC, Stratford KJ, Moore DR. Duration and recurrence of otitis media with effusion in children from birth to 3 years: prospective study using monthly otoscopy and tympanometry. BMJ 1997;314:350.

21. Zeisel SA, Roberts JE, Gunn EB, et al. Prospective surveillance for otitis media with effusion among black infants in group child care. J Pediatr 1995;127:481–9.

22. Zeisel SA, Roberts JE, Neebe EC, et al. A longitudinal

study of otitis media with effusion among 2- to 5-year-old African-American children in child care. Pediatrics 1999;103:15–9.

23. Gravel JS, Wallace IF. Effects of otitis media with effusion on hearing in the first three years of life. J Speech Lang Hear Res 2000;43:631–44.

24. Stephenson H, Haggard M, Zielhuis G, et al. Prevalence of tympanogram asymmetries and fluctuations in otitis media with effusion: implications for binaural hearing. Audiology 1993;32:164–74.

25. Webster DB. Neuroscience of communication. 2nd ed. San Diego (CA): Singular Publishing Group, Inc.; 1999.

26. Marsh RR, Baranak CC, Potsic WP. Hearing loss and visco-elasticity of middle ear fluid. Int J Pediatr Otorhinolaryngol 1985;9:115–20.

27. Wiederhold ML, Zajtchuk JT, Vap JG, Paggi RE. Hearing loss in relation to physical properties of middle ear effusion. Ann Otol Rhinol Laryngol 1980;89 Suppl 68:185–9.

28. Brown DT, Marsh RR, Potsic WP. Hearing loss induced by viscous fluids in the middle ear. Int J Pediatr Otorhinolaryngol 1983;5:39–46.

29. Lupovich P, Bluestone CD, Paradise JL, Harkins MT. Middle ear effusions: preliminary viscometric, histologic and biochemical studies. Ann Otol 1971;80:342–6.

30. Majima Y, Hamaguchi Y, Hirata K, et al. Hearing impairment in relation to viscoelasticity of middle ear effusions in children. Ann Otol Rhinol Laryngol 1988;97:272–4.

31. ASHA: American Speech Language Hearing Association. Guidelines for audiologic screening. Rockville (MD): ASHA; 1997.

32. Haggard RS, Primus MA. Parental perceptions of hearing loss classification in children. Am J Audiol 1999;8:83–92.

33. Rosenfeld RM, Goldsmith AJ, Madell JR. How accurate is parent rating of hearing for children with otitis media? Arch Otolaryngol Head Neck Surg 1998;124:989–92.

34. Stewart MG, Ohlms LA, Friedman EM, et al. Is parental perception an accurate predictor of childhood hearing loss? A prospective study. Otolaryngol Head Neck Surg 1999;120:340–4.

35. Anteunis LJ, Engel JA, Hendriks JJ, Manni JJ. A longitudinal study of the validity of parental reporting in the detection of otitis media and related hearing impairment in infancy. Audiology 1999;38:75–82.

36. Fria TJ, Cantekin EI, Eichler JA. Hearing acuity in children with effusion. Arch Otolaryngol 1985;11:10–6.

37. Li Y, Hunter LL, Margolis RH, et al. Prospective study of tympanic membrane retraction, hearing loss, and multifrequency tympanometry. Otolaryngol Head Neck Surg 1999;121:514–22.

38. Gravel JS. Potential pitfalls in the audiological assessment of infants and young children. In: Seewald RC, Gravel JS, editors. A sound foundation through early amplification 2001. Proceedings of the Second International Conference. UK: St. Edmundsbury Press; 2002. p. 85–101.

39. Stapells DR, Gravel JS, Martin BA. Thresholds for auditory brainstem responses to tones in notched noise from infants and young children with normal hearing or sensorineural hearing loss. Ear Hear 1995;16:361–71.

40. Kokko E. Chronic secretory otitis media in children.

41. Hunter LL. Auditory sequelae of recurrent and persistent otitis media with effusion in children [dissertation]. Minneapolis (MN): University of Minnesota; 1993.

42. Pringle MB, Thompson A, Reddy K. A comparison of speech audiometry and pure tone audiometry in patients with secretory otitis media. J Laryngol Otol 1993;107:787–9.

43. Roland PS, Finitzo T, Friel-Patti S, et al. Otitis media: incidence, duration, and hearing status. Arch Otolaryngol Head Neck Surg 1989;115:1049–53.

44. Margolis RH, Saly GL, Hunter LL. High-frequency hearing loss and wideband middle ear impedance in children with otitis media histories. Ear Hear 2000;21:206–11.

45. Hunter LL, Margolis RH, Rykken JR, et al. High frequency hearing loss associated with otitis media. Ear Hear 1996;17:1–11.

46. Ryding M, Konradsson K, Kalm O, Prellner K. Auditory consequences of recurrent acute purulent otitis media. Ann Otol Rhinol Laryngol 2002;111:261–6.

47. Laitila P, Karma P, Sipilä M, et al. Extended high frequency hearing and history of acute otitis media in 14-year-old children in Finland. Acta Otolaryngol (Stockh) 1997;Suppl 529:27–9.

48. Fria TJ, Sabo DL. Auditory brainstem responses in children with otitis media with effusion. Ann Otol Rhinol Laryngol 1979;89:200–6.

49. Owen MJ, Norcross-Nechay K, Howie VM. Brainstem auditory evoked potentials in young children before and after tympanostomy tube placement. Int J Pediatr Otorhinolaryngol 1993;25:105–17.

50. Stapells DR, Mackersie CL. Auditory brainstem response wave I prediction of conductive component in infants and young children. Am J Audiol 1994;3:52–8.

51. Nozza RJ. Infant speech-sound discrimination testing: effects of stimulus intensity and procedural model on measures of performance. J Acoust Soc Am 1987;81:1928–39.

52. Penn TO, Grantham W, Gravel JS. Effects of OME on speech recognition. Presented at the Annual Meeting of the American Academy of Audiology. Philadelphia (PA); 2002. J Am Acad Audiol [Submitted].

53. Petinou KC, Schwartz RG, Gravel JS, Raphael LJ. A preliminary account of phonological and morphological perception in young children with and without otitis media. Int J Lang Commun Dis 2001;36:21–42.

54. Eimas PD, Clarkson RL. Speech perception in children: are there effects of otitis media? In: Kavanaugh J, editor. Otitis media and child development. Parkton (MD): York Press; 1986. p. 139–59.

55. Clarkson RL, Eimas PD, Marean GC. Speech perception in children with histories of recurrent otitis media. J Acoust Soc Am 1989;85:926–33.

56. Groenen P, Crul T, Maassen B, van Bon W. Perception of voicing cues by children with early otitis media with and without language impairment. J Speech Hear Res 1996;39:43–54.

57. Mody M, Schwartz RG, Gravel JS, Ruben RJ. Speech perception and verbal memory in children with and

A clinical study. Acta Otolaryngol 1974;327 Suppl:1–44.

without histories of otitis media. J Speech Lang Hear Res 1999;42:1069–79.

58. DeMarco S, Givens GD. Speech sound discrimination pre- and post-tympanostomy: a clinical case report. Ear Hear 1989;10:64–7.

59. Rosenfeld RM, Madell JR, McMahon A. Auditory function in normal-hearing children with middle ear effusion. In: Lim DJ, Bluestone CD, Casselbrandt M, et al, editors. Recent advances in otitis media: proceedings of the 6th international symposium, Hamilton (ON): BC Decker, Inc.; 1996. p. 354–6.

60. Jerger S, Jerger J, Alford BR, Abrams S. Development of speech intelligibility in children with recurrent otitis media. Ear Hear 1983;4:138–45.

61. Gravel JS, Wallace IF. Listening and language at 4 years of age: effects of early otitis media. J Speech Hear Res 1992;35:588–95.

62. Schilder AGM, Snik AFM, Straatman H, van den Broek P. The effect of otitis media with effusion at preschool age on some aspects of auditory perception at school age. Ear Hear 1994;15:224–31.

63. Gunnarson AD, Finitzo T. Conductive hearing loss during infancy: effects on later auditory brain stem electrophysiology. J Speech Hear Res 1991;34:1207–15.

64. Hall JW, Grose JH. The effect of otitis media with effusion on the masking-level difference and the auditory brainstem response. J Speech Hear Res 1993;36:210–7.

65. Ferguson MO, Cook RD, Hall JW, Grose JH, Pillsbury HC. Chronic conductive hearing loss in adults. Effects on the auditory brainstem response and masking-level difference. Arch Otolaryngol Head Neck Surg 1998;124:678–85.

66. Moore DR, Hutchings ME, Meyer SE. Binaural masking level differences in children with a history of otitis media. Audiol 1991;30:91–101.

67. Hall JW, Grose JH, Pillsbury HC Long-term effects of chronic otitis media on binaural hearing in children. Arch Otolaryngol Head Neck Surg 1995;121:847–52.

68. Hall JW, Grose JH, Dev MB, Ghassi S. The effect of masker interaural time delay on the masking level difference in children with history of normal hearing or history of otitis media with effusion. Ear Hear 1998;19:429–33.

69. Hall JW, Grose JH, Dev MB, et al. The effect of otitis media with effusion on complex masking tasks in chil-

dren. Arch Otolaryngol Head Neck Surg 1998;124:892–6.

70. Pillsbury HC, Grose JH, Hall JW. Otitis media with effusion in children: binaural hearing before and after corrective surgery. Arch Otolaryngol 1991;117:718–23.

71. Hutchings ME, Meyer SE, Moore DR. Binaural masking level differences in infants with and without otitis media with effusion. Hear Res 1992;63:71–8.

72. Besing J, Koehnke J. A test of virtual auditory localization. Ear Hear 1995;16:220–9.

73. Morrongiello B. Infant's binaural localization of sounds: effects of unilateral ear infection. J Acoust Soc Am 1989;86:597–602.

74. Nozza RJ, Wagner EF, Crandell MA. Binaural release from masking for a speech sound in infants, preschoolers, and adults. J Speech Hear Res 1988;31:211–8.

75. Hall JW, Grose JH. The masking level difference in children. J Am Acad Audiol 1990;1:81–8.

76. Gravel JS, Wallace IF. Audiologic management of otitis media. In: Bess F, editor. Children with hearing impairment. Contemporary trends. Nashville (TN): Vanderbilt Bill Wilkerson Center Press; 1998. p. 215–27.

77. Bluestone CD, Beery QC, Paradise JL. Audiometry and tympanometry in relation to middle ear effusion in children. Laryngoscope 1973;83:594–604.

78. Folsom RC, Weber BA, Thompson GT. Auditory brainstem responses in children with early recurrent middle ear disease. Ann Otol Rhinol Laryngol 1983;92:249–53.

79. Lenhardt ML, Shaia FT, Abedi E. Brain-stem evoked response waveform variation associated with recurrent otitis media. Arch Otolaryngol 1985;111:315–6.

80. Anteby I, Hafner H, Pratt H, Uri N. Auditory brainstem evoked potentials in evaluating the central effects of middle ear effusion. Int J Pediatr Otorhinolaryngol 1986;12:1–11.

81. Chambers RD, Rowan LF, Matthies ML, Novak MA. Auditory brain-stem responses in children with previous otitis media. Arch Otolaryngol Head Neck Surg 1989;115:452–7.

82. Hogan SC, Meyer SE, Moore DR. Binaural unmasking returns to normal in teenagers who had otitis media in infancy. Audiol Neurootol 1996;1:104–11.

83. Stollman MH, Snik AF, Schilder AG, van den Broek P. Measures of binaural hearing in children with a history of asymmetric otitis media with effusion. Audiol Neurootol 1996;1:175–85.

CHAPTER 23

Speech, Language, Pragmatics, and Attention

Lynne Vernon-Feagans, PhD, Adele W. Miccio, PhD, and Kristine M. Yont, PhD

*If one cannot state a matter clearly enough so that even an intelligent twelve-year-old can understand it,
one should remain within the cloistered walls of the university and laboratory
until one has a better grasp of one's subject.*
Margaret Mead

OBJECTIVES

On completing this chapter, the reader will be able to
1. Understand the possible pathways through which otitis media (OM) may affect development.
2. Appreciate how mediators and moderators affect developmental outcomes.
3. Summarize the impact of OM on speech, language, pragmatics, and attention.
4. Recognize methodologic differences that have prompted controversy in the literature on OM.

This chapter updates research on how otitis media (OM) affects child development, emphasizing recent prospective studies. In the first edition of this book, we reviewed a broader range of effects, but we now focus on three aspects of development that need greater research emphasis and can help better understand how and when OM may impact development: (1) speech processes and phonologic development in early life, (2) receptive and expressive language, especially using language in narratives and to interact with others (pragmatics), and (3) attention to language and its implications for school-age children.

We begin by reviewing and summarizing the historic literature of how OM affects development. Next, we examine second-generation studies of the Global Language Model and third-generation studies using more detailed models to explain how OM affects development in different ways under certain conditions. In this way, we hope to develop a newer conceptual model that argues for understanding how OM impacts the three areas noted above. Evidence tables are updated with prospective studies published since the first edition and now include columns describing sample characteristics with respect to ethnicity and socioeconomic status. Last, we discuss the importance of these characteristics and implications for future research.

THEORETIC MODELS OF OTITIS MEDIA AND CHILD DEVELOPMENT

First-Generation Models and Research

Over the past 30 years, hundreds of research articles have examined whether OM affects child development. From the early speculation of clinicians and researchers, such as Marion Downs, Jerry Northern, and Paula Menyuk,[1,2] that very young children with persistent OM in early life were likely to experience prolonged periods of intermittent hearing loss that might affect the development of language, researchers have studied children's development in relation to their OM histories. The proposed causal variable that affected language, however, was intermittent hearing loss, not OM, per se. The initial model of effects that was postulated by these early pioneers in the field is depicted in Figure 23-1.

In the Global Language Model the causal (intermediate) variable for poor language-related outcomes is hearing loss. The hearing loss accompanying OM is intermittent between and within episodes, varies from child to child, and has been one of the most difficult constructs to assess (see Chapter 22, "Hearing and Auditory Function"). Early pioneers postulated that intermittent hearing loss might affect early language acquisition because OM is most frequent in the first years of life. Further, ample evidence suggested that even a mild sensorineural hearing loss could affect language and academic development. Gravel and Nozza[3] concluded that a permanent sensorineural hearing loss of the same magnitude as conductive loss during OM could cause poor speech, language, and academic outcomes. Similarly, children with unilateral and bilateral permanent hearing loss of 25 to 50 dB have short- and long-term problems with speech, language, and social and academic functioning.[4,5]

In this Global Language Model, the speech and language problems were not well specified but were thought to occur early and later in development because of intermittent hearing loss. This model was influenced

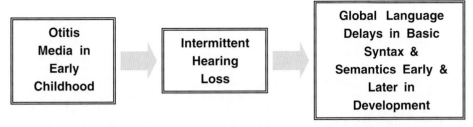

Figure 23-1   Global Language Model of otitis media and developmental outcomes. Intermittent hearing loss is the intervening variable, associated with both the independent variable (otitis media) and the dependent variable (developmental outcomes).

by the fact that speech and language develop relatively quickly, and almost miraculously, in children around the globe in the first 2 or 3 years of life. The incidence of OM and the prevalence of middle ear effusion (MEE) are also highest during these critical first 2 or 3 years of speech and language development.

Animal and some human studies[6,7] suggest that auditory deprivation during early brain development can lead to underdeveloped auditory pathways and early auditory deprivation, even in rather mild forms in humans, and permanent speech and language problems. Further, certain neural and auditory paths may develop later and abnormally without optimal auditory input early in life.[3] Thus, much theoretic work was based on a "critical period" during which normal hearing was necessary. Consequently, experts agreed that even a mild intermittent hearing loss early in life could cause both short- and long-term effects on speech and language because of the timing of the hearing loss in the developing child.

The question with respect to OM was and still continues to be: "Can an intermittent hearing loss during the early years of life that is not permanent in nature lead to poor developmental outcomes early and later in development?" This early speculation led a number of experts to compare children who had a history of persistent OM with similar children who did not have a history of OM. These initial retrospective studies[8–11] found that children with a history of persistent OM in early childhood had language and academic problems later in childhood.

Retrospective studies argued for possible effects of OM on development but had fundamental flaws because they relied on parent reports or medical records for measuring OM experience, which are both unreliable.[12] Moreover, many initial studies examined children already diagnosed with a learning problem. These samples did not represent the larger population, making it difficult to conceptualize appropriate comparison groups. Further, none of these initial studies documented hearing associated with the OM episodes and, therefore, lacked critical data that were expensive and difficult to ascertain in very young children. Despite these and other methodologic flaws,[12,13] retrospective studies were important first steps in understanding the possible effects of OM on development.

Second-Generation Models and Research

The second generation of studies that examined the effects of OM on development improved on earlier retrospective studies in many ways but, as will be pointed out in this chapter, also had deficiencies that hampered the field in understanding the precise impact of persistent OM in early life. Like the first-generation studies, most second-generation studies used the theoretic model depicted in Figure 23-1 to guide their hypotheses and choice of measures. Studies reviewed here are prospective and used otoscopy and tympanometry to diagnose OM. Most report some hearing loss data.

Understanding how hearing loss is measured is important because the frequency and/or duration of OM are often used as proxies. All the studies reported in this chapter used pneumatic otoscopy or otoscopy in diagnosing OM; some also used tympanometry. Combining pneumatic otoscopy and tympanometry is best for detecting OM.[14] Reported studies vary in their ability to differentiate among different types of OM (eg, acute OM, chronic MEE), so this aspect is not emphasized. Although otitis media with effusion (OME) is presumed in many of these research articles, it is not always carefully explained. Overall, OM will be used as the more global term in discussing this body of research literature and in describing the "models" that hypothesize the possible short- and long-term effects of OM.

Some children with OM experience hearing loss; however, it has been very difficult to obtain adequate hearing data on infants and young children who do not often cooperate with testing, especially when suffering from OM. Sound field audiometry is possible in infants, but cooperation is crucial for validity, and even under optimal testing conditions, only hearing in the better ear can be assessed. Testing using headphones is usually not possible until after age 2 years, when the frequency of OM decreases. Although auditory brainstem response (ABR) and other related measures can assess broad

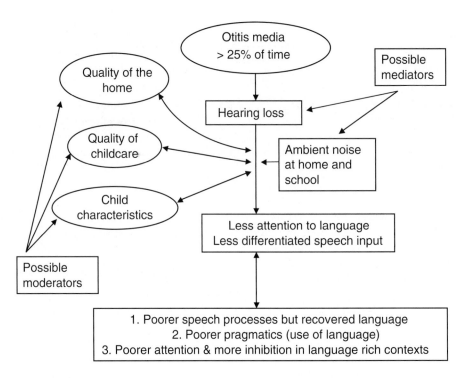

Figure 23-2 Contextual Transactional Model of otitis media and developmental outcomes. Note the bidirectional relationship of possible moderator variables and adverse outcomes.

hearing acuity without the child's direct cooperation, children usually must be sedated for the procedure, making it unlikely that this type of testing would be performed on a regular basis during episodes of OM. Consequently, the hearing loss data in many studies are scant or missing. The proxy for hearing loss is often the number of episodes of OM or an estimate of the OM duration.

In the first studies of the effects of OM, most attention was focused on developmental outcomes linked in some way to speech and language outcomes. These included not only language test performance early in life but also later more distal measures of children's language. Several studies showed that early oral language problems could lead to poorer performance on intelligence quotient (IQ) tests and especially reading.[15,16] Thus, OM studies have often examined school achievement measures as the distal outcome measure of early language problems.

Third-Generation Models and Research

At the time of the previous edition, few research projects used an interaction or transactional model of development to understand the impact of OM (Figure 23-2). Two current projects use these models to help understand the multiple factors in early childhood that affect development in conjunction with OM experi-

ence. These models are much more complex and place OM as just one of many factors in early childhood that can affect development. For example, Roberts and colleagues,[17,18] who studied primarily low-income African American children, have stressed the influence of the home environment and OM on development. Bidirectional effects are stressed, suggesting that early infant characteristics influence parental and adult input to the child, which, in turn, affect the child in a transactional process over time. This kind of model helps place the role of the OM experience in the larger context of early development.

The model of effects proposed here is an updated version of the one presented in this chapter in the earlier edition. The logic of this model is somewhat different from that of the Global Language Model in two important ways. First, this model conceptualizes the OM effects using a threshold effect, and second, this model uses mediating and moderating variables to better understand other causal variables in development along with the conditions under which OM may have effects on development. As we lay out these features of the model, we emphasize the importance of our three outcome variables: speech, language, and attention. Thus, before we discuss the mechanisms in the model, we explain why there may be effects in these three domains of development.

THREE DOMAINS OF CHILD DEVELOPMENT

Speech and Language

Our model suggests few long-term effects of OM on basic language processes, except effects on basic speech processes. We argue this because the hearing loss from OM is intermittent and, for most children, becomes much less frequent after 3 years of age. Thus, the long-term effects of OM may not be directly linked to language per se.

Lenneberg[6] and Rubin[7] present evidence for the resiliency of the early period. Even with large brain insults and environmental deprivations, most children eventually acquire functional vocabulary and syntax. As in the Global Language Model, speech and language are postulated to be affected early in life because of the hearing loss experienced by numerous and lengthy bouts of OM. But because of the redundant and frequent cues in language input, the contextual model hypothesizes that most language functions will be recovered as children mature biologically in a protective environment that buffers them against lasting problems.

If children cannot hear some of the sounds of the language, the transactional model suggests that unlike syntactic and lexical development, phonologic development may not be impervious to negative effects. Both the chronicity of OM and the amount of hearing loss negatively affect phonologic acquisition in recent research.[19,20] Although typically developing children produce atypical utterances periodically during early development, these features disappear rather quickly.[21] In our sample, atypical productions persisted in children with the most bouts of OM. Thus, we expect that these phonologic problems could persist into school age as emergent reading problems.

Attention to Language

Vernon-Feagans has used the Contextual Transactional Model (see Figure 23-2),[13,22,23] to argue that children with an intermittent mild hearing loss in early childhood eventually learn the basic grammatical rules and vocabulary of their language and may not appear to have global language deficits later in childhood on standardized tests. Yet, these long periods of hearing loss during early life may affect the child's attention to language input. Children with chronic problems may learn to "tune out" language and attend to other nonauditory signals from the environment. This lack of attention to language may become a persistent coping strategy and lead to less and less attention to language in situations where sustained attention is needed in order to comprehend information. Consequently, children with per-

sistent OM in early childhood may have a much harder time comprehending extended discourse, storytelling, or extended topic elaborations that occur in school.

Lack of attention to language may also affect social interactions with peers and adults.[24,25] Young children with hearing loss may be able to understand language in a quiet environment or in a one-to-one interaction but may have difficulty in and avoid situations where many children are talking or in situations with background noise. Thus, these children appear to have attention problems and also may be more likely to withdraw from language-rich situations and become inhibited in these contexts. They may also have atypical or immature speech production patterns that hinder their ability to participate in conversation, resulting in communication breakdowns.[26] Speech and language difficulties may also impair phonologic awareness and cause subsequent problems learning to read and spell.[19,20] Using the bidirectionality depicted in our model, poorer initial use of language may affect the kind of input children receive from others and may set up a pattern of interaction that can persist over time.

Pragmatics

Pragmatics is the use of language in context, including knowing when and how to use certain language forms and nonverbal communicative cues. Early communication is highly pragmatic,[27] involving the purposeful expression of communicative intents using gestures, vocalizations, and words.[28,29]

Recent research suggests that early gestures and gesture-word combinations predict children's later verbal ability.[30–33] The literature of typically developing children has focused much attention on pragmatics; however, few studies have investigated this domain in children with OM, despite the fact that early intentional communication may serve as a predictor for these children's later communication development. In addition, pragmatic differences may be evident in preschoolers and school-age children with histories of OM, as their earlier hearing loss may result in learned patterns of reduced attention to auditory input; thus, skills requiring sustained attention, such as pragmatics, may be less developed.

Pragmatics also includes using language in conversation with others and the comprehension and expression of oral narratives. Children with OM may have syntactic and semantic skills resembling those of their non-OM peers, as measured by standardized tests. Roberts and colleagues have reported recovered language skills.[17] More likely, children with histories of OM may attend less to language in the preschool years and, therefore, may not have developed discourse skills required to interact successfully with conversational partners. Some recent studies reviewed later in this chapter have suggested that this is the case in both early and later childhood.[25,34]

Two Processes in the Contextual Transactional Model

Threshold Effects

A threshold model suggests that individuals can experience adverse life events without any significant negative outcomes because of both internal and external compensatory mechanisms that help buffer individuals from negative events. Yet, when this experience reaches a critical level, at one point in time or a critical amount over time, negative effects do result. For example, small amounts of air pollution have negligible effects on development because the lungs and other organs can absorb and eliminate pollutants; however, at certain levels of pollution, adverse health effects occur. This could also be the experience with OM. In the Contextual Transactional Model, OM is hypothesized to only have an effect in young children who have the disease for substantial amounts of time in early childhood. Conversely, children with infrequent or transient OM do not have detrimental outcomes.

Figure 23-3 illustrates a threshold effect for children's pragmatic skills in kindergarten in relationship to early experience with OM.[35] There was no relationship between OM and language use until the children had at least nine episodes of OM in the first 3 years of life. After that threshold had been reached, there was an important relationship between OM and our pragmatic variable of paraphrasing a story: additional episodes substantially reduced the child's ability to paraphrase effectively.

Another example of threshold effect can be found in research we reported on children's attention behavior

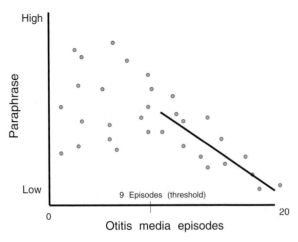

Figure 23-3 Scatterplot of a child's ability to paraphrase a story versus otitis media episodes experienced in the first 3 years of life. The regression line indicates a significant negative correlation after the threshold of nine episodes is surpassed. Data from Vernon-Feagans et al.[35]

at age 2 years in relation to their OM histories (Table 23-1).[13] Children were divided into those with OM less than 20% of the time in early childhood, based on weekly pneumatic otoscopy and tympanometry (nonchronic OM group), and those with OM greater than 20% in early childhood (chronic OM group). The relationship between OM and nonattention was not significant for the nonchronic children who had OM less than 20% of the time, but there was a strong relationship between OM and nonattending behaviors once this threshold was surpassed.

A threshold effect can be seen in hearing data (Figure 23-4) from 66 children in the first 3 years of life tested in sound field when they were well and during episodes of bilateral OM (data from 322 ears). Two groups were identified using a median split: chronic

Table 23-1 Maternal Ratings of Behavior at 24 Months of Age versus Prior OM History

Variables	Correlation of Negative Behavior with OM Proportion		
	Chronic OM*	Nonchronic OM	Overall
General negative affect	0.18	0.03	0.08
Nonattentional behaviors	[†]0.44	0.20	[‡]0.43
Poor communication	0.22	0.00	0.09
Poor intelligent behavior	0.28	− 0.37	− 0.08

OM = otitis media.

*Chronic OM is an OM prevalence of 20% or higher in early childhood.

[†]$p < .05$.

[‡]$p < .01$.

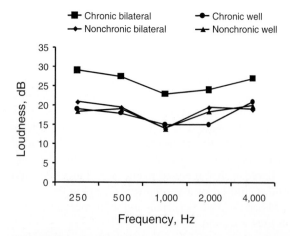

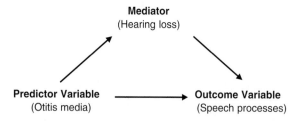

Figure 23-5 Example of a mediator effect, with hearing loss as the primary mediating variable between otitis media and negative outcomes.

Figure 23-4 Sound field thresholds for chronic ears (bilateral otitis media versus well) and nonchronic ears (bilateral otitis media versus well) for children under 24 months of age. Only the chronic bilateral group had elevated hearing thresholds at all speech frequencies compared with their thresholds when well. Data from Vernon-Feagans.[45]

(> 20% of the time) versus nonchronic. The chronic OM group had elevated hearing thresholds during episodes of OM across all the speech frequencies compared with their thresholds when well. Conversely, the nonchronic group had hearing thresholds during episodes of bilateral OM that did not differ from their thresholds when well. Since hearing is assumed to be the variable that may cause developmental problems, developmental problems should not be apparent for the half of the sample that had nonchronic OM.

Not examining threshold effect may mask important negative effects for subgroups of children with OM: the overall relationship between OM and outcomes may be nonsignificant because the effect was only present in the most chronic group. In many studies, OM is used as a continuous variable, and an extreme group that might show effects is not analyzed for threshold effects. For example, Paradise and colleagues[36] excluded children who were most affected by OM in a correlation study because they were enrolled in a clinical trial. Therefore, the modest effects they found excluded children with the most extreme OM experience in early life. Since it is unclear where the threshold effect for OM might be for young children, it is important to think about studies that might use an extreme group comparison or a median split on experience with OM to examine threshold effects.

Mediators and Moderators and Cumulative Risk

The second way in which the model differs is by methodologic concepts that specify the conditions under

which OM might lead to negative outcomes. In the Contextual Transactional Model, there are *mediating and moderating* variables through which OM effects development. *Mediators* can be conceived as possible causal variables that intervene between a predictor and outcome variable and account for more of the variance in the outcome variable than the initial predictor variable. Hearing loss, for example, is thought to be the primary mediating variable between OM and negative outcomes. Figure 23-5 depicts this mediating relationship.

Mediator Variables

Parental input and the quality of the home environment is another possible mediating variable that has been conceptualized here and elsewhere as being a powerful variable that affects all aspects of children's development.[17,18] While typically developing infants appear to be well buffered against variations in parental input, children with mild-to-moderate hearing loss may have to learn language without the availability of some of this buffering.[16] Because children with OM attend less to language input, they are at risk of missing many of the meaningful language experiences available to typically developing children.[13,22,35] Consequently, these children may be more dependent than their typically developing peers on the availability of optimal parent input if they are to show normal patterns of language acquisition.

Parents interact differently with children with chronic OM than with healthy children. For example, Roberts and colleagues[18] found that quality and responsiveness of the home environment was significantly lower at 9 and 18 months for children with OM than healthy peers, and Black and colleagues[37] reported that mothers displayed less social behavior with children who had OM than did mothers of healthy children. Similarly, Yont and colleagues[25] found that parents of 12-month-old children with chronic OM engaged in significantly fewer joint attention episodes and were more directive in their play with their infants than were parents who had children without chronic OM.

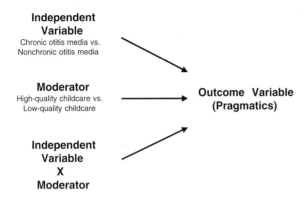

Figure 23-6 Example of a moderator effect, whereby effects of the independent variable (otitis media) on pragmatics are moderated by the quality of childcare.

Current research on language development has implications for this finding. Normally developing children's language development appears to be facilitated when parents engage in discussions of joint attention[38] and when parental directives are associated with less-developed language.[39] Enriched parent talk may buffer the potentially negative language outcomes associated with OM because children with OM may depend more on optimal parental input than their healthy counterparts to achieve typical patterns of language development.[17,18,37,40]

Moderator Variables

There are also moderating variables that represent the conditions under which good or bad outcomes occur. Moderators partition the predictor or independent variable to examine interactions between independent or predictor variables. Understanding the conditions under which OM can have effects is extremely important and has been valuable in our work.[34,41,42]

Figure 23-6 depicts how moderators work in examining interactions. The independent variable (OM) is partitioned such that the interest was in whether chronic and nonchronic OM may affect children differently depending on whether they are in high- or low-quality childcare. Thus, it depicts whether there would be an interaction between OM and quality of care in understanding its effects on pragmatics. In our work, we have been interested in whether children with chronic OM in low-quality care would have greater problems than the other three groups.

Moderator variables are a theoretic underpinning of our Contextual Transactional Model, called by some "the cumulative risk" model.[43] Moderator variables can interact with OM in producing effects. The model postulates that children with persistent OM and hearing loss can be buffered against bad effects in environ-

ments where there is greater one-to-one interaction with adults, there is little or no background noise, and adults are sensitive to the child's reduced hearing. Conversely, the effects of OM may be exacerbated in environments where the child has little one-to-one interaction with adults, there is persistent background noise, and there is little sensitivity in caregivers to the child's hearing loss. In our earlier study, the variable that significantly interacted with OM was the quality of the day care environment: high-quality day care buffered against many of the negative outcomes from OM. Children in low-quality day care with chronic OM had the most persistent and severe negative effects in preschool and school.[41,42,44]

Developmental psychologists interested in children at risk of poor developmental outcomes support the Cumulative Risk Model, which postulates that many moderate risk factors for poor outcomes, if seen alone in a child's life, are unlikely to produce poor outcomes. Garmezy[45] and Rutter[46] have articulated this model in a series of studies to identify factors associated with child development. For example, Rutter[46] examined risk factors including poverty, overcrowding, marital discord, and maternal psychotic disorders. Children who were exposed to none of the stressors or to one, despite the poverty of the family, shared only a 1% increase in psychological problems as compared with a group without stressors. Exposure to two stressors resulted in a fourfold increase in risk of psychological problems, while exposure to four or more stressors raised the psychological problems to 21%.

Sameroff and Fiese[43,47] reported similar findings using IQ as the outcome in children followed up from infancy to age 13 years. A list of 10 risk factors was used to predict intellectual outcomes. These included such factors as few positive maternal interactions, parental rigidity, maternal education, and stressful life events. The authors reported that each risk factor cost a child four IQ points, especially when there were multiple risks involved. Many of these risk or protective factors were those that related to the quality of caregiving, in addition to other life events. In the more complex models, some of these factors can be weighted more heavily than others and may actually interact with each other in producing poorer outcomes.

EPIDEMIOLOGY OF OTITIS MEDIA IN YOUNG CHILDREN

In other chapters in this book (see Chapters 10, "Epidemiology" and 12, "Natural History of Untreated Otitis Media"), the reader will find more detailed information about the incidence and epidemiology of

OM, but some of the information will be summarized here to understand the studies reviewed and to identify those children at greatest risk.

Incidence

Two reviews[48,49] suggested that many factors relate to incidence, but that OM in early childhood was almost universal. Rates in the United States are between 49 and 97% in the first year of life.[50,51] Children who experience their first episode of OM in the first months of life are two to eight times more likely to experience chronic OM than children who experience their first episode later.[48] The peak period for the incidence of OM is between 1 and 2 years of age, with a dramatic decrease among the older children. Most of the children who experience OM will have fluid or effusion during an episode, but this resolves rapidly over a 3-month period in about 70 to 80% of cases.[52,53]

Risk Groups

Although OM is almost universal in the first 2 or 3 years of life, certain groups are more at risk than others and, in turn, experience developmental problems. Recent reviews of these factors can be found in the literature[13,48,49] and in this book (see Chapter 10).

Host and environmental factors relate to OM susceptibility. An important endogenous factor is age: children in the first 2 or 3 years of life are more likely to experience many bouts of OM compared with older children. Anatomic features related to birth defects, such as cleft palate and Down syndrome, also increase the risk of OM. Ethnic groups, including Native Americans and Aborigines, also have increased risk. Although some studies have shown that boys have more episodes of OM than girls, the issue is unresolved.[13] Probably the most important endogenous factor is upper respiratory infection, which causes Eustachian tube dysfunction and accompanies most OM. Exogenous factors include breast-feeding, which protects against OM, and bottle-propping, which has an adverse impact, as does exposure to environmental tobacco smoke. Otitis media is more frequent in the winter months than in the summer months.

Most important for the studies reported here is the effect of exposure to many people in a crowded environment. Children living in large families, those who live in crowded conditions, and those who are in large childcare situations, like a day care center, are more likely to experience bouts of OM. Children in day care have been reported to experience up to four times the number of OM episodes as children who are cared for at home. In a study of 70 children in day care,[42] examined weekly with tympanometry and pneumatic otoscopy, the overall prevalence of OM was 30%. Half the children experienced OM greater than 20% of the time, with a mean of almost 5 months annually. Many of the studies discussed in the next section of this chapter examined children in day care and the effects of OM on their development. Consequently, it is important to understand the frequency of OM in this population of children.

Lower socioeconomic status (SES) may increase the family experience of OM. This may be caused by the strong association among lower SES and crowding, large families, less breast-feeding, and poorer nutrition and health care. In all these studies, many of the factors that put children at risk are found in combination with each other, putting certain children at much higher risk than others. A study from Pittsburgh[54] reported that children spent 56% of their first year of life with OM and 48% of their second year. Children in urban areas experienced the most persistent OM, suggesting an association with lower SES and other risk factors.

These confounding risk factors often occur naturally and are difficult to understand individually. Studies examining the effects of OM on development must deal with these confounding factors and multiple risks, which add to the complexity of interpreting results.

PROSPECTIVE STUDIES OF THE EFFECTS OF OTITIS MEDIA ON DEVELOPMENT

This section reviews prospective studies that have monitored children carefully through the early years of life to examine their experience with OM. In addition, almost all used pneumatic otoscopy to diagnose OM, and some used tympanometry. The number of times that each child was examined by the researchers to diagnose OM ranged greatly from once a week to four or five times a year. The list of developmental outcome measures used also varies greatly. Some studies do report hearing data, but most use experience with OM as the proxy for hearing loss. Even with these limitations, valuable information is available about the effects of OM on development.

In the tables that follow, studies are divided on the basis of whether the effect of OM was examined in the preschool years when OM is most frequent (infancy to 5 years of age) or at school age when the frequency of OM is very low (6 years and older). This dichotomy looks at the short-term or concurrent effects of OM versus the long-term effects after the child's hearing has presumably been normal for some time. The tables also include the reference for each study, the sample size, the age of the children, and whether or not the study found significant effects for that domain of development. An asterisk indicates that a pragmatic task was studied. Ethnicity and SES are summarized because of their important role as exogenous risk factors.

Table 23-2 Speech Perception Outcomes in Prospective Studies of Children with Otitis Media

Age Group First Author, Year	N	Test* Age	Ethnicity	SES	Nonsignificant Test Outcomes	Significant Test Outcomes (p < .05)
Preschool Children						
Gravel[55] 1992	23	4 yr	Af Am, Hispanic, Caucasian	Low; low birthweight	—	PSI
School Age Children						
Nittrouer[56] 1996	12	7–11 yr	NS	Low, middle	—	Phonemic awareness & perceptual weighting

Af Am = African American; NS = not specified; PSI = Pediatric Sentence Intelligibility test; SES = socioeconomic status.
*Age at time of measurement.

Effects of Otitis Media on Speech Development

As shown in Table 23-2, there are very few controlled studies of the effects of OM on speech perception. Perceptual evidence suggests that insufficient and inappropriate auditory input, such as may result from chronic OM, affects young children's ability to categorize or comprehend speech input. Using the Pediatric Sentence Intelligibility (PSI) test, Gravel and Wallace[55] found that 4-year-old children with chronic OM performed more poorly compared with controls when trying to comprehend sentences in background noise (no differences were found in quietness). Nittrouer[56] examined phonemic awareness in children with OM in comparison with children with OM from low SES backgrounds and with children with low SES backgrounds but no history of OM. The children with chronic OM performed worse than the comparison group. The low SES children, however, had the poorest performance, and children with chronic OM and low SES performed similarly to the low SES group without OM.

Very few large-scale prospective studies have examined the development of speech sound production during the first few years of life (Table 23-3). The first peer-reviewed case studies of infants and toddlers with OM followed the phonologic development of toddlers with chronic OM.[57,58] Donahue[57] reported that her child used mostly vowels from 9 to 22 months. When her child started producing consonants in words she used "consonant harmony," where all consonants in a word are similar. The child had delayed phonologic development, but this could not be attributed exclusively to OM. Robb and colleagues[58] conducted monthly phonetic analyses on a toddler with chronic OM. Results of phonetic inventory analyses revealed simple phonetic inventories that resembled those of children with severe hearing impairments.

Teele and coworkers[59] found that OM was not associated with lower scores on the Goldman-Fristoe Test of Articulation (GFTA)[60] at age 3 years, but an association between OM and the number of articulation errors was found at age 7 years.[61] Roberts and colleagues[62] found phonologic processes were suppressed more slowly after 4.5 years of age; however, there was no effect of OM on the GFTA at 2.5 or 4.5 years. More recently, McCormick and colleagues[63] found a significant relationship between the duration of bilateral OM and scores on the GFTA at age 5 years in 294 subjects monitored for OM every 2 to 4 weeks until the age of 3 years.

Recently, Paradise and colleagues[36] correlated children's cumulative durations of OM in the first year of life and the percent of consonants produced correctly (Percentage of Consonants Correct-Revised [PCC-R]) on language samples at age 3 years in comparison with healthy children. No significant differences were found. Further, PCC-R scores did not differ significantly between children with tympanostomy tubes inserted early versus later.[64]

A number of factors contribute to the restricted information available on how OM affects speech production. Early speech development is not easily quantifiable, and consequently, attempts to do so may not capture differences. Standardized tests of speech production, such as the GFTA, simply count the number of errors children make when naming pictures in comparison with a normative sample. The nature of the error is not taken into account in the standard score. Although a more sensitive measure of severity in preschool children, counting the number of correctly produced consonants in a spontaneous speech sample also does not reveal specific aspects of speech production problems. A developmental substitution, for example, producing a /t/ for an /s/ is viewed equivalent to producing a non-English phoneme, such as a click. Although phonologic

Table 23-3 Speech Production Outcomes in Prospective Studies of Children with Otitis Media

Age Group First Author, Year	N	Test* Age	Ethnicity	SES	Nonsignificant Test Outcomes	Significant Test Outcomes (p < .05)
Preschool Children						
Abraham[67] 1996	16	2 yr	Hispanic (most)	Low	—	No. consonants
Luloff[66] 1991	138	1 yr	NS	Low, middle	Articulation, % variegated babble, number true words	No. consonants, proportion consonants to vowels
McCormick[63] 2001	294	5 yr	NS	NS	—	GFTA
Miccio[19] 2001	6	1–4 yr	Caucasian	Middle	—	Phonetic inventories and phonotactics
Miccio[20] 2002	10	6 mo–2 yr	Caucasian	Middle	—	Phonetic inventories and phonotactics
Paradise[36] 2000	241	3 yr	Af Am, other, Caucasian	Low, middle	PCC-R	—
Paradise[64] 2001	402	3 yr	NS	Low, middle	PCC-R	—
Robb[58] 1993	1	11–21 mo	NS	NS	—	Phonetic inventories
Roberts[62] 1988	55	2.5–4 yr	Af Am, Caucasian	Low	GFTA	—
Rvachew[65] 1999	18	≤ 18 mo	NS	NS	—	Canonical babbling ratios
Teele[59] 1984	205	3 yr	NS	Low, middle	GFTA	—
School Age Children						
Roberts[62] 1988	55	5–8 yr	Af Am, Caucasian	Low	GFTA	—
Teele[61] 1990	194	7 yr	Caucasian	Low, middle	—	GFTA

Af Am = African American; GFTA = Goldman-Fristoe-Woodcock Test of Articulation; NS = not specified; PCC-R = Percent Consonants Correct-Revised; SES = socioeconomic status.
*Age at time of measurement.

process assessments identify patterns of error, they are also based on typical developmental processes, not unusual error patterns. Effects of a typical developmental error on intelligibility are quite different when errors deviate from normal patterns.

Infants and toddlers present an even greater challenge because of difficulties discerning babbling from early meaningful speech. Infants begin to produce consonant vowel combinations around age 6 months and continue to babble when acquiring words. Rvachew and colleagues[65] found a consistently lower rate of canonical babble among infants with early-onset OM compared with healthy peers. Luloff and colleagues[66] found a significantly reduced number of different consonants produced by 1-year-old children with chronic OM. Similarly, Abraham and coworkers[67] found significantly fewer initial consonants in eight 2-year-olds with chronic OM compared with otitis-free toddlers.

These results encouraged Miccio and colleagues[19] to examine longitudinally the influence of OM on the range and types of consonants produced by six children using repeated measures at nine intervals between 12 and 48 months. Four children with a high incidence of OM had delayed phonologic development at the earlier analyses and produced non-English fricatives at various periods during acquisition. A child with a low incidence of OM, however, showed only a mild delay in acquisition of fricatives (eg, /s/, /f/, and so on). Another child with a low incidence of OM had an atypical phonologic system that resembled that of young deaf children. This child also had more hearing loss during bouts of OM.

Miccio and colleagues[20] monitored the consonant acquisition of 10 children for 2 years. The OM status was documented weekly, and speech production was sampled every 2 weeks. After 2 years, 3 children had minimal episodes of OM, and 2 had chronic OM throughout the study. Of the remaining 5 children, 3 were affected chronically during the first year of life and 2 had chronic OM during the second year of life. Children with a low incidence of OM had typical phonologic development. Children with chronic OM for 2 years, however, did not babble until the second year of life and were nearly 2 years of age at the onset of meaningful speech; both milestones occurred simultaneously with periods of wellness. Throughout the study, declines in the amount of vocalizations coincided with elevated hearing levels. The remaining children also showed delays in development and some atypical speech production characteristics during periods of chronic OM.

The specific effects of OM on speech development are unclear. Studies of the effect of OM on speech perception or production continue to have mixed results. Longitudinal studies using repeated measures have noted more differences between children with chronic OM compared with their healthy peers or with children with a low incidence of OM. Larger studies using more controlled designs and quantitative measures of speech sound productions have not observed differences in children's speech production as a result of OM in early childhood. More longitudinal studies are needed that monitor children from infancy to school age. Quantitative measures are needed that are sensitive to qualitative differences in speech production errors.

Effects of Otitis Media on Overall Language

The relationship between OM and language has been the area of focus in most studies because it is such an important skill for all children and because the "Global Language Model" has been the guiding model for most of the large-scale OM studies. All studies reported here are prospective but use varying language outcome measures. The receptive and expressive language outcomes include language samples, standardized receptive and expressive language tests, and vocabulary tests. Some studies looked specifically at pragmatics (indicated by an asterisk in the tables), but others developed tasks that include expressive language variables that tap

the use of language, such as narratives. We believe this new category of studies may help elucidate where children with chronic OM may have problems.

Preschool Receptive Language

This area of language continues to have few effects (Table 23-4). The ability to understand language is very difficult to measure in the first few years of life when children are too young to actually say whether they understand something. Thus, most of the tests administered to infants under age 2.5 years rely on nonverbal measures (pointing, looking, and so on) of comprehension of language and parent or caregiver reports. The most frequently reported measure in the OM literature has been the language reception score on the Sequenced Inventory of Communication Development (SICD-R), which relies on parental report, examiner presented tasks, and direct observation.

For the SICD, there is strong evidence for an OM effect on receptive language at age 1 year but scant evidence at later preschool ages. Three studies[17,68,69] reported a significant negative effect for experience with OM at age 1 year, of which two showed a strong relationship between OM and hearing loss. They included children with a range of SES and ethnicity, and all included good measures of experience with OM. Studies reporting data on children up to 2 years of age have mixed results. One small study reported a significant effect at 2 years of age[68] but others do not.[18,42,69] Roberts and colleagues[70] reported a significant effect for OM on the SICD at age 3 years, which disappeared when controlling for demographic and home variables. By ages 4 and 5 years, there was no longer any relationship with OM. Gravel and Wallace[55] also found no effect of OM on the receptive portion of the SICD at 4 years of age.

More recent studies have examined receptive language over the preschool years using the Peabody Picture Vocabulary Test (PPVT) and the Clinical Evaluation of Language Functions (CELF). Paradise and colleagues[36] found a significant relationship at age 3 years, but Roberts and colleagues[70] found no relationship at 3, 4, or 5 years of age. Roberts' study also found no relationship on other receptive language measures over the preschool years.

In summary, there is strong evidence for an effect of OM on receptive language at 1 year of age that diminishes over the preschool years. The evidence may be equivocal later because there is less of an effect with age, but it also could be caused by the difficulty in devising valid instruments for young children. In addition, equivocal results may have occurred because many of the studies did not or were not able to examine factors that might interact with OM to produce effects. Only some of the studies were able to examine hearing loss (the real

Table 23-4 Receptive Language Outcomes in Prospective Studies of Children with Otitis Media

Age Group / First Author, Year	N	Test* Age	Ethnicity	SES	Nonsignificant Test Outcomes	Significant Test Outcomes (p < .05)
Preschool Children						
Friel-Patti[68] 1982	35	1 yr	NS	Middle, low; low birthweight	—	REEL, SICD-R
Friel-Patti[69] 1990	483	1–2 yr	NS	Middle, high	SICD-R (1.5 yr, 2 yr)	SICD-R (1 yr)
Feagans[41] 1994	46	2 yr	Caucasian	Middle	SICD-E	—
Gravel[55] 1992	23	4 yr	Af Am, Hispanic, Caucasian	Low; low birthweight	SICD-R	—
Paradise[36] 2000	241	3 yr	Af Am, Caucasian	Inclusive	—	PPVT-R
Rach[73] 1988	65	2–4 yr	Dutch	NS	RDSL-r	—
Rach[84] 1991	102	4 yr	Dutch	NS	RDSL-r	—
Roberts[72] 1991	63	4.5–6 yr	Af Am, Asian, Caucasian	Low, middle	M-Y, BLST, PPVT, CELF	—
Roberts[17] 1995	61	1 yr	Af Am	Low (62%)	—	SICD-R[†]
Roberts[18] 1998	86	2 yr	Af Am	Low (most)	SICD-R	—
Roberts[70] 2000	85	3–5 yr	Af Am	Low (73%)	PPVT (3 yr, 4 yr, 5 yr), SICD-R (4 yr, 5 yr), CELF-R (4 yr, 5 yr)	SICD-R (3 yr)[†]
Teele[59] 1984	205	3 yr	Caucasian	Inclusive	—	PPVT, ACQ
Vernon-Feagans[42] 1997	67	2 yr	Caucasian	Middle, high	SICD	—
Wright[74] 1988	156	2–4 yr	Af Am, Caucasian	Low (88%)	VAQ, PPVT, PLS, REEL, Boone	—
School Age Children						
Lous[71] 1988	52	8 yr	Danish	Inclusive	PPVT	—
Teele[61] 1990	194	7 yr	Caucasian	Inclusive	PPVT, WUG	—

Af Am = African American; ACQ = Auditory Comprehension Quotient (Zimmerman Preschool Language Scale); BLST = Bankson Language Screening Test; Boone = Boone Infant Speech and Language Development; CELF = Clinical Evaluation of Language Functions; CSBS = Communication and Symbolic Behavior Scales; M-Y = Miller-Yoder Language Comprehension Test; NS = not specified; PPVT-R = Peabody Picture Vocabulary Test Revised; REEL = Receptive-Expressive Emergent Language Scale; SES = socioeconomic status; SICD-R = Sequenced Inventory of Communication Development, Receptive; VAQ = Verbal Ability Quotient (Zimmerman Preschool Language Scale); WUG = "WUG" Test.

*Age at time of measurement.

†After controlling for SES and other demographic variables, significance disappeared.

causal variable), and only the most recent studies were able to test the moderating influence of such factors as the home environment and the day care environment.

School Age Receptive Language

There are no new studies of receptive language at school age (see Table 23-4) since the first edition of this book. Seven measures of receptive language have been administered to children ranging in age from 4.5 to 8 years. These measures assessed vocabulary and certain areas of grammatical development in three separate studies.[61,71,72] None of the measures showed an effect of OM, thus giving no evidence of a long-term negative effect of OM on receptive language.

Preschool Expressive Language

Children's ability to produce language may be the most objective measure of overall language, but in young children who are just beginning to talk, it is often difficult to capture their level of language production because it may not be displayed in formal testing situations.

There are several validated measures of a child's ability to produce language. The expressive portion of the SICD, the SICD-E, has been used in seven studies and a few others used the Reynell Developmental Language Scales–revised (RDLS-r), the CELF, or the Receptive-Expressive Emergent Language Scale (REEL). Two other articles examined language samples and used the number of morphemes per utterance, or mean length of utterance (MLU), as a major measure. MLU is a good reflection of the grammatical complexity of children's talk in the preschool years. A variety of other measures have been used that reflect grammatical development or vocabulary.

Not including the study of pragmatics, OM appears to affect expressive language (Table 23-5) more than receptive language (see Table 23-4), but effects may diminish over the preschool years. Of the studies that used the SICD, there was a significant effect for two of the three at age 1 year.[17,68,69] Three studies found a significant effect at 2 years of age while one did not, although this study did find a significant effect at 18 months.[42,68,69] The two studies that did find an effect examined mediating or moderating effects, and both measured hearing loss.

Vernon-Feagans and colleagues[42] found that middle-class children in low-quality childcare with chronic OM did poorer on the SICD-E than children in low-quality childcare. Children in high-quality day care with chronic and nonchronic OM appeared buffered against the effects of OM. Only children with chronic OM had hearing loss during bouts of OM, whereas others did not. Roberts and colleagues[18] studied low-income African American children in day care. They found a

significant direct relationship between OM, hearing loss, and the SICD-E at age 1 year, but this relationship was confounded by quality of day care and the home environment. Therefore, it was difficult to interpret whether OM or the caregiving environment caused poorer expressive language. Similar findings were noted at age 3 years, but by ages 4 and 5 years, there were no effects of OM on the SICD-E.[70] Gravel and Wallace[55] found no effects of OM on the SICD-E in a small group of 4-year old children.

Roberts and colleagues[70,72] used the CELF and found no effects for OM. Of the other well-known language tests used over the preschool period (Reynell, McCarthy Scales, and REEL), three of the five showed a significant effect for OM.[36,68,73,74] Another study[74] used two other less well-known tests, the Zimmerman Preschool Language Scale (PLS) and the Boone Infant Speech and Language Scale (Boone). Teele and colleagues[61] did find an effect for the PLS, but Wright and colleagues[74] did not find an effect on the PLS at 2 or 3 to 4 years of age. Nor did they find effects on the Boone or REEL at 3 to 4 years of age. Conversely, a large recent study found moderate effects of bilateral OM on the CELF at 5 years of age.[63] A 20% increase in duration of bilateral OM was associated with a decrease in the CELF score of about 22% of 1 standard deviation.

Language samples have been used in a number of studies to examine basic grammatical complexity and vocabulary. Wallace and colleagues[40] found OM effects on MLU, verbosity, and grammatical complexity at 2 years of age from a mother/child language session. Roberts and colleagues[70] found a significant effect at 3 and 4 years of age on the percentage of different word types and no effects at 5 years of age. In a previous study, Roberts and colleagues[72] found no effects of OM on MLU or vocabulary for children from age 4.5 to 6 years. Teele and colleagues[61] also found no effect of OM on MLU at 3 years of age. Paradise and colleagues[36] found no effects on the number of different words or MLU at 3 years of age. Vernon-Feagans and colleagues[34] found very significant differences (effect sizes of 1) on MLU, number of total words, and number of different words between children with chronic OM who were in low-quality childcare and all other children, but their study used a bookreading task to elicit language.

Overall, it does appear from these studies that expressive language, as measured on standardized tests, shows a consistent pattern of effects for OM experience in the early preschool years but much less in the later preschool period. These results support the Global Language Model of effects and the more recent studies of mediating and moderating variables that may interact with OM in producing poorer outcomes. Results from language samples are minimal. Very few studies at 3 and 4 years of age show

Table 23-5 Expressive Language Outcomes in Prospective Studies of Children with Otitis Media

Age Group First Author, Year	N	Test* Age	Ethnicity	SES	Nonsignificant Test Outcomes	Significant Test Outcomes (p < .05)
Preschool Children						
Friel-Patti[68] 1982	35	1–2 yr	NS	Low, middle	—	REEL (1 yr, 2 yr), SICD-E (1 yr, 2 yr)
Friel-Patti[69] 1990	483	1–2 yr	NS	Middle, high	SICD-E (1 yr), SICD-E (2 yr)	SICD-E (1.5 yr)
Gravel[55] 1992	23	4 yr	Hispanic (most)	Low	SICD-E	—
McCormick[63] 2001	698	5 yr	Caucasian, Af Am, Hispanic	Inclusive	—	CELF
Paradise[36] 2000	241	3 yr	Af Am, Caucasian	Inclusive	NDW, MLU (LS)	McCarthy Verbal Scores
Pearce[85] 1988	43	2–4 yr	NS	NS	SICD-E	—
Rach[73] 1988	65	2–4 yr	Dutch	NS	—	RDSL-r
Rach[84] 1991	102	2–4 yr	Dutch	NS	RDSL-r	—
Roberts[72] 1991	63	4.5–6 yr	Af Am, Caucasian, Asian	Low, middle	CELF, BLST, MLU (LS), syntax & vocabulary (LS)	—
Roberts[17] 1995*	61	1 yr	Af Am	Low, middle	—	SICD-E,‡ CSBS
Roberts[18] 1998*	86	2 yr	Af Am	Low	—	SICD-R,‡ CSBS, CDI
Roberts[70] 2000	85	3–5 yr	Af Am	Low (73%)	SICD-E (4 yr, 5 yr), CELF-E (4 yr, 5 yr), % word type LS (5 yr)	SICD-E‡ (3 yr), word type LS (4 yr, 5 yr)
Teele[59] 1984	205	3 yr	Caucasian	Low, middle	MLU (LS)	PLS
Vernon-Feagans[42] 1997	67	2 yr	Caucasian	Middle	—	SICD-R
Vernon-Feagans[77] 1996*	36	1.5–4 yr	Caucasian	Middle	—	Verbal initiations

Table 23-5 Expressive Language Outcomes in Prospective Studies of Children with Otitis Media (continued)

Age Group / First Author, Year	N	Test* Age	Ethnicity	SES	Nonsignificant Test Outcomes	Significant Test Outcomes (p < .05)
Vernon-Feagans[34] 2002*	41	4 yr	Caucasian	Middle	—	Bookreading (LS), MLU, NDW, TNW, abstract questions, ALI
Wallace[86] 1988	65	1 yr	Af Am, Hispanic, Caucasian	Low (most)	—	SICD-R
Wallace[40] 1996*	26	2 yr	NS	Low	—	MLU, verbosity (LS), SCS for different caregiver styles
Wright[74] 1988	156	2–4 yr	Af Am, Caucasian	Low	PLS, Boone, REEL	—
Yont[25] 2001*	40	1 yr	Caucasian	Middle	Verbal communicative intents (LS)	Nonverbal communicative intents (LS)
School Age Children						
Creps[44] 1999*	37	7 yr	Caucasian	Middle	—	Verbal expression composite
Feagans[35] 1987*	44	5–7 yr	Af Am	Low	MLU (5 yr, 7 yr)	Paraphrase (5 yr, 7 yr)
Fischler[87] 1985	167	6–8 yr	Apache Natives	Low	TOLD	—
Grievink[88] 1993	270	7 yr	Dutch	NS	LTC	—
Teele[61] 1990	194	7 yr	NS	Low, middle	Grammar (LS), vocabulary diversity (LS), WUG, Boston	Morphology (LS)

Af Am = African American; ALI = Adaptive Language Inventory; BLST = Bankson Language Screening Test; Boone = Boone Infant Speech and Language Development; Boston = Boston Naming Test; CBI = Classroom Behavior Inventory; CELF = Clinical Evaluation of Language Functions; CSBS = Communication and Symbolic Behavior Scales; LS = Language Sample; LTC = language testing for children; MLU = mean length of utterance; NDW = number of different words; NS = not specified; PCC-R = percentage of consonants correct-revised; PLS = Zimmerman Preschool Language Scale; RDLS = Reynell Developmental Language Scales (-r, revised); REEL = Receptive-Expressive Emergent Language Scale; SCS = Syntax Complexity Score; SES = socioeconomic status; SICD-E = Sequenced Inventory of Communication Development, Expressive; TNW = total number of words; TOLD = Test of Language Development; WUG = "WUG" Test.

*Studies of pragmatics.

†Age at time of measurement.

‡After controlling for SES and other demographic variables, significance disappeared.

any effects of OM. The only study that had large effects used a bookreading task to gather the language sample, and their results may be caused by demands of the task that differed from an elicited language sample.

School Age Expressive Language

There are very few studies of expressive language at school age. Two tests were administered in one study,[61] and neither showed an effect of OM. Language samples show mixed results. Teele and colleagues[61] reported that children who had a history of chronic OM had less developed grammar as measured by morphology. Feagans and colleagues[35] reported that children's MLU in kindergarten and second grade was not related to OM.

A more recent study by Creps and coworkers[44] used a composite score of verbal language with an expressive language test (parent and teacher ratings) and conversational language with a friend. At 7 years of age, there was an additive effect of OM on verbal behavior. These results support the Global Language Model early in life, but there was also support for a Transactional Model later that would predict recovered basic language skills.

Pragmatics or Using Language at Preschool and School Age

Pragmatics may be most affected by OM because basic language skills are so impervious to environmental insults. It is hypothesized that children with chronic OM withdraw more from verbal interactions when they have difficulty hearing and that this pattern of behavior may lead to less ability to use language effectively in interaction with others and in narrative tasks.

Preschool Pragmatics

Several preschool pragmatic measures are explained in this section. Some involve parent report, but most use coding schemes to measure language use. One relatively new standardized pragmatic measure, the Communication and Symbolic Behavior Scale (CSBS), was given to North Carolina parents when their children were 1 year of age[17] and 2 years of age.[18] This measure showed an effect of OM at 1 year of age and 2 years of age, but the effect at 2 years may be mediated by the caregiving environment.

Yont and colleagues[25] analyzed mother-father-child toy-play interactions for children's early intentional communication using the Inventory of Communicative Acts-Abridged (INCA-A).[75] The INCA identifies and codes communicative intent at two different levels—the level of the *verbal interchange* (ie, social context) and the level of the *utterance* (ie, speech act). An interchange is defined as one or more rounds of talk, all of which serve a unitary interactive function. Examples of inter-

changes include discussing a joint focus of attention, directing attention, or negotiating an immediate activity. The utterance level is embedded within the level of the interchange. Examples of utterance level codes include making a statement, asking a yes/no question, or requesting or proposing action. There were no differences in children's expression of verbal intents, which is a reasonable finding, given the individual variability in children's early lexical development at 12 months. Children with chronic OM did, however, use fewer types of nonverbal strategies to help parents interpret their otherwise unintelligible vocalizations than did the nonchronic children.

Vernon-Feagans and colleagues[76] observed children in their day care classroom during free play on two different days (mean child age 2 years, range 14 months to almost 4 years), revealing that children with a history of chronic OM verbally initiated half as much talk to peers and adults compared with same-age peers without chronic OM. Similarly, they[34] presented 4-year-old children with a bookreading task,[81] in which mothers read a wordless picture book titled "A Boy, A Dog, and a Frog." On each page were concrete and abstract questions, totaling 32, about the story. A priori planned comparisons showed that chronic OM children in low-quality childcare answered fewer abstract questions correctly. When mothers followed up on incorrect answers to help their children get them correct, children with chronic OM in low-quality day care produced half as many total words and half as many different words compared with all other children.

Overall, of the few studies that have examined preschool pragmatics, all found effects of OM on using language. These studies support the Contextual Transactional Modal that argues language use should be most affected by experience with OM.

School Age Pragmatics

One previous study by Feagans and colleagues[35] examined children's ability to paraphrase a story they were told. Children with chronic OM were less able to produce a good paraphrase in comparison with children with nonchronic OM at 5 and 7 years of age. This sample was the same one that Roberts and colleagues had used in many of her previous studies.[17]

More recently, Creps and Vernon-Feagans[44] examined children's verbal ability and behavior at 7 years of age. They used a composite score, including measures geared to examining pragmatics, but did include a language test. The measures were the transcription of a play and a 30-minute videotape of friends in their homes or neighborhoods using a transcription coding system. This yielded MLU, total words, and number of different words. Additional measures included the expressive portion of the Assessing Semantic Skills through Everyday Themes (ASSET), in which children describe and label pictures of everyday events important to them, and the Adaptive Language Inventory (ALI), which measures children's pragmatics in the classroom. Children with early chronic OM were significantly poorer on this composite measure of expressive language use.

Attention-Related Behaviors

In our model, we hypothesize that children with chronic OM in early childhood may have less attention to language and, thus, interact less with others verbally (Table 23-6). Thus, they may later develop attention problems in school, and they may also withdraw from social interactions and have characteristics that include "inhibition," "shyness," and "introversion."

Preschool Attention Behaviors

Actual behavior in the day care classroom is the subject of two studies. The first examined children's attention to language at 12 to 18 months of age during a bookreading situation in day care, both when the child was well and during a bout of OM.[13] When children had OM, they attended to bookreading half as much as when well, if the children were in a low-quality day care. Even with a rather small sample, the effect size was over 1 standard deviation. There were no differences on this measure in a high-quality day care. Further, children with OM, no matter what the quality of the day care, spent much less time in bookreading. At 24 months of age, there was a significant correlation between parents' ratings of lack of attention in their children and experience with OM for those children who were classified as chronic. At an older age, these same children (with chronic OM over the first 3 years of life) were found to play more by themselves in the preschool classroom during free play, suggesting that they may withdraw in language-demanding situations.[77] These children also initiated less verbally to both peers and adults in the classroom.

Minter and colleagues[78] reported rating scales that tap attention-related behaviors in early childhood. Instruments were filled out by parents and/or teachers and testers and included the Behavior Rating Scale (BRS) that accompanies the Bayley; the Distractibility/Hyperactivity Subscale of the Parenting Stress Index (PSI), the Social Skills Rating System (SSRS), and the Hyperactivity Index of the Conners' Teacher/Parent Ratings Scale. Over the infancy and preschool period, only two relationships were found. At 1 year of age, OM was significantly correlated with the BRS, and at preschool, OM was correlated with the Conners Rating Scale; but these effects disappeared when controlling for demographic and home variables.

These studies suggest a real discrepancy in results that may be caused by varying factors, some of which will be discussed later. Ethnicity, SES, and whether observation or rating scales were used differ in these studies. Another important factor is that attention to language was the focus of the observational studies while overall attention was the focus of the rating scales.

School Age Attention-Related Behaviors

Information on school-age behavior is limited, but three new studies add new information. In previous studies Roberts and colleagues[62,79,80] reported that children's experience with OM in the first 3 years of life was related to less task orientation in the classroom on the Classroom Behavior Inventory (CBI), as rated by their class teachers at 7 years of age and 8 to 9 years of age. At 12 years of age, the CBI was not given but the Child Behavior Checklist (CBCL), a child psychopathology scale, was administered. This showed no effect of OM. Feagans and colleagues[35] observed the same children in the classroom at 5 and 7 years of age and found that children with chronic OM in the first 3 years of life were twice as often off task in the regular classroom during teacher-directed activities as children without chronic OM.

In the following studies, there is some evidence for continued effects of OM on attention. Minter and colleagues[78] report no effects of OM on the Conner Rating Scale and the SSRS (filled out by parents and teachers) at 6 years of age, but two studies have found effects. Creps and Vernon-Feagans[44] used a composite of behavior including the Teacher's Rating Scale of Children's Social Behavior[81] and the Introversion Subscale of the CBI. They also scored inhibition in a videotaped session of the target child playing with a friend for 30 minutes in the home. Shyness and inhibition interacted with OM and quality of day care at age 7 years, with 30% of the variance accounted for by a three-way interaction between OM, age of entry into day care, and quality of day care. Children in low-quality day care when young tended to display more shy and withdrawn behaviors with their friends at age 7 years, but this relationship was moderated by OM and age of entry into care. Children with high-quality care plus chronic OM and early age of entry into day care were much less withdrawn than their peers who experienced low-quality day care, chronic OM, and later age of entry into day care.

Another recent large-scale study[82] of 962 children examined data from the Dunedin, New Zealand, using the Rutter Parent and Teacher Behavior Scales and parent-reported behavior problems at 11, 13, and 15 years of age. After adjusting for covariates, children's OM experience through 9 years of age was related to hyperactive and inattentive behavior problems at 11, 13, and 15 years of age.

Table 23-6 Attention and Behavior Outcomes in Prospective Studies of Children with Otitis Media

Age Group First Author, Year	N	Test* Age	Ethnicity	SES	Nonsignificant Test Outcomes	Significant Test Outcomes (p < .05)
Preschool Children						
Feagans[41] 1994	35	1–1.5 yr	Caucasian	Middle	—	Length of bookreading, attention to bookreading
Feagans[41] 1994	46	2 yr	Caucasian	Middle	—	GOFS: Parental report of distractibility
Feagans[77] 1996	36	1.5–4 yr	Caucasian	Middle	—	Observed solitary play
Minter[78] 2001	85	≤5 yr	Af Am	Low (73%)	Infancy: PSI; Preschool: Conners-T, SSRS-P, SSRS-T	Infancy: BRS; Preschool: Conners-P
School Age Children						
Bennett[82] 2001	962	11–15 yr	New Zealand	Inclusive	—	Rutter-P (11 yr, 13 yr, 15 yr), Rutter-T (11 yr, 13 yr)
Creps[44] 1999	37	7 yr	Caucasian	Middle	—	Shyness
Feagans[35] 1987	44	5 yr	Af Am	Low	—	SCAN observation, distractibility
Minter[78] 2001	85	6 yr	Af Am	Low (73%)	Conners-T, Conners-P, SSRS-P, SSRS-T	—
Roberts[89] 1989	44	8 yr	Af Am	Low	—	CBI: task orientation/independence
Roberts[80] 1995	51	8–9 yr	Af Am	Low	—	CBI: task orientation

Af Am = African American; BRS = Behavioral Rating Scale; CBI = Classroom Behavior Inventory; GOFS = Goodness of Fit Scale; PSI = Pediatric Sentence Intelligibility Test; SCAN Observation = Schedule of Classroom Activity Norms; SES = socioeconomic status; SSRS = Social Skills Rating System (-P, parent; -T, teacher).
*Age at time of measurement.

The findings were particularly consistent for inattention. These findings strongly support our model of effects by indicating that at school age, some of the major effects of OM may be inattention, distractibility, and inhibition.

ETHNICITY, SES, AND OTITIS MEDIA EXPERIENCE

One of the really puzzling issues that plagued the literature on the effects of OM on development has been the inconsistency in the results. Whereas some inconsistencies stem from a myriad of measures, procedures, and time points, others may relate to sample characteristics and confounding.

In examining Tables 23-2 through 23-6 for ethnicity and SES, there are many differences among OM studies. Only a few have samples that include a range of SES and ethnicity (inclusive studies). Studies vary in outcome, but some are from the United States, New Zealand, or the Netherlands. Within the American studies, the North Carolina studies contain almost all African American children born in low-income families. The Pennsylvania State studies contain mostly Caucasian children with middle SES. Both Roberts and Vernon-Feagans study children in day care with much higher rates of OM, while most other investigators have community samples where day care experience was not examined as a factor.

The largest and most inclusive study has been the Pittsburgh study,[54,64] but even this sample has limitations. For example, children who entered clinical trial were excluded from analysis in the language outcomes. Although the rationale for this exclusion is scientifically sound (the clinical trial was as a separate study), in effect, those children with the early-onset OM had to be excluded. Thus, in the normal distribution of OM experience in the first year of life, those children with the most experience were those eligible for random assignment to early versus late tube insertions in the clinical trial. Thus, even this large study has not been able to report the effects on development using the full range of experience with OM of the children they studied.

SYNTHESIS AND NEED FOR FURTHER STUDIES

Speech

In the area of speech processes, there are still very few good prospective studies. Although a few standardized tests have been used, qualitative analyses may be most important in understanding the particular effects of OM on speech. Some recent studies suggest delayed onset of consonants in children with chronic OM; however, the long-term consequences of such delays in speech production for children are unknown. Since phonologic awareness and the ability to decode is a critical aspect of learning to read, it would be important to longitudinally monitor children with chronic OM who have had particular speech production problems early in life to examine whether these early problems are related to early reading skills. It would also be important to understand how phonologic processes might be affected for children who use African-American English and who may be bilingual because this may put an additional burden on the child who may have to learn two dialects or two languages early in life.

Language

There is fairly convincing evidence that OM in early life affects both receptive and expressive language in the first 2 years of life, when children experience OM most frequently. Later in early childhood when OM is less common, receptive language appears to recover. Expressive language also seems to recover, but there are still conflicting results, with some studies showing effects of OM in the later early childhood period and some studies showing no effects. These results were based on standardized tests and language samples. At school age, there are few studies of language but most of these did not show an effect, although there were some that did find effects on expressive language.

It would be important in future studies to monitor children using both language samples and standardized tests. It is particularly important to understand children's basic language skills with respect to vocabulary, since this has been shown to predict success in school.[16]

Pragmatics

The area that has been of unique interest in this chapter is pragmatics. We have argued that basic language skills are fairly impervious to environmental insult but the use of language is not. In addition, it is really the use of language in interacting with others and in narratives that may be of most importance to children's daily success. Parents and teachers expect children to comprehend lengthy interchanges and communicate effectively with others. Being competent in these areas has been related to school success[83] much more than basic language skills.

Children with chronic OM did much poorer tasks requiring use of language or on dialogue codes that tapped the language use skills both early in life and later in childhood. Yet, there were very few studies that included pragmatics as an area of study. We have argued that children with chronic OM may learn early in life not to attend to language and may consequently have less experience than other children in interacting with others and in understanding and producing lengthy dialogues and narratives. These pragmatic skills are critical for school success, and it would be very important to better understand how children with chronic OM use language at home and at school.

Attention

Attention-related processes are another area of concern. Children with chronic OM may attend less to language, and this may result in less interaction with others and less attention to oral language at home and at school. Most of the studies do find some effects on attention, although the North Carolina study, which has focused on low-income African American children, has found that many effects disappear when controlling for demographics and the quality of the home environment. The Pennsylvania study of middle-class Caucasian children has found effects in early childhood and at school age, and the Dunedin studies have shown consistent effects on attention. Attention problems may mediate the effects on later achievement. More research is needed to understand the exact processes affected and the role of SES and ethnicity.

Threshold Effects and Cumulative Risks

There are very few studies of the effect of OM that suggest there might be threshold effects. Our work has used this technique successfully in identifying children most at risk. We believe this is a very important issue in future research studies. Viewing OM and hearing loss as continuous variables may mask effects at the extreme end of the distribution. We suggest that studies try to examine this by using regression techniques that look for a breakline in the regression or by using extreme groups comparison. Both these techniques might be helpful in understanding the group at most risk for the effects of OM.

Of course, the truth in OM research is even more complicated than a mere threshold effect. We still know so little about how much OM a young child must experience early in life to lead to effects, how much hearing loss is associated with this experience, and at what point in development must this occur. For instance, even if we hypothesize a threshold effect, no studies have examined whether OM is most detrimental to development when experienced in the first year of life versus the second year of life. We also do not know whether intermittent OM is more detrimental than long bouts of OM over the early years.

Looking for moderators is very important because OM may only have effects under certain conditions. Children who experience multiple risks early in life, with one of them being OM, may be at very high risk of poor outcomes. We have used this cumulative risk notion in our work. In the Pennsylvania State studies, two different samples revealed an interaction between OM and the quality of childcare: children with chronic OM who were in high-quality care had few developmental sequelae and appeared buffered from the effects of OM and hearing loss. Conversely, children with OM in low-quality day care showed very significant effects on a variety of measures. Although these studies show almost no main effects for OM, the children with chronic OM in low-quality day care were almost 1 standard deviation below all others. Studies are needed to examine other conditions under which OM might have its greatest impact, such as the home environment or other critically important contexts for children.

CONCLUSION

The review of literature in this chapter supports many conclusions from the chapter in the previous edition, but we have tried to emphasize particular aspects of development that might be most affected by OM. Research on the effects of OM remains controversial, and there are still many issues to resolve because of the different populations of children studied. Despite some consistent effects on pragmatics and attention, there are still many unanswered questions about whether and under what conditions OM affects child development.

From a scientific perspective, there are two ways we believe research on the effects of OM on development can be improved. First, better models are needed to specifically predict which children will be affected by OM and under what conditions. Many studies use a myriad of measures without any hypotheses about why these measures were used and how they relate to their theories or models. It would help to know whether the authors predicted effects of OM on particular measures because it appears that many of the studies would actually predict no effects on many of the measures used. Models that specify mediating and moderating variables would be extremely helpful in understanding the exact nature of the predictions. This information would facilitate future systematic reviews and meta-analyses.

Second, and most importantly, the best way to resolve these differences would be a multisite prospective study of infants, where investigators from different areas of this country and with different perspectives used the same procedures and measures over the early infancy period and monitored the children as they go into school. Investigator sites would need to vary as to whether they included children in day care, children from different SES groups, and children of different ethnic backgrounds. This kind of study is critically important if we ever want to make definitive statements about the effects of OM.

Although this may seem like a large undertaking, the National Institutes of Child Health and Development (NICHD) Study of Early Childcare undertook a similar kind of study to understand the effects of early day care on children's development. This 10-site study of children from birth into early adolescence was undertaken because of the same issues that are problematic in OM. That is, the studies used different measures with different populations of children and found conflicting results. The NICHD study of Early Childcare (2000, 2002) has resolved many issues around the effects of early childcare that have made a difference for future research and for national policy related to childcare. A similar effort needs to take place for OM if we are really to make significant advances in our understanding of which children are affected by OM and under what conditions.

REFERENCES

1. Menyuk P. Effect of persistent otitis media on language development. Ann Otol Rhinol Laryngol 1980;89:257–63.
2. Northern JL, Downs MP. Hearing in children. 2nd ed. Baltimore (MD): Williams & Wilkins; 1978.
3. Gravel JS, Nozza RJ. Hearing loss among children with otitis media with effusion. In: Roberts JE, Wallace IF, Henderson FW, editors. Otitis media in young children. Baltimore (MD): Paul H Brookes Publishing Co; 1997. p. 63–92.
4. Blair JC, Peterson ME, Verheg SH. The effects of mild sensorineural hearing loss on academic performance of young school-age children. Volta Review 1985;87:87–93.
5. Oyler RF, Oyler AL, Matkin ND. Unilateral hearing loss: demographics and educational impact. Lang Speech Hear Service School 1988;19:201–10.
6. Lenneberg EH. Biological foundations of language. New York (NY): Wiley; 1967.
7. Ruben RJ. An inquiry into the minimal amount of auditory deprivation which results in a cognitive effect in man. Acta Otolaryngol 1984;414:157–64.
8. Brandes PJ, Ehinger DM. The effects of early middle ear pathology on auditory perception and academic achievement. J Speech Hear Dis 1981;46:301–7.
9. Lewis N. Otitis media and linguistic incompetence. Arch Otolaryngol 1976;102:387–90.
10. Sak RJ, Ruben RJ. Recurrent middle ear effusion in childhood: implications of temporary auditory deprivation for language and learning. Ann Otol Rhinol Laryngol 1981;90:546–55.
11. Zinkus PW, Gottlieb MI. Patterns of perceptual and academic defects related to early chronic otitis media. Pediatrics 1980;66:246–53.
12. Ventry IM. Effects of conductive hearing loss: fact or fiction? J Speech Hear Dis 1980;45:143–56.
13. Feagans LV, Proctor A. The effects of mild illness in infancy on later development: the sample case of the effects of otitis media (middle ear effusion). In: Fisher CB, Lerner RM, editors. Applied developmental psychology. Cambridge (MA): McGraw-Hill; 1994. p. 139–73.
14. Stool SE, Berg AO, Berman S, et al. Otitis media with effusion in young children: clinical practice guideline No. 12 (AHCPR Publication No. (4-0622). Rockville (MD): Agency for Health Care Policy and Research; 1994.
15. Feagans LV, Short EJ. Developmental differences in the comprehension and production of narratives by reading-disabled and normally achieving children. Child Dev 1984;55:1727–36.
16. Snow C, Barnes WS, Chandler J, et al. Unfulfilled expectations: home and school influences on literacy. Cambridge (MA): Harvard University Press; 1991.
17. Roberts JE, Burchinal MR, Medley LP, et al. Otitis media, hearing sensitivity, and maternal responsiveness in relation to language during infancy. J Pediatr 1995;126:481–9.
18. Roberts JE, Burchinal MR, Zeisel S et al. Otitis media, the caregiving environment, and language and cognitive outcomes at 2 years. Pediatrics 1998;102:346–53.
19. Miccio AW, Gallagher E, Grossman C, et al. Influence of chronic otitis media on phonological acquisition. Clin Linguist Phonet 2001;15:47–51.
20. Miccio AW, Yont KM, Clemons HL, Vernon-Feagans L. Otitis media and the acquisition of consonants. Windsor F, Kelly M, Hewlett N, editors. Investigations in clinical phonetics and linguistics. Mahwah (NJ): Lawrence Erlbaum; 2002. p. 429–36.
21. Stoel-Gammon C. Phonetic inventories, 15–24 months: a longitudinal study. J Speech Hear Res 1985;28:505–12.
22. Feagans LV. Otitis media: a model for long term effects with implications for intervention. In: Kavanaugh JF, editor. Otitis media and child development. Parkton (MD): York Press; 1986. p. 192–208.
23. Vernon-Feagans L. Impact of otitis media on speech, language, cognition and behavior. In: Rosenfeld RM, Bluestone CD, editors. Evidence-based otitis media. Hamilton (ON): BC Decker Inc.; 1999. p. 353–73.
24. Vernon-Feagans LV. Children's talk in communities and classrooms. Cambridge (MA): Blackwell Publishers; 1996.
25. Yont KM, Snow CE, Vernon-Feagans L. Early communicative intents in 12-month-old children with and without chronic otitis media. First Lang 2001;21:265–88.
26. Yont KM, Hewitt LE, Miccio AW. 'What did you say'?: understanding conversational breakdowns in children with speech and language impairments. Clin Linguist Phonet 2002;16:265–85.
27. Bates E. Language and context: the acquisition of pragmatics. New York (NY): Academic Press; 1976.
28. Fenson L, Dale PS, Reznick JS, et al. Variability in early communicative development. Monogr Soc Res Child Dev 1994;242:1–183.
29. Ninio A, Snow CE. Pragmatic development: essays in developmental science. Boulder (CO): Westview Press; 1996.

30. Bates E, Thal D, Whitesell K, et al. Integrating language and gestures in infancy. Dev Psychol 1989;25:1004–9.

31. Capirci O, Iverson JM, Pizzuto E, Volterra V. Gestures and words during the transition to two-word speech. J Child Lang 1996;23:645–73.

32. Goldin-Meadow S. The development of gesture and speech as an integrated system. In: Iverson J, Goldin-Meadow S, editors. The nature and functions of gesture in children's communication. New directions for child development (no. 79). San Francisco (CA): Jossey-Bass; 1998.

33. Laakso ML, Poikkeus AM, Katajamaki J, Lyytinen P. Early intentional communication as a predictor of language development in toddlers. First Lang 1999;19:207–31.

34. Vernon-Feagans L, Hurley MM, Yont KM. The effect of otitis media and daycare quality on mother/child bookreading and language use at 48 months. Appl Dev Psychol 2002;23:113–33.

35. Feagans LV, Sanyal M, Henderson F, et al. Relationship of middle ear disease in early childhood to later narrative and attention skills. J Pediatr Psychol 1987;12:581–94.

36. Paradise JL, Dollaghan CA Campbell TF, et al. Language, speech sound production, and cognition in three-year-old children in relation to otitis media in their first three years of life. Pediatrics 2000;105:1119–30.

37. Black MM, Gerson LF, Freeland CA, et al. Language screening for infants prone to otitis media. J Pediatr Psychol 1988;13:423–33.

38. Tomasello M, Farrar MJ. Joint attention and early language. Child Dev 1986;57:1454–63.

39. Barnes S, Gutfreund M, Satterly D, Wells G. Characteristics of adult speech which predict children's language development. J Child Lang 1983;10:65–84.

40. Wallace IF, Gravel JS, Schwartz RG, Ruben RJ. Otitis media, communication style of primary caregivers, and language skills of 2 year olds: a preliminary report. Dev Behav Pediatr 1996;17:27–35.

41. Feagans LV, Kipp EK, Blood I. The effects of otitis media on the language and attention skills of daycare attending toddlers. Dev Psychol 1994;30:701–8.

42. Vernon-Feagans L, Emanuel DC, Blood I. The effect of otitis media and quality of daycare on children's language development. J Appl Dev Psychol 1997;18:395–409.

43. Sameroff AJ, Feise BH. Transactional regulation: The developmental ecology of early intervention. In: Shonkoff JP, Meisels SJ, editors. Handbook of early childhood intervention. 2nd ed. Cambridge (UK): Cambridge University Press; 2000. p. 135–59.

44. Creps CL, Vernon-Feagans L. Preschoolers social behavior in day care: links with entering day care in the first year. J Appl Dev Psychol 1999;20:461–79.

45. Garmezy N. Resilence in children's adaptation to negative life events and stressed environments. Pediatr Ann 1991;20:459–60, 463–6.

46. Rutter M. Psychosocial resilience and protective mechanisms. Am J Orthopsych 1987;57:316–31.

47. Sameroff AJ. Environmental context of child development. Ann Prog Child Psych Child Dev 1987;109:113–29.

48. Daly KA. Definition and epidemiology of otitis media. In: Roberts JE, Wallace IF, Henderson FW, editors. Otitis media in young children. Baltimore (MD): Paul H Brookes Publishing Co.; 1997. p. 3–41.

49. Maw R, Counsell A. An international perspective on otitis media with effusion: incidence, prevalence, management, and policy guidelines. In: Roberts JE, Wallace IF, Henderson FW, editors. Otitis media in young children. Baltimore (MD): Paul H Brooks Publishing Co.; 1997. p. 267–86.

50. Casselbrant ML, Mandel EM, Rockette HE, Bluestone CD. Incidence of otitis media and bacteriology of acute otitis media during the first two years of life. In: Lim DJ, Bluestone CD, Klein JO, et al, editors. Recent advances in otitis media. Toronto (ON): Decker Periodicals; 1993. p. 1–3.

51. Owen MJ, Baldwin CD, Luttman D, Howie VM. Universality of otitis media with effusion detected by tympanometry on frequent home visits in Galveston, Texas. In: Lim DJ, Bluestone CD, Klein JO, et al, editors. Recent advances in otitis media. Toronto (ON): Decker Periodicals; 1993. p. 17–20.

52. Rosenfeld RM, Vertrees JE, Carr J, et al. Clinical efficacy of antimicrobial drugs for acute otitis media: meta-analysis of 5400 children from thirty-three randomized trials. J Pediatr 1994;124:355–67.

53. Schwartz RH, Rodriguez WJ, Grundfast KM. Duration of middle ear effusion after acute otitis media. Pediatr Infect Dis 1984;3:204–7.

54. Paradise JL, Rockette HE, Colborn DK, et al. Otitis media in 2253 Pittsburgh-area infants: prevalence and risk factors during the first two years of life. Pediatrics 1997;99:318–33.

55. Gravel JS, Wallace IF. Listening and language at 4 years of age: effects of early otitis media. J Speech Hear Res 1992;35:588–95.

56. Nittrouer S. The relation between speech perception and phonemic awareness: evidence from low-SES children and children with chronic otitis media. J Speech Hear Res 1996;39:1059–70.

57. Donahue M. Early phonological and lexical development and otitis media. J Child Lang 1993;20:489–501.

58. Robb MP, Psak JL, Pang-Ching GK. Chronic otitis media and early speech development: a case study. Int J Pediatr Otorhinolaryngol 1993;26:117–27.

59. Teele DW, Klein JO, Rosner B, and the Greater Boston Otitis Media Study Group. Otitis media with effusion during the first three years of life and the development of speech and language. Pediatrics 1984;74:282–7.

60. Goldman R, Fristoe M. Goldman-Fristoe Test of Articulation. Circle Pines (MN): American Guidance Service; 1986.

61. Teele DW, Klein JO, Chase C, Menyuk P, Rosner B, and the Greater Boston Otitis Media Study Group. Otitis media in infancy and intellectual ability, school achievement, speech, and language at age 7 years. J Infect Dis 1990;162:685–94.

62. Roberts JE, Burchinal MR, Koch MA, et al. Otitis media in early childhood and its relationship to later phonological development. J Speech Hear Dis 1988;53:416–24.

63. McCormick DP, Baldwin CD, Klecan-Aker JS, et al. Association of early bilateral middle ear effusion with language at age 5 years. Ambul Pediatr 2001;1:87–90.

64. Paradise JL, Feldman HM, Campbell TF, et al. Effect of early or delayed insertion of tympanostomy tubes for persistent otitis media on developmental outcomes at the age of three years. New Engl J Med 2001;344:1179–87.

65. Rvachew S, Slawinski EB, Williams M, Green C. The impact of early onset otitis media on babbling and early language development. J Acoust Soc Am 1999;105:467–75.

66. Luloff A, Menyuk P, Teele D. Effects of persistent otitis media on the speech sound repertoire of infants. In: Recent advances in otitis media with effusion. Proceedings of the Fifth International Symposium. Toronto (ON): BC Decker Inc.; 1991. p. 178–9.

67. Abraham S, Wallace I, Gravel J. Early otitis media and phonological development at age 2 years. Laryngoscope 1996;106:727–32.

68. Friel-Patti S, Finitzo-Hieber T, Conti G, Brown KC. Language delay in infants associated with middle ear disease and mild, fluctuating hearing impairment. Pediatr Infect Dis 1982;1:104–9.

69. Friel-Patti S, Finitzo T. Language learning in a prospective study of otitis media with effusion in the first two years of life. J Speech Hear Res 1990;33:188–94.

70. Roberts JE, Burchinal MR, Jackson SC et al. Otitis media in childhood in relation to preschool language and school readiness skills among black children. Pediatrics 2000;106:725–35.

71. Lous J, Fiellau-Nikolajsen M, Jeppesen, AL. Secretory otitis media and verbal intelligence: a six-year prospective case control study. In: Lim DJ, Bluestone CD, Klein JO, Nelson JD, editors. Recent advances in otitis media. Proceedings of the fourth international symposium. Toronto (ON): BC Decker Inc.; 1988. p. 393–5.

72. Roberts JE, Burchinal MR, Davis BP, et al. Otitis media in early childhood and later language. J Speech Hear Res 1991;34:1158–68.

73. Rach GH, Zielhuis GA, van den Broek P. The influence of chronic persistent otitis media with effusion on language development of 2- to 4-year-olds. Int J Pediatr Otorhinolaryngol 1988;15:253–61.

74. Wright PF, Sell SH, McConnell KB, et al. Impact of recurrent otitis media on middle-ear function, hearing and language. J Pediatr 1988;113:581–7.

75. Ninio A, Snow CE, Pan BA, Rollins PR. Classifying communicative acts in children's interaction. J Communic Dis 1994;27:157–88.

76. Vernon-Feagans L, Emanuel D, Blood I. Otitis media and daycare: factors that affect children's language. In: Lim DJ, Bluestone CD, Casselbrant M, et al, editors. Recent advances in otitis media. Toronto (ON): BC Decker Inc.; 1996. pp. 331–4.

77. Vernon-Feagans L, Manlove EE, Volling BL. Otitis media and the social behavior of day care-attending children. Child Dev 1996;67:1528–39.

78. Minter KR, Roberts JE, Hooper SR, et al. Early childhood otitis media in relation to children's attention-related behavior in the first six years of life. Pediatrics 2001;107:1037–42.

79. Roberts JE, Burchinal MR, Campbell F. Otitis media in early childhood and patterns of intellectual development and later academic performance. J Pediatr Psychol 1994;19:347–67.

80. Roberts JE, Burchinal MR, Clarke-Klein SM. Otitis media in early childhood and cognitive, academic and behavior outcomes at 12 years of age. J Pediatr Psychol 1995;20:645–60.

81. Cassidy J, Asher SR. Loneliness and peer relations in young children. Child Dev 1992;63:350–65.

82. Bennett KE, Haggard MP, Silva PA, Stewart IA. Behaviour and developmental effects of otitis media with effusion into the teens. Arch Dis Child 2001;85:91–5.

83. Feagans LV, Merriwether AM, Haldane D. Goodness of fit in the home: its relationship to school behavior and achievement in children with learning disabilities. J Learn Disabil 1991;24:413–20.

84. Rach GH, Zielhuis GA, van Baarle PW, van den Broek P. The effect of treatment with ventilating tubes on language development in preschool children with otitis media with effusion. Clin Otolaryngol 1991;16: 128–32.

85. Pearce PS, Saunders MA, Creighton DE, Sauve RS. Hearing and verbal-cognitive abilities in high-risk preterm children prone to otitis media with effusion. Dev Behav Pediatr 1988;9:346–51.

86. Wallace IF, Gravel JS, McCarton CM, Ruben RJ. Otitis media and language development at one year of age. J Speech Hear Dis 1988;53:245–51.

87. Fischler RS, Todd NW, Feldman CM. Otitis media and language performance in a cohort of Apache Indian children. Am J Dis Child 1985;139:355–60.

88. Grievink EH, Peters SAF, van Bon WHJ, Schilder AGM. The effects of early bilateral otitis media with effusion on language ability: a prospective cohort study. J Speech Hear Res 1993;36:1004–12.

89. Roberts JE, Burchinal MR, Davis BP, et al. Otitis media in early childhood and cognitive, academic and classroom performance of the school-aged child. Pediatrics 1989; 83:477–85.

CHAPTER 24

Meta-analysis of Speech and Language Sequelae

Joanne E. Roberts, PhD, Susan A. Zeisel, EdD,
Richard Rosenfeld, MD, MPH, and Patricia Reitz, MA

Children are one-third of our population and all of our future.
Select Panel for the Promotion of Child Health, 1981

OBJECTIVES

On completing this chapter, the reader will be able to

1. Appreciate the methodology for systematic review and meta-analysis of otitis media (OM) speech and language sequelae.
2. Identify prospective studies suitable for statistical pooling to estimate effect size.
3. State if OM in early childhood is related to later receptive language, expressive language, speech, vocabulary, and syntax in children aged 1 to 5 years.
4. State if hearing loss cause by OM in early childhood is related to later receptive language or expressive language in children under age 2 years.
5. Identify implications of developmental findings for health care practices.

Considerable controversy continues to surround whether a history of otitis media with effusion (OME) during the first few years of life, a critical period for learning language, causes later speech and language difficulties.[1-3] A child with OME typically experiences a mild to moderate fluctuating hearing loss and, thus, receives a partial or inconsistent auditory signal. This may interfere with rapid language processing, causing a child to encode information inefficiently, incompletely, or inaccurately into the database from which language develops.[3] Persistent (prolonged) or recurrent (varied) hearing loss during the formative years of language and learning, which interferes with or prevents completing this processing in a timely manner, could reduce language information and subsequently delay aspects of language development, such as vocabulary or grammar.

The developmental consequences of OME influence management because OME is highly prevalent in young children. One of the major reasons for intervention,

including insertion of tympanostomy tubes, is to prevent potential developmental consequences related to OME. Over 100 original studies have examined the linkage of a history of OM (including OME and acute OM) to difficulties in later speech and language development. Compared with children who infrequently experienced OM, those with a history of OME scored lower on measures of speech and language development in some studies,[4-6] whereas others found no differences in children's speech and language development caused by a history of OME.[7-9]

Earlier studies[10] of the OME language learning relationship were retrospective, first identifying children with or without language or learning disabilities and then examining the amount of OME in both groups. Methodologic problems included inadequate recall of OME. Other studies[11] in this time period were cross-sectional, measuring OME and language together, making it impossible to infer dynamic linkages. In the last two decades, investigators monitored children prospectively to examine how OME impacts later language development,[7,12,13] providing the best evidence attainable without randomized control trials (RCTs).[14] Recently, children with persistent OME were randomized in three studies[6,8,9] to have tympanostomy tubes inserted promptly or at a later point while monitoring language development. The design of RCT is the gold standard for studies examining how OME affects children's development.

To examine the controversy surrounding the OME development linkage, we used meta-analysis to test whether a history of OME in early childhood is related to children's later speech and language skills. Meta-analysis is a form of systematic literature review whereby studies are identified, analyzed, and evaluated using specified statistical procedures to minimize bias. We included only prospective studies and RCTs because they provide the highest scientific rigor for clinical recommendations. We examined the following speech and language outcomes: (1) receptive language or language comprehension, (2) expressive language or language production, (3) speech production or how the individual sounds are said, and (4) two commonly studied language domains—vocabulary and grammar.

Our analyses include children tested between 1 and 5 years of age. We initially included studies of children through the age of 12 years but found insufficient combinable data to complete analyses after age 5 years. Two recent meta-analyses[15,16] examined how OME impacts children's later speech and language development. Building on these analyses, this chapter will interpret conflicting findings on the OME language linkage in light of new studies, analyze how the hearing loss associated with OME affects language development, discuss how OME impacts a broad range of outcomes (speech, syntax, vocabulary, plus receptive and expressive language), and suggest clinical implications for health care practices.

METHODOLOGY

Selection of Studies

First, we searched MEDLINE, Cochrane Library, and PsycINFO as well as the bibliographies of OME original data studies and OME language reviews for articles published between January 1966, and October 2002, examining the relationship of OME in early childhood to later speech and language skills. The MeSH terms and keywords used in our computerized search strategy were "otitis media/otitis media with effusion/ear infections; infant, preschool, child, adolescent; and speech/language development/disorder, child language/development, speech perception/production, and language comprehension/production, receptive/expressive language, and communication/disorders." Manual searches included the bibliographies of original OME data studies and review articles.

Two investigators independently assessed the initial data set for original research studies that (1) used a prospective or RCT study design; (2) measured outcomes of receptive language, expressive language, vocabulary, syntax, language use, and speech; and (3) documented OME or associated hearing loss before age 4 years. We excluded studies on children with biologic or genetic conditions that increased the risk of OME, such as Down syndrome, craniofacial anomalies, or pre-existing speech, language, or learning disorders. We also excluded original research studies presented in case reports, letters, reviews, chapters, and conference proceedings.

Two investigators independently reviewed 38 articles meeting inclusion criteria and abstracted descriptive information and quantitative data. Any disagreements were settled by consensus after re-examining the article. Next, we eliminated articles in several steps. First, we excluded studies that included the same children at the same age in multiple studies.[17–22] Second, we excluded studies that used such measures as parent report[23,24] instead of standard means of assessing speech and language. Third, we excluded studies without usable data for the meta-analysis (as described below),[13, 25–32] including correlation studies that did not report a correlation coefficient or R-squared, and group comparison studies that did not report means and standard deviations (SDs), standard or mean group differences, T values, or p values.

To identify groupings for meta-analysis, we classified studies by design (correlational versus independent group comparisons), independent variable in early childhood (OME versus direct measure of hearing), and by age at outcome assessment: infancy (1 to 2 years), preschool (2 to 5 years), or school age (5 to 8 years). The major dichotomy into correlational versus group studies was mandated by practical issues in data pooling because the two types of data are not interchangeable. Correlational studies associated an independent variable (OM or hearing) with one or more outcomes. Group studies compared outcomes in two or more independent and parallel groups of children with varying levels of OM on the basis of historic experience of OME or randomization to tympanostomy tubes versus watchful waiting.

Several a priori assumptions were made to facilitate data grouping and pooling. Within an age grouping, a study could contribute data from a given cohort of children only once to maintain statistical independence. This excluded one study of later outcomes in the same age grouping on a previous cohort.[33] For infants we used the oldest test age if a study reported multiple outcomes (eg, ages 1 and 2 years). For preschoolers, we used test data from age 3 years, if available, because this was available for most studies and would help maintain consistency. If all studies in a preschool grouping did not provide test results at age 3 years, we again used the oldest test age reported (eg, age 5 years for a study giving outcomes at ages 3, 4, and 5 years).

A final criterion for meta-analysis was that data be available from three or more studies to justify statistical pooling. We therefore excluded studies[5,34–39] in meta-analyses that would contain data from only one or two cohorts (eg, only two correlation studies examined OME and receptive language in infancy). The remaining groups with at least three studies on a particular outcome that were available for analysis were as follows:

1. Infancy: receptive language versus hearing loss (correlation studies)
2. Infancy: expressive language versus hearing loss (correlation studies)

3. Preschool: receptive language versus OME (correlation and group studies)
4. Preschool: expressive language versus OME (correlation and group studies)
5. Preschool: vocabulary comprehension (Peabody Picture Vocabulary Test [PPVT])[40] versus OME (correlation and group studies)
6. Preschool: expressive vocabulary (number of different words [NDW]) versus OME (correlation studies)
7. Preschool: expressive syntax (mean length of utterance [MLU]) versus OME (correlation studies)
8. Preschool: speech versus OME (group studies)

The final data set included 14 studies.[4,6,7–9,12,41–48] For each included study, Table 24-1 describes the study population, procedures for documenting OME, speech and language tests administered, age of children when tested, and to which specific meta-analyses the study contributed data.

Statistical Methods

Data from individual studies were combined (pooled) using a random-effects model of meta-analysis,[49] which assumes a population (distribution) of true effect sizes with each source article representing one member of this population. Under this model, results are expected to vary from study to study, with differences caused by experimental error and differences in populations (between-study variability). Because of this additional variability, the 95% confidence interval (CI) for the pooled result is wider (less precise) than for a fixed-effect model. Therefore, the random-effects model gives a more conservative estimate of association.

For correlation studies, data were pooled using the Pearson correlation coefficients (R) and sample sizes from source articles. Adjusted coefficients were used whenever available, to account for the impact of modifying factors on effect size (eg, maternal education, socioeconomic status). If a study gave separate coefficients for low-income versus middle-income families, we used the middle-income data as a more conservative estimate. The combined R is statistically significant ($p < .05$) if the 95% CI does not contain zero; negative values indicate poorer outcomes with OME. A statistically significant R less than .25 suggests little or no relationship, .25 to .49 is a fair relationship, .50 to .74 is a moderate relationship, and .75 or higher is a good relationship. The coefficient of variation (R^2) gives the variability in effect size that is explained by changes in the independent variable (OME or hearing levels).

For studies comparing independent groups (randomized or observational) with different levels of OME, data were pooled using the p values or group means and

SDs from source articles. If more than two groups were available, we designated the group with the least OM as "OM–" and the one with the most OM as "OM+" (data from intermediate groups were not used). Effect sizes for individual and combined studies were calculated using the standard difference, defined as the mean difference between the OM+ versus OM– groups divided by the common within-group SD. This allows comparison between studies because the metric of comparison is the number of SD units that the groups differ. The effect size is statistically significant ($p < .05$) if the 95% CI does not contain zero; negative values indicate poorer outcomes with OM. A statistically significant effect size less than 0.20 standard difference suggests little or no effect, .20 to .49 standard difference is a small effect, .50 to .79 standard difference is a moderate effect, and .80 standard difference or higher is a large effect. Analysis of variance (ANOVA) was used, whenever possible, to assess the impact of study design (randomized vs. observational) on outcomes.

Statistical analysis was performed using Comprehensive Meta-Analysis,[50] a computer program for research synthesis developed with funding from the National Institutes of Health. The program weights study results with the inverse of variance and calculates a random effects estimate of the combined effect and 95% CI. A test of heterogeneity is performed using the Q statistic to evaluate constancy of effect across strata. Significant heterogeneity exists if $p < .05$, although the test has low power and important variations may be present even with a nonsignificant result. For this reason, the random effects model is used regardless of the test of heterogeneity, although test results are still stated and explored.

All meta-analyses with statistically significant results include a graphic display of results to aid interpretation. The forest plot is a widely used form of presentation that plots point estimates (black squares) from different studies along with their error bars (horizontal lines).[51] Because the eye is drawn to longer error bars, data from smaller studies have a relatively greater visual effect. To compensate for this distortion, boxes are drawn proportional to study sample size. The combined result is depicted below the studies with a black diamond spanning the 95% CI. When most or all of the individual studies' 95% CIs contain the combined RD (center of the black squares), the studies are relatively homogeneous.

RESULTS

Results are organized by language outcomes relative to previous OME or associated hearing loss. Receptive language outcomes are described first, followed by expressive language, specific aspects of language (vocabulary and

Table 24-1 Characteristics of Final Data Set for Meta-analysis

Author Year Location	Description of Study Sample Source; Ethnicity; SES	OME and Hearing Documentation	Meta-analyses Using Study Data (Test Used, Child Age at Testing)
Teele[47] 1984 Boston, MA	Neighborhood health centers and private practice; ethnicity unknown; SES middle and lower	Otoscopy, age 0–3 yr (well and sick office visits)	Correlational analyses Rec language 3 yr vs. OME (PLS, 3 yr) Exp language 3 yr vs. OME (PLS, 3 yr) Vocabulary 3 yr vs. OME (PPVT, 3 yr) OM+ group vs. OM– group analyses Rec language 2–5 yr vs. OME (PLS, 3 yr) Exp language 2–5 yr vs. OME (PLS, 3 yr) Vocabulary 3 yr vs. OME (PPVT, 3 yr)
Pearce[43] 1988 Alberta, Canada	Hospital, < 37 wk gestation and 1,500 g or complicated ventilation; IQ > 70; OM+ had tubes before age 3.5 yr or abnormal tymp x2; OM– had normal tymp; 88% White; SES unknown	Tymp at 0, 4, 8, 12, 18, and 36 mo	OM+ group vs. OM– group analyses Rec language 2–5 yr vs. OME (SICD, 2–4 yr)
Rach[44] 1988 Nijmegen, Netherlands	Community birth cohort, matched sample; OM+ had OME > 5 mo; OM– was normal; SES unknown; Dutch speaking	Tymp every 3 mo, age 2–4 yr	OM+ group vs. OM– group analyses Rec language 2–5 yr vs. OME (Reynell, 31–36 mo) Exp language 2–5 yr vs. OME (Reynell, 31–36 mo)
Wallace[48] 1988a New York, NY	Hospital, high risk and full-term infants; 52% Hispanic, 44% Black; SES mostly low	Otoscopy, age 0–1 yr (mean 8–9 visits); ABR at 0, 3, 6, 9, and 12 mo	Correlational analyses Rec language 1–2 yr vs. hearing (SICD, 1 yr) Exp language 1–2 yr vs. hearing (SICD, 1 yr)
Friel-Patti[41] 1990 Dallas, TX	Private pediatric practice, typically developing; ethnicity unknown; SES middle–high	Otoscopy, tymp every ≤ 6 wk, age 6–18 mo, then every 12 wk	Correlational analyses Rec language 1–2 yr vs. hearing (SICD, 18 mo) Exp language 1–2 yr vs. hearing (SICD, 18 mo)
Roberts[45] 1991 North Carolina ABC Study	University-based child care; 60% Black, 38% White; SES 52% low, 48% middle	Otoscopy, tymp every 2–4 wk, age 0–3 yr	Correlational analyses: Vocabulary 3–5 yr vs. OME (NDW, 54 mo) Syntax 3–5 yr vs. OME (MLU, 54 mo)
Gravel[42] 1992 New York, NY	Hospital, 61% high risk, 39% full-term infants; 52% Black, 39% Hispanic; SES low	Otoscopy, 0–1 yr (10 routine visits plus illness visits)	OM+ group vs. OM– group analyses Rec language 2–5 yr vs. OME (SICD, 4 yr) Exp language 2–5 yr vs. OME (SICD, 4 yr)
Roberts[46] 1998 North Carolina COMP Study	Childcare centers; 100% Black; SES mostly low	Otoscopy, tymp every 2–4 wk, age 6–24 mo	Correlational analyses Rec language 1–2y vs. hearing (SICD-R, 2y) Exp language 1–2y vs. hearing (SICD-R, 2y)

Study	Diagnostic criteria	Setting/sample	Analyses
Maw[6] 1999 Bristol, UK	Otoscopy; tymp; bilateral OME documented ≥ 3 mo	Otolaryngology clinic; if bilateral chronic OME randomized to no tubes (OM+) vs. tubes (OM−); 96% White; SES unknown	OM+ group vs. OM− group analyses Rec language 2–5 yr vs. OME (Reynell, 3.8–4.5 yr) Exp language 2–5 yr vs. OME (Reynell, 3.8–4.5 yr)
Paradise[7] 2000 Pittsburgh, PA	Otoscopy, tymp at least monthly, age 0–3 yr	Urban hospitals or private practice; 83% White, 16% Black; SES 32% low, 66% private insurance	Correlational analyses Vocabulary 3 yr vs. OME (PPVT-R, 3 yr) Vocabulary 3–5 yr vs. OME (NDW, 3 yr) Syntax 3 yr vs. OME (MLU, 3 yr) OM+ group vs. OM− group analyses Vocabulary 3 yr vs. OME (PPVT-R, 3 yr) Speech 3 yr vs. OME (PCC, 3 yr)
Roberts[12] 2000 North Carolina COMP Study	Otoscopy, tymp every 2–4 wk, age 6–48 mo	Childcare centers; 100% Black; SES mostly low	Correlational analyses Rec language 3 yr vs. OME (SICD-R, 3 yr) Exp language 3 yr vs. OME (SICD-R, 3 yr) Vocabulary 3 yr vs. OME (PPVT, 3 yr) Vocabulary 3–5 yr vs. OME (NDW, 3 yr) Syntax vs. 3–5 yr OME (MLU, 3–5 yr)
Rovers[9] 2000 Utrecht, Netherlands	Otoscopy, tymp, audiogram every 3 mo, age 9–19 mo	Birth cohort failed hearing screen age 9 mo; if OME 4–6 mo randomized to no tubes (OM+) vs.tubes (OM−); SES unknown; Dutch speaking	OM+ group vs. OM− group analyses Rec language 2–5 yr vs. OME (Reynell, 2.5 yr) Exp language 2–5 yr vs. OME (Reynell, 2.5 yr)
Shriberg[4] 2000 Dallas, TX	Otoscopy, tymp every ≤ 6 wk, age 6–24 mo, then every ≤ 12 wk; ABR at 6 mo; VRA at 12, 18, and 24 mo	Private practice, typically developing; ethnicity unknown; SES 100% middle–high	Correlational analyses Rec language 3 yr vs. OME (SICD, 3 yr) Exp language 3 yr vs. OME (SICD, 3 yr) Vocabulary 3 yr vs. OME (PPVT, 3 yr) OM+ group vs. OM− group analyses Rec language 2–5 yr vs. OME (SICD, 3 yr) Exp language 2–5 yr vs. OME (SICD, 3 yr) Vocabulary 3 yr vs. OME (PPVT, 3 yr) Speech 3 yr vs. OME (PCC, 3 yr)
Paradise[8] 2001 Pittsburgh, PA	Otoscopy, tymp every ≤ 3 mo	Urban hospitals or private practice; if OME threshold, randomized to late tubes (OM+) vs. early tubes (OM−); 83% White, 16% Black; SES 32% low, 66% private insurance	OM+ group vs. OM− group analyses Vocabulary 3 yr vs. OME (PPVT, 3 yr) Speech 3 yr vs. OME (PCC, 3 yr)

ABR = auditory brainstem response; Exp = expressive; IQ = intelligence quotient; MLU = mean length of utterance; NDW = number of different words; OME = otitis media with effusion; PCC = percent consonants correct; PLS = Preschool Language Scale; PPVT = Peabody Picture Vocabulary Test; Rec = receptive; Reynell = Reynell Development Language Scales; SES = socioeconomic status; SICD = Sequenced Inventory of Communication Development; SICD-R = Sequenced Inventory of Communication Development–Revised; Tymp = tympanometry; VRA = visual response audiometry.

Table 24-2 Correlation Meta-analysis of Receptive Language at Age 3 Years versus OME

Author Year	N	Dir[†]	Test (age, yr)	R (95% CI)[‡]
Teele[47] 1984	205	E	PLS (3)	−.14 (−.27, 0)
Roberts[12] 2000	79	E	SICD (3)	−.15 (−.36, .07)[§]
Shriberg[4] 2000	67	R	SICD (3)	.23 (−.01, .45)
Combined	351	E	Various (3)	−.03 (−.27, .22)*

OME = otitis media with effusion; PLS = Preschool Language Scale; SICD = Sequenced Inventory of Communication Development.
*Random effects combined $p = .811$; test of heterogeneity $Q = 7.44$, df = 2, $p = .024$.
[†]Direction of effect, expected (E) or reverse (R).
[‡]Pearson correlation coefficient, $p < .05$ if 95% CI does not contain zero.
[§]Adjusted correlation coefficient.

syntax), and speech. Each section and corresponding tables report analyses separately for correlation and group studies. Tables include data abstracted from individual studies for statistical pooling plus a combined estimate of effect size based on random effects meta-analysis. The direction of effect (expected versus reverse) is also given for individual studies and the combined estimate (eg, an "expected" effect would imply poorer developmental outcomes for children with greater OME or hearing loss).

Receptive Language versus OME and Hearing Loss

Three correlational studies[4,12,47] examined the relationship between OME and receptive language using a standardized measure of receptive language, either the Preschool Language Scale (PLS)[52] or Sequenced Inventory of Communication Development (SICD)[53] during the preschool years (Table 24-2). Because all these studies were done with the subjects at 3 years of age, the analysis will be considered a 3-year outcome analysis. All studies were prospective cohorts. At 3 years of age, OME was unrelated to receptive language, and the R of −.03 (95% CI, −.27, .22) does not suggest a problem with low statistical power. The studies were heterogeneous ($p = .024$).

Seven studies[4,6,9 42–44,47] used a group design to examine the relationship of OME to children's receptive language during the preschool years (ages 2 to 5 years) (Table 24-3 and Figure 24-1). The outcome measures were standardized tests, the PLS, SICD, or Reynell Development Language Scales (Reynell).[54] Two studies were RCTs,[6,9] and five were prospective cohorts.[4,42–44,47] There was a statistically significant association between OME and receptive language during the preschool years with a standard difference of −.25 (95% CI, −.41, −.09). The magnitude of relationship, −.25 standard difference, suggests a small effect, although the 95% CI cannot exclude a trivial effect

(−.09) or almost a good effect (−.41 standard difference). The studies are relatively homogeneous ($p = .564$). The two RCT studies had a smaller effect size (−.22 standard difference) than did the observational studies (−.28 standard difference), but the difference was small and was not significant using ANOVA ($p = .729$).

Three correlation studies[41,46,48] examined the relationship between hearing loss associated with OME and children's receptive language during infancy (age 1 to 2 years) using the SICD (Table 24-4 and Figure 24-2). All studies were prospective. There was a significant association between hearing loss and receptive language, with an R of −.17 (95% CI, −.29, −.05). Although the effect size is small (explains 2.9% of variance), the 95% CI cannot exclude a trivial (−.05) or a fair correlation (−.29). The studies are relatively homogeneous ($p = .516$).

Expressive Language versus OME and Hearing Loss

Three correlation studies[4,12,47] examined the relationship between OME and expressive language with the PLS[52] or SICD[53] with subjects at age 3 years (Table 24-5). All studies were prospective. There was not a significant association between OME and expressive language at 3 years of age, and the R of −.07 (95% CI −.22, .08) does not suggest a problem with low statistical power. The studies are relatively homogeneous ($p = .201$).

Six studies[4,6,9,42,44,47] examined the relationship of OME to children's expressive language during the preschool years (age 2 to 5 years) with the PLS,[52] SICD,[53] or Reynell[54] using a group design (Table 24-6 and Figure 24-3). Two studies were RCTs,[6,9] and four were prospective cohorts.[4,42,44,47] There was a statistically significant association between OME and expressive language during the preschool years with an standard difference of −.24 (95% CI, −.41, −.07). The magnitude of relationship, −.24 standard difference, suggests a small effect, although the 95% CI cannot exclude a trivial effect

Table 24-3 Group Data Meta-analysis of Receptive Language at Age 2 to 5 Years versus OME

Author Year	OM+ Group: N; Mean (SD)	OM– Group: N; Mean (SD)	p Value	Dir[†]	Test (age, yr)	Std Difference (95% CI)[‡]
Teele[47] 1984	88; 119.9(18.6)	54; 123.4(21.7)	.30	E	PLS (3)	−.18 (−.52, .16)
Pearce[43] 1988	23; 17.8	20; 26.0	.02	E	SICD (2–4)	−.73 (−1.37, −.09)
Rach[44] 1988	36	13	.13	E	Reynell (2.5–3)	−.49 (−1.15, .17)
Gravel[42] 1992	35.5(5.4)	13; 37.8(5.3)	.342	E	SICD (4)	−.42 (−1.37, .53)
Maw[6] 1999[§]	71	71	.14	E	Reynell (4.5)	−.25 (−.58, .09)
Rovers[9] 2000[§]	86	87	.18	E	Reynell (2.5)	−.20 (−.51, .10)
Shriberg[4] 2000	8; 43.0(4.1)	59; 42.0(4.3)	.534	R	SICD (3)	.23 (−.52, .99)
Combined	320	317	.003	E	Various (2–4.5)	−.25 (−.41, −.09)*

OM = otitis media; OME = otitis media with effusion; PLS = Preschool Language Scale; Reynell = Reynell Development Language Scales; SICD = Sequenced Inventory of Communication Development.

*Test of heterogeneity Q = 4.84, df = 6, *p* = .564.

[†]Direction of effect, expected (E) or reverse (R).

[‡]Standardized difference between groups, *p* < .05 if 95% CI does not contain zero.

[§]Groups differentiated by random assignment to tympanostomy tubes.

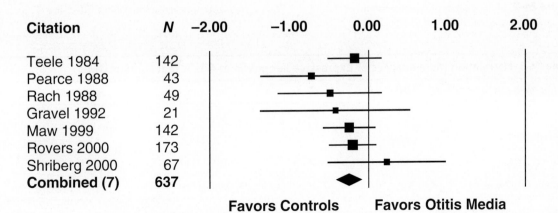

Figure 24-1 Meta-analysis of receptive language at age 2 to 5 years versus OME for group studies. Effect size is expressed as standard difference.

(−.07) or almost a good effect (−.41 standard difference). The studies are relatively homogeneous (*p* = .432). The two RCT studies had a smaller effect size (−.23 standard difference) than did the observational studies (−.25 standard difference), but the difference was trivial and was not significant using ANOVA (*p* = .908).

Three correlation studies[41,46,48] examined the relationship between OME associated hearing loss and children's expressive language during infancy (age 1 to 2 years) using the SICD[53] (Table 24-7 and Figure 24-4). There was a significant association between hearing loss and expressive language in the correlation analyses, R = −.30 (95% CI −.43, −.16). The magnitude of relationship is fair, explaining 9% of variance. The 95% CI

cannot exclude a trivial relationship (R = −.16) or an almost good relationship (R = −.43). Studies are relatively homogeneous (*p* = .295). Although the Wallace and colleagues' study[48] included low-birth-weight children and had a stronger relationship between hearing and language (R = .55) than the other studies, this did not alter the combined results because the small sample size (*N* = 25) of this study reduced its relative contribution.

Vocabulary versus OME

Four correlation studies[4,7,12,47] examined the relationship between OME and receptive vocabulary using the PPVT[40] with subjects at age 3 years (Table 24-8).

Table 24-4 Correlation Meta-analysis of Receptive Language at Age 1 to 2 Years versus Hearing

Author Year	N	Dir[†]	Test (age, yr)	R (95% CI)[‡]
Wallace[48] 1988	25	E	SICD (1)	−.03 (−.42, .37)
Friel-Patti[41] 1990	151	E	SICD (2)	−.23 (−.38, −.07)
Roberts[46] 1998	85	E	SICD (2)	−.11 (−.32, .11)
Combined	261	E	SICD (1–2)	−.17 (−.29, −.05)*

OME = otitis media with effusion; SICD = Sequenced Inventory of Communication Development.
*Random effects combined p = .005; test of heterogeneity Q = 1.32, df = 2, p = .516.
[†]Direction of effect, expected (E) or reverse (R).
[‡]Pearson correlation coefficient, p < .05 if 95% CI does not contain zero.

Citation	N	−1.00	−0.50	0.00	0.50	1.00

Wallace 1988   25
Friel-Patti 1990   151
Roberts 1998   85
Combined (3)   261

Favors Better Hearing   Favors Poorer Hearing

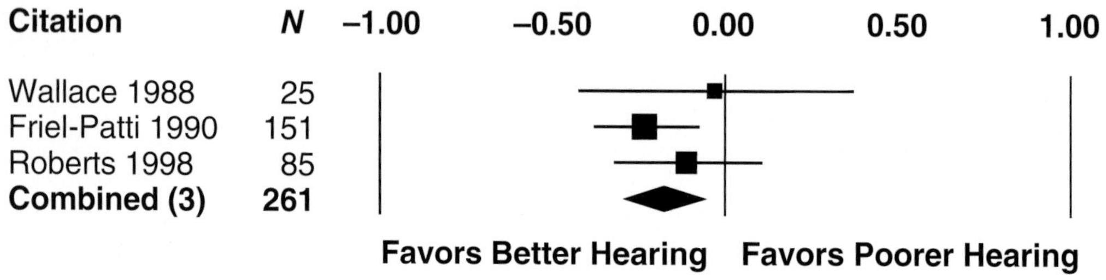

Figure 24–2 Meta-analysis of receptive language at age 1 to 2 years versus OME for correlation studies. Effect size is expressed as Pearson correlation coefficient.

Table 24-5 Correlation Meta-analysis of Expressive Language at Age 3 Years versus OME

Author Year	N	Dir[†]	Test (age, yr)	R (95% CI)[‡]
Teele[47] 1984	201	E	PLS (3)	−.14 (−.27, 0)
Roberts[12] 2000	79	E	SICD (3)	−.13 (−.34, .09)[§]
Shriberg[4] 2000	67	R	SICD (3)	.11 (−.13, .34)
Combined	347	E	Various (3)	−.07 (−.22, .08)*

OME = otitis media with effusion; PLS = Preschool Language Scale; SICD = Sequenced Inventory of Communication Development.
*Random effects combined p = .350; test of heterogeneity Q = 3.21, df = 2, p = .201.
[†]Direction of effect, expected (E) or reverse (R).
[‡]Pearson correlation coefficient, p < .05 if 95% CI does not contain zero.
[§]Adjusted correlation coefficient.

All studies were prospective cohorts. There was not a significant association between OME and receptive vocabulary during the preschool years (R = −.05) and the 95% CI (−.23, .13) does not suggest a problem with low statistical power. The studies are heterogeneous (p = .012).

Four studies[4,7,8,47] used a group design to examine the relationship of OME to children's receptive vocabulary on the PPVT at age 3 years (Table 24-9). One study was an RCT,[8] and the others were prospective cohorts.[4,8,47] There was no statistically significant association between OME and receptive vocabulary during the preschool years with a standard difference of −.16

(95% CI, −.37, .05). The 95% CI suggests possible low statistical power because the upper limit (−.37 standard difference) cannot exclude a fair to good effect size. The studies are relatively homogeneous (p = .195).

Three correlation studies[7,12,45] examined the relationship between OME and children's expressive vocabulary using NDW on a language sample during preschool years (age 3 to 5 years) (Table 24-10). All were prospective cohort studies. There was no significant association between OME and NDW in the correlation analyses (R = −.05), and the 95% CI (−.16, .05) does not suggest a problem with low statistical power. Studies are relatively homogeneous (p = .837).

Table 24-6 Group Data Meta-analysis of Expressive Language at Age 2 to 5 Years versus OME

Author Year	OM+ Group: N; Mean (SD)	OM– Group: N; Mean (SD)	p Value	Dir[†]	Test (age, yr)	Std Difference (95% CI)[‡]
Teele[47] 1984	86; 116.0(24.6)	53; 120.6(23.7)	.28	E	PLS (3)	−.19 (−.54, .16)
Rach[44] 1988	35	13	.02	E	Reynell (2.5–3)	−.77 (−1.44, −.10)
Gravel[42] 1992	8; 36.0(5.2)	12; 39.0(6.2)	.274	E	SICD (4)	−.49 (−1.47, .48)
Maw[6] 1999[§]	81	71	.11	E	Reynell (4.5)	−.26 (−.58, .06)
Rovers[9] 2000[§]	86	87	.18	R	Reynell (2.5)	−.20 (−.51, .10)
Shriberg[4] 2000	8; 42.0(3.0)	59; 43.1(4.4)	.452	R	SICD (3)	.28 (−.47, 1.04)
Combined	304	295	.006	E	Various (2.5–4.5)	−.24 (−.41, −.07)*

OM = otitis media; OME = otitis media with effusion; PLS = Preschool Language Scale; Reynell = Reynell Development Language Scales; SICD = Sequenced Inventory of Communication Development.

*Test of heterogeneity Q = 4.87, df = 5, p = .908.

[†]Direction of effect, expected (E) or reverse (R).

[‡]Standardized difference between groups, $p < .05$ if 95% CI does not contain zero.

[§]Groups differentiated by random assignment to tympanostomy tubes.

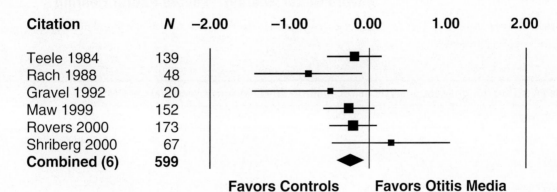

Figure 24-3 Meta-analysis of expressive language at age 2 to 5 years versus OME for group studies. Effect size is expressed as standard difference.

Syntax versus OME

Three correlation studies[7,12,45] examined the relationship between OME and children's syntax as measured by MLU on a language sample in the preschool years (age 3 to 5 years) (Table 24-11). There was no significant association between OME and MLU in the correlation analyses (R = −.07), and the 95% CI (−.18, .04) does not suggest a problem with low statistical power. The studies are relatively homogeneous (p = .718).

Speech versus OME

Three studies[4,7,8] used a group design to examine the relationship of OME to children's speech development at age 3 years (Table 24-12). One study was an RCT,[8] and two

were prospective cohorts.[4,7] There was no statistically significant association between OME and speech development at 3 years of age with an standard difference of −.15 (95% CI, −.32, .01). The 95% CI suggests possible low statistical power because the upper limit (−.32 standard difference) cannot exclude a fair effect size and the lower limit (.01) just missed statistical significance. The studies are relatively homogeneous (p = .472).

CLINICAL IMPLICATIONS

The analyses of OME versus receptive and expressive language in the correlation studies, as well as all the analyses for OME versus vocabulary, syntax, and speech during the preschool years, show no significant relationships between

Table 24-7 Correlation Meta-analysis of Expressive Language at Age 1 to 2 Years versus Hearing

Author Year	N	Dir[†]	Test (age, yr)	R (95% CI)[‡]
Wallace[48] 1988	25	E	SICD (1)	−.55 (−.78, −.20)
Friel-Patti[41] 1990	151	E	SICD (2)	−.26 (−.40, −.11)
Roberts[46] 1998	85	E	SICD (2)	−.27 (−.46, −.06)
Combined	261	E	SICD (1–2)	−.30 (−.43, −.16)*

SICD = Sequenced Inventory of Communication Development.
*Random effects combined $p < .001$; test of heterogeneity Q = 0.24, df = 2, $p = .295$.
[†]Direction of effect, expected (E) or reverse (R).
[‡]Pearson correlation coefficient, $p < .05$ if 95% CI does not contain zero.

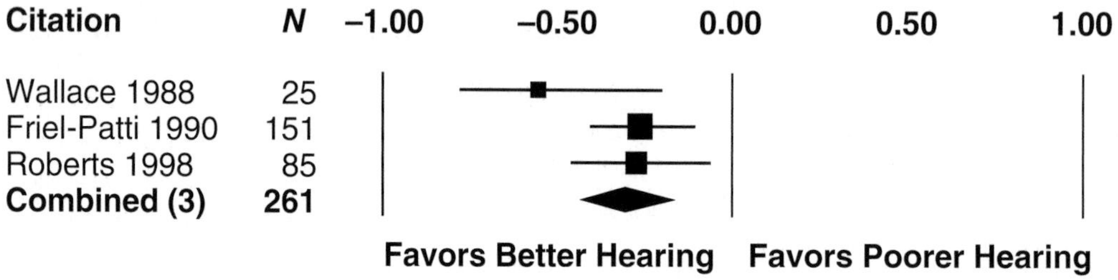

Figure 24-4 Meta-analysis of expressive language at age 1 to 2 years versus OME for correlation studies. Effect size is expressed as Pearson correlation coefficient.

Table 24-8 Correlation Meta-analysis of Vocabulary (PPVT) at Age 3 Years versus OME

Author Year	N	Dir[†]	Test (age, yr)	R (95% CI)[‡]
Teele[47] 1984	200	E	PPVT (3)	−.22 (−.35, −.08)
Paradise[7] 2000	237	E	PPVT (3)	−.13 (−.25, 0)
Roberts[12] 2000	79	E	PPVT (3)	−.01 (−.23, .21)[§]
Shriberg[4] 2000	67	R	PPVT (3)	.23 (−.01, .45)
Combined	583	E	PPVT (3)	−.05 (−.23, .13)*

OME = otitis media with effusion; PPVT = Peabody Picture Vocabulary Test.
*Random effects combined $p = .564$; test of heterogeneity Q = 10.98, df = 3, $p = .012$.
[†]Direction of effect, expected (E) or reverse (R).
[‡]Pearson correlation coefficient, $p < .05$ if 95% CI does not contain zero.
[§]Adjusted correlation coefficient.

OME and speech or language outcomes. Conversely, the analyses of group studies show a statistically significant association in preschoolers for OME versus receptive and expressive language (.24 and .25 standard difference, respectively). Further, the analyses of correlation studies for hearing versus receptive and expressive language suggest a slight negative relationship (3 to 9% of variance).

Although effect sizes are small, most of the data were unadjusted for known confounders (maternal education, socioeconomic status [SES], and so on). Thus, our results

may overestimate the true impact of OME on outcomes. The negligible impact of OME on developmental outcomes suggests that differences are detectable only by large studies or by meta-analysis to increase statistical power.

Are the Results Valid and Generalizable?

Two meta-analyses[15,16] of OME versus receptive and expressive language reported results similar to most of the above analyses but are inconsistent with the results

Table 24-9 Group Data Meta-analysis of Vocabulary (PPVT) at Age 3 Years versus OME

Author Year	OM+ Group: N; Mean (SD)	OM– Group: N; Mean (SD)	p Value	Dir[†]	Test (age, yr)	Std Difference (95% CI)[‡]
Teele[47] 1984	80; 96.4(15.3)	52; 101.4(17.1)	.082	E	PPVT (3)	–.31 (–.67, .04)
Paradise[7] 2000	64; 98.4(14.8)	84; 104.0(16.9)	.037	E	PPVT (3)	–.35 (–.68, –.02)
Shriberg[4] 2000	8; 113.0(10.9)	51; 112.1(10.8)	.809	R	PPVT (3)	.09 (–.67, .85)
Paradise[8] 2001[§]	203; 92.0(13.0)	192; 92.0(15.0)	1.00	R	PPVT (3)	0 (–.20, .20)
Combined	355	379	.144	E	PPVT (3)	–.16 (–.37, .05)*

OM = otitis media; OME= otitis media with effusion; PPVT = Peabody Picture Vocabulary Test.
*Test of heterogeneity Q = 4.71, df = 3, p = .195.
[†]Direction of effect, expected (E) or reverse (R).
[‡]Standardized difference between groups, p < .05 if 95% CI does not contain zero.
[§]Groups differentiated by random assignment to tympanostomy tubes.

Table 24-10 Correlation Meta-analysis of Vocabulary (NDW) at Age 3 to 5 Years versus OME

Author Year	N	Dir[†]	Test (age, yr)	R (95% CI)[‡]
Roberts[45] 1991	26	E	NDW (5)	0 (–.39, .39)
Paradise[7] 2000	237	E	NDW (3)	–.04 (–.17, .09)
Roberts[12] 2000	79	E	NDW (3)	–.11 (–.32, .11)[§]
Combined	342	E	NDW (3–5)	–.05 (–.16, .05)*

OME = otitis media with effusion; NDW = number of different words (from a language sample).
*Random effects combined p = .330; test of heterogeneity Q = .35, df = 2, p = .837.
[†]Direction of effect, expected (E) or reverse (R).
[‡]Pearson correlation coefficient, p < .05 if 95% CI does not contain zero.
[§]Adjusted correlation coefficient.

Table 24-11 Correlation Meta-analysis of Syntax (MLU) at Age 3 to 5 Years versus OME

Author Year	N	Dir[†]	Test (age, yr)	R (95% CI)[‡]
Roberts[45] 1991	26	E	MLU (5)	–.22 (–.56, .18)
Paradise[7] 2000	237	E	MLU (3)	–.07 (–.20, .06)
Roberts[12] 2000	79	E	MLU (3)	–.03 (–.25, .19)[§]
Combined	342	E	MLU (3–5)	–.07 (–.18, .04)*

OME = otitis media with effusion; MLU = mean length of utterance (from a language sample).
*Random effects combined p = .192; test of heterogeneity Q = .66, df = 2, p = .718.
[†]Direction of effect, expected (E) or reverse (R).
[‡]Pearson correlation coefficient, p < .05 if 95% CI does not contain zero.
[§]Adjusted correlation coefficient.

of the OME group studies or hearing studies for receptive and expressive language. Neither of these meta-analyses included OME-related hearing loss as an independent predictor variable.

The Agency for Healthcare Research Quality (AHRQ)[16] examined the relationship of OME to children's receptive and expressive language as measured by standardized tests in six cohorts of children. No associations were found for expressive language, receptive language, or cognitive verbal intelligence, but heterogeneity and wide 95% CIs could not exclude that an effect was missed (low power). Although they did not

Table 24-12 Group Data Meta-analysis of Speech at Age 3 Years versus OME

Author Year	OM+ Group: N; Mean (SD)	OM– Group: N; Mean (SD)	p Value	Dir[†]	Test (age, yr)	Std Difference (95% CI)[‡]
Paradise[7] 2000	64; 84.6(7.8)	84; 86.5(6.6)	.111	E	PCC (3)	−.26 (−.59, .07)
Shriberg[4] 2000	8; 87.4(3.6)	59; 86.3(4.8)	.535	R	PCC (3)	.23 (−.52, .99)
Paradise[8] 2001[§]	205; 85.0(7.0)	193; 86.0(7.0)	.155	E	PCC (3)	−.14 (−.34, .06)
Combined	277	336	.065	E	PCC (3)	−.15 (−.32, .01)*

OM = otitis media; OME = otitis media with effusion; PCC = percent consonants correct.

*Test of heterogeneity Q = 1.50, df = 2, p = .472.

[†]Direction of effect, expected (E) or reverse (R).

[‡]Standardized difference between groups, $p < .05$ if 95% CI does not contain zero.

[§]Groups differentiated by random assignment to tympanostomy tubes.

find evidence that OME history in the first 3 years of life was related to receptive or expressive language in children age 3 years and older, they concluded they could neither support nor refute the possible effect of OME on children's language development.

Casby[15] reviewed 22 studies of the effects of OME on children's receptive and expressive language through the elementary school years and reported the magnitude of an effect of OME to be markedly low. Children with histories of early OME scored an average of .16 standard difference below their peers without OME histories (95% CI, −.23, −.10) in receptive language and −.23 standard difference lower in expressive language (95% CI, −.30, −.16). Although Casby[15] completed a separate analysis for receptive and expressive language, validity may be compromised because analyses used multiple outcomes from a single cohort, combined results from group and correlation studies, did not stratify by age groups, and included studies that looked at both specific (eg, vocabulary) and overall measures of language.

Validity of our results is supported by an a priori meta-analysis protocol, explicit criteria for study selection, and use of random effects methods for data pooling. All studies were prospective cohorts[4,7,12,41–48] or RCTs.[6,8,9] For each analysis, we pooled studies with similar data formats (correlational versus group statistics), similar speech or language outcomes, similar speech or language assessment age ranges, and a consistent predictor variable (OME or hearing loss). The studies were generally homogeneous, although there was heterogeneity in two of the seven analyses, including Shriberg and colleagues,[4] who studied the same cohort from Dallas, Texas, as Friel-Patti and Finitzo.[41] There did not appear to be differences in the populations of children, OME documentation method, or study design of the Shriberg[4] as compared with the other studies.

Documentation of OME varied among studies (see Table 24-1), but most used tympanometry, with or without otoscopy. The age of documentation also varied and included the first year of life,[42,48] the first 2 years,[4,9,28,46] the first 3 years,[7,8,12,43,45,47] and after age 2 years.[6,44] Despite the variations noted, all documentation was prospective and done on multiple occasions, which suggests adequate validity. Few studies obtained baseline or serial assessments of hearing status, thereby limiting the ability to relate hearing to outcomes.

Generalizability of our findings is limited by the study samples (see Table 24-1), but the diversity of children studied suggests reasonable external validity. Children were recruited from pediatric/primary care practices,[4,7,8,41,47] hospitals,[42,43,48] childcare centers,[12,45,46] community cohorts,[44] and otolaryngology clinics.[6,9] Because of the recruitment site, many of the studies included a select group of children[12,46] rather than a random or broad sample. Further, some included children who had specific characteristics, such as low birth weight,[42,43,48] OME histories and speech, language, behavior, or learning problems,[6] or OME histories and failed hearing screenings.[9]

Comparing the significant versus nonsignificant meta-analyses is useful. First, there appears to be little difference among studies in the subject characteristics or OME documentation methods. Two RCTs[6,9] contributed to the significant OME group analyses of receptive and expressive language, and one RCT[8] contributed to the nonsignificant analyses of vocabulary, syntax, and speech. Second, the results may suggest an association for hearing and language development since only two hearing analyses were done and both were significant. This would conceptually make sense because hearing loss, not OME, is hypothesized to affect children's language development. The hearing analyses, however, were done on infant language outcomes, whereas all other analyses were done on preschool speech and language assessments.

Interestingly, the analyses of group data for OME as compared with the correlation studies suggested an association between OME and receptive and expressive language. The group analyses compared children with more severe OME with those with less severe OME, but the correlation analyses considered the distribution of the whole cohort. These data suggest a threshold amount where having OME may place a child at greater risk for language differences.

Are the Results Clinically Important?

Otitis media with effusion and associated hearing loss that children experienced during early childhood explained none to a very small amount of the observed variation in children's language skills. We did not find significant association for specific aspects of language, including vocabulary or syntax or speech. As noted above, most of the data were not adjusted for known confounders (maternal education, SES, childcare environment) that have been shown to explain a considerably larger portion of children's language development. Therefore, our meta-analysis results may overestimate the true impact of OME on speech and language outcomes.

Results should be interpreted cautiously because of the limitations inherent in a meta-analysis based on primarily observational studies. We cannot infer causality from studies that examine associations between OME and language. Moreover, meta-analysis is a form of retrospective research and is prone to certain biases. For example, authors and editors may preferentially publish studies with positive results, causing the published literature to overestimate true effects. We do not consider publication bias a problem because the small number of researchers in this field, who communicate regularly, would make it unlikely that null effects were unpublished or overlooked. Similarly, the likelihood of missing a significant study because of language bias (eg, including only English-language articles) would be minimal.

The small effect sizes we found may be unimportant for most otherwise healthy children with OME, but the impact may be disproportionate on children with developmental delays, those from special populations (eg, Down syndrome, fragile X syndrome, cleft palate), or those with hearing loss independent of OM. For these "at-risk" populations, even minor auditory degradation from OME could be problematic. Unfortunately, these same children are often systematically excluded from prospective studies and RCTs because of ethical concerns. Further, the meta-analyses presented in this chapter only assessed the effects of OME on speech and language during the preschool years and OME-related

hearing loss and language during infancy; other age groupings may be more sensitive to the effects of OME and associated hearing loss.

These results leave many clinicians in a dilemma of what to with a child who experiences persistent OME. It may suggest that just ignoring the OME and associated hearing loss for a young child is a reasonable approach; however, this is not always the case. The relative risk, for example, for a particular child, of not screening for hearing and missing a moderate degree of hearing loss caused by OME must be weighed against the advantages of giving the child the optimal language and learning environment. The data reviewed above reflect outcomes for an "average" otherwise healthy child; individual host susceptibility must also be considered.

Children from special populations or with developmental delays, who are at risk of language and learning difficulties and experience hearing loss related to persistent OME, would benefit from preventive strategies. The strategies that follow are appropriate for all children but are particularly important for children who are at increased risk of language and learning problems and experience persistent OME in early childhood:

- *Monitor for hearing loss.* A child's hearing should be screened (1) after 3 months of bilateral OME,[55] (2) after four to six episodes of OM in a 6-month period, with follow-up every 3 months until the effusion has resolved, (3) if parents or teachers have concerns about their children's hearing or if there are speech and language delays or a disorder, or (4) if they are under age 5 years and at increased risk of OME (eg, children with Down syndrome, cleft palate). See the American Speech-Language-Hearing Association[56] for published guidelines for screening the middle ear and hearing status of preschool and school-age children.

- *Screen for language and other developmental delays.* A child's speech and language should be screened for delay if (1) persistent OME and hearing loss are present, or (2) when families or caregivers express concerns regarding a child's development. Speech and language skills can be screened as young as 6 months of age with the *Early Language Milestone Scale*[57] or a parent report form, such as *MacArthur Communication Development Inventories.*[58] A child who fails a communication screening should be referred to a speech-language pathologist, and a child who fails a developmental screening should be referred to a psychologist, developmental pediatrician, or special educator.

- *Encourage a responsive language learning environment.* Children who experience recurrent or persistent OME and associated hearing loss will benefit from a highly responsive language- and literacy-enriched environment using strategies similar to those recommended for language development. Practical strategies for care-

Table 24-13 Language Learning Strategies for Children with Persistent Middle Ear Effusion*

Get down to the child's eye level when talking.

Talk about familiar things in the child's environment (eg, pets, toys) and interests.

Talk with the child during mealtimes, baths, and throughout the day.

Play interactive games, such as pat-a-cake, with the child to encourage talking.

Ask simple questions and pause for the child to respond.

Respond to what the child is talking about immediately and with interest.

Add to what the child is saying by using more words.

*From Roberts JE and Zeisel SA.[59]

givers are listed in Tables 24-13 to 24-15.[59] Children showing language and other developmental difficulties should receive speech and language intervention.

FUTURE RESEARCH

There continues to be a need for study of the relationship of OME to children's later speech and language development. Meta-analyses were only done on the effects of OME in early childhood on speech and language during the preschool years and the effects of hearing loss on language during infancy. Meta-analyses were not performed in all age groupings of interest, such as hearing loss and receptive language during the preschool years, because of sparse data not suitable for statistical pooling. Thus, as additional studies examine the linkage of OME and associated hearing loss to speech and language development, a broader spectrum of meta-analyses will be possible.

Table 24-14 Listening Strategies for Children with Persistent Middle Ear Effusion*

Help children hear and understand your speech

Get within three feet of the child before speaking.

Get the child's attention before speaking.

Face the child and speak clearly with a normal tone and normal loudness.

Use visual cues, such as moving your hands and showing pictures, in addition to using speech.

Seat the child near adults and children who are speaking.

Speak clearly and repeat important words, but use natural speaking tones and pattern.

Check often to make sure the child understands what is being said.

Stand still when talking to the child to decrease distractions.

Praise the child for talking even if the speech is unclear.

Take the child lots of places (library, supermarket, the park) and talk about what you see.

Say the names of things the child sees or plays with and describe things that happen.

Talk with the child about what he did and will do, why things happen, and feelings.

Encourage the child to talk to other children.

Decrease background noise

Turn off unnecessary music and TV in the background.

Fix noisy appliances, such as heaters or air conditioners.

Limit play with noisy toys.

Encourage teachers to create quiet areas, such as dividers for small group play and reading.

Close windows and doors when it is noisy outside.

*From Roberts JE and Zeisel SA.[59]

Table 24-15 Promoting Early Literacy Learning for Children with Persistent Middle Ear Effusion*

Read often to the child, describing and explaining pictures and referring to the child's own experiences ("Spot is like your dog.").

Read slowly to the child, pausing at times to ask questions ("What will happen next?").

Give the child books and magazines to look at.

Read out loud, such things as traffic and store signs, labels on packages, and words on a menu.

Let the child draw and write using crayons, markers, and pencils.

Sing simple songs with repeated words and phrases.

Talk about sounds and names of letters.

Play sound, alphabet, and word games that focus on beginning and ending sounds of words.

Play word and listening games so the child will listen to familiar patterns and fill in words.

For older preschoolers, play rhyming games, such as hat, cat, and bat.

*From Roberts JE and Zeisel SA.[59]

Table 24-16 Pointers and Pitfalls

1. For infants and toddlers, meta-analysis shows small negative correlation between receptive language (−.17) and expressive language (−.30) at age 1 to 2 years and OM-associated hearing loss. The correlations explain 2.9% and 9% of variance in outcomes, respectively.

2. For preschoolers, meta-analysis shows small adverse effects of OM on receptive language (.24 standard difference) and expressive language (.25 standard difference) at age 2 to 5 years in OM+ children versus OM− controls. Conversely, there is no correlation between syntax, speech, vocabulary, or language (expressive or receptive) at age 3 to 5 years and OM history. There are no differences in vocabulary or speech production at age 3 years for OM+ children versus OM− controls.

3. The small effect sizes noted above may overestimate the impact of OM on developmental outcomes because most data were not adjusted for confounders (eg, maternal education, socioeconomic status).

4. The small effect sizes may be unimportant for most otherwise healthy children, but the impact may be disproportionate on children with developmental delays, from special populations (eg, Down syndrome, fragile X syndrome, cleft palate), or with hearing loss independent of OM.

5. The negligible to small impact of OM on developmental outcomes suggests that differences are detectable only by large studies or by meta-analysis to increase statistical power.

6. Children at risk of adverse language learning sequelae of OM should be monitored for hearing loss, screened for language delay, and be placed in a highly responsive language- and literacy-enriched environment using strategies similar to those recommended for normal language development.

7. Studies of OM and developmental sequelae should measure hearing loss as the predictor variable, adjust for factors that may mediate or moderate outcomes, use a prospective or randomized design, and address special populations of children at risk of OM and language learning difficulties.

OM = otitis media.

Future research efforts should measure hearing loss and other variables that may affect the OME developmental linkage. Most studies used OME, not hearing, as the independent variable, although hearing loss, rather than OME, is hypothesized to affect language. Factors must also be studied that may mediate (ie, explanatory intervening variable, such as hearing loss) or moderate (ie, interact with OME, such as a highly responsive childcare environment) developmental outcomes. Randomized controlled trials are optimal, but well-planned prospective cohorts can suffice when randomization is unethical. Last, the impact of persistent OME and associated hearing loss should be carefully studied in different populations, including special populations of at-risk children (eg, those with Down syndrome).

Meta-analysis provides a systematic review of the evidence but cannot substitute for assessing and treating each child on an individual basis. We found small effects of OM on speech and language development in most children, but existing evidence is not always combinable or generalizable (Table 24-16). Managing young children with histories of OME must consider a particular child's hearing status, language skills, and development.

ACKNOWLEDGMENT

Research supported in part by the National Institute of Health (NIDCD) 01 R01-CD03817-01 and Maternal and Child Health Program (5 R40 MC 00145) Health Resources and Services Administration, U.S. Department of Health and Human Services

REFERENCES

1. Paradise JL. Otitis media and child development: should we worry? Pediatr Infect Dis J 1998;17:1076–83.
2. Roberts JE, Wallace IF. Language and otitis media. In: Roberts JE, Wallace IF, Henderson F, editors. Otitis media in young children: medical, developmental, and educational considerations. Baltimore (MD): Paul H. Brookes; 1997.
3. Roberts J, Hunter L, Gravel J, et al. Otitis media and language learning: controversies and current research; Pediatrics [In review].
4. Shriberg LD, Friel-Patti S, Flipsen P Jr, Brown RL. Otitis media, fluctuant hearing loss, and speech-language outcomes: a preliminary structural equation model. J Speech Lang Hear Res 2000;43:100–20.
5. Roberts JE, Burchinal, MR, Zeisel, SA. Otitis media in early childhood in relation to children's school-age language and academic skills. Pediatrics 2002;110:696–706.
6. Maw R, Wilks J, Harvey I, et al. Early surgery compared with watchful waiting for glue ear and effect on language development in preschool children: a randomised trial. Lancet 1999;353:960–3.
7. Paradise JL, Dollaghan CA, Campbell TF, et al. Language, speech sound production, and cognition in three-year-old children in relation to otitis media in their first three years of life. Pediatrics 2000;105:1119–30.
8. Paradise JL, Feldman HM, Campbell TF, et al. Effect of early or delayed insertion of tympanostomy tubes for persistent otitis media on developmental outcomes at the age of three years. N Engl J Med 2001;344:1179–87.
9. Rovers MM, Straatman H, Ingels K, et al. The effect of ventilation tubes on language development in infants with otitis media with effusion: a randomized trial. Pediatrics 2000;106:e42.
10. Hagerman RJ, Fakkenstein AR. An association between recurrent otitis media in infancy and later hyperactivity. Clin Pediatr 1987;26:253–7.
11. Silva PA, Kirkland C, Simpson A, et al. Some developmental and behavioral problems associated with bilateral otitis media with effusion. J Learn Disabil 1982;15:417–21.
12. Roberts JE, Burchinal MR, Jackson SC, et al. Otitis media in childhood in relation to preschool language and school readiness skills among black children. Pediatrics 2000;106:725–35.
13. Vernon-Feagans L, Emanuel D, Blood I. The effects of otitis media and quality of daycare on children's language development. J Appl Dev Psychol 1997;18:395–409.
14. Rockette HE. Design considerations for clinical studies. In: Rosenfeld RM, Bluestone CD, editors. Evidence-based otitis media. Hamilton (ON): BC Decker Inc; 1999. p. 23–34.
15. Casby MW. Otitis media and language development: a meta-analysis. Am J Speech Lang Pathol 2001;10:65–80.
16. Takata GS, Chan LS, Shekelle P, et al. Diagnosis, natural history, and late effects of otitis media with effusion. Evidence Report/Technology Assessment: Number 55. AHRQ Publication Number 02-E026. Rockville (MD): Agency for Healthcare Research and Quality; June 2002.
17. Peters SA, Grievink EH, van Bon WH, et al. The contribution of risk factors to the effect of early otitis media with effusion on later language, reading, and spelling. Dev Med Child Neurol 1997;39:31–9.
18. Rach GH, Zielhuis GA, van Barrle PW, van den Broek P. The effect of treatment with ventilating tubes on language development in preschool children with otitis media with effusion. Clin Otolaryngol 1991;16:128–32.
19. Schilder AG, van Manen JG, Zielhuis GA, et al. Long-term effects of otitis media with effusion on language, reading and spelling. Clin Otolaryngol 1993;18:234–41.
20. Schilder AG, Hak E, Straatman H, et al. Long-term effects of ventilation tubes for persistent otitis media with effusion in children. Clin Otolaryngol 1997;22:423–9.
21. Wallace IF, Gravel JS, McCarton CM, Ruben RJ. Otitis media and language development at 1 year of age. J Speech Hear Disord 1988a;53:245–51.
22. Zielhuis GA, Rach GH, van den Broek P. Screening for otitis media with effusion in preschool children. Lancet 1989;1(8633):311–4.
23. Abraham SS, Wallace IF, Gravel JS. Early otitis media and phonological development at age 2 years. Laryngoscope 1996;106:727–32.
24. Feldman HM, Dollaghan CA, Campbell TF, et al. Parent-reported language and communication skills at one and two years of age in relation to otitis media in the first two years of life. Pediatrics 1999;104:e52.
25. Creps CL. Infant daycare and otitis media: multiple influences on children's later development. J Appl Dev Psychol 2000;21:357–78.
26. Feagans L, Sanyal M, Henderson F, et al. Relationship of middle ear disease in early childhood to later narrative and attention skills. J Pediatr Psychol 1987;12:581–94.
27. Feagans LV, Kipp E, Blood I. The effects of otitis media on the attention skills of day-car-attending toddlers. Dev Psychol 1994;30:701–8.
28. Friel-Patti S, Finitzo-Hieber T, Conti G, Brown KC.

Language delay in infants associated with middle ear disease and mild, fluctuating hearing impairment. Pediatr Infect Dis 1982;1:104–9.

29. Harsten G, Nettelbladt U, Schalen L, et al. Language development in children with recurrent acute otitis media during the first three years of life. Follow-up study from birth to seven years of age. J Laryngol Otol 1993;107:407–12.

30. Lous J. Linguistic and cognitive sequelae to secretory otitis media in children. Scand Audiol Suppl 1986;26: 71–5.

31. Roberts JE, Burchinal MR, Koch MA, et al. Otitis media in early childhood and its relationship to later phonological development. J Speech Hear Disord 1988;53:424–32.

32. Wright PF, Sell SH, McConnell KB, et al. Impact of recurrent otitis media on middle ear function, hearing, and language. J Pediatr 1988;113:581–7.

33. Roberts JE, Burchinal MR, Medley LP, et al. Otitis media, hearing sensitivity, and maternal responsiveness in relation to language during infancy. J Pediatr 1995;126:481–9.

34. Grievink EH, Peters SA, van Bon WH, Schilder AG. The effects of early bilateral otitis media with effusion on language ability: a prospective cohort study. J Speech Hear Res 1993;36:1004–12.

35. Lous J, Fiellau-Nikolajsen M, Jeppesen AL. Secretory otitis media and language development: a six-year follow-up study with case-control. Int J Pediatr Otorhinolaryngol 1988;15:185–203.

36. McCormick DP, Baldwin CD, Klecan-Aker JS, et al. Association of early bilateral middle ear effusion with language at age 5 years. Ambul Pediatr 2001;1:87–90.

37. Teele DW, Klein JO, Chase C, et al. The Greater Boston Otitis Media Study Group. Otitis media in infancy and intellectual ability, school achievement, speech, and language at age 7 years. J Infect Dis 1990;162:685–94.

38. Vernon-Feagans L, Manlove EE, Volling BL. Otitis media and the social behavior of day care-attending children. Child Dev 1996;67:1528–39.

39. Wallace IF, Gravel JS, Schwartz RG, Ruben RJ. Otitis media, communication style of primary caregivers, and language skills of 2 year olds: a preliminary report. J Dev Behav Pediatr 1996;17:27–35.

40. Dunn LM, Dunn LM. Peabody Picture Vocabulary Test—Revised. Circle Pines (MN): American Guidance Service; 1981.

41. Friel-Patti S, Finitzo T. Language learning in a prospective study of otitis media with effusion in the first two years of life. J Speech Hear Res 1990;33:188–94.

42. Gravel JS, Wallace IF. Listening and language at 4 years of age: effects of early otitis media. J Speech Hear Res 1992;35:588–95.

43. Pearce PS, Saunders MA, Creighton DE, Sauve RS. Hearing and verbal-cognitive abilities in high-risk preterm infants prone to otitis media with effusion. J Dev Behav Pediatr 1988;9:346–51.

44. Rach GH, Zielhuis GA, van den Broek P. The influence of chronic persistent otitis media with effusion on language development of 2- to 4-year-olds. Int J Pediatr Otorhinolaryngol 1988;15:253–61.

45. Roberts JE, Burchinal MR, Davis BP, et al. Otitis media in early childhood and later language. J Speech Hear Res 1991;34:1158–68.

46. Roberts JE, Burchinal MR, Zeisel SA, et al. Otitis media, the caregiving environment, and language and cognitive outcomes at 2 years. Pediatrics 1998;102:346–54.

47. Teele DW, Klein JO, Rosner BA, The Greater Boston Otitis Media Study Group. Otitis media with effusion during the first three years of life and development of speech and language. Pediatrics 1984;74:282–7.

48. Wallace IF, Gravel JS, McCarton CM, et al. Otitis media, auditory sensitivity, and language outcomes at one year. Laryngoscope 1988b;98:64–70.

49. DerSimonian R, Laird N. Meta-analysis in clinical trials. Control Clin Trials 1986;17:177–88.

50. Borenstein M, Rothstein H. Comprehensive Meta-Analysis: a computer program for research synthesis (v. 1.0.25). Englewood (NJ): Biostat Inc; 2000.

51. Sutton AJ, Abrams KR, Jones DR. An illustrated guide to the methods of meta-analysis. J Eval Clin Pract 2001;7:135–48.

52. Zimmerman, IL, Steiner VG, Pond, RE. Preschool Language Scale-3. San Antonio (TX): Psychological Corporation; 1992.

53. Hedrick DL, Prather EM, Tobin AR. Sequenced Inventory of Communication Development. Seattle (WA): University of Washington Press; 1984.

54. Reynell J, Huntley M. Reynell development language scales manual. 2nd ed. Windsor (UK): NFER-NELSON; 1985.

55. Stool SE, Berg AO, Berman S, et al. Otitis media with effusion in young children. Clinical practice guideline, Number 12. AHCPR Publication No. 94-0622. Rockville (MD): Agency for Health Care Policy and Research, Public Health Service, US Department of Health and Human Services; July 1994.

56. American Speech-Language-Hearing Association. Guidelines for audiologic screening. Rockville (MD): American Speech-Language-Hearing Association; 1997.

57. Coplan J. The early language milestone scale. 2nd ed. Austin (TX): Pro-Ed; 1993.

58. Fenson L, Dale P, Reznick S, et al. MacArthur communication development inventories. San Diego (CA): Singular Publishing Group, Inc; 1993.

59. Roberts JE, Zeisel SA. Ear infections and language development. Rockville (MD): American Speech-Language-Hearing Association and the National Center for Early Development and Learning; 2000.

CHAPTER 25

Quality of Life and Child Behavior

Mark P. Haggard, PhD, Sarah C. Smith, PhD, and Elaine E. Nicholls, PhD

No one ever keeps a secret so well as a child.
Victor Hugo

OBJECTIVES

On completing this chapter, the reader will be able to
1. Understand the main issues in measuring patient-centered health outcomes, particularly quality of life, in the light of the difficulty in obtaining systematic verbal responses from young children.
2. Integrate this understanding within general scientific concepts, such as anchored measurement, measurement error, and economy in explanation, so as to pursue good standards of method and measurement in clinical research.
3. Critically appraise future literature in terms of the expected and obtained magnitudes of outcomes in children with otitis media (OM) histories, both from the disease and from treatments.
4. Deploy a critical understanding of quality of life in decisions on treatment policies and individual cases, and in counseling families.
5. Judge the appropriateness of existing and future instruments purporting to measure "broad" outcomes, both in research and the routine monitoring of health care.
6. Collaborate effectively with researchers specializing in measurement issues.

In the absence of large quantities of good evidence on its topic, this chapter concentrates on principles that would help make evidence better. Our goal is to clarify concepts and questions and to encourage rigor, rather than follow the formulaic steps of systematic review. Until recently, there has been little systematic research on quality of life (QoL) in children and, in particular, for OM, so meta-analyses of the effects of disease or treatment on QoL are not yet profitable to attempt.

We begin with a long general section on measurement issues, with examples in OM. Appraising a QoL instrument requires an understanding of the main methods and criteria by which various types of "broad" outcome measures, including QoL scales, are developed,

validated, and evaluated. After illustrating the importance of a theoretic framework, we then review, in the final two sections, the existing literature on OM measures and applications. Our separation cannot be complete, as it is not complete in the literature; therefore, studies of the QoL domain in children with OM are reviewed allowing for the interplay of issues of content and of method.

Chapters 22 through 24 address the impact of OM on *performance* measures of hearing and language. The performance aspects of health status are sometimes called "functional status," but that term is ambiguous as to whether the measure itself is reported or performance based. A disability in performance may be presumed to have some relation to QoL; however, objectively, the two may not be closely related because individuals and families place differing values on the fruits of good or normal performance. Nevertheless, false decoupling of the mental world from the physical and social worlds of activity should be avoided. For this reason, questions probing QoL should be concrete and maximally oriented to cover the individual's interplay with the physical and social environments.

DEFINITIONS

The term "quality of life" is used in two slightly differing senses. The first, loose sense, covers almost any measure of outcome that stands in contrast to the specific symptoms and pathology that have traditionally attracted most medical interest in seeking to quantify impact. For brevity, we call these "broad" outcomes here. The second, more precise sense, concerns measuring *directly* the abstract or aggregate concept of quality of life, on the assumption that the individual can access a quantitative concept (construct) of it. These different usages imply only a slight disagreement over purpose. We here embrace the first usage but distinguish and include the second within it.

In the context of health care, the term "health-related quality of life" (HRQoL) is often used to *restrict* the definition of QoL to those aspects directly affected by a physical health condition, but there are practical difficulties in this restriction. The term HRQoL is often used interchangeably with "health status," although its scope is meant to be broader. The available conceptual work[1] confirms QoL as the individual's subjective perception of a global, multidimensional entity. It is an aggregate, incorporating aspects of physical, functional, psychological, social, and economic well being that may be influenced by disease, injury, treatment or health policy.[1]

The definition sits well within the World Health Organization (WHO) definition of health as multidimensional: "A state of complete physical, mental and social well being and not merely the absence of disease or infirmity."[2,3] One response to this multidimensionality is to develop subscores on several more readily defined constituent dimensions and then aggregate them. Potentially, a score on any outcome measure for which people desire the value to be high and that, in principle, can be linked to disease or treatment may contribute potentially to HRQoL, but there is a potential gradient of relevance among subscores, which will be discussed later.

The WHO recently added a fourth component—autonomy—with both a rights and a performance aspect.[4] In children, the relevance of autonomy increases with developmental age. Hence, there are limits to the extent to which work on HRQoL in OM, a disease mostly of young children, can draw on the largely adult literature. In children, the notion of health as reserve or potential for the future also has particular importance, but this is also difficult to deploy in practice. It explains why sequelae studies in OM have attempted to quantify any *long-term* effects on the ear or developing nervous system, even though the disease mostly resolves in the medium term. A fuller review of the conceptual issues surrounding a QoL definition is available elsewhere.[5,6]

There is growing demand for value for money in both public- and insurance-funded health care systems; this, plus the reorientation of priorities as captured by the WHO definition, has led to the burgeoning introduction of (HR)QoL measures in research and in clinical audit (routine outcome monitoring). The relative paucity of work, to date, on QoL in OM may represent an opportunity to not repeat others' errors. One review[7] noted 62 different existing measures and 13 new ones introduced in 48 trials. Such anarchy is worth avoiding. Where the measures are at least similar in their underlying construct, meta-analysis (see Chapter 4, "Meta-analysis and Systematic Literature Review") can often achieve some accumulation of information using standardised effect sizes, but this is far from ideal.

The problem lies largely with the great need for and the relative ease of producing something fairly sensible in specific measures. The general solution is strategic research and developing critical mass that is publicly funded for partnerships of independent methodologists with health care purchasers, providers, and patients. The task would be to produce measures that meet a range of requirements, but would carry more authority than incidental products from investigators whose interest is primarily in the application because their development used large reference samples. In the context of sparse literature on QoL in OM, we illustrate some points below with unpublished data from the generally large samples in our own studies. However, because of the need for greater formality in endorsing quality in studies of treatment effectiveness, we do not report QoL effects from treatment.

METHODOLOGIC ISSUES IN PATIENT-BASED MEASURES

The reader already highly familiar with psychometrics or outcome measurement, or the general reader on first skim, may choose to skip this long section and go to Tables 25-2 and 25-3, where two checklists summarize appropriate characteristics in a QoL outcome instrument. These tables capture the spirit of the recent systemization by the Medical Outcomes Trust[8] of the criteria for good measures, in response to some recent proliferation. An introduction is needed, however, as to why measurement problems must be solved, and how this can best be done so that the criteria in these tables can be meaningfully applied.

Generic and Specific Measures

Health status or outcomes can be reported generically, or in the specific context of the effects on an individual of a condition, such as OM, or its treatment. The two types of measure have different purposes. *Generic measures* are broad in scope and apply to a wide range of conditions, but, consequently, cannot be sensitive to specific effects of a particular disease. *Disease-specific measures* are focused on a narrower range of health outcomes in the particular condition; therefore, for a given reliability, this type is more sensitive to disease-related events, such as deterioration or treatment ("sensitivity" and "specificity" of a screening test do not apply here). Specific measures, however, do not enable any meaningful comparison of health states between diseases. Recently, a further "site-specific" category of measure has been postulated to allow for an instrument covering all the symptoms of an organ system (the ear) not necessarily associated with one disease (eg, OM).[9]

In QoL instruments that rely on aggregating constituent subscores, some scheme of weighting is at least implicit to balance up the contributions of the constituent domains: social communication (not always given adequate weighting in the past) versus mobility, pain, worry, discomfort, energy, and so on. It is necessary to make such weightings explicit, partly so that they can be debated or substituted to reflect differing perspectives.

Quality-of-life measures have disadvantages for some purposes. If one set of symptoms is readily coped with by personal adaptation, global questions will inevitably be insensitive to the direct effect from disease and, for example, reflect coping ability and other aspects of personal circumstances. Depending on the purpose of the enquiry, this may be seen as a good reason to choose, or to avoid, a QoL measure. In specific instruments the dilemma is less because the scope is narrower. They often include traditional questions, born of the need for diagnosis, that are known to be useful clinically, as well as new ones developed with questionnaires or interviews. Studies intending to be a base for recommending treatment policies should include both specific and generic measures.

Quality of life is by definition generic, but this is not the only type of generic construct. For example, child behavior problems also qualify; they are not linked to any specific disease but are potentially influenced by many diseases. The balance between specific and generic sits not only in the instrument but also in the respondent, who may spontaneously adopt a semispecific or highly specific disease-centered mindset, despite the investigator's intent. Clear instructions and illustrative examples at the top of the questionnaire can help reduce this source of error, or "tune" the degree of specificity. Deliberately introducing a context to focus the mindset may help reduce measurement error and improve statistical power. Even if the question items are about global QoL, however, the instrument can be tuned back toward being specific by references to a particular disease in the introductory rubric. This may lose calibration for the magnitude of scale units across disease conditions, compromising the main purpose of having a generic measure.

The context set for the respondent by the introductory instructions (generic or disease specific) should, therefore, be clearly reported in research publications because the magnitude of impact or treatment may be inflated through a contextual bias toward being specific. Mistuning can be nonintentional, and instructions usually seek to minimize this. A current acute pain may distort a respondent's awareness or valuation of various health states. More seriously, items from standard instruments are sometimes detached from their form or booklet, and, hence, the assumption that the standard instructions and context are in play will be false. This may also undermine absolute calibration of magnitudes, although usually retaining the ability to show differences. Where items are detached in this way, a good reason for doing so should be stated, as should caution over the interpretation of the mean scores and correlations.

The Role of Subjective Measurement

The ideal characterization of OM as a disease would include objective measures at frequent time points on many aspects of the clinical presentation, so as to span the known disease fluctuations and probe the mysteries of their temporal structure. Even for a few aspects of OM, however, frequent measurement is usually unaffordable. For broader aspects of impact, objective measures do not exist.

The challenge of measuring QoL— to be systematic about what is subjective— is particularly pertinent in OM because information must be time integrated. In a fluctuating and generally mild condition, reported information can bring the singular advantage (clinically and even in research) of integration over time. Audiometry and tympanometry are certainly useful; however, in OM, there is increasing recognition that an outcome measure of treatment impact and the effectiveness must reflect what results from hearing loss, rather than what causes it.

"Broad" outcome measures are mostly report based and inevitably subjective. Self-reports or proxy reports, however, can be elicited and combined in systematic and minimally bias-prone ways. This individual perspective or subjectivity is inherent to QoL but does not excuse poor measurement; rather, it obliges large samples and explicit decision as to the degree of acceptable subjectivity in relation to study aims. Errors and biases are reduced by psychometric development (item selection and optimum scoring) plus experimental and statistical control. The format and style of questions require further attention. Emphasizing concrete signs helps minimize differences of interpretation and valuation. Similarly, clearly defined modular and recent time periods (eg, the last 3 months) minimize biases exacerbated by faulty memory. Standard sources address how items are best presented to respondents.[10,11]

To boost objectivity, a generic QoL measure can be supplemented by other broad measures. Those may be specific, or partly objective, marker variables in the same domain, such as the frequency of physician consultations.[12] Data on uptake of health care are unambiguous if record-keeping is comprehensive and the database or sample is large; however, outside acute pain or physical system failure, the probability of consultation differs greatly across income levels, health beliefs, and lifestyles. The reasons for consultation can be complex, with many subjective determinants, so interpretation remains ambiguous. Data on health care uptake are usually gathered to estimate economic costs (see Chapter 21, "Economic Costs"), against which effectiveness (eg, in QoL terms) is to be compared when judging cost-effectiveness. Such data can also reflect effectiveness of prior treatment and can complement QoL data.

Logical circularity can be avoided here, provided that the patient's seeking of a solution to their problem, when used as an outcome measure, is not used also as the definition of the problem in the same analysis. As an illustration of the danger, clinically judged "need" for treatment has been used as a broad measure (eg, reduced re-insertions of ventilation tubes in OME following adenoidectomy). Although it is potentially sensitive to more complex realities and is relevant to practice, accepting a judgment of "need" may simply be replacing the patient's biases with the clinician's. A better method of studying timely treatment as a way to avoid further treatment, especially with a small sample, is to specify a criterion measure (eg, hearing levels) for intervention.

Diversity of Information—Direct and Indirect Measures

The use of multiple instruments, for example, when evaluating a treatment, is generally better than using one alone. There are trade-offs, however, among the burden or cost, the diversity of information required, and the reliability of each type. In clinical trials, one extreme contrary view used to predominate—that a multiplicity of measures is burdensome to patients, costly to acquire, and potentially confusing to the practitioners who would apply the results. Ultrasimplicity held sway for many years with some good cause. An obtained large divergence over the treatment effect size between two outcome measures could allow uncertainty to continue or prompt selective quoting of the more positive (or negative) result to bolster preconceptions.

An a priori publicly declared strategy for conduct, analysis, and interpretation of a clinical trial is important but does not preclude diversity and multiplicity in outcome measurement. The possibility of biased interpretation from the mishandling of multiple outcomes is not sufficient reason to suppress the desirably rich description of a rich clinical reality. Using multiple outcomes, however, does require an unbiased statistical procedure for aggregating several measures into one or two "bottom-line" summaries for drawing overall conclusions (see below).

The need to weight constituent subscores into an aggregate is avoided when using a direct rating, such as a global numerical estimate or a visual analogue scale (VAS), to obtain a direct judgment of the overall QoL

(Figure 25-1). Such "top-down" direct judgments should not be the sole source of data. Analogue scales are less popular than before in clinical research because single responses are unreliable and because direct quantitative judgments are bias prone. However, for light clinical audit or within an already burdensome protocol, a VAS seen as one type of question format does make efficient use of patient time, compared with multiple verbal items. A VAS can also, in a large sample, help determine the weighting of constituent domains.

We favor the "indirect" approach to reduce bias, with a large number of items using "Likert-type" format (Table 25-1). Each item addresses only one clearly defined manifestation of health status, for example, one sign or symptom, referring to an appropriate time period. When quantified and totaled raw or when combined in subtler ways, the set of items leads to an overall QoL score. Instruments with many items usually offer separate subscales for each of a few known dimensions. The essentially multidimensional definition of QoL implies using appropriate weightings of importance or valuation, to combine various subscale scores into an overall QoL score. Generalized weighting requires us first to equalize the weightings by correcting the (false) assumption that unspecified weightings are equal; this is done by standardizing (dividing each subscore by its standard deviation). The appropriate relative weighting can then be imposed if it is known.

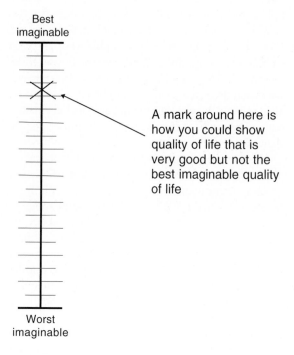

Figure 25-1 Visual analogue scale (VAS) for quality of life (see text for explanation).

Table 25-1 Example of a Likert-Type Question for Behavior*

Since your child first developed an ear or hearing problem, **how concerned have you been** about **behavior** that may be related to your child's ear problem?

Examples could be being fidgety, squirmy, overactive, uncooperative, isolated from other children, having difficulties at school, though there may be others.

(Please draw a circle round your answer.)

Extremely concerned (1)　　**Very concerned (2)**　　**Slightly concerned (3)**　　**Not at all concerned (4)**　　**Not applicable (5)**

---

*This item illustrates the response options for an item using verbal quantifiers, such as "slightly" and so on. The particular item illustrates a catch-all domain of behavior rather than one concrete aspect, for example, fidgetiness. This variant would favour test brevity, but at the likely expense of precision and freedom of bias (see text).

Direct judgments of overall QoL are not necessarily continuous and quantitative; bottom-up items for aggregation do not necessarily involve a small number of response options in the Likert fashion. The reasons why these tendencies are, nevertheless, seen are explained in the next few sections. The issue of whether to measure a construct directly (top-down, abstract) or indirectly (bottom-up, concrete) has both philosophic and practical aspects. The best solution will depend on the constraints within the application.

Multioption items may be of the Likert categoric or ordinal type, or they may have a more explicit quantitative structure, such as the familiar five- and seven-point scales. The latter are mostly used with direct measurements, where there will be little accumulation of multiple items. The particular issue of optimum number of response levels in an item is not straightforward. "Yes" or "no" dichotomies pose problems of choice of dichotomization point and are extremely wasteful;[13] however, they may be advised when the scaling problems are insoluble or the need for simplicity is overriding. Most respondents can transmit much more information, making responses of the VAS type or its numeric equivalent more efficient per minute of completion time.

Most people can reliably recall or identify only about seven or eight levels on a continuous dimension, even although they can discriminate many more with simultaneous presentation. Although seven-point scales are widespread and their use assumes little about the judgements, scoring can carry a false hidden assumption about the meaning of the numbers resulting (next section). Where the dimension being rated is familiar and is intrinsically one of degree (eg, rated "to a great extent" and so on), seven-point scales are probably an efficient compromise, but assumptions about the interval properties of the units still need to be checked. Where some more challenging property, such as probability or frequency ("nearly always," etc), has to be judged, the use of fewer categories may be preferable.

The optimum number of response options may depend on the intrinsic item content. Where fewer than seven are chosen, even numbers may be preferable to odd ones, so as to force the respondent out of the neutral middle category. One good reason for having between three and five response options relates to the size of reference sample necessary when using the correlation patterns within the data to quantify the appropriate score-value contribution from each of the item's response levels.

Item Format and Scaling

Item scales should have equal-interval properties with known spread and discriminative precision for the resulting score. A single-scaled number for the utility of any health state is required if across-disease comparisons are to be meaningful, and there are increasing pressures for such comparisons. This implies a formula to trade off units in the outcome measure used, against units in a valued quantity having accepted equal-interval properties, such as cash or time. Utility studies ideally compare treatments and their costs across varying conditions and health care domains, which may not be presently achievable for OM. Nevertheless, the assurance that one unit separating two values, such as 3.5 and 4.5 equals the unit between 7.5 and 8.5, enables more robust comparisons. Equal-interval scales also enable meaningful tests for interaction effects, which are important because a suggested indicator for a treatment is not evidence based, unless it interacts with treatment at a respectable p value.

One way to ensure equal-interval properties is to obtain parallel data on an objective equal-interval scale, which relates closely to the subjective one being developed. For example, responses to an item in the subjective dimension (eg, reported hearing difficulties) can be scaled to (further) optimize association (regression) with the objective one (eg, hearing levels). The assumption that this regression should be linear can be imposed or alternatives explored, but the effect of linearity on item scaling is less than might be supposed. Importantly, a rational basis has been introduced for saying, for example, precisely where an intermediate option, such as "somewhat," should fall on the continuum that is being constructed between "not at all" and "very much."

Where a pairing with an objective measure is not available, the place of the objective measure can be taken by a count of positive responses on other similar items, but the details of how this is done are beyond the present scope. Where a continuum is not available, internally constructable items can still be scaled by using a single dichotomous variable, such as living/dead, did/did not re-consult, and so on, as the criterion (dependent variable). Scaling has then to be done by logistic regression, and the underlying dimension is the log odds ratio.

Large reference sample sizes are required for item scaling, but realistically achievable samples are usually only a few hundred. This means that with numbers of response levels up to four or five per item, it is more feasible than with seven levels to obtain enough responses in each response-level category to then reliably estimate the appropriate scale values for each category in the regression. This is a limitation of seven-point scales; testing the assumption of equal-interval scoring may be difficult, and a judgment has to be formed on whether the distortion of the intervals or the loss of precision through making a false assumption is doing important harm to the measure.

Beyond assisting with linearity issues and equal-interval properties, scaling of item response levels assists precision of measurement and avoids errors caused by unequal spacing. Though it may not always seem so to busy clinical personnel, respondent time and burden are precious resources in clinical research, sometimes more precious than a few minutes of staff time scoring to make the best use of whatever sophistication of response can be elicited. Respondent burden requires the number of items and alternatives to be few. Investment in item scaling and weighting, when built on large sample reference data, is, therefore justified in instruments that are to be used widely. Item scaling can make a measure more efficient in terms of fewer items required, and offers developers of instruments a margin for attending to other desirable properties. Developing instruments without recognizing and exploiting these known principles fails to maximize the options for the application stage and is, therefore, an antistrategic underinvestment on the part of medical science.

Valuation of Resulting Scale Values

Using a total measure within a clinical or policy decision requires a criterion for important magnitude, not just equivalence of units. We do not act on trivial findings.

Much clinical research only goes as far as showing statistically reliable differences. The magnitude of a disease effect or treatment effect is sometimes called "clinical significance," though standards for usage of this concept and methods of defining a cutoff remain poorly defined. To avoid confusion with statistical reliability (p value), the word "significance" is best avoided altogether. The term "clinically important difference" on a particular measure better represents the magnitude of shift considered worth achieving via treatment.[14]

In theory, a generic instrument could define what magnitude of difference for the overall QoL or related construct is important at the outset with a single exercise; doing this for the full range of scale values obviously assumes that an equal-interval measurement exists. Paradoxically, with a more specific measure, which might be used with differing diseases of the same organ system, differing values of the clinically important difference may be considered. This is because a specific instrument could be limited to a particular organ system and might not attempt any unifying reduction to a common scale incorporating valuation, instead relying on fixed meaning for the measured values and other properties offered by the specific scale.

Utility Approach to Scaling

The motivation for considering QoL and related broad outcomes arises from clinical and health-economic pressures (see Chapter 21). This sets the context for defining what is "large" and what is "worthwhile." The predominant methodology—cost utility—for evaluating relative impact of health conditions and comparing treatments across different conditions has been imported from economics.[15] The utility approach has most point when applied to *generic* scales, going beyond clinical effectiveness to comparative utility, that is, although utility could also be scaled for specific health states.

Cost utility requires interval-level scaling of health states. The most used decision metric, the quality-adjusted life-year (QALY), also emphasizes the *duration* of those states; it is the result of summing multiple component durations, multiplied by the qualities of life experienced during those durations. The QoL is scaled as a utility between 0.00 (death) and 1.00 (perfect). Utilities are scaled by panels of impartial judges stating preferences between health states defined as fairly gross category bands on a small number of dimensions of QoL, for example, "too deaf to communicate without a hearing aid." In other types of study, judges trade hypothetic health states for such variables as *duration* of vacation, *quantity* of cash, or the *probability* of a well-defined undesirable event, such as death.

A comparative scaling or trade-off of direct numeric ratings presupposes that people can judge the health concept or QoL on a scale on which the units have defined meaning. Preferences between health states provide a more robust basis for scaling, as they do not assume this mental dimension. A particular distribution of errors in comparative judgment has then to be assumed to convert preferences into scale values. A problematic assumption underlying this approach lies in a judge only being able to directly experience one state at the time of judgment, his or her own. The judges only have access to the states being compared via relatively crude categoric verbal descriptions or stereotypes. Such states have personal and social, as well as pathophysiologic determinants, so different judges will likely have differing experiences, if any, of them. Therefore, the panel of scaling judges must be large.

Distributional Approach to Scaling

Historically, economists adopted Rational Numerate Man as a calculator of trade-offs in the manner of an entrepreneur or a currency speculator. In contrast, psychologists had to face the overwhelming fact of variability in biologic measures and demographic statistics. They adopted the Gaussian statistical distribution of errors for a large population as also applying to systematic, but obscurely determined, differences between individuals. This is sometimes called "the bell curve." When a distribution is near-Gaussian, its standard deviation (SD) can provide the unit of measurement.

The Gaussian (normal) distribution (Figure 25-2) is often obtained when the main knowable determinants of

the measure have been removed experimentally or statistically and the remaining influences are small or unknowable, hence apparently random. A less well-recognized prerequisite is that there be no constraint on the values, such as a floor or ceiling effect that would prevent symmetry. In clinical work, such a constraint is frequently met because a measure that grades well among patients may have a peak of "no-problem" responses near zero in the unaffected controls (floor effect). Conversely, it may fail to distinguish among the more severely affected patients if it grades well among controls (ceiling effect). When taking the SD across individuals' measure-values to use as the scaled unit magnitude, symmetry of the distribution is desirable to give similar meaning to a percentile shift at each end of the distribution.

Before transforming data to achieve a normal distribution, the possibility that a major source of variance could still be extracted should be considered. First, this may avoid or reduce the need for transformation and help distribute discriminatory power more equally throughout the range than would a fierce transformation. Second, the resulting model would have reduced error and greater power. In clinical trials, this is often and best done by fitting a term for the score at baseline into the treatment analysis using the analysis of covariance. This has a somewhat similar effect to using difference scores but poses fewer limitations both in options for analysis and in representation of the raw data. With a near-Gaussian shape achieved, the p value can be interpreted literally. When the results are marginal

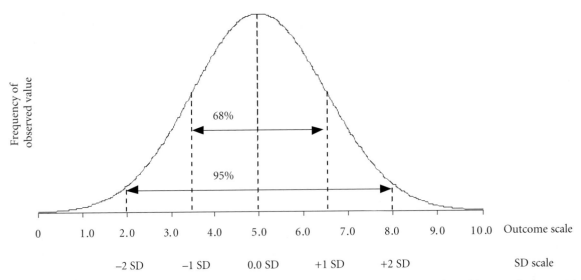

Figure 25-2 Gaussian (normal) distribution for a hypothetic outcome measure with a range of 10 arbitrary units (mean 5.0, standard deviation 1.5). Nearly all observations fall within ±3.0 standard deviation (SD) units, although this limit is never formally reached. Arrows indicate the percentages within the ranges ±1.0 SD and ±2.0 SD. There is no agreed international standard for clinical importance of cutoff values in SD units that is independent of the particular outcome measure. Describing shifts > 1.00 SD as large and those around 0.33 SD as small, however, is a rough guide. The text describes percentile competition for assigning verbal labels to define magnitudes for data without a Gaussian distribution.

(.10 > *p* > .01) the distribution shape is important for consistency of the logic of hypothesis testing.

The distributional approach to defining units is applicable to all types of continuously distributed data: generic/specific, direct/indirect, and so on. It makes no assumptions about the judges' ability to trade off disease severity or consequences against other types of value. Scaling psychological measures, such as QoL, via SDs does make four assumptions, usually not too heroic:

1. The measure is continuous.
2. The distribution of the raw measure can be transformed to near-Gaussian (see Figure 25-2).
3. The reference sample is large.
4. The measurement error is low enough to not make the SD for individual differences seem much wider than it is.

If the SD is materially inflated by measurement error (as with few items in a score), false enlargement of the unit will occur because the true variance across individuals is augmented by the error variance. This will make mean differences appear to comprise fewer SD units and be conservative as to standardized effect size. With very small studies, or where the measures have very few items, SDs and standardized effect sizes should, therefore, be compared only with caution.

Where the SDs in the effect size denominator are derived from *new* small data sets, rather than from a previous large reference sample, particular care is required. The essential element in "standardization" is the large reference sample. By necessity or association, available standardized measures have, often justly, come to be thought crude (for population robustness) or undersensitive to particular rare or subtle problems (for justifiability of the investment). Nevertheless, standardization is necessary to make medical science a cumulative, communicative, and beneficial enterprise.

Utility versus Distributional Scaling

One potential advantage of both utility and distributional approaches to scaling is that a single-scale definition makes easier the desirable multiway communication of magnitudes among clinicians, policy makers, managers, and patients. These groups would otherwise differ in their understanding of scale values and hence would need to learn new systems of anchors. However, with either definition of unit, magnitudes can be widely appreciated and compared, on a common scale after its simple explanation, irrespective of individual stakeholders' knowledge of the specific symptom scores or pathophysiologic measures used in diabetes, cancer, OM, and so on.

Improved communication from the generality of a common scale does not presuppose a detailed understanding of exactly how the scale is composed or distributed. The two types of scale give compatible but not identical information.[16] Where between-disease comparisons are not required, the distributional approach has slight advantages. No extra scaling exercise is required to define the scale units for a new related measure. Transformation may be required but involves only algebra and arithmetic. Obtaining utilities by the preference or trading approach may require a new scaling exercise for each new measure, at least by plotting the relationship of the new measure against an accepted measure. Determining new utility values for newly defined health states is a major effort.

The fundamental idea behind the distribution approach does not even require a Gaussian or other symmetric distribution. Via the ranking of states within any distribution, we can understand the force of and provide benchmark values for a "large" or "small" effect. Any variable that can be ordered (whether based on signs, symptoms, abilities, or global health status measurements), can be scaled in terms of a shift along a distribution from a reference point in a reference sample; this is usually a "normal," "control," or "unselected" population. The reference point is usually the median (ie, the value exceeded by 50% of the population). The shift may occur to any other point, for example, to the value that is exceeded by only 40%, or 30%, or 1% of the population. For a measure defined in the direction where high percentiles are "bad" (ie, exceeded only by few), a desired therapeutic shift will obviously take a negative sign, that is, back toward or to below the reference group's median.

In the Gaussian distribution, the median and mean coincide and the percentile shift corresponding to a shift of one population SD from the mean is +34 percentile points (to the 16th or 84th percentile). In competitive Western societies, everyone understands the idea of being able to overtake 34% of the competition. In health care issues, this concept of "overtaking the competition" is unacceptable, but it can be acceptably reworded as "achieving better outcomes than cases that would have an equivalent, or not knowably differing, average prognosis if left untreated." This rewording gives some basis for comparing results between measures with different types of distribution or quantifying as percentile shift within a style distribution. If percentile shifts or differences are to be quoted, the reference baseline percentile (eg, 50th percentile) must be specified. These absolute percentiles and shifts are more informative than counts of cases above/below some arbitrary cutoff.

The distribution approach meets difficulties when dealing with rare cases or those having extreme scores from severe symptoms and signs. The prevalence of the index state in the normal controls may be so close to zero that it is impossible to estimate. With several insufficiently sensitive items in succession, "zero" responses may become habitual, even if some nonzero responses should be made. The between-group difference can then appear very large, or only the clinical group may have a near-symmetric distribution. Transforming the reference group distribution into a near-Gaussian one may then be impossible; worse, the percentile rankings may become indeterminate.

Defining a state relative to states of other people is not ethically appropriate for serious and life-threatening illness. For this reason, reference distributions for health states have been alien to the Hippocratic tradition. This important restriction acknowledged, a general resistance to the comparative (distributional) view of clinical severity would be illogical because health care embraces much more than serious life-threatening illness. Indeed, the traditional idea of subclinical severity already contains an implicit reference to a distribution and control population data, whether or not these exist or are used formally.

Clinical versus Statistical Significance

Whatever the particular outcome measure used, statistical reliability (p value) should only be a first step to the goal of considering magnitude. Treatment is only justifiable if the magnitude of effect is large enough to be worthwhile in relation to cost and risks. Generally, existence of some difference or correlation is all that small-sample studies can establish. The next step is the justified taking of a larger sample to address magnitude. More precisely, a large sample enables a sufficiently narrow confidence interval on the magnitude estimate to usefully compare magnitudes among different treatments or studies. Sample size is discussed further below.

Differences in magnitude caused by treatment need to be compared with a benchmark for what is worthwhile. For a generic utility scale, it may sometimes be possible to provide a simple overall value for the clinically important difference.[14] However, for the distributional approach, the valuation that people would place on an effect of a certain magnitude and on finding it is a separate and further step. The economic utility approach builds this in from the start. The distributional approach already addresses value to some extent because of the implicit competitive reference, although it does so in a less comprehensive way.

Step 0 should importantly establish that the dimensions to be measured are at least, generally speaking, the relevant and valued ones and not merely those that happen to be feasible to measure. The effort in scaling of magnitude and valuation will then be productive.

Validity—Can It Be Easily Achieved and Measured?

The main types of validity include "face" or content validity, construct validity, validity by comparison of

known groups, and concurrent validity plus responsiveness. Concurrent may be further subdivided into convergent (ie, mutual), when there is not an obvious basis for assuming that one measure is more basic, reliable, or accepted than the other and is criterion related where such a basis does exist. This range is at first confusing to the nonpsychometrician. It must also be acknowledged that usage of some terms, particularly "discriminant" and "divergent," has not been unique and consistent. The range and terminologic confusion signals that the issue of validity cannot be as simple as it is sometimes portrayed in glib quotation of a validity index or when questioning the validity information on a particular measure.

An instrument offering some validity information is more likely to have been systematically developed for a defined purpose, and possibly, to be more valid than one that does not, but little more than this may be reasonably inferred by the reader. Articles on applications give, at best, sketchy validity information in the justification of instrument choice, for example, one or two differences between groups, shown as being in their expected directions, and the fault is often at the source. From the limited-quality and limited-quantity evidence given in primary description of the instrument, it may not be possible to place instruments on a generalizable ranking as to degree of validity, so claims and criticisms about validity are often questionable.

Components of Psychometric Validity

Face or *content validity* is a fairly obvious prerequisite. In health care, it is usually guaranteed by prior clinical insight and interviews plus piloting with clinicians and patients. It is not usually formally quantified but is of some importance, not least to the cooperation of the respondent.

Concurrent validity is the easiest to quantify: a high correlation value with an accepted measure (criterion) of the same construct (concept or dimension) that the new instrument attempts to measure. But this makes progress appear, if not circular, at least spiral; if there is a suitable criterion measure, why develop a new one? The scope of this type of validity is largely limited to the instrument development stage. This includes the particular task of generating a short form where an accepted long form exists. More generally, it is good to start with a very large pool of items, some of which have accrued general item validity and reliability in previous work, and then select the very few "best" for the purpose in hand. Here, what is "best" is most easily demonstrated on the basis of item consistency.

Internal (item) consistency may be shown using average item-total correlation, factor loading, principal component loading, or Cronbach's alpha. An item (question) is discarded if doing so increases consistency. Internal consistency is often portrayed as a form of reliability; however, reliability implies stability and precision, whereas a set of similar items could be perfectly internally consistent yet neither stable nor precise for any desired construct. In practice, inter-item correlations reflect both validity and reliability, so selecting items on the basis of internal consistency brings reliability and validity. The strongest items with a secure place determine what the weaker items have to be consistent with, but apart from this, combinations are rarely considered. The extent and the basis of reduction in number of items are what confer validity on the eventual scale.

Known-groups validity implies the ability to discriminate groups (or occasionally conditions ranged along certain reference dimensions) that are known to differ in terms of the construct to be measured. The groups are usually patients and controls (the difference giving a disease effect). A merely significant *p* value for some group difference is hardly world-shaking, and the occasional absence of such differences is perhaps more (provocatively) informative. With a clearly defined clinical sample, a significant *p* value for a patient-control difference on a specific measure can usually be purchased for the price of a modest sample size, and the effect may contain large comorbidity or consultation biases.

Validation for known groups ideally shows a *large* disease effect size, that is, only a small overlap remaining of the distributions for the two groups on the score(s) from the instrument. Usefulness can then be compared with other possible methods of separating the groups. An alternative is to set a more severe test of a known difference to be discriminated, smaller than a typical difference between patients and unaffected controls. For a generic measure, and setting aside devastating systemic disease, the task of showing differences is already harder, so these cautions do not apply. This issue of magnitude addressed, demonstrating a disease effect in known-groups validity is probably the most widely useful type of validation in health care. The most general direction in which we want to help patients change their health status is back toward the state unaffected by disease.

Construct validity is a part theoretic, part empiric idea. If a measure enters well into a set of relationships where the particular construct it measures should participate, then the measure is considered to be valid for that construct. Those relationships may simply be known, in which case this is concurrent validity removed once, avoiding the problem of a defining criterion measure. For example, a behavior-problems instrument may generate strong factors (and hence good subscores) for antisocial (aggressive) behavior and for anxiety and may show more of the first for boys as expected and more of the second for girls. It is then shown to have construct validity. This is so because we already know from several studies with several measures that these are the chief dimensions underlying differences in children's behavior patterns and the directions of the gender differences. The relationships may also be more genuinely theoretic than these examples. Usually, construct validity accrues gradually through use, as well as being demonstrated in deliberate efforts for the launch of a new instrument.

Responsiveness to treatment or other change (such as development or resolution) is of clear practical relevance to health care. The same caution, however, applies to the quoted information as for known-groups validity: a significant *p* value may say rather little. In addition, if items are selected on the basis of responsiveness, the reason may not be that they are intrinsically sensitive and quasiobjective items reflecting the intended construct. It may be because they are prone to expectancy bias or other components of placebo response to treatment. In the pre-/post-treatment paradigm, there are, therefore, two selection pressures on items. If it is wished to reflect placebo-related biases within the measure as being related to effectiveness, as well as to reflect efficacy, this type of validity criterion and the properties to which it leads become acceptable, but that decision should be explicit.

Predictive and divergent validity complete our battery of necessary concepts. Taking the word "prediction" literally, as referring to future events or attributes, rather than multiple correlation, predictive validity should have much to offer to QoL measurement in children because the developmental sequelae tend to lag behind the impairment. For practical reasons, such as complexity of analysis and the cost of longitudinal studies, time-series analysis has been little used in the OM field. Nevertheless, in development, validation over time may be especially relevant.

Divergent validity, in one usage, means showing that a measure does *not* reflect something you do not want it to. The sophistication of also showing some desirably *low* correlations is rare in health outcome measurement. Choosing items for their loadings on factors from a rotated factor analysis builds in some divergence; this is done by not using items that load highly on more than one factor. Divergent validity offers some insurance against overgeneral or abstract concepts and, hence, against finding effects or correlations caused by pervasive underlying response biases.

Assessing Instrument Validity

The different types of validity are a response to limited availability of validation paradigms. For example, developing an instrument on clinical and population samples enables discriminatory properties of the scale to be enhanced by high weighting of those items differing most between cases and controls. Thus, selecting and weighting for known-groups validity maximizes the ratio of between-group to within-group variance. This will not necessarily enhance discriminatory ability in portions of the range of scores away from the midpoint between the two group means. Such conflicts between possible goals of development (and there are others) illustrate the limitations of a single validity coefficient, quoted as an *output* of the development process and the difficulties quantifying the final validity absolutely.

The difficulties seen in maximizing types of validity and in setting up a satisfactory ways to quantify them, teach us that the *processes* tending to create validity should also be reported. For example, initial item pools should be large and should be quoted alongside the final number in the set selected. It is useful to know whether item selection has consistently maximized one or more types of validity in developing the instrument, via the way in which selection, scaling, and weighting of items was constrained.

Indices of the various types of validity are often quoted from previous work as if they were a fixed property of an instrument offered. This is succinct but superficial and can be misleading. A concurrent validity *r* value will be specific to the sample used. Additionally, a single known-groups or responsiveness *p* value is insufficient for choosing the best instrument for the purpose in hand. To indicate an amount of information that would help critical appraisal, the next four items illustrate how the OM7-27, referred to later in more detail, could be usefully reported as to validity, without quoting an entire article.

1. A construct validity framework was employed in the final reduction of 83 items to 27 for the OM7-27.
2. An explanatory model for OM impact interrelating the six summary dimensions of the original 13 was introduced, constrained a priori, but was refined and validated on repeated measures of a large data set (N = 432).
3. Chosen within this framework, were the best few items for each of the six variables as they enter into this explanatory model to maximize concurrent criterion validity.
4. Concurrent validity of the short-form against the full pool of 83 items was r > 0.93 on all of five occasions of repeated measurement.

Citing the appropriateness of the samples and the sample sizes in known-groups validity, the initial and final item numbers, and the final completion time taken would also be relevant and would help the choice of best instrument for an application. It is particularly necessary to state whether the quoted coefficients were achieved in an independent cross-test (preferable) or on the test development sample itself (only informative if the sample was very large).

Differing Respondent Perspectives

Clinicians' judgments can diverge from those of patients concerning an individual's health state, over the relative importance of particular symptom domains, or of pathology versus disability.[17]

Consider the relative importance of the following seven aspects of presentation in otitis media with effusion (OME): (1) hearing, (2) physical "illness" signs and symptoms, (3) social behavior, (4) concentration and communicative behavior, (5) speech and language, (6) balance, and (7) educational progress. On samples of parents and various professional groups (including general practitioners, community pediatricians, and otolaryngologists), their importance ordering differs substantially.[18] These differences are not arbitrary but relate to the types and severity of case seen, as well as to professional stakes and specific roles. The secondary-care physician concentrating on accurate diagnoses, including those of uncommon conditions, can become distanced from the full range of human impact of even common conditions.

Discrepancies of perspective can be large in the disabilities and in those complex conditions that tend also to receive multidisciplinary care or cross-referral, and this raises a practical problem. The link between a diagnostic label and presumed need for treatment is the chief currency of interprofessional communication. This fact tends to hide the discrepant stereotypes of impact that pose a threat to communication about broader patient needs. Discrepancies need to be taken into account in routine interprofessional activity; however, they also imply that if different groups of professionals appraise the item content of a measure, they could arrive at differing judgments on the face validity of that measure.

In developing and using a measure, consideration should be given to whether there exists sufficient divergence of perspective that separate weighting judgments should be sought from possibly conflicting parties (say, parents versus professionals). This is worthwhile to consider for three reasons:

1. Some divergence may be obtained between effect sizes for different measures, among less-than-overwhelming overall results for effectiveness of a treatment. Where this occurs, each result may need to be shown to hold true according to the parent's and the professional's perspectives. This can be done using the same raw score data for the dimensions but differing systems of weighting. From the literature, the most likely divergence to be expected is between the

perspective of medical clinicians (higher weighting to treatable pathology[17]) because of their professional understanding of it and that of rehabilitation professionals or parents (higher weighting on function, participation and QoL).

2. Treatments generally have more capacity to influence pathology and the proximal specific measures of disease than they have to work through to QoL, which many other factors and events can also influence. Without a formal evaluation framework, clinicians may, therefore, be more readily impressed as to treatment effectiveness than are patients or parents; this makes crucial the definition of a gradient of weighting mentioned earlier.

3. Under an important principle of multiattribute evaluation, once there are six or more dimensions, results become very robust between differing perspectives (ie, over different sets of weightings) because scores aggregate over the constituents, which generally have positive intercorrelations. Some specific health problems are inherently limited to fewer dimensions than six. In QoL, however, the main approach involves contribution from about six constituent scores, because multiplicity is essential to the multifactorial nature of QoL.

Thus, differing respondent perspectives are needed only where there is prior reason to believe major discrepancy or explicit conflict exists. Even where it does, there is reasonable chance that with six or more outcome measures to be aggregated, or with a generic measure such as QoL having six or more components across which perspective is defined by a weighting profile, the robustness of a particular result across the perspectives can be demonstrated.

In OM, there is a major problem in accessing the perspective of young children, although this would ideally be the main arbiter of item content and weightings in outcomes. There are differences in reports of children's health behavior and attitudes among child, parent, and teachers as respondents.[19,20] It is usually impractical to obtain judgments of QoL from young children, so parental proxy reports are used as a surrogate measure. In the domain of adult health measurement, it has been suggested that patient–proxy agreement is usually high, although exceptions occur in particular domains or cases.[21] For dimensions concerned with less observable, individual domains of satisfaction about health and emotional status, agreement is particularly low. Patients may only selectively reveal emotions and attitudes, or the proxy may overweight negative information.

The child health literature suggests that some older children have more knowledge of their recent functional status than do adults.[22] In addition, some types of information are nonobservable (eg, about pain, such as earaches in acute otitis media [AOM] or tinnitus in OME); these can be elicited from the older child via explicit report but require careful nonleading questioning. In very young children, inferences from observed behavior (for example, tugging of the ears) have to be used; although potentially less bias prone, such observations may still be bias prone in practice. There is a need for detailed studies on articulate older children still suffering from OM, but, mostly, there is no alternative to parents as proxies. This is true both of the items acquired on individual children and of the generalized weightings for the component dimension scores that are aggregated to give QoL.

What risks of bias arise from proxy parental report? Proxy reporting for adults with such concepts as QoL is problematic. However, there are legal and philosophic reasons to accord higher credibility to parental report on children, at least for large sample data, than to adult proxy report. Comprehensive evaluation of impact and treatment also increasingly includes knock-on effects on the "significant other" person. Proxy report is, therefore, more than an acceptable second-best; some reflection in the score for the patient of the impact on the respondent is acceptable in a pragmatic framework.

There was greater parenting stress and perceived demandingness of children in a recurrent AOM group[23] compared with controls; these differences were small, on the order of 0.25 SD of the control distribution. But in the absence of substantial literature on children themselves, such findings, even on small groups (N = 52) contribute to the overall picture of the impact of OM on families' QoL. The raw data items from the parent's judgment can be structured to minimize projecting parental impact onto the child but not to preclude it; the best that can be achieved is statistical adjustment by taking some objective measures on the child and other subjective measures on the parents themselves, using large samples.

Reliability and Size of Sample Required

Sample size has been mentioned informally at several points. The sample size relates inversely to the size of effect that it is feasible or desired to show. Statistical power is usually defined as a percentage: $100(1-\beta)$, where β is the probability of a type II error (false-negative conclusion). Power also depends on the intended significance level used, expressed as α, the probability of a type I error (false-positive), which the obtained p value is desired not to exceed. This is usually taken as .05, although .01 is wiser if scientific replicability, rather than competitive publication, is the aim. Conventional precalculated power levels often used include 80%, 90%, 95% or 99%, that is, a 1/5, 1/10, 1/20, or 1/100 chance of missing a true difference or association; 80% is most commonly adopted. Many small studies on examination turn out to have much lower power.

Low power undermines the potentially high information value of any null result and also makes any positive results subject to caution over replication. Selection or publication bias applied to a body of underpowered studies will underscore convention and miss important novelty. Studies need enough power to show that an observed effect size represents some genuine effect and is not due to chance alone. Usually, this means the sample size is large enough, but strictly speaking, large sample size is not an end in itself and is not required if measurement error is low. Within practical limits, questionnaires should have many items, objective measures should be repeated, and measurement errors reduced in other ways. In clinical research, however, the need to sample types of patients, and consider homogeneity versus potential subgroups, has placed the emphasis firmly on sample size for this extra reason.

Although "effect size" is a general concept, as used here, it describes the difference between two groups divided by the reference sample SD (also called *standardized* effect size). A further advantage of the distribution-based approach is that provided the measure is reliable enough for the sample SD not to be heavily contaminated with measurement error, sample size calculation becomes a very simple matter of looking up a table. For a small effect size of 0.33 SD, large sample sizes of about $N = 125$ per group are required to achieve 80% power at $p = .05$. If the plausible effect size is 0.33 SD or smaller, then special justification would be required for undertaking or publishing smaller studies; for example, they would have to be a pilot for something greater to follow, or to be worth airing for early replication by others because, if true, the preliminary positive findings would be especially important.

Sample size is particularly relevant to QoL in OM. We cannot possibly expect the disease or treatment effects to be large when dealing with a mild, fluctuating condition (OM) and a multiplicity of other determinants of such a broadly defined outcome measure. Notional group sizes of the order of 100 at least are going to be necessary. Conversely (though a rarer fault), where an effect size is justifiably expected to be large, it is wasteful to overrecruit; group sizes of 15 achieve conventional power for a 1.0 SD (large) effect.

An a priori *large* expected effect size can be used as the justification for undertaking only a *small* study; but to do this, there must be good scientific justification. There must also be a fairly precise estimate of the SD, preferably from a large preceding study or from piloting on similar patients to those in view, and with a reliable (generally long) instrument. The reason is to ensure that the SD from the reference sample is mostly summarizing reliable differences in individuals' health status or prognoses. This provides a second reason for taking large samples. From a small study, there may still be inaccuracy of any estimated statistical parameters, in either direction; that, for the SD, is no exception. Use of the SD as a unit of measurement assumes that it has been accurately estimated in the first place, that is, that a large sample has been available.

Clearly, the ideals outlined in this and other sections will be moderated in practice by limitations of time, patient numbers, and funding.

Summary of Criteria for Measures, Their Choice, and Reporting

Table 25-2 offers the reader a checklist for evaluating the development of outcome measures and Table 25-3 one for evaluating applications in OM studies, based on the principles outlined in this didactic section. Further details of psychometrics of outcomes in the context of health care are described elsewhere.[24]

UNDERSTANDING THE INTERRELATIONSHIP OF OUTCOME MEASURES IN OTITIS MEDIA

As described previously, a broad outcome measure could be validly achieved by aggregation, instead of by eliciting highly abstract judgments. Internal consistency is the accepted basis for selecting and totaling items into constituent dimension scores, but this can only work weakly, and subject to some cautions, when attempting to aggregate heterogeneous items, that is, ones giving low internal consistency. For an aggregate construct, such as general health, heterogeneity may be inevitable or even intended. At the item-to-score or score-to-aggregate level, attention to weightings for aggregation avoids the flawed assumption that weightings will automatically turn out to be equal.

Often, there are no data from which to place an a priori valuation on the constituent scores in an aggregate measure (for example, coming from a professional standard or previous data). Where a basis for such valuation is lacking, but, reduction to a single overall measure is necessary, consistency-based techniques provide a useful compromise. Principal components analysis, for example, summarizes intercorrelation by underlying dimensions that are linear combinations of the raw scores. Defining the principal component from the data available helps select and weight the most mutually consistent scores, which defines the aggregate weightings automatically without bias. Weightings based on principal component analysis can weight scores into an aggregate, such as QoL

Table 25-2 Investigator Checklist for Appraising and Choosing Otitis Media Outcome Measures

1   *Purposes*—does the defining publication include a clear statement of the specific purposes for which the instrument was developed? This should include an acknowledgement of trade-offs, rather than a nonspecific assertion of fitness for all purposes.

2.   *Process*—is there a clear and reasoned statement of the processes through which the instrument was developed, and were these careful and extensive?

3.   *Generalizability and reliability*—were the reference samples large enough to reliably optimize item selection and scoring? Are they relevant to your potential application, and has some cross-testing been reported on other samples or independent data other than the data on which development was based? Is information on reliability given (test-retest correlation, or error of measurement)?

4.   *Validity*—is there a clear statement of attempts to quantify validity of two or more of the recognised types? Is there acknowledgement of issues that may not yet have been fully addressed and a clear statement of the basis of comparison between instruments that would define "sufficient" validity?

5.   *Body of application data*—for an instrument that is at least reasonably good psychometrically, is there so much data published that not using it (eg, as an anchor or comparator) would seem perverse or wasteful?

6.   *Scaling*—is distribution information supplied and are scaling and transformation issues addressed?

7.   *Acceptability*—is the instrument (or the authorized subsection of it that you would use) long enough to give the required reliability, yet short enough to ensure high completion rates? Are the items personally and culturally acceptable and unambiguous to your patients or participants?

Table 25-3 Reader Checklist for Appraising, Choosing, and Applying Outcome Measures in Otitis Media Research

1.   Does the instrument measure the construct particularly relevant to the research question in the study?

2.   Has the choice of measures used been clearly justified in terms similar to those of Table 25-2, with the author going back to source?

3.   Has more than one outcome measure been used—of complementary types (eg, objective plus subjective, generic plus specific)? (Where the purpose is validation, complementarity need not apply.)

4.   Do the research design and features of the chosen measure, such as the report period, respect the singular features of otitis media? (These would include diversity of presentation, fluctuation and resolution, varying parental awareness, and health beliefs.)

5.   Have likely sources of bias been considered and attempts made to reduce them? Except where obviously constrained, has the issue of respondent perspective been addressed?

6.   Are averages and variability measures for the sample briefly compared with the reference values for those from other studies?

7.   Does the article offer (attempted) replication of known or obvious effects by way of supplementary validation as well as the results relevant to the current research question?

8.   Are issues of magnitude addressed, not just statistical reliability (p value), including mention of an a priori postulated or expected effect size, or a clinically important difference?

(Figure 25-3), where some rational basis is required for producing a single bottom-line number for each patient. This approach, however, remains a compromise because it lacks valuation or causal structure.

A single principal component from scores relevant to OM cannot do justice to the diverse developmental impacts of OM. It cannot reflect causal dependencies between different types of outcome (construct validity) nor a desired gradient of weighting between proximal outcomes, such as hearing level and physical health, and ultimate ones, such as QoL. A set of dimension subscores cannot be relied on to yield homogeneous treatment effects, that is, effects falling within a narrow range of effect sizes. Even with more than one principle component or component or factor extracted, this diversity will be blurred by aggregating. An example is the gradient between specific (large effect sizes expected) and generic (small effect sizes expected).

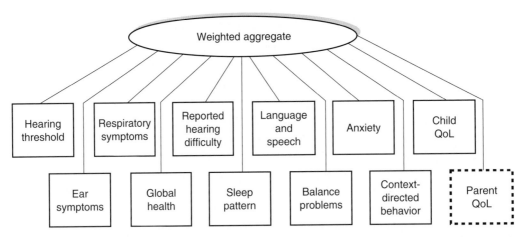

Figure 25-3 Simple aggregation model for a set of outcome measures to obtain a single "bottom-line" number, based on the full set of TARGET measures. Such a model can exist in two main versions: (1) with the weights of each measure determined by a priori valuation, or (2) weighted on the basis of at least modest internal consistency (a mixture of validity and reliability) within the data, by using principal component analysis (see text). Aggregation models are better than arbitrary or conventional lists of measured outcomes. General and explicit models are needed for an abstract construct like quality of life (QoL) to clarify constituent domains when selecting, based on high internal consistency, which items best reflect the domains. For generic QoL, a smaller number of broader domains would be used, rather than the range seen here, of which several are specific to ear, nose, and throat disease.

Thus, aggregation loses some of the reality in the data, and we need a better principle for integrating effects on multiple outcome measures. In the previous edition of this book, we had to draw a purely conceptual model for causation of developmental sequelae in OM. Fortunately, we can now provide a causal path model, arrived at by a partly interactive, but highly constrained, modeling strategy on a large set of relevant data. The causal cascade in the model bears some resemblance to the WHO cascade of distinctions: pathology (disease) → impairment → disability → handicap.[25] The data modeled can be of three types: (1) natural variation (severities and spectrum of symptoms, differing between individuals at one time); (2) naturally occurring longitudinal shifts in these; or (3) differences due to treatment. Ideally, very similar models would hold for all three types of data, and this is what we have found.

Figure 25-4 models the time-averaged postrandomization data from a clinical trial on surgical treatment in OME, for a subset of children on whom parental judgments of child QoL were also obtained. Children were aged 3.5 to 7 years at the start. The analysis is still blinded as to treatment (ie, randomization code unbroken, treatment terms with link to physical health and hearing loss not fitted), so no claims about treatment effects are made. The covariation modeled is mixed, incorporating two types of the above, (1) and (3).

The latent variable (factor) structures for behavior and physical health in Figure 25-4 were determined a priori, as were the main links, before structural equation modeling (SEM). All loading of observed markers on latent variables for these data from the Trial of

Alternative Regimens for Glue Ear Treatment (TARGET) are greater than 0.5. With SEM, the data were used to fine-tune, for example, to determine whether hearing thresholds were cross-linked to behavior and speech language directly and whether speech/language was linked to QoL. The desired *high p* value of .329 shows a *good* fit for the model. Three stronger coefficients could likely have been obtained for the QoL determinants had a more reliable measure been used than the VAS estimate. Nevertheless, the approximately equal weightings of 0.24, 0.21, and 0.19 are all highly significant, and their ratio is unlikely to differ greatly for other QoL measures. This particular finding justifies the inclusion of items on reported hearing difficulties, behavior, and sleep in a QoL measure for OME in the 3- to 9-year age group, and it justifies the weightings they would receive.

Structural equation modeling provides causal path models. Good-practice guidance on conventions of reporting SEM analyses exists,[26] but these are exhaustive and not covered here. In SEM, the variables are of two types: latent factors (ellipses), which summarize a small set of measured variables, and single measured variables (boxes representing scores that are the sole marker variable for the construct). Figure 25-4 is a particular conceptual model for understanding OM impact on QoL (and how this can be reduced by treatment); as such, overall, it is well supported by both the baseline and the postrandomization data. When a good summarization of the observed measures by the latent factors is taken into account, it fits the data extremely well.

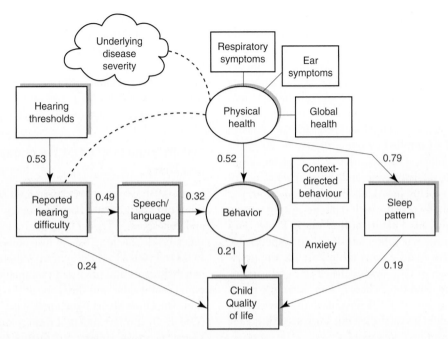

Figure 25-4 Path model obtained by structural equation modeling (SEM) for developmental outcome measures in otitis media with effusion (OME) applied to postrandomization TARGET data blinded as to treatment (goodness of fit = 32.86, df = 30, *p* = .329, *N*=157; adjusted goodness of fit index = 0.93). The model expresses the interrelationships between domains of outcome and the dominant aspects of how these aggregate into quality of life. Scores for observed measures acting only as markers for latent variables are in boxes with no 3-D effect. Straight-directed arrows represent modeled regression relationships, with residual correlation as dotted nondirected curves. The path coefficients are standardized regression weights; all paths included are highly statistically reliable after controlling for all other relationships in the model.

Models of process are not just an academic game. A basically well-fitting model offers a framework of tight statistical control for testing differences of interest, tighter than with the usual partialing to control for potential confounding variables one at a time. We do not always need to know absolutely *why* treatments work; however, it is worth showing that they do work in terms of known processes. For developmental outcomes, this would mean the treatment effects working along a rational set of paths as shown in Figure 25-4. We can, then, be more confident that the treatment process involves physiologic or psychological realities (therapeutic efficacy), and that outcomes measured are less likely to reflect biases or artefacts.

Process models help in two other ways. First, they provide the construct validity framework for selecting items and formulating the overall scoring for a particular short-form outcome instrument, the OM7-27, mentioned elsewhere in this chapter. Second, the model confirms, in the OM context, that QoL is predictable from a structured set of subscores in developmental, functional, or psychological domains that intervene between the specific markers of disease and QoL. The constituent approach to QoL requires the constituent domains to be defined rationally. With one that is fur-

ther supported by data, we do not need to rely on a purely intuitive or taxonomic system of five or six abstract aspects of QoL. The model structure defines more precisely what we mean by "intervening." Relying excessively on (specific) disease symptom or impairment scores (those near the top of the model) would undermine the claim that QoL is being measured, so the issue of a gradient of weighting remains.

Any construct of negligible importance would, of course, drop out of the model because it would not underlie any of the covariation modeled. Balance, insofar as this is reportable by parents, did, indeed, drop out of the model of the TARGET data. The model supplies path strength coefficients, which express the relative proportions of variance in a variable explained by its inward paths. This offers one basis for relative weighting of the three paths into the child QoL, the ultimate variable, out of which no paths flow (see legend for Figure 25-4). A decision still has to be made on what additional gradient of weighting for a priori valuation is imposed between the top and bottom of the cascade of variables (roughly specific to generic), to generate a single bottom-line number reflecting QoL. This argues for acquiring directly some independent a priori data on the importance ascribed to domains in the model.

The evidence-based model in Figure 25-4 merits a comment on attaining scientific generalization and explanation. Evidence-based health care emphasizes data, but data that are not made meaningful by theory can be barren or misinterpreted. The costs of gathering good data have to be justified by those data being potentially relevant to rational action, which, in turn, implies generalization and explanation. "Theory" is not fanciful speculation, as implied by one everyday usage of the term but is a logical framework of related propositions that permits interpretation and specifies relevance of data; theory helps in asking the right question and can occasionally reveal which data are simply wrong. The plausibly causal nature of the links in Figure 25-4 show that some scientific maturity of correspondence between theory and data is achievable for the detrimental impact of OM, despite the elusive and variable nature of the condition. There is some scientific parsimony (economy): of the 21 possible paths between the 7 main variables, 13 can be left out when accounting for the relations among the variables.

QoL Instruments for OM and General Health

Like all outcomes instruments, measures of QoL should be valid and reliable. For a discriminating measure in a relatively mild condition, such as OM, generically oriented items need to distinguish among symptoms or behaviors within the "normal" range, rather than among extremes. As QoL usually relies on parental proxy reports, the items will best refer to concrete behavior traits in actions observable by a parent.

Acute OM has greatest prevalence between ages 1 and 3 years and OME between 2 and 7 years. Within these ranges, children experience large natural developmental changes. Reference samples for developing an instrument should specify and include the full range of applicable ages. Furthermore, a change can only be interpreted as improvement after considering normal development, which can be rapid in some areas of health and behavior. This requires at least cross-sectional norms to document the age function, even if the longitudinal ideal cannot be met.

Some reviewers might regret the paucity of instrument development for QoL studies in OM, and the limited use of truly generic measures. Recent trends, however, have been encouraging. Two developments in pediatric otolaryngology—rhinoconjunctivitis in older children using self-report[27] and general infections in young children[28]—illustrate a parallel trend but are insufficiently concentrated on OM to merit detailed attention here. Several studies in OM have developed scales to quantify symptoms and broader impact in a way that approaches health-related QoL, specifically for children with middle ear problems. They go some way to meeting the above criteria. We also summarize below the properties of a highly generic child health status instrument, which is likely to prove insensitive to OM impact but can complement more specific measures in certain types of study.

OM-FSQ and OMD: OM Functional Status and Diary

For AOM, three instruments of clinical severity and functional otitis health status have been developed by Alsarraf and colleagues.[29] Their Otitis Media Clinical Severity Index (OM-CSI) is a 10-item instrument for recurrent AOM completed by the physician. Although it integrates parental report and physician examination in an interesting way, it is beyond the scope of the present discussion. The Otitis Media Functional Status Questionnaire (OM-FSQ) involves parental ratings and consists of a 14-item general health status evaluation based on a modification[20] of the Functional Status II-R.[30] The second part addresses health status based on presence of episodes of otitis, associated pain, and sleep loss. The third scale is an Otitis Media Diary (OMD) completed by the parent. The parent is asked to record the daily instances of the presence and severity of AOM symptoms, the time spent caring for the child, and medication taken by the child.

The OM-FSQ and OMD are highly internally consistent and have also been reported to demonstrate good test-retest reliability and to show concurrent validity with other functional health instruments, such as a parental play rating, and with clinician judgments of overall severity. As to particular purpose (and hence the appropriate form of validation), this is stated somewhat generally by the authors. Because of a declared emphasis on cost-effectiveness of treatments, the aim can be assumed to center on measuring change. Apparently large change scores are reported, with highly significant trend tests, but the samples are very small and no indication of variability is given.

In the physical health and symptoms domain of QoL, the work with the OM-FSQ and OMD[29] has suggested that there is a difference in scores between children with recurrent AOM and children with well-controlled OM, though the magnitude of this difference cannot be calibrated, as the samples are small and their SDs are not reported. In considering cross-sectional data on sensitivity to change, children with AOM scored higher than those with well-controlled OM, but the magnitude of difference was not quantified. The OM-CSI, OM-FSQ, and the OMD all showed reasonable sensitivity and specificity, suggesting reliable between-groups differences.

OM-6: Checklist-Based Six-Domain Questionnaire

Rosenfeld and colleagues[31] developed the OM-6, a specific symptom and QoL measure for children with OM. This six-item HRQoL instrument accesses one whole domain per item: physical suffering, hearing loss, speech impairment, emotional distress, activity limitations, and caregiver concerns. Each domain takes the form of a short checklist. A global rating of HR QoL is also made in OM-6.

The OM-6 uses a seven-point response scale rating of the extent (combining frequency and severity) to which any of the impacts of OM within the particular exemplified domain may have occurred in the report period. Given the nature of judgment involved, assuming equal intervals on the seven-point scales possibly does not decrease precision. The division into domains respects a natural factor structure according to existing knowledge of OM impact and makes highly efficient use of parental time. The instrument achieves some of the totaling for scoring within the parental judgment itself that a separation of items within domains would impose on the user. This makes it even more attractive for routine clinical use.

Reference clinical data have been published on 186 children, of whom 74% had chronic OM, 46% had recurrent OM, and 20% of the sample had both. With this sample, all items showed good test-retest reliability coefficients of > .70. Good construct validity is suggested by intercorrelation between the overall score (sum of the 6 domain scores ÷ 6) and the global rating of ear-related QoL made by visual analogue scale (r = −0.64; p < .001).

Of the six prompting categories, caregiver concern, physical suffering, and hearing loss contributed most highly to the overall score. This suggests that the others—speech impairment, emotional distress, and activity (at least when measured in this way)—may be less focal to the impact of OME. There are other possible reasons for their lower weightings: mismatch of the degree of severity, which the item format can reflect, or the typical severity range in the clinical sample, low frequency and low reliability of speech problems in the cases seen, and so on.

Construct validity of the OM-6 categories is supported by the primacy of hearing and physical health in Figure 25-4, and the British "Symptom Concern" study described earlier.[18] "Caregiver concern" as an overall construct could not be directly compared in this international corroboration as it was part of the basis of response, not a domain pinned on parents, rather than on the children. Across the remaining domains, however, the importance ordering across symptom area agreed well with those for OM-6. The agreement occurred even though in the Symptom Concern study, parents were being asked to generalize in a global way, rather than to rate the current health status of their child.

Magnitudes of treatment effects can be judged provisionally from the percentile scores, by assuming that the SDs are homogeneous. Benchmark categories for magnitudes of shift are offered with OM-6. The OM-6 was developed to be particularly sensitive to change. The change scores for 50 cases for whom both pre- and postintervention data were available (the minimum time between pre- and postintervention was 4 weeks) are, therefore, of particular interest. Change in the total of scores was moderately correlated with the change in the global rating scores (r = 0.52; p < .001). Despite its simplicity, this instrument demonstrates good reliability and sensitivity to change and shows potential for widespread use in the audit of otolaryngology practice.

In research where time for a lengthier coverage of OM is not available, or where the primary emphasis was on objective outcomes, OM-6 would offer a low-burden supplement. However, for a pragmatic trial on OM, the precision required for a chief outcome measure is not compatible with the brevity of OM-6. The small number of items and the reliance on a nonexhaustive list must limit precision; the "any of" grouping would be expected to be more bias prone than a separate listing of occurrence and severity of each of the listed aspects of OM would be.

A version of the OM-6 has been reported, expanded to 22 items with a more comprehensive closed-format symptom inventory, also registered as a seven-point scale.[32] These features probably make it more reliable and less bias prone than OM-6. The reliability is a possible contributor to the very large before-after differences reported. However, few details are given on the composition or properties of the resulting measure or the N-values that might permit back-calculation of SD effects. Accordingly, the supplemented instrument is not entered in Tables 25-4 and 25-5.

OM7-27: Seven-Domain, 27-Item Questionnaire

The present authors, with clinical colleagues in the U.K. Multicenter Otitis Media Study Group have investigated QoL-related outcomes in OM on a large (> 700) general population sample and on entrants to the TARGET randomized controlled trial (RCT). That trial was undertaken specifically to fill the gap in clinical trials in respect of broad outcome measures but on the slightly older children (3 to 7 years) forming the bulk of secondary-care referrals in the less interventionist British health care system. It was obliged first to develop new outcome measures,[33] as appropriate ones for the condition and age group were not available in the mid-1990s. A large unaffected general population

Table 25-4 Summary of Descriptive Characteristics of Specific Quality-of-Life (QoL) Measures for Otitis Media

	Rosenfeld et al[31,58]	Alsarraf et al[29]		UK Multicentre Otitis Media Study Group
Name of instrument	OM-6	Otitis Media Functional Status Questionnaire (OM-FSQ)	Otitis Media Diary (OMD)	OM7-27
Length	6 items + 1 global rating	17 items	3 items	27 items
Breadth (constructs included)	(1) Physical suffering (2) Hearing loss (3) Speech impairment (4) Emotional distress (5) Activity limitations (6) Caregiver concerns + global rating	(1) *General well being* (2) *Otitis specific health* —presence of episodes associated pain, sleep loss	(1) Presence of episodes (2) Associated pain (3) Loss of sleep	(1) Hearing difficulty (2) Symptoms of associated URT infection or airway problems (3) Sleep patterns (4) Behavior problems (5) ENT-related parent QoL (6) Global physical health (7) Speech/Language impairment
Respondent	Parent	Parent	Parent	Parent
Style of QoL measure	Hybrid direct and indirect	Indirect	Indirect	Indirect
Age range	6 mo–12 yr	1–3 yr	1–3 yr	3–9 yr
AOM/OME	OME or recurrent AOM	Recurrent AOM	Recurrent AOM	OME

AOM = acute otitis media; ENT = ear, nose, and throat; OME = otitis media with effusion; QoL = quality of life; URT = upper respiratory tract.

Table 25-5 Application of Criteria for Scale Evaluation to Otitis Media Quality-of-Life (QoL) Measures

	OM-6	Otitis Media Functional Status Questionnaire (OM-FSQ)	Otitis Media Diary (OMD)	OM7-27
Basis of item choice	Clinical a priori	Adaptation of existing broader instrument	Open-ended	Clinical a priori and factor analysis of a large pool of items on behaviors within the normal range
Internal consistency (Cronbach's alpha)	Not applicable to heterogeneous total	$\alpha = 0.89$	$\alpha = 0.96$	Not applicable to heterogeneous total
Reliability, test-retest	r = 0.71 to 0.86	—	≥ 0.73 over 6 months	≥ 0.73 over 3 months
Face validity	Items developed with wide range of contributions	—	—	Development informed by questionnaire studies with professionals and open-ended studies with parents
Construct or responsiveness validity	High responsiveness to change and change scores associated with clinical change	—	—	Items selected from fuller set within a specified model of outcome relationships
Known-groups validity	—	78–83% sensitivity and 89–98% specificity	78–100% sensitivity and 61–73% specificity	—
Concurrent validity	—	Correlated with PPSC (0.68)	Correlated with PPSC (0.27–.030)	Correlation with long-form > .93 on five occasions
Reference data	Clinical group only group	Clinical and control group	Clinical and control	Clinical group only in most domains

PPSC = Play performance scale for children.

to develop and scale the behavior and QoL measures was a further requirement.

The trial included an indirect (item-based) measure referring to the parent's own QoL and a direct (VAS) for the child's QoL (Figure 25-5). The preceding context items and the instructions for this QoL estimate on the child were based on the WHO definition of health. This encourages the parent to think about physical, social, and emotional aspects of the child's QoL, but the rubric ensures that they are thinking about this in relation to an ear condition that might affect QoL.

Figure 25-6 illustrates the disease effect obtained with this instrument. The original data were acquired on a continuous QoL scale (see Figure 25-1), with high values meaning good quality of life because this is how respondents mostly think. Partly because most problem scores

come the other way up, and partly to aid symmetry of the distributions from Figure 25-5, the transformation contains an inversion (reflection) plus an additive constant, prior to taking a natural logarithm. As a result, good QoL now takes low values and the distribution becomes nearly symmetric for both groups, reflected by the approximate equidistance of the medians (heavy black lines) from the edges both of boxes and whiskers. Formal tests for near-Gaussian distribution are available in packages for parametric statistics (*t*-test, *F*-test, and so on). The transformation enables these more powerful tests than the nonparametric type otherwise necessary.

There was no test-retest reliability estimate for the child QoL VAS scale to calculate the extent to which the individual family variance is contaminated by measurement error because intervals between test occasions for both the unaffected and trial samples were long; for the latter, by the second and third occasion of administering the VAS, two-thirds of children had been treated. It is, therefore, possible that the true effect of OM on child QoL is larger than that suggested at around 0.5 SD.

The population and trial samples also received a four-domain generic behavior instrument, to discriminate degree of problem within the normal range; these cover the domains of antisocial behavior, social confidence,

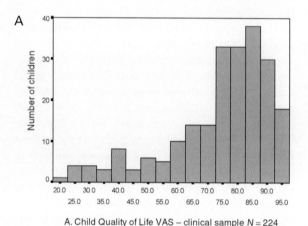

A. Child Quality of Life VAS – clinical sample *N* = 224

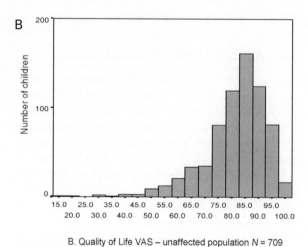

B. Quality of Life VAS – unaffected population *N* = 709

Figure 25-5 Raw distributions of child quality of life visual analogue scale (VAS) as a percentage of best imaginable for the Trial of Alternative Regimens for Glue Ear Treatment (TARGET) clinical sample *(A)* and unaffected control children *(B)*. Although the mode (peak) is similar (around 85%) a material proportion fall below 50% only in the clinical sample.

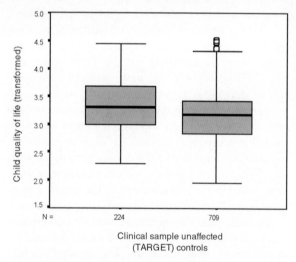

Clinical sample unaffected
(TARGET) controls

Figure 25-6 Box plot for child quality of life in clinical and control groups, measured using the direct visual analogue scale in Figure 25-1. The box plot is useful for reporting outcomes with Gaussian or irregular distributions, permitting generalized comparisons. The box represents the subrange from the 25th to the 75th percentile, heavy black lines the medians, and whiskers the full range excluding outliers (plotted as circles 1.5 box lengths or more from the box edge). Although statistically reliable for large numbers, the difference between distributions is modest (see text), a fact clearly communicated by the graphic alignments of all five features of the two distributions, as reflected in the box plot.

anxiety, and context-directed behavior. All have strong internal consistency and test-retest reliability, but the last two are the more strongly OM-related behavior scores with disease effect over 0.5 SD; that is, they demonstrate known-groups validity. Recurrent AOM and upper respiratory tract infection scores were also derived on the clinical sample but are not reported here in detail.

Standardized disease effect sizes for the domain scores contributing to QoL were the starting point for the broadly based OM7-27 questionnaire (27 items). This is a short form of the "superaggregate" (83 items) of all the "full" reported measures as used in the trial analysis. For construct validity, between three and five items were chosen for each domain that best substituted in the model for the scored full set (having between five and seven items) of which the items are members. The domains are hearing difficulty, respiratory infection, ear problems (AOM), sleep problems, behavior problems, speech/language problems, global physical health (only one item) and parent QoL. OM-7-27 is based entirely on bottom-up aggregation and selection of verbal Likert items, and includes five items from the 17 in the full parent QoL measure but *not* the VAS child QoL as described above.

Developing the OM7-27 also illustrates several other points from this chapter, precisely because it was a strategic development intended to implement many of the general principles of psychometrics in health outcome measurement. For example, the pattern of intercorrelations among measures as modeled in Figure 25-4 involves severity of disease impact among patients, rather than distinguishing patients from unaffected cases. This is an appropriate, more stringent than usual, way of showing known-groups validity. As to overall concurrent validity, OM7-27 produces correlations with its 83-item ancestor always > 0.93 over five post-treatment occasions in the trial. The dimension weighting problem was solved by fine-tuning optimally to predict the long form aggregate with its a priori weighting determined by the importance of all the dimensions as rated by otolaryngologists and public health doctors.

The obligation between instrument developers and users in stating and judging fitness for purpose requires dispassionate claims about the range of applicability. Reduction to a short form for clinical outcome monitoring was one original declared goal of OM7-27. The goal of clinical monitoring, however, cannot realistically be achieved with as many as 27 items, and so, for that purpose OM-6 will be preferable. The comprehensive development process does appear to have made OM7-27 relatively efficient and nonburdensome but only by the more exacting metric standards required for research instruments. Research and routine clinical goals are sufficiently different, especially in respect of respondent burden, that they cannot be met in a single instrument.

Neither OM7-27 nor OM-6 can be called a measure of QoL in the narrower sense of a direct abstract measure. Furthermore, although both have breadth via including some QoL items and variables known to predict QoL, their concentration of items makes them largely specific. The inclusion of some disease-proximal and intervening developmental variables may make them less bias prone than direct QoL judgments, and both are able to accumulate reliability across differing item contents, which cannot be done by a set of virtually identical abstract direct QoL questions.

The descriptive characteristics of the scales from these disease-specific measures by researchers in OM are summarized in Table 25-4. The declared purpose of each development was broadly similar, including outcome measures for clinical trials or routine outcome monitoring. But we have seen a profound conflict between the reliability requirement for research and the brevity requirement for routine practice.

The most basic criteria for derived outcome measures and the extent to which these are met by the scales discussed above are summarized in Table 25-5. In addition, stable factor structure, data on developmental trends, and demonstrated adequacy across the intended age range are desirable. Given the differing purposes and conditions (recurrent AOM, unspecified OM, OME) and the differing lengths of instrument, a direct evaluative comparison of these measures is unlikely to be useful. Choice is better dictated by demonstrated fitness for stated purpose and by general acceptability in context. There may be no single "best buy." The growing recognition of QoL issues in OM is at least fostering measures that address explicit standards for QoL measurement in children with OM.

Generic Child Health Status Instrument

The requirement for a generic health status instrument to compare outcomes across several different health conditions has been met by the Child Health Questionnaire (CHQ).[34] The CHQ as described here consists of 50 items (shorter forms exist) and is intended to fill the same role that the well-known SF-36 does for adults. The CHQ-50 is specifically designed for children aged 5 years and older and is reported (pencil and paper) by the child's parent or caregiver. Work has also been undertaken to develop self-reported versions for older children.

The CHQ yields scores for each of its 12 dimensions (general health perceptions [GH], physical functioning [PF], bodily pain/discomfort [BP], limitations in school work and activities with friends due to physical problems [RP], limitations in school work and activities with friends due to emotional/behavioral difficulties [REB], behavior [BE], mental health [MH], self esteem [SE], emotional impact on the parent [PE], time impact on the parent [PT], limitations on family activities [FA], and family cohesion [FC]). The choice of CHQ scales was made a priori, based on the dimensions most frequently reported in the literature and in current theories of health status. A two-factor model of health (physical/psychosocial) is supported giving some construct validity, each scale score contributing to one or other of these factors (aggregates); in addition, an overall summary score is defined.

Items in CHQ include positive and negative states, representing objective functioning and subjective feeling. The items are scored positively such that a higher score always indicates a better health state. On United States standardization data, all 12 scales showed reasonable internal consistency, though this was relatively low for the subscale PE. The CHQ potentially meets the need for a generic measure of health-related QoL. Exercises with panels of judges making preference judgments of health are likely to be undertaken to map CHQ into utilities. In pediatric cancer, a study has been conducted relating the CHQ to the Health Utilities Index (HUI) Mark 2 giving correlations between 0.38 and 0.64 for the various constituent scores.[16]

As with the preceding specific measures, a contrast is seen between more elaborate instruments appropriate for research and those in which ingenious compromises are made to achieve usefulness despite brevity. The multipurpose PedsQL scale[35] applies to ages 2 to 18 years, with self-report forms for older children. The 15-item core, with extra modules for specific domains, contributes to low burden of completion. Like much of the QoL work in children, PedsQL originated in cancer where differences can be gross but may not necessarily place emphasis on differences in communication. The 15-item core has satisfactory overall internal consistency, and information on construct validity is also given. We are unaware of parallel comparisons with CHQ on pairings of groups, where there is a priori reason to believe in modest overall QoL differences. However, for OM studies, PedsQL has the advantage over CHQ of a generally lower end to the age range covered, even if the claimed age range is optimistic or leads to sacrifice in precision.

QUALITY OF LIFE AND BEHAVIOR IN OTITIS MEDIA

Behavior Outcomes

Developmental sequelae studies in OM have mainly been in the domains of speech and language or cognitive performance, but behavior problems have also been included as a generic child-centered marker, which feeds into the QoL for family members (see Figure 25-4). Early studies used off-the-shelf behavior instruments without establishing their specific appropriateness for a mild condition or have used a piecemeal undocumented selection of items and usually rather small clinical samples, but some consensus emerges.

Many of the studies addressing the behavioral impact and sequelae of OME have been retrospective and and/or small scale.[23,36–38] Some studies demonstrate an effect of OME on behavior, but small samples (< 50 per group) restrict more detailed conclusions. Prospective studies of behavioral effects of OME are contradictory, which may be caused by low statistical power and genuine differences of age of sample or due to the particular construct being measured.

Results from a North Carolina cohort of low socioeconomic status (SES) children from a university-based day care center, followed up at 24, 36, and 48 months, suggest no association between duration of OME and attention.[39] At age 9 years, a significant association was found between OME and task orientation[40,41] and independence.[40] The association had disappeared by the time the children were aged 12 years,[42] which is credible in terms of developmental dilution with time. This cohort was relatively small ($N = 70$ at initial recruitment, and smaller at follow up visits because of drop-out) and, therefore, underpowered for all but gross effects intimately connected with a major path to developmental deficit.

One important issue raised by the multivariable cohort studies and the detailed aspects of behaviors studied in the North Carolina work is the need for a theoretic model to predict effects in the particular aspects of behavior to be examined. Rather detailed aspects of behavior are being examined in the latter and the question arises of whether there is good reason to expect effects restricted to the behaviors examined, *not* on some 20 or 30 equally detailed aspects of behavior that could be suggested at this level of detail.

In earlier studies,[43] attentive behaviors were identified as a problem during current OM in 1- and 2-year olds, establishing a prior reason for concentrating on these as sequelae after remission of OM. Similarly, in studies where an investigator concentrates on only two or three comprehensive aspects of behavior and only affords tests or questionnaires on those, inflated probability of finding some variable that is affected is not a severe problem. Where a larger number of outcome measures are examined, however, it may become impossible to interpret the p value or to adjust it in any precise way for the number of hypotheses tested. There is no universal solution to this problem but four preventive steps can be taken: (1) prior hypothesis from a theoretic model, (2) use of large samples, (3) adopting conservative p values before any strong interpretation, and (4) requiring replication.

In a clinical sample, reasonable certainty can be achieved about whether the patient has had the disease in question, but it is hard to rule out co-presence of relevant factors (eg, hypochondria, income level, comorbidity, or particular alertness to the developmental outcomes in question) that may have led the family to consult. The first two will tend to reduce and the second to increase the disease effect size. At the very least, rigorous prospective case definitions are required, with control for the most likely confounding variables.

The most convincing evidence for behavior outcomes of OM comes from large prospective longitudinal population cohorts because of statistical control and minimal comorbidity bias. There is, however, a disadvantage: not all of the large numbers in a population cohort are located at severities efficient for drawing a conclusion, and cohort studies have to be very large to contain sufficient index "cases" of severe enough disease to show what may be relatively small effects. Also, the markers of middle ear disease that such general-purpose (ie, extensive rather than intensive) studies include are often less than perfect, and may require specific within-sample validation. This will tend to underestimate the disease effect. An ideal strategy is to proceed from more cost-efficient explanatory clinical studies with matched population controls to the more completely controlled comorbidity-free population sampling and, especially, to avoid categoric preconceptions about the validity or otherwise of particular types of study. Strengths of one design tend to complement weaknesses in another.

Detailed analyses of the 1970 British birth cohort[44] have used derived scores on a small number of dimensions on existing behavior instruments. They demonstrate that a history of early ear discharge is associated at age 5 years with parent-reported antisocial, neurotic, and hyperactive behavior. Similarly, a history of early reported hearing difficulty is associated with antisocial, neurotic, or hyperactive behavior and poor conduct. This hearing difficulty is not permanent (of which the rare cases were excluded from analysis), and it can be safely ascribed to middle ear disease. Similar associations were also found with reported ear discharge at age 10 years. Neurotic, clumsy, and hyperactive behaviors were significantly associated with hearing difficulty, though no significant effect was found at age 10 years for antisocial behavior.

The effect sizes for behavior varied over age between 0.25 and –0.01 SD for hearing difficulty and between 0.14 and 0.01 SD for ear discharge as the OM markers, after adjusting for maternal malaise and SES. These effects are mostly small but some were still significant at age 10 years. This highlights the need for the several

thousand cases with complete data on the variables for adequate statistical power. Clinical diagnoses were not available, but obtaining such information is neither practicable nor affordable when documenting the mass population effects of early OM histories.

Similar behavior effects for OME have been demonstrated within the Dunedin (New Zealand) cohort,[45] for which the otologic definition of disease from age 5 years was much more satisfactory. There was no significant difference between cases and controls when all age groups were considered together. Parents of 5-year-old children with OME, however, reported their children to be significantly more restless, fidgety, destructive, less liked by other children, and more often disobedient.[46] Between-group effect sizes for parent-reported behavior were found to decrease with age. When assessed at ages 5, 7, 9, and 11 years, the respective effect sizes were 0.35, 0.30, 0.20, and 0.10 SD, respectively, confirming the expected dilution with time caused by final remission of the OME. For these earlier findings, the single classification as OM or control was made only at age 5 years and not reclassified on the basis of later reassessment.

Sufficient length of exposure to the disease and the associated hearing loss is necessary for a communication deficit, but eventually the disease remits, leading to difficulty tracking the few cases with very long histories. Consequently, the age range of 4 to 6 years is probably the most appropriate when obtaining a general picture of the impact of OME's effects in childhood. A later Dunedin follow-up defined the index group as those children still showing OM history between ages 5 and 9 years.[47] The results showed deficits into the teens on a reading test. Secondary sources will almost certainly misquote this finding in an alarmist way to suggest long-term effects from mild transitory conditions in young children that happen to achieve the OME diagnostic label. In fact, what the analysis shows is that if the years of disease exposure period are many and the test period is separated from exposure by no longer an interval than the duration of the exposure itself, then effects are measurable.

Although these studies suggest that behavior is a pertinent outcome in OM, the 1970 British cohort and the Dunedin cohort used the Rutter behavior scale for parents. Despite its good psychometric properties, the Rutter behavior scale was originally developed to discriminate extremes, that is, the behaviorally disordered from the majority of children and for distinguishing among different forms of clinical disorder.[48] In a relatively mild condition, such as OM, a scale designed to discriminate beyond the ninetieth percentile is suboptimal. Any behavioral effect of OM is likely to be within the normal range and would, therefore, be more appropriately assessed with an instrument designed to address this range of behaviors, rather than the psychiatric extreme. This again suggests that studies with such instruments as the Rutter scale may slightly underestimate the behavior impact of OM.

An alternative source of data on OM outcomes comes from clinical trials, which are useful in two ways. First, the cases are usually well specified, which can clearly document disease effects relative to an unaffected population and often permit internal tests for comorbidity bias. Second, the intervention may permit a tightly controlled experimental test of a therapeutic hypothesis, whereas experiments on disease effects are obviously ruled out ethically. This test regards the therapy as a simple inverse of the developmental deficit from the disease (or from its associated hearing impairment). A disadvantage, however, is that ethical constraints make it difficult to recruit severe cases and to achieve a long-term or major therapeutic effect that might have major knock-on developmental effects.

Reported RCTs on younger children have included broader outcomes relevant to aspects of behavior and QoL. In one conducted in Bristol, in the United Kingdom,[49] bilateral insertion of ventilation tubes reduced some behavioral difficulties in preschool children with OME. On a sample of younger children in Pittsburgh (age 1 and 2 years), parental ratings of parent/child stress were not associated with extent of the child's middle ear effusion (MEE) during the first 2 years, after adjusting for race, gender, maternal education, and meaningful percentage of time spent with unilateral MEE.[50,51] A similar lack of association was found between the duration of MEE up to age 2 years and behavioral ratings at age 2 years. Part of the difference could be caused by overadjustment or by unreliability of the behavior ratings at the very young age in question. These latter studies come from the early stages of the major Pittsburgh trial, which was selectively nested in a population cohort. The subsequent RCT[52] showed no benefits of ventilation tubes on behavior and language outcomes, and only modest and short-term benefit on disease markers. The behavior measure used, however, was a brief checklist for screening purposes and may have been undersensitive to small differences.

At the categoric level, the Bristol and Pittsburgh findings appear in conflict; a deficit cannot be reduced by remedial treatment, unless a real deficit exists. Differences in age may be responsible for the discrepancy (mean 2 years and 9 months at entry in the Bristol trial, versus 15 months when randomized in the Pittsburgh trial). The age difference could influence the tendency for the condition to resolve and the validity of the outcome instrument. Critical appraisal of findings has to consider a range of such discrepancies before concluding whether there is a genuine conflict or paradox to be resolved or sufficient homogeneity of cases and outcomes measured to attempt informal or formal (meta-analytic) synthesis.

The most likely difference in the Bristol and Pittsburgh trials is the severity/persistence of OME characterizing the children accessible to randomization in the British and American health care systems, respectively. Many of the children in the American trial would not have reached secondary care in the British health care system. The authors of the Pittsburgh trial properly acknowledge that more selected (ie, symptomatic) children still might display beneficial effects of intervention. Unfortunately, secondary media, such as newspapers, and even professional digests do not draw attention to differences on the basis of case inclusion in this way but fixate on the thing most easily described as characterizing a study—in this case, placing ventilation tubes.

Balance (Vestibular) Outcomes

The tradition of clinical physiologic measurement in otolaryngology has led to several studies addressing the extent to which children with middle ear disease are susceptible to balance problems. In adults, balance disorders can have a severe effect on QoL (falls, vertigo, nausea), at least over the short term. Many published balance studies of children with OME have reported a significant disease effect, and this appears to reduce after inserting ventilation tubes; however, some studies have very small samples and should, therefore, be interpreted with caution. The methodologically stronger studies[53–55] suggest some between-groups effect (deficit in OME), but the effect size is uncertain. Sensitive diagnostic tests, which are appropriate for some purposes, may be less relevant in a QoL context.

Parents attribute low importance to balance problems, and feasible questions to parents on balance-related abilities in their children (although displaying adequate internal consistency) did not correlate with OM disease severity in the TARGET sample. A possible explanation of the discrepancy is vicarious central adaptation to vestibular disturbance, which is known to occur in adult vestibular pathologies and would make effects on abilities or reported symptoms detectable only on short-term deterioration or improvement. Whereas the pathophysiologic findings are of interest within a clinically rich portrayal of OME, balance is not an obligatory dimension within a "bottom-up" approach to QoL. The nausea and vertigo from vestibular pathology in adults lead to profound QoL effects; however, their magnitude and form in OME are greatly diminished.

Application Data with QoL Instruments in Otitis Media

Although not primarily concerned with OM, two studies of candidates for tonsillectomy and adenoidectomy illustrate related QoL issues. In the first,[56] back-calculation of the SD effect sizes is possible from group sizes and confidence intervals, resulting in domains of large versus modest impact on the 28-item CHQ. Adenotonsillar disease had large effect sizes for pain, physical functioning, parental impact, and family activities. Assuming these associations are reliable (despite the small sample of 55), the pattern is credible in terms of known clinical characterization of the disease group. The study exemplifies a useful extension of traditional clinical characterization by using a well-standardized measure, with at least an implicit control group in the reference sample for the instrument. For example, it could be used as a pilot and baseline variability assay in planning a randomized trial.

In another study on a similar population[57] with adenotonsillar disease, the Child Behavior Checklist was run in parallel with the OSA-18, a short questionnaire on sleep-disordered breathing in children. The two measures had moderate correlation at baseline and on the change scores after intervention. As a before-and-after study, it is unclear clear how much of the correlation in the change scores was caused by correlated biases to perceive an improvement after treatment and how much to their intrinsic relatedness. The true correlation in change scores may be higher because of a confounding from variance introduced by differencing measures of finite reliability. Regardless, the moderate correlation at baseline supports a link between physical health and behavior problems, which may manifest to a milder extent in OM. Similarly, hearing impairment should not be expected as the only, or even main, influence on behavior. This observation supports the strong physical health-to-behavior link in Figure 25-4.

In a multicenter before-and-after study of children scheduled for ventilation tubes, a consortium of American otolaryngologists[58] gave the OM-6 to 248 children with a median age of 1.4 years. This study differed from a clinical trial in several important respects: the entry criteria were not prespecified, there was no randomized control group, and the follow-up period was short and unspecified (although within the range of 2 to 4 months from pre- to postoperative consultation, not enough developmental trend would be expected to undermine the conclusion). Standardized effect sizes of 0.52 to 1.20 were obtained for change scores in the various domains, which is equivalent in the simple instance to the recommended procedure of modeling absolute postintervention scores with the baseline as a covariate. Conversely, effect sizes were trivial between the initial consultation visit and the day of planned surgery.

A contrast is seen between these large reported benefits and an RCT from the Netherlands.[59] The contrast is stark and merits analysis because despite the Dutch case finding having begun in formal screening, rather than pediatrician vigilance, the age (19.5 months mean in the Dutch study) the clinical characteristics of the children appear similar. This is unusual for unconnected studies in a new field. The Dutch study ($N = 187$) used a well-developed and standardized generic QoL scale, plus an observational analysis of video of parent-child interaction. Despite a substantial reduction in OME, the mean values on all the QoL dimensions were very nearly identical for the ventilation tube and the watchful waiting groups. Other outcome measures in this trial supported the nullity of result found in the Pittsburgh study summarized earlier. The null result and conclusions are particularly of note because the study was conducted by impartial epidemiologists and analyzed in the ways recommended for clinical trials.

Smaller treatment effect sizes are more common in RCTs than in otherwise well-controlled nonrandomized studies, for a mixture of reasons hard to disentangle. In conventionally prescribed systematic reviewing, specialized insight and understanding have to be suspended in many respects because these are held to introduce interpretative bias and be counterproductive. As long as certainty is not overclaimed for interpretation, however, bringing to bear that an understanding of psychometric principles and of the evaluation literature can help avoid uninformative desperation at the difficulty of reconciling two studies with such differing results.

The two main factors favoring the large reported benefit in the American study are a disease-specific (nongeneric) measure and a very short follow-up period. In addition, the framework of the American study, with questions about client satisfaction, does not minimize expectancy (placebo) bias. Nevertheless, the American effect sizes are believable *for the methods and follow-up period used*. The implications of the study for health gain and clinical policies need to be expressed precisely, to avoid overgeneralization and overinterpretation. The American consortium study documents satisfaction with services, a worthwhile objective, but separate from efficacy or effectiveness. Differences between the Netherlands and the United States in the economic relationship between the family and health care provider may also have colored how subjective QoL-related judgments were formed.

To avoid the conflict seeming larger than it need be, the Dutch study might have also included a reported OM-specific measure, more likely to illustrate therapeutic efficacy beyond reduced MEE. Another favorable American before-and-after outcome monitoring study[32] cited *only* insensitivity of generic measures in the Dutch study, without addressing other measurement issues. For example, there must be difficulty with parental rating of attributes in any questionnaire on the youngest children. The Dutch instrument, however, was specifically developed for very young children, whereas the OM-6 is for ages up to 12 years. The authors[32] also ignored the policy implications of the null result from the well-conducted Dutch study and sought to undermine RCTs as the best basis for evaluating health care. This antievidence stance may best be discouraged by educating readers and helping them revise their belief systems. As noted earlier, one good way is to facilitate findings consistent with the known therapeutic mechanism (ie, positive) and to a be able to, nevertheless, show that the magnitude of effect on the valued outcome is below a previously agreed clinically important difference (as here proved to be the case). This two-part strategy ensures a power margin using specific and generic measures.

As described earlier, issues of known-groups validity in relation to controls can be stood on their head to ask whether the impact of OM is important in the first place but also to set a context for judging plausible and worthwhile treatment effects. The baseline data on the TARGET behavior and QoL outcome measures offer some indications of these effect sizes, although these are not available for all components of OM7-27. The directly rated child QoL score (see Figure 25-6) demonstrated a disease effect size of 0.51 SD. TARGET baseline data show a disease effect size of 0.62 for a general behavior scale. Effect sizes of this magnitude equate to shifts of 15 to 20 percentile points in the population distribution.

Index cases in the TARGET study were a stringently selected sample of children with OME (inclusion criteria: B + B or B + C_2 tympanograms and ≥ 20 dB hearing levels) on two occasions 3 months apart. The control group was unselected 3.5 to 7 year olds from the general population in schools. The OM effect sizes obtained are appreciable, probably reflecting the age/persistence and the inclusion criteria on better markers of OME than used in cohort studies. A degree of comorbidity bias, which would not be seen in a prospective population study, cannot be ruled out because the cases were those who had consulted clinically in a health care system with relatively restricted access.

None of these studies is perfect or able to construct a watertight defense to criticisms that generic instruments are undersensitive, that specific instruments are oversensitive, or that some of the disease effects or treatment effects seen are bias prone. Nevertheless, there is no need to conclude that results are inconsistent such as to permit no conclusions, when there are rational bases for explaining the discrepancies among them. Whereas effect magnitudes are ideally ascertained with greater precision than has yet been done, we have reason to believe that disease and treatment effects on QoL are seen in OM.

Implications of QoL for Clinical Policies— Magnitudes Revisited

Evidence on prevalence, morbidity, general impact, burden of care, and QoL is often used in discussions of health care policy. Effect sizes, both for impact of disease and benefits of treatment, must contribute to the importance ascribed to health care provision in OM, and both have implications for the health care resources allocated to, or chargeable by, a health care provider, as well as for a nation's research budget. Interpreting and evaluating these data can be subject to the bias of an author's professional or financial interest, which should be properly declared. Disease effect sizes 0.51 to 0.62 SD in the QoL domain (ie, shifts of 15 to 20 percentile points of the population distribution) entail that OM impact on well-defined cases cannot be dismissed as trivial. Nor should it be exaggerated as "devastating."[60]

An alternative perspective is that the skewed distribution reflects a long tail in the distribution of cases (see Figure 25-5B), much less evident in the controls. This tail becomes censored when a transformation is applied to make both the case and the control distributions symmetric for statistical analysis (see Figure 25-6). This view implies that the true "cases" reside in this tail of the distribution. Although counting cases below (or above) some cutoff comprises less precise measurement, we are happy with a tail view of "caseness" and with its implied reduction in the prevalence of cases regarded as treatable.

Considering "cases" as the tail of a distribution, however, creates a practical obstacle: disease assessed by conventional clinical measures may be unable to adequately select these "cases," because impact may be highly synergistic in ways not yet understood and not determined by disease severity and persistence alone. The tail could be defined in terms of extreme *impact*, and some clinicians' informal assessment when balancing decisions at the margin does respect this idea. But reorientation is required before physicians will, in general, replace formal diagnostic measurements with formal outcome measures for the early stages decisions in the clinical process, that is, referral or first surgical intervention.

An effective treatment is most unlikely to remove all of the disease effect, though it might quite plausibly remove 50 to 75%. Bringing treatment effects into correspondence with disease effects for reported measures is problematic. Without special steps in control, treatment effects on repeated measures will be susceptible to expectancy biases (placebo effects), which disease effects are not, producing the contradiction that something seems to be more fixable than it was broken in the first place.

The TARGET trial with 376 cases randomized was powered to detect mean group effect sizes of one-third

Table 25-6 Pointers and Pitfalls: Five Criteria for Articles Claiming Differences or Shifts in Quality of Life*

1. Are the cases and any controls clearly defined, especially as to degree of selection for severity and persistence of otitis media history?

2. Are the balance of items and their weighting in the instrument, between disease-specific symptoms and generic impact of disease, made clear, and is any unintentional tuning by the rubric or context toward a highly disease-specific interpretation precluded, specified, or at least considered?

3. Are sources of bias considered and minimized?

4. Are magnitude issues addressed, via reference populations or explicit benchmarks for the instrument and/or the clinical population?

5. Is the magnitude of difference claimed credible, in the light of the existing literature and the particular patients and/or interventions?

*When there is no time for detailed methodologic critique, readers should at least apply these five criteria to the claimed conclusion of an article before believing or generalizing it.

(0.33) SD, on the grounds that if an overall treatment effect of only this magnitude were found, and the interpretation was therapeutically sound, it could just influence practice. A 0.33 SD therapeutic effect equates to moving from the fiftieth to the sixty second percentile (or vice versa, if improvement takes a score down, rather than up), bypassing 12% of "the competition." From the point of view of detecting a plausible two-thirds amelioration of the disease effect (0.33/0.51) in QoL, TARGET power is, therefore, marginal, unless expectancy biases are admitted.

Among the reasons for carrying a reserve of power (ie, building the smaller effect size into the trial design) is the need to be relatively precise about magnitudes. Further, predicted effects smaller than the importance cutoff can be confirmed. This avoids mistrust of a trial that fails to show effects. The policy decision must then be based on a magnitude in relation to a clinically important difference (CID), rather than on existence of some unspecified nonzero effect (reaching conventional *p* value). Unfortunately, most trial designs do not bother to make this important distinction. Trial design and interpretation also fail to distinguish between a metric magnitude and the differing valuations that may be put on it. In other words, existing design does not drive the CID and the sample size calculation by utility values for *what would be worth finding* and hence worth funding to find. But let us learn to walk before we attempt to run.

Conclusion

Usable measures with specified properties in the QoL domain now exist for AOM and OME, although the quantitative sophistication is not high and the literature making use of them is still very small. From a recent systematic review of the reporting of QoL-domain measures in the general clinical research literature,[7] it is clear that the term

"QoL" has been used chiefly as a default label for a vast and heterogeneous range of measures that happen to be novel in not reflecting pathophysiology or abnormal anatomy. There has been little attention to type, fitness for purpose, profile of domains, or psychometric properties.

We decided to review issues and measurement principles here in an informative and encouraging style, rather than to summarize other reviews of work extending outside of OM that have only been unproductively critical of quality. We hope that this will enable readers to critically appraise further instruments and applications in the years to come. To that end, we offer a minimal summary checklist (Table 25-6) for quality of claims about magnitude of QoL effects applicable to studies of disease and treatment. Many challenges remain, including that of reducing biases in report (including the expectancy bias—placebo effect) so as to bring disease effects and treatment effects into a more logical alignment.

References

1. Patrick D, Erickson P. Health Status and health policy. Quality of life in health care evaluation and resource allocation. Oxford (UK): University Press; 1993.
2. World Health Organization. The constitution of the World Health Organization. WHO Chronicles, 1, 29. Geneva: WHO; 1947.
3. World Health Organization. Official records of the World Health Organization, No. 2, 100. Geneva: WHO; 1948.
4. World Health Organization. Uses of epidemiology in ageing; report of a scientific group, 1983. Technical report series, No. 706. Geneva: WHO; 1984.
5. Patrick D, Erickson P. What constitutes quality of life? Concepts and dimensions. J Drug Therapy Res 1988; 13:152–8.
6. Levine S. The meanings of health, illness and quality of life. In: Quality of life and health: concepts, methods and applications. Oxford (UK): Blackwell; 1995.

7. Sanders C, Egger M, Donovan J, et al. Reporting on quality of life in randomized controlled trials: bibliographic study. BMJ 1998;317:1191–4.

8. Scientific Advisory Committee of the Medical Outcomes Trust. Assessing health status and quality-of-life instruments: attributes and review criteria. Qual Life Res 2002;11:193–205.

9. Fitzpatrick R, Davey C, Buxton MJ, Jones DR. Evaluating patient-based outcome measures for use in clinical trials. Health Technol Assess 1998;2:i–iv, 7–24.

10. Oppenheim AN. Questionnaire design and attitude measurement. London (UK): Heinemann; 1966.

11. Stone DH. How to do it: design a questionnaire. BMJ 1993;307:1264–5.

12. Facione N. Quality of life issues in chronic otitis media with effusion: parameters for future study. Int J Pediatr Otorhinolaryngol 1991;22:167–79.

13. McCallum RC, Zung S, Preacher KJ, Rucker DD. On the practice of dichotomization of quantitative variables. Psychol Methods 2002;7:19–40

14. Samson G, Edelman D, Rothman ML, et al. Determining clinically important differences in health status measures. Pharmacoeconomics 1999;15:141–55.

15. Fenny DH, Torrance GW, Labelle R. Integrating economic evaluations and quality of life assessments. In: Spilker B, editor. Quality of life and pharmacoeconomics in clinical trials. New York (NY): Lippincott-Raven; 1996.

16. Nixon SK, Maunsell E, Desmeules M, et al. Mutual concurrent validity of the Child Health Questionnaire and the Health Utilities Index: an exploratory analysis using survivors of child cancer. Int J Cancer Suppl 1999;12:95–105

17. Browning GG. Do patients and surgeons agree? Clin Otolaryngol 1997;22:485–96.

18. Higson JM. Parent and professional health beliefs about otitis media with effusion: impact on parent behavior [PhD thesis]. Nottingham: University of Nottingham; 1998.

19. Parcel GS, Meyer MP. Development of an instrument to measure children's health locus of control. Health Educ Monogr 1978;6:149–59.

20. Lewis CC, Pantell RH, Kieckhefer GM. Assessment of children's health status. Med Care 1989;27 Suppl: S54–65.

21. Sneeuw KC, Sprangers MAG, Aaronson NK. The role of health care providers and significant others in evaluating the quality of life of patients with chronic disease. J Clin Epidemiol 2002;55:1130–43.

22. Pantell RH, Lewis CC. Measuring the impact of medical care on children. J Chron Disabil 1987;40 Suppl:S99–108.

23. Forgays DK, Hasazi JE, Wasserman RC. Recurrent otitis media and parenting stress in mothers of two year-old children. Develop Behav Pediatr 1992;13:321–5.

24. Streiner DL, Norman GR. Health measurement scales: a practical guide to their development and use. New York (NY): Oxford University Press Inc; 1995.

25. World Health Organization. International classification of impairments, disabilities and handicaps. Geneva: WHO; 1980.

26. McDonald RP, Moon-Ho RH. Principles and practice in reporting structural equation analyses. Psychol Methods 2002;7:64–82.

27. Juniper E, Howland WC, Roberts NB, et al. Measuring quality of life in children with rhinoconjunctivitis. J Allerg Clin Immunol 1998;101:163–70.

28. Berdeaux G, Hervie C, Smajda MP. Rhinitis Survey Group. Parental quality of life and recurrent ENT infections in their children: development of a questionnaire. Qual Life Res 1998;7:501–12.

29. Alsarraf R, Jung CJ, Perkins J, et al. Otitis media health status evaluation: a pilot study for the investigation of cost effective outcomes of recurrent acute otitis media treatment. Ann Otol Rhinol Laryngol 1998;107:120–8.

30. Stein REK, Jessop DJ. Functional status II(R) a measure of child health status. Med Care 1990;28:1041–55.

31. Rosenfeld RM, Goldsmith AJ, Tetlus L, Balzano A. Quality of Life for children with otitis media. Arch Otolaryngol Head Neck Surg 1997;123:1049–54.

32. Richards M, Giannoni C. Quality-of-life outcomes after surgical intervention for otitis media. Arch Otolaryngol 2002;128:776–81.

33. Smith SC. Measurement of quality of life, behavior and health outcomes in children with otitis media with effusion [PhD thesis]. Nottingham: University of Nottingham; 1998.

34. Landgraf J, Abetz L, Ware JE. The CHQ users manual. 1st ed. Boston (MA): The Health Institute, New England Medical Center; 1996.

35. Varni JW, Seid M, Kurtin PS. PedsQLTM 4.0: reliability and validity of the Pediatric Quality of Life Inventory TM Version 4.0 generic core scales in healthy and patient populations. Med Care 2001;39:800–12.

36. Black MM, Sonnenschein S. Early exposure to otitis media: a preliminary investigation of behavioral outcome. Develop Behav Pediatr 1993;14:150–5.

37. Adesman AR, Altshuler LA, Lipkin PH, Walco GA. Otitis media in children with learning disabilities with attention deficit disorder with hyperactivity. Pediatrics 1990;85:442–6.

38. Funk JB, Jurs SG. A preliminary investigation of associations between disorders of behavior and language in children with chronic otitis media. Child Study J 1986; 16:255–64.

39. Arcia E, Roberts JE. Otitis media in early childhood and its association with sustained attention in structured situations. Develop Behav Pediatr 1993;14:181–3.

40. Roberts JE, Burchinal MR, Collier AM, et al. Otitis media in early childhood and cognitive, academic and classroom performance of the school-aged child. Pediatrics 1989;83:477–85.

41. Roberts JE, Burchinal MR, Campbell F. Otitis media in early childhood and patterns of intellectual development and later academic performance. J Pediatr Psychol 1994;19:347–67.

42. Roberts JE, Burchinal MR, Clarke-Klein SM. Otitis media in early childhood and cognitive, academic and behavior outcomes. J Pediatr Psychol 1995;20:645–60.

43. Feagans LV, Kipp E, Blood I. The effects of otitis media on the attention skills of day-care-attending toddlers. Dev Psychol 1994;30:701–8.

44. Bennett KE, Haggard MP. Behavior and cognitive outcomes from middle ear disease. Arch Dis Child 1999; 80:28–35.

45. Chalmers D, Stewart I, Silva P, Mulvena A. Otitis media with effusion in children—the Dunedin study. Clin Develop Med 108. Oxford (UK): Blackwell Scientific Publications Ltd.; 1989.

46. Silva PA, Kirkland C, Simpson A, et al. Some developmental and behavioral problems associated with bilateral otitis media with effusion. J Learn Disabil 1982;15:417–21.

47. Bennett KE, Haggard MP, Silva PA, Stewart IA. Behavior and developmental effects of otitis media with effusion into the teens. Arch Dis Child 2001;85:91–5

48. Boyle MH, Jones SC. Selecting measures of emotional and behavioral disorders of childhood for use in general populations. J Child Psychol Psych 1985;26:137–59.

49. Wilks J, Maw R, Peters T, et al. Randomized controlled trial of early surgery versus watchful waiting for glue ear: the effect on behavioral problems in pre-school children. Clin Otolaryngol 2000;25:209–14.

50. Paradise JL, Feldman HM, Bernard BS, et al, and the Pittsburgh-area Child Development/Otitis Media Study. Parent-related behavior in a mixed population of 2-year olds in relation to otitis media in their first 2 years of life. Pediatr Res 1995a;37(4):18A.

51. Paradise JL, Feldman HM, Bernard BS, et al, and the Pittsburgh-area Child Development/Otitis Media Study. Parent-child stress in 1003 two year olds in relation to otitis media (OM) during their first 2 years of life. Pediatr Res 1995b;37(4):142A.

52. Paradise JL, Feldman HM, Campbell TF, et al. Effect of early or delayed insertion of tympanostomy tubes for persistent otitis media on developmental outcomes at the age of three years. N Engl J Med 2001;344:1179–87.

53. Golz A, Angel-Yeger B, Parush S. Evaluation of balance disturbances in children with middle ear effusion. Int J Pediatr Otorhinolaryngol 1998;43:21–6.

54. Grace ARH, Pfleiderer AG. Dysequilibrium and otitis media with effusion: what is the association? J Laryngol Otol 1990;104:682–4.

55. Casselbrant ML, Furman JM, Rubenstein E, Mandel EM. Effect of otitis media on the vestibular system in children. Ann Otol Rhinol Laryngol 1995;104:620–4.

56. Stewart MG, Friedman EM, Sulek M, et al. Quality of life and health status in pediatric tonsil and adenoid disease. Arch Otolaryngol 2000;126:45–8.

57. Goldstein, Fatima M, Campbell TF, Rosenfeld RM. Child behavior and quality of life before and after tonsillectomy and adenoidectomy. Arch Otolaryngol 2002;128:770–5.

58. Rosenfeld RM, Bhaya MH, Bower CM, et al. Impact of tympanostomy tubes on child quality of life. Arch Otolaryngol 2000;126:585–92.

59. Rovers M, Krabee P, Straatman H, et al. Randomized controlled trial of the effect of ventilation tubes (grommets) on quality of life at age 1–2 years. Arch Dis Child 2001;84:45–9.

60. Leviton A, Bellinger D. Consequences of unremitting middle-ear infection in early life (with reply). N Engl J Med 1985;313:1353–4.

CHAPTER 26

Bacterial Resistance and Antimicrobial Drug Selection

Jerome O. Klein, MD

To regard any form of life merely as slave or foe will one day be considered poor philosophy,
for all living things constitute an integral part of the cosmic order.
René Dubos[1]

OBJECTIVES

On completing this chapter, the reader will be able to

1. State the current incidence of resistance of bacterial pathogens.
2. Distinguish among mechanisms of bacterial resistance.
3. Select an antimicrobial agent for initial therapy of acute otitis media (AOM).
4. Select an antimicrobial agent for AOM relapse and recurrence.
5. Define strategies for limiting the incidence of bacterial resistance.

EDITORIAL COMMENT

This chapter begins with the premise that a clinician has elected to treat a particular child with antibiotics for otitis media (OM) and then summarizes evidence regarding optimal drug selection. Judicious use of antibiotics is also emphasized as a primary strategy for controlling bacterial resistance. An obvious method of reducing antibiotic-induced bacterial resistance is simply not to prescribe an antibiotic at all. Most otitis media with effusion (OME) can be managed without antibiotics (see Chapter 19, "Clinical Pathway for Otitis Media with Effusion"), and some children with AOM are suitable for initial observation (see Chapter 18, "Clinical Pathway for Acute Otitis Media"). Therefore, as much intellectual effort should be expended on deciding whether to treat at all as on which drug is best for treatment.

INTRODUCTION

Developing resistance to antimicrobial agents has been a constant feature of drug therapy since the sulfonamides were introduced in the mid-1930s. Identifying beta-lactamase–producing strains of *Haemophilus influenzae*

and *Moraxella catarrhalis* in the 1970s and the increased incidence of multidrug-resistant pneumococci in the 1980s were important in managing OM. Resistance is increasing, but there are differences among and within countries.

Clinicians should be aware of data for drug resistance in their community, risk features associated with increased resistance, and its clinical implications. Clinicians also need to be cognizant of measures that will limit bacterial resistance. These include avoiding trivial use of antimicrobial agents, improving accuracy of diagnosis of AOM, increased use of preventive techniques, such as immunoprophylaxis and chemoprophylaxis, and educating parents and other consumers on the appropriate use of antimicrobial drugs.

BACTERIAL PATHOGENS RESPONSIBLE FOR AOM

Streptococcus pneumoniae

Clinical resistance of pneumococci to penicillin was first identified in 1965 in Boston. Resistance of *S. pneumoniae* to multiple antibacterial drugs was identified in South Africa in the 1970s and is now a worldwide problem. Pneumococcal strains are designated susceptible and nonsusceptible. The former are termed intermediate or resistant, according to the minimum inhibitory concentration (MIC) of penicillin required to inhibit growth of the organism.

- Susceptible strains are inhibited by MICs less than 0.1 µg per mL.
- Intermediate strains are inhibited by MICs of 0.1 to 1.0 µg per mL.
- Resistant strains are inhibited by MICs of 2.0 µg per mL or higher.

The clinical relevance of these numbers lies in comparing the MIC of the strain of bacteria with levels of antibiotic achievable at the site of infection. Because pneumococci show incremental levels of resistance to beta-lactam drugs (including penicillins and cephalosporins), some infections caused by intermediate strains of pneumococci may be treated adequately with routine or increased doses of this family of drugs. Clinical failure may result if infections caused by resistant strains are treated with usual dosage schedules.

Mechanism of Resistance

Penicillin resistance in pneumococci is caused by changes in the penicillin-binding proteins in the cell wall of the bacteria resulting in reduced affinity for beta-lactam drugs. Penicillin resistance in a community usually begins with the identification of intermediate strains that increase and are followed by resistant strains. Penicillin-resistant pneumococci often resist other antimicrobial agents, including other beta-lactam drugs and such drugs as macrolides and sulfonamides, whose mode of resistance differs from that of penicillin.

Incidence

Rates of penicillin resistance of pneumococci vary worldwide: Spain, France, Hungary, and Israel reported rates exceeding 40%; Korea and the Far East reported the highest to date, exceeding 80%; and The Netherlands, in contrast, reported < 1%.[2] Current rates of penicillin resistance in the United States are approximately 25%, but regional differences range between < 10% and > 40%.[3]

Pneumococcal resistance to other agents varies. The large proportion of pneumococci resistant to trimethoprim-sulfamethoxazole (TMP-SMX) is of particular concern. The proportion of resistant strains is usually lower for the parenteral cephalosporins (cefotaxime and ceftriaxone). Resistance to the macrolides (erythromycin, azithromycin, and clarithromycin) is increasing and approximates the rates of penicillin resistance in most communities. Rates of resistance to clindamycin remain low. Although the rate of resistance to fluoroquinolone is less than 1% in most regions of the United States, rates of 5% have been reported from Massachusetts and Colorado.[4,5] To date, there are no vancomycin-resistant pneumococci.

All pneumococci isolated from body fluids, including ear aspirates, or usually sterile sites should be screened for susceptibility to penicillin. Most laboratories now use the E (ellipse)-test based on application of paper strips with graded concentrations of drug placed on the agar plate seeded with the test organism. The E-test provides data about MICs of the test organism. The physician should be aware of contemporary susceptibility data in the community so that optimal decisions may be made for initial therapy.

Risk Features

Risk factors for colonization and infection with resistant pneumococci include prior exposure to antibacterial agents, young age, day care attendance, and hospitalization. Isolates from mucosal surfaces, such as the throat and nasopharynx, yield higher rates of resistance than do isolates from body fluids, such as blood and cerebrospinal fluid (CSF). No clinical features distinguish infection with resistant organisms from infection with susceptible organisms, and there does not appear to be increased virulence of the disease caused by the former.[6,7]

Haemophilus influenzae

The mechanism of resistance of *H. influenzae* to beta-lactam drugs is production of plasmid-mediated beta-lactamase. The enzyme produced by the bacteria hydrolyzes ampicillin, amoxicillin, and penicillins G and V, which confers resistance to these drugs. In contrast with penicillin resistance, which is incremental and can be overcome by achieving higher concentrations of drug at the site of infection, resistance caused by beta-lactamase production is more likely to be absolute. The beta-lactam ring is cleaved, rendering the susceptible penicillin inactive. Resistance of *H. influenzae* not associated with beta-lactamase production, such as that occurring from alterations in penicillin-binding proteins, currently remains below 5%.[8]

Incidence

Beta-lactamase–producing strains of *H. influenzae* were first identified in the early 1970s. The rate of resistant strains increased steadily and now varies between 20 and 50% in the United States. In Pittsburgh, beta-lactamase–producing strains of *H. influenzae* isolated from middle ear fluid in children rose from under 20% to over 40% during the 1980s.[9]

Moraxella catarrhalis

Before 1970, virtually all strains of *M. catarrhalis* were susceptible to penicillin. In the 1970s, beta-lactamase–producing strains were identified, and within a decade, the vast majority of strains isolated from patients were beta-lactamase positive. The mechanism of resistance is similar to that of other beta-lactamase–producing bacteria including *H. influenzae, Staphylococcus aureus,* and gram-negative enteric bacilli.

Group A Streptococci

Although group A streptococci (GAS) became resistant to the sulfonamides within a decade after the introduction of the drugs, these streptococci remain universally susceptible to penicillins and cephalosporins. No strain resistant to a beta-lactam drug has ever been identified. Resistance to erythromycin and the newer macrolides, however, has increased over the past years but remains low in the United States at 2 to 4%.[10]

The current concern with invasive and toxin-producing strains of GAS causing toxic shock syndromes and tissue necrosis is not associated with a change in the antimicrobial susceptibility pattern of the streptococci. The changes appear to result from re-introduction of selected M types of streptococci in the community, which produce exotoxins with the potential to cause tissue necrosis and shock. Group A streptococci remain an uncommon cause of AOM in the United States.

PHARMACOKINETICS OF ANTIBIOTICS IN AOM

Middle Ear Concentration versus Minimum Inhibitory Concentration

The clinical and microbiologic efficacies of antimicrobial agents are optimal when concentrations of the drug at the site of infection exceed the MIC of the bacterial strain. For some mechanisms of bacterial resistance, increasing the concentration of drug at the site of infection may not prevent clinical and microbiologic failure. If an organism produces beta-lactamase, a susceptible penicillin, such as amoxicillin, will be ineffective, even if a high concentration of drug is achieved at the site of infection. In contrast, penicillins and cephalosporins may be effective against resistant pneumococci if the concentration is increased at the site of infection (Table 26-1).

The physician can predict the clinical and microbiologic efficacies of a drug by knowing the concentration of the drug achieved at the site of infection and the MIC of the organism. Craig and Andes[11] collated data about the pharmacokinetics and pharmacodynamics of antibiotics in OM, including extensive data about the penetration of antimicrobial drugs into middle ear fluids (MEF). The authors noted that 80 to 85% eradication of *S. pneumoniae* was achieved when the MEF:MIC ratio was between 3.2 and 6.3. As a corollary, bacteriologic cure of 80 to 85% was achieved when serum concentrations exceeded the MIC for 40 to 50% of the dosing interval.

Penetration of Antimicrobial Agents into Middle Ear Fluid

Significant concentrations of most drugs approved for AOM appear promptly in MEF (Table 26-2). The concentrations of drug are generally parallel to, though lower than, concentrations of drug in serum. Penicillins and cephalosporins achieve concentrations in MEF approximately 10 to 40% that of the levels present in serum. Sulfonamides cross biologic membranes efficiently and achieve concentrations in MEF that are approximately one-quarter to one-half the serum concentrations. Clarithromycin and azithromycin have concentrations in MEF greater than concentrations in serum because the macrolides have high intracellular concentrations.

Concentrations in excess of 30 µg/mL are produced in the MEF at peak following a single dose of ceftriaxone intramuscularly (IM) (50 mg per kg); concentrations in serum are approximately 170 µg/mL.[12] Increasing the

---

Table 26-1 Bug and Drug Issues When Managing Otitis Media

1. Resistance of bacterial pathogens to available antimicrobial drugs has been, is now, and will be a continuing problem.

2. Resistance of *Streptococcus pneumoniae* to penicillins and cephalosporins is caused by altered penicillin and cephalosporin binding proteins and is identifiable by increased amounts of drug needed to inhibit the resistant strains. As a corollary, increasing the concentration of drug at the site of infection *can result* in clinical and microbiologic cure.

3. Resistance of *Haemophilus influenzae* to susceptible penicillins (including amoxicillin, penicillins G and V) is caused by production of beta-lactamase, which cleaves the beta-lactam ring of the susceptible penicillin, rendering it ineffective. Increasing the concentration of drug at the site of infection *does not result* in clinical or microbiologic cure.

4. There are no penicillin- or cephalosporin-resistant strains of group A *Streptococcus*.

5. Microbiologic efficacy is achieved when concentrations of beta-lactam drugs in middle ear fluids exceed the MIC of the pathogen by three- to sixfold or concentrations of drug in serum exceed the MIC for at least 50% of the dosing interval.

6. Risk features for colonization and disease due to resistant strains include prior exposure to antibacterial drugs, young age, day care attendance, and prior hospitalization.

MIC = minimum inhibitory concentration.

dose of amoxicillin increased the concentration of drug in MEF, leading to a recommendation of 80 mg/kg/d in two doses as the standard for therapy of AOM, rather than the previous use of 40 mg/kg/d in three doses.[13]

The "In Vivo Sensitivity Test"

The in vivo correlate of in vitro studies of susceptibility of bacterial strains causing AOM is the "in vivo sensitivity test." Howie and Ploussard[14] developed a technique using dual aspirates of MEFs of children with AOM to determine the ability of antibacterial drugs to eradicate organisms in the MEF. The initial aspirate identified the bacterial pathogen. The second aspirate, performed several days after the onset of therapy, documented absence or persistence of the organism.

The double-tap technique has been used since 1969 to document the microbiologic effectiveness of old and new antibacterial drugs for AOM and to correlate clinical and microbiologic results. Dagan and colleagues[15] in Beersheva have provided information of value about sterilization of MEFs for recently introduced antimicrobial agents. The results demonstrate consistently that a drug effective in eradicating the bacterial pathogen almost always leads to early resolution of clinical signs and that drugs failing to eradicate the pathogen have lower rates of clinical success.

The results of the "in vivo sensitivity test" correlate with the susceptibility of the organism to the drug and the concentration of drug achieved in the MEF. Marchant and colleagues[16] collated their data and found that clinical success was usually achieved when the bacterial pathogen was eradicated from the middle ear (93%). Clinical success was still evident in a majority of patients (62%) when the drug failed to sterilize the middle ear infection. When a bacterial pathogen was not isolated from the MEF (which was presumably due to a viral infection), clinical success occurred in 80% of patients.

Some bacterial infections are cleared from the MEF without an antimicrobial agent.[14] When dual aspirates were performed with placebo given instead of an antibacterial drug, 19% of MEFs initially infected with *S. pneumoniae* became sterile, and 48% of fluid initially infected with *H. influenzae* became sterile. This discrepancy among bacteria indicates that a simple mechanical effect (drainage of the infected fluid via a patent Eustachian tube or a perforated tympanic membrane) was unlikely to be responsible for the microbiologic effect. Humoral or cellular immune factors likely acted preferentially to rid the ear of *H. influenzae* more frequently than in the case of *S. pneumoniae*.

These studies document the lack of bacteriological efficacy of drugs that were evaluated for presumed resistant organisms: amoxicillin failed to sterilize MEF of beta-lactamase–producing organisms more efficiently than placebo. At this time, the proportion of intermediate and resistant pneumococci are few in number, and data using the "in vivo sensitivity test" are inadequate to establish the efficacy of the antimicrobial agents against resistant pneumococci causing AOM.

CHOICE OF ANTIMICROBIAL DRUGS FOR AOM

Amoxicillin

Amoxicillin remains the drug of choice for treating AOM (Table 26-3) because of its 25-year record of clinical success, acceptability, limited side effects, and relatively low cost. Amoxicillin is degraded by beta-lactamase from *H. influenzae* and *M. catarrhalis*. The expected clinical failure rate in children with AOM who are given amoxicillin is less than 10%, based on current incidence of resistant strains of *S. pneumoniae* and nontypeable *H. influenzae*. Physicians should substitute susceptibility data from their community in the model outlined

Table 26-2 Penetration of Selected Antimicrobials into Middle Ear Fluids*

Drug	Dose	Serum µg/mL	MEF µg/mL
Amoxicillin	15 mg/kg PO	13.6	5.6
Cefaclor	15 mg/kg PO	8.5–16.8	0.5–3.8
Cefpodoxime	5 mg/kg PO	2	0.2
Sulfamethoxazole	20 mg/kg PO	44.6–70.3	8.2–18.7
Clarithromycin	7.5 mg/kg PO	1.7	2.5
Ceftriaxone	50 mg/kg IM	170	34

IM = intramuscularly; MEF = middle ear effusion; PO = by mouth.
*Data adapted from Craig WA and Andes D[11] and Gudnason T et al.[12]

below to determine the continued value of amoxicillin or the need to choose an alternative antimicrobial agent.

The pneumococci cause about 40% of cases of AOM, and roughly 20% of these middle ear infections are sterilized and respond clinically without an antimicrobial agent. Since most intermediate-resistant strains are inhibited by concentrations of amoxicillin achieved in MEFs, clinical failure is likely to occur only with the resistant strains with MICs of > 2 μg/mL. Given the above, the expected failure rate of children receiving amoxicillin for AOM due to a resistant pneumococci would be 40% less the spontaneous cure rate of 20% divided by a 10% resistance rate, or about 3%.

The same calculations can be applied to *H. influenzae*. Roughly 25% of AOM is caused by nontypeable strains of *H. influenzae*, and about 50% of strains respond clinically and microbiologically without antimicrobial agents. Roughly 40% of *H. influenzae* produce beta-lactamase that would render amoxicillin ineffective. Therefore, the expected failure rate for children receiving amoxicillin for AOM due to a beta-lactamase–producing *Haemophilus* would be 25% less the spontaneous cure rate of 50% divided by the 40% resistance rate, or about 5%.

Doubling the dosage of amoxicillin to 80 mg/kg/d in two doses provides increased concentrations of drug in serum and MEF (up to 8 μg/mL) and would inhibit additional intermediate and resistant strains of *S. pneumoniae*. The increased dose, though, would have no effect on beta-lactamase–producing organisms.[13]

Alternatives to Amoxicillin

Each of the 16 drugs approved by the U.S. Food and Drug Administration (FDA) has documented clinical efficacy for AOM. Because of the small proportion of pneumococci with MICs of > 2 μg/mL, there is a paucity of data about the efficacy of drugs in cases due to resistant strains; none has been approved for use in multidrug-resistant pneumococcal infections. All drugs

other than amoxicillin are unaffected by beta-lactamase but have varying activity against strains of *H. influenzae*.

Opinions vary about the optimal agent for AOM if amoxicillin fails (see Table 26-3). An expert panel convened by the Centers for Disease Control and Prevention (CDC) suggested an increased dosage schedule of amoxicillin-clavulanate, cefuroxime axetil, or intramuscular ceftriaxone for children who fail amoxicillin at day 3 or days 10 to 14.[17] Alternative oral cephalosporins include cefpodoxime and cefdinir. Because of the bitter taste of cefuroxime axetil and cefpodoxime, cefdinir may be the preferred oral cephalosporin.

For children who are allergic to penicillins and cephalosporins, macrolides (erythromycin plus sulfisoxazole, clarithromycin, or azithromycin) are preferable to trimethoprim-sulfamethoxazole because of high rates of resistance to the latter. For some children who are septic, immunosuppressed, or have had multiple recurrences, use of tympanocentesis to identify the bacterial pathogen and susceptibility pattern may be appropriate.

TECHNIQUES FOR LIMITING ANTIBIOTIC RESISTANCE

Pointers and pitfalls for limiting antibiotic resistance are summarized in Table 26-4. Readers should also consult Chapters 27, "Judicious Use of Systemic Antimicrobials" and 28, "Judicious Use of Ototopical Antimicrobials, which deal comprehensively with the judicious use of systemic and topical antimicrobials, respectively.

Fostering Judicious Use of Antimicrobial Agents

Development of resistance has been associated with extensive use of one or more families of antimicrobial agents. As a corollary, withholding the drug has often led to renewed efficacy. Several studies have documented increased colonization and disease caused by

---

Table 26-3 Pointers and Pitfalls in Choosing Antimicrobials for AOM

1. Amoxicillin remains the drug of choice for AOM.

2. Increasing the dosage of amoxicillin (80 mg/kg/d in two doses) is warranted in communities with high rates of pneumococcal resistance.

3. Choice of antimicrobial agents for children who fail when AOM is treated with amoxicillin is controversial; amoxicillin-clavulanate, intramuscular ceftriaxone, and an oral cephalosporin (cefuroxime axetil, cefpodoxime, or cefixime) have been suggested.

4. Patients allergic to penicillins and cephalosporins should receive a macrolide (erythromycin, azithromycin, or clarithromycin); trimethoprim-sulfamethoxazole is less useful because of high rates of resistance.

AOM = acute otitis media.

Table 26-4 Pointers and Pitfalls for Decreasing Bacterial Resistance

1. Reduce inappropriate use of antimicrobial agents for colds, cough/bronchitis, purulent rhinorrhea, nonstreptococcal pharyngitis, and otitis media with effusion.

2. Increase accuracy of pneumatic otoscopy by increased availability of tympanometry and acoustic reflectometry.

3. Use materials for parent education about appropriate use of antibiotics.

4. Use chemoprophylaxis *selectively* for children with recurrent AOM; breakthrough episodes may be caused by pathogens resistant to the prophylactic drug.

5. All infants should receive the conjugate pneumococcal vaccine. Consider using the pneumococcal conjugate vaccine, followed 8 weeks later by the pneumococcal polysaccharide vaccine, for children 2 to 5 years of age.

6. Consider using influenza virus vaccine for children who had recurrent AOM the previous winter or are born into families with histories of recurrent AOM.

AOM = acute otitis media.

resistant *S. pneumoniae* in children who recently completed a course of antibiotics. Studies of antibiotic resistance patterns have also shown a correlation between countries and regions with low rates of antibiotic use and low rates of penicillin-resistant pneumococci.

Expert committees from the CDC and American Academy of Pediatrics (AAP) have provided recommendations to limit the increase in incidence of bacterial pathogens. The guidelines stress limiting antimicrobial agents for diseases that are likely caused by viral agents, such as colds, cough/bronchitis, nonstreptococcal pharyngitis, and OME (see Table 26-4).[18]

Increasing Accuracy of Diagnosis

Acute OM is defined as the presence of middle ear effusion with an acute sign of ear and systemic illness. Pneumatic otoscopy is the primary mode of diagnosis but is a difficult part of the physical examination of the infant or young child, even in the hands of expert pediatricians and otolaryngologists.[19] Because of the importance of accurate diagnosis, the academic physician and the practicing physician should re-examine techniques for improving otoscopic skills. Use of a teaching otoscope permits student and teacher to simultaneously perform the examination and is an effective technique for introducing students to otoscopy. Examiner skills can be increased by comparing the results of otoscopic examination with the results of tympanometry[20] and/or acoustic reflectometry.[21,22]

Decreased Antibiotic Prescribing in Infants and Children

Surveys of antibiotic use in different areas of the United States and using different databases indicate a substantial decrease in the volume of antibiotic used in pediatrics over the past 10 years. In northern Wisconsin, a community program to promote judicious antibiotic use resulted in a decline of 19% of solid antibiotic prescriptions per clinician in the intervention region and 8% in the control region.[23] In Knox County, Kentucky, antibiotic prescribing rates for children declined 19% after a community-wide campaign; a decline of 8% was identified in the control group.[24] In rural Alaska, antibiotic courses per person decreased by 31% after an educational program.[25]

McCaig and colleagues[26] compared rates of antimicrobial prescribing for children by office-based physicians during two 2-year periods, 1989–1990 and 1999–2000, using data from the National Ambulatory Medical Care Survey. The mean population-based rate of annual antimicrobial prescriptions per 1,000 children and adolescents younger than 15 years decreased by an astounding 40%. Similarly, office-based prescribing decreased by 29%. The decrease occurred in diagnoses of upper respiratory tract infection *but not* for OM or sinusitis.

The preceding trends were corroborated by a survey of antibiotic usage in children who received care from organizations of the Health Maintenance Organization (HMO) Research Network.[27] Antibiotic prescriptions decreased by approximately 20% in the 5-year period beginning in 1995 for each pediatric age category.

Chemoprophylaxis

Chemoprophylaxis using antibacterial drugs has been effective in reducing episodes of asymptomatic AOM in children with severe and recurrent disease by 40 to 90%.[28] Meta-analysis confirms the efficacy of antimicrobial prophylaxis for recurrent AOM,[29] but the absolute impact on outcomes is modest (see Chapter 13, "Clinical Efficacy of Medical Therapy"). Chemoprophylaxis uses a modified dosage of the drug administered over a prolonged period of time. Amoxicillin or sulfisoxazole have been used most frequently at half the therapeutic dose (20 mg/kg and 50 mg/kg, respectively) administered once a day. The dosage should prevent implantation of organisms on the upper respiratory mucosa that might lead to subsequent invasion of the middle ear space.

The increased incidence of antibiotic resistance raises concern that low concentrations of drug might eliminate or prevent implantation of susceptible organisms and permit colonization by resistant strains. Use of antimicrobial chemoprophylaxis may, therefore, foster development of a resistant flora. Although this is a reasonable concern, data indicating that children on chemoprophylaxis suffer more episodes of AOM caused by resistant strains than children not receiving chemoprophylaxis are lacking.

Extrapolation of data from the use of chemoprophylaxis for children with sickle cell disease may provide insight into concerns of use of chemoprophylaxis for children with recurrent AOM. Children on penicillin V prophylaxis had a lower rate of colonization with pneumococci than children not on prophylaxis. Among the children on prophylaxis who were colonized, however, the rates of resistant strains of pneumococci were higher than among those not on antibiotic prophylaxis.[29,30] These data suggest that chemoprophylaxis may diminish colonization with bacterial pathogens in the nasopharynx, but breakthrough episodes of AOM, if they occur, might be caused by an organism resistant to the prophylactic drug. The antimicrobial drug used for breakthrough episodes should include optimal activity against organisms resistant to the prophylactic agent.

Prevention

If disease is prevented, the amount of antibiotic is decreased in the child and the community, and the pressure of antibiotic selection for resistant strains is reduced. This section presents a brief overview of modes of prevention relevant to judicious antibiotic therapy of AOM. Additional background and details are presented in Chapter 17, "Vaccine Prevention".

Pneumococcal Polysaccharide Vaccines

Pneumococcal polysaccharide vaccines were effective in preventing type-specific pneumococcal AOM when a sufficient concentration of antibody was achieved consistent with previously documented levels of protection.[31] Because of the limited number of pneumococcal types to which children younger than 2 years of age produced an adequate response, the overall decrease in incidence of AOM was not significantly different in immunized and unimmunized children. Children older than 2 years of age respond to selected pneumococcal polysaccharides, with a greater number of responses in older children.

Pneumococcal Conjugate Vaccine

Conjugation of polysaccharides to various proteins alters the nature of the immune response from T-cell independent to T-cell dependent. This stimulates an active T-helper cell response even in infants as young as 2 months of age and also elicits a strong booster response on re-immunization. The currently available conjugate pneumococcal vaccine (PCV7) is a heptavalent vaccine, in which individual polysaccharides are directly conjugated to the protein carrier CRM 197, a nontoxic variant of the diphtheria toxin.

Two large clinical trials, in Northern California[32] and Finland,[33] show a 7% decrease in AOM in immunized children. In children who completed the primary series of three doses at 2, 4, and 6 months of age in Northern California, otitis visits decreased by 7.8%, antibiotic prescriptions by 5.7%, and tube placement by 24%. Microbiologic data are available from the Finnish trial because each enrolled child had an MEF aspirate when AOM occurred after completing the primary series. Vaccination decreased pneumococcal AOM from any serotype by 34% and from vaccine serotypes by 57%. Of concern was a 33% increase in AOM caused by nonvaccine serotype pneumococci and an 11% increase in episodes caused by nontypeable *H. influenzae* in vaccinated children.

Influenza Virus Vaccines

Children in day care who received the influenza virus vaccine have fewer episodes of AOM,[34,35] suggesting that vaccination be considered each fall for children with recurrent and severe AOM the previous winter. The AAP and the Advisory Committee on Immunization Practices in the summer of 2002 issued statements that encouraged annual immunization for infants 6 months to 24 months of age. The groups will likely recommend universal immunization with influenza virus vaccine, depending on availability and overcoming logistic problems in immunizing many infants during a short period after the vaccine becomes available and before the virus enters the community. An intranasal cold-adapted influenza virus vaccine in the near future may increase the use of influenza virus vaccines in children.

Surgery and Mechanical Techniques

Results of three clinical trials during the past decade demonstrated that myringotomy and tympanostomy tube insertion were effective in preventing recurrent AOM (see Chapter 14, "Clinical Efficacy of Surgical Therapy"). Casselbrant and coworkers[36] reported that amoxicillin prophylaxis and myringotomy and tympanostomy tube insertion were more effective than placebo in preventing recurrent AOM. Adenoidectomy is also an effective preventive strategy in children with middle ear infections after prior tube extrusion.[37] Children randomized to adenoidectomy had a significant reduction in the rate of AOM at the end of the second year of the trial when compared with the control group (tympanostomy tubes were inserted into ears of children in both groups if middle ear effusion was present).

Although inflation of the Eustachian tube–middle ear system, using Politzer's method or Valsalva's maneuver, has been advocated to promote middle ear drainage for more than a century, there are no data demonstrating consistent clinical success using these techniques.

Parent Education

Parents influence decisions by primary-care physicians to use antimicrobial agents, often requesting a specific antibiotic. To respond to the need for parents to understand concerns about inappropriate use of antimicrobial drugs, parent education programs are being considered by the various professional groups. Informative brochures have been prepared by the CDC/AAP and the Alliance for the Prudent Use of Antibiotics (P.O. Box 1372, Boston, MA 02117-13723).

REFERENCES

1. Dubos R. Pasteur in his time. In: McKeen JE, editor. The Pasteur fermentation centennial, 1857–1957. New York (NY): Charles Pfizer; 1958. p. 193.
2. De Neeling AJ, Van Leeuwen WJ, Van Klingeren B, et al. Epidemiology of resistance of *Streptococcus pneumoniae* in The Netherlands. Abstracts of the 36th Interscience Conference on Antimicrobial Agents and Chemotherapy; 1996 Sept; New Orleans, LA. Abstract No. C57. p. 44.
3. Committee on Infectious Diseases, American Academy of Pediatrics. Therapy for children with invasive pneumococcal infections. Pediatrics 1997;99:289–99.
4. Zenni MK, Cheatham SH, Thompson JM, et al. *Streptococcus pneumoniae* colonization in the young child: association with otitis media and resistance to penicillin. J Pediatr 1995;127:533–7.
5. Ferraro MJ, Brown S, Harding I. Prevalence of fluoroquinolone resistance amongst *Streptococcus pneumoniae* isolated in the United States during the winter of 2000–2001. Abstract C2-650. Program and abstracts of the 42nd Interscience Conference on Antimicrobial Agents and Chemotherapy; 2002 September 27–30; San Diego, CA. Abstract C2-650.
6. Arnold KE, Leggiadro RJ, Breiman RF, et al. Risk factors for carriage of drug-resistant *Streptococcus pneumoniae* among children in Memphis, Tennessee. J Pediatr 1996; 128:757–64.
7. Friedland IR, McCracken GH. Management of infections caused by antibiotic-resistant *Streptococcus pneumoniae*. N Engl J Med 1994;331:377–82.
8. Doern GV, Jorgensen JH, Thornsberry C, et al. National collaborative study of the prevalence of antimicrobial resistance among clinical isolates of *Haemophilus influenzae*. Antimicrob Agents Chemother 1988;32:180–5.
9. Bluestone CD, Stephenson JS, Martin LM. Ten-year review of otitis media pathogens. Pediatr Infect Dis J 1992;11:S5–S11.
10. Wittler RR, Yamada SM, Bass JW, et al. Penicillin tolerance and erythromycin resistance of group A beta-hemolytic streptococci in Hawaii and the Philippines. Am J Dis Child 1990;144:587–9.
11. Craig WA, Andes D. Pharmacokinetics and pharmacodynamics of antibiotics in otitis media. Pediatr Infect Dis J 1996;15:255–9.
12. Gudnason T, Gudbrandsson F, Barsante F, Kristinason KG. Penetration of ceftriaxone into the middle-ear fluid of children. Pediatr Infect Dis J 1998;17:258–60.
13. Seikel K, Shelton S, McCracken GH. Middle-ear fluid concentrations of amoxicillin after large dosages in children with acute otitis media. Pediatr Infect Dis J 1997; 16:710–1.
14. Howie VM, Ploussard JH. The "in-vivo sensitivity test": bacteriology of middle-ear exudate during antimicrobial therapy in otitis media. Pediatrics 1969;44:940–4.
15. Dagan R, McCracken GH Jr. Flaws in design and conduct of clinical trials in acute otitis media. Pediatr Infect Dis J 2002;21:894–902.
16. Marchant CD, Carlin SA, Johnson CE, et al. Measuring the comparative efficacy of antibacterial agents for acute otitis media: the "Pollyanna phenomenon." J Pediatr 1992;120:72–7.
17. Dowell SF, Butler JC, Giebink SE, et al. Acute otitis media: management and surveillance in an era of pneumococcal resistance—a report from the Drug-resistant *Streptococcus pneumoniae* Therapeutic Working Group. Pediatr Infect Dis J 1999;18:1–9.
18. Dowell SF. Principles of judicious use of antimicrobial agents for pediatric upper respiratory tract infections. Pediatrics 1998;101 Suppl:163–84.
19. Pelton SI. Otoscopy for the diagnosis of otitis media. Pediatr Infect Dis J 1998;17:540–3.
20. Brookhouser PE. Use of tympanometry in office practice for diagnosis of otitis media. Pediatr Infect Dis J 1998;17:544–51.
21. Kimball S. Acoustic reflectometry: spectral gradient analysis for improved detection of middle-ear effusion in children. Pediatr Infect Dis J 1998;17:552–5.
22. Barnett ED, Klein JO, Hawkins KA, et al. Comparison of spectral gradient acoustic reflectometry and other diagnostic techniques for detection of middle-ear effusion in children with middle-ear disease. Pediatr Infect Dis J 1998;17:556–9.
23. Belonga EA, Sullivan BJ, Chyou P-H et al. A community intervention trial to promote judicious antibiotic use and reduce penicillin-resistant *Streptococcus pneumoniae* carriage in children. Pediatrics 2001;108:575–83.
24. Perz JF, Craig AS, Coffey CS, et al. Changes in antibiotic prescribing for children after a community-wide campaign. JAMA 2002;287:3103–9.

25. Hennessy TW, Petersen KM, Bruden D, et al. Changes in antibiotic-prescribing practices and carriage of penicillin-resistant *Streptococcus pneumoniae*: a controlled intervention trial in rural Alaska. Clin Infect Dis 2002;34:1543–50.

26. McCaig LF, Besser RE, Hughes JM. Trends in antimicrobial prescribing rates for children and adolescents. JAMA 2002;287:3096–102.

27. Finkelstein J, Stille C, Nordin J, et al. Decreasing antibiotic use in United States children: 1995–2000. Pediatr Res 2002;51:213A.

28. Klein JO. Preventing recurrent otitis: what role for antibiotics? Contemp Pediatr 1994;11:44–60.

29. Williams RL, Chalmers TC, Stange KC, et al. Use of antibiotics in preventing recurrent acute otitis media and in treating otitis media with effusion. JAMA 1993;270:1344–51.

30. Steele RW, Warrier R, Unkel PJ, et al. Colonization with antibiotic resistant *Streptococcus pneumoniae* in children with sickle cell disease. J Pediatr 1996;128:531–5.

31. Teele DW, Klein JO, Bratton LW, et al. Use of pneumococcal vaccine for prevention of recurrent acute otitis media in infants in Boston. Rev Infect Dis 1981;3:S113–8.

32. Fireman B, Black SB, Shinefield HR, et al. Impact of the pneumococcal conjugate vaccine on otitis media. Pediatr Infect Dis J 2002;22:1–7.

33. Eskola J, Kilpi T, Palmu A, et al. Efficacy of a pneumococcal conjugate vaccine against acute otitis media. N Engl J Med 2001;344:403–9.

34. Heikkinen T, Ruuskanen O, Waris M et al. Influenza vaccination in the prevention of acute otitis media in children. Am J Dis Child 1991;145:445–8.

35. Clements DA, Langdon L, Bland C, Walter E. Influenza A vaccine decreases the incidence of otitis media in 6- to 30-month-old children in day care. Arch Pediatr Adolesc Med 1995;149:1113–7.

36. Casselbrant ML, Kaleida PH, Rockette HE, et al. Efficacy of antimicrobial prophylaxis and of tympanostomy tube insertion for prevention of recurrent acute otitis media: results of a randomized clinical trial. Pediatr Infect Dis J 1992;11:278–86.

37. Paradise JL, Bluestone CD, Rogers KD, et al. Efficacy of adenoidectomy for recurrent otitis media in children previously treated with tympanostomy-tube placement: results of parallel randomized and nonrandomized trials. JAMA 1990;263:2066–73.

CHAPTER 27

Judicious Use of Systemic Antimicrobials

Richard E. Besser, MD

There are really no "safe" biologically active drugs. There are only "safe" physicians
Harold A. Kaminetzky

I find the medicine worse than the malady.
John Fletcher[1]

OBJECTIVES

On completing this chapter, the reader will be able to
1. Understand the relationship between antibiotic use and antibiotic resistance.
2. Describe the contribution of antibiotic prescriptions for otitis media (OM) to overall antibiotic use in children.
3. Apply principles of appropriate antibiotic use to clinical encounters.
4. Describe strategies for promoting appropriate antibiotic use for OM in the community.

ANTIBIOTIC RESISTANCE

During the 1990s, penicillin resistance among invasive isolates of *Streptococcus pneumoniae* increased dramatically from 8% in 1992 to 27% in 2000 (Figure 27-1).[2,3] Even higher rates of resistance have been reported for noninvasive isolates.[4] While resistance is often discussed in terms of penicillin, increasing proportions of pneumococci are resistant to all antibiotic classes except vancomycin.[5]

Pneumococcal resistance has relevance for treating acute otitis media (AOM). Three bacteria account for most AOM in the United States: *S. pneumoniae* (40–50%); nontypeable *Haemophilus influenzae* (20–30%); and *Moraxella catarrhalis* (10–15%).[6,7] Resistance has also been increasing for nontypeable *H. influenzae* and *M. catarrhalis* because of beta-lactamase produced by 35 to 90% of current isolates.[7] AOM caused by pneumococci is least likely to resolve without antibiotics.[8,9] Treating resistant pneumococcal infections requires higher doses of amoxicillin, and, at times, more expensive broader-spectrum antibiotics are needed.[7]

RISK FACTORS FOR ANTIBIOTIC RESISTANCE

Among persons with pneumococcal infections, recent antibiotic use is the leading risk factor for having a resistant infection. This is true for carriage of pneumococci in the nasopharynx as well as invasive disease.[10] Nasopharyngeal carriage can be interpreted as a proxy for organisms causing AOM because the pathophysiology of infection usually involves organisms ascending through the Eustachian tube.

Simplistically, the relationship between antibiotic use and resistance can be viewed as a case of selective pressure. If resistant strains are present in the community, any antibiotic use, whether appropriate or inappropriate, will favor their proliferation at the expense of susceptible strains.[11] The more antibiotics are used, the greater will be the selective pressure and the more likely the strains circulating within a community will be resistant.

Given the relationship between antibiotic use and resistance, it is important that antibiotics be reserved for conditions for which patients are likely to benefit. Several articles in the 1990s highlighted discordance between antibiotic prescribing and likely patient benefit.[12–14] Analysis of data from the 1992 National Ambulatory Care Survey, a population-based survey of prescribing in physicians' offices in the United States, found that 31% of antibiotic prescriptions were for the common cold and acute bronchitis, conditions that are caused primarily by viruses against which antibiotics are not effective. Antibiotics were prescribed most often for OM, with 27 million prescriptions in 1992.[12] What proportion of antibiotics prescribed for OM were appropriate is unknown. However, the sheer volume of prescribing makes it an attractive target for efforts to reduce inappropriate prescribing.

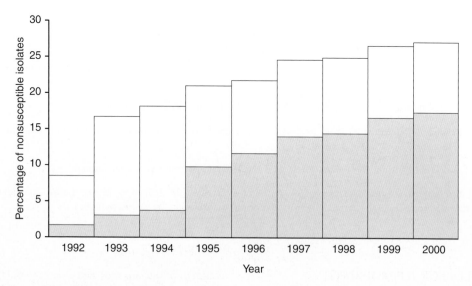

Figure 27-1 Proportion of pneumococcal isolates resistant to penicillin, United States, 1992–2000, as reported to the sentinel surveillance (1992–1994) and the Active Bacterial Core Surveillance (1995–2000). The dark portion of each bar indicates high-level resistance; the white portion indicates intermediate-level resistance.

GET SMART: KNOW WHEN ANTIBIOTICS WORK

In 1994, Centers for Disease Control and Prevention (CDC) convened the Drug Resistant *Streptococcus Pneumoniae* Working Group to develop a plan to combat pneumococcal resistance.[15] This group consisted of public health practitioners, health care providers, and clinical laboratorians representing state and federal agencies and various professional organizations, all of whom recognized the role played by inappropriate antibiotic prescribing in the promotion of antimicrobial resistance. As part of their plan, they called for promoting judicious use of antimicrobials. Since that time, the CDC has launched a National Campaign for Appropriate Antibiotic Use in the Community.[16] In 2002, the campaign took on a new name, "Get Smart: Know When Antibiotics Work."

The goal of the Get Smart campaign is to decrease inappropriate antimicrobial use and thereby slow the rise in bacterial resistance. Appropriate antibiotic use is defined as

- prescribing antibiotics only when treatment is likely to benefit the patient;
- selecting agents that target likely pathogens; and
- using these agents at the appropriate dose and for the correct duration.

The campaign is targeting the five respiratory conditions that, in 1992, accounted for more than 75% of all office-based prescribing: OM, sinusitis, pharyngitis, bronchitis, and the common cold.[12] There are four major arms of the campaign:

1. Developing materials to promote appropriate use that can be used by programs around the country
2. Forming partnerships with other groups committed to promoting appropriate use, thereby combining resources and maximizing impact
3. Developing, implementing, and evaluating interventions
4. Serving as a resource to other groups with similar missions

Partnerships are an essential component of the campaign and partners come from many different areas. Traditional CDC partners include state and local health departments, professional medical societies, and the academic community, but the CDC has reached beyond these groups to include managed-care organizations and health care insurers, pharmacy benefit companies, large health care purchasers, and pharmaceutical manufacturers. Each partner has a role to play and a vested interest in promoting appropriate antibiotic use in the community.

To assist coalitions that are promoting appropriate antibiotic use, the CDC provides extensive resources. The campaign Web site (<http://www.cdc.gov/drugresistance/community>) contains background on the issue of antibiotic prescribing and its relationship to antimicrobial resistance, a quiz for the public on indications for antibiotic use, technical resources for providers, educational materials for the public, and links to groups around the country that are working on this topic. In addition, the CDC hosts two national meetings each year, during which training is provided, ideas are shared among programs, and scientific updates are given.

Table 27-1 Principles of Appropriate Antibiotic Use for Acute Otitis Media in Children

1. Episodes of otitis media should be classified as acute otitis media (AOM) or otitis media with effusion (OME).

2. Antimicrobials are indicated for treating AOM; however, diagnosis requires documented middle ear effusion and signs or symptoms of acute local or systemic illness.

3. Uncomplicated AOM may be treated with a 5- to 7-day course of antimicrobials in certain patients.

4. Antimicrobials are not indicated for initial treatment of OME; treatment may be indicated if effusions persist for 3 months or longer.

5. Persistent middle ear effusion after therapy for AOM is expected and does not require retreatment.

6. Antimicrobial prophylaxis should be reserved for control of recurrent AOM, defined by three or more distinct and well-documented episodes in the past 6 months or four or more episodes in the past 12 months.

PRINCIPLES FOR APPROPRIATE ANTIBIOTIC USE IN CHILDREN WITH OTITIS MEDIA

In 1998, the CDC and the American Academy of Pediatrics (AAP) published principles for judicious antibiotic use in children with OM (Table 27-1).[17] One of the key contributions was a focus on distinguishing between AOM, for which antibiotics were recommended, and otitis media with effusion (OME), for which antibiotics were not recommended routinely. In assigning diagnoses, clinicians rarely distinguish between AOM and OME. Given that anti-biotics are not recommended routinely for the latter, this distinction is critical. The principles clarify the diagnostic criteria for AOM, requiring both middle ear effusion, as demonstrated by pneumatic otoscopy, tympanometry, or acoustic reflectometry, and signs of an acute infection referable to the ear.

There are no reliable studies looking at what proportion of OM is diagnosed correctly, what proportion of OM represents AOM versus OME, and what proportion of children who truly have AOM are prescribed an appropriate, targeted antimicrobial agent. These studies would be next to impossible to perform for many reasons: (1) there is no easily applied gold standard for diagnosing AOM; (2) administrative coding rarely differentiates between the two conditions; and (3) the act of observing a physician examining a child would likely change the evaluation itself. Nonetheless, the CDC/AAP principles stress distinguishing AOM and OME.[17]

The CDC/AAP principles became the scientific basis for developing educational materials. These include a viral prescription pad used by clinicians to indicate symptomatic relief for patients not receiving an antibiotic (Figure 27-2); information sheets teaching the difference between AOM and OME (Figure 27-3); instructional, or "detailing" sheets for small group edu-

cation of physicians modeled after materials used by the pharmaceutical industry (Figure 27-4); and posters for display in waiting rooms.

INTERVENTIONS PROMOTING APPROPRIATE ANTIBIOTIC USE FOR RESPIRATORY TRACT INFECTIONS

The principles for appropriate prescribing have been incorporated into many broad-based programs to promote appropriate antibiotic use for respiratory infections in the community. Analyses of these projects have not separated out reductions in prescribing for otitis from other targeted infections. However, it is worthwhile to understand the components of projects that have successfully reduced antibiotic prescribing for respiratory tract infections in general.

Since 1998, five broad-based, controlled trials promoting appropriate antibiotic use for outpatient respiratory tract infections in a variety of settings in the United States have been published (Table 27-2).[18–22] Each trial has recognized the important role played by providers and patients in promoting the overprescription of antibiotics and the necessity of addressing both groups. Although it is not possible to discern from these interventions what components are essential to include if one is to be successful, the results are clear: it is possible to reduce inappropriate prescribing for respiratory tract infections. The impact in terms of reduced antibiotic prescribing has ranged from 5 to 32% over the control setting. The impact has varied by patient age group, conditions targeted, and practice setting.

None of the trials that have reported success at improving prescribing has attempted to change prescribing for an entire state. Nevertheless, there are some characteristics of these successful smaller scale trials that

Name:_____ **Date:**____/____/____

Diagnosis: o Cold or Flu   o Middle ear fluid (Otitis Media with Effusion, OME)
              o Cough   o Viral sore throat
              o Other: _____

R℞

You have been diagnosed as having an illness caused by a virus. **Antibiotic treatment does not cure viral infections.** If given when not needed, antibiotics can be harmful. The treatments prescribed below will help you feel better while your body's own defenses are defeating the virus.

General instructions:
o Increase fluids.
o Use cool mist vaporizer or saline nasal spray to relieve congestion.
o Soothe throat with ice chips, or sore throat spray; lozenges for older children and adults.

Specific medicines:
o Fever or aches:
o Ear pain:

o _____:_____

o _____:_____

Use medicines as directed by your doctor or the package instructions. Stop the medication when the symptoms get better.

Follow up:
o If not improved in ____ days, if new symptoms occur, or if you have other concerns, please call or return to the office for a recheck.

o Other:_____

_____

Signed:_____

CDC
Centers for Disease
Control and Prevention

U.S. GPO: 2000-533-020/26013

Figure 27-2 Viral illness prescription pads.

A Guide for Parents

Fluid in the Middle Ear

(Otitis Media with Effusion)

Questions and Answers

A doctor said your child has fluid in the middle ear, also called otitis (oh-TIE-tus) media with effusion (uh-FEW-zhun) (OME). Fluid usually does not bother children, and it almost always goes away on its own. This does not have to be treated with antibiotics, unless it lasts for a few months. Here are some facts about OME and ear infections.

What are the main kinds of ear infections?
♦ Swimmer's ear (otitis externa) is an infection of the ear canal that can be painful and is treated with eardrops.
♦ A middle ear infection, which a doctor might call "acute otitis media" (AOM) may cause ear pain, fever, or an inflamed eardrum, and is often treated with oral antibiotics.

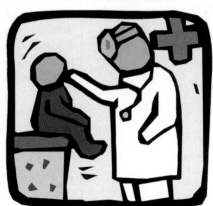

What causes OME?
Fluid may build up in the middle ear for two reasons. First, when a child has a cold, the middle ear makes fluid just as the nose does – it just doesn't run out as easily from the middle ear. Second, after a middle ear infection, fluid may take a month or longer to go away.

Are antibiotics ever needed for OME?
Sometimes antibiotics may be needed if the fluid is still present after a few months and is causing decreased hearing in both ears. For this reason, your child will need an ear check in a few months. If there is still fluid in the middle ear, your child may need a hearing test.

What should I do?
♦ The best treatment is to wait and watch your child. Since fluid in the middle ear rarely bothers children, it is best to let it go away on its own. Right now, your child does not need antibiotics.

♦ On your next routine visit, the doctor will be able to tell you if the fluid has gone away.
-OR-
♦ You may need to schedule a visit to see the doctor again in a few months to be sure the fluid is gone.

Why not try antibiotics now?
Taking antibiotics when they are not needed can be harmful. Each time someone takes antibiotics, they are more likely to carry resistant germs in their noses and throats. These resistant germs cannot be killed by common antibiotics. Your child may need more costly antibiotics or antibiotics given by needle, or may even need to be in the hospital to get antibiotics. Since OME will almost always get better on its own, it is better to wait and take antibiotics only when they are needed.

Figure 27-3 Otitis media with effusion fact sheet—fluid in the middle ear.

CAREFUL ANTIBIOTIC USE

Otitis media with effusion does not require antibiotic treatment

OTITIS MEDIA

Differentiating Acute Otitis Media (AOM) from Otitis Media with Effusion (OME):
A tool for promoting appropriate antibiotic use.[1]

Always use pneumatic otoscopy or tympanometry to confirm middle ear effusion → **No effusion** Not OME or AOM

Yes effusion present

Signs or symptoms of AOM-including ear pain, fever, and bulging yellow or red TM

Yes ← → **No**

AOM	**OME**
Presence of effusion (always use pneumatic otoscopy or tympanometry) **with** signs or symptoms of acute infection (ear pain, fever, or bulging yellow or red TM).	Presence of effusion (including immobility of the tympanic membrane) **without** signs or symptoms of acute infection. Nonspecific signs and symptoms (rhinitis, cough, diarrhea) are often present.
↓	↓
Treatment *Choose narrow spectrum drugs first.* Amoxicillin, especially at high doses (80-90 mg/kg/day)[5], remains highly effective and is recommended as the first-line antibiotic by most experts.[2, 3, 4]	**Treatment** *Antibiotics are not required for initial treatment.*[5] Meta-analysis of all known studies showed only marginal short term benefit, and no long term benefit (>1 month) of antibiotic treatment.[6]

Only consider antibiotic prophalaxis for recurrent AOM as defined by ≥ 3 distinct, well documented episodes in 6 months (or ≥ 4 in 12 months).

Residual effusion after AOM normally persists for up to 6 weeks - no evidence of benefit from treatment in these cases.

Share this algorithm with parents. Explain when the risks of using antibiotics outweigh the benefits.

Avoiding unnecessary treatment of OME would save up to 6 - 8 million courses of antibiotics each year.[5]

References

1. Dowell SF, Marcy SM, Phillips WR, Gerber MA, Schwartz B. Principles of judicious use of antimicrobial agents for pediatric upper respiratory tract infections. Pediatrics 1998;101:165-171.
2. McCracken GH. Considerations in selecting an antibiotic for treatment of acute otitis media. Pediatr Infect Dis J. 1994;13:1054-1057.
3. Barnett ED, Klein JO. The problem of resistant bacteria for the management of acute otitis media. Ped Clin N America 1995;42:509-17.
4. Dowell SF, Butler JC, Giebink GS. Acute otitis media: management and surveillance in an era of pnemococcal resistance-a report from Drug-resistance *Streptococcus pneumoniae* Therapeutic Working Group. Pediatr Infect Dis J 1999;18:1-9.
5. Stool SE, Berg AO, Berman S, et al. Otitis media with effusion in young children. Clinical practice guideline. AHCPR Publication no 94-0622 1994.
6. Williams RL, Chalmers TC, Stange KC, Chalmers FT, Bowlin SJ. Use of antibiotics in preventing recurrent acute otitis media and in treating otitis media with effusion. A meta-analytic attempt to resolve the brouhaha. JAMA 1993;270:1344-51.

Figure 27-4 One-on-one educational sheets—otitis media.

Table 27-2 Controlled Interventions Promoting Appropriate Antibiotic Use for Respiratory Tract Infections, United States, 1997–99

Author (Years)	Location; Setting	Patient Component	Provider Component	Scope	Prescription Rate Decline	
					Intervention	Control
Gonzalez[18] (1997–98)	Denver; HMO	Brochures and informational magnets mailed to homes; letter from clinic director	Posters for examination rooms, information sheets for patients; site-specific prescribing rate feedback; small group presentations; practice tips for withholding antibiotics*	Adult; bronchitis only	35%*	3%
Finkelstein[19] (1997–98)	Boston/ Seattle; HMO	Brochures mailed to homes; waiting room materials	Small group office presentations; prescribing profiling	5 respiratory conditions	18.6% (age 3–35 mo) 15% (age 36–72 mo)	11.5% (age 3–35 mo) 9.8% (age 36–72 mo)
Perz[20] (1997–98)	Tennessee; metropolitan area	Brochures to parents of newborns, children in day care, and K–3rd grade; pamphlets to persons receiving flu vaccine; pamphlets through pharmacies; public service announcements	Lectures to targeted providers in multiple settings (primary care clinics, grand rounds, hospital staff meetings); guideline distribution; articles in county health journal; distribution of patient education materials	5 respiratory conditions	19%	8%
Belongia[21] (1998)	Wisconsin; rural communities	Presentations to community groups; brochures distributed through clinics, pharmacies, schools, childcare facilities	Grand rounds presentations; practice-based small group presentations; guideline distribution; CDC fact sheets, patient education materials, viral prescription pad	5 respiratory conditions	19.6%	1%
Hennessy[22] (1999)	Alaska; multiple rural villages	Presentations at village-wide meetings; health newsletters mailed to homes; high school education; health fairs	Targeted community health aides; otitis media workshops for aides and physicians; follow-up visits to clinics	5 respiratory conditions	31%	9.5%

CDC = Centers for Disease Control and Prevention; HMO = Health maintenance organization.

*Provider component for full intervention practices only.

are being applied around the country. Table 27-3[23–28] summarizes the lessons learned from these trials; these should serve as a good starting point for other groups that wish to promote appropriate prescribing.

Control groups are very important in these studies. Nationally, antibiotic prescribing for children has been declining.[29] Between 1989 and 1990 and 1999 and 2000, the average population-based annual rate of antimi-crobial prescriptions per 1,000 children younger than 15 years decreased by 40%. Control groups are necessary to avoid crediting an intervention with a decline that is caused simply by secular trends. In addition, many states are undertaking activities to promote appropriate antibiotic use (Figure 27-5). Failure to control for these activities will also overestimate the impact of a more local intervention. Whereas control groups are needed

Table 27-3 Strategies Used by Successful Appropriate Use Campaigns

Strategy/Characteristic	Rationale
Form a state-appropriate antibiotic use coalition consisting of a large variety of stakeholders. Hire a dedicated coordinator.	The coalition partners can share the work and reach different audiences. The in-kind support provided by coalition members will expand the reach of the campaign.
Focus major attention on curbing antibiotic use for respiratory ailments and for promoting selection of targeted agents when antibiotics are indicated.	Respiratory infections account for the largest proportion of antibiotic overuse.[23] While overall prescribing is declining, a shift is occurring to selection of broad-spectrum agents.[24]
Target health care providers and consumers.	Antibiotic overuse is promoted by patients (demand) and providers (limited time, overestimating demand, diagnostic uncertainty, communication skills deficits).[16]
Deliver messages over a sustained period of time using multiple modalities.	Reinforcement is important.[25]
Identify and change policies and practices that fuel inappropriate antibiotic prescribing.	Day care, school, and work policies requiring antibiotics are often cited by parents and patients as reasons for requesting antibiotics.[26]
Evaluate what you do so you can show you are using resources effectively and are on track for changing behavior.	A well-done evaluation can help determine how to allocate funds efficiently and can be used to justify continued funding of successful activities.[27,28]

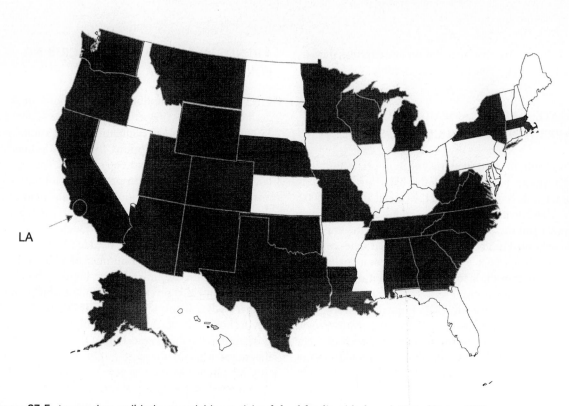

Figure 27-5 Appropriate antibiotic use activities receiving federal funding (*dark gray*), United States, 2002.

Table 27-4 Examples of Partners for Appropriate Use Activities*

Partner Type	Partner	State	Program Name
Health insurer organizations	Council for Affordable Quality Healthcare	GA	Georgia United Against Antibiotic Resistant Diseases (Guard)
Health care purchasers	Daimler Chrysler Corporation; Ford Motor Company; General Motors Corporation	MI	Michigan Antibiotic Resistance Reduction Network (MARR)
Professional societies	American Academy of Pediatrics, District IX; California Academy of Family Physicians; California Medical Association (CMA); Association of California Nurse Leaders; California School Nurses Organization; California Hispanic Healthcare Association; California Pharmacists Association; California Primary Care Association	CA	Alliance Working for Antibiotic Resistance Education (AWARE)
Parent-teacher associations	South Carolina Parent-Teacher Association	SC	South Carolina Careful Antibiotic Use (SC Cause)
Pharmacists	Oregon State Pharmacists Association	OR	Oregon's Campaign to Promote Judicious Use of Antibiotics
Medical and public health schools	State University of New York, School of Public Health and Albany Medical College	NY	Wise Antibiotics Information Team (WAIT)

*A complete listing is available at (<http://www.cdc.gov/drugresistance/community/partners.htm>).

to help discern what interventions are effective, they are unnecessary outside the research setting.

STATE-BASED CAMPAIGNS TO PROMOTE APPROPRIATE ANTIBIOTIC USE

The results of controlled trials of appropriate antibiotic prescribing have provided the basis for developing larger scale activities around the United States. In 2002, the CDC divided $2.8 million among 26 states to help implement these programs. To maximize the impact of these limited funds, we have encouraged states to hire a coordinator whose main job is to form a coalition of groups within the state with an interest in improving antibiotic prescribing.

A complete list of CDC-funded projects, with descriptions of activities, can be found at <http://www.cdc.gov/drugresistance/community/partners.htm>. The list of partners varies by state. Table 27-4 provides examples of the types of partners with whom states are working. In addition to the partners listed here, there has been active participation by some pharmaceutical companies who view appropriate antibiotic use as a means of prolonging the life of their products and as good corporate citizenship.

TRENDS IN ANTIBIOTIC PRESCRIBING FOR OTITIS MEDIA

The total number of antibiotic prescriptions for AOM declined during the 1990s.[29] In the years 1989–1990 and 1999–2000, the average population-based annual rate of antimicrobial prescriptions for AOM declined by 47%, from 347 to 184 per 1,000 children. This was, by far, the largest reduction in prescribing for any diagnostic category. However, looking at what went on in the physician's office itself, there was no change. Roughly 80% of children diagnosed with OM received an antibiotic during the entire decade.

The decline in the total number of visits coded as OM accounts for the entire decline in prescribing. This could be caused by several factors, all of which require further study: patients with milder ear infections may be staying home; physicians may be applying stricter diagnostic criteria to the diagnosis of AOM, coding as other diagnoses what in the past might have been coded as OM; physicians may be following guidelines that recommend delaying or abolishing follow-up "ear check" visits after an episode of AOM; or perhaps the overall incidence of AOM is declining.[29]

The lack of decline in visit-based prescribing is not surprising. Antibiotics are currently recommended for the initial management of AOM in the United States.[7,17] That this rate is not closer to 100% is probably a reflection of the fact that the coding for OM contains cases of OME for which antibiotics are not routinely indicated. The nearly universal prescription of antibiotics for AOM in the United States may be on the verge of changing. Such a change could have a major impact on overall antibiotic use for children.

THE OBSERVATION OPTION FOR ACUTE OTITIS MEDIA

Improved prescribing for colds, the flu, and bronchitis could be considered the low-lying fruit for appropriate antibiotic use campaigns. There is fairly widespread agreement within the medical community that viruses primarily cause these conditions and that antibiotics have little role in their treatment. However, it is clear from a look at overall antibiotic prescribing for children that OM accounts for the lion's share (Figure 27-6).

Recently, the Agency for Healthcare Research and Quality (AHRQ) convened a meeting to assess outstanding issues in promoting appropriate antibiotic use for AOM.[30] In addition to recognizing the need to improve diagnosis, the group acknowledged that for many children, the benefit of antibiotic therapy for confirmed infections was quite small. A formal assessment of the role of antibiotics for AOM, commissioned by AHRQ, was recently published.[31] Within 24 hours, two-thirds of all children with AOM recover, whether treated with antibiotics or placebo.[32]

The meeting addressed the feasibility of implementing an observation or "watchful waiting" approach to selected patients with AOM. The observation option refers to deferring antibiotic treatment of selected children with uncomplicated AOM for up to 72 hours, during which time management is limited to analgesics and symptomatic relief (see Chapter 18, "Clinical Pathway for Acute Otitis Media").[33] Adopting this approach could potentially reduce antibiotic use in children by 25% (see Figure 27-6). Endorsement of this approach is being considered by the AAP, the American Academy of Family Physicians, and the CDC.

In 1997, the New York State Department of Health formed the New York Region Otitis Project to look at the evidence supporting an observation option. This stemmed from recognition that OM accounted for the largest share of antibiotic prescribing and that the approach to AOM varied dramatically by country. In the Netherlands, for example, where watchful waiting is applied, only 31% of children with AOM receive an antibiotic (see Chapter 20, "International Perspective on Management").[34] The committee endorsed the obser-

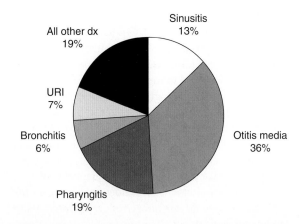

Figure 27-6 Antibiotic prescribing to children < 15 years old in doctors' offices, by condition, United States, 1999–2000 average. Total prescriptions = 29 million.

vation option and developed a toolkit for physicians who wished to implement this strategy in their practices.[33,35] It will be important to evaluate the impact of this approach on antibiotic use, patient satisfaction, and medical complications, such as mastoiditis.[34]

IMPROVING THE DIAGNOSIS OF ACUTE OTITIS MEDIA

There is no debate regarding the importance of applying firm criteria to diagnosing AOM. Clearly, there is room for improved training in diagnosis.

Two studies assessed the training and proficiency of pediatric residents in performing middle ear examinations.[36,37] Forty percent of residency programs provided no formal training related to diagnosing or treating OM. Of those that provided some training, most consisted of lectures by primary-care physicians. Only 15% provided premyringotomy otoscopic examinations with an otolaryngologist, one method of providing extensive exposure to diseased ears in a controlled setting.[38] Not surprisingly, a subsequent study by the same investigators found a very poor correlation between the findings of resident otoscopic examinations and those of tympanometry or diagnostic examinations by an otolaryngologist.[36]

The Accreditation Council for Graduate Medical Education (ACGME) oversees residency training in the United States. Given the limited time for postgraduate medical education, many programs determine what will be included in their curricula on the basis of what is required by the ACGME. There is no mention of otoscopy or pneumatic otoscopy in the requirements for training in Family Medicine or Pediatrics of the ACGME or the Educational Guidelines for Training in General Pediatrics of the Ambulatory Pediatric Association, the leading professional organization for pediatricians involved in medical education.[39–41]

Pediatric residency programs, however, are required to document and certify their residents' proficiency at such rarely performed procedures as chest tube and intra-osseous line placement. An important step in improving how primary-care physicians diagnose ear infections would be to have proficiency in the diagnosis of OM included as a requirement for residency training by the ACGME. This would encourage residency programs to develop curricula designed to provide hands-on, super-vised training in pneumatic otoscopy.

The CDC has developed a curriculum for teaching medical students about antimicrobial resistance and appropriate antibiotic prescribing.[42] This curriculum contains three modules: lectures, small group exercises, and Web-based case studies. In 2002–2003, the curricu-lum was pilot tested in six medical schools across the country to determine whether student knowledge had improved and whether the material was acceptable to teachers and administrators. The curriculum will now be revised, updated, distributed, and promoted for inclusion in all medical schools in the United States. It will then form the basis for a curriculum for primary-care residents and for physicians in practice.

In addition to curricula that improve knowledge, students and residents need training that will improve their ability to communicate with patients. Many stud-ies have demonstrated that physicians overestimate patient demand for antibiotics and that this overesti-mation leads to overprescribing.[43,44] To counter this misperception, efforts must be undertaken to improve physician-patient communication.

CONCLUSION

Antibiotic resistance has been rising during the past decade, driven, in large part, by antibiotic prescribing. While it is clear that antibiotic prescribing has begun to decline, there is room for further improvement in gen-eral and for OM in particular. Individual practitioners should make sure they are familiar with the diagnostic criteria for AOM and OME. Persons lacking skills in pneumatic otoscopy should acquire them by attending continuing medical education workshops. When decid-ing on the management of AOM for individual patients, clinicians should consider both the risks and the bene-fits of antibiotic therapy.

Nationwide, coalitions have formed and campaigns have begun with a focus on antibiotic use for respiratory infections. New strategies are being directed at AOM, including interventions to improve diagnosis and to implement the observation option. These two approaches could dramatically reduce the number of antibiotics pre-scribed to children. While it may be too late to regain the effectiveness of those antimicrobial agents for which resistance is already high, appropriate use activities may be able to safeguard and prolong the life of new agents as they are introduced.

REFERENCES

1. The Columbia world of quotations (last update: 1996). Columbia University Press, 1996. Available at: www.bartleby.com (accessed Oct 7, 2002).
2. Centers for Disease Control and Prevention. Active bacterial core surveillance (ABCs) report. Emerging Infec-tions Program network, Streptococcus pneumoniae 2000. Available at: www.cdc.gov/abcs (accessed Aug 27, 2002).
3. Breiman R, Butler J, Tenover F, et al. Emergence of drug-resistant pneumococcal infections in the United States. JAMA 1994;271:1831–5.
4. Jacobs MR, Bajaksouzian S, Zilles A, et al. Susceptibi-lities of Streptococcus pneumoniae and Haemophilus influenzae to 10 oral antimicrobial agents based on pharmacodynamic parameters: 1997 U.S. surveillance study. Antimicrob Agents Chemother 1999;43:1901–8.
5. Whitney CG, Farley MM, Hadler J, et al. Increasing prevalence of multidrug-resistant Streptococcus pneu-moniae in the United States. N Engl J Med 2000;343:1917–24.
6. Bluestone C, Klein J. Otitis media in infants and children. Philadelphia (PA): WB Saunders; 1995.
7. Dowell SF, Butler JC, Giebink GS, et al. Acute otitis media: management and surveillance in an era of pneu-mococcal resistance—a report from the Drug-Resistant Streptococcus pneumoniae Therapeutic Working Group. Pediatr Infect Dis J 1999;18:1–9.
8. Jacobs MR, Dagan R, Appelbaum PC, Burch DJ. Preva-lence of antimicrobial-resistant pathogens in middle ear fluid: multinational study of 917 children with acute otitis media. Antimicrob Agents Chemother 1998;42:589–95.
9. Howie VM, Ploussard JH. Efficacy of fixed combination antibiotics versus separate components in otitis media. Effectiveness of erythromycin estolate, triple sulfonamide, ampicillin, erythromycin estolate-triple sulfonamide, and placebo in 280 patients with acute otitis media under two and one-half years of age. Clin Pediatr 1972;11:205–14.
10. Dowell S, Schwartz B. Resistant pneumococci: pro-tecting patients through judicious use of antibiotics. Am Fam Phys 1997;55:1647–54.
11. Lipsitch M, Samore MH. Antimicrobial use and anti-microbial resistance: a population perspective. Emerg Infect Dis 2002;8:347–54.
12. McCaig LF, Hughes JM. Trends in antimicrobial drug prescribing among office-based physicians in the United States. JAMA 1995;273:214–9.

13. Gonzales R, Steiner JF, Sande MA. Antibiotic prescribing for adults with colds, upper respiratory tract infections, and bronchitis by ambulatory care physicians. JAMA 1997;278:901–4.

14. Nyquist AC, Gonzales R, Steiner JF, Sande MA. Antibiotic prescribing for children with colds, upper respiratory tract infections, and bronchitis. JAMA 1998;279: 875–7.

15. Jernigan DB, Cetron MS, Breiman RF. Minimizing the impact of drug-resistant *Streptococcus pneumoniae* (DRSP). A strategy from the DRSP Working Group. JAMA 1996;275:206–9.

16. Emmer C, Besser R. Combating antimicrobial resistance: intervention programs to promote appropriate antibiotic use. Infect Med 2002;19:160–73.

17. Dowell SF, Marcy SM, Phillips WR, et al. Otitis media—principles of judicious use of antimicrobial agents. Pediatrics 1998;101:165–71.

18. Gonzales R, Steiner JF, Lum A, Barrett PH Jr. Decreasing antibiotic use in ambulatory practice: impact of a multidimensional intervention on the treatment of uncomplicated acute bronchitis in adults. JAMA 1999;281:1512–9.

19. Finkelstein JA, Davis RL, Dowell SF, et al. Reducing antibiotic use in children: a randomized trial in 12 practices. Pediatrics 2001;108:1–7.

20. Perz JF, Craig AS, Coffey CS, et al. Changes in antibiotic prescribing for children after a community-wide campaign. JAMA 2002;287:3103–9.

21. Belongia EA, Sullivan BJ, Chyou PH, et al. A community intervention trial to promote judicious antibiotic use and reduce penicillin-resistant *Streptococcus pneumoniae* carriage in children. Pediatrics 2001;108:575–83.

22. Hennessy TW, Petersen KM, Bruden D, et al. Changes in antibiotic-prescribing practices and carriage of penicillin-resistant *Streptococcus pneumoniae*: a controlled intervention trial in rural Alaska. Clin Infect Dis 2002;34: 1543–50.

23. Gonzales R, Malone DC, Maselli JH, Sande MA. Excessive antibiotic use for acute respiratory infections in the United States. Clin Infect Dis 2001;33:757–62.

24. McCaig LF, Besser RE, Hughes JM. Trends in antimicrobial prescribing in ambulatory care settings in the United States. Emerg Infect Dis J. [In press]

25. Trepka MJ, Belongia EA, Chyou PH, et al. The effect of a community intervention trial on parental knowledge and awareness of antibiotic resistance and appropriate antibiotic use in children. Pediatrics 2001;107:E6.

26. Barden LS, Dowell SF, Schwartz B, Lackey C. Current attitudes regarding use of antimicrobial agents: results from physicians' and parents' focus group discussions. Clin Pediatr 1998;37:665–72.

27. Centers for Disease Control and Prevention. Framework for program evaluation in public health. MMWR Morb Mortal Wkly Rep 1999;48(No. RR-11). p.1–40.

28. MacDonald G, Starr G, Schooley M, et al. Introduction to program evaluation for comprehensive tobacco control programs. Atlanta (GA): Centers for Disease Control and Prevention; 2001. p. 139.

29. McCaig LF, Besser RE, Hughes JM. Trends in antimicro-

bial prescribing rates for children and adolescents. JAMA 2002;287:3096–102.

30. Bauchner H, Besser R. Promoting the appropriate use of oral antibiotics: there is some very good news [commentary]. Pediatrics 2003. [In press]

31. Takata GS, Chan LS, Shekelle P, et al. Evidence assessment of management of acute otitis media: I. The role of antibiotics in treatment of uncomplicated acute otitis media [review]. Pediatrics 2001;108:239–47.

32. Glasziou P, Hayem M, Del Mar C. Antibiotics for acute otitis media in children. The Cochrane Library. 1999; (last update: October 7, 2002).

33. Rosenfeld RM. Observation option toolkit for acute otitis media. Int J Pediatr Otorhinolaryngol 2001;58:1–8.

34. Van Zuijlen DA, Schilder AG, Van Balen FA, Hoes AW. National differences in incidence of acute mastoiditis: relationship to prescribing patterns of antibiotics for acute otitis media? Pediatr Infect Dis J 2001;20:140–4.

35. New York State Department of Health. WAIT New York State: Wise Antibiotics Information Team (last update: August 2002). New York State Department of Health; August 2002. Available at http://www.health.state.ny. us/nysdoh/antibiotic/antibiotic.htm (accessed October 10, 2002).

36. Steinbach WJ, Sectish TC, Benjamin DK Jr, et al. Pediatric residents' clinical diagnostic accuracy of otitis media. Pediatrics 2002;109:993–8.

37. Steinbach WJ, Sectish TC. Pediatric resident training in the diagnosis and treatment of acute otitis media. Pediatrics 2002;109:404–8.

38. Silva AB, Hotaling AJ. A protocol for otolaryngology-head and neck resident training in pneumatic otoscopy. Int J Pediatr Otorhinolaryngol 1997;40:125–31.

39. Accreditation Council for Graduate Medical Education. Program requirements for residency education in pediatrics (last update: July 2001) 2001. Available at: http://www.acgme.org (accessed September 25, 2002).

40. Accreditation Council for Graduate Medical Education. Program requirements for residency education in family medicine (last update: July 2001) 2001. Available at: http://www. acgme. org (accessed September 25, 2002).

41. Ambulatory Pediatric Association. 1996 Educational guidelines for residency training in general pediatrics (last update: Ambulatory Pediatric Association) 1996. Available at: http://www.ambpeds.org/guidelines/10-ch7.pdf. (accessed September 25, 2002).

42. Centers for Disease Control and Prevention. Promoting appropriate antibiotic use in the community: Medical school curriculum (last update: Centers for Disease Control and Prevention) 2002. Available at: http://www. cdc.gov/drugresistance/community/#medschool. (accessed October 1, 2002).

43. Hamm R, Hicks R, Bemben D. Antibiotics and respiratory infections: are patients more satisfied when expectations are met? J Fam Pract 1996;43:56–62.

44. Mangione-Smith R, McGlynn E, Elliott M, et al. The relationship between perceived parental expectations and pediatrician antimicrobial prescribing behavior. Pediatrics 1999;103:711–8.

CHAPTER 28

Judicious Use of Ototopical Antimicrobials

Joseph E. Dohar, MD, MS

Eighty percent of all questions are statements in disguise.
Phil McGraw
If you can see a bandwagon, it's too late to get on it.
James Goldsmith

OBJECTIVES

On completing this chapter, the reader will be able to
1. Distinguish between acute otitis media (AOM) with an intact and nonintact tympanic membrane.
2. Recognize the advantages of topical antimicrobials over systemic antimicrobials.
3. Assess microbial profiles of the most common ototopical agents.
4. Understand important formulation concepts that impact safety and efficacy.
5. Evaluate the contribution of elements for combination formulations.

A decade ago, a chapter such as this could not have legitimately been included in an evidence-based text. Little data existed supporting formulation, safety, and efficacy of ototopical antimicrobials, and little research and development of new ototopical preparations had occurred since the 1970s. Lore and anecdote led most practices. Of the several otic preparations (Table 28-1) listed in the Physician's Desk Reference (PDR), the U.S. Food and Drug Administration (FDA) approved all except one for use only in the external auditory canal. Product labels had contraindications or cautions for use in the middle ear. This changed in the 1990s because of several new developments and some that are currently evolving. Otic formulations of one of the newest classes of antibiotics, the quinolones, led to the first FDA-approved ototopical antimicrobial in the middle ear, 0.3% topical ofloxacin.

Treating otorrhea through a tympanostomy tube is a common problem for clinicians. In the United States alone, it is estimated that one million tympanostomy tube insertions are performed annually.[1] Current data suggest that the incidence of this disease is increasing.[2–5] Although it has traditionally been stated that the rate of post-tympanostomy tube otorrhea is 5 to 15%, the

Table 28-1 Topical Otic Preparations

Americaine Otic Topical Anesthetic Ear Drops (Medeva)
Auralgan Otic Solution (Wyeth-Ayerst)
Cerumenex Drops (Purdue Frederick)
Cipro HC Otic Suspension (Alcon)
Cortisporin–TC Otic Suspension (Monarch)
Decadron Phosphate Sterile Ophthalmic Solution (Merck & Co., Inc.)
Floxin Otic Solution (Daiichi)*
Otic Domeboro Solution (Bayer)
Pediotic Suspension Sterile (Monarch)
Vosol HC Otic Solution (Wallace)
Vosol Otic Solution (Wallace)

*FDA-approved for middle ear infections (November 2002).

number has varied by study, and an average of 20% had been estimated.[6] Herzon reported that of 140 patients with tympanostomy tubes who were followed up for at least 1 year, 21% developed otorrhea one or more times, whereas McLelland reported that drainage developed in 19.9% of 697 ears with tympanostomy tubes.[7,8]

Recent reports suggest up to an 84% incidence of tube otorrhea.[2–5] Mandel and colleagues reported that of 34 subjects with chronic middle ear effusion (MEE) who were treated with tympanostomy tubes and observed for 3 years, 68% developed at least one episode of tube otorrhea.[2] The most recent data suggest post-tympanostomy tube otorrhea rates as high as 84% within an 18-month follow-up.[5] This trend is caused by several factors, although day care attendance has been highlighted as most significant. Physicians should anticipate much more of this disease in the future and must devise the most appropriate, cost-effective, safe, and efficacious treatments. Today, the most common initial treatment for otorrhea through a tympanostomy tube is systemic antimicrobial therapy, ototopical medication, or both.[9]

This review will distinguish between AOM with both intact and nonintact tympanic membranes, discuss the advantages of topical therapy in otitis media (OM), assess microbial profiles of the commonly available agents, highlight important formulation concepts that impact safety and efficacy, and finally, review the contribution of elements for combination formulations.

AOM in Intact versus Open Tympanic Membrane

A critical distinction relates to otorrhea through a tympanostomy tube (AOT) versus AOM with an intact tympanic membrane. Although histopathologically similar, the two are distinct clinical entities (Table 28-2). Too often, they are thought to be identical, and errors in management result.

In middle ear infections, ototopicals are only useful if the tympanic membrane is not intact. Children with AOT rarely have fever, unless there is a concomitant viral or bacterial infection in another site or, more rarely, drug fever or a suppurative complication. Also rare are other symptoms and signs of AOM, such as otalgia or an erythematous and edematous tympanic membrane. Thus, acute purulent otorrhea, often without other signs or symptoms of middle ear infection, is the primary symptom of AOT in children.

The microbiology of AOT and AOM also differ (Table 28-3). The three pathogens most commonly isolated from children with AOM are *Streptococcus pneumoniae*, *Haemophilus influenzae*, and *Moraxella catarrhalis*. In AOT, regardless of whether the drainage is acute or chronic, *Pseudomonas aeruginosa* and *Staphylococcus aureus* are the primary pathogens. For example, *P. aeruginosa* was the most common pathogen isolated from AOT in children aged 1 to 12 years.[10] To avoid colonizers of the external auditory canal, the investigators suctioned or dry-mopped the external auditory canal, and obtained the culture from the tympanostomy tube lumen. Further, pathogens were only considered valid if their growth index was 2+ or greater. Aerobic, fungal, and mycobacterial cultures were performed.

Many clinicians have assumed that AOT is caused primarily by the acute pathogens found in AOM. They have often, therefore, treated this condition with standard oral antibiotics from the penicillin, cephalosporin, sulfa, or macrolide classes and excluded additional topical therapy. On the basis of the microbiology of this disease, this treatment would be expected to fail in a substantial number of cases. Since most clinicians are not going to delay treatment until culture and sensitivity results are obtained, they must select an empiric antibiotic that will cover all five major pathogens found in this disease.

Of the available ototopical preparations, only the fluoroquinolone class of antibiotics, with monotherapy, can cover all five pathogens noted above. Although fluoroquinolones are currently not FDA approved for systemic use in children because of potential joint toxicity, clinicians can, nonetheless, benefit from the topical use of this remarkably broad-spectrum class of anti-infectives. Human evidence of joint arthropathy in children given systemic fluoroquinolones, however, is lacking.[11] Consequently, these agents may gain FDA approval for systemic use. Until then, the standard of care in the United States will likely be continued avoidance of systemic use of this class of agents in children; therefore, the topical agent is a welcome addition to the armamentarium of agents in pediatric medicine.

Systemic absorption of quinolones used topically in the ear is negligible.[12] Further, there has been no demonstrated toxicity resulting from topical use to any of the middle ear structures, including the ossicular joints.[13] Intuition would suggest that there are likely also natural history differences between AOM and AOT, though no human data are available for untreated patients.

Topical versus Systemic Therapy

All five significant pathogens most commonly isolated from draining ears, *P. aeruginosa*, *S. pneumoniae*, *S. aureus*, *H. influenzae*, and *M. catarrhalis*, are major threats to developing antimicrobial resistance. This fact, coupled with the relatively high prevalence of OM and the substantial public health concern that the issue

Table 28-2 Acute Otorrhea through a Tympanostomy Tube versus Acute Otitis Media

	AOT	AOM
Fever	Rare	Common
Drainage	Common	Rare
Otalgia	Rare	Common
TM inflammation	Less intense	More intense

AOM = acute otitis media; AOT = acute otorrhea through a tympanostomy tube; TM = tympanic membrane.

Table 28-3 Microbiology of Acute Otitis Media versus Tympanostomy Tube Otorrhea

	Streptococcus pneumoniae	Haemophilus influenzae	Moraxella catarrhalis	Pseudomonas aeruginosa	Staphylococcus aureus
AOM	Common	Common	Common	Rare	Rare
AOT	Select children*	Select children*	Select children*	Common	Common

AOM = acute otitis media ; AOT = acute otorrhea through a tympanostomy tube.
*Children less than age 6 years during respiratory infection season.

of bacterial resistance has become, strongly support developing topical antibiotic strategies.

There are many advantages of using topical, rather than systemic, antibiotics (Table 28-4). First, topical medications are delivered directly to the target organ. By bypassing the systemic circulation, pharmacokinetic factors, such as solubility, intestinal absorption, and hepatic first pass effect, do not affect ultimate tissue concentrations. More importantly, topical antibiotics have not been associated with the development of resistance. In 1982, the FDA stated that it "...is unaware of any evidence that...topical antibiotics...have led to an increase in infection in the general population by resistant organisms....The agency believes that if resistance were a problem...it would have been known by now."[14]

A recent Pittsburgh study corroborates the inability of topical antimicrobials to induce bacterial resistance when used in the short term, provided that drug delivery is effective. The authors studied 231 consecutive outpatient children with culture-proven *P. aeruginosa* otorrhea.[15] Of these, 99.6% showed sensitivity to polymyxin B, one of the active ingredients in Cortisporin-TC Otic Suspension (Monarch) used very commonly in the community since the 1970s. Only one strain of *P. aeruginosa* proved resistant to polymyxin B. Despite widespread community use of ototopical drops containing polymyxin B for nearly three decades, *P. aeruginosa*, which is known to be quite facile in developing resistance strategies, nonetheless remained susceptible.

The inability of ototopical antibiotics to induce bacterial resistance also applies to topical eye and skin preparations. This most likely occurs because the concentrations of topical antibiotics exceed the minimal inhibitory concentrations (MIC) at the site of infection to such a degree that eradication is more rapid and complete. Also, topical therapy is generally used in relatively shorter treatment courses.

When reports of resistance to a topical agent are made, a critical reviewer must carefully examine why that occurred. For example, a recent report concluded that an increased resistance to ciprofloxacin (available as an ototopical formulation Cipro HC Otic Suspension, Alcon

Table 28-4 Topical versus Systemic Antimicrobials

	Topical	Systemic
Local concentration	High	Low
Bacterial resistance	Rare	Common
Adverse reactions	Rare	Common
Cost (expense)	Lower	Higher

Laboratories, Inc.) by *P. aeruginosa* was observed in a select population of otitis externa patients.[16] Ciprofloxacin, however, is often used systemically, and its systemic, not ototopical, use is likely responsible for increased resistance. Another common explanation for bacterial resistance to topical antibiotics is inadequate drug delivery. This has occurred in lower respiratory tract and sinus infections, where a substantial difference exists between the amount of drug administered and that which actually reaches the target organ. This is not anticipated in middle ear infections.

The next major advantage of a topical over a systemic strategy is less adverse events. Side effects of systemic antibiotics typically include diarrhea, nausea, rash, vomiting, abdominal pain, and headache, among others. Far more severe side effects, such as Steven S-Johnson syndrome, aplastic anemia, seizure, and anaphylaxis, can also occur. With the newer topical agents, however, only minor local irritative and allergic effects are common— a marked advantage. A recent efficacy trial of topical ofloxacin versus systemic amoxicillin/clavulanate found an incidence of 6% treatment-related side effects associated with the ototopical agent compared with 31% for the systemic agent.[17] The improved safety profile of topical over systemic antimicrobials is unequivocal.

A higher incidence of adverse events has been reported for older, as compared with newer, ototopical agents. Most of these were local sensitivity responses and, by and large, were seen with neomycin-containing products. The major disadvantage of products containing neomycin is its propensity to lead to sensitization. This manifests as allergic inflammation, most often of the skin of the external auditory canal and pinna. Van Ginkel and coworkers[18] stated that "because of the high risk of sensitization, topical preparations containing neomycin... should not be used routinely."

In patients with otitis who have been treated topically, neomycin is invariably the most important sensitizer.[18–23] Neomycin sensitization is vastly underestimated. When used in the external auditory canal, the package insert of Cortisporin-TC Otic Suspension (Monarch) (PDR, 1995) states that the manifestation of sensitization to neomycin is usually a low-grade reddening with swelling, dry scaling, and itching. It may manifest as failure to heal. Given the experience in nasal allergy, we know that the mucosa responds to allergic triggers with edema and drainage. In both the skin and mucosa, the inflammatory manifestations of allergy and infection are clinically similar, if not indistinguishable.

The final advantage of topical antibiotics is that, in general, they cost less than their systemic counterparts.

TOPICAL THERAPY IN AOT

Given that topical therapy has clear advantages over systemic therapy, what is the evidence supporting use in the middle ear?

A multicenter, open-label trial by Dohar and colleagues[24] demonstrated the clinical efficacy and safety of topical 0.3% ofloxacin in treating AOT in children. This evaluator-blind trial enrolled children between 1 and 12 years of age and randomized them into one of two treatment groups: systemic amoxicillin/clavulanate or topical ofloxacin. Importantly, if subjects had *P. aeruginosa* or fungus as the sole pathogen, they were excluded from further study because *P. aeruginosa* is generally resistant to the systemic agent chosen in this study, and fungus is resistant to both. Nonetheless, topical 0.3% ofloxacin alone resulted in a 76% overall cure rate versus 68% with amoxicillin/clavulanate ($n = 145$). A significantly higher percentage of ofloxacin-treated subjects (96.5%) had an overall microbiologic response (eradication of all baseline pathogens) than did amoxicillin/clavulanate-treated subjects (66.7%).

Parents and guardians were more satisfied with ototopical versus systemic treatment (55% versus 40%; $p = .002$). Further, if the patients with *P. aeruginosa* as a sole baseline pathogen had not been withdrawn from the study, the topical quinolone would likely have outperformed the systemic agent. In patients without systemic signs of infection, therefore, initial treatment for AOT should be with a topical agent alone, reserving culture-directed oral antibiotics for treatment failures.

A topic for future study is whether there is an additional benefit associated with using a systemic agent plus a topical agent. Any such advantage would have to be considered in light of the disadvantages of added cost, increased morbidity (side effects), and, possibly, increased development of treatment-related resistance.

Formulation Issues

When evaluating systemic drugs, most emphasis is on the active ingredients of the formulation. A broader spectrum of issues must considered in selecting an ototopical agent, including viscosity, preservatives, antimicrobial(s), anti-inflammatory agent, and other vehicle additives. Vehicular components may possess antimicrobial activity, either primarily or synergistically, in combination with other compounds. Further, vehicular components may contribute as significantly or even more significantly to the side-effect profile of the compound. Lastly, the biocompatibility of the drug may be heavily influenced by these components.

The Role of pH

A fundamental consideration in formulating an ototopical agent is pH. Most traditional preparations are formulated as acidic solutions and suspensions with an average pH of 3.0 to the low 4.0s. According to the PDR, for example, the pH of Cortisporin-TC Otic Solution is 3.0.

It is unclear from the literature as to why older ototopical agents were formulated at such low pH. This was probably because they were steroid-containing combinations and acidic pH is needed to solubilize the steroid. From an anti-infective standpoint, however, two additional benefits were realized as a result of the degree of acidity. First, acetic acid is bactericidal to *P. aeruginosa*, the major pathogen isolated from otorrhea.[25] Consequently, Vosol (Wallace), a 2% solution of acetic acid with 3% propylene glycol, is effective in treating some discharging ears. Second, adding aluminum to acetic acid to form aluminum acetate (Burow's solution) results in an even greater inhibition of the growth of *P. aeruginosa* and also of *S. aureus*, *Proteus mirabilis*, and *Streptococcus pyogenes* because of a synergistic effect.[25]

The antibiotic effect of acid against *P. aeruginosa* applies to other pathogens. Certain fungi, for example, are suppressed by acid in vitro.[26] The role of fungi in ear disease is debated, and there is question as to whether they warrant specific treatment. Also, fungi are known pathogens in other regions of the body. On the other hand, because the environment is humid, dark, and warm in a draining ear—conditions known to ideally support the growth of fungi—their presence in aural drainage may only be as saprophytes and not as opportunistic primary pathogens. If this second hypothesis is correct, simply drying up the ear should eliminate the fungi that are present. Curiously, fungi are rarely isolated in AOT. One recent study found that fungi were isolated from children with AOT in only 2% of cases.[24]

The physiologic pH of the external auditory canal is acidic. Restoring the pH of the external auditory canal, which is often altered by otorrhea, may prevent the opportunistic proliferation of yeast, which, in turn, results in a secondary superinfection. This hypothesis has recently been supported by finding increased isolation of yeast in ears treated with topical ofloxacin (pH 6.8).[27] The chief disadvantage of an acidic formulation is the discomfort associated with acid that may compromise compliance. Until additional studies are done, the decision of whether to use a nonacidic formulation that is less likely to burn as opposed to an acidic one with theoretic antimicrobial advantages is left to the individual clinician. For acute infection requiring a short duration of treatment, the evidence supports the former.

Viscosity

The key to effectively using topical agents is adequate drug delivery. Clearly, the concentration effect would be completely irrelevant if the drug is not effectively delivered to the infected site.

Conceptually, the more viscous the preparation, the less likely it is to overcome the high surface tension of a tympanostomy tube and gain access to the middle ear. In general, suspensions are more viscous than solutions. Because of pH issues (and, thus, comfort), otic suspensions (for combination steroid-containing formulations) are far more commonly used than their solution counterparts. No pharmacokinetic studies have been performed in which delivery of solutions and suspensions to the middle ear through a tympanostomy tube has been measured. It is likely that this issue is less relevant in treating otitis externa, but unless comparative delivery studies are done, it would seem that, all things being equal, less viscous agents would be preferable when delivery to the middle ear is the goal.

A second adverse consequence of higher viscosity may relate to their use with otowicks. Though less often used with middle ear infections, there are instances where a cannulated otowick may be useful in treating AOT. Since the principle of otowicks relies on drug delivery via capillary action, solutions with all components solubilized would be absorbed and delivered most evenly and efficiently. Again, no comparative trials of solutions and suspensions with otowicks are available.

Other Components

Components of the vehicle may act opposite to the desired clinical outcome. For example, many older ototopical formulations contained propylene glycol, a compound sold as antifreeze. Though seemingly irrelevant, there is a considerable irritative effect on the mucosa by such a compound. Barlow and colleagues found that Cortisporin-TC Otic Suspension, produced moderate to severe middle ear mucosal thickening, moderate periosteal thickening, and inflammatory cell infiltration and resultant thickening of the tympanic membrane.[13]

More recent attention has been given to the excipient preservatives of newer topical agents. Most of the research has focused on topical intranasal steroids though there is little reason to believe that a significant difference would exist between the middle ear and nasal mucosa. Benzalkonium chloride is the most widely used preservative in topical nasal corticosteroids and newer ototopical preparations, such as Floxin Otic Solution, (Daiichi Pharmaceutical Corporation). It may be found in ophthalmic, pulmonary, and dermatologic topical products as well.

Benzalkonium chloride is a quaternary ammonium compound, first introduced in 1935 as an antiseptic agent. Mucosal contact may induce squamous metaplasia, loss of cilia, loss of goblet cells, and lack of mucus-covering epithelium.[28] Ciliostasis was promoted, and a reduction in mucociliary transport was measured. Reflex mucosal congestion was also noted with long-term use. Additionally, systemic reactions to topical exposures, such as hypersensitivity lung syndrome with circulating immune complexes, were seen. As an aside, benzalkonium chloride found in most Dutch ototopical preparations, hardly elicited any allergic reaction at all, with only 1 of 34 patients demonstrating a positive skin test.[18]

Polyvinyl alcohol is yet another preservative found in more recent ototopical preparations (Cipro HC Otic Suspension). Anecdotes of polymerization of this substance leading to obstructed tympanostomy tubes and cast formation within the external auditory canal have been discussed. Though suspected to be, in part, a function of higher than recommended dosages or longer than recommended treatment courses, neither mechanism explained some cases.

The critical point for all these examples is that no ototopical agent is FDA approved for prolonged use. Though it is likely that preservative effects, such as those described above, are reversible when a short-treatment course (ie, less than 14 days) is prescribed, longer off-label use may present a variety of problems with those attributable to the preservative being among them. Future research efforts are focusing on compounds with intrinsic properties obviating the need for a preservative. Until such products are available, judicious use of such agents must be practiced.

Ototoxicity Secondary to Ototopical Compounds

Undoubtedly, few subjects are greeted with more controversy and debate than secondary ototoxicity from using ototopical compounds.

Reversible and irreversible ototoxicity and nephrotoxicity have long been associated with systemic aminoglycoside antibiotics.[29] Whether such antibiotics, when applied topically to the middle ear, are toxic to the cochlea and labyrinth is less certain. A growing concern exists that substances in the middle ear cavity can cause inner ear damage. Meniere's disease may be treated with topical gentamicin, which chemically ablates the labyrinth and, in a significant percentage of cases, results in hearing loss.[30] Animal studies convincingly demonstrate that the round window membrane is semipermeable and allows passage of substances known to damage the inner ear. Yet, other animal studies have concluded the opposite, demonstrating the relative safety of these same ototopicals. Thus, conclusive evidence does not exist that ototoxicity can occur from active or inactive vehicular components of ototopical agents during infection.

One of the primary problems in proving causality between ototopical agents and hearing loss is the difficulty in distinguishing between sensorineural hearing loss from the primary disease (OM) and that of the treatment for it.[31] Several anecdotal reports exist.[32–34] Podoshin and colleagues[35] found that in patients with chronic suppurative otitis media (CSOM) who received topical steroid alone ($n = 24$), the mean sensorineural hearing loss was only 0.9 dB as opposed 6.0 dB ($p < .025$) in those treated with a combination of topical dexamethasone, neomycin, and polymyxin B ($n = 124$).

Given that there are ethical issues in designing a study to prove ototoxicity, alternative strategies have been used to gain insight. A very recent investigation described a novel human labyrinthine sampling model that measured in vivo gentamicin absorption through the round window.[36] They found that intratympanic gentamicin diffuses rapidly through the round window membrane and achieves significant levels in the inner ear.

Although the incidence of ototoxicity secondary to the use of ototopicals is likely quite rare, it can occur. In a recent survey of otolaryngologists, 3.4% of the respondents indicated that they had witnessed irreversible inner ear damage following the use of anti-infective ototopical formulations.[34] Of course, this does not include the instances of reversible toxicity or the instances of unidentified ototoxicity.

There are several reasons to explain why clinicians may not identify ototoxicity. First, the effect may be reversible. This is significant, as the high-risk population for otorrhea through a tympanostomy tube—children 1 to 3 years of age—are often not walking or just beginning to walk. Vestibular insults may be interpreted as age-appropriate "clumsiness." Only recently have labyrinthine effects been recognized as a result of MEE in this age group, likely for the same reason.[37,38] Further, most people, especially younger individuals, centrally compensate for a unilateral vestibular insult. When vestibular symptoms occur in a patient being treated with a topical aminoglycoside for otorrhea, they are often attributed to a complication of the middle ear infection, rather than to the ototopical medication. Only histopathologic examination of the temporal bones would distinguish between the two causes. Finally, if hearing loss occurs as a result of topical aminoglycosides in the middle ear, the highest frequencies are at greatest risk. Ultra-high-frequency audiometry may be needed to detect such a sensorineural hearing loss, a test not routinely performed.

One reason it is difficult to refute that ototoxicity ever occurs relates to recent advances in treating and managing Meniere's disease, which include applying a topical aminoglycoside to the middle ear.[30] A standard 10-day treatment course for a middle ear infection would result in 30 mg of gentamicin administered to the middle ear. In contrast, the concentration of gentamicin in a standard solution used to treat Meniere's disease is 10-fold more concentrated, containing an average dose of 0.25 cc to 0.45 cc per application. The average number of applications is three over a 2- to 3-week span, resulting in a total of 22.5 mg to 40 mg of gentamicin administered to the middle ear. Note that this dose range includes the dose given for infection and is intended to completely ablate the labyrinth. Hearing loss secondary to this dose has also been reported in about one-third of the patients treated.[30]

Further evidence supporting this claim comes from a recent report by Kaplan and colleagues[39] demonstrating that commercially available gentamicin sulfate and betamethasone sodium phosphate eardrops completely ablate vestibular function. There are admitted differences between the uses of topical aminoglycoside for infection as opposed to Meniere's disease. The most significant difference is that the round window membrane is expected to be more permeable when not inflamed.[40–42] Brummet and colleagues demonstrated that the topical administration of neomycin, an aminoglycoside found in Cortisporin-TC Otic Suspension, directly into an otherwise healthy and uninflamed ear at concentrations found in the commercially available product resulted in the loss of cochlear hair cells in a guinea pig model.[41]

The extent of the damage was related to the frequency of administration. Myerhoff and colleagues demonstrated that Cortisporin-TC Otic Suspension resulted in middle ear injury in the chinchilla.[43,44] Several other studies in both rodent and primate models also show inner ear toxicity and middle ear effects.

On the basis of collective evidence from both animal studies and clinical experience, ototoxicity may be said to occur secondary to the application of aminoglycosides, components of vehicles, or other antiseptics to the middle ear. Although rare, the true incidence of such toxic outcomes may be underestimated, and safer alternatives, such as the quinolones, should be used, whenever possible.

CONTRIBUTION OF ELEMENTS

Until recently, the standard of care was to formulate combination agents with more than one antibiotic, a steroid with the antibiotic, or both. The FDA has become much more stringent and less likely to approve combination preparations unless a significant contribution of each component is shown. Although this regulatory attitude has been more recently adopted in the United States, it has long been a standard in other countries. This approach is prudent because as the number of agents increases, so does the potential for toxicity—and cost—in most cases. Further, it makes little sense to risk sensitization to a compound that may benefit the patient later in life if including it in a combination product does not make a significant contribution.

Steroids

The need for a steroid has become one of the most hotly debated issues of ototopical preparation. The rationale for including a steroid in ototopical preparations is theoretically sound. The problem, however, is that there are no conclusive published clinical trials demonstrating the added benefit.

Studies that lend support, albeit weak, for including a steroid with an antibiotic, will be discussed initially. The first study compared treating otorrhea with gentamicin alone to a colistin/neomycin/hydrocortisone combination.[45] The authors concluded that the steroid/antibiotic combination was more effective in relieving inflammation in a shorter period of time, while gentamicin alone was more effective in eradicating the infecting organisms. There were several problems with this study. The sample size was small, and the comparators were unmatched. The study design would have produced more meaningful data had the same antibiotic been used in both groups, adding the steroid to one arm.

In another study of 163 patients with chronic otitis media, combined gentamicin/steroid therapy was compared with placebo, and more clinical cures (52% versus 30%) resulted with the combination.[40] Again, the study would have been more meaningful had the combined-gentamicin/steroid group been compared with a gentamicin-only group.

Roland[46] recently presented the best clinical data available to date. The investigators demonstrated in a multi-institutional prospective, randomized, blinded clinical trial, enrolling 201 pediatric patients with AOT, a net difference of 1.09 days shortening of mean time to cessation of drainage when treated with topical ciprofloxacin plus dexamethasone as compared with treatment with topical ciprofloxacin alone.

On the other side of the debate are clinical trials that lead one to question the need for a combination steroid/antibiotic in all cases. Again, though far from conclusive, these are the only data available and will be detailed below. A multicenter, prospective, open-label trial examined the safety and efficacy of topical 0.3% ofloxacin to treat CSOM .[12] Adolescents and adults (12 years of age or older) with purulent otorrhea through a chronic perforation in the tympanic membrane were studied. Importantly, the defining clinical feature of CSOM in this trial was not by the duration of drainage as others have defined it but by the fact that the drainage occurred through a chronic perforation of the tympanic membrane, present $\geq$ 21 days. In other words, the duration of drainage could have been 1 day if it occurred through a chronic perforation. In spite of this definition, the mean duration of drainage in the United States was 50.5 $\pm$ 142.0 days and a median of 10 days. In patients from Latin America, the mean duration of drainage was 214.3 $\pm$ 265.7 days and a median of 100 days. Overall, therefore, the mean duration of drainage for all sites combined was 97.8 $\pm$ 199.7 days and a median of 28.5 days.

This comparative trial[12] is important because chronic inflammation is one of the clinical circumstances for which most feel the contribution of a steroid is significant, especially if an obvious manifestation of the inflammation, such as granulation tissue, is present. Most infections in the study were unilateral. The overall clinical response in topical ofloxacin-treated subjects was cure (meaning "dry ear") for 91% of the subjects. Pathogens eradicated included *S. aureus*, *Proteus mirabilis*, and *P. aeruginosa*. Though there was no steroid-containing comparator in this trial, it would be hard to improve this cure rate with the addition of a steroid. The evidence, therefore, seems to suggest that the contribution of a steroid added to an antibiotic would be something other than improving overall cure rates.

The clinically meaningful outcome measure that is most likely to be impacted by the addition of a steroid is time to cessation of otorrhea, as was the case for the study discussed earlier for AOT.[46] In the trial for CSOM, however, this was difficult to assess post hoc, as the second visit was not until days 4 to 6, likely too late to have measured an effect. The study did reveal that at visit 2 (days 4 to 6), 94% of clinically evaluable subjects from Latin American sites and 85% of those from American centers showed improvement. Another interesting finding in this study was that only 59% of the American subjects had valid pathogens at baseline. One would suspect that the drainage in these subjects was a result of continued inflammation and not persistent infection.

One final point to be stressed is the misassumption that adding a steroid "may help but cannot hurt." In a warning for Cortisporin-TC Otic Suspension regarding the steroid component, the PDR states that "since corticosteroids may inhibit the body's defense mechanism against infection, a concomitant antimicrobial drug may be used when this inhibition is considered to be clinically significant in a particular case."[47] Moreover, steroid sensitization may induce inflammation, despite intrinsic anti-inflammatory activity.[18] For example, 6 of 34 patients (18%) with chronic otorrhea (ie, > 3 months) treated with a steroid-containing ototopical agent had positive patch tests to steroids.[18] Consequently, some patients with CSOM persisting despite a steroid-containing topical agent may, in fact, have allergic inflammation perpetuated by continued steroid exposure. Otolaryngologists also use steroids for protracted lengths of time to treat other diseases, such as allergic rhinitis. The question again is whether sensitization to the steroid causes the symptoms to persist.

Clearly, much more study is necessary, but until better data are available, the evidence supports treating with single-antibiotic monotherapy without a steroid in most routine cases of AOT, unless an associated vigorous inflammatory host response is present (ie, obstructing aural granuloma and so on). The other clinical setting in which steroids may play a prominent role might be chronic otorrhea. The data suggest that these cases may have no pathogen present or a sole fungal isolate. Both scenarios would benefit from treatment with an anti-inflammatory agent.

Presently, most of the available steroid-containing combination ototopical agents contain hydrocortisone, which has relatively weak anti-inflammatory properties. If a clinician judges that anti-inflammatory action is necessary, use of a more potent steroid than hydrocortisone seems optimal. More potent topical steroids are available, and still others are currently under investigation.

Multiple Antimicrobial Agents

The last issue relating to combination products is the need for more than one antimicrobial agent in any single formulation. Cortisporin-TC Otic Suspension, Pediotic Suspension, and Coly-Mycin (Monarch) are all examples of combination topical otic preparations that contain one or more antibiotics and an anti-inflammatory agent.

The rationale for combining antibiotics in topical otic preparations is unclear. Polymyxin B sulfate (10,000 units per mL), found in most preparations, is effective against *P. aeruginosa* and other gram-negative bacteria, including strains of *Escherichia*.[16] Similarly, colistin sulfate (3 mg/mL) is effective against most gram-negative organisms, notably *P. aeruginosa*, *Escherichia coli*, and *Klebsiella* species.[24] Neomycin sulfate (3.3 mg/mL) is an aminoglycoside, again with primary effectiveness against many gram-negative organisms and some activity against *S. aureus* as well. Surprisingly, from an anti-infective perspective, the activity against the gram-positive staphylococci led to including neomycin, an activity not generally emphasized for antibiotics belonging to the aminoglycoside class.

Another rationale for including neomycin in ototopical preparations was providing a second antibiotic with activity against gram-negative bacteria, such as the pseudomonads. Traditional teaching is that "dual" antibiotic therapy is necessary for treating *Pseudomonas* infections causing pneumonia or infections in immunocompromised patients.[48] This premise is based on the rationale that the synergy of two drugs with different modes of activity reduces the likelihood of treatment-induced resistance and more effectively eradicates the organism. As stated earlier, it is likely that, in part, this rationale led to the development of combination ototopical agents containing an aminoglycoside (ie, neomycin) and a member of the polymyxin class of antibiotics (ie, polymyxin B sulfate).

The data on treating aural *Pseudomonas* infections, however, have not supported dual therapy. A recent study from Pittsburgh revealed excellent in vitro susceptibility of aural isolates of *P. aeruginosa* to the semisynthetic penicillins. Single-agent intravenous therapy from this class of antibiotics has been the standard treatment for CSOM caused by *P. aeruginosa* in children, refractory to outpatient management, with excellent results.[49] The fluoroquinolones, as mentioned previously, achieve the appropriate coverage of both the gram-postive and gram-negative bacterial pathogens commonly recovered in AOT. Studies have shown that 0.3% ofloxacin used topically eradicated 94% or more of *P. aeruginosa*, *H. influenzae*, *S. pneumoniae*, *S. aureus*, and *M. catarrhalis*, the five major pathogens isolated in AOT in children aged 1 to 12 years.[24]

None of the antibiotic components of Cortisporin-TC Otic Suspension or Pediotic Suspension provides adequate effectiveness against *S. pneumoniae*,[50] which is one of the three most common AOT pathogens in younger children, especially during the respiratory infection season.[10] In a real-life situation, a physician is likely to treat a child with a draining ear by empirically selecting an antibiotic. Choosing one that does not cover a primary potential pathogen would clearly be unwise. In such a setting, Cortisporin-TC Otic Suspension, would have to be combined with a systemic antibiotic that covered the important pathogens that the Cortisporin-TC Otic Suspension did not, defeating the purpose of treating with a topical agent alone.

CONCLUSION

The evidence presented herein will hopefully instill greater appreciation for the often taken for granted category of ototopicals. With respect to the use of these medications, we have entered a new era. As is often the case in medicine, more questions have been raised than evidence-based answers. Research remains active in hopes that progress will continue. Pointers and pitfalls are given in Table 28-5.

Table 28-5 Pointers and Pitfalls

1. Acute otorrhea through a tympanostomy tube (AOT) is clinically and microbiologically distinct from acute otitis media with an intact tympanic membrane.

2. Ototopical therapy is recommended as first-line treatment of uncomplicated AOT because of marked advantages over systemic therapy.

3. Formulation considerations and vehicular components of ototopical preparations are significant both in terms of efficacy and safety.

4. Topical fluoroquinolone drops obviate the need for multiple antibiotic combination products.

5. Topical fluoroquinolone has distinct safety advantages over aminoglycoside.

6. Insufficient data exist to recommend the routine use of a steroid in all cases of uncomplicated AOT.

REFERENCES

1. Theone DE, Johnson CE. Pharmacotherapy of otitis media. Pharmacotherapy 1991;11:212–21.

2. Mandel EM, Rockette HE, Bluestone CD, et al. Myringotomy with and without tympanostomy tubes for chronic otitis media with effusion. Arch Otolaryngol Head Neck Surg 1989;115:1217–24.

3. Baker RS, Chole RA. A randomized clinical trial of topical gentamicin after tympanostomy tube placement. Arch Otolaryngol Head Neck Surg 1988;114:755–7.

4. Mandel EM, Casselbrant ML, Kurs-Lasky M. Acute otorrhea: bacteriology of a common complication of tympanostomy tubes. Ann Otol Rhinol Laryngol 1994;103:713–8.

5. Ah-Tye C, Colborn DK, Paradise JL. Prevalence, incidence, and duration of otorrhea in young children with tympanostomy tubes for persistent otitis media with effusion. Pediatr Res 1997;41:89–95.

6. Lusk RP. Tympanostomy membrane-ventilating tubes. In: Cummings CW, editor. Otolaryngology—head and neck surgery. 1st ed. St. Louis (MO): Mosby-Year Book; 1986. p. 3064.

7. Herzon FS. Tympanostomy tubes. Infectious complications. Arch Otolaryngol 1980;106:645–7.

8. McLelland CA. Incidence of complications from use of tympanostomy tubes. Arch Otolaryngol 1980;106:97–9.

9. Nelson JD. Management of chronic suppurative otitis media: a survey of practicing pediatricians. In: Bluestone CD, Kenna MA, Scheetz MD, editors. Workshop on chronic suppurative otitis media: etiology and management. Ann Otol Rhinol Laryngol 1988; 97 Suppl 131:26–8.

10. Dohar JE, Garner ET, Nielsen RW, et al. Topical ofloxacin treatment of otorrhea in children with tympanostomy tubes. Arch Otolaryngol Head Neck Surg. 1999;125:537–45.

11. Schaad UB, Salam MA, Aujard Y, et al. Use of fluoroquinolones in pediatrics: consensus report of an International Society of Chemotherapy Commission. Pediatr Infect Dis J 1995;14:1–9.

12. Argo AS, Garner ET, Wright JW III, et al. Clinical trial of ototopical ofloxacin for treatment of chronic suppurative otitis media. Clin Ther 1998;20:744–59.

13. Barlow DW, Duckert LG, Kreig SC, Gates GA. Ototoxicity of topical otomicrobial agents. Acta Otolaryngol (Stockh) 1994;115:231–5.

14. Langford JH, Benrimoj SI. Clinical rationale for topical antimicrobial preparations. J Antimicrob Chemother 1996;37:399–402.

15. Dohar JE, Kenna MA, Wadowsky RM. In vitro susceptibility of aural isolates of *P. aeruginosa* to commonly used ototopical antibiotics. Am J Otol 1996;17:207–9.

16. Berenhold L, Katzenell U, Harrell M. Evolving resistant *Pseudomonas* to ciprofloxacin in malignant otitis externa. Laryngoscope 2002;112(9):1619–22

17. Goldblatt EL, Dohar JE, Nozza RJ, et al. Topical ofloxacin versus systemic amoxicillin/clavulanate in purulent otorrhea in children with tympanostomy tubes. Int J Pediatr Otorhinolaryngol 1998;46:91–101.

18. Van Ginkel CJ, Bruintjes TD, Huizing EH. Allergy due to topical medications in chronic otitis externa and chronic otitis media. Clin Otolaryngol 1995;20:326–8.

19. Rasmussen PA. Otitis externa and allergic contact dermatitis. Acta Otolaryngol 1974;77:344–7.

20. Holmes RC, Johns AN, Wilkinson JD, et al. Medicament contact dermatitis in patients with chronic inflammatory ear disease. J R Soc Med 1982;75:27–30.

21. Fraki JE, Kalimo K, Tuohimaa P, Aantaa E. Contact allergy to various components of topical preparations for treatment of external otitis. Acta Otolaryngol 1985;100:414–8.

22. Smith IM, Keay DG, Buxton PK. Contact hypersensitivity in patients with chronic otitis externa. Clin Otolaryngol 1990;15:155–8.

23. Pigatto PD, Bigardi A, Legori A, et al. Allergic contact dermatitis prevalence in patients with otitis externa. Acta Derm Venereol 1991;71:162–5.

24. Dohar JE, Alper CM, Rose EA, et al. Treatment of chronic suppurative otitis media with topical ciprofloxacin. Ann Otol Rhinol Otolaryngol 1998;107:865–71.

25. Thorp MA, Kruger J, Oliver S, et al. The antibacterial acidity of acetic acid and Burow's solution as topical otological preparations. J Larynol Otol 1998;12:925–8.

26. Glassman JM, Pillar J, Soyka JP. Otitis externa: comparative in vitro sensitivities of clinical isolates of bacteria and fungi to nonantibiotic and antibiotic otic preparations. Curr Ther Res Clin Exp 1978;23:S29–S38.

27. Jackman A, Bent J, April M, Ward R. Topical antibiotics induced otomycosis [unpublished]. Abstracted in: American Society of Pediatric Otolaryngology Seventeenth Annual Meeting, 2002; May 11–14; Boca Raton, FL.

28. Berg OH, Lie K, Steinsvag SK. The effects of topical nasal steroids on rat respiratory mucosa in vito, with special reference to benzalkonium chloride. Allergy 1997;52:627–32.

29. Waisbren BA, Spink WW. Clinical appraisal of neomycin. Ann Intern Med 1950;33:1099–119.

30. Monsell EM, Cass SP, Rybak LP. Therapeutic use of aminoglycosides in Meniere's disease. Otolaryngol Clin North Am 1993;26:737–49.

31. Hunter LL, Margolis RH, Rykken JR, et al. High frequency hearing loss associated with otitis media. Ear Hear 1996;17:1–1.

32. Tommerup B, Moller K. A case of profound hearing impairment following the prolonged use of framycetin ear drops. J Laryngol Otol 1984;98:1135–7.

33. Lelìever WC. Topical gentamicin-induced positional vertigo. Otolaryngol Head Neck Surg 1985;93:553–5.

34. Lundy LB, Graham MD. Ototoxicity and ototopical medications: a survey of otolaryngologists. Am J Otol 1993;14:141–6.

35. Podoshin L, Fradis M, David JB. Ototoxicity of ear drops in patients suffering from chronic otitis media. J Laryngol Otol 1989;103:46–50.

36. Becvarovski Z, Michaelides EM, Kartush JM, et al. Rapid evaluation of gentamicin levels in the human labyrinth following intravenous administration. Laryngoscope 2002;112:1163–657.

37. Casselbrant ML, Furman JM, Rubenstein E, Mandel EM. Effect of otitis media on the vestibular system in children. Ann Otol Rhinol Laryngol 1995;104:620–4.

38. Casselbrant ML, Redfern MS, Furman JM, et al. Visual-induced postural sway in children with and without otitis media. Ann Otol Rhinol Laryngol 1998;107:401–5.

39. Kaplan DM, Hehar SS, Bance ML, Rutka JA. Intentional ablation of vestibular function using commercially available topical gentamicin-betamethasone eardrops in patients with Meniere's disease: further evidence for topical eardrop ototoxicity. Laryngoscope 2002;112(4): 689–95.

40. Browning GG, Gatehouse S, Calder IT. Medical management of active chronic otitis media: a controlled study. J Laryngol Otol 1988;102:491–5.

41. Brummett RE, Harris RF, Lindgren JA. Detection of ototoxicity from drugs applied topically to the middle ear space. Laryngoscope 1976;86:1177–87.

42. Linder TE, Zwicky S, Brandle P. Ototoxicity of ear drops: a clinical perspective. J Otol 1995;16:653–7.

43. Myerhoff WL, Morizono T, Wright CG, et al. Tympanostomy tubes and otic drops. Laryngoscope 1983;93:1022–7.

44. Morizono T. Toxicity of ototopical drugs: animal modeling. Ann Otol Rhinol Laryngol 1990;99:42–5.

45. Gyde MC, Norris D, Kavalec EC. The weeping ear: clinical re-evaluation of treatment. J Int Med Res 1982; 10:333–40.

46. Roland, PS. Topical Dexamethasone enhances resolution of acute otitis media with a tympanostomy tube [unpublished]. Presented in: Combined Otolaryngological Spring Meetings of the Triological Society and the American Society of Pediatric Otolaryngology annual meeting, 2001; May 14, 2001; Boca Raton, FL.

47. Physician's Desk Reference. 49th Ed. Montvale (NJ): Medical Economics Data Production Company; 1995. p. 741–52.

48. Menzies B, Gregory DW. *Pseudomonas*. In: Schlossberg D, editor. Current therapy of infectious disease. St. Louis (MO): Mosby-Year Book; 1996. p. 446–50.

49. Dohar JE, Kenna MA, Wadowsky RM. Therapeutic implications in the treatment of aural *P. aeruginosa* infections based on in vitro susceptibility patterns. Arch Otolaryngol Head Neck Surg 1995;121:1022–5.

50. Physician's Desk Reference. 51st ed. Montvale(NJ): Medical Economics Data Production Company; 1997. p. 1076–7.

CHAPTER 29

Tympanostomy Tube Care and Consequences

Richard M. Rosenfeld, MD, MPH, and Glenn Isaacson, MD

In chronic catarrhal otitis media, thickened membrana tympani from hyperplasia with obstruction of the Eustachian tube is often present. The drumhead may be incised as a temporary measure, or a portion of the drumhead may be removed with a knife or cautery to admit air into the middle ear. All such measures have met with but partial or temporary success, since the opening usually closes within a few days. The relief is often pronounced while the perforation remains open, but quickly disappears after it closes.

W.L. Ballenger

OBJECTIVES

On completing this chapter, the reader will be able to
1. Appreciate the history of middle ear ventilation.
2. Understand how a tympanostomy tube functions.
3. Care for children with indwelling tympanostomy tubes.
4. Manage common tube consequences and complications.
5. Use patient education to optimize outcomes.
6. Understand the importance of regular follow-up in minimizing morbidity.

Tympanostomy tube insertion is the second most common operative procedure in childhood, exceeded in frequency only by neonatal circumcision.[1] In 1996, about 512,000 children in the United States, under age 15 years had tubes inserted, accounting for more than 20% of all ambulatory surgery in this group.[2] About 7% of American children have tubes inserted by age 3 years,[3] with rates up to 30% reported in a managed-care cohort attending day care.[4] These already high rates may increase further, given concerns about multidrug-resistant bacteria and the appeal of tubes as a preventive strategy to limit systemic antibiotics.[5] From the perspective of insurers and health care payers, such figures have raised the specter of an "epidemic" of tympanostomy tubes.[6] The public health implications are obvious.[7]

Tube insertion rates vary greatly within and between countries. Coyte and colleagues[8] reported a 10-fold difference in rates for 49 Ontario counties. Similarly, rates in The Netherlands are 10 times higher than those in the United Kingdom (see Chapter 20, "International Perspective on Management").[9,10] These variations imply considerable uncertainty about who benefits most from tube insertion. Randomized trials show that tubes reduce infection incidence, effusion prevalence, and improve hearing (see Chapter 14, "Clinical Efficacy of

Surgical Therapy"), but these trials have been less helpful in establishing objective operative criteria. The impact of effusion, infection, and hearing loss on a given child and family has enormous variability because of host susceptibility issues (see Chapter 31, "Host Susceptibility to Sequelae"). Further, considering the favorable natural history of most otitis media (OM) (see Chapter 12, "Natural History of Untreated Otitis Media"), the low incidence of serious sequelae, and the diagnostic difficulties, the surgical variability is not surprising (and possibly not modifiable).

This chapter provides an evidence-based overview of the care and consequences of tympanostomy tubes in children. We begin by assuming that an appropriate decision has been made to proceed with tube insertion based on the specific circumstances of the child and family. Consequently, we do not discuss in detail patient selection or surgical indications. Rather, the emphasis is on maximizing patient satisfaction during the period of intubation and minimizing sequelae once the tubes extrude. Patient education and routine tube surveillance are essential for optimal outcomes.

HISTORY OF TYMPANOSTOMY TUBES

Inadequate ventilation of the middle ear and mastoid caused by Eustachian tube dysfunction is central to developing acute otitis media (AOM) and otitis media with effusion (OME).[11] It was observed in the 18th century that some patients with tympanic membrane perforations had experienced stabilization of their middle ear disease. Sir Astley Cooper, a British surgeon and expert anatomist, capitalized on this observation, reporting his success with paracentesis of the tympanic membrane (myringotomy) in 1801. The relief of deafness, however, was only transient because iatrogenic perforations of the tympanic membrane tend to close rapidly,[12] with early relapse of middle ear fluid and conductive hearing loss.

Adam Politzer noted, "Around the turn of the 18th century, another procedure was added to practical otology. Though it had been devised quite rationally, it was soon discredited because of indiscriminate, improper use. We are referring to paracentesis of the tympanic membrane, which was first practiced on a larger scale by Astley Cooper."[13] Politzer realized correctly that prolonged, not transient, ventilation of the middle ear was needed. He cited numerous attempts, all of which were unsuccessful, to prolong ventilation by inserting catgut, fish bones, lead wires, and gold rings into the myringotomy incision.[14] Such attempts persisted into the later part of the 19th century, after which adenoidectomy superseded myringotomy as the method in vogue for treating chronic OME.

Ventilation of the middle ear by stenting open a perforation in the tympanic membrane failed to gain popularity until 1954, when Armstrong published his initial successful series of five patients treated by myringotomy with polyethylene tube insertion.[15] He used a straight, narrow plastic tube that remained in place for only a few weeks. This was, however, long enough for symptom improvement, and the tube could be replaced if relapse occurred. Armstrong and many others subsequently modified this initial design to achieve a greater duration of tube placement and lower rates of permanent perforation after extrusion.

Armstrong correctly cautioned that tubes are not "a panacea in the management of secretory otitis media," and are appropriate only in "chronic cases that have resisted treatment."[15] Over 45 years later, the appropriate use of tympanostomy tubes remains the subject of considerable debate. Allegations of injudicious use appear periodically in the medical literature[16] but are not substantiated by methodologically sound investigations.[17] In contrast, well-designed, randomized controlled trials (RCTs) have documented the efficacy of tympanostomy tubes in treating OME and preventing recurrent AOM. Large-scale studies in Pittsburgh,[18–20] San Antonio,[21] and Minneapolis[22] have shown tube placement to be highly efficacious in carefully selected children. Details of these studies are presented in Chapter 14.

Appreciating the history of tympanostomy tubes is important when evaluating alternative treatments. For example, laser-assisted myringotomy, which avoids the "care and consequences" described herein, has been promoted as an alternative to tube insertion.[23] After 200 years of efforts to prolong the ventilation period, however, the likelihood of achieving successful outcomes with only a few weeks of ventilation appears tenuous. Despite promising short-term results in uncontrolled studies, the efficacy of laser myringotomy is unsupported by large-scale randomized trials with parallel treatment groups (see Chapter 14). Until such trials are forthcoming (which is highly unlikely), tympanostomy tubes remain the proven intervention for children with refractory OM.

Deciding whether or not a given child will benefit from tympanostomy tubes is complex (see Chapters 18, "Clinical Pathway for Acute Otitis Media" and 19, "Clinical Pathway for Otitis Media with Effusion"). Some of the variables are (1) the frequency, duration, and severity of AOM and OME; (2) whether or not the child has any underlying comorbid conditions that predispose to developmental or behavioral sequelae of middle ear effusion (eg, sensorineural hearing loss, speech delay, developmental delays, or cognitive deficits); (3) suitability of the child for general anesthesia; (4) degree of associated hearing loss; (5) impact of OM on equilibrium and balance; (6) structural integrity of the tympanic membrane; and (7) impact of OM on child and family quality of life. For the specifics of decision making, readers should refer to the clinical pathways in Chapters 18 and 19.

CARE OF THE CHILD WITH TYMPANOSTOMY TUBES

Once tubes have been placed, follow-up care is required to ensure that the tubes are functional, hearing loss has been corrected, and potential complications are properly diagnosed and managed. This has traditionally been the job of the operating otolaryngologist, but increasingly, this burden has been placed on the primary-care physician.

Tube Design and Function

There are numerous different tube designs and materials. This bewildering array of devices can be reduced to two general types (Table 29-1): (1) short-term tubes (intended to remain in the eardrum for 8 to 18 months), and (2) long-term tubes (intended for more than 15 months). Short-term tubes are recommended for most children because long-term tubes (T-tubes) are associated with high rates of otorrhea and persistent perforation of the tympanic membrane.[24–26] Although the prolonged ventilation offered by long-term tubes is theoretically desirable, only about 30 to 40% of children initially treated with short-term tubes require additional tubes or surgery for OM.

Tympanostomy tubes stay in position, spanning the eardrum because they have flanges on both inner and outer surfaces (grommet tubes) or have shafts too long to fit in the middle ear (T-tubes). A tube will ultimately extrude as migrating keratin from the tympanic mem-

Table 29-1. Common Tympanostomy Tubes

Type	Eponym	Duration	Notes
Short-term tube	Shepard	8 months	Shortest term
	Armstrong	8–18 months	Teflon
	Paparella I	8–18 months	Silastic
	Sheehy	8–18 months	Teflon
	Reuter bobbin	8–18 months	Steel
Long-term tube	Goode T-tube	> 15 months	High perforation rates
	Butterfly		
	Paparella II		

brane accumulates between the surface epithelium and the outer flange of the tube.[27] Therefore, small amounts of keratin debris adjacent to a functioning tube are a normal and expected finding. The debris requires no attention, unless it obstructs the tube lumen or causes a local inflammatory response (granulation tissue). To resist extrusion, long-term tubes have very large inner flanges, no outer flange to collect epithelial debris, or both.

A tympanostomy tube must be patent to function. The middle ear is a closed space that requires periodic replenishment of mucosally absorbed air to remain healthy. This process normally occurs unnoticed during yawning or swallowing, as the palatal musculature contracts and briefly opens the pharyngeal end of the Eustachian tube. In infants and young children, however, the Eustachian tube is too short, too floppy, and often works poorly (see Chapter 11, "Eustachian Tube Function and Dysfunction"). The result is underventilation of the middle ear (negative pressure) leading to aspiration of nasopharyngeal secretions (AOM) and transudation of intracellular fluid (OME).

The small, approximately 1 mm, opening in a tympanostomy tube prevents pressure gradients from developing in the middle ear by permitting direct air entry from the ear canal. The tube itself does not "cure" OM but equalizes middle ear and atmospheric pressures by preventing early closure of the initial myringotomy opening. In effect, a patent tube serves to effectively bypass the child's own immature and poorly functioning Eustachian tube. Relapse of AOM or OME when a tube extrudes or is obstructed reflects persistent inadequate function of the child's Eustachian tube and should not be interpreted as a surgical "failure."

As with any prothesis, tube materials are selected for maximum biocompatibility and include metals (stainless steel, titanium, gold), plastics (silicon elastomer [Silastic], polytetrafluoroethylene [fluoroplastic or Teflon]), and calcium phosphate–based ceramic (hydroxylapatite).[28] No one material has been proved superior, but fluoroplastic tubes have been used in most RCTs of tube safety and efficacy. Conversely, a variety of modifications have been proposed that are of uncertain value. Silver-oxide–impregnated Silastic tubes slightly reduce postoperative otorrhea,[29] but long-term benefits are poorly studied. Bacterial biofilms (see Chapter 7, "Molecular and Translational Research") can develop on silver-oxide tubes, but ion-bombarded silicone tubes and phosphorylcholine-coated fluoroplastic tubes resist *Staphylococcus aureus* and *Pseudomonas aeruginosa* biofilm formation.[30,31] Lastly, tube coating with human serum albumin may reduce occlusion.[32]

Most tubes are placed in the pars tensa of the tympanic membrane, in any location except the posterosuperior quadrant, which overlies the incus and stapes. Although the anterior half of the drum is generally chosen, location does not correlate with duration of intubation.[33] In children with extensive atelectasis or atrophy of the tympanic membrane, the anterosuperior portion may be the only area into which a tube can be inserted.[34] Routine placement in the anterosuperior quadrant, however, does not prolong intubation compared with anteroinferior quadrant insertion.[35] Rarely, tubes are placed between the tympanic annulus and bony ear canal as permanent devices.[36] Details of surgical technique for tympanostomy tube placement and related procedures are covered elsewhere.[37]

Ensuring Tube Function

Proper function of a tympanostomy tube is ensured if it is seen to span the eardrum, its lumen is unobstructed, and no middle ear effusion (MEE) is present. When these three features are observed, ventilation of the middle ear through the tube lumen will maintain good hearing and reduce the frequency, duration, and severity of subsequent OM episodes. Visualization of a tympanostomy tube may be difficult if the child is struggling, cerumen obstructs the external canal, a long-shafted tube has been used, the tube is oddly angulated, or the tube is placed in the anterosuperior quadrant of the tympanic membrane. Adequate cerumen removal and appropriate restraint are needed for any good ear examination. The techniques are reviewed elsewhere.[38]

When tube function cannot be confirmed by visual inspection, pneumatic otoscopy and tympanometry are helpful. If an eardrum is immobile and translucent on pneumatic otoscopy, with no other signs of middle ear effusion, the tube is probably functioning. A flat (type B) tympanogram with a large volume measurement (static compliance) confirms that a functioning tube (or a perforation) connects the ear canal and middle ear. A peaked (type A or C) tympanogram suggests a clogged or extruded tube without MEE. A flat tympanogram with small volume measurement indicates a nonfunctioning tube with MEE.[39] The acoustic reflectometer cannot be used to assess tube patency because it measures tympanic membrane vibration. A patent tube reduces vibration and will provide a low reading despite no MEE.

The lumen of a tympanostomy tube can become plugged with mucus, blood, or suppurative secretions. Elution profiles of hydrolyzed plugs are most often consistent with mucoid MEE as the obstructing substance.[40] Tube blockage may occur in the immediate postoperative period or after an initial period of patency. If a tube becomes blocked, it can sometimes be cleared by applying an ototopical drop for 5 to 7 days. Otic suspensions are preferable to solutions because their mildly acidic pH is less irritating to the middle ear mucosa. If the child tastes the drops or complains of stinging (with acidic drops), the drops are likely reaching the middle ear or Eustachian tube, indicating that the tympanostomy tube is functioning.

In a randomized trial of 110 British patients aged 27 months or older with obstructed tubes, Spraggs and colleagues[41] found higher rates of reopening with active therapy (55 to 70%) versus observation alone (0%). The treatment groups received eardrops containing 3% hydrogen peroxide solution or 5% sodium bicarbonate. Patients filled the ear canal with drops twice daily for 14 days and remained supine, with the ear upright for 5 minutes before draining the solution. Mild pain developed in 17% of patients but did not prevent them from completing 14 days of therapy.

Using an experimental model of tube obstruction, Westine and colleagues[40] found that hyaluronidase solution and dilute vinegar (1:1 with water) were best at dissolving dried mucoid MEE. Although vinegar is not ototoxic, there are no data on in vivo efficacy, and perox-

ide may be superior for treating plugs composed mainly of dried blood. Altman and colleagues[42] randomized 208 patients to ototopical antibiotics with or without four drops of 0.025% phenylephrine hydrochloride at tube insertion. Phenylephrine reduced tube obstruction from 8.6% to 2.3% (multivariate odds ratio, .25; 95% confidence interval [CI], .08, .79). More recently, Kumar, Szermeta, and Isaacson (unpublished data, submitted to *Laryngoscope*) compared ciprofloxacin eardrops and oxymetazoline eyedrops given at surgery and for 3 days after in 488 consecutive children. Rates of tube occlusion and otorrhea were equivalent after 2 to 4 weeks.

A skilled otolaryngologist can often unclog a plastic grommet, which is not nearing extrusion, by sliding a 3-French metal suction catheter through the tube lumen using the binocular microscope for visualization. Alternatively, an 18-gauge spinal needle can be used. This should not be attempted without magnification and is usually unsuccessful with metal or long-shafted tubes.

Preventing Tympanostomy-Tube Otorrhea

Early Postoperative Tube Otorrhea

Otorrhea occurs in the early postoperative period in about 10 to 20% of children after placement of tympanostomy tubes (Tables 29-2 and 29-3). Surgical technique and ear canal preparation have no effect on rates of early postoperative otorrhea.[43,44] The relative risk of otorrhea is higher for children with inflamed middle ear mucosa at surgery and mucoid effusion and for those with bacterial pathogens in the ear canal or MEE.[44] About 30% of effusions cultured at the time of tube insertion are culture positive for bacterial pathogens.[45] Risk factors for antimicrobial resistance include young age, day care attendance, and the number of prior antibiotic courses.

Gross and colleagues[46] reduced early postoperative otorrhea by saline irrigation at tympanostomy tube placement. Of 145 enrolled children, 84 with MEE were randomized to topical antibiotic drops or saline irrigation. Irrigation was performed twice with 1 mL of sterile normal saline through the myringotomy incision via suction catheter on a tuberculin syringe. Otorrhea rates at 7 to 14 days were 36% with otic drops versus 19% with saline irrigation (*p* = .04). Validity may be compromised, however, because of low precision, an unusually high otorrhea rate, and no follow-up information on 26% of enrolled patients. Nonetheless, saline irrigation is a benign means of potentially reducing early postoperative otorrhea.

The efficacy of antimicrobial eardrops given during or shortly after surgery in reducing early postoperative otorrhea has been studied in 11 RCTs.[47–57] Overall, otorrhea rates are 7% lower (see Table 29-2) when out-

Table 29-2 Randomized Trials of Antibiotic Eardrops for Early Postoperative Tube Otorrhea (by Child)

Author Year	Drugs	Otorrhea Rate, N(%)[‡]		Absolute RD (95% CI)[†]	Statistically Significant?
		Ear Drops	No drug		
Balkany[47] 1983	NEO,PMX,HCT	2/34 (6)	5/26 (19)	−.13 (−.30, .04)	No
Baker[48] 1988	GEN	0/56 (0)	9/46 (20)	−.19 (−.31, −.08)	Yes
Epstein[49] 1992	SFC,PRD	23/218 (11)	28/212 (13)	−.03 (−.09, .04)	No
Cannon[50] 1997	GEN	7/50 (14)	4/50 (8)	.06 (−.06, .18)	No
Combined*		32/358 (9)	46/334 (14)	−.07 (−.18, .04)	No

CI = confidence interval; GEN = gentamicin; HCT = hydrocortisone; NEO = neomycin; PMX = polymyxin B; PRD = prednisolone; RD = rate difference; SFC = sulfacetamide.
*Random effects meta-analysis, $p = .235$; test for heterogeneity Q = 10.33, df = 3, $p = .016$.[171]
[†]Absolute change in otorrhea attributable to therapy; negative values favor treatment.
[‡]Number of children with otorrhea divided by the total number of evaluable children.

Table 29-3 Randomized Trials of Antibiotic Eardrops for Early Postoperative Tube Otorrhea (by Ear)

Author Year	Drugs	Otorrhea Rate, N(%)[‡]		Absolute RD (95% CI)[†]	Statistically Significant?
		Ear Drops	No drug		
Ramadan[51] 1991	PMX,NEO,SFC,HCT	5/60 (8)	8/60 (13)	−.05 (−.16, .06)	No
Scott[52] 1992	GEN	2/36 (6)	4/34 (12)	−.06 (−.19, .07)	No
Younis[53] 1992	PMX,NEO,HCT	22/200 (11)	26/200 (13)	−.02 (−.08, .04)	No
Salam[54] 1993	NEO,BET	3/162 (2)	14/162 (9)	−.07 (−.12, −.02)	Yes
Hester[55] 1995	NEO,PMX,HCT	16/198 (8)	32/195 (16)	−.08 (−.15, −.02)	Yes
Welling[56] 1995	PMX,NEO,HCT	4/50 (8)	4/50 (8)	0 (−.11, .11)	No
Shinkwin[57] 1996	GEN,HCT	2/161 (1)	15/161 (9)	−.08 (−.13, −.03)	Yes
Combined*		54/867 (6)	103/862 (12)	−.06 (−.09, −.04)	Yes

BET = betamethasone; CI = confidence interval; GEN = gentamicin; HCT = hydrocortisone; NEO = neomycin; PMX = polymyxin B; RD = rate difference; SFC = sulfacetamide.
*Random effects meta-analysis, $p < .0001$; test for heterogeneity Q = 4.08, df = 6, $p = .665$.[171]
[†]Absolute change in otorrhea attributable to therapy; negative values favor treatment.
[‡]Number of children with otorrhea divided by the total number of evaluable children.

comes are analyzed by patients (not ears), but the result is not statistically significant (95% CI contains zero). Moreover, the studies have significant heterogeneity. When outcomes are analyzed by ears instead (see Table 29-3), the overall decrease in otorrhea is 6%, which is statistically significant (95% CI, −9,−4%) and homogeneous. The clinical significance, however, of this marginal benefit can be questioned.

Although prophylactic eardrops administered after tube insertion may slightly decrease early otorrhea rates, there is no impact on subsequent rates of delayed otorrhea or other long-term outcomes. Further, prophylaxis of about 17 children with antibiotic eardrops is required (see Table 29-2) to prevent otorrhea in one (see Chapter 2, "Critical Evaluation of Journal Articles"). We believe that the risks of ototoxicity, drug reactions, and drug allergies exceed this small benefit and, therefore, do not recommend *routine* topical prophylaxis for all children receiving tympanostomy tubes. *Selective* prophylaxis may be of benefit for ears with purulent

Table 29-4 Prospective Studies of Tube Otorrhea Rates in Nonswimmers versus Swimmers[†]

Author Year	Otorrhea Rate, N(%)[‡]		Absolute RD (95% CI)[§]	Statistically Significant?
	Nonswimmers	Swimmers		
Smelt[59] 1984	6/40 (15)	3/43 (7)	.08 (−.05, .22)	No
Sharma[60] 1986	12/58 (21)	11/72 (15)	.05 (−.08, .19)	No
Becker[61] 1987	9/30 (30)	5/32 (16)	.14 (−.06, .35)	No
Parker[62] 1994	18/30 (60)	42/62 (68)	−.08 (−.29, .13)	No
Salata[63] 1996	41/116 (35)	44/138 (32)	.03 (−.08, .15)	No
Combined*	86/274 (31)	105/347 (30)	.05 (−.02, .12)	No

CI = confidence interval; RD = rate difference.

*Random effects meta-analysis, $p = .133$; test for heterogeneity $Q = 2.46$, df = 4, $p = .651$.[171]

[†]Data extracted from Lee D et al[70] and pooled using random-effects meta-analysis.

[‡]Number of children with otorrhea divided by the total number of evaluable children.

[§]Absolute change in otorrhea attributable to not swimming; negative values favor nonswimmers.

effusion, bleeding from the myringotomy incision or middle ear mucosa, or with a prior history of intubation and tube plugging or troublesome otorrhea.

All antimicrobials in Tables 29-2 and 29-3 are potentially ototoxic. Topical quinolones (ciprofloxacin and ofloxacin) have no reported ototoxicity but have not been compared with placebo for prophylaxis against post-tympanostomy otorrhea. In one double-blind RCT,[58] however, ciprofloxacin otic drops had equivalent efficacy to a suspension of neomycin, polymyxin B, and hydrocortisone. Therefore, topical quinolones have a theoretic advantage when antibiotic drops are administered after tube insertion.

Delayed Tube Otorrhea

Approximately 30% of children have at least one episode of tympanostomy-tube otorrhea (TTO) while the tube remains in place (Table 29-4),[59–63] with published rates ranging from 4 to 68% (Table 29-5).[64] For most patients, the otorrhea is brief, painless, and nonrecurrent; only about 4% develop chronic TTO (reported range of 1 to 10%).[63–66] Infants and young children with tubes inserted to control recurrent infection are more likely than older children to experience delayed otorrhea.[49,67] In temperate climates, tube otorrhea occurs most often in the winter, coinciding with the upper respiratory infection season, and in the summer, coinciding with the external otitis (swimmer's ear) season.

Mandel and colleagues[68] pooled data from three RCTs and reported TTO for 123 (50%) of 246 Pittsburgh children after a median of 4.8 months. Multiple episodes were reported for 22% of children, and 9% had three or more discrete bouts (four children had six or

more new episodes). Another RCT reported a 75% incidence of TTO after 12 months and 83% after 18 months.[69] These rates are much higher than the mean rates in other studies (see Table 29-5) and most likely reflect intense and regular surveillance. Although many episodes were prolonged (mean 17 days), the management protocol states that aural toilet was "usually not feasible," topical antimicrobial drops were begun only after 2 weeks of oral antimicrobials, and cultures were obtained only for topical therapy failures. This protocol is suboptimal (see below) and likely explains the protracted TTO observed.

Preventing delayed otorrhea has largely focused on measures to avoid water entry into the ear canal during bathing or swimming. Such measures may empirically "make sense," but their effectiveness is *not* supported by prospective, controlled studies (see Table 29-4). When data from individual studies are pooled using meta-analysis, swimmers and nonswimmers have statistically equivalent rates of otorrhea.[70] Similarly, routine use of earplugs, swimming caps, or prophylactic otic drops to prevent otorrhea after water exposure is ineffective.[71] Consequently, it is hard to justify aggressive measures to keep water from entering the ear canal (ear plugs, head bands) and even harder to justify depriving children of swimming pleasure or participation in water sports just because they have tympanostomy tubes.

Table 29-4 shows the individual and pooled results for five studies[59–63] comparing the incidence of acute otorrhea in swimmers (with tubes) versus nonswimmers (with tubes). All studies analyzed results by patients, not ears, and the children studied did not use

Table 29-5 Otorrhea Incidence with Indwelling Tubes*

Type of Otorrhea	No. of Studies	Unit of Analysis	Incidence, %	
			Mean	Range
Unspecified	29	Ears	17.0	3.0–74.0
	23	Patients	26.2	4.3–68.2
Early postoperative	25	Ears	9.1	1.7–26.3
	7	Patients	16.0	8.8–42.0
Recurrent acute	3	Ears	2.1	1.7–2.9
	7	Patients	7.4	0.7–19.6
Chronic	6	Ears	3.3	1.9–7.7
	3	Patients	3.8	1.4–9.9
Requiring tube removal	14	Ears	4.0	0–34.3

*Data adapted from Kay DJ et al.[64]

ear plugs, eardrops, or concomitant oral antimicrobials. No significant differences in otorrhea rates were noted individually or on aggregate, and all studies except one[62] had a trend toward less otorrhea among swimmers. These results are not surprising, considering that most otorrhea is caused by inflammation secondary to a viral upper respiratory infection, not from direct water penetration through the tube.[63] For the same reason, aggressive medical therapy at the time of tube insertion does not reduce the incidence of delayed otorrhea.[72]

We recommend providing parents of all patients with an information sheet (Table 29-6) about tube-associated otorrhea at the time of their children's surgery. Unless parents are educated in advance about the causes and consequences of otorrhea, they are likely to experience undue worry and concern over what is usually a transient condition with minimal associated morbidity. Approximate otorrhea rates that can be anticipated by most children with tubes are summarized in Table 29-5.

Managing Tympanostomy-Tube Otorrhea

Acute Tube Otorrhea

Acute TTO in children aged 2 years or younger is usually caused by typical AOM pathogens, *Streptococcus pneumoniae*, *Moraxella catarrhalis*, and *Haemophilus influenzae*.[68,73,74] Conversely, *P. aeruginosa* and *Staphylococcus aureus* are more prevalent in older children, after TTO induced by water penetration or when TTO persists despite an oral antibiotic.[68,74,75] The natural history of untreated acute TTO is unknown, but, anecdotally, many episodes resolve spontaneously within several days. Similarly, viral myringitis (tympanic membrane erythema without purulent infection) or a very early AOM

may abort spontaneously without drainage occurring because the tube provides middle ear ventilation. Active therapy may be withheld pending visible otorrhea in the tube orifice or in the external auditory canal.

An expert panel convened by the American Academy of Otolaryngology–Head and Neck Surgery recommended ototopical antibiotics alone as first-line treatment for patients with TTO and no systemic infection or serious underlying disease.[76] The panel concluded that (1) systemic antibiotics, as sole therapy or combined with topical drops, did not improve treatment outcomes compared with topical antibiotics alone; and (2) nonototoxic preparations be considered for TTO. Similarly, a meta-analysis of otorrhea with a nonintact tympanic membrane found topical antibiotics better than systemic agents (odds ratio .46), topical quinolones better than nonquinolones (odds ratio .26), and ototopical antibiotics plus aural toilet better than toilet alone (odds ratio .31).[77] Generalizability of this review is limited, however, because most subjects were adults, children with tubes were excluded, and studies were heterogeneous.

Ofloxacin (Floxin Otic) is presently (January 2003) the only topical antimicrobial approved by the U.S. Food and Drug Administration (FDA) for treating otorrhea with a nonintact tympanic membrane. Clinical efficacy suggested in pilot studies[78,79] has been confirmed in a multicenter open-label study[74] and a comparative RCT with amoxicillin-clavulanate.[80] Overall cure for clinically evaluable subjects (60% of the intent-to-treat population) was 76 to 84% and baseline pathogens were eradicated in 96% of microbiologically evaluable patients (40 to 45% of the original population). Amoxicillin-clavulanate had comparable clinical efficacy, but bacterial eradication

Table 29-6 Patient Information: Tympanostomy Tubes and Ear Infections

Although uncommon, children can still get an ear infection (otitis media) with a functioning tube; discharge from the ear canal is the most common symptom.

Pain is usually minimal or absent when the ear infection begins; pain may occur later because of local skin irritation as the infection drains through the tube.

If your child gets an ear infection with visible drainage or discharge from the ear canal:

1. Do not worry: there is no danger to hearing. Ear drainage can be clear, cloudy, or even bloody. The drainage indicates that the tube is working to eliminate infection.

2. Use a cotton ball to prevent discharge from building up and irritating the skin of the ear canal and outer ear. Clean any crusts with a Q-tip dipped in hydrogen peroxide.

3. Prevent water entry into the ear canal during bathing by using cotton saturated with Vaseline to cover the opening; do not allow swimming until the drainage stops.

4. Most discharge results from a cold or viral illness; antibiotics are unnecessary, unless drainage lasts more than a few days, your child is very ill, or has another illness.

5. Persistent drainage is treated with antibiotic drops alone, placed in the ear canal twice daily for 3 to 5 days. Clean any discharge before placing the drops, and "pump" the skin in front of the canal after placing the drops so they enter properly.

6. An oral antibiotic is sometimes necessary, especially if your child is very young or ill.

If your child gets an ear infection without visible drainage from the ear canal:

1. Ask your primary doctor if the tube is open; if it is, the infection should resolve without a need for oral antibiotics or antibiotic eardrops.

2. If your doctor gives you an antibiotic or eardrop prescription anyway, ask if you can wait a few days before filling it; chances are high that you will not need the medication. Use acetaminophen (Tylenol) or ibuprofen (Advil) to relieve pain during the first few days.

3. If the tube is not open, the ear infection is treated as if the tube was not there; the blocked tube does not do any harm, but it also does not do any good.

Contact the physician who inserted the tubes if the discharge persists longer than 7 days or tends to recur frequently

---

was only 67% (excluding children with *P. aeruginosa* as the sole baseline pathogen). About 65% of children studied were age 2 years or older.

Ofloxacin offers several advantages over older drops (polymyxin, neomycin, aminoglycosides), including no demonstrable ototoxicity and a broader antimicrobial spectrum.[81] Because this spectrum includes *S. pneumoniae* and *H. influenzae*, children with acute TTO can often be managed topically without oral antimicrobials. For infants and young children (less than age 2 years), in whom the bacteriology more closely mirrors AOM, an alternative approach is to treat initially with oral antimicrobials followed by culture-guided topical therapy of failures. Any child with TTO and other bacterial illness (eg, persistent sinonasal infection) or serious underlying disease should also receive an oral antimicrobial, with concurrent topical therapy if *P. aeruginosa* is suspected (eg, older child or after water contamination).

Ciprofloxacin ophthalmic solution (Ciloxan) is used empirically to treat TTO, although it is not FDA approved for this purpose. A multicenter (unblinded) RCT of children aged 6 months to 12 years showed TTO cure rates of 70% and 84% in clinically evaluable subjects (83% of the intent-to-treat population) after 7 days of ciprofloxacin alone or ciprofloxacin plus dexamethasone (CiproDex Otic), respectively.[82] Mean days of otorrhea decreased significantly from 5.3 to 4.2 when dexamethasone was added, but bacterial efficacy was statistically unchanged. In another multicenter (unblinded) RCT of acute TTO,[83] ciprofloxacin plus dexamethasone suspension had clinical and bacteriologic cure rates of 90 to 92%, which were 10 to 12% higher than ofloxacin solution. These two studies suggest a need to treat about 7 to 10 children with dexamethasone-containing drops to achieve one additional cure over quinolone drops alone.

Despite the potential for drug-resistant *P. aeruginosa* induced by quinolones,[84,85] the high local concentrations of topically administered agents make this more of a theoretic concern.[74] Significant treatment-emergent resistance has not been reported, to date, with topical quinolone use. Increasing pseudomonal resistance over time, however, has occurred with ciprofloxacin-treated malignant otitis externa.[86] Methicillin-resistant *S. aureus* TTO, which is usually resistant to fluoroquinolones, has been reported de novo[87] and following topical quinolone drops (Glenn Isaacson, personal communication, September 2003). Prolonged use of drops may also result in fungal overgrowth (see below). These observations support judicious use of topical quinolone drops for the minimal time needed to resolve acute TTO.

A variety of non-FDA approved drops are used to treat TTO, including aminoglycoside ophthalmic drops and combination products with neomycin, polymyxin B, and hydrocortisone (Cortisporin Otic Suspension and others). These products, however, should be used judiciously because sensorineural hearing loss occurs when they are placed in the *noninfected* middle ear of rodents.[88] Whereas ototoxicity has not been shown in humans or in nonhuman primates,[89] it would seem prudent to instill these agents only during the period of active ear drainage. When monkeys with *P. aeruginosa* otorrhea received topical tobramycin for 7 weeks, there was no detectable drug in perilymph samples nor any outer hair cell damage.[90] Dexamethasone added to the drops improved clinical efficacy.

Regardless of which particular otic preparation is used by the clinician, certain principles should be observed to optimize efficacy:

- A clean ear canal facilitates passage of drops through the tube into the middle ear. Prior to instilling drops, parents are instructed to blot thin secretions with a cotton wick or to remove thick secretions with a nasal aspirator (small bulb syringe available in most drug stores).
- Drops must completely enter the ear canal. If, instead, the drops "float" in the external auditory meatus or conchal bowl, the parent should pull the pinna laterally with a gentle circular motion until the drops disappear into the canal.
- Drops must penetrate the tympanostomy tube and reach the middle ear. Parents are instructed to "pump" the tragus several times to generate the slight pressure needed for otic solutions and suspensions to penetrate the tube.[91,92]
- Children should refrain from swimming and water sports when otorrhea is present. Until the discharge resolves, a cotton plug moistened with petroleum jelly should be placed in the outer ear canal during bathing or showering to prevent water entry.

The above principles are best illustrated by demonstrating the process at the time of the office visit. Prior to this, the clinician should remove any crusted or dried otorrhea from the conchal bowl and external auditory canal meatus using cotton applicators moistened with hydrogen peroxide solution.

Recurrent or Persistent Tube Otorrhea

Recurrent, acute otorrhea with minimal associated symptoms often resolves promptly with dry ear precautions and cleaning of the ear canal. The most frequent cause is secondary inflammation of the middle ear during a viral upper respiratory infection, with or without reflux of nasopharyngeal secretions. External water entry is also possible, and routine dry ear precautions, if not already instituted, are advised. If the acute otorrhea persists or is associated with signs and symptoms of AOM, treatment with ototopical or systemic antimicrobials, as described above, is indicated. Recurrent acute TTO that is unresponsive to water precautions should prompt a search for underlying factors including gastroesophageal reflux, repetitive viral illness (eg, day care syndrome), daytime pacifier use, adenoid vegetations, and untreated food or inhalant allergies. Immunologic evaluation may also be appropriate for selected children.

Children may present to the otolaryngologist with persistent TTO for up to several weeks despite initial treatment with an ototopical antimicrobial. The usual cause is inadequate penetration of the drops because of inspissated or accumulated debris in the ear canal. Most cases resolve promptly after thorough cleaning, suctioning of the tube, and application of a steroid-antibiotic topical drop for 5 to 7 days. Although not based on RCTs, adding a steroid (preferably dexamethasone) for second-line therapy is empirically useful for the inflammatory response that invariably accompanies several weeks of TTO. Children with untreated clinical sinusitis (nonimproving rhinorrhea, nasal congestion, or daytime cough after 10 to 14 days) are candidates for oral antimicrobial therapy.

When otorrhea becomes chronic or refractory, selecting ototopical drops, on the basis of culture and sensitivity of organisms from the ear canal, is recommended. This is particularly important after prolonged antibiotic therapy (topical or oral) to detect fungal overgrowth. We prefer to directly suction the tube orifice under magnification to obtain material for culture and to ensure adequate cleaning (aural toilet).[93] If this is impossible because of equipment limitations or an apprehensive child, drying the ear canal with multiple cotton applicators and suctioning with an 8-French catheter are alternative ways to clear debris and permit entry of ear drops.[94]

Prolonged use of any topical antimicrobial, particularly broad-spectrum quinolones, may result in fungal overgrowth.[95] Children present with thick fungal debris and clogged, itchy, or painful ears. Of 18 consecutive cases treated by Schrader and Isaacson[96] in the summer months, 11 had culture-proven fungal otitis externa (10 *Candida albicans*, 1 *Aspergillus* species), 4 grew bacterial contaminants, and 3 had results unavailable. Most were treated successfully by thorough cleaning under the binocular microscope and application of topical clotrimazole solution. Several needed multiple treatments for control, and 2 required systemic antifungal therapy (fluconazole orally for 7 days). One child was refractory to topical and systemic drugs. An alternative topical therapy, used with success by one author (RMR) in several cases of fungal TTO, is natamycin 5% suspension (Natacyn), an ophthalmic antifungal.

Recurrent or chronic TTO may cause localized fungal dermatitis of the concha, lobule, external auditory meatus, or intertragal incisura. Children present with dry, flakey lesions, often associated with excoriation caused by scratching. Nystatin; triamcinolone cream is applied twice daily after removing any dried crusts or debris with hydrogen peroxide solution. Although the clinical response is often rapid, treatment should be continued for at least 10 to 14 days to prevent recurrence.

Otorrhea persisting despite aural toilet, dry ear precautions, and intensive medical management may be caused by a cholesterol granuloma, an occult cholesteatoma, or unusual pathogens, such as *Candida albicans*,[97] actinomyces,[98] or *Aspergillus*.[99] Referral to an otolaryngologist is warranted for binocular microscopy and early intervention to prevent development of more serious sequelae. Refractory otorrhea caused by *P. aeruginosa* or other resistant organisms may require parenteral antimicrobials for adequate control. In-patient therapy based on culture of the tube orifice, combined with daily aural toilet and ototopical drops, will control almost all infectious otorrhea.[100–102]

Removing a tympanostomy tube is occasionally necessary to stop refractory otorrhea (see Table 29-5),[64,103] but recurrent otitis requiring an additional anesthetic for tube reinsertion is common. Bacterial biofilms (see Chapter 7) may form on mucosal surfaces and implanted prostheses, including tympanostomy tubes.[104] These bacterial aggregates are resistant to therapy with systemic antibiotics and to standard culture methods. Biofilm formation may help explain why tube removal is sometimes curative in treating refractory otorrhea. Ion-bombarded silicone tubes and phosphorylcholine-coated fluoroplastic tubes resist biofilm formation,[30,31] but their impact on refractory otorrhea, if any, has not been studied in prospective clinical trials.

Table 29-7 Adverse Events with Indwelling Tubes*

Outcome (Ears)	No. of Studies	Incidence, %	
		Mean	Range
Blockage of tube lumen	17	6.9	0–37.3
Granulations, no surgery required	5	4.2	0.5–8.0
Granulations, surgery required	8	1.8	0.6–4.4
Granulations, unknown severity	11	1.0	0–12.0
Premature extrusion of tube	3	3.9	1.1–8.3
Tube displacement into middle ear	8	0.5	0–1.3

*Data adapted from Kay DJ et al.[64]

Adverse Events with Indwelling Tubes

Adverse events are uncommon with indwelling tubes (Table 29-7) and rarely necessitate tube removal. Management of the most common problems—otorrhea (see Table 29-5) and blockage of the tube lumen—has been addressed earlier in this chapter. This section deals with granulation tissue and highlights the important relation between tube type (short-term versus long-term) and outcomes.

Granulation tissue develops adjacent to the tympanostomy tube in up to 8% of children (see Table 29-7) and often presents with painless *bloody* otorrhea. The tissue results from focal irritation of the tympanic membrane adjacent to the tube and a foreign body reaction to the tube itself or to accumulated squamous debris around the tube shaft. A small focus of granulation may be visible only with the binocular microscope, or a large granuloma (discrete, well-formed granulations) may fill the external auditory canal. Granulations detected during a routine office examination or as part of tube surveillance require intervention because the natural history is often progressive enlargement with eventual obstruction, infection, or bloody otorrhea. Early detection and treatment are a primary reason for routine tube surveillance by the operating otolaryngologist.

When granulation tissue is present, ototopical drops containing an anti-inflammatory agent (corticosteroid) in addition to an antimicrobial are preferred. Dexamethasone is the preferred steroid component, and the antimicrobial should ideally be nonototoxic. Most granulomas resolve after 7 to 14 days of topical therapy

Table 29-8 Impact of Tube Type (Short Term versus Long Term) on Incidence of Sequelae*

Sequelae	Long Term Tube, %	Short Term Tube, %	Relative Risk[†] (95% CI)	p Value
Otorrhea, unspecified type	32.5	14.8	2.2 (2.0, 2.4)	< .001
Otorrhea needing tube removal	13.5	0.9	14.4 (9.9, 21.0)	< .001
Chronic perforation	16.6	2.2	7.7 (6.5, 9.1)	< .001
Cholesteatoma	1.4	0.8	1.7 (1.1, 2.7)	.041
Atrophy or retraction at tube site	23.3	25.5	0.9 (0.8, 1.1)	.366
Tympanosclerosis	21.0	25.1	0.8 (0.7, 1.1)	.132
Blockage of tube lumen	9.1	7.4	1.2 (0.9, 1.5)	.125

*Data adapted from Kay DJ et al.[64]

[†]Ratio of sequelae incidence for long-term tubes vs. short-term tubes; values greater than 1.0 indicate greater risk with long-term tubes.

Table 29-9 Meta-analysis of Tympanostomy Tube Sequelae*

Outcome Assessed	No. of Studies	Rate Difference, % (95% CI)[†]	Relative Risk (95% CI)[‡]
Increase in otorrhea from long-term tube vs. short-term tube	6	13.7 (−0.7, 28.0)	2.1 (1.0, - 4.0)
Increase in chronic perforation from long-term tube vs. short-term tube	8	7.3 (1.3, 13.3)	3.5 (1.5, 7.1)
Increase in cholesteatoma from long-term tube vs. short-term tube	6	1.3 (0.4, 2.2)	2.6 (1.5, 4.4)
Increase in atrophy/retraction from tube vs. no surgery or myringotomy alone	10	11.0 (2.6, 19.3)	1.7 (1.1, 2.7)
Increase in tympanosclerosis from tube vs. no surgery or myringotomy alone	13	29.9 (21.9, 38.0)	3.5 (2.6, 4.9)

*Data adapted from Kay DJ et al.[64]

[†]Absolute difference in outcomes between groups; $p < .05$ when the 95% CI does not include zero.

[‡]Ratio of sequelae incidence between groups; $p < .05$ when the 95% CI does not include one.

and water precautions. Persistent or large granulomas can be débrided under the binocular microscope using a suction or cup forceps; cauterization with silver nitrate may be helpful. Tube removal or surgical débridement is rarely necessary. Follow-up after treatment is important to ensure complete resolution of the granuloma and patency of the tympanostomy tube.

Long-term tubes should be used judiciously because of significantly higher rates of adverse events and sequelae compared with short-term tubes.[64] Granuloma development is related to the intubation period and is, therefore, more commonly seen with long-term tubes (12 to 21% incidence)[25,105] than with short-term ones (2 to 4% incidence).[106–108] Otorrhea is twice as com-

mon with a long-term tube, and the necessity to remove the tube because of refractory otorrhea increases by more than 14-fold (Tables 29-8 and 29-9). The risk of cholesteatoma more than doubles with long- versus short-term tubes, and the incidence of chronic perforation is more than three times as high. Sequelae *not* significantly associated with choice of tube include tympanosclerosis, blockage of tube lumen, and atrophy or retraction at the tube site after extrusion.

A commonly used long-term tube is the Silastic T-tube (Goode tube). We recommend using this tube (instead of a short-term grommet tube) when (1) the ear canal is too narrow to pass a short-term tube (eg, in most Down syndrome children), (2) there are structural changes in the tympanic membrane (atrophy or atelectasis) that impair placing a short-term tube or interfere with tube retention, (3) the physician wishes to more precisely control the duration of ventilation (soft T-tubes can be readily removed in the office setting), or (4) a prolonged period of ventilation is specifically desired. Because of the aforementioned complications and sequelae, we advise strongly *against* using a long-term tube at a preset interval (eg, the second or third tube placement) or for routine management of all children with craniofacial syndromes or disorders.

CONSEQUENCES OF TYMPANOSTOMY TUBES

Changes in Health Status

The impact of chronic or recurrent OM on children can be profound, and most parents report improved quality of life shortly after tube placement. Rosenfeld and colleagues[109] developed a disease-specific quality-of-life survey for children with OM (OM-6) designed to quantify changes in parent perceptions of their child's health status. The survey consisted of six global questions representing the broad domains of physical symptoms—hearing loss, speech problems, activity limitations, emotional distress, and caregiver concerns. When 37 children were surveyed before and after tympanostomy tube placement, 76% had a moderate or large improvement in quality of life, 19% had a small improvement, and 5% experienced a trivial degree of change.

In a multicenter follow-up study using the OM-6, the short-term impact of tympanostomy tubes on quality of life was measured in 248 children (median age 1.4 years).[110] Changes in quality of life before surgery were trivial and were smaller than changes observed after surgery. Improved quality of life occurred after surgery (median 30 days) in 79% of children (56% had large improvement). Physical symptoms, caregiver concerns, emotional distress, and hearing loss were most improved, but significant changes were also seen for activity limitations and speech impairment. Predictors of poorer quality of life (4% of children) were otorrhea 3 or more days (10% of variance), and low satisfaction with surgical decision (3% of variance). Hearing loss, child age, type of OM (recurrent versus chronic), and satisfaction with office visit were unrelated to outcomes.

The quality-of-life improvements noted after tubes for *symptomatic* children are not seen when tubes are placed for persistent but *asymptomatic* MEE. Paradise and colleagues[111] showed no effect of early versus delayed tympanostomy tubes for persistent MEE on developmental outcomes at the age of 3 years. Children qualified for study inclusion if they exceeded an arbitrary threshold of cumulative MEE on the basis of

intense screening from infancy; most were asymptomatic and had unilateral or discontinuous effusions. Rovers and coworkers[112,113] found no effect of tubes versus no tubes for chronic bilateral OME on language development and general (*not* otitis specific) child quality of life. They identified subjects by population-based auditory screening at 9 to 12 months. Although these two studies argue strongly against *routine* tube insertion for asymptomatic children with persistent MEE,[114] they *cannot* be extrapolated to children with pre-existing symptoms, complaints, or developmental delays.

Changes in subjective quality of life after tube insertion do not necessarily correlate with changes observed in objective health status. Improvements in hearing status and tympanic membrane integrity (eg, resolution of a retraction pocket) may not be accurately perceived by parents.[115] Similarly, postoperative changes in speech, language, cognition, or behavior following resolution of chronic middle ear effusion may also be subtle. Many parents, however, do report their children to be less clumsy and accident prone after tube insertion, which relates to the detrimental effects of OME on vestibular function.[116] Several longitudinal studies have demonstrated significant improvements in balance,[117] vestibular function,[118] and gross motor ability[119] after treatment of chronic OME with tympanostomy tubes. Protracted vomiting in infants may also resolve after middle ear ventilation.[120]

Water Precautions

Routine water precautions are *not* a routine consequence of tympanostomy tube insertion. As with tube-related otorrhea (see Table 29-5), water precautions with tubes are another area in which patient education is strongly advised (Table 29-10). There is *no convincing evidence* to justify routine water precautions or abstention from swimming because of indwelling tympanostomy tubes.[121] As noted previously, most TTO results from young age and concurrent respiratory illness, not water penetration. Precautions in the form of earplugs, ear molds, or headbands are appropriate for *selected* children for three reasons: (1) child comfort, (2) prevention of recurrent otorrhea, and (3) treatment of acute otorrhea.

Some children with patent tympanostomy tubes complain of otalgia or discomfort when water enters their ear canal during bathing, hair washing, or swimming. The otalgia is of varying intensity and not associated with otorrhea or signs of acute infection. Although no prospective studies have documented the incidence of this complaint, in our experience it affects less than 5% of intubated children. Parents should be advised that the water entry is not harmful, but that earplugs or headbands may be used for child comfort.

Table 29-10 Patient Information: Tympanostomy Tubes, Earplugs, and Water Precautions

Earplugs, head bands, or other special efforts to prevent water from entering the ear canal are *unnecessary* for most children with tympanostomy tubes.

In theory, the small opening in the tube (about 1/20th of an inch) may permit water to enter the normally dry middle ear space, leading to bacterial infection and ear discharge.

In practice, however, the pressure needed to force water through the tube is very high and is not reached unless a child swims 6 feet or deeper under water.

Medical studies have shown *no difference* in the frequency of ear discharge when children with tubes swim (without earplugs) or when they stay out of the water.

Special efforts to prevent water from entering the ear canal are only necessary when

1. water entry in the ear canal causes pain or discomfort,

2. active discharge or drainage is observed coming out of the ear canal, or

3. frequent or prolonged episodes of ear discharge occur.

Other situations in which routine water precautions should be considered, but are not mandatory, are when

1. swimming more than 6 feet under water,

2. swimming in lakes or nonchlorinated pools, or

3. head dunking in the bathtub (soapy water has a lower surface tension).

A variety of soft, fitted earplugs and neoprene bands are available for water precautions, if needed. Never use Playdoh or Silly Putty as an earplug.

Once the tube becomes blocked or extrudes, water precautions may be stopped unless the eardrum has a perforation

When a child has frequent bouts of acute TTO, water precautions are instituted as a preventive measure. As noted above, less than 10% of children with tubes have three or more discrete otorrhea episodes. *Routine* water precautions in children *without* frequent otorrhea are optional because controlled studies show equivalence for swimmers and nonswimmers (see Table 29-4). The small lumen of a tympanostomy tube requires relatively high external water pressure for entry into the middle ear. This pressure is *not* reached with surface swimming or shallow diving, nor with head submersion in soapy bath water (despite the decreased surface tension).[122,123] Swimming more than 6 feet under water does increase the chance of water penetration, but this rarely occurs at the age most children have tubes.

Children who swim in lakes, ponds, or rivers are exposed to higher bacterial counts than those exposed only to chlorinated pools or salt water. Although a definitive benefit of water precautions has not been shown in such situations, avoiding gross contamination of the middle ear by pathogen-containing water appears prudent.[124,125] A similar situation exists for children who enjoy dunking their head in dirty bath water.

During exposure to contaminated water, earplugs or a headband may be used to decrease the probability of water entry.

Water precautions are also mandatory when a child develops otorrhea. In this situation, we recommend avoiding all elective water exposure (eg, swimming) until the discharge has ceased for 24 to 48 hours. Unless the child has frequent otorrhea or is regularly exposed to contaminated water, water precautions may be discontinued once the acute otorrhea subsides.

Tube Extrusion and Removal

Extrusion of most tubes is initiated by the continual shedding of squamous debris from the epithelium of the tympanic membrane. As debris accumulates under the outer flange of a grommet tube, the pressure causes the flange to lift up from the surface of the tympanic membrane. The inner flange of the tube becomes visible as it presses against the eardrum and begins to extrude as the tube tips posteriorly. When both flanges are clearly in view, extrusion is complete. A long-shafted tube (T-tube) will often accumulate a column of migrating epithelium along its length, although it is still in place and functioning. The absence of an outer flange on a long-shafted tube prevents the above sequence of events from occurring.

The duration of tympanostomy tube function is largely dependent on tube design. Grommet tubes with right angle or bevelled flanges (Armstrong-type tubes) normally last about 13 months, with 95% extruding between 6 and 18 months.[18–20,126] Shepard-type grommets with an hour-glass shape extrude sooner, after a mean duration of about 8 months.[127] Long-shafted tubes (T-tubes) last 20 months or more and frequently require active removal.[128] Earlier extrusion may occur when tubes are inserted into tympanic membranes that have been previously intubated or have been weakened focally by atrophy or atelectasis.[129]

A small percentage of short-term tubes and many long-term tubes will not extrude spontaneously from the tympanic membrane, thereby necessitating surgical removal. Most otolaryngologists will wait at least 2 to 3 years before considering the surgical removal of an uncomplicated short-term (grommet) tube and 4 years for a long-term tube.[130–132] Intubation periods of 3 years or longer have much higher rates of otorrhea, granulation tissue, and persistent perforation than when tubes are removed electively before 3 years.[133,134] Flexible silicone tubes may occasionally be removed in the office setting, but, for rigid materials, general anesthesia is usually necessary. An additional advantage of anesthesia is that epithelial debris or ingrowth can be removed from the perforation edges under microscopic visualization.

Indications for removing a tympanostomy tube are subjective but well described.[130,131,135] Children aged 6 years or older are the best candidates because OM declines rapidly as the immune system and Eustachian tube reach maturity. Younger children, however, may also benefit from removal based on the frequency and severity of associated morbidity. Specific indications for tube removal include the following:

1. Failure of spontaneous tube extrusion after 3 years
2. Retained unilateral tympanostomy tube in a child aged 6 years or older, when the contralateral tympanic membrane is intact and has been free of AOM or OME for at least 1 year
3. Retained bilateral tympanostomy tubes in a child with normal Eustachian tube function, resulting from growth, medical therapy, or surgery (adenoidectomy or cleft palate repair)
4. Frequently recurrent otorrhea despite medical management, particularly in older children with long-standing tubes
5. Chronic otorrhea, unresponsive to topical and systemic antimicrobials

6. Tube-associated granulation tissue or granuloma, topical therapy, or débridement

Myringoplasty with a paper-patch,[131] steri-strip,[135,136] Silastic sheeting,[137] or absorbable gelatin film[138] at the time of tympanostomy tube removal may increase the rate of perforation closure. Although not all children require myringoplasty when the tubes are removed, reasonable indications include long-term tubes, a history of multiple prior intubations, and short-term tubes with epithelial ingrowth or an intubation period of > 2 years.

A rare complication of tympanostomy tubes is displacement into the middle ear, either at the time of insertion or later because of infection or external trauma. The mean incidence of medial tube displacement is 0.5%, ranging from 0 to 1.3% in the literature (see Table 29-7).[65,139,140] Although tubes are inert and unlikely to cause damage if left in the middle ear, removal should be attempted because of potential for foreign body reaction and progressive pathologic changes.[130] Alternatively, the child may return annually for otologic surveillance and binocular microscopy. Surgical removal entails wide myringotomy and extraction, but perseverance may be required if the tube moves beyond the visible confines of the mesotympanum. An exploratory tympanotomy may be necessary on rare occasions.

Complications after Tube Extrusion

A child with middle ear disease severe enough to require tympanostomy tubes remains at risk for recurrent infection and middle ear effusion and for several late complications of tube placement (see Tables 29-8 and 29-9). Although most of these complications are uncommon, early detection and management are necessary to reduce long-term morbidity. Therefore, we advise routine examination of the tympanic membrane by the otolaryngologist after tube extrusion, preferably at approximately 6 and 12 months.

Persistent perforation after tube extrusion related to tube type, duration of intubation, and initial structural integrity of the tympanic membrane.[26,141] Perforation rates in large series are 0.5 to 2% for short-term tubes[18–20,65,142] and about 9% (range 3 to 48%) for long-term tubes[24–26,143,144] Mean perforation rates for short- versus long-term tubes are 2.2 versus 16.6%, respectively (see Table 29-8), with 3.5-fold increase in relative risk for the latter (see Table 29-9). A 6- to 12-month observation period is recommended before surgical closure because most postintubation perforations will close spontaneously.[145] Persistent small, central perforations are plugged with adipose tissue harvested from the posterior aspect of the lobule (80 to

90% success).[146,147] The best results are achieved when the child has been free of active middle ear disease for 1 year, to avoid having to re-intubate a tympanic membrane that has been grafted successfully.[148]

Tympanostomy tubes are associated with structural changes of the tympanic membrane.[149,150] About 40% of tympanic membranes develop asymptomatic whitish plaques of calcium and phosphate crystals, (tympanosclerosis) ranging from 11 to 59%.[108] For every 3.3 children who receive tubes, 1 additional case of tympanosclerosis will occur compared with nonintubated OM controls (rate difference of 30% in Table 29-9). The plaques may be localized or diffuse and are of uncertain etiology. Boys are affected more often than girls,[151] and larger plaques are associated with multiple intubations.[152] Although such plaques may theoretically cause hearing loss if they involve the ossicles, this phenomenon has not been associated with tubes. The hearing impairment caused by tympanosclerosis is less than 0.5 dB, which is inconsequential and cannot serve as an argument against the use of ventilation tubes.[149]

After a tympanostomy tube has extruded, the resultant perforation (about 1 to 2 mm diameter) heals as a dimer composed of only the squamous and mucosal layers of the tympanic membrane (the middle fibrous layer does not regenerate).[153] This potential area of weakness is more susceptible to subsequent retraction or perforation. For every 9 children who receive tubes, 1 additional case of focal atrophy or retraction will occur compared with nonintubated OM controls (rate difference of 11% in Table 29-9). Focal atrophy at the site of a prior tube has an estimated incidence of 18% (13 to 25%),[154–157] and pars tensa retraction pockets have been observed in 1 to 2% of ears.[65,140,157] Most of these changes are nonprogressive, and tympanoplasty is rarely required. Generalized atrophy or tympanic membrane collapse (atelectasis) is caused by poor Eustachian tube function, not by prior intubation.

Acquired cholesteatoma is a rare tube sequela,[65,108,139,158–161] but tubes may have an overall protective effect on cholesteatoma formation in children with OM.[162] Long-term tubes are 3.5 times more likely to result in a cholesteatoma compared with short-term tubes (see Tables 29-8 and 29-9). Retraction pockets are the first step in the genesis of an acquired cholesteatoma. If a deep or narrow-mouthed pocket at a prior tube site begins to collect squamous debris and egress of the material is impossible, granulation tissue formation and secondary infection ensue. Expansion of the pocket causes recurrent infection and bone destruction. Cholesteatoma is best prevented by routine follow-up of all children by an otolaryngologist after tube extrusion so that precursor retractions can be detected and appropriately monitored. Established cholesteatoma requires surgical intervention.

Tube Follow-Up and Aftercare

Regular and timely follow-up of all children with tympanostomy tubes is essential for optimum outcomes.[132,163,164] The initial postoperative follow-up visit should be performed by the otolaryngologist to verify the patency and functional status of the tube. Subsequent tube "check-ups" are scheduled with the otolaryngologist at 4- to 6-month intervals *regardless* of how well the child is doing. The purpose of these check-ups is to

- confirm tube patency and middle ear status,
- detect granulation tissue and foreign body reaction *before* problems ensue,
- institute measures, when necessary, to control recurrent or chronic otorrhea,
- reassess the need (if any) for water precautions (see Table 29-10),
- reinforce principles of managing otorrhea (see Table 29-6) and the importance of tube follow-up (Table 29-11) even if the child is asymptomatic, and to
- implement strategies for judicious use of antimicrobials (see below).

Only an ear specialist has the training, expertise, and equipment (eg, binocular microscope) to achieve the above objectives. Evaluation *only* by the child's primary-care practitioner is inadequate, regardless of the stipulations by third-party payers or managed-care insurance companies. Similarly, absence of symptoms does not imply absence of problems with a tube; granulation tissue, tube displacement, or tube obstruction (with or without OME relapse) may have a prolonged asymptomatic interval. Early detection and management are the best means of minimizing short-term morbidity and long-term sequelae. Routine and regular follow-up is particularly important for children with pre-existing sensorineural hearing loss or documented language or developmental delay and for those with special needs, in whom the additional conductive hearing compromise associated with a nonfunctional tube could be debilitating.[163]

An audiologic evaluation should be performed postoperatively,[165,166] especially if normal hearing was not established prior to surgery.[163] The purpose of this assessment is to detect children with persistent conductive or sensorineural hearing loss, independent of OME, who require additional diagnostic evaluation. Rarely, the tube itself may cause a mild conductive hearing loss (about 10 to 20 dB), which resolves if the tube is occluded temporarily with a paper patch.[167] Extended follow-up of children with tubes, however,

Table 29-11 Patient Information: Tympanostomy Tube Follow-Up

Children with tympanostomy tubes should be seen by the physician who inserted the tube on a regular basis, usually every 4 to 6 months, until the tube falls out.

Regular follow-up is required to detect the following conditions, which may have no readily apparent symptoms but do benefit from early diagnosis and treatment:

1. Blockage or obstruction of the tube opening with relapse of middle ear fluid

2. Displacement or extrusion of the tube from the eardrum

3. Irritation of the eardrum by the edge of the tube, producing a small pimple (also called a granuloma or granulation tissue)

Follow-up examinations by the primary care physician alone are insufficient; only an ear specialist has the proper training and equipment to optimally monitor tube status.

An absence of symptoms or apparent problems does not imply that the tube is intact and functioning properly; all children need follow-up regardless of how well they are doing.

After your child's tubes fall out, you should return for a final recheck after 6 to 12 months to check for relapse of middle ear fluid and abnormalities of the eardrum.

Some children develop a whitish mark or "scar" on the eardrum after a tube comes out; the scar usually persists but does not impair hearing or require any medical attention.

Table 29-12 Indications for Otolaryngologic Referral after Tympanostomy Tubes

Suggested	*Strongly Recommended*
Every 4 to 6 months after tube placement	Postoperative audiogram
Six to 12 months after tube extrusion	When unable to visualize the tube
Recurrent or chronic otorrhea	Bloody otorrhea
Occluded tube	Otorrhea not controlled by antibiotics
Tympanic membrane perforation	Worsening hearing
Tympanic membrane structural defect	Persistent otalgia
Imbalance	Granulation tissue
	Retention of tube for more than 2 years

shows no evidence of persistent hearing loss directly attributable to intubation.[168] Because one-third of ears in this series continued to have middle ear sequelae, the authors advocate proper follow-up and restoration of middle ear ventilation with repeat tubes, if not otherwise achieved.

Strategies for judicious use of antimicrobials should be discussed at all tube follow-up visits for children who continue to have frequent AOM. Oral antimicrobials are *unnecessary* for most intubated children with nonsevere AOM and no otorrhea because a functioning tube promotes early resolution through direct ventilation and drainage of the middle ear. In contrast, antimicrobials are appropriate for very young or severely ill children with AOM, especially when otorrhea or concurrent ill-

ness is present (eg, rhinosinusitis). Otorrhea without other systemic symptoms or signs of toxicity generally responds to topical antimicrobial drops alone without any need for oral therapy.

Indications for otolaryngologic referral after tympanostomy tubes are summarized in Table 29-12. Of note is the need for a routine follow-up visit approximately 6 to 12 months *after* extrusion of both tubes, to detect abnormalities of the middle ear and tympanic membrane.[156] Children without significant pathology at this visit no longer require specialist evaluation. In contrast, children with OME, atrophy, atelectasis, or retraction pockets require ongoing otologic surveillance to prevent adhesion, cholesteatoma, and hearing loss. Tympanic membrane pathology progressively increases in many children for at least 7 years after tube treatment of chronic OME.[157] These changes are not a "complication" of tube placement but, rather, reflect the inability of the tubes to alter underlying poor Eustachian tube function and middle ear hypoventilation.

BEYOND TUBE CONSEQUENCES

A chapter on the consequences of tympanostomy tubes must, by necessity, emphasize potential complications and sequelae. A problem-oriented approach, however, belies the fact that tubes are relatively problem-free for most children. The impact on quality of life can be profound,[110,169] with a dramatic increase in well being and an equally dramatic reduction in otitis-related physi-

cian visits and antibiotic use. Qualitative comments from parents whose children receive tubes are that the results have been wonderful—improved appetite, less irritability, improved awareness, improved social interaction, and a much happier child.[170]

Tympanostomy tubes are safe and effective for carefully selected children with OM. We again emphasize that tubes are not a panacea but simply a means of reliably bypassing a dysfunctional Eustachian tube while the child grows and develops. Ongoing communication among the patient, otolaryngologist, and primary-care physician will minimize the potential morbidity from tubes and the underlying factors that originally resulted in OM. We hope that this chapter and the pointers in Table 29-13 will help facilitate such communication.

Table 29-13 Pointers and Pitfalls

1. Tympanostomy tubes are not a panacea for OM; they simply bypass a dysfunctional Eustachian tube and ventilate the middle ear while a child grows and develops.

2. Most tubes extrude spontaneously because of epithelial debris and migration; because this occurs independent of Eustachian tube function, OM may subsequently recur.

3. About one-third of intubated children experience otorrhea, but less than 10% have frequent or chronic drainage; most otorrhea can be managed with ototopical antimicrobials.

4. Prophylactic antibiotic eardrops administered during or shortly after tube insertion have a minor impact on rates of early postoperative otorrhea.

5. Most otorrhea is secondary to viral illness, not external water entry; routine water precautions or swimming restrictions are unnecessary for most children with tubes.

6. Bloody otorrhea is usually caused by granulation tissue adjacent to the tube.

7. Parents usually report large improvements in their child's quality of life after tubes; poorer outcomes occur with prolonged otorrhea and with lower satisfaction when opting for tubes.

8. Short-term (grommet-type) tubes are preferred for children because long-term (T-type) tubes cause more otorrhea, perforation, granulation tissue, and structural changes.

9. Tympanosclerosis or "scarring" after tubes is common but is generally a cosmetic issue; intervention is rarely needed, and there is no discernible impact on hearing levels.

10. Focal atrophy or retraction may occur at the intubation site after tube extrusion; generalized atrophy or atelectasis, however, is caused by poor Eustachian function, not by a prior tube.

11. Intubated children should be seen by an otolaryngologist every 4 to 6 months; primary-care physicians do not have the equipment or expertise for early detection of complications.

12. A follow-up visit with the otolaryngologist is needed between 6 to 12 months after extrusion of both tubes; children with structural changes in the TM require ongoing surveillance.

13. Children with Eustachian tube dysfunction of sufficient severity to require tubes are at risk of progressive structural changes in the TM for at least several years after tube extrusion.

OM = otitis media; TM = tympanic membrane.

REFERENCES

1. Derkay CS. Pediatric otolaryngology procedures in the US: 1978-1987. Int J Pediatr Otorhinolaryngol 1993;25:1–12.

2. Vital and Health Statistics. Ambulatory and inpatient procedures in the United States, 1996. Series 13: Data From the National Health Care Survey No. 139. Hyattsville (MD): US Department Health and Human Services Publication no. (PHS) 99-1710; p. 13.

3. Kogan MD, Overpeck MD, Hoffman HJ, Casselbrant ML. Factors associated with tympanostomy tube insertion among preschool-aged children in the United States. Am J Public Health 2000;90:245–50.

4. Myer CM, France A. Ventilation tube placement in a managed care population. Arch Otol Rhinol Laryngol 1997;123:226–8.

5. Rosenfeld RM. Surgical prevention of otitis media. Vaccine 2001;19:S134–9.

6. Black N. Surgery for glue ear: the English epidemic wanes. J Epidemiol Community Health 1995;49(3):234–7.

7. Coyte PC, Asche CV, Ho E, et al. Comparative cost analysis of myringotomy with insertion of ventilation tubes in Ontario and British Columbia. J Otolaryngol 1998;27:69–75.

8. Coyte PC, Croxford R, Asche CV, et al. Physician and population determinants of rates of middle-ear surgery in Ontario. JAMA 2001;286;2128–35.

9. Engel JAM, Anteunis LJC, Hendriks JJT. Treatment with grommets in The Netherlands: incidence in children from birth to 12 years. In: Tos M, Thomsen J, Balle V, editors. Otitis media today. The Hague/The Netherlands: Kugler Publications; 1999. p. 451–5.

10. Mason J, Freemantle N, Browning G. Impact of effective health care bulletin on treatment of persistent glue ear in children: time series analysis. BMJ 2001;323:1096–7.

11. Bluestone CD, Paradise LJ, Berry QC. Physiology of the Eustachian tube in the pathogenesis and management of middle ear effusions. Laryngoscope 1972;82:1654–70.

12. Berger G. Nature of spontaneous tympanic membrane perforation in acute otitis media in children. J Laryngol Otol 1989;103:1150–3.

13. Politzer A. History of otology. Vol I. Phoenix (AZ): Columella Press; 1981. p. 198–200.

14. Alberti PW. Myringotomy and ventilating tubes in the 19th century. Laryngoscope 1974;84:805–15.

15. Armstrong BW. A new treatment for chronic secretory otitis media. Arch Otolaryngol 1954;59:653–4.

16. Kleinman LC, Kosecoff J, Dubois RW, Brook RH. The medical appropriateness of tympanostomy tubes proposed for children younger than 16 years in the United States. JAMA 1994;271:1250–5.

17. Bluestone CD, Klein JO, Gates GA. 'Appropriateness' of tympanostomy tubes: setting the record straight. Arch Otolaryngol Head Neck Surg 1994;120:1051–3.

18. Mandel EM, Rockette HE, Bluestone CD, et al. Myringotomy with and without tympanostomy tubes for chronic otitis media with effusion. Arch Otolaryngol Head Neck Surg 1989;115:1217–24.

19. Mandel EM, Rockette HE, Bluestone CD, et al. Efficacy of myringotomy with and without tympanostomy tubes for chronic otitis media with effusion. Pediatr Infect Dis J 1992;11:270–7.

20. Casselbrant ML, Kaleida PH, Rockette HE, et al. Efficacy of antimicrobial prophylaxis and of tympanostomy tube insertion in the prevention of recurrent acute otitis media: results of a randomized clinical trial. Pediatr Infect Dis J 1992;11:278–86.

21. Gates GA, Avery CA, Cooper JC, Prihoda TJ. Chronic secretory otitis media: effects of surgical management. Ann Otol Rhinol Laryngol 1989;98 Suppl 138:2–32.

22. Giebink GS. Preventing otitis media. Ann Otol Rhinol Laryngol 1994;163:20–3.

23. Siegel G, Brodsky L, Waner M, et al. Office based laser assisted tympanic membrane fenestration in adults and children: pilot data to support an alternative to traditional approaches to otitis media. Int J Pediatr Otorhinolaryngol 2000;53:111–20.

24. Siegel MT, Parker MY, Goldsmith MM, et al. A prospective randomized study of four commonly used tympanostomy tubes. Laryngoscope 1989;99:252–6.

25. Von Schoenberg M, Wengraf CL, Gleeson M. Results of middle ear ventilation with Goode's tubes. Clin Otolaryngol 1989;14:503–8.

26. Goode RL. Long-term middle ear ventilation with T tubes: the perforation problem. Otolaryngol Head Neck Surg 1996;115:500–1.

27. van Baarle PWL, Wentges RT. Extrusion of transtympanic ventilating tubes, relative to site of insertion. ORL J Oto Rhino Laryngol Relat Spec 1975;37:35–40.

28. Soderberg O, Hellstrom SOM. Effects of different tympanostomy tubes (Teflon and stainless steel) on the tympanic membrane structures. In: Lim DJ, Bluestone CD, Klein JO, Nelson JD, editors. Recent advances in otitis media, Toronto (ON): BC Decker Inc; 1988. p. 280–2.

29. Gourin CG, Hubbell RN. Otorrhea after insertion of silver oxide-impregnated Silastic tympanostomy tubes. Arch Otolaryngol Head Neck Surg 1999;125:446–50.

30. Saidi IS, Biedlingmaier JF, Whelan P. In vivo resistance to bacterial biofilm formation on tympanostomy tubes as a function of tube material. Otolaryngol Head Neck Surg 1999;120:621–7.

31. Berry JA, Biedlingmaier JF, Whelan PJ. In vitro resistance to bacterial biofilm formation on coated fluoroplastic tympanostomy tubes. Otolaryngol Head Neck Surg 2000;123:246–51.

32. Kinnari TJ, Salonen EM, Jero J. New method for coating tympanostomy tubes to prevent tube occlusions. Int J Pediatr Otorhinolaryngol 2001;58:107–11.

33. April MM, Portella RR, Orobello PW, Naclerio RM. Tympanostomy tube insertion: anterosuperior vs. anterioinferior quadrant. Otolaryngol Head Neck Surg 1992;106:241–2.

34. Bluestone CD, Klein JO. Otitis media, atelectasis, and Eustachian tube dysfunction. In: Bluestone CD, Stool SE, Kenna MA, editors. Pediatric otolaryngology. 3rd ed. Philadelphia (PA): WB Saunders; 1996. p. 545–9.

35. Hern JD, Jonathan DA. Insertion of ventilation tubes: does the site matter? Clin Otolaryngol 1999;24:424–5.

36. Jahn AF. Middle ear ventilation with HydroxlVent tube: review of the initial series. Otolaryngol Head Neck Surg 1993;108:701–5.

37. Bluestone CD. Tympanostomy tubes and related procedures. In: Bluestone CD, Rosenfeld RM, editors. Surgical atlas of pediatric otolaryngology. Hamilton (ON): BC Decker Inc; 2002.

38. Bluestone CD, Klein JO. Method of examination: clinical examination. In: Bluestone CD, Stool SE, editors. Pediatric otolaryngology, Philadelphia (PA): WB Saunders Co.; 1990. p. 111–24.

39. Bluestone CD, Klein JO. Otitis media in infants and children. Philadelphia (PA): WB Saunders Co.; 1988. p. 89.

40. Westine JG, Giannoni CM, Gajewski B, Antonelli PJ. Opening plugged tympanostomy tubes. Laryngoscope 2002;112:1342–5.

41. Spraggs PDR, Robinson PJ, Ryan R, et al. A prospective randomised trial of the use of sodium bicarbonate and hydrogen peroxide ear drops to clear a blocked tympanostomy tube. Int J Pediatr Otorhinolaryngol 1995;31:207–14.

42. Altman JS, Haupert MS, Hamaker RA, Belenky WM. Phenylephrine and the prevention of postoperative tympanostomy tube obstruction. Arch Otolaryngol Head Neck Surg 1998;124:1233–6.

43. Scott BA, Strunk CL. Posttympanostomy otorrhea: the efficacy of canal preparation. Laryngoscope 1992;102:1103–7.

44. Giebink GS, Daly K, Buran DJ, et al. Predictors for postoperative otorrhea following tympanostomy tube insertion. Arch Otolaryngol Head Neck Surg 1992;118:491–4.

45. Sutton DV, Derkay CS, Darrow DH, Strasnick B. Resistant bacteria in middle ear fluid at the time of tympanostomy tube surgery. Ann Otol Rhinol Laryngol 2000;109:24–9.

46. Gross RD, Burgess LP, Holtel MR, et al. Saline irrigation in the prevention of otorrhea after tympanostomy tube placement. Laryngoscope 2000;110:246–9.

47. Balkany TJ, Barkin RM, Suzuki BH, Watson WJ. A prospective study of infection following tympanostomy and tube insertion. Am J Otol 1983;4:288–91.

48. Baker RS, Chole RA. A randomized clinical trial of topical gentamicin after tympanostomy tube placement. Arch Otolaryngol Head Neck Surg 1988;114:755–7.

49. Epstein JS, Beane J, Hubbell R. Prevention of early otorrhea in ventilation tubes. Otolaryngol Head Neck Surg 1992;107:758–62.

50. Cannon CR. Early otorrhea following ear tube insertion. J Miss State Med Assoc 1997;38:39–43.

51. Ramadan HH, Tarazi T, Zaytoun GM. Use of prophylactic otic drops after tympanostomy tube insertion. Arch Otolaryngol Head Neck Surg 1991;117:537.

52. Scott BA, Strunk CL Jr. Post-tympanostomy otorrhea: a randomized clinical trial of topical prophylaxis. Otolaryngol Head Neck Surg 1992;106:34–41.

53. Younis RT, Lazar RH, Long TE. Ventilation tubes and prophylactic antibiotic ear drops. Otolaryngol Head Neck Surg 1992;106:193–5.

54. Salam MA, Cable HR. The use of antibiotic/steroid ear drops to reduce post-operative otorrhoea and blockage of ventilation tubes. A prospective study. J Laryngol Otol 1993;107:188–9.

55. Hester TO, Jones RO, Archer SM, Hayden RC. Prophylactic antibiotic drops after tympanostomy tube placement. Arch Otolaryngol Head Neck Surg 1995;121: 445–8.

56. Welling DB, Forrest LA, Goll F III. Safety of ototopical antibiotics. Laryngoscope 1995;105:472–4.

57. Shinkwin CA, Murty GE, Simo R, Jones NS. Per-operative antibiotic/steroid prophylaxis of tympanostomy tube otorrhoea: chemical or mechanical effect? J Laryngol Otol 1996;110:531–3.

58. Morpeth JF, Bent JP, Watson T. A comparison of Cortisporin and ciprofloxacin otic drops as prophylaxis against post-tympanostomy otorrhea. Int J Pediatr Otorhinolaryngol 2001;61:99–104.

59. Smelt GJ, Yeoh LH. Swimming and grommets. J Laryngol Otol 1984; 98:243–5.

60. Sharma PD. Swimming with grommets. Scand Audiol 1986;Suppl 26:89–91.

61. Becker GD, Eckberg TJ, Goldware RR. Swimming and tympanostomy tubes: a prospective study. Laryngoscope 1987;97:740–1.

62. Parker GS, Tami TA, Maddox MR, Wilson JF. The effect of water exposure after tympanostomy tube insertion. Am J Otolaryngol 1994;15:193–6.

63. Salata JA, Derkay CS. Water precautions in children with tympanostomy tubes. Arch Otolaryngol Head Neck Surg 1996;122:276–80.

64. Kay DJ, Nelson M, Rosenfeld RM. Meta-analysis of tympanostomy tube sequelae. Otolaryngol Head Neck Surg 2001;124:374–80.

65. McLelland CA. Incidence of complications from use of tympanostomy tubes. Arch Otolaryngol 1980;106:97–9.

66. Herzon FS. Tympanostomy tubes: infectious complications. Arch Otolaryngol 1980;106:645–7.

67. Debruyne F, Jorissen M, Poelmans J. Otorrhea during transtympanal ventilation. Am J Otol 1988;9:316–7.

68. Mandel EM, Casselbrant ML, Kurs-Lasky M. Acute otorrhea: bacteriology of a common complication of tympanostomy tubes. Ann Otol Rhinol Laryngol 1994;103:713–8.

69. Ah-Tye C, Paradise JL, Colborn K. Otorrhea in young children after tympanostomy-tube placement for persistent middle-ear effusion: prevalence, incidence, and duration. Pediatrics 2001;107:1251–8.

70. Lee D, Youk A, Goldstein NA. A meta-analysis of swimming and water precautions. Laryngoscope 1999;109:536–40.

71. Carbonell R, Ruiz-Garcia V. Ventilation tubes after surgery for otitis media with effusion or acute otitis media and swimming. Systematic review and meta-analysis. Int J Pediatr Otorhinolaryngol 2002;66:281–9.

72. Daly KA, Giebink GS, Lindgren B, et al. Randomized trial of the efficacy of trimethoprim-sulfamethoxazole and prednisone in preventing post-tympanostomy tube morbidity. Pediatr Infect Dis J 1995;14:1068–74.

73. Schneider ML. Bacteriology of otorrhea from tympanostomy tubes. Arch Otolaryngol Head Neck Surg 1989;115:1225–6.

74. Dohar JE, Garner ET, Nielsen RW, et al. Topical ofloxacin treatment of otorrhea in children with tympanostomy tubes. Arch Otolaryngol Head Neck Surg 1999;125:537–45.

75. Fliss DM, Dagan R, Meidan N, Leiberman A. Aerobic bacteriology of chronic suppurative otitis media without cholesteatoma in children. Ann Otol Rhinol Laryngol 1992;101:866–9.

76. Hannley MT, Denneny JC, Holzer SS. Use of ototopical antibiotics in treating 3 common ear diseases. Otolaryngol Head Neck Surg 2000;122:934–40.

77. Acuin J, Smith A, Mackenzie I. Interventions for chronic suppurative otitis media (Cochrane Review). In: the Cochrane Library, Issue 2, 2002. Oxford (UK): Update Software; 2002.

78. Wintermeyer SM, Hart MC, Nahata MC. Efficacy of ototopical ciprofloxacin in pediatric patients with otorrhea. Otolaryngol Head Neck Surg 1997;116:450–3.

79. Force RW, Hart MC, Plummer SA, et al. Topical ciprofloxacin for otorrhea after tympanostomy tube placement. Arch Otolaryngol Head Neck Surg 1995;121:880–4.

80. Goldblatt EL, Dohar J, Nozza RJ, et al. Topical ofloxacin versus systemic amoxicillin/clavulanate in purulent otorrhea in children with tympanostomy tubes. Int J Pediatr Otorhinolaryngol 1998;46:91–101.

81. Gates GA. Safety of ofloxacin otic and other ototopical treatments in animal models and in humans. Pediatr Infect Dis J 2001;20:104–7.

82. Roland PS, Anon JB, Conroy PJ et al, for the CiproDex study group. Topical ciprofloxacin/dexamethasone is superior to ciprofloxacin alone in pediatric patients with acute otitis media with tympanostomy tubes. Laryngoscope. [In press]

83. Roland PS, Kreisler L, Reese B, et al. Topical ciprofloxacin/dexamethasone otic suspension is superior to ofloxacin otic solution in the treatment of children with acute otitis media with otorrhea through tympanostomy tubes. Alcon Laboratories; unpublished data.

84. Martinez-Martinez L, Pascual A, Jacoby GA. Quinolone resistance from a transferable plasmid. Lancet 1998;351:797–9.

85. Pina SE, Mattingly A. The role of fluoroquinolones in the promotion of alginate synthesis and antibiotic resistance in *Pseudomonas aeruginosa*. Curr Microbiol 1997;35:103–8.

86. Berenholz L, Katzenell U, Harell M. Evolving resistant *Pseudomonas* to ciprofloxacin in malignant otitis externa. Laryngoscope 2002;112:1619–22.

87. Hartnick CJ, Shott S, Willging P, Myer CM III. Methicillin-resistant *Staphylococcus aureus* otorrhea after tympanostomy tube placement. Arch Otolaryngol Head Neck Surg 2000;126:1440–3.

88. Wright CG, Meyerhoff WL. Ototoxicity of otic drops applied to the middle ear in the chinchilla. Am J Otolaryngol 1984;5:166–76.

89. Welling DB, Forrest LA, Goll F. Safety of ototopical antibiotics. Laryngoscope 1995;105:472–4.

90. Alper CM, Dohar JE, Gulhan M, et al. Treatment of chronic suppurative otitis media with topical tobramycin and dexamethasone. Arch Otolaryngol Head Neck Surg 2000;126:165–73.

91. Saunders MW, Robinson PJ. How easily do topical antibiotics pass through tympanostomy tubes?—an in vitro study. Int J Pediatr Otorhinolaryngol 1999;50:45–50.

92. Herbert RL II, Vick ML, King GE, Bent JP III. Tympanostomy tubes and otic suspensions: do they reach the middle ear space? Otolaryngol Head Neck Surg 2000;122:330–3.

93. Supance JS, Bluestone CD. Medical management of the chronic draining ear. Laryngoscope 1983;93:661–2.

94. Nelson JD. Management of chronic suppurative otitis media: a survey of practicing pediatricians. Workshop on chronic suppurative otitis media: etiology and management. St. Louis (MO): Annals Publishing Co.; 1988. p. 26–7.

95. Cohen SR, Thompson JW. Otitic candidiasis in children: an evaluation of the problem and effectiveness of ketoconazole in 10 patients. Ann Otol Rhinol Laryngol 1990;99:427–31.

96. Schrader N, Isaacson G. Fungal otitis externa—its association with fluoroquinolone eardrops [letter to the editor]. Pediatrics. [In press]

97. Cohen SR, Thompson JW. Otitic candidiasis in children: an evaluation of the problem and the effectiveness of ketoconazole in 10 patients. Ann Otol Rhinol Laryngol 1990;99:427–31.

98. Shelton C, Brackmann DE. Actinomycosis otitis media. Arch Otolaryngol Head Neck Surg 1988;114:88–9.

99. Hall PJ, Farrior JB. Aspergillus mastoiditis. Otolaryngol Head Neck Surg 1993;108:167–70.

100. Poole MD. Treatment of otorrhea associated with tubes or perforations. Ear Nose Throat J 1993 72:225–6.

101. Kenna MA, Bluestone CD, Reilly JS, Lusk RP. Medical management of chronic suppurative otitis media without cholesteatoma in children. Laryngoscope 1986;96:146–51.

102. Arguedas AG, Herrera JF, Faingezicht I, Mohs E. Ceftazidime for the therapy of children with chronic suppurative otitis media without cholesteatoma. Pediatr Infect Dis J 1993;12:246–7.

103. Luxford WM, Sheehy JL. Myringotomy and ventilation tubes: a report of 1568 ears. Laryngoscope 1982;92:1293–7.

104. Post JC. Direct evidence of bacterial biofilms in otitis media. Laryngoscope 2001;111:2083–94.

105. Mangat KS, Morrison GAJ, Ganniwalla TM. T-tubes: a retrospective review of 1274 insertions over a 4-year period. Int J Pediatr Otorhinolaryngol 1993;25:119–25.

106. Lildholdt T. Ventilation tubes in secretory otitis media. A randomized, controlled study of the course, the complications, and the sequelae of ventilation tubes. Acta Otolaryngol 1983;398 Suppl:1–28.

107. Bernard PAM, Stenstrom RJ, Feldman W, Durieux-Smith A. Randomized, controlled trial comparing long-term sulfonamide therapy to ventilation tubes for otitis media with effusion. Pediatrics 1991;88:215–22.

108. Goldstein NA, Roland JT Jr, Sculerati N. Complications of tympanostomy tubes in an inner city clinic population. Int J Pediatr Otorhinolaryngol 1996;34:87–99.

109. Rosenfeld RM, Goldsmith AJ, Tetlus L, Balzano A. Quality of life for children with otitis media. Arch Otolaryngol Head Neck Surg 1997;123:1049–54.

110. Rosenfeld RM, Bhaya MH, Bower CM, et al. Impact of tympanostomy tubes on child quality of life. Arch Otolaryngol Head Neck Surg 2000;126:585–92.

111. Paradise JL, Feldman HM, Campbell TF, et al. Effect of early or delayed insertion of tympanostomy tubes for persistent otitis media on developmental outcomes at the age of three years. N Engl J Med 2001;344:1179–87.

112. Rovers MM, Straatman H, Ingels K, et al. The effect of ventilation tubes on language development in infants with otitis media with effusion. A randomized trial. Pediatrics 2000;106:E42.

113. Rovers MM, Krabbe PFM, Straatman H, et al. Randomised controlled trial of the effect of ventilation tubes (grommets) on quality of life at age 1-2 years. Arch Dis Child 2001;84:45–9.

114. Hartman M, Rovers MM, Ingels K, et al. Economic evaluation of ventilation tubes in otitis media with effusion. Arch Otolaryngol Head Neck Surg 2001;127:1471–6.

115. Rosenfeld RM, Goldsmith AJ, Madell JR. How accurate is parent rating of hearing for children with otitis media? Arch Otolaryngol Head Neck Surg 1998;124:989–92.

116. Casselbrant ML, Redfern MS, Furman JM, et al. Visual-induced postural sway in children with and without otitis media. Ann Otol Rhinol Laryngol 1998;107:401–5.

117. Golz A, Angel-Yeger B, Parush S. Evaluation of balance disturbances in children with middle-ear effusion. Int J Pediatr Otorhinolaryngol 1998;43:21–6.

118. Casselbrant ML, Furman JM, Rubenstein E, Mandel EM. Effect of otitis media on the vestibular system in children. Ann Otol Rhinol Laryngol 1995;104:620–4.

119. Orlin MN, Effgen SK, Handler SD. Effect of otitis media with effusion on gross motor ability in preschool-aged children: preliminary findings. Pediatrics 1997;99:334–7.

120. Feinmesser R, Segal K, Granot E. Minimal middle ear effusion: an indication for ventilation tubes in infants with protracted vomiting. J Otolaryngol 1993;22:108–9.

121. Giannoni C. Swimming with tympanostomy tubes. Arch Otolaryngol Head Neck Surg 2000;126:1507–8.

122. Marks NJ, Mills RP. Swimming and grommets. J R Soc Med 1983;76:23–6.

123. Pashley NRT, Scholl PD. Tympanostomy tubes and liquids: an in vitro study. J Otolaryngol 1984;13:296–8.

124. Jaffe BF. Are water and tympanostomy tubes compatible? Laryngoscope 1981;91:631–4.

125. Johnson DW, Mathog RH, Maisel RH. Tympanostomy tube protection with ear plugs. Arch Otolaryngol 1977;103:377–80.

126. Weigel MT, Parker MY, Goldsmith MM, et al. A prospective randomized study of four commonly used tympanostomy tubes. Laryngoscope 1989;99:252–6.

127. Hussain SS. Extrusion rate of Shah and Shepard ventilation tubes in children. Ear Nose Throat J 1992;71:273–5.

128. Moore PJ. Ventilation tube duration versus design. Ann Otol Rhinol Laryngol 1990;99:722–3.

129. Leopold DA, McCabe BF. Factors influencing tympanostomy tube function and extrusion: a study of 1,127 ears. Otolaryngol Head Neck Surg 1980;88:447–54.

130. Cunningham MJ, Eavey RD, Krouse JH, Kiskaddon RM. Tympanostomy tubes: experience with removal. Laryngoscope 1993;103:659–62.

131. Pribitkin EA, Handler SD, Lawrence WCT, et al. Ventilation tube removal: indications for paper patch myringoplasty. Arch Otolaryngol Head Neck Surg 1992;118:495–7.

132. Derkay CS, Carron JD, Wiatrak BJ, et al. Postsurgical follow-up of children with tympanostomy tubes: results of the American Academy of Otolaryngology—Head and Neck Surgery Pediatric Otolaryngology Committee National Survey. Otolaryngol Head Neck Surg 2000;122:313–8.

133. Lentsch EJ, Goudy S, Ganzel TM, et al. Rate of persistent perforation after elective tympanostomy tube removal in pediatric patients. Int J Pediatr Otorhinolaryngol 2000;54:143–8.

134. El-Bitar MA, Pena MT, Choi SS, Zalzal GH. Retained ventilation tubes: should they be removed at 2 years? Arch Otolaryngol Head Neck Surg 2002;128:1357–60.

135. Bluestone CD. Otologic surgical procedures. In: Bluestone CD, Stool SE, editors. Atlas of pediatric otolaryngology. Philadelphia (PA): WB Saunders; 1995. p. 38–41.

136. Saito T, Iwaki E, Kohno Y, et al. Prevention of persistent ear drum perforation after long-term ventilation tube treatment for otitis media with effusion in children. Int J Pediatr Otorhinolaryngol 1996;38:31–9.

137. Courteney-Harris RG. Ford GR, Ganiwalla TMJ, Mangat KS. Closure of tympanic membrane perforations after the removal of Good-type tympanostomy tubes: the use of Silastic sheeting. J Laryngol Otol 1992;106:960–2.

138. Hekkenberg RJ, Smitheringale AJ. Gelfoam/Gelfilm patching following the removal of ventilation tubes. J Otolaryngol 1995;24:362–3.

139. Hughes LA, Warder FR, Hudson WR. Complications of tympanostomy tubes. Arch Otolaryngol 1974;100:151–4.

140. Birck HG, Mravec JJ. Myringotomy for middle ear effusions. Ann Otol Rhinol Laryngol 1976;85 Suppl 25:263–7.

141. Nichols PT, Ramadan HH, Wax MK, Santrock RD. Relationship between tympanic membrane perforation and retained ventilation tubes. Arch Otolaryngol Head Neck Surg 1998;124:417–9.

142. Paradise JL, Bluestone CD, Rogers KD, et al. Efficacy of adenoidectomy for recurrent otitis media in children previously treated with tympanostomy-tube placement. JAMA 1990;263:2066–73.

143. Buckley WJ, Bowes AK, Marlowe JF. Complications following ventilation of the middle ear with Goode T tubes. Arch Otolaryngol Head Neck Surg 1991;117:895–8.

144. Per-Lee JH. Experience with a "permanent" wide flange middle ear ventilation tube. Laryngoscope 1981;91:1063–73.

145. Koch WM, Friedman EM, McGill TJE, Healy GB. Tympanoplasty in children. Arch Otolaryngol Head Neck Surg 1990;116:35–40.

146. Gross CW, Bassila M, Lazar RH, et al. Adipose plug myringoplasty: an alternative to formal myringoplasty techniques in children. Otolaryngol Head Neck Surg 1989;101:617–20.

147. Deddens AE, Muntz HR, Lusk RP. Adipose myringoplasty in children. Laryngoscope 1993;103:216–9.

148. Bluestone CD, Cantekin EI, Douglas GS. Eustachian tube function related to the results of tympanoplasty in children. Laryngoscope 1979;89:450–8.

149. Tos M, Stangerup SE. Hearing loss in tympanosclerosis caused by grommets. Arch Otolaryngol Head Neck Surg 1989;115:931–5.

150. Pichichero ME, Berghash LR, Hengerer AS. Anatomic and audiologic sequelae after tympanostomy tube insertion or prolonged antibiotic therapy for otitis media. Pediatr Infect Dis J 1989;8:780–7.

151. Koc A, Uneri C. Sex distribution in children with tympanosclerosis after insertion of a tympanostomy tube. Eur Arch Otorhinolaryngol 2001;258:16–9.

152. Friedman EM, Sprecher RC, Simon S, Dunn JK. Quantitation and prevalence of tympanosclerosis in a pediatric otolaryngologic clinic. Int J Pediatr Otorhinolaryngol 2001;60:205–11.

153. Schuknecht HF. Pathology of the ear. Cambridge (MA): Harvard University Press; 1974. p. 256–7.

154. Brown MJKM, Richards SH, Ambegaokar AG. Grommets and glue ear: a five-year follow-up of a controlled trial. J R Soc Med 1978;71:353–6.

155. Karma P, Sipila M, Kokko E. Long-term results of tympanostomy tube treatment in chronic secretory otitis media. Acta Otolaryngol Stockh 1982;94 Suppl 386: 163–5.

156. Sederberg-Olsen JF, Sederberg-Olsen AE, Jensen AM. Late sequelae related to treatment with ventilation tubes for secretory otitis media in ENT practice. In: Mogi G, Honjo I, Tetsuo I, Takasaka T, editors. Recent advances in otitis media. Amsterdam: Kugler Publications; 1994. p. 843–6.

157. Giebink GS, Daly KA, Lindgren B, et al. Seven-year prospective study of tympanic membrane pathology after tympanostomy tube treatment of chronic otitis media with effusion. In: Lim DJ, Bluestone CD, Casselbrant M, Klein JO, Ogra PL, editors. Recent advances in otitis media: proceedings of the Sixth International Symposium. Hamilton (ON): BC Decker; 1996. p. 380–3.

158. Klingensmith MR, Strauss M, Conner GH. A comparison of retention and complication rates of large-bore

159. (Paparella II) and small-bore middle ear ventilating tubes. Otolaryngol Head Neck Surg 1985;93:322–30.

159. Mawson SR, Fagan P. Tympanic effusions in children. J Laryngol Otol 1972;86:105–19.

160. Pappas JJ. Middle ear ventilation tubes. Laryngoscope 1974;84:1098–116.

161. Tos M, Stangerup SE, Larse P. Dynamics of eardrum changes following secretory otitis—a prospective study. Arch Otolaryngol Head Neck Surg 1987;113:380–5.

162. Rakover Y, Keywan K, Rosen G. Comparison of the incidence of cholesteatoma surgery before and after using ventilation tubes for secretory otitis media. Int J Pediatr Otorhinolaryngol 2000;56:41–4.

163. Isaacson GC, Rosenfeld RM. Care of the child with tympanostomy tubes: a visual guide for the pediatrician. Pediatrics 1994;93:924–9.

164. Cunningham MJ, Darrow DH, Goldstein MN, et al. American Academy of Pediatrics Section on Otolaryngology and Bronchoesophagology. Follow-up management of children with tympanostomy tubes. Pediatrics 2002;109:328–9.

165. Manning SC, Brown OE, Roland PS, Phillips DL. Incidence of sensorineural hearing loss in patients evaluated for tympanostomy tubes. Arch Otolaryngol Head Neck Surg 1994;120:881–4.

166. Emery M, Weber PC. Hearing loss due to myringotomy and tube placement and the role of pre-operative audiograms. Arch Otolaryngol Head Neck Surg 1998;124:421–4.

167. Estrem SA, Batra PS. Conductive hearing loss associated with pressure equalization tubes. Otolaryngol Head Neck Surg 2000;122:349–51.

168. Valtonen HJ, Qvarnberg YH, Nuutinen J. Otological and audiological outcomes five years after tympanostomy in early childhood. Laryngoscope 2002;112:669–75.

169. Asmussen L, Olson LM, Sullivan SA. 'You have to live it to understand it…' Family experiences with chronic otitis media in children. Ambul Child Health 1999;5:303–12.

170. Facione N. Quality of life issues in chronic otitis media with effusion: parameters for future study. Int J Pediatr Otorhinolaryngol 1991;22:167–79.

171. Borenstein M, Rothstein H. Comprehensive meta-analysis: a computer program for research synthesis. Version 1.0.25. Englewood (NJ): Biostat Inc; 2000.

CHAPTER 30

Suppurative Complications

Charles D. Bluestone, MD

The course of acute mastoiditis lasts from days to weeks and may end in spontaneous recovery,
or there may be necrosis of the temporal bone with a fatal outcome.
Francis L. Lederer

OBJECTIVES

On completing this chapter, the reader will be able to

1. Understand that current management decisions are based on expert opinion despite the lack of evidence-based clinical trials.
2. Realize that chronic suppurative otitis media (CSOM) without cholesteatoma usually responds to medical management that may require intravenous antimicrobial therapy.
3. Distinguish between the three stages of acute mastoiditis and manage accordingly.
4. Tailor management of acute apical petrositis related to the severity of the disease.
5. Realize that acute facial paralysis is a frequent complication of acute otitis media (AOM), especially in infants, and that myringotomy and antimicrobial therapy are usually effective treatment.
6. Be aware that acute suppurative labyrinthitis may be due to a congenital defect in the round window, stapes, or both.
7. Be aware of the signs and symptoms associated with the suppurative intracranial complications and manage them at the earliest stage possible.

Unfortunately, we do not have evidenced-based data to determine the safest and most effective management options for the suppurative complications of otitis media (OM) and its related diseases. Despite this, the best available information currently available is presented here to help the clinician in the decision-making process when confronted with a patient in whom such a complication is suspected or present.

Suppurative complications of OM can be either within the temporal bone and termed *intratemporal* or in other parts of the body, such as the neck. Thus, an alter-native term to intratemporal is *extracranial*. When a suppurative complication of OM is within the cranial cavity, it is termed an *intracranial* complication. Another disease or disorder that is concurrent with OM is considered a *complication*, whereas a *sequela* of OM is a disease or disorder that follows, is a consequence of, or is caused by OM.

This chapter will not deal with the sequelae of OM, that is, hearing loss, perforation of the tympanic membrane (without OM), atelectasis of the middle ear (including retraction pocket), cholesteatoma, cholesterol granuloma, tympanosclerosis, adhesive OM, or ossicular discontinuity and fixation. The reader is referred to Bluestone and Klein[1] for a discussion of these sequelae. The intratemporal complications are CSOM, facial paralysis, mastoiditis, petrositis, and labyrinthitis. The intracranial complications are meningitis, extradural abscess, subdural empyema, focal otitic encephalitis, brain abscess, dural sinus thrombosis, and otitic hydrocephalus.

INTRATEMPORAL (EXTRACRANIAL) COMPLICATIONS

The most common intratemporal complication is CSOM, although acute mastoiditis and facial paralysis are also relatively common, especially in children. Petrositis and labyrinthitis are uncommon complications in all age groups.

Chronic Suppurative Otitis Media

Chronic suppurative otitis media is the stage of ear disease in which there is chronic inflammation of the middle ear and mastoid and a nonintact tympanic membrane (chronic perforation or tympanostomy tube) is present. This complication of OM has also been called *chronic otitis media,* but this term can be confused with *chronic otitis media with effusion,* which is not a complication of OM and in which there is no perforation of the tympanic membrane.[2] The term *chronic otitis media* has also been inappropriately used when a chronic perforation of the tympanic membrane is present, but the middle ear and mastoid are free of infection (see Chapter 8, "Definitions, Terminology, and Classification"). *Otorrhea* may or may not be evident. A discharge may be present in the middle ear, mastoid, or both, but otorrhea is not evident through the perforation (or tympanostomy tube) or in the external auditory canal.

There is no consensus regarding the duration of OM to be designated *chronic suppurative otitis media.* Even though three or more months appears appropriate, some clinicians consider a shorter duration of OM as being chronic, especially when the causative organism is *Pseudomonas.* When a cholesteatoma is also present, the term *cholesteatoma with chronic suppurative otitis media* is appropriately used. However, because an acquired aural cholesteatoma does not have to be associated with CSOM, cholesteatoma is not part of the pathologic features of the type of ear disease described in this chapter. Chronic suppurative otitis media without cholesteatoma is preceded by AOM, in which a perforation of the tympanic membrane or tympanostomy tube is present.[3]

A purulent, mucoid, or serous discharge through a perforation of the tympanic membrane, or tympanostomy tube, for at least 2 or 3 months is evidence of CSOM. Frequently, a polyp will be seen emerging through the perforation or tympanostomy tube. The size of the perforation has no relation to the duration or severity of the disease, but, frequently, the defect involves most of the pars tensa. There is no otalgia, mastoid or pinna tenderness, vertigo, or fever. When any of these signs or symptoms is present, the examiner should look for a possible suppurative intratemporal complication, such as mastoiditis or labyrinthitis or an intracranial complication. The disease must be distinguished from cholesteatoma or a neoplasm, both of which may also cause chronic otorrhea. When either is suspected, computed tomographic (CT) scans should be obtained.

Nonsurgical Management

Uncomplicated CSOM is initially treated medically. Since most frequently cultured bacteria are gram negative, antimicrobial agents should be selected to be effective against these organisms, but the antibiotic treatment should be culture directed. As described below, medical treatment consists of aural toilet, ototopical medication, and possible administration of systemic antimicrobial agents, first orally and, if this fails, then intravenously. Tympanomastoid surgery is reserved for those patients in whom intensive medical treatment has failed or when cholesteatoma or neoplasm is diagnosed or suspected. Evidence of these disease entities may not be apparent from CT scans.

An important part of managing CSOM is frequent *aural toilet.* The most effective manner of cleaning the external auditory canal is by carefully and completely aspirating the discharge with the aid of an otomicroscope. Thoroughly cleaning the ear canal will enhance the use of ototopical agents. Aural toilet as the sole method of treating CSOM had been advocated for management of this disease in the developing nations, but a study failed to show that it was as effective as combining this treatment with ototopical agents (see below)[4].

Regarding *ototopical medications,* a suspension containing polymyxin B, neomycin sulfates, and hydrocortisone (Pediotic) and one that has neomycin, polymyxin E, and hydrocortisone (Coly-Mycin S) have been used in the past but are no longer used in the United States. Caution is advised owing to the concern over the potential ototoxicity of these agents.[5] Some clinicians use topical tobramycin with dexamethasone (Tobradex) or gentamicin (Garamycin) ophthalmic drops instilled into the ear when *Pseudomonas* is isolated, but these agents are aminoglycosides and may be ototoxic.[6] More importantly, none of these popular medications is approved for use when there is a nonintact tympanic membrane. Nevertheless, these ototopical agents are used widely and appear to be effective for treating CSOM.[4] Clinicians who have employed them with apparent success think that if the infection is not eliminated, it too may cause damage to the inner ear.

Ofloxacin (Floxin Otic) is the only ototopical agent approved by the U.S. Food and Drug Administration (FDA) when the tympanic membrane is not intact. It is used in children when AOM with otorrhea occurs while a tympanostomy tube is in place. At present, it is the only topical antimicrobial agent that has been demonstrated to be safe and effective and approved for this indication in children.[7–10] It is also approved for adults who have CSOM, but it is currently not approved for this indication in children, even though it has been reported to be effective in this age group.[11,12] The common bacterial pathogens isolated from these infections are susceptible to this topical agent.[13] Also, topical ofloxacin has been shown to be more effective than the combination of neomycin, polymyxin B, and hydrocortisone otic drops in adults with CSOM.[14] Thus, the lack of reported clinical trials in children notwithstanding, it seems reasonable today to use ofloxacin initially in children who have uncomplicated CSOM.

Ciprofloxacin with hydrocortisone (Cipro HC) is approved by the FDA to treat external otitis in both children and adults. Even though ciprofloxacin is not approved for CSOM, it appears to be effective.[15–18] One study showed that topical ciprofloxacin was more effective than topical gentamicin for CSOM in adults and another showed that this antibiotic was as equally effective as tobramycin in adults with this infection.[19,20] No apparent ototoxicity has occurred after using this ototopical agent in patients with CSOM.[21] In addition, topical ciprofloxacin did not cause ototoxicity in the monkey model of CSOM.[22] There is still no consensus about the potential efficacy of adding a corticosteroid component to the antimicrobial agent, but steroids may hasten resolution of the inflammation.[23]

Some clinicians, especially in the developing countries that have limited health care financial resources, recommend antiseptic drops as an alternative to antibiotic topical agents. An antiseptic ototopical agent (aluminum acetate) was found to be as effective as topical gentamicin sulfate for otorrhea in a randomized clinical trial reported from the United Kingdom.[24] Thorp and colleagues[25] evaluated the in vitro activity of acetic acid and aluminum subacetate (Burow's solution) and found both to be effective against the major pathogens causing CSOM. Burow's solution was somewhat more effective than acetic acid. Antiseptic drops (eg, acetic acid) are commonly used in developing countries and are reputed to be effective. Due to cost and availability,

antibiotic ototopical agents are used when antiseptic drops are ineffective.

Ototopical agents currently approved by the FDA (2002) for ear infections are listed in Table 30-1. As stated above, only ofloxacin otic solution is approved for children when the tympanic membrane is non-intact and then only when a tympanostomy tube is present. Nevertheless, other agents, such as ciprofloxacin with hydrocortisone, may be beneficial for use inchildren with middle ear and mastoid infection. The advantage of quinolone topical agents is that there is no evidence of ototoxicity in animal models, which had been reported using the aminoglycosides. Also, with the growing concern regarding the emergence of multidrug-resistant bacterial otic pathogens, the use of an ototopical agent is desirable, because using a high concentration of the drug directed at the site of infection will hopefully prevent emergence of resistant organisms.

Ideally, when ototopical antibiotic medications are elected, the patient should return to the outpatient facility daily to have the discharge thoroughly aspirated or swabbed (ie, *aural toilet*, *ear mopping*) and to have the ototopical medication directly instilled into the middle ear through the perforation or tympanostomy tube using an otoscope or otomicroscope. Frequently, the discharge will rapidly improve within a week with this type of treatment. After a week, the eardrops may be administered at home until there is complete resolution of the middle ear–mastoid inflammation. When daily administration by the

Table 30-1 Ototopical Agents Used in the Treatment of Chronic Suppurative Otitis Media*

Generic Name	Trade Name (Company)
Acetic acid (2%) otic solution	Vosol (Wallace Laboratories)
Acetic acid (2%) and hydrocortisone (1%) otic solution	Vosol HC otic Solution (Wallace Laboratories)
Acetic acid 2% in aqueous aluminum acetate otic solution	Otic Domeboro Solution (Bayer Corporation, West Haven, CT)
Ciprofloxacin hydrochloride and hydrocortisone otic suspension	Cipro HC Otic Suspension (Alcon, Humacao, PR)
Colistin sulfate-neomycin sulfate-thonzonium bromide-hydrocortisone acetate otic suspension	CortisporinTC Otic Suspension (Monarch Pharmaceuticals, Bristol, TN)
Neomycin, polymycin B sulfate, and hydrocortisone otic suspension	Pediotic Suspension Sterile (Monarch Pharmaceuticals, Bristol, TN)
Ofloxacin otic solution 0.3%	Floxin Otic Solution (Daiichi Pharmaceutical Corp., Montvale, NJ)

*Agents listed are commonly used in children and adults. Only Floxin Otic has U.S. Food and Drug Administration approval for this indication, but only for adults.

physician is not feasible, a family member or caregiver can administer the drops.

Oral antibiotics that are approved to treat AOM may be effective if the bacterium is susceptible, but as the organism is usually *Pseudomonas aeruginosa*, agents that are currently approved for children will usually not be effective. Currently, systemic quinolone antibiotics are not FDA approved in the United States. However, orally administered ciprofloxacin has been shown to be effective in adults and children who had CSOM.[26,27] Despite the potential drawbacks of prescribing oral antibiotics that are not effective when *Pseudomonas* is the causative organism, many clinicians still administer a broad-spectrum oral antibiotic hoping that the underlying infection is caused by the usual bacteria that are isolated from ears with AOM.

In a randomized clinical trial conducted in Kenya, Smith and colleagues[4] compared oral amoxicillin-clavulanate, *dry mopping* of the ear, and ototopical antibiotic-cortisone drops; *dry mopping* alone; and no treatment, and they found that the combination of oral antibiotic and topical agents were statistically more effective than dry mopping alone or no treatment. One randomized clinical trial found that topical ofloxacin was more effective than systemic amoxicillin-clavulanate (without eardrops) in adults with CSOM.[28]

The patient should be re-examined in about 7 to 10 days when ototopical agents, oral antimicrobial agents, or both are used. At this time, any adjustments can be made in the medications following the results of the microbiologic studies. After approximately 1 week, there should be cessation of the discharge or marked improvement. If the otorrhea is improving, the child should be re-examined periodically thereafter until resolution occurs. If after 1 to 2 weeks there is no improvement, other treatment options should be considered, such as parenteral antimicrobial therapy.

Parenteral antimicrobial agents should be used if the child is a treatment failure following the administration of ototopical agents with or without an oral antimicrobial agent. Of 173 children followed up prospectively after tympanostomy tube placement, Ah-Tye and colleagues[29] reported that 5 (3%) required parenteral antibiotic therapy to eliminate chronic infection that was unresponsive to ototopical and oral antimicrobial therapy. When intravenous therapy is indicated, the patient should receive a parenteral beta-lactam antipseudomonal drug, such as ticarcillin, piperacillin, or ceftazidime. Empirically, ticarcillin-tazobactam is usually selected because *Pseudomonas*, with and without *Staphylococcus aureus*, is frequently isolated.

The results of the culture and susceptibility studies dictate the antimicrobial agent ultimately chosen.[30,31]

Dagan and colleagues[32] in Israel and Arguedas and associates[33] in Costa Rica reported excellent results using ceftazidime. In Finland, Vartiainen and Kansanen[34] also recommend a trial of intravenous antimicrobial therapy before considering mastoid surgery. The regimen can be altered when results of culture and susceptibility tests are available. Also, purulent material and debris from the external canal (and middle ear, if possible) are aspirated and the ototopical medication instilled daily. This method of treatment is usually performed on an ambulatory basis.[32,35] Hospitalization may be required on an individualized basis, such as when daily aural toilet is inconvenient or compliance in giving the medication as an outpatient is uncertain.

In approximately 90% of children, the middle ear will be free of discharge, and signs of CSOM will be greatly improved or absent within 5 to 7 days. We conducted a study in 36 pediatric patients with CSOM in which all received parenteral antimicrobial therapy and daily aural toilet.[30] Medical therapy alone resolved the infection in 32 patients (89%). Four children required tympanomastoidectomy. We later increased the study group to 66 children and reported similar short-term results. Eighty-nine percent had *dry* ears following intravenous antibiotic therapy.[36] In a follow-up of that study, 51 of the original 66 were evaluated for their long-term outcomes.[31] Of these 51 children, 40 (78%) had resolution of their initial or recurrent infection following medical treatment and 11 (22%) had to eventually have mastoid surgery. Failure was associated with older children and early recurrence. If the patient had recurrence of the otorrhea with the same type, medical therapy usually failed and the patient required mastoid surgery.

If resolution does occur with intravenous antimicrobial therapy, and hospitalization is required, the child can be discharged and receive the parenteral antibiotic and eardrops (given by the parent or caregiver) for 10 to 14 days at home. The patient should be followed up at periodic intervals to watch for signs of spontaneous closure of the perforation, which frequently happens after the middle ear and mastoid are no longer infected. Appropriate intensive medical treatment should be attempted before recommending major ear surgery because the outcome of surgery is not as favorable when medical treatment is withheld.[37]

Surgical Management

Placement of a tympanostomy tube may be helpful if the CSOM is associated with a perforation that is too small to permit adequate drainage or one that frequently closes but reopens with episodic drainage. If the chronic infection is related to a tympanostomy tube (ie, the middle ear *air cushion* is absent), some clinicians advocate removing the tube hoping that the infection will subsequently subside. However, the recurrent/chronic ear infections for which the tube was originally inserted frequently recur. There may be some merit in attempting this approach in a patient who has had a longstanding retained tube.

When CSOM fails to respond to intensive medical therapy (ie, intravenous antibiotics, aural toilet, and ototopical medications) within several days, surgery on the middle ear and mastoid, that is, *tympanomastoidectomy*, may be required to eradicate the infection. A CT scan should be obtained (see above). Failures usually occur when there is an underlying blockage of the communication between the middle ear and mastoid (ie, aditus ad antrum), irreversible chronic osteitis, cholesteatoma (or tumor), or an early recurrence with the same causative organism.[31]

The preferred tympanomastoidectomy procedure combines a complete (simple, cortical) mastoidectomy with middle ear surgery to remove the infection (eg, purulent material, granulation tissue, and the involved mastoid bone) and frequently includes a tympanoplasty, that is, *tympanomastoidectomy with tympanoplasty*.[38] Cultures of all infected tissue (including infected bone) are assessed for Gram stain, aerobic and anaerobic bacteria, fungi, and susceptibility testing. In addition to eradication of the disease process, the goals of this surgery are to maintain the intact posterior and superior canal walls and maintain or reconstruct the tympanic membrane and ossicular chain. This procedure is preferred over performing a modified radical or radical mastoidectomy, especially in children. Peri- and postoperative culture-directed intravenous antimicrobial therapy is advised to aid in eliminating the chronic infection and to prevent postoperative wound breakdown. Placement of a tympanostomy tube is optional but preferred, at least in the immediate postoperative course. A tube provides adequate middle ear and mastoid drainage if the infection has been particularly long-lasting.

Prevention of Recurrence

The most effective way to prevent recurrence of otorrhea when the tympanic membrane is intact and an attack of AOM occurs is to promptly, appropriately, and adequately treat the infection with the usual oral antimicrobial agents recommended for AOM. If the tympanic membrane is not intact (ie, a perforation or a tympanostomy tube is present without evidence of infection), early treatment of acute otorrhea, that is, AOM, should likewise be effective. Treatment with an oral antimicrobial agent may be enhanced by adding an ototopical agent(s) to prevent a secondary infection with external ear canal organisms, such as *Pseudomonas*.

A recent meta-analysis of post-tympanostomy tube otorrhea revealed that approximately 16% will have otorrhea in the immediate postoperative period, 26% will develop it later, 7% have recurrent episodes, and about 4% will develop chronic otorrhea.[39] It is important to remember that chronic infection is always preceded by acute infection: if the acute infection is eliminated, chronic infection does not occur.[40]

If a perforation or tympanostomy tube is present without a middle ear–mastoid infection and it is desirable to maintain middle ear ventilation through a nonintact eardrum, recurrent episodes of otorrhea can usually be prevented with *antimicrobial prophylaxis*, for example, amoxicillin. If a tympanostomy tube is present and the middle ear is now disease free, its removal may restore middle ear–Eustachian tube physiology (ie, prevent *reflux* or *insufflation* of nasopharyngeal secretions). Removal of tympanostomy tubes may not be desirable in infants and young children, and, in these cases, antimicrobial prophylaxis, despite the current concern about emergence of antibiotic resistant bacteria, should also be considered until the tubes spontaneously extrude.

If the patient has a chronic perforation and OM (and mastoiditis) has been eliminated, *tympanoplastic surgery* should be considered. The same factors should be considered when deciding to repair an eardrum perforation in children as described above related to removing a tympanostomy tube.[41]

Mastoiditis

Mastoiditis may be acute, subacute, or chronic.

Acute Mastoiditis

Since the widespread use of antimicrobial agents, the incidence of acute mastoiditis with osteitis has dramatically fallen, but the clinician should always be aware that this disease is a common suppurative complication of AOM.[3,42–44] In addition, there is some evidence that the incidence of acute mastoiditis has recently increased in the United States[45] and in other countries in which antibiotics are employed on a routine basis.[46] This is apparently not due to an increase in the rate of antibiotic-resistant pneumococcus but occurs in geographic areas in which antimicrobial agents are withheld in children who have AOM.[47–49] Acute mastoiditis still causes suppurative intracranial complications in the developed nations of the world.[50]

The following classification of the stages of this suppurative complication has recently been revised on the basis of an understanding of the pathogenesis and pathology and on the more recent availability of CT scans.[51] Acute mastoiditis can be staged as follows (see Chapter 7):

1. Acute mastoiditis without periosteitis/osteitis
2. Acute mastoiditis with periosteitis
3. Acute mastoid osteitis

In *acute mastoiditis without periosteitis/osteitis*, most likely, all episodes of OM are associated with some inflammation of the mastoid, because the mastoid gas cell system is connected to the distal end of the middle ear. Thus, mastoiditis can be a natural extension and part of the pathologic process of middle ear inflammation—the mastoid may be involved in AOM or otitis media with effusion (OME) (of any duration). The diagnosis is commonly made after CT scans or magnetic resonance imaging (MRI) studies are obtained for another problem (eg, sinusitis, head trauma, and so on) in a child who has no signs or symptoms referable to the ears. In these cases, it is an incidental finding. No specific signs or symptoms of mastoid infection, for example, protrusion of the pinna, postauricular swelling, tenderness, pain, and erythema, are present in this most common stage of mastoiditis. Imaging of the mastoid area frequently reveals *cloudy* mastoids indicating inflammation, but no mastoid *osteitis* (ie, bony erosion of the mastoid air cells) is evident. This stage is commonly reversible as the middle ear–mastoid infection resolves either as a natural process or as a result of medical management, for example, antimicrobial therapy. With no periosteal involvement of the postauricular region, osteitis of the mastoid, or subperiosteal abscess, this stage of mastoiditis is *not* a suppurative complication of OM.

When this stage of mastoiditis is diagnosed in a child who has an episode of AOM, the management is the same as recommended for AOM because the involvement of the mastoid is a natural extension of the middle ear infection. Indications for tympanocentesis (diagnostic aspiration of the middle ear) are the same as when AOM is diagnosed and the status of the mastoid is undetermined (by CT/MRI), such as when the patient is severely ill or toxic, fails to improve rapidly while on appropriate and adequate antibiotic treatment, develops OM while receiving antimicrobial agents, develops OM in the newborn period, is immunologically deficient, or has a suppurative complication.[52]

Myringotomy is indicated when drainage of the middle ear is desirable, such as when the child has severe otalgia or when a suppurative complication is suspected or is present. When acute infection in the mastoid (and usually middle ear) does not resolve at this stage, the disease can rapidly progress to *acute mastoiditis with periosteitis*, with the next stage being *acute mastoid osteitis*, which can occur with or without the presence of a *subperiosteal abscess.*

When infection within the mastoid spreads to the periosteum covering the mastoid process, *acute mastoiditis with periosteitis* can develop. The route of infection from the mastoid cells to the periosteum is by venous channels, usually the mastoid emissary vein. The condition should not be confused with the presence of a subperiosteal abscess, whereas the management of the latter condition usually requires a mastoidectomy, the former frequently responds to medical treatment and tympanocentesis/myringotomy.

The patient may be managed on an ambulatory basis if the infection is not severe. However, hospitalization is usually necessary because parenteral antimicrobial therapy is frequently needed and most patients require an immediate tympanocentesis (for aspiration and microbiologic assessment of the middle ear–mastoid effusion) and myringotomy to drain the middle ear. In the absence of an aditus ad antrum *"block,"* this should also drain the mastoid. If the child has had recurrent attacks of AOM or has the current episode of AOM superimposed on chronic OME, inserting a tympanostomy tube is indicated. Inserting a tympanostomy tube is desirable and will enhance drainage over a longer period of time than myringotomy alone. Even though there have been reports revealing that antibiotic treatment was successful in curing some children without the benefit of tympanocentesis or myringotomy, aspirating the middle ear is an important diagnostic (and therapeutic) procedure today.[53] This is because an antibiotic-resistant bacterial pathogen, such as multidrug-resistant pneumococcus, may be the causative organism, which may require an antimicrobial agent not frequently used for AOM/mastoiditis, for example, vancomycin.[42,54–58] Also, unusual pathogens, such as *Mycobacterium tuberculosis*, may be encountered in some geographic areas of the world.[59]

Cultures for bacteria from the middle ear are required to identify the causative organism(s). Antimicrobial susceptibility studies are important to select the most effective antibiotic agent. For empiric parenteral antimicrobial therapy, cefuroxime sodium, ticarcillin disodium with clavulanate potassium, or ampicillin-sulbactam can be initiated until the Gram stain, culture, and susceptibility studies of the middle ear aspirates are available. If a penicillin-resistant *S. pneumoniae* is the possible pathogen, some clinicians today would also add vancomycin while awaiting the culture and susceptibly report.

The periosteal involvement should resolve within 24 to 48 hours after the tympanic membrane has been opened for drainage and adequate and appropriate antimicrobial therapy has begun. A mastoidectomy should be performed if the symptoms of the acute infection, such as fever and otalgia, persist; the postauricular involvement does not progressively improve; or a subperiosteal abscess develops.

A CT scan can be helpful in the decision to surgically intervene or not. A mastoidectomy is also indicated if an intratemporal (extracranial) suppurative complication of OM (eg, facial paralysis, labyrinthitis, petrous apicitis) or an intracranial complication from OM (eg, meningitis, lateral sinus thrombosis, or abscess of the epidural or subdural space or brain) is present.

In the review by Goldstein and colleagues[42] cited above, of the 72 infants and children with acute mastoiditis at the Children's Hospital of Pittsburgh, 54 (75%) were managed conservatively with broad-spectrum intravenous antibiotics and myringotomy with and without tympanostomy tube insertion. The other 18 (25%) required mastoidectomy. Of these 18 children, 14 (78%) had one or more of the following: mastoid osteitis, subperiosteal abscess, cholesteatoma, or another suppurative complication, for example, facial paralysis. A review from Australia by Harley and associates[55] had approximately the same experience as in Pittsburgh. Between 1982 and 1993, 58 infants and children were admitted to the Royal Children's Hospital of Melbourne, and of these, 45 (78%) were treated conservatively with intravenous antimicrobial therapy with or without tympanostomy tube insertion. The remaining 13 patients required mastoidectomy. Other centers have recently reported treating most children conservatively and not requiring mastoidectomy.[44,53,60,61] Other centers have reported that most of their patients required a mastoidectomy.[54,62–68] Most likely the reasons for these conflicting reports are the lack of uniform definition of the disease, dissimilarity in presentation of the cases, and variation in management. Our opinion is that most patients with acute mastoiditis with only periosteitis recover without the need for mastoidectomy.

Immediate treatment at this stage of acute mastoiditis is mandatory because failing to do so may result in acute mastoid osteitis (with or without a subperiosteal abscess) developing or, potentially more life-threatening to the child, a suppurative complication, such as meningitis or brain abscess.[43]

In the absence of mastoid osteitis (with or without subperiosteal abscess), the primary-care physician or pediatric infectious disease specialist can provide the initial medical care for patients with acute mastoiditis with periosteitis. However, tympanocentesis/myringotomy is required, and an otolaryngologist will be needed if the medical specialists are untrained in this procedure. Referral to an otolaryngologist is appropriate if a mastoidectomy is indicated, as described above. Also, immediate referral for surgical evaluation and management is indicated when acute mastoid infection develops in a child with CSOM or cholesteatoma or both.

Acute mastoiditis with osteitis has also been called *acute coalescent mastoiditis* or *acute surgical mastoiditis,* but the pathologic process is really *acute mastoid osteitis.* A *subperiosteal abscess* may or may not be present.[2] The infection can spread to the neck, which is termed a Bezold's abscess.[69] The child usually has the same signs and symptoms as those associated with AOM, such as fever and otalgia, though the fever may be low grade with occasional temperature spikes. Some patients may have toxic symptoms. The signs and symptoms referable to the mastoid infection are swelling, erythema, and tenderness to touch over the mastoid bone; displacement of the pinna outward and downward; and swelling or sagging of the postero-superior external auditory canal wall. The diagnosis should be suspected on the basis of clinical signs and symptoms. Computed tomographic scans of the mastoid area usually reveal one or more of the following: haziness, distortion, or destruction of the mastoid outline; loss of sharpness of the shadows of cellular walls due to demineralization, atrophy, and ischemia of the bony septa; decrease in density and cloudiness of the areas of pneumatization due to inflammatory swelling of the air cells; or in longstanding cases, a chronic osteoblastic inflammatory reaction that may obliterate the cellular structure. Small abscess cavities in sclerotic bone may be confused with pneumatic cells.

Antonelli and colleagues[70] reviewed CT scans of 21 patients with acute coalescent mastoiditis (with osteitis) or acute noncoalescent mastoiditis (without osteitis) and 12 patients with chronic mastoiditis. They found that erosion of the cortical plate overlying the sigmoid sinus was the most sensitive and specific CT finding to distinguish osteitis from nonosteitis acute disease.

As part of the diagnostic work-up, cultures to determine the causative bacterial organisms should be obtained, either before or at the time of mastoid surgery. When otorrhea is present, cultures for bacteria from the ear drainage must be taken with care to discern fresh drainage from debris in the external canal. The canal must be initially cleaned. Then, if fresh pus is exuding through a perforation in the tympanic membrane, the discharge is cultured at the point of exit from the tympanic membrane with a cotton-tipped, wire swab or, preferably, a needle and syringe under direct view. A Gram stain of the pus provides immediate information about the organisms responsible. When the mastoidectomy is performed, portions of mucosa and bone of the mastoid should be sent for Gram stain, culture, and antibiotic susceptibility testing. The differential diagnosis between this stage of mastoiditis and other disease entities (eg, acute external otitis with postauricular periosteitis or postauricular lymphadenitis) that involve the postauricular area is described above.

Management consists of parenteral antimicrobial therapy, as described above for acute mastoiditis with periosteitis. To ensure that drainage of the middle ear and mastoid is adequate, in the absence of a large perforation and otorrhea, a wide-field large myringotomy should be done immediately. Insertion of a tympanostomy tube, in addition to a large myringotomy incision, can provide more prolonged drainage from the middle ear–mastoid than myringotomy alone. Also, the tympanostomy tube placement will help prevent AOM (and mastoiditis) from recurring.

A cortical (simple) mastoidectomy will usually be required when there is evidence of acute mastoid osteitis, especially when the mastoid empyema has extended outside the mastoid bone and a subperiosteal abscess is present. The procedure should be considered an emergency, but the timing of the operation depends on the condition of the child. Ideally, sepsis should be under control and the patient must be able to tolerate a general anesthetic. The principle is to clean out the mastoid infection, to drain the mastoid air cell system into the middle ear by eliminating any obstruction caused by edema or granulation tissue in the aditus ad antrum, and to provide external drainage.[41] Surgical intervention for these conditions may also be required if another suppurative intratemporal or intracranial complication is also present.

Subacute Mastoiditis (Masked Mastoiditis, Occult Mastoiditis)

A condition called *masked mastoiditis,* for which a complete simple mastoidectomy has been advocated, has been described.[71] The disease appears to be a subacute stage of OM and mastoiditis (without osteitis) characterized by the same signs and symptoms as AOM (such as persistent fever and ear pain), except that they are persistent and less severe. The progression to this stage is attributed to failure of the initial antimicrobial agent to resolve the middle ear and mastoid infection within a short period. Persistent otalgia and fever in a patient receiving an antimicrobial agent is an indication for tympanocentesis and myringotomy to identify the causative organism and promote drainage. In selected children, especially those who have had frequently recurrent episodes of AOM in the past, inserting a tympanostomy tube (in addition to the appropriate antimicrobial therapy) will resolve the problem. Mastoid surgery is not indicated, unless inserting the tympanostomy tube and intravenous antimicrobial therapy are ineffective.

From France, Denoyelle and colleagues[72] reported having 165 children over a 2-year period with *subacute mastoiditis,* which was defined as an attack of AOM that did not resolve with 10 days of antibiotic treatment, despite intravenous therapy. Middle ear aspiration (or

cultures of otorrhea) revealed *Haemophilus influenzae* (28%), *P. aeruginosa* (23%), and *S. pneumoniae* (16%). Of these 165 children, 31 (19%) had mastoidectomy. It is likely that tympanostomy tube insertion would have prevented mastoidectomy in most, if not all, of these children.

The condition described above is usually a failure of initial antimicrobial treatment that frequently resolves following adequate middle ear drainage and identifying the causative organism, followed by administration of a culture-directed antibiotic. In contrast, infants and children may have a suppurative process in the mastoid that is not clinically obvious, that is, occult. This mastoid infection may even result in an intratemporal or intracranial complication, in which the middle ear may not appear to be diseased and the patient lacks the classic signs and symptoms of OM and mastoiditis. This condition can be called *masked mastoiditis.* The diagnosis is usually made by CT scan or by obtaining a bone scan.[73] Children who have intracranial suppurative disease or disease of the temporal bone that could possibly be due to mastoid infection should have a CT of the temporal bones included in the work-up, even though there is no evidence of middle ear disease on otoscopy. It is rare, but children who have fever of unknown origin may have masked mastoiditis.

On occasion, older children or adolescents will complain of persistent or recurrent postauricular pain, but the middle ear appears to be free of disease. The communication between the middle ear and the mastoid air cells (ie, the aditus ad antrum) may be blocked, causing mastoiditis. These children usually have had a history of recurrent AOM, recurrent/chronic OME, or CSOM, and mastoiditis is diagnosed when a CT scan is obtained. Medical treatment (eg, antimicrobial therapy) is indicated, but if the symptoms are severe or a trial of medical management fails, a mastoidectomy is indicated to relieve the aditus ad antrum blockage and eliminate the infected cells. More rarely, a child with these symptoms may have relatively normal-appearing mastoid cellular architecture on CT scan. In this case, the patient could have negative pressure within the mastoid due to an aditus ad antrum obstruction. Again, mastoidectomy may be the only method of eliminating the blockage and relieving the symptoms.

Chronic Mastoiditis (with and without Chronic Suppurative Otitis Media/Cholesteatoma)

Chronic mastoiditis that develops after an episode of acute mastoiditis has also decreased during the past 50 years of widespread antibiotic use. But chronic mastoiditis is still a major problem when *chronic suppurative otitis media* is present, especially in certain racial groups and geographic areas in which this disease is common.[74] Also, both acute and chronic mastoiditis can occur in the presence of cholesteatoma.[75] Thus, acute and chronic mastoiditis still occur and may be responsible for significant morbidity and life-threatening infection, especially from intracranial extension of the disease.[76]

An occasional child will develop acute mastoiditis, which is either untreated or inappropriately treated, or the child is neglected and the infection progresses to a chronic stage in which no perforation (or tympanostomy tube) is present in the tympanic membrane; no CSOM, with or without otorrhea, is present. Nevertheless, the disease in the mastoid progresses to the chronic stage and OM may or may not be present. These children can present with a fever of unknown origin or chronic/recurrent otalgia and tenderness over the mastoid process. Similar to the description of a child who has subacute or *masked* mastoiditis, patients who have chronic mastoiditis may have another intratemporal or intracranial complication. A child with an intracranial infectious process, such as a brain abscess, who has no clinical evidence of OM or mastoiditis, may have chronic mastoiditis as the focus of the intracranial infection.

If it can be reversed, chronic mastoiditis may be brought under control by medical treatment with antimicrobial agents (similar to those recommended above for acute mastoiditis without periosteitis or osteitis). A tympanocentesis for Gram stain, culture, and susceptibility studies and myringotomy for drainage should be performed. When there are extensive amounts of granulation tissue and osteitis in the mastoid (ie, irreversible mastoid disease) or the child fails to improve on medical therapy, referral to an otolaryngologist will be needed because a tympanomastoidectomy is required to eliminate the chronic mastoid osteitis. When another suppurative complication is present in addition to the chronic mastoiditis, such as brain abscess, dural sinus thrombosis, or otitic hydrocephalus, mastoidectomy is indicated.

Chronic mastoiditis can also be caused by a cholesteatoma, which is usually manifested by chronic otorrhea through a defect in the tympanic membrane. A cholesteatoma requires definitive surgical treatment.

Petrositis

Petrositis is secondary to an extension of infection from the middle ear and mastoid into the petrous portion of the temporal bone. All the inflammatory and cellular changes described as occurring in the mastoid can also occur in the pneumatized petrous pyramid. About 80% of mastoids are aerated in adults, but only approximately 30% of petrous apex cells are aerated. About 7% can have asymmetric pneumatization of the petrous apex.[77] Petrositis may be more frequent than appreciated by clinical and roentgenographic signs, because there is communication of the petrosal gas cells with the mastoid–middle ear system. Pneumatization usually does not occur before age 3 years.

This suppurative complication of OM may be either acute or chronic. In the acute stage, there is extension of AOM and mastoiditis into the pneumatized petrous air cells. Like acute mastoiditis, the condition is usually self-limited, with resolution of the acute middle ear and mastoid infection. Occasionally, the infection in the petrous portion of the temporal bone does not drain due to mucosal swelling or because granulation is obstructing the passage from the petrous air cells to the mastoid and middle ear. This results in acute petrous osteomyelitis.[78,79] The widespread use of antimicrobial agents has made this a rare complication. Chronic petrous osteomyelitis, however, can be a complication of CSOM or cholesteatoma or both.[80] Pneumatization of the petrous portion of the temporal bone does not have to be present because the infection can invade the area by thrombophlebitis or osteitis or along fascial planes.[81] When there is sixth nerve palsy and OM but no identifiable petrositis and without increased intracranial pressure, the palsy may be related to phlebitis along the inferior petrosal sinus.[82] The infection may persist for months or years with mild and intermittent signs and symptoms or may spread to the intracranial cavity and result in one or more of the suppurative complications of ear disease, such as meningitis or extradural or intracranial abscess. The infection can also spread to the skull base with involvement of cranial nerves IX, X, and XI (Vernet's syndrome).[83]

The patient who develops acute petrositis usually presents with pain behind the eye, deep ear pain, persistent ear discharge, and sixth nerve palsy. This classic triad is known as the Gradenigo's syndrome.[84] However, in the four patients who were admitted to Children's Hospital of Pittsburgh during a recent 15-year period with this complication of OM, neither eye pain, deep ear pain, nor persistent otorrhea were all consistently present.[42] This has also been the experience in other reviews.[85] Eye pain is due to irritation of the ophthalmic branch of the fifth cranial nerve. On occasion, the maxillary and mandibular divisions of the fifth nerve will be involved, and pain will occur in the teeth and jaw. A discharge from the ear is common with acute petrositis but may not be present with chronic disease. Paralysis of the sixth cranial nerve leading to diplopia is a late complication.[80] Acute petrous osteomyelitis should be suspected when persistent purulent discharge follows a complete simple mastoidectomy for mastoid osteitis.

The diagnosis of acute petrous osteomyelitis is suggested by the unique clinical signs. Standard radiographs of the temporal bones may show clouding with loss of trabeculation of the petrous bone. The visualization is uncertain, however, because of normal variation in pneumatization (including asymmetry) and the obscuring of the petrous pyramids by superimposed shadows of other portions of the skull. Computed tomographic scans of the temporal bones can lead to diagnosis and should be obtained if there might be the possibility of an extension of infection into the cranial cavity. Thin-section (1.5 mm) axial and coronal CT scans with a bone algorithm are recommended.[86] This complication must be distinguished from destructive lesions of the petrous apex due to such conditions as cholesteatoma, cholesterol granuloma, arachnoid cysts, and chronic granulomatous disease. Computed tomographic scans and MRI can be diagnostic in distinguishing between these diseases.[87–91] Radioisotope bone scan, which will show increased uptake in the petrous apex, has also shown to be helpful.[92]

When acute petrositis is diagnosed, prompt and appropriate treatment is indicated to prevent spread into the intracranial cavity. If acute petrositis is confined to the temporal bone and osteitis of the temporal bone is not evident on the CT scans, tympanocentesis to identify the causative organism, culture-directed intravenous antimicrobial therapy, and tympanostomy tube placement may be effective in reversing the disease process. Thus, conservative management can be effective in selected cases. Surgical drainage of the mastoid and opening of the readily available perilabyrinthine cells is indicated if there is osteitis of the petrous apex (other portions of the temporal bone) identified on the CT scans or if the patient fails to rapidly improve with conservative management.[40,93,94] The procedure should be a complete (simple, cortical) mastoidectomy that provides adequate drainage through the aditus ad antrum and free flow of irrigation fluid from the mastoid to the middle ear at the end of the procedure. A tympanostomy tube should also be placed. All four of the patients who had this diagnosis at the Children's Hospital of Pittsburgh (see above) were successfully treated with high-dose broad-spectrum intravenous antibiotic therapy and cortical (simple) mastoidectomy without entering the petrous apex. The petrous apex disease most likely drained into the mastoid cavity during the postoperative period. The three children with intracranial complications also had specific management of that complication.[42]

Some surgeons have advocated mastoidectomy for patients who have a sixth nerve palsy and OM but no demonstrable evidence of petrositis on the CT scans,[82] but a more conservative approach (eg, tympanocentesis, tympanostomy tube insertion, and intravenous antimicrobial therapy) is a more appropriate initial therapeutic approach. This reserves mastoidectomy for those patients who fail to rapidly improve.

In more severe cases of acute petrous osteomyelitis and acute mastoid osteitis, a more aggressive surgical approach to management may be required. Coker and Jenkins advocate the infracochlear approach, in which a tympanomeatal flap is created through a postauricular approach.[86] A transmastoid infralabyrinthine approach can also be used, in which a complete mastoidectomy is performed and the infralabyrinthine gas cells opened inferior to the posterior canal, superior to the jugular bulb, and medial to the facial nerve. If the infection has caused complete loss of cochlear and labyrinthine function, a petrosectomy through a radical mastoidectomy is also an alternative. Neely and Wallace[95] recommend a staged approach. The first stage is a modified radical mastoidectomy (the ossicular chain remains intact), and cell tracts to the petrous apex are opened, if possible. If this procedure is not effective in reversing the disease process, a second stage is performed through the middle cranial fossa. For patients whose disease extends into surrounding structures, such as the pericarotid area, an infralabyrithine retrofacial route has been successful in eliminating the disease.[85] As an alternative for these complicated cases, the middle cranial fossa approach has been advocated.[96,97]

Facial Paralysis

Infants and young children are the most affected by facial paralysis as a complication of AOM. This is because the facial nerve is frequently exposed in its horizontal portion within the middle ear from a congenital bony dehiscence. It can also occur as a complication of acute mastoiditis with osteitis[42] or CSOM.[98] When it occurs as a complication of CSOM, a cholesteatoma is also frequently present. On rare occasions, it can occur in children as a complication of OME,[99] be bilateral after the onset of AOM,[100,101] or as a complication of acute mastoiditis.[102] When facial paralysis develops during an attack of OM, an underlying disease such as leukemia may be present.[42,103]

The vast majority of children who develop facial paralysis that is not associated with acute mastoiditis or a concomitant underlying disease can be treated successfully with conservative management. When it occurs as an isolated complication, tympanocentesis (to identify the causative organism) and a myringotomy (to provide immediate drainage) should be performed, and parenteral antibiotics effective for *S. pneumoniae* and *H. influenzae* should be administered. Inserting a tympanostomy tube is indicated when the child has had recurrent episodes of AOM, when the attack of AOM is superimposed on pre-existing chronic OME, and whenever prolonged drainage of the middle ear and mastoid is desirable. The paralysis will usually improve rapidly without the need for further surgery (eg, mastoidectomy or facial nerve decompression). Mastoidectomy is not indicated, unless acute mastoiditis with osteitis (acute "coalescent" mastoiditis), CSOM, or cholesteatoma is present. However, if there is complete loss of facial function and electrophysiologic testing indicates the presence of degeneration or progressive deterioration of the nerve, then facial nerve decompression may be necessary to achieve complete return of function. Immediate surgical intervention is indicated when a facial paralysis develops in a child who has CSOM or cholesteatoma or both.

The successful outcome of conservative management in most infants and children has been reported by Goldstein and colleagues[42] in a review of 22 infants and children who had facial paralysis associated with OM or related infections at the Children's Hospital of Pittsburgh between 1980 and 1995. Facial weakness, otalgia, otorrhea, concomitant upper respiratory tract symptoms of infection, and fever were the most common symptoms. The mean duration of ear symptoms and duration of facial weakness on presentation was 6 and 4 days, respectively. Two children had acute mastoiditis with periosteitis, and 1 patient had acute mastoiditis with osteitis and subperiosteal abscess. In 18 patients (80%), initial treatment consisted of antimicrobial therapy and in all but 1 child, a myringotomy with or without tympanostomy tube placement was also performed. Of these 22 children, 4 patients (18%) had further surgery. Two patients had a cortical (simple) mastoidectomy for acute mastoiditis; 1 child who had lymphoblastic leukemia underwent facial nerve decompression, radical mastoidectomy, and a labyrinthectomy; and another child who had had a prior mastoidectomy for cholesteatoma later developed an acute mastoiditis with subperiosteal abscess and a facial paralysis and had to have a revision tympanomastoidectomy.

In Washington, D.C., in a smaller series of 10 patients who developed facial paralysis after the onset of AOM, Elliott and associates[104] reported that 8 had an incomplete paralysis, which resolved with only myringotomy and intravenous antibiotic. Two children who had complete paralysis and persistent fever and otorrhea despite antibiotic treatment had a mastoidectomy. None required decompression of the facial nerve. Others have reported similar success with conservative management.[105]

Labyrinthitis

Labyrinthitis as a complication of OM or mastoiditis occurs when infection spreads from the middle ear cleft into the cochlear and vestibular apparatus. The usual portal of entry is the round window and, less commonly, the oval window. Invasion may take place from an infectious focus in an adjacent area, such as the mastoid antrum, the petrous bone, the meninges, or as a result of bacteremia. Schuknecht[106] has reclassified labyrinthitis into three types:

1. Serous (toxic) labyrinthitis, in which there may be bacterial toxins or biochemical involvement but no bacteria
2. Suppurative (acute and chronic otogenic suppurative) labyrinthitis, in which bacteria have invaded the otic capsule
3. Meningogenic suppurative labyrinthitis, which is the result of invasion of bacteria from the subarachnoid space into the labyrinth. Labyrinthitis ossificans (labyrinthine sclerosis), in which there is replacement of the normal labyrinthine structures by fibrous tissue and bone, is the end stage of this complication, if arrested.

An acceptable classification of labyrinthitis today is the following[2]:
1. Acute labyrinthitis
2. Subacute labyrinthitis
3. Chronic labyrinthitis
4. Labyrinthitis ossificans

Acute Labyrinthitis

Acute labyrinthitis can be classified as being either serous or suppurative, and each of these entities can be either localized or generalized.

Acute serous (toxic) labyrinthitis (with or without perilymphatic fistula) is one of the most common suppurative complications of OM. Paparella and associates[107] described the histopathologic evidence of serous labyrinthitis in most of the temporal bone specimens from patients who had OM. Bacterial toxins from the infection in the middle ear may enter the inner ear, primarily through an intact round window or through a congenital defect between the middle ear and inner ear. The portal of entry may also be through an acquired defect of the labyrinth, such as from head trauma or previous middle ear or mastoid surgery. Biochemical changes within the labyrinth have also been found. The cochlea is usually more severely involved than the vestibular system.

Paparella and coworkers[108] reviewed the audiograms of 232 patients who had surgery for chronic OM and found a significant degree of bone-conduction loss in the younger age groups. There was also a marked difference in the presence and degree of sensorineural hearing loss in the affected ear compared with the normal ear in patients of all age groups who had unilateral disease. They postulated that the high-frequency sensorineural hearing loss that frequently accompanies this disease is due to a pathologic insult to the basal turn of the cochlea. In the review of intratemporal complications of OM from the Children's Hospital of Pittsburgh between 1980 and 1995, there were three children admitted with a diagnosis of acute serous labyrinthitis that were complications of an attack of AOM.[42]

Fluctuating sensorineural hearing loss has been described in patients with OM and has been thought to be due to either endolymphatic hydrops[109] or to a perilymphatic fistula.[110–112] However, fluctuating/progressive sensorineural hearing loss can be due to a variety of other hereditary and acquired etiologies.[113]

The signs and symptoms of serous labyrinthitis (especially when a perilymphatic fistula is present) are a sudden, progressive, or fluctuating sensorineural hearing loss or vertigo, or both, associated with OM or one or more of its complications or sequelae, such as mastoid osteitis. When serous labyrinthitis is a complication of OM, the loss of hearing is usually mixed, meaning there are both conductive and sensorineural components. The hearing may be normal between episodes in some children who have recurrent middle ear infections. In other children, only a mild or moderate sensorineural hearing loss will be present at all times.

Vertigo may not be obvious in children, especially infants. Older children may describe a feeling of spinning or turning, while younger children may not be able to verbalize the symptoms but manifest the dysequilibrium by falling, stumbling, or being clumsy. The vertigo may be mild and momentary, and it may tend to recur over months or years. Onset of vertigo, progressive sensorineural hearing loss, or both in a patient who has a pre-existing hearing loss is frequently due to a fistula.[114] Spontaneous nystagmus may also be present, but the signs and symptoms of acute suppurative labyrinthitis, such as nausea, vomiting, and deep-seated pain, are usually absent. If present, fever is usually due to a concurrent upper respiratory tract infection or AOM. If congenital perilymphatic fistula is present, nystagmus may be present during the course of the episode of AOM in addition to the mixed hearing loss. In a review of 47 infants and children who had exploratory tympanotomy for possible fistula at the Children's Hospital of Pittsburgh, 30 children (64%) had a past history of OM. Of these 30 patients, 28 (93%) had a fistula diagnosed at surgery.[115]

When this complication occurs during an attack of AOM, tympanocentesis and myringotomy should be performed for microbiologic assessment of the middle ear effusion (MEE) and drainage. If possible, a tympanostomy tube should also be inserted for more prolonged drainage and in an attempt to ventilate the middle ear. Antimicrobial agents with efficacy against *S. pneumoniae, H. influenzae,* and *M. catarrhalis,* such as amoxicillin, should be administered. Other organisms, such as *S. aureus* and *Pseudomonas,* have also been isolated from middle ears of children who have acute labyrinthitis.[42] Following resolution of the OME, the signs and symptoms of the labyrinthitis should rapidly disappear. Sensorineural hearing loss may persist.

If the diagnostic assessment indicates a possible congenital or acquired defect of the labyrinth, an exploratory tympanotomy should be performed as soon as the middle ear is free of infection. The most common malformations are abnormal round window and niche, such as a laterally facing round window, deformities of the stapes superstructure and footplate, deformed long process of the incus, or some combination of these congenital defects. More rarely, a congenital fissure between the round and oval windows is present.[111,112] If a perilymphatic fistula is found, it should be repaired using temporalis muscle grafts.[116] When no defect of the oval or round window is identified but a fistula is still suspected, the stapes footplate and round window should be covered with connective tissue because a leak may not be present at the time of the tympanotomy but may recur.[110,111] A tympanostomy tube should be re-inserted if recurrent OM persists.

When acute mastoid osteitis, CSOM, or cholesteatoma is present, definitive medical and surgical management of these conditions is essential in eliminating the labyrinthine involvement. A careful search for a labyrinthine fistula must be performed when mastoid surgery is indicated. However, a labyrinthectomy is not indicated for serous labyrinthitis. The surgical procedure to repair aperilymphatic/cerebrospinal fluid (CSF) fistula is described in detail by Bluestone.[41]

Acute suppurative (purulent) labyrinthitis may develop as a complication of OM or may be one of its complications and sequelae when bacteria migrate from the middle ear into the perilymphatic fluid through the oval or round window, a pre-existing temporal bone fracture, an area where bone has been eroded by cholesteatoma or chronic infection, or a congenital defect, such as a congenital perilymphatic (cerebrospinal) fistula, as described above. The most common way that bacteria enter the labyrinth is from the meninges, but migration by this route is usually not a complication of OM.

The incidence of suppurative labyrinthitis as a complication of OM is unknown, but it is rare due to the widespread use of antibiotics. When acute suppurative labyrinthitis occurs in a patient who has an episode of AOM that is appropriately and adequately treated with an antimicrobial agent, either the patient has an underlying anatomic defect (eg, congenital or acquired abnormal communication between the middle and inner ears) or a medical condition (eg, impaired immunity) that predisposes to this relatively infrequently encountered complication. In a series of 96 cases of suppurative intratemporal and intracranial complications of acute and chronic OM that were treated from 1956 to 1971, there were only 5 cases of suppurative labyrinthitis, and all were secondary to cholesteatoma that had caused a labyrinthine fistula[117] Nonetheless, suppurative labyrinthitis still occurs.

When suppurative labyrinthitis occurs in children who have an episode of AOM and who are apparently treated appropriately and adequately, a congenital (or acquired) perilymphatic fistula must be ruled out to prevent further hearing loss and recurrence, which can be life threatening due to meningitis. Conversely, when a child develops bacterial meningitis, especially recurrent episodes, a congenital defect of the inner and middle ears must be ruled out. Recently, Rupa and associates[118] reported on two children who had recurrent meningitis and were found to have a congenital perilymph fistula at the time their middle ears were explored. A congenital or acquired defect between the paranasal sinuses and the anterior cranial cavity can also cause meningitis. In the review of children who had intratemporal complications of OM, Goldstein and colleagues[42] found two patients who had a suppurative labyrinthitis during a recent 15-year period. One child had a congenital defect of the labyrinthine windows that was considered to be a perilymphatic/CSF fistula.

The sudden onset of vertigo, dysequilibrium, deep-seated pain, nausea and vomiting, and sensorineural hearing loss during an episode of AOM or an exacerbation of CSOM indicates that labyrinthitis had developed. The hearing loss is severe, and there is loss of the child's ability to repeat words shouted in the affected ear, with masking of sound in the opposite ear. Often, spontaneous nystagmus and past pointing can be observed. Initially, the quick component of the nystagmus is toward the involved ear, and there is a tendency to fall toward the opposite side. However, when there is complete loss of vestibular function, the quick component will be toward the normal ear.

Management of suppurative labyrinthitis without meningitis consists of otologic surgery combined with intensive antimicrobial therapy. If this complication is

due to AOM, immediate tympanocentesis and myringotomy with tympanostomy tube insertion are indicated, as described when serous labyrinthitis is present. If acute mastoid osteitis is present, a cortical (simple) mastoidectomy should be performed. However, because this complication can be secondary to cholesteatoma, a radical mastoidectomy or modified radical mastoidectomy may be required. A modified radical mastoidectomy may also be required when CSOM is present without cholesteatoma.

When meningitis coexists with suppurative labyrinthitis, then otologic surgery other than a diagnostic and therapeutic tympanocentesis-myringotomy may have to be delayed until the meningitis is under control and the child is able to tolerate a general anesthetic. It is important to control the source of the infection in the middle ear and labyrinth as soon as possible. A labyrinthectomy should be performed only if there is complete loss of labyrinthine function or if the infection has spread to the meninges in spite of adequate antimicrobial therapy. Initially, parenteral antimicrobial agents appropriate to manage the primary middle ear and mastoid disease present should be administered. However, because cholesteatoma and CSOM are frequent causes of suppurative labyrinthitis, antimicrobials effective for the gram-negative organisms (*P. aeruginosa* and *Proteus*) are frequently required. The results of culturing the MEE, purulent discharge, or the CSF may alter the selection of the antibiotics.

Chronic Labyrinthitis

The most common cause of chronic labyrinthitis as a complication of middle ear disease is a cholesteatoma that has eroded the labyrinth, resulting in a fistula.[119] Osteitis may also cause bone erosion of the otic capsule. The fistula most commonly occurs in the lateral semicircular canal and is filled by squamous epithelium of a cholesteatoma, granulation tissue, or fibrous tissue entering the labyrinth. The middle ear and mastoid are usually separated from the inner ear by the soft tissue at the site of the fistula, but acute suppurative labyrinthitis may develop when there is continuity. However, chronic labyrinthitis may be caused by CSOM or even chronic OME, especially if the child has a congenital defect between the middle and inner ears (congenital perilymphatic fistula).

The signs and symptoms of chronic labyrinthitis are similar to those of the acute forms of the disease (eg, sensorineural hearing loss and vertigo) except that their onset is subtler. The disease is characterized by a slowly progressive loss of cochlear and vestibular functions over a prolonged period of time. The fistula test may be helpful in diagnosing a labyrinthine fistula, an MRI may reveal labyrinthitis, and CT scans may reveal a bony defect. When there is complete loss of function, there may be no signs or symptoms of labyrinthine dysfunction.

Management consists of middle ear and mastoid surgery, since a cholesteatoma is the most common cause of this type of labyrinthitis. A tympanomastoidectomy may be required when a labyrinthine fistula due to a cholesteatoma is present. A modified radical mastoidectomy may be required when labyrinthine function is still present; the cholesteatoma matrix overlying the fistula should be left undisturbed because removal can result in total loss of function. Even though there are advocates of performing an intact canal wall procedure and surgeons who prefer to remove the cholesteatoma matrix during the initial surgery or in a second-stage procedure, the approach that is the most safe is recommended when a cholesteatoma has caused a labyrinthine fistula in a child. Failure to diagnose this complication and perform the surgery as soon as possible may result in complete loss of cochlear and vestibular functions with possible development of labyrinthine sclerosis or an acute suppurative labyrinthitis. The latter can cause a life-threatening intracranial complication, such as meningitis.

Labyrinthitis Ossificans (Labyrinthine Sclerosis)

Labyrinthitis ossificans is caused by fibrous replacement or new bone formation (labyrinthitis ossificans) in part or all of the labyrinth with resulting loss of labyrinthine function. Today, this end stage of labyrinthitis is most commonly the result of meningitis, not OM. But, as found in the review of CT scans by Weber and colleagues,[112] one child was found to have labyrinthitis ossi-

ficans associated with a congenital perilymphatic fistula, presumably secondary to OM, as meningitis had not occurred. Because this condition is the end stage of healing after acute or chronic labyrinthitis, prevention of disease of the middle ear is the most effective way to prevent this complication. Recently, Hartnick and colleagues[120] reported that steroids may prevent this unfortunate sequela following pneumococcal meningitis.

INTRACRANIAL COMPLICATIONS

Intracranial complications of OM are relatively rare since the availability of antimicrobial therapy for treatment of AOM in the developed countries of the world. These complications are still frequently encountered in populations that have limited resources or poor access to health care. These complications may occur again in the developing nations, with the current trend to withhold antimicrobial agents for the treatment of AOM in an effort to reduce the rate of antibiotic-resistant otogenic bacteria.[121] As shown in Tables 30-2,[122] and 30-3,[123] meningitis is the most commonly encountered intracranial complication in children and adults. Brain abscess is more frequent than meningitis in some countries, such as South Africa (Table 30-4[124]).

Meningitis

Inflammation of the meninges is termed *meningitis*. When a suppurative complication of OM or certain

Table 30-2 Distribution of 48 Suppurative Intracranial Complications of Otitis Media* in 37 Children—Children's Hospital of Pittsburgh, 1980–1997

	Number of Patients
Meningitis	20
Epidural abscess	7
Brain abscess	1
Lateral sinus thrombosis	9
Otitic hydrocephalus	9
Cavernous sinus thrombosis	1
Carotid artery thrombosis	1
Total	48[†]

Adapted from Don DM et al.[122]

*Acute otitis media and chronic suppurative otitis media.

[†]9 (24.3%) patients had coexisting complications.

Table 30-3 Intracranial Complications of Otitis Media in 43 Patients from Thailand, 1983–1990

	No. of Cases*	Percentage
Meningitis	22	51
Brain abscess	18	42
Lateral sinus thrombosis	8	19
Extradural abscess	7	16
Perisinus abscess	5	12
Cerebellitis	2	5
Internal jugular vein thrombosis	2	5
Otitic hydrocephalus	2	5
Encephalitis	1	2
Cavernous sinus thrombosis	1	2

Adapted from Kangsanarak J et al.[123]

* Some patients had more than one complication.

Table 30-4 Intracranial Complications of Otitis Media and Mastoiditis in 181 Patients in South Africa, 1985–1990

| Cholesteatoma | Intracranial Complications | | | | | |
	Brain Abscess	Subdural Empyema	Lateral Sinus Thrombosis	Meningitis	Extradural Empyema	Total Complications
Yes	54	25	19	9	11	118 (57%)[†]
No	39	11	17	13	8	88 (43%)
Total complications	93 (51%)[*]	36 (20%)	36 (20%)	22 (12%)	19 (10%)	206

Adapted from Singh B et al.[124]

[†]Percentage with and without cholesteatoma of 206 complications.

[*]Percentage with complications of 181 patients.

related conditions, such as labyrinthitis, it is usually caused by a bacterium associated with infections of the middle ear or mastoid or both. Most commonly, meningitis is not a result of OM but is blood borne. When due to *S. pneumoniae*, it is also possible that the infection can spread from the nasopharynx (and middle ear) to the meninges without evidence of invasion of the bloodstream.[125] When due to OM, the infection may spread directly from the middle ear–mastoid through the dura and extend to the pia-arachnoid causing generalized meningitis.[126] Other suppurative intracranial complications in an adjacent area may also cause inflammation of the meninges, such as a subdural abscess, brain abscess, or lateral sinus thrombophlebitis.[127] The patient with meningitis presents with classic clinical features: fever, headache, neck stiffness, and altered consciousness.

Meningitis should be treated initially with high doses of antimicrobial agents. The antibiotic chosen should be culture directed from results of the tympanocentesis and spinal fluid, which should be obtained as soon as possible when the diagnosis is suspected. If the causative agent is unknown, a third-generation cephalosporin (ceftriaxone or cefotaxime) or a combination of ampicillin and chloramphenicol is administered on an empiric basis.[52] Because of concern for multidrug-resistant *S. pneumoniae* as a cause of otogenic meningitis in the United States, vancomycin (with uniform efficacy for pneumococcus) should be added to the cephalosporin regimen in communities where resistant strains are prevalent.[128] Otogenic meningitis caused by a cephalosporin-resistant pneumococcus has been reported in Japan.[129] The regimen may be modified after results of CSF cultures are known. If cultures are negative and there is concern that the aseptic process may be caused by a suppurative focus, diagnostic tests should be performed to identify the focus, obtain material for culture, and clear the local infection, usually by incision and drainage. If an AOM or OME is present, tympanocentesis and myringotomy (for drainage) should be performed immediately to identify the causative organism within the middle ear. If otorrhea is present, a culture should be obtained from the middle ear, if possible. If CSOM is present, the purulent material from the middle ear should be aspirated and sent for Gram stain, culture, and susceptibility tests.

When acute mastoiditis with osteitis is the underlying cause, a complete simple mastoidectomy is indicated as soon as the child can tolerate a general anesthetic. If CSOM or cholesteatoma, or both are present, then tympanomastoidectomy is frequently required and should be performed when the patient is stable.[95] If there is bilateral middle ear disease and the offending side is uncertain, then bilateral tympanomastoidectomy is a reasonable choice.[130] Most otologic surgeons attempt to perform hearing preservation surgery for these patients today, instead of the radical or modified radical mastoidectomy recommended in the past. However, appropriate management of any of the suppurative intratemporal complications (eg, petrositis, labyrinthitis) or intracranial complications (eg, extradural abscess) may require surgical management and consultation with a neurologist or a neurologic surgeon or both.

Tympanocentesis and myringotomy should be performed immediately for culture and drainage and any otorrhea should be cultured if there has been trauma to the temporal bone and AOM that is complicated by meningitis develops. However, exploration of the middle ear and mastoid may be necessary later to search for and repair possible defects in the dura, especially if CSF is present.

Extradural Abscess

A suppurative infection that occurs between the dura of the brain and the cranial bone is an extradural abscess (epidural abscess). It usually results from the destruction of bone adjacent to the dura by cholesteatoma or CSOM or both. This occurs when granulation tissue and purulent material collect between the lateral aspect of the dura and the adjacent temporal bone. Dural granulation tissue within a bony defect is much more common than an actual accumulation of pus. When an abscess is present, a dural sinus thrombosis or subdural or brain abscess may also be present.

Patients with an extradural abscess may have symptoms that include severe earache, low-grade fever, and headache in the temporal region with deep local throbbing pain. The more common extradural abscess encountered today may produce no signs or symptoms. An asymptomatic extradural abscess can be found in patients undergoing elective mastoidectomy for cholesteatoma. Otorrhea may be present when an extradural abscess is diagnosed and is characteristically profuse, creamy, and pulsatile. Compression of the ipsilateral jugular vein may increase the rate of discharge and the degree of pulsation. There is usually no accompanying fever, but malaise and anorexia may be observed. Generally, there are no neurologic signs, intracranial pressure is normal, and it is difficult to detect any displacement of the brain. The CSF cell count and pressure are normal, unless meningitis is also present. A CT scan may demonstrate a sizable extradural abscess.

Treating an extradural abscess consists of surgical drainage, even though identification of the infecting organism and appropriate antimicrobial therapy can help prevent the development of an intradural complication from an extradural abscess. A mastoidectomy is performed, enough bone is removed so that the dura of the middle and posterior fossae may be inspected directly, the extradural abscess is identified and removed (in some instances a drain is also inserted), and the otologic procedure that provides optimal exteriorization of the diseased area is completed by removing all the granulation tissue until normal dura is found.

Subdural Empyema

When purulent material collects within the potential space between the dura externally and the arachnoid membrane internally, it is a subdural empyema. Because the pus collects in a preformed space, it is correctly termed *empyema*, rather than *abscess*. Subdural empyema may develop as a direct extension or, more rarely, by thrombophlebitis through venous channels. In this antibiotic era, it is one of the rarer complications of

OM and mastoiditis in the highly developed nations. When subdural empyema is diagnosed, sinusitis is usually the origin.[131] In a review of 19 patients with this diagnosis at Duke University Hospital from 1979 to 1988, sinusitis was the cause in 9 patients (53%) and OM in only 2, both of whom were infants.[132]

In the underdeveloped and developing countries, OM is still a relatively frequent cause of subdural empyema.[133,134] A child who has a subdural empyema is extremely toxic and febrile. There are usually signs and symptoms of a locally expanding intracranial mass along with severe headache in the temporoparietal area. Central nervous system findings may include seizures, hemiplegia, dysmetria, belligerent behavior, somnolence, stupor, deviation of the eyes, dysphagia, sensory deficits, stiff neck, and a positive Kernig's sign. Hemiplegia and jacksonian epilepsy in a child with suppurative disease of the middle ear and mastoid usually indicate a subdural empyema.

Management of subdural empyema includes intensive intravenous antimicrobial therapy, anticonvulsants, and neurosurgical drainage of the empyema through burr holes or craniotomies. Percutaneous needle aspiration in infants has also been successful.[133,135] Corticosteroids are occasionally needed to diminish severe edema in spite of their effects on the inflammatory response. Mastoid surgery to locate and drain the source of infection is usually delayed until after neurosurgical intervention has yielded some improvement in neurologic status. The type of mastoid surgery to eradicate the focus of infection depends on the pathology and extent of the disease within the middle ear and mastoid. Chronic suppurative otitis media may only require a tympanomastoidectomy, whereas a more radical mastoid procedure may be indicated in the presence of an extensive cholesteatoma.

Focal Otitic Encephalitis

Focal otitic encephalitis (cerebritis) is a localized area of the brain that becomes edematous and inflamed as a complication of AOM, CSOM, cholesteatoma, or another suppurative complication, such as an extradural abscess or dural sinus thrombophlebitis. The signs and symptoms may be similar to those that are characteristic of a brain abscess, except there is no suppuration within the brain. Ataxia, nystagmus, vomiting, and giddiness indicate a possible focus within the cerebellum. Drowsiness, disorientation, restlessness, seizures, and coma may indicate a cerebral focus. Headache may be present in both sites. However, because these signs and symptoms are also commonly associated with a brain abscess or subdural empyema, needle aspiration may be necessary to rule out an abscess. Computed tomography or MRI can help make this distinction.

Focal encephalitis should be treated by administering therapeutic doses of antimicrobial agents and by an appropriate otologic surgical procedure to remove the infection if an abscess is not thought to be present. This should be performed as soon as possible because failure to control the source of the infection within the temporal bone and the focal encephalitis may result in a brain abscess. Anticonvulsive medication is given when there is cerebral involvement.

Brain Abscess

Otogenic brain abscess is a potential intracranial suppurative complication of cholesteatoma or CSOM or both.[136] It may also be caused by AOM or acute mastoiditis. In addition, an intratemporal complication, such as labyrinthitis or apical petrositis, may be the focus or the abscess may follow the development of an adjacent intracranial otogenic suppurative complication, such as lateral sinus thrombophlebitis or meningitis. Signs and symptoms of central nervous system invasion usually occur about 1 month after an episode of AOM or an acute exacerbation of chronic OM.

Most patients are febrile, although systemic signs, such as fever and chills, are variable and may be absent. Signs of a generalized central nervous system infection include severe headache, vomiting, drowsiness, seizures, irritability, personality changes, altered levels of consciousness, anorexia and weight loss, and meningismus. In addition to these signs of an expanding intracranial lesion, there may be specific signs of involvement of the temporal or cerebellar lobes. Temporal lobe abscesses are associated with seizures in some children and may be associated with visual field deficits (optic radiation involvement) or may be silent. Cerebellar abscesses cause vertigo, nystagmus, ataxia, dysmetria, and symptoms of hydrocephalus. There may be persistent purulent ear drainage, suggesting the primary site of infection. Terminal signs include coma, papilledema, and cardiovascular changes.

Management of brain abscess includes the use of antimicrobial agents, drainage or resection of the brain abscess, and surgical débridement of the primary focus, the mastoid, or adjacent infected tissues, such as in thrombophlebitis of the lateral sinus. Initial tympanocentesis to identify the causative organisms and myringotomy (and tympanostomy tube placement, if possible) to provide drainage should be performed on admission.[52] Aspiration of the abscess to define the cause is most helpful. The decision to either excise the lesion or perform stereotactic aspiration may depend on the depth of the abscess,[137] but some centers have

reported more sequelae, primarily epilepsy, after partial or total removal.[137,138]

The choice of the most appropriate antimicrobial regimen is difficult because of the varied bacteriology of otogenic brain abscesses. Initial therapy should include administration of a penicillin for Gram-positive cocci, an aminoglycoside for Gram-negative enteric pathogens, and chloramphenicol to combat Gram-negative organisms and anaerobic bacteria. A penicillinase-resistant penicillin should be substituted as the penicillin if the Gram stain suggests a staphylococcal infection. The use of a beta-lactam agent combined with chloramphenicol or metronidazole for 2 months has also been recommended. The parenteral route of administration for the first 2 weeks is usually advised.

Some centers recommend adding dexamethasone to the antimicrobial treatment because this drug may potentially decrease cerebral edema, lower intracranial pressure, restore capillary permeability, stabilize cellular membranes, and have a regulatory effect on the blood–brain barrier.[139] However, in the 39 cases reported from Switzerland by Seydoux and Francioli,[140] 28 (72%) received corticosteroids, but these authors could not detect any difference in outcome between patients who were given the drug and those who were not. The authors recommended the drug only for cases of massive cerebral edema. After a review of their 41 cases in children and adults, Sennaroglu and Sozeri recommend a combination of ampicillin-sulbactam and metronidazole with steroids (to reduce edema of the brain) and anticonvulsants (to reduce the risk of seizures).[136]

Several reports have described successful medical treatment of brain abscess without neurosurgical intervention.[141–143] When indicated, mastoid surgery is usually withheld until the patient's condition improves, but concurrent craniotomy and mastoidectomy appear to be safe and effective in selected patients, even in the developing countries.[144,145]

Lateral Sinus Thrombosis

Lateral and sigmoid sinus thrombosis or thrombophlebitis can develop as a result of AOM, an intratemporal complication (eg, acute mastoiditis or apical petrositis), or another suppurative intracranial complication of OM, such as otitic hydrocephalus. The superior and petrosal dural sinuses are intimately associated with the temporal bone but are rarely affected. An infection of the mastoid is frequently in contact with the sinus walls and produces inflammation of the adventitia, followed by penetration of the venous wall. Formation of a thrombus occurs after the infection has spread to the intima. The mural thrombus may become infected and may propagate, occluding the lumen. Embolization of

Table 30-5 Pointers and Pitfalls

1. Current management of suppurative complications must be based on available expert opinion and experience since clinical trials are lacking.

2. Chronic suppurative otitis that is not associated with cholesteatoma can initially be treated by nonsurgical methods, such as aural toilet, ototopical medications, and oral antimicrobial agents.

3. Cultures of the external auditory canal in patients with CSOM can be misleading. Aspirates of the middle ear are preferred.

4. When cholesteatoma is absent, CSOM that is unresponsive to aural toilet, ototopical drugs, and oral antibiotics can be treated successfully with intravenous antimicrobial therapy in many patients, especially children, reserving tympanomastoid surgery for failures.

5. Acute mastoiditis without periosteitis or osteitis is a natural extension of OM and does not require mastoidectomy.

6. Acute mastoiditis with periosteitis, but without osteitis, as shown by CT scans, will usually respond favorably to myringotomy (with or without tympanostomy tube insertion) and culture-directed parenteral antimicrobial therapy.

7. Mastoid surgery is indicated when acute mastoiditis progresses to osteitis.

8. When acute petrositis is diagnosed, extensive surgery of the petrous apex is usually not necessary when osteitis of the apex is absent. However, myringotomy with tympanostomy tube placement and culture-directed parenteral antimicrobial therapy are recommended. Tympanomastoidectomy is reserved for medical treatment failures and when mastoid osteitis, osteitis of the petrous apex, or both are present.

9. When an infant develops facial paralysis during an attack of AOM, mastoid surgery and decompression of the facial nerve is rarely indicated.

10. When acute suppurative labyrinthitis occurs in a patient who has an episode of AOM that is appropriately and adequately treated with an antimicrobial agent, either the patient has an underlying anatomic defect (eg, congenital or acquired abnormal communication between the middle and inner ears) or a medical condition (eg, impaired immunity) that predisposes to this relatively rare complication.

11. Even though suppurative intracranial complications are rare in the highly industrialized nations of the world, they still occur. Clinicians in these countries must be aware of their early signs and symptoms so that effective management can be rapidly instituted to prevent a fatal outcome.

AOM = acute otitis media; CSOM = chronic suppurative otitis media; CT = computed tomography; OM = otitis media.

septic thrombi or extension of infection into the tributary vessels may produce further disease.

Bilateral lateral sinus thrombosis has been reported, even though it is usually a unilateral complication.[146] A patient with this complication will frequently present with spiking fever, chills, headache, malaise, altered states of consciousness and seizures secondary to increased intracranial pressure, and papilledema. Infected thrombi can spread to the lungs (causing pneumonia) and joints (causing an empyema). A contralateral abducens palsy may also be associated with this complication.[147]

Management of thrombosis of the dural sinuses includes using appropriate antimicrobial agents. Penicillin, an aminoglycoside, and clindamycin (or metronidazole) are recommended to manage brain abscess. Some clinicians advocate using anticoagulant medication, but there is no consensus on this treatment today.[148,149] Those who advise against anticoagulation medication cite the risk that septic emboli could be released from a lateral sinus that has septic thrombophlebitis.[150]

Deciding to perform middle ear and mastoid surgery depends on the disease status in these anatomic sites. If only OM is present, myringotomy and tympanostomy tube insertion may be effective without the need for mastoid surgery.[149] Tympanomastoidectomy is usually indicated if acute mastoid osteitis, CSOM, cholesteatoma, or a combination of these conditions coexist. When mastoidectomy is required, the sinus should be uncovered and any perisinus abscess drained. Some surgeons recommend opening the lateral sinus and removing any thrombus. Others recommend only needle aspiration, and still others recommend neither procedure.[149] The internal jugular vein rarely requires ligation, although it is still performed by some surgeons.[151]

Otitic Hydrocephalus

Otitic hydrocephalus describes a complication of OM—mastoiditis, in which there is increased intracranial pressure without abnormalities of the CSF.[152] The pathogenesis of the syndrome is unknown, but because the ventricles are not dilated, the term *benign intracranial hypertension* also seems appropriate. The disease is frequently associated with lateral sinus thrombosis, which can be diagnosed with MRI.[153] The symptoms of otitic hydrocephalus include intractable headache, blurred vision, nausea, vomiting, and diplopia. Signs include otorrhea, abducens paralysis of one or both lateral rectus muscles, and papilledema.

Management is similar to that recommended above for lateral sinus thrombosis, for example, antimicrobial agents; myringotomy, tympanostomy tube insertion, and possible tympanomastoid surgery; medication (acetazolamide or furosemide); repeated lumbar punctures; or a lumboperitoneal shunt to normalize intracranial pressure. An aggressive surgical approach is warranted because of the possibility of optic atrophy.

CONCLUSION

Suppurative complications of OM are still common. However, those that occur in the intracranial cavity are encountered less frequently than complications that develop in the temporal bone and adjacent structures and should be managed in the safest and most effective manner. Unfortunately, we do not have clinical trials available today that provide evidence-based management options. We do have expert opinion based on experience to guide therapy. These complications are encountered in many different medical centers making clinical trials that address the most effective management options unfeasible. Other more common complications, such as CSOM, should be subjected to appropriately designed clinical trials at more than one center in the future. Table 30-5 lists the pointers and pitfalls for these complications despite the lack of evidence from such trials.

REFERENCES

1. Bluestone CD, Klein JO. Intratemporal complications and sequealae of otitis media. In: Bluestone CD, Stool SE, et al, editors. Pediatric otolaryngology. 4th ed. Philadelphia (PA): WB Saunders; 2003. p. 687–763.
2. Bluestone CD. Eustachian tube function and dysfunction. In: Rosenfeld RM, Bluestone CD, editors. Evidence-based otitis media. Hamilton (ON): BC Decker; 1999. p. 137–56.
3. Bluestone CD. Clinical course, complications and sequelae of AOM. Pediatr Infect Dis J 2000;19:S37–46.
4. Smith AW, Hatcher J, Mackenzie IJ, et al. Randomized controlled trial of treatment of chronic suppurative otitis media in Kenyan schoolchildren. Lancet 1996;348:1128–33.
5. Perry BP, Smith DW. Effect of cortisporin otic suspension on cochlear function and efferent activity in the guinea pig. Laryngoscope 1996;106:1557–61.
6. Ikeda K, Morizono T. Effect of ototopic application of a corticosteroid preparation on cochlear function. Am J Otolaryngol 1991;12:150–3.
7. Goldblatt EL. Efficacy of ofloxacin and other otic preparations for AOM in patients with tympanostomy tubes. Pediatr Infect Dis J 2001;20:116–9.
8. Goldblatt EL, Dohar J, Nozza RJ, et al. Topical ofloxin versus systematic amoxicillin/clavunate in purulent otorrhea in children. Int J Pediatr Otorhinolaryngol 1998;46:91–6.
9. Dohar JE, Garner ET, Nielsen RW, et al. Topic ofloxacin treatment of otorrhea in children with tympanostomy tubes. Arch Otolaryngol Head Neck Surg 1999;125:537–45.
10. Gates GA. Safety of ofloxacin otic and other ototopical treatments in animal models and in humans. Pediatr Infect Dis J 2001;20:104–7.
11. Agro AS, Garner ET, Wright JW III, et al. Clinical trial of ototopical ofloxacin for treatment of chronic suppurative otitis media. Clin Ther 1998;20:744–59.
12. Kaga K, Ichimura K. A preliminary report: clinical effects of otic solution of ofloxacin in infantile myringitis and chronic otitis media. Int J Pediatr Otorhinolaryngol 1998;42:199–205.
13. Klein JO. *In vitro* and *in vivo* antimicrobial activity of topical ofloxacin and other ototopical agents. Pediatr Infect Dis J 2001;20:102–3.
14. Tong MCF, Woo JKS, van Hasslet CA. A double-blind comparative study of ofloxacin otic drops versus neomycin-polymyxin B-hydrocortisone otic drops in the medical treatment of chronic suppurative otitis media. J Laryngol Otol 1996;110:309–14.
15. Dohar JE, Alper CM, Bluestone CD et al. Treatment of chronic suppurative otitis media with topical ciprofloxacin. In: Lim DJ, Bluestone CD, Casselbrant ML, et al, editors. Recent advances in otitis media—proceedings of the Sixth International Symposium. Hamilton (ON): BC Decker; 1996. p. 525–8.
16. Esposito S, D'Errico G, Montanaro C. Topical and oral treatment of chronic otitis media with ciprofloxacin. Arch Otolaryngol Head Neck Surg 1990;116:557–9.
17. Esposito S, Noviello S, D'Errico G, Montanaro C. Topical ciprofloxacin vs. intramuscular gentamicin for chronic otitis media. Arch Otolaryngol Head Neck Surg 1992; 118:842–4.
18. Aslan A, Altuntas A, Titiz A, et al. A new dosage regimen for topical application of ciprofloxacin in the management of chronic suppurative otitis media. Otolaryngol Head Neck Surg 1998;118:883–5.
19. Tutkun A, Ozagar A, Koc A, et al. Treatment of chronic ear disease: topical ciprofloxacin vs. topical gentamicin. Arch Otolaryngol Head Neck Surg 1995;121:1414–6.
20. Fradis M, Brodsky A, Ben-David J, et al. Chronic otitis media treated topically with ciprofloxacin or tobramycin. Arch Otolaryngol Head Neck Surg 1997;123:1057–60.
21. Ozagar A, Koc A, Ciprut A, et al. Effects of topical otic preparation on hearing in chronic otitis media. Otolaryngol Head Neck Surg 1997;117:405–8.

22. Alper CM, Doyle WJ. Repeated inflation does not prevent OME in a monkey model. Laryngoscope 1999;109:1074–80.

23. Crowther JA, Simpson D. Medical treatment of chronic otitis media: steroid or antibiotic with steroid ear-drops? Clin Otolaryngol 1991;16:142–4.

24. Clayton MI, Osborne JE, Rutherford D, Rivron RP. A double-blind, randomized, prospective trial of a topical antiseptic versus a topical antibiotic in the treatment of otorrhea. J Otolaryngol 1990;15:7–10.

25. Thorp MA, Kruger J, Oliver S, et al. The antibacterial acidity of acetic acid and Burow's solution as topical otological preparations. J Laryngol Otol 1998;112:925–8.

26. Piccirillo JF, Parnes SM. Ciprofloxacin for the treatment of chronic ear disease. Laryngoscope 1989;99:510–3.

27. Lang R, Goshen S, Raas-Rothschild A, et al. Oral ciprofloxacin in the management of chronic suppurative otitis media without cholesteatoma in children: preliminary experience in 21 children. Pediatr Infect Dis J 1992;11:925–9.

28. Yuen PW, Lau SK, Chau PY, et al. Ofloxacin eardrop treatment for active chronic suppurative otitis media: prospective randomized study. Am J Otol 1994;15:670–3.

29. Ah-Tye C, Paradise JL, Colburn DK. Otorrhea in young children after tympanostomy-tube placement for persistent MEE: prevalence, incidence, and duration. Pediatrics 2001;107:1251–8.

30. Kenna MA, Bluestone CD, Reilly J. Medical management of chronic suppurative otitis media without cholesteatoma in children. Laryngoscope 1986;96:146–51.

31. Kenna MA, Rosane BA, Bluestone CD. Medical management of chronic suppurative otitis media without cholesteatoma in children-update 1992. Am J Otolaryngol 1993;14:469–73.

32. Dagan R, Fliss DM, Einhorn M, et al. Outpatient management of chronic suppurative otitis media without cholesteatoma in children. Pediatr Infect Dis J 1992;11: 542–6.

33. Arguedas AG, Herrera JF, Faingezicht I, Mohs E. Ceftazidime for therapy of children with chronic suppurative otitis media without cholesteatoma. Pediatr Infect Dis J 1993;12:246–8.

34. Vartiainen E, Kansanen M. Tympanomastoidectomy for chronic otitis media without cholesteatoma. Otolaryngol Head Neck Surg 1992;106:230–4.

35. Esposito S. Outpatient parenteral treatment of bacterial infections: the Italian model as an international trend? J Antimicrob Chemother 2000;45:724–7.

36. Kenna MA, Bluestone CD. Medical management of chronic suppurative otitis media without cholesteatoma. In: Lim DJ, Bluestone CD, Klein JO, Nelson JD, editors. Proceedings of the Fourth International Symposium on Otitis Media. Burlington (ON): BC Decker; 1988. p. 222–6.

37. Vartiainen E, Vartiainen J. Effect of aerobic bacteriology on the clinical presentation and treatment results of chronic suppurative otitis media. J Laryngol Otol 1996;110:315–8.

38. Bluestone CD. Mastoidectomy and cholesteatoma. In: Bluestone CD, Rosenfeld RM, editors. Surgical atlas of pediatric otolaryngology. Hamilton (ON): BC Decker; 2002.

39. Kay DJ, Nelson M, Rosenfeld RM. Meta-analysis of tympanostomy tube sequelae. Otolaryngol Head Neck Surg 2001;124:374–80.

40. Bluestone CD. Extracranial complications of otitis media. In: Alper CM, Myers EN, Eibling DE, editors. Decision making in ear, nose and throat disorders. Philadelphia (PA): WB Saunders; 2001. p. 40–2.

41. Bluestone CD. Otologic procedures. In: Bluestone CD, Rosenfeld RH, editors. Atlas of pediatric otolaryngology. Hamilton (ON): BC Decker Inc; 2002. p. 1–136.

42. Goldstein NA, Casselbrant ML, Bluestone CD, Kurs-Lasky M. Intratemporal complications of AOM in infants and children. Otolaryngol Head Neck Surg 1998;119:444–54.

43. Dhooge IJM, Albers FWJ, Van Cauwenberge PB. Intratemporal and intracranial complications of acute suppurative otitis media in children: renewed interest. Int J Pediatr Otorhinolaryngol 1999;49 Suppl 1: S109.

44. Ghaffar FA, Wordemann M, Mccracken GH. Acute mastoiditis in children: a seventeen-year experience in Dallas, Texas. Pediatr Infect Dis J 2001;20:376–80.

45. Bahadori RS, Schwartz RH, Ziai M. Acute mastoiditis in children: an increase in frequency in Northern Virginia. Pediatr Infect Dis J 2000;19:212–5.

46. Spratley J, Silveira H, Alverez I, Pais-Clemente M. Acute mastoiditis in children: review of the current status. Int J Pediatr Otorhinolaryngol 2000;56:33–40.

47. Kaplan SL, Mason EO, Wald ER, et al. Pneumococcal mastoiditis in children. Pediatrics 2000;106:695–9.

48. Hoppe JE, Koster S, Bootz F, Niethammer D. Acute mastoiditis—relevant once again. Infection 1994;22:178–82.

49. Van Zuijlen DA, Schilder AGM, Van Balen FAM, Hoes AW. National differences in incidence of acute mastoiditis: relationship to prescribing patterns of antibiotics for AOM. Pediatr Infect Dis J 2001;20:140–4.

50. Go C, Bernstein JM, de Jong AL, et al. Intracranial complications of acute mastoiditis. Int J Pediatr Otorhinolaryngol 2000;52:143–8.

51. Bluestone CD. Acute and chronic mastoiditis and chronic suppurative otitis media. Semin Pediatr Infect Dis 1998a;9:12–26.

52. Bluestone CD, Klein JO, editors. Otitis media in infants and children. 3rd ed. Philadelphia (PA): WB Saunders; 2001.

53. Luntz M, Brodsky A, Nusem S, et al. Acute mastoiditis—the antibiotic era: a multicenter study. Int J Pediatr Otorhinolaryngol 2001;57:1–9.

54. Nadol D, Herrmann P, Baumann A, Fanconi A. Acute mastoiditis: clinical, microbiological, and therapeutic aspects. Eur J Pediatr 1990;149:560–4.

55. Harley EH, Sdralis T, Berkowitz RG. Acute mastoiditis in children: a 12-year retrospective study. Otolaryngol Head Neck Surg 1997;116:26–30.

56. Breiman RF, Butler JC, Tenover FC, et al. Emergence of drug-resistant pneumococcal infections in the United States. JAMA 1994;271:1831–5.

57. Welby PL, Keller DS, Cromien JL, et al. Resistance to penicillin and no-beta-lactam antibiotics of *Streptococcus pneumoniae* at a children's hospital. Pediatr Infect Dis J 1994;13:281–7.

58. Antonelli PJ, Dhanani N, Giannoni, C, Kublis PS. Impact of resistant pneumococcus on rates of acute mastoiditis. Otolaryngol Head Neck Surg 1990;120:190–4.

59. Lee E-S, Chae S-W, Lim H-H, et al. Clinical experiences with acute mastoiditis—1988–1998. Ear Nose Throat J 2000;79:890–2.

60. Cohen-Kerem R, Uri N, Rennert H, et al. Acute mastoiditis in children: is surgical treatment necessary? J Laryngol Otol 1999;113:1081–5.

61. Kvestad E, Kvaerner KJ, Mair IWS. Acute mastoiditis: predictors for surgery. Int J Pediatr Otorhinolaryngol 2000;52:149–55.

62. Hawkins DB, Dru D, House JW, Clark RW. Acute mastoiditis in children: a review of 54 cases. Laryngoscope 1983;93:568–72.

63. Rubin JS, Wei WI. Acute mastoiditis: a review of 34 patients. Laryngoscope 1985;95:963–5.

64. Ogle JW, Lauer BA. Acute mastoiditis. Diagnosis and complications. Am J Dis Child 1986;140:1178–82.

65. Rosen A, Ophir D, Marshak G. Acute mastoiditis: a review of 69 cases. Ann Otol Rhinol Laryngol 1986; 95:222–4.

66. Luntz, M, Keren G, Nusem S, Kronenberg J. Acute mastoiditis—revisited. Ear Nose Throat J 1994;73:648–54.

67. Gliklich RE, Eavey RD, Iannuzzi RA, Camacho AE. A contemporary analysis of acute mastoiditis. Arch Otolaryngol Head Neck Surg 1996;122:135–9.

68. Petersen CG, Ovesen T, Pedersen CB. Acute mastoidectomy in a Danish county from 1977 to 1996 with focus on the bacteriology. Int J Pediatr Otorhinolaryngol 1998;45:21–9.

69. Marioni G, de Filippis C, Tregnaghi A, et al. Bezold's abscess in children: a report and review of the literature. Int J Pediatr Otorhinolaryngol 2001;61:173–7.

70. Antonelli PJ, Garside JA, Mancuso AA, et al. Computed tomography and the diagnosis of coalescent mastoiditis. Otolaryngol Head Neck Surg 1999;120:350–4.

71. Mawson SR, Ludman H. Diseases of the ear: a textbook of otology. Chicago (IL): Year Book; 1979. p. 378–80.

72. Denoyelle F, Garabedian FN, Roelly P, et al. Protracted AOM and subacute mastoiditis: a prospective study of 165 cases. In: Lim DJ, editor. Recent advances in otitis media. Burlington (ON): BC Decker; 1993. p. 264–7.

73. Tovi F, Gatot A. Bone scan diagnosis of masked mastoiditis. Ann Otol Rhinol Laryngol 1992;101:707–9.

74. Bluestone CD. Epidemiology and pathogenesis of chronic suppurative otitis media: implications for prevention and treatment. Int J Pediatr Otol 1998b;42:207–23.

75. Osma U, Cureoglu S, Hosoglu S. The complications of chronic otitis media: report of 93 cases. J Laryngol Otol 2000;114:97–100.

76. Leiberman A, Lupu L, Landsberg R, Fliss DM. Unusual complications of otitis media. Am J Otolaryngol 1994;15:444–8.

77. Brachman DE, Giddings NA. Drainage procedures for petrous apex lesions. In: Brachman DE, Shelton C, Arriaga MA, editors. Otologic surgery. 2nd ed. Philadelphia (PA): WB Saunders; 2001. p. 466–77.

78. Chole RA, Donald PJ. Petrous apicitis: clinical considerations. Ann Otol Rhinol Laryngol 1983:92:544–51.

79. Stamm C, Pinto JA, Coser PL, Marigo C. Nonspecific necrotizing petrositis: an unusual complication of otitis in children. Laryngoscope 1984;94:1218–22.

80. Glasscock ME. Chronic petrositis. Ann Otol Rhinol Laryngol 1972;81:677–85.

81. Allam AF, Schuknecht HF. Pathology of petrositis. Laryngoscope 1968;78:1813–32.

82. Homer JJ, Johnson IJM, Jones NS. Middle ear infection and sixth nerve palsy. J Laryngol Otol 1996;110:872–4.

83. Motamed M, Kalan A. Gradenigo's syndrome. Postgrad Med J 2000;76:559–60.

84. Gradenigo G. Ueber die paralyse des Nervus abducens bei Otitis. Arch Ohrenheilunde 1907;774:149–87.

85. Somers TJ, De Foer B, Govaerts P, et al. Chronic petrous apicitis with pericarotid extension into the neck in a child. Ann Otol Rhinol Laryngol 2001;110:988–91.

86. Coker NJ, Jenkins HA. Atlas of otologic surgery. Philadelphia (PA): WB Saunders; 2001. p. 522–32.

87. McHugh K, de Silva M, Isaacs D. MRI of petrositis in chronic granulomatous disease. Pediatr Radiol 1994;24:530–1.

88. Hardjasudarma M, Edwards RL, Ganley JP, Aarstad RF. Magnetic resonance imaging features of Gradenigo's syndrome. Am J Otolaryngol 1995;16:247–50.

89. Jackler RK, Parker DA. Radiographic differential diagnosis of petrous apex lesions. Am J Otol 1992;13:561–74.

90. Murakami T, Tsubaki J, Tahara Y, Nagashima T. Gradenigo's syndrome: CT and MRI findings. Pediatr Radiol 1996;26:684–5.

91. Chang P, Fagan PA, Atlas MD, Roche J. Imaging destructive lesions of the petrous apex. Laryngoscope 1998;108:599–604.

92. Gillanders DA. Gradenigo's syndrome revisited. J Otolaryngol 1983;12:169–74.

93. Minotti AM, Kountakis SE. Management of abducens palsy in patients with petrositis. Ann Otol Rhinol Laryngol 1999;108:897–902.

94. Al-Ammar AY. Recurrent temporal petrositis. J Laryngol Otol 2001;115:316–8.

95. Neely JG, Wallace MS. Surgery of acute infections and their complications. In: Brachman DE, Shelton C, Arriaga MA, editors. Otologic surgery. 2nd ed. Philadelphia (PA): WB Saunders; 2001. p. 155–65.

96. Hendershott EL, Wood JW, Bennhoff D. The middle cranial fossa approach to the petrous apex. Laryngoscope 1976;86:658–63.

97. Chang CYJ. Petrous apex lesions. In: Alper CM, Myers EN, Eibling DE, editors. Decision making in ear, nose and throat disorders. Philadelphia (PA): WB Saunders; 2001. p. 72–3.

98. Altuntas A, Unal A, Aslan A, et al. Facial nerve paralysis in chronic suppurative otitis media: Ankara Numune Hospital experience. Auris Nasus Larynx 1998;25: 169–72.

99. Prior AJ. Facial palsy caused by OME: the pathophysiology discussed. ORL J Otorhinolaryngol Relat Spec 1995;57:348–50.

100. Edmond CV, Antoine G, Yim D, et al. A case of facial diplegia associated with acute bilateral otitis media. Int J Pediatr Otorhinolaryngol 1990;18:257–62.

101. Smith V, Traquina DN. Pediatric bilateral facial paralysis. Laryngoscope 1998;108:519–23.

102. Fukuda T, Sugie H, Ito M, Kikawada T. Bilateral facial palsy caused by bilateral masked mastoiditis. Pediatr Neurol 1998;18:351–3.

103. Almadori G, Del Ninno M, Cadoni G, et al. Facial nerve paralysis in acute otomastoiditis as presenting symptom of FAB M2, T8;21 leukemic relapse. Case report and review of the literature. Int J Pediatr Otorhinolaryngol 1996;36:45–52.

104. Elliott CA, Zalzal GH, Gottlieb WR. AOM and facial paralysis in children. Ann Otol Rhinol Laryngol 1996;105:58–62.

105. White N, McCans KM. Facial paralysis secondary to AOM. Pediatr Emerg Care 2000;16:343–5.

106. Schuknecht HF. Pathology of the ear. 2nd ed. Philadelphia (PA): Lea & Febiger; 1993. p. 223–30.

107. Paparella MM, Oda M, Hiraide F, Brady D. Pathology of sensorineural hearing loss in otitis media. Ann Otol Rhinol Laryngol 1972;81:632–47.

108. Paparella MM, Goycoolea MV, Meyerhoff WL. Inner ear pathology and otitis media: a review. Ann Otol Rhinol Laryngol 1980;89:249–53.

109. Paparella MM, Goycoolea MV, Meyerhoff WL, Shea D. Endolymphatic hydrops and otitis media. Laryngoscope 1979;89:43–58.

110. Grundfast KM, Bluestone CD. Sudden or fluctuating hearing loss and vertigo in children due to perilymph fistula. Ann Otol Rhinol Laryngol 1978;87:761–71.

111. Supance JS, Bluestone CD. Perilymph fistulas in infants and children. Otolaryngol Head Neck Surg 1993;91:663–71.

112. Weber PC, Perez BA, Bluestone CD. Congenital perilymphatic fistula and associated middle ear abnormalities. Laryngoscope 1993;103:160–4.

113. Brookhouser PE, Worthington DW, Kelly WJ. Fluctuating and/or progressive sensorineural hearing loss in children. Laryngoscope 1994;104:958–64.

114. Fitzgerald DC. Perilymphatic fistula in teens and young adults: emphasis on preexisting sensorineural hearing loss. Am J Otol 1996;17:397–400.

115. Bluestone CD. Otitis media and congenital perilymphatic fistula as a cause of sensorineural hearing loss in children. Pediatr Infect Dis J 1988;7:S141.

116. Bluestone CD. Perilymphatic fistula and Eustachian tube surgery. In: Bluestone CD, Rosenfeld RM, editors. Surgical atlas of pediatric otolaryngology. Hamilton (ON): BC Decker; 2002a.

117. Juselius H, Kaltiokallio K. Complications of acute and chronic otitis media in the antibiotic era. Acta Otolaryngol (Stockh) 1972;74:445–50.

118. Rupa V, Rajshekhar V, Weider, DJ. Syndrome of recurrent meningitis due to congenital perilymph fistula with two different clinical presentations. Int J Pediatr Otorhinolaryngol 2000;54:173–7.

119. Jang CH, Merchant SN. Histopathology of labyrinthine fistulae in chronic otitis media with clinical implication. Am J Otol 1997;18:15–25.

120. Hartnick CJ, Kim HY, Chute PM, Parisier SC. Preventing labyrinthitis ossificans. Arch Otolaryngol Head Neck Surg 2001;127:180–3.

121. Spandow O, Gothefors L, Fagerlund M, et al. Lateral sinus thrombosis after untreated otitis media: a clinical problem-again? Eur Arch Otorhinolaryngol 2000;257:1–5.

122. Don DM, Goldstein NA, Alper CM, et al. Intracranial complications of acute and chronic suppurative otitis media in children [abstract]. Presented at the American Society of Pediatric Otolaryngology; 1999 April; Palm Desert, CA.

123. Kangsanarak J, Fooanant S, Ruckphaopunt K, et al. Extracranial and intracranial complications of suppurative otitis media. Report of 102 cases. J Laryngol Otol 1993;107:999–1004.

124. Singh B. The management of lateral sinus thrombosis. J Laryngol Otol 1993;107:803–8.

125. Marra, A, Brigham D. *Streptococcus pneumoniae* causes experimental meningitis following intranasal and otitis media infections via a nonhematogenous route. Infect Immun 2001;69:2318–25.

126. Perry BP, Rubinstein JT. Meningitis due to AOM and arachnoid granulations. Ann Otol Rhinol Laryngol 2000;109:877–9.

127. Barry B, Delattre J, Vie F, et al. Otogenic intracranial infections in adults. Laryngoscope 1999;109:483–7.

128. Ryan MW, Antonelli PJ. Pneumococcal antibiotic resistance and rates of meningitis in children. Laryngoscope 2000;110:961–4.

129. Sakamoto M, Ito K, Sugasawa M, Taniguchi M. Otogenic meningitis cause by the *Pneumococcus* that had acquired resistance to cephalosporins. Otolaryngol Head Neck Surg 2001;124:250–1.

130. Job A, Kurien K, Jacob A, Mathew J. Bilateral simultaneous hearing preservation mastoidectomy in otogenic meningitis. Ann Otol Rhinol Laryngol 1998;107:872–5.

131. Dill SR, Cobbs CG, McDonald CK. Subdural empyema: analysis of 32 cases and review. Clin Infect Dis 1995;20:372–86.

132. Hoyt DJ, Fisher SR. Otolaryngologic management of patients with subdural empyema. Laryngoscope 1991;101:20–4.

133. Pathak A, Sharma BS, Mathuriya SN, et al. Controversies in the management of subdural empyema. A study of 41 cases with review of literature. Acta Neurochir (Wien) 1990;102:25–32.

134. Bok APL, Peter JC. Subdural empyema: burr holes or craniotomy? J Neurosurg 1993;78:574–8.

135. de Falco R, Scarano E, Cigliano A, et al. Surgical treatment of subdural empyema: a critical review. J Neurosurg Sci 1996;40:53–8.

136. Sennaroglu L, Sozeri B. Otogenic brain abscess: review of 41 cases. Otolaryngol Head Neck Surg 2000;123:751–5.

137. Rousseaux M, Lesoin F, Destee A, et al. Long term seque-lae of hemispheric abscesses as a function of the treat-ment. Acta Neurochir (Wein) 1985;74:61–7.

138. Mampalam TJ, Rosenblum ML. Trends in the manage-ment of bacterial brain abscesses: a review of 102 cases over 17 years. Neurosurgery 1988;23:451–8.

139. Pasaoglu A, Yildizhan A, Kandemir B. Treatment of experimental brain abscess. Acta Neurochir (Wien) 1989;100:79–83.

140. Seydoux CH, Francioli P. Bacterial brain abscesses: factors influencing mortality and sequelae. Clin Infect Dis 1992;15:394–401.

141. Berg B, Franklin G, Cuneo R, et al. Nonsurgical care of brain abscess: early diagnosis and follow-up with computerized tomography. Ann Neurol 1978;3:474–8.

142. Keven G, Tyrell LJ. Nonsurgical treatment of brain abscess: report of two cases. Pediatr Infect Dis J 1984;3:331.

143. Rennels MB, Woodward CL, Robinson WL, et al. Medical cure of apparent brain abscesses. Pediatrics 1983;72:220–4.

144. Nalbone VP, Kuruvilla A, Gacek RR. Otogenic brain abscess: the Syracuse experience. Ear Nose Throat J 1992;71: 238–42.

145. Kurien M, Job A, Mathew J, Chandry M. Otogenic

146. Samaha M, Prudencio JA, Tewfik TL, Schloss MD. Bilat-eral lateral sinus thrombosis associated with otitis media and mastoiditis. J Otolaryngol 2001;30:250–3.

147. Marzo SJ. Sigmoid sinus thrombosis with contralateral abducens palsy: first report of a case. Ear Nose Throat J 2001;80: 869–70.

148. Hawkins DB. Lateral sinus thrombosis: a sometimes unexpected diagnosis. Laryngoscope 1985;95:674–7.

149. Garcia RDJ, Baker AS, Cunningham MJ, Weber AL. Lateral sinus thrombosis associated with otitis media and mastoiditis in children. Pediatr Infect Dis J 1995;14:617–23.

150. Samuel J, Fernandes CMC. Lateral sinus thrombosis: a review of 45 cases. J Laryngol Otol 1987;101:1227–9.

151. Kuczkowski J, Mikaszewski B. Intracranial complica-tions of acute and chronic mastoiditis: report of two cases in children. Int J Pediatr Otorhinolaryngol 2001; 60:227–37.

152. Symonds CP. Otitic hydrocephalus. Brain 1931;54:55.

153. Tovi F, Hirsch M. Computed tomographic diagnosis of septic lateral sinus thrombosis. Ann Otol Rhinol Laryngol 1991;100:79–81.

intracranial abscess: concurrent craniotomy and mas-toidectomy—changing trends in a developing country. Arch Otolaryngol Head Neck Surg 1998;124:1353–6.

CHAPTER 31

Host Susceptibility to Sequelae

Robert J. Ruben, MD

All animals are equal, but some animals are more equal than others.
George Orwell

The rich get richer, and the poor get poorer.
Gus Kahn and Raymond Egan

The sum is greater than its parts.
Anonymous

OBJECTIVES

On completing this chapter, the reader will be able to
1. Determine the individual (host) *intrinsic* susceptibility of a child for each of the various deleterious sequelae of otitis media (OM).
2. Determine the individual (host) *extrinsic* susceptibility of a child for each of the various deleterious sequelae of OM.
3. Identify which child will have more than one susceptibility characteristic for the various deleterious sequelae of OM.
4. Use the susceptibility characteristic(s) of the individual child to determine intervention.

Disease manifests itself as a result of the interaction of the person—the host—and the causative agent(s)—the vector(s). Tuberculosis exemplifies this interaction. Most often, there is an immune-competent host (a typical medical student) and a modest vector (exposure to tuberculosis in a public clinic). Almost all medical students will acquire a tuberculosis infection that is only noted by skin test conversion from negative to positive. The host, because of a competent immune system, is able to contain the effects of the mycobacterium so as not to be overtly affected. In contrast, a patient with acquired immune deficiency syndrome (AIDS), similarly exposed as the immune-competent medical student, will likely manifest clinical tuberculosis, which may be fatal.

The impaired host (AIDS patient) is highly susceptible to infection, and his impaired immune system allows the infection to spread and severely injure the person. The same vector, a modest exposure to tuberculosis, results in two very different outcomes depending on the host. There are vectors, such as a gunshot wound to the head, which are so overwhelming that there is little that a host can do

to prevent or ameliorate the outcome. OM, however, is not such an overwhelming vector. This chapter will provide information as to which children (impaired hosts) are susceptible to disease (OM).

OM (the vector) causes diseases that are manifested as sequelae (Table 31-1).[1] These are increased severity and frequency of infection, diminished communication abilities, adverse intervention outcomes, and social and economic underachievement. The effect of each of these sequelae will vary as to the greater or lesser susceptibly of each child (host).

INTRINSIC SUSCEPTIBILITIES

Numerous intrinsic conditions make a child (host) more susceptible to the detrimental sequelae of OM (vector). These deleterious conditions can be classified into eight groups (Table 31-2)[2–85]: anatomic, cognitive, enzymatic, immune, linguistic, physiologic, psychiatric, and sensory. Each of these inherent states increases the morbidity of one or more OM sequelae (Table 31-3). Evidence for these effects is based on clinical observations, clinical reports, retrospective analyses, and a few prospective longitudinal natural history studies. Studies were identified by MEDLINE search using Pub MED (<http://www.ncbi.nlm.nih.gov/entrez/query.fcgi>), PaperChase (<http://www.paperchase.com>), and Science Direct (<http://www.sciencedirect.com>). These heterogeneous data sources are consistent in that each of the intrinsic and extrinsic conditions appears to exacerbate the deleterious sequelae of OM. The effect of the host characteristic for increased susceptibility, manifested as a sequelae, has been subjectively scaled as mild, moderate, or severe (see Table 31-3) based on the available information.

Table 31-1 Sequelae of Otitis Media

Sequela	Manifestations
Infection	General
	Ear pathology
	Middle
	Inner
	Hearing loss, sensorineural
	Balance
Communication abilities	Hearing
	Voice and speech
	Language
	Receptive
	Expressive
Interventions	Medical
	Surgical
Social	Activities
	Swimming
	Bathing
	Interpersonal
	Isolation
	Acting out nonverbally (behavioral)[1]
	Juvenile delinquency (?)
Economic	Family
	Society

Anatomic Abnormality

Anatomic abnormalities are those of the skull base and are seen in children with cleft palate (overt or submucosal) and malformations of the middle ear and/or Eustachian tube. Syndromic children are included in this group, such as those with Treacher Collins a 5q31.3-32 anomaly, velocardiofacial (VCF) syndrome, and Shprintzen's syndrome, a 22q11 deletion. Many of these patients, especially those whose skull base angle is acute, have almost constant OM (acute otitis media [AOM] or otitis media with effusion [OME]) from earliest life. Untreated, these children will have severe hearing loss, moderate to severe linguistic difficulties, and severe infections. In some children, the effect of OME is compounded because of additional defects that increase their susceptibility.

All children with cleft palate have speech and voice problems, which combined with intermittent or constant hearing loss will add to their communication disability. The children with VCF syndrome have associated language and psychiatric disorders and are more affected by the OM-induced hearing loss that exacerbates their communication disability. Additionally, VCF syndrome children have occult submucosal clefts of the palate and many have their internal carotid artery medially displaced. They will have increased susceptibility to the adverse sequelae of interventions in that an adenoidectomy will, in many, result in velopharyngeal insufficiency and, in a few, severe hemorrhage from carotid artery injury.

Cognitive Deficiency

The effect of hearing loss in children with cognitive deficiencies, such as those with Down syndrome, has been associated with decreased language function. Much of the hearing loss in Down syndrome children is from OM caused by anatomic abnormalities and immune defects. Data suggest that alleviating the hearing loss from OM will reduce the linguistic defect.[86–88]

Many of the cognitive deficit syndromes or anomalads have an associated increased incidence of OM, and the resulting hearing loss can exacerbate linguistic dysfunction. A child with diminished cognitive ability has less "mental redundancy" and is less able to cope with sensory deficits than a normal child. A normal child will show little or no measurable effect from the hearing loss of OM, but the mentally challenged child will exhibit a greater effect because of greatly diminished ability to compensate for the lack of input. Many mentally challenged children have additional host factors, such poverty that is often associated with fetal alcohol syndrome, or primary linguistic defects as found in VCF and Williams syndromes. Each cognitively delayed child will usually be at risk of more than one host susceptibility trait.

Enzymatic Deficiency

Some children have inborn errors of metabolism that increase their susceptibility to the effects of OM. There are two general categories. The first, in the area of adverse sequelae of intervention, comprises those who have an increased sensitivity to aminoglycosides. They can have severe hearing loss as a result of any medical therapy, especially the use of eardrops, which contain an aminoglycoside. The second, in the sequelae categories of infection and communication abilities, comprises those patients with the various forms of mucopolysaccharidoses (see Table 31-2). These children have prolonged OME with moderate to severe conductive or mixed hearing loss. Further, they acquire skull base malformations that increase their propensity to ear infection and persistent middle ear effusion. The situation is further compounded in these children because as they become older, the abnormal metabolic products

Table 31-2 Intrinsic Host Factors Resulting in Increased Susceptibility to Otitis Media

GENERAL DEFICIENCY *Specific Examples*	*Comment*
Anatomic abnormalities	
Craniofacial malformations[2-5]	
Eustachian tube (trisomy 22)[6,7]	
Submucosal cleft palate (Native American)[8-11]	Synergy with low socioeconomic rank
Turner's syndrome[12-14]	
Cognitive deficiencies	
22Q11.2 microdeletion syndrome[15]	
Down syndrome[16-20,86]	Immune deficit, skull base anomaly
Fetal alcohol syndrome[21-24]	Synergy with low socioeconomic rank
Kabuki make-up syndrome[25]	
Learning disabled[26,27]	
Velocardiofacial syndrome[28-31]	Submucous cleft palate, linguistic deficit, and psychiatric disorder
Williams syndrome[90,91]	Craniofacial abnormality
Wolf-Hirschhorn syndrome[32]	Craniofacial abnormality
Enzymatic defects	
Aminoglycoside sensitivity[33-36]	Rare but serious
Beckwith-Wiedemann syndrome[37]	Synergy with cognitive deficiency and craniofacial abnormality
Mucopolysaccharidoses[38-41]	Synergy with cognitive deficiency and craniofacial abnormality
Immune deficiencies	
Human immune deficiency virus[42-44]	
Immotile cilia syndrome[45-47]	
Specific immune deficiencies, life long[48]	Immunoglobin A most common of many
Specific immune deficiencies, transitory (developmental, prematurity)[49-54]	
Linguistic deficiencies	
Asperger's syndrome[55]	
Pervasive developmental delay (autism)[55-58]	
Specific language impairment, mixed[59-60]	
Specific language impairment, receptive[61-63]	
Specific language impairment, expressive[61-63]	
Physiologic abnormalities	
Muscular dystrophy[64,65]	
Neurologic impairments	Increased infection with anerobic bacteria[66]
Psychiatric disorders	
Fragile X syndrome[67-71]	Also cognitive and linguistic

Table 31-2 Intrinsic Host Factors Resulting in Increased Susceptibility to Otitis Media (continued)

GENERAL DEFICIENCY Specific Examples	Comment
Sensory deficiencies	
Stickler syndrome (auditory combined)[72,73]	Abnormal palate, sensorineural hearing loss, visual deficit
CHARGE sequence (auditory combined)[74,75]	Abnormal palate, mixed hearing loss
Central auditory[58,76]	
Auditory, neural	
Hearing loss, mild–moderate[77–80]	
Hearing loss, moderate–severe[77,80–82]	
Hearing loss, profound[80,81]	
Hearing loss, unilateral[83,84]	
Visual impairment[85]	
Speech dysfunction	
Speech dysfunction[63]	

Table 31-3 Interactions of Intrinsic Host Factors and Otitis Media Sequelae

| Intrinsic Host Factor | Sequelae Category and Interaction Level | | | | |
	Infection	Communication Abilities	Interventions	Social	Economic
Anatomic abnormality	Severe	Moderate	Moderate	Moderate	Moderate
Cognitive deficiency	Mild	Severe	Mild	Severe	Severe
Enzymatic defect	Severe	Moderate	Severe	Moderate	Moderate
Immune deficiency	Severe	Moderate	Severe	Moderate	Moderate
Linguistic deficiency	Mild	Severe	Mild	Severe	Severe
Physiologic abnormality	Severe	Moderate	Moderate	Moderate	Moderate
Psychiatric	Mild	Moderate	Mild	Severe	Severe
Sensory deficiency	Mild	Severe	Mild	Severe	Severe
Speech dysfunction	Mild	Severe	Mild	Severe	Severe

accumulate and cause voice and speech deficiencies and, in many, mental retardation.

Immune Deficiency

Immune deficits may be temporary or permanent. The most common are those of early childhood that are self-correcting. There is also the acquired immune defect of the child who is not breast fed. Children with temporary defects are more susceptible to infections in the first year or two of life. This early-life OM and associated hearing loss may, if associated with other predisposing factors, result in adverse linguistic and social/economic outcomes.

Children with permanent immune defects (eg, AIDS, Kartagener's syndrome) are highly susceptible to the adverse sequelae of OM and usually have persistent middle ear effusion with constant hearing loss and language deficits. Recurrent AOM is also common. As they grow older, their educational opportunities may be limited by their intrinsic immune deficiency and exacerbated by their otologic and linguistic handicaps. Interventions may also increase morbidity because of surgical risk and sequelae of frequent antibiotic therapy (allergies, gastrointestinal problems, and colonization with antibiotic-resistant pathogens).

Linguistic Deficiency

Specific language impairment (SLI) is a common intrinsic linguistic deficit found in 5 to 10% of the population.[89] There is a strong genetic component, and the deficit may be expressive, receptive, or mixed. Retrospective uncontrolled studies suggest that the hearing loss associated with OM will exacerbate the linguistic defects in these children. The ubiquity of this disorder makes SLI an important predisposing condition, which is sensitive to the deleterious effect of the vector of the hearing loss of OM.

Linguistic deficiencies found in the spectrum of disorders that include Asperger's syndrome and pervasive developmental delay (PDD, autism), appear to be inordinately adversely affected by the hearing loss of OM. These children may also have substantial psychiatric and/or cognitive pathology that appears to further increase the deleterious effect of impaired hearing. Children with Williams syndrome have, in addition to their intrinsic linguistic and cognitive abnormalities, an increased incidence of OM.[90,91] This can undermine their language abilities and result in infectious morbidity of the middle ear.

On the basis of limited information, children with any intrinsic language morbidity appear to be both the largest and most seriously affected group by the deleterious effects of OM on communication abilities and language skills. Many of these children have other intrinsic pathologies that compound the negative effects of OM.

All children who have repeated OM with effusion and hearing loss need language screening as a routine and essential part of their medical evaluation. If it is determined that a child has language delay, appropriate intervention should be planned considering the linguistic effect.[92]

Physiologic Abnormality

Eustachian tube function is compromised in patients with generalized neuromotor disorders, including various muscular dystrophies and cerebral palsies. Many of these patients have an almost continual OME with associated hearing loss and middle ear pathology. Anerobic ear infections are more common with neurologic impairments. Some children with neuromotor disorders will have cognitive impairments and are consequently highly susceptible to the infectious and communication sequelae of OM.

Psychiatric Disorders

Inborn psychiatric disorders, such as fragile X syndrome and others, appear to increase the negative effects of OM on communication abilities. Boys with fragile X syndrome may have an increased incidence of OM that adds to the morbidity caused by OM. A number of the other disorders associated with increased susceptibility to OM have a psychiatric component, and this will also increase their OM-related morbidity.

Sensory Deficiency

Any child with one sensory defect may be at increased risk of morbidity caused by reducing another sensory input or degrading already impaired function. Children with sensorineural hearing loss are particularly vulnerable to OM-induced hearing loss. A 20-dB average conductive hearing loss of the speech frequencies in a normal-hearing child needs only an increase of .02 dynes to achieve threshold detection and discrimination. Conversely, if the child has a 60-dB baseline deficit, adding 20-dB of conductive loss from OM requires a sound increase of 1,000 times (2 dynes) for detection threshold. For a sensorineural loss of 80 dB, the required increase is 10,000 times or 20 dynes.

Increased sound pressure levels impair sound amplification and, most importantly, distort complex signals and speech. Although the amplified signal is detected, discrimination is reduced because of degraded input. The child with a unilateral hearing loss may be similarly affected, as an increased threshold in the only hearing ear will add to the difficulties of localizing sound and detecting speech in background noise. All children with intrinsic hearing loss have a greater susceptibility for communication difficulties (hearing and language related) when hearing loss accompanies OM. Consequently, frequent monitoring for middle ear disease is appropriate, with timely and effective intervention to minimize the effusion prevalence.

Children with severe visual impairments appear to be more susceptible to the deleterious effects of OM because they depend on hearing more than children with normal vision. Any decrease in their most important remaining sensory input for language—hearing—may significantly compromise language development and their ability to interact and communicate with others. This is compounded in such syndromes as Stickler's syndrome, in which there are primary visual defects, increased incidence of OM, and intrinsic speech and voice defects caused by palatal abnormalities. All children with severe visual defects are to be considered as more susceptible to the morbidities of OM, especially in the area of communication abilities.

Table 31-4 Extrinsic Host Factors Resulting in Increased Susceptibility to Otitis Media

GENERAL DEFICIENCY Specific Examples	Comment
Low socioeconomic class (poverty)	
Low income[61,93]	Malnutrition can cause immune deficiency
Poverty and Native American[22,94]	
Australian Aborigine[95]	
Inadequate parental language input	
Inner city[100]	
Native American[99,100]	
Sensory deprivation	
Orphanage[96,97]	Associated with a depressed immune system
Prolonged hospitalization[98]	

Table 31-5 Interactions of Extrinsic Host Factors and Otitis Media Sequelae

Extrinsic Host Factor	Sequelae Category and Interaction Level				
	Infection	Communication Abilities	Interventions	Social	Economic
Low socioeconomic class	Moderate	Moderate	Moderate	Moderate	Moderate
Inadequate parental language input	Mild	Severe	Mild	Severe	Severe
Sensory deprivation	Mild	Severe	Mild	Severe	Severe

EXTRINSIC SUSCEPTIBILITIES

Extrinsic host factors that increase a child's susceptibility to the adverse effects of OM (Tables 31-4 and 31-5) can be categorized as low socioeconomic class (poverty), inadequate parental language input, and sensory deprivation.[93–98] Medical evaluation and diagnosis usually does not take into account these aspects of the patients' extrinsic environment in considering the care of disease. OM differs from some of the other conditions encountered in medicine in that these environmental host factors create a negative synergy when they occur in association with the intrinsic deleterious host factors. They play an especially important role in the adverse sequelae of deficient language.

Clinicians must consider not only the biologic make up of the patient but also what has and is occurring in the environment that will influence the extent, both qualitatively and quantitatively, of the OM-related morbidity.

For many, this factoring of extrinsic condition(s) will be a new dimension in caring for a patient and deciding what, if any, interventions for OM are appropriate.

Low Socioeconomic Class (Poverty)

The prevalence of OM may be higher in children living in poverty because of numerous factors, including poor nutrition, overcrowding, exposure to other children (day care), environmental tobacco smoke, and so on. These environmental insults, combined with inadequate access to and receipt of medical care, result in prolonged episodes of inadequately or untreated OM. If a child has other intrinsic or host factors, increased morbidity will result. The child in poverty is at greater risk and is more susceptible to the sequelae of OM than the child who is cared for in a resource-ample environment. This is seen in the studies of the Native American, who have not only anatomic risk factors but may also live in poverty.

Table 31-6 Pointers and Pitfalls

1. Manifestations of disease result from interactions of the person (host) and the causative agent (vector). The impact of OM (vector) on a given child depends largely on host susceptibility factors.

2. Potential sequelae of OM include increased severity and frequency of infection, diminished communication abilities, adverse intervention outcomes, and social and economic underachievement.

3. The effect that OM will have on an individual child is a complex amalgam of intrinsic and extrinsic susceptibility characteristics.

4. Intrinsic host factors that predispose to adverse sequelae can be categorized as anatomic, cognitive, enzymatic, immunologic, linguistic, physiologic, psychiatric, and sensory.

5. Extrinsic host factors that predispose to adverse sequelae can be categorized as low socioeconomic class (poverty), inadequate parental language input, and sensory deprivation.

6. Extrinsic host factors create a negative synergy when they occur in association with intrinsic host factors.

7. Intrinsic and extrinsic host factors must be considered when assessing the effect of OME, the likelihood of developmental sequelae, and the need for intervention.

OM = otitis media; OME = otitis media with effusion.

Inadequate Parental Language Input

Numerous prospective and retrospective studies have demonstrated a negative synergy between OM early in life and inadequate parental language input.[99,100] The child who has even a modest amount of OM during the first year or so of life and is exposed to a limited linguistic environment has diminished language function later in life. Clinicians must consider the linguistic environment of a child with OM as part of management. If the environment is satisfactory, then the child will be more resistant to the negative linguistic effect of OM than a child who is placed in a language-diminished home.

Sensory Deprivation

Extreme sensory deprivation is found in many children who are kept in orphanages, especially those from the developing or former "iron curtain" countries. Children are adopted and brought into a family in a developed nation usually between the ages of 6 to 24 months. Many have experienced malnutrition and inadequate prior medical care in addition to sensory deprivation. The sensory deprivation is manifested by substantial language delay and failure to thrive. Chronic, untreated OME and hearing loss are also highly prevalent. The extreme sensory deprivation, combined with the multitude of other issues described, increases susceptibility to the linguistic sequelae of OM. Another group that may have a similar sensory deprivation comprises those infants and young children with prolonged hospitalization and inadequate sensory stimulation.

CONCLUSION

The effect that OM will have on an individual child is a complex amalgam of intrinsic and extrinsic susceptibly characteristics (see Tables 31-2 and 31-4). There are negative synergies both within and between the host factors (see Tables 31-3 and 31-5). Studies of the effect of OM must take into account these various vectors. One study of intervention came to the following conclusion:

"Our results are particularly applicable to the commonly encountered child of less than three years who is otherwise healthy and who has had effusion for the intervals that we studied, with its usual, attendant mild-to-moderate hearing loss, but who has no other, less debatable indications for the insertion of tympanostomy tubes, such as a severe retraction pocket of the tympanic membrane or a recent history of frequent episodes of acute otitis media. For such a child, our results indicate that the insertion of tympanostomy tubes cannot be expected to result in improved developmental outcome at the age of three years."[101]

This was claimed after excluding the following infants from the study:

"In brief, we excluded infants who met any of the following criteria: a birth weight of less than 2,270 g (5 lb), a small size for gestational age, a history of neonatal asphyxia or other serious illness, a major congenital malformation or chronic illness, or the product of a multiple birth. Infants were also excluded if they had a sibling enrolled in the study; they were in foster care or adopted; their mother was dead, seriously ill, a known drug or alcohol abuser, or (in the judgment of study personnel) too limited socially or intellectually to give informed consent or adhere to the study protocol; their mother was younger than 18 years of age; or English was not the only language spoken in the household."[101]

The above list includes most of the intrinsic and extrinsic host factors that cause a child to be more susceptible to the deleterious effects of OM. Additionally, 91% of the children in this study had minimal hearing loss because OME was intermittent or unilateral, and hearing loss was defined as a threshold greater than 20 to 25 dB before age 23 months or 15 dB in older children. Not surprisingly, this study showed no effect of the intervention because subjects had minimal otitis—a small vector occurring in very resistant hosts.

Intrinsic and extrinsic host factors must be considered when assessing the effect of OM and the efficacy of any intervention. Failure to do so may mislead many and inadvertently deny care to those for whom it would be beneficial. The decision for an intervention in a child with a form of OM depends primarily on the intrinsic and extrinsic host characteristics (Table 31–6).

References

1. Bennett KE, Haggard MP, Silva PA, Stewart IA. Behaviour and developmental effects of otitis media with effusion into the teens. Arch Dis Child 2001;85:91–5.

2. Liu L, Sun Y, Zhao W. The effects of otitis media with effusion and hearing loss on the speech outcome after cleft palate surgery. Chung Hua Chiang Hsueh Tsa Chih Chin J Stomatol 2001;36:424–6.

3. Rynnel-Dagoo B, Lindberg K, Bagger-Sjoback D, Larson O. Middle ear disease in cleft palate children at three years of age. Int J Pediatr Otorhinolaryngol 1992;23:201–9.

4. Schonweiler R, Schonweiler B, Schmelzeisen R. Hearing capacity and speech production in 417 children with facial cleft abnormalities. HNO 1994;42:691–6.

5. Gould HJ, Caldarelli DD. Hearing and otopathology in Apert syndrome. Arch Otolaryngol 1982;108:347–9.

6. Miura M, Sando I, Haginomori SI, Casselbrant ML. Histopathological study on temporal bone and Eustachian tube in trisomy 22. Int J Pediatr Otorhinolaryngol 2000;56:191–8.

7. Poe DS, Abou-Halawa A, Abdel-Razek O. Analysis of the dysfunctional Eustachian tube by video endoscopy. Otol Neurotol 2001;22:590–5.

8. Gregg JB, Zimmerman L, Clifford S, Gregg PS. Craniofacial anomalies in the Upper Missouri River over a millennium: archeological and clinical evidence. Cleft Palate J 1981;18:210–22.

9. Croen LA, Shaw GM, Wasserman CR, Tolarova MM. Racial and ethnic variations in the prevalence of orofacial clefts in California, 1983-1992. Am J Med Genet 1998;79:42–7.

10. Fischler RS, Todd NW, Feldman CM. Otitis media and language performance in a cohort of Apache Indian children. Am J Dis Child 1985;139:355–60.

11. Beery QC, Doyle WJ, Cantekin EI, et al. Eustachian tube function in an American Indian population. Ann Otol Rhinol Laryngol 1980;89 Suppl:28–33.

12. Stenberg AE, Nylen O, Windh M, Hultcrantz M. Otological problems in children with Turner's syndrome. Hear Res 1998;124:85–90.

13. Van Borsel J, Dhooge I, Verhoye K, et al. Communication problems in Turner syndrome: a sample survey. J Commun Disord 1999;32:435–46.

14. Watkin PM. Otological disease in Turner's syndrome. J Laryngol Otol 1989;103:731–8.

15. Solot CB, Knightly C, Handler SD, et al. Communication disorders in the 22Q11.2 microdeletion syndrome. J Commun Disord 2000;33:187–204.

16. Dahle AJ, McCollister FP. Hearing and otologic disorders in children with Down syndrome. Am J Ment Defic 1986;90:636–42.

17. Iino Y, Imamura Y, Harigai S, Tanaka Y. Efficacy of tympanostomy tube insertion for otitis media with effusion in children with Down syndrome. Int J Pediatr Otorhinolaryngol 1999;49:143–9.

18. Marcell MM, Cohen S. Hearing abilities of Down syndrome and other mentally handicapped adolescents. Res Dev Disabil 1992;13:533–51.

19. Selikowitz M. Short-term efficacy of tympanostomy tubes for secretory otitis media in children with Down syndrome. Dev Med Child Neurol 1993;35:11–5.

20. Tomasevic P, Vinayak B, Jones J, Freeland A. Management of hearing impairment in children with Downs syndrome. Aust J Otolaryngol 1998;3:25–8.

21. Abkarian GG. Communication effects of prenatal alcohol exposure. J Commun Disord 1992;25:221–40.

22. Carney LJ, Chermak GD. Performance of American Indian children with fetal alcohol syndrome on the test of language development. J Commun Disord 1991;24:123–34.

23. Church MW, Eldis F, Blakley BW, Bawle EV. Hearing, language, speech, vestibular, and dentofacial disorders in fetal alcohol syndrome. Alcohol Clin Exp Res 1997;21:227–37.

24. Church MW, Kaltenbach JA. Hearing, speech, language, and vestibular disorders in the fetal alcohol syndrome: a literature review. Alcohol Clin Exp Res 1997;21:495–512.

25. Niikawa N, Matsuura N, Fukushima Y, et al. Kabuki make-up syndrome: a syndrome of mental retardation, unusual facies, large and protruding ears, and postnatal growth deficiency. J Pediatr 1981;99:565–9.

26. Bennett FC, Ruuska SH, Sherman R. Middle ear function in learning-disabled children. Pediatrics 1980;66:254–60.

27. Reichman J, Healey WC. Learning disabilities and conductive hearing loss involving otitis media. J Learn Disabil 1983;16:272–8.

28. Ardinger HH, Ardinger J. Clinical presentation of velocardiofacial syndrome. Progr Pediatr Cardiol 2002; 15:93–7.

29. Reyes MR, LeBlanc EM, Bassila MK. Hearing loss and otitis media in velo-cardio-facial syndrome. Int J Pediatr Otorhinolaryngol 1999;47:227–33.

30. Shprintzen RJ. Velocardiofacial syndrome: a distinctive behavioral phenotype. Ment Retard Dev Disabil Res 2000;6:142–7.

31. Vantrappen G, Rommel N, Cremers CWRJ, et al. The velocardiofacial syndrome: the otorhinolaryngeal manifestations and implications. Int J Pediatr Otorhinolaryngol 1998;45:133–41.

32. Lesperance MM, Grundfast KM, Rosenbaum KN. Otologic manifestations of Wolf-Hirschhorn syndrome. Arch Otolaryngol Head Neck Surg 1998;124:193–6.

33. Lehtonen MS, Uimonen S, Hassinen IE, Majamaa K. Frequency of mitochondrial DNA point mutations among patients with familial sensorineural hearing impairment. Eur J Hum Genet 2000;8:315–8.

34. Casano RA, Johnson DF, Bykhovskaya Y, et al. Inherited susceptibility to aminoglycoside ototoxicity: genetic heterogeneity and clinical implications. Am J Otolaryngol 1999;20:151–6.

35. Fischel-Ghodsian N. Genetic factors in aminoglycoside toxicity. Ann N Y Acad Sci 1999;884:99–109.

36. Fischel-Ghodsian N. Mitochondrial deafness mutations reviewed. Hum Mutat 1999;13:261–70.

37. Schick B, Brors D, Prescher A, Draf W. Conductive hearing loss in Beckwith-Wiedemann syndrome. Int J Pediatr Otorhinolaryngol 1999;48:175–9.

38. Ohlemiller KK, Hennig AK, Lett JM, et al. Inner ear pathology in the mucopolysaccharidosis VII mouse. Hear Res 2002;151:69–84.

39. Motamed M, Thorne S, Narula A. Treatment of otitis media with effusion in children with mucopolysaccharidoses. Int J Pediatr Otorhinolaryngol 2000;53: 121–4.

40. Komura Y, Kaga K, Ogawa Y, et al. ABR and temporal bone pathology in Hurler's disease. Int J Pediatr Otorhinolaryngol 1998;43:179–88.

41. Wallace SP, Prutting CA, Gerber SE. Degeneration of speech, language, and hearing in a patient with mucopolysaccharidosis VII. Int J Pediatr Otorhinolaryngol 1990;19:97–107.

42. Glorieux J, Samson J, Lapointe N. Neurodevelopmental evaluation in relation to clinical outcome in children of HIV seropositive mothers: baseline findings. Int Conf AIDS 1992;8:B206.

43. Nedelcu I. AIDS in Romania. Am J Med Sci 1992;304: 188–91.

44. Retzlaff C. Speech and language pathology and pediatric HIV. J Int Assoc Phys AIDS Care 1999;5:60–2.

45. Greenstone M, Rutman A, Dewar A, et al. Primary ciliary dyskinesia: cytological and clinical features. QJM 1988;67:405–23.

46. Ernstson S, Afzelius BA, Mossberg B. Otologic manifestations of the immotile-cilia syndrome. Acta Otolaryngol 1984;87:83–92.

47. Fischer TJ, McAdams JA, Entis GN, et al. Middle ear ciliary defect in Kartagener's syndrome. Pediatrics 1978;62:443–5.

48. Buckley RH. Clinical and immunologic features of selective IgA deficiency. Birth Defects Original Article Series 1975;11:134–42.

49. Gravel JS, McCarton CM, Ruben RJ. A prospective study of otitis media in infants born at very-low birthweight. Acta Oto Laryngol 1988;105:516–21.

50. Pearce PS, Saunders MA, Creighton DE, Sauve RS. Hearing and verbal-cognitive abilities in high-risk preterm infants prone to otitis media with effusion. J Dev Behav Pediatr 1988;9:346–51.

51. Seidman S, Allen R, Wasserman GA. Productive language of premature and physically handicapped two-year-olds. J Commun Disord 1986;19:49–61.

52. Engel J, Mahler E, Anteunis L, et al. Why are NICU infants at risk for chronic otitis media with effusion? Int J Pediatr Otorhinolaryngol 2001;57:137–44.

53. Gravel JS, McCarton CM, Ruben RJ. Otitis media in neonatal intensive care unit graduates: a 1-year prospective study. Pediatrics 1988;82:44–9.

54. Holmes N, Conway MJ, Flood L, et al. Language development in a group of very low-birth-weight children whose postauricular myogenic response was tested in infancy. Pediatrics 1983;71:257–61.

55. Shriberg LD, Paul R, McSweeny JL, et al. Speech and prosody characteristics of adolescents and adults with high-functioning autism and Asperger syndrome. J Speech Lang Hear Res 2001;44:1097–115.

56. Gordon AG. Debate and argument: interpretation of auditory impairment and markers for brain damage in autism. J Child Psychol Psychiatry 1993;34:587–92.

57. Rosenhall U, Nordin V, Sandstrom M, et al. Autism and hearing loss. J Autism Dev Disord 1999;29:349–57.

58. Konstantareas MM, Homatidis S. Ear infections in autistic and normal children. J Autism Dev Disord 1987;17:585–94.

59. Paul R, Lynn TF, Lohr-Flanders M. History of middle ear involvement and speech/language development in late talkers. J Speech Hear Res 1993;36:1055–62.

60. Psarommatis IM, Goritsa E, Douniadakis D, et al. Hearing loss in speech-language delayed children. Int J Pediatr Otorhinolaryngol 2001;58:205–10.

61. Brookhouser PE, Goldgar DE. Medical profile of the language-delayed child: otitis-prone versus otitis-free. Int J Pediatr Otorhinolaryngol 1987;12:237–71.

62. Rollins PR, Pan BA, Conti-Ramsden G, Snow CE. Communicative skills in children with specific language impairments: a comparison with their language-matched siblings. J Commun Disord 1994;27:189–206.

63. Schonweiler R. Synopsis of results with 1,300 children with language developmental delay from the etiopatho-genetic, audiologic and speech pathology viewpoint. Folia Phoniatr Logop 1994;46:18–26.

64. Bilgen C, Bilgen IG, Sener RN. Oculopharyngeal muscular dystrophy: clinical and CT findings. Comput Med Imaging Graph 2001;25:527–9.

65. O'Brien TA, Harper PS. Course, prognosis and complications of childhood-onset myotonic dystrophy. Dev Med Child Neurol 1984;26:62–7.

66. Brook I. Anaerobic infections in children with neurological impairments. Am J Ment Retard 1995;99:579–94.

67. Abbeduto L, Hagerman RJ. Language and communication in fragile X syndrome. Ment Retard Dev Disabil Res 1997;3:313–22.

68. Berry-Kravis E, Grossman AW, Crnic LS, Greenough WT. Understanding fragile X syndrome. Curr Paediatr 2002;12:316–24.

69. Hagerman RJ, Altshul-Stark D, McBogg P. Recurrent otitis media in the fragile X syndrome. Am J Dis Child 1987;141:184–7.

70. Goldson E, Hagerman RJ. The fragile X syndrome. Dev Med Child Neurol 1992;34:826–32.

71. Hagerman RJ. Fragile X syndrome—molecular and clinical insights and treatment issues. West J Med 1997; 166:129–37.

72. Admiraal RJ, Brunner HG, Dijkstra TL, et al. Hearing loss in the nonocular Stickler syndrome caused by a COL11A2 mutation. Laryngoscope 2000;110:457–61.

73. Nowak CB. Genetics and hearing loss: a review of Stickler syndrome. J Commun Disord 1998;31:437–54.

74. Admiraal RJ, Joosten FB, Huygen PL. Temporal bone CT findings in the CHARGE association. Int J Pediatr Otorhinolaryngol 1998;45:151–62.

75. Shah UK, Ohlms LA, Neault MW, et al. Otologic management in children with the CHARGE association. Int J Pediatr Otorhinolaryngol 1998;44:139–47.

76. Moore DR, Hogan SC, Kacelnik O, et al. Auditory learning as a cause and treatment of central dysfunction. Audiol Neuro Otol 2001;6:216–20.

77. Bess FH, DoddMurphy J, Parker RA. Children with minimal sensorineural hearing loss: prevalence, educational performance, and functional status. Ear Hear 1998;19:339–54.

78. Margolis RH, Hunter LL, Rykken JR, Giebink GS. Effects of otitis media on extended high-frequency hearing in children. Ann Otol Rhinol Laryngol 1993;102:1–5.

79. Margolis RH, Saly GL, Hunter LL. High-frequency hearing loss and wideband middle ear impedance in children with otitis media histories. Ear Hear 2000;21:206–11.

80. Ruben RJ, Math R. Serous otitis media associated with sensorineural hearing loss in children. Laryngoscope 1978;88:1139–54.

81. Wilber LA. Significance and detection of conductive lesions in children with multiple handicaps. J Commun Disord 1974;7:31–44.

82. Shishiyama F, Tsuchihashi N, Kawashiro N. Recognition of previously undiagnosed moderate hearing loss during an episode of otitis media with effusion. Int J Pediatr Otorhinolaryngol 1996;34:288–9.

83. Skotnicka B, Topolska M,]gorzata, Hassmann-Poznanska E. Incidence of coexisting sensorineural hearing loss and secretory otitis media. Otolaryngol Pol 2002;56:195–8.

84. Vartiainen E, Karjalainen S. Prevalence and etiology of unilateral sensorineural hearing impairment in a Finnish childhood population. Int J Pediatr Otorhinolaryngol 1998;43:253–9.

85. Voutilainen R, Jauhiainen T, Linkola H. Associated handicaps in children with hearing loss. Scand Audiol 1988;30 Suppl:57–9.

86. Shott SR, Joseph A, Heithaus D. Hearing loss in children with Down syndrome. Int J Pediatr Otorhinolaryngol 2001;61:199–205.

87. Whiteman BC, Simpson GB, Compton WC. Relationship of otitis media and language impairment in adolescents with Down syndrome. Ment Retard 1986;24:353–6.

88. Cunningham C, McArthur K. Hearing loss and treatment in young Down's syndrome children. Child Care Health Dev 1981;7:357–74.

89. Rice ML. Specific language impairments: in search of diagnostic markers and genetic contributions. Ment Retard Dev Disabil Res 1997;3:350–7.

90. Klein AJ, Armstrong BL, Greer MK, Brown FR III. Hyperacusis and otitis media in individuals with Williams syndrome. J Speech Hear Dis 1990;55:339–44.

91. Morris CA, Demsey SA, Leonard CO, et al. Natural history of Williams syndrome: physical characteristics. J Pediatr 1988;113:318–26.

92. Ruben RJ. Language screening as a factor in the management of the pediatric otolaryngic patient. Effectiveness and efficiency. Arch Otolaryngol Head Neck Surg 1991;117:1021–5.

93. Castagno LA, Lavinsky L. Otitis media in children: seasonal changes and socioeconomic level. Int J Pediatr Otorhinolaryngol 2002;62:129–34.

94. Gissler M, Rahkonen O, Jarvelin MR, Hemminki E. Social class differences in health until the age of seven years among the Finnish 1987 birth cohort. Social Sci Med 1998;46:1543–52.

95. Latzel S, Hunter G. Prevalence of otitis media in Aboriginal school children on Groote Eylandt. Aust J Otolaryngol 2002;5:14–6.

96. Jenista JA, Chapman D. Medical problems of foreign-born adopted children. Am J Dis Child 1987;141:298–302.

97. Johnson DE. Adoption and the effect on children's development. Early Hum Dev 2002;68:39–54.

98. Singer L. Long-term hospitalization of failure-to-thrive infants: developmental outcome at three years. Child Abuse Negl 1986;104:479–86.

99. Shriberg LD, Flipsen P Jr, Thielke H, et al. Risk for speech disorder associated with early recurrent otitis media with effusion: two retrospective studies. J Speech Lang Hear Res 2000;43:79–99.

100. Wallace IF, Gravel JS, Schwartz RG, Ruben RJ. Otitis media, communication style of primary caregivers, and language skills of 2 year olds: a preliminary report. J Dev Behav Pediatr 1996;17:27–35.

101. Paradise JL, Feldman HM, Campbell TF, et al. Effect of early or delayed insertion of tympanostomy tubes for persistent otitis media on developmental outcomes at the age of three years. N Engl J Med 2001;344:1179–87.

Index